BUSINESS POLICY

Text and Cases

BUSINESS POLICY

Text and Cases

Edmund P. Learned, D.C.S.
Charles Edward Wilson Professor of
Business Policy Emeritus

C. Roland Christensen, D.C.S.
George Fisher Baker, Jr., Professor of
Business Administration

Kenneth R. Andrews, Ph.D.
Donald Kirk David Professor of
Business Administration

All of the
GRADUATE SCHOOL OF BUSINESS ADMINISTRATION
Harvard University

William D. Guth, D.B.A.
Professor of Business Administration
Columbia University

Revised Edition • 1969
Richard D. Irwin, Inc., Homewood, Illinois
Irwin-Dorsey Limited, Nobleton, Ontario

Revised Edition

First Printing, January 1969

Case material of the Harvard Graduate School of Business Administration is made possible by the cooperation of business firms who may wish to remain anonymous by having names, quantities, and other identifying details disguised while maintaining basic relationships. Cases are prepared as the basis for class discussion rather than to illustrate either effective or ineffective handling of administrative situations.

Library of Congress Catalog Card No. 68–56877

Printed in the United States of America

To
Donald K. David

Preface

Business Policy: Text and Cases (Revised Edition) provides the materials, as did its predecessor edition, for a complete course in business policy. The case material and text may also be supplemented with separate cases available from the Intercollegiate Case Clearing House and with readings selected from the growing literature in the business policy field. This edition carries forward the format of the first edition, incorporating changes suggested by our policy colleagues teaching in many institutions throughout the world. We are appreciative of their interest in, and use of, this book.

The basic administrative processes and problems with which business policy is concerned have been part of organizational life for centuries; the academic history of business policy as a field dates back less than six decades.

This volume builds on the substantial contributions made by our former policy colleagues; it carries their efforts but one step forward along the way to greater understanding. The specific core idea—the concept of corporate strategy—and case organization used in this book began to be developed in the early 1960's under the leadership of Professors Andrews and Christensen and with the strong encouragement of Professor Learned. Maintaining traditional course interests in a generalist–top management orientation and in the administrative and organizational problems of the enterprise as a totality, the course emphasis concentrated on the definition of corporate strategy (Book I) and the implementation of strategy (Book II). Professor Guth's leadership of the field research program meant that the conceptual framework of strategy formulation and administration could be applied to the richness of real-life case situations.

Despite its incompleteness, the concept of corporate strategy provides both a teaching and a research framework. As Professor Andrews has stated:

This concept is far from complete. But its early development shows it to be an organizing perspective that makes possible the development of research projects which build upon one another, as for instance in a series devoted to the problems of scanning the environment. The process of planning thus defined can be studied in firms, in industries, or in the French economy, where the relation of the French national plan and strategic planning in private firms, for example, has been studied in detail. But besides providing a special focus and study for a general field (as we have seen a central problem in professional education) this framework allows all other fields to be brought to bear upon the highest function of the general manager—supervision of the continuous process of determining the nature of the enterprise and setting, revising, and attempting to achieve its goals. So far the development of organizational behavior fits well into the framework of implementation. The sophisticated developments in quantitative analysis are not yet readily available to policy problems, but if all goes well, this will come.

The utility of the policy framework, which mostly articulates and raises to the level of conscious analysis the intuitive approaches developed over years of close attention to concrete situations, is such that some adaptation of it will surely remain after present attempts to develop and test it have been completed. It may prove, indeed, the answer to the conceptual need of the environmental studies. One alternative, at least, is to examine repeatedly the economic, social, technological, and political aspects of the American and international scenes from the perspective of the chief executive in an expanding firm in one industry after another, stressing constantly perception of relevant developments and opportunities for innovation. The skill exercised would be the imaginative identification of opportunity, something quite different from merely looking.

The idea of corporate strategy constitutes a simple practitioner's theory, a kind of Everyman's conceptual scheme. It is nonetheless capable of including the most extensive combination of interrelated variables involved in the most important of all business decisions. It is a definition of the manager's central function, whether he is a staff specialist contributing in depth and detail to the identification of alternatives and to the predicted return on investment for each of these alternatives, or the senior executive who must finally make or complete the decision.[1]

And, of course, the business policy subject area continues to evolve and develop. The need for professionally trained generalists—the men who make our organized society's critical decisions—is great; our present efforts are limited. Sir Eric Ashby has put the challenge well:

But the world needs generalists as well as specialists. Indeed you have only to read your newspapers to know that the big decisions on which the fate of nations depends are in the hands of generalists. I do not think that universities, American or British, are satisfied with the education they give to the man who is to become a generalist. Some believe he should have a rigorously specialist training in some field which he then abandons for life. Others believe he should have a synoptic acquaintance with the ways of thinking of humanists, social scientists, and natural scientists. And I suppose there are still a few antique persons who cling to the view that generalists need no higher education at all. We can with some confidence prescribe the minutiae of curriculum for doctors, physicists, and lawyers. The unpalatable fact is that we have no such confidence in prescribing curricula for men who will become presidents of industries, newspaper editors, senior civil servants, or Congressmen.[2]

---

[1] Kenneth R. Andrews, "The Progress of Professional Education for Business," unpublished remarks presented for discussion at the Centennial Convocation on Graduate Professional Education at the Episcopal Theological School, Cambridge, Massachusetts, January 27–29, 1967.

[2] Sir Eric Ashby, Master, Clare College, Cambridge, "Centennial Convocation Address," delivered at the 100th anniversary of the granting of the charter to Cornell University, October 9, 1964.

We believe that the challenge will be met, at least in part, by all of us who work in the policy area in countless colleges and universities throughout this country and the world.

The authors of this book are in debt to former and present colleagues. Former colleagues—now numbering more than 100—cannot each be individually recognized, but we are grateful to them for their multiple contributions. We wish to especially thank Professor Emeritus M. T. Copeland; Professor Geo. Albert Smith, Jr.; Professor John D. Glover; Professor Emeritus Richard S. Meriam; and former Dean and Professor Emeritus Donald K. David, to whom this book is dedicated.

Present members of the policy area have contributed substantially to the recent developments of the field. Professors Francis J. Aguilar, Robert W. Austin, Norman A. Berg, Joseph L. Bower, John B. Matthews, Robert W. Merry, Malcolm S. Salter, Bruce R. Scott, Howard H. Stevenson, and Hugo E. R. Uyterhoeven have made major contributions to the ongoing developments in the teaching and research efforts of this area.

We are indebted to Professor Andrews for the text sections of this book.

Our sincere appreciation goes to the authors of the cases included in this edition. To the following our thanks: John F. Archer for East-West Trade; Norman A. Berg for Acoustic Research (D); Joseph L. Bower for the NEFCO series, with which he was assisted by Miss Audrey Barrett; Peter Brengel for Solartron; Paul Donham and David C. D. Rogers for Multi-Products; James S. Garrison for the Note on the Metal Container Industry and for Crown Cork and Seal; Richard G. C. Hanna for Univis, the Litton series, and his contribution to the Olivetti series; Charles W. Hofer for the Note on the Farm Equipment Industry, Deere & Company, Massey-Ferguson Ltd., and Heublein, Inc. (A) and (B); David F. Hawkins for Olivetti (E–1); John B. Matthews for Xerox; John Priedeman for the Note on Portland Cement, and The Rugby Portland Cement Company; John W. Rosenblum for Basic Industries, and Associated Petroleum; Mrs. Audrey T. Sproat for J. I. Case Company, and A Note on the United States Drug Industry; Howard H. Stevenson for American Motors (D), Head Ski, the Dennison series, and his major contribution to the Olivetti series; Bruce R. Scott for American Motors and for Acoustic Research (A), (B), and (C); Robert C. K. Valtz for revisions of the Note on Portland Cement and The Rugby Portland Cement Company; and H. Edward Wrapp (assisted by L. A. Guthart) for Texas Instruments cases.

We owe special thanks to Miss Priscilla Winslow who, with a "general management point of view," has directed the entire production of this book. Her combination of efficiency and good humor is most appreciated. Miss Winifred I. Barnard and Miss Karen L. Peters contributed secretarial assistance, and Miss Josepha M. Perry a critical and helpful editorial and proofing review.

To Enrico Bignami and Jean-C. Corthésy, Vice Chairmen of Nestlé Alimentana Company and Co-Chairmen of the Board of Trustees of IMEDE in

Lausanne, Switzerland, we acknowledge our debt for their support of the IMEDE case-gathering effort and of research in European problems in national and business policy. They have permitted us to use a number of IMEDE cases which were prepared while three of us were temporary members of the IMEDE faculty. The coordination of IMEDE and our own studies of policy has been most productive.

On September 1, 1967, Professor Edmund P. Learned became the Charles E. Wilson Professor of Business Policy Emeritus. During his 40-year career at the Harvard Business School, Professor Learned has made major contributions to many course areas. His coauthors wish to acknowledge not only his significant academic contribution to the policy area, but also those personal qualities of loyalty, integrity, and compassion which have gained for him the respect and affection of his associates. We are pleased that his retirement will not interfere with our continuing collaboration.

Dean George P. Baker and Associate Dean George F. F. Lombard, together with their predecessors Stanley F. Teele and Russell H. Hassler, have provided steady support for our efforts to make progress in our field. The McKinsey Foundation for Management Research gave marked impetus to the joint efforts of the large group named here, and many more who are teaching in this field in other institutions, by sponsoring at Harvard a Symposium in Business Policy in 1963. This occasion marked the beginning of a new chapter in an old study; its influence continues. Andrew R. Towl, Director of Case Development and Distribution, and Director of the Intercollegiate Case Clearing House at the Harvard Business School, has lent his support generously to this effort. We hope this book, in which the effort of so many good people is compressed, will contribute to constructive concern for corporate purposes and accomplishments and to the effective study and practice of business policy.

Harvard University
December 1968

EDMUND P. LEARNED
C. ROLAND CHRISTENSEN
KENNETH R. ANDREWS
WILLIAM D. GUTH

Table of contents

INTRODUCTION

BOOK ONE: DETERMINING CORPORATE STRATEGY

The Company and Its Social Responsibilities: Relating Corporate
Strategy and Moral Values 485

The Moral Aspect of Strategic Choice. Relevance of the Public Good. Conflict of Responsibilities. Corporate Responsibility and Individual Self-
Expression. The Problem of Final Choice.

BOOK TWO: IMPLEMENTING CORPORATE STRATEGY

The Accomplishment of Purpose: Organizational Structure
and Relationships 571

Interdependence of Formulation and Implementation. Strategy and Organizational Structure. Subdivision of Task Responsibility. Coordination of
Divided Responsibility. Effective Design of Information Systems.

The Accomplishment of Purpose: Organizational Processes and
Behavior 629

Establishment of Standards and Measurement of Performance. Motivation
and Incentive Systems. Systems of Restraint and Control. Recruitment and
Development of Management.

The Role of Leadership in the Achievement of Purpose 759

The General Manager as Architect of Strategy. The General Manager as Organization Leader. The General Manager as Personal Leader. The Quality of Leadership.

Effecting Major Changes in Strategy and Organization 857

INDEX OF CASES

Introduction

Introduction

Business policy as a field of study

This book is intended as an instrument for the study of Business Policy. As a field in business administration, Policy is the study of the functions and responsibilities of general management and the problems which affect the character and success of the total enterprise. The problems of policy in business, like those of policy in public affairs, have to do with the choice of purposes, the molding of organizational character, the definition of what needs to be done, and the mobilization of resources for the attainment of goals in the face of competition or adverse circumstance. On occasions when more urgent but less important operating problems permit, policy is what the president of a country or a corporation is likely to think about at night.

In Business Policy, the problems considered and the point of view assumed in analyzing and dealing with them are those of the chief executive or general manager, whose primary responsibility is the enterprise as a whole. But while the study of Business Policy (under whatever name it may be called) should be the capstone of professional business education, its usefulness goes far beyond the direct preparation of future general managers and chief executives for the responsibilities of office. In an age of increasing complexity and advancing specialization, and in companies where no person knows how to do what every other person does, it becomes important that the specialist possess the ability to discern corporate purpose, to make recommendations for its clarification or development, and to shape his own contributions, not by the canons of his specialization, but by his perception of the needs of the organization as a whole. The special needs of individuals and the technical requirements of specialized groups and disciplines inevitably develop points of view that ultimately come into conflict with one another and with the central purposes of the organization they serve. The specialist who is able to exercise control over this tendency in organizational life and to keep his deference to the conventions of his own specialty subordinate to the needs of his company becomes free to make creative contributions to its progress

3

and growth. To be thus effective in his organization, he must have a sense of its mission, of its character, and of its importance. If he does not know the purposes he serves, he can hardly serve them well. Most users of this book will neither be nor become corporation presidents, but virtually all can benefit from the detachment implicit in the presidential point of view.

The purposes of organized effort, in business as elsewhere, are usually neither clear, fixed, nor unchanging. Except in abstract language they cannot be communicated once and for all to the variety of persons whose effort and commitment are required. It is not enough, therefore, for senior executives to issue statements of policy and for junior managers to acquiesce and proceed. In each subunit of an organization and in each individual, corporate purpose must become meaningful in ways that announcement cannot accomplish. It must be brought into balance with individual and departmental needs, satisfactions, and noneconomic aspirations. But if corporate purpose is to be reconciled with rather than subordinated to individual and departmental purposes, then there must be widespread knowledge of the considerations on which corporate policy is based, and widespread understanding of the risks by which it is threatened. In addition, the adaptation of corporate purpose to changing circumstances, to tactical countermoves by competitors, or to newly identified opportunities, is assisted if there can be *informed* participation in policy thinking by subordinate executives from different ranks and groups. This advantage, however, can be realized only if these subordinates are capable of looking beyond the narrow limits of their own specializations. Thus the study of Policy is not as remote from the immediate concerns of the apprentice manager or the student of business as at first appears. In fact, whenever a man is challenged—in business or out—by the problem of establishing goals *for himself* that will shape a productive and satisfying life, he will find the study of the process of determining strategy of central relevance. It is helpful to personal as well as to corporate decision, and to the discovery of the individual's own powers and the purposes to which they might well be devoted.

The study of Business Policy provides, therefore, a direct if distant preparation for performance as a general manager, and a less direct but more immediate broadening of the provincial perspective of the specialist. In addition, it may be viewed as resulting in certain *knowledge, attitudes,* and *skills*. Some of these are unique to Policy studies. Others may have germinated in other activities and learning. But the latter are brought to fruition by examination of the most fundamental issues and problems that confront the professional manager in the course of a business career. It may prove useful to characterize briefly the expected outcomes.

Objectives in knowledge

The choice of objectives and the formulation of policy to guide action in attainment of objectives depend upon many variables unique to a given organization and situation. It is not possible to make useful generalizations about the nature of these variables or to classify their possible combinations in all situations. Knowledge of what, *in general*, Policy is and should be is incomplete and inconclusive. The knowledge to be gained from Policy studies is therefore primarily a familiarity with an approach to the policy problems of business and public affairs which makes it possible, in conjunction with attitudes and skills to be discussed later, to combine these variables into a pattern valid for one organization. This pattern may then be examined against accepted criteria and tested for its quality.

The basic concept that the student of Policy will in time come to understand is the concept of *strategy*, since the design and implementation of strategy provide the intellectual substance of this study. What is meant by *strategy* and, more important, how this concept may be usefully employed in the choice and accomplishment of purpose is the subject of the rest of this book. Strategy will be the idea unifying the discussions in which the student will engage. These discussions will involve cerebral activities more important than simply acquiring information.

An abundance of information about business practice is, nonetheless, a by-product of the study of Business Policy—and other—cases. In their deliberately planned variety, the cases in this book encompass many industries, companies, and business situations. Although the information contained in these cases is provided mainly to permit consideration of policy issues, the importance of this incidental knowledge should not be underestimated. Breadth of exposure to the conventions, points of view, and practices of many industries is inoculation against the assumption that all industries are basically the same or that all businessmen share the same values and belief. Thus consideration of the policy problems of a number of different industries guards against distraction by the particular in seeking out the nature of the universal.

For this reason it is hoped that the student—although he may be, or plan to be, an engineer in a utility or the vice president of a railroad—will not resent learning about the economics of the cement industry of England or the problems of allocating research funds in an electronics firm. Knowledge of the environment and problems of other industries and companies is something that the student may never consciously use. It will nevertheless widen the perspective which he brings to his own problems. It may stimulate the imagination he puts to work in introducing innovation into the obsolescent practices of his own industry. It should provide a broader base for his powers of generalization.

The study of strategy as a concept will be relatively systematic; the acquisition of information about the management problems of the many firms and industries whose strategic problems are presented in this book will be less orderly. Both are important. In particular the time spent in mastering the detail of the cases will ultimately seem to be of greater value than at first appears.

A considerable body of literature purporting to make general statements about policy making is in existence. It generally reflects either the unsystematically reported experience of individuals or the logical projection to general management of concepts taken from engineering, economics, psychology, sociology, or mathematics. Neither suffices. What men wise in practice have to say is often instructive, but intuitive skill cannot be changed into conscious skill by exposition alone. The disciplines cited have much to do with business, but their purposes are not ours. Knowledge generated for one set of ends is not readily applicable to another. Besides reported experience and borrowed concepts, the literature of the field also includes some first fruits of independent research, guided by designs derived from the idea of strategy. Such research has been for some time under way, but it is not yet advanced enough to make more than a modest claim on our attention. Thus, though we shall often allude to the expository literature of Policy and shall, where appropriate, acknowledge our considerable indebtedness to it, yet the most valid literature for our purpose is not that of general statements but case studies.[1] These present, not illustrations of principle, but data from which generalizations may to a limited degree be derived and to which the idea of strategy may be usefully applied.

Objectives in attitudes

Knowledge of either concepts or cases is less the objective of the study of Policy than certain attitudes and skills. What a manager knows by way of verifiable fact about management appears to us less important than the attitudes, aspirations, and values that he brings to his tasks. Instructors in Policy do not have a dogma which they force upon their students, but most of them, like their students, appear to be influenced in their analysis and conclusions by characteristic assumptions. Thus indoctrination is implicit in the study of the ideas and cases included in this book; this indoctrination —tempered by the authors' exhortation to the student to think always for himself—is comprised of some important beliefs of which the student should be aware.

The attitudes appropriate to the resolution of policy problems are several. First, the frame of mind which the student will be encouraged to adopt and which will influence the outcome of his thinking is that of the *generalist* rather than the specialist. Breadth, it follows, takes precedence over depth. Since attitudes appropriate for the generalist are not always appropriate for the specialist, the two will sometimes come into conflict. Efforts to resolve this conflict in practice should help to prove that breadth which is shallow is no more satisfactory than depth which is narrow.

---

[1]In addition to the cases in this book, the reader is referred to such volumes as G. A. Smith, Jr., C. R. Christensen, and N. A. Berg, *Policy Formulation and Administration;* E. P. Learned, C. R. Christensen, and K. R. Andrews, *Problems of General Management;* and E. P. Learned, F. J. Aguilar, and R. C. K. Valtz, *European Problems in General Management* (all published by Richard D. Irwin, Inc., Homewood, Illinois). Many other cases from a variety of sources are listed in the bibliographies of the Intercollegiate Case Clearing House, Soldiers Field, Boston, Mass. 02163.

A second outlook encountered in the study of Business Policy is the point of view of the *practitioner* as opposed to that of the researcher or scientist. A willingness to act in the face of incomplete information and to run the risk of being proved wrong by subsequent events will be developed in the classroom as pressure is brought to bear on the student to make decisions on the problems before him and to determine what he, as the manager responsible, would do about them. Despite the explosion of knowledge and the widely heralded advance of electronic data processing, it is still true that decisions affecting the business firm as a whole must almost always be made in the face of incomplete information. Uncertainty is the lot of all thoughtful leaders who must act, whether they are in government, education, or business. Acceptance of the priority of risk-taking and the problem resolution over completeness of information is sometimes hard for students of science and engineering to achieve. Though natural and understandable, hesitation in the face of the managerial imperative to make decisions will impede the study of Policy. At the same time, rashness, overconfidence, and the impulse to act without analysis will be discouraged.

The third set of attitudes to be developed is the orientation of the professional businessman as distinct from the self-seeking contriver of deals. The energetic opportunist sometimes has motives which are inconsistent with the approach to policy embodied in this book. This is not to say that quick response to opportunity and entrepreneurial energy are not qualities to be admired. Our assumption will be that the role of the businessman includes but goes beyond the entrepreneurial function. We shall examine what we acknowledge to be the obligations of the business community to the rest of society. We shall be concerned with the quality as well as the clarity of the alternative purposes we consider and of our final choice. Maximum short-run profit is not what we mean when we consider the purpose of business enterprise. At the same time it is assumed that profit is desirable and indispensable. It is one of the necessary *results* of business activity.

A fourth set of attitudes to be evoked is one that attaches more value to creativity and innovation than to maintenance of the status quo. We have grown accustomed to innovation stemming from new inventions and advancing technology. But suiting policy to changing circumstances includes also the application of a firm's long-established strengths to unexplored segments of the market via innovations in price, service, distribution, or merchandising.

In any course of study that has as its object enabling practitioners to learn more from subsequent experience than they otherwise might, the attitudes appropriate to the professional activity being taught are as important as knowledge. It is therefore expected that the student will take time to determine for himself the particular point of view, the values, and the morality which he feels are appropriate to the effective exercise of general management skills. Much more could be said about the frame of mind and qualities of temperament that are most appropriate to business leadership, but we will do better to let these exhibit themselves in the discussion of case problems.

Objectives in skills

Extensive knowledge and positive attitudes, desirable as both are, come to little if not effectively applied. The skills that a course in Business Policy seeks to develop and mature are at once analytical and administrative. Since even with a variety of simulation and the use of case situations drawn from life, the reality of responsibility can only be approximated in a professional school, we may look to make most progress in analytical power and to use it in actual experience to develop executive ability.

The study of Policy cases, unlike, for example, the effort to comprehend these expository notes, requires the student to develop and broaden the analytical ability he brings to the task from other studies. The policy problems of the total enterprise are not labeled as accounting, financial, marketing, production, or human relations problems. The student is not forewarned of the kind of problem he can expect and of which tool kit he should have with him. He must now consider problems in relation to one another, distinguish the more from the less important, and consider the impact of his approach to one problem upon all the others. He will bring to the cases his knowledge and abilities in special fields, but he will be asked to diagnose first the total situation and to persist in seeking out central problems through all the distraction presented by manifest symptoms.

The study of Policy, besides having its own jurisdiction, has an integrative function. It asks the analyst to view a company as an organic entity comprising a system in itself, but related also to the larger systems of its environment. In each diagnostic situation, the student must pull together the separate concepts he has studied in functional and basic discipline courses and adapt them to a less structured set of problems. He must be able to see and to devise patterns of information, activities, and relationships. If he deals one at a time with the facts he is given or the problems he observes, he will be overwhelmed.

Besides extending to the company as a multifaceted whole the knowledge and analytic skills developed in his less comprehensive studies, the student of Policy must acquire some additional abilities. These are abilities particularly needed to deal with the concept of strategy. Under the heading of thinking about strategy, the student will be asked to examine the economic environment of the company, to determine the essential characteristics of the industry, to note its developments and trends, and to estimate future opportunity and risks for firms of varying resources and competence. He will be asked to appraise the strengths and weaknesses of the particular firm he is studying when viewed against the background of its competition and its environment, and he will be asked to estimate its capacity to alter as well as to adapt to the forces affecting it. Finally, he will be asked to make a decision putting market opportunity and corporate capability together into a suitable entrepreneurial combination. At this point he will realize the full measure of the new skill required. The strategic decision is the one that determines the nature of the business in which a company is to engage and the kind of company it is to be. As such, it is the most important decision to be made for the company. It requires the best judgment and analysis that can be brought to it. Practice in making this decision while still safe from most of the consequences of error is one of the most important advantages offered by an education for business.

But analysis is not the whole of the task implied by the concept of strategy. Once the entrepreneurial decision has been determined, the resources of the organization must be mobilized to make it effective. Devising organizational relationships appropriate to the tasks to be performed, determining the specialized talents required, and assisting and providing for the development of individuals and subgroups are essential tasks of strategy and policy implementation. These tasks, together with those of prescribing a system of incentives and controls that will be appropriate to the performance required, and determining the impetus that can be given to achievement by the general manager's personal style of leadership, demand of the student that he bring to the discussion of Policy everything he has learned about administrative processes.

Administrative skills can be approached, though not captured, in the classroom. Patterns of action will be judged as consistent or inconsistent with the strategy selected according to criteria which must be developed. The student approaches the study of Business Policy with skills nurtured in his studies of accounting and control, personnel and human relations, financial management, manufacturing, and marketing; the balanced application of these skills to the accomplishment of chosen purpose in a unique organizational situation is the best test of their power. Any failure to see the impact on the program as a whole of a decision based on the tenets of a special discipline will be sharply called to its proponent's attention by the defenders of other points of view.

General management skills center intellectually upon relating the firm to its environment and administratively upon coordinating departmental specialties and points of view. Some students of business and even some students of Policy believe that these skills cannot be taught. General management is indeed an art to be learned in the last analysis only through years of responsible experience. And even through experience it can be learned only by those with the necessary native qualities: intelligence, a sense of responsibility, and administrative ability.

But if education means anything at all, a student with the requisite native qualities can learn more readily and more certainly from experience, and can more readily identify the kinds of seminal experience to seek, if he has at his disposal a conceptual framework with which to comprehend the analytical and administrative skills he will require and the nature of the situation in which he will find himself. If, in addition, he has had practice in making and debating the merits of policy decisions, he will be more likely to grow in qualification for senior management responsibility than if he is submerged in operational detail and preoccupied by the intricacies of technique.

This book is not a manual for policymakers or a how-to-do-it checklist for corporate planners. In fact it virtually ignores the mechanisms of planning on the grounds that they often miss their mark. The authors do not believe that the conceptual framework described here can take the place of informed judgment. All the knowledge, professional attitudes, and analytical and administrative skills in the world cannot fully replace the intuitive genius of some of the natural entrepreneurs the student will encounter in this book. Native powers cannot be counterfeited by book learning.

We do not even propose book learning in the usual sense. We plan instead to give men with latent imagination the opportunity to exercise it in a disciplined way under critical observation. We expect to prepare men for the assumption of responsibility by exposing them to the temptation of expediency. We plan to press for clarification of personal purposes and to challenge shoddy or ill-considered values. We expect to affect permanently analytical habits of mind in a way that will permit assimilation of all, rather than part, of experience. The ideas, attitudes, and skills here discussed are adequate for a lifetime study of one of the most vitally important of all human activities—leadership in organizations. Education is the prelude to true learning, which often does not take place without it.

The need for general management ability is far too acute to be left to chance. The ideas, attitudes, and skills that comprise this study are much in demand not only throughout our own economy but also—in this age of rapid economic development abroad—throughout the world. In addition to their utility, these ideas are their own reward. For those who wish to lead an active life, or to provide for themselves and their families the material comfort and education that make culture possible, or to make substantial contributions to human welfare, the acquisition of policy skills is essential. Not all who turn to business are called to leadership, to be sure, but all are affected by it. No one suffers from study of its place in business.

The nature of the text and cases

The vehicles here provided for making progress toward these objectives are the text and cases that follow. All the cases are drawn from real life; none is selected to prove a point or draw a moral. Accuracy has been attested to by the sources from which information was taken; disguise has not been allowed to alter essential issues.

The text is designed to assist in the development of an effective approach to the cases. Its content is important only if it helps the student to make his analysis, to choose and defend his conclusions, and to decide what ought to be done and how it can be accomplished.

The text is dispersed throughout the book so as to permit a step-by-step consideration of what is involved in corporate strategy and in the subactivities required for its formulation and implementation. The order of cases is only partially determined by the sequence of ideas in the text. Each case should be approached without preconceptions as to what is to come. To make conceptual progress possible without predetermining the student's analysis of the problem or the nature of his recommendations, the cases focus initially on problems in strategy formulation and later on problems of building the organization and leading it to the accomplishment of the tasks assigned. As the course unfolds, considerations pertinent to previous cases are included in the new cases, at the end, a long case series encompasses the full range of policy considerations. Students should not feel constrained in their analysis by the position of the case in the book; they are free to decide that an apparent problem of strategy implementation is actually a problem of strategy choice. However, the increasing complexity of the material provided will enable most students to feel a natural and organic evolution of subject matter, in keeping with their own evolving understanding, perspective, and skill.

The text suggests only that order is possible in approaching the enormous purview of Policy. The concept of strategy is an idea that experience has shown to be useful to researchers and practitioners alike in developing a comprehension of, and an approach to, policy problems. It is not a "theory" attended in the traditional sense by elegance and rigor. Only a very kindly "management scientist" will call it a "model," inasmuch as the relationships designated by the concept are not quantifiable. But in lieu of a better theory or a more precise model, it will serve as an informing idea to which we can return again and again with increasing understanding after dealing with one unique case situation after another. The idea is intended to sharpen the analytical skills developed in the process of case discussion, and to serve as the basis for identifying uniformities and generalizations that will be useful later on, in practice. Our energies should be spent not so much on perfecting the definition of the concept as on using it in preparing to discuss the cases and in coming to conclusions about their issues. The student will not really learn how to distinguish effective from ineffective recommendations and good from bad judgment by his study of the "word," but rather by active argument with his classmates. Such discussion should always end in the clarification of his own standards and criteria. The cases, we know from experience, provide stimulating opportunity for productive differences of opinion.

Book One

determining corporate strategy

The concept of corporate strategy

I t is the purpose of this text to make clear the idea of corporate strategy, the uses and limitations of the concept, the criteria that may be used to test the soundness and viability of a strategy, and the problems of evaluation that we may expect to encounter in considering strategic alternatives.

Definition

Our use of the term corporate strategy comprises more than the usual military connotations of this term. For the military, strategy is most simply the positioning of armed forces on the battlefield to accomplish the defeat of the enemy. Less simply, it is the deployment of resources against an enemy in pursuit of goals prescribed by the leaders of the state. When we pass, as we must, from the military to the political sphere, strategy becomes the application of national resources to the accomplishment of national goals.

Our use of the term strategy extends its meaning still further to encompass the choice of goals, as well as the plans for attaining goals. The economist speaks often of strategy as the allocation of scarce resources; we intend more than the closely related selection of product-market relationships. For us strategy is the pattern of objectives, purposes, or goals and major policies and plans for achieving these goals, stated in such a way as to define what business the company is in or is to be in and the kind of company it is or is to be.

Because we are less concerned with exactness of language than we might be if development of theory were our first objective, we do not argue the question whether the term strategy should include the selection of goals or denote only the deployment of resources marshaled in pursuit of these goals. It is to us a matter of indifference. Little confusion results so long as we make clear what we are doing. In our experience, simplicity and convenience are served by combining the choice of goals and the formulation of major

15

policy into one activity. The choice of goals and the formulation of policy cannot in any case be separate decisions. The Stanford Research Institute takes a different path when it equates strategy with the ways in which the firm, reacting to its environment, deploys its principal resources and marshals its main efforts in pursuit of its purpose. Alfred Chandler, in *Strategy and Structure*, takes the direction we favor when he called strategy, ". . . the determination of the basic long-term goals and objectives of an enterprise, and the adoption of courses of action and the allocation of resources necessary for carrying out these goals."[1]

A more important effort to subdivide the idea of strategy seeks to segregate those aspects that are enduring and unchanging over relatively long periods of time from those that are necessarily more responsive to changes in the marketplace and the pressures of other environmental forces. The strategic decision is concerned with the long-term development of the enterprise. The central character of a business organization and the individuality it has for its members and its various publics may, in the instance of mature and highly developed corporations, be determined with some clarity.

Thus the "personality" of firms like Polaroid, Xerox, Control Data, IBM, and General Motors clearly reflects aspects of company intent that are manifested only partially in such activities as research expenditures, choice of product line, and the recruitment and development of organization members. It would be likely to persist through substantial changes in the allocation of resources and in product policy, in part because the basic determinants of organization character would tend to prevent sharp discontinuity. The central character of *The New York Times* is likely to be unchanged, even if the services it offers are altered drastically in the direction of increased emphasis on its news service or on the development of other outlets for its news-processing capacity. In this view, the basic character of an enterprise and the core of its special competence would be considered separately from the manifestation of these long-range characteristics in changing product lines, markets, and policies designed to make activities profitable from year to year.

Our primary interest in isolating the need for strategic decision in concrete instances and in determining the most satisfactory pattern of goals and policies makes further refinement of definition or defense of our own preference of little importance. The student will wish to develop the definition presented here in directions which are useful to him. But before we proceed to clarification by application, we should comment on the terms in which strategy is usually expressed.

A complete summary statement of strategy will in fact say less about what the word means than it does about the company involved. First, it will define

---

[1] Alfred D. Chandler, Jr., *Strategy and Structure: Chapters in the History of the Industrial Enterprise* (Cambridge, Mass.: The M.I.T. Press, 1962), p. 13.

extent to which present profits will be forgone to prepare for larger profits at a later time is unspecified. The desirability of profit, like that of survival, good health, and growth, does not make it a magnetic pole establishing a directed course among many alternatives.

In an era of rapid change and intense interindustry and intereconomy competition, improvisation, however brilliant, cannot suffice as a company's sole weapon against the negative effects of change. The range of activities planned in advance is generally wider than that determinable on the spur of the moment. Many moves, because they require long preparation, cannot be made at all without forward planning. When new product development requires years and a new distribution network may cost millions of dollars, purpose must necessarily be considered in detail well in advance of investment.

Colorful intuitive leadership may seem to render conscious planning unnecessary. For example, the elder Mr. Baker of Baker Metal and Foil[3] repeatedly confounded his subordinates by buying plants and equipment on the spur of the moment. He planned his moves in the solitude of his study during the early hours of the morning, and he doubtless reached a clear decision in his own mind about where he wanted to go. His vision was responsible for his company's status as a leader in its industry. But had he been able to articulate his goals, his associates—relieved of the frustration occasioned by continued chaos—could have more easily performed the financial planning to make them feasible. The forward look which Mr. Baker took in solitude did not in itself constitute the formulation of a coherent strategy that would permit his organization to know what he was up to and what was required of them.

Planned purpose can affect and change the character of future developments which otherwise might endanger even the healthiest organization. Reliance upon adaptation alone leaves the company at the mercy of the strongest currents. Innovation, and the creativity which supports it, can enable a company to carve out its own future rather than simply to depend on favorable circumstances. But such a course requires predetermination of what must be done. Thus at least one manufacturer of small radios and another of camera equipment, apparently about to be overwhelmed by Japanese imports, stemmed the tide and reversed a trend by a program comprising cost reduction, product restyling, and improved marketing, all of which took time and predetermined purpose to perfect.

From the point of view of implementation, the most important function of strategy is to serve as the focus of organizational effort, as the object of commitment, and as the source of constructive motivation and self-control in the organization itself. We shall have ample opportunity to see later that it is a common understanding of the goals to be served and a widespread acceptance of their importance, persisting through the inevitable distortions

---

[3]See G. A. Smith and C. R. Christensen, *Policy Formulation and Administration* (rev. ed.; Homewood, Ill.: Richard D. Irwin, Inc., 1955), p. 453.

products in terms more functional than literal, saying what they do rather than what they are made of. At the same time, it will designate clearly the markets and market segments for which products are now or will be designed, and the channels through which these markets will be reached. The means by which the operation is to be financed will be specified, as will the emphasis to be placed on safety of capital versus income return. Finally, the size and kind of organization which is to be the medium of achievement will be described. It is, of course, more important that the identification of strategy capture the present and projected character of the organization than that it elaborate the categories of purpose just cited.

Thus of Continental Watchmakers Company,[2] a Swiss firm, we could say:

It is Mr. Keller's present plan to produce watches of the highest quality—in a price range between the hand-made ultra-exclusive level and Omega and Rolex. He aims to distribute his watches to all markets of the free world via exclusive wholesale agents and carefully chosen retailers, who are expected to convince customers of the particular value of the product. His growth of about 10% per year is not geared to demand but is deliberately restricted to the productivity of available skilled labor, and to his recognition of cyclical fluctuations in the industry. He aims to maintain within the rules of the industry a stable organization of highly skilled, fully trained workers and a management organization of some breadth, but he apparently wishes to retain personal direction over marketing and a close familiarity with the whole organization.

Companies seldom formulate and publish as complete a statement as we have just illustrated, usually because conscious planning is not carried far enough to achieve the agreement or clarification which publication presumes. These cases enable the student of Policy to do what the managements of the companies usually have not done. In the absence of explicit statements, the student may deduce from operations what the goals and policies are, on the assumption that all normal human behavior is purposeful. Careful examination of the behavior described in the cases will reveal what the strategy must be. At the same time, it is desirable not to infer a degree of conscious planning which does not in fact exist. The current strategy of a company may almost always be deduced from its behavior, but a strategy for a future of changed circumstance may not always be distinguishable from performance in the present.

Corporate strategy has two equally important aspects, interrelated in life but separated to the extent practicable in our study of the concept. The first of these is formulation; the second is implementation. Deciding what strategy should be is, at least ideally, a rational undertaking. Its principal subactivities include identifying opportunities and threats in the company's environment and attaching some estimate of risk to the discernible alternatives. Before

---

[2]See E. P. Learned, C. R. Christensen, and K. R. Andrews, *Problems of General Management—Business Policy* (Homewood, Ill.: Richard D. Irwin, Inc., 1961), p. 88.

a choice can be made, the company's strengths and weaknesses must be appraised. Its actual or potential capacity to take advantage of perceived market needs or to cope with attendant risks must be estimated as objectively as possible. The strategic alternative which results from a matching of opportunity and corporate capability at an acceptable level of risk is what we may call an *economic strategy*.

The process described thus far assumes that the strategist is analytically objective in estimating the relative capacity of his company and the opportunity he sees or anticipates in developing markets. The extent to which he wishes to undertake low or high risk presumably depends on his profit objective. The higher he sets the latter, the more willing he must be to assume a correspondingly high risk that the market opportunity he sees will not develop or that the corporate competence required to excel competition will not be forthcoming.

So far we have described the intellectual processes of ascertaining what a company *might do* in terms of environmental opportunity, of deciding what it *can do* in terms of ability and power, and of bringing these two considerations together in optimal equilibrium. The determination of strategy also requires consideration of what alternative is preferred by the chief executive and perhaps by his immediate associates as well, quite apart from economic considerations. Personal values, aspirations, and ideals do, and in our judgment quite properly should, influence the final choice of purposes. Thus what the executives of a company *want to do* must be brought into the strategic decision.

Finally, strategic choice has an ethical aspect—a fact much more dramatically illustrated in some industries than in others. Just as alternatives may be ordered in terms of the degree of risk that they entail, so may they be examined against the standards of responsibility that the strategist elects. Some alternatives may seem to the executive considering them more attractive than others when the public good or service to society is considered. What a company *should do* thus appears as a fourth element of the fateful decision we have called strategic.

The ability to identify the four components of strategy—(1) market opportunity, (2) corporate competence and resources, (3) personal values and aspirations, and (4) acknowledged obligations to segments of society other than the stockholders—is nothing compared to the art of reconciling their implications in a final choice of purpose. Taken by itself, each consideration might lead in a different direction.

For example, the manager of a radio station that is declining in ratings and income may decide that in his community the teen-age clientele is his best market, especially given the programming practices of competing stations. His program directors, announcers, and advertising salesmen are experienced, however, only in providing a mixture of news, music, and commercials addressed to the adult commuter-motorist, with housewife fare broadcast between rush hours. The manager may hate rock-and-roll music and com-

mercials addressed to the skin problems of adolescents, and ... have no real rapport with younger listeners. He may believe that ... granted his station to make profit-making use of a publicly owne... as well as the policies of the Federal Communications Commissic ... him to some degree of public service more substantial than ai... and roll.

Something will have to give before a unified strategy can be achie... of this divergence. At first glance it appears that making a convention... and-roll approach to teen-agers is out, unless personal taste and se... responsibility are to be wholly ignored. Some innovations will be req... to end the impasse—either a new approach to teen-age listeners or ... successful programming for the audience preferred. A pioneering reconc... tion is required, for the conventional alternatives in radio programming... inadequate for this problem. Furthermore, the balance finally struck mu... be adaptable to further changes in the community environment.

The implementation of strategy is comprised of a series of subactivities which are primarily administrative. Once purpose is determined, then the resources of a company must be mobilized to accomplish it. An organizational structure that is appropriate for the efficient performance of the required tasks must be made effective by information systems and relationships permitting coordination of subdivided activities. The organizational processes of performance measurement, compensation, management development—all of them enmeshed in systems of incentives and controls—must be directed toward the kind of behavior required by organizational purpose. The role of personal leadership is important and sometimes decisive in the accomplishment of strategy. Since effective implementation can make a sound strategic decision ineffective or a debatable choice thoroughly successful, it is as important to examine the processes of implementation as to weigh the advantages of the available strategic alternatives.

The functions of strategy

It is relatively rare, although in substantial organizations less and less so, to encounter the conscious attention to strategy which our definition suggests is appropriate. The many reasons need not detain us now. At the moment, we should consider whether the advantages of a consciously considered strategy are worth the effort it obviously requires. Four considerations suggest an affirmative answer. These are the inadequacy of stating goals only in terms of maximum profit, the necessity of planning ahead in undertakings with long lead times, the need of influencing rather than merely responding to environmental change, and the utility of setting visible goals as an inspiration to organizational effort.

The age-old assertion that the only true purpose of business is profit is no substitute for a more detailed program. To specify how much profit in terms of "as much as possible" leaves unanswered questions about how it is to be made and whether any restraints are to be observed in the quest. The

of individual and departmental needs, that are the soundest bases of cooperative action.

The limitations of strategy

These claims regarding the value of formulating a strategy are stated as ideas to be examined and tested, for the practice is not without its limitations. One objection sometimes voiced is that strategy involves planning, ✓ and that planning ahead poses serious obstacles. With increasing complexity and an accelerating rate of change, it grows more and more difficult to predict the future in detail. Long-range plans cannot be detailed quantitatively with much confidence. Accuracy in forecasting is impossible. These complaints are not real limitations, however, for strategy does not require more knowledge of the future than we have. The extent to which a variety of alternatives is studied in advance reduces the possibility of surprise and permits the preparation of alternative plans for a range of possibilities. The more uncertain the future, in fact, the more necessary it is to contemplate what can happen and what is likely to happen and to assign probabilities to the imaginable possibilities.

A more serious limitation is that overdedication to plan may result in ✓ lost opportunity. The rise of research expenditures and the impossibility of knowing in advance what research will bring forth often lead opponents of planning to say with some justice that maintenance of flexibility to take advantage of unanticipated opportunity is more important than commitment to fixed plans over long time periods. One must admit at once that the determination of strategy must not be so rigid that unexpected opportunity cannot be considered. But it is possible to conceive of strategy as being firm and influential without its being cast in concrete. We shall ultimately be able to conceive of strategy as performing all that we ask of it without ever becoming finally solidified. To accommodate uncertainty and to preserve flexibility are not the easiest activities in the world, but a strategy formulated without regard for these necessities would indeed be folly. What is needed is the concept of a moving balance among the considerations on which strategy is based, the concept of a strategy that progressively evolves in the direction of improving the match between the company's resources and the opportunities in its environment. To design a strategy that is *optimal* is a challenge ✓ to insight and intelligence which simply lies beyond the capacity of many an effective operator. The skill required in the use of an idea may be a limitation to its usefulness.

A third set of limitations and problems which requires us to say at once ✓ that the concept of strategy is no panacea is the inevitability of conflict between corporate and departmental goals and between organizational and personal goals. We shall have more to say about these impediments to effective implementation at a later time. In the meantime we must accept as a fact of life that the most articulate, specific, and persuasive definition of strategy by the president of a company, ratified by the board of directors and promptly emulated by competitors, will never have the same meaning or appeal to all parts of the organization to which it is announced. To communicate a strategy requires as much trouble and time as to conceive it. To adhere to it wisely under the temptations posed by expediency is difficult. To adhere to it blindly when changing circumstance has made it obsolete is no more preferable than thoughtless opportunism. New opportunities, unexpected innovations, sudden emergencies, competitive pressures, and incomplete programming of action required by the strategy selected all constitute real problems in adhering to a plan once it has been made clear.

The limitations of the concept of strategy consist principally of the inherent difficulties of conceiving a viable pattern of goals and policies and implementing them wisely. Dealing with these limitations effectively means not abandoning the concept, but learning to use it successfully with reasonable perspective on what is possible. We cannot expect the concept of strategy to be a substitute for judgment or a shortcut to wisdom. It does not in itself point out the course of action to be taken in difficult situations. Nevertheless, it is the strategic decision to which judgment must be applied. Wisdom cannot be brought to a decision that is not recognized as needed. No consideration of the limitations of this idea invalidates the proposition that the essential business and character of an enterprise should be determined well in advance of shifting circumstances (which will otherwise become the determining factors), if the future of the corporation is to be kept to an appreciable extent within the control of its management.

Criteria for evaluation

The attempt to identify the actual or optimal strategy for a business firm raises at once the question of how the actual or proposed strategy is to be judged. How are we to know that one strategy is better than another in advance of validation by experience? As is already evident, no infallible indicators are available. A number of important questions can regularly be asked.[4] With practice they will lead to intuitive discriminations.

1. *Is the strategy indentifiable and has it been made clear either in words or practice?*

The degree to which attention has been given to the strategic alternatives available to a company is likely to be basic to the soundness of its strategic decision. To cover in empty phrases ("our policy is planned profitable growth in any market we can serve well") an absence of analysis of opportunity or actual determination of corporate strength is worse than to remain silent, for it conveys the illusion of a commitment when none has been made. The unstated strategy cannot be tested or contested and is likely therefore to be weak. If it is implicit in the intuition of a strong leader, his organization is likely to be weak and the demands his strategy makes upon it are likely to remain unmet.

---

[4]For an earlier statement of most of the criteria discussed here, see Seymour Tilles, "How to Evaluate Corporate Strategy," *Harvard Business Review*, July-August 1963, p. 111.

2. *Does the strategy exploit fully domestic and international environmental opportunity?*

An unqualified yes answer is likely to be rare even in the instance of global giants like General Motors. But the present and future dimensions of markets can be analyzed without forgetting the limited resources of the planning company in order to outline the requirements of balanced growth and the need for environmental information. The relation between market opportunity and organizational development is a critical one in the design of future plans. Unless growth is incompatible with the resources of an organization or the aspirations of its management, it is likely that a strategy that does not purport to make full use of market opportunity will be weak also in other respects. Vulnerability to competition is increased by lack of interest in market share.

3. *Is the strategy consistent with corporate competence and resources, both present and projected?*

Although additional resources, both financial and managerial, are available to companies with genuine opportunity, the availability of each must be finally determined and programmed along a practicable time scale. The decision of the Wilkinson Sword Company to distribute stainless steel razor blades in the United States must have raised the question whether the company could in effect takes yes for an answer from this market—that is, whether its productive capacity could be increased fast enough to fend off the countermoves of large competitors.

4. *Are the major provisions of the strategy and the program of major policies of which it is comprised internally consistent?*

A foolish consistency is the hobgoblin of little minds, and consistency of any kind is certainly not the first qualification of successful corporation presidents. Nonetheless, one advantage of making as specific a statement of strategy as is practicable is the resultant availability of a careful check on coherence, compatability, and synergy—the state in which the whole can be viewed as greater than the sum of its parts. For example, a manufacturer of chocolate candy who depends for two-thirds of his business upon wholesalers should not follow a policy of ignoring them or of dropping all support of their activities and all attention to their complaints. Similarly, two engineers who found a new firm expressly to do development work should not follow a policy of accepting orders that, though highly profitable, in effect turn their company into a large job shop, with the result that unanticipated financial and production problems take all the time that might have gone into development. An examination of any substantial firm will reveal at least some details in which policies pursued by different departments tend to go in different directions. Where inconsistency threatens concerted effort to achieve budgeted results within a planned time period, then consistency becomes a vital rather than merely an aesthetic problem.

5. *Is the chosen level of risk feasible in economic and personal terms?*

Strategies vary in the degree of risk willingly undertaken by their designers. For example, the Midway Foods Company,[5] in pursuit of its marketing strategy,

[5]See Learned, Christensen, and Andrews, *op. cit.*, p. 143.

deliberately courts disaster in production slowdowns and in erratic behavior of cocoa futures. But the choice is made knowingly and the return, if success is achieved, is likely to be correspondingly great. Temperamentally the president is willing to live under this pressure and presumably has recourse if disaster strikes. At the other extreme, a company may have such modest growth aspirations that the junior members of its management are unhappy. A more aggressive and ambitious company would be their choice. Although risk cannot always be assessed scientifically, the level at which it is set is, within limits, optional. The riskiness of any future plan should be compatible with the economic resources of the organization and the temperament of the managers concerned.

6. *Is the strategy appropriate to the personal values and aspirations of the key managers?*

Until we consider the relationship of personal values to the choice of strategy, it is not useful to dwell long upon this criterion. But, to cite an extreme case, the deliberate falsification of warehouse receipts to conceal the absence of soybean oil from the tanks which are supposed to contain it would not be an element of competitive strategy to which most of us would like to be committed. A strong attraction of leisure, to cite a less extreme example, is inconsistent with a strategy requiring all-out effort from the senior members of a company. Or if, for example, the president abhors conflict and competition, then it can be predicted that the hard-driving firm of an earlier day will have to change its strategy. Conflict between the personal preferences, aspirations, and goals of the key members of an organization and the plan for its future is a sign of danger and a harbinger of mediocre performance or failure.

7. *Is the strategy appropriate to the desired level of contribution to society?*

Closely allied to the value criterion is the ethical criterion. As the professional obligations of business are acknowledged by an increasing number of senior managers, it grows more and more appropriate to ask whether the current strategy of a firm is as socially responsible as it might be. Although it can be argued that filling any economic need contributes to the social good, it is clear that a manufacturer of cigarettes might well consider diversification on grounds other than his fear of future legislation.

8. *Does the strategy constitute a clear stimulus to organizational effort and commitment?*

For organizations which aspire not merely to survive but to lead and to generate productive performance in a climate that will encourage the development of competence and the satisfaction of individual needs, the strategy selected should be examined for its inherent attractiveness to the organization. Some undertakings are inherently more likely to gain the commitment of able men of goodwill than others. Given the variety of human preferences, it is risky to illustrate this difference briefly. But currently a company that is vigorously expanding its overseas operations finds that several of its socially conscious young men exhibit more zeal in connection with its work in developing countries than in Europe. Generally speaking, the bolder the choice of goals and the wider the range of human needs they reflect, the more successfully they will appeal to the capable membership of a healthy and energetic organization.

9. *Are there early indications of the responsiveness of markets and market segments to the strategy?*

Results, no matter how long postponed by necessary preparations, are, of course, the most telling indicators of soundness, so long as they are read correctly at the proper time. A strategy may pass with flying colors all the tests so far proposed, and may be in internal consistency and uniqueness an admirable work of art. But if within a time period made reasonable by the company's resources and the original plan the strategy does not work, then it must be weak in some way that has escaped attention. Bad luck, faulty implementation, and competitive countermoves may be more to blame for unsatisfactory results than flaws in design, but the possibility of the latter should not be unduly discounted. Conceiving a strategy that will win the company a unique place in the business community, that will give it an enduring concept of itself, that will harmonize its diverse activities, and that will provide a fit between environmental opportunity and present or potential company strength is an extremely complicated task, so we cannot expect simple tests of soundness to tell the whole story. But an analytical examination of any company's strategy against the several criteria here suggested will nonetheless give anyone concerned with making, proving, or contributing to corporate planning a good deal to think about.

Problems of evaluation

The evaluation of strategy is as much an act of judgment as is the original conception, and may be as subject to error. The most common source of difficulty is the misevaluation of current results. When results are unsatisfactory, as we have just pointed out, a reexamination of strategy is called for. At the same time, outstandingly good current results are not necessarily evidence that the strategy is sound. For example, a candy manufacturer made more money from his newly established retail stores just after the war than from the rest of his operations, but these profits were poor evidence that he was doing what he should have been doing. With the end of sugar rationing and the return of a buyers' market, he went bankrupt. Extrapolation of present performance into the future, overoptimism and complacence, and underestimation of competitive response and of the time required to accommodate to changes in demand are often by-products of success. Usually high profits may blind the unwary manager to impending environmental change. His concern for the future can under no circumstances be safely suspended. Conversely, a high-risk strategy that has failed was not necessarily a mistake, so long as the risk was anticipated and the consequences of failure carefully calculated. In fact, a planning problem confronting a number of diversified companies today is how to encourage their divisions to undertake projects where failure can be afforded but where success, if it comes, will be attended by high profits not available in run-of-the-mill, low-risk activities.

Although the possibility of misinterpreting results is by far the commonest obstacle to accurate evaluation of strategy, the criteria previously outlined suggest immediately some additional difficulties. It is as easy to misevaluate corporate resources and the financial requirements of a new move as to misread the environment for future opportunities. To be overresponsive to industry trends may be as dangerous as to ignore them. For example, if a manufacturer of jeweled-lever watches should switch his production to pin-lever watches because of the success of Timex in the United States and the faster growth rate of inexpensive watches in other countries, his course would not necessarily be correct. The correspondence of the company's strategy with current environmental developments and an overreadiness to adapt may obscure the opportunity for a larger share of a declining market or for growth in profits without a parallel growth in total sales. The decision of American Motors not to follow trends toward big cars in the middle 1950's provides us with an opportunity to examine the strategic alternatives of adapting to, or running counter to, massive current trends in demand.

The intrinsic difficulty of determining and choosing among strategic alternatives leads many companies to do what the rest of the industry is doing rather than to make an independent determination of opportunity and resources. Sometimes the companies of an industry run like sheep all in one direction. The similarity among the strategies, at least in some periods of history, of insurance companies, banks, railroads, and airplane manu-facturers may lead one to wonder whether strategic decisions were based upon industry convention or upon independent analysis. When the student examines the farm equipment industry he may wish to inquire whether the similarity of timing, decision, and reaction to competition constituted inde-pendent appraisals of each company's situation, or whether imitation took the place of independent decision. At any rate, the similarity of one company's strategy to that of its competitors does not constitute the assurance of soundness which it might at first suggest.

A strategy may manifest an all-too-clear correspondence with the personal values of the founder, owner, or chief executive. Like a correspondence with dominant trends and the strategic decisions of competitors, this may also be dysfunctional. For example, a personal preference for growth beyond all reasonable expectations may be given undue weight. It should be only one factor among several in any balanced consideration of what is involved in designing strategy. Too little attention to a corporation's actual competence for growth or diversification is the commonest error of all.

It is entirely possible that a strategy may reflect in an exaggerated fashion the values rather than the reasoned decisions of the responsible manager or managers and that imbalance may go undetected. That this may be the case is a reflection of the fact that the entire business community may be domi-nated by certain beliefs of which one should be wary. A critic of strategy must be at heart enough of a nonconformist to raise questions about gen-erally accepted modes of thought and the conventional thinking which serves as a substitute for original analysis. The timid may not find it prudent to challenge publicly some of the ritual of policy formulation. But even for them it will serve the purposes of criticism to inquire privately into such sacred propositions as the one proclaiming that a company must grow or die.

Another canon of management that may engender questionable strategies is the idea that cash funds in excess of reasonable dividend requirements should be reinvested either in revitalization of a company's traditional activities or in mergers and acquisitions that will diversify products and services. Successful operations, a heretic might observe, sometimes bring riches to a company which lacks the capacity to reemploy them. Yet a decision to return to the owners large amounts of capital which the company does not have the competence or desire to put to work is an almost unheard-of development. It is therefore appropriate, particularly in the instance of very successful companies in older and stable industries, to inquire how far strategy reflects a simple desire to put all resources to work rather than a more valid appraisal of investment opportunity in relation to unique corporate strengths. We should not forget to consider an unfashionable, even if utimately also an untenable alternative—namely, that to keep an already large worldwide corporation within reasonable bounds, a portion of the assets might well be returned to stockholders for investment in other enterprises.

The identification of opportunity and choice of purpose are such challenging intellectual activities that we should not be surprised to find that persistent problems attend the proper evaluation of strategy. But just as the criteria for evaluation are useful, even if not precise, so the dangers of misevaluation are less menacing if they are recognized. We have noted the inexactness of the concept of strategy, the limits to its usefulness in practice, the problems of making resolute determinations in the face of uncertainty, the necessity for judgment in the evaluation of the soundness of strategy, and the misevaluation into which human error may lead us. None of these alters the fact that a business enterprise guided by a clear sense of purpose rationally arrived at and emotionally ratified by commitment is more likely to have a successful outcome, in terms of profit and social good, than a company whose future is left to guesswork and chance. Conscious strategy does not preclude brilliance of improvisation or the welcome consequences of good fortune. Its cost is principally thought and hard work which, though often painful, are seldom fatal.

Application to cases

As the student attempts to apply the concept of strategy to the analysis of cases, he should try to keep in mind three questions:

1. What is the strategy of this company?
2. In the light of (a) the characteristics and developments of its environment and (b) its own strengths and weaknesses, is the strategy sound?
3. What recommendations for changed strategy might advantageously be made to the president?

Whatever other questions the student may be asked or may ask himself, he will wish constantly to order his study and structure his analysis of case information according to the need to *identify, evaluate,* and *recommend.* ⏤

By now the student has an idea, which discussion of the cases will greatly clarify, of what is meant by corporate strategy. He knows how it is derived and some of its uses and limitations. He has been given some criteria for evaluating the strategies he identifies and those he proposes. And he has been properly warned about errors of judgment which await the unwary.

The cases which immediately follow will permit the student to consider in the context of real situations what this text has been talking about. What contribution, if any, would the concept of strategy, mostly missing as a conscious formulation, have made to these companies? What strategic alternatives can be detected in the changing circumstances affecting their fortunes? Which ones would the student choose if he were responsible or were asked to advise? By the time these introductory cases have been examined, the student will be ready to turn from the nature and uses of strategy to a study in sequence of its principal components—environmental opportunity, corporate capability, personal aspirations, and moral responsibility.

J. I. CASE COMPANY (REVISED)*

^^

J. I. Case during its fiscal year ending October 1952 achieved a sales volume of $153.5 million resulting in a profit before taxes of $15.2 million. Gross assets on October 31, 1952, amounted to $174.4 million of which $128.5 million was financed internally. Debt financing contributed $27.6 million with the remaining $18.3 million coming from suppliers, tax liabilities, and other sources.

Nine years later, the 1961 fiscal year closed with sales of $128.7 million resulting in a net loss of $32.3 million. Gross assets on October 31, 1961, amounted to $234.7 million of which $81.5 million was financed internally. Debt financing contributed $127.4 million (not counting the obligations of Case's credit subsidiary) with the remaining $25.8 million coming from suppliers, tax liabilities, and other sources.

By the end of the nine-year period, J. I. Case's earned surplus had dropped by $80.6 million to a negative figure of $26.8 million. The following material, all drawn from published sources, bears on policies, policy implementation, and results achieved as three successive administrations wrestled during this period with the problem of working out a viable strategy for Case: (1) Mr. John T. Brown from 1953 to 1956, (2) Mr. Marc B. Rojtman (pronounced Roitman) from 1957 to 1959, and (3) Mr. William J. Grede during 1960 and 1961.

Background

Stepping up from executive vice president to president of Case in mid-1953,[1] Mr. Brown assumed direction of a 111-year-old company. Its general offices (a careful reproduction of the Boston Public Library, with a roll-top desk and brass cuspidor in the president's office)[2] were at Racine, Wisconsin. Manufacturing operations were conducted in eight plants in five states. Some 4,000 dealers were served through 49 company-operated branches: 36 in the United States, 8 in Canada, and 5 in South America. Manufacturing facilities, ex-

---

*Copyright © 1963 by the President and Fellows of Harvard College. Reprinted by permission.

[1] Appendix A provides some background information on J. I. Case during the period 1945–1952.

[2] "The Rojtman's Tractor Race," *Fortune*, February 1958, p. 107.

panded and modernized since World War II at a cumulative cost of some $30 million,[3] contained about eight million square feet—enough to support sales of over $300 million a year.[4] Except for a small volume of tractors for the industrial market ($3.2 million in 1953)[5] the company's whole peacetime business was in agricultural machinery.[6]

The John T. Brown administration

Policies. In response to flagging sales and profits, Mr. Brown's policies included: (1) cutting costs; (2) increasing the sales effectiveness of dealers; (3) accelerating product development; and (4) remaining as financially liquid as possible.

Implementation. To implement the policy of cutting costs, Mr. Brown's administration carried on a continuing program of reviewing expenses, installing new and improved machinery, and scrutinizing manufacturing methods. In 1956 it closed two plants and cut the number of domestic sales branches from 36 in 28 states to 28 in 24.

To implement the policy of improving the sales effectiveness of dealers, the Brown administration continued past programs of training dealers and modernizing branches; held the line on prices in 1954 in spite of cost increases; engaged in multimedia advertising in 1955 and 1956; and overhauled dealerships in 1956, making 345 additions or replacements.[7] The most important sales change, however, was increased use of company financing to carry dealers' inventories and a limited amount of farmers' paper. Reflecting an industry-wide trend, customers' accounts and notes receivable rose $26 million, or 70%, from 1952 through 1956. In the latter year, according to the Annual Report, the contract offered dealers was changed to increase their "opportunity and effectiveness in obtaining greater retail volume," while the contract offered farmers was changed to gear payments to the farm-income cycle.

To implement the policy of accelerated product development, which Mr. Brown, according to *Fortune*, saw as the most needed feature of his program, the company brought out three new tractors as well as new models of other machines and equipment. Reflecting an industry trend, the new tractors were relatively large: a five-plow diesel, "first with power steering" in August 1953; a "completely new four-plow model with more speeds, more usable power," and an engine adaptable to three types of fuel in February 1955, and a "revolutionary" three-plow model completed and marketed in 1956.[8] Other new models included grain combines, hay balers, and a corn picker.[9] (After tractors and related equipment, these three lines made the greatest contribution

---

[3]J. I. Case, Annual Report, 1952, p. 5.
[4]*Implement & Tractor*, February 9, 1957, p. 76.
[5]J. I. Case, Prospectus, October 1958, p. 9.
[6]See Appendix B for some data on the farm equipment industry.
[7]Annual Reports.
[8]Annual Reports.
[9]For pictures of these and other items, see Appendix C.

to Case volume.)[10] Commenting on this development program, *Fortune* stated:

Brown wanted to put more money into research. Like its competitors, Case was still producing prewar machines in 1946. Unlike its competitors, Case was not developing very much that was new. In 1949, its research budget was only $1 million, far less than 1 per cent of sales. Brown kept raising his research budget until, by 1956, it was $2,500,000.[11]

To implement the policy of remaining as liquid as possible in spite of rising needs for working capital to use in the sales end of the business, an effort was made to limit short-term debt to its traditional function of meeting seasonal needs, and to reduce inventories mainly by holding production below sales. From a peak of $80.8 million in March 1953, inventories declined to $35.9 million at the end of fiscal 1956.[12]

Further attesting Mr. Brown's interest in staying liquid are the following figures for current ratios and net working capital:

	1952	1953	1954	1955	1956
Current ratio	2.5	4.7	6.5	6.8	5.1
Net current assets (millions)	$68.6	$88.2	$85.2	$84.5	$84.9

Source: Annual Reports.

Overall achievements and a new approach. Results for the Brown administration seesawed between profit and loss, with the cumulative four-year net after taxes falling to only $146,000, in contrast to almost $50 million during the previous four years. (For financial statements, see Exhibits 1 and 2.) Explaining these results, management stressed the need for continuing its "corrective action" and the impact of such unfavorable factors as the end of the postwar boom, poor crops and weather, political uncertainties about the farm program, shifts in foreign sales, and the downswing that carried net farm income from $14.3 billion in 1951 and 1952 to a low of $11.3 billion in 1955. When 1956 turned unprofitable despite the relatively good results achieved with the Brown program in the more depressed farm market of the previous year, management decided to try a new approach, even though still retaining faith in the long-run future of farm equipment as the only answer to the cost-price squeeze on farmers.[13]

The new approach was merger. According to *Fortune*, talks were under way for a time with two of Case's smaller full-line competitors, but what Mr. Brown really wanted was "a merger that would give him a growth product." A possibility that seemed to fill this need was the American Tractor Corporation, a small but fast expanding maker of crawler tractors for varied industrial

[10]Prospectus, 1952, p. 8; 1953, p. 6; 1956, p. 8.
[11]*Fortune, op. cit.*, p. 188.
[12]*Annual Report*, 1956.
[13]Annual Reports.

Exhibit 1
J. I. CASE COMPANY
Operating and Surplus Reconciliation Statements for Years Ending October 31, 1952–1961
(Dollars in Millions)

	1952	1953	1954	1955	1956	1957	1958	1959	1960	1961
Sales	$153.5	$111.5	$92.4	$94.8	$87.1	$123.9	$177.9	$200.6	...	...
Gross	...	...	...	...	...	...	...	...	$111.5	$128.7
Net	...	...	...	...	...	...	...	...	...	...
Cost of goods sold	...	...	...	...	...	...	...	...	111.1	117.7
Selling, general and administrative expense	...	...	...	...	...	...	...	...	32.8	29.7
Total	137.4	108.6	92.5	92.3	87.7	120.9	166.4	182.7	143.9	147.4
Operating profit or (loss)	$ 16.1	$ 2.8	$(0.2)	$ 2.6	$(0.6)	$ 3.0	$ 11.5	$ 17.9	$(32.4)	$(18.7)
Other income										
Discounts on purchases	0.4	0.3	0.2	0.2	0.2	0.3	0.7	...	...	...
Interest and financial charges earned	...	0.2	0.3	0.4	0.6	1.1	1.9	1.3	1.7	1.3
Earnings, Case Credit Corp.	...	...	...	...	...	...	...	4.4	4.8	2.6
Miscellaneous	...	...	0.2	...	...	0.4	0.2	0.2	...	...
Other expenses										
Case Credit financial charges*	...	...	...	...	...	...	3.3	6.5	9.0	7.5
Interest paid	1.4	1.7	1.5	1.4	1.7	2.8	3.0	4.3	5.6	7.2
Losses, French subsidiary	...	...	...	...	...	...	...	...	6.0	1.2
Miscellaneous	...	...	...	0.1	...	...	...	...	...	1.6
Income before taxes	15.2	1.6	(1.0)	1.7	(1.6)	2.0	8.0	13.0	(46.4)	(32.3)
Taxes	8.1	0.8	(0.5)	0.8	(0.6)	0.7	3.7	6.8	(6.6)	...
Net profit	$ 7.0	$ 0.8	$(0.5)	$ 0.9	$(1.0)	$ 1.3	$ 4.3	$ 6.2	$(39.8)	$(32.3)
Surplus, beginning	39.4	40.8	36.4	34.1	34.1	32.7	45.9	49.1	54.1	13.1
Dividends										
Preferred	0.6	0.6	0.6	0.8	0.4	1.0	1.2	1.2	1.2	...
Common	5.0	4.5	1.1	...	...	...	...	...	...	...
Other charges	...	...	...	...	...	...	...	...	...	7.6‡
Special credits	...	...	...	...	...	12.9†	...	...	...	...
Surplus, ending	$ 40.8	$ 36.4	$ 34.1	$ 34.1	$ 32.7	$ 45.9	$ 49.1	$ 54.1	$ 13.1	$(26.8)

Note: (1) Consolidated figures, except for French subsidiaries and J. I. Case Credit Corporation. (2) Figures may fail to add because of rounding.

*Less interest received from Case Credit Corporation.

†Restoration of special reserves.

‡Includes $2.95 million for taxes applicable to 1947–1954; $3.2 million for losses on plants, etc., and $1.4 million for additional loss on French subsidiaries.

Source: Annual Reports.

and construction markets. Under the leadership of its founder and president, Mr. Marc B. Rojtman, ATC had grown from a volume of under $1 million in 1951 to over $10 million in 1956.[14] This success, in the face of competition from industry giants, seemed due in the main to Mr. Rojtman's flair for product development and merchandising. He had seen the advantages of putting out a crawler with a tank-type automatic transmission, had lured away a top engineer from Allis-Chalmers to work out the design, had been first with such a tractor on the market, and had exploited his position through a novel but dramatic promotional device, the "Tractorama," or tractor tug-of-war, in which the new transmission guaranteed that ATC would out-tug its competition.

If ATC seemed to Case to offer growth prospects, Case, according to *Fortune*, offered ATC needed cash and space for manufacturing. Mr. Rojtman, therefore, responded favorably to Case feelers. Terms of merger were worked out, calling for exchange of stock, Case paying one-half share of common and one share of second preferred for each common share of ATC. At current market values, the price approximated $15 million, or $12.4 million more than ATC's book value. The excess was to be amortized over 20 years.

The Marc B. Rojtman administration: 1957-1959

Objective and policies. Following the merger, Mr. Rojtman became chief executive of the combined company, as had previously been agreed. His policies—outlined in a series of rapid-fire pronouncements and changes—were: (1) maximizing factory and dealer sales both at home and abroad; (2) enlarging emphasis on R.&D. "as the very foundation . . . of future growth and prosperity"; (3) increasing diversification; (4) relying on high volume to bring down costs in relation to income; and (5) utilizing debt to meet the capital needs of this program. Something of the tone and emphasis of the new administration emerged in an address made by Mr. Rojtman at the Case annual meeting shortly after he took office:

First and foremost . . . will come an aggressive sales program. Sales will take the No. 1 order of importance, and we will not rest until sales volume has filled all seven existing Case plants to maximum capacity [over $300 million]. . . .

Second . . . will be a strong emphasis on engineering and development of new products. . . . We will develop more products, more diversified products, and products that are technically well ahead of the industry. . . .

The third factor to be given major emphasis is the strengthening of the present worldwide network of over 3,500 Case dealers and factory-owned branches. . . .[15]

Implementation under Mr. Rojtman

Sales. To implement the policy of maximizing sales from the factory to dealers and from dealers to the field, Mr. Rojtman made a variety of moves,

---

[14]J. I. Case, Prospectus, 1958, p. 9.
[15]*Implement & Tractor*, February 9, 1957, p. 76.

Exhibit 2

J. I. CASE COMPANY

Balance Sheets as of October 31, Selected Years, 1952–1961
(Dollars in Millions)

ASSETS	1952	1956	1959	1960	1961
Current assets					
Cash	$ 6.6	$ 5.2	$ 12.0	$ 13.2	$ 5.7
Accounts receivable					
Customers	37.7	63.9	33.8	20.7	19.6
Sundry	0.5	1.2	1.7	1.2	2.7
Reserve for doubtful accounts	(0.5)	(0.7)	(0.5)	(1.0)	(1.5)
Claim for income tax refund	...	...	...	4.6	...
Prepaid expenses	...	...	1.5	1.3	0.7
Due from Case Credit Corporation	...	...	13.4	4.7	...
Inventories	70.1	35.9	56.7	65.9	59.0
Total current assets	$114.5	$105.6	$118.5	$110.6	$ 86.0
Investments and other assets					
American Tractor Corporation	...	$ 1.0	...	...	...
Case Credit Corporation*	...	...	$ 44.9	$ 52.2	$ 53.4
French subsidiaries†	...	...	0.7	0.8	1.6
Deferred charges					
Engineering expense	...	...	4.1‡	...	...
Other	$ 0.6	0.9	0.6	0.6	...
Miscellaneous	0.2	0.3	1.4	2.5	2.8
	$ 0.8	$ 2.2	$ 51.8	$ 56.0	$ 57.7
Properties					
Land	$ 2.3	$ 2.4	$ 2.3	$ 2.5	$ 2.1
Building and equipment	56.9	64.2	81.1	83.7	77.9
Less depreciation reserve	27.1	35.4	43.3	45.4	44.7
Net	$ 32.0	$ 31.2	$ 40.0	$ 40.7	$ 35.3
Excess of cost of assets§	...	...	11.9	11.5	11.0
Total assets	$147.2	$138.9	$222.3	$218.9	$190.1

*At equity in underlying assets.
†At cost, 1959. Less reserves of $6.0 million in 1960 and $8.5 million in 1961.
‡Charged to cost of goods sold in 1960, less related deferred income taxes.
§Excess of acquisition cost over assigned value, American Tractor Corporation.

initiating most of them during his first year. His sales drive looked not only to the domestic market but also to markets abroad, and it involved many additions to field and home-office sales management for both the agricultural and industrial divisions.

One of Mr. Rojtman's earliest moves was setting up the J. I. Case Credit Corporation[16] (Exhibit 3) to provide sales financing facilities "equal to those offered by competing manufacturers."[17] Loans to farmers would be greatly increased, while existing aids for dealers would be both continued and ex-

---

[16]*Fortune, op. cit.,* p. 191, explained the reason for creating a separate subsidiary company to handle this business: "Lenders will balk when a manufacturing company like Case pushes its borrowing above 50% to 60% of net worth but they will loan a credit corporation 300% to 400% of its net worth."

[17]Prospectus, October 1958, p. 4.

Exhibit 2—Continued

LIABILITIES	1952	1956	1959	1960	1961
Current liabilities					
Notes payable, banks	$ 27.6	$ 15.4	$ 36.8	$ 82.3	$ 85.1
Accounts payable	6.1	2.7	13.4	8.0	8.0
Accrued liabilities	4.3	1.8	4.8	5.1	5.0
Federal and other income taxes	8.0	0.8	3.7	0.4	3.4
Current portion, long-term debt	...	...	0.8	0.8	1.0
Due to Case Credit	...	...	...	...	3.7
Discounts, allowance, etc.	...	...	...	3.2	5.6
Total current liabilities	$ 45.9	$ 20.7	$ 59.5	$ 99.9	$111.9
Deferred income tax	...	...	$ 2.4	...	...
Long-term debt					
Debentures due 1978	...	$ 25.0	$ 22.0	$ 21.0	$ 19.8
Subordinated debentures—due 1983	...	...	20.1	20.1	20.1
Mortgages payable	...	...	0.5	1.1	1.4
Total	...	$ 25.0	$ 42.6	$ 42.2	$ 41.3
Stockholders' equity					
7% cum. pf.	$ 9.3	$ 9.3	$ 9.3	$ 9.3	$ 9.3
6½% cum. 2nd pf.	...	...	8.4	8.4	8.4
Common	28.3	28.3	35.8	35.8	35.8
Capital in excess of par value	10.0	10.0	10.2	10.2	10.2
Special reserves	13.0	13.0	...	...	...
Surplus	39.7	32.7	54.1	13.1	(26.8)
	$101.3	$ 93.2	$117.8	$ 76.8	$ 36.9
Total liabilities	$147.2	$138.9	$222.3	$218.9	$190.1

Note: Figures may fail to add because of rounding.
Source: Annual Reports.

panded. Said a Prospectus issued the next year:

Case Credit also finances allied equipment of other manufacturers attached to or sold and used with company products as well as used units of any make when traded against the purchase of new Case equipment. . . . The company contemplates that either it or Case Credit may finance to a limited degree retail repair contracts involving Case parts, and also sales of shop equipment to company dealers.[18]

The increased scope of lending under Mr. Rojtman appears in the following figures:

NOTES AND CUSTOMERS' ACCOUNTS RECEIVABLE
(Dollars in Millions)

	1956	1957	1958	1959
J. I. Case Company $63.9		$ 62.2	$ 37.1	$ 33.8
Case Credit Corporation				
Retail		23.7	83.9	100.7
Wholesale		20.6	61.4	112.8
Total $63.9		$106.5	$182.4	$247.3

Source: Annual Reports; Prospectus, October 1958, p. 11.

[18]*Ibid.*, p. 11.

Exhibit 3

J. I. CASE CREDIT CORPORATION
Statement of Financial Condition, 1959 and 1961
(Dollars in Millions)

ASSETS

	1959	*1961*
Cash	$ 18.3	$ 8.7
Due from Case	...	3.7
Notes receivable		
Wholesale	112.8	74.1
Retail	100.7	88.1
Unearned financial charges	(12.6)	(9.7)
Provision for losses	(2.0)	(4.4)
Total notes (net)	$198.9	$148.2
Other	1.8	0.9
Total assets	$219.1	$161.5

LIABILITIES AND CAPITAL

Short-term notes payable	$105.4	$ 33.7
Accounts payable	0.1	...
Due to Case	13.4	...
Taxes	2.0	0.1
Withheld from dealers	3.3	3.9
Long-term notes		
Due 1964–1973	25.0	} 70.0
Due 1965–1974	25.0	
Total	$174.2	$108.1
Subordinated notes and equity		
Notes due Case	$ 22.0	$ 22.0
Capital stock	20.0	25.0
Surplus	2.9	6.4
Total	$ 44.9	$ 53.4
Total liabilities and capital	$219.1	$161.5

INCOME AND ACCUMULATED EARNINGS

Income from financing charges		
To Case wholesale notes	$ 8.1	$ 8.8
From retail notes	5.6	6.7
Other	0.2	0.3
Total income	$ 13.9	$ 15.8
Interest expense	$ 7.9	$ 8.4
Provision for possible losses	1.3	4.4
Other	0.3	0.4
Total	$ 9.6	$ 13.2
Income before taxes	$ 4.4	$ 2.6
Provision for, or in lieu of, taxes	2.4	1.4*
Net income	$ 2.0	$ 1.2

*Paid to parent company, which had no tax liability because of losses.
Source: Annual Reports.

Additional marketing moves aimed mainly at increasing factory sales to dealers included: (1) a campaign to sell agricultural dealers on carrying a "12-month line," i.e., one comprising not only seasonal farm equipment, but also Case light industrial equipment to "blanket" the requirements of the "home builder, remodeler, general purpose builder, sewer and waterworks contractor, landscaper, logger, and . . . municipalities"; (2) a campaign to attract stronger dealers—although not increasing the total number—using the 12-month line as one incentive, Case's stepped-up program of product development as another; and (3) a campaign to stimulate dealer enthusiasm through a series of annual "World Premiers," where dealers could review new Case equipment and place their orders for the coming year.

Owing to the interest they aroused, the yearly World Premiers merit more attention. Four in all were held: at Phoenix, Arizona; Nassau, the Bahamas; Bal Harbor, Florida; and in Hawaii. *Fortune* provides the following description of the prototype at Phoenix:

Last November and December the once staid J. I. Case . . . put on a million dollar extravaganza to dramatize its comeback in the farm-machinery business. . . . Amidst the blare of a fifteen-piece band, . . . Case unveiled sixty carloads of dazzling new equipment. . . .

The first of over 3,000 guests who poured in to see the show were financial men. . . . Then came the farm-machinery dealers. Over a period of six weeks, 2,000 Case dealers and 700 more from competition were flown to Phoenix for a stay of three days.

* * * * *

. . . the whoop-de-do staged in Phoenix was pure Rojtman. . . . Farm machinery makers are conservative in their sales tactics. Normally, new products are simply presented in catalogues by the salesmen when they call on dealers, or they are exhibited none too dramatically at a regional meeting. . . .[19]

Reviewing the results of the World Premiers, Case claimed that dealers placed orders for over $150 million at Phoenix; over $200 million at Nassau; over $218 million at Bal Harbor.[20] Besides producing orders, the World Premiers reportedly also helped the company "in planning orderly production," and the dealer "to receive needed seasonal merchandise according to a definite prearranged schedule."[21]

Marketing moves aimed mainly at increasing dealers' sales to farmers included the following: (1) a greatly increased advertising budget—reportedly over $2.5 million in 1958, and up to $2.9 million budgeted in 1959 for 1960;[22] (2) addition of novel promotional devices, including movies of the World Premiers, tractor tugs-of-war, and a Case "service and sales patrol" truck introduced in 1959 as a means for enabling dealers to carry the Case story

[19]*Fortune, op. cit.*, pp. 107, 191.
[20]Annual Report, 1957; *Implement & Tractor*, January 10, 1959, p. 36; *Business Week*, April 30, 1960, p. 57.
[21]Annual Report, 1958.
[22]*Implement & Tractor*, January 25, 1958, p. 28; *Business Week*, April 30, 1960, p. 57.

right to the customers' barn door; and (3) assistance to dealers in meeting their new building requirements through the Case Building Corporation established in 1959.

Moves designed to increase foreign sales included: (1) setting up new European and Canadian export divisions under new managing directors; (2) creating J. I. Case International S.A., under the recently retired president of Massey-Harris Ferguson, Inc., in order to "gain entry into some of the most lucrative overseas markets" by establishing manufacturing operations abroad;[23] (3) buying a controlling interest in a French tractor manufacturer;[24] and (4) setting up a British subsidiary, "scheduled to begin operating in the construction, roadbuilding, and materials handling field in 1960."[25] In 1959, Case's net assets in foreign countries, "principally . . . current," peaked at a reported $29.8 million, while earnings of Case International S.A. were reportedly $826,000.[26]

Product development. To implement the policy of basing sales expansion on new products, Mr. Rojtman emphasized (1) automation; (2) more attention to styling and comfort; (3) increased size and equipment capacity; and (4) more rapid introduction of new products. Owing in part to the start in this direction made by Mr. Brown, Mr. Rojtman was able to push through several projects in 1957.[27] In the following year, he initiated a "four-year plan of new product development and diversification."[28]

The emphasis on automation was designed "to make the machine perform the big chores automatically, thus relieving the operator from excessive fatigue. . . ."[29] It was exemplified in the late 1957 introduction of the "Case-O-Matic Drive," a hydrostatic torque converter for use with conventional direct transmission. Pushed through by Mr. Rojtman in "eleven frantic months,"[30] the new drive, it was said, "matches power output with requirements; reduces jerking, gear shifting, and engine stalling; and increases 'pull power.' "[31] Introduced at first on only a few models, Case-O-Matic Drive, like power steering, was subsequently made available on other tractor series and self-propelled units.

The emphasis on styling was designed to bring "our farm tractors at a par with the luxury look of the modern car which the farmer is buying today."[32] It was exemplified by two-tone paint jobs and recessed headlights

---

[23] Annual Report, 1957.
[24] Annual Report, 1958. A new president and manufacturing director were hired the next year from Remington-Rand of France; a new controller from General Motors of France.
[25] Annual Report, 1959.
[26] *Ibid.*
[27] *Fortune, op. cit.,* p. 188.
[28] Annual Report, 1958.
[29] *Implement & Tractor,* January 25, 1958, p. 25.
[30] *Fortune, op. cit.,* p. 108.
[31] Prospectus, October 1958, p. 8.
[32] *Implement & Tractor,* January 25, 1958, p. 25.

by mid-1957,[33] and in "new streamlined all-weather cabs" readied in 1959 for 1960.[34]

The emphasis on size was designed, in the agricultural line, to reflect the well-publicized trend toward larger farms, and was exemplified in the introduction of new farm tractor series with four, five, and five-six plow ratings for 1958; in the introduction of two new self-propelled grain combines claimed to have "the largest capacity in the industry"[35] for 1959; and in the introduction of a new two-row mounted corn picker for 1960, as well as other large implements and machines.

The emphasis on an increased flow of new products was exemplified in the new introductions made yearly at successive World Premiers—32, for example, at Bal Harbor 1958–1959. According to *Business Week*, Mr. Rojtman "revamped 60% of Case's traditional line" in three years.[36]

While the agricultural product line was being thus overhauled, the industrial line was by no means left standing. Besides introducing new loaders, shovels, and backhoe loaders in a wider range of sizes, the company was working on a pull-type scraper in 1958, a self-propelled scraper in 1959, and on a new rubber-tired fork lift for heavy-duty materials handling.[37] Even larger models for many lines were planned for introduction after 1959, as indicated by the following figures:

Line	Top Capacity of Models in or Nearing Production	Top Capacity of Models Planned
Crawler-tractor	100 hp.	135–150 hp.
Self-propelled scraper	6½ cu. yds.	21 cu. yds.
Rubber-tired fork lift	4,000 lbs.	8,000 lbs.
Four-wheel unit loader	2½ cu. yds.	"larger"
Crawler-tractor loader	2 cu. yds.	"larger"

Source: Annual Report for 1959, pp. 6-9.

Like the stepped-up program in marketing, the stepped-up program in development brought changes in structure and personnel. For the first time, control of R.&D. was taken out of the various plants, each of which had previously engineered its own products (to the detriment of family resemblance among them).[38] A new centralized engineering department was created under the direction of Mr. Theodore Haller, who had some years past been lured by Mr. Rojtman from Allis-Chalmers to ATC.[39] Into Mr. Haller's old

[33]*Fortune, op. cit.; Implement & Tractor*, January 25, 1958, p. 25.
[34]Annual Report, 1959.
[35]Annual Report, 1958.
[36]*Business Week*, April 30, 1960, p. 57.
[37]Annual Reports.
[38]*Fortune, op. cit.*, p. 110.
[39]*Fortune, op. cit.*, p. 110.

job as head of crawler-tractor engineering went an outsider—the former chief of research and testing for Caterpillar Tractor Company.[40]

The extent of Mr. Rojtman's commitment to a policy of increased R.&D. is suggested by the report in *Business Week* that his administration laid out "about $28 million for engineering, new product development and tooling."[41] This contrasts with $12 million reported for the period 1950–1955.[42]

Further diversification. Following its union with ATC, Case emerged as a diversified company serving agriculture, roadbuilding, and construction. Mr. Rojtman, however, had ambitions to enter other fields. Accordingly, by 1959, Case was in materials handling with two fork lifts and a tractor shovel; in commercial construction with Case Building Corporation; and in purchasing and selling small tools to farmers through a new Small Tools Division.

Costs. Mr. Rojtman indicated that his main approach to the problem of achieving a more favorable ratio of costs and income was one of spreading overhead through high volume:

> With minor capital expenditures . . . Case has the capacity to produce $335 million annual volume. The fundamental thing in my program was that the best way to make money for the company and its stockholders was to use that capacity.[43]

Bringing down unit costs through volume operation was also a key to one of Mr. Rojtman's plans for competing pricewise in the small (30–40 horsepower) tractor market with rising European imports. Believing that Case was losing sales to companies importing small tractors from affiliates abroad, Mr. Rojtman decided not only to try this game himself by purchasing a French subsidiary, but also to try making a competitive American tractor through exploiting techniques of mass production. To this end he equipped the Case Rock Island plant with high-production machines—many of them inexpensively converted to special purposes within his own shop—and planned through volume operation (20,000 units a year) to put out a U.S. tractor with a newly developed "Dynaclonic" diesel engine in the $2,700 price range, as compared with about $5,000 for the lowest listed current Case Diesel. Such a tractor was duly pictured in the next Case Annual Report, which described it as being "the first United States-manufactured small diesel tractor to compete pricewise with European imports." In contrast, the plan for a French import fizzled when it was found that the subsidiary's product was "inferior."[44]

Finance. For financing his program, Mr. Rojtman relied mainly on debt, which increased as follows:

---

[40]*Implement & Tractor*, November 2, 1957, p. 212.

[41]*Business Week*, April 30, 1960, p. 57.

[42]Annual Report, 1955.

[43]*Business Week*, April 30, 1960, p. 57.

[44]*Wall Street Journal*, July 2, 1959; *Implement & Tractor*, July 25, 1959, p. 80; *Automotive Industries*, February 15, 1959, p. 61; Annual Report, 1959.

	1956	1959	
	Case Company	Case Company	Case Credit
		(Dollars in Millions)	
Short-term notes payable	$15.4	$36.8	$105.4
Current portion of long-term debt	...	0.8	...
Long-term debt	25.0	42.6	50.5
	$40.4	$80.2	$155.9

Source: Balance sheets.

Overall achievement under Mr. Rojtman. Helped by a good market in 1959, Case's net profits in three years under Mr. Rojtman totaled $11.8 million, compared with under $150,000 for four years under Mr. Brown. The value of Case common, which had hit a low of $11½ in 1956, climbed to $26⅝.

Back of the encouraging rise in profits was the fastest growth rate in the industry in terms of factory sales to dealers. Farm and industrial equipment both showed gains, as follows:

FACTORY SALES

	1956	1957	1959	Per Cent Increase
	(Dollars in Millions)			1956–1959
Agricultural	$83.8	$97.7	$137.6	+ 63
Industrial and utility	12.4*	26.1	63.0	+400

*Includes $2.3 million in industrial sales for Case, $10.1 million for ATC.
Source: Annual Reports; Prospectus, October 1958, p. 9.

Reporting on the effort to increase retail sales, Mr. Rojtman told stockholders that in 1957, "Agricultural sales to dealers showed an increase of over 15% and, significantly, retail sales by dealers increased by more than 20%."[45] For 1958 he told dealers that retail sales were up 57%.[46] Then in 1959, as was later revealed, dealers' sales were $174.9 million compared with factory sales of $200.6 million.[47]

Looking forward in 1959, Mr. Rojtman planned, by taking a bigger share of the market, to achieve his goal of capacity production—or sales of $335 million by 1964.[48]

The William J. Grede administration

In February 1960, Mr. Rojtman was replaced as president of Case by Mr. William J. Grede, previously head of Grede Foundries (a Case supplier), a

[45]Annual Report, 1957.
[46]From a statement by Mr. Rojtman at the Nassau World Premier, cited in *Implement & Tractor*, January 10, 1959, p. 36.
[47]Annual Report, 1960.
[48]*Business Week*, April 30, 1960, pp. 55, 57.

Case board member since 1953, and a past ally of President Brown in pushing for more liberal development expenditures.[49]

Reason for the change, soon made clear at the Case annual meeting, was a fundamental divergence of objectives between Mr. Rojtman and the more conservative members of his board. As *Business Week* reported, "The farm-equipment maker's board thinks ex-President Rojtman was expanding too fast, making the company top-heavy on debt and inventory."[50] Causes of the board's financial jitters were summarized by *Forbes* as follows:

> Out of the $502 million worth of sales that Case rang up between 1956 and 1960, only about $400 million . . . went into the hands of the ultimate customers. Most of the rest remained in dealers' inventory. Case, which had a rock-solid current ratio of 5 to 1 before Rojtman took over, was down to just 2 to 1 at the end of 1959. Its debt had risen from just $25 million to $216.8 million—counting obligations of its credit subsidiary. Total interest charges had climbed from just over $1.7 million to $12.2 million.[51]

Summing up, *Business Week* remarked, "The real question is whether Rojtman wheeled and dealed too much, or whether the company panicked too soon. . . . Now that Rojtman is out there is no way of knowing whether he could have succeeded."[52]

Objectives and policies under Mr. Grede. Shortly after stepping into his new role, Mr. Grede explained Case's changed objectives at the stockholders' annual meeting. After pointing out that Mr. Rojtman had resigned because the new thinking of the board was a "complete reversal of all he had stood for," Mr. Grede went on to say that goals for the present would be reducing debt, inventory, and receivables, even though these measures would lead to a temporary cut in both sales and profits. Common stockholders were, however, assured that resumption of dividends (passed since 1955) would come about sooner than if expansion had gone on unchecked. In a more precise early statement of his target, reported by *Business Week*, Mr. Grede indicated that he aimed to cut at least $15 million out of inventory and $10 million out of receivables by the end of the year and to apply this $25 million to the bank debt.[53]

Mr. Grede's major policies, as inferred from his first Annual Report, might be summarized as follows: (1) shifting sales emphasis to the retail level to help work down dealers' inventories; (2) cutting back production below retail sales with the same purpose in mind; (3) slashing costs; yet (4) continuing to do some product development; and (5) attempting to work down short-term debt.

Implementation under Mr. Grede

Sales. Granting special allowances to move dealers' inventories, especially

[49]*Fortune, op. cit.,* pp. 110, 188.
[50]*Business Week,* April 30, 1960, p. 54.
[51]*Forbes,* July 1, 1960, p. 23.
[52]*Business Week,* April 30, 1960, p. 54.
[53]*Ibid.*

of noncurrent models, was a prominent feature of Case sales policy under Mr. Grede. Along with losses from the liquidation of receivables, this program cost $8.70 million in 1960 and $16.35 million in 1961, including reserves for 1962.

Other marketing measures described by Mr. Grede in his first Annual Report included establishing an overall marketing division and hiring a single marketing vice president in place of Mr. Rojtman's parallel sales organizations for industrial and agricultural lines, and setting up a program of market research. Speaking of these changes and of the shift in emphasis to retail sales, Mr. Grede remarked, "These are fresh concepts which are expected to increase the effectiveness of our product-development, production, and sales effort."[54]

Still other selling moves, as reported seriatim by the trade or business press, included a 1960 advertising program—much reduced, however, from Mr. Rojtman's $2.9 million budget; a special advertising campaign to scotch a rumor originating in Mr. Rojtman's day that Case was about to shift from independent dealers to direct selling; addition of accessory items (such as oil) to the line, reportedly in response to dealer and customer demand; limiting the already scheduled Hawaiian World Premier to dealers who had met stepped-up sales quotas, and eliminating World Premiers thereafter; revising the sales organization so that regional divisions followed major crop areas with the stated aim of improving service to dealers; and initiating an "aggressive promotional campaign" about mid-1961 "in an effort to maintain a proper balance between production, sales to dealers, and dealers' net sales."[55]

Reducing production. Besides emphasizing retail sales, Mr. Grede's two-pronged attack on dealer inventories included cutting factory production and shipments. Thus in 1960, with retail sales reportedly only $6 million off from the peak of 1959, factory production was cut $65 million and factory sales $74 million. (The resultant $9 million rise in factory inventory was explained as a deliberate move to make new equipment "available to our dealers in time for the selling season.")[56]

In 1961 factory sales and factory production were off again, by $17 and $24 million respectively, and factory inventory also fell.

Results achieved under this program were a $39 million reduction in Case and Case Credit wholesale receivables in 1960, and a further decline of $14 million in 1961. This contrasted with an $89 million rise under Mr. Rojtman. "Unusual costs" were, however, attributed to the cut-back program—almost $30 million in 1960 alone (including the estimated effects of two plant strikes).[57]

---

[54] Annual Report, 1960.

[55] *Business Week*, April 30, 1960, p. 54; *Implement & Tractor*, July 9, 1960, p. 24; October 10, 1960, p. 46; December 12, 1960, p. 79; March 15, 1961, p. 42; June 15, 1960, p. 50.

[56] Annual Report, 1960.

[57] Annual Reports.

Cutting costs. Early moves to cut costs, as reported by *Business Week*, included slashing more than $1 million from the advertising budget ("Grede says he came in too late to turn off the ad spigot entirely") and "eyeing" Case's parallel sales and service organizations for farm and industrial products with a view to consolidating these "as much as possible."[58] Still other steps were taken in 1961 when Case shut down two plants (the original ATC facility, and the unit converted to mass-produce small tractors in 1959); deactivated Case International S.A.; sold its assets in Argentina; dissolved the central engineering department, resorting instead to a liaison officer to coordinate engineering at the plants; and terminated the World Premiers.[59]

Product development. While Mr. Grede promised to continue development, "recognizing its importance to the future of the company," he reduced its scale. Wrote *Forbes*, "Where Rojtman boasted of budgeting half his operating profits for engineering, Grede fired more than 100 engineers, according to some estimates."[60] New developments were not reported in detail, the 1960 Annual Report simply stating, "New products introduced are proving very popular."

By far the biggest news in the engineering area was the revelation in 1961 that the company had costs of $9.76 million for "reworking certain models of one product line,"[61] including a reserve $1.28 million for anticipated future costs in this connection.

Reducing short-term debt. In keeping with the goal of debt reduction, short-term bank loans to Case Credit were cut by $72 million by the end of October 1961, in part by means of placing a $20 million 15-year note with four institutional investors. The total short-term debt of the parent company, however, went not down but up—from $37 to $85 million—reflecting the fact that Case had to borrow under lines of credit from the banks to meet its working capital needs.

Overall results under Mr. Grede. The need to borrow for working capital reflected losses in the two years under Mr. Grede that totaled over $79 million. Not only was the earned surplus wiped out, but part of the common stock values as well, and Case was forced to seek extension of its bank loans in order to stay alive.

Explaining these results in its Annual Reports, the company ascribed the drop from a $13 million pretax profit in 1959 to a $46 million pretax loss in 1960 largely to "unusual costs" and "nonrecurring charges" of $59 million, while the loss of $32 million in 1961 was traced almost entirely to "costs attributable to inventories and receivables built up in prior years, their reduction in 1961, and the rework of certain models of our product line" (Exhibit 4). It was explicitly stated, however, that the 1961 tabulation of losses "was not intended to be construed as a listing of nonrecurring costs."

---

[58]*Business Week*, April 30, 1960, p. 54.
[59]*Implement & Tractor*, March 15, 1961, p. 58; July 1, 1961, p. 55; July 7, 1961, p. 91.
[60]*Forbes*, October 1, 1961, p. 13.
[61]A tractor (*Wall Street Journal*, December 31, 1962).

Exhibit 4

J. I. CASE COMPANY
Explanation of Losses, 1960 and 1961
(Dollars in Millions)

1960 Operations Compared with 1959

Unusual costs attributable to reduced wholesale sales volume of $73,000,000 and reduced production level of $65,000,000 (including the estimated effects of strikes at Racine and Bettendorf plants) $29.9

Nonrecurring charges:

Increase in research and development expense, primarily as a result of change in accounting policy to write off such expense as incurred (before adjustment for related taxes on income) 5.5

Other, principally special allowances to move dealer inventories and losses on liquidation of receivables 8.7

Adjustment of carrying value of investment in French subsidiaries 6.0

Added costs during 1960 such as increases in interest and selling expenses 8.9

Difference in taxes on income, 1960/1959 ....(13.0)

Difference in net profit, 1960/1959 .... $46.0

1961 Operations

Losses incurred in collection of retail and wholesale receivables and provision for estimated future losses thereon $6.68

Scrapping of obsolete materials and provision for estimated obsolescence remaining in our inventories 3.96

Cost of reworking certain products and provision for estimated future rework .. 9.76

Reductions in the retail selling price of goods (primarily noncurrent models) granted to dealers during 1961, and estimated reductions to be granted in 1962 applicable to products in dealers' inventories at October 31, 1961 ...... 9.67

	$30.07

Other 2.27

Total $32.34

Source: Annual Reports.

By the time the Annual Report for 1961 was published, some 91 bank creditors had decided to extend their loans to Case and thus allow the company "a three-year lease on life." As one senior lending officer explained, "We had no choice. We either had to give Case an extension or take responsibility for putting the company into bankruptcy." Lines of credit were rewritten under the terms that called for (1) a maximum loan figure of $140 million for Case and its credit subsidiary, with the maximum declining over a three-year period; (2) greatly scaled down interest rates; and (3) payment of additional compensation to the banks contingent upon profits until 1972. Nonfinancial conditions of the loan included, according to *Business Week*, a proviso that both Mr. Grede and Mr. Brown (then vice chairman of the board) should resign, thus making way for a new administration.[62]

Case in 1962

Following conclusion of the loan extension in 1961, Mr. Grede and Mr. Brown resigned, and the board, now chairmanned by Mr. Samuel B. Payne,

---

[62]*Business Week,* January 6, 1962, p. 100.

a Morgan Stanley partner, began the search for a new president. Meanwhile, into the newly created post of executive vice president went Mr. J. C. Freeman, formerly vice president for domestic operations at Allis-Chalmers Corporation, who had joined Case in 1961.

Initial statements by these two leaders indicated that the banks had both a "plan" and an "action program" for Case. Mr. Payne stated that the plan put primary emphasis on debt repayment, but should make it possible to operate profitably. Profitable operations, he said, would enable the company to use a substantial amount of its tax loss carry-forward to aid in the reduction of debt.

Included in the action program were moves designed to "streamline and strengthen" the still profitable J. I. Case Credit Corporation; to continue reducing inventories and receivables; and to effect plant consolidations which were expected to reduce overhead by $5 million or 43% when completed. Marketing emphasis would continue to be placed on retail sales.[63]

Reported actions of the new interim administration included sale of the Churubusco plant for about $1 million; an advertising campaign urging dealers to take a "new look" at Case on the grounds of its retail record and its combined farm-utility line; and a new promotional device—the dealer's open house with door prizes supplied in part by the company.[64]

At the end of the first quarter, sales and profits were down from 1961, but reportedly were better than original targets:

. . . Sales to dealers were about 20% over those projected by the plan, and net loss was about 37% below anticipated. Retail sales by dealers to customers were encouraging, and were 21% above the plan.[65]

Shortly after this report was issued, Mr. Payne announced that the board had succeeded in its search for a new president—someone who would be "a man with a record of accomplishment in the farm machinery industry, someone who could promise something constructive and who could provide vigorous leadership for our new executive group."[66] This man was Mr. Merritt D. Hill, formerly a vice president of the Ford Motor Company and general manager of the Ford Implement and Tractor Division.

As had happened in previous administrations, the new president used the occasion of the annual stockholders' meeting in April for his first major public policy statement. The following account appeared in *Implement & Tractor:*

My interest is only in the future. . . . I didn't take on this assignment with the idea of assisting in carrying out an orderly liquidation of the company.

---

[63]*Implement & Tractor*, January 15, 1962, p. 107.
[64]*Implement & Tractor*, January 15, 1962, pp. 39, 44; March 1, 1962, p. 44; March 15, 1962, p. 43.
[65]*Implement & Tractor*, March 15, 1962, p. 48.
[66]*Implement & Tractor*, April 1, 1962, p. 14.

I came here to try and do a job which I am firmly convinced can be done.
I accept no responsibility for what has taken place before I joined it. . . .
On the other hand, I have assumed responsibility for correcting the problems
which I find here. It is evident to me at this time that major changes in the
organization structure here at the general offices are imperative and steps are
being taken now to revamp it for the purpose of getting it properly set up to
do a more effective and efficient job starting at the top.

Mr. Hill credited Freeman and other top-echelon personnel for their good
work of the past few months, "which is now starting to show up on the financial statements of both Case and Case Credit Corporation":

For example . . . real progress has been made in reducing inventory—most
of the old products have been moved out of the distribution system. Warranty
expense is down sharply this year. Accounts receivable from both wholesale and
retail customers have been brought down to manageable proportions.

While confident of the industrial and utility market for Case, Hill was
not as optimistic regarding farm machinery, stating, "The possibility of increasing our sales volume in the United States and Canadian markets is
limited in view of the overall reductions in farm machinery volume during
the past several years and the prospects for the future. United States tractor
production has decreased by 60% (in units) in the past ten years, and other
items of farm equipment in a similar ratio."

Hill concluded, "It is my job to put this Case machine together properly,
making certain that the right men are in the right places and that they clearly
understand their duties and responsibilities. These fundamentals and proper
motivation will provide the kind of environment where men will want to
do their best. From this combination will come a profitable organization."[67]

Competition in 1962

Serving the domestic farm equipment market in 1962 were 1,050 firms,
of which only seven were full-line manufacturers; i.e., producers of both
tractors and a complete line of equipment, attachments, and other agricultural
machines. These seven companies reportedly shared some 65% of the total
industry volume. (See Exhibit 5 for some financial data.) Another 12 to 15
long-line concerns produced specialized equipment that was widely marketed
and comprised about 10% of the total. The balance of the manufacturers, all
smaller companies, built specialty items sold locally.[68]

Included in the seven full-line manufacturers was one newcomer, the White
Motor Company, which between 1960 and 1962 had acquired all the farm
equipment business of three small full-line makers: the Oliver Corporation,[69]

---

[67]*Implement & Tractor*, May 15, 1962, pp. 84, 85.

[68]Standard & Poor's *Industry Surveys: Machinery, Agricultural–Basic Analysis*, March
15, 1962, p. M-11.

[69]1959 sales, $114.6 million; profits, 3% on sales during 1959 and same or lower during
previous six years. White acquired Oliver assets producing $88 million in farm equipment
sales.

Exhibit 5

SALES AND PROFIT MARGINS, SELECTED COMPANIES, 1945–1961

Year	Allis-Chalmers Sales*	Allis-Chalmers Profit Margin†	J. I. Case Sales*	J. I. Case Profit Margin†	Deere Sales*	Deere Profit Margin†	International Harvester Sales*	International Harvester Profit Margin†	Massey-Ferguson Sales*	Massey-Ferguson Profit Margin†	Motec Industries Sales*	Motec Industries Profit Margin†
1945	98	10.6%	61	17.9%	47	13.2%	72	7.1%	82	5.9%	...	...
1946	32	def.	28	1.4	49	14.9	56	5.4	50	7.9	...	...
1947	71	5.2	60	12.8	72	16.2	86	10.1	59	11.5	...	...
1948	110	8.9	114	14.7	105	17.2	109	9.3	94	15.0	110	15.8%
1949	118	10.4	125	21.2	123	21.5	105	11.0	113	19.8	111	16.0
1950	116	14.5	107	23.3	114	24.5	109	13.9	116	23.4	120	17.6
1951	154	15.8	123	17.3	147	23.9	148	15.5	139	18.7	138	16.5
1952	173	12.8	115	13.8	130	18.8	139	10.8	159	13.2	140	9.0
1953	173	9.8	84	6.3	129	15.6	145	8.9	134	9.9	160	6.4
1954	166	11.8	74	4.0	100	16.8	115	8.6	237	6.4	117	3.0
1955	180	11.0	76	6.8	115	20.1	135	11.0	293	7.7	110	4.7
1956	184	9.5	70	3.8	106	14.6	145	8.9	283	5.4	85	def.
1957	180	8.8	99	6.0	132	18.8	137	9.5	311	3.6	87	0.6
1958	179	9.7	143	9.1	160	22.1	127	10.2	335	8.4	81	3.7
1959	182	10.0	161	11.4	185	21.5	199	14.0	379	9.6	81	9.4
1960	178	6.1	89	def.	159	10.5	195	11.0	391	9.3	75	8.3
1961	169	3.9	103	def.	173	16.7	186	10.0	414	8.8	88	6.6
Average sales in 1947-49 base period, millions of dollars	$297.0		$124.6		$294.5		$865.2		$125.5		$66.0	

*Index form, 1947–1949 = 100.

†Operating income as a percentage of sales. Operating income is usually the balance left from sales after deducting operating costs, selling, general, and administrative expenses; local and state taxes; provision for bad debts and pensions; but before other income and before deducting depreciation charges, debt service charges if any, federal taxes, and any special reserves.

Source: Standard & Poor's *Industry Surveys: Machinery, Agricultural—Basic Analysis*, March 15, 1962, p. M–13.

Cockshutt Farm Equipment, Ltd.,[70] and Motec Industries, Inc. (formerly named Minneapolis-Moline Company).[71] A spokesman for White indicated both the reasons leading his company to enter this business and certain main features of the strategy by which it meant to compete:

Heavy farm machinery has a lot in common with trucks. . . . Also we wanted to move into a stable industry—one that involves essential income-producing, food-producing equipment that is the basis for our everyday living. We'll always have farms, and farmers will need machinery. We're counting on a replacement business in heavy tractors in which Oliver will increase its share. We're looking for an overall increase of about 15% in farm-equipment industry sales in the next five years and there's room for Oliver to pick up an increasing per cent as the market expands.

* * * * *

What's Sam White's formula? The main factor is dealer development. "We, along with others in this business, used to be concerned mainly with moving our production to dealers. We had a wholesale concept of sales. Now, we are mainly concerned with what happens at retail. We are embarked on a program of strengthening our ties with dealers and helping them to do a more efficient, profitable job of selling our line of equipment."

* * * * *

Sam White's second cardinal principle is prudent market management with an eagle eye on inventory. . . . The third point . . . is decentralized management for more effective use of executive talent.[72]

Of the remaining six full-line companies, three were heavily diversified (International Harvester, Allis-Chalmers, and Ford), while the three others were largely specializing in farm equipment (Deere, Massey-Ferguson, and J. I. Case). Highlights in the recent history of these six full-line companies were summarized by *Fortune* as follows during the summer of 1961:

Deere & Co. displaced International Harvester in 1958 as leader in U.S. sales. Nonetheless, to protect its competitive position, Deere felt obliged last year to invest $50 million for an entire new line of tractors and implements. President William A. Hewitt is also trying hard to expand sales of light industrial equipment ($40 million last year vs. total Deere sales of $468,500,000) and is committed to greater foreign expansion. A five-year-old investment in Germany may show a profit this year, and Deere will soon manufacture tractors in France.

International Harvester, no longer leader in the United States, is second to Toronto-based Massey-Ferguson outside North America. Its combined sales in all markets are still larger than those of any other farm-equipment company. Though Harvester's business traces its ancestry to McCormick's reaper, trucks and industrial equipment now dominate the company's sales and profit picture.

---

[70]Certain assets, mainly fixed, of Cockshutt's farm equipment business were purchased by White for $8 million in 1962. White thereby expected to add about $25 million to its sales.

[71]Motec's farm equipment sales in 1962 amounted to approximately $50 million, with the company about breaking even. The company's farm equipment assets and liabilities were purchased for $21 million at 60% of book value.

[72]*Implement & Tractor*, January 15, 1962, pp. 82, 83.

Farm equipment last year made up only 35% of Harvester's $1.7 billion sales, continuing a long-term downward trend.

Massey-Ferguson, Ltd., leading in sales outside North America, is battling for third place in United States sales with Allis-Chalmers and Ford's Tractor & Implement Division. . . . The overseas market accounted for 58% of the company's $490-million sales last year.

Allis-Chalmers now does only about one-third of its business in the farm field. By far the largest share of total sales . . . is equipment for the electric-power industry, for mining and construction. A-C's sales to American farmers are declining while exports and sales from plants in Britain, France, and Australia gain.

Ford is much stronger in the farm market abroad than at home. . . . In the U.S., Ford's Tractor & Implement Division . . . nearly ran into disaster last year. Ford was handicapped by having no tractor to sell in the upper power ranges that American farmers now demand, also by a limited selection of implements. This year Ford introduced tractors in the 70-hp class, and its implement line is fatter.

J. I. Case is on the critical list. Last year the company lost $40 million, a deficit of $14.32 a share. Flamboyant sales tactics introduced by President Marc B. Rojtman (replaced in 1960) piled huge inventories on dealers' lots, which Case carried on credit. But final sales to farmers came nowhere near matching the factory sales to dealers. As a result, J. I. Case is now in debt $178 million to a group of 90 banks. The caretaker president, William J. Grede, former head of an iron-foundry company, says bravely, "We'll do our damndest to share in any increase in the market," but everyone else in the industry is watching with fascination to see if Case can stay alive.[73]

APPENDIX A

SUMMARY OF J. I. CASE OPERATIONS, 1945-1952

As World War II hostilities ended in 1945, about two-thirds of J. I. Case's sales were in farm machinery and one-third in special war materials, military tractors, and equipment. The 1945 Annual Report stated that "sales for the year were determined by production rather than by market demand. The demand exceeded the supply by a substantial volume." Even though peacetime reconversion of the manufacturing facilities was immediately started, shortages and controls on manpower, raw materials, and prices restricted sales.

Then, on December 26, 1945, a strike was called. (Some, but not all, of the farm equipment manufacturers were also affected by shorter strikes.) According to the 1946 Annual Report:

In addition to the demand for company-wide bargaining, the UAW-CIO demanded a "closed shop," "irrevocable check-off of union dues, fines and assessments," "compulsory arbitration," "payment by the Company for union participants in the grievance machinery," "preferred seniority and other preferences for union officers." The acceptance of these confiscatory demands by the Company

---

[73]George Bookman, "Farm Machinery Shifts Gears," *Fortune*, July 1961, pp. 130, 131.

would have meant that the authority of the owners of the business over the conduct of its operations would have been transferred to the UAW-CIO.

Even though some of the Case plants never fully closed and others gradually resumed work, it took until March 10, 1947, for the strike to be formally settled for the major Racine plant. As a result, fiscal year 1946 closed with an operating loss. As to J. I. Case's dealer organization, the 1946 Annual Report stated:

> The Company expresses its sincere appreciation to the thousands of loyal dealers who, in spite of the shortage of certain machines and repair parts because of the strikes at Racine and Rockford plants, have carried on their sales and service programs in an efficient manner. They have cooperated fully with the Company in support of its efforts to retain the management of its business, rather than to permit control by union officials.
>
> Due to their steadfastness, the Company today faces the future with virtually an intact dealer organization capable of handling future sales and service.

With the strike being settled, Case sales increased rapidly. Yet the 1948 Annual Report stated that "the demand for Case farm machinery exceeded the available supply." To meet this demand the company since 1945 invested significantly in additional plants, equipment, and inventories, accomplishing simultaneously a factory modernization program. The heavy demand, with some minor cyclical variations, persisted so that the 1951 Annual Report commented: "The demand for farm machinery in 1952 should continue strong. Whether such demands can be met will depend largely upon the materials available and whether a balanced supply of materials can be obtained early enough to manufacture the machinery in time for seasonal use." At the same time working capital requirements, both for inventories and dealer credit, increased. In 1952, however, sales declined by 7.2%, due, according to the Annual Report, "principally to the drought . . . , a decline in sales in foreign countries . . . , and the inability to complete certain harvesting machines in time to meet the harvest season because of the strike in steel plants."

During the 1945–1952 period selling prices were mentioned yearly in the J. I. Case Annual Report. The following quote in 1950 is representative:

> Selling prices follow costs. During the year costs of materials, wages, freight, taxes, and other important elements continued to rise. It is apparent that the inflationary pressure of these added costs will force prices still higher, and, furthermore, unless the inflationary trend is reversed, the results ultimately will be disastrous.
>
> It is the established policy to keep selling prices as low as practicable, consistent with high quality products, and the cost of production and distribution, including taxes. This is the American way of raising living standards, and, further, it is recognized that this is desirable because high prices invariably restrict sales volume.
>
> Reports issued by the Bureau of Labor Statistics show that the percentage of increase in farm machinery prices is relatively lower than on other products

made from similar materials. This means that price increases have not kept pace with the increases in wages and other costs, and farmers for many years have had the benefit of such lower prices. This has been made possible only because of the larger volume of business done and improved methods of manufacture.

In contrast to selling prices and factory production, research and new product developments were not specifically mentioned in the Annual Reports from 1945 to 1952 with the exception of the following quote in 1945:

It has been a long established policy of the Company to carry on an extensive program of research and development work on machines for use on farms. It is no longer necessary to give attention to engineering of special war materials. It is therefore possible for the Company's staff of agricultural engineers to devote their entire time to its regular line of product. New items which have been developed and tested, and which are ready for production, include a nine-foot and a twelve-foot self-propelled combine, a forage harvester, and a small shop tractor for industrial use.

In 1953, however, the tune changed. The Annual Report mentioned that "engineering and development work on new products and on the improvement of other products was intensified during the year. It was the judgment of the Management that the cost of this increased program in engineering and development work was in the best long-term interest of the Company." Also, the 1953 Annual Report explained a $42 million sales decrease as follows:

This large reduction in sales volume is very disappointing. In appraising its significance it should be pointed out that a large unfilled demand for farm equipment was built up during World War II when severe restrictions were placed on manufacturers. This accumulation of unfilled demand, stimulated by inflation and the Korean war development, resulted in a higher than normal demand for farm machinery which continued well into the year of 1952. Beginning in the latter part of 1952 the dealers and distributing organization were confronted with the complete return of a highly competitive market.

It was during this year that Mr. John T. Brown, who had joined J. I. Case as vice president on January 1, 1948 (formerly vice president of the Chain Belt Company for a number of years), became president.

Included below are some selected financial figures on J. I. Case for the 1945–1952 period.

J. I. CASE COMPANY
Income Statements and Balance Sheets, 1945–1952
(Dollars in Millions)

	1945	1946	1947	1948	1949	1950	1951	1952
Net sales	$79.6	$38.2	$75.3	$142.9	$156.4	$133.0	$154.1	$143.4
Cost of goods sold	62.5	38.9	62.0	114.3	114.7	93.3	116.3	112.1
Depreciation				2.5	3.0	3.2	3.3	3.6
Selling, general and administrative expense	4.9		5.5	7.5	8.6	8.4	10.7	11.1
Operating profit (or loss)	12.3	(0.7)	7.8	18.1	29.6	27.8	23.2	16.1
Other income	0.3	0.3	0.3	0.4	0.4	0.3	0.5	0.5
Other expenses	...	(0.4)	...	0.1	0.1	0.2	0.4	1.4
Income before taxes	12.6	(0.4)	8.1	18.4	29.9	27.9	23.3	15.2
Taxes	9.5	[1.9]	3.2	8.0	12.3	12.8	13.5	8.2
Net profit	3.1	1.5	4.9	10.4	17.6	15.1	9.8	7.0
Surplus, beginning	10.0	9.7	8.9	12.0	18.1	28.5	38.7	39.4
Dividends								
Preferred	0.6	0.6	0.6	0.6	0.6	0.6	0.6	0.6
Common	1.7	1.6	1.2	1.5	1.7	4.3	4.7	5.0
Other charges (mostly appropriation to reserves)	1.0	...	...	2.0	4.9	...	3.8	...
Surplus, ending	9.7	8.9	12.0	18.1	28.5	38.7	39.4	40.8
Cash and securities	$29.8	$ 8.4	$ 7.0	$ 7.0	$ 16.1	$ 10.0	$ 7.8	$ 6.6
Receivables (net)	4.3	1.3	2.4	4.2	2.3	20.8	30.3	37.7
Inventory	20.2	27.7	32.6	42.7	52.3	52.6	71.3	70.1
Gross fixed assets	26.0	29.2	37.7	44.4	48.3	50.1	54.1	59.2
Other assets	0.3	2.2	0.4	0.8	0.6	0.5	0.7	0.8
Total gross assets	$80.6	$68.8	$80.1	$ 99.1	$119.6	$134.0	$164.2	$174.4
Supplier, tax, and other credits	$16.1	$ 4.4	$11.4	$ 20.5	$ 23.2	$ 25.4	$ 31.0	$ 18.3
Debt	...	...	...	...	...	...	17.8	27.6
Equity (depreciation, reserves, retained earnings, and capital stock)	64.5	64.4	68.7	78.6	96.4	108.6	115.4	128.5
Total	$80.6	$68.8	$80.1	$ 99.1	$119.6	$134.0	$164.2	$174.4

Source: Annual Reports.

APPENDIX B

Charts 1–7

MAJOR TRENDS IN THE FARM MARKET

1. THE COST/PRICE SQUEEZE ON FARMERS

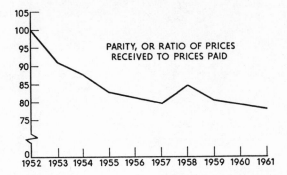

PARITY, OR RATIO OF PRICES
RECEIVED TO PRICES PAID

2. FAT AND LEAN YEARS IN NET FARM INCOME

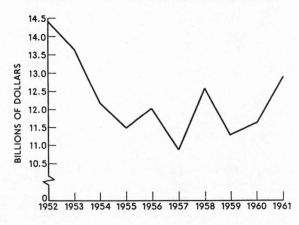

Charts 1-7—Continued

3. FAT AND LEAN YEARS IN THE FARM EQUIPMENT BUSINESS

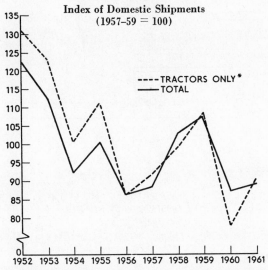

Index of Domestic Shipments
(1957–59 = 100)

- - - - TRACTORS ONLY*
——— TOTAL

*Includes garden-type tractors and parts, excluded from Chart 7.
Source: Charts 1 and 2, U.S. Bureau of Census figures, cited *Statistical Abstract of the United States*; Chart 3, Farm Equipment Institute.

4. PERCENT CHANGE, 1954/1959: FARMS*

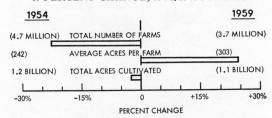

1954   **1959**

(4.7 MILLION)   TOTAL NUMBER OF FARMS   (3.7 MILLION)

(242)   AVERAGE ACRES PER FARM   (303)

1.2 BILLION)   TOTAL ACRES CULTIVATED   (1.1 BILLION)

-30%   -15%   0   +15%   +30%

PERCENT CHANGE

*Not adjusted for changes in the definition of a farm, which accounted for about two-thirds of the decline, mainly in the smallest size class.

5. PERCENT CHANGE, 1954/1959: NUMBER OF FARMS BY SIZE CLASS IN ACRES*

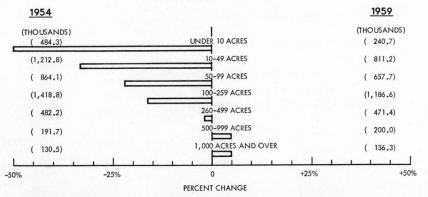

1954   **1959**

(THOUSANDS)   (THOUSANDS)
(484.3)   UNDER 10 ACRES   (240.7)

(1,212.8)   10-49 ACRES   (811.2)

(864.1)   50-99 ACRES   (657.7)

(1,418.8)   100-259 ACRES   (1,186.6)

(482.2)   260-499 ACRES   (471.4)

(191.7)   500-999 ACRES   (200.0)

(130.5)   1,000 ACRES AND OVER   (136.3)

-50%   -25%   0   +25%   +50%

PERCENT CHANGE

*See note, Chart 4 above.

Charts 1–7—Continued

6. PERCENT CHANGE, 1954/1959: NUMBER OF FARMS BY VALUE OF PRODUCTS SOLD*

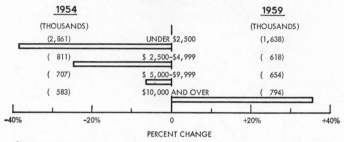

1954		1959
(THOUSANDS)		(THOUSANDS)
(2,861)	UNDER $2,500	(1,638)
(811)	$ 2,500–$4,999	(618)
(707)	$ 5,000–$9,999	(654)
(583)	$10,000 AND OVER	(794)

–40%   –20%   0   +20%   +40%

PERCENT CHANGE

*See note, Chart 4 above.
Source: Charts 4, 5, and 6, U.S. Bureau of the Census figures, cited *Statistical Abstract of the United States.*

7. PERCENT CHANGE, 1953/1960 VALUE OF MANUFACTURERS' SHIPMENTS FOR DOMESTIC FARM USE

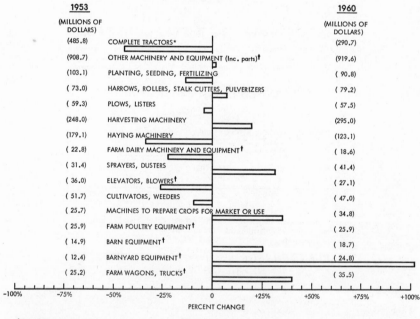

1953		1960
(MILLIONS OF DOLLARS)		(MILLIONS OF DOLLARS)
(485.8)	COMPLETE TRACTORS*	(290.7)
(908.7)	OTHER MACHINERY AND EQUIPMENT (Inc. parts)†	(919.6)
(103.1)	PLANTING, SEEDING, FERTILIZING	(90.8)
(73.0)	HARROWS, ROLLERS, STALK CUTTERS, PULVERIZERS	(79.2)
(59.3)	PLOWS, LISTERS	(57.5)
(248.0)	HARVESTING MACHINERY	(295.0)
(179.1)	HAYING MACHINERY	(123.1)
(22.8)	FARM DAIRY MACHINERY AND EQUIPMENT†	(18.6)
(31.4)	SPRAYERS, DUSTERS	(41.4)
(36.0)	ELEVATORS, BLOWERS†	(27.1)
(51.7)	CULTIVATORS, WEEDERS	(47.0)
(25.7)	MACHINES TO PREPARE CROPS FOR MARKET OR USE	(34.8)
(25.9)	FARM POULTRY EQUIPMENT†	(25.9)
(14.9)	BARN EQUIPMENT†	(18.7)
(12.4)	BARNYARD EQUIPMENT†	(24.8)
(25.2)	FARM WAGONS, TRUCKS†	(35.5)

–100%   –75%   –50%   –25%   0   +25%   +50%   +75%   +100%

PERCENT CHANGE

*Excludes garden tractors and tractor parts and accessories for domestic farm use valued as follows (dollars in millions):

	1960	1961
Garden tractors	$43,926	$ 51,920
Attachments (wheel and garden)	42,534	46,056
Parts (wheel and garden)	93,204	125,228

†Includes items not necessarily made by "full-line" producers.
Source: U.S. Burean of the Census, "Tractors" and "Farm Machinery and Equipment," *Current Industrial Reports.*

APPENDIX C

WHEEL-TYPE TRACTORS, SELECTED PULL-TYPE, MOUNTED, AND SELF-PROPELLED FARM EQUIPMENT

CASE® the PLUS-POWERED Tractor Line
with DIESELS IN EVERY POWER CLASS
... revolutionary Dynaclonic, famous Powrcel engines

6 Power Sizes • 32 Models

430 3-Plow Tractor. 4-speed, 12-speed Tripl-Range, shuttle. Gasoline or Dynaclonic diesel. 3 models.

530 3-4 Plow Tractor. Case-o-matic Drive, 4-speed, 12-speed, shuttle. Gas, LP-gas or Dynaclonic diesel. 4 models.

630 4-Plow Tractor. Case-o-matic Drive, 4-speed, 12-speed, shuttle. Gasoline or Dynaclonic diesel. 5 models.

730 5-Plow Tractor. Case-o-matic or 8-speed Dual-Range. Gas, LP-gas, Powrcel diesel. 5 models.

830 5-6 Plow Tractor. Case-o-matic or 8-speed Dual-Range. Gas, LP-gas, Powrcel diesel. 6 models.

930 6-Plow Tractor. 6 speeds. Powrcel diesel or LP-gas. Dual-Control hydraulics. Wide-swing drawbar.

171 fuel, transmission and front-end options

A COMPLETE LINE OF **CASE®** PULL-TYPE EQUIPMENT

MOLDBOARD PLOWS

Case CH series plow is available with 3 to 5 bottoms, 14 and 16-inch sizes. Big 27x24-inch throat swallows heavy trash.

TANDEM DISKS

Case S series disk harrow is available in 7 to 17-foot sizes, with sealed anti-friction or steelite bearings. Transport wheels control depth.

DRAWBAR CARRIER

The HD-100 hydraulic drawbar carrier handles from 3 to 7 spring tooth, spike tooth or rotary hoe sections ... up to 42-foot working width.

ROTARY HOES

WT wheel-type rotary hoe is available in 2, 4 and 6-row models ... B trail-type in 7 to 42-foot widths ... BE Eagle Hitch mounted in 7 to 10½-foot sizes.

PLANTERS

Pull-type corn planters are available in 4 and 6-row models. Attachments for pre-emergence weedicide, liquid or dry fertilizer.

DRILLS

D series plain grain drill is available in 6, 8, 10 and 12-foot sizes. Also fertilizer models, lister and plow press drills.

MOWERS

T-10 trail-type mower equipped with 7-foot cutter bar ... also 5 or 6-foot. Easy hook-up to any tractor with standard PTO.

RAKES

281 side delivery rake handles full 8-foot, 4-inch swath. Easy and gentle raking, short hay travel saves valuable leaves.

CONDITIONER

222 hay conditioner handles 7-foot swath. Saves leaves ... speeds hay drying time 40 to 50%. Both crimps and crushes.

BALERS

New Case 200 Sweep Feed baler. Twine-ties up to 10 tons per hour. Simple power train ... fewer parts, less maintenance. Smooth, gentle baling ... no surging.

FLAIL-TYPE CHOPPER

Case 640 flail-type chopper cuts a 60-inch swath, 2½ to 6 inches high. Clips pastures ... chops standing and windrowed crops, stalks and brush.

CHOPPER

200 series forage harvester is available with 4 or 6-knife cutter wheel. Three quick-change heads: row-crop, windrow pick-up, 60-inch cutter bar.

COMBINES

New Case 80 combine with 7-foot cut features straight-thru design. Big 32-bushel bin. Adjustable wheel spacing for row crops.

SPREADERS

New 100, 115 and 135-bushel spreaders with exclusive V-belt drive, give 20% wider spread. Also 75 and 95-bushel ground-drive models.

MIXER-BLENDER

Case-Helix auger unloader mixer-blender blends and transfers a ton of feed in 5 minutes ... hauls up to 3 tons in one trip. 90 and 125-bushel.

BUNK FEEDER

Case-Helix power unloading wagon with bunk feeder has exclusive, self-cleaning Convey-o-matic floor. Unloads 6 to 7 tons in 2½ minutes.

JOB-MATCHED MOUNTED TOOLS

Your Case dealer has a complete line of front and rear-mounted tools, quickly attached and hydraulically controlled, for your Case 730 tractor. These include 4 and 6-row planters and cultivators, disk and moldboard plows, tandem and offset disk harrows, pickers and loaders, etc. — all designed to give your tractor greater versatility, quick maneuverability on many jobs.

PLANTERS...

Case 400-E series 4-row corn planters check row, hill drop and drill 36-42 inch rows. High speed valves assure accurate drop. Fertilizer attachment available.

CULTIVATORS

The 700 series cultivators include: 2-row to work 28-48 inch rows; 4-row for 28, 36, 38, 40 and 42-inch rows. Convenient drive-in attaching and detaching.

DISK PLOWS

Case 300 series disk plow is available in 2, 3 and 4-furrow sizes with 24-inch disks. Ideal for tough, heavy or sticky gumbo soils. Plows up to 16 acres a day.

Case 400 series reversible disk plow is available in 2 or 3-disk, 26 or 28-inch sizes. Designed for deep plowing (down to 14 inches) in irrigated areas — up to 10 acres a day. Leaves land level ... no ridges or furrows.

DISK HARROWS

Case SE and SEA disk harrows are available in 7, 8, or 9-foot widths. Sealed anti-friction or steelite bearings. Pivot action; adjustable gangs; heavy semi-rigid bolted frame.

Case D toolbar planters are available in nine different units, both rigid and flexible beams. Wide choice of bottoms, openers, seed cans and plates for cotton, corn, sorghum, peanuts, beets.

PICKERS .. STRIPPERS

Case 426 2-row corn picker mounts easily. Exclusive forward gathering design gets more down ears. Long 48-inch picking rolls are adjustable from tractor seat. Picking points and elevator raise together for faster, safer turns.

Case 2-row cotton stripper harvests clean in storm-resistant, tight-locked varieties. Handles high yield irrigated cotton at normal speeds. Fits many tractors.

SUBSOILERS...

Case T-620 series subsoiler available in 1 and 2-point models. Tough steel points on strong narrow standards. Gauge wheels assure constant depth down to 22 inches.

LOADERS...

Case 190 series loaders with 10½ cubic foot capacity handle any loading job fast and easy. Sturdy, compact design ... 3,000-lb. break-out power. Lifts 9 feet. Manure fork, dirt or snow buckets available.

SCRAPERS...

Case-Danuser all-purpose blade available in 6 and 8-foot sizes. Ideal for barn or feed lot cleaning, ditching and backfilling, leveling and grading.

CASE. | SELF-PROPELLED WINDROWERS

CASE. | SELF-PROPELLED COMBINES

Courtesy J. I. Case Company.

AMERICAN MOTORS CORPORATION (A)*

American Motors was formed on May 1, 1954, through the merger of two faltering automobile companies, Nash-Kelvinator Corporation and the Hudson Motor Car Company. Combined sales for the fiscal year ended September 30, 1954, showed unit sales off 42% from the preceding year of separate operations, and the combined statement of earnings showed a net loss of slightly more than $11,000,000 after receipt of a tax loss credit of $11,500,000, i.e., a total operating loss of more than $22,000,000 (see Exhibits 1 and 2).

In the three succeeding years sales volume declined about 25%, and market share fell to less than 2%. Successive operating losses of $16,700,000; $30,000,000; and $11,000,000 forced the company to borrow heavily from various banks in order to maintain minimal working capital balances. Near the nadir of its fortunes, sometime financier Louis E. Wolfson began buying shares, and by early 1958 was believed to be within easy reach of a controlling interest in the company. In July 1957 one of his nominees joined the board of directors, and another in February 1958.

Then as the columnists began writing obituaries for the company, AMC made a spectacular comeback. By the end of 1960 unit sales had risen about 300% from their low, market share had more than tripled, the company had an operating profit of $105 million, and all bank indebtedness had been repaid. With its "compact" cars the company had become a leader in the low-price field, and the "Big Three" were taking preliminary steps toward following AMC's lead in making cars with a "unitized" body.

Commenting on the company's comeback, and on the public acceptance of compact cars, George Romney, AMC's chairman and president since 1954, noted that there was a long lead time between the development of a new basic concept, the acceptance of this concept by the organization, and finally its acceptance by the public.

> . . . it seems to require about seven years for a good idea to really catch on. It took seven years to develop the Rambler idea internally (1943–50)—and it wasn't sold internally at the end of seven years. Only three men in top management believed in the Rambler at that point.
>
> It was just seven years—(1950–1957)—before the Rambler took hold pub-

---

licly. It was in the Spring of 1957, just seven years after it was introduced, that Rambler's sales began to move up.[1]

Mr. Romney noted on other occasions that confidence in the Rambler had been anything but universal in the company up through 1956, thirteen years after the original experiments on a lightweight, compact car were begun. During this period, a handful of members of top management had built a strategy around this new idea, had merged two companies, closed factories, retired a number of key executives who were "big car minded," and borrowed to the limit of the company's capacity in order to put over this new concept. Perhaps most important of all, the company had discontinued its Nash and Hudson lines, and had concentrated all its efforts on the remaining line, the Rambler. By 1957 the company had bet all of its chips on the next roll, the 1958 models, and Mr. Romney conceded to members of his organization that if they didn't bring the company into the black in 1958 the game was up.

As the company's fortunes improved during 1958, the strategy shifted to one of expansion in the compact field. But despite its rapidly increasing output, the company was unable to meet the total demand for its cars for almost a year. Then as the Big Three brought out directly competitive cars, company strategy shifted once again, as AMC sought to hold its share of market.

Mr. Romney frequently described AMC's strategy in terms of this seesaw between offense and defense, likening it to a sequence of "campaigns" where a campaign was a program of action stretching over a period of years. On one occasion he reviewed the campaigns following the founding of the company as follows:

On many occasions I have discussed our program in terms of campaigns. Between 1954 and 1957 we won our "campaign for survival." Between 1957 and 1958 we won our "campaign opportunity" and since 1959, as our competitors imitated Rambler, we have successfully faced their "campaign counterattack." We have shown those financial advisors and those who said we could not compete successfully with the Big Three head-on that they were wrong. We have demonstrated this by our success in competing with them head-on. We expect conclusively to win in this year [1962] by selling the largest number of Ramblers in our history despite all-out compact car competition. Next year we expect to resume the offensive with "campaign leadership." In the years ahead, we can expect to begin a long-range battle for the number one brand name position in the automobile industry in this country.

*   *   *   *   *

This case describes the automotive strategy of American Motors in relation to market conditions and the strategies of its major competitors in the American market. It omits the appliance business, in which AMC's Kelvinator division was a participant, and it also omits all but the briefest consideration

[1] Report to Stockholders, February 7, 1962.

Exhibit 1

AMERICAN MOTORS CORPORATION

Consolidated Statements of Profit and Loss
(In Thousands)

	1954		1955		1956		1957	
Sales		$416,845		$468,773		$429,074		$383,175
Less: Excise taxes......		16,502		27,646		20,666		20,941
Net sales.............		$400,343		$441,127		$408,407		$362,234
Other income:								
Dividends from subsidiaries*	$ 1,043		$ 2,900		$ 202		$ 133	
Interest on securities	120							
Sundry income	1,748	2,912	2,801	5,701	2,099	2,302	2,104	2,327
		$403,255		$446,828		$410,709		$364,472
Costs and expenses:								
Cost of product sold .	$363,437		$395,950		$377,102		$323,009	
Depreciation (Plant) (Tools & dies)	6,342		5,307		5,033		5,088	
Cost of pensions	4,267		5,278		6,272		3,127	
Selling, advertising & administration ..	48,339		54,100		50,508		41,004	
Refrigerator warranties	586		187		182		370	
Interest	2,202		2,119		2,502		1,842	
Sundry expenses	740	425,913	541	462,085	969	442,571	973	375,507
Net profit or loss on operations		$(22,658)		$(15,257)		$(32,362)		$(11,035)
Credits on income tax .		11,590		9,700		1,453		502
Nonrecurring income or (loss)		......		......		10,662		(1,300)
Income tax		......		......		......		
Net Income after Tax ..		$(11,071)		$ (6,956)		$(19,746)		$(11,833)

*Changed in 1960 to reflect equity in subsidiaries rather than dividends received.
Note: Failure of figures to add is due to rounding.
Source: Annual Reports.

of the foreign markets for automobiles. The case focuses on the seven-year period following the formation of American Motors, i.e., from 1954 to 1961. In particular, the case describes the competitive position of AMC at three points in time (1954, 1957, and 1961), and the AMC "campaign" strategy for dealing with each situation. In conclusion, it describes the situation in 1962 and poses the question of what "campaign leadership" might consist.

The situation in 1954

As the postwar seller's market in automobiles changed to a buyer's market in 1953, the independents (Packard, Studebaker, Kaiser-Willys, Hudson, and Nash) began merger talks. Amid the varying combinations and deals, several considerations stood out.

First, the independents were producing too many body styles relative to

1958		1959		1960		1961		1962	
$502,788		$935,738		$1,139,508		$938,599		$1,135,190	
32,439		65,888		81,791		62,876		78,795	
$470,349		$869,849		$1,057,716		$875,723		$1,056,395	
$ 1,163		$ 1,567		$ 2,858		$ 1,009		$ 2,568	
2,413	3,577	5,040	6,607	5,574	8,433	3,556	4,565	6,475	8,944
	$473,926		$876,458		$1,066,849		$880,290		$1,065,439
$391,188		$684,198		$862,899		$726,529		$870,701	
4,787		4,717		7,239		10,608		9,744	
		11,933		10,892		18,041		19,876	
5,893		6,852		6,738		7,420		10,144	
42,896		62,543		72,003		67,101		81,731	
647		......		......		......		......	
993		390		300		210		120	
350	446,756	379	771,017	631	960,706	......	829,911	......	992,299
	$ 27,170		$105,441		$ 105,443		$ 50,378		$ 73,140
	515		......		......		......		......
	(1,600)		......		......		......		......
			45,100		57,200		26,800		38,900
	$ 26,085		$ 60,341		$ 48,243		$ 23,578		$ 34,240

the volume of cars for their unit costs to remain competitive with the big three. Packard, Nash, and Hudson together marketed only eight series of cars, yet required five basic body styles. In contrast, Ford made seven series from two basic body shells, while Chrysler made eleven series from four shells, and GM made fourteen from only four shells.[2] The difference in tooling costs thus gave the Big Three a sizable advantage with each model change-over, and the greater volume of each model allowed the Big Three to spread the tooling costs over more cars. The advantage was thus twofold, and in a style-conscious market it was a compelling one.

Second, and less tangible, none of the independents could count on gener-ating enough sales volume for their dealer organizations to keep the dealers

[2]Tom Mahoney, *The Story of George Romney* (New York: Harper & Bros., 1960).

Exhibit 2

AMERICAN MOTORS CORPORATION

Consolidated Balance Sheets
(In Thousands)

ASSETS	1954		1955		1956		1957	
Current Assets:								
Cash and government securities	$ 45,402		$37,859		$26,517		$22,600	
Accounts receivable (net)	19,996		20,925		23,624		23,788	
Due from subsidiaries	1,949		2,589		3,101		351	
Income tax refund due	16,853		9,683		......		......	
Inventories (net)	80,616		89,553		83,980		67,965	
Miscellaneous items	5,023	$169,841	4,078	$164,690	3,504	$140,728	3,300	$118,006
Investments in subsidiaries		13,957		12,888		7,355		8,563
Miscellaneous assets		774		6,741		3,524		3,467
Property, plant and equipment (net)		82,138		75,960		73,297		65,934
Total Assets		$266,711		$260,281		$224,905		$195,972
LIABILITIES AND NET WORTH								
Current Liabilities:								
Bank notes, and amount due on long-term debt	$ 31,200		$38,500		$36,000		$28,569	
Accounts payable	48,834		56,338		43,795		37,072	
Accrued expenses	2,212		2,251		2,172		2,731	
Warranties on refrigerators	4,729		4,096		3,491		2,886	
Income tax	......		......		......		......	
Miscellaneous	781	$ 87,756	1,097	$102,283	624	$ 86,084	504	$ 71,768
Long-term debt		16,000		14,000		14,569		13,000
Stockholders Investment:								
Common stock	$ 28,352		$28,352		$28,352		$27,939	
Additional paid-in capital	27,136		27,136		27,136		26,334	
Retained earnings	107,465	162,954	88,509	143,998	68,763	124,251	56,930	111,204
		$266,711		$260,281		$224,905		$195,972

Source: Annual Reports.

profitable and strong. Declining dealer strength would lead to reduced service as well as reduced sales, and might sooner or later spell disaster. As a real buyer's market developed, and price wars developed, this would hasten the plight of the weak, "off-brand" dealer.

Thus the independents knew the days of "independent" operations were numbered. While various proposals were tried, the results were a merger between Hudson and Nash, and later a belated merger between Packard and Studebaker. In the aftermath of these mergers, three of the famous names in American automotive history disappeared. Nash and Hudson cars suc-

	1958		1959		1960		1961		1962
$44,553		$ 60,041		$ 43,762		$ 69,752		$ 87,058	
28,757		33,177		38,856		36,239		45,579	
2,352		1,633		1,688		3,968		4,815	
......		......		......		......		......	
59,931		98,070		115,569		93,254		96,078	
3,010	$138,586	2,938	$195,861	3,938	$203,815	3,697	$206,913	3,916	$237,448
	10,603		24,428		33,416		34,635		40,946
	5,509		5,546		6,367		5,676		7,891
	51,484		58,617		94,792		85,731		88,789
	$206,184		$284,453		$338,392		$332,957		$375,076
$ 3,000		$ 3,000		$ 3,000		$ 4,000		0	
50,367		73,243		78,314		67,805		$ 86,998	
2,125		2,725		21,609		24,069		28,207	
2,669		2,570		......		......		......	
......		4,102		4,735		7,888		5,761	
508	$ 58,670	990	$ 86,631	3,442	$111,102	3,507	$107,207	4,654	$125,522
	10,000		7,000		4,000		......		......
$28,068		$ 29,694		$ 29,981		$ 30,096		$ 31,199	
26,429		34,052		34,518		34,866		44,772	
83,015	137,514	127,074	190,821	158,790	223,290	160,724	225,687	173,482	249,454
	$206,184		$284,453		$338,392		$332,957		$375,076

cumbed to the American Motors Rambler, and the Packard disappeared in favor of the Studebaker.

While the independents were working on their tooling and dealer problems, GM had returned to its strategy of the 1930's. It marketed progressively longer, lower, more powerful cars. Unlike the earlier era, however, Ford and Chrysler now followed suit. And as the 1954 model year got under way, Ford and Chevy were once more running neck and neck for leadership in total new car registrations.

In 1958 Mr. Romney, in discussing the background of these competitive developments, reviewed the industry's history as follows:[3]

I think as further background we might review some of the basic changes that have taken place in the automobile market since the start of the industry. At the beginning, of course, a lot of companies went into the business. Then Ford emerged as the dominant factor as Henry Ford developed the concept of building a dependable piece of transportation within the reach of the mass market. He succeeded by 1921—his peak year—in securing 62% of total industry sales. In that year there were 88 companies manufacturing automobiles. At that time the Ford was a 100-inch wheelbase vehicle—in wheelbase, the same size as this Rambler American we have which is at the top end of the small-car field. From 100 inches, other makes went as high as 145 inches in wheelbase, 10 inches beyond anything on the market today. There was an assortment of vehicles in terms of size and engines and various components, and so on, of a very widespread character indeed.

With the growth in American prosperity and with the growth that the Ford success helped to bring about, American car buyers began to indicate a desire for more than just bare transportation. General Motors excelled in its recognition of the change that was taking place in consumer preference. The result was that by 1927 they had succeeded in capturing about a third of the market, and Ford at that time still had a third. But a third of the market was not enough to permit Ford to operate profitably; so he shut down to convert over to the Model A in an effort to meet this new-type consumer demand.

General Motors continued and adopted the basic philosophy that has dominated the automobile industry in the United States, from a product standpoint, until the last few years. As a matter of fact, you'd almost have to say it still dominates in terms of current product volume. But General Motors adopted the policy—clearly stated by their technical people and policy people—of building cars each year a little bit bigger, a little bit more stylish, for the purpose of progressive, dynamic obsolescence. That product philosophy, coupled with other contributions they made—because General Motors has made many very substantial and significant contributions to the concepts of large industrial management—made General Motors the largest industrial corporation in the world.

Ford never quite came back. Under Henry Ford, Sr., the company never really adopted the product philosophy of General Motors. But following World War II the new management, in an effort to recapture first place, literally jumped onto the General Motors bandwagon, and basically adopted the General Motors product philosophy.

Then five years ago, when there was a change in the Chrysler management, [1953–54] Chrysler did the same thing. By 1954, therefore, at the time of the formation of American Motors, you had the three dominant factors in the automobile industry all going down substantially the identical product road.

As a result of this philosophy of making their cars a little bigger and more powerful each year, they kept moving them up in size and reducing the degree of variation and distinction. The result was that they created a vacuum back of them in the market and they created a concentration of competition as between their own models, with effects that we're beginning to see.

---

[3]Tobé and Associates, *The Tobé Lectures in Retail Distribution, 1958–1959* (Boston, Mass.: Harvard Graduate School of Business Administration).

American Motors set out to fill this vacuum. But it took several years to produce a car to fill the need, and still longer to convince the mass market that there was indeed something "below" the low-priced three. While working to develop the product and the market, the company very nearly succumbed to competitive pressures. Its strategy was one of fighting for survival.

Campaign survival: 1954–57

American Motors' long-run objectives were to become a leading competitor in the automotive field. To accomplish this, the company was relying primarily on (1) its conception of the unfilled need in the American market, the need for a car between the big cars of the big three and the small cars imported from Europe; and (2) its belief that its concept of a "compact" car filled this need.

The evidence of need was supported by a survey of transportation habits which showed "that 85% of all [automobile] trips in the United States were 13 miles or less in length, and that the bulk of them were for essential purposes."[4] The automobile was not primarily a vehicle of transcontinental travel, nor one of pleasure cruising. It was becoming a part of everyday urban and suburban living. From this knowledge sprang the conviction that there was a real market for a comfortable car with improved economy and maintenance which could be maneuvered easily, parked easily, and for which styling changes for change's sake might be avoided. It was this conception which lay behind the experimental development of the compact car.

In the design itself, the principles of aircraft engineering had been successfully applied by Nash-Kelvinator for almost a decade, permitting the company to make the car strong but light while at the same time preserving the riding comfort of which Americans are so fond. The resulting development was called a unitized or a single unit body, where the parts were welded together rather than being bolted to a strong, heavy frame, as was the universal practice in the United States at the time.

With this conception of a need and of a product to fill the need, American Motors faced the formidable task of devising a strategy which could (1) get the idea of this need across to the public, (2) gain the commitment of the organization to the product concept, and (3) keep the company from going under while management tried to get the first two steps accomplished. American Motors strategy from 1954–57 was called a campaign for survival, since the short-run problems were so acute that long-range goals had to be tempered if the company was to survive. The strategy included the following major steps.

Product line. Effective with the consolidation of 1955 model production at Nash's Wisconsin facilities in December 1954, the product line was made up of three basic elements: the standard automobiles (with approximately a 116-inch wheelbase), the Rambler (some with 108-inch and some with

---

[4]Mahoney, *op. cit.*, p. 197.

100-inch wheelbase), and the Metropolitan (with an 85-inch wheelbase). There were four models of the standard autos, two sold under the Hudson name (Hornet and Wasp) and two under the Nash name (Ambassador and Statesman). The Ramblers were sold under both brand names, giving the two surviving dealer organizations identical products to sell under different brand names. Sales of standard automobiles and Ramblers developed opposite trends over the first three years, as indicated by the following figures:

Year	Unit Total Sales	Hudson and Nash Standard	Hudson and Nash Rambler	Rambler as % of Total
1954	99,774	61,995	37,779	38%
1955	194,175	110,323	83,852	43
1956	104,189	25,023	79,166	77

Even more significant, however, was the fact that by 1955 sales of the 108-inch Ramblers were running four to one over the 100-inch model. It was on this basis that management decided to discontinue the 100-inch Rambler for 1956, and to concentrate on the larger model. But the problem of defining a clear product policy remained. The Hudson and Nash cars were just "above" the low-priced three in retail price, while the Ramblers were intended to be just below the low-priced—even though they were only slightly lower in price at this point. At any rate, the company did not market a car which was directly competitive in size and price with the low-priced three, but rather it straddled this market segment by being on both flanks. Was AMC going to compete with the low-priced three directly, or be above and below them, or just below them, or what?

Mr. Romney spoke on this question in September 1956, in a speech entitled "In League with the Future" at a meeting introducing the 1957 models:

Sales of compact cars will continue to grow, but more big cars than compact cars will be sold during the transition period. For that reason American Motors has no plans to drop its big car program.

American Motors is wedded to the program of supplying its dealers cars for each major segment of the future car market. For 1957 you have a big Nash or Hudson, the compact Rambler, and the small and increasingly popular Metropolitan. In 1958, Nash dealers will have an all new big car with the Nash name to sell and the Hudson dealers will have an all new big car with the Hudson name to sell.

Our 1958 cars will be the first ones resulting from combined Nash and Hudson engineering. Our 1958 program will be the first one to basically reflect the new management's product philosophy.

Product styling. In a speech to the dealer organization, Mr. Romney pointed out that company policy on automobile styling was being changed:

We have changed the company's previous styling policy. Under the old policy, styling distinction was sought to the point of production designs with high controversial and sometimes unacceptable features. Looking ahead, American Motors cars will be styled in the basic advanced patterns of future cars with elements of distinction that are not so extreme as to be controversial. We should avoid styling controversy or pioneering because our cars themselves are basically advanced, distinct, and superior.

Marketing. The marketing program faced the twofold task of selling the organization as well as the public:

The biggest difficulty we had in the early marketing and merchandising of the Rambler concept was internal, not external. The biggest problem was to change the attitude of our own vice president in charges of sales and of our sales organization and of our dealers. As late as the spring of 1954, just following the merger—at a meeting of all the Nash zone managers—I asked how many of them thought the Rambler would ever become a bread-and-butter car for American Motors. There were only two out of twenty-three zone managers who thought that was even a remote possibility. Our vice president in charge of sales was insisting internally that what we had to have was a car directly competitive with the Chevrolet, Ford, and Plymouth. And our biggest dealers were taking the same position.

*   *   *   *   *

The first thing that happened after I succeeded to the presidency (in October of 1954) of the company was that I brought in a new man (Roy Abernethy, now president of the corporation) to head up our sales effort who believed in this product approach. The second thing we did was to use the new model announcement meetings in the fall of 1954 to stress this theme with our dealers. The theme of my talk to our dealers across the country was "Get your sights up on the Rambler."

*   *   *   *   *

As a result of a lot of effort, we succeeded in convincing our dealer body that this product concept had merit in the market place. What convinced them as much as anything else that first year was that in the spring of 1954, the resale value of used Ramblers moved ahead of the resale value of Chevrolet, Ford, and Plymouth models. And it has remained above ever since. That was conclusive evidence that in one vital aspect of automotive marketing—namely, what the buyer can expect when he takes his car back in to buy a new car—we had a competitive advantage.

We also had public attitudes to deal with, as well as the internal attitudes. We were faced with a difficult public attitude created by the failure of all independent companies except two. And in the fall of 1954 somebody was giving us a mock burial almost every day in the press.

*   *   *   *   *

There was also a frozen big-car mentality in this country that had been built up almost from the beginning of the automobile industry, but particularly as the new product philosophy took over in the late 1920's.

Now how did we [try to] change that public attitude? Well, we went to work to tell the basic product advantage story of Rambler, and to tell it not only in terms of calling attention to the product specifically, but also by way of comparison. At that point people were not inclined to pay any attention to us.

So we had to be dramatic, and we had to make people stop, look, and listen. And probably the biggest break we had was one day when I happened to read an article by an automotive editor, who talked about dinosaurs. And I said, "That's it, we're competing against gas-guzzling dinosaurs." And that stuck.[5]

Later Mr. Romney took to giving speeches where he used scale model dinosaurs as props. At a meeting of the National Parking Association in 1957 he led off as follows:

This fellow is called a Brontosaurus. He was about seventy feet long. . . . He weighed a good many tons. His fuel consumption was tremendous. His mouth was relatively so small that he had to spend all of his waking hours eating. This streamlined fellow here was called Dimetrodon and is considered a predecessor of the modern horse. One of his problems was he began developing a fin on his back to a point where it became larger and larger and finally upset his equilibrium.

This handsome model was known as Stegosaurus. He perhaps represented the highest development of the dinosaur in terms of useless, nonfunctional decorative treatment.[6]

*   *   *   *   *

While moving with this concept of the competitors' "dinosaurs," American Motors also moved to change the way its own products were advertised and promoted. Mr. Romney pointed out that—

We . . . changed our advertising policy, and that was a tough one. Boy, Madison Avenue has got fixed ideas. . . . It took us three years to get our advertising agency not only to agree that our policy should be different on advertising, but also to reach the point where they could reflect accurately our product story in ads that would command the attention of the American people.[7]

He went on to stress that American Motors advertising must henceforward meet standards such as the following:

1. American Motors copy must be as simple, informational, and factual as possible. Banish the superlatives . . . rule out conventional advertising language [and], use new language to the greatest extent possible.

2. Every advertisement must be centered on a dominant idea that is validated by a quality or feature in the product.[8]

Dealer organization. American Motors had a combined total of 2,800 Nash and Hudson dealers in 1954. In less than two years this had declined to 1,900, largely through dealer resignations. While the downward trend was reversed following the consolidation of the Nash and Hudson franchises, a weak distribution organization remained a key problem for the company. In 1956, with unit sales slipping almost 50% from the previous year, the

---

[5]Tobé, *op. cit.*, pp. 30, 34.
[6]Mahoney, *op. cit.*, p. 21.
[7]Tobé, *op. cit.*, p. 34.
[8]*Ibid.*

company instituted a dealer bonus plan which credited the dealer with from $30 to $50 extra per car on all domestic sales. Over a two-year period, the plan cost the company more than $7 million, but it was credited with being instrumental in keeping the dealer organization together during these lean years.

Finance and control. At the time of the merger the company was losing about $2 million a month. On the one hand this called for drastic cost cutting, and on the other it called for a campaign to turn nonessential resources into cash so the company could carry forward long enough to give its compact car concept a chance to prove itself in the marketplace. Backing up this move meant betting the company's last chips on automobiles, just at a time when some of the most vocal stockholders were recommending the company bow out of the automotive field altogether.

In addition to securing a loan from an insurance company and increased credit from a group of banks, the company sold its Hudson body plant, its West Coast assembly plant, and its 60% interest in Ranco, Inc., a highly successful manufacturer of thermostatic controls for appliances. The three sales gave the company an additional $15 million in "chips" to put behind Rambler. Part of these funds was used to tool the company's own V-8 engine (introduced in March 1957) to replace the very expensive V-8 engine and transmission bought from Packard and used in the 1955 and 1956 models. Still, as 1956 progressed, it became clear that more drastic measures were required. With working capital down almost 50% in two years, and only a few million dollars above the minimum required by bank loans, heroic cost cutting measures were taken.

In the management echelons, it meant selling the company airplanes, a new policy urging managers to take more modest hotel accommodations when traveling, and an "end to the two-hour lunches." The company resigned from the NAM, went through a systematic curtailment of magazine subscriptions, and to bring the point home to all concerned, Mr. Romney and other top executives took "voluntary" salary reductions up to 40%.

At lower levels, the company advertising agency was required to pay rent for its office space at the company headquarters. Company garages stopped giving free gas and service to executive cars.

At one point, offices were cleaned only every other day, for a saving of forty thousand dollars a year. Another forty thousand dollars a year was deferred by delaying the customary gifts of watches or clocks to employees with thirty years of service. . . . Offices went unpainted, and sheet toilet paper replaced rolls.[9]

Consolidation

Besides the consolidation of production into the Nash plants and the sale of the Hudson facilities, American Motors was able to effect economies from utilizing common tooling for the 1955 models, and from running all

---

[9]Mahoney, *op. cit.*, p. 191.

of the 1956 models on the same assembly lines. Following consolidation, disposal of the surplus plants, and write-downs of $12 million of other Hudson facilities, the company entered the 1957 model year with an estimated break-even point at below 150,000 units. The 1956 annual report noted: "The primary automotive objective since the merger has been to reduce the automotive break-even point, and simultaneously, to develop new lines of cars needed to increase sales to profitable levels."

The significance of the consolidation is easily seen by comparing performance from 1955 through 1958:

Year	Unit Sales	Pretax Earnings
1955	194,000	$(16,700,000)
1956	104,000	(30,000,000)
1957	119,000	(11,000,000)
1958	189,000	26,000,000

By 1958 the break-even had been reduced to a point where a volume smaller than the one achieved in 1955 was adequate to generate a sizable pretax profit (American Motors Corporation was not able to fill all of its orders in 1958), and this even though 1955 had been a good year in the industry, whereas 1958 was one of the worst in the postwar period. Survival was to be based in large measure on keeping the break-even low, and the low break-even was to be maintained by manufacturing only the bare essentials (motors, bodies, transmissions, and a few other items), by purchasing the remaining items from outside suppliers, and by maintaining a single assembly center. By the end of 1957 American Motors had become the least integrated manufacturer in the business, and had thereby helped prepare a flexible base from which to operate in the ups and downs of the auto business. So much for "campaign survival."

The situation in the fall of 1957

While American Motors was retrenching and proceeding largely unnoticed by others in the industry, a battle was shaping up in the medium-priced cars between General Motors and Ford. The battle came to a climax with the introduction of the 1958 models in the fall of 1957. As reported by *Fortune*,[10] the giants prepared for the clash in the following manner:

The Big Three were caught off base in the shifting markets of 1956 and 1957 because of some decision making back in 1954. That year, G.M.'s President Harlow Curtice and the high command at Chevrolet were disturbed by reports that Ford was planning to attack Chevrolet with a car "as big as Buick." It was to be ready for introduction in 1957.

Indeed, G.M. heard that Ford was committing itself to big cars in all its

---

[10]"Detroit Shoots the Works," *Fortune*, June 1959. Reproduced by permission.

brands. Ford's Edsel division was being set up to swing across all price lines except at the very bottom and top of the market. This was as wide a market as Buick had carved out. The G.M. high command also knew that Ford was designing a bigger body shell for Mercury which would interchange with the larger Edsels, and that smaller Edsels would interchange with the big Ford.

What had happened was this: Ford had tested the lower end of the medium-price market with luxury-model Fords. It had found no resistance and raked in some nice profits. With this experience, and with the knowledge that consumer income was up sharply, Ford had every reason to believe that the markets of the future would favor the medium-price entries at the expense of the low-price cars. Also, Ford division officials were worried by the tremendous sales surge of Buick, which had recently pushed Plymouth out of third place. They believed that if the market continued to demand big cars, Buick might push the Ford for second place.

It seemed apparent to the bosses at Ford that the medium-price Mercury was no match for Buick. This meant that far too much of the burgeoning medium-price market would be captured by G.M., which had not only Buick in that arena but Pontiac, Olds, and the top end of Chevrolet. What to do? Fight Buick with Ford. How? By making Ford as big as a 1954 Buick.

By early 1955, G.M. knew that Ford had definitely committed itself to this strategy. Curtice and his officers also learned that Chrysler, with no one division capable of achieving the savings that accrue to a factory that can make and sell a million units, had committed itself to one line of body shells for all of its cars. Watching their own labor costs mounting, G.M. officials reflected that one body shell for all their brands would save scores of millions of dollars. Late in 1955, G.M. decided on one big body shell for all its brands by 1958. It had to be big so that Chevrolet could meet the threat the big Ford would pose. And to hedge the bet on bigness, G.M. shortly put into motion plans for the compact Chevrolet that will be introduced this fall [1959], as related above, and Ford and Chrysler felt obliged to follow.

(While it takes eighteen months' to two years' lead time to make a major model change on a current car, it takes three years for a complete re-engineering job.)

Work had hardly been started on the big Chevrolet before G.M. statisticians pointed out that something odd was happening to Buick and Olds. Both had broken their records in 1955 (738,000 for Buick and 590,000 for Olds), but sales in the metropolitan areas had not kept pace with total sales. What could this mean? The big cities were normally the principal volume markets for these luxurious cars, for no other markets had enough upper-middle incomes. Evidently buyers outside the big cities had used three-year credit, which was widely available in 1955, to trade themselves up to Buicks and Oldsmobiles. This was apparently the reason for the 1955 increase in sales for these brands, for they were unable to hold their gains.

By the end of the first half of 1956, Buick and Olds were limping. Was the move to suburbia bad for Buick because more people needed two cars and couldn't afford two Buicks? Surveys showed that this might be one factor. Another factor might be the size of the new Buicks and Olds, which made them awkward to park in the cities. G.M. concluded that size and high price were in some way at the root of Buick's and Olds' problem, so the company also put compact models for these two cars in work. And again Ford and Chrysler followed.

The figures show how radically the market changed between 1956 and 1957.

In 1956, 61 per cent of domestic sales were in the $1,800 to $2,300 range; the medium-price markets, which spread from $2,300 to $4,000, took about 35 per cent of the business; 4 per cent went to high-price cars. Buick had dropped back nearly 210,000 units to 529,000; and Olds, at 438,000, was off more than 150,000. This was the reverse of the sales pattern Ford had predicted for Buick —a fact that gave Ford, with the medium-priced Edsel poised for introduction the next year, something to ponder.

In 1957, when Ford began its fight against G.M. with big Fords, low-price cars tobogganed down from 61 per cent to a little under 20 per cent of the market. (The larger Fords were classed as medium-priced automobiles.) High-price cars went up to almost 6 per cent. Buick slid still further, to 395,000 units, Olds to 372,000, while the medium-price market soared to an astonishing 75 per cent. Imports more than doubled, to nearly 200,000 units—a figure that looked impressive for the first time. Ford trounced Chevrolet for the first time in a generation. Chrysler, which since 1953 had been on a feast-or-famine diet, did nicely with the Plymouth and its other lines. [See Exhibit 3.]

The sobering fact of the 1957 market was that the invasion of the medium-price field by the former low-price three had murdered the old-timers in that market. Buick will never forget the slaughter of 1957, and neither will Ford, for in the process the big new 1957 Mercury lost business, and the brand-new Edsel fizzled in the market that wasn't there.

When 1958 and recession rolled around, G.M. offered a Chevrolet bigger than a Ford, as big, in fact, as a Cadillac.

It was the Cadillac-sized Chevrolet pitted against the almost as large Ford and Chrysler models which gave American Motors its opening for "campaign opportunity."

Campaign opportunity

American Motors faced its crucial test just at the time when the medium-priced cars were being squeezed the hardest. Sales of Buick and Olds were declining, Edsel was unable to get rolling, and the medium-priced cars of American Motors—the Nash and Hudson lines—were declining sharply. Thus it was that in early 1957 a decision was made to stop production and to withdraw these lines from the market. American Motors made a historic decision to bet all of its chips on the Rambler, believing that the "Rambler concept" was the key to an opportunity. To back up its bet, the company took the following steps:

Product line. The Nash and Hudson lines were dropped after a stormy meeting of the board of directors, and two names of long-standing tradition disappeared from the market. The company made special allowances to dealers to help them move the last of these cars off the showroom floors.

Instead of introducing new Nash and Hudson models, as previously planned, the company introduced a 117-inch Ambassador by Rambler. By

Exhibit 3

PER CENT OF INDUSTRY NEW CAR REGISTRATIONS BY MAKES CALENDAR YEARS 1954–62

	1954	1955	1956	1957	1958	1959	1960	1961	1962
Chevrolet	25.6	22.9	26.3	24.3	26.6	23.5	25.8	27.2	29.9
Pontiac	6.5	7.4	6.0	5.4	4.9	6.3	6.1	6.4	7.6
Oldsmobile	7.3	8.2	7.4	6.2	6.6	6.0	5.4	5.6	6.4
Buick	9.3	10.3	8.9	6.6	5.7	4.1	4.1	5.0	5.8
Cadillac	2.0	2.0	2.2	2.4	2.6	2.2	2.2	2.4	2.2
GM	50.7	50.8	50.8	44.9	46.4	42.1	43.6	46.6	51.9
Ford	25.3	21.9	23.1	25.0	22.1	24.4	21.6	22.7	21.2
Edsel	...	...	...	0.4	0.8	0.7	...	...	...
Mercury	4.9	5.2	4.6	4.4	2.9	2.6	4.7	5.3	4.6
Lincoln	0.7	0.5	0.7	0.6	0.6	0.5	0.3	0.5	0.5
Ford Motor Co.	30.9	27.6	28.4	30.4	26.4	28.2	26.6	28.5	26.3
Plymouth	6.9	9.0	8.1	10.0	8.4	6.4	6.8	5.1	4.4
Dodge	2.8	4.0	3.7	4.3	2.9	2.8	5.4	3.9	3.4
De Soto	1.4	1.6	1.7	1.7	1.0	0.7	0.4	...	...
Chrysler	1.8	2.0	1.8	1.8	1.3	1.1	1.2	1.6	1.6
Imperial	...	0.2	0.2	0.5	0.3	0.3	0.2	0.2	0.2
Chrysler Corp.	12.9	16.8	15.5	18.3	13.9	11.3	14.0	10.8	9.6
Hudson	0.6	0.3	0.2	0.1	...	...	...	...	...
Nash	0.9	0.6	0.5	0.2	...	...	...	...	...
Rambler	0.6	1.0	1.2	1.5	4.0	6.0	6.4	6.3	6.1
AM*	2.1	1.9	1.9	2.0	4.3	6.0	6.4	6.3	6.1
Studebaker	1.7	1.4	1.3	1.0	1.0	2.2	1.6	1.2	1.1
Packard	0.7	0.7	0.5	0.1	0.1	...	...	...	...
S-P	2.4	2.1	1.8	1.1	1.1	2.2	1.6	1.2	1.1
Crosley	...	...	...	...	...	...	...	...	...
Frazer	...	...	...	...	...	...	...	...	...
Henry J.	...	...	...	...	...	...	...	...	...
Kaiser	0.4	0.2	...	...	...	...	...	...	...
Willys	0.3	0.1	...	...	...	...	...	...	...
Others	0.3	0.6	1.6	3.3	7.9	10.2	7.8	6.6	5.0
Industry	100.0	100.0	100.0	100.0	100.0	100.0	100.0	100.0	100.0

*Includes imported Metropolitan 1958 and prior years, but not 1959–62.
Source: *Ward's Automotive Yearbook, 1963*, p. 145. Reproduced by permission.

design this model used the same body shell as the 108-inch Rambler. At the same time the company reintroduced the 100-inch Rambler American, using largely the same dies and tooling as when the car had been discontinued in 1955.

When asked why American Motors had discontinued the 100-inch Rambler for almost three years and then revived it, Mr. Romney pointed out that the company had tried both the two-door 100-inch model and the four-door 108-inch model, and found that the latter had outsold the "more compact" model about four to one. He went on to point out that he believed there was a very good reason why the larger model had achieved greater acceptance:

I think there's a very logical reason for that having happened. I once read that if you ever wanted to start a revolution—and after all, that's what we were trying to start in products—you should sell the basic idea with the least possible departure from existing forms. Now the 108-inch model was a smaller departure from the big-car concept in this country than the 100-inch model. And our figures indicated you could probably sell that size car, and break through the big-car mentality, quicker than you could with a 100-inch.

Later the American public was not only accepting the compact car idea but also accepting the small car idea; and therefore we not only decided to have our Metropolitan model, which is an 85-inch small model, but also decided to bring back the 100-inch model because we were convinced that the small car idea had taken hold well enough to do that. And we brought it back in February of this year [1958], just the two-door model, and that two-door model is now second only to the Volkswagen in small car sales in America.[11]

Later that same day, asked why the 1958 Rambler had tail fins, Mr. Romney returned to the same theme, answering to the effect that "it's the basic idea that counts. If we have to use tail fins to get people to try compact cars, we'll use tail fins. Later on we will certainly be able to do away with them, and to build clean, simple, uncluttered cars."

Marketing. With the reintroduction of the 100-inch car, and with a restyled 108-inch car, 1958 was the "do or die" year for American Motors. In the fall of 1957:

Romney felt constrained . . . to tell his deficit ridden [organization] that if the new year didn't see the corporation in the black, there could be a change in management. In consequence, 1958 [began] with Romney and every other executive who could grab a lapel, seize an ear, or clamber on a rostrum, hammering home the points that this was American Motors' year, this time the big three had gone too far, this was the moment when common sense in car buying could stretch the recession's "skimpy pay-checks."

We resorted to something akin to shock treatment [one executive recalled], in an effort to shatter the prevailing myth that the greatest car values were to be found in products built by the Big Three.[12]

Not only did top executives take to the road selling and promoting,

Celebrated cartoonists like William Steig, Whitney Darrow, and Chon Day were put to work on full page American Motors ads featuring . . . "Siegfried Slays the Dragon . . . Again" (he'd stabbed his fire breathing monster in the gas tank, after finding it unparkable and ungarageable). . . .[13]

With the "dinosaurs of the driveway" larger and longer than ever, the lampooning spread. and numerous cartoons appeared in magazines and

---

[11]Tobé, *op. cit.,* p. 43.
[12]"Will Success Spoil American Motors?" *Fortune,* January 1959, p. 98. Reproduced by permission.
[13]*Ibid.*

newspapers all over the country. The spontaneous cartoons, plus the success of the Volkswagen, plus the persistent drumfire of American Motors, finally turned the tide.

In March, Consumer Reports, a monthly buyer's guide, hit the stands with the news it had selected the Rambler Ambassador V-8 as the "consultant's choice," the one U.S. car that year which could "serve as the foundation for a hypothetical but eminently desirable automobile."

In June, Ford became so alarmed over the success of American Motors propaganda that it devoted an entire advertising campaign to counter "talk about gas-guzzling monsters . . . claims of big car room with small car economy."

In September, with . . . 26 million [in] profit (for the fiscal year just ended) George Romney announced he expected to sell 300,000 of his 1959 Ramblers, and to get 6 per cent [of the] market (vs. 4.4 per cent of 1958's).

In October . . . sales were nearly triple those of October 1957.

In December, the corporation started a $10 million expansion program that would permit an increase in Rambler capacity to 450,000 units by the end of 1959.[14] [See Exhibit 4.]

Exhibit 4

MARKET SHARES: 1953–62

Year	Imports	Independents	Big Three
1953	0.5	9.0	90.5
1954	0.6	5.0	94.4
1955	0.8	4.0	95.2
1956	1.7	3.6	94.7
1957	3.4	3.0	93.6
1958	8.1	5.1	86.8
1959	10.2	8.3	81.5
1960	7.6	8.1	84.3
1961	6.5	7.7	85.8
1962	4.9	7.3	87.8

Source: *Ward's Automotive Yearbook, 1963,* p. 145. Reproduced by permission.

Dealer organization. Beginning early in 1957 the company was able to turn the tide in its dealer organization. Having slipped from 2,700 to about 1,900, the company lost 368 more, but was able to sign 741 new ones to finish the year with 2,300. By September 1958 the number had reached 2,636. From this point on the effort was to upgrade the quality of the dealerships, and to see that the dealers earned enough to provide both the working capital and the incentives needed to provide good service for the cars being sold.

Finance and control. The first fruits of operating in the black went for the repayment of bank debt. By September, the bank debt had been completely

[14] *Ibid.*

repaid, and working capital rose from less than $50 million the preceding year to $80 million. It was under these circumstances that the company appropriated $10 million to make provisions for a 50% increase in auto capacity, the $10 million going primarily for expanded assembly facilities. The company had reduced its break-even point to an estimated 125,000 units, and was in no mood to add the bricks and mortar necessary for a full-blown expansion of facilities. In addition, management could feel some satisfaction in the fact that though volume exceeded 1954, the number of salaried employees was only 50% as large as when the company had been formed.

The situation in 1961

Strategies for 1959 differed little from those of 1958, as the Big Three played out their biggest, longest, most expensive models, appropriately adorned with the high watermark in fins and ornamentation. The serious business of new strategy formulation began to show up that fall, as four compacts were introduced in the 1960 product lines. The real punch came in the fall of 1960, however, as four more compacts were introduced in the 1961 lines, thus giving GM four and Chrysler and Ford two each. The competitive pressure generated by the proliferation of new models was particularly acute because the automobile market had, according to some estimates, settled down to being largely a replacement market, a market which fluctuated with purchasing power and grew with the population rather than one which expanded in reflection of rising living standards. The significance of this development was that if the overall market was no longer basically a growth market, then the flood of new models was competing for shares of a relatively stable pie. One could get a bigger share only if someone else got a smaller share. As *Fortune* remarked,[15]

When the pie was getting bigger all the time, a manufacturer could accept a smaller slice and still come out ahead. Today, however, quite a different situation prevails. Automobile manufacturing in the U.S. has become primarily a replacement industry. The ratio of cars per person has changed only slightly since 1955; the car population itself stands at a whopping 61 million. Last year there was roughly one automobile for every three Americans, compared to one for five in 1945 and one for every seven in the middle Twenties. This does not mean thin pickings for Detroit from now on, but it does mean that in an average annual market of even 6,750,000 units between 1961 and 1965, a relatively small number will represent absolute growth. Some of the long-range forecasts: General Motors, most bullish of the Big Three, foresees a 3 per cent annual increase in new car sales, the trend line passing the seven-million mark in 1965. Ford's forecast is for a 2.8 per cent increase, a difference of some 80,000 cars in a seven-million car market.

Those estimates show that the automobile manunfacturer of 1961 has virtually given up the push for the bigger pie. Not very much can be done today about the total size of the market, summed up a Big Three economist this

---

[15]"Detroit Is Flying by the Seat of Its Pants," *Fortune*, January 1961. Reproduced by permission.

November. We measure success by per cent of penetration. Thus American Motors, Studebaker-Packard, and the imports are out to maintain, or better, their 17.4 per cent of the market (September registrations), three-fourths of which was wrung from G.M., Ford, and Chrysler between 1955 and 1960. As for the major manufacturers, G.M. with 42.7 per cent of the market is pressing to regain the 50.8 per cent it had in 1955; Ford at 26.9 per cent has set its sights on the 30.4 per cent of 1957; Chrysler's hope is to move its percentage from 12.9 to 20.

As far as Big Three strategies were concerned, *Fortune* had the following to say:

The briefest summary of future strategies is this: Ford and Chrysler place prime emphasis on a generally lower-priced market, which includes the compacts, and Ford is strongly impressed by the "segmented" character of the over-all market. General Motors appears much less committed to the new emphasis on the bottom of the price range. It seems to be pulling for the standard-sized machine, and a rejuvenation of the middle-price brackets, with the compacts a fringe or supplemental market. With those very broad strategic patterns in mind, we can look more closely at the thinking of each company.

At Ford, the central element is its concept of the new U.S. market. "The most important thing to remember about selling automobiles today," said the company's new president, Robert S. McNamara, in early December, "is that this isn't a single or homogeneous market. Ford's product strategy is based on a segmented market where different groups of consumers want different types of cars. We believe the general-purpose car will become a thing of the past; the expanding need is for specialized vehicles designed to fill a particular requirement."

In putting this concept into operation, Ford has undergone perhaps the most extensive transformation within the Big Three. The number of models it offered in the medium and high-price field was sharply cut, the Edsel being discontinued in 1960 and Lincoln's twelve models reduced to two for the 1961 market. At the same time Mercury was given six new models, raising its total to nineteen. These were heavily concentrated in the low-priced area; indeed, one of them was simply the Ford Galaxie, wearing the Mercury name plate and a slightly higher price tag. [See Exhibits 5 and 6.]

* * * * *

Ford's strategic posture, though committed to the compacts and to Mercury's new positioning in the low-price field, nevertheless preserves considerable flexibility. The company is acutely aware of the squeeze on profits that would occur should the proportion of compacts to standard-sized machines move from its present one-to-three ratio to parity or better. Any switch in public preference back to standard-sized machine, such as some of its executives now discern, will find Ford more than ready. What won't be altered is the impetus given interchangeability and cost control by a public in search of better but cheaper cars. Body stampings of the Continental and the Thunderbird are already interchangeable. So are those of the Falcon and the Comet, the latter being fundamentally a "stretched"—i.e., pieced-out amidships—version of the Falcon. Further economies of interchangeability can be expected to follow the centralizing

Exhibit 5

1961 MODEL PRICES

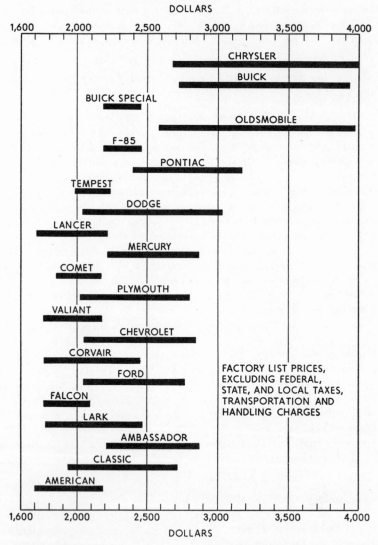

Ford and Chrysler, as the chart above reveals, are committed to the compacts and a generally lower-priced market; General Motors seems to be trying to husband its strength in Chevrolet, revitalize the middle-priced bracket, and give little play to the compacts.

Source: *Fortune*, January 1961. Reproduced with permission.

of all car production under one manager, announced last November. Eventually there may be consolidations between the lines themselves.

. . . and as the two grand divisions come more and more to duplicate each other's products, their own consolidation into a single division may follow.

Exhibit 6

A.M.A. SPECIFICATION COMPARISON FOR 1961 AUTOMOBILES

	Compact Cars											Low-Priced Standard-Size Cars		
	Rambler American	Studebaker Lark	Chevrolet Corvair	Ford Falcon	Plymouth Valiant	Olds F-85	Buick Special	Dodge Lancer	Pontiac Tempest	Rambler Classic	M-L Comet	Chevrolet Biscayne	Plymouth Savoy	Ford Fairlane
Overall length	173.1	175.0	180.0	181.2	183.7	188.2	188.4	188.8	189.3	189.8	194.8	209.3	209.5	209.9
width	70.0	71.4	67.0	70.6	70.4	71.5	71.3	72.3	72.2	72.4	70.4	78.4	80.0	79.9
height	56.2	56.5	51.5	54.5	53.3	52.6	52.5	53.3	53.5	57.3	54.5	55.5	54.4	55.0
Wheelbase	100.0	108.5	108.0	109.5	106.5	112.0	112.0	106.5	112.0	108.0	114.0	119.0	118.0	119.0
Engine type	LHD-6	OHV-6	Flat-6	OHV-6	Slant-6	Alum V/8	Alum V/8	Slant-6	Slant-4	OHV-6	OHV-6	Inline	Slant	Inline
horsepower	90	112	80	85	101	155	155	101	110	127	85	135 (6) 170 (V/8)	145 (6) 230 (V/8)	135 (6) 175 (V/8)
Price*	$1,730 1,809	$1,822 1,961	$1,800 1,860	$1,803 1,875	$1,838 1,927			$1,889 1,968	$1,975†	$1,918 2,071	$1,880 1,961	$2,106 2,106	$2,106 2,169	$2,105 2,213
Price: V/8 engine		$1,940 2,079				$2,175 2,300	$2,175 2,300			$2,038 2,191		$2,206 2,206	$2,169	$2,213

*Factory list price: four-door sedan, six-cylinder engine.

†Four-cylinder.

The Compacts have sharpened many old questions such as whether a car's interior dimensions would have to be reduced when overall length was cut. The above table provides answers to some of these, plus comparisons with the "low-priced three," Ford, Plymouth, and Chevrolet.

Source: *Fortune*, January 1961. Reproduced by permission.

Interestingly enough, where the divisions have in a sense been combined, with one dealer offering both the Falcon and the Comet, sales of each compact have showed marked improvement—a point that would gain force if the compacts took over more of the car market.

General Motors' over-all strategy, like that of Ford, recognizes the concept of a segmented market. This year in particular the variety of its 119 models —it was the only Big Three company to raise rather than lower the total—is the gauge of its efforts to offer something to virtually every segment. At the same time there are important differences in outlook and situation that differentiate G.M.'s strategy from Ford's, indeed from that of any other automobile manufacturer. To begin with, G.M.'s drop in total share of the market from 50.8 per cent in calendar 1955 to 42.1 per cent in 1959 came fundamentally from a decline of its middle-price makes. Chevrolet managed to do a little better than hold its own at 23 to 24 per cent, in part because G.M. permitted it to push up into the middle-priced market. But Buick declined steadily from 10.3 in 1955 to 4.1 in 1959, Oldsmobile slid from 8.2 to 6, Pontiac from 7.4 to 6.3. The actual unit volumes tell an even sadder story, Buick falling from 738,000 units to 246,000. On the other hand, Buick-Oldsmobile-Pontiac commanded 16.4 per cent of the 1959 market even after their slump and this made their representation in the middle-priced class five times more important than Ford's, more than triple Chrysler's. Thus the prime strategic question facing General Motors was how the company could move with the current trend toward cheaper, smaller cars at the least possible sacrifice of its B-O-P strength and profitability.

A partial answer was provided in the 1960 model year with the introduction of the Corvair by the Chevrolet Division. Nobody could reasonably conceive of Corvair's being a threat to B-O-P or to Chevrolet, either. For one thing, the car's rear engine—most radical engineering innovation since the Cord of 1934— made it an automotive novelty. Production of 250,000 did go higher than one might have expected of a novel machine making its way against no-nonsense competition in the economy field, but it merely emphasized the probability that G.M.'s strategy had been to get token participation in the compact-car market without injury to Chevrolet sales. Competitive figures tend to support this view. Ford Division production was off 1.6 per cent in the 1960 model year, while its Falcon volume reached a whopping 436,000 cars; conversely Chevrolet Division sales were up 11.7 per cent, with Corvair volume at only 250,000.

The complete tip-off on G.M.'s strategy came, however, with the introduction of its new small B-O-P cars in 1960. The Buick Special and the Olds F-85 extended B-O-P lines further down toward the low-price field, but a good $100 short of the most expensive Falcon, $17 short of the highest-priced Comet. Pontiac's Tempest alone touched the top of the Falcon range. Moreover, the term "compact" was sedulously avoided in describing them; they were billed as smaller versions of B-O-P cars. G.M.'s strategy, in essence, was to give the public what it wanted (i.e., smaller, cheaper, more economical cars) while at the same time trying to lead the buyers back to the standard-sized, middle-priced market, where G.M. still possessed so much competitive strength. Pointedly, G.M. refused to follow Ford's formula of concentrating on the lower-priced segments of the market with compacts and middle-priced cars at sharply reduced price tags. The G.M. strategy of going only part of the way down with the market was based on the hope that the "man who had always wanted an Oldsmobile" (or

Buick or Pontiac) would buy one of the new less expensive models and eventually trade up in the line, to the rejuvenation of the middle-priced market. Chevrolet, in the meantime, would be expected to hold the fort in its own area. [See Exhibit 7.]

*   *   *   *   *

General Motors' power to implement its strategy is, of course, immense and it can be expected to use that power to the fullest. No fear of antitrust prosecution is likely to inhibit G.M.'s efforts to push its market percentages as high as they will go. Nor is it likely to pay much attention to the recent outcry against "planned obsolescence" in automobiles. For G.M. the cost of model changes is minimal: old body dies would wear out anyway after a couple of years' production at the huge volumes attained by G.M.; new dies with new designs can be had for little more than the cost of replacing the worn-out ones. Thus G.M. is attracted naturally to a two-year model cycle. By talking of such a cycle it may compel its competitors, most of whom would prefer a three-year cycle, to follow suit, even though a two-year cycle would often force them to discard dies that have not worn out simply because they lack G.M.'s high levels of production. G.M. initiative, in consequence, may force its competitors to bear model-change costs that G.M. itself wll not bear.

The strategy of the remaining member of the Big Three, Chrysler, is focused on one overriding objective: remaining a member of the Big Three rather than joining American Motors and Studebaker-Packard in a Little Three. In calendar 1959, Chrysler's percentage of the market (in registrations) dropped to 11.3 per cent, the lowest level since 1930. Last year the company managed a significant gain; its percentage of the market rose to 14.4 for the first nine months, and it even turned in a third-quarter profit of $1,400,000, the first in that period since 1957.

The strategy employed was much like Ford's. Chrysler moved an increasing number of its entries down into the low-priced sector of the market, and put its main emphasis there. The Plymouth Division got a new compact, the Valiant. The Dodge Division models were concentrated in the lower-price areas, leaving only a single series of cars in the upper brackets. Then the destructive competition between Dodge dealers (who also handled Plymouth) and the Plymouth dealers themselves was mitigated by taking the Plymouth out of the Dodge agencies and replacing it with the new Dart, essentially a Plymouth under another name. With the Dart going very well indeed, Chrysler further strengthened Dodge dealerships by giving them a new compact, the Lancer. This car was really a Valiant with slightly better upholstery, five inches added to trunk space, and a few dollars to the price tags, but it gave Chrysler two compacts to push. And push them it has. By mid-November, 34 per cent of Chrysler's 1961 model production was devoted to Valiant and Lancer. This performance was topped by the 39 per cent of Ford output going to its compacts, but way ahead of the 19 per cent of G.M.'s smaller car volume. With its share of the market (registrations) rising, Chrysler had grounds for hoping that by the first quarter of this year it would be back to 15 per cent.

What Chrysler's strategy will be from here on out is not too difficult to foresee. It estimates that the compacts of all companies will take 33.4 per cent of the whole 1961 market, and that this figure will rise only slightly (34.7 per cent) in 1962. At the same time the company expects the Plymouth-Ford-

Exhibit 7

MOTORS A LA MODE: THE STYLING RACE PICKS UP SPEED

While the horsepower race has petered out and the size race appears to be running backward, it is clear from the chart at right that the style race is hotter than ever. More models were offered by Detroit for 1961 than at any time in automotive history. G.M. alone spent $480 million for new tooling. Next year (1962) the pace is expected to slacken somewhat as the industry waits for its second wind. Ford will probably bring out a new standard-sized machine, to fit in between the Fairlane and the Comet. Chevrolet may follow suit with a smaller Chevy. Chrysler will likely strengthen its all-important low-price divisions with a new body for Plymouth and one for Dodge. But another big push for the industry is expected for 1963. Probabilities then are for three new G.M. cars (assigned to the Buick, Oldsmobile and Pontiac divisions and intended to compete against the Thunderbird) and a new Ford, a "subcompact" approximating the Volkswagen in size. Should Ford go ahead on its subcompact, G.M. stands ready to turn out a competitive car, built at its West German Opel plant. However some of the other companies might yearn for a three-year cycle, nobody can chance one so long as General Motors sticks to its two-year push.

Model Years	1949	1950	1951	1952	1953	1954	1955	1956	1957	1958	1959	1960	1961	1962	1963
Chevrolet	B		M		B		B	M	M	B	B	M	B	M	B
Corvette						C							M		M
Corvair												C		M	C
?															
Pontiac	B				B		B	M	M	B	B	M	B	M	B
Tempest													C		C
?															
GENERAL MOTORS CORPORATION Oldsmobile 88	B		B		M	B	M	M	B	M	B	M	B	M	B
Super 88			B		M	B	M	M	B	M	B	M	B	M	M
98		B		B	B	B	M	M	B	M	B	M	B	M	M
F-85				B									C		B
?															
Buick Special Century	B	B	B		M	B	M	M	B	M	B	M	B	M	C
Super Roadmaster	B	B			M	B	M	M	B	M	B	M	B	M	B
Special									M	B		C	C		B
?							C								C
Cadillac	M	B				B	M	M	B	M	B	M	B	M	B
FORD MOTOR COMPANY Ford	B			B			B		B	M	B	B	B	C	B
Thunderbird							B		B	B		B	B	C	B
Falcon							C		M			C		M	B
?															C
Mercury	B		M	B		B	B		B	M	M	M	B	M	B
Comet												C		M	M
Lincoln	B			B			B		M	B		M	B		
Continental Mk. II								B	M						
Edsel								C		C		M			
CHRYSLER CORPORATION Plymouth	B	M	M		B		B	M	B	C	B	B	M	B	M
Valiant												C	C		M
Dodge	B	M	M		B		B	M	B		M	B	B	B	M
Lancer													C		M
De Soto	B	M	M		B		B	M	B		M	B	B		M
Chrysler	B	M	M		B		B	M	B		M	B	M	M	
Imperial		M			B		B	M	B		M	M	M	M	
AMERICAN MOTORS American											B	B	B		B
Rambler		C					B			C	M	C		B	
Nash	B	M	M	B		M		B							
Studebaker	B	M	M	B	B	M		M			C		M		M

NEW CAR—C   NEW BODY—B   MAJOR CHANGE—M

Source: *Fortune*, 1961. Reproduced by permission.

Chevrolet-Dart sector to rise to 46 per cent this year and hold that percentage in 1962. Best bet is that Chrysler will make only minor changes in its compacts this coming September. With DeSoto discontinued, its fighting money will likely go into new bodies for Dodge and Plymouth, and even greater emphasis on the low end of the market.[16]

In summary, the counterattack by the Big Three included the following major steps. First, they reversed the trend toward longer, lower, more orna-mented automobiles throughout their entire line. Second, they offered a greater variety of sizes, styles, and horsepower ratings, giving the public a much wider range of choice, particularly in the low-priced ranges. Third, they brought out eight new automobiles aimed specifically at the "compact" car market, the market where American Motors had been largely unopposed in 1958–59. Beyond this, their strategies appeared to diverge, with Ford and Chrysler appearing to bet that compacts were here to stay, while GM appeared to be betting that it could lead the public back up to larger cars in due time through its "B-O-P" compacts, on the one hand, and through keeping its Corvair out of the styling race and thereby de-emphasizing it. Taken together, these strategies put the squeeze on American Motors, though at the same time they involved a significant change in industry competition. While attack-ing AMC (and each other) with their compacts, the Big Three were now playing on AMC's home ground, and they were advertising the values of compactness, economy, and durability—long the bywords at American Motors. The counterattack stood to help as well as hurt AMC.

Facing up to the counterattack: 1959–62

During the years 1959–62, American Motors reached and maintained about a 6% share of the market (Exhibit 8). Pretax profits reached a high of $105 million in 1959 and 1960, and then tapered off, owing in part to the rigors of immediate competition and in part to increasing outlays for auto-motive styling changes, including a significant redesign of the Rambler American for 1961. In facing the counterattack, then, the company had a profitable operation with a relatively stable market share, i.e., a much stronger position than in the days of the "campaign for survival."

Product line. The American Motors product line consisted of the 117-inch Ambassador, the 108-inch Rambler Classic, the 100-inch Rambler American, and the 85-inch Metropolitan, with the two larger models accounting for approximately 70% of sales, the American about 20%, and the Metropolitan about 5%.

Forbes,[17] in discussing the product line, made the following observations:

The product that American sends to compete in the market place shows interesting similarities to the facilities that bore it. As a car, the Rambler could

---

[16]*Fortune,* January 1961.
[17]"Can George Do It Again?" *Forbes,* August 1, 1961. Reproduced by permission.

Exhibit 8

1962 MODEL YEAR U.S. CAR PRODUCTION BY $100 PRICE GROUPS*
(Entire Model Year)

$100 Price Groups	Chevrolet	Chevy II	Corvair	Pontiac	Tempest	Oldsmobile	F-85	Buick	Special	Ford Galaxie	Fairlane	F
$1,601–$1,700	.....	.....	.....	.....	.....	.....	.....	.....	.....	.....	.....	
1,701– 1,800	.....	11,457	16,245	.....	.....	.....	.....	.....	.....	.....	.....	6
1,801– 1,900	.....	63,479	53,842	.....	.....	.....	.....	.....	.....	.....	23,511	17
1,901– 2,000	.....	168,044	.....	.....	52,903	.....	.....	.....	.....	.....	65,282	3
2,001– 2,100	135,692	1,663	199,797	.....	51,981	.....	.....	.....	42,384	.....	91,550	6
2,101– 2,200	72,195	40,467	3,716	.....	.....	.....	15,983	.....	.....	26,114	99,804	5
2,201– 2,300	174,591	41,497	18,931	.....	38,309	.....	18,736	.....	40,202	66,810	17,969	
2,301– 2,400	226,104	.....	.....	14,263	.....	.....	32,461	.....	7,382	93,178	.....	2
2,401– 2,500	430,298	.....	13,491	68,620	.....	.....	6,864	.....	36,874	288,126	.....	
2,501– 2,600	197,469	.....	.....	75,275	.....	.....	6,861	7,418	18,712	55,548	.....	
2,601– 2,700	138,607	.....	.....	.....	.....	108,143	9,898	56,783	8,913	47,217	.....	
2,701– 2,800	38,707	.....	.....	27,760	.....	53,438	3,765	62,997	.....	70,802	.....	
2,801– 2,900	10,345	.....	.....	50,158	.....	24,125	.....	.....	.....	15,385	.....	
2,901– 3,000	.....	.....	.....	42,345	.....	12,212	.....	13,471	.....	28,412	.....	
3,001– 3,100	.....	.....	.....	44,015	.....	38,712	.....	20,698	.....	.....	.....	
3,101– 3,200	.....	.....	.....	51,777	.....	6,417	.....	9,131	.....	13,183	.....	
3,201– 3,300	.....	.....	.....	4,527	.....	.....	.....	12,717	.....	.....	.....	
3,301– 3,400	.....	.....	.....	.....	.....	3,837	.....	.....	.....	.....	.....	
3,401– 3,500	.....	.....	.....	.....	.....	.....	.....	.....	.....	.....	.....	
3,501– 3,600	.....	.....	.....	.....	.....	7,653	.....	22,445	.....	.....	.....	
3,601– 3,700	14,531	.....	.....	.....	.....	47,006	.....	16,734	.....	.....	.....	
3,701– 3,800	.....	.....	.....	.....	.....	40,641	.....	.....	.....	.....	.....	
3,801– 3,900	.....	.....	.....	.....	.....	.....	.....	7,894	.....	.....	.....	
3,901– 4,000	.....	.....	.....	.....	.....	3,691	.....	15,395	.....	.....	.....	
4,001– 4,100	.....	.....	.....	.....	.....	.....	.....	.....	.....	.....	.....	
4,101– 4,200	.....	.....	.....	.....	.....	.....	.....	.....	.....	.....	.....	
4,201– 4,300	.....	.....	.....	.....	.....	7,149	.....	.....	.....	.....	.....	
4,301– 4,400	.....	.....	.....	.....	.....	.....	.....	.....	.....	.....	.....	
4,401 & Over	.....	.....	.....	.....	.....	.....	.....	.....	.....	.....	.....	
Totals	1,438,539	326,607	306,022	378,740	143,193	353,024	94,568	245,683	154,467	704,775	298,116	41

*Based on suggested factory list prices before excise tax, dealer handling charges and optional equipment installat[ion]. 1962 model prices include deduction of heater prices for General Motors Corp. and Ford Motor Co. car lines to [bring] industry-wide prices on an equal basis with entire 1961 model year. Source: Ward's Statistical Dept.

Source: *Ward's Automotive Yearbook, 1963*, p. 22. Reproduced by permission.

be described as a sound whole made up of frequently improvised parts. Most Ramblers, for example, are powered with a basically old-fashioned six-cylinder engine first designed in the 1930's. (There is also a quite modern V-8 that is used on one Rambler Classic line and on the larger Rambler Ambassador.) However, in typical Rambler fashion this engine was converted in 1956 from L-head to valve-in-head design for use on most Ramblers, and in addition is now being offered with an ultra-modern aluminum cylinder block.

Nevertheless, management believed that continued successful participation in "economy runs" by this engine contributed significantly to Rambler's reputation for economy and quality.

To continue with *Forbes:*

Yet the Rambler has consistently had elements of solid and often unique worth. Its unit-body-and-frame construction is miles ahead of the traditional technique followed on U.S. cars, although all the new compacts have come over to Rambler's side. Its ceramic-coated muffler promises to remedy at last an almost

sun-bird	Mercury Monterey	Meteor	Comet	Plymouth	Valiant	Dodge	Lancer	Chrysler	Cadillac Lincoln Imperial	Rambler	Stude-baker	Total All Cars Units	% of Total
.....	.....	.....	.....	.....	.....	.....	.....	.....	.....	29,948	.....	29,948	0.45
.....	.....	.....	.....	.....	21,803	.....	7,327	.....	.....	44,352	15,793	181,243	2.71
.....	.....	.....	62,491	.....	32,413	.....	16,775	.....	.....	62,071	23,897	512,345	7.66
.....	.....	.....	60,701	.....	47,967	.....	19,024	.....	.....	106,816	14,277	566,573	8.47
.....	.....	11,230	.....	47,682	34,303	35,457	14,140	.....	.....	5,521	3,115	736,931	11.02
.....	.....	30,603	29,128	27,885	8,867	13,648	2,699	.....	.....	76,793	9,599	512,757	7.67
.....	.....	21,524	10,667	21,344	.....	8,753	4,306	.....	.....	61,482	9,811	554,932	8.30
.....	641	5,695	.....	13,083	.....	19,138	.....	.....	.....	21,893	5,393	461,855	6.91
.....	5,328	.....	2,318	29,090	.....	27,743	.....	.....	.....	21,281	2,861	937,189	14.01
.....	26,435	.....	.....	14,115	.....	12,907	.....	.....	.....	4,379	1,149	420,268	6.28
.....	46,501	.....	.....	12,566	.....	21,963	.....	50,832	.....	6,401	.....	507,824	7.59
.....	8,932	.....	.....	2,410	.....	15,862	.....	10,313	.....	1,289	320	296,595	4.43
.....	15,085	.....	.....	3,959	.....	5,564	.....	7,705	.....	.....	8,467	140,793	2.11
.....	.....	.....	.....	.....	.....	3,933	.....	.....	.....	.....	.....	100,373	1.50
.....	.....	.....	.....	.....	.....	.....	.....	21,337	.....	.....	.....	124,762	1.87
.....	2,772	.....	.....	.....	.....	893	.....	3,319	.....	.....	.....	87,492	1.31
.....	.....	.....	.....	.....	.....	.....	.....	2,371	.....	.....	.....	19,615	0.29
.....	1,315	.....	.....	.....	.....	.....	.....	.....	.....	*	.....	5,152	0.08
.....	.....	.....	.....	.....	.....	.....	.....	.....	.....	.....	.....	.....	...
.....	.....	.....	.....	.....	.....	.....	.....	1,786	.....	.....	.....	31,884	0.48
.....	.....	.....	.....	.....	.....	.....	.....	.....	.....	.....	.....	78,271	1.17
.....	.....	.....	.....	.....	.....	.....	.....	12,083	.....	.....	.....	52,724	0.79
7,845	.....	.....	.....	.....	.....	.....	.....	6,638	.....	.....	.....	72,377	1.08
9,282	.....	.....	.....	.....	.....	.....	.....	.....	.....	.....	.....	29,368	0.44
.....	.....	.....	.....	.....	.....	.....	.....	.....	.....	.....	.....	.....	...
.....	.....	.....	.....	.....	.....	.....	.....	.....	.....	.....	.....	7,149	0.11
8,457	.....	.....	.....	.....	.....	.....	.....	781	.....	.....	.....	9,238	0.14
4,427	.....	.....	.....	.....	.....	.....	.....	1,374	206,238	.....	.....	209,039	3.13
8,011	107,009	69,052	165,305	172,134	145,353	165,861	64,271	118,539	206,238	442,226	94,682	6,686,697	100.0

scandalous piece of automotive misdesign; its dip-coating of the entire body shows how to prevent the moth-eaten appearance around the bottom that marks so many five-year-olds and up among U.S. cars; and Rambler bodies now get the benefit of a water spray test that should at least keep them from leaking when brand new, as many U.S. cars do.

Given this combination of homemade improvisations plus specific technological leads over major competitors, American Motors' timing of introducing new models was of particular interest. On several occasions the company employed what has been called a "Notre Dame" strategy, a strategy of introducing major model changes one year after its competitors. *Forbes* illustrated this in the case of the Rambler Classic, the company's bread-and-butter model:

This quiet, almost sedate vehicle plays a crucial part in American Motors strategy. The company feels that to date it has had practically no direct competition for its major product, the 108-inch wheelbase Rambler Classic that Romney describes as a "family-sized compact." For the two leading competitive compacts are nearer in size to the 100-inch wheelbase Rambler American (an "economy compact," in Romney lingo). But within the next few months (fall 1961) both Ford and Chevy will introduce brand new lines, slightly larger than the Falcon and Corvair, that will meet the Rambler Classic head-on.

Romney expects to take on this new competition with only slightly face-lifted versions of the present Ramblers, praying that the car's general reputation will carry it through. Meantime, however, he is preparing new 1963 models whose tooling alone will cost considerably more than this year's entire $20 million–$25 million capital outlay for tooling, expansion, plant modernization and whatnot. American's future will hinge on how much ground (if any) it must give in the fiscal year just ahead, and how much it gains back as a result of its 1963 counterattack.

Thus Romney displays a strategy of timing not unlike that Notre Dame once used in football, namely, employing the second team to take the initial shock before putting the first team in.

The second team was aided, however, by across-the-board price cuts. Thus the company advertised that every single model had been reduced in price for 1962. The following fall, when the new Classic and Ambassador models were introduced, prices were raised some $30 to $50 per car. Meanwhile, American Motors was able to maintain its market share in 1962, choosing to do this at the expense of substantially lowered profits for that year. As the 1963 models were introduced and the price increases became effective, profits improved sharply, up 30% from the preceding year.

Mr. Romney explained this strategy to the AMC shareholders in the following way: ". . . we sharply increased product value without a corresponding increase in prices in 1962 models. This was a very calculated decision because we thought it was more important to increase our penetration of the market—more important in terms of the interests of stockholders and others associated with this company—then to make maximum current profits our primary objective."[18]

Marketing. With acceptance of the compact car idea, AMC advertising and promotion focused increasingly on specific product features, such as the unit-body construction, deep-dip rust prevention, and the ceramic muffler. The company also took the lead in extending the warranty on its automobiles, a move which spread rapidly, and led competitors to extend 90-day warranties up to five years in some cases. Longevity had become a selling point—a development which would have seemed unthinkable only a few years previously.

Dealer organization. Having rebuilt its dealer organization during the previous campaign adroitly captained by the aggressive Roy Abernethy, who succeeded George Romney in 1962 as president of the corporation, the company now attempted to maintain existing numbers and to strengthen individual dealerships. To implement this, the company once again resorted to granting extra discounts to dealers when the going got tough. Thus as the United States slid into a recession in 1961, the company sales and profits slipped, but at the same time dealer discounts were increased $30–$40 per car, causing corporate profits to slide still more. By paying an extra $6 to

---

[18]Report to Stockholders, February 7, 1962.

$8 million in dealer commissions (while operating profits dropped from 105 to 50 millions), the company was able to report a net loss in dealers of 1.3% in the first six months of 1961 while its competitors reported losses as follows:[19]

G.M. 1.0%
Ford 1.7
Chrysler 4.3
Studebaker-Packard 7.9

This left the company's dealer strength relatively unimpaired, though AMC's dealer organization was still weaker than those of its major competitors. *Forbes* noted that AMC's dealers

were outnumbered six-to-one by G.M.'s dealers and nearly three-to-one by Ford's and Chrysler's. But old sales boss Abernethy has some factors working for him, too. The rapidly increasing number of Ramblers on the road—now close to 2 million—means an equally rapid increase in the parts-and-service business that provides the dealer's bread and butter. And Rambler leads all U.S. cars except Cadillac in owner loyalty, as measured by the percentage of Rambler owners who become repeat buyers. The latest score: 67%. Thus American has the distinction of being the only carmaker that is increasing its dealer corps, though its map is not still without blank spots.

Finance and control. In 1961 the company became the only U.S. automobile manufacturer to be completely free of long-term debt. The company maintained, however, a standing line of credit of approximately $50 million which it could call upon in an emergency.

The company's elimination of all debt had been accompanied by an expansion of capacity to an estimated 600,000 cars per year. To accomplish the debt reduction and the expansion of output at the same time, the company had maintained its policy of not integrating its operation to include any but the essential elements. Thus, capacity was doubled from 300,000 to 600,000 at an estimated investment of about $30 million, mere peanuts compared to the outlay for a comparable expansion of an integrated operation.

That American could get so much additional capacity at this relatively small cost is partly because of the company's style of play and partly because of a fortunate break. The style of play refers to American's preference for making maximum use of its suppliers' investment rather than pouring its own money into integrated facilities. If G.M. were given an index number of 100 on an "integration scale," then Ford would rank perhaps a little above 100 (with its steel and glass plants more than offsetting certain other components that Ford does not make) and American Motors probably at about 70. Thus new capacity will obviously cost American less per unit (the degree of integration remaining unchanged) than its two biggest competitors.

The lucky break was the sudden availability in Kenosha, Wisconsin cheek by jowl with American's main plant, of a 2-million square-foot plant where Simmons once made metal beds. The Simmons plant was quite capable of be-

[19] *Forbes*, August 1, 1961, p. 17.

ing converted into the building of Rambler bodies, one of American's worst bottlenecks. Precisely this was done, at an annual rental cost (with options to buy) of only $450,000. And while it took nearly $15 million to equip it for production, the company still got by with a fraction of the capital cost it would have taken to build a new facility from scratch.[20]

Corresponding to this lack of integration, the company was estimated to have a smaller profit margin per car than GM or Ford, but a higher return on the capital invested, as below:

1960 RESULTS*

	Pretax Profits		Capital Employed per Vehicle Produced	Return on Capital before Income Taxes
	Per Vehicle Produced	As a % of Auto Sales		
General Motors $400	16%		$1,000	40%
Ford 240	15		825	29
American 200	11		400	50

*In American's case the fiscal year ends September 30; for the other two it ends December 31.

All figures are *Forbes'* estimates. In each case they represent earnings and capital employed in the auto business on a worldwide basis. Nonautomotive activities have been screened out. In GM's case, GMAC earnings and capital are included in automotive results.[21]

With this approach, the company was able to maintain a low break-even point even with its sharply expanded scale of operations. Thus *Forbes* estimated the break-even in 1961 to be 150,000 units, up only slightly from 1959 despite the increase in productive capacity from 300,000 to 600,000 units. On the other hand, one American Motors executive noted that with this approach the company was not able to attain significant economies of scale in the 400,000–600,000-car range. Unit costs were about the same over the entire range. Strategy remained essentially unchanged, then, with the company placing heavy emphasis on safety (via a low break-even) at the expense of the opportunities for rising profits per unit from integrated operations (with their attendant fixed costs).

Production. As for the strength of American's production sinews, the company's car output takes place in two Kenosha, Wis., plants and a third in Milwaukee, 40-odd miles away. Little about any of the plants represents a production man's dream of efficiency. For example, the very thought of trucking Rambler bodies from the Milwaukee body plant to Kenosha for assembly, at a $5 cost per car, would flabbergast the average factory boss. But American's production heads are hardened to the practice. They insist that in view of the huge capital costs that would be involved it would not prove economical to

---

[20]*Ibid.*, p. 16.
[21]*Ibid.*

move the Milwaukee operation to Kenosha. They take much the same view toward the frequent multi-story sections in American's plants: conveyor belts simply run upstairs and down, in fine disregard of auto industry dogma that only single-story plants make sense.

All of American's auto production operations have an air of artful and thrifty improvisation, as though new equipment is added only when absolutely essential, or when it is a leadpipe cinch to pay back its cost in a matter of months. Thus, fine, new automated tools operate side by side with virtual clunkers—a practice perhaps necessary for a company in American's spot, but one that always carries the danger of falling too far behind.

American also contravenes industry—or at least Big Three—practice by crowding all its auto output into one Wisconsin area, instead of seeking a calculated scatter of component and assembly plants across the country. In fact, measured in unit output American's Kenosha assembly plant is the industry's largest, outranking even Ford's River Rouge.

Romney explains: "In 1948, we made a study which showed that a volume of 200,000 cars assembled on the West Coast yielded a saving of $60 per unit, which justified the use of east and west coast plants. However, a 1958 study, assuming a volume of 400,000 cars, showed that freight rates on components vs. completed vehicles had changed so much in the meantime that a West Coast assembly plant meant a penalty of $59 per car." American is, therefore, quite content with its current concentration—though its executives readily grant that it might not pay other companies to change their own established patterns.[22]

Labor relations. In keeping with its strategy of maintaining a low break-even for safety in bad years at the expense of possible economies and profits in good years, the company negotiated an unusual labor contract in 1961. Called a "progress sharing" agreement, the contract provided for profit sharing in lieu of a certain portion of the straight hourly increase granted by the Big Three.

Mr. Romney explained the concepts involved in the 1961 agreement as follows:

While much has been written about this historic Progress Sharing labor agreement, which we negotiated with the UAW last summer, we find continuing public interest in this subject. Since my written report to you on the agreement, all of our nonrepresented salaried employees also are now participating in this program.

The management of your company is convinced that the progress sharing approach—founded on the principle of sharing progress equitably among employees, stockholders, consumers, dealers and suppliers—will make it possible to expand our sales, increase our earnings and substantially benefit our stockholders. If you had been familiar with the internal operation of the company, you would realize that this dedication to progress sharing has been as fundamental in this company's growth as has the pioneering of the compact Rambler.

Let me tell you why this contract with the union is important:

First, in the initial paragraph of our new union contract, it is recognized by

---

[22]*Ibid.*

the union as well as the management that for employees to enjoy high wages and good working conditions, they must make progress *and it must be shared with customers.* In other words, our contract repudiates the idea that you can turn over to workers, or workers and stockholders, *all* of the progress—and still make progress. It's premised on the concept that if you're going to make progress, you must share that progress with the customer. This is sound. Without progress sharing, the American economy would not be what it is today. But this was a unique principle to write into our labor contract in face of national policies that are of an opposite character.

Second, our unique contract with the UAW is designed specifically to meet the needs and opportunities of American Motors. It is not a pattern settlement imposed on us—it was our idea—nor a pattern settlement to be imposed on others. We weren't trying to say what others ought to have. Flexibility and freedom of action and choice are great principles. It is based on the opportunities of American Motors and the needs of American Motors.

Third, the fixed-cost increases are *lower* for American Motors than for any other automobile company. In other words, while the employee benefit increases which all the companies have provided for in their labor contracts are generally similar, their method of financing is not the same. All the benefit increases granted by the Big Three represent fixed-cost increases. Virtually all the increased benefits granted under our contract will come out of profits, and therefore our fixed-cost increases are *lower* than those of our major competitors. And "if there ain't no profits, there ain't no sharing." It's just that simple.

Fourth, a large share of our cost increases is placed on a variable basis—subject to actual earnings. This is a distinct advantage to us because the determinations are to be made after the facts instead of before the facts are known. This permits more realistic forecasting, sounder fiscal approaches and greater mutuality of interest in progress.

While the "Progress Sharing Agreement" has been described previously as "unusual," consideration of this plan must include the entire 1961 labor agreement of which the plan was only a portion. Additional considerations in the contract affecting such matters as paid time not worked, seniority benefits, and production standards resulted in tangible savings of several millions per year, and intangible, but nonetheless significant benefits, which have improved the company's competitive position.

The situation at the end of 1962

In its 1962 Annual Report, American Motors described its competitive position in part as follows:

Setting a new Rambler world-wide record, wholesale sales of Rambler cars in the U.S. and foreign markets increased to 478,132 units. This was a 24.2% gain over the 1961 fiscal period.

With several new entries attracted to the compact car segment of the U.S. car market in 1962, Rambler experienced the most vigorous onslaught to date on its domestic market position [see table]. Our strengthened distribution and dealer organization, however, demonstrated full capability for meeting the competitive challenge. Rambler U.S. wholesale sales increased 18.5% over the previous fiscal year.

Year	U.S. Only	Outside U.S.	Total
1961	366,384	18,445	384,829
1962	434,486	43,646	478,132

Rambler's percentage of U.S. industry registrations was 6.7%, virtually unchanged from the previous year.

*   *   *   *   *

Advertising and selling expense increased during the fiscal year as Rambler made a successful bid for larger volume. Additional customer benefits were provided by the extension of warranty terms.

The building of a stronger distribution system to meet the requirements of a growing business is a continuing activity. To provide better service to dealers and retail customers, we added a new automotive zone office in Newark, N.J., and a new parts warehouse at Queens, L.I., during the fiscal year. Additional parts warehouses have since been opened in Houston and San Francisco. We also expanded our financial program of assisting the development of Rambler franchises in important markets.

A net of ninety-six new Rambler dealers was franchised in the U.S. during the fiscal year, bringing our total automotive dealer count as of September 30 to 3,076 dealers.

Increased strength of our Rambler dealers is reflected in their aggregate net worth of $216,714,000 currently which compares to $100,877,000 in 1957.

*   *   *   *   *

In line with our policy of making changes only when they truly benefit the customer, American Motors introduced major engineering and structural improvements in the 1963 Classic and Ambassador models which permitted wholly restyled cars.

An advanced method of unit construction, which contributes greater strength, solidity, precision and quality to Rambler bodies, made feasible the attractive new styling of the 1963 models. The new Rambler car body was designed to use curved glass side windows with doors that curve into the roof. This feature is available only on a few expensive U.S. cars. Combined with these exterior appearance changes is a new development in power transfer—the Tri-Poised engine mount—which provides a quieter Rambler ride at all speeds.

The Rambler American line has been broadened and enhanced with the addition of new hardtop models. A new Twin-Stick floor shift transmission with overdrive is available as optional equipment on the top line of all series. U.S. prices were maintained at the same level as a year ago on fifteen of the 1963 models, were reduced on two models and increased modestly on 12 models.

Rambler remains the leader in the segment of the U.S. market that continues to be the fastest growing. We believe the compact car will take an ever greater share of total car sales in the 1963 calendar year. The factors that have contributed to Rambler's rapid growth are accelerating: the dispersal of population to suburban areas, the dependence of more and more people upon the motor car for personal mobility, and the traffic congestion, parking problems and other trends arising from increasing urbanization.

Cars that are more practical and convenient to use, while equally comfortable and attractive, are in the ascendency in the American market. Rambler's present and future product programs are well timed and ideally adapted to those strong trends in customer preference.

*   *   *   *   *

American Motors also launched major moves overseas during 1962. The annual report noted, for instance, that the company's overseas investment increased fivefold during the year. Continuing, the report had this to say about AMC's international operations:

More Rambler cars are appearing throughout the world.

American Motors now accounts for 18% of shipments of new cars from the United States. Sales of these cars, plus Ramblers produced by foreign plants, increased 136% over unit sales in the prior year.

American Motors of Canada is developing a firm position in the Canadian market. The subsidiary recorded a 75% gain in sales, reaching a level of 19,000 units, and substantially increased its percentage of industry registrations over the previous year. Our Canadian automobile manufacturing plant has under construction at Brampton, Ontario a new addition which will enlarge its work space by two-thirds. The new building is scheduled to be completed in the March quarter. The cost of this expansion will be paid for out of the subsidiary's earnings.

Rambler is now the best selling car of American origin in Latin America. Production of Rambler cars has been under way since January 1962 in Argentina. Despite political unrest in that nation, the output of our cars by Industries Kaiser Argentina S.A. is at a highly satisfactory rate. Rambler is now taking 40% of U.S. car sales in that country.

Rambler assembly for distribution in Common Market countries commenced in March 1962 in the Renault plant at Haren, Belgium. Since then a steady monthly step-up in Rambler output has been achieved, and further growth is indicated as Rambler gains the benefit of added distribution through Renault's wide network of dealers.

In sum, then, American Motors was maintaining its domestic position and expanding abroad. With the introduction of restyled Ambassadors and Classics for 1963, it was hoping to move ahead in the domestic market as well.

Reviewing these events in February 1962, Mr. Romney noted that the company had successfully weathered "campaign counterattack." Looking to 1963, he stated that "next year we expect to resume the offensive with 'campaign leadership.' In the years ahead, we expect to begin a long-range battle for the number-one brand-name position in the automobile industry in this country."

AMERICAN MOTORS CORPORATION (D)*

^^^

On January 9, 1967, Mr. Roy Chapin, automotive manager and executive vice president of American Motors Corporation (AMC), was named as chairman and chief executive officer. *The Wall Street Journal* reported as follows:

His election' highlighted a top management realignment and was the latest development in AMC's tangled financial affairs. William V. Luneburg was selected as president and chief operating officer. Roy Abernethy resigned as president and Robert B. Evans stepped down as chairman to clear the way for the executive changes. The most urgent problems confronting the new officers are the company's car sales slump, and the need to arrange new financing to replace a $75 million credit line that expires May 31.[1]

One of Mr. Chapin's first tasks was to explain to the stockholders' annual meeting the cause and the cure for the $12.6 million deficit which AMC had incurred in fiscal 1966. This was the first deficit since 1957. (For financial statements, see Exhibits 1 and 2.) Mr. Chapin also took immediate steps to rebuild public confidence in AMC through buying full page ads in most leading newspapers and periodicals to explain how the company was tackling its problems. "People, product, and plant," said the text, "we've moved on all three fronts." As the fourth and final major step, "We intend to expand the number of dealers."

Mr. Chapin's appointment as chairman came at a time when many analysts were beginning once again to write obituary notices for AMC as a car producer. Few could see a chance for the company to stage another comeback like the one it had achieved between 1954 and 1962. Just prior to the management switch, *Forbes* gave the following gloomy appraisal:

. . . Detroit's American Motors Corp., once a stunning success with its Rambler compact car, now [is] fighting for its life. In just three years its volume has fallen more than 40% . . . its sales have dropped from $1.1 billion in fiscal 1963 to $870 million in the year through September 30th; and its earnings have been wiped out, from $2.01 per share to a 66 cent deficit. Perhaps most perilous, AMC is in danger of losing the confidence of the auto buying public.

---

[1] *Wall Street Journal*, January 10, 1967.

Exhibit 1

AMERICAN MOTORS CORPORATION AND CONSOLIDATED SUBSIDIARIES

Consolidated Statement of Net Loss
(Year Ended September 30, 1966)

Revenues:

Sales	$901,952,773
Less excise taxes	31,503,717
Net Sales	$870,449,056
Equity in net loss—earnings of unconsolidated subsidiaries	872,424
Other income	6,812,033
	$876,388,665

Costs and Expenses:

Cost of products sold, other than items below	$737,333,860
Selling, advertising, and administrative expenses	106,608,321
Amortization of tools and dies	32,320,889
Depreciation and amortization of plant and equipment	15,199,329
Cost of pensions for employees	13,369,235
Interest	2,319,192
Minority interest in net earnings of Kelvinator of Canada Limited	156,009
	$907,306,835
Loss—Earnings before taxes on income and special credit	$ 30,918,170
Taxes on income—credit	15,200,000
Loss—Earnings before special credit	$ 15,718,170
Special credit—tax provisions of prior years no longer required	3,070,000
Net loss—earnings	$ 12,648,170

Per Share of Capital Stock:

Loss—earnings from ordinary operations	$.82
Special credit	.16
Net loss—earnings	$.66

To make the task all the harder . . . [the management] must attempt to turn AMC around in a model year whose sales are now running significantly below the record level of 1966.

. . . Time is running short for American Motors. It is not—at least not yet—a question of staying solvent: AMC is still strong financially despite its loss in fiscal 1966. But it will grow progressively weaker if its sales are not quickly brought back to a profitable level.[2]

The table on page 98 highlights the steady decline which had occurred. Mr. Chapin himself added a note of urgency when he reported to the stockholders' meeting:

Mr. Chapin said the new team is "very conscious" of "time as a key factor." He said that "the new management has started off on the run, and don't expect to stop running until we have the kind of results in the form of restored profits

[2]*Forbes,* December 1, 1966.

Exhibit 2

AMERICAN MOTORS CORPORATION AND CONSOLIDATED SUBSIDIARIES

Consolidated Balance Sheets
(September 30, 1966)

Current Assets:

Cash	$ 17,157,562
Marketable securities—at cost and accrued interest (approximately market)	3,098,744
Accounts receivable, less allowance of $700,000 for doubtful accounts	54,067,374
Accounts receivable from affiliated companies	14,242,287
Refundable taxes on income	22,568,848
Inventories—at lower of cost (first-in, first-out method) or market	135,562,936
Prepaid insurance, taxes, and other expenses	7,237,335
Total current assets	**$253,935,086**

Investments and Other Assets:

Investments in and advances to unconsolidated subsidiaries	$ 44,923,325
Miscellaneous advances and investments	9,551,062
Total investments and other assets	**$ 54,474,387**

Property, Plant, and Equipment—at cost, less accumulated depreciation:

Land	$ 4,369,546
Buildings and improvements	59,425,901
Machinery and equipment, including tools and dies	209,986,197
	$273,781,644
Less accumulated depreciation	122,689,205
Total property, plant, and equipment	**$151,092,439**
	$459,501,912

Liabilities and Stockholders' Investment

Current Liabilities:

Notes payable	$ 73,176,160
Accounts payable	90,363,242
Salaries, wages, and amounts withheld from employees	8,126,020
Accrued expenses, including excise and miscellaneous taxes	26,107,674
Taxes on income	3,372,441
Total current liabilities	**$201,145,537**

Other Liabilities:

Executive compensation payable after one year, less applicable income taxes	$ 113,800
Deferred income taxes	1,639,641
Total other liabilities	**$ 1,753,441**

Minority Interest (27.51% at September 30, 1966) in Kelvinator of Canada Limited ... 2,002,098

Stockholders' Investment:

Capital Stock, par value $1.66-2/3 a share:
Authorized 30,000,000 shares

Issued—19,268,359 shares	$ 32,113,932
In treasury—202,895 shares	338,158
Outstanding—19,065,464 shares	$ 31,775,774
Additional paid-in capital	50,069,529
Earnings retained for use in the business	172,755,533
Total stockholders' investment	**$254,600,836**
	$459,501,912

Year	Share of Market (%)	AMC Unit Sales (000)	AMC Dollar Sales ($000,000)	Profit ($000)	Return on Sales (%)	Dividends Share ($)	No. of Dealers	E.P.S. ($)
1960	6.6	478	$1,057	$ 48,243	4.6	$1.05	...	$ 2.63
1961	6.7	392	$ 875	$ 23,579	2.7	$1.10	2,980	$ 1.28
1962	6.7	478	$1,056	$ 34,241	3.2	$1.00	3,076	$ 1.85
1963	5.8	511	$1,132	$ 37,807	3.3	$1.00	3,000	$ 2.01
1964	5.1	455	$1,009	$ 26,227	2.6	$1.00	3,100	$ 1.38
1965	3.7	412	$ 990	$ 5,205	0.5	$0.625	2,967	$ 0.27
1966	3.2	346	$ 870	$(12,648)	...	...	2,629	$(0.66)

and dividends you have every right and reason to expect." He said that "in present circumstances there is no time to spare," but added that "we also believe there is time enough." Mr. Luneburg said that "time is short, but all this means is we have to think and act faster. Urgency is the password."[3]

This case describes the events that led from the prosperous years before 1962 to the situation inherited by Mr. Chapin in January 1967. The case describes in particular the strategy of AMC and its competitors during the period of Mr. Abernethy's chairmanship, the interregnum of Mr. Evans, the problems and alternatives facing Mr. Chapin and Mr. Luneburg when they assumed control, and the first actions initiated by these men in order to restore both profits and financial viability.

The Abernethy era

On November 15, 1962, Roy Abernethy was appointed president and chief executive officer of American Motors Corporation. He was to fill the vacancy created when George Romney resigned to serve as governor of Michigan.[4] The "Abernethy Era" was ushered in with an aura of optimism. The company's 1962 Annual Report described the year just passed in glowing terms:

The results for the year are particularly gratifying in the light of the solid advances we are continuing to make in strengthening our competitive position.

Without borrowing, and, in fact, while paying off a $89,600,000 debt, we have put $161,000,000 into plant modernization and expansion during the past few years, and paid our stockholders $71,600,000 since the resumption of dividend payments in January, 1959.

Our 1962 net earnings represent 15.2% on stockholder investment. Profit margins were improved through higher volumes and greater operating economies in 1962. . . .

The strengthening of our engineering and research organizations has become a vital part of our program to build for the future. Larger expenditures for forward planning than ever before were authorized in the 1962 fiscal year.[5]

Results in 1962 seemed to all concerned to justify this optimism. Rambler

---

[3] *Wall Street Journal*, February 2, 1967.
[4] Romney had been on leave of absence since February 1962.
[5] AMC Annual Report 1962, p. 10.

sales had set new records, showing a 24.2% gain over the previous year. In the domestic market, in spite of added competition arising from the entry of several new compacts, Rambler realized an 18.5% gain over the previous year. Market penetration was 6.7% up from less than 2% eight years earlier.

1963

Although Abernethy had held effective control at AMC during 1962, 1963 was the first model year for which he had had formal responsibility.[6] Results in 1963 did not repeat the spectacular gains of 1959–1962, but the Annual Report could still point to new highs:

This annual report to you is a brief summary of a year of substantial advance for American Motors in further strengthening its competitive position.

The immediate gains are related in the financial results. American Motors earnings in the 1963 fiscal year increased 10.4% while dollar sales increased 7.2%.

Net sales for American Motors and its consolidated subsidiaries totaled $1,132,356,298, a new high, against $1,056,395,059 for the previous year.

Rambler sold 511,038 units at wholesale in world markets in the fiscal year, a 6.9% increase over the previous year. It was the first year that Rambler had passed the half-million mark in annual world sales.

Rambler led all compact cars in sales with wholesale deliveries of 454,532 in the United States market, up 4.6% over the previous year.

American Motors' owner count now is in excess of 2,700,000, an all-time peak, providing an enlarged basis for repeat sales. Rambler's parts and accessory business has reached a new high, having tripled in the past six years.[7]

Mr. Abernethy attempted during 1963 to broaden and upgrade the product line. He had the company introduce new hardtop models and floor-mounted stick shifts, and he tried to emphasize the luxury appointments on its top-of-the-line models. The hope was to "broaden the range of choice offered to customers." Although locked into body sizes and styles by production requirements for body shells, he made every effort to exercise the options available to him for upgrading the Rambler.

Mr. Abernethy was hoping to take advantage of a trend toward a "personalized" car. *Business Week* discussed this trend as follows:

Last model year [1962], 76% of Chevy Corvair buyers ordered the sporty, more expensive Monza: This model year [1963], 79% are specifying the Monza. Chevy's standard-sized Impala and intermediate-sized Chevy II introduced super sport models last fall, with high performance and bucket seats. Since October, 32% of all Impala sales and 35% of Chevy II Nova sales have been for these models. It is much the same at Ford. Premium priced Galaxie 500 and 500 XL a year ago accounted for 54% of the Ford Division's sales of standard-sized cars; this year they account for 64%. . . . Ford Division's economy-oriented

---

[6]Automobile design generally took three years from initial drawings to product introduction. Significant changes could be made as late as 1½ years into the production cycle.
[7]AMC Annual Report 1963, p. 3.

Falcon declined 28% last year and is still falling behind larger and plusher compacts. Ford notes, though, that 37% of Falcon buyers are paying extra for deluxe vinyl interior trim this year, compared to 15% last year.[8]

1964

Much of the effort in 1964 was directed toward making the consumer think of Rambler as a small but luxurious car, rather than as an economical compact. One executive explained the objective as follows:

Because Rambler became distinctively known for its trimmer length and for its unusual operating economy, and, because the earliest competitive imitations of Rambler stressed these characteristics excessively, the word "compact" tended to become associated with "small, economy." However, the Rambler idea is that maximum consumer benefit is best achieved through a balance of all elements in car design that makes for total usefulness. In summary, the Rambler compact car concept is the balanced combination of the major elements of car design, packaged to meet the new problems of more intensive car use while squarely meeting American standards of interior roominess, riding comfort, performance, luxury, and pride of ownership.[9]

The results of 1964 were a disappointment. Sales fell only slightly, about 2%, but earnings dropped more than 30%. Mr. Abernethy explained the lack of success to the stockholders as follows:

To some extent buyers continue to identify Rambler primarily with conservative design and economy in a period of increased customer interest in extra options, luxury features and higher performance. Rambler has been moving with this trend and the lag in identity should be amply corrected by the 1965 models, which represent the most sweeping changes in our history. While maintaining the basic virtues that established Rambler popularity, all three Rambler lines are now dramatically in the three divisions of the most active segment of the automobile market.[10]

The year 1964 was the year of the Mustang. Introduced in April 1964, it still captured 3.92% of the total car market for the model year. The Mustang sold 450,000 units, the most ever for a new car. Ford Motor Company products captured 23.6% of the market. Chrysler's market share increased as well, owing at least in part to the introduction of the fastback Barracuda late in the spring. These two companies made a serious impact on General Motors and definitively halted the rise in AMC's market penetration. In spite of the trend towards the "personalized" car, 1964 proved to be the year of the low-priced car for AMC. The completely restyled Rambler American, the low-priced model, was the only car which saved AMC from a completely disastrous year. The higher priced Classic and Ambassador suffered declines

---

[8]*Business Week*, May 4, 1963, p. 33.

[9]*The Changing Car Market: Phase II*, American Motors Corporation, September 19, 1963, p. 1.

[10]AMC Annual Report 1964, p. 3.

of 33% and 50% respectively. Sales of the American line went up 50%, leaving the company with an overall sales drop of 70,000 units and a loss in market share of 1.2%.

1965

Steps taken by the company for the 1965 model year were the complete separation and restyling of the Classic and Ambassador series, the introduction of the Marlin into the "sporty car" market, and the introduction of an expanded range of accessories and options. Looking forward, Mr. Abernethy expressed confidence:

The basic challenge, of course, is in the attitude of people. We have a very powerful economy image . . . one we are proud of.

But there has been a swift change toward buying up in recent months. During this market transition period, we have continued to have a strong appeal for conservative owners, as in the past. We have not adequately made the public aware of the extent to which we have broadened our appeal. Our challenge is to create a new picture of Rambler in the minds of the public—a picture that contains the best of both, the best of the established Rambler concept and the best of the new. We will move toward this challenge with the best tools I think we ever had for the breadth of appeal to buyers of every type.

As you have seen, we will have three distinctly different Rambler lines, each with fresh and strong curbstone identification and each with a different appeal to a different segment of the market—all within our basic concept of sense and balance.

The big visible change in the Rambler line—beauty and size of package— gives us a positive and realistic basis for the enlargement of our product image. The American will compete in price, size, roominess, style and power with the Falcon, Valiant and Chevy II. The Classic will compete with the Fairlane, Chevelle, Dart and Comet. Their power range with their sixes runs from 170 for the Comet to 200 for the Fairlane, while we will have 199–232. The Ambassador will compete with the Tempest, Special, F-85, Plymouth Belvedere, Dodge Coronet, and so on. In addition to an excellent power position, with the edge in most cases, we'll have a roominess advantage. And we'll have the options, trim, luxury and looks to match their best.

How do we meet this challenge of 1965 from a policy and advertising approach?

As I emphasized, we must enlarge our identity, not trade it in for an all new one. We have roughly 2.4 million Ramblers on the road. A large share of our owners bought the established Rambler image. Essentially, what most of them bought was common sense.

They represent a great potential backlog of repeat sales. It would be a stupid business decision to desert them and millions more like them who moved toward the Rambler idea. You don't sneeze at a mass of buyers who account for close to 40% of the total market and who have made their moves in a very short space of time because of the excitement of a fresh new appealing idea.

Our objective is to keep them and add their cousins. We're in a green pasture that we've plowed and fertilized and dropped some sweat and blood into and we're not going to jump the fence and run to a pasture that just looks greener. The idea is to move the fence.[11]

The year's sales figures gave some evidence that consumers were responding to Mr. Abernethy's efforts to push the sales mix toward more luxurious, more powerful cars. When sales breakdowns for 1961 and 1965 were compared, gains showed up in the proportion of higher priced cars and cars sold equipped with expensive options. In both respects, however, AMC fell below the industry average. (See Exhibit 3.)

Exhibit 3

CHANGES IN AMC AND INDUSTRY SALES MIX, 1961, 1965, AND 1966

Percentage of Car Sales by Price Class

Factory List Price	AMC 1961	Industry 1961	AMC 1965	Industry 1965	AMC 1966	Industry 1966
$2,000 or Less	38.8	19.8	25.5	5.6	15.6	3.0
2,001–2,500	58.2	47.4	60.3	41.8	70.5	37.5
2,501–3,000	3.0	22.8	14.2	39.2	13.9	43.0
3,001–over	0.0	10.0	0.0	13.4	0.0	16.5
Total	100.0	100.0	100.0	100.0	100.0	100.0
Total units (000) ..	377.9	5,408.6	391.4	8,842.7	295.9	8,606.1

Percentage of Cars Sold with Options

Item	AMC 1961	AMC 1965	AMC 1966	Industry 1965	Industry 1966
V-8 engine	0.0	27.6	31.3	71.4	80.0
Power steering	15.7	32.9	40.1	59.6	59.6
Power brakes	7.9	17.9	26.4	32.2	32.3
White sidewalls	18.8	65.6	64.1	75.0	76.5
Wheel covers	7.5	50.2	53.9	71.0	74.2
Bucket seats	2.0	11.5	21.7	23.2	22.4

Source: *Ward's Automotive Yearbook, 1961, 1965, 1966.*

Near the end of the third fiscal quarter, Mr. Abernethy summarized achievements to date in a June speech before the Automobile Analysts of New York, as follows:

American Motors is like no independent automobile manufacturer that ever existed before. We have the kind of volume base that no other independent has ever reached before . . . and we have done and are continuing to do the right things to move ahead.

Our position in automotive history is unique.

---

[11]"The Challenge of 1965," remarks by Roy Abernethy, *1965 Product Review*, May 27, 1964.

We've come through more than half a century of competitive battles in an area that has seen more than a thousand companies come and go.

Sales of a billion dollars a year is the new plateau on which we are building. Our sales this year (1965) should again be in that area.

We have a far better foundation than ever before. At the end of our fiscal year, last September 30th, assets totaled $421 million. Five years ago the figure was $288 million.

Going into the current fiscal year, our investment in property, plant and equipment was more than $125 million. Five years ago, it was $59 million.

Over the past five years, the company invested $90 million in capital improvements . . . $127 million in new model tooling . . . and $26 million in subsidiaries.[12] In addition, we paid off some staggering debts. Meanwhile we have paid stockholders $115 million in dividends—more than half of this in the past three years. Since we resumed dividend payments in 1959, we have paid our stockholders $17 million more than Chrysler has.

All of our expansion to date has been paid for completely out of earnings retained in the business. Working capital as a result was down somewhat going into our current fiscal year. But the total figure of $94.6 million is far above the $46 million we showed in 1957, when so many people were writing American Motors off.

Nevertheless, 1965 closed amid indications of trouble. In the last fiscal quarter there was speculation that AMC, which in 1965 was the only automaker without long-term debt, would soon have to borrow:

. . . A feeling [exists] both in Detroit and on Wall Street that American Motors will have to borrow money to reshape its products and image successfully. Mr. Abernethy says there is "nothing at the moment" planned, but adds that "whether we have future financing or not remains to be seen."[13]

Other problems included a decline in the number of dealers from 3,100 late in 1963 to 2,900 late in 1965 (see Exhibit 4), and a steep rise in dealers' inventories. These rose to 123 days' supply, compared with 90 days a year earlier and 44 days for the industry. In early August, *The Wall Street Journal* took a serious view of AMC's condition:

With profits falling, its share of the U.S. auto market down to little more than half what it was five years ago, and its Rambler being outsold in America even by Volkswagen, American Motors Corporation yesterday took its most drastic step yet to loosen a growing financial squeeze: it cut its quarterly dividend in half. On September 20 it will pay 12½ cents a share to common stockholders of record August 20; previously it had paid 25 cents quarterly.

The move was hardly unexpected. For the last two years AMC has been raising eyebrows in Detroit and on Wall Street by reporting slipping sales while the bigger three U.S. automakers were pushing sales to undreamed of heights. Its latest profit report released yesterday with news of the dividend cut makes it plain the trend is continuing.

---

[12]In comparison, Ford spent $629 million in 1965, $692.5 million in 1966, and planned to spend $780 million in 1967 on plant expansion, modernization, and replacement.

[13]*New York Times,* July 25, 1965.

Exhibit 4

AMERICAN MOTORS CORPORATION

Selected Data on Dealer Franchises and Market Share, 1962 67
(Franchises* as of January 1)

Make or Company	1962	1963	1964	1965	1966	1967
Total GM	18,742	18,662	18,591	18,469	18,305	18,147
Chevrolet	6,856	6,791	6,739	6,669	6,600	6,507
Total Ford Motor Co.	12,226	10,086	10,042	9,921	9,830	9,810
Ford	6,623	6,550	6,454	6,368	6,263	6,170
Total Chrysler Co.	9,786	9,721	10,906	11,484	11,882	11,702
Plymouth	3,265	3,093	3,462	3,666	3,821	3,704
AMC	2,980	3,095	3,100	2,968	2,629	2,462
Studebaker Corp.	2,084	2,092	1,832	1,690	1,500	N.A.
Total*	45,818	43,656	44,471	44,532	44,151	42,421

Percentage Market Shares by Calendar Year, 1962–66

Make or Company	1962	1963	1964	1965	1966
Total GM	51.9	51.0	49.1	50.0	48.0
Chevrolet	24.9	28.6	26.3	26.0	23.7
Total Ford Motor Co.	26.3	24.9	26.0	25.5	26.2
Ford	21.2	20.7	21.7	21.4	22.1
Total Chrysler	9.6	12.4	13.8	14.7	15.4
Plymouth	4.4	5.7	6.1	6.7	6.7
Total Big Three	87.8	88.3	88.9	90.2	92.6
AMC	6.1	5.7	4.7	3.5	3.0
Studebaker Corp.	1.1	0.8	0.3	0.2	—
Other (mainly imports)	5.0	5.2	6.1	6.1	7.4

*Includes intracompany duals.
Source: Franchise data from Ward's Statistical Department, market-share data from *Ward's Automotive Yearbooks*.

But if the dividend cut startled few, it is bound to stir debate over AMC's future role. Fresh in the minds of many, of course, is the decision by Studebaker Corporation 18 months ago to close its U.S. auto plants after nearly five decades and move all output to Canada.[14]

By the end of the 1965 model year, Rambler's market share had dropped to 3.7%. Earnings fell precipitously as well. From over $26 million in 1964, they fell to $5.2 million in 1965. Even with consolidation of the Canadian subsidiary, total corporate sales fell to under $1 billion. To conserve capital, dividends were eliminated by the vote of the Board on November 17, 1965.

1966

Looking ahead to 1966, the 1965 AMC Annual Report analyzed the company's problems and indicated remedial steps:

[14] *Wall Street Journal,* August 3, 1965.

Domestic sales of American Motors automobiles were lower than expectations for the fiscal year, with the decline almost entirely in the lowest-priced categories which also declined for the industry as a whole. For 1966, the company made major changes in its merchandising approach. American Motors cars are backed by a new aggressive merchandising and national advertising program.

American Motors has made significant price reductions in its 1966 cars, even allowing for the additional cost of certain safety features that were optional extras last year but are now standard in the industry. . . . To emphasize the broadening of the company's car lines certain luxury models are being marketed under their own identity. The American and Classic series will continue to be identified as Ramblers, but both the luxury Ambassador series and the sporty Marlin will be identified separately as American Motors makes, without the Rambler designation. This is a further step to strengthen the public awareness of the new breadth of choice provided the consumer by the variety of product appeals incorporated in the new lines of American Motors cars.

The new merchandising effort includes greater emphasis on built-in rather than added-on quality, and on safety. The American Motors position on safety was commended during Congressional hearings in Washington, which highlighted the extra safety features the consumer gets from American Motors.[15]

In addition, the 1965 Annual Report revealed that a short-term loan for $50 million had been negotiated late in the summer with a group of 24 banks. According to a company spokesman, this loan had become necessary when a three-week strike closed the company's auto plant in August. The loan was secured by company notes; the covenant imposed dividend restrictions, and the principal would become payable on September 30, 1966.

As early results came in on the 1966 model year, it became clear that the face-lifts and interior improvements which AMC had made were not sufficient to reverse the downward trend of sales. AMC hired a new advertising agency, Benton and Bowles, which fashioned an $8.5 million advertising campaign featuring Rambler dealers as the "Friendly Giant Killers." This campaign was dropped early in 1966. It was believed by the trade that it had been based too heavily on an "inside joke," and that it was confused with the "Jolly Green Giant" trademark of canned and frozen vegetable fame. Some thought was also given to the problem created by identifying AMC with "killer" in the face of the well-publicized Congressional inquiry into automobile safety.

Some of the models that had been expected to perform well were disappointments. The Marlin, which was AMC's response to the Mustang and Barracuda, did poorly. Dealers believed that the price was too high. The first Marlins shipped had been deluxe models made to sell in the $4,000 range. *Time* reported that of 9,000 Marlins produced in 1965, 2,000 remained unsold as of late January 1966. Only 1,701 Marlins were produced in the first half of 1966, and the line was dropped completely late in the year.

The top-of-the-line Ambassador was the only series to show improved sales

---

[15]AMC Annual Report 1965, p. 5.

in late 1965 and early 1966. The Classic, the largest selling car, dropped 30%, and the American 10%.

The company's dealers were reportedly suffering severely. By the end of January 1966, AMC was down to 2,629 outlets, compared with 2,967 a year before and about 3,100 at the beginning of 1964. Of this number, 700 were reportedly carrying other lines. These dealers, comprising more than 25% of the total, contributed less than 10% of sales.

In February 1966, AMC inaugurated a plan whereby the company rebated one-half of the dealers' expenditure on local advertising. In addition AMC started a $10 million program to finance dealerships in 37 key market areas. This move would quadruple the investment which AMC had previously had in dealers. This policy was similar to the programs of other manufacturers, who had established well-run and well-financed key dealerships in major markets.[16]

Although there was a small profit in the first quarter of fiscal 1966, the last quarter of fiscal 1965 and the second quarter of fiscal 1966 showed losses. In March 1966, AMC negotiated a new loan agreement to replace the former one, on which $25 million had been repaid. The new loan for $75 million came from the same group of bankers, and was due May 31, 1967. According to *The Wall Street Journal*, the new loan covenant, unlike the old, required mortgages on substantially all the company's properties. The paper quoted "financial sources connected with the creditors" as saying, "The banks are staying in . . . [American Motors] has a tough period ahead of it, but it has a lot of fine people in that organization." The new funds, the company indicated, would be used for new product development and promotion.

The Evans interregnum

During the winter of 1965–66, Robert Evans, a Detroit financier, entrepreneur, and investor, began acquiring AMC stock. By the February stockholders' meeting he had acquired over 200,000 shares at an average price some 40% below book value. *Forbes* reported reactions as follows:

. . . The first reaction in the company was surprise followed quickly by uneasiness. But Evans had, in effect, given management a tremendous vote of confidence by betting some $2 million of his own fortune on AMC.

The next surprise came when the new man began telling everyone who would listen that he had complete confidence in the ability of the present management to turn AMC around.

Behind closed doors, Evans was far more critical than he had been in front of his fellow stockholders. But he did not denounce or threaten. Rather he spoke calmly but frankly in his Tidewater drawl, outlining what he thought could be done.

"If you walk into a meeting, start talking and tell people where you think

---

[16]For example, on April 12, 1967, Chrysler announced plans to put some company-owned dealer properties into a new subsidiary and then arrange up to $150 million of financing for the new unit.

they are making mistakes and what they can do about them, you're bound to create confidence," Evans says. However debatable the proposition, that is apparently what he achieved. Lacking the voting power to make demands, he proceeded quite literally to talk his way into the company. His dramatic stock purchase had made him a rallying point for demoralized directors and executives; by following that up with a palatable blend of persistence, frankness and persuasion, he gradually became the man they looked to for direction. Says a long-time Evans associate: "Working with Bob is like being pushed along by a bale of feathers."[17]

On June 7, 1966, *The Wall Street Journal* reported that Robert Evans had been elected chairman of AMC's board. He assumed this position after the company had reported a sales decline from $563.8 million in the first half of fiscal 1965 to $479.1 million in the first half of fiscal 1966. Market share had fallen to 3.2% for the six months ending in June, and AMC had shown a loss of $7.9 million before taxes. By the end of the fiscal year in September, the Annual Report showed the sales had fallen $876.4 million from $997.6 million, and that there had been a $12.6 million loss after taxes.

By October, certain personnel changes had occurred. Bernard Chapman, executive vice president in charge of auto operations, had left, and former chairman Cross had returned to his law practice. Roy Chapin, who had been in charge of international operations, had been made head of automotive operations, and Victor Raviolo, former head of Ford engineering, had become AMC group vice president for product planning.

Forbes interviewed Evans on the direction he hoped AMC would take, and reported as follows:

Evans' product push will be on several fronts. "First," he says, "we must have [a] fuller line of standard cars that are at least as good as those of the Big Three and hopefully better." The new 1967 line is a big step in that direction, encouraging Evans to believe that AMC can appeal to a wider range of potential car-buyers than the economy bugs who bought its cars of the past. It improves AMC's mathematical chances of making more sales.

"Next," he goes on, "we must have so-called personality cars, or glamour girls to appeal to all segments of the market. For example, we have been negligent of the youth market in the past. So we must now build cars that will attract and excite youth, such as the AMX, which will be in the line next year, and other cars I can't discuss right now."

The fastback AMX is one of four experimental cars that Evans insisted be shown around the United States last summer to sound out their appeal. The public reaction was such that Evans ordered its introduction stepped up from model year 1969 to 1968, and hang the extra cost. The AMX will probably sell at a higher price than Big Three sports cars like the Mustang, Cougar and Camaro.

Evans also hopes to tap other potential markets. Among the cars in last summer's nationwide tour, called project IV, was a subcompact model almost

---

[17]*Forbes*, December 1, 1966, p. 35.

in the Volkswagen class dubbed the Cavalier. Evans is convinced AMC is missing a good bet in this lower end of the auto market. AMC almost certainly will enter it two years from now (the design and tooling will take that long). . . .

Says Evans, "There are two areas in the auto market that have not been touched by the American manufacturers, the sub-compact car and the super-duper car that sells for $10,000 to $15,000. Those areas are wide open for someone who can get in there. They haven't attracted the big fellows so much, first because the volume hasn't been there, and second because it costs perhaps $100 million to put a brand-new car into the line.

This is where the next phase of Evans' product plan comes in. Says he: "You might ask, 'How can American Motors afford to spend that kind of money?' Well, we can't. So it must be done through new approaches to things like tooling."

"The thing that has been putting the independent automotive producers out of business is the tooling factor," Evans goes on. "It costs from $26 million to $30 million to make a new shell for a car. The Big Three will make maybe 2 or 3 million cars off their tools. The most we would run would be maybe 150,000 to 300,000. Now it doesn't make sense to make tools for 3 million parts when you need only 300,000. So we are exploring maybe half a dozen different areas to see what we can do about tooling costs."

One possible answer, plastic bodies, was a natural one for Evans to explore. But Evans admits plastic has its limitations. "Structurally, it's fine," he explains. "But from a cost standpoint you can only use plastic for from 20,000 to 40,000 cars before steel once again becomes the lowest cost material. To tool a Volkswagen type car from the ground up—power train, suspension, the works—would cost you maybe $100 million. But if you use the component you already have and don't exceed 40,000 units, you're in pretty good shape with a plastic body. Then instead of needing, say, $35 million for a new steel body, you would need only about $5 million or $6 million. So this has some intriguing possibilities."[18]

At the time of Evans' introduction as chairman of the board, there was considerable debate as to the future role of Roy Abernethy. Many both in the company and outside saw him as the architect of the strategy calling for head-on competition with the Big Three. Some publications hinted that his future lay with the results of the 1967 models. Others felt that he had already had five years to prove himself. He had started with adequate financing and a solid market base, and thus had been to blame for the lack of success. For exponents of this view, said *Forbes*, "It is tempting to suspect that Evans is keeping Abernethy around as a convenient goat, waiting until success looks surer before moving his man Chapin up to chief executive."[19]

The guessing ended on January 9, 1967, when Abernethy and Evans resigned from their positions. The board of directors named Roy Chapin chairman and chief executive officer with William Luneburg president and chief operating officer.

---

[18]*Ibid.*, p. 36.
[19]*Ibid.*, p. 35.

The Chapin era

By the time of Mr. Chapin's appointment, the situation at AMC had deteriorated even further. First quarter results for fiscal 1967 showed a net loss of $8,459,917 and dollar sales had slipped 10%. Unit auto sales were off 15% as compared with one year earlier. At the annual stockholders' meeting in February, Chapin announced some of the steps which the management was contemplating. These were reported in the press as follows:

Cost cutting, with $27 million in savings already found. "By next fall this rate will be at the level of $30 million. The bulk of this is a reduction in administrative and commercial expense. This gears our expenses to lower sales-volume levels, but we don't accept for one minute our present level of sales as our proper objective," said Mr. Chapin.

New officers, including the chairman, president, a group vice president for manufacturing, treasurer, controller and plant manager in Milwaukee. "There will be further management changes," Mr. Luneburg said. "An 'A' is given for results, and not for effort. Nonperformance will not be tolerated."

Minor product changes, already in the works. Major changes are not accomplished in weeks or even months, "but we have made some product moves—and contemplate more," Mr. Luneburg said. "Three unique station wagon models will be introduced later this month." Details weren't given, but it is understood the changes are in trim and appearance. . . .

Also there was no Marlin car among the autos exhibited for stockholders. The Marlin is a sporty, fastback model that had been a slow seller. It was learned that production of this car is being ended.

New advertising program. One part is a confidence building campaign costing $300,000.

Racing, with AMC entering cars in a major Canadian road rally, or race, the first time the company has ever officially entered any type of road competition other than an economy run.[20]

Also announced at the stockholders' meeting was the addition of $20 million to the amount due to the banks on May 31, 1967. The additional sum had been raised by pledging accounts receivable and inventories, and brought the total due to $95 million.

Production

At the time the new management took over, it found itself the legatee of sundry past decisions affecting the resources with which it had to work. Among these decisions were those regarding plant, labor relations, expansion abroad, and diversification.

The plant which Mr. Chapin had to operate was old, but had a low break-even point estimated to be between 345,000 and 375,000 units.[21] Of these facilities *Fortune* wrote as follows:

---

[20] *Wall Street Journal,* February 2, 1967.
[21] *Forbes,* December 1, 1966, p. 32.

Some of American Motors' production facilities are behind the times, the critics say. The charge is leveled not at the company's Kenosha assembly line, which is modern enough, but at such operations as the Milwaukee body shop. This plant is a five-story affair, so crammed with uphill and downhill conveyer lines that it looks like an amusement-park fun ride. The same could be said for a former Simmons Co. plant at Kenosha that American Motors has leased since 1959. The company insists that these facilities are as efficient as any brand-new one-story plant; if they weren't it would replace them. But it has a long-standing policy against investing in bricks and mortar except where it is absolutely unavoidable. Just to prove the company can build when necessary, officials cite the brand-new, $34 million engine plant at Kenosha, finished last February. The new facility, as up to date as anything the Big Three have, turns out the company's complete new six-cylinder engine.[22]

Fortune also quoted Roy Abernethy as estimating that the most efficient automobile production volume was between 330,000 and 440,000 cars a year. Beyond that, it was easier to go to multiplant operations such as the Big Three had done. Romney had earlier been quoted as estimating that it was cheaper to assemble the finished car in Kenosha and ship it to the final destination than it was to ship components to various plants for final assembly.

Labor relations

Labor relations had been a difficult area at AMC since Romney's departure. Some blamed labor problems on the failure of the profit-sharing program in recent years. Others felt the major factor was the change in leadership when Romney left, soon to be followed by his vice president of labor relations.

Whatever the cause, AMC had suffered strikes at the most inconvenient times: i.e., during model changeovers and new product introductions. Also, the work rules had never been fully brought up to date, leading to excessive costs. There were rumors that workers' dissatisfaction had led to sabotage which in turn affected quality control.

Although as of early March 1967 all car makers had closed plants temporarily to cut their inventories, AMC had given work holidays for almost half the time since New Year's Day. There was some speculation that the union would renew its 1966 demands that AMC should lower its production rate and lay off more workers permanently in preference to these periodic shutdowns. Management had resisted on the grounds that such a procedure would seriously and permanently increase costs.

Expansion abroad

According to the Annual Report for 1966, AMC sales abroad just missed setting a record for the eighth consecutive fiscal year with 45,991 units exported and total foreign sales of 74,420. New assembly plants were opened in Peru and Iran, bringing the total number to 14, of which 7 were in Latin

---

[22]Edmund Faltermayer, "The Squeeze in American Motors' Road," *Fortune*, September, 1964, p. 170.

America. Floor space in facilities abroad totaled 770,000 square feet (compared with 62.3 million for GM, 48.6 million for Ford, and 16.1 million for Chrysler).

AMC's share of total U.S. units sold abroad was 2.6%. The company far exceeded this average, however, in Latin America where its share of U.S. business was 15%.

Unlike the Big Three, AMC sold abroad substantially the same car that it sold at home. Some parts for assembly abroad were supplied knocked-down by the U.S. plant, while others might be of local manufacture. Local content in production ranged up to 60% in Mexico and 90% in Argentina. Except in Canada, AMC participated in foreign manufacturing operations as a minority partner in joint ventures.

As of early 1967, AMC had two major nonautomotive assets: its Kelvinator Division, which made appliances, and Redisco, Inc., its sales finance subsidiary.

Kelvinator, estimated by *Forbes* to account for $100 million to $200 million sales in 1966, had enjoyed volume gains in five of the preceding six years. Besides producing the Kelvinator line of stoves, refrigerators, etc., the division had taken on contracts to produce Norge refrigerators for Borg-Warner, and compressors and ranges for two other companies.[23] Kelvinator nevertheless remained much smaller than the appliance divisions of Westinghouse, GE, GM, and Whirlpool.

Though Kelvinator was believed profitable,[24] there had been problems in the past of maintaining efficient enough operations to meet competitors' prices. As a result, the product had remained middle- to high-priced, and the division had come to rely on a reputation for quality and style. For example, AMC had attempted to introduce product differentiation by bringing out an "Originals" series of refrigerators. These appliances were decorated with "pop" art, "op" art, and other decorative motifs so that they could be used as pieces of furniture besides providing functional utility. There had been wide interest in this approach and exhibits of new "originals" at trade fairs had been crowded.

Early in 1967, with car sales continuing to slide, it became clear that AMC was offering the two nonautomotive subsidiaries for sale. On May 3 it was announced that Redisco had been sold to Chrysler for an estimated $30 million. Industry sources estimated that if a buyer could be found for Kelvinator it might bring $45 to $50 million.[25]

Chapin's response

Given the difficult situation which he had inherited, Roy Chapin made a dramatic move. On February 21, on a stage with foreign cars to the left, American cars to the right, and a white sheet in the center, Chapin stood before his assembled dealers. Then, with a blare of trumpets, an AMC American was driven into the gap, and a new price of $1,839 was announced. Full-

---

[23]*Forbes*, December 1, 1966, p. 34.
[24]*Wall Street Journal*, April 5, 1967.
[25]*Wall Street Journal*, April 6, 1967.

page ads were taken in most major papers to announce the cut to the general public. (See Exhibit 5.) *Business Week* analyzed this move as follows:

American Motors Corporation this week chopped prices on its compact Rambler American by an average of $200 in a marketing maneuver that it hoped would stem the rapid decline in its sales position.

The Rambler series now will start at an advertised price of $1,839, compared with $2,073 when the new models were introduced in the fall of 1966. This compares with a price for the four-cylinder Chevy II, the nearest domestic competitor.

Behind AMC's announcement was a partial return to the marketing policy that once made it prosperous: Find a niche in the auto market the Big Three are overlooking and clutch it fiercely.

"That niche," announced AM Chairman Roy D. Chapin, Jr., "is between the imports and the domestic compacts, where a gap as wide as $434 exists." Chapin said this market segment has rapidly been developing around a growing consumer need reflecting the rising cost of car ownership, increasing traffic congestion, the trend to multicar families, and a revolt by the "nonaverage" American against stereotyped choices in car design.

"We are convinced," he said, "this is not just a temporary phenomenon, but a continuing market opportunity."

In the past several years, AM has been challenging the Big Three head on, asserting that it had cars equal to those of its competitors. Now, with the price cuts on the American, the company's smallest car, AM apparently is going in the other direction.

To recover some of the costs of the price cut, Chapin said AM will abandon the annual model appearance change in the American, following the example of the foreign producers.

So far there has been no official reaction from the other auto companies on AM's price cut. But one highly placed auto executive did say: "I'd sure as hell hate to have to cut my prices $200 today. But I hope AMC can solve its problems."[26]

Other reports characterized this move as "returning to Romneyism." *The Wall Street Journal* saw in it some possible problems:

. . . The announced price cuts likely are much larger than the savings to car buyers. This is because the actual price cuts in the wholesale car price to dealers was much smaller than the announced cuts in "sticker" prices.

The company also narrowed the percentage spread between the "sticker" price and the factory price. "I'm stunned," said one Big Three vice president and car division chief. "This could have a far-reaching effect on the price structure of the industry. This is because the dealers like a large spread between their car costs and the sticker price so they can appear to give their customers a bargain and have more room to negotiate a price."

Whether the price cuts and other Chapin efforts will help the company is still unknown. Even the attempts to crack the economy market may cause big problems. Three-fourths of AMC's sales are in its larger, more costly cars that

---

[26]*Business Week*, February 25, 1967, p. 39.

Exhibit 5

COMPARATIVE PRICE AND OTHER DATA, RAMBLER AMERICAN AND COMPETING CARS

(As of February 21, 1967)

Make	Price (Lowest-Priced Model)	Curb Weight (In Pounds)	Overall Length (In Inches)	Overall Width (In Inches)	Wheelbase (In Inches)	Passenger Capacity	Usable Trunk Capacity (Cubic Ft.)	Standard Horsepower & No. of Cylinders	Automatic Transmission Available	Turning Circle (Diameter in Ft.)	No. of Models Available	Warranty
Simca 1000 4-dr. sedan	$1,639*	1,609	149.5	58.5	87.3	4	5.1	52 hp./4 cyl.	No	28.9	4	5/50,000 & 2/24,000
Volkswagen 2-dr. sedan	$1,639*	1,764	160.6	60.6	94.5	4	5.0	53 hp./4 cyl.	No	36.0	6	6 months/ 6,000 miles
Opel Kadett 2-dr. sedan	$1,695*	1,614	161.6	61.9	95.1	4	11.6	54 hp./4 cyl.	No	34.8	4	2/24,000
Ford Cortina Model C 2-dr. sedan	$1,815*	1,923	168.0	64.9	98.0	5	12.0	65 hp./4 cyl.	Yes	30.0	5	2/24,000
RAMBLER AMERICAN 220 2-dr. sedan	$1,839†	2,000	181.0	70.8	100.0	6	12.0	128 hp./6 cyl.	Yes	36.0	9	5/50,000 & 2/24,000
Valiant 100 2-dr. sedan	$2,117†	2,780	188.4	71.1	108.0	6	12.4	115 hp./6 cyl.	Yes	37.8	4	5/50,000 & 2/24,000
Falcon Standard 2-dr. sedan	$2,118†	2,638	184.3	73.2	111.0	6	12.3	105 hp./6 cyl.	Yes	39.8	7	5/50,000 & 2/24,000
Corvair 500 2-dr. H.T.	$2,128†	2,525	183.3	69.7	108.0	5	7.0	95 hp./6 cyl.	Yes	37.0	5	5/50,000 & 2/24,000
Chevy II 100 2-dr. sedan	$2,152†	2,765	183.0	71.3	110.0	6	13.0	120 hp./6 cyl.	Yes	38.4	7	5/50,000 & 2/24,000

*Port of Entry, East Coast. Ocean freight, Import duty and 7% U.S. excise tax included. State or local taxes if any, optional equipment extra.
†Manufacturer's suggested retail price for model named, federal taxes included. State or local taxes if any, destination charges, optional equipment extra.
Source: Company advertisement, *Boston Globe*, March 10, 1967.

the company has attempted to build up in the past four years. There were no price cuts on these cars—and none currently is planned. The attempt to emphasize the economy market while most of the business is still pointed in the other direction could cause merchandising difficulties.[27]

Dealers reportedly were enthusiastic, however:

"It's a positive move," said one dealer. "They're taking positive action. When I was in Officers' Candidate School in the 1940's and we practiced the attack, we'd bog down and lie there. The officer would come to us and yell: 'What are you doing? I don't care if it's right or wrong. Just do something.' They've got to just do something."

In fact, dealers were highly enthusiastic about the price revisions as they brought the hope of increasing sales of the laggard American series.

"Fabulous, tremendous," said Ed Bailey, a Detroit AMC dealer. "I'd have to be an idiot not to be excited. We've got good headlines now. This puts us right in competition with Volkswagen."

"The most fantastic thing to happen in this country," said Ernie Boch, a Norwood, Mass., dealer. "At our meeting announcing the change, dealers got up and clapped and cheered."[28]

The price cut initiated by Chapin brought about the following ranking of prices in the low-price compact and import market.

Advertised Delivered Price as of Feb. 21	Make	Price Difference over (under) Rambler American	
		Before Feb. 21	After Feb. 21
$2,187	Dart 6	$114	$348
2,152	Chevy II 6	79	313
2,128	Corvair 6	55	289
2,118	Falcon 6	45	279
2,117	Valiant 6	44	278
2,090	Chevy II 4	17	251
1,839	American 6	—	—
1,815	Cortina 4 (Ford)	(258)	(24)
1,760	Toyota 4	(313)	(79)
1,695	Opel 4 (GM)	(378)	(144)
1,666	Datsun 4	(407)	(173)
1,639	Volkswagen 1,300	(434)	(200)
1,639	Simca 4 (Chrysler)	(434)	(200)

Source: *Ward's Weekly Automotive Reports*, February 24, 1967.

In 1966 the Rambler American models accounted for 28% of the company's total unit sales, down from 38% in 1964. Mr. Luneburg said, "A 50% sales increase would be a fair test of the drastic restructuring of prices." He made no comment on the potential effect of the reduction of dealer margins from 21% to 17%.

---

[27] *Wall Street Journal*, February 23, 1967.
[28] *Ibid.*

One factor encouraging the move by AMC was the behavior of foreign car sales. In 1966, when domestic sales were off almost 8% from the record year of 1965, foreign car sales were up 10% and surpassed even the record year of 1959. Whereas forecasts for 1967 showed total sales off another 10%, manufacturers predicted that foreign sales would rise to 700,000 units. This would mean an 8% penetration of the market, up from 7% in 1966.[29]

Some experts were predicting that foreign cars sales would reach 1,000,000 by 1970. Their appeal was considered to be largely to young people, mainly students and young marrieds, with a strong secondary attraction for multiple car families. (See Exhibit 6 for data on car purchasers.)

Exhibit 6

CONSUMER DATA

Percentage of Households Owning One or More Cars

Year	Number of Households (Millions)	Per Cent Owning Cars	Per Cent Multicar Households
1955	47.9	73.5	10.1
1960	53.3	75.5	13.4
1961	53.7	75.8	13.8
1962	54.5	77.1	14.4
1963	55.9	77.5	15.6
1964	56.4	78.1	17.9
1965	56.9	79.6	20.6

Percentage of Car-Owning Households by Income Groups

Income Groups	Per Cent of All Households	Per Cent Owning Cars	Per Cent Owning 2 or More Cars
Under $4,000	26.0	52.5	2.7
4,000– 4,999	8.6	78.5	10.8
5,000– 6,999	19.8	84.9	17.4
7,000– 9,999	23.2	94.0	27.2
10,000–14,999	16.2	94.7	45.9
15,000 and over	6.3	95.6	53.7

Percentage of Car-Owning Households by Age Group

Age of Household Head	Per Cent of All Households	Per Cent Buying New Cars	Per Cent Owning Multiple Cars
Under 25	6.1	9.7	3.7
25–34	19.4	20.8	19.1
35–44	23.3	25.5	27.4
45–54	21.5	25.3	31.2
55 or over	29.7	19.0	18.6

Source: National Automobile and Tire Survey, sponsored by *Look Magazine. Statistical Abstract of the United States,* 1966.

[29] *Wall Street Journal,* February 24, 1967.

A look toward the future

The year 1967 was not shaping up as a good one for automobiles. Sales of domestic makes in the first two months of the calendar year ran at about the same pace as in 1963 when the industry sold 7.7 million units. February sales fell 24% from the year before; AMC reported sales off 29%, and GM, Ford, and Chrysler were each down more than 20%.[30]

AMC reported that the price reduction had increased dealer traffic substantially. Mr. Chapin was quoted as saying that the price cut had helped sales "beyond our expectations."[31]

Even though sales were beyond expectation, they did not pull the second quarter of 1967 back into the black. The results for the second quarter showed a loss of $21,599,836, bringing the loss for the first half to over $30 million. The loss was the largest on AMC's 13-year history. In addition AMC was in technical default on its loan as working capital shrank to less than $29 million, down from almost $85 million the previous year.[32] The banks holding the loan granted an extension to December 31, 1967, apparently on the condition that $25 million of the proceeds from the sale of Redisco be applied to the reduction of the loan.

According to published reports, AMC helped to achieve a new advance by introducing a new sporty car:

Two sporty cars are being readied at American Motors Corporation.

One is called the Javelin and is built along lines of Ford Motor Co.'s Mustang, according to sources close to the company, which means a longish hood and short trunk. This car is being rushed; dealers have been told it may be out by late summer—before introduction of 1968 models. AMC officials wouldn't confirm any proposed introduction date but did say that the Javelin program is "on schedule."

The second model is tentatively called AMX after a small, sleek experimental model American Motors showed last year called the AMX. Plans call for this model to be brought out some time after the Javelin, the sources say, perhaps early next year.[33]

As plans for the Javelin firmed, additional details became available on both the car and the company's expectations:

The price is expected to be close to that of the Mustang, which carries a suggested retail list price of $2,461.

The Javelin is 190 inches long, six inches longer than the 1967 Mustang. The Javelin carries what Detroit stylists call a split grille, reminiscent of the grille on Pontiac cars.

Only one model of the Javelin, a two-door hardtop, will be offered for sale.

---

[30] Wall Street Journal, March 6, 1967.
[31] New York Times, March 28, 1967.
[32] Wall Street Journal, May 2, 1967.
[33] Wall Street Journal, February 23, 1967.

American Motors believes that Javelin can add 35,000 to 50,000 unit sales annually to its total sales.[34]

In addition to moving into the subcompact field and redesigning its station wagon, AMC might follow the advice, with which it was being bombarded, to merge. Frequently mentioned partners were International Harvester, Litton Industries, and Ling-Temco-Vought:

Ling-Temco-Vought is reportedly eyeing further diversification through American Motors. A man close to Jim Ling quotes him as saying: "I don't know anything about the automobile business, but in the end these things always boil down to a balance sheet." Besides assets carried on the books at well over the market price of its stock, AMC has a thriving appliance division (Kelvinator), a prosperous foreign business and a chance to make a comeback as a manufacturer of semicompact cars. To this comeback presumably Ling's outfit could contribute fresh working capital and new borrowing power.[35]

In answer to this and other speculation, Mr. Luneburg issued a categorical denial that AMC was currently engaged in merger negotiations or even thinking in that direction. He implied that he and Roy Chapin saw the company continuing on as an independent producer of cars with a successful future to be achieved by a careful follow-through on the moves that they had already projected.

---

[34]New York Times, March 28, 1967.
[35]Forbes, February 15, 1967, p. 1.

HEAD SKI COMPANY, INC.*

The Head Ski Company, Inc., of Timonium, Maryland, was formed in 1950 to sell metal skis which had been developed by Howard Head during three years of research. In the first year six employees turned out 300 pairs of skis. By the 1954–55 skiing season, output reached 8,000 pairs, and by 1965 it passed 133,000. Growth in dollar sales and profits was equally spectacular. When Head went public in 1960, sales were just over $2 million and profits just under $59,000. By 1965 sales were up to $8.6 million and profits to $393,713. In the next two years, volume continued upward, though growth was less dramatic. In the 53 weeks ended April 30, 1966, sales were $9.1 million and profits $264,389. For a like period ending April 29, 1967, sales were $11.0 million and profits $401,482. (For financial data, see Exhibit 1.)

The industry

Head was an enthusiastic participant in the growing market generated by leisure-time activities, of which skiing was one of the most dynamic segments. The industry association, Ski Industries America (SIA), estimated that skiing expenditures—including clothing, equipment, footwear, accessories, lift tickets, travel, entertainment, food and lodging—rose from $280 million in 1960 to $750 million in 1966–67. Gross sales were expected to reach $1.14 billion by 1969–70. This growth was attributed to both the rising number of skiers and greater per capita expenditures. In 1947 it was estimated that there were fewer than 10,000 active skiers in the United States. SIA estimated that there were 1.6 million in 1960, 3.5 million in 1966–67 and predicted 5 million for 1970. Another industry source estimated that the number of skiers was increasing by 20% a year.

As of 1966–67 the $750 million retail expenditures on skiing were estimated to be divided into $200 million going for ski equipment and ski wear, and $550 million going to the 1,200 ski areas and the transportation companies carrying skiers to their destinations. Ninety-eight manufacturers belonged to the SIA. *Skiing International Yearbook* for 1967 listed 85 brands of wooden skis available in 260 models, 49 brands of metal skis in 101

Exhibit 1

HEAD SKI COMPANY, INC.

Consolidated Balance Sheet, 1965–67

ASSETS

	As of April 24, 1965	As of April 30, 1966	As of April 29, 1967
Current assets			
Cash	$ 162,646	$ 233,330	$ 263,896
Short-term commercial paper receivable	1,200,000	800,000	1,200,000
Notes and accounts receivable—less reserve	334,503	174,127	242,632
Inventories—valued at lower of cost or market	2,815,042	3,522,235	3,102,069
Prepayments and miscellaneous receivables	207,279	223,864	402,879
Total current assets	$4,719,470	$4,953,556	$5,211,476
Fixed assets, at cost			
Building—pledged under mortgage	$1,014,738	$1,012,085	$1,010,149
Machinery and equipment	847,974	1,059,274	1,540,707
Other	147,336	213,692	715,089
	$2,010,048	$2,285,051	$3,265,945
Less accumulated depreciation	822,255	892,153	1,123,203
Total fixed assets	$1,187,793	$1,392,898	$2,142,742
Other assets			
Unamortized bond discount and expenses	$ 277,636	$ 263,564	$ 252,004
Cash surrender value of life insurance	103,117	120,589	133,568
Other	28,583	22,364	70,194
Total other assets	$ 409,336	$ 406,517	$ 455,766
Total assets	$6,316,599	$6,752,971	$7,809,984

LIABILITIES AND STOCKHOLDERS' EQUITY

	As of April 24, 1965	As of April 30, 1966	As of April 29, 1967
Current liabilities			
Accounts payable	$ 521,031	$ 299,040	$ 829,826
Current portion of long-term debt	20,600	21,000	23,100
Accrued expenses	451,062	413,865	549,720
Income taxes payable	39,102	299,452	333,514
Other	94,899	91,271	51,120
Total current liabilities	$1,126,694	$1,124,628	$1,787,280
Long-term debt			
Mortgage on building—5⅜%, payable to 1978	$ 396,646	$ 376,036	$ 331,115
Convertible subordinated debentures	2,125,000	2,125,000	2,125,000
	$2,521,646	$2,501,036	$2,456,115
Less current portion	20,600	21,000	...
Total long-term debt	$2,501,046	$2,480,036	$2,456,115
Commitments and contingent liabilities, stockholders' equity			
Common stock—par value 50c per share (authorized 2,000,000 shares; outstanding 1966, 915,202 shares; 1965, 882,840 shares adjusted for 2-for-1 stock split-up effective September 15, 1965)	$ 220,710	$ 457,601	$ 459,401
Paid-in capital	1,820,323	1,679,700	1,694,700
Retained earnings	647,826	1,011,006	1,412,488
Total stockholders' equity	$2,688,859	$3,148,307	$3,566,589
Total liabilities and stockholders' equity	$6,316,599	$6,752,971	$7,809,984

Source: Company records.

Exhibit 1—Continued

Consolidated Statement of Earnings

	52 Weeks Ended* April 25, 1964	52 Weeks Ended* April 24, 1965	53 Weeks Ended* April 30, 1966	52 Weeks Ended April 29, 1967
Net sales	$6,018,779	$8,600,392	$9,080,223	$11,048,072
Cost of sales	4,033,576	5,799,868	6,357,169	7,213,188
Gross profit	$1,985,203	$2,800,524	$2,723,054	$ 3,834,884
Expenses:				
Selling, administrative and general	$1,169,392	$1,697,659	$2,029,531	$ 2,756,939
Research and engineering	102,358	303,884	239,851	327,857
Total expenses	$1,271,750	$2,001,543	$2,269,382	$ 3,084,796
Income before income taxes and nonrecurring charges	$ 713,453	$ 798,981	$ 453,672	$ 750,088
Federal and state income taxes	367,542	392,515	221,034	348,606
Income before nonrecurring charges	$ 345,911	$ 406,466	$ 232,638	$ 401,482
Nonrecurring debt expense—after giving effect to income taxes		$ 63,678		
Net earnings	$ 345,911	$ 342,788	$ 232,638	$ 401,482
Net earnings as restated	$ 376,788	$ 393,713	$ 264,389	$ 401,482
Earnings per share before nonrecurring charges	$ 0.40	$ 0.51	$ 0.26	$ 0.44
Earnings per share after nonrecurring charges	$ 0.40	$ 0.43	$ 0.26	$ 0.44
Earnings per share as restated	$ 0.48	$ 0.49	$ 0.29	$ 0.44

Earnings per share are based on average shares outstanding of 904,237 in 1966 and 801,196 in 1965 after giving effect to the 2-for-1 stock split-up effective September 15, 1965, and the 3-for-1 stock split on July 7, 1964.

*Earnings restated April 29, 1967, to give effect to an adjustment in the lives of depreciable assets for federal income tax purposes.

Exhibit 1—Continued

	52 Weeks Ended April 27, 1963	52 Weeks Ended April 25, 1964	52 Weeks Ended April 24, 1965	53 Weeks Ended April 30, 1966	52 Weeks Ended April 29, 1967
Net sales	$4,124,445	$6,018,779	$8,600,392	$9,080,223	$11,048,072
Net earnings	$ 191,511	$ 376,788	$ 393,713	$ 264,389	$ 401,482
Expenditures for plant and equipment	$ 272,154	$ 513,130	$ 558,865	$ 304,102	$ 1,027,854
Depreciation	$ 79,719	$ 132,497	$ 211,683	$ 238,161	$ 249,961
Working capital	$654,676	$1,525,015	$3,542,857	$3,828,928	$3,424,196
Plant and equipment and other assets, net	$ 701,875	$1,187,246	$1,745,839	$1,799,415	$ 2,598,508
Long-term debt	$ 287,245	$1,176,647	$2,501,046	$2,480,036	$ 2,456,115
Shareholders' equity	$1,069,306	$1,535,614	$2,787,650	$3,148,307	$3,566,589
Earnings per share	$ 0.25	$ 0.48	$ 0.49	$ 0.29	$ 0.44
Average shares outstanding	777,600	777,600	801,196	904,237	916,542

Average shares outstanding reflect the 2-for-1 stock split-up effective September 15, 1965, and 3-for-1 stock split on July 7, 1964.
Statistical data for the years 1963 to 1966, inclusive, have been adjusted to reflect retroactive adjustments.

models, and 53 brands of fiberglass skis in 116 models. For each model there could be as many as 15 sizes. Many manufacturers made all three types of skis and some had multiple brands, but even so the industry was divided into many competing units.

The table which follows illustrates the division of the market by price and type:

Type	Number of Brands of Skis by Price Range		
	$0—$49.99	$50—$99.99	$100 and up
Wood (85 brands)	69	27	3
Metal (49 brands)	0	22 (28 models)	28 (73 models)
Fiberglass (53 brands)	0	24 (35 models)	39 (81 models)

Source: *Skiing International Yearbook, 1967*, pp. 90–91. Copyright by Ziff-Davis Publishing Co.

Ski Business summed up an analysis of industry trends as follows:

Imports of low-priced adult wood skis into the United States are skidding sharply.

U.S. metal skis are gaining faster than any other category.

The ski equipment and apparel market is experiencing an unusually broad and pronounced price and quality uptrend.

Ski specialty shop business appears to be gaining faster than that of the much publicized department stores and general sporting goods outlets.

The growth in the national skier population is probably decelerating and may already have reached a plateau.[1]

Supporting these statements of trends, *Ski Business* made some other observations.

Foreign skis clearly lost in 1966 at the gain of domestic manufacturers. (The total of imported and domestic skis sold in the United States is believed to be running at over 900,000 pairs annually.) By conservative estimate, U.S. metal ski production in 1966 (for shipment to retail shops for the 1966–67 selling season) was up by at least 40,000 pairs from 1965. . . .

But far more important than the domestic American ski gain (which will continue now that American fiberglass ski makers are entering the market) is the remarkable upward price shift. Thus while 10 per cent fewer foreign skis entered the United States in 1966, the dollar value of all the skis imported actually rose by more than 10 per cent or $700,000. . . . Here was the real measure of growth of the ski market; it was not in numbers, but in dollars.

The principal beneficiary of this remarkable upward shift in consumer pref-

---

[1]John Fry, *Ski Business*, May–June 1967, p. 25.

erence for higher product quality is, of course, the ski specialty shop. The skier bent on purchasing $140 skis and $80 boots will tend to put his confidence in the experienced specialist retailer. The ski specialist shops themselves are almost overwhelmed by what is happening. Here's one retailer's comment: "Just two or three years ago, we were selling a complete binding for $15. Now skiers come into our shop and think nothing of spending $40 for a binding. . . ."

. . . Most of the department store chains and sporting goods shops contacted by *Ski Business* were also able to report increased business in 1966–67, but somehow the exuberant, expansionist talk seems to have evaporated among non-specialty ski dealers. Montgomery Ward, for instance, says that ski equipment sales have not come up to company expectations. Ward's has specialized in low end merchandise for beginning and intermediate skiers. . . . Significantly, department stores or sporting goods shops which reported the largest sales increases tended to be those which strive hardest to cast their image in the ski specialist mold. . . .[2]

Ski imports for 1966 served both the low-priced and high-priced market. More than half the Japanese imports of 530,000 pairs of skis were thought to be children's skis which helped to explain the low valuation of the Japanese skis. This value of $6.84 a pair was the f.o.b. price at the door of the Japanese ski factory and does not include shipping, duty, importer's or retailer's margins.[3] *Ski Business* reported imports into the United States as follows:

1966 SKI IMPORTS INTO THE UNITED STATES
(By Country of Origin)

Country of Origin	No. of Pairs	Change: 1966 vs. 1965	$ Value	Average $* Value per Pair 1965	Average $* Value per Pair 1966
Canada	7,091	+6,350	149,961	23	21.14
Sweden	2,767	+1,131	22,386	9	8.09
Norway	1,125	−698	18,221	6	16.20
Finland	10,184	+5,411	98,275	9	9.65
Belgium	129	+129	6,327	...	49.05
France	5,257	+2,828	265,018	49	50.41
West Germany ...	44,736	+9,959	1,010,354	18	22.58
Austria	72,536	−20,872	1,511,563	21	20.84
Switzerland	2,835	+1,155	124,068	39	43.76
Italy	7,494	+351	195,723	14	26.12
Yugoslavia	22,540	+5,122	254,962	11	11.31
Japan	529,732	−89,632	3,625,639	5.54	6.84
Australia	2,307	+2,307	114,091	...	49.45
1965 total	785,746	...	$6,692,451	...	$8.52
1966 total	708,733	−77,013	$7,396,588	$8.52	$10.44

*The average value per pair of skis represents an f.o.b. plant price and does not include charges for shipping and handling, tariff, excise tax, or profit for trading company or wholesaler. Tariff on skis was 16 2/3%.

Source: *Ski Business*, May-June 1967, p. 31.

---

[2]*Ibid.*
[3]*Ibid.*

In the high-price market segment, where skis retailed at $100 or more, the annual market was estimated by industry sources to be approximately 250,000 pairs of skis. Here estimates of the leading contenders according to these industry sources were:

Brand	Type	Estimated Sales	Price Range
Head (United States)	Metal	125,000 pairs	$115.00 — $175.00
Hart (United States)	Metal	44,000 pairs	$ 99.50 — $175.00
Kniessl (Austria)	Epoxy	20,000 pairs	$150.00 — $200.00
Yamaha (Japan)	Epoxy	13,000 pairs	$ 79.00 — $169.00
Fischer (Austria)	Wood } Metal } Epoxy }	13,000 pairs	$112.00 — $189.00

Source: *Skiing International Yearbook, 1967*, pp. 90–91. Copyright by Ziff-Davis Publishing Co.

Fischer was believed to have $15–$18 million sales worldwide. Kniessl was believed to be about the same size as Head worldwide, but only about one-tenth Head's size in the United States. In addition Voit, the recreational products division of AMF, was entering the market with a fiberglass ski. Voit also manufactured water skis, a wide variety of aquatic equipment, and rubber products. AMF's total 1966 sales were $357 million. Recreational equipment accounted for approximately 20%, not including bowling equipment which accounted for an additional 22% of sales.

The skier's skill level was one determining factor in his choice of skis. (For those unfamiliar with the differences among skis designed for each group, a discussion of ski construction is included as Appendix A.) Of the 3.5 million active skiers, 17,000 were regarded as racers, another 75,000 were considered to be experts, and another 100,000 were classed as sufficiently skillful to be strong recreational skiers.

The market

Skiing was considered to be a sport which attracted the moderately well-to-do and those on the way up. This conception was borne out by the following market data:

A statistical study released early this year [1965] by the Department of Commerce disclosed that the American skier has a median age of 26.2 and a median annual income of $11,115. Moreover, it showed that about two-thirds of all skiers are college graduates.

How do these young, affluent and intelligent men and women spend their skiing dollars? At a typical resort, a person might spend each day $10 for accommodations, $10 for food, $5.00 for a lift ticket and $10 for renting everything needed to attack the slopes from pants and parka to skis, boots, poles and bindings. . . .

The initial purchases of a person determined to have his or her own good equipment and to look well while skiing could easily be about $200. For this amount, a skier could buy everything from winter underwear to goggles and perhaps even have a bit left over for a rum toddy in the ski lodge the first night of his trip.

For instance, ski boots cost from $20 to $150 and average $50 a pair. Skis range from $30 to $200 and poles from $5 to $35.

When it comes to apparel, costs vary considerably. Snow jackets or parkas might cost as little as $20 or as much as $1,000 for those made with fur. Many jackets are available, though, at about $30.

Stretch pants have an average price of about $20. Other apparel requirements for skiing include sweaters which retail from $10 to $50, winter underwear which costs about $5, and ski hats and caps which sell for $3 and up.[4]

There was an apparent fashionability to skiing. Fashion consciousness was apparent in the design of ski equipment, ski wear, and the influx of a new type of skier. Under the headline "The Nonskiers: They Flock to Ski Resorts For The Indoor Sports," *The Wall Street Journal* reported as follows:

Want to take up a rugged, outdoor sport?

Cross skiing off your list.

The sport has gone soft. Ski resorts now have all the comforts of home— if your home happens to have a plush bar, a heated swimming pool, a padded chair lift, boutiques and a built in baby sitter. . . . Skiing, in fact, has become almost an incidental activity at some ski resorts; indeed, some of the most enthusiastic patrons here at Squaw Valley and other resorts don't even know how to ski. They rarely venture outdoors.

So why do they come here? "Men, M-E-N. They're here in bunches, and so am I, baby," answers slinky, sloe-eyed Betty Reames as she selects a couch strategically placed midway between the fireplace and the bar. . . .

Squaw Valley houses half a dozen bars and restaurants and often has three different bands and a folksinger entertaining at the same time. Aspen, in Colorado, throws a mid-winter Mardi Gras. Sun Valley, in Idaho, has a shopping village that includes a two-floor bookstore and boutique selling miniskirts.

Life has also been made softer for those skiers who ski. . . . Also some resorts are making their chair lifts more comfortable by adding foam padding. But even that isn't enough for some softies. "What? Me ride the chair lift? Are you crazy? I'd freeze to death out in the open like that," says blond Wanda Peterson as she waits to ride up the mountain in an enclosed gondola car. She doesn't stand alone. The line of the gondola is 200 strong; the nearby chair lift, meanwhile, is all but empty. . . .

. . . for beginning skiers most resorts offer gentle, meticulously groomed inclines that make it almost impossible to fall. "We try to make it so that the person who has no muscle tone and little experience can't be fooled, can't make a mistake," says one resort operator. "Then we've got him. He's a new customer as well as a happy man."

Once he gets the hang of it—whether he's any good or not—the happy man starts spending lots of money, and that's what the resorts love.[5]

---

[4]*The New York Times*, December 12, 1965. © 1965 by The New York Times Company. Reprinted by permission.

[5]*The Wall Street Journal*, February 1967.

In line with the concern for style, some manufacturers of skiwear and ski equipment developed new colors and annual model changes to inspire annual obsolescence and fad purchases.

Head Company history

Howard Head, chairman and founder of the company bearing his name, was the man responsible for the development of the first successful metal ski. Combining the experience of an aircraft designer with dedication to a sport which he enjoyed, he spent more than three years developing a ski which would not break, turned easily, and tracked correctly without shimmying and chattering. Others had tried to produce metal skis, but Head succeeded almost five years before his nearest competitors, Hart and Harry Holmberg, introduced the Hart metal skis. *Ski Magazine* described the reason behind Howard Head's success:

. . . He was obsessed, to be sure, and being relatively unencumbered by stockholders, high overhead and strong yearnings for luxurious living, he was well braced for the long haul. . . .

"I made changes only where I had to make them," he has said of the days when his skis were undergoing trial by fire. "When they broke, I made them stronger only where they broke. . . ."[6]

In 1960 Howard Head described the early years of his enterprise and the trials which surrounded it as follows:

Twelve years ago I took six pairs of handmade metal skis to Stowe, Vermont, and asked the pros there to try them out. It had taken about a year to make those six pairs of skis. The design, based on engineering principles of aircraft construction, was radically different from any ever tried before. I thought it was sound but the pros weren't a bit surprised when all six pairs promptly broke to pieces. After all, others before me had tried to make metal skis and all they had proved was what everyone knew anyway—a ski had to be made of wood.

That was in January 1948. Today about 60% of all high-grade skis sold in the United States are metal skis. The reasons for this revolution in ski manufacturing industry are simple. People like the way metal skis ski, they like their durability, and they like their easy maintenance. . . .

Many small refinements and changes in design have been introduced through the years because of our continued testing and development program and to meet the advances in technique and changes in skiing conditions. But the basic structural design hasn't changed, which speaks well for the original concept.[7]

Mr. Head further indicated that his personal interest in technical problems played a major part in leading him to create his business:

When I started out, I was a mechanical design engineer—the whole origin of the business was the feeling that it should be possible to build a better ski. What started as an engineering puzzle ended as a business.

[6]*Ski Magazine*, January 1964.
[7]"On Metal Skis" (manuscript by Howard Head, 1960).

I distinctly remember wondering at that time whether we would ever grow to the point where we would be making 5,000 pairs of skis a year.

Price-volume considerations exerted small influence over initial marketing policy. Mr. Head priced his first metal skis at $75 in spite of the fact that most skiers were using war surplus skis that cost $20, including bindings. Mr. Head discussed his early ideas on quality, costs, and prices as follows:

The great disadvantage of all metal skis is simply their high price. This became apparent to us when we were pioneering the original metal ski and found it was going to cost a good bit more than a wood ski. We didn't let that stop us because we believed the striking advantages of a metal ski more than compensated for its high price. As it turned out, even with a higher initial price, Head Skis proved to cost less in the long run because they are so durable. . . .

In the early days people had no way of knowing the skis would last so long that they actually ended up costing less than cheaper skis. They simply liked them enough to go ahead and buy them in spite of the price.[8]

Mr. Head found a market which was quite unexpected. In spite of the high price, Head skis appealed more to the average beginner or slightly better skier than to racers. Among skiers, Heads became known as "cheaters." This designation grew out of the skis' ability to make almost anyone look good. "They practically turned themselves." Soon the black plastic top of the Head ski became a ubiquitous status symbol on the slopes.

Product policy

The keynote of Mr. Head's product policy was quality. His fundamental belief was that the consumer should get all he pays for and pay for all he gets. The 17-year history of the company had seen considerable upgrading of the products. Several times in the past the company had called in particular models or production runs of skis which had been found to be defective. One executive commented that this had been done without hesitation, even when the company was in precarious financial condition.

Asked what set Head apart from its competition, Mr. Head replied as follows:

I believe that it is a tradition of attention to detail which grew out of its entrepreneurial history. In every aspect we attempt to follow through. Service, dealer relations, product quality, style, advertising are all important and must be done in the best way we know how.

We stress continued emphasis on quality of product and quality of operating philosophy. We pay meticulous attention to the individual relationships with dealers and the public.

I have attempted to make creativity, imagination, and standards of perfection apply across the board. This was always our desire, and we only failed to live up to it when the business got too big for the existing staff. The philosophy remained constant, and now we have the people to live up to it.

---

[8]*Ibid.*

We get a return on this attention to detail. The feedback from success allows us to maintain the necessary staff to insure continuation of this philosophy. We allow no sloppiness.

Head skis came in one color—black. There was no special trim to designate the model, only a modification in the color of the name "Head" embossed on the top of the ski and a change in the color of the case: red for some models, yellow or black for others. Although at one time a chrome top was considered, it was rejected because of the glare, and because it was difficult to see against the snow. In addition to these factors, one executive described black as being a conservative color which would go with anything. Howard Head explained that he "did not want to complicate the consumer's choice."

I deeply believe in sticking to function and letting style take care of itself. We have stuck so rigorously to our black color because it is honest and functional that it has become almost a trademark. While we constantly make minor improvements, we never make an important model change unless there is a performance reason for it. In other words, we skipped the principle of forced obsolescence, and we will continue to skip it.

This policy had been consciously chosen and maintained, in spite of competition which had introduced six or eight different colors and yearly color changes to keep up with fashion.

Apart from color and style, skis had to perform well on the slopes. There were three fundamental things which a ski had to do. It had to "track,"[9] "traverse,"[10] and "turn."[11] The need to perform these functions imposed certain constraints on ski design, and the necessity to both track and turn required some compromises in design. *Ski Magazine* listed some of the characteristics which this balancing involved:

1. The tip must be pointed and turned up in a gradual curve to permit the ski to climb over obstacles without changing directions, to prevent it from diving beneath soft snow, and to help prevent the skis from crossing. (Splay)
2. The bottom should be flat and perfectly flush with its steel edges, except for a narrow groove extending the length of the ski which increases tracking stability.
3. The skis must be straight without warp or twist, each side must have the same curve to it, and the groove must be straight and in the middle.
4. The bottom surface must be slippery so that it will run smoothly.
5. To distribute the skier's weight over the length of the ski, a cambered or arched shape is necessary.
6. A ski must be flexible.

---

[9]Track: If you point a ski down a slope and allow it to run freely, it should hold a straight course—over bumps and through hollows and on every type of snow surface.

[10]Traverse: A ski should be able to hold a straight line while moving diagonally across a slope over obstacles and various snow conditions.

[11]Turn: When a skier releases the edges of his skis, the skis must be capable of slipping sideways, and, when edged, they must bite into the snow evenly. (A skiing turn is nothing more than a slideslip carved into an arc by the controlled bite of the edges.)

7. The shape or "sidecut" of the ski must be correlated to the flexibility of the ski and the torsional rigidity of the material used. A flexible ski will have difficulty holding if the sidecut is too straight, for the ends will barely touch the snow. Only a correct sidecut will tolerate a momentary twist of the skis, reducing the effect of edges just enough to allow smooth passage over bumps yet not enough to pull the ski out of line.

8. A sharp edge is needed to hold on hard surfaces.

9. For maximum stability, the skier must choose the proper length ski.[12]

Mr. Head found a proper combination of these elements for the recreational skier in his earliest metal ski. Designated the "Standard," this model underwent substantial improvement over its 17-year history. Until 1960, however, the goal of providing the best ski for experts eluded Head and other metal ski makers. Mr. Head said of this period, "During the early years at Head Ski, we were too busy making the best ski we could for the general public to spend much time developing a competition ski."

For experts, the basic complaint against metal skis was that they were too "soft" and tended to vibrate badly at racing speeds. This problem was substantially solved in 1960, when Head introduced its "Vector" model, to be followed in 1962 (and later entirely replaced) by the "Competition." In these skis, an imbedded layer of neoprene dampened vibrations and considerably improved performance. Whereas in 1960 most competitors in the Squaw Valley Olympics had stuck to their wooden skis, by the end of 1962 Head skis were in wide use, and they had carried 77 racers out of 141 to positions among the top six contenders at races conducted by the International Professional Ski Race Association in Canada and the United States. Also about half the skis used in the U.S. National Junior and Senior Championships that year were Heads.

By 1966 Head had established itself as an important factor in the ski racing world. Two Americans had set the world speed record—106.527 m.p.h.—on Head skis. In major international competition in 1966, one-third of all finishers in the top ten places at all events were on Head skis, and Head was the outstanding single manufacturer on the circuit with 18 gold medals, 15 silver medals, and 15 bronze medals.

The 1968 Head line included a ski for every type of skier from the unskilled beginner to the top professional racer. The line was described in Head's *Ski Handbook* as follows:

. . . the most important design consideration is you—the type of skier you are and where you ski. That's why your dealer was able to offer you nine different models of Head Skis to choose from. You can be sure the model he helped you select was the optimum—for you.

STANDARD—THE MOST FORGIVING SKI: For beginners of average size and athletic ability up to intermediates learning stem christies. Also for the better, occasional skier who prefers an easy-going, lively, light-weight ski that practically turns for him.

---

[12]*Skiing International Yearbook 1967*, pp. 62–63. Copyright by Ziff-Davis Publishing Co.

The *Standard* is medium soft in flex overall for easy turning and responsiveness. Engineered side camber and relative overall width contribute to ease and slow-speed stability. Its light weight and torsional rigidity make traversing and other basic maneuvers simple. Thin taper in the tip allows the *Standard* to cut easily through the heaviest snow instead of ploughing.

Standard. $115. Thirteen sizes from 140 to 215 cm. Black top, sidewalls and bottom; white engraving.

MASTER—MORE OF A CHALLENGE: For the skier who has mastered the basic techniques and wants to begin driving the skis and attacking the slope. As lively as the *Standard*, this is also the ski for the heavier, more athletic beginner who wants more "beef" underfoot.

The *Master* is like the Standard in basic shape but thicker and heavier. The tip radius is longer for extra shock absorption. Slightly stiffer flex overall acts as a heavy-duty shock absorber over bumps.

Master. $135. Nine sizes from 175 through 215 cm. Black top and sidewalls; blue base and engraving.

THE FABULOUS 360—THE MOST VERSATILE SKI: Finest all-around ski ever made—for the skier beginning stem christies on through the expert class. Remarkable for its ease of turning as well as its steadiness and precision, the *360* is the serious skier's ski for attack or enjoyment on the slope, under any condition of snow or terrain.

With its smooth-arcing flex pattern, the *360* has the supple forebody of the other recreational skis, but is slightly stiffer at the tail. Its side camber is similar to that of the *Giant Slalom*. Narrower overall than the *Standard* or *Master*. Rubber damping in the lightweight top-skin unit makes the *360* a very responsive ski, allowing the expert to control his turns beautifully and set his edges precisely. Tip splay is designed to give easiest entrance through snow and to provide excellent shock absorption, particularly in heavily moguled areas.

The Fabulous 360. $155. Eleven sizes from 170 to 220 cm. Black top and sidewalls; yellow base and engraving.

SLALOM—THE HOT DOG: For the expert skier who likes to stay in the fall-line, slashing through quick short-radius turns on the steepest, iciest, slopes. The *Slalom* has been totally redesigned this year to fit the special needs of the expert recreational skier, who wants the lightest, fastest-reacting, and best ice-holding ski possible.

Slalom is Head's narrowest ski overall. And, thanks to the lightweight top-skin unit and core, it is also one of Head's lightest skis. Lightness and narrowness allow for carved or pivoted turns, reflex-fast changes in direction. Special engineered side camber and relative softness at the thin waist give the ultimate in "feel" and control on ice. Neoprene rubber gives the damping and torque necessary for a top-performance ice ski.

Slalom. $160. Five sizes from 190 to 210 cm. Black top and sidewalls. Racing red base and engraving.

DOWNHILL—BOMB!: Widest and heaviest Head ski, the *Downhill* is for the advanced skier—recreational or competitor—who wants to blast straight down the slope. It offers the ultimate in high-speed performance, tracking ability, and stability over bumps and moguls.

The long tip splay and supple forebody is the secret of the *Downhill's* exceptional speed advantage. It virtually planes over the surface of the slope. With its firm midsection and tail acting like the rudder of a hydroplane, the

Downhill affords the skier utmost control coupled with great turning ability at slower speeds. Heavy duty topskin unit and added rubber damping contribute to the stability and high-speed "quietness" of the *Downhill*. This is the elite international-class racing ski, and experts have found it an excellent powder ski as well.

Downhill. $175. Seven sizes from 195 to 225 cm. Black top and sidewalls. Yellow base and engraving.

GIANT SLALOM—GRACE PLUS SPEED: The *"GS"* incorporates the best features of the *Downhill* and *Slalom* models. It offers the expert skier—recreational and/or competitor—the optimum in stable all-out speed skiing, combined with precise carving and holding ability in high-speed turns. It is another favorite on the international racing circuit.

The *Giant Slalom's* stability and precision come from a unique combination of sidecut and relatively stiff flex. The *"GS"* is similar to the *360* in overall dimensions, but has a stiffer flex pattern than the *360*, particularly underfoot. This gives the *"GS"* the versatility of the *360* but with greater control at high speeds. Tip splay is designed for maximum shock absorption and easy riding.

Giant Slalom. $165. Nine sizes from 175 to 215 cm. Black top and sidewalls. Yellow base and engraving.

YOUNGSTER'S COMPETITION—JUNIOR HOT DOG: Carrying the *Giant Slalom* engraving, this ski is designed for expert youngsters who want, and can handle, a faster, more demanding ski than the small size *Standard*. Similar in cut and performance characteristics to the *Giant Slalom*, but without the *"GS's"* neoprene damping, to provide the junior racer with easier turning ability.

Youngster's Competition. $120. Two sizes, 160 and 170 cm. Black top and sidewalls; yellow bottom and engraving.

SHORTSKI—FUN WITHOUT EFFORT: Not just a sawed-off *Standard*, but a totally different ski with totally different proportions. Very wide for its length, quite stiff overall, the *Shortski* is the only ski of its kind with an engineered side camber. Ideal for quick learning of the fundamentals of skiing. Also for the older or more casual skier who enjoys being on the slopes and wants the easiest-possible tracking and turning ski ever built.

Shortski. $115. Four sizes from 150 to 190 cm. Black top, sidewalls and bottom. White engraving.

DEEP POWDER—SHEER BUOYANCY ON THE SLOPES: Super soft flexibility and buggy-whip suppleness allow this specialized ski to float in powder, while maintaining easy turning plus full control and tracking ability on packed slopes.

The *Deep Powder* is very wide and soft overall, with a "hinge-like" effect in the forebody that enables it to glide through the deepest powder.

Deep Powder. $115. Five sizes from 195 to 215 cm. Black top, sidewalls and bottom. White engraving.

Head was constantly experimenting with new designs and introducing minor modifications to improve the performance and durability of its product. When asked about a major change in product construction, such as to the fiber-reinforced plastic type ski, Mr. Head gave the following reply:

We think that the metal sandwich construction is the best material. We do not see this situation changing in the foreseeable future. Certainly now the

other exotic materials are not gaining ground. They lack the versatility of application of the metal sandwich ski. The epoxy or fiber reinforced plastic have
low durability and don't have the wide performance range of our skis.

We believe that the advantage of the metal ski is that you can build in any
performance characteristic which you desire. Naturally, we have a research department investigating other materials, but until a major improvement is found,
we should stick to our basic material. We can always build the best ski for
beginners, and we can adapt that ski to get the performance required by experts.

Marketing policies

Head's emphasis on quality extended beyond the product to the dealer
and service network. The company sold through only a limited number of
franchised dealers, who had satisfied management that "they know something
about skis and skiing." Ten district sales managers were employed, who sold
to about 900 dealers throughout the United States. Of these about 85%
were ski specialty shops, 12% were large full-line sporting goods stores, and
the remainder were full-line department stores (see Exhibit 2). Head skis
were distributed in Europe through an exclusive distributor, Walter Haensli
of Klosters, Switzerland. In 1964 he sold 19% of Head's output. This figure
appeared to be declining gradually.

Exhibit 2

HEAD SKI COMPANY, INC.

Dealer Organization, 1962–67
(Franchised Dealers)

Year	Number at Beginning	Newly Franchised	Terminated or Not Renewed	Number at End
1962	390	105	41	454
1963	454	136	30	560
1964	560	167	57	670
1965	670	96	39	727
1966	727 (est.)	N.A.	N.A.	900
1967	900 (est.)	30	N.A.	—

N.A.—Not available.
Note: In addition the franchised dealers had approximately 300 branches which are not included in the
above figures.
Source: Company records.

Head believed that a Head franchise was valuable to a dealer. Many large
stores had wanted to sell Heads, but had been turned down. Saks Fifth
Avenue had waited eight years before it was given a franchise. Mr. Head
commented on dealer selection as follows:

Getting Saks Fifth Avenue as a dealer is consistent with our operating philosophy of expecting the same quality from our dealers as from ourselves.

Once they become a dealer, however, we get to know the people involved
and work closely with them. Increasingly, we are recognizing the business value

of providing more assistance and leadership to our dealers in helping them to do a better job for their customers.

Even a large, well-managed department store or sporting goods store may need help in the specialized area of skis. They may need help in display stock selection, or even personnel selection. We are increasingly concerned about the type of personnel who sell skis. There is a high degree of dependence on the salesman. He must be a good skier himself.

We have seen instances of two department stores of essentially identical quality in the same area where one store could sell eight pairs of skis a year and the other three hundred simply because of a different degree of commitment to getting the right man to sell. Skis can only be sold by a floor salesman who can ski and who can sell from personal experience.

The company was committed to the belief that selling skis was an exacting business. The ski size had to be matched to the individual's height and body weight, flexibility had to be chosen correctly depending on use, and bindings had to be mounted properly.

Following up on the initial sale, Head offered extensive customer service. Dealers were expected to have service facilities for minor repairs and the factory had facilities for sharpening edges, rebuilding the plastic portion of the ski, and matching a single ski if the mate had been broken beyond repair. Even in the busiest part of the season, service time was kept under three weeks.

In March 1967, Mr. Harold Seigle, the newly appointed president and chief operating officer of Head, sent out a "management news bulletin" outlining Head's marketing philosophy:

Marketing Philosophy

1. Our current selective dealer organization is one of Head Ski Company's most valuable assets, next to the product itself.
2. Our continued sales growth will be based on a market-by-market approach aimed at increasing the effectiveness of our present dealers and by the very selective addition of new dealers wherever present dealers prove to be inadequate rather than by mass distribution and merchandising techniques.
3. Our future marketing efforts, particularly personal selling, advertising, merchandising, and sales promotion, will be geared to the specific needs of our dealers to sell all Head Ski products.
4. We want and will have the finest sales forces in the industry . . . who rely upon personal integrity, service, and hard work to do a professional selling job rather than inside deals and short cuts.
5. We feel that, next to quality products, strong personal selling at the manufacturer's level and the retail level is paramount to our continued success and tends to transcend other facets of marketing that contribute to the sale of merchandise.

Advertising was done on a selective basis. An outside source reported as follows:

The company invests about 2% of gross sales in advertising, split between the skiing magazines (50%) and *Sports Illustrated, The New Yorker,* and *Yachting*—"the same kind of people like to sail."

The most effective promotion, however, is probably the ski itself. Head is delighted at the growing demand for his skis in the rental market. "We sold 10,000 pairs—almost 10% of our business—for rental last year," he points out, "and everyone who rents those skis becomes a prospect."[13]

To aid in placing rental skis, Head gave an additional 12%-15% discount on skis which a dealer purchased for rental. Ski rental was seen as the best way to introduce a customer to the ease of skiing on Heads.

The Head Ski Company approach was a "soft sell." Unlike many sporting-goods companies, Head did not rely on personal endorsements of famous skiers. According to one executive, it was impossible under American Amateur rules even to have posters featuring an amateur skier. Professional endorsements were probably ineffective anyway, since so many other sporting goods companies used them, and most of the public knew that such endorsements could be bought. Head tried to get actual news pictures of famous skiers or racers using Head skis and winning. To make certain that top skiers would use Head skis, the company did lend skis to racers for one year. Even this practice was expensive and had to be tightly controlled. A good skier might need upwards of nine pairs of skis a year, which would represent an expenditure of nearly $1,000. Head did feel this type of promotion yielded a secondary benefit of product development information which could not be overlooked.

Head had received many requests for a promotional film made in conjunction with United Airlines showing famous ski slopes. Head was mentioned in the title, at the end, and in a few identifiable spots in the body of the show. This film was used by ski clubs and other organizations to promote interest in the sport.

Other Head promotion came as a result of skiwear and resort advertisements. As *Sales Management* put it:

So great is the worldwide prestige of Head skis that although Howard Head claims he makes no promotional tie-in deals, the ski buff can hardly miss seeing the familiar black skis in ads for anything from parkas to ski resorts. They're status symbols.[14]

Production

Head skis were produced in three steps. The Detail Department made up the various components which were to go into the assembly, including the core, the nose piece, the tail piece, the top plastic, the top and bottom skins, the running surface, and the edges. The separate pieces were then taken to the Cavity Department, where they were assembled. Here, too, the various layers were laid into a mold and heated and bonded under controlled time,

---

[13]*Sales Management,* February 5, 1965.
[14]*Ibid.*

temperature, and pressure. At this point the skis were roughed out on a band saw. From that time on, all work was done on the skis as a pair. In the Finishing Department, the skis were ground to final form, buffed, polished, and engraved.

Manufacture involved a great deal of handwork, of which 70% was characterized as requiring a high degree of skill. The basic nature of the assembly process meant that operations did not lend themselves to mass production techniques.

In May 1967, Head completed the fifth addition to the plant since its construction in 1959. Prior to the new addition, the plant contained 105,668 square feet, of which 93,040 was devoted to manufacturing and warehouse facilities, and 12,628 to office space. Included were a cafeteria, locker rooms, and shower areas for the workers.

Howard Head commented on the difficulty of the manufacturing process and on the relationship between costs and price:

[There are] approximately 250 different operations, involving a great number of specially developed machines, tools, and processes. None of the processes is standard. It all had to be developed more or less from scratch.

Some of the special-purpose machines involved are those for routing the groove in the bottom aluminum, for attaching the steel edges, and for profiling the ski after it comes out of the presses. Also there are the bonding procedures which require an unusual degree of control of heat and pressure cycles.

Supplementing all the special-purpose machines, we have learned to make rather unusual use of band saws. A good example of a demanding band-saw operation is the profiling of the plywood and plastic core elements. Since the stiffness of a ski at any point goes up as the square of the spacing between the top and bottom sheets—i.e., the core thickness—a normal band-saw tolerance of about 0.010″ would grossly affect our flexibility pattern and would be out of the question. However, by special adapters and guides, we are actually able to band saw these parts in high production at about ten seconds apiece to a tolerance of plus or minus 0.002″ over the entire contour.

An example of effective but low cost equipment in our factory is the press used to laminate 3′ x 10′ sheets of plywood core material to their corresponding sheets of sidewall plastic. This operation requires a total load of some 90,000 pounds. By using a roof beam as the reaction point, the floor for a base, and three screw jacks for pressure, we are able to produce enough material for 600 pairs of skis at one shot with equipment costing a total of about $250.

It's been our policy from the start to put absolute emphasis on quality of product. We never compromise on old material, nor reject a new one on the basis of cost. In principle, if better skis could be made out of sheet platinum, I suspect we would wind up with it. In other words it is our policy to make the best product we can regardless of cost and then price it accordingly to the trade.

Production at Head was on a three-shift basis throughout the year, with skis being made for inventory during the slow months. There were over 600 employees.

Six attempts had been made to unionize the plant, but all had been rejected, several times by three-to-one majorities. One warehouse employee with 12 years' seniority said, "It's a nice place to work. We don't need a union. If you have a problem, Mr. Head will listen to you."

All employees received automatic step raises based on seniority, as well as merit reviews and raises. In addition there was a profit-sharing trust plan which in the past had generally added 6%–7% to the employees' salaries. These funds became fully vested after three years.

Another important benefit in which exempt salaried employees participated was the year-end bonus plan. Under this plan, three groups received different bonus rates. For the lowest paid group, the rate was 3% if pretax profits on sales were under 2%, but 10%–11% if profits were 8%–12%. For the middle group, no bonus was paid if profits were 2% or below, but the rate was 20%–22% if profits ranged between 8% and 12%. For the top group rates were not disclosed, but it was indicated that their bonus plan was even more steeply peaked. For most of the past several years, the payoffs had been at or near the upper range.

Finance

The initial financing of Head Ski Company was $6,000 from Howard Head's personal funds. In 1953 Mr. Head sold 40% of the stock in the company for $60,000. This, together with retained earnings and normal bank debt, financed expansion until 1960 when common stock was issued. Additional financing was required to continue the rapid expansion, and in January 1965 a $3,527,500 package was sold, made up of 5½% convertible subordinated debentures in face amount of $2,125,000, and 42,500 shares of common stock. Until the stock issue of 1965, Howard Head had owned 42.4% of the common stock, and the other directors and officers had owned 46.1%. At no time had there been any question about the commanding role of Howard Head when important decisions were made. Full conversion of the new issue would represent 17.1% ownership.

Expansion was viewed by many in the company as a defensive tactic. The belief was expressed that "if you do not grow as fast as the market will allow you to, you are taking substantial risk that someone else will come in and take that market away from you." In addition, the new funds provided capital for two diversifications started in 1966: The Head Ski and Sportswear Co., and the Head plastics division.

In spite of the drop in earnings growth, the stock market continued to evaluate Head's prospects at 29 to 60 times previous years' earnings. During the period January 1966 to July 1967, its stock sold in the range from 9⅜ to 17¾. As late as January 1965, however, the stock had sold at 22¾.

Organization

As of June 1967, the Head Ski Company was organized along functional lines. Reporting to the president were the vice president for operations, the treasurer, and the directors of marketing, quality control, and the director of personnel. This organization pattern had been introduced by Mr. Harold Seigle when he was named chief operating officer on January 16, 1967 (see Exhibit 3).

Of the 26 men shown on the organization chart, 12 had been with Head one year or less. When asked about the potential difficulties of that situation, Mr. Head responded,

I would only say that if you are to have a lot of new people, you must have one man in command who is an experienced and gifted professional at utilizing people. My job is to support and use that man.

Mr. Head reviewed the history of the organization which had led to the current structure as follows:

I think that this is typical of the kind of business that starts solely from an entrepreneurial product basis, with no interest or skills in management or business in the original package. Such a business never stops to plan. The consuming interest is to build something new and to get acceptance. The entrepreneur has to pick up the rudiments of finance and organizational practices as he goes along. Any thought of planning comes later. Initially he is solely concerned with the problems of surviving and building. Also, if the business is at all successful, it is so successful that there is no real motivation to stop and obtain the sophisticated planning and people-management techniques. Such a business is fantastically efficient as long as it can survive. One man can make all of the important decisions. There is no pyramidal team structure.

In our case this approach worked quite successfully until about 1955 when we sold 10,000 pairs of skis and reached the $500,000 sales level. The next five years from 1955 to 1960 saw a number of disorganized attempts to acquire and use a more conventional pyramidal organizational system. To put it succinctly, what was efficient at the $500,000 level was increasingly inefficient as we reached $1 million, then $2 million in sales. One man just couldn't handle it. I made too many mistakes. It was like trying to run an army wtih only a general and some sergeants. There were just no officers, to say nothing of an orderly chain of command.

In 1960 came the first successful breakthrough, where I finally developed the ability to take on a general manager who later became an executive vice president. It was hard for me to learn to operate under this framework. The most striking thing missing from this period was a concept of people-management. I spent five years gradually learning not to either over- or under-delegate.

Let me interject that the final motivation necessary to make a complete transition to an orderly company came because the company got into trouble in 1965–66. Even five years after the beginning of a team system, the company got into trouble, and this was the final prod which pushed me to go all the way. It is interesting that it took 12 years. Up until 1960 the company was totally under my direction. From 1960 to 1965 we stuttered between too much of my direction and not enough.

The chief difficulty for me was to learn to lay down a statement of the results required and then stay out of details. The weakness was in finding a

Exhibit 3
HEAD SKI COMPANY, INC.
Organization Chart
(June 1967)

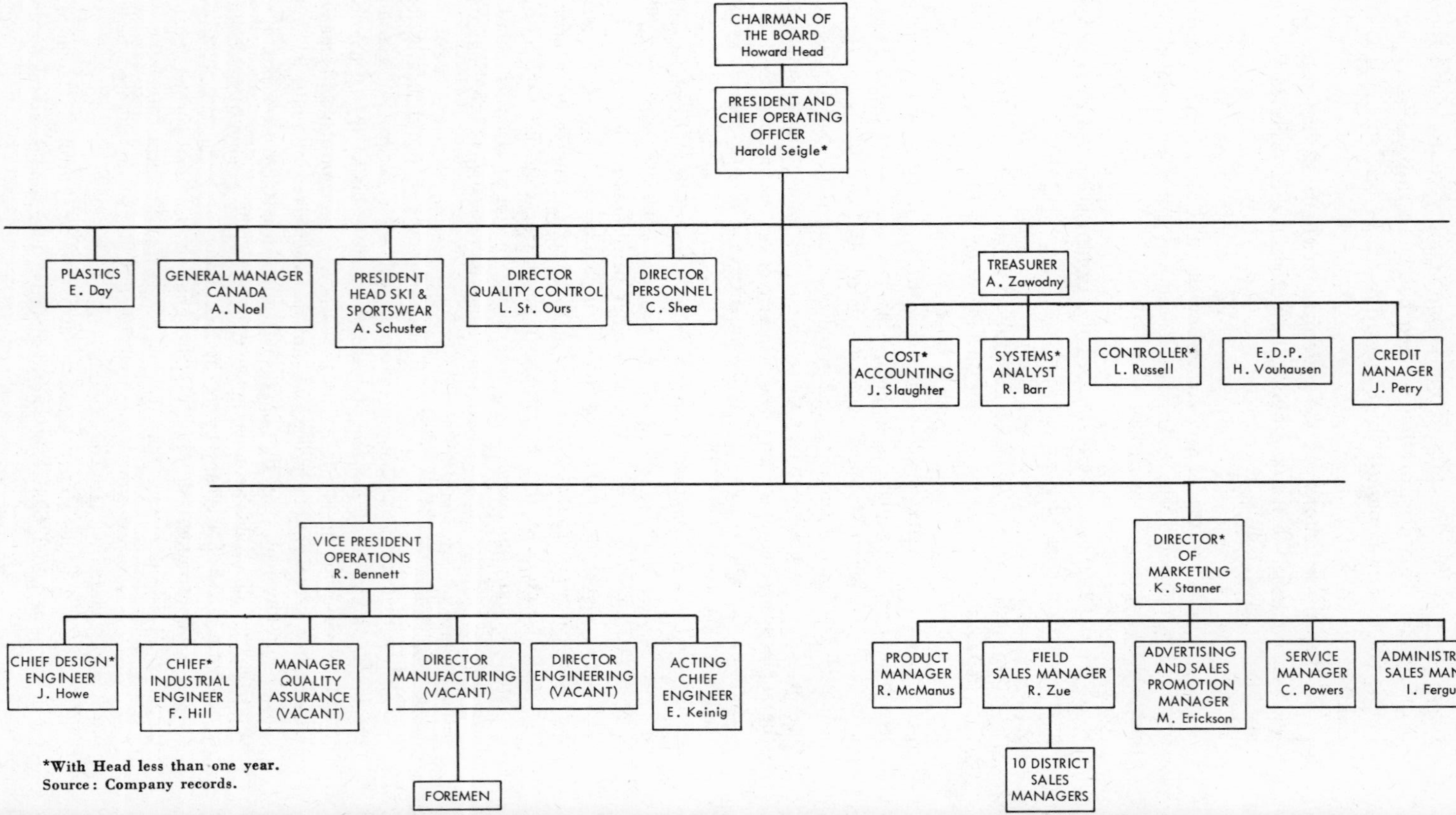

CHAIRMAN OF THE BOARD
Howard Head

PRESIDENT AND CHIEF OPERATING OFFICER
Harold Seigle*

TREASURER
A. Zawodny

COST* ACCOUNTING
J. Slaughter

SYSTEMS* ANALYST
R. Barr

CONTROLLER*
L. Russell

E.D.P.
H. Vouhausen

CREDIT MANAGER
J. Perry

DIRECTOR* OF MARKETING
K. Stanner

PRODUCT MANAGER
R. McManus

FIELD SALES MANAGER
R. Zue

10 DISTRICT SALES MANAGERS

ADVERTISING AND SALES PROMOTION MANAGER
M. Erickson

SERVICE MANAGER
C. Powers

ADMINISTRATION SALES MANAGER
I. Fergusson

PLASTICS
E. Day

GENERAL MANAGER CANADA
A. Noel

PRESIDENT HEAD SKI & SPORTSWEAR
A. Schuster

DIRECTOR QUALITY CONTROL
L. St. Ours

DIRECTOR PERSONNEL
C. Shea

VICE PRESIDENT OPERATIONS
R. Bennett

CHIEF DESIGN* ENGINEER
J. Howe

CHIEF* INDUSTRIAL ENGINEER
F. Hill

MANAGER QUALITY ASSURANCE
(VACANT)

DIRECTOR MANUFACTURING
(VACANT)

FOREMEN

DIRECTOR ENGINEERING
(VACANT)

ACTING CHIEF ENGINEER
E. Keinig

*With Head less than one year.
Source: Company records.

formula of specifying objectives, then giving freedom as long as the objectives were met.

The appointment of Hal Seigle as president brought us a thoroughly sophisticated individual who can bring us the beginning of big business methods. On my part, this change has involved two things: first, my finally recognizing that I wanted this kind of organization; second, the selection of a man with proven professional management skills.

Unfortunately, with an entrepreneur, there are only two courses which can be taken if the company is to grow beyond a certain size. He can get the hell out, or he can really change his method of operation. I am pleased that this company has made the transition.

Now more than ever the company is using my special skills and abilities, but I am no longer interfering with an orderly and sophisticated management and planning system. We have given the company new tools to operate with, and I have not pulled the rug out from under them.

I am reserving my energies for two things. First, there is a continuation of my creative input—almost like a consultant to the company. Second, I have taken the more conventional role of chairman and chief executive officer. In this role I devote my efforts to planning and longer range strategy.

I feel that I can serve in both capacities. I can only be successful in the role of creative input if I can be solely a consultant without authority. It has to be made clear in this role that anything said is for consideration only. It has been demonstrated that this role is consultative, since some of my suggestions have been rejected. I like this role because I like the freedom. I can think freer, knowing that my suggestions will be carefully reviewed.

Of course, in areas of real importance like new product lines such as binding or boots, adding new models to the ski line, or acquisitions, etc., I must exert authority, channeled through the president.

Prior to coming to Head, Mr. Seigle had been vice president and general manager of a $50 million consumer electronics division of a $150 million company. His appointment was viewed as "contributing to a more professional company operating philosophy." He hoped to introduce more formalized methods of budget control and to "preside over the transition from a 'one man' organization to a traditionally conceived functional pattern."

Mr. Seigle introduced a budgeting system broken down into 13 periods each year. Reports were to be prepared every four weeks comparing target with actual for each of the revenue or expense centers, such as marketing, operations, the staff functions, and the three subsidiaries. The hope was eventually to tie the bonus to performance against budget. Previously statements had been prepared every four weeks, but only to compare actual results against previous years' results.

Being new to the company, Mr. Seigle found that much of his time was being spent on operating problems. He believed, however, that as the budget system became completely accepted and operational, he would be able to devote more of his time to looking ahead and worrying about longer term projects. He said: "Ideally, I like to be working six to eighteen months ahead of the organization. As a project gets within six months of actual operation, I will turn it over to the operating managers." He had hired a manager for corporate planning with whom he worked closely.

Under the previous organization from March 1966 until Mr. Seigle's appointment, Howard Head had presided directly over the various departments and marketing functions. There was no overall marketing director at that time. Even in the period from 1960 to 1966 when there was an executive vice president, Mr. Head indicated that he had concerned himself with the operating details of the business.

A view toward the future

Head's first diversification was to ski poles. These were relatively simple to manufacture and were sold through existing channels. As with the skis, Head maintained the highest standards of quality and style. The poles were distinguished from competition by their black color and adoption of the tapered shape and extra light weight which at the time were unavailable on other high-priced, quality ski poles. Head's prices were well toward the upper end of the spectrum: $24.50, as compared with as little as $5 for some brands. Success in selling poles encouraged the company to look at other products it might add.

Two further steps taken were toward diversification in late 1966 when Head formed a plastics division and established a subsidiary, Head Ski and Sportswear, Inc.

The plastic division's activity centered on high molecular weight plastics. In March 1967 a press release was issued concerning this activity:

Head Ski Co., Inc., has signed a license agreement with Phillips Petroleum Company . . . to use a new method developed by Phillips for extruding ultra-high molecular weight high density polyethylene into finished products. . . .

Developmental equipment has been installed at the Head plant here and limited quantities of sheet have been extruded and tested in the running surface of Head skis with excellent results. . . . Production of ski base material is scheduled for this Spring. . . .

In addition to its own running surface material, the Head plastics division has been developing special ultra-high molecular weight high density polyethylene compound to serve a variety of industrial applications. . . .

Ultra-high molecular weight high density polyethylene is an extremely tough abrasion-resistant thermoplastic capable of replacing metal and metal alloys in many industrial areas. Compared with regular high density resins, the ultra-high molecular weight material has better stress-cracking resistance, better long-term stress life and less notch sensitivity.

The diversification into skiwear was considered by company executives to be the more important move. Howard Head talked about the logic of this new venture as follows:

Skiwear is "equipment" first and fashion second. We are satisfied that our line of skiwear is better than anything done before. It represents the same degree of attention to detail which has characterized our hardware line.

The president of the new subsidiary, Alex Schuster, said:

Many people thought that Head should stay in hardware such as poles, bindings, and wax. As I see it, however, by going into skiwear we are taking advantage of ready-made distribution and reputation. There is no reason why the good will developed through the years can't be related to our endeavor.

This new market offers a greater potential and reward than the more hardware oriented areas. Any entry into a new market has difficulties. These can only be solved by doing things right and by measuring up to the Head standards. Having a Head label commits us to a standard of excellence.

Assuming that we live up to those standards, we shall be able to develop into a supplier in a small market but with formidable potential. We are creating a skill base for further diversification.

Our products are engineered, not designed. We are concerned with the engineered relationship among fabric, function, and fit. The engineering details are not always obvious, but they are related to functional demands. Emphasis is placed on function over fashion, yet there is definite beauty created out of concern for function. We are definitely in tune with fashion trends.

[See Exhibit 4 for examples of the new products.]

We will provide a complete skiing outfit—pants, parkas, sweaters, accessories, sox, and gloves. We will offer a total coordinated look.

Along with the design innovations, we shall offer innovations in packaging, display and promotion. We have to go beyond simply preparing the proper apparel.

Head Ski and Sportswear did both manufacturing and subcontracting. The products which had the highest engineering content were made in the Head plant. Sweaters, with less engineering, were contract-made to Head specifications by one of Europe's leading sweater manufacturers.

The collection was first shown to dealers in April 1967 and was scheduled for public release for the 1967–1968 skiing season. Initial response by dealers and by the fashion press had been extremely encouraging. *Ski Business* reported:

HEAD'S UP.

. . . way up, in fact 194% ahead of planned volume on its premier line of skiwear.

Anyone who expected Howard Head's entry into the world of fashion to be presented in basic black was in for a surprise. Ironically the skiwear collection that blasted off with the hottest colors in the market is offered by a man who is totally color blind. . . .

On pants: The $55 pant was the big surprise. It was our top seller—way beyond expectations—and the basic $45 pant came in second in sales. Another surprise was the $70 foam waisted pant for which we only projected limited sales—it's a winner. . . .

On orders: Way beyond expectations. Ninety per cent of the orders are

Exhibit 4

Exhibit 4

SAMPLES OF THE NEW HEAD SKIWEAR

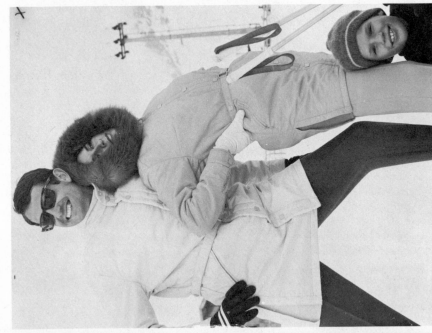

Exhibit 4—Continued

SAMPLES OF THE NEW HEAD SKIWEAR

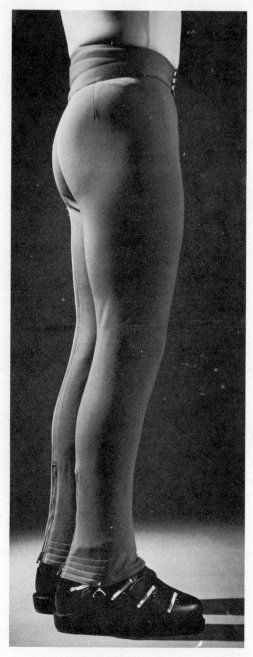

with ski shops and 10% with the department stores. Naturally we are committed to selling Head Ski dealers but it definitely is not obligatory.[15]

The sportswear subsidiary had been set up in a separate plant five miles from Head's Timonium headquarters. It was an autonomous operation with a separate sales force and profit responsibility. The initial premise was that the sportswear would be distributed through current Head dealers, although according to Mr. Seigle the marketing decisions of the sportswear division would be made independently of decisions in the ski division. Although Head dealers were offered the Head sportswear line, it was not sold on an exclusive basis. Distribution would be directly from factory salesmen to the dealer. Within the company, the necessity for a separated and different type of sales force was acknowledged. As one executive phrased it, "I can't imagine our ski salesmen trying to push soft goods. Our salesmen got into the business first and foremost because they were excellent skiers." As with skis and poles, the product line was to be maintained at the high end of the spectrum in both quality and price.

When asked about future growth potential, Mr. Seigle replied that he believed Head would continue to grow rapidly in the future. He saw the potential of doubling the ski business in the next five years. Although he characterized the sportswear business as a "good calculated risk," he believed it offered the potential of expanding to $5 to $8 million per year. Beyond that he felt that Head might go in three possible directions. First, he believed that Head should once again explore the opportunities and risks of moving into the other price segments of the ski market, either under another brand or with a nonmetallic ski. Although he believed that by selling in a lower price range Head could sell 50,000 or more pairs of skis, the risks were also high. Second, he felt that Head should explore the opportunity in other related ski products, such as boots or bindings. Third, he felt that eventually Head should expand into other specialty sporting goods, preferably of a contraseasonal nature.

In looking to these new areas, Mr. Seigle had formulated a two-part product philosophy as follows:

Any new product which Head will consider should:
1. Be consistent with the quality and prestige image of Head Skis.
2. Should entail one or more of the following characteristics:
    a) High innovative content.
    b) High engineering content.
    c) High style appeal.
    d) Be patentable.

We will consider getting into new products through any of the normal methods such as internal product development, product acquisition, or corporate acquisition. If we are to move into a new area we definitely want to have a product edge. For example, if we were to manufacture a boot, we would want to be

---

[15]*Ski Business*, May-June, 1967.

different. We would only seriously consider it if we had a definite product advantage such as if we were to develop a high quality plastic boot.

Howard Head, in speaking of the future, voiced the following hopes:

I would like to see Head grow in an orderly fashion sufficient to maintain its present youth and resiliency. That would mean at least 20%–25% per year. This statement does not preclude the possibility that we might grow faster. We believe the ski business alone will grow 20%–25% per year. As our staff capabilities grow, we will probably branch out into other areas.

As to our objectives for the next five years, I would say that the first corporate objective is to maintain healthy growth in the basic ski business. It is the taproot of all that is good in Head. Second, we must be certain that any new activity is carefully selected for a reasonable probability of developing a good profit and an image platform consistent with the past activity of Head.

APPENDIX A*

TYPES OF SKIS

ELEMENTS OF A WELL-DESIGNED SKI

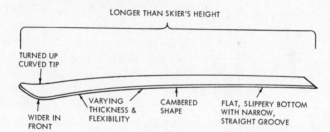

LONGER THAN SKIER'S HEIGHT

TURNED UP
CURVED TIP

VARYING THICKNESS & FLEXIBILITY

CAMBERED SHAPE

FLAT, SLIPPERY BOTTOM WITH NARROW, STRAIGHT GROOVE

WIDER IN FRONT

PHOTO IMPRESSION SHOWS HOW SKI MUST TORQUE OVER BUMPS

Wood skis

If you are on a tight budget, well-designed wood skis at low prices are available from domestic and foreign manufacturers. Wood is a bundle of tubular cellulose cells bound together in an elastic medium called lignin. The internal slippage of wood skis not only lets them torque over the bumps in traverse, but damps any tendency to vibrate or chatter on hard rough surfaces. There are wood skis for any snow, any speed, and they are fun to ski on. Their only problem is a lack of durability. Wood skis are fragile. Besides, as wood skis are used, the internal slippage of the fibers increases, and they lose their life.

In choosing a wood ski, it is probably wise to pay more than the minimum price. Multiple laminations of hickory or ash, a soft flex pattern, interlocking

---

*Source: *Skiing International Yearbook,* 1967, pp. 63–68. Copyright by Ziff-Davis Publishing Co.

edges, polyethylene base, plastic top and sidewalls, tip and tail protectors are some of the features a beginner or intermediate should look for in a better wood ski. When you get past the $40 to $70 range, your own dealer's recommendations will be your best guarantee of value.

WOOD SKI CROSS-SECTION

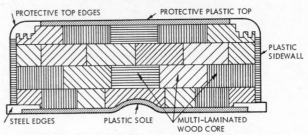

FRP skis

A few years ago there were only a handful of "epoxy" skis on the market, and skiers were eyeing them with mixed interest and distrust. Now the available models have multiplied almost unbelievably. New companies have been formed, and many of the established manufacturers have now brought out versions of their own. The plastic skis are still new enough for most skiers to be confused about their true nature—and with good reason, since there are so many types.

The word epoxy is part of the confusion. The true family resemblance of all the skis that are currently being lumped under that designation is the use of glass fibers locked into a plastic medium to create layers of great strength. The plastics engineers use the term fiber-reinforced plastic (FRP) to designate this type of structural solution. It is very strong.

The reinforcing layers used in these new designs derive their strength from the combined strength of millions of fine glass fibers or threads locked in the plastic layer. The potential strengths of materials in this family of structural plastics can exceed those of aluminum or steel. Unfortunately, there is no simple way to evaluate them or describe the materials actually in use. The wide variety of glass fibers, resins, and systems of molding and curing the fiber-reinforced layer produces a wide range of results. These can be evaluated only by laboratory tests or, finally, by actual in-service results.

FRP materials are being used for all sorts of sporting goods, industrial, and space-age applications. The strength-to-weight ratio is attractively high, and the possibility of creating new reinforced shapes by means of molding operations has proved to be attractive enough to encourage a great deal of experimentation. Skis seem to adapt to this structural technique.

Metal skis

In the search for more durable skis, the metal skis took over the quality market about a decade ago, and are widely accepted as ideal for both recreational skier and expert. Except for specialized racing uses, the wooden skis have been largely outmoded in the better ski market. Today, the fiber-reinforced plastic designs are the only challengers to the primacy of the metals.

Metal skis obtain their strength from aluminum sheets that are light in weight but very strong. The structure of a metal ski is somewhat like an "I" beam; when the ski is bent, the bottom sheet is stretched and the top sheet is compressed. The core material serves as the web—the vertical portion of the "I"—and must be attached to the top and bottom metal sheets securely enough to resist the shearing stress that occurs when the ski is bent.

Service potential of metal skis

The possibility of rebuilding and refinishing metal skis has been one of the key sales attractions of the metal ski in this country. So long as bonding remains intact, only the effects of wear and tear—rocks, skis banging together, rough treatment in transportation, etc.—limit the life of the skis. The possibility of having the plastic surfaces and edges, or even the structural members themselves, replaced has strong appeal for the skier investing well over $100 in his skis. The rebuilding potential also tends to keep the trade-in and used resale value of the skis higher, making it less expensive for the skier to move to higher performance or more recent models as his skiing ability—or his desire for something new—dictates. The American companies were the first to develop rebuilding techniques, but more recently European factories have been establishing service centers in the U.S.

METAL SKI CROSS-SECTIONS

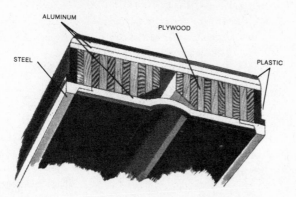

Northland Golden Jet—Cross-laminated fir plywood core with no filler in center, full-length bonded steel edge, aluminum sheets on both the top and the bottom.

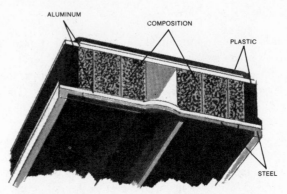

Hart Javelin—Grainless core of pressed particles, continuous full-length steel L edge welded to steel sheet, revealed aluminum top edge, phenolic plastic top.

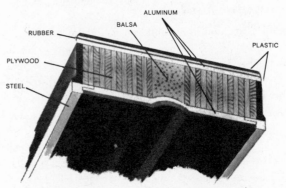

Head Competition—Cross-laminated fir plywood core, rubber damping layer on top of structure, full-length bonded steel L edge, high-density plastic base.

FRP CROSS-SECTIONS

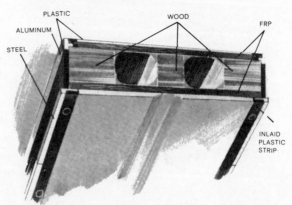

Kneissl White Star—Epoxy sandwich with interrupted wood core for lightness, sectional steel L edge screwed-in, aluminum top edge, two-color inlaid base.

A&T K2—Vestigial core of pine, full wrap-around construction, bonded full-length L edge. ABS plastic top sheet. Bonded edges have tab construction for strength.

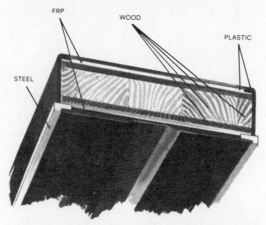

Yamaha Hi-Flex—FRP sandwich, hardwood core with grain running lengthwise, full-length bonded stainless steel L edges on bottom, with top edges of celluloid.

There are three basic elements of FRP construction: the plastic material or resin; the glass fibers themselves; and the method of combining, curing, and shaping the composite reinforcing layer. Variation of any of these three elements affects the characteristics of the end product.

Service potential of FRP skis

One of the problems facing the manufacturers of fiber-reinforced plastic skis has been how to service and rebuild them—once the normal wear and tear of skiing has taken its toll. Only the metal skis, it has seemed, could be refinished and rebuilt.

Though it is true that you cannot heat up an FRP ski, melt the glue, resand, recoat, and reconstruct it quite as easily as you can a metal ski, progress has been made in this direction during the past season. Several manufacturers have set up regional service centers.

What these various service centers can accomplish is considerable. They are replacing bases and edges. They are renewing and refinishing top surfaces. In some cases, the structural fiberglass members can be separated from the wood core and replaced, producing in effect a brand-new ski. The sum of all this is real benefit to the average skier, who is unwilling to discard a pair of skis every season or so. The gap between metal and FRP skis, as far as service potential is concerned, is being narrowed. You will find that the costs range over approximately the same spread as the metal skis and that guarantee provisions are similar.

UNIVIS, INC.*

^^

During 1966 Univis, Inc., a Ft. Lauderdale, Florida, firm primarily engaged in the ophthalmic lens and frame business, published a booklet for the financial community that included the following statement about the company's business philosophy:

A formalized philosophy underlies our planning and operations at all levels, indicative excerpts from which are presented below for your further Univis orientation.

OBJECTIVE
Acknowledging the limitations thereto, it is is our contention that over a reasonable period, the single most comprehensive indicator of a public company's performance, though not the only one, is the price-earnings ratio of its common stock share. Thus as a reflection of intended long-run excellence, our fundamental objective is to:

maximize owners' common share price.

PURSUIT OF GROWTH
Within the context of our circumstances, we feel it appropriate that:

We identify ourselves, through adherence to requisite prudent performance standards, as a *growth company*, and contend that this will cause our common share, through continuity in earnings increases, to be viewed as a *growth stock*.

We intend to maintain such superior performance first through excellence in generalized *professional management*, whereby specialized endeavor is subordinated and utilized as deemed desirable to achieve fundamental corporate-wide goals.

Furthermore, in view of our resource, risk, and yield propensities, we will pursue growth primarily through compatible exploitation of ongoing *environmental change*, although opportunities otherwise commensurate with our standards will be considered.

FLEXIBILITY
To further clarify our managerial stance, two additional precepts are embraced.

We view our organization resources as an *homogeneous* pool, untied to specific endeavors except by limitation in skills and commitments, neither of which we underestimate.

Thus, while we acknowledge ophthalmics as our core industry, we feel that our organization resources are applicable to *any business opportunity* which meets our standards of desirability, and these include preference for activities characterized by common interests.

DIVIDEND POLICY

Recognizing the inverse relationship between self-generated funds to finance expansion, and cash dividend payout to provide current income to shareholders, and given the ultimate precedence of our fundamental objective and its supporting commitment to growth, we consider it desirable to:

Maintain cash dividend payout at the dollar quantity already established, increasing this when permitted by ability to sustain such increments.[1]

This explicit statement of business philosophy was one of the more recent steps taken by Univis to improve corporate performance through the use of "business planning." Although the company had talked in terms of business planning ever since its new management took over in late 1955, it was with the decision to set up a department of formal corporate planning in September 1963 that steps were made toward formalizing the objectives and philosophy in "the way they should have been."[2]

Of the company's commitment to formal planning, Mr. R. O. Barber, president of Univis, said in 1965,

In 1955, we had no one devoting full attention to formal planning. Today our corporate planning department is composed of three professional planners and three service personnel, and is headed by a company officer.

Is there a secret to growth? We don't think so. But there is a best way to grow. We call it corporate planning.[3]

The company

Background. Univis, Inc., began in 1911 as the Stanley Optical Company of Dayton, Ohio. This company, which was privately owned, subsequently changed its name to the Univis Lens Company. In 1955 working control was purchased from the founding family by four of the company's staff. Sales at the time were slightly over $4 million and in the first year of the new management the company suffered an operating loss of $290,000. Figures for the company's sales and profit from 1950–55 were as follows:

Sales and Net Profit, Univis Lens Company—1950–55
(Dollars in Thousands)

	1950	1951	1952	1953	1954	1955
Sales	$4,497	$4,749	$4,909	$5,163	$4,360	$4,220
Net profit	293	257	131	257	(89)	(292)

Source: Moody's *Industrials.*

[1]Excerpts from *Facts about Univis 1966.*
[2]Robert O. Barber, "Plan Those Profits," *The Presidents Forum,* Fall/Winter 1965, p. 29.
[3]*Ibid.,* p. 32.

In 1960 the company changed its name to Univis, Inc., and moved its headquarters from Dayton, Ohio, to Ft. Lauderdale, Florida. In 1966 three of the original four purchasers—Robert O. Barber (president), Arthur J. Sowers (vice president and treasurer), and Stanley A. Emerson (first vice president)—were still with the company. Together they formed Univis' executive committee. In 1966, 35% of the company's common stock was held by the directors and officers. The rest, traded over the counter, was widely distributed among approximately 2,000 shareholders.

From the small beginning in 1955, sales had climbed to $16.3 million in 1966; net earnings had risen to $1,005,118. These figures represented the latest in a series showing continuous growth in both sales and earnings since the new management had acquired control. Only in 1960, when the company moved its corporate headquarters from Dayton to Ft. Lauderdale, and again in 1963 did the earnings show a temporary decline. Since 1960 net earnings had grown at an average yearly compounded rate of 18.9% on an average yearly compounded sales growth of 14.8%. Exhibit 1 shows comparative income statement items for the years 1956–66. Exhibit 2 is a similar comparison for balance sheet items while Exhibit 3 shows market data on stock as well as the growth comparison of selected parameters.

Product line. The company produced both glass and plastic lenses. It offered a complete range of glass lenses from single vision, through bifocal to cataract,[4] and had introduced the industry's first straight-top bifocal *plastic* lens in 1963. Expansion into the frame business took place in 1961 with the acquisition of the Bishop Company. This commitment was further increased with the inclusion of the Zylite Corporation into the Univis group in 1962. Univis was then able to offer a complete line of men's, women's and children's frames, comprising in all about 2,000 different items.

Production facilities. The company had four production facilities. The Ft. Lauderdale plant made special-purpose and single-vision glass lenses. A factory in Guayama, Puerto Rico, specialized in producing the standard range of bifocal glass lenses. A facility in West Babylon, New York, made plastic lenses and another in North Attleboro, Mass., manufactured Univis spectacle frames. The combined output of these factories, comprising nearly 10,000 different items, was warehoused and shipped from the Ft. Lauderdale headquarters. The total number of employes in 1965 had risen to 1,398.

Management. Exhibit 4 gives some information on the background and experience of the company's corporate officers while Exhibit 5 shows the company's organization chart. Although there was no formal management development program, the company encouraged interested personnel to

---

[4]Single vision lenses have only one power of magnification.

Bifocal lenses combine two powers of magnification in a single lens. Straight-top bifocals have the break in magnification running in a straight line horizontally across the lens face.

Cataract lenses are designed for patients who suffer from aphakia, a condition resulting from the absence of the eye's crystalline lens.

Exhibit 1

UNIVIS, INC.

Comparative Income Statements, 1956–1966

(Dollars in Thousands)

	1956	1957	1958	1959	1960	1961	1962	1963	1964	1965	1966
Sales and Other Income											
Net sales	$5,030	$5,665	$5,675	$6,449	$7,141	$8,844	$10,378	$12,258	$13,944	$15,456	$16,293
Discounts earned, etc. (net)	14	33	26	30	42	34	64	73	66	58	95
Total	$5,044	$5,698	$5,701	$6,479	$7,183	$8,878	$10,442	$12,331	$14,010	$15,514	$16,388
Costs and Expenses											
Cost of sales	3,116	3,415	3,222	3,259	3,682	4,849	5,846	7,251	8,360	8,896	9,856
Selling, general and administrative	1,707	1,871	1,994	2,338	2,950	3,317	3,318	3,918	4,231	4,659	4,500
Depreciation	167	174	111	116	133	138	143	190	165	158	167
Interest and debt	48	39	38	20	13	8	8	22	10	—	—
Total	$5,038	$5,499	$5,365	$5,733	$6,778	$8,312	$9,315	$11,381	$12,766	$13,713	$14,523
Earnings before taxes on income	$ 6	$ 199	$ 336	$ 746	$ 405	$ 565	$ 1,127	$ 950	$ 1,244	$ 1,801	$ 1,865
Taxes on income	(31)	65	145*	285*	49*	126*	522†	468†	622	842	860
Net earnings	$ 37	$ 134	$ 191	$ 461	$ 356	$ 439	$ 575	$ 482	$ 622	$ 959	$ 1,005
Shares outstanding‡	635,250	635,250	635,250	646,447	646,447	646,447	661,484	667,252	674,300	702,425	712,272
Earnings per share§	0.06	0.21	0.30	0.72	0.55	0.68	0.88	0.72	0.93	1.38	1.42
Dividends per share	0.02	0.04	0.11	0.30	0.21	0.24	0.26	0.26	0.38	0.54	.625

*Restated 1958 through 1961 for elimination of deferred taxes on undistributed earnings of Puerto Rican subsidiary.

†Restated to reflect adjusted Federal income tax provisions needed in earnings reinvested in the business in 1965.

‡Adjusted for 1-for-2 stock distributions (same adjustment as for 3-for-2 split) July 31, 1964 and July 31, 1965, and 2% stock dividends December 31, 1962 and December 31, 1963

§Earnings per share adjusted 1959 through 1964 for issuance of 11,197 shares in 1965 for the minority interest in a subsidiary.

Source: Company records.

Exhibit 2

UNIVIS, INC.

Comparative Balance Sheet Items, 1956–1966
(Dollars in Thousands)

	1956	1957	1958	1959	1960	1961	1962	1963	1964	1965	1966
Cash and marketable securities	$ 211	$ 339	$ 432	$1,111	$ 314	$ 657	$ 531	$ 542	$ 885	$1,467	$1,456
Receivables	681	759	892	768	901	910	976	1,383	1,365	1,697	1,681
Inventories	1,463	1,562	1,272	1,429	1,861	1,773	2,138	2,556	2,803	2,915	3,159
Current assets	2,355	2,660	2,596	3,308	3,076	3,340	3,645	4,481	5,053	6,079	6,296
Current liabilities	258	304	131	405	647	600	653	1,233	1,589	1,726	1,760
Total assets	3,571	3,592	3,328	3,913	3,929	4,066	4,797	5,694	6,309	7,412	8,033
Gross plant	1,176	1,187	1,120	1,203	1,442	1,549	1,886	2,198	2,371	2,500	3,084
Net plant	674	592	488	469	631	606	789	950	1,007	1,069	1,510
Long-term liabilities*	860	752	566	715	433	491	673	770	643	188	154
Common equity†	2,453	2,536	2,631	2,793	2,849	2,976	3,471	3,691	4,076	5,498	6,119
Book value per share	$ 3.86	$ 3.99	$ 4.14	$ 4.32	$ 4.40	$ 4.60	$ 5.25	$ 5.72	$ 6.27	$ 7.12	$ 8.59
Common equity return	1.5%	5.2%	6.1%	12.3%	7.2%	9.3%	16.5%	13.1%	15.3%	17.4%	16.5%
Total net assets return	1.0%	3.7%	4.8%	8.8%	5.2%	6.8%	12.0%	8.5%	9.9%	12.9%	12.5%

*Prior to 1965 includes deferred Puerto Rican taxes, deferred executive compensation, and long-term notes payable.
†1965 and 1966, following a ruling by the U.S. Internal Revenue Service, includes $500,000 of previously deferred Puerto Rican taxes.
Source: Company records.

Exhibit 3

UNIVIS, INC.

Information on Common Share Market Valuation, 1956–1966

Year	Stock Price—Adjusted			Thousand Shares Transferred	Price/Earnings		Price/Cash Flow		Yield	
	High	Low	Close		High	Low	High	Low	High	Low
1956	2⅛	1⅛	1⅜	...	35	19	7	4	1.8	0.9
1957	2	1⅜	1⅜	...	10	7	4	3	2.8	2.0
1958	3½	1⅜	3¼	...	14	6	8	3	8.0	3.1
1959	7¼	2¾	7¼	...	14	5	10	4	10.9	4.1
1960	7½	4	5⅛	440,817	23	12	14	8	5.2	2.8
1961	7¼	4¾	7⅞	338,295	17	11	11	7	5.1	3.3
1962	8⅞	6⅛	8⅞	263,166	10	7	8	6	4.2	2.9
1963	9½	7¼	7½	237,785	13	10	9	7	3.6	2.7
1964	16½	7½	16¼	327,985	18	8	14	6	5.1	2,3
1965	35¼	16½	27	286,680	26	12	22	10	3.3%	1.5%
1966	31½	13¾	...	...	...	...	...	...	...	...

Source: Company records.

Exhibit 3—Continued

Selected Growth Comparisons

	% Average Yearly Compound 1960 QII–1965 QIII
U.S. gross national product	6.1%
U.S. personal consumption expenditures	5.3
U.S. ophthalmic market revenue	7.8
Univis revenue	16.6
U.S. manufacturing corporations profit, post-tax	14.3
Univis profit, post-tax	33.5
Standard and Poor's composite earnings per share	10.7
Univis earnings per share	29.9

Source: Company records.

attend management seminars and to develop their experience and training as each one saw fit.

Ophthalmic industry and market

The U.S. retail market for ophthalmic goods and related services was estimated by the Better Vision Institute at over $1 billion per year. Factory sales of conventional eyeglass products plus imports amounted to over $150 million annually. At the consumer level this was equivalent to $1,050 million annually.

The potential of the industry was outlined by the Better Vision Institute which estimated that, although nearly 54% of the American population over the age of six utilized some form of corrective lenses, about 40 million

Exhibit 4

UNIVIS, INC.
Management Profile

Person	Age	Education	Length of Service	Experience
A	60	College	15	Marketing
B	62	Graduate degree	30	Optical and scientific
C	55	College	15	Diversified-finance
D	45	College	15	Marketing
E	45	College	10	Manufacturing
F	55	College	15	Scientific
G	45	College	15	Market research
H	45	High school	27	Production
I	54	College	28	Sales and personnel
J	47	College	6	Scientific
K	43	College	6	Scientific
L	50	College	5	Finance and accounting
M	36	Graduate degree	3	Business

Average age: 49.3 yrs. Average length of service: 14.6 yrs.

Source: Company records.

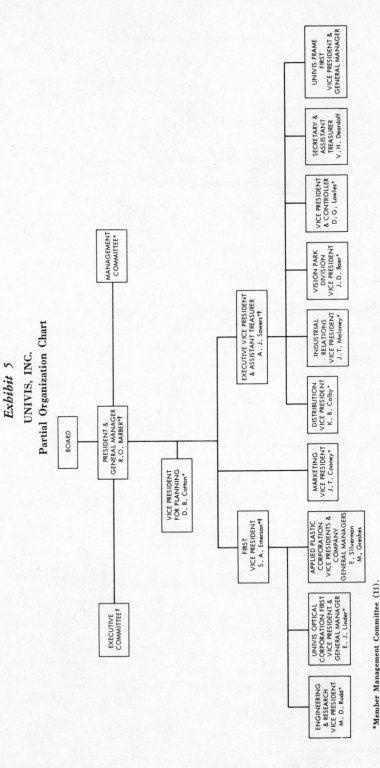

Exhibit 5

UNIVIS, INC.

Partial Organization Chart

BOARD

MANAGEMENT COMMITTEE*

EXECUTIVE COMMITTEE†

PRESIDENT & GENERAL MANAGER
R. O. BARBER*†

VICE PRESIDENT FOR PLANNING
D. B. Cotton*

EXECUTIVE VICE PRESIDENT & ASSISTANT TREASURER
A. J. Sowers*†

FIRST VICE PRESIDENT
S. A. Emerson*†

DISTRIBUTION VICE PRESIDENT
K. B. Colby*

MARKETING VICE PRESIDENT
J. T. Cooney*

INDUSTRIAL RELATIONS VICE PRESIDENT
J. T. Maloney*

VISION PARK DIVISION VICE PRESIDENT
J. D. Boer*

VICE PRESIDENT & CONTROLLER
D. G. Lowles*

SECRETARY & ASSISTANT TREASURER
V. H. Deardoff

UNIVIS FRAME FIRST VICE PRESIDENT & GENERAL MANAGER

APPLIED PLASTIC CORPORATION VICE PRESIDENTS & COMPANY GENERAL MANAGERS
E. Silverman
M. Greshes

UNIVIS OPTICAL CORPORATION FIRST VICE PRESIDENT & GENERAL MANAGER
E. J. Linder*

ENGINEERING & RESEARCH VICE PRESIDENT
M. D. Rudd*

*Member Management Committee (11).
†Member Executive Committee (3).
Source: Company records.

eyeglass wearers had not had their eyes examined in the last four years; and that, of these, 28 million needed new prescriptions. Univis' corporate planning department estimated that the 1970 Optical Manufacturers Association ophthalmic lens sales would probably be 40.8 million pairs or 39% above 1965's figures. This represented an average annual compounded growth rate of 6.8%.

The ophthalmic industry was dominated by four firms—American Optical (who because of their size effectively set the prices), Bausch & Lomb, the Shuron-Continental Division of Textron, and Univis. Each company produced and sold ophthalmic lenses, spectacle frames, and associated products, although Univis' major competitors were more highly diversified in terms of technology, industry, and product. Because of the consolidation of divisional figures in annual reports, Univis was the only company for which sales data were available. Univis' sales were made through wholesalers or, occasionally, directly to the United States or a state government.

Planning at Univis

Prior to the introduction of a formal corporate planning department, the company had always emphasized planning as a key aspect of effective management. The first decision to institute a series of formal controls was made when the new management took over working control of the company in 1955. The president, Mr. Barber, explained the decision as follows:

. . . but our immediate concern was to put Univis in the black. As a start, we established a cost-cutting program that eliminated most of the fat while sparing most of the muscle. We wrote job descriptions for all jobs and set up performance standards for key people. (For the past several years these standards have been the basis for payment of incentive bonuses.)

We spelled out our company creed [see Exhibit 6], the first in our history, and defined our business:

"Univis, Inc., is engaged in providing products and services used in the protection and improvement of human vision."

This statement changed management's concepts and broadened the horizon for future planning and growth.

*   *   *   *   *

Because we believe that decisions are never any better than the information on which they are based, we set up controls to give managers at all levels timely and adequate, but not excessive, information about the jobs for which they were responsible.[5]

In line with this early emphasis on formal control the company had written job descriptions for all the major functions in the company. These descriptions, 124 in all, were kept in a three-inch thick organization manual that was broken down into eight company divisions. Each of the divisions, such as top management, marketing, engineering, and research, etc., had an organi-

---

[5]Barber, *op. cit.,* p. 29.

Exhibit 6

UNIVIS CREED

*We at Univis believe that we owe a responsibility to our Customers,
Personnel, Shareholders, Community and our Nation.
In accepting this responsibility we specifically
detail our obligations in each of these areas as follows:*

I. To bring to our Customers, products and services of such merit and so competitively priced that the Customer will find his Univis Distributorship to be valuable both from a profit as well as a prestige standpoint; to remain constantly aware that the sale of our goods and services to our Customers is not enough but that we must make available to them the kind of programs and assistance which will assure the adequate movement of these goods and services from our Customers to their Customers; to create and support constructive marketing policies which will strengthen our Customers' position in the industry and justify their continuing confidence in Univis as a supplier; to constantly upgrade the quality of our Distribution to the end that the climate in which our Customers function is of the highest order.

II. To pay our Personnel as high a wage as their skills merit in the labor market in which they offer their services; to maintain a benefit program consistent with our industry and our area; to support programs inside and outside the Company organization which will help develop the inherent capabilities of our Personnel; and to so select, train, supervise, control and motivate our Personnel that the job will be performed with maximum efficiency with a full measure of satisfaction going to those who perform it.

III. To recognize that our Shareholders are individuals or institutions who have shown confidence in the management of this Company and its products, and that it is our responsibility to conduct our Corporate affairs in such a manner that they will receive a fair return on their investment; to keep our Shareholders properly informed through Annual and interim reports and such other communications as are necessary regarding Company progress and condition.

IV. To make a sensible allotment of our time and abilities to the service of our Community to the end that our Community receives support for those activities which contribute to its material progress, spiritual growth and cultural environment.

V. To take advantage of opportunities to actively interest ourselves as individuals, or as a Company, in State and National issues so that our contribution may also be made in the continuing struggle for survival of our freedom and our way of life.

---

zation chart showing the positioning of all the people in that division and a series of job descriptions for the relevant tasks. Exhibit 7 illustrates a typical job description format for the assistant vice president for corporate planning. Most of these descriptions were written by the personnel department and involved talking to both the person involved and his "boss" in order to produce an accurate prescription of the task to be performed.

In addition to the detailed organization manual, the company also set "standards of performance" for managerial and administrative functions and determined a "job rating" for all the factory tasks.

The "standards of performance" were negotiated between the superior and subordinate and were aimed at ensuring that the particular person under review played his role in achieving the division objectives set for the year. Consequently each person was set a "performance standard" for the ensuing year. The actual performance of the individual versus this standard was evaluated four times a year and if the subordinate was not measuring up to requirements he would be asked to write his superior a memo describing how he planned to do a better job. As an incentive to meet the standard, a dollar bonus was calculated by comparing *actual* managerial performance with the standard. To calculate the size of the bonus the person under review was rated by his superior along several dimensions, and a point number was obtained somewhere in the range between 0–15, with 9 being the average. The bonus was then obtained by using the score obtained as a percentage of the base pay (i.e., if the score was 9 then the bonus for the period would be + 9% of the salary).

Because the nature of some tasks made them either harder to evaluate effectively or else because they carried more responsibility, there were two special incentive "clubs" in operation. The first, the "Key Club," was for staff people and members of it were evaluated more informally owing to the difficulty of setting meaningful performance standards. The maximum bonus here was one month's pay or a maximum of an $8\frac{1}{3}\%$ increase on the base pay. The second, the "Fulcrum Club," was set up for individuals like the advertising or data processing manager who could more directly affect the company's profitability. In addition to their evaluation against a performance standard, which held out the possibility of achieving a maximum bonus of 15%, they also participated in a scheme based on return on investment. If the return on investment goal for the year had been set at 10% and the actual achieved was 26%, then members of the "Fulcrum Club" would receive an additional 16% bonus.

Factory positions, on the other hand, were all "job rated." This was done along such dimensions as education required, experience required, complexity of the task, supervision received, and the possibility of errors. People were then hired to suit particular jobs or classes of jobs. In this way the personnel department attempted to match people to the formalized system of job requirements. Factory personnel did not receive a bonus. They were, however, presented with a Christmas turkey every year.

Under the old planning system that was in effect until 1963, the executive committee[6] formulated the objectives once each year for the coming year. These were based upon budget forecasts from the division and upon top management's understanding of business conditions and market opportunity in the period ahead. This overall plan was passed down to the division heads in the form of division objectives. These objectives were then translated

---

[6]See Exhibit 5 for membership.

Exhibit 7

UNIVIS, INC. POLICY, ORGANIZATION AND PROCEDURE BULLETIN TITLE: Assistant Vice President for Corporate Planning	NUMBER: 0-1025 DATE EFFECTIVE 7/12/65 PAGE 1 OF 2

Reporting	The Assistant Vice President for Corporate Planning, reports directly to the President, to assist in development and control of corporate goals, policies, and plans.
General Responsibility	The Assistant Vice President for Corporate Planning, furnishes expertise, coordination, and integration for design of corporate goal attainment activity. He applies management science, executes management research, and performs management consulting relevant to corporate planning. These endeavors will be characterized by a total systems concept resting in identification, description, and manipulation of substantive social, technological and pecuniary parameters.

Duties	In carrying out his general responsibilities, the Assistant Vice President for Corporate Planning, performs the following duties:
	1. Develops objectives, policies, and programs for approval of the President.
	2. Confers in relevant situations in all functions, echelons, and locales, encompassed by the Corporation.
	3. Executes assignments from the President regarding:
	   a) Formulation of corporate goals, policies, and plans.
	   b) Impact simulation of major corporate alternatives.
	   c) Macro- and micro-economic analyses.
	   d) Macro-organization structure and process.
	4. Offers, in a consistent and timely manner:
	   a) Surveillance of the general macro-economic environment.
	   b) Interindustry comparisons.
	   c) Commentary on capital markets.
	5. Administers corporatewide long-range planning activities.

into the "standards of performance" just described for each and every managerial position. Thus the growth and progress of the company and the bonuses paid were directly related to the original objective and goal setting determined by the executive committee. As the company grew, Mr. Barber came to believe that it was becoming important to improve upon the methods of goal setting.

Clearly [he wrote], the company's progress since 1955 was primarily the result of planning. However, much of our planning was intuitive.

Forecasts were not sufficiently sophisticated and our objectives were not formalized the way they should have been. We realized that the employment of capital in the years ahead would assume a new and greater significance and we needed constraints which would help guide future decisions.[7]

[7]Barber, *op. cit.*, p. 29.

Exhibit 7—Continued

<table>
<tr><td colspan="2">UNIVIS, INC.
POLICY, ORGANIZATION AND PROCEDURE BULLETIN</td><td>NUMBER: 0-1025</td></tr>
<tr><td colspan="2" rowspan="2">TITLE: Assistant Vice President for Corporate Planning</td><td>DATE EFFECTIVE
7/12/65</td></tr>
<tr><td>PAGE 2 OF 2</td></tr>
<tr><td></td><td colspan="2">6. Participates in relations with the Financial Community in general, and specifically is responsible for:
   a) Development, interpretation, and communication of underlying technical analyses.
   b) Liaison, with relevant personnel internal to and external to the Corporation, in which comprehensive knowledge of the aforementioned is desirable.
7. For the above purposes, serves in the collateral capacities of:
   a) Member, Corporatewide Planning Committee
   b) Member, Management Committee</td></tr>
<tr><td>Scope and Limits of Authority</td><td colspan="2">The Assistant Vice President for Corporate Planning, has authority derived from the President. He plans, organizes, directs, and controls the activities of his office. He is limited in the exercise of this authority in the following ways:
1. Current established company objectives, policies, and procedures.
2. Changes in objectives, policies, or procedures must be approved by the President.
3. All expenditures are limited by approved budgets. Expenditures for any amount in excess of $150 must be approved by the President.
4. Employment, promotion, transfer, and release of department personnel are limited by approved organization plans.
5. Compensation of personnel is limited by pay policy with any exception therefrom to be approved by the Executive Committee.</td></tr>
<tr><td>Supervisory Relationship</td><td colspan="2">The Assistant Vice President for Corporate Planning directly supervises the activities of the following positions:
1. Corporate Planning Analyst (General)
2. Corporate Planning Analyst (Marketing)
3. Research Assistant</td></tr>
</table>

The decision was made in September 1963 to institute a corporate planning department.

Corporate planning

The corporate planning department was located in the organization structure so that it reported directly to the president (see Exhibits 5 and 7). All the material, in the form of reports and requests, that was produced by the planning department was either specifically addressed to or approved by the president. The company felt that this support by the president was the key to the successful functioning of the department. Mr. Barber appointed Donald B. Cotton to the position of director of corporate planning in 1963.

Gradually [he said], Cotton's professional skills and top management back-

ing (he reported directly to me) won him the confidence of our top management team and the cooperation of divisions.[8]

The Purpose of Planning[9]

The primary purpose of corporatewide planning is to increase the probability
that corporatewide objectives will be attained. Toward this end, plans for future
deployment of corporate resources are appraised to assure their compatability
with the basic corporate objectives.[10]

This view of corporatewide planning was restated in the more fundamental
terminology of the organization as follows:

We view *planning* as a prescriptive process, intended to guide decision making in the deployment of organization resources, through continuing surveillance
and adjustment of goal attainment behavior.

In their full capacity, these endeavors are characterized by a total systems
concept resting in identification, description, and manipulation of substantive
behavioral, technological, and pecuniary parameters.

In our opinion, the paramount phase in the planning process is in the reduction of preferences, insofar as useful, into a clear, precise, and formal goal
statement, with due regard to priority order and consistency in the arrangement of
its multiple facets.[11]

As can be seen from the diagram on page 165, planning was aimed at determining the "gap" that existed between the company's objectives and the
expected performance over the period of the planning cycle. The expected
performance could come from two sources: (1) the existing business in which
the firm was engaged after making due allowance for "normal" growth (the
passive projection)[12] or from planned expansion in this business, or (2) from
planned diversification into other industries. If the plan showed that a gap
existed between the objectives and the expected performance, the theory was
that management could then either change the objectives or improve the
performance so as to close the gap.

Conceptual Background of the Plan

A particular organization is delineated from the general social system by its
participants' (1) interrelations and (2) *goal orientation*.

The integration of human behavior can be viewed as a process which occurs
in three decisional depths: (1) *substantive* planning prescribes the values and
boundaries for subsidiary decisions, (2) *procedural* planning establishes mech-

---

[8]Barber, *op. cit.*, p. 30.

[9]The remainder of this section on "Corporate Planning" is drawn from material
generated by Mr. Cotton as he set up Univis' planning function. Only specific quotations
from this material will be fully referenced.

[10]*Corporatewide Planning Guide*, November 1, 1965, Section 1, p. 1.

[11]Donald B. Cotton, *Our Management Philosophy, Report 1*, August 20, 1964, p. 1.

[12]A passive projection is an estimate of future business generated from the normal
growth of existing product lines. It does *not* include the possibility of expanding into other
product categories or markets.

UNIVIS, INC.
Comprehensive Planning System

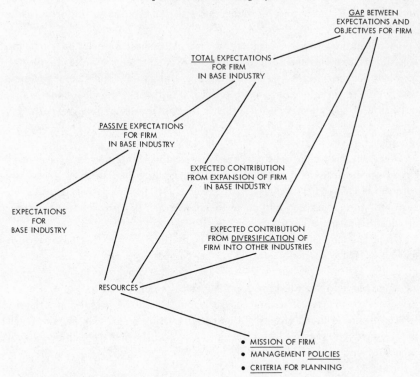

Source: D. ·B. Cotton.

anisms which channel subordinate activities into conformance, (3) *routine* endeavors are executed within the framework structured by the procedural plan.

In consonance, the goal structure of the organization can be visualized as a pyramid wherein three horizontal hierarchical layers, from the top down, are (1) *substantive goals*, (2) *procedural goals*, and (3) *routine goals*.

Substantive goals are *fundamental*, procedural goals are *strategic*, and routine goals are *tactical*. In that order value content diminishes and fact content, especially as regards immediate environment and resources, increases.[13]

In *Organization Study, Report 3*, it was amplified that the behavior of large U.S. corporations suggests derivation from the institutional assumptions of private enterprise ideology, capitalistic economics, and bureaucratic administration, and that these have their common focus in *rational economic productivity of capital*. On this basis, it was submitted that, therefore, substantive goal parameters would be amount, risk, time, and yield of capital employed. Further, acceptable bounds would be specified through circumscription of activity scope and depth.[14]

---

[13]Donald B. Cotton, *Organization Study, Report 3*, p. 1.
[14]Donald B. Cotton, *Our Capital Markets Viewpoint*, August 20, 1964, p. 2.

In addition to this report regarding basic substantive goal parameters, other reports defined the company's concept of risk, time, capital employed and yields. Of these four perhaps the risk concept most requires further clarification here.

To obtain some measure of useful risk categories, Mr. Cotton performed a series of experiments with the executive committee in order to gain an idea of what they meant by risk. He used several gaming and chance analogies with which to classify their concept of risk into three categories: conservative, normal, and speculative. See Exhibit 8 for the results of these experiments. This table was used by the executive committee to help appraise the risk inherent in new ventures.

Given the risk category of a new project the committee then assigned a "yield on assets employed" figure that the venture had to meet (see "Corporatewide Goals" below for yield requirements). Knowing the yield that was required, the committee had to evaluate whether the project would in fact provide this yield on the assets employed.

Using the substantive goal parameters outlined above, this basic requirement was more formally stated in the company's organization study as: given the assets employed (active and/or passive), achieve the yield on the assets employed over the time span for assets employment and at the appropriate risk category all within the scope and depth of prescribed behavior. It was proposed that "properly aligned supporting statements should [then] be assigned component organization units"[15] in order to achieve overall corporatewide goals.

Corporatewide goals

From the fundamental corporatewide objective of maximizing owners' common share price through the medium of growth company behavior, management had derived a set of quantitative goals. These goals were expressed in terms of four variables related to the assets employed: (1) amount, (2) risk, (3) yield, and (4) time span. Specifically these corporatewide goals had been tentatively formulated as follows:

1. Expected yield on assets employed will be at least 20% at the standard risk mix, wherein
   a) Expected yield on conservatively employed assets will be at least 17%,
   b) Expected yield on normally employed assets will be at least 21%,
   c) Expected yield on speculatively employed assets will be at least 25%.
2. Earning per share will increase at an average annual compounded rate of at least 7%.[16]

By late 1966 these quantitative goals had undergone minor clarification to include the word *pretax* after each of the yield percentages, and to change the wording of part 2 to read:

---

[15]Donald B. Cotton, *Organization Study, Report 3*, p. 3.
[16]*Univis Five-Year Plan*, second estimation, October 1, 1965, p. 6.

Exhibit 8

UNIVIS, INC.

Our Standards for Risk Classification

The purpose of this typology is to prescribe broad magnitude categories wherein risk judgments on projects throughout the organization would be cast into more consistent and precise channels so as to facilitate the systemwide comparison of alternatives in the deployment of organization resources.

If risk is considered, as herein, through the parallel aspects of *probability of success* and *confidence in data*, then one of these may cause rejection of a decision alternative when its characteristics in these respects are deemed beyond the tolerances implied by preset value preferences for risk.

CLASS		CONSERVATIVE	NORMAL	SPECULATIVE
	probability requisites	More than 85 but less than 100 chances of success in 100.	More than 70 but less than 85 chances of success in 100.	More than 50 but less than 70 chances of success in 100.
	confidence requisites			
infor-mation		Quite confident of all estimates, due comprehensive experience in same circumstances.	Fairly confident of most estimates, based upon reasonably complete knowledge.	Little confidence in estimates, because of fragmentary knowledge.
		Satisfactorily reliable and complete. Routinely available and processed in standard manner.	With some reservations, adequately reliable and complete. Requires some nonroutine selectivity, integration, and synthesis.	Questionably reliable and incomplete. Data preponderantly unavailable and/or unprocessed.
tech-niques		Existing techniques satisfactory.	Some nonroutine analysis and/or modification of existing techniques.	Present techniques untried in new circumstances and/or new techniques.
con-straints		Acceptance of nondiscretionary constraints, with no contest.	Questioning recognition of non-discretionary constraints, with some peripheral maneuvering.	Recognition of nondiscretionary constraints, with active confrontation.

The rationale underlying differentiation of confidence requisites is that confidence decreases as innovation relative to in-company routine increases. While it is recognized that this is not necessarily so, the probability is deemed sufficient to warrant this hypothesis in most cases.

Source: D. B. Cotton, *Our Concept of Risk*, July 21, 1964.

2. Earnings per share will increase at a rate, on the average over a significant period of time, substantially greater than that characterizing the broad stock market averages.[17]

Progress to date. The first step toward relating the planning concepts and objectives with actual performance projections was accomplished on March 18, 1966 with the completion of the "Univis Passive Projections, 1966–70." The "passive projections" were simply estimates of business activity resulting from an extension of the existing operations through the ensuing five-year period.

The projections were based on the assumptions of normal market growth without diversification into other lines and industries. These passive projections were in the process of being replaced by the first five-year plan covering the period 1967–1971.

The purpose of the Univis Five-Year Plan, 1967–71, is to present estimates of the *most probable* expected Univis performance during the period, with respect to Univis management objectives and parameters, subject to the assumptions and constraints specified subsequently in this text.

Acknowledging the compromises induced in this corporatewide planning effort by resource limitations, personnel availabilities, and schedule deadlines, it is intended that:

The Univis Five-Year Plan, 1967–71, is a *working document* for operations during that period.[18]

This "first" plan was different from the passive projections in that it allowed the division managers to exploit the opportunities in the environment as they saw fit, subject of course to certain specified constraints and later management approval. The corporate planning department supplied information regarding economic trends and the basic guidelines upon which the plan was to be built.

Each division was required to produce an *operations* plan for its own activities during the period while marketing and distribution, in particular, were to produce *function* plans (prior to the development of operation plans) as a guide in the construction of these operation plans. Exhibit 9 shows the planning cycle in more detail. It will be seen there how the industry assumptions preceded the marketing and distribution division's function plans which in turn preceded the division's operation plans.

Analysis and discussion of the gap between expected performance and corporate objectives by the executive committee was scheduled for early February while the final presentation of the plan was to be held on March 13, 1967.

Executive comment and reaction. Although the actual cost involved in instituting the planning function was not known, estimates of the figure

---

[17]Donald B. Cotton, *Standards for Expected Performance Illustration*, September 1, 1966.

[18]*Univis Five-Year Plan, 1967-1971, Context, Requirements and Schedule*, Corporate Planning Department, August 18, 1966, p. 3.

Exhibit 9

UNIVIS, INC.

Corporatewide Planning Cycle Plan

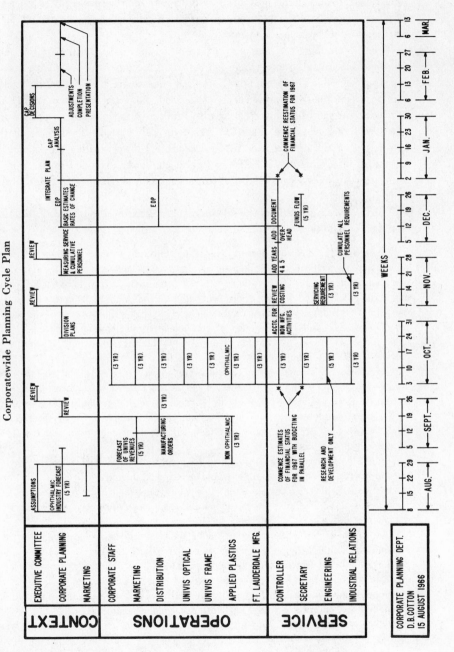

suggested that it was somewhere in the range of $75,000–$100,000 a year. This range included the cost of the additional man-hours required in each division to generate the planning information which was estimated at 300–600 man-hours a year per division.

Reaction amongst the management group to the formalization of company planning was mixed. Some people felt the planning department's requirements had been introduced too quickly. Some felt that as yet no worthwhile results had been obtained. Almost everybody agreed, however, that the setting up of a five-year plan had forced people to think and to question aspects of the status quo that had been taken for granted. Although the final form of the five-year plan had not yet been set (see Exhibit 9 for schedule), the managers seemed to take pleasure in the freedom and challenge provided by the opportunity to plan five years ahead and to thus take an active role in determining their *own* future.

The following quotations are all comments regarding the planning function by different members of the top management group.

EXECUTIVE 1: The plan forced people to think, to estimate things for themselves, and to participate for themselves. It gives a goal and a sense of accomplishment. In fact it's funny how it makes the men in my department think more about life, what it's all about and where they're going from here. I guess they'd never thought of those things before. In a roundabout way you could say that it gives a fellow a sense of confidence in the company, also he tends to be an expert in his own field. Strangely enough they all fought it originally, now they love planning.

EXECUTIVE 2: Formal planning puts you in a frame of thinking that unconsciously makes you think further ahead and puts you in a position to question things. We've been operating for 46 years and we did O.K. However, this really increased thought. On your question of the plan causing some rigidity, this is always a problem, but its effect will depend upon top management's administration of the plan.

It could've been sold a little more carefully in the initial stages probably through better communication. I would've tried to avoid a directive type approach myself, but I'm not sure that this would've been any more effective.

EXECUTIVE 3: The plan lacks personality. It doesn't portray the feelings of the people and what they achieve.

EXECUTIVE 4: The first reaction was "We're bringing the brains trust in." No one discounted the activity. I'm not sure what they're doing but if Bob Barber thinks it's worth doing then it must be worth doing.

EXECUTIVE 5: It helped personnel expand horizons. It made us list our assumptions and constraints. Forced us to realize areas of responsibility. Really sharpened up on forecasting. Excellent management training.

EXECUTIVE 6: It hasn't provided us yet with too much more than we were getting previously with the 12 months' forecast, even though it now projects out into the future. There is a lack of sophistication down the line and, because of the difficult terminology, they can't understand what's going on. In any event I'm not yet convinced that the form of corporate planning we have is necessarily the best. I'm not negative on planning but some people feel that less sophistication would have achieved the same results.

EXECUTIVE 7: There are several benefits that the introduction of planning has brought us. It has helped educate division management by broadening their horizons and clarifying what is happening. It has pointed out areas that need improvement to maintain our past growth and it has emphasized the need to think logically. On the other hand, however, it is very time-consuming although not all the time is extra. I feel it has really just formalized what we were doing before, but I definitely hope that the plan will initiate new policies.

The president, Mr. Barber, summed up his feelings when he said:

I think the introduction of corporate planning is a very good investment. However, we have always planned to one degree or another. I guess I just really believe in it.

The company and its environment:
relating opportunity and resources

Determination of a suitable strategy for a company begins in identifying the opportunities and risks in its environment. This text is concerned with the identification of a range of strategic alternatives, the narrowing of this range by recognizing the constraints imposed by corporate capability, and the determination of one or more economic strategies at acceptable levels of risk. We shall examine the complexity and variety of the environmental forces which must be considered and the problems in accurately assessing company strengths and weaknesses. Economic strategy will be viewed as the match between qualification and opportunity which relates a firm to its environment. We shall attempt in passing to categorize the kinds of economic strategies that result from the combination of internal capability and external market needs, and to relate these categories to the normal course of corporate development.

The nature of the company's environment

The environment of a company in business, like that of any other organic entity, is the pattern of all the external conditions and influences that affect its life and development. The environmental influences relevant to strategic decision operate in industry, business community, city, country, and world. They are technological, economic, social, and political in kind. Technological developments are, of course, among the most far-reaching and fastest un-
√ folding. They include the discoveries of science, the impact of related product development, and the progress of automation. We see in technical progress a continually accelerating rate of change—with new developments piling up before the implications of yesterday's changes can be assimilated. Industries hitherto protected from obsolescence by stable technologis or by the need for huge capital investment become vulnerable to new processes or to cross-industry competition. Science gives the impetus to change not only in technology but also in all the other aspects of business activity.

Economic influences include the extension of the Industrial Revolution to the underdeveloped countries of the world, which has in turn created a vast expansion of demand and an unprecedented upward surge in standards of living. Other major economic trends that affect a company's potential markets are the internationalization of competition, the increased importance of the large corporation, and new interrelationships between private and public sectors of the economy and between privately owned and state-owned enterprises. Social developments include such influential forces as the increasingly insistent quest for equality by minority groups, the changing patterns of work and leisure, the Americanization of taste and culture throughout the world, the urbanization of fully industrialized countries, and the changing composition of an increasing world population. Political forces important to the business firm include the relation between communist and noncommunist countries, the regulation of business by government, the impact of changing legislation and administrative law, the attitude of courts, and the impact of national planning on private corporate planning.

Because so much of what is changing in the world affects the markets for a company's present products, the prospects for future products, and the success of product and market choices, it is, of course, impossible for us to describe or even to know for all business the relevant characteristics of today's world, to say nothing of tomorrow's. We know that a firm—itself a system —is bound in a variety of interrelationships to other larger systems that comprise its economic, technological, social, and political environment. We may conclude that the changes taking place in these larger systems bode both good and ill for the firm. Change threatens all established strategies and requires the businessman to be alert to the possibility that the opportunity he has seized will expire. At the same time, change brings new opportunity for the application of developed expertness and new market needs which entrepreneurial energy may seek to satisfy. No matter how secure a company's position, obsolescence of strategy is a continuous threat. At the same time, new opportunities are emerging everywhere as relative affluence puts unprecedented discretionary income into the hands of consumers in developing countries, and as rising income introduces underdeveloped countries to material conveniences.

If environmental developments are destroying and creating business opportunities, advance notice of this fact in specific instances is essential to intelligent planning. Fortunately, the fundamental characteristics of any industry can be determined and the requirements of success can be identified and their implications noted, so that responsive action can be taken. The behavior of competitors, for example, is impossible to conceal completely. It can be appraised for the influence it will have and for the assumptions about the future by which it seems to be determined. The identification of new opportunity or of impending threat therefore depends upon knowing what kind of information is relevant. Surveillance of developments becomes more practicable once the critical elements to look for have been determined.

Identification of opportunities and risks

It follows then, despite the staggering difficulty of foreseeing what is to come or even of recognizing what is already at work in the total environment of business, that some means must be found for organizing systematic intelligence about the changing nature of those forces that most vitally affect a given industry and company. For the man who cannot know everything and whose firm may never reach the size of the global giants, a few simple questions kept constantly in mind will serve to highlight changing opportunity and risk. For the student of cases, who is conveniently presented with the most important information needing interpretation, these questions will lead in short order to an estimate of opportunities and dangers in the present and predictable company setting.

1. *What are the essential economic and technical characteristics of the industry in which the company participates?*

Whether these are in flux or not, they may define the restrictions and opportunities confronting the individual company, and will certainly suggest strategy for it. For example, knowledge that the cement industry requires high investment in plant, proximity to a certain combination of raw materials, a relatively small labor force, and enormous fuel and transportation costs, suggests where to look for new plant sites and what will constitute competitive advantage and disadvantage. The nature of this product may suggest for a given company the wisdom of developing efficient pipeline and truck transportation and cheap energy sources rather than engaging in extensive research to achieve product differentiation or aggressive price competition to increase market share.

2. *What trends suggesting future change in economic and technical characteristics are apparent?*

Changes in demand for the product of one industry in competition with the products of another, and changes in the product itself, occurring as a result of research and development, affect the chance for growth. For example, the glass container industry's development of strong, light, disposable bottles recouped part of the market lost by glass to the metal container. The need for the glass industry to engage in this development effort was made apparent by the observable success of the metal beer can. Similarly the easy-opening metal container suggested the need for an easily removable bottle cap. The physical characteristics of any product can be examined against the master trend toward simplicity, convenience, and serviceability in consumer goods and against competitive innovations.

3. *What is the nature of competition both within the industry and across industries?*

A small rubber company in an industry led by U.S. Rubber, Goodyear, Goodrich, and Firestone, will not, under the economic condition of overcapacity, elect to provide the automobile business with original tires for new cars. The structure of competition, quite apart from the resources of the firm, may suggest that a relatively small firm should seek out a niche of relatively small attraction to the majors, and concentrate its powers on that limited segment of the market.

Present and developing competition usually extends, of course, beyond the industry in which a company finds itself. For example, the competition for the cement industry from producers of asphalt road-building materials is as important as that from other cement producers.

4. *What are the requirements for success in competition in the company's industry?*

In every industry some critical tasks must be performed particularly well to insure survival. In the ladies' belt and handbag business style and design are critical, but so (less obviously) are relationships with department store buyers. In the computer business, a sales force able to diagnose customer requirements for information systems, to design a suitable system, and to equip a customer to use it, is more important than the circuitry of the hardware.

Although the question of what tasks are most critical may be chiefly useful as a means of identifying risks or possible causes of failure, it may also suggest opportunity. Imagination in perceiving new requirements for success under changing conditions, when production-oriented competitors have not done so, can give a company a leadership position. For example, opportunity for a local radio station and the strategy it needed to follow changed sharply with the rise of television, and those who first diagnosed the new requirements paid much less for stations than is now necessary.

5. *Given the technical, economic, social, and political developments that most directly apply, what is the range of strategy available to any company in this industry?*

The force of this question will become obvious when we look at the drug industry. The speed and direction of pharmaceutical research, the structure of the industry, the characteristics of worldwide demand, the different and changing ideas about how adequate medical care should be made available to the world's population, the concern about price, and the nature of government regulation suggest some constraints within which a range of opportunity is still vividly clear. Similarly, in a more stable industry, there is always a choice. To determine its limits, an examination of environmental characteristics and developments is essential.

Opportunity as a determinant of strategy

Awareness of the environment is necessarily a continuing requirement for informed choice of purposes, not a special project to be undertaken only when warning of change becomes deafening. Planned exploitation of changing opportunity ordinarily follows an orderly course which both permits and provides increasing awareness of areas to which a company's capabilities may be profitably extended. For a typical company, which is governed by the determination that after a dividend adequate to maintain stockholder confidence profits will be reinvested, the search for opportunity appears to take a variety of forms. First, within its domestic market, a company will try to increase its volume, to expand the market, and to increase its market share. This step does not require a changed strategy but a more intensive implementation. Policies regarding quality, service, price, promotion, and sales management will be shaped in detail to reflect extensive knowledge of a relatively specialized area of business. In response to detailed awareness of market need, the product will appear in a variety of forms and will proliferate into a family of related items, like a full range of small motors or a series of breakfast foods. The opportunity for growth stems from increase of demand, and competitive success is measured by increased market share.

If the original strategy proves workable in its original sphere, the growing company will typically move next into new geographical areas, either within a large domestic market like the United States or overseas. The product-market combinations remain the same. Macroeconomic and political developments have opened the world to companies not confined by law to their domestic markets. The American firm no longer limits its search for opportunity to the continental United States. The growth of free trade, the relative stability of East-West relations, the appearance of the management contract as an opportunity for free enterprise in socialist economies, and the development abroad of consumer purchasing power means a marked geographical expansion of opportunity. The consequence is that the strategist's interests and information must henceforth be global in extent. Geographical expansion of the sphere of the original strategy thus introduces the problem of systematizing intelligence to which we have already alluded.

A growing company that has successfully extended its activities to wider geographic areas is thereafter likely to enlarge its operations and the scope of its strategy by reaching forward toward the ultimate consumer or backward to the sources of supply. Vertical integration is logically the next step, since the firm's knowledge of its environment will naturally focus its attention on opportunities in those areas that are most closely related to original activities. Furthermore, geographical expansion may well involve acquisitions and mergers of firms that are integrated in varying degrees. The growth of the oil industry is a classic example of both geographical expansion and vertical integration.

Once a company has successfully come to terms with its original milieu, has expanded its market geographically, and has extended the range of the related functions it performs in its markets, then it is likely to seek still further growth by diversifying its product line horizontally. Product diversification of this type imposes the most severe requirements, since it calls for knowledge of present situations and future possibilities in industries where the company has no prior experience to guide it.

Theoretically, then, the course of growth finally spans the full range of business activity for any firm not limited by special legislation. The identification of opportunity in the context of risk is simplest in the instance of the manufacturer of a single product sold within a clearly defined geographical area to meet a known demand. As geographical coverage is extended, or more stages are added in the making of a product, or the product becomes a line of related products via vertical integration, more attention to a more complex pattern of environmental forces is required. For example, the proprietor of a small engineering company specializing in electromechanical devices—unless he wishes to grow greatly—need not concern himself with anything besides meeting the demand for his highly specialized products and making sure that, whatever happens, enough demand remains to sustain his company. He need spend on the state of the world less time than the few minutes he devotes every hour to overseeing his entire production operation. The president of General Electric, on the other hand, would be hard put to it to identify any significant political, social, economic, or technological development in the world that did not have some influence on the future strategic opportunity of his company.

The multiplication of strategic alternatives which accompanies the progress of a single enterprise along the course just sketched presents, finally, problems which escape solution. The more one finds out what might be done, the harder it is to make the final choice. The demonstrated existence of an opportunity is not an adequate basis for the decision to seek it out. Before we pass to the other factors that must be considered, two consequences of the development pattern we have described should be clearly defined. They will be of great importance for a growing company in pondering its proper decision.

First, the sheer number of alternatives which will be disclosed by a well-directed scrutiny of world markets constitutes an embarrassment of riches. Some large firms, slow to make the decision to become multinational, seem now to have Klondike fever on a global scale. Those who refuse to go everywhere at once do not find choice easy. For example, the McGraw-Hill Book Company has the good fortune to have an economic opportunity of enormous proportions for its future expansion. Its distinctive strategy of furnishing technical and scientific information to particular groups previously identified as having a special need for these data is obviously applicable to all countries of the world where education is transforming the life of the people and technical progress is nurturing a growing need for more information. The problem for McGraw-Hill is not where opportunity exists for expansion overseas—it is everywhere—but which opportunity to pursue first. This choice begins in the determination of potential return, and though it does not end there, the ranking of alternatives in order of their economic significance is probably the first step.

The objective assessment of opportunity is difficult because of the unreliability of statistical information in developing countries and the hazards of predicting the political, social, and technical developments in a given area. But with the assignment of sufficient analytical brainpower to the task, a degree of order can be imposed upon the range of alternatives available. The investment in this activity is preferable to opening up operations in all countries at once on the grounds that some will succeed, or to acquiring any business that foreign nationals decide to sell to Americans at what their local competitors consider an outrageous price.

The diversified company has another problem different from that of trying to make the best choice among many. If it has divisionalized its operations and strategies, as sooner or later in the course of diversification it must, then divisional opportunities come into competition with each other.

The corporate management will wish to invest profits not distributed to stockholders in those opportunities that will produce the greatest return to the corporation, and, if need be, management will be willing to let an individual division decline if its future looks less attractive than that of others. √The division will wish to protect its own market position, ward off adverse developments, prolong its own existence, and provide for its own growth. The division manager, who is not rewarded for failures, will program projects of safe but usually not dramatic prospects. The claims regarding projected return on investment, which are submitted in all honesty as the divisional estimate of future opportunity, can be assumed to be biased by the division's regard for its own interest and the manager's awareness of measurement.

The corporate management cannot be expected to be able to make independent judgments about all the proposals for growth which are submitted by all the divisions. On the other hand, all divisions cannot be given their heads, if the corporation's needs for present profit are to be met and if funds for reinvestment are limited. In a decentralized organization, it is inappropriate to centralize planning. In any case, the greatest knowledge about the opportunities for a given technology and set of markets should be found at the divisional level.[1]

The strategic dilemma of a conglomerate world enterprise is one that may not have a satisfactory solution. When the range of what must be known exceeds the capacity—as these days it soon does—of a single mind, and when the range of a company's activities spans many industries and technologies, the problems of formulating a coherent strategy get out of hand. If the identification of opportunity results in its being pursued without regard for any consideration other than return on investment, then total performance is apt, in the long run, to become at best mediocre.

We have said that the identification of opportunities and risks in the environment of a company committed to growth will lead it to increase its volume in a given market, to develop products related to its original product, to expand geographically, to integrate vertically, and ultimately to diversify its product line. From the point of view of maintaining control of strategy, the critical step is diversification away from the company's original business. Guided by a strategic concept of the nature of the enterprise and the unity of its businesses, a company may successfully enter fields that appear to be different but are fundamentally related. Guided only by the entrepreneurial estimate of attractive return on investment or by the opportunistic impulse to embark on a new venture, the large diversified enterprise may find itself unable to compete effectively with more specialized firms which are better able to know what they should do. Though it may be equal to capitalizing

[1]See Norman Berg: "Strategic Planning in Conglomerate Companies," *Harvard Business Review*, May-June 1965.

on the present opportunity, it may not be able to solve the problem of resource allocation posed by future requirements.

To decide which is the best among several opportunities identified by informed examination is a task that requires more than economic analysis. If the difficulties inherent in following through on new undertakings in a swiftly changing world are to remain manageable, then some criterion for choice besides the opportunity for profit must be observed. Economic opportunity abounds, but not the ability to capture it. For example, a company jaded by shrinking margins may be tempted by the fortunes to be made in land development in Australia. But the fact that there is much money to be made in a new field or in a strong growth industry does not mean that a company with abilities developed in an unrelated field is going to make it. We must turn now to the critical factors which for an individual company make one good opportunity better than another.

Determining corporate competence and resources

The first step in validating a tentative choice among several opportunities✓ is to determine whether the organization has the capacity to prosecute it successfully. The capability of an organization is its demonstrated and potential ability to accomplish, against the opposition of circumstance or competition, whatever its sets out to do. Every organization has actual and potential strengths and weaknesses. Since it is prudent in formulating strategy to extend or maximize the one and contain or minimize the other, it is important to try to determine what they are and to distinguish one from the other.

The strengths of a company which constitute a resource for growth and diversification accrue primarily through experience in making and marketing a product line. They inhere as well in (1) the developing strengths and weaknesses of the individuals comprising the organization, (2) the degree to which individual capability is effectively applied to the common task, and (3) the quality of coordination of individual and group effort.

The experience gained through successful execution of a strategy centered upon one goal may unexpectedly develop capabilities which could be applied to different ends. Whether they should be so applied is another question. For example, a manufacturer of salt can strengthen his competitive position by offering his customers salt-dispensing equipment. If, in the course of making engineering improvements in this equipment, a new solenoid principle is perfected that has application to many industrial switching problems, should this patentable and marketable innovation be exploited? The answer would turn not only on whether economic analysis of the opportunity shows this to be a durable and profitable possibility, but also on whether the organization can muster the financial, manufacturing, and marketing strength to exploit the discovery. The former question is likely to have a more positive answer than the latter. In this connection, it seems important to remember that individual and unsupported flashes of strength are not as dependable as the gradually accumulated product- and market-related fruits of experience.

Even where competence to exploit an opportunity is nurtured by experience in related fields, the level of that competence may be too low for any great reliance to be placed upon it. Thus a chain of children's clothing stores might well acquire the administrative, merchandising, buying, and selling skills that would permit it to add departments in womens' wear. Similarly, a sales force effective in distributing typewriters may gain proficiency in selling office machinery and supplies. But even here it would be well to ask what distinctive ability these companies could bring to the retailing of soft goods or office equipment to attract customers away from competitors.

The "distinctive competence"[2] of an organization is more than what it can do; it is what it can do particularly well. Thus a hapless manufacturer of chocolate candy who finally lost his chain of candy stores was not really a surpassingly efficient retailer of candy. He just thought he was. His real skill lay in production, in his ability to design special machinery to permit quality production at low cost. The proper application of his real strengths would probably have confined him to manufacturing for wholesalers and supermarket chains.

To identify the less obvious or by-product strengths of an organization, which may well be transferable to some more profitable new opportunity, one might well begin by examining the organization's current product line and by defining the functions its serves in its markets. Almost any important consumer product has functions which are related to others into which a qualified company might move. The typewriter, for example, is more than the simple machine for mechanizing handwriting that it appears to be when looked at only from the point of view of its designer and manufacturer. If closely analyzed from the point of view of the potential user, the typewriter will be found to contribute to a broad range of information processing functions. Any one of these might suggest an area to be exploited by a typewriter manufacturer. Thus the definition of product that would lead to identification of transferable skills must obviously be expressed in terms of the market needs it may fill rather than the engineering specifications to which it conforms.

Besides looking at the uses or functions to which his present product line contributes, the would-be diversifier might profitably identify the skills that underlie whatever success he has achieved. A watch manufacturer, for example, must have design and engineering skills, and he could apply these to other small precision products. It might be more likely, however, that success in this competitive industry turns less on design and engineering (obvious requirements, whose incidence is widespread) than on special skills in international marketing (a more subtle need, and a capability that seems relatively rare in the watch industry). Perhaps, then, merchandising skill could provide a basis for diversification by a successful manufacturer

---

[2]This phrase is used by Philip Selznick, *Leadership in Administration* (Evanston Ill.: Row, Peterson & Co., 1957), p. 42.

of watches. If so, it is again something quite different from the physical characteristics of a product that provides the clue a company should follow in seeking new areas for growth.

The insight required to perceive in the humdrum qualifications of an organization efficient at performing its long-accustomed tasks the essential strength to justify new ventures does not come naturally. Its cultivation can probably be helped by recognition of the need for analysis. In any case, we should look beyond the company's capacity to invent new products. Product leadership is not possible for a majority of companies, so it is fortunate that patentable new products are not the only major highway to new opportunities. Other avenues include new marketing services, new methods of distribution, new values in quality-price combinations, and creative merchandising. The effort to find or to create a competence that is truly distinctive may hold the real key to a company's success or even to its future development. For example, the ability of our cement manufacturer (to spare our candy manufacturer this time) to run a truck fleet more effectively than his competitors may constitute one of his principal competitive strengths in selling an undifferentiated product. Similarly, the ability of Crown Cork and Seal to provide prompt delivery on specialty containers sets this company apart from its larger competitors whose forte is to provide standard cans at lower prices. Unless Crown's skill in giving fast service on nonstandard items proves limited to specialty containers, it might be extended to other products and activities—for instance to fast service on equipment breakdowns. But even if the company never leaves the container industry, there are many additional markets overseas in which it can employ its inconspicuous but highly valuable abilities.

The way, then, to narrow the range of alternatives is to match opportunity to competence, once each has been accurately identified and its future significance estimated. It is this combination which establishes a company's economic mission and its relationship to its environment. The match is designed to minimize organizational weakness and to maximize strength. In any case, risk attends it. And when opportunity seems to outrun present distinctive competence, the willingness to gamble that the latter can be built up to the required level is almost indispensable to a strategy that challenges the organization and the people in it.

Before we leave the creative act of putting together a company's unique internal capability and evolving opportunity in the external world, we should note that—aside from distinctive competence—the principal resources found in any company are money and people—technical and managerial people. At this stage of economic development, money seems less a problem than technical competence, and the latter much less critical than managerial ability. In reading the cases that follow, by all means look carefully at the financial records of each company and take note of its success and its problems. Look also at the apparent managerial capacity and, without underestimating it, do not assume that it can rise to any occasion. The recent vigorous diversification of American industry is marked by hundreds of instances in which a company strong in one endeavor lacked the ability to manage an enterprise requiring different skills. The right to make handsome profits over a long time period must be earned. Opportunism without competence is a garden path. Where it leads cannot be predicted, but in any case it is beyond the confines of a sober essay in praise of predetermined purpose.

Besides equating an appraisal of market opportunity and organizational capability, the decision to make and market a particular product or service should be accompanied by an identification of the nature of the business and the kind of company management desires. Such a guiding concept is a product of many considerations, including the management's personal values. As such, this concept will change more slowly than other aspects of the organization, and it will give coherence to all the various company activities. For example, a president who is determined to make his firm into a worldwide producer and fabricator of a basic metal, through policies differentiating it from the industry leader, will not be distracted by excess capacity in developed markets, low metal prices, and cutthroat competition in certain markets. Such a firm should not be sidetracked into acquiring, for example, the Pepsi Cola franchise in Africa, even if this business promised to yield a good profit. (That such a firm should have an experimental division exploring offshoot technology is, however, entirely appropriate.)

In each company, the way in which distinctive competence, organizational resources, and organizational values are combined is unique. Differences among companies are as numerous as differences among individuals. The combinations of opportunity to which distinctive competencies, resources, and values may be applied are equally extensive. Generalizing about how to make an effective match is less rewarding than working at it. The effort is a highly stimulating and challenging exercise. The outcome will be unique for each case and each situation, but each achievement of a viable economic strategy will leave the student of strategy better prepared to take part in real-life strategic decisions.

Application to cases

The student could profitably bring to the cases he studies not only the questions suggested earlier, but the following as well:

What really is our product? What functions does it serve? To what additional functions might it be extended or adapted?

What is happening to the market for our products? Is it expanding or contracting? Why?

What are our company's major strengths and weaknesses? From what source do these arise?

What is our strategy? Is the combination of product and market an optimum economic strategy? Is the central nature of our business clear enough to provide us with a criterion for product diversification?

What, if any, better combinations of market opportunities and distinctive competence can our company effect, within a range of reasonable risk?

These questions will prove helpful throughout the course in the task of designing an economic strategy. However, they are never wholly sufficient, for the strategic decision is never wholly economic in character.

A NOTE ON THE FARM EQUIPMENT
INDUSTRY (REVISED)*

Almost from the beginning of recorded history, man has farmed the land to produce food. Many historians consider the change from nomadic societies, in which man hunted game and gathered various forms of plant life, to pastoral societies, in which he raised animals and cultivated the soil, as one of the key events in man's history. Agriculture continued to be the base of most societies until the industrial revolution. With the coming of industry, farming declined in importance in the nations of Northern Europe and North America. Nevertheless, farming still occupied a key role in the economies of these nations even in 1965. According to Mr. William A. Hewitt, chairman of Deere & Company, the world's largest manufacturer of farm equipment:

United States agriculture employs about six million people—seven times as many as the steel industry—and has total assets of $250 billion—more than ten times the assets of the steel industry. In fact, the investment in agriculture is about three-fourths of the total investment in all manufacturing industries combined. By many measures, agriculture is the world's largest industry.[1]

In the 1960's, various forces and trends were developing that promised to influence significantly both world agriculture and the industries that served its needs. *Forbes* described some of these forces and their implications as follows:

One billion people, a third of the world's population, drag themselves through the day weak from hunger, an easy target for disease and frequently for death from starvation. Another billion are badly malnourished, almost on the borderline of starvation. What we call progress, civilization, prosperity is meaningless to two-thirds of the human race. These people are only half alive. They are half dead from hunger.

While the United States, Western Europe, Japan and a few other nations get richer, the hungry get hungrier, because, in the underdeveloped part of the world, human fecundity is outstripping agricultural fecundity. In Asia and Latin America in the past five years, the population has risen by 12% and 17%, respectively. In contrast, production of food has risen by only 10%. The result

---

*Copyright © 1966 by the President and Fellows of Harvard College. Reprinted by permission.

[1]Remarks by William A. Hewitt, chairman of Deere & Company, before the American Agricultural Editors' Association, Chicago, Illinois, December 1, 1965, p. 1.

184

is that per-capita food production has fallen by 3% in Asia, by 7% in Latin America.

*   *   *   *   *

Almost in desperation, the United States plans to escalate its efforts to deal with the world hunger problem. In so doing it will create tremendous opportunities for businesses that have the knowhow, the foresight and the capital to help end hunger.

*   *   *   *   *

As Chairman Robert S. Stephenson of Allis-Chalmers puts it: "The United States, Canada and Australia are going to have to feed the world, or we're going to have to help the world feed itself."[2]

In order to facilitate a better understanding of the future problems and opportunities that these trends and forces promise to create for farm equipment manufacturers, this note will discuss the following topics: (1) trends in population growth, economic and technical development, and government policy that will affect the world supply of and demand for food; (2) the characteristics of and changes occurring in world agriculture as a result of these and other forces; and (3) the structure of and changes occurring in the world farm equipment industry. In addition, a brief description of the light industrial equipment industry will be given, since most of the full-line farm equipment manufacturers had entered this additional field in the late 1950's and early 1960's.

World food supply and demand

According to the U.S. Department of Agriculture (USDA), the world food budget was not in balance in 1963. The USDA estimated that it would require the additional consumption of 1.1 billion bushels of wheat (11% of the 1963 world supply), 7.0 billion pounds of vegetable oils (8%), 3.5 million bags of dry edible beans (4%), and 3.3 billion pounds of nonfat dry milk (4%) to raise to a minimum nutritional standard the diets of the two billion people who lived in the 70 underdeveloped countries.

According to most agricultural experts, there would be an increasing worldwide shortage of food during the next 15 years if present population and agricultural trends continued. (See Exhibit 1 for an estimate of population growth and Exhibit 2 for estimates of food production and consumption in the developed and underdeveloped countries of the world.) Although the forecasts differed in the magnitude of the shortage, they did agree on four points: (1) there would be a worldwide shortage of food in 1980; (2) it would be of sufficient magnitude to be a major worldwide political and economic issue; (3) neither the developed nor the underdeveloped countries would be able to solve the problem by themselves; and (4) new forms of action to attack the problem should be developed as soon as possible.

Factors affecting world food demand. Agricultural and economic experts predicted that the worldwide demand for food was going to increase tremendously during the remainder of this century. The forecasts varied some-

Exhibit 1

WORLD POPULATION: ACTUAL AND FORECAST, 1800–2000

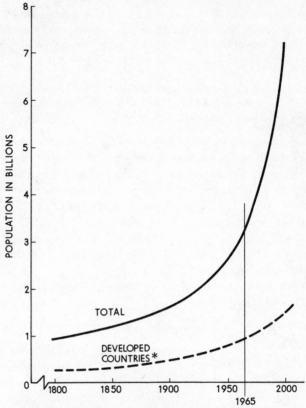

*United States, Australia, Canada, New Zealand, Europe, U.S.S.R.
Source: UN Statistics, cited in *Fortune*, June 1966, p. 110.

what because of different assumptions about population growth and minimum per capita nutritional needs. The forecast by Mr. Willard Cochrane,[3] contained in the following tabulation and explained in more detail in Exhibit 2, was typical.

WORLD FOOD DEMAND

	1960	1980	2000
Demand (1960 dollars in billions)	$146	$225–$247	$371–$475

Projected population growth was the principal cause of the increased demand. This factor alone would require an increase in food supply of 43% between 1960 and 1980 and an increase of over 130% between 1960 and 2000. Two other factors contributed to the forecast increases, however. One was projected increases in per capita food consumption in both the developed

---

[3]Director of Agricultural Economics for the United States Department of Agriculture.

Exhibit 2

WORLD FOOD SUPPLY AND DEMAND, ACTUAL AND FORECAST, 1960–2000

	1960		1980		2000	
	Developed Countries	Under-developed Countries	Developed Countries	Under-developed Countries	Developed Countries	Under-developed Countries
Population (billions)	1.00	2.00	1.19	3.10	1.50	5.40
Income, per capita (dollars*)	900	100	1,337	129,[a] 146,[b] 164[c]	1,987	149,[a] 209,[b] 268[c]
Income total (billion dollars*)	900	200	1,591	400,[a] 451,[b] 508[c]	2,980	805,[a] 1,129,[b] 1,450[c]
Food consumption per capita (dollars*)	79	34	85	40,[a] 44,[b] 47[c]	90	44,[a] 54,[b] 63[c]
Food consumption total (billion dollars*)	79	67	101	124,[a] 135,[b] 146[c]	135	236,[a] 291,[b] 340[c]
Food production per capita (dollars*)	80	33	93,[d] 121[e]	38,[a] 40,[b] 38[c]	110,[d] 174[e]	42,[a] 48,[b] 42[c]
Food production total (billion dollars*)	80	66	111,[d] 144[e]	119,[a] 125,[b] 119[c]	165,[d] 261[e]	226,[a] 261,[b] 226[c]
Food surplus or (deficit) (billion dollars*)	1	(1)	11,[d] 43[e]	(5[a]), (10[b]), (27[c])	30,[d] 126[e]	(10[a]), (30[b]), (114[c])

*1960 U.S. dollars.

[a]Assumes a balanced food budget with moderate rates of food production and imports, and a low rate of economic development.

[b]Assumes a balanced food budget with high rates of food production and imports, and a moderate rate of economic development.

[c]Assumes a rapid rate of economic development with an increasing food deficit.

[d]Assumes a balanced food budget with output restricted to domestic demand plus large exports.

[e]Assumes unrestricted food production with a large food surplus.

Source: Willard W. Cochrane, Director of Agricultural Economics, USDA, "The World Food Budget: A Forward Look to 2000 and Beyond," May 1962.

and underdeveloped countries resulting from increased per capita income. The second was the additional per capita increase needed in underdeveloped countries to bring consumption up to minimum nutritional levels.

Factors affecting world food supply. In 1965 most of the underdeveloped countries were net importers of grains and other foodstuffs. This had not always been the case, however. Before World War II, most of these areas were net exporters of foodstuffs. The change was caused partially by increased internal consumption resulting from increased populations and partially by programs of economic development that placed much greater emphasis on the development of the industrial sectors than on the agricultural sectors of these countries' economies.

In these underdeveloped countries, experts saw three principal factors as limiting agricultural production in 1965: governmental agricultural policies, inefficient farming techniques, and limited amounts of food-producing land. Many experts regarded the use of inefficient farm techniques as the most important of these factors, and believed that the application of U.S. methods would enable many of these countries to become self-sufficient. These same experts felt, however, that there would have to be changes in various cultural values and increased government support of agriculture before such techniques could be effectively applied. Even with modern farming methods, most agricultural experts felt that limited amounts of food-producing land would limit supply in the long run.

In the developed countries, government agricultural policies were the principal factor limiting farm production in 1965. In the longer run, however, the limited amounts of food-producing land promised to become the primary restrictive factor.

Forecasts of total world food production depended largely on assumptions concerning the agricultural policies followed by various governments. The forecast by Mr. Cochrane, which is summarized in the following tabulation and explained in more detail in Exhibit 2, was typical.

WORLD FOOD SUPPLY

	1960	1980	2000
Supply (1960 dollars in billions)	$146	$230–$269	$391–$522

The projected world food deficit. Even though the forecasts prepared by Mr. Cochrane and other experts indicated that it was theoretically possible to meet the world demand for food in the coming decades, most experts felt there would be deficits in the underdeveloped countries unless drastic steps were taken. Without these steps, the deficits forecast for 1980 ranged from $6 to $17 billion worth of foodstuffs, while for 2000 they ranged from $35 to $84 billion.

Methods of meeting the food deficit. In 1965 the proposals advanced for meeting the food deficit fell into three broad groups: (1) those that recommended a redistribution of existing food supplies; (2) those that recommended population control; and (3) those that aimed at increasing food production, primarily in the underdeveloped countries. Most agricultural and economic experts felt that all three types of programs would be needed to meet the projected food deficit.

Proposals to redistribute existing food supplies generally recommended that the developed countries expand their agricultural production as much as possible, and export their surplus to the underdeveloped countries. These proposals were complicated by the fact that few of the underdeveloped countries were able to pay for these exports in dollars or other hard currencies. Nevertheless, in the middle 1960's, such exports were increasing. They were usually paid for in local currency at less than world market rates.[4] Even so, many experts felt that the economic and political problems associated with expanding food production in the developed countries and disrupting the world food market would probably limit the magnitude of these exports. Furthermore, while some experts and most manufacturers of agricultural equipment felt that redistribution could meet the world food deficit if pursued to the limit, most experts felt that the solution would not suffice beyond 1975, if at all, and that it would therefore inevitably be necessary to increase food production in the underdeveloped countries.

Since the rapid growth of population was one of the primary factors causing the world food problem, some form of population control was often recommended as a solution. Some form of limitation certainly appeared desirable in addition to the traditional war, pestilence, and famine, since, at the rates of increase of the mid-1960's, the world population would reach 4.4 billion in 1980, 7.4 billion by 2000, and over 50 billion by 2100.

The main factor behind the rapid increase in population in most of the world appeared to be declining death rates rather than rising birth rates. Historically, societies often passed through three stages: (1) with high birth and death rates (40–50 per thousand annually) and little growth in population; (2) with high birth rates and declining death rates, as public health measures and living conditions were gradually improved, and rapid growth in population; and (3) with low birth and death rates (10–20 per thousand annually) and slow growth. Largely as a result of the rapid introduction of public health measures into the underdeveloped areas following World War II,[5] most of these areas were in the early part of the high-growth middle stage. The developed countries, on the other hand, tended to be in the more stable third stage.

In 1965, it seemed unlikely that birth control measures would provide a

[4]Such currency generally could not be spent, however, because of the inflationary pressures it would put on these developing economies. For example, in India the U.S. holdings of these counterpart funds reputedly approximated half the total circulation of Indian currency in 1965.

[5]For example, it took about 300 years to bring malaria under control in England as opposed to about 6 years in Ceylon.

significant part of the answer by 1980, since it would be necessary to reduce the rate of population growth quickly from 1.9%[6] per year to 1.5% per year in order for the projected food supply to be sufficient to meet the forecast needs in 1980.[7] Not only were the cultural and religious values in many of these countries opposed to population control, but the medical means of providing acceptable and effective birth control measures were not available in sufficient quantities in these countries in 1965.

Most agricultural experts, therefore, felt that increased agricultural production, primarily in the underdeveloped countries, would be the most important method of meeting the food deficit from 1970 until population growth could be more effectively controlled. Various means of expanding production had been proposed by 1965. Two of these, increased land tillage and farming the sea, were applicable to both developed and underdeveloped countries. Other means, such as agricultural reforms and the increased use of better tools, fertilizers, seeds, and weed and pest controls, were more applicable to the underdeveloped countries.

The need for increased land tillage was caused by the limited amount of food-producing land. In 1965 only 3.5% of the world's land surface of 110 billion acres, or less than 4 billion acres, was arable food-producing land, and most of this was already under cultivation. According to Mr. Thomas Ware, chairman of the Freedom from Hunger Foundation and chairman of the International Minerals & Chemical Corporation:

> Even with the most imaginative and energetic program of land reclamation and development, optimists agree that the amount of food producing land cannot be pushed beyond 5.5 billion acres.[8]

In addition to more intensive cultivation of the land, some experts recommended increased utilization of the sea as a means of increasing food production. According to testimony before the Senate Commerce Committee,[9] the oceans were able to provide 400 million tons of animal protein annually without depletion of their resources, while only 10 million tons of animal protein were taken from the sea in 1965. That same year, there was a worldwide shortage of 80 million tons of animal protein for food.

According to most agricultural experts, the key to increased production in the underdeveloped countries was agricultural reforms, principally making the farmer the owner of the land he tilled.[10] Absentee ownership of land, whether by individuals or the state, and usurious rates of interest on agricultural credit appeared to stifle individual initiative to such an extent that

---

[6]This percentage represents a doubling of total population every 36.5 years.

[7]This calculation assumes that the present rate of increase of 1.25% in the developed countries will be lowered to 1.2% by 1970.

[8]Hearing before the Consultative Subcommittee on Economic and Social Affairs of the Committee on Foreign Relations, U.S. Senate, 89th Cong., 1st sess., June 29, 1965, p. 4.

[9]*Ibid.*, p. 14.

[10]*Ibid.*, pp. 6-11, 14, and Simon Williams, "Private Investment in World Agriculture," *The Harvard Business Review*, November–December 1965, pp. 98-99.

other forms of agrarian reforms had proved unsuccessful when tried. Another prerequisite for the success of improved farming techniques in the under-developed countries was the education of the farmer, who was usually illiterate and ignorant of modern farming practices.

As immediate steps in improving methods, most experts recommended the use of fertilizers, new seeds and crops, and weed and pest killers. Each of these measures was usually capable of increasing output 50% to 100%—enough to return a profit to the farmer after paying for the cost of the materials. When these methods had proved successful, the introduction of better tools, such as tractors and cultivators, and more intensive farming methods could begin.

The U.S. role in meeting the food deficit. Forbes discussed U.S. plans as follows:

The United States plans to fight the war against hunger on two fronts. The first will be a crash program to supply the underdeveloped countries with food. The United States has been giving away $1.5 billion worth of food abroad every year under Public Law 480. If Congress approves the President's new program—as seems all but certain—food shipments could rise to $3.3 billion by 1967–1968. This move is designed to cope with such emergencies as the recent drought in India which already has led to Communist-organized riots in the state of Kerala.

In the long run, the second front will be the decisive one. This is the self-help part. Every nation receiving U.S. aid will have to promise to build up its own agriculture as swiftly as possible. Not only *promise*, but show results. The reason for this is simple. "We don't have enough capacity to feed all these people," says Secretary of Agriculture Orville L. Freeman. "Unless they learn to feed themselves, there will be world famine."

Along with the food, therefore, the United States will send the underdeveloped nations fertilizer and farm equipment. It will also encourage U.S. companies to build fertilizer plants and farm equipment factories abroad. It will teach farmers in Asia and Africa and Latin America how to make the most of the land they have. It will urge—and even arm-twist—governments to re-rig archaic policies in the field of price incentives, farm credit, and land reform. This will also be done under the Agency for International Development (AID).

Increasing food shipments abroad will mean increasing production at home, for, according to Freeman, the reserves in the government storage don't come anywhere near the world's requirements.

This means that millions of acres of land that have been retired under the present farm program eventually will be brought back into production as needed. . . . In short, to change the very nature of U.S. agricultural policy but without causing chaos on the farm and in the marketplace.

*   *   *   *   *

Robert W. Engle, manager of marketing of Allis-Chalmers' farm equipment division, believes that increased production will have to come from improved farm equipment and improved farm techniques, as well as from greater acreage.

*   *   *   *   *

In the fight to increase production of foodstuffs abroad, the United States will count particularly on the manufacturers of fertilizer. Says David E. Bell, Administrator of the Agency for International Development: "Fertilizers will be our biggest need."

AID's Bell is also counting on farm-equipment manufacturers and food processors to help beef up the agriculture of the underdeveloped countries. The farm-machinery makers will have to develop equipment especially designed for their needs, he says, pointing out that in India, for example, "the land holdings are very small. Farming takes on the characteristics of gardening. You need small power units, hand equipment almost."[11]

Characteristics and trends in world farming

In 1960 the United States produced over 13% of the world's total supply of food, or 302 million of the 2,276 million metric tons produced. The other 29 developed countries produced 1,073 million metric tons, or 47%, while the underdeveloped countries, which accounted for 67% of the world's population, produced only 900 million tons, or 40%, of the world's production.

Characteristics and trends in U.S. farming. In 1964, there were an estimated 3.5 million farms of all sizes and types in the United States. An average farm in 1964 contained 333 acres and earned a net income of about $3,634 in value of product sold.[12] Such a farm would probably need one large and two middle-sized tractors at $8,000 and $6,000 respectively (if purchased new at 1965 prices), plus about $45,200 worth of other farm equipment.[13]

The machinery available for food production on U.S. farms included plows, listers, harrows, rollers, pulverizers, and stalkcutters for preparing the soil or the fields; planters, drills, and seeders for planting; loaders, applicators, and spreaders for fertilizing; cultivators and weeders for improving the soil while crops were growing; sprayers and dusters for applying pesticides; combines, pickers, diggers, shakers, and harvesters for gathering crops; shellers, grinders, cutters, mixers, and driers for preparing crops for use or market; and mowers, rakes, stackers, pick-up balers, and waferers for haying. This equipment was purchased from the full-line and the long-line farm equipment manufacturers (who served primarily grain, tobacco, cotton and other field crop farms, general and miscellaneous farms, and livestock and dairy farms raising hay and grain for feed) as well as from smaller, more specialized firms. In addition, the specialized firms produced equipment for animal feeding, milking, chicken raising, and ranching.

The major trends in the U.S. farm market in 1965 were: (1) the decrease in the total number of farms, with a corresponding increase in average farm size and in the number of farms containing over 500 acres or grossing more than $10,000 a year (see parts [a] and [b] of Exhibit 3); (2) the cost-price squeeze on farmers, which increased their need for more efficient machinery

---

[11]"World Hunger: Enemy of U.S. Prosperity," *Forbes*, March 1, 1966, p. 20.

[12]U.S. Department of Agriculture figures, cited in *Agricultural Statistics*, 1965.

[13]Conversation with Samuel White, Jr., president of Oliver Corporation, in May 1966.

(see parts [c] and [d] of Exhibit 3); and (3) the changing pattern of farm machinery purchases caused by changes in technology and/or changes in the demand for particular products (see Exhibit 4).

Exhibit 3

MAJOR TRENDS AND CHARACTERISTICS OF THE U.S. FARM MARKET, 1950-65

(a) Decrease in the Number of Farms and Increase in the Size of Each Farm

	Number and Size of Farms*			
	Number of Farms (Thousands)	Land in Farms (Millions of Acres)	Acres per Farm	Average Value of Production Assets per Farm
1950	5,648	1,202	212	$18,700
1955	4,654	1,202	258	28,600
1960	3,949	1,174	297	43,200
1965†	3,376	1,151	341	60,200

*48 states.
†Preliminary.
Source: Donaldson, Lufkin & Jenrette, Inc., "Agricultural Equipment Industry: An Improving Environment for Above Average Profit Growth," May 1966, p. 6.

(b) Increasing Number of Large Farms, by Value of Product Sold, 1954-64

	Number of Farms (in Thousands)		
Value of Products Sold	1954	1959*	1964*
Under $2,500	2,861	1,922	1,522
$ 2,501 to $ 4,999	811	654	380
$ 5,000 to $ 9,999	707	693	560
$10,000 to $19,999 .... } 583	503	573
$20,000 and over .... }	325	437
Total	4,962	4,097	3,452

*Adjusted for changes in the definition of a farm.
Source: For 1954: U.S. Department of Commerce, *Statistical Abstract of the United States, 1966*, Table 903, p. 169.
For 1959 and 1964: U.S. Department of Agriculture, Economic Research Service, "Farm Income Situation," FIS-199, p. 72.

(c) The Cost/Price Squeeze on Farmers: Parity, or Ratio of Prices Received to Prices Paid, 1950-65

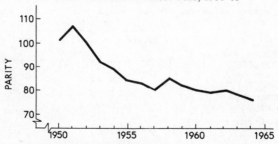

Source: U.S. Department of Agriculture, *Agricultural Statistics, 1965*, Table 626, p. 430.

Exhibit 3—Continued

(d) Increasing Percentage of Farm Income Spent for Capital Equipment, 1950–1965

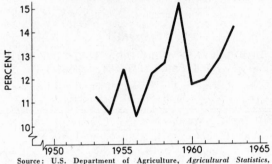

Source: U.S. Department of Agriculture, *Agricultural Statistics*, *1965*, Tables 626, 645, and 691, pp. 430, 443, and 483.

(e) Gross Cash Receipts of U.S. Farmers and Domestic Farm Machinery Sales, 1950–1967

Source: U.S. Department of Agriculture, *Agricultural Statistics, 1965*, Tables 645 and 686, pp. 443 and 479, cited in Donaldson, Lufkin & Jenrette, Inc., *"Agricultural Equipment Industry,"* May 1966, p. 5.

(f) Farm Inputs for the Period 1949–1951 and 1962–1964, and Per Cent of Change

	Index of Expenditures (1957–1959 Average = 100)		
Input	1949–1951 Average	1962–1964 Average	Per Cent Increase or (Decrease)
Farm labor	145	82	(43)
Farm real estate	97	101	4
Mechanical power and machinery	86	99	15
Fertilizer and lime	67	140	109
Feed, seed, and livestock purchases*	74	123	66
Miscellaneous	85	116	36
Total input	102	102	0

*Nonfarm portion of feed, seed, and livestock purchases.
Source: U.S. Department of Agriculture, *Agricultural Statistics, 1965*, Table 661, p. 456.

Exhibit 3—Continued

(g) Farm Outputs for the Periods 1949–1951 and 1962–1964, and Per Cent of Change

	Index of Production (1957–1959 Average = 100)		
Output	1949–1951 Average	1962–1964 Average	Per Cent Increase or (Decrease)
Livestock and products	88	110	25
Meat animals	89	110	24
Dairy products	93	113	22
Poultry and eggs	78	104	33
All crops	91	115	26
Feed grains	79	109	38
Hay and forage	88	102	16
Food grains	88	105	19
Vegetables	93	107	15
Fruits and nuts	99	103	4
Sugar crops	81	144	78
Cotton	112	123	10
Tobacco	122	133	9
Oil crops	66	126	91
Farm output	87	110	26

Source: U.S. Department of Agriculture, *Agricultural Statistics, 1965*, Table 662, p. 456.

Exhibit 4

FARM MACHINES AND EQUIPMENT

Value of Shipments by Classes for the Periods 1953–1955 and 1962–1964, and Per Cent of Change

Classes	1953 to 1955 Average (Dollars in Millions)	1962 to 1964 Average (Dollars in Millions)	Per Cent Increase or (Decrease)
Tractors for farm use	$520.2	$ 691.6*	33%
Other machinery and equipment ...	850.5	1,072.1	26
Plows and listers	58.4	71.4	22
Harrows, rollers, pulverizers, and stalk cutters	67.9	107.3	58
Planting and fertilizing equipment ..	92.5	106.4	15
Cultivators and weeders	46.9	55.0	17
Sprayers and dusters	33.0	42.4	28
Harvesting machinery	230.4	339.3	47
Machinery for preparing crops for market use	28.3	45.2	60
Haying machinery	158.1	114.8	(27)
Farm wagons and trucks	26.7†	46.6	75
Elevators and blowers	36.4†	26.8	(26)
Dairy equipment	20.4	19.1	(6)
Poultry equipment	25.7	34.9	36
Barn and barnyard equipment	25.8	62.5	142

*Average of 1962 and 1963 figures.
†Average of 1953 and 1955 figures.
Source: U.S. Department of Agriculture, *Agricultural Statistics, 1966*, Table 645.

The total number of farms in the United States decreased from 4.8 million in 1954 to 3.5 million in 1964 and was projected to decrease to 2.8 million in 1975, according to the USDA. However, the number of large farms, those producing more than $10,000 in value of product sold, increased from an estimated 617,000 in 1954 to 1,010,000 in 1964. These farms, about 29% of the U.S. total, accounted for 78% of all farm production and purchased about 40% of all new farm equipment in 1964. The 350,000 largest farms (10% of the total number) produced 60% of all farm products, grossed $50,000 a year on the average, and gave their owners an annual return of about $17,000. This handful of big farmers produced more food in 1964 than all of the six million American farmers were able to produce 50 years ago. These farmers had a net worth of $200,000 per farm, up 50% since 1954. They were more than just traditional tillers of the soil; they were businessmen and capitalists.[14]

With the increasing cost/price squeeze,[15] the larger farmers had been increasing both the total amount and the percentage of their incomes that they spent on capital equipment. Between 1953 and 1964, farmers increased the percentage of income they spent on equipment from 10.5% to 14.0% (see part [d] of Exhibit 3). However, because of the fluctuating nature of farm income, it was not possible to predict accurately what the year-to-year level would be, but only that it would increase, on the average, over a period of years. Thus, there were fat and lean years in equipment purchases (see part [f] of Exhibit 3).

During the decade preceding 1965, two changes occurred in the nature of farm equipment purchases. First, shifts occurred in the relative demand in each of the machinery categories as a result of changing technology and changes in demand for agricultural products (see Exhibit 4). Relatively more was being spent in 1965 than in 1955 on equipment to prepare the soil for planting, to harvest the crop, and to prepare the crop for market use, and relatively less on equipment for fertilizing, improving the soil while crops were growing, and for haying. Second, in each product category, there was a tendency toward larger and more specialized equipment in order to obtain greater operating efficiencies, and wherever self-propelled machinery was feasible, there was a tendency to use it.

While some observers felt that the changes in the U.S. agricultural policy, which encouraged the expansion of farm output, would prevent or retard the decline of the small farmer, most experts did not believe that the small farmer could compete economically with the larger farmers, who had lower operating costs. In the past, the government had maintained price supports high enough to allow the marginal producer to survive. However, because of the necessity of "giving away" much of the subsidized produce to the

---

[14]"Agribusiness: The Revolution's Just Beginning," *Forbes*, November 1, 1965, pp. 18–21.

[15]The extension of the minimum wage laws to farm workers, who in 1965 often received only half the federal standard, promised to increase this squeeze even more.

underdeveloped countries, and because of a growing differentiation of the economic and social aspects of the farm problem, the government was becoming increasingly unwilling to continue these price supports. The declining political strength of farmers, caused by the movement of people to the cities, and the one-man, one-vote Supreme Court ruling of 1965 had served to speed up the process.

Characteristics and trends in farming in the developed countries. Farming in most of the developed countries provided adequate basic support of their population. Nevertheless, because of their large populations and limited farming area, Eastern and Western Europe and Japan had to import foodstuffs in 1965. These imports were provided by the other developed areas—North America, the area of the River Plate,[16] the U.S.S.R., and Oceania[17]—which were net exporters of food. The USDA projections indicated that these basic relationships would continue into the 1970's, with South Africa joining the group of exporting regions.

In the River Plate area, South Africa and Oceania, farming in 1965 was very similar to contemporary farming in the United States. The farms were about the same size and, in some cases, even larger than most U.S. farms. Except for variations caused by different types of crops, these farmers used the same kinds and sizes of equipment as the U.S. farmer. The farms, however, did not usually have as much capital equipment per acre as U.S. farms.

In Western Europe and Japan, farming in 1965 was similar to U.S. farming in the early 1950's, except for the level of mechanization, which was lower. According to Mr. Comart Peterson, vice president for international marketing of Deere & Company, the principal difference between farming in Western Europe in 1965 and farming in the United States in the early 1950's was that the Western European farmer used far fewer implements and power-oriented accessories than his U.S. counterpart. In both Western Europe and Japan, however, the size of farms and the amount of machinery in use were increasing more rapidly than in the United States.

Characteristics and trends in farming in the underdeveloped countries. In those underdeveloped countries with low man-land ratios, such as Mexico, Brazil, the other countries of Central and South America,[18] and the countries of North Africa, West Central Africa, East Africa, and West Asia, imports and exports of food were about in balance. Most of the countries in these areas in 1965 had diets that approached minimum standards and had land available for further development.

In the underdeveloped countries with high man-land ratios, which included Communist Asia, India, and other countries in East and South Asia, there was a chronic food deficit. Half the world's people lived in these areas in 1965, and they could neither grow enough to feed themselves nor obtain the purchasing power to buy what they wanted.

[16]Argentina, Uruguay, Chile, and Paraguay.
[17]Australia, New Zealand, and New Guinea.
[18]Except for the River Plate area.

In most of the underdeveloped countries, 60% to 80% of the population was engaged in farming in 1964, compared to 7% in the United States. Farms were usually small, often only a few acres, and seldom yielded much more than was necessary to sustain the farmer. The USDA attributed these low yields mainly to inadequate fertilizer inputs, technological backwardness, and a lack of economic incentives.

Structure of the U.S. farm equipment industry

According to the 1963 U.S. Census of Manufactures, the farm machinery and equipment industry had 1,568 establishments in 1963, an increase of 6% over the number in 1958. Of these, 1,010 had under 20 employees. These companies fell into three broad groupings: (1) the full-line manufacturers; (2) long-line firms; and (3) small firms which produced a few items of specialized equipment.

Full-line manufacturers. In 1965 there were only seven full-line manufacturers, i.e., producers of a complete line of agricultural machinery, including tractors, and other equipment and attachments. One of the seven was a newcomer, the White Motor Company, which diversified into farm equipment in the early 1960's through acquisitions.

The full-line manufacturers dominated the industry and its retailers. Their combined share of industry volume was reputed to be 70% in 1963. Their individual sales of farm equipment ranged from $214 million to $795 million in 1965. They generally distributed their products through company-owned branch sales offices and warehouses to independent retail dealers, who sold the machinery to the farmers.

All the full-line manufacturers were diversified to some extent, both horizontally and geographically. As a result, rank by sales of farm equipment—domestically, internationally, or total—did not necessarily correspond to rank in total company sales, as shown in the table on page 199.

Although the companies were quite different, a few generalizations could be made from a study of their annual reports: (1) since 1960 all the companies had experienced annual increases in their domestic shipments of tractors and equipment because of the high level of farm income, the demand for new types of equipment caused by rapidly changing farm technology, and the replacement of existing equipment with larger units as farms became larger (see Exhibits 5 and 6); (2) since 1950 the larger companies showed more stability in sales and profits than the smaller ones; and (3) Deere consistently led the group in terms of profit margins.

Highlights of the recent history and activities of these seven full-line manufacturers are summarized below:[19]

Deere & Company displaced International Harvester in 1958 as the leader in U.S. farm equipment sales and in 1964 as the leader in worldwide farm

---

[19]The sources of this information were various case writer interivews and company annual reports.

COMPARISON OF THE FULL-LINE FARM EQUIPMENT MANUFACTURERS,
1965
(Dollars in Millions)

Company	Farm Equipment Sales		Total Sales, Worldwide	Rank by Farm Equipment Sales		
	North American	Worldwide	Worldwide	North American*	Overseas	Worldwide
Deere & Company	$617	$745	$887	1	4	1
International Harvester Company	est. 630†	795†	2,337	2	2	2
Massey-Ferguson Ltd.	209†	581	752	3	1	3
Ford Motor Company‡ ..	est. 175	est. 350	11,537	7	3	4
J. I. Case Company	240†	274†	274	3	5	5
Allis-Chalmers Manufacturing Company	est. 200	est. 214	714	3	6	6
White Motor Company ..	189	195	638	3	7	7

*The four companies ranked third were all very close in 1965; a more precise ranking was difficult because of the inaccurate nature of statistics.
†Includes light industrial equipment sales.
‡Excludes implements sold under Ford name but manufactured by other companies.
Source: 1965 company annual reports and case writer's estimates.

equipment sales. In 1955, Deere decided to strengthen its domestic farm equipment position, establish overseas manufacturing facilities, and expand its light industrial equipment business. One of the prinicpal steps to increase its domestic position was the introduction of a completely new line of tractors and equipment in 1960. In 1962 Deere decided to expand its overseas farm equipment business significantly. As a result of increased capital investment, these operations were not profitable between 1962 and 1965. In 1963, Deere entered the lawn and garden equipment market. In 1965, the company sold its chemical division, which produced fertilizer and had accounted for 2% of its 1964 sales.

International Harvester Company traced its history in farm equipment to the McCormick reaper, although trucks and construction equipment accounted for over 60% of the company's sales in 1965. Worldwide, IHC was the second largest producer of construction equipment, and the third largest producer of trucks. In addition, IHC produced steel, baler twine, lawn and garden equipment, gas turbine engines, aircraft components, and light industrial equipment. Although IHC's farm and light industrial equipment sales had increased steadily between 1955 and 1965, IHC's share of the U.S. market had declined. In an effort to reverse this trend, IHC introduced a completely new line of farm equipment in 1964.

Massey-Ferguson Ltd.'s operations extended to all continents in 1965, and were especially strong in the British Commonwealth. In the United States, Massey was battling for third place in market share with the farm equipment subsidiaries of Case, Allis-Chalmers, and White. To aid in this battle, Massey had introduced a completely new line of tractors and equipment in 1964 and 1965, had moved the executive offices of its North American subsidiary to Des Moines in 1965, and planned to complete a new plant in Des Moines in 1966

Exhibit 5

COMMERCIAL FARM EQUIPMENT DEMAND IN THE UNITED STATES, 1955-67

| | Factory Sales of Wheel Tractors | | | Wheel Tractor Wholesale Prices per Horsepower | Domestic Tractor* Sales (Millions) | Other Farm Equipment Sales (Millions) | Total Farm Equipment Sales (Millions) |
	Units (Thousands)	Value (Millions)	Average Price per Unit				
1955	286	$450	$1,573	$41	$ 627	$ 844	$1,471
1956	191	327	1,712	41	527	778	1,305
1957	204	365	1,789	46	524	826	1,350
1958	216	440	2,037	48	632	1,017	1,649
1959	227	485	2,137	49	706	1,051	1,757
1960	137	308	2,248	50	509	920	1,429
1961	153	380	2,483	51	590	928	1,518
1962	169	462	2,733	53	668	964	1,632
1963	177	518	2,926	55	737	1,085	1,822
1964	170	551	3,241	56	775	1,168	1,943
1965E	209	690	3,301	57	930	1,270	2,200
1966E	215	738	3,433	58	995	1,359	2,354
1967E	217	775	3,571	59	1,045	1,427	2,472

E: estimated.

*Wheel, tracklaying under 60 net engine horsepower, and riding garden types. Wheel tractor attachments and parts included.

Source: U.S. Bureau of the Census, cited in Donaldson, Lufkin & Jenrette, Inc., "Agricultural Equipment Industry," May 1966, p. 8.

Exhibit 6

VALUE OF SHIPMENTS OF AGRICULTURAL MACHINERY FOR DOMESTIC USE, SELECTED ITEMS, 1964

	Units Shipped	Total Value (Thousands)	Per Unit Value
Tractors			
Wheel-type tractors*			
9–34 hp.	8,807	$ 15,472	$ 1,757
35–49 hp.	41,023	98,247	2,395
50–69 hp.	36,901	127,475	3,455
70–89 hp.	19,633	70,685	3,600
90 hp. up	35,883	172,318	4,802
Tracklaying tractors	1,923	25,142	13,074
Garden tractors and motor tillers	397,390	76,606	193
Other machines and equipment			
Corn planters, drawn and mounted	40,545	16,449	405
Loaders—Manure and general utility	27,550	11,376	413
Tandem disk harrow	82,547	40,145	486
Combines			
Pull-type (over 6 feet)	2,910	6,123	2,104
Self-propelled			
Without heads ⎰ under 14 feet	13,214	53,347	4,037
14–16 feet	6,380	30,857	4,836
16 feet plus	6,294	40,934	6,504
Grain heads for combines	25,659	13,647	532
Corn heads for combines	16,857	21,402	1,270
Corn pickers, 2–row			
Drawn and mounted	11,239	19,789	1,761
Cotton pickers	3,696	33,961	9,189
Cotton strippers	2,561	3,757	1,467
Pick-up hay balers†			
Wire	6,283	12,590	2,004
Twine	36,536	44,969	1,231
Hay conditioners	10,355	6,047	584
Field forage harvesters	20,821	22,474	1,079

Note: Value of shipments is defined as net selling value, f.o.b.
*Except garden-type.
†Tractor power take-off type.
Source: U.S. Bureau of the Census, "Farm Machines and Equipment," *Current Industrial Reports*, 1965.

which would assemble most of the farm implements sold by Massey in North America. Massey was also one of the world's largest manufacturers of high-speed diesel engines in 1965. In addition, Massey manufactured light industrial equipment, lawn and garden equipment, and office furniture. In total, nonfarm products accounted for about 22% of Massey's 1965 sales.

Ford Tractor and Implement Division was much stronger in the farm market abroad than in the United States, where its penetration was limited by its relatively short product line. In 1964, however, Ford took steps to strengthen both its domestic and international operations. Domestically, it introduced a new tractor line with higher horsepower and broadened its implement line. Ford also dropped its 24 U.S. distributors in 1964 and began to sell directly to its 2,000 farm and light industrial equipment dealers. Internationally, Ford reorganized its tractor operations and invested over $40 million in new facilities in Europe in 1964. In 1965, Ford became the seventh farm equipment manufacturer to enter the lawn and garden tractor market.

J. I. Case Company manufactured crawler tractors, attachments, and other industrial equipment for the construction, earthmoving, and roadbuilding fields, in addition to a full line of tractors and implements for the farm market. Late in 1964, a line of small garden tractors with related accessories was added. During 1964, the Kern County Land Company acquired 54.6% of Case's common stock. Kern County Land was a corporate farm that had discovered oil on its land and had diversified into other fields, e.g., electronics, auto parts, minerals, real estate development, and oil wildcatting.

White Motor Corporation was the second largest manufacturer of heavy-duty trucks in the United States in 1965, which accounted for over 60% of White's total sales. White diversified into the farm equipment business between 1960 and 1963 by acquiring the farm equipment assets of three small, full-line manufacturers: the Oliver Corporation (1960); Cockshutt Farm Equipment Ltd. (1962), and Motec Industries, Inc. (formerly the Minneapolis-Moline Company, 1963). White maintained the separate names of the companies it acquired, although it consolidated manufacturing operations in order to achieve production economies. Farm equipment accounted for nearly 30% of sales in 1965. Stationary diesel engines and rebuilt auto parts accounted for the remaining sales.

Allis-Chalmers Manufacturing Company was one of four firms battling for third place in the sale of farm equipment domestically. Overseas, A-C manufactured tractors in England, France, Australia, and Mexico. In total, farm equipment accounted for about 30% of A-C's 1965 sales. A-C was also the third largest manufacturer of construction equipment and the second largest producer of materials handling equipment in the United States. In addition, A-C manufactured electrical equipment, lawn and garden equipment, stationary diesel engines, and atomic reactor components. Export sales of products manufactured in the United States and Canada accounted for about 12% of total sales in 1965.

Long-line manufacturers. The number of long-line manufacturers of farm equipment in 1965 was estimated at 15. These concerns produced a long line, but not a full line, of farm equipment. Usually they did not produce tractors or tractor-mounted implements, although they made most other widely demanded pieces of farm equipment. In total, they sold about 15% of the agricultural equipment in the United States in 1965. Individually, their sales ranged from $30 million to $100 million annually. Like the full-line manufacturers, they distributed their products through company-owned branch sales offices and warehouses to independent retail equipment dealers (see Exhibit 7).

They competed primarily by developing technically advanced products in specialized areas.[20] New Holland, for example, was a specialist in haying tools, with 26 models. The company also produced crop elevators and conveyers. New Idea, a division of Avco Corporation, specialized in corn pickers and shellers, but had recently added a semiautomated line of bulk feeders,

---

[20]"The Farm Sees a New Revolution," *Business Week*, October 24, 1964.

Exhibit 7

FULL-LINE AND LONG-LINE DISTRIBUTION CHANNELS FOR FARM
EQUIPMENT

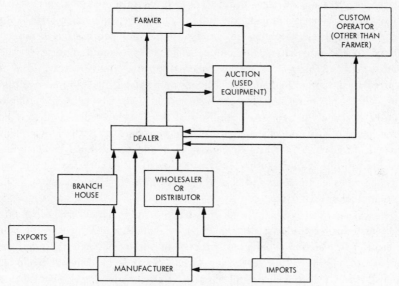

Source: Survey data reported in *Implement & Tractor*, June 21, 1964, pp. 25–29.

silo unloaders, and barn cleaners. Food Machinery and Chemical Corporation had developed a $20,000 pea and lima bean combine in 1964, which the company believed reduced costs 75% over older stationary machines. Other FMC machines harvested prunes, nuts, peaches, and raspberries. Chisholm-Ryder made a $13,000 snap beaner that did the work of 80 men, and the company had been working for a decade on a $10,000 machine for harvesting cucumbers that it hoped to market in 1966.

Short-line manufacturers and small firms. The third group of manufacturers ranged in size from small welding shops which produced single items for localized demand to highly efficient manufacturers producing a few items of specialized equipment and realizing annual sales up to $15 million. The pattern of this group's distribution was by no means standardized. Generally, however, the welding shops sold direct to the farmer while the smaller and medium-sized manufacturers sold to dealers in a one- or two-state area. The larger manufacturers used either a combination of direct sales to dealers in their immediate areas with wholesalers in other geographical areas, or sold entirely through wholesalers in a wide geographical area.

Trends in the U.S. farm equipment industry

As a result of the trend toward fewer but larger and more mechanized farms, several changes had been taking place in the farm equipment industry during the decade preceding 1965. These included: (1) changes in industry structure; (2) changes in products; and (3) changes in the channels of distribution.

Changes in industry structure. The changes in industry structure concerned the relationships among the full-line, long-line, and other farm equipment manufacturers. Because of heavy competition and a slackening of demand in the late fifties, the number of full-line manufacturers declined from ten to seven, as the weaker manufacturers either merged or were acquired by larger manufacturers. During this period, the full-line manufacturers allocated increasing resources to product development in order to meet the demand for new products. Most of this development was directed at increasing the size and efficiency of existing products. The long-line manufacturers, faced with increasing competition in their traditional product lines from the full-line manufacturers, began to diversify into very specialized, self-propelled field equipment and into the development of automated or semi-automated farmstead equipment.

Changes in farm equipment. Three basic changes had occurred in farm machinery during the past decade. First, tractors became larger and more powerful, yet also more versatile, in response to a demand for improved economy of operation on the larger farms. Second, implements tended to become larger, self-propelled, and capable of performing more operations at one time. Finally, manufacturers began to develop more mechanized farmstead equipment such as barn cleaners and automatic silos.

According to an article in an industry magazine,[21] there were several clear trends in tractor design. These included trends toward: (1) larger but more compact machines (less weight per unit of output); (2) bigger and more powerful engines; (3) more efficient engines, i.e., engines with higher compression ratios and faster speeds that yielded more stable fuel consumption; (4) diesel-powered units, particularly on the larger tractors; and (5) more versatile transmissions with a greater number of travel speeds to allow greater and more versatile working range.

In addition to these developments in field tractors, changes occurred in the lawn and garden tractor market. Since 1960, when International Harvester became the first full-line manufacturer to enter that market, sales growth had been rapid. By 1964 shipments of these tractors totaled $50 million, slightly over 9% of the total tractor market, and an increase of $37 million over 1959, when lawn and garden tractors represented only 3% of tractor sales.

Between 1954 and 1963, the sales of farm implements used in crop production increased from $742 million to $928 million.[22] Two changes occurred in these products during this period. First, the units became larger and performed more operations at one time and an increasing percentage were

---

[21]Mark Zimmerman, "The Farm Tractor: A Case Study in Mechanical Evolution," *Implement & Tractor*, November 21, 1964, pp. 28–31.

[22]These are three-year averages centered about 1954 and 1963.

self-propelled. Grain combines illustrated all three characteristics. In 1954 the average self-propelled grain combine had a cutting width of 12 feet, and a large percentage cut the grain without shelling it. About 57% of the grain combines sold between 1953 and 1955 were self-propelled. By contrast, in 1963 the average self-propelled grain combine had a cutting width of 15 feet and the overwhelming majority both cut and shelled the grain. In addition, nearly 91% of the grain combines sold between 1962 and 1964 were self-propelled.[23]

The second change in implements used for crop production was an increase in the demand for equipment that prepared the soil for planting and harvesting the crop relative to equipment for fertilizing, for improving the soil while crops were growing, and for haying.

The greatest percentage increase in farm equipment sales between 1955 and 1964 occurred in farmstead materials handling equipment, however. The USDA estimated that during the early 1960's, nearly one-half of all farm labor was expended for work in the barnyard. Farmstead equipment was designed to reduce this workload and/or to make it more efficient by mechanical and electrical means. Within the broad group of farm production equipment that would be labeled "farmstead equipment," there were three distinct types:

1. *Self-contained units*, which consisted primarily of movable equipment that, by itself, would perform some handling or processing task. This equipment was usually on wheels and was powered by a tractor power take-off. Examples were auger wagons, bulk-filling wagons, portable chain and slat or auger elevators, forage blowers, pail-type milking machines, etc.
2. *Installations*, which consisted primarily of equipment that had to be permanently or semipermanently installed in conjunction with other components to form a complete handling or processing system. This equipment was usually powered by electric motors. Examples were electric grinders and mixers, feed-metering devices, silo unloaders, automatic hog feeders, water systems, etc.
3. *Structures and buildings*, which could be built on the site or could be prefabricated and assembled on the site. Examples were grain elevators, hog houses, cattle sheds, utility buildings, etc.

While no industry figures were available for most of these farmstead equipment items in 1965, *Implement & Tractor* selected 17 items in the self-contained and installation categories from the 150 items reported by manufacturers to the U.S. Bureau of the Census and showed that manufacturers' domestic shipments increased from $44 million in 1950 to $80 million in 1958, or from 3.7% to 7.0% of all farm equipment and tractors shipped. And, according to USDA estimates, "post-harvest crop preparation equipment" and "farmstead and livestock equipment" made up 18% of all farm equipment, excluding tractors, sold during the 1953 to 1957 period, and will probably increase to 35% during the 1967–1975 period.

Those items of equipment in the "self-contained" category were similar

---

[23]Percentage of dollar value of shipments.

to field equipment or tractor attachments in their marketing characteristics. They were sold on a single product basis through farm equipment dealers. On the other hand, those items in the "installations" and "structures" categories required adaptation to and installation at the site of use. Since they did not lend themselves to over-the-counter selling, they were not popular items with product-oriented farm equipment dealers.

It was the general consensus among the speakers at the May 24, 1960, meeting of the Farm Equipment Institute that installations and structures could not be effectively merchandised by retail farm equipment dealers as the latter were constituted at that time, and that there was no other class of retailers in existence that could adequately engineer, sell, install, and service such equipment. It was also generally agreed by those in attendance, including many executives of the full-line tractor and equipment companies, that the market would be too specialized and require too many small items to interest the full-line companies, and that no company, either larger or small, could profitably manufacture all the needed components.

A list of opportunities for new developments, ranked according to priority of need or usefulness, was developed in 1961 by an advisory committee to the U.S. Department of Agriculture. It called for new methods and/or equipment for performing the following tasks: (1) harvesting the highly valuable citrus and vegetable crops; (2) pest control and pesticide application; (3) irrigation; (4) sugar-beet production; (5) harvesting deciduous fruits and tree-nuts; and (6) providing farmstead water-supply and water-disposal systems.[24]

According to industry sources, many product innovations were contributed by farmers or by the industry's smaller manufacturers. One of these sources explained that this was partly due to the nature of farming:

> In recent years, the full-line manufacturers have increased the amount of resources they have allocated to product development. Much of this money has been spent to improve existing products such as tractors and combines. A significant proportion, however, has been spent on the development of new technology in crops that offer a large potential market. For example, most full-line manufacturers are working on methods to harvest citrus fruits, particularly oranges.
>
> On the other hand, there are many crops requiring new technology that do not offer large markets. The full-line manufacturers seldom, if ever, try to develop products for these markets because of the restricted demand. Nevertheless, the development, manufacture, and sale of equipment to serve these specialized needs sometimes provide highly profitable opportunities for the smaller, more flexible companies. If demand for a product of this type increases significantly, however, the larger manufacturers would probably enter the market.

The same source indicated that patent protection was of minor value with regard to most product developments, and that there was wide use of cross-

---

[24]*Implement & Tractor*, April 1, 1961, p. 38, ff.

licensing of patents that were important.[25] He also indicated that the lead time for most product developments (or adaptations) was only one or two years.

A number of other sources agreed and indicated that although in any given year there were variations in the characteristics, quality, and price of the products of the major manufacturers these differences were seldom substantial or lasting. In addition, many of the product differences that did in fact exist were often regarded as being of more importance from a marketing viewpoint than a functional viewpoint.

Perhaps the greatest advantage in product differentiation in recent years had accrued to Deere & Company, which had introduced a full line of equipment for the large commercial farms in 1960. Most other full-line manufacturers did not introduce a comparable line until 1964 or 1965.

Changes in channels of distribution. Besides undergoing changes in structure and products, the domestic farm equipment industry was also experiencing changes in the channels of distribution.

Both full- and long-line manufacturers serviced the farmers through independent dealers and company-owned stores. These outlets were, in turn, supplied by company branch warehouses and independent wholesalers (see Exhibit 7).

Farm equipment dealers generally handled the lines of one full-line manufacturer on an exclusive franchise basis, even though they legally had the right to handle competing major lines. However, they generally did carry individual products of smaller manufacturers which sometimes competed with similar items in their major line.

Farm equipment wholesalers almost defied classification. They ranged in size from organizations handling the products of a single or very few manufacturers within a state or part of a state to multistate organizations with many warehouses handling hundreds of items of farm equipment as well as many farm supply items. They seldom handled competing lines, but generally attempted to maintain an identity separate from that of their principal suppliers.

The two principal changes taking place in the distribution systems utilized by the full-line and long-line manufacturers in the early 1960's were (1) a shortening of the distribution channels, and (2) a decrease in the number of independent dealers.

The shortening of the distribution channels was generally achieved by bypassing the farm equipment wholesalers and serving dealers from branch warehouses. Ford was the last full-line manufacturer to use wholesalers and it switched to using branch warehouses in 1964. Thus, by 1965, all the full-line manufacturers supplied their dealers and company stores directly.

---

[25]Industry sources also stated that there was a very high degree of interchangeability among the products of all the manufacturers. Hitches, hydraulic systems, and even power take-offs from tractor to implements were either standardized, or compatible with the addition of simple converting attachments.

Between 1958 and 1963, the number of retail dealers handling principally farm equipment decreased from 19,008 to 16,362. The average dealer's sales, however, increased from $167,000 in 1958 to $222,000 in 1964, according to the U.S. Bureau of the Census. Industry sources expected these trends to continue through the 1960's because of manufacturer's programs designed to develop fewer, but stronger dealers.

The operation of company-owned stores was viewed differently by different full-line manufacturers. Some, such as Deere and White, were trying to decrease the number of their stores by getting independent dealers to take over these operations. Others, such as International Harvester, Massey-Ferguson, and Ford, were building company-store operations where they had been unable to establish independent dealers. Overall, the number of retail outlets owned and operated by the full-line manufacturers increased slightly during the 1960's.

Although farm equipment dealers had been getting stronger, they still needed help in financing inventories and customer sales because of the high cost of the equipment, the low rate of inventory turnover, and the long credit terms they had to extend to farmers. Since 1948, the meeting of this need had been increasingly faced by manufacturers, some of whom also provided lease agreements. According to *Fortune:*

> The credit terms, both to dealers and to farmers, are probably the most liberal in all industry. The manufacturer may carry the dealer's inventory of new machines on his sales floor for as long as eighteen months; often, the manufacturer will also help the dealer carry the used merchandise he has to take in trade. . . . Retail credit is also easy—farmers traditionally get three or even four crop-years to pay for a large purchase.[26]

Banks in rural areas also extended liberal credit to farmers.

One of the reasons the full-line manufacturers wanted fewer but larger dealers, in the case writer's opinion, was the desire to stabilize prices. Although *Standard & Poor's* reported that "the industry is relatively free from unstable prices and bad competitive conditions" because the establishment of relations with and confidence in responsible dealers was a slow process,[27] trade sources reported that dealers complained of cut-throat pricing, dumping in one another's territories, and discounters' invasion into the relatively lucrative field of merchandising fast-moving parts.[28] In the case writer's opinion, the large dealers serving the full- and long-line manufacturers generally did not cut prices or engage in other "bad" competitive practices. However, the case writer felt that the marginal dealers serving the full- and long-line manufacturers and many of the outlets in the short-line distribution system did engage in such practices.

---

[26]George Bookman, "Farm Machinery Shifts Gears," *Fortune,* July 1961, p. 132.
[27]Standard & Poor's, *Machinery, Agricultural,* 1966, p. M–12.
[28]*Implement & Tractor,* April 1, 1962, p. 17.

Another reason the full-line manufacturers wanted fewer but larger distributors was their desire to offer more service to the farmer. Some dealers, for example, even went to the expense of maintaining an airplane fully equipped with tools, spare parts, and a two-way radio. During the harvesting season, such a plane might be flown to a dozen farms a day in order to give service to customers.[29] In addition to improving service during the crop-growing season, most full-line manufacturers were beginning to promote the idea of regular maintenance and pre-use checkup during the off season.

There were some differences among the full-line manufacturers in dealer orientation, however. Deere & Company and Oliver Corporation wanted their dealers to handle only farm equipment so that they would devote full attention to that line. International Harvester, on the other hand, encouraged some of its dealers to handle other products such as refrigerators, air conditioners, trucks, etc. so that the farmer might make all his capital equipment purchases from the International dealer.

The distribution channels utilized by the short-line manufacturers were longer and more complex than those of the full-line and long-line manufacturers. These channels generally carried the products of many manufacturers. Consumable products often accounted for more than 50% of their total sales. In some cases, these distribution organizations were larger and more powerful than the manufacturers who served them. The two principal trends occurring in this distribution system were (1) the increasing concentration of power in the hands of distribution organizations, and (2) an increasing tendency on the part of the short-line and smaller manufacturers to sell directly to the farmer.

The attention that farm equipment manufacturers gave to product-line development, pricing practices, and distribution systems indicated the importance they attached to farmers' buying motives. These motives included (1) those factors which caused him to buy rather than hold off the market; (2) those factors which caused him to choose one brand and/or dealer rather than another; and (3) those factors which caused him to buy larger equipment. A study of farmers' reasons for purchasing produced the following answers: (1) needed more power, or previous machinery old fashioned: 39%; (2) did not have machine previously, needed one: 27%; (3) previous machine worn out: 19%; (4) dealer offered a good deal: 9%; and (5) previous machine "no good": 7%.[30] A more recent study indicated that the reasons for selecting one dealer rather than another were: (1) brand of equipment sold by dealer: 34%; (2) dealer's parts and service policies: 27%; and (3) price, cost, or best deal: 25%.[31] In the same study, farmers

[29]"Agribusiness: The Revolution's Just Beginning," *Forbes*, November 1, 1964, p. 21.

[30]Ohio Agricultural Experimental Station; findings cited in *Implement & Tractor*, September 3, 1960, p. 21.

[31]Nationwide study sponsored by the National Farm and Power Equipment Dealers Association, conducted by Drs. J. M. Bolen and G. M. Beal of Iowa State University, reported in *Farm & Power Equipment*, February 1965, pp. 48–51 and March 1965, pp. 32–34.

indicated the following reasons for buying their largest tractor: (1) more power needed: 78%; (2) ability to perform job faster: 57%; (3) farming more land: 44%; and (4) old tractor worn out: 42%. Thus, it appeared that farmers bought equipment primarily because of economic or technological need rather than because of physical obsolescence, and that farmers selected dealers more on the basis of product brand and service than because of price concessions.

The international farm equipment industry

In 1965 worldwide[32] sales of farm machinery and equipment exceeded $5 billion, an increase of 67% over the $3 billion sold a decade earlier (see Exhibit 8). The world market could be divided into four basic markets according to industry structure. Each of these basic markets could be further subdivided into different national markets. The four basic markets were the North American market, the European market, the market consisting of the other developed countries, and the underdeveloped countries market.

Exhibit 8

WORLD DEMAND FOR FARM EQUIPMENT, BY MAJOR MARKETS, 1955–67

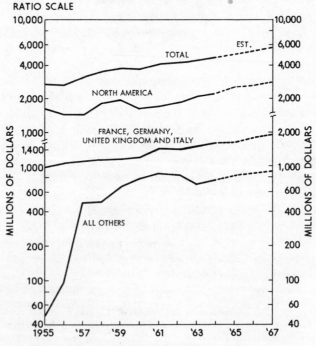

Source: U.S. Bureau of the Census and General Statistical Bulletin
E.E.C., Massey-Ferguson Ltd., cited in Donaldson, Lufkin & Jenrette,
Inc., "Agricultural Equipment Industry," May 1966, p. 4.

---

[32]Excluding the Soviet Union, Communist China, Eastern Europe, and Communist Southeast Asia.

The North American market consisted of the United States and Canada. This market was served primarily by the seven full-line farm equipment manufacturers, all of whom had their corporate headquarters in this market. Sales in the North American market totaled about $2.1 billion in 1965, with the United States accounting for $1.8 billion of that total. While this market was growing and changing in the 1960's, it was not growing as rapidly or changing as dramatically as the European market or the market for the other developed countries.

The European market consisted of all the non-Communist countries in Europe. Total 1965 farm equipment sales to this area exceeded $1.7 billion. France, Germany, Italy, and the United Kingdom accounted for the major portion of this market, however (see Exhibit 9 for farm equipment sales in these countries).

The European market was served by four different groups of manufacturers (see Exhibit 10 for market share of various manufacturers by country). The largest group, which accounted for over 41% of total sales, consisted of the seven North American full-line manufacturers. Their combined share of the market depended on the country, however, ranging from a low of 19% in Italy to a high of 80% in the United Kingdom. Massey-Ferguson, International Harvester, Ford, and Deere, who collectively accounted for almost all the sales of the seven full-line manufacturers in Europe, all had European factories (see Exhibit 11). Allis-Chalmers had factories in England and France, but was not a large factor in either market. Case and White served the European market only through exports from the United States.

The second group, which accounted for almost 40% of total sales, was composed of large, well-financed European companies such as Renault (France), Deutz and Claas (Germany), Fiat (Italy), David Brown and Nuffield (England), and Claeys (Belgium). These companies generally manufactured their products in one or two countries and exported them to the remaining European countries. In addition, in most cases, farm equipment only represented part of their total business (often less than 50%). These companies usually had equal or better distribution than the North American full-line manufacturers and sometimes benefited from national feelings on the part of the European farmers. They were at a disadvantage in product line, however, since they did not have a full line of farm equipment. Claas and Claeys, for example, manufactured only combines.

The third group, which accounted for 10% to 15% of the market, consisted of moderate-sized manufacturers who produced mostly farm equipment. These manufacturers, who were mostly German or Italian, included Fendt, Hanomag, Guldner, Eicher, Carraro, and Steyr. Although these manufacturers had been successful in the past, they were losing ground to the first and second groups because they were not able to afford the capital expenditures necessary to update their product line and maintain their distribution facilities.[33]

---

[33]Donaldson, Lufkin & Jenrette, Inc., *The European Agricultural Equipment Industry and Competitive Positions of North American Producers*, April 1966, p. 4.

Exhibit 9

ESTIMATED EUROPEAN AGRICULTURAL EQUIPMENT DOLLAR SALES, 1958–65
(Dollars in Millions)

	France		Germany		Italy		U.K.		Four Country Total	
		% Change		% Change		% Change		% Change		% Change
1958	$482	+ 5.9	$385	+14.9	$110	(4.8)	$192	+25.3	$1,169	+10.4
1959	409	(15.2)	430	+11.8	115	+ 4.2	205	+ 6.7	1,159	(0.9)
1960	380	(7.0)	500	+16.3	154	+33.9	185	(9.9)	1,219	+ 5.2
1961	469	+22.1	597	+19.2	168	+ 9.6	213	+15.0	1,446	+18.7
1962	481	+ 2.5	541	(9.3)	213	+26.4	210	(1.3)	1,444	(0.1)
1963	550	+14.3	538	(0.5)	226	+ 6.1	216	+ 3.1	1,531	+ 6.0
1964	605	+10.0	540	+ 0.3	244	+ 8.2	214	(0.9)	1,604	+ 4.8
1965E	639	+ 5.6	570	+ 5.0	250	+ 2.3	212	(1.3)	1,635	+ 2.2
Compound annual per cent change, 1960–64	+12.3%		+1.9%		+12.2%		+3.7%		+7.1%	

E: estimated

Source: General Statistical Bulletin, E.E.C. Massey-Ferguson Ltd., cited in Donaldson, Lufkin & Jenrette, Inc., "The European Agricultural Equipment Industry and Competitive Positions of North American Producers," April 1966, p. 2.

Exhibit 10

TRENDS IN AGRICULTURAL TRACTOR MARKET SHARE POSITIONS OF MAJOR PRODUCERS FOR FRANCE, GERMANY, BELGIUM, AND SWEDEN, 1960–65
(Per Cent of Domestic Tractor Sales)

	1960	1961	1962	1963	1964	1965
France						
Massey-Ferguson	25%	24%	22%	20%	21.3%	21.7%
Renault	22	19	19	18	18.9	19.5
Someca/Fiat	10	11	11	10	11.1	11.5
International Harvester	18	16	16	15	12.8	11.0
Ford	3	5	7	10	10.1	9.7
Deutz	3	4	4	5	6.4	6.6
David Brown	1	1	2	2	2.3	3.1
Deere-Lanz	1	1	1	2	2.6	3.0
Others	17	19	18	18	14.5	13.9
Germany						
Deutz	15.7%	15.8%	17.1%	20.3%	20.8%	20.8%
International Harvester	11.4	11.2	12.5	12.3	12.2	12.0
Fendt	10.8	9.6	11.1	10.7	11.1	12.3
Massey-Ferguson	3.8	5.3	7.1	7.7	7.9	7.2
Deere-Lanz	3.6	4.3	3.9	5.5	6.8	5.5
Hanomag	7.2	6.8	7.1	5.4	6.7	7.2
Eicher	8.8	7.5	8.3	7.2	7.0	NA
Guldner	8.0	8.5	4.9	5.5	5.9	6.0
Ford	2.4	3.2	3.4	4.1	4.3	4.6
Others	28.3	27.8	24.6	21.3	17.3	24.4
Belgium*						
Massey-Ferguson	10.0%	16.3%	11.2%	10.8%	13.1%	...
Ford	5.7	7.4	7.9	10.2	10.1	...
David Brown	17.4	13.2	17.4	14.8	7.8	...
International Harvester	4.0	2.9	1.6	3.2	6.6	...
Fiat/Someca	1.3	2.0	2.1	5.8	5.0	...
Deere-Lanz	3.9	4.4	2.7	4.0	5.0	...
Others	57.7	53.8	57.1	51.2	52.4	...
Sweden†						
Volvo	43.1%	39.0%	37.3%	38.0%	39.9%	...
Massey-Ferguson	25.6	30.2	28.6	26.9	28.7	...
Ford	11.5	12.1	11.4	11.8	9.5	...
Nuffield	2.7	3.8	5.2	4.5	6.1	...
David Brown	3.0	2.3	4.2	5.7	5.2	...
International Harvester	6.6	6.5	6.8	5.8	4.6	...
Others	7.5	6.1	6.5	7.3	6.0	...

*In 1964, Belgium's estimated agricultural equipment sales were $22 million.

†In 1964, Sweden's estimated agricultural equipment sales were $94 million.

Source: *Inlassung von neue Zugmaschinen (Gewohnliche) nach Hersteller*, 1963; *Tatsachen und Zahlen aus der Kraftverkehrswirtschaft*, 1964/65, *Statistique des vehicules a motor neufs mis en circulation année*, 1964; *Motor Traffic in Sweden*, 1965; cited in Donaldson, Lufkin & Jenrette, Inc., *The European Agricultural Equipment Industry and Competitive Positions of North American Producers*, April 1966, p. 17.

The fourth group, which accounted for 4% to 9% of the market, was composed of small, local manufacturers, similar to the short-line manufacturers in the United States. They generally produced only a few types of equipment. They were also losing ground to the first and second groups.[34]

---

[34] *Ibid.*

Exhibit 11

EUROPEAN AGRICULTURAL EQUIPMENT PRODUCTION POINTS AND ESTIMATED TRACTOR CAPACITY OF NORTH AMERICAN COMPANIES IN 1965

	Massey-Ferguson	*Ford*	*International Harvester*	*Deere*
U.K.	T(100*), C, E	T(80), E	T(30†), E	
France	T(40‡), C, E		T(7§)	E
Germany	C		T(15§)	T(18ᵉ), C
Italy	T(4)			
Belgium		T(30)		
Spain	[T]		[T]	T(7ᵉ)

T = Tractor (capacity in thousands of units)
C = Combine
E = Diesel engine
[] = Factory under construction
ᵉ = Rough estimate
*Expansion to 125,000–135,000 units expected in 1966.
†Expansion to 40,000–45,000 units expected in 1966–67.
‡Expansion to around 50,000 units expected in 1967; excludes partial subassemblies.
§Total E.E.C. production capacity of around 40,000 units should be available to IHC by 1967.
Source: Donaldson, Lufkin & Jenrette, Inc., *The European Agricultural Equipment Industry and Competitive Positions of North American Producers*, April 1966, p. 15.

During the 1960's, the European market was growing more rapidly and changing more dramatically than any of the others. Two basic causes were at work: (1) a rapid increase in the size of the European farm, and (2) a cost-price squeeze on the European farmer. During the early part of this century, the average European farm had been much smaller than its American counterpart. According to Deere's Mr. Peterson, small farms were the result of the cultural practice of dividing the family farm equally among a family's sons. After World War II, this practice waned under the impact of changing values and the movement of population to urban areas. As a result, small farms were consolidated into larger units which required larger, more modern equipment for efficient operation. This trend was accentuated by a cost-price squeeze on farmers which made the substitution of capital equipment for labor more attractive. While these same forces were operating in the U.S. market, the European market appeared to be about 10 years behind the United States in size of farm and degree of mechanization. However, the European market was changing faster than the U.S. market did during the 1950's. For example, in 1960 only 3% of the tractors in France exceeded 49 hp., yet by 1965 over 13% exceeded this rating. Although the relative degree of mechanization varied according to country, similar changes were occurring throughout the European market. Donaldson, Lufkin, and Jenrette, Inc., commented on the European agricultural situation as follows:

While unit demand for tractors and other agricultural equipment will probably only increase at a rate of 2 to 3% [per year], product mix upgrading in terms of larger, more powerful units amounting to perhaps 3% per year (in terms of value) and expected price inflation of 2% per year should lead to

European agricultural equipment growth in terms of value of 7 to 8% per year—a figure in line with historical experience from 1960–64. However, we do not expect this growth to be uniform for all manufacturers. We anticipate that the international producers, particularly Massey-Ferguson and Ford, and to a lesser extent International Harvester and John Deere, will increase their market penetration at the expense of the smaller and marginal companies.[35]

Australia, South Africa, Argentina, Mexico, and Japan accounted for most of the $500 million in farm equipment sold to other developed countries. These markets were generally served by two groups of manufacturers. The first group, which provided almost all of the tractors and self-propelled equipment, consisted of the seven North American full-line manufacturers. Since these markets were geographically separated and, individually, were only large enough to support one or two modern tractor factories, only one or two of the seven full-line manufacturers usually produced equipment locally. The others would ship machinery to these markets from either the United States or Europe. Massey-Ferguson, International Harvester, Deere and Ford were the companies that had such local factories. In some of these markets, unlike Europe, Deere was as strong as or stronger than Massey-Ferguson, International Harvester, and Ford. The second group of manufacturers serving these markets were small local companies that built specialized tools and implements. Although these local manufacturers would compete on a price basis because they operated on lower margins and did not maintain expensive marketing organizations, Mr. Peterson felt that they would lose market share to the full-line manufacturers as the latter companies developed more modern products and improved their service organizations. (For U.S. exports to various areas, see Exhibit 12.)

While the farm equipment markets in the other developed countries had grown rapidly during the 1960's, Mr. Peterson did not expect the future growth in these areas to be as rapid or the changes to be as dramatic as in the European market. The primary reason, according to Mr. Peterson, was that agriculture in these markets was more similar to that of the United States than European agriculture was, i.e., farms were quite large and therefore had begun to use large, mechanized equipment before the European market had. The table on page 216 summarizes the sources of farm equipment in these markets.

The remaining $700 million in world farm equipment sales was accounted for by the underdeveloped countries in Africa, Asia, and South America. The agricultural potential of most of these countries was not large because of climatic and soil conditions. Most of the farming was done by crude implements manufactured by local companies or by the farmer himself. Modern implements were not economically feasible in many of these countries because of the small size of the farms and the overabundance of cheap manual labor. The modern machinery that was used, however, was usually imported from the United States and Europe.

[35] *Ibid.*

MARKET SHARE OF VARIOUS SOURCES OF FARM EQUIPMENT
IN NON-EUROPEAN DEVELOPED COUNTRIES

Country	Full-Line Manufacturers with Local Production	Full-Line Manufacturers' Share from Local Output	Full-Line Manufacturers' Share from Imports	Local Manufacturers' Share
Australia	IHC, M.-F., A.-C.	Over 25%	50%	Under 25%
South Africa ..	IHC, M.-F., Deere	Over 50%	25%–40%	10% to 25% (mostly implements)
Argentina	Deere (Fiat and Deutz)	About 60%	Few imports	About 40%
Mexico	IHC, Deere	All tractors; some implements	Few imports	Mostly implements
Japan	None	None	Majority of products	Just started licensing operations from full-line manufacturers

Brazil and India were different from the other countries in this group, however. Both had farming lands that would benefit from the introduction of modern equipment. Both also had cultural problems that made such mechanization difficult, however. In addition, both suffered from another problem common to most of the underdeveloped countries: the lack of distribution facilities not only for selling and servicing modern farm equipment, but also for efficiently transferring agricultural produce from the farm to the city markets.

The light industrial equipment industry in the United States

By 1965 all the full-line farm equipment manufacturers were engaged in the manufacture and marketing of light industrial equipment. They generally entered this business through the production of tractors for nonagricultural purposes. In 1963, *Business Week* described this market as follows:

Just how big this new market [light industrial equipment] is still is uncertain—because the manufacturers themselves disagree on how it should be defined. It's estimated this year anywhere from $220 million to $500 million. The market is generally labeled "light industrial," and the companies vying for it are all farm equipment manufacturers; it is largely ignored by the makers of big, heavy earthmoving machinery.

Entries in the race include Allis-Chalmers Mfg. Co.; Ford Tractor Div. of Ford Motor Co.; Deere & Co.; International Harvester Co.; Massey-Ferguson, Ltd.; and Minneapolis-Moline, Inc., and Oliver Corp., both White Motor Co. subsidiaries.

Exhibit 12

U.S. EXPORTS OF AGRICULTURAL MACHINERY AND IMPLEMENTS, TRACTORS, ACCESSORIES, AND PARTS, 1956–64*

Destination	1956	1960	1961	1964	1964 Sales as a Per Cent of Total
Canada	$196	$198	$183	$304	39.3
American Republics	135	123	113	136	17.6
Western Europe					
Common Market		36	46	64	8.3
U.K.		9	11	25	3.2
Total, including other ..	48	74	85	129	16.7
Near East	22	14	17	23	2.9
Far East	33	37	40	47	6.1
Australia, Oceania	†	33	21	64	8.3
Africa	45	44	39	56	7.2
Total†	516	532	503	773	100.0

Note: U.S. imports of agricultural machinery were about $80 million between 1950 and 1957, rose to a high of $169 million in 1959, but fell to $114 million in 1961. Between 1960 and 1964, they averaged about $155 million a year. Canada supplied about 77% of the total during this period.

*Tractors accounted for about 70% of the total, but 68% of these (49% of total) were crawler types which had limited use in agriculture.

†Total includes areas not separately shown.

Source: U.S. Bureau of Foreign Commerce, "U.S. Trade with Major Trade Areas," *World Trade Information Service, Statistical Reports,* 1957, 1961, 1963, and 1965.

"Light industrial" means equipment of roughly 30 hp. to 70 hp., designed for jobs too small for a big contractor's machinery. These jobs range from landscaping, mowing, logging, trenching, and snow removal to gravedigging and straightening of freight cars.

Though manufacturers disagree on defining the market, they are united in seeing in it a growing potential. Some industrial tractors were introduced as early as the 1930's, and after World War II, with an increase of hydraulic applications to hitches, the market began to take form. But it's just now beginning to be tapped, and each manufacturer sees steady gains ahead over the next five years.

For farm machinery makers, traditionally bound to the agricultural field with its discouragingly slow growth, industrial equipment provides a new outlet. A-C and IH are both widely diversified, and Ford's tractor business is only a small part of its total volume. But for such manufacturers as Deere, Case, and Massey-Ferguson, the light industrial market represents a significant area of diversification.

The new market breaks down into two general segments—wheel tractors and crawler tractors—and their attachments. Ford claims domestic leadership in wheel tractor and equipment sales; but Deere, leading U.S. producer of farm machinery, says flatly it has the overall lead in the light industrial field.

Regardless of who's ahead, Deere's growth is indicative of the exploding market. At the last Road Show in 1957, Deere's light industrial line totaled eight models; now it has 85. Sales of such equipment were $11 million for the quarter ended January 31—up more than 50% from $7 million a year earlier. Last year, industrial tractor and equipment sales accounted for 10% of Deere's

$540 million domestic volume. President William A. Hewitt says Deere has invested over $15 million in the line.

Deere got into the market after a specialty manufacturer in northwest Washington started buying Deere chassis, putting crawler tracks on them, and selling the units to loggers. Deere bought the facility in 1948 and began marketing a small crawler in its farm line; in the early 1950's dealers reported crawler sales to small contractors. Other farm implement makers also were discovering that not all tractors were ending up on the farm.

By the middle 1950's the producers were committed to a market that had been dumped in their laps. It was a natural form of diversification. Deere's executive vice president, Ellwood F. Curtis, says: "We used the same engineering talent in most cases, the same distribution setup, and a similar manufacturing facility."

But the market was a vague one. One manufacturer says that "60% of our industrial customers . . . two or three years ago weren't listed in the yellow pages of the phone book."

Ill-defined or not, the market boomed. Oliver in 1962 showed a 30% increase in industrial sales over 1961. S. F. Beatty, manager of its Industrial Div., sees another 30% increase this year, says: "We're just getting under way." Deere's marketing vice president, E. W. Ukkelberg, sets a bench mark for its industrial tractor and equipment sales of $100 million by 1968, foresees $150 million in the future.

International Harvester's manager of tractor and industrial equipment sales, Richard W. Hough, says industrial tractors may account for half of its Farm Equipment Div.'s unit output in three to five years. Massey-Ferguson's marketing vice president, J. H. Shiner, expects "a minimum 20% increase in light industrial volume in North America in the next five years."

Ford keeps light industrial tractors within its existing network of dealers. The combination carries through marketing, sales, research and development, and manufacturing.

Deere takes a different tack, draws a distinct line all the way through between its farm and industrial lines. Its 500-plus dealer organization splits 55-to-45 between combination and straight industrial outlets—but the trend is to the latter. Gerstenberger says the 45% figure could climb to 80% in five years.

International, A-C, Case, Massey-Ferguson, and Oliver have combination dealers, with some straight industrial dealers in urban areas. Most also see a trend to more straightline industrial dealers.

The combination dealer setup followed naturally when farm tractors were first modified for nonfarm tasks. But a heavier, more durable tractor was needed for the new market. Besides removing the tag of "warmed-over farm tractor," says Deere's Gerstenberger, one with heavier axles and a tougher chassis was required.

Equipment had to be specially designed, too. Deere came up with a hydraulic grappling device—called the Rotoboom—that can be rear-mounted on either a crawler or wheel tractor. The first model was designed for handling pulpwood 4 ft. to 8 ft. long; where it used to take four men 10 hours to load 100 cords of 4 ft. pulpwood by hand, a Rotoboom and two men do the job in 5½ hours. The device also handles sand and gravel, removes brush and debris, and—

in unusual modifications used by the Southern Pacific Co.—straightens the ends of railroad cars or raises cars for truck spring changes.

Says Gerstenberger: "I don't really know where the lid is on industrial equipment and its applications."[36]

[36]"Offbeat Market Lures Farm Tractor Makers," *Business Week*, March 16, 1963, pp. 98–103.

DEERE & COMPANY*

∧∧

In 1965 Deere & Company was the largest seller of farm equipment in the world, with total sales of over $886 million. Since 1956, both sales and profits had increased by about 180% (see Exhibit 1). During this period, Deere consistently led the industry in return on investment. Assets more than doubled during this time, increasing from $454 to $981 million (see Exhibit 2). Nearly half this increase was allocated to the development of overseas operations, primarily in Western Europe and Latin America. By 1965, overseas operations accounted for 21% of Deere's total assets and 16% of total sales.

Deere was one of seven full-line farm equipment manufacturers in the world. Although the company produced and/or marketed farm equipment in Western Europe, Latin America, South Africa, Australia, and the Far East, most of its production, sales, and profits were derived from the United States and Canada. In addition to farm equipment, Deere also manufactured and sold light industrial equipment and lawn and garden tractors (see Exhibit 3). These products were marketed primarily in the United States and Canada, and together they accounted for about 14% of Deere's 1965 sales. However, Deere, to a greater extent than most other full-line farm equipment manufacturers, devoted most of its energy to the farm equipment business.

Mr. William Hewitt, Deere's board chairman and chief executive officer, analyzed the company's current problems and opportunities as follows:

At the present time, there are several problems and also several opportunities facing Deere & Company. Some of these are relatively immediate, while others are more long range.

An example of a short- to medium-run problem is the question of what Deere must do to substantially increase its domestic market share again. Our totally new tractor line, called the "New Generation of Power," enabled us to increase our share when it was introduced in 1960. By now, however, most of our competitors have learned the new rules and are offering similar products. If we want to achieve another major increase in market penetration, we will probably have to come up with another major innovation.

Industrial equipment, on the other hand, presents us with an excellent op-

---

Exhibit 1

DEERE & COMPANY

Eleven-Year Summary of Consolidated Income and Earned Surplus, Years Ended October 31, 1955–65

(Dollars in Millions)

	1955	1956	1957	1958	1959	1960	1961	1962	1963	1964	1965
Sales and other income:											
Net sales	$339.6	$313.8	$424.4	$507.4	$577.3	$511.9	$561.6	$572.8	$688.9	$816.6	$886.6
Interest and finance charges	2.3	3.5	5.7	8.4	7.0	7.7	9.2	9.6	9.5	9.2	8.0
Net income of credit company subsidiaries	...	...	...	(0.1)	0.3	1.4	3.0	3.0	3.0	3.3	3.1
Miscellaneous income	1.1	0.5*	0.8	1.4	2.0	2.3	2.1	2.1	3.2	3.5	4.2
Total	$343.0	$317.7	$430.9	$517.0	$586.7	$523.2	$575.9	$587.6	$704.7	$832.6	$901.9
Less:											
Cost of goods sold	242.5	236.8	309.9	352.5	405.1	409.5	423.3	418.2	505.1	591.6	659.8
Selling, administrative and general expenses	41.4	45.4	54.2	63.7	69.2	67.0	71.2	70.6	80.6	98.4	99.9
Provision for income taxes	28.7	13.3	33.5	52.6	53.6	15.1	33.0	44.4	58.4	69.4	69.3
Interest	2.2	2.2	3.7	4.9	7.9	11.2	10.7	10.1	9.7	11.9	19.2
Foreign exchange loss (gain)	(0.2)	(0.2)	(0.04)	(0.2)	(0.3)	(0.2)	0.6	4.8	0.9	0.4	0.5
Miscellaneous charges	0.1	0.1	0.4	0.2	0.4	0.3	1.2	1.5	1.7	1.5	2.2
Total	$314.7	$297.7	$401.7	$473.6	$535.8	$502.9	$540.0	$549.6	$656.4	$773.2	$850.9
Gain on sales of chemical company assets	...	...	...	...	...	...	...	...	...	...	4.8
Net income for the year	28.3	20.1	29.2	43.4	50.9	20.3	36.0	38.0	48.4	59.4	55.8
Earned surplus at beginning of year	194.5	207.3	215.2	230.5	234.9	261.6	268.0	290.2	313.0	343.4	382.1
Total	$222.9	$227.4	$244.4	$274.0	$285.8	$281.8	$304.0	$328.1	$361.3	$402.8	$437.9
Less:											
Cash dividends on preferred stock	2.2	2.2	2.2	1.4	...	...	...	...	...	...	...
Cash dividends on common stock	13.4	10.1	11.7	13.4	13.4	13.8	13.8	15.2	17.9	20.7	21.5
Stock dividend—3%	...	...	...	...	10.8	...	...	...	...	...	...
Charge to earned surplus arising from conversion of preferred stock to debentures	...	...	...	24.2	...	...	...	...	...	...	...
Total	15.6	12.2	13.9	39.1	24.2	13.8	13.8	15.2	17.9	20.7	21.5
Earned surplus at end of year	$207.3	$215.2	$230.5	$234.9	$261.6	$268.0	$290.2	$313.0	$343.4	$382.1	$416.4

Notes: Figures may fail to add because of rounding.

Figures for the years 1956 through 1963 differ from those previously reported because of a change in the basis for consolidation. In this summary all significant subsidiaries throughout the world with the exception of John Deere Credit Company are consolidated. The company's share of net income or loss and retained income or accumulated deficit of unconsolidated subsidiaries including John Deere Credit Company is combined with those of the consolidated group.

*Includes special credit of $53,061 representing restoration to income of depreciation reserves no longer required of $7,553,061 and a special provision for pensions of $7,500,000.

Source: Company records.

Exhibit 2

DEERE & COMPANY

Eleven-Year Summary of Consolidated Balance Sheets, 1955-65
(Dollars in Millions)

	1955	1956	1957	1958	1959	1960	1961	1962	1963	1964	1965
					(As of October 31)						
ASSETS:											
Current assets:											
Cash and government securities	$99.8	$50.2	$37.9	$13.8	$15.5	$27.9	$14.7	$23.7	$17.4	$22.1	$21.2
Receivables from John Deere Credit Company	...	...	...		9.1	0.5	12.7	55.5	44.2	31.3	9.4
Trade receivables—net	146.4	185.9	237.3	313.1	299.1	233.6	258.9	240.3	269.9	342.6	390.4
Inventories	113.0	127.2	123.1	130.7	179.8	177.7	172.3	162.0	175.9	235.5	282.4
Total current assets	$359.3	$363.3	$398.3	$457.6	$503.5	$439.6	$458.6	$481.5	$507.5	$631.5	$703.4
Property and equipment—at cost	172.7	195.8	205.2	218.3	238.6	269.8	284.3	305.3	329.3	385.3	413.4
Less reserves for depreciation	83.6	94.2	106.3	118.2	130.4	136.8	149.1	167.0	185.0	207.0	206.0
Property and equipment—net	$89.1	$101.7	$98.9	$100.2	$108.2	$133.0	$135.1	$138.3	$144.4	$178.3	$207.4
Investments in and advances to unconsolidated subsidiaries:											
John Deere Credit Company	...	...	...	0.01	20.3	41.6	44.4	47.2	50.0	53.1	41.1
Other	0.3	0.3	0.3	1.8	3.1	4.5	10.9	12.8	16.3	2.9	5.3
Total investments in and advances to unconsolidated subsidiaries	$0.3	$0.3	$0.3	$1.8	$23.5	$46.1	$55.3	$59.9	$66.3	$56.0	$46.4
Other assets	1.2	2.8	3.4	4.2	5.4	5.0	6.8	7.3	8.8	10.4	15.1
Deferred charges	4.1	4.1	4.2	4.2	4.3	4.4	6.4	5.5	6.1	6.6	8.4
Total assets	$454.0	$472.3	$505.1	$568.1	$644.9	$628.2	$662.3	$692.5	$733.0	$882.8	$980.6

Exhibit 2—Continued

	1955	1956	1957	1958	1959 (As of October 31)	1960	1961	1962	1963	1964	1965
LIABILITIES:											
Current liabilities:											
Notes payable	$ ...	$ 9.6	$ 8.3	$ 23.0	$ 43.8	$ 52.8	$ 9.4	$ 24.4	$ 11.7	$ 37.2	$112.4
Accounts payable and other	22.1	24.2	27.2	38.4	50.6	58.0	54.6	58.0	78.3	117.8	109.0
Accrued taxes	32.4	15.7	35.3	45.5	55.0	17.0	35.7	41.7	47.1	55.2	56.1
Total current liabilities	$ 54.5	$ 49.4	$ 70.8	$107.0	$149.4	$127.7	$ 99.7	$124.1	$137.1	$210.2	$277.5
Long-term debt	66.1	71.7	68.0	123.5	120.9	119.0	159.0	144.9	142.9	181.5	176.1
Pension and miscellaneous reserves	14.2	21.3	22.1	20.3	19.8	20.3	19.5	17.0	15.9	15.0	16.0
Minority interest	...	2.8	1.6	1.4	1.4	1.3	2.1	1.7	1.8	1.6	1.3
Capital stock and earned surplus:											
Preferred stock	$ 30.9	$ 30.9	$ 30.9	...	...	...	...	...	...	...	...
Common stock	$ 81.1	$ 81.1	$ 81.1	$ 81.1	$ 91.9	$ 91.9	$ 91.9	$ 91.9	$ 92.0	$ 92.5	$ 93.4
Earned surplus	207.3	215.2	230.5	234.9	261.6	268.0	290.2	313.0	343.4	382.1	416.4
Total capital stock and earned surplus	$319.2	$327.1	$342.4	$315.9	$353.4	$359.9	$382.0	$404.8	$435.4	$474.6	$509.8
Total liabilities	$454.0	$472.3	$505.1	$568.1	$644.9	$628.2	$662.3	$692.5	$733.0	$882.8	$980.6

Note: Figures may fail to add because of rounding.
Source: Company records.

Exhibit 3

SALES BY PRODUCT TYPE, 1958–65

(Dollars in Millions)

Type	1958*	1959*	1960*	1961*	1962*	1963*	1963	1964	1965
Farm machinery									
North America	$424.8	$471.3	$396.5	$439.9	$454.6	$535.9	$539.9	$580.0	$617.3
Overseas	13.3	14.8	24.6	24.0	24.9	28.1	65.7	116.0	128.0
Total	$438.1	$486.1	$421.1	$463.9	$479.5	$564.0	$605.6	$696.0	$745.3
Industrial machinery	26.5	48.1	39.7	33.0	45.7	60.5	68.7	93.1	112.1
Lawn and garden tractors	...	...	...	...	...	...	...	9.5	15.7
Chemical products	6.7	8.3	7.7	12.7	16.3	14.6	14.6	18.0	13.5†
Total nonconsolidated	$471.4‡	$542.5	$468.5	$509.6	$541.5	$639.1	...	...	...
Total consolidated	$507.4	$577.3	$511.9	$561.6	$572.8	$688.9	$688.9	$816.6	$886.6

*Reported on a nonconsolidated basis; unconsolidated subsidiaries, other than Deere Credit Company, sold only farm and industrial machinery; overseas sales did not include exports from North America sold overseas.

†Includes seven months' sales only. The assets of the John Deere Chemical Company were sold effective June 1, 1965.

‡Excludes $1.2 million of military products.

Source: Various company annual reports and internal reports.

portunity. Presently, we have one of the more complete lines of industrial equipment and an excellent distribution system for these products. This gives us the opportunity to increase our share of this rapidly growing market before our competition can duplicate our resources in this area.

The most important opportunities and challenges facing us in the next decade, however, are in our overseas operations. These represent a major opportunity because half of the free world's sales of farm equipment takes place outside of North America, and our share of this market has been extremely low. Our overseas operations are a problem currently because they have required a great deal of time and money and are still not profitable.

The basis of our current problem can probably be traced to our late entry into these markets. Massey-Ferguson and International Harvester, for example, had been operating overseas for more than 40 years when we entered these markets in 1956. Initially, we tried to grow into these markets slowly. By 1962, we decided that we had to move rapidly, however, if we were going to be able to achieve the volume necessary to become competitive in costs in time to take advantage of the major changes toward U.S.-type farming we saw ahead in overseas—and particularly European—agriculture. This decision presented us with several problems. Should we acquire existing companies or build our own facilities? To date we have followed both approaches.

Personnel was another problem. Should we take John Deere men and let them gain overseas experience, or should we take overseas men and make them John Deere men? We decided on the former course, because we felt it would enable more rapid initial growth. At the same time, we picked nationals to work side by side with these men so that we would have nationals in overseas management positions eventually. This created a further problem, since we felt we needed to send our very best men overseas, while, at the same time, we needed these men to help meet competitive challenges at home. There were also the problems of different languages, laws, customs, and people that are present in all overseas operations.

We have come a long way since 1956, but there is a long way to go. Shortly, we will have modern, efficient plants and a competitive product line. We will still have the important task of building distribution and sales, however, to utilize our new capacity. This will be complicated by the diversity and complexity of the overseas markets and particularly by the fact that trade practices vary widely from country to country. In Germany, for example, dealers generally carried a number of lines, and each dealer negotiated with the factory on the price he should pay. We have expended a lot of effort to try to create a more logical dealer system in this market. We still have a way to go, however, and will have to repeat this effort in each market.

There are other problems which we also face in our overseas operations. Should we insist on 100% ownership? Should we ever settle for less than 50%? Why not just licensing agreements if we cannot get 50%? Whom should we get as the other stockholders? The government, a few influential locals, or a wider group? Presently we do not know the answers to these questions, although we try for 100% ownership and then negotiate downward.

Perhaps more important for the long run, though, is the challenge of mechanization of agriculture in the underdeveloped countries. If you try to leapfrog to modern equipment, you must figure out how to finance the sale of this equipment and what to do with the people displaced from the farm. If you use the type of equipment utilized 50 years ago in the developed countries, you have no way to utilize your present marketing, manufacturing, and engineering skills. The problem is very complex. At present, we feel it is more of a problem for governments than for companies, and that our best present contribution is to focus attention on the problem. Nevertheless, we must continuously be aware of trends in these markets so that we may take advantage of them when it appears profitable to do so.

You've perhaps noted that I have concentrated almost entirely on our present businesses rather than on additional diversification. This is because I feel there are enough challenges and opportunities in these businesses over the next decade so that we do not need to look elsewhere in order to make full use of both our financial and managerial resources.

History: 1837–1954

Deere & Company was founded in 1837 by John Deere, a blacksmith who developed the first commercially successful steel plow. While John Deere sold these plows to farmers in the area surrounding Moline, Illinois, it was his son Charles who built the Deere business by developing first regional, then national distribution facilities for the company's plant at Moline.

This distribution system, which was substantially completed by 1890, consisted of wholesale branch houses located throughout the United States. These branch houses were originally run as partnerships between Deere and local businessmen. They stocked Deere's plows and harvesters, in addition to farm products of other manufacturers that complemented the Deere line.

During the 1890s, farm equipment was manufactured by a large group of companies, none of whom had more than 10% of the market. In the United States John Deere, International Harvester, McCormick, Deering, and Champion were among the larger manufacturers.

In 1902, International Harvester (IHC) fashioned an amalgamation of several grain-harvesting companies, including McCormick, Champion, and Deering, to control the supply of grain binders to the farm market. IHC thus became the dominant company in the farm equipment business with over 30% of the total market and a substantially higher percentage of the grain binder business.

In response to IHC's "grain binder trust,' in 1902 Deere tried to create a "plow trust," consisting of the leading plow manufacturers and tillage equipment producers. This effort failed. However, in 1911, Deere consolidated its selling effort by acquiring complete ownership of its branch houses. At the same time, Deere merged with several of the other manufacturers who were supplying its branch houses with farm equipment. The presidents of these companies became officers, directors, and factory managers in Deere & Company. This enlarged company became IHC's main competitor in the farm equipment market.

Beginning in 1915, with the introduction of the first commercially successful farm tractors, the farm equipment market began to change dramatically as mechanical power began to replace animal power. Not only did this allow the use of larger implements, but it also released vast tracts of land which had formerly been required to feed draft animals. Between 1915 and 1940, Deere, IHC and a few other large farm equipment manufacturers increased in size, while numerous smaller companies went out of business. During the same period, Ford and Allis-Chalmers entered the farm equipment business.

A second agricultural revolution, which began during the second World War and accelerated after the war ended, was the substitution of mechanized equipment for manual labor. This substitution was the result of the tremendous increase in the cost of farm labor, which was caused by the continuing withdrawal of workers from rural areas. This withdrawal was started by the draft during the war, and continued after the war because of the relatively higher wage rates in industry.

At the end of World War II, IHC was the largest producer of farm equipment in the world. IHC had the most modern product line and the largest number of dealers. Shortly after the war, however, Deere began a series of planned moves that, according to company officials, were eventually responsible for Deere displacing IHC as the major farm equipment producer in the United States. While most farm equipment manufacturers, including IHC, began expanding the number of dealers they served, Deere began a deliberate reduction in the number of dealers it served. This policy, pursued over the next 20 years, reduced Deere's farm equipment dealers from 7,000 just after World War II to only 3,550 in 1965.

Behind this policy was an intensive study of the farm market which had convinced Deere that, although sales were booming after World War II, the long-run trends of a reduction in the number of farms and an increase in the size of equipment sold would make fewer but larger dealers a competitive asset. Accordingly, the company instituted its "key dealer plan." Under this plan, Deere analyzed farming areas throughout the nation to determine an optimal network of dealers to serve these areas. Deere then established and discontinued dealerships in selected locations over a period of several years to conform to this network.

In addition, Deere extended retail credit to farmers even though many purchases were for cash and many of its competitors, including International Harvester, were urging farmers to finance their purchases through banks.

However, in the early 1950's, Deere's farm equipment sales, like those of other manufacturers, began to drop as a result of the end of the postwar selling boom. Deere, therefore, began to look for other businesses which would offer a growth opportunity. After an intensive investigation and in response to government urging, Deere decided in 1952 to build a chemical plant for the production of fertilizers, and achieved volume production in 1954. Shortly thereafter, however, the farm equipment business began to improve.

At the same time, some top management changes were taking place at Deere. In 1954, Mr. William Hewitt was named executive vice president.

The next year, Mr. Charles Deere Wiman, who had been president of Deere for 26 years and had seen sales increase from $61 million to $340 million, died and was succeeded by Mr. Hewitt. He thus became the fifth of an unbroken line of family presidents at Deere since its founding in 1837.[1]

History: 1954–65

In the decade after Mr. Hewitt assumed the presidency, several key decisions were made. First, Deere decided to strengthen its farm equipment operations by continuing its key dealer program and by updating its product line, especially tractors. Second, Deere decided to expand its overseas operations significantly by increasing its export activities and by establishing manufacturing operations overseas. Third, Deere decided to develop further its newly created industrial equipment operations.

Farm equipment expansion: 1954–65. When farm equipment sales began to expand in 1954, Deere's distribution system was one of the strongest in the industry. However, even though Deere had improved its tractor line periodically and offered a variety of horsepower ratings, the company was still producing only two-cylinder models—the same engine type Deere utilized on its first tractor built in 1918. Deere's competitors, however, had long been building four-cylinder models.

Accordingly, in late 1954, Deere initiated a substantial research and development effort to update its product line, including the construction of a tractor R.&D. center in Waterloo, Iowa. Deere's principal competitive activity through 1958, when it displaced IHC as the largest farm equipment manufacturer in the United States, however, was the continuation of its key dealer program. During this period, Deere also offered relatively liberal retail financing terms compared to the rest of the industry. This policy was explained in the 1957 Annual Report:

The new terms benefit the dealers and benefit the company by permitting the dealers to concentrate on selling without concern about financing any customer who is a good credit risk.

As a result, Deere's retail notes increased from $38 million at the beginning of 1956 to $132 million at the end of 1958. (At the same time, IHC, which was encouraging its dealers to finance time sales through banks and finance companies, experienced an increase in retail notes from $8 million in 1956 to $30 million in 1959). In 1958 Deere organized the John Deere Credit Company to handle its retail farm notes. It was in this year that Deere's domestic sales reached $473 million, and exceeded those of IHC for the first time.

In 1960, Deere introduced its new line of four- and six-cylinder agricultural and industrial tractors. This "New Generation of Power" was the first

---

[1]Except for a two-year period during World War II, when a nonfamily member served as interim president while Charles Deere Wiman served as a colonel in U.S. Army Ordnance.

clearly visible evidence of the heavy investment Deere had been making in product development since 1954. At the same time, Deere also introduced a new line of tools and attachments to complement its new tractors. Nevertheless, Deere's 1960 farm sales decreased 13% to $421 million because of a general industry decline caused by the reduction in farm income that occurred in 1959 and early 1960 and because of a shortage of products caused by the five-month plant shutdown required to permit tooling for the "New Generation of Power."

In 1961, however, Deere's farm equipment sales increased to $464 million. During this year and the next, Deere added to its new line by introducing the John Deere 5010, the first two-wheel-drive tractor with over 100 horsepower, and a new self-propelled combine. Deere also improved its parts handling program by using computer techniques for the first time. In 1962 and 1963, farm equipment sales continued to rise.

In 1964, Deere revamped its tractor and combine lines and introduced attachments designed specifically for the new minimum tillage farming techniques. Most of the new tractor models were more powerful than those they replaced, while the combines were the first in the industry to utilize hydraulic transmissions. Deere also spent $65 million on capital expenditures in 1964, nearly double the amount spent in 1963. This included $16 million for a new engine plant and engineering center in Dubuque, Iowa, and a major addition to the combine plant. Sales rose in 1964 and again in 1965, when Deere introduced the John Deere 5020, the most powerful two-wheel tractor ever produced for agricultural use.

Overseas operations. Deere's reasons for expanding overseas were described in the 1956 Annual Report as follows:

It is becoming more difficult to sell in foreign countries farm machinery manufactured in the United States, because many nations want to develop their own industries and others are short of dollar exchange. Sales to the company's overseas dealers in the future will be increasingly dependent upon our foreign manufacturing facilities.

The foreign buildup started in a small way with the establishment of a wholly owned sales subsidiary in Venezuela in 1955 and the acquisition of Heinrich Lanz Company, a German maufacturer of tractors and combines, in 1956. Between 1956 and 1962, manufacturing operations on a limited scale were established in France, Argentina, Mexico, Spain, and South Africa. Deere's overseas activities, which are described in detail in Exhibits 4 and 5, continued on this relatively limited scale until 1962. In that year, Deere decided it had to expand its overseas operations significantly if it was to attain a competitive position in these markets. Mr. Hewitt explained this decision before the New York Society of Security Analysts in 1963:

Here at home experience has taught us that we have usually made better progress in the long run by feeling out the situation slowly, step by step, and building upon the basis of gradual success. Overseas markets are changing too

Exhibit 4

FOREIGN OPERATIONS

Year	Country	Comment
1955	Venezuela	Organized a wholly owned sales subsidiary, John Deere C.A., to sell Deere products outside the U.S. and Canada.
1956	Germany	Acquired 74½% of the stock of Heinrich Lanz Company for $7.5 million. Lanz, whose 1956 sales were approximately $40 million, had had an excellent prewar reputation for the performance and quality of its products.
	Mexico	Established a sales branch in Mexico City and began constructing a manufacturing plant in Monterrey.
1957	Germany	Increased ownership in Lanz to 78%.
	Argentina	Began plans to build a tractor plant with 3,000 unit annual capacity.
1958	Germany	Increased ownership in Lanz to 85%. Began an extensive R.&D. program to update product line.
	Mexico	Monterrey factory began assembling tractors and manufacturing implements.
	Argentina	Construction started on tractor factory.
1959	Australia	Established a sales branch in Sydney to distribute Deere and Lanz products to established dealers in Australia and New Zealand.
1960	Germany	Lanz introduced a new tractor line.
	Switzerland, France	Established a subsidiary, John Deere, S.A., in Switzerland, which owned a controlling interest in a French company, Compagnie Française John Deere. The latter company assembled tractors in France which sold through a sales company it owned jointly with three French implement manufacturers.
1961	Argentina	Construction was completed on the tractor plant.
	France	Construction was begun on an engine plant near Orléans.
	Spain	Increased holdings in Lanz Iberica, a Spanish tractor manufacturer.
	England	Purchased a majority interest in Lundell, Ltd., a British manufacturer which has been producing forage harvesters under license from Deere.
1962	France	Purchased a majority interest in Ets. R. Rousseau, one of the three French implement manufacturers with which Deere had been associated since 1960.
	South Africa	Acquired a majority interest in South African Cultivators (Proprietary), Ltd., a South African implement manufacturer.
1963	Germany	Began expanding Lanz tractor plant.
	Japan	Signed licensing agreement with Hitachi, Ltd., Japan's largest manufacturing concern, under which Hitachi would produce John Deere farm and industrial tractors and equipment for the Japanese, South Korean, and Okinawan markets and would supply the Deere organization with tractors and equipment in other parts of the Far East.
	All countries	Reorganized overseas organizational structure to correspond to the structure that had proved successful in the U.S. and Canada.
1964	Germany	Began expanding the Lanz foundry in Mannheim.
	Mexico	Was designated by Mexican government as one of two companies permitted to manufacture tractors in Mexico.

Exhibit 4—Continued

Year	Country	Comment
1964 (*Cont.*)	Argentina	Introduced a new line of tractors and began expanding the tractor plant.
	France	Completed construction on the engine plant at Orléans.
	Spain	Introduced new tractor models.
1965	Germany	Introduced four new tractor models and an entire line of combines.
	Mexico	Plant expansion nearly completed. A new Mexican administration has decided to allow at least three and possibly more companies to manufacture tractors in Mexico.
	Argentina	Completed plant expansion. Government required 90% local manufacturing content.

Source: Company annual reports.

rapidly for this kind of approach to success. Consequently we are now engaged in a major effort to broaden rapidly our overseas product lines, to build aggressive distribution systems, and establish large, modern, efficient production facilities, particularly in Europe. Unfortunately it does not seem possible to carry through a program of this scope and at the same time make a current profit on the operations involved. Unpalatable as they may seem our losses, insofar as they are attributable to operations rather than to changes in relative currency values, are part of the investment required to put our overseas business on a sound economic footing for the basis of future profits.

The 1962 Annual Report described additional details of the problems Deere faced overseas:

Although we have now manufacturing operations in countries which account for about three-fourths of the free world farm equipment market and have established the nucleus of a worldwide marketing organization, much remains to be done. Our foreign manufacturing plants and sales branches must be integrated with our North American plants and branches into a truly international operation. Progress may be uneven until we have gained sufficiently in experience and skill and until we have developed a broader worldwide product line.

Exhibit 5

LOCATION OF ASSETS BY GEOGRAPHICAL AREA, 1960–65

(Dollars in Millions)

Area	1960	1961	1962	1963	1964	1965
United States }	$560	$581	$596	$582	$674	$668
Canada ..... }				39	53	65
Western Europe }				59	94	145
Latin America }	68	81	97	43	46	73
Other .... }				10	16	30
Total	$628	$662	$693	$733	$883	$981

Source: Various company annual reports.

Exhibit 6

DEERE & COMPANY
1965 Organizational Chart

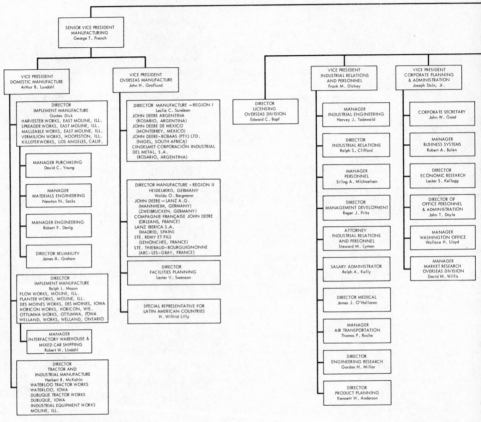

Source: Company records

In order to handle the growth it expected overseas, Deere in 1963 realigned its overseas organization to correspond to the structure that had proven successful in North America (see Exhibit 6).

Although Deere's overseas sales rose substantially after 1962 (a depressed year in several foreign markets, as was 1965), losses were sustained in 1962, 1963, 1964 and 1965 and were forecast for 1966 and 1967 (see Exhibit 7). In the 1965 Annual Report, management discussed these losses:

The company's two plants in Germany experienced considerable delay in achieving scheduled production of four new John Deere tractor models and an entire line of new combines before the spring selling season. Marketing conditions in France, Spain, and Australia were not favorable. Drought conditions slowed sales in Spain and Australia, while uncertainty over eventual Common

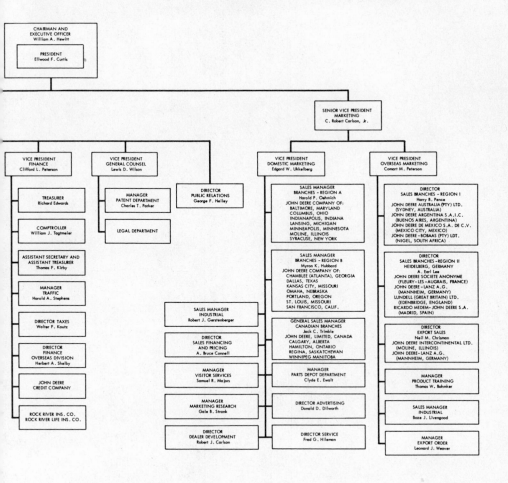

Market agricultural policies is exerting a continuing drag on the market for farm machinery in France.

In Argentina the John Deere plant in Rosario experienced some production delays when, in compliance with government regulations, it stepped up its use of components of Argentine manufacture to 90 per cent of total product content.

In Mannheim, Germany, it will take another year to complete the modernization of the foundry. During 1965 engine assembly and some machining operations were started at the company's new engine plant near Orléans, France, and in 1966 full manufacturing operations are scheduled to begin. In Monterrey, Mexico, where the John Deere plant soon will be manufacturing tractors with 60 per cent national content, construction work to expand the factory is nearly completed. At the time this expansion started, the Mexican government planned to allow only two companies to manufacture tractors in that country. The gov-

Exhibit 7

OVERSEAS OPERATIONS, 1956–67

(Millions of Dollars)

Category	1956	1957	1958	1959	1960	1961	1962	1963	1964	1965	1966	1967
Sales	$12.5	$51.5	$49.0	$50.0	$68.0	$76.0	$56.0	$78.0	$131.0	145.0	$180*	$205*
Profit or loss	n.a.	0.5	Tot. $1.3 L ($1.2)	Tot. $2.1 L $0.0	Tot. $1.1 $ ($1.7)	$ 1.0	($1.3)	($9.7)	($9.1)	($18.0)*	($15)*	($10)*
Assets	40.0	41.0	41.0	49.0	68.0	81.0	97.0	112.0	156.0	248.0	n.a.	n.a.
Investment†	14.7	22.2	22.4	28.5‡	36.6	43.3	59.4	81.3	96.9	162.7	n.a.	n.a.

n.a.—Not available.

L—Heinrich Lanz profits or losses.

*Estimates by Donaldson, Lufkin, & Jenrette, Inc.

†Carried at cost less any deficit accumulated since date of acquisition.

‡Accumulated losses in Heinrich Lanz Company totaled $4 million to October 31, 1959.

Source: Company records.

ernment has since modified that plan, and it now appears there eventually will be several manufacturers of tractors there.

In the same report, however, Mr. Hewitt sounded a cautious but optimistic note in his letter to the stockholders:

Progress has been slower than expected and overseas losses in the last three years have reduced earnings severely. Still ahead are many heavy expenses related to starting up these new facilities which will expand our product line and improve our distribution organization. Despite delays and larger losses than anticipated, we strongly believe that our long-range program is soundly based and that our overseas operations will benefit greatly from the new facilities and the operating experience acquired in the past three years.

Industrial equipment. At about the same time that Deere began expanding overseas, it also concentrated more effort on its industrial equipment. This equipment was sold principally to the logging, construction, and materials handling industries. In 1956, sales of these products were only $11.0 million. In 1957, however, Deere introduced several new wheel and crawler tractors designed specifically for industrial use and a line of implements to accompany these tractors. As a result, sales more than doubled in 1957. With this new line, plus improvements in distribution, industrial equipment sales increased through 1960, when Deere shut down its tractor plants for five months for the changeover to the new four- and six-cylinder models. Sales of industrial equipment remained low in 1961 because Deere gave priority to building farm tractors.

Nevertheless, Deere doubled the floor space of its Industrial Equipment Works in Moline in 1961 to provide room for increased capacity and for a new industrial equipment engineering and design group. In 1962, Deere introduced a new 52-horsepower crawler tractor, started a program to strengthen its industrial equipment dealers, and established a product-engineering center for industrial tractors in Dubuque, Iowa.

By 1963 sales of industrial equipment had reached $60.5 million, and the Annual Report indicated that many potential markets had not yet been tapped:

The potential market is very promising. It includes all nonfarm operations which can be performed at lower cost by using tractors and auxiliary equipment. New work applications are being found continually. The company anticipates that in the next five years its volume of industrial business should at least double.

In order to better utilize manufacturing space and tooling, the company has restricted itself to some extent by limiting the size of industrial tractors to approximately the same horsepower as agricultural tractors. For example, the company's industrial line was expanded to include a 127-horsepower wheel tractor . . . this tractor is the industrial counterpart of the 121-horsepower agricultural tractor introduced a year ago.

In 1964, Deere introduced four new industrial tractors and began to put more emphasis on developing products needed for the industrial equipment market. Deere was also trying to increase the number of and strength of dealers who sold exclusively industrial equipment. In 1965, when sales of industrial equipment had increased to $112 million, Deere began expanding industrial tractor capacity at its Dubuque tractor works.

Lawn and garden equipment. In 1963, Deere entered a new business— the manufacture and sale of lawn and garden tractors and equipment. These products were manufactured at Deere's plant in Horicon, Wisconsin, and were sold through existing Deere farm and industrial equipment dealers, and by other retail outlets, such as hardware stores, in urban areas where the company felt additional retail representation was needed.

In 1964, Deere's first full year of operations in this market, sales reached $9.5 million. Sales increased to $15.7 million in 1965, as the implement line was enlarged (see Exhibit 3, page 224).

Chemical operations. Shortly after Deere had achieved volume production with its chemical plant in 1954, the farm equipment business began to improve. Consequently, Deere did not place much emphasis on its chemical operations until 1961, when it began a three-year program to double the capacity of its chemical facilities. The first step in this program was the acquisition of the mixed fertilizer business of the Ozark-Mahoning Company in April 1961.

This acquisition not only increased plant capacity, but also improved Deere's dealer organization for the sale of chemical products to farmers. The second step was the construction of a $3 million addition to its chemical facilities in 1962 for additional ammonia and urea production. As a result of these additions, Deere's sales of chemical products increased from $7.7 million in 1960 to $18 million in 1964 (see Exhibit 3, page 224).

In 1965, however, Deere sold the assets of its chemical company to Nipak, Inc., a subsidiary of Lone Star Producing Company, for about $24 million, which resulted in a profit of $4.8 million. According to Mr. Joseph Dain, Jr., vice president of corporate planning and administration, there were several reasons for this decision:

First, the fertilizer business was no longer needed as a growth hedge as it was in 1952. In addition, the opportunity was not as great in fertilizers in 1965 as in 1952, since industry capacity had increased roughly 16% a year while demand only increased 14% a year during this period. More important, the nature of the business was changing. New technology was developing that cut production costs 40%, but required larger plants capable of producing 1,000 tons per day, which was far in excess of our existing capacity of 350 tons a day. Channels of distribution were changing also. We never did try to sell fertilizer through farm equipment dealers since to do so would have reduced the selling effort made on equipment. In addition, after the oil companies entered the business, selling tended to be done on a price basis for bulk quantities. As a result of all these factors, when we were faced with the need to invest $100 to $150 million over the next seven to eight years in order to remain competitive, we decided to invest our resources in our primary business—the manufacture and sale of farm equipment instead.

The new administrative center. As Deere began expanding its operations in overseas and industrial equipment markets, the need for a new administrative center for the growing corporate staffs became apparent. Mr. Hewitt felt the new administrative center should be more than just a new and efficient office building, however. He felt it should help to create a new image for Deere and the farm equipment industry. Therefore, in 1957 Deere bought a square mile of land outside Moline, Illinois, and commissioned Mr. Eero Saarinen, one of the nation's leading architects, to design the center.

The design was completed and construction begun in 1961. Early in 1964, Deere moved into its new headquarters, which consisted of three buildings: a seven-story office building, which could be entered only through a glass-enclosed bridge from the product display building, where current and historical John Deere products were permanently on view, and a 387-seat auditorium. The buildings were constructed of a corrosion-resistant steel that was left unpainted and a special type of glass that inhibited glare in much the same manner as a one-way mirror. Very attractively situated in a slight valley, the buildings attracted considerable national attention in architectural circles. In 1965, the center won the Capital Gold Medal Award of the American Institute of Architects.

1965 strategy

According to Mr. Elwood F. Curtis, Deere's president since 1965,[2] Deere's strategy in 1966 was divided into four parts:

First and most important, we plan to maintain and hope to increase our share of the farm equipment market in the United States and Canada. We feel we can do this by foreseeing the future needs of the farmer in time to develop products to meet these needs, which we will then sell through our superior marketing organization. We will, of course, maintain sufficient financial and production resources to support this effort.

Second, we plan to increase our sales in the rapidly growing industrial equipment market by developing a longer line of products designed to meet customer needs and by strengthening our dealer organization. At present no company has a full line, although there may be companies which have a longer line than Deere. We plan to expand our line by developing equipment that will perform functions not performed now and by developing equipment of different sizes in the present areas of performance. When designing this equipment, we'll try to make it as close as possible to our agricultural products in order to achieve production economies, but as different as needed to meet customer requirements. In addition, we hope to develop more dealers who sell only industrial equipment. At present we have 200 industrial equipment dealers and 550 dealers who sell both industrial and agricultural equipment. Yet the 200 exclusive dealers sell about two-thirds of all our industrial equipment. Even-

---

[2]Mr. Curtis was not a member of the Deere family.

tually, we may have separate distribution networks for agricultural and industrial equipment.

Third, we must develop both our agricultural and industrial equipment businesses overseas by getting into the right places so that we can develop sufficient volume to have profitable operations. We want to sell products wherever there is a market, but we do not want to get trapped in every small country that wants a tractor plant. Presently, we have operations in Europe, Latin America, and South Africa, and are trying to build distribution and get production costs down. In Europe, we've specialized by products in each country, e.g., we produce tractors and combines in Germany which we export to the rest of Europe. At the same time, we produce implements in our French plants which we export to the rest of Europe. In the rest of the world, we'll probably build plants for local production only. The basic strategy, then, is to develop Europe and have it supply export markets that cannot be served as well from the United States and Canada. For pocket areas that cannot be reached any other way, we will develop single factories. It will take time to implement this plan, however. For example, we presently supply Southeast Asia from the United States, but we eventually plan to serve it from Europe or possibly Japan or Australia. At the present time, we produce primarily agricultural equipment in our overseas plants, but we plan to build industrial equipment in these same plants eventually.

Finally, we plan to expand our sales of lawn and garden equipment. Last year, this line accounted for about 2% of our total sales, but the market is growing rapidly and we plan to grow with it. At present, we must expand our line of products and secure new distribution besides gaining general experience in the market.

Mr. Curtis subsequently described the major strengths that he felt would enable Deere to accomplish this strategy:

The most important is that we have the best dealer organization in the industry. The difference is not easy to make explicit, but somehow our dealers seem to be more loyal and productive than is usual for the industry. I even think that most people familiar with the industry would agree with me on this point.

I think our tractor line also gives us a significant advantage. Ours was brand new in 1960, and competitors have been copying us since then. We have built a reputation for quality, and have never tried to sell on price alone. We are generally not much higher than our competitors, but we don't mind if we are a little higher.

A third factor which helps us is the reputation we have built up with respect to our customer finance policies. In the depression years, when farmers were unable to meet payments to dealers, we switched our financing plan and took over farmers' notes without recourse to dealers. During this time, we granted very long credit terms and forgave many loans when both farmers and our dealers were in trouble. Interestingly enough, some of these farmers voluntarily repaid some of these written-off loans during the prosperous years during and after World War II. We even received some payments in the early 1950's.

1965 organization

At the end of 1965, Deere was organized along functional lines, a structure basically similar to that used since the acquisition of the sales branches and equipment manufacturers in 1911 (see Exhibit 6). The 1963 Annual Report described the company's organization as follows:

Manufacturing and marketing operations have been split into separate lines of responsibility. A senior vice president is responsible for both overseas and domestic manufacturing operations, and another senior vice president is responsible for both overseas and domestic marketing. Reporting to these senior vice presidents are a vice president for manufacturing and a vice president for marketing in the overseas areas, and a vice president for each of these two functions in the United States and Canada. The result is a functional integration of domestic and overseas business into one worldwide operation.

Mr. Dain elaborated on Deere's present organization:

Although Deere has maintained its philosophy of decentralized operations which date back to the acquisition of its sales branches, this does not mean that headquarters does not know what is happening in the branches. As a matter of fact, we probably have greater awareness of the activities of our overseas operations today than our predecessors in 1911 had in the activities of a factory only a hundred miles away.

Some of our competitors have recently restructured their organizations in an effort to achieve the same benefits we have gotten from decentralization. There are still two aspects of our organization that are unique, however.

First, our sales branches are responsible for both sales *and* collections. The sales branch manager is evaluated on the basis of the profits he makes, not just on sales. This disciplines him not to overstock the dealers with inventories to reach quotas, but rather focuses his attention on helping the dealer to sell the equipment to the farmer.[3]

The second unique feature of our organization is that we have no central product development function. Our factories, which usually make entire products, are responsible for product design and development. We feel this is beneficial because the product design engineer becomes a specialist in one product and because it creates a close liaison between the product design and the production engineering people, which is valuable in terms of costs and feasibility of manufacture. There is the weakness that the product design people don't have as much formal contact with marketing as we would like, however. We are considering the possibility of having marketing specify performance requirements as a means of correcting this.

If there were no central coordination, however, our products might not have a family resemblance. We achieve this in two ways. First, there is an annual product review at each factory in which the local people present their new product ideas to the corporate officers. Second, we employ Henry Dreyfuss, the noted industrial stylist, to give our products a pleasing and unified theme.

To make sure we keep abreast of the industry, we also have a corporate engineering research department, consisting of about 130 people, which is technologically oriented and searches for new developments that can be applied to our product lines. As soon as these principles are proven out, they are turned over to the plants for the actual product development.

---

[3]Deere, like most farm equipment manufacturers, considered a product sold, from an accounting standpoint, when it was transferred to a dealer's inventory.

1965 domestic[4] farm equipment operations

In 1965 Deere sold $617 million in farm equipment in the United States and Canada, which represented about 28% of the domestic market. This total was more than double Deere's estimated 1956 domestic farm equipment sales of $302 million, which represented about 20% of the market.[5]

Mr. Dain indicated that he expected the farm equipment market in the United States and Canada to grow 4% to 6% a year for the next 10 years. During this period, he expected Deere's market share to increase, although not as much as during the preceding decade. Mr. Dain felt Deere would achieve these results by anticipating and leading the market in both product and distribution:

> We try to forecast the structure and needs of the industry 10 to 15 years out: the number of farms; their location, size, profits, and needs; the kind of dealers needed to service them; the number of dealers needed in each location; and the type and size of products needed. Then we try to develop our product line and distribution system in these directions before the need arises. In this manner, Deere is able to maintain and increase its market leadership.

Product line. In 1965 Deere manufactured a full line of farm equipment that included wheel tractors ranging from 38 to 132 horsepower, crawler tractors of 43 and 59 horsepower, tillage tools, seeding equipment, harvesting machinery, soil improvement tools, crop handling equipment, and barnyard and maintenance equipment. In total, Deere's farm equipment line included some 513 different items.

According to Mr. C. R. Carlson, Jr., senior vice president of marketing, Deere tried to design its products primarily for the half-million or so big farmers who produced 80% of the annual agricultural output of the United States. An example of this policy was the 132-horsepower John Deere 5020 tractor introduced in 1965, which was the most powerful two-wheel drive farm tractor ever marketed in the world. Nevertheless, Deere also served the two and a quarter million small farmers who purchased smaller equipment.

Product development. In order to maintain and improve its market position, Deere had been making large expenditures for product development since the early 1950's. After 1962, these expenditures had averaged about 4.1% of Deere's sales (see Exhibit 8). As a result, over 80 of Deere's domestic products were redesigned for 1966, and substantially all the products in the line had been introduced or significantly improved since 1960.

According to Mr. Dain, these product changes were closely related to the changes taking place in American agricultural methods of production, and were primarily evolutionary rather than revolutionary. They represented new ways of applying existing technology rather than the development of

---

[4]United States and Canada.
[5]Percentage of dollar value of factory shipments.

Exhibit 8

SELECTED RATIOS OF WORLDWIDE OPERATIONS, 1955–1965

Ratios	1955	1956	1957	1958	1959	1960	1961	1962	1963	1964	1965
Cost of goods sold*	71.5	75.6	73.1	69.6	70.8	79.9	75.4	73.0	73.5	72.5	74.3
Product development*	3.0	4.1	3.4	3.3	3.4	4.5	4.0	4.0	3.9	4.0	4.4
Advertising*	1.2	1.6	1.2	1.1	1.1	1.3	1.2	1.3	1.0	1.1	1.1
Capital facilities expenditures	$9.7†	$12.0†	$10.8†	$14.8†	$22.3†	$40.0†	$21.8†	$29.0†	$32.7	$64.9	$67.9
Per cent of sales	...	3.8‡	2.8‡	3.1‡	4.1‡	8.5‡	4.3‡	5.3‡	4.8	7.9	7.7
Return on equity	8.8	6.1	8.6	13.8	14.4	5.6	9.4	9.4	11.1	12.5	11.0

*As a per cent of worldwide consolidated sales.
†On a nonconsolidated basis.
‡As a per cent of nonconsolidated sales.
Source: Company records.

new technology. The nature of changes in the market coupled with Deere's strong marketing organization led Mr. Dain to conclude that Deere's future appeared secure:

There is really nothing that I can see on the horizon, barring some drastic technological change in the traditional nature of producing food, i.e., with dirt, water, and sunshine, that can really hurt Deere. And even a new method of producing food might not hurt too much because of the magnitude of the demand for food and the difficulty of getting people to change established eating patterns.

Marketing. According to Mr. Carlson, good dealers and good products were the keystones to success in the farm equipment business. Mr. Carlson also felt service was relatively important, and that the farmer, particularly the big farmer, did not mind paying for it:

Farm equipment products are capital goods, not consumer products. The farmer needs maximum productive time, i.e., minimum breakdowns and efficient equipment, when harvesting his crop. Just as in a factory, down-time is costly. Therefore, the farmer is willing to pay for reliability and service.

For these same reasons, Mr. Carlson felt that price was less important to the farmer than other factors and could be compensated for by high quality.

Another factor that Mr. Carlson believed to be of growing importance in marketing farm equipment was operator comfort:

We are including more comfort features, such as airconditioned cabs, radios, and hydraulic transmissions, on tractors and self-propelled equipment because these features make it possible for the operator to work longer hours at a time. They are also necessary if the farmer is to successfully compete for labor against the modern factory. In addition, we make a deliberate effort to style our products in a pleasing way since this is indicative of good overall design and increases customer acceptance of the product.

Mr. Carlson also indicated it was necessary to acquaint farmers with the uses of new products. To achieve this end, Deere conducted company and dealer demonstrations, and also made use of various other advertising media.

To assist dealers, Deere also had maintained over the years territory managers who were well trained in basic business operations. These men worked closely with dealers in all areas of management, including market planning service, credits, and the various facets of management which were pertinent to profitable retail operations.

Channels of distribution. In 1965 Deere distributed its products through 18 wholly owned sales branches that operated 37 subbranches, warehouses, and parts depots. These branches in turn distributed the equipment to 3,000 independent farm equipment dealers, 550 independent farm equipment and industrial equipment dealers, and 16 retail stores operated by the branches. In 1965, a "typical" Deere farm equipment dealer had total sales (at dealer prices) between $450,000 and $500,000. According to Mr. Carlson, this "typical" Deere dealer derived 54% of his gross sales from new equipment, 17% from used equipment, 18% from parts sales, 5% from service charges, and 6% from other items. He realized a margin approaching 18% on his gross sales and made a net profit before taxes of 4% to 6% on total sales. His return on net worth exceeded 20%.

Unlike some farm equipment manufacturers, Deere's contracts with dealers were for a one-year term. According to Deere officials, the company rarely declined to offer a new contract to the dealer when the old one expired, but used the contract meeting as a time to review the dealer's whole business with him. If there were glaring weaknesses, Deere insisted that a soundly planned effort be made to remedy them. In connection with the contract meeting, dealers were asked to analyze carefully their expected needs for the coming year and to place orders for a substantial portion of them.

Geographically, Deere's distribution was the strongest in the central corn and wheat belt, which produced the majority of the agricultural output of the United States. Nevertheless, Deere's dealers in the other agricultural regions maintained about the same market share as the dealers in the central region. In some parts of the South, however, Deere's share of market was slightly less than it was in other regions.

According to industry sources, Deere's distribution system, particularly its independent retail dealers, was Deere's strongest asset. In the case writer's opinion, Deere's dealers were different from those of the other farm equipment manufacturers in several ways. First, most Deere and IHC dealers, unlike other dealers, did not sell the products of other farm equipment manufacturers, except for specialized noncompeting lines recommended by the respective companies. Second, Deere dealers, unlike IHC dealers, did not sell other products such as refrigerators, air conditioners, or trucks. In addition, Deere dealers were, as a group, the most loyal in the industry. In fact, more than 25% of Deere's dealers in 1965 were second or third generation.

Credit policies. High unit value of equipment, seasonal and cyclical demand, and the need to keep plants operating throughout the year all contributed toward making the farm equipment industry one of unusually heavy financing requirements. Besides their factory inventories, manufacturers financed inventory in dealers' hands and time sales to dealers' customers. Thus, many farm equipment companies were deeply in the business of extending credit.

In financing dealer purchases, Deere required no down payment and no interest until the maturity date, which usually allowed for two selling seasons for agricultural products. These terms were designed to permit dealers to carry representative inventories of tractors and equipment for supplying farmers' needs.

In financing retail sales, Deere purchased the sales contracts from its dealers, and in turn sold these contracts to the John Deere Credit Company (see Exhibit 9). In 1965, the average contract was for 33 months, and the minimum down payment was 30%.

Exhibit 9

SEVEN-YEAR SUMMARY OF JOHN DEERE CREDIT COMPANY BALANCE SHEETS, 1959-65

(Dollars in Millions)

	First Year of Operation 1959	1960	1961	1962	1963	1964	1965
			(As of October 31)				
ASSETS							
Current assets:							
Cash	$ 2.0	$ 5.0	$ 7.0	$ 6.7	$ 4.9	$ 4.9	$ 3.2
Receivables—net	91.6	166.2	181.9	182.1	191.1	207.4	244.5
Prepaid interest and insurance	0.5	1.1	0.2	0.1	...	0.2	0.7
Total current assets	$94.1	$172.3	$189.1	$188.9	$196.0	$212.5	$284.4
Unamortized debt discount and expense	...	0.1	1.7	1.6	1.5	1.4	1.6
Total	$94.1	$172.3	$190.7	$190.5	$197.5	$214.0	$250.0
LIABILITIES							
Current liabilities:							
Bank borrowings and commercial paper	$64.1	$128.0	$ 52.6	$ 5.0	$ 22.0	$ 47.5	$ 96.8
Payables to Deere & Company	9.1	0.5	12.7	55.5	44.2	31.3	9.4
Other payables and accrued expenses	0.5	2.2	5.9	7.8	6.3	7.0	7.7
Total current liabilities	$73.7	$130.7	$ 71.3	$ 68.3	$ 72.5	$ 85.9	$113.9
Long-term debentures	...	...	$ 75.0	$ 75.0	$ 75.0	$ 75.0	$ 75.0
Long-term subordinated notes	...	...	...	...	...	...	$ 20.0
Subordinated notes payable to Deere & Company	$ 5.0	$ 15.0	$ 15.0	$ 15.0	$ 15.0	$ 15.0	...
Capital stock and earned surplus:							
Capital stock	$15.0	$ 25.0	$ 25.0	$ 25.0	$ 25.0	$ 25.0	$ 25.0
Earned surplus	0.3	1.6	4.4	7.2	10.0	13.1	16.1
Total capital stock and earned surplus	$15.3	$ 26.6	$ 29.4	$ 32.2	$ 35.0	$ 38.1	$ 41.1
Total	$94.1	$172.3	$190.7	$190.5	$197.5	$214.0	$250.0

Note: Figures may fail to add because of rounding.
Source: Company records.

Production. In 1965 Deere owned and operated 13 plants in the United States and one in Canada for the production of agricultural and industrial equipment. These plants were relatively modern, according to George French, senior vice president of manufacturing. Manufacturing methods in the tractor plants were as modern as those of any automobile plants. In the implement factories, because the quantities of production varied tremendously according to the type of product, the methods of manufacture varied from mass production with the most up-to-date machinery available to batch production with relatively simple methods. The locations of these plants and the products they produced are shown in the following table:

DEERE & COMPANY

North American Production Facilities

Location	Products
1. Dubuque, Ia.	Agricultural and industrial tractors
2. Waterloo, Ia.	Agricultural tractors
3. East Moline, Ill.	Combines
4. Moline, Ill.	Plows, bedders, listers, and harrows
5. Moline, Ill.	Planters and disk harrows
6. Des Moines, Ia.	Corn and cotton pickers, corn harvesters, cultivators, crop dryers, and rotary hoes
7. Ottumwa, Ia.	Haying machinery
8. East Moline, Ill.	Other farm equipment
9. Horicon, Wis.	Other farm equipment and lawn and garden equipment
10. Los Angeles, Calif.	Other farm equipment
11. Welland, Ont. (Canada)	Other farm equipment
12. Moline, Ill.	Other industrial equipment
13. East Moline, Ill.	Iron castings
14. Hoopeston, Ill.	Iron castings

According to Mr. French, Deere was as highly integrated as any farm equipment manufacturer in the world. He commented:

Deere has integrated as far as return on investment would indicate it should go. As a result, we produce nearly 100% of the end product. We make engines, hydraulics, and transmissions. The products we buy the most of are steel, pig iron, and tires.

Mr. French indicated that the most crucial factor in the manufacturing area during 1966 was keeping up to date in the design of products. As a result, he felt it was necessary to maintain a close liaison between the product engineers who designed the products and the production engineers who developed the manufacturing processes to produce them. It was also important, in Mr. French's opinion, to maintain high quality while meeting standard cost targets.

Overseas farm equipment operations

In 1965 Deere sold $128 million in agricultural machinery products outside of the United States and Canada. This total was more than four times

Exhibit 10

SHARE OF VARIOUS MARKETS: 1964

Market Area	Deere's Market Share
United States and Canada	26.2
France	2.6
Germany	6.8
Italy	less than 0.5
United Kingdom	less than 2.0
Belgium	5.0
Sweden	less than 2.0
Spain	8-12
Mexico	unknown
Argentina	unknown
World Market	14.9

Note: Company officials indicated that market share estimates by country were sometimes unreliable since definitions of the market varied.

Sources: Donaldson, Lufkin, & Jenrette, Inc., *Agricultural Equipment Industry— An Improving Environment for Above-Average Profit Growth*, May 1966, p. 17, and Donaldson, Lufkin, & Jenrette, Inc., *The European Agricultural Equipment Industry and Competitive Positions of North American Producers*, April 1966, p. 10.

the amount sold by Deere in 1956, the first full year of international manufacture. It placed Deere far behind Massey-Ferguson, IHC, and the Tractor Division of Ford Motor Company, and well ahead of the other full-line farm equipment manufacturers. Most of Deere's overseas sales were in Europe, where Deere had about 4% of the total market (see Exhibit 10). However, Deere had lost money on these operations since 1962, when it decided to increase substantially the magnitude of its activities abroad. An independent appraisal of the competitive strengths of these companies in the European agricultural market is contained in Exhibit 11.

According to Mr. Dain, Deere's overseas strategy was to develop high-volume manufacturing facilities in Europe which would be used to supply internal consumption and export requirements, and to establish single factories in other markets that were capable of supporting a plant and could not be reached by exports. Mr. Dain indicated that most large equipment would be exported from the United States for the next several years. He commented further:

I don't see Deere getting into the production of small, inexpensive tractors for developing countries, since our strength is in the production of large, highly engineered farm equipment. Rather, Deere will concentrate on the developed countries and on the major farming areas of the world. To get an idea of what this means for us, draw a strip around the world between 30° North latitude and 55° North latitude and then do the same in the Southern hemisphere. These two bands encompass, with few exceptions, the world's principal farming areas. This includes the United States, Canada, Europe, North Africa, Russia, China, Argentina, South Africa and Australia.

At the present time, Deere has operations in most of these areas. Brazil and Australia are probably the next areas in which we will establish plants. We are not interested in India, though, unless she solves some of her social and political

Exhibit 11

APPRAISAL OF COMPARATIVE COMPETITIVE STRENGTHS OF EUROPEAN AGRICULTURAL EQUIPMENT OPERATIONS: MASSEY-FERGUSON, FORD, INTERNATIONAL HARVESTER, AND DEERE

Company	Product Line	Distribution	Production Efficiency and Flexibility
Massey-Ferguson	Above average, improving	Above average	Above average
Ford	Above average	Average, improving	Above average
International Harvester ..	Average, improving	Average	Average, improving
Deere	Average, improving	Below average	Below average, improving

Note: These rough estimates of relative competitive positions are based on a theoretical average of the international companies and large national firms. If all companies in the industry were considered, including the large number of small and marginal manufacturers, all four firms mentioned above would rate in the above-average category in most sectors of competitive activity.

Source: Donaldson, Lufkin, & Jenrette, Inc., *The European Agricultural Equipment Industry and the Competitive Positions of North American Producers*, April 1966, p. 12.

problems. As you can see, most of these major agricultural areas are already fairly well developed economically. They need the type of equipment we produce. The developing countries, on the other hand, need the type of equipment that was used in America 25 to 30 years ago. We aren't good at making products like that anymore. The major fertilizer companies can help them more at present than Deere can.

Our major goal overseas, then, is to strengthen ourselves in the markets we already compete in, particularly in Europe. At the present time, we're behind Massey-Ferguson, International Harvester, and Ford in Europe, but we have increased our assets in this area by more than $100 million since 1962 in an effort to catch up.

It will be difficult, however, because these other companies were there in strength at least 10 years before us. We do have a kind of an advantage, though. This is the fact that European farming is just beginning to undergo the same type of revolution that occurred in the United States 10 to 15 years ago. There are presently small farms, but these are being consolidated into larger units as the owners retire, since most of the younger people have been drawn into industry and thus do not want to keep the family farm. In addition, there is a cost-price squeeze on the farmers because of rising labor costs and stable prices. As a result, the farmers are beginning to use larger equipment, e.g., the average horsepower of a tractor in Germany was 20 ten years ago; it is 38 now, and will be 70 ten years from now. We, therefore, have the advantage of moving from strength into a market which is 10 or 15 years behind us. In many respects, I think this will be easier than trying to move from those markets to the United States would be.

Thus, while Massey-Ferguson and the others were in Europe before us, we have new plant in addition to product design and distribution skills these companies do not have. While we need to build distribution, we will be helped because distribution will change and become similar to that in the United States.

At the present time, we are broadening our product line and beginning to shake down our new production facilities. We should complete these tasks by 1967. We are also trying to build a better distribution system by strengthening our present dealers and adding new ones. Eventually, we hope to gain 10% of this market.

Overseas product line. In 1965, Deere's overseas product line was neither so broad as the domestic line nor exactly like it in design. For example, the Lanz tractor in the 40-horsepower range was different from the Deere tractor in the 40-horsepower range. The design difference was primarily caused by Deere's policy of designing products to fit the needs of the local market. Massey-Ferguson, on the other hand, had developed one standardized product line for the entire world, although items could be modified somewhat to meet local market needs.

Although tractors and combines accounted for about two-thirds of Deere's overseas sales in 1965, Deere was rapidly broadening its overseas product line, particularly in Europe. To speed this work and to help transfer United States methods abroad, Deere was using product development people from the United States overseas, even though ovrseas product development was the responsibility of the overseas plants.

Overseas channels of distribution. In 1965 Deere served its overseas markets through exports from the United States and by local manufacture. Products were distributed to nearly 1,000 independent dealers in six countries, as follows:

OVERSEAS DEALER NETWORK

Country	Number of Dealers
Germany	350
France	250
Spain	90
United Kingdom	80
Argentina	150
Mexico	75
Total	995

In addition, Deere served Australia and other countries through distributors who served the dealers in these areas. Deere also licensed Hitachi, Ltd. to produce certain John Deere tractors and implements in Japan for sale in Japan, South Korea, and Okinawa.

In 1965 Deere was engaged in an aggressive effort to increase the number of and strength of its overseas dealer network.

Overseas production. At the end of 1965, Deere owned and operated seven manufacturing plants outside the United States and Canada—two in Germany and one each in France, Spain, Argentina, Mexico, and South Africa. The French, Argentine, and Mexican plants had been constructed after 1956, while the German plants had been expanded and extensively modernized during the same period. According to Mr. Dain, Deere preferred to have each factory specialize in the manufacture of a total product rather than to produce the parts in one factory, then ship them to another for assembly.

1965 industrial equipment operations

In 1965 Deere sold $112 million worth of industrial tractors and equipment. This represented a 20% increase over 1964 sales and a 420% increase over 1958 sales. Because of this growth, Deere was quite interested in expanding its industrial operations, even though the market was somewhat different from the agricultural market. Mr. Dain commented as follows:

The industrial equipment market has grown at better than 20% per year for the past ten years and I foresee similar growth for the next five or ten years. The principal cause of this growth is the same factor causing growth in the farm equipment market—declining labor supply and increasing wage rates. The industrial equipment market does not have the same seasonal or cyclical swings as the farm equipment market, however. This is because it is not really a single market but a series of markets. It is lumbering operations, grave digging, highway repairing, landscaping, materials handling, and myriad other operations. This means that it is necessary to design the products to entirely different customer needs. On the other hand, it also means that total demand is not limited by the number of customers we can sell to. Thus, over the short run, at least, total demand is elastic rather than inelastic, as in the farm equipment industry.

We plan to expand our market initially by broadening our product line, which we can do by building present equipment in new sizes. Later we will develop new equipment that performs different functions.

Product line. In 1965 Deere manufactured small- and medium-sized construction equipment, including wheel and crawler tractors ranging between 40 and 143 horsepower, and equipment used in logging, earthmoving, materials handling, and landscaping. According to Mr. Dain, Deere tried to limit the size ranges of its industrial tractors to the size ranges of its agricultural tractors in order to use common parts and to realize other manufacturing efficiencies. However, he felt that recently industrial and agricultural products had grown more dissimilar because of the differing customer requirements.

Distribution. Deere distributed its industrial equipment and service parts through the same 18 sales branches that it used to distribute its agricultural equipment. These branches redistributed to 200 dealers who handled only industrial equipment and to 550 dealers who handled both industrial and agricultural equipment. In 1965, the average exclusive industrial equipment dealer sold about $375,000[6] in new Deere equipment, in addition to used equipment, repair parts, service, and other items. The 550 combination dealers sold an average of $67,000[6] in industrial equipment. Deere eventually

---

[6]At manufacturer's selling prices.

hoped to convert the combination dealers into either agricultural or industrial equipment dealers, since management believed that carrying both lines reduced the dealer's selling effort on at least one of them.

Credit policies. According to Mr. Dain, Deere recommended tighter credit policies on industrial equipment than on agricultural equipment, largely because the former was used more intensely than the latter and therefore wore out faster. The higher down payments and shorter terms helped to protect Deere's value in equipment sold on credit.

Production. In 1965 Deere produced its industrial equipment in two factories, one in Moline, Illinois, the other in Dubuque, Iowa. According to the 1965 Annual Report, production at both factories exceeded planned capacity. As a result, Deere was constructing an addition to the Dubuque tractor works, and planned to move production of items such as loaders and bulldozers from Moline to Dubuque in order to make room for new products that it planned to produce at Moline.

1965 lawn and garden equipment operations

In 1965 Deere sales of lawn and garden equipment totaled $15.7 million, an increase of more than $6 million over the $9.5 million sold in 1964, Deere's first full year in this market. As a result of this growth, Deere planned to broaden its lawn and garden equipment line and increase the production capacity of the Horicon plant, where these products were made, in 1966.

The 1965 product line included one lawn and one garden tractor plus a line of implements to use with these tractors. These implements included a mower, a snow-thrower, a wagon, and a rotary tiller. In addition, dealers could obtain a plow, a cultivator, a dish harrow, a rotary rake, and a garden cart from an allied manufacturer. In early 1966, Deere added another, smaller tractor size with an associated line of implements.

Distribution of Deere's lawn and garden equipment was through its farm equipment and industrial products dealers. In addition, Deere sold these products to retail outlets, such as hardware stores, in certain urban areas.

A look ahead

In a talk before the American Agricultural Editor's Association in December 1965, Mr. Hewitt, Deere's board chairman and chief executive officer, commented:

As a world leader in our industry, we shoulder a special responsibility in serving agriculture's future needs. Never before has world agriculture faced such a challenge in providing the basic necessities of food and fiber as it will in the next 15 years. The challenge comes from the strain that world population is putting on the capacity of world agriculture—a strain that will reach awesome proportions in the 1970's at today's rate of population increase.

Much of the food and fiber needed to meet this skyrocketing demand must come from the United States, Canada, and Western Europe. A quick survey of this map I have before me will show you why I say this. [The world's principal agricultural belt lies] between the 30th and 55th parallels of north latitude. Outside these latitudes, productive agricultural capacity falls off sharply due to inadequate soils or climate, or both. Below the equator, in the Southern Hemisphere, the 30 to 55 degree belt is mostly ocean. Of course, there are some scattered, highly productive farming areas around the world that I have not mentioned, but they are quite limited in size. Some other areas that have good natural resources, but which now are limited by other constraints, may be able eventually to develop a productive agriculture. This takes time, and the population explosion won't wait.

Adding up the *arable* land—that is, the *primary* land for farm production—in the key "green-belt" areas I have identified, we arrive at this startling conclusion: the world must depend for a major portion of its agricultural production, at least in the next 15 years, primarily on four per cent of the earth's land area—that is, the *arable* land in these key "green-belt" areas between 30 and 55 degrees latitude.

One of the most alarming facts of the population explosion is that a major portion of the increase is developing in these very regions which are least equipped to feed themselves.

Thus, it becomes clear that if monumental famine is to be avoided, the key agricultural areas I identified earlier—particularly North America and Western Europe—must provide an increasing proportion of the world's food supplies in the critical period of the 1970's.

We have all seen how the mechanical revolution changed American agriculture. Now a *new* revolution is unfolding in the United States, forged by a new kind of farmer—the businessman farmer. The key word of this new revolution is *management*—it might well be called a farm management revolution.

The new businessmen farmers have a big job ahead in operating larger, more productive farms with fewer workers. Their demands for farm machinery reflect it—they want big machines. They demand not simply larger physical size but greater capacity measured in productivity—in the ability to get more work done faster, cheaper, and easier.

In addition to increased capacity, the new businessmen farmers are demanding equipment to simplify farming operations—minimum tillage for fewer trips over the field, attachments which in one planting trip through the field will also apply herbicide and insecticide, as well as fertilizer and seed.

The patterns of change I have described for American agriculture are being repeated the world over. The key agricultural countries of the world that I pinpointed in the green bands on this map will soon follow these same paths.

The next 15 years in agriculture, as I have described them for you here today, have profound meaning for all of us—meaning that goes well beyond our everyday concerns as businessmen.

The question we must squarely face today is this. "What can and should we in the United States do to help the developing countries achieve this 'decent, dignified existence'?" We, in John Deere, consider it not only a challenge but a privilege to do our part as we serve to the best of our abilities the growing capital goods requirements of world agriculture needed in the enormous task of adequately feeding the exploding population of the world.

MASSEY-FERGUSON LIMITED*

^^

In 1965 Massey-Ferguson Limited of Toronto, Canada, was the third largest farm equipment manufacturer in the world (in dollar sales)[1] and the largest tractor manufacturer in the world (in units produced). Outside of the United States, MF was the largest producer of farm equipment, having surpassed International Harvester (IHC) in the early 1960's. In the United States, MF, with 1965 farm equipment sales estimated at $190 million, trailed Deere and IHC by a considerable margin, even though it had moved from seventh to third place in market share between 1953 and 1965 according to company officials. Although farm equipment accounted for almost 80% of total sales of $808 million in 1965, MF was one of the world's leading manufacturers of high-speed diesel engines and was also a producer of light industrial equipment (see Exhibits 1 and 2 for financial statements and Exhibit 3 for sales by product type). The company employed about 40,000 people throughout the world.

At the end of 1965, top management was faced with two major challenges. The first was the increasing competition from Deere, Ford, and IHC in overseas markets, and the second was the major effort of MF to increase its market share in the important central corn and wheat belt of the United States farm market. A related issue was the question of a suitable organization structure in view of the increasing importance of MF's nonfarming activities such as diesel engines and industrial and construction equipment.

Because MF had a long history of successful operations as well as a leading position in most important farm equipment markets outside the United States, management felt that it could successfully meet the increasing competition in these markets. Increasing its penetration of the rich U.S. corn and wheat belt, a market long dominated by Deere and IHC, was seen as a more difficult problem. Achieving greater sales and penetration in this large and important market was regarded by management as particularly essential in meeting overall corporate growth objectives because MF was already so large in a number of other markets that significant growth through increased market share in these markets seemed unlikely.

---

*Copyright © 1966 by the President and Fellows of Harvard College. Reprinted by permission.

[1]All figures given in this case are in Canadian dollars. In 1965, U.S. $1.00 was equivalent to $1.07 Canadian.

Exhibit 1

MASSEY-FERGUSON LIMITED

Statement of Consolidated Income for Years Ending October 31, 1953–1965

(Canadian Dollars in Millions)

	1953	1954	1955	1956	1957	1958	1959	1960	1961	1962	1963	1964	1965
Sales and Other Income													
Net income	$189.1	$297.7	$285.7	$372.1	$412.4	$420.2	$475.5	$490.4	$519.3	$596.1	$685.7	$772.0	$808.5
Interest and finance charges	...	0.7	0.8	1.4	3.0	2.6	3.7	4.3	7.8	10.6	9.9	10.5	14.0
Profit on disposal of capital assets	0.3	0.5	0.1	0.5	0.6	0.3	0.2	(0.6)	1.4	1.7	0.1	0.3	0.4
Dividends from subsidiaries not consolidated and other income	1.1	0.6	(0.2)	...	...	...	...	...	...	...	...	...	...
Total sales and other income	$190.5	$299.5	$286.4	$374.0	$415.9	$423.2	$479.4	$494.1	$528.5	$608.4	$695.7	$782.9	$822.9
Deduct													
Cost of goods sold	$173.0	$281.8	$271.0	$359.9*	$406.9†	$341.3	$378.6	$390.5	$411.1	$468.3	$531.0	$590.0	$630.7
Marketing, general and administrative expense						45.3	54.8	61.3	68.5	78.3	88.2	93.1	101.4
Engineering expenses						7.1	8.6	11.7	13.1	14.0	16.1	17.4	19.1
Interest on long-term debt	1.9	2.0	1.8	3.0	3.4	3.4	3.4	4.8	5.1	5.1	6.6	7.1	8.7
Interest on bank and other short-term debt	0.6	0.2	0.2	1.9	1.9	2.6	4.6	8.8	9.9	12.0	11.3	11.5	15.4
Exchange adjustments	...	...	...	1.5	3.0	1.4	1.9	(3.0)	(4.8)	(2.4)	(0.1)	1.9	(1.0)
Minority interests	...	...	...	0.2	0.2	0.3	0.2	0.2	0.2	0.7	0.8	1.0	0.9
Total deductions	$175.5	$283.9	$273.0	$366.4	$415.3	$401.4	$452.2	$474.3	$503.3	$576.0	$654.0	$722.0	$775.4
Profit before income taxes	$ 15.0	$ 15.6	$ 13.4	$ 7.6	$ 0.6	$ 21.7	$ 27.2	$ 19.8	$ 25.3	$ 32.4	$ 41.8	$ 60.9	$ 47.5
Income taxes	7.6	8.4	5.9	4.4	5.3	8.7	6.1	6.6	10.0	14.3	17.7	15.8	7.5
Net income for the year	$ 7.4	$ 7.2	$ 7.5	$ 3.2	$ (4.7)	$ 13.0	$ 21.1	$ 13.2	$ 15.2	$ 18.1	$ 24.1	$ 45.0	$ 40.1

*Includes inventory writeoffs and liquidation losses of $8.2 million.

†Includes inventory writeoffs and liquidation losses of $8.7 million and a cost of changing from dual to single product line distribution of $2.6 million

Source: Various company annual reports.

Exhibit 2

MASSEY-FERGUSON LIMITED

Consolidated Balance Sheets for Years Ended October 31, 1953–1965
(Canadian Dollars in Millions)

Assets	1953	1954	1955	1956	1957	1958	1959	1960	1961	1962	1963	1964	1965
Current Assets													
Cash	$ 11.0	$ 15.2	$ 13.3	$ 13.1	$ 22.4	$ 13.3	$ 8.2	$ 3.9	$ 6.7	$ 4.0	$ 9.6	$ 19.2	$ 9.0
Government securities—at cost	4.0	...	1.8	3.9	7.9	...	...	...	...	...	...	...	...
Notes and accounts receivable													
Retail notes—net	25.7	53.9	59.4	14.2	12.9	20.0	30.1	10.8*	11.6*	192.5*	193.5*	203.5*	245.6*
Wholesale notes—net				58.5	61.9	71.3	98.4	129.0	145.1				
Sundry—net	2.3	0.4	1.5	7.4	6.2	5.2	13.2	13.5	25.6				
Subsidiary companies—net	4.3	3.3	9.1										
Inventories at lower cost or market	81.3	87.1	96.5	133.7	106.6	124.9	194.2	171.9	178.2	193.3	201.4	218.3	284.9
Prepaid expenses, etc.	1.1	1.5	1.4	1.4	1.0	1.1	1.0	1.5	3.9	3.8	7.3	8.0	7.5
Total current assets	$129.6	$161.3	$183.0	$232.3	$218.9	$235.7	$345.1	$330.5	$371.1	$393.6	$411.9	$448.9	$547.0
Investments													
Wholly owned finance company†								$ 9.5	$ 11.8	$ 15.9	$ 17.7	$ 22.5	$ 21.5
Associated companies at cost	24.7	6.9	8.8	7.7	8.1	10.5	1.5	3.6	3.1	1.8	2.0	5.0	4.9
Total investments	$ 24.7	$ 6.9	$ 8.8	$ 7.7	$ 8.1	$ 10.5	$ 1.5	$ 13.1	$ 15.0	$ 17.7	$ 19.7	$ 27.4	$ 26.4
Fixed Assets													
Land	$ 50.7	$ 61.5	$ 69.3	$101.6	$109.3	$ 4.8	$ 4.8	$ 4.4	$ 5.2	$ 5.3	$ 5.3	$ 6.0	$ 6.8
Buildings						47.6	54.3	56.9	59.2	63.3	70.8	76.3	88.9
Machinery, equipment, and tooling						61.1	126.1	130.9	141.2	152.3	167.2	193.8	217.5
Total fixed assets at cost	$ 50.7	$ 61.5	$ 69.3	$101.6	$109.3	$113.5	$185.1	$192.3	$205.6	$220.9	$243.2	$276.1	$313.2
Less accumulated depreciation	25.8	30.8	35.3	46.7	51.8	51.4	67.9	80.1	88.7	104.1	119.1	135.3	153.1
Total fixed assets—net	$ 24.9	$ 30.7	$ 34.0	$ 54.9	$ 57.6	$ 62.1	$117.2	$112.2	$116.9	$116.8	$124.2	$140.8	$160.1
Other Assets and Deferred Charges	0.0	0.0	0.0	1.2	1.6	1.6	1.6	2.2	5.0	5.4	4.9	4.3	8.1
Total assets	$179.2	$198.9	$225.8	$296.0	$286.1	$310.0	$465.4	$458.0	$507.9	$533.5	$560.8	$621.4	$741.6

*Does not include the notes held by the North American finance companies, but does include accounts receivable from the North American finance companies.

†At equity value, i.e., investment plus profits or minus losses.

Exhibit 2—Continued

Liabilities and Stockholders' Equity	1953	1954	1955	1956	1957	1958	1959	1960	1961	1962	1963	1964	1965
Current Liabilities													
Bank loans and overdrafts	...	...	...	$ 6.1	$ 5.3	$ 12.9	$ 72.0	$ 55.3	$ 57.6	$ 59.8	$ 22.2	$ 21.8	$ 85.4
Short-term notes payable	...	...	...						22.5	20.2	2.2	2.2	15.4
Accounts payable and accrued charges	$12.1	$18.6	$21.1	36.2	40.1	47.0	79.8	83.8	93.1	92.5	107.6	129.4	141.1
Income, sales, and other taxes payable	7.0	10.6	14.4	15.7	13.3	15.0	15.5	11.7	10.4	23.7	18.4	14.1	16.7
Advance payments from customers	0.2	5.7*	2.1	2.7	2.5	6.1	2.2	2.5	6.6	6.1	9.0	14.2	9.8
Dividends payable	1.4	1.4	1.7	1.3	1.2	1.2	1.6	1.6	1.6	1.6	2.0	2.2	3.8
Due subsidiary companies	2.1	...	...	...	...	...	...	...	...	...	...	...	...
Total current liabilities	$ 22.8	$ 36.3	$ 39.2	$ 62.0	$ 62.5	$ 82.2	$171.1	$155.0	$191.7	$203.9	$161.5	$183.9	$272.2
Deferred income taxes and other charges	$ 2.1	$ 6.2	$ 7.0	...	...	...	...	$ 5.1	$ 6.8	$ 6.0	$ 4.9	$ 5.2	$ 1.5
Reserves for inventories, pensions, and contingencies	23.6	22.3	22.4	...	...	...	...	...	...	...	...	...	...
Long-Term Debt													
Bonds, debentures, notes and loans	49.8	49.1	46.8	78.5	78.0	74.2	100.8	98.4	95.8	94.5	133.7	133.7	136.2
Less: installments due in one year, included with accounts payable	1.8	1.9	1.9	2.6	2.7	3.1	3.8	4.8	4.2	4.3	4.0	3.5	3.1
	$ 48.0	$ 47.2	$ 44.9	$ 75.9	$ 75.3	$ 71.1	$ 97.0	$ 93.6	$ 91.6	$ 90.1	$129.8	$130.2	$133.2
Minority Interest in Subsidiaries	...	...	...	3.4	3.4	3.4	3.4	3.4	7.1	10.7	11.1	11.8	11.3
Shareholders' Equity													
Preferred share capital†	...	...	$ 24.8	$ 24.6	$ 24.4	$ 24.3	$ 26.0	$ 26.0	$ 26.0	$ 25.5	$ 25.5	...	...
Common share capital	$ 33.6	$ 33.6	34.0	35.5	35.5	35.7	58.6	58.7	59.7	60.4	70.9	$ 97.1	$103.6
Retained earnings	49.1	53.3	53.4	94.8	85.1	93.3	109.3	116.2	125.2	136.9	157.1	193.3	219.9
Total equity	$ 82.8	$ 87.0	$111.9	$154.8	$145.0	$153.3	$193.9	$200.9	$210.8	$222.8	$253.5	$290.4	$323.4
Total liabilities and equity	$179.2	$198.9	$225.8	$296.0	$286.1	$310.0	$465.4	$458.0	$507.9	$533.5	$560.8	$621.4	$741.6

*Includes $4.5 million prepayment on a U.S. government defense contract.

†Preferred shares converted to common in 1964 on a one-for-one basis.

Source: Various company annual reports.

Exhibit 3

SALES BY PRODUCT CATEGORY, 1956–65
(Per Cent)

Product Category	1956	1957	1958	1959	1960	1961	1962	1963	1964	1965
Tractors	45%	48%	46%	46%	45%	47%	48%	47%	45%	44%
Grain-harvesting equipment	23	23	23	21	17	16	14	14	17	18
Hay-harvesting equipment	4	4	6	6	6	5	5	5	5	4
Diesel engines	...	...	...	5	10	10	12	12	12	12
Other products	17	14	14	12	12	11	11	11	11	12
Parts	11	11	11	10	10	11	10	11	10	10
Total	100	100	100	100	100	100	100	100	100	100

Source: Various company annual reports.

Mr. Albert A. Thornbrough, MF's president and chief executive officer, explained Massey's 1966 goals and its strategy for achieving them:

Our primary objective is to increase our penetration in the worldwide farm machinery industry. To do this, we must maintain our position in those areas where we presently enjoy a leading position and increase our penetration in those areas where we are presently less strong.

Our present organizational structure helps us accomplish these two tasks. We have a centralized product development activity which has created a standardized, but extremely modern product line. This does not mean that ideas are not developed in local areas, but rather that these ideas are presented to a central product development group. This is necessary in order that other parts of the company may benefit from them and to insure that there is sufficient worldwide demand to allow profitable manufacture of the product. We also have a centralized planning and procurement activity. It is the function of this activity to assist in the scheduling of our production to insure that we shall have sufficient products of the right type in each area to meet the demand and that these products will be produced in a manner to maximize the utilization of our manufacturing capacity. This procurement function also assists in the selection of new plant sites for lowest possible operating costs. Our marketing is decentralized by geographic region, however, so that we can better meet the needs of each local area.

We are presently considering other organizational structures, however, because of the growing importance of our diesel engine and industrial and construction equipment activities. Any new structure, however, must not diminish the efficiency of our farm machinery operations.

Also in the future is the possibility of adding new activities. Although I expect our present operations to require most of our time and effort for at least the next five years, we might take on new activities as our present ones plateau.

History

Massey-Ferguson Limited was an outgrowth of a farm equipment business begun in 1830 in Canada by Daniel Massey. The company was first incorporated in 1847, and the firm's international orientation began with the exhibition of Massey farm machinery at the Paris Exhibition in 1867. Headquarters were established in Toronto in 1879, and by 1883 yearly sales had reached $1 million. A London office was opened in 1887, and by 1890 European sales had reached $125,000. Mergers with the A. Harris Son and Company and the Patterson-Wisner Company in 1891 made the newly named Massey-Harris organization the largest company of its kind in the British Empire, with sales volume of about $3 million and a full line of agricultural implements.

Between 1892 and 1941, Massey-Harris sales increased from $3 million to $35 million. Although many events affected the company's fortunes during this period, three stood out as particularly significant. The first was the formation of IHC in 1902 which brought together a number of the leaders of the American implement industry in a $120-million corporation. Soon after the consolidation, the new company announced itself a convert to the full-line principle pioneered by Massey-Harris a decade earlier. For the next 40 years, IHC was to be Massey-Harris' chief competitor in the overseas farm markets.

The second "event" was the increasing volume of business Massey-Harris received from overseas markets and the corresponding buildup of overseas experience and facilities.

The third event was the development of the self-propelled combine in 1938. This innovation revolutionized farming as much as the development of the tractor. Most of the early combines were sold in the Argentine wheat lands, where the machine was developed. In 1944, however, Massey-Harris persuaded the U.S. government to allocate enough scarce wartime materials to build 650 of these machines. The government agreed, but, in order to insure full use of these combines, required that they be sold to custom wheat threshers, who had agreed to start in Texas and cut the crop north into Canada as the grain ripened. The 650 machines, tagged the Harvest Brigade, were kept running 24 hours a day with the help of special repair crews sent along by Massey-Harris. By the end of the 1944 harvest season, the Harvest Brigade had harvested 1,019,500 acres, saved 500,000 gallons of fuel vitally needed in the war effort, and added upwards of 25 million bushels of wheat and other foods to America's larder. The remarkable performance of this machine helped Massey-Harris make its first serious penetration into the U.S. farm equipment market.

Immediately after World War II, Massey-Harris was able to increase its exports, since its principal facilities were undamaged by the war and had been improved for wartime operations. Dollar limitations restricted exports somewhat, however, so the company began developing overseas manufacturing plants. By 1952, worldwide sales had reached $293 million, of which $224.8 million was derived from the company's North American markets. Total assets were $162.6 million and the company had 14 factories located in five countries. Sales were primarily derived from the implement line, however, which was relatively more modern and more complete than the tractor line at that time.

In 1953 Massey-Harris took steps to remedy this problem by acquiring the assets of the Ferguson Company through an exchange of stock. Ferguson's principal asset, in addition to its $119 million sales base, was the Ferguson tractor; by 1953, more Ferguson tractors had been sold throughout the world than any other kind. Developed by Harry Ferguson in the middle thirties, this tractor had an outstanding worldwide reputation for durability, economy, and simplicity. Even more significantly, this tractor incorporated the first three-point linkage and related hydraulic developments, which subsequently strongly influenced worldwide tractor development. The tractor had originally been produced and marketed in the United States by Ford as the Ferguson Ford, but Harry Ferguson had terminated this agreement after World War II to set up his own company in Detroit. Until the purchase of Ferguson by Massey-Harris, Standard Motor Company of England had produced and sold the Ferguson Tractor outside the North American markets.

During 1954 and 1955, efforts were made to consolidate the operations of the two companies as one factory was closed and production in several others rearranged. Massey-Harris-Ferguson also continued its efforts to expand overseas operations. The principal step in this program was the purchase of H. V. McKay Massey-Harris Proprietary Ltd., the leading farm implement manufacturer in Australia, for $1.2 million in 1955.

At the same time that the company was trying to consolidate the operations of both companies, the North American farm equipment market was contracting after the boom of the early postwar years. During this period, the company's profit after tax dropped from 5.6% on sales in 1952 to 2.6% in 1955. This decrease, coupled with expenditures for plant expansion and modernization and rapid inventory buildups because of declining sales, drastically reduced the company's cash position.

A critical situation was reached in 1956. Even though sales continued to decline at the beginning of the year, management continued to operate the factories at capacity. By May the company's inventory reached $182 million, an increase of $53 million in six months. When sales remained depressed in May and early June, the cash position became precarious. According to *Fortune*,[2] the company faced bankruptcy within a matter of weeks. Colonel W. Eric Phillips and Mr. Edward P. Taylor, members of the executive committee of the board and senior partners of the Argus Corporation, which owned 20% of the company's common stock, were unable to convince the president that drastic measures were needed. Under these circumstances, the president resigned in July, and Mr. Albert Thornbrough was subsequently appointed president.

Mr. Thornbrough immediately shut down the company's large plants in Racine, Detroit, and Toronto, and closed for good a high-cost plant in Batavia,

---

[2]William B. Harris, "Massey-Ferguson Back from the Brink," *Fortune*, October 1958, p. 146.

New York, which had been the company's second largest U.S. facility. Then he mounted a bargain-sales campaign in which product prices were written down to $8 million less than cost of manufacture. As a result, equipment began to move and within four months nearly $50 million in cash was received. By October 1956, worldwide inventory had been reduced to $134 million and the company was solvent again, though its longer term problems remained.

Although $9 million in additional writedowns had to be taken in 1957 and total losses in the North American market totaled $15.7 million in that year, the immediate crisis was over. The company emerged from 1956–1957 with a net loss on total operations of only $1.5 million for the two-year period.

Looking back, Mr. Thornbrough commented on his handling of the crisis as follows:

Our first steps were designed to allow the company to survive the short-run cash shortage. Once this was cleared up, however, we had to decide how Massey was to compete successfully in the long run. After looking at this problem for a while, two facts became evident. First, it wasn't enough simply to be the number one farm equipment manufacturer in Canada. The market wasn't big enough to support a company of our size. Second, it didn't make sense to try to concentrate all our efforts in the U.S. market at this time because we didn't have the appropriate product line or distribution; this was particularly so in the central corn and wheat belt where Deere and Harvester were strong, and where over 70% of all U.S. farm machinery was sold. These facts indicated that we had to become international to survive.

This was easier said than done, though, since we were only slightly more experienced than International Harvester and were certainly far weaker financially. Fortunately, however, Harvester left us alone overseas for five or six years. By then we had strengthened ourselves sufficiently to meet the increasing competition they subsequently offered. Ford maintained its specific competition against us all along, but we progressed nevertheless.

Having made the decision to emphasize our international operations more strongly, our long-term actions were aimed toward this goal. Before 1958, however, we were unable to make significant progress because of the necessity to straighten up our operations in the North American market. By a series of major actions in 1959, including the purchasing of the tractor manufacturing facilities of Standard Motors of Coventry and the F. Perkins group of companies, together with the establishment of a new worldwide organizational structure, we undertook to consolidate our position abroad.

The year 1958 marked something of a turning point. The company introduced a completely new line of tractors; assumed a new name (Massey-Ferguson Limited); initiated steps toward the parallel development of integrated, worldwide manufacturing capacity, and integrated, worldwide product planning and development; embarked on programs to strengthen its worldwide marketing organization and distribution facilities; decided to increase the percentage of its product that it manufactured; and decided to continue to commit substantial resources to product research and development.

Implementation of the plan to strengthen worldwide marketing and distribution began in 1958, when MF reorganized its North American distribution system by purchasing the 17 Ferguson distributors.

In 1959, MF substantially increased its manufacturing capacity and the per cent of product it manufactured by acquiring F. Perkins, Ltd., in April for $12.5 million and the tractor interests and assets of the Standard Motor Company, Ltd., in August for about $40 million. F. Perkins, a British manufacturer, was one of the world's largest producers of high-speed diesel engines, while Standard, a large British automobile manufacturer, was the company licensed to produce the Ferguson tractor outside North America. Included in the Standard purchase were two plants of Standard's French subsidiary.

During the next four years, many other steps were taken to increase worldwide manufacturing capacity and penetrate markets abroad. These included the reorganization of the export division into an international marketing agency with headquarters in Coventry, England, in 1960; the acquisition of the Landini Company, which was one of the leading farm equipment manufacturers in Italy, in 1960; and the construction of a new tractor plant in Beauvais, France, in 1961. In addition, MF established a tractor plant in Brazil in 1960; set up an associated company to manufacture tractors in India in 1961; and participated in the creation of a jointly owned implement manufacturer in South Africa in 1961.

In 1963, the Annual Report summarized some of the benefits of the company's international orientation:

Because of the vulnerability of the farm machinery industry to unfavorable economic cycles and weather, the directors have placed emphasis on securing sales volume in many different world markets in order to minimize local unfavorable situations that might arise and affect individual operations units. The 1963 harvest, for example, ranged from excellent in North America and in Australia to near failures in Eastern Europe and in parts of Asia.

Meanwhile some of the other objectives of 1958 had also been pushed forward, including more "making" and less "buying," increased R.&D., and increased integration of manufacturing facilities. By 1961, the percentage of value added by the company's own manufacture had risen to over 80%, compared with 25% in 1956. By 1962, several types of large, new, relatively specialized equipment were ready for market, and 85% of sales were obtained from products that had not been in the line in 1957. The 1963 Annual Report described the improvements in manufacturing facilities:

Since 1958 our manufacturing facilities worldwide have been greatly expanded and improved. Over this period 13 additional plants have been acquired or constructed and considerable improvement in production toolage and equipment has been made in all factories. A most important aspect of these manufacturing developments, now aggregating 27 plants in all continents, has been the unusual extent to which integration and interchangeability of components has been achieved. This has provided opportunities both for cost control and flexibility in markets.

During this period, MF had also improved its U.S. position. By 1961, it had moved into third place in U.S. sales according to company officials (moving up from seventh place in 1956), and prospects for further growth were improved by new equipment introduced in 1962 and 1964.

Sales reached $782 million in 1964, the eleventh consecutive increase. Profits increased for the fifth consecutive year and reached an all time high of $45 million. In addition, sales of the Export Division reached an all time high of $126 million.

Organization: 1965

The corporate headquarters of MF's worldwide operations were located in the top of a large, modern office building in downtown Toronto, Canada. Even though almost three-fourths of the present top corporate management were U.S. citizens, the atmosphere seemed decidedly European to the case writers (for example, executives usually wore suits with vests and occasionally vests with lapels). The researchers also had the impression that fluency in several languages was more the rule than the exception. This appeared necessary since the company had a policy of using nationals to operate its subsidiaries, and the executive group spent at least 50% of its time working overseas with these subsidiaries.

Reporting to the president were ten senior corporate staff officers, all but two of whom were in Toronto, and eight line managers, as shown in Exhibit 4. The staff group, about 100 people in total (including secretaries), was responsible for assisting the president in setting general corporate policy and evaluating the operations of the divisions against objectives derived from this policy. Although these men were not responsible for the operations of any division, they could provide help to the divisional general managers on matters in their field of specialty.

Most of the operating divisions were based on geographical and/or national boundaries. Each of the major agricultural regions was served by a separate division. The developing markets of Brazil and South Africa were served by special operations. The Export Division was responsible for serving the remaining countries in Europe, Africa, Asia, the Middle East, and Latin America.[3] The International Division was set up to take advantage of various favorable tax situations throughout the world. Because of its worldwide operations and the different nature of its products, the Perkins engine operation was also set up as a separate division.

Each of these divisions, with the exception of the Export Division and the International Division, had both marketing and manufacturing operations. The Export Division had a marketing staff but no manufacturing capacity. There was a tremendous amount of product transshipped between divisions, which led to complicated sourcing and transfer-pricing problems. Within a

---

[3]The Export Division's sales consisted of all sales made to areas not under the jurisdiction of an operating division; sales of one operating division to another were not considered to be export sales.

Exhibit 4

MASSEY-FERGUSON LIMITED

1965 Corporate Organizational Plan

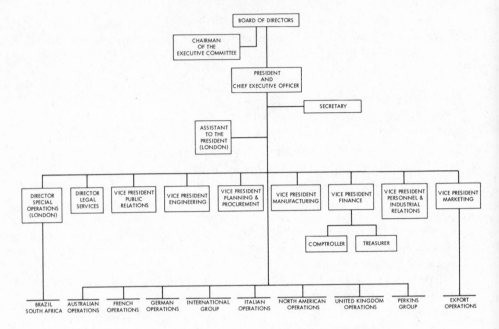

division, for example, the marketing operation would usually obtain some of the products needed to serve its local area from other divisions, while the manufacturing operation would ship a significant portion of its output to other divisions. As a result, MF's corporate staff exerted a strong influence over some planning activities of the operating divisions. After yearly plans had been set, however, each division operated relatively independently of corporate headquarters and was responsible for earning adequate profits and meeting other performance measures.

There were two activities that were centralized, however: finance, and planning and procurement. Although MF tried to do as much debt financing as possible for local subsidiaries from local capital markets, the finance function was centralized in order to maintain close control over the company's liquidity. The other centralized activity—planning and procurement—was a major coordinating activity. In 1965, it was responsible for new product development and logistics. Logistics included sourcing and supply, i.e., the determination of where a unit ought to be made and where plants should be located in the future; inventory control; program planning; general purchasing; and shipping and traffic, i.e., the determination of how a product should be transported from the place of manufacture to the place of sale. This division also included parts provisioning and warehousing.

The farm equipment business in 1965

Product line. In 1965, MF produced a full line of farm equipment for the world market. Its line included more than 500 different pieces of equipment, even though tractors and self-propelled harvesting equipment accounted for more than three quarters of total farm sales. Since the company introduced a new tractor line in 1965 and had introduced a new line of self-propelled harvesting equipment in 1964, its product line was one of the most modern in the industry. Certainly "pressure control,"[4] an innovation in its 1965 line of tractors, was one of the most up-to-date developments in the industry. MF's automatic transmission was also one of the best in the industry, according to company sources. On the other hand, some of the tractor-attached implements were not as modern as those carried by the other full-line manufacturers.

Unlike Deere and IHC, which produced different products in Europe than they did in the United States, MF's product line was standardized throughout the world, except for small differences caused by local marketing needs. Because of this worldwide orientation, its product line had not been as broad as that of Deere and IHC in some markets, principally the United States. MF's line had been particularly weak in the larger equipment used in the central U.S. corn and wheat belt and similar areas throughout the world. In recent years, however, the company had considerably broadened its line, and in 1965 the line was almost as broad as those of Deere and IHC. For example, the new tractor line included seven models ranging from 25 to 120 horsepower. This range allowed MF to cover every market in the world, from India to the United States.

Many industry sources felt that with this modern, broad line of farm equipment, MF had the strongest line of products in every market area in which it competed, except possibly for North America.

Product development. The identification of product needs in each local market was the responsibility of a product development manager in each operating division. This manager, who was part of the marketing function in the operating division, was in continuous communication with the corporate product development manager about his future product needs. In order to have a standard line of products throughout the world, however, MF had a product development meeting under the direction of the president once a year in either North America or Europe. All the people concerned with new product development—the president, all the corporate staff, all the general managers, all product planning managers, and most of the directors of marketing and/or engineering in the operating units—attended this meeting. Involving about 70 people in total, this was the major top-level worldwide meeting each year. Together they would decide on the products to be manufactured during the coming year and the broad guidelines for products to

---

[4]A method of transferring effective weight from the front wheels and attached implement to the drive wheels by means of hydraulic cylinders. Under conditions of poor traction, this increased the pulling capacity of the tractor.

be developed or discontinued for future years. Sufficient latitude was usually allowed so that the local product development manager could develop modifications to the standard line so it would better fit local market needs.

Once a product's specifications and its modifications were agreed upon, they were turned over to the development engineers in the operating division primarily responsible for manufacturing the product for the development of engineering designs. Inasmuch as engineering was a line function, with all engineering groups, worldwide, reporting to the corporate vice president of engineering, company sources felt there was in fact complete central control of all engineering development.

Mr. Hal Wallace, vice president of manufacturing, summarized the product development process as follows:

Marketing people estimate the type of products that will be needed and then try to estimate the demand. Product engineers then make cost estimates to determine whether the product can be built at a cost that will permit profitable manufacture. Sometimes, with a crucial product, they even propose to build a prototype to be sure about costs and workability. The procurement people monitor all of this so they can program facilities for the production of the product.

Mr. William Reed-Lewis, assistant to the vice president of marketing, evaluated MF's product development as follows:

Although Massey-Harris did develop the first self-propelled combine, I feel we have tended to be a year or two behind the leaders in introducing new farm products. In hydraulics, however, we have been the innovators in the industry— from the superior hydraulics of the "Fergy" tractor to "pressure control." This is consistent with our philosophy of trying to build equipment that will get maximum mileage out of available horsepower.

Between 1961 and 1965, MF spent over $79 million, about 2.4% of sales, on engineering development. As a result of this effort, over 85% of MF's 1965 farm equipment sales were accounted for by products developed between 1961 and 1965.

Manufacturing. In 1965, MF manufactured farm equipment and/or parts in 26 factories located in 11 different countries throughout the world. This gave MF a production network that was more extensive and was located closer to most major markets than any other farm equipment manufacturer in the world. Company officials felt that because of nearly $250 million in capital improvements between 1959 and 1965, these plants were relatively modern and efficient. In addition, MF was one of the most highly integrated farm equipment manufacturers when viewed on a worldwide basis, as the company produced over 85% of its total product in 1965.

MF's manufacturing policy, according to Mr. Wallace, was as follows:

The optimum location of manufacturing facilities depends entirely on the product. With tractors, for example, the economies of mass production are such that it would be economically most desirable to produce all the world's requirements in one plant and then ship them to the various markets. Politically, it is not possible to do this and even if it were, we'd probably want at least two locations in order to have some flexibility if, for any reason, one plant were shut down. On some other products, however, it would be economically more desirable to produce in every major market area because transportation costs would be so high relative to manufacturing costs.

The manufacturing strategy that has evolved to meet the many economic and political constraints we face is complex. First, we try to design our products in order to achieve the greatest possible interchangeability of parts and of major subassemblies. This allows us to mass produce all these parts and subassemblies in one or two locations. Then we try to set up two or three assembly plants for each major product, if it is economically desirable to have a few plants, and export the finished product to the rest of the world. We try to satisfy political concerns by locating a different product assembly plant in each country. For example, we manufacture most of our tractors for the European market in Beauvais, France. However, we manufacture our self-propelled harvesting equipment in Eschwege, Germany. For each product there we get the benefit of mass production and yet we also satisfy political considerations.

With many of the developing countries, it is necessary for us to manufacture locally if we wish to compete in the market. If we deem the market potential good enough, we will usually set up local tractor assembly operations. We are thus able to compete but still enjoy mass-production of parts and subassemblies, which we export to those countries. Generally, we have to increase local content, but we try to point out the economic disadvantage of this to the country whenever possible.

This manufacturing strategy resulted in a considerable amount of transshipment. In 1965, for example, $300 million of MF's products, about 37% of total sales, were sold in markets other than the one where the product was produced. The degree of parts and subassembly shipment was indicated in a *Forbes* article:

A gleaming red farm tractor roared off an assembly line at a huge plant in Coventry [England] one day last month boasting an English frame, a diesel engine made in France, transmission and axle assemblies made in Detroit, and other components made in Italy.[5]

In 1965, MF produced about 160,000 tractors in its five tractor factories and about 23,000 combines in its four combine factories. Exhibit 5 describes the products produced at each of the factories.

Planning and procurement. Because the worldwide operations of MF required a great deal of coordination, there existed in Toronto a planning and procurement department whose function was to help determine where and how products ought to be made. Planning and procurement was a centralized function which tried to meet the sometimes contradictory demands of marketing and manufacturing, both decentralized functions.

The process of deciding where a product ought to be produced was de-

---

[5] "Massey-Ferguson's Common Market," *Forbes,* September 1, 1962, p. 26.

Exhibit 5

SYNOPSIS OF MF'S WORLDWIDE OPERATIONS

Country	Per Cent of MF's 1965 Sales	Estimates of MF's Rank and Share of Market in 1964*	MF's Principal Competitors and Estimates of Their Market Share in 1964*	MF's Manufacturing Facilities	Other Comments
United States	28%	#3 12% (14%)	Deere: 26% IHC: 20%	1 Tractor assembly plant 1 Transmission and axle plant 2 Implement plants 2 Farmstead equipment plants 1 Industrial products plant	See text.
Canada	11%	#1 24% (24%)	Deere: 23% IHC: 20% Cockshutt: 14%	1 Combine plant 1 Harvesting equipment plant 2 Implement plants 1 Foundry 2 Office furniture plants	See text.
United Kingdom	11%	#1 25% (38%)	Ford: (33%)	2 Tractor plants 1 Implement plant 1 Component plant 3 Diesel engine plants 1 Diesel engine component plant	Revamped distribution system between 1960–62. Decreased number of outlets, but increased volume per dealer. Had 100 dealers and 200 sub-dealers versus 700 for Ford in 1964. Expected to regain market share lost during transition.

*Figures in parentheses ( ) were estimated 1964 tractor penetrations; figures not in parentheses were estimated 1964 total farm equipment penetrations.

Exhibit 5—Continued

Country	Per Cent of MF's 1965 Sales	Estimates of MF's Rank and Share of Market in 1964*	MF's Principal Competitors and Estimates of Their Market Share in 1964*	MF's Manufacturing Facilities	Other Comments
France	12%	#1 (21%)	Renault: (19%) IHC: (13%) Fiat: (11%) Ford: (10%)	1 Tractor plant 1 Combine and implement plant 1 Diesel engine plant	Unprofitable for several years, but between 1960 and 1963 had built new plants, introduced new product line, and strengthened distribution system. Network of 230 exclusive dealers was strongest in France. Renault relied on factory branches and subdealers, while Ford and IHC only started to strengthen distribution in 1965.
Germany	6%	#4 (8%)	Deutz: (21%) IHC: (12%) Fendt: (11%)	1 Combine and implement plant	Distribution system inefficiently organized as most dealers carried multiple lines and had little product loyalty. Deutz exclusive dealer organization was strongest in country. MF used cooperatives and independent dealers to serve this market; about 20% of the latter were exclusive.

*Figures in parentheses ( ) were estimated 1964 tractor penetrations; figures not in parentheses were estimated 1964 total farm equipment penetrations.

Exhibit 5—Continued

Country	Per Cent of MF's 1965 Sales	Estimates of MF's Rank and Share of Market in 1964*	MF's Principal Competitors and Estimates of Their Market Share in 1964*	MF's Manufacturing Facilities	Other Comments
Italy	3%	#2 12% (15%)	Fiat: (49%)	1 Agricultural and industrial tractor plant 1 Diesel engine plant	Increased penetration since 1960 when acquired local manufacturing facilities. MF served this market through independent dealers and also through Landini dealers.
Europe not listed above:	About 8%			None	These markets were served through MF's export division.
(a) Belgium		#1 (13%)	Ford: (10%)		
(b) Sweden		#2 (30%)	Volvo: (40%); Ford: (10%)		
(c) Spain		#4 (4%)	Ford: (22%); Deere: (10%)		
(d) Other		Usually in top 4	Usually Ford, IHC, or a larger national firm		
Australia	7%	#1 20% (25%)	IHC Ford Chamberland	1 Combine and implement plant 1 Diesel engine assembly plant 1 Noncurrent spare parts plant	Distributed products through 600 dealers. Product line well received. Expected strong long-term growth. Expected to maintain penetration.

*Figures in parentheses ( ) were estimated 1964 tractor penetrations; figures not in parentheses were estimated 1964 total farm equipment penetrations.

Exhibit 5—Continued

Country	Per Cent of MF's 1965 Sales	Estimates of MF's Rank and Share of Market in 1964*	MF's Principal Competitors and Estimates of Their Market Share in 1964*	MF's Manufacturing Facilities	Other Comments
South Africa	4%	#1 40% (50%)	IHC Ford	1 Implement plant	Distributed products through independent dealers. Expected strong long-term growth. Expected to maintain penetration.
Brazil	3%	#1 30% (40%)	IHC Ford Fendt	1 Tractor assembly plant 1 Diesel engine plant	Only full-line manufacturer with a factory in the country. Low economic level limited primary demand. Expected to grow with the country; therefore anxious to protect favored position.
India	1%	#1	No other large company	1 Tractor assembly plant	Low economic level limited primary demand. MF hoped to get best position to capitalize on long-run potential.
Remainder of world	8%	#1	Ford IHC	Rhodesia: 1 plant that produces animal draft implements, hoes, and groundnut shellers	Served by Export Division which operated through 130 distributors located in these and the other European countries.
Total	102%	#3 12.5% (21.0%)	Deere: 14.7% IHC: 14.3%	36 plants	

*Figures in parentheses ( ) were estimated 1964 tractor penetrations; figures not in parentheses were estimated 1964 total farm equipment penetrations.
Sources: (1) Company annual reports. (2) Donaldson, Lufkin, & Jenrette, Inc., *The European Agricultural Equipment Industry and Competitive Positions of North American Producers,* April 1966. (3) Donaldson, Lufkin, & Jenrette, Inc., *Agricultural Equipment Industry: An Improving Environment for Above-Average Profit Growth,* May 1966.

scribed by Mr. Francis Bouilliant-Linet, corporate product programming coordinator:

We generally start by determining where the product ought to be produced because of economic considerations. Then we look at the constraints imposed by manufacturing capacity and sourcing of parts. After determining a desired place of production from these factors, we check to see whether this violates any religious or other discriminatory trade barriers. For example, even though it might be most desirable to supply farm equipment to African countries from our South African plant, we cannot do this since these countries have set up trade barriers against the Union of South Africa because of its race policies. Sometimes we also consider the manufacturing facility we would like to have in the future; that is, we will sometimes subsidize a present high cost producer in order to develop that operation for the future.

At times, the determination of where to produce a product also affects product design. For example, there are differences between axles made in the U.K. and those made in France although both will fit any of our tractors.

Mr. Bouilliant-Linet also discussed the advantages of MF's manufacturing policies and practices:

We feel our approach to manufacturing—i.e., standardizing parts and sub-assemblies so that they can be mass-produced, assembling the end product in a few locations, and then shipping the finished product to various marketing areas— allows us to minimize our total cost of supplying finished goods to the world markets.

It is the function of planning and procurement to see that this objective is met by determining the most efficient utilization of our own and our suppliers' capacity, and by ensuring that the finished goods are physically distributed to the end-user in the most economical manner possible.

In the short run, however, our system may sometimes result in higher manufacturing costs because of differences in materials costs and labor rates from area to area. Since we also participate in determining the transfer prices on internal shipments and have an influence on the establishment of profit goals and the interpretation of performance, it all works out, however.

Marketing and distribution. In 1965 over 28% of MF's farm equipment sales were derived from the United States, where MF was the third largest farm equipment marketer according to company officials, with about 11% of the market. MF's strongest penetration was in the southeastern part of the United States where the Ferguson small- and medium-sized tractors had long been popular. During recent years, the company had strengthened its distribution in this area, primarily at the expense of Ford. MF's penetration in the Far West was also above its national average. In the midwestern wheat belt, MF's penetration was about the same as its national average, primarily because of its well-known line of self-propelled combines. In the central corn belt, however, an area which included only about 27% of all U.S. farms, but which accounted for 35% of all tractor sales and 42% of all combine sales, MF's penetration was far below its national average. Historically, one of the reasons for MF's poor performance in this area had been a lack of the large tractors and corn pickers required in this market. MF's new product line, however, had gained increasing acceptance in this area in 1964 and 1965.

In total Massey had 1,720 independent farm equipment dealers in the United States at the end of 1965. Of these dealers, 646 also sold MF's industrial and construction equipment line. MF also had 48 dealers who sold exclusively industrial and construction equipment. The average MF dealer in the United States sold about $92,500 (at retail prices) worth of new MF farm equipment, which accounted for about 50% of his total sales. According to Mr. Larry Pomeroy, vice president of North American marketing, the average MF dealer had about the same margins as the average industry dealer. The statistics for the average industry dealer, as contained in the *1964 Cost of Doing Business Study* of the National Farm and Power Equipment Dealers Association, are shown below:

AN AVERAGE DEALER'S OPERATING STATISTICS

	New Equipment	Used Equipment	Repair Parts	Service Labor	All Other Lines
Sales percentage	52.2	17.0	17.8	5.5	7.5
Gross margin	13.1%	(4.1%)	26.7%	27.3%	15.7%

MF also operated 42 company stores in the United States in 1965. These were primarily set up in regions where MF had been unable to secure effective dealers, but also provided the company with the opportunity to train their own people and to try new merchandising techniques. According to some industry sources, these company stores had caused MF some problems in its dealer relations; however, these problems had been corrected, according to company officials. Exhibit 6 contains data on the cost of establishing a company store.

Canada provided 11% of MF's 1965 farm equipment sales. MF had about 25% of this market, the largest share of any farm equipment manufacturer. Its 720 dealers, who sold both farm and industrial and construction equipment, were among the strongest in the country. On the average, an MF dealer in Canada sold about $143,000 worth of new MF equipment (at retail prices). Unlike their U.S. counterparts, however, MF's Canadian dealers generally were not inclined to sell new equipment produced by competitive manufacturers. According to Mr. Pomeroy, except for making slightly higher margins, their operating statistics were similar to those of the average U.S. dealer. Because of MF's strong position in the Canadian market, some industry sources felt it would be difficult for MF to increase its penetration much further in this area.

MF's market position and distribution system for the remaining countries of the world are summarized in Exhibit 5. In most countries outside of North America, MF was either first or second in market share. In some areas,

Exhibit 6

ESTIMATED COST TO ESTABLISH VARIOUS SIZED COMPANY STORES

	Store Sizes	
Cost Category	Annual Sales: $150,000*	Annual Sales: $500,000*
Land and building	$ 50,000	$120,000
Furniture and fixtures	10,000	25,000
Inventory of equipment	75,000	250,000
Customer receivables	10,000	40,000
Cash	6,000	15,000
Total assets	$151,000	$450,000
Cumulative losses†	40,000	100,000
Total assets and losses	$191,000	$550,000

*Sales of new equipment only. Does not include sales of used equipment, repair parts, service labor, or other items.

†There will be development losses during the first few years of operations in a new trade area. These development costs are related to the market involved. Where the local competitive position has been strong for some time, these development costs could exceed income for as long as five years, depending on product acceptance.

Source: Estimates by Mr. V. Tracy, assistant director of marketing-retail development, Massey-Ferguson, Inc.

however, MF was only third or fourth. MF averaged about 14% of the market in these countries and almost always had more than 9% of the market. In most of these countries, MF's principal competition came from Ford, IHC, and/or a large local company.

MF served these markets in three ways in 1965. In the larger farm equipment markets, MF usually had an operating subsidiary with manufacturing facilities and a network of independent dealers, which was sometimes supplemented with other types of retail outlets. The smaller markets were served by MF's export division which operated through 130 independent distributors who served the dealers in these countries. MF served Brazil and India through special operations set up specifically for those countries.

Exhibits 7 through 11 contain data on MF's sales, income, and assets by geographical area. Exhibits 12 and 13 show MF's European and worldwide market share over time.

Exhibit 7

SALES BY GEOGRAPHICAL AREA, 1956–65
(Per Cent)

Geographical Area	1956	1957	1958	1959	1960	1961	1962	1963	1964	1965
North America ...	40%	34%	41%	46%	42%	36%	35%	36%	35%	39%
Europe	40	47	43	39	39	45	45	41	41	39
Australia	9	9	7	6	8	7	7	7	8	7
Africa	5	6	4	4	5	4	5	6	6	6
Asia	3	2	3	3	4	4	4	5	3	4
Latin America	3	2	2	2	2	4	4	5	7	5
Total	100	100	100	100	100	100	100	100	100	100

Source: Various company annual reports.

Exhibit 8

SALES BY GEOGRAPHICAL AREA, 1956–65
(Canadian Dollars in Millions)

Geographical Area	1956	1957	1958	1959	1960	1961	1962	1963	1964	1965
North America	$142.9	$131.0	$170.6	$217.7	$206.2	$189.2	$207.9	$243.0	$269.9	$314.6
Europe	142.8	183.4	181.3	186.8	191.1	234.3	268.3	282.8	319.7	318.4
Australia	30.3	33.0	27.8	29.8	37.9	34.7	38.7	47.5	57.7	55.2
Africa	19.0	24.3	20.0	18.4	23.4	20.3	31.2	43.0	44.8	47.5
Asia	9.1	9.2	11.0	14.6	18.8	22.2	24.0	32.7	27.1	31.6
Latin America	11.0	9.8	9.5	8.2	12.9	18.7	26.0	36.7	52.8	41.2
Total ...	$355.1	$390.8	$420.2	$475.5	$490.4	$519.3	$596.1	$685.7	$772.0	$808.5

Source: Various company annual reports.

Exhibit 9

NET INCOME BY GEOGRAPHICAL AREA
(Canadian Dollars in Thousands)

Geographical Area	1956	1957	1958	1959	1960	1961	1962	1963	1964	1965
North America ...	$(7,377)	$(15,931)	$ 5,729	$13,627						
Europe	9,150	10,748	6,216	5,613		Breakdowns Not				
Australia	1,356	1,075	506	1,267		Available for				
South Africa	(124)	(467)	422	489		These Years.				
India	132	106	91	(11)		See Note Below.				
Latin America ...	22	(268)	61	33						
Total	$ 3,159	$ (4,737)	$13,025	$21,018	$13,154	$15,247	$18,074	$24,056	$45,016	$40,067

Note: MF earned profits in each country in which it operated between 1960 and 1965, except in France between 1960 and 1962 and Brazil in 1962. According to a 1966 prospectus, MF's net profit margin on sales was higher in Canada and the U.K. than in other areas.
Source for figures: Company annual reports.

Exhibit 10

ASSETS EMPLOYED BY GEOGRAPHICAL AREA, 1956–65
(Canadian Dollars in Millions)

Geographical Area	1956	1957	1958	1959	1960	1961	1962	1963	1964	1965
North America ...	n.a.	n.a.	$183.3	$263.2	$237.6	$234.5	$230.5	$253.3	$277.4	$317.3
Europe	n.a.	n.a.	95.6	173.6	184.3	228.4	233.8	230.4	255.2	321.3
Australia	n.a.	n.a.	26.1	23.9	28.1	28.0	29.6	30.6	38.1	42.7
Africa	n.a.	n.a.	3.9	3.5	3.3	4.1	20.2	20.8	20.5	27.0
Asia	n.a.	n.a.	0.6	0.6	0.6	0.2	1.1	1.1	2.3	2.2
Latin America ...	n.a.	n.a.	0.4	0.5	4.1	12.7	18.3	24.6	27.9	31.1
Total	$296.0	$286.1	$309.9	$465.3	$458.0	$507.9	$533.5	$560.8	$621.4	$741.6

n.a. Not available.
Source: Various company annual reports.

Exhibit 11

1965 SALES BY GEOGRAPHICAL AREA AND PRODUCT TYPE
(Canadian Dollars in Millions)

Product Type	North America	Europe	Australia	Africa	Asia	Latin America	Total
Diesel engines ...	$ 14	$ 60	$ 8	$ 2	$11	$11	$106
Light industrial equipment	36	26	1	1	0	1	65
Furniture	10	0	0	0	0	0	10
Total nonfarm	$ 60	$ 86	$ 9	$ 3	$11	$12	$181
Farm equipment ..	255	232	46	45	21	29	627
Total	$315	$318	$55	$48	$32	$41	$808

Source: Case writer's estimates derived from data in company annual reports.

Exhibit 12

MASSEY-FERGUSON VALUE SALES OF AGRICULTURAL EQUIPMENT AS PER CENT OF TOTAL AGRICULTURAL MACHINERY SALES IN LEADING EUROPEAN MARKETS, 1956–64

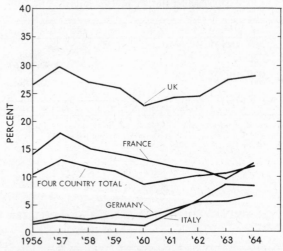

Source: Donaldson, Lufkin, & Jenrette, Inc., *The European Agricultural Equipment Industry and Competitive Positions of North American Producers*, April 1966.

Special opportunities facing Massey-Ferguson at the end of 1965

North American operations. Although MF was the largest marketer of farm equipment outside of the United States and had moved from seventh to third place in market share in the United States according to company officials, the company had not significantly increased its penetration of the central corn and wheat belt, which was the largest single market for farm equipment in the world.

Exhibit 13

GROWTH IN WORLD FARM MARKET SHARE (EXCLUDING PARTS),
1959–67
(Canadian Dollars in Millions)

	1959	1960	1961	1962	1963	1964	1965	1966	1967
Industry sales	$3,588	$3,715	$4,093	$4,084	$4,481	$4,684	$5,050[e]	$5,400[e]	$5,700[e]
MF farm equipment sales	402	393	410	463	534	599	632	735[e]	805[e]
MF market share .	11.2%	10.6%	10.0%	11.3%	11.9%	12.8%	12.5%	13.6%[e]	14.1%[e]

[e]estimate

Source: Donaldson, Lufkin, & Jenrette, Inc., *Agricultural Equipment Industry: An Improving Environment for Above-Average Profit Growth*, May 1966, p. 11.

The more important recent moves that had contributed to the $63 million increase in MF's U.S. sales between 1959 and 1965 were as follows: reorganizing the U.S. and Canadian operations into one North American operation with headquarters in Toronto in 1959; entering the heavy tractor market (100 horsepower and up) in 1962; establishing the industry's largest dealer-employee service and product training facilities at Indianapolis, Indiana, in 1963; building a $13.5 million combine plant in Brantford, Ontario, Canada (two-thirds of its annual output was for the U.S. market) in 1963; introducing a new line of grain and corn harvesting equipment (an MF 300 combine won the U.S. National Corn Picking Contest and three others placed among the top eight) in 1964; introducing a completely new line of agricultural tractors (one model, the MF 150, achieved the highest score for fuel economy in the 45-year history of such tests conducted by the Nebraska Tractor Test Laboratory) in 1965; expanding into the forage harvesting and farmstead market with the purchase of Badger Northland, Inc., of Kaukauna, Wisconsin, for $10 million in 1965; and reorganizing its marketing operations in the U.S. to make its marketing management more sensitive to customer needs in 1965. Throughout this period, MF also worked to strengthen its distribution system, particularly its independent dealers.

As a further step in its efforts to penetrate the central corn and wheat belt, MF acquired the Solar Aircraft plant in Des Moines, Iowa, in 1965. MF relocated the executive offices of its U.S. subsidiary, Massey-Ferguson, Inc., in this building, and planned to convert the facility into a new farm implement plant.

Mr. J. G. Staiger, president of Massey-Ferguson, Inc., described MF's plans to increase its penetration of the North American market as follows:

The two factors most responsible for our sales increase in the United States over the past six years were our new product line, which was introduced in 1964 and 1965, and our move to Des Moines. To be sure, all of our efforts since 1959 helped, but we could not really make serious inroads in this market until we had a competitive product line. I think our new product line gave us as much of a boost as Deere's new tractor line gave it in 1960. Perhaps more important for the long run, though, was our move to Des Moines. Prior to this move, many farmers felt MF was a foreign company and, as a result, were reluctant to buy MF products. Now, even though we've only moved the headquarters of our North American operations to Des Moines, our customers feel that we've moved our corporate headquarters to Des Moines and are a U.S. company. Consequently, they are now more willing to buy our products.

These actions will not be sufficient for us to reach our goal of $500 million in sales in North America by 1970, however. To gain the additional $190 million in sales needed to reach this goal will require a major effort. We feel we can do it, though.

Basically, our plan is to maintain our position where we are strong and to strengthen our position where we are weak. For example, in Canada we have 25% of the market. We do not expect to increase our share of this market, but do plan to maintain our present 25%. In the United States, however, we presently only have 11% of the market. We plan to increase this to 15%. Within the United States we plan to increase our share by boosting our penetration in the central corn and wheat belt, while maintaining our share of the southeastern and western markets. By products, this will mean a sales increase of five percentage points in tractor penetration, three percentage points in grain harvesting equipment, and at least four percentage points in the penetration of most other lines.

Increased penetration will only bring us part of our goal, however. The additional sales will come from a growth in the total market for farm products and from an increase in our industrial and construction equipment sales. We were the first farm machinery company to enter the light industrial markets in the late 1950's, but we neglected the area and didn't keep our lead. This market has traditionally been an offshoot of the farm equipment business, but as you move up in product size you get into different types of products, customers, dealers, and competitors. The question now is basically how far up we should go in this market in terms of the size of equipment, how fast, and by what means.

Of course, it is one thing to say where we plan to get additional sales, and another to actually accomplish those results. We think we have some strengths that will help us, though. These include a superior product line, a superior parts handling and service organization, and an ability to identify the needs of the farmer. The latter is one of the benefits of the reorganization of our U.S. marketing organization. Basically, what we did was to centralize staff services for all of North America and decentralize line operations by geographical areas within North America.

As I see it, our two major weaknesses at present are our distribution system and our financial position. Presently, we are using nearly all of our cash inflow to build capital facilities, since some of our existing facilities are somewhat old and most are operating near capacity. In addition to this, however, it generally requires an increased dollar in assets (generally inventory and credit) to support each new sales dollar because of the "cradle to grave" financing practices in this industry. [See Exhibit 14 for balance sheets of Massey-Ferguson's North American Finance Companies.] That means we would need to add nearly $190 million in additional assets over the next five years to support our sales goal, without allowing for facility requirements. Even if we achieve our objective of doubling the return we make on our assets, we would not be able to generate this kind of money internally. This means that we may have to find some way of breaking with industry tradition on financing. I'm not prepared to say how we might do this, but we have been testing out some ideas on a mathematical model we developed. If these ideas appear to be workable, we will then test them out in selected market areas.

Our most important task, however, will be to strengthen our distribution system. This will involve four things: filling key areas where we presently lack dealers; replacing unsatisfactory dealers with better ones; upgrading most existing dealers; and allowing the natural attrition of marginal dealers to occur in areas of low potential or overlapping double coverage. In 1970, we should have about the same number of dealers we presently have, although we may have 10% more dealers in the corn and wheat belt than we have now and, of course, correspondingly fewer in other areas. Each dealer in 1970 should handle a greater volume of MF business than now. To achieve our future sales objectives, each dealer's penetration must increase substantially, but some of Massey's sales increase also has to come from displacing other manufacturers. Unlike Deere or International dealers, many of our dealers presently carry the products of other full-line or the various long-line manufacturers. Increasing the degree of concentrated sales effort in any dealer group is a lengthy process.

We obtain few new dealers from other manufacturers. Usually, our sources of new dealers are farmers or auto dealers who want to invest extra capital, long-line dealers who want to get the MF line, or employees of present dealers.

We have set some ambitious goals for ourselves, but I think we can achieve them. We are going to meet well-entrenched and financially stronger competitors head-on, but we have a long history of operations in this country and know the market and its problems well. We will simply have to do everything as well as, and a few things a little better than, our competitors. I do not anticipate any competitive product changes or breakthroughs that could hurt us. The only major risk we run is that of a serious product catastrophe.

Expanding in the United States, now that we have a more acceptable and competitive product line, will certainly be easier for us than establishing large and profitable operations overseas will be for Deere. They will have to either learn the language and customs all over again in every country, or else try to superimpose American practices everywhere they go. It has been our experience that the latter seldom succeeds.

Motor Iberica. Through the end of 1965, MF sold its farm equipment in Spain through its export division. During 1965, however, the opportunity arose to merge the MF activities in Spain with those of Motor Iberica, S.A., the leading Spanish manufacturer of trucks and tractors. Mr. H. G. Kettle, vice president of public relations, described the proposal as follows:

We did not expect to get an opportunity to manufacture in Spain. However, Ford and Motor Iberica, which for many years had had a close association through licensing agreements, decided to terminate this arrangement.

After joint discussions, a new arrangement was proposed in which the existing Perkins diesel factory in Madrid, together with a small combine assembly operation in Northern Spain, would be integrated with the existing Motor Iberica tractor and truck operations. Under the agreement, the Motor Iberica brand name "Ebro" on their tractors and trucks will continue to be used, but the sheet metal configuration and the colors will be similar to the worldwide MF line. In addi-

Exhibit 14

MASSEY-FERGUSON LIMITED

Consolidated Balance Sheets of North American Finance Companies
For Years Ended October 31, 1960–1965
(Canadian Dollars in Millions)

Assets	1960	1961	1962	1963	1964	1965
Cash	$ 0.9	$ 2.0	$ 0.1	$ 0.0	$ 0.0	$ 0.3
Retail notes receivable*	40.3	67.8	81.1	96.7	119.7	149.0
Current account receivable from Massey-Ferguson Industries Limited	...	...	...	...	...	1.6
Prepaid expenses	0.2	0.2	0.3	0.3	1.3	2.3
Total assets	$41.4	$69.9	$81.5	$97.0	$121.1	$153.2
Liabilities and Shareholders' Equity						
Short-term notes payable — banks	$31.9	$47.0	$37.3	$34.4	$ 52.8	$ 59.4
— other	...	2.5	21.2	39.4	39.2	41.1
Accrued charges	...	0.4	0.5	0.6	0.6	0.7
Income taxes	...	0.1	1.0	2.3	2.2	3.4
Current accounts payable — Massey-Ferguson, Inc.	0.1	8.0	5.0	2.6	2.4	0.7
— Massey-Ferguson Industries Limited	...	...	...	...	1.5	...
	$31.9	$58.1	$65.5	$79.2	$ 98.6	$105.2
Long-term debt	...	...	...	...	...	26.5
Equity of Massey-Ferguson Limited and its subsidiaries						
Interest-bearing notes payable	$ 3.0	$ 1.0	$ 4.0	$ 4.1	$ 8.2	5.0
Share capital	7.0	11.0	11.0	10.9	10.9	10.9
Retained earnings	(0.5)	(0.2)	0.9	2.8	3.3	5.6
	$ 9.5	$11.8	$15.9	$17.8	$ 22.5	$ 21.5
Total liabilities and equity	$41.4	$69.9	$81.5	$97.0	$121.1	$153.2

*The following table gives the approximate per cent of receivables maturing beyond one year:

Year	1960	1961	1962	1963	1964	1965
Per cent	n.a.	43%	46%	47%	50%	57%

n.a.: Not available.
Source: Various company annual reports.

tion, MF tractors and equipment in limited amounts, as controlled by import restrictions, will be sold through the Motor Iberica dealers.

As a net result of all this, MF will have a 38% interest in the new company.

The FAO project. In 1965, MF was supporting a series of FAO (The Food and Agriculture Organization of the United Nations) conferences on food production. According to Mr. Kettle:

Two years ago, we realized that as a substantial Canadian corporation we would be expected to make some significant contribution toward the country's centennial celebration in 1967. Rather than put money into a number of local projects, we decided to look around and see if we could find some way of applying the money that might be more in keeping with the international operations of our company.

We were of course aware of the problems that developing countries were facing in trying to increase food production. After some thought, we decided to contribute $500,000 to support a series of seven seminars held by the FAO in various parts of the world during 1966 and 1967 which would focus on these problems of food production. We planned to make this gift our contribution to the Canadian centennial celebration.

The first seminar covering Asia will take place in September in Bangkok. It will be attended by representatives from 4-H type organizations in neighboring countries, plus FAO officials, of course. Subsequent seminars will be held in Addis Ababa, Lima, Beirut, Des Moines, and Rome. They will cover Africa, Latin America, the Near East, North America, and Europe. These seminars will culminate in a worldwide conference in Toronto in September 1967. It is our hope that action programs to strengthen these developing farm and rural organizations will be developed from these seminars and that we may be able to profitably assist in some of the programs that result.

Incidentally, we will also be participating with the FAO in a worldwide rice seminar in England and Italy in September of 1966, and early in 1967 we will be officially opening a mechanization school in Cali, Colombia, in cooperation with the FAO and the Colombian government.

The nonfree world. According to Mr. Kettle, there were three types of market areas for farm machinery in the nonfree world. Russia itself constituted one major agricultural area, but had minor imports and exports of farm machinery. Russia had several huge farm equipment plants, but their equipment tended to be somewhat larger and heavier than was customary in most world markets.

China was another major area, and Mr. Kettle felt that it could conceivably become a major market in the distant future, but that neither sales of equipment nor manufacturing agreements seemed likely to be significant in the foreseeable future.

Many countries in the "fringe areas" had been worthwhile markets for MF, however. Trade with Yugoslavia, for example, had started shortly after World War II, and had involved both sale of equipment and joint manufacturing agreements.

Mr. Kettle indicated that MF had continuing contacts in most of the nonfree world. Partly because Russia and Canada had historically had some common agricultural problems, visits and exchanges of ideas and information with Russia, in particular, had been frequent at the governmental and technical level. Several of the MF headquarters staff officers, for example, had visited the larger Russian farm equipment plants.

Other Massey-Ferguson operations

In addition to its farm equipment operations, MF was in three other businesses. The largest of these, in 1965, was its Perkins Division, which manufactured and marketed high-speed diesel engines for marine, automotive, agricultural, and industrial purposes. In 1965 Perkins sold $106 million worth of diesel engines, about 12% of Massey's total sales, in addition to producing engines for Massey's agricultural and industrial equipment. Slightly over half of this output was for general industrial use; the remainder was sold to competing tractor and combine manufacturers. The majority of Perkins' sales were made in the United Kingdom and Europe. Massey maintained a separate marketing and distribution effort for these products.

The sale of industrial and construction equipment was rapidly becoming a major segment of MF's total operations. Between 1962 and 1965, Massey's sales of industrial equipment increased from $20 million to $65 million and were expected to show continuing growth. Nevertheless, the majority of this equipment was sold through dealers who also carried farm equipment in 1965. MF was, however, considering the establishment of a separate division to handle this business, since it was basically different from the farm equipment business. Unlike Deere, MF derived a substantial proportion of its industrial and construction equipment sales outside of North America—about 45% in 1965.

MF also manufactured and marketed steel and wooden office furniture in Canada. In 1965, sales of these products reached $10 million, slightly over 1% of MF's total sales.

Exhibit 15 indicates increasing U.S. ownership of Massey-Ferguson common stock.

Exhibit 15

OWNERSHIP OF MASSEY-FERGUSON COMMON STOCK
BY COUNTRY OF RESIDENCE, 1957–1965

Nationality	1957	1959	1961	1962	1963	1964	1965
Canada	90	84	80	78	80	71	68
United States	4	12	16	19	16	26	29
Other	6	4	4	3	4	3	3
Total	100	100	100	100	100	100	100

Source: Company statistics.

HEUBLEIN, INC. (A)*

∧∧

With growth in sales and profits since 1959 far outstripping the liquor industry's "Big Four," Heublein, Inc., producer of Smirnoff vodka and other liquor and food items, had moved up to become the fifth largest liquor company in the United States by 1965. (See Exhibits 1 and 2 for Heublein financial statistics.)

Industry Rank in 1965	Company	1964 Liquor Sales (Millions)	1965 Total Sales (Millions)	Total Sales Gain 1959–65 (Per Cent)	Profit Gain 1959–65 (Per Cent)
1	Distillers Corporation	$718	$1,005	37%	52%
2	Hiram Walker	498	530	28	46
3	National Distillers	430	829	44	33
4	Schenley Industries (est.)	390	461	0	33
5	Heublein, Inc.	123	166	89	259

*Derived from various company annual reports.

Mr. Hart, Heublein's president since 1960 and a former executive vice president of international marketing for the Colgate-Palmolive Company, commented on the company's business as follows:

Although liquor products account for most of our sales at the present time, we consider ourselves in the consumer goods business, not the liquor business. Liquor is a consumer good just like toothpaste and is sold the same way.

To be successful in this business, you need three things: a good product, distribution, and advertising. You must have a good product. If you don't, the consumer will find you out and you will not get any repeat purchases. You also need good distribution, so the consumer will be able to get your product easily and conveniently. Finally, you must have a good convincing story to tell the consumer about why he should buy your product and you tell it through advertising.

In 1965, Heublein's management had three long-range goals: (1) to make Smirnoff the number one liquor brand in the world; (2) to continue a sales growth of 10% a year through internal growth, acquisitions, or both; and (3) to maintain Heublein's return on equity above 15%.

Exhibit 1

HEUBLEIN, INC.
Consolidated Balance Sheets as of June 30
(Dollars in Thousands)

Assets

Current assets:	1955	1960	1963	1964	1965
Cash	$ 2,298	$ 3,925	$ 2,744	$ 3,357	$ 3,338
Time deposits	...	...	6,000	1,750	...
Marketable securities	9	4,883	1,000	...	4,048
Investment in whiskey certificates ...	...	593	1,069	150	...
Accounts and notes receivable	5,157	12,426	17,835	18,668	19,010
Inventories	5,825	8,269	9,127	13,347	16,323
Prepaid expenses	297	382	356	325	548
Total current assets	$13,586	$30,479	$38,130	$37,597	$43,267
Long-term assets:					
Property, plant and equipment—net ..	$ 3,254	$ 5,793	$ 6,363	$ 7,339	$ 7,502
Deferred charges, other assets and goodwill	223	416	1,068	3,659	5,383
Total long-term assets	$ 3,477	$ 6,209	$ 7,431	$10,998	$12,885
Total assets	$17,063	$36,688	$45,561	$48,595	$56,152

Liabilities and Stockholders' Equity

Current liabilities:	1955	1960	1963	1964	1965
Notes payable to banks	$ 2,000	...	...	...	...
Accounts payable	687	$ 1,933	$ 2,078	$ 2,417	$ 3,584
Federal income tax	531	2,857	3,607	4,129	4,701
Accrued liabilities	513	2,688	4,044	5,175	5,774
Cash dividends payable	98	299	733	721	986
Long-term debt due within one year ..	301	631	777	850	1,013
Total current liabilities	$ 4,129	$ 8,408	$11,239	$13,292	$16,059
Long-term liabilities:					
Long-term debt due after one year ..	$ 4,699	$ 5,388	$ 3,239	$ 2,416	$ 1,403
Deferred federal income tax	...	...	154	248	316
Minority interest	...	...	...	272	...
Total long-term liabilities	$ 4,699	$ 5,388	$ 3,393	$ 2,936	$ 1,719
Stockholders' equity	8,235	22,892	30,929	32,368	38,374
Total liabilities and stockholders' equity	$17,063	$36,688	$45,561	$48,595	$56,152

Source: Heublein records.

Some industry observers, however, predicted a more normal growth rate for Heublein over the coming years because of the increasing competition from the four largest distillers in the vodka and other nonwhiskey markets from which Heublein derived the majority of its sales.

Exhibit 2

HEUBLEIN, INC.

Consolidated Statement of Income for Year Ending June 30

(Dollars in Thousands)

	1955	1956	1957	1958	1959	1960	1961	1962	1963	1964	1965
Net sales	$37,222	$68,543	$82,064	$87,839	$87,647	$103,169	$108,281	$116,142	$121,995	$135,848	$165,595
Cost of sales*	29,503	53,219	63,234	67,231	67,276	78,028	80,419	85,793	89,500	99,575	121,503
Gross profit	$ 7,719	$15,325	$18,830	$20,608	$20,372	$ 25,140	$ 27,862	$ 30,349	$ 32,495	$ 36,273	$ 44,092
Expenses:											
Selling and advertising ..	$ 4,650	$ 8,013	$10,617	$12,613	$12,710	$ 14,276	$ 16,089	$ 16,444	$ 18,271	$ 20,477	$ 24,551
Administrative and general	1,479	2,288	2,699	2,822	2,561	2,783	3,205	4,111	3,710	3,485	4,257
	$ 6,130	$10,301	$13,315	$15,434	$15,271	$ 17,060	$ 19,293	$ 20,555	$ 21,981	$ 23,962	$ 28,808
	$ 1,590	$ 5,024	$ 5,515	$ 5,176	$ 5,100	$ 8,080	$ 8,569	$ 9,794	$ 10,514	$ 12,312	$ 15,284
Other†	$ 189	$ 316	$ 407	$ 519	$ 638	$ 293	$ 168	$ 199	$ (339)	$ (18)	$ (112)
	1,401	4,708	5,109	4,654	4,462	7,788	8,401	9,595	10,852	12,330	15,397
State and federal income taxes	733	2,531	2,697	2,524	2,399	4,232	4,587	5,188	5,830	6,516	8,021
Net income	$ 667	$ 2,177	$ 2,411	$ 2,130	$ 2,063	$ 3,556	$ 3,814	$ 4,407	$ 5,022	$ 5,814	$ 7,376

*Cost of sales includes federal excise taxes on the withdrawal of distilled spirits from bond. For the fiscal year 1965, these totaled $90 million.

†Interest income, interest expense, and miscellaneous.

Source: Heublein records.

The liquor industry[1]

Product. Ten categories of liquor (distilled spirits, excluding beer and wine) were listed by the U.S. Department of Commerce in 1964. Of these, five were whiskeys and five were nonwhiskeys.

Whiskeys	*Nonwhiskeys*
Straight	Gin
Blended	Vodka
Bonded	Rum
Scotch (100% imported)	Brandy
Canadian (100% imported)	Other (cordials, aperitifs, bottled cocktails, etc.)

The labeling of liquor products within these categories was subject to federal standards, as follows:

Product	*Requirements*
Straight whiskey	Aged not less than 24 months in new charred-oak barrels; distilled from not less than 51% of the designated grain (corn,* rye, or wheat).
Bonded whiskeys	Straight whiskeys; aged at least four years, bottled at 100 proof; the product of a single distiller, a single distillery, and a single season and year.
Blended whiskey	A mixture of two or more straight whiskeys.
Scotch and Canadian	Aged not less than 24 months,† straight or blended; if blended, then designated as such.
Gin	No aging requirement;‡ at least 80 proof; containing the juniper berry flavor; made by direct distillation of mash or redistillation of distilled spirits.
Vodka	:No aging requirement;‡ no distinctive character, flavor, or taste; approved by the federal government;§ usually made by filtering grain neutral spirits through activated charcoal.
Rum	Produced from sugar cane; no federal requirements regarding method of production.
Brandy	Obtained solely from the fermented juice, mash, or wine of fruit; distilled at less than 190 proof.‖
Other	Requirements depend on the product type.

*Of the straight whiskeys, 98% were bourbons distilled from corn.
†Usually aged four or more years.
‡Gin and vodka were unique among the distilled spirits since they required no aging. The principal distinction between gin and vodka was that the juniper berry flavor was added to grain neutral spirits to produce the former, while as many flavor-producing ingredients as possible were filtered out from grain neutral spirits to produce the latter.
§Federal requirements complex, but essentially as stated above.
‖Usually produced from white grapes and bottled at 80 proof or higher.

---

[1]Several terms in common use in the industry require definition:
Proof is a term used to specify the proportion of alcohol in a product. The proof number is equal to twice the per cent of alcohol (by volume) in the product.
A *proof gallon* is any volume which contains the same amount of alcohol as a gallon of 100-proof spirits.
A *wine gallon* is a gallon by volume (regardless of proof). Thus, a gallon (five fifths) of 80-proof vodka would be one wine gallon but only 8/10 proof gallons.

Exhibit 3

LIQUOR CONSUMPTION VS. POPULATION

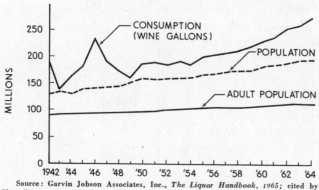

Source: Garvin Jobson Associates, Inc., *The Liquor Handbook, 1965*; cited by Glore Forgan, Wm. R. Staats Inc., in *Heublein, Inc.* (December, 1965).

Market. Between 1955 and 1964, U.S. consumption of distilled spirits increased from 199 million to 277 million wine gallons, or 39% (see Exhibit 3). By the latter year, some 60 million Americans—about 53% of the adult population—drank some sort of alcoholic beverage. These Americans spent about $6.5 billion for liquor, about one third of the amount spent for public elementary and secondary school education. Excise taxes[2] on these sales provided the federal government with about $2.5 billion in 1964, more than any other single source of revenue, except for personal and corporate income taxes. According to *Barron's*,[3] illegal distilling was increasing as a consequence of these taxes. In 1964, an estimated 50 million wine gallons of liquor was "bootlegged," representing about 18% of the 277 million wine gallons of legally produced liquor.

Rising sales of liquor could be attributed to various causes, including a rising population; increased personal discretionary income contributing to higher per capita consumption; changing social mores; the declining proportion of people in "dry" states; and changes in the population makeup by age groups.

Exhibits 4, 5, 6, and 7 contain the best publicly available information on some of these trends. Mr. Edward Kelley, Heublein's executive vice president, cautioned that statistics about liquor consumption by demographic groups were not as dependable as for some other consumer goods. Mr. Kelley felt the growth in liquor consumption between 1955 and 1965 was primarily the result of the increase in per capita consumption, which appeared to be related to the growth in personal discretionary income, and the spread of drinking to more segments of the population and on more occasions, resulting from the trends of social living habits.

[2] The federal excise tax on distilled spirits was $10.50 per proof gallon in 1965.
[3] Dana L. Thomas, "Flush of Success: New Competitive Spirit Has Given a Healthier Glow to the Distillers," *Barron's* (July 20, 1964), p. 3.

Exhibit 4

THE ORIGINS OF DEMAND BY AGE GROUP
(Urban Family Expenditures for Alcoholic Beverages,* 1960–61)

SHARE OF MARKET PERCENT DISTRIBUTION

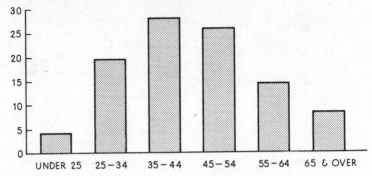

AVERAGE ANNUAL EXPENDITURES: DOLLARS

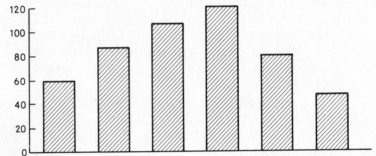

*Includes beer and wine.
Source: Department of Labor; The Conference Board; cited by Glore Forgan, Wm. R. Staats Inc., in *Heublein, Inc.* (December, 1965).

Predicting the future in relation to income and demographic changes, industry sources looked forward to an even faster growth in consumption from 1965 to 1970 than from 1955 to 1964: 4.5% or more a year, compared with 3.6%. Since the Bureau of the Census forecast that the 25 to 54 age groups would increase an average of nearly 17% between 1970 and 1980, many industry observers felt the picture beyond 1970 looked better than that between 1965 and 1970.

Market changes. Demand for the various categories of liquor was changing as well as growing between 1955 and 1964 (see Exhibits 8, 9, 10, and 11). Thus there was a dramatic shift in consumer preference to straight whiskeys, imported whiskeys, and the nonwhiskeys, and away from the blended and bonded whiskeys. While some observers felt this represented a return to the pre-World War II relationship, which provided straight

Exhibit 5

TOTAL POPULATION BY AGE
(Millions)

Year	Total	Under 15	15–19	20–24	25–34	35–44	45–54	55–64	65 and Over
1950	151.7	40.6	10.8	11.7	24.0	21.6	17.4	13.3	12.3
1960	180.7	56.1	13.4	11.1	22.9	24.2	20.6	15.6	16.7
1965	195.1	60.6	17.0	13.6	22.4	24.5	22.1	17.0	18.1
1970	211.4	65.7	18.9	17.1	25.2	23.0	23.4	18.5	19.6
1980	252.1	81.9	21.4	20.6	36.1	25.3	22.2	21.5	23.1

Per Cent Increase (Decrease)

1950–60 ...	19.1	38.2	24.1	(5.1)	(4.6)	12.0	18.4	17.3	35.8
1960–65 ...	8.0	8.0	26.9	22.5	(2.2)	1.2	7.3	9.0	8.4
1965–70 ...	8.4	8.4	11.2	25.7	12.5	(6.1)	5.9	8.8	8.3
1970–80 ...	19.3	24.7	13.2	20.5	44.8	10.0	(5.1)	16.2	17.9

Source: Department of Commerce, Bureau of the Census, figures updated as of July 9, 1964; cited by Glore Forgan, Wm. R. Staats Inc., in *Heublein, Inc.* (December, 1965).

Exhibit 6

THE ORIGINS OF DEMAND BY INCOME CLASS
(Urban Family Expenditures for Alcoholic Beverages,* 1960–61)

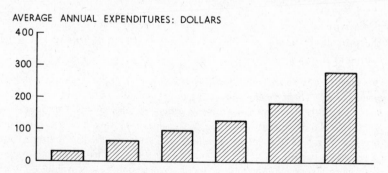

*Includes beer and wine.
Source: Department of Labor: The Conference Board; cited by Glore Forgan, Wm. R. Staats Inc., in *Heublein, Inc.* (December, 1965).

Exhibit 7

LIQUOR CONSUMPTION

(Wine Gallons)

Year	Total (Millions)	Per Capita	
		Total Pop.	Adults
1934	58.0	0.46	0.75
1935	89.7	0.70	1.14
1936	122.1	0.95	1.53
1937	135.4	1.05	1.67
1938	126.9	0.98	1.55
1939	134.7	1.03	1.62
1940	145.0	1.10	1.72
1941	158.2	1.19	1.85
1942	190.3	1.42	2.20
1943	145.5	1.09	1.68
1944	166.7	1.26	1.95
1945	190.1	1.44	2.23
1946	231.0	1.65	2.51
1947	181.7	1.27	1.94
1948	171.0	1.17	1.80
1949	169.6	1.14	1.76
1950	190.0	1.26	1.95
1951	193.8	1.26	1.97
1952	183.7	1.18	1.85
1953	194.7	1.23	1.94
1954	189.5	1.18	1.87
1955	199.6	1.22	1.95
1956	215.2	1.29	2.08
1957	212.1	1.25	2.03
1958	215.5	1.24	2.05
1959	225.5	1.28	2.12
1960	234.7	1.31	2.17
1961	241.5	1.33	2.21
1962	253.7	1.37	2.30
1963	259.0	1.38	2.32
1964	276.0	1.44	2.44

Source: Distilled Spirits Institute and U.S. Department of Commerce; cited by Gavin Jobson Associates, Inc., in *The Liquor Handbook, 1965.*

whiskeys with a slight edge over blended whiskeys, most industry sources felt the shift in consumption reflected a trend toward lightness in liquor taste. According to Roger Bensen:

The most probable reason [for the trend toward lightness] is that people drink mainly to satisfy social and status needs and for effect and not inherently for taste. The taste of many liquors is something which new drinkers find difficult to assimilate. Hence, they turn to various cocktails or mixed drinks to disguise the original flavor of the liquor product. And to complete the pattern, people achieve further fulfillment of social and status needs by using the newer, more current, more exotic liquor and cocktail formulations as a vehicle for their drinking.[4]

---

[4]Roger Bensen, *Heublein, Inc.,* Investment Research Dept., Glore Forgan, Wm. R. Staats Inc. (December, 1965), p. 21.

Some of the most important of these changes are reflected in the following figures for distilled spirits entering trade channels:

Product Type	Volume (Millions of Wine Gallons)		Market Share (Per Cent)		Change in Volume (Per Cent)
	1955	1964	1955	1964	1955 to 1964
Whiskeys:					
Bonded	12.9	7.9	6.3%	2.8%	(39)%
Straight	46.1	69.6	22.7	24.3	51
Blend	81.5	74.7	40.0	26.1	(8)
Scotch	12.3	28.3	6.0	9.9	130
Canadian	9.2	17.2	4.5	6.0	87
Total all whiskeys	161.5	197.9	79.5%	69.1%	22%
Nonwhiskeys:					
Gin	20.7	31.1	10.2	10.9	50
Vodka	7.0	28.1	3.4	9.8	302
Rum	2.7	5.9	1.3	2.1	119
Brandy	4.6	8.7	2.3	3.0	89
Other (cordials, etc.)	6.6	14.6	3.3	5.1	121
Total nonwhiskeys	41.8	88.4	20.5%	30.9%	111%
Total distilled spirits ..	203.3	286.3	100.0%	100.0%	41%

Note: For greater detail, see Exhibit 8.

According to many liquor observers, one of the more important developments in the liquor industry between 1960 and 1965 was the growth of bottled cocktails. Although bottled cocktails had been on the market for over 50 years, they had shown little growth until 1960. In that year, Heublein, which had almost 100% of the market at that time, developed a new product formulation, package, and promotional campaign for its line of bottled cocktails. By 1965, volume had increased 100% to an estimated 1.9 million wine gallons, as Distillers Corporation, Hiram Walker, Schenley, and others entered the market. Nevertheless, Heublein, whose volume increased 60% during the period, still had 55% of the market in 1965. The convenience, low consumer price (only a few pennies more than comparable drinks mixed at home), and trend toward lightness caused one liquor authority to predict that bottled cocktails might represent close to 10% of the industry's volume by 1975.

Bulk imports were also expected to be an area of potential future growth. Bulk imports consisted of Scotch or Canadian whiskeys that were imported in barrels rather than bottles. They were then reduced to the desired proof by the addition of water and bottled in the United States. Since Scotch and Canadian whiskeys imported in bottles were taxed at a rate of $10.50 a proof gallon while the same whiskeys imported in barrels were taxed at a rate of $10.50 a wine gallon, bulk importing resulted in a tax saving of from $0.30 to $0.42 a fifth. This tax savings, coupled with lower transportation costs and reduced markups by the wholesaler and retailer, resulted in a

Exhibit 8

ESTIMATED DISTILLED SPIRITS ENTERING TRADE CHANNELS

Class and Type	1955 Gallons (Millions)	1955 Market Share (Per Cent)	1960 Gallons (Millions)	1960 Market Share (Per Cent)	1964 Gallons (Millions)	1964 Market Share (Per Cent)	Growth, 1964 from 1955 (Per Cent)
Domestic whiskey							
Bonded	12,869	6.3%	9,394	3.9%	7,911	2.8%	(38.5)%
Straight	44,838	22.1	58,939	24.6	68,802	24.0	53.5
Blend of straights	1,249	0.6	793	0.3	758	0.3	(39.2)
Blend of neutral spirits	81,494	40.0	74,074	31.0	74,731	26.1	(8.0)
Other	(449)	(0.2)	(119)	...	...	...	...
Total	140,001	68.9%	143,082	59.8%	152,203	52.2%	8.9%
Imported whiskey							
Scotch	12,284	6.0	20,585	8.6	28,249	9.9	130.5
Canadian	9,158	4.5	12,552	5.3	17,170	6.0	87.5
Other*	13	...	79	...	251	...	1,822.0
Total	21,455	10.6%	33,215	13.9%	45,670	16.0%	113.0%
Total whiskey	161,457	79.5%	176,297	73.7%	197,873	69.2%	22.5%
Gin							
Domestic	20,447	10.1	22,001	9.2	28,963	10.1	41.5
Imported	291	0.2	1,149	0.5	2,167	0.8	645.0
Total	20,738	10.2%	23,150	9.7%	31,130	10.9%	50.0%
Vodka	6,968	3.4	19,406	8.1	28,130	9.8	304.0

Exhibit 8—Continued

Class and Type	1955 Gallons (Millions)	1955 Market Share (Per Cent)	1960 Gallons (Millions)	1960 Market Share (Per Cent)	1964 Gallons (Millions)	1964 Market Share (Per Cent)	Growth, 1964 from 1955 (Per Cent)
Rum							
Puerto Rican, Virgin Islands	1,873	0.9	2,724	1.2	4,189	1.4	124.0
Other domestic	663	0.3	804	0.3	1,543	0.5	133.0
Total domestic	2,537	1.3%	3,528	1.5%	5,731	1.9%	126.0%
Imported	181	...	219	0.1	186	...	3.0
Brandies							
Domestic	3,726	1.8	5,300	2.2	7,575	2.6	103.0
Imported	893	0.4	1,163	0.5	1,113	0.4	24.5
Total	4,619	2.3%	6,463	2.7%	8,688	3.0%	88.0%
Cordials and specialties							
Domestic	6,173	3.0	9,156	3.8	12,761	4.5	106.0
Imported	455	0.2	812	0.4	1,052	0.4	131.5
Total	6,629	3.3%	9,968	4.2%	13,813	4.9%	109.0%
Not elsewhere specified	178	...	342	...	750	0.3	320.0
Grand total	203,306	100.0%	239,373	100.0%	286,301	100.0%	41.0%
Total domestic	179,916	88.5	202,594	84.6	235,743	82.2	41.0
Total imported	23,390	11.5	36,779	15.4	50,559	17.7	121.0
Grand total	203,306	100.0%	239,373	100.0%	286,301	100.0%	41.0%

*Mainly Irish and Belgian.
Source: Distilled Spirits Institute: cited by Glore Forgan, Wm. R. Staats Inc., in *Heublein, Inc.* (December, 1965).

Exhibit 9

WHISKEY CONSUMPTION TREND, 1955–64
(Expressed as a Three-Year Moving Average)

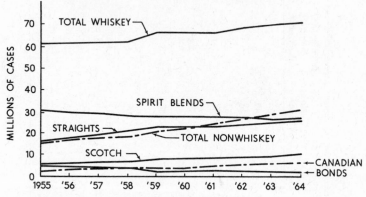

Source: Gavin Jobson Associates, *The Liquor Handbook, 1965*; cited by Glore Forgan, Wm. R. Staats, Inc., in *Heublein, Inc.* (December, 1965).

Exhibit 10

NONWHISKEY CONSUMPTION TREND, 1955–64
(Expressed as a Three-Year Moving Average)

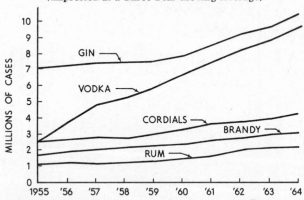

Source: Gavin Jobson Associates, *The Liquor Handbook, 1965*; cited by Glore Forgan, Wm. R. Staats, Inc., in *Heublein, Inc.* (December, 1965).

price savings of as much as $1 per fifth to the consumer. Although the demand for bulk whiskeys increased during the early sixties, some bulk importers felt their gains were made primarily at the expense of American straight and blended whiskeys rather than the higher priced, bottled imported whiskeys.

Trends in competition. Between 1955 and 1965, the majority of the companies in the liquor industry followed one of two broad strategies. Most of the medium-sized companies aggressively marketed their products in tradi-

Exhibit 11

PROJECTED 1968 SALES OF LIQUOR
(Millions of Cases)
(Based on Extension of 1960–64 Sales)

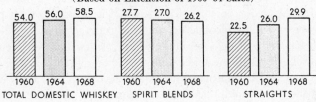

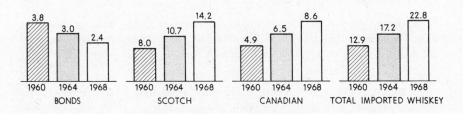

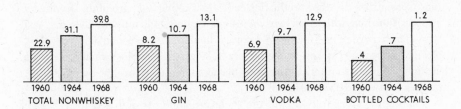

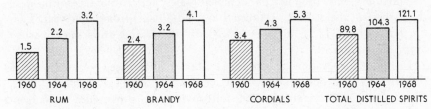

Source: Gavin Jobson Associates, *The Liquor Handbook, 1965*; cited by Glore Forgan, Wm. R. Staats Inc., in *Heublein, Inc.* (December, 1965).

tional ways. They did not increase, decrease, or change their product line, nor did they attempt to diversify out of the liquor business. None of these companies had a complete line of liquor products, and some had only one or two products. Several of these companies, however, experienced extremely rapid growth during this period. Their success could generally be attributed to having a leading product in one or two or the more rapidly growing segments of the liquor market.

The four major distillers also marketed their products in traditional ways. However, with the exception of Hiram Walker, each of these companies attempted to diversify out of the liquor industry through acquisitions between 1955 and 1965. Even with this diversification, however, liquor accounted for the major portion of the sales of each of these companies in 1965. Moreover, with the possible exception of National Distillers, the major distillers no longer seemed to be interested in further diversification outside of the liquor business in the middle 1960's. Rather they began to compete more vigorously in all segments of the liquor market during 1964 and 1965, particularly the more rapidly growing segments. This increased competition, coupled with the trend toward lightness, caused John Shaw of Equity Research Associates to predict that:

Marketing efforts will become more consumer-oriented, stressing "appetite appeal" in much the same way as the food industry. Over all, advertising and promotional costs can be expected to trend higher, as brand competition remains intense.[5]

Thumbnail sketches of a few of the companies that have grown rapidly or that competed directly with Heublein are given below:

James B. Beam Distilling Company was a medium-sized liquor company that specialized in the production and marketing of premium Kentucky straight bourbon whiskey. Nearly 80% of Beam's $92 million sales in 1965 were derived from its Jim Beam brand, which was the second largest selling straight bourbon whiskey in the country. As a result of the expansion of the straight whiskey market, Beam was able to increase its profits by over 20% per year between 1953 and 1965.

Paddington Corporation[6] was the exclusive importer of J & B Rare Scotch whiskey, the number two brand of Scotch in 1964. Although J & B was Paddington's only product, the company sales and earnings growth were the highest in the industry between 1960 and 1964. In the latter year, Paddington earned 37.5% on its stockholders' equity, and gross sales reached over $125 million.

Distillers Corporation–Seagram's, Ltd., a Canadian-based corporation, was the largest worldwide producer and marketer of distilled spirits in 1965. Although 80% of Seagram's $897 million in 1964 gross sales came from whiskeys, the company also had a complete line of the nonwhiskeys. The breadth of its product line allowed Seagram to take advantage of changing consumer preferences. Seagram's VO, for example, was the major recipient of the growing demand for Canadian whiskey. However, the company also

---

[5] John Shaw, "Trends in the Liquor Industry," *Equity Research Associates* (August 30, 1965), p. 6.

[6] Paddington Corporation was acquired by Liggett & Myers Tobacco Company in April, 1966. L & M also acquired Star Industries, a wholesale liquor distributor, liquor importer, and owner of 40% of Paddington's voting securities, at the same time. In 1964, Star's net sales (sales less federal and state excise taxes) were $82 million. During the same year, L & M had net sales of $293 million and total assets of $401 million.

changed old products or introduced new products in response to changing consumer preference. When sales of Calvert Reserve had declined for over seven consecutive years, Seagram's replaced it with a restyled "soft whiskey," Calvert Extra, in the spring of 1963, and experienced an immediate sales gain of over 17%. In 1964, Seagram's withdrew Lord Calvert, a premium blended whiskey, and replaced it with Canadian Lord Calvert, a moderately priced Canadian whiskey bottled in the U.S., to take advantage of the trend toward bulk imports. In addition, Seagram's introduced nine new liquor products between 1961 and 1964 to capitalize on the trend toward lightness. Among these were two Scotches (100 Pipers and Passport) and four liqueurs as well as a gin, a vodka, the first Hawaiian rum, and a line of Calvert bottled cocktails.

Schenley, the fourth largest liquor company in 1964 with gross sales of $406 million, had one of the lowest growth rates in the liquor industry between 1955 and 1964. The company's gross sales decreased about 3% during that period, even though Schenley had three of the top 10 straight whiskey brands and had made several nonliquor acquisitions. However, in 1964, Schenley acquired Buckingham, the importer of Cutty Sark, the number one brand of Scotch, and introduced a line of bottled cocktails. As a result of these actions, several industry observers were predicting a turn around at Schenley by 1967.

Methods of distributing. Distribution of liquor took two basic forms at the beginning of 1966. In 18 "control states," a state-regulated agency was responsible for the distribution and sale of distilled spirits. In these states, the marketer usually sold the product to the state agency at the national wholesaler price and allowed the state to redistribute the products as it saw fit. These states often had laws which restricted the type of point of promotion advertising that a company could undertake. In the other 32 states, called "open states," distribution was accomplished through wholesalers who redistributed the product to the retailers who sold the product to the ultimate consumer. From 1958 to 1964, the number of these independent wholesalers declined almost 43%, so there were only 2,305 wholesalers left in 1964 who were licensed by the Federal Alcohol Administration to deal in distilled spirits. This trend, which was similar to that in other consumer product industries, was primarily caused, according to industry observers, by a serious profit squeeze on the wholesaler as his costs of operation increased while the retail prices of inexpensive liquors declined because of intense competition—a situation which was aggravated by the spread of private labels. While distillers had not felt the effects of this squeeze by 1964, there was a feeling among some industry observers that distillers might have to lower their prices to wholesalers or lose lower volume lines if the trend continued.

Cost structure. The cost of producing liquor products, excluding federal and state taxes on the raw materials, was relatively low compared to the retail selling prices. For example, high-quality vodka reportedly cost about 61 cents a fifth to produce, and retailed at $5.75. Federal taxes on raw materials (assuming an 80-proof product) were $1.68 per fifth. In addition, the costs of production, excluding federal and state taxes on raw materials, were often not much different for high-priced and low-priced liquors, even though they were often made by different processes. The different methods of production resulted in differences in taste and quality between the high-priced and low-priced liquors, however.

Heublein's history

The House of Heublein was founded in 1859 in Hartford, Connecticut, by Andrew Heublein, a painter and weaver by trade. At that time, the House of Heublein was a combination restaurant, cafe, and small hotel. By 1875, Andrew's two sons, Gilbert and Lewis, were running the business. They branched out by conducting a wholesale wine business in addition to expanding the original operations. In 1892, through a combination of fortuitous circumstances, Heublein invented the bottled cocktail. From this time until the start of national prohibition, Heublein's principal business was the production and sale of distilled spirits.

In 1907, Heublein began importing Brand's A-1 steak sauce and later, when World War I disrupted the importation, acquired the manufacturing rights to the product in the United States. When prohibition forced Heublein to close down its liquor plant in 1920, the company transferred key personnel to food operations. Until the repeal of prohibition in 1933, A-1 steak sauce was Heublein's principal product.

In 1939, John Martin, Heublein's president and one of the company's principal stockholders, acquired the rights to Smirnoff vodka from Mr. Rudolph Kunett. Although Heublein sold only 6,000 cases of Smirnoff that year, a carefully planned promotional campaign, which was put into operation immediately after World War II, aided in boosting the sales of Smirnoff to over one million cases per year by 1954. As the vodka market expanded, Heublein introduced Relska vodka in 1953 and Popov in 1961 to have entries in the middle-price and low-price segments of the market.

Although Smirnoff's remained Heublein's principal product from 1959, when it accounted for over 67% of sales, to 1965, when it accounted for 51% of sales, Heublein began to diversify its product line and to expand its international operations in the former year.

Heublein used both internal growth and acquisitions to broaden its product line. In 1960, Heublein began a campaign to increase the sales of its bottled cocktails by introducing new kinds of cocktails and promoting the entire line more heavily. As Heublein's sales began to increase, other distillers, principally Distillers Corporation, began to market their own cocktails. By 1965, bottled cocktail sales exceeded 850,000 cases a year, more than double the 1960 sales. At that time, Heublein still claimed 55% of the market.

In 1961, Heublein made two acquisitions which strengthened its specialty food line. Timely Brands, which manufactured and marketed a complete line of ready-to-use, home dessert decorating products, including Cake-Mate icing and gels, was acquired in June. In July, Heublein acquired Escoffier, Ltd., of London, England, makers of 23 famed gourmet sauces and specialties.

Heublein made two more acquisitions during this period, both of which were designed to broaden and strengthen Heublein's liquor line. In April, 1964, Heublein acquired Arrow Liquors Corporation for an estimated cost of $5.7 million. Arrow's principal products were its line of cordials, including Arrow Peppermint Schnapps, Arrow Blackberry Brandy, and its domestically bottled, bulk-imported Scotch, McMaster's. According to Mr. Edward Kelly, the three principal reasons for the Arrow acquisition were that Heublein expected the cordial and Scotch markets to grow in the future, that Arrow had products that were among the leaders in these markets in the control states, and that Arrow had a small but extremely competent management.

In January, 1965, Heublein acquired Vintage Wines for approximately $2.2 million. Vintage, whose sales were about $4 million at the time of the acquisition, was integrated with the Heublein Liquor Division. Vintage's principal product was Lancers Vin Rose, an imported Portuguese wine that accounted for about 50% of the company's sales.

The expansion which occurred in Heublein's international operations consisted primarily of the establishment of franchise operations in 21 additional foreign countries. This raised the number of such operations from 11 in 1959 to 32 in 1965.

Heublein's present operations

Financial situation. During the 1965 fiscal year, Heublein earned $7.4 million on sales of $166 million, which represented about a 19% return on stockholders' equity. Between 1959 and 1965, Heublein's sales growth, profit growth, and return on equity far exceeded the average of the four major distillers (see page 281). In addition, even though Heublein was spending nearly twice as much (as a percentage of sales) on advertising as the average of the four major distillers, and had increased the company's dividend payout ratio to 50% of earnings, the company had a cash flow of $8.6 million in 1965, about 22% on equity, which compared favorably to the 9% average of the four major distillers.

Product line. At the end of 1965, Heublein was marketing well over 50 products through its four divisions. While vodka was the company's principal product, accounting for 62% of 1965 sales, the company's product base had been broadened considerably since 1960 by acquisitions, internal growth, and new marketing agreements (see Exhibit 12 for sales-mix trends). Heublein's product-line strategy was to market high-quality consumer products which provided the high margins necessary to support intensive advertising.

Exhibit 12

HEUBLEIN SALES MIX FOR SELECTED YEARS

Year	Smirnoff Vodka	Other Vodka	Total Vodka	Other Alcoholic Beverages	Food	Total
1950	27%	...	27%	63%	10%	100%
1955	61	2%	63	31	5	100
1960	67	9	76	18	6	100
1961	64	11	75	19	6	100
1962	63	11	74	16	10	100
1963	62	12	74	16	10	100
1964	58	12	70	21	9	100
1965	51	11	62	30	8	100

Source: Heublein records.

Heublein aimed its promotions of these products at the growing, prosperous, young adult market. The company was also interested in phasing out some of its less profitable lines whenever possible.

The liquor products division accounted for over 80% of Heublein's 1965 sales. Its principal product was Smirnoff vodka, the fourth largest selling liquor brand in the United States in 1965, with estimated annual sales of 2.3 million cases. Company officials expected that Smirnoff, with its faster rate of growth, would move ahead of the third place brand (Canadian Club: 2.4 million cases) and second place brand (Seagram's VO: 2.5 million cases) within three years.

In 1965, Smirnoff had 23% of the total vodka market and outsold the second place vodka brand by over four to one. In addition, Smirnoff was the only premium-priced vodka on the market in 1965, since Wolfschmidt, formerly another premium-priced vodka, had lowered its wholesale price in 1964 in an effort to stimulate sales. After considering this action, Mr. Hart decided the appropriate response was to raise Smirnoff's wholesale price $1 per case and to put the additional revenue into advertising. Although Wolfschmidt's sales more than doubled, this increase appeared to come from the middle-priced segment of the vodka market, since Smirnoff's sales also increased 4% over the previous year and was running over 10% ahead in 1966. Smirnoff also appeared to be immune to the spread of the hundreds of private label vodkas, since company officials felt that these products obtained their sales from the 15% to 30% of the vodka market that was price conscious.

As a result, many industry observers expected Smirnoff to dominate the vodka market well into the future, particularly since Smirnoff could, on the basis of its sales volume, afford to spend $7 million to $8 million on advertising, while its closest rival could afford to spend only $2 million before putting the brand into the red.[7, 8]

Relska, a medium-priced vodka, and Popov, a low-priced vodka, were produced and sold primarily to give Heublein's distributors a full line of vodka products. They accounted for 11% of company sales in 1965. They were cheaper to produce than Smirnoff but were not as smooth to the taste, according to company officials.

Heublein bottled cocktails sold an estimated 500,000 cases in 1965, about 55% of the bottled cocktail market. Nevertheless, Heublein was beginning to receive competition from the national distilling companies, particularly Distillers Corporation, whose United States subsidiary, Seagram's, was marketing a similar line. Mr. Hart, however, welcomed this competition. He commented to the Los Angeles Society of Security Analysts in 1965:

> We believe the idea of bottled cocktails has not been completely sold to the American public. We were therefore delighted when we learned that one of the major companies in the liquor industry was introducing a new line of cocktails and that there would be heavy expenditures in advertising and merchandising to promote their usage to the public.[9]

> We are of the opinion that, as the cocktail market expands, our share will decrease, but Heublein cocktails will continue to be the leader, and that our sales will show remarkable increases.

Mr. Hart explained to the case writer that distribution was one of the principal reasons Heublein would keep its number one position:

> We secured distribution in 1960 when the other companies weren't too interested in cocktails. Since a distributor will usually carry only two or three lines, this means that he will have Heublein and Calvert or Heublein and Schenley: in other words, Heublein and somebody else. . . . In addition to being first, Heublein's wide line will also help us get and maintain distribution.

In 1965, Heublein's bottled cocktail line included Manhattans, Vodka Sours, Extra Dry Martinis, Gin Sours, Whiskey Sours, Side Cars, Vodka Martinis, Daiquiris, Old Fashioneds, and Stingers.

During 1964, the liquor products division reintroduced Milshire gin. For years, Milshire had been a regional gin selling about 100,000 cases a year. However, in 1963 the promotional budget was deemed sufficient to devote some real attention to Milshire. To prepare for this, the old inventory was sold off, the product was reformulated, and the package was redesigned.

---

[7]Roger D. Bensen, *Heublein, Inc.*, Glore Forgan, Wm. R. Staats Inc. (December 1965), p. 25.

[8]In 1963, according to the *Liquor Handbook*, Heublein spent $1.4 million to advertise Smirnoff, while total advertising for all other vodka brands during the same years was $1.2 million.

[9]Heublein spent $2 million advertising its line of bottled cocktails in 1965. Seagram's spent $1.5 million advertising its Calvert line the same year.

The principal difference in the product was that its botanical and aromatic content was lowered since it was filtered through activated charcoal in a process similar to that used to make Smirnoff. The net effect of this was to make the gin "lighter." Sales for 1964 increased to 150,000 cases, a significant jump, but still very far behind the 2.1 million cases of Gordon's, the leading brand.

In 1966, Heublein reached an agreement with Tequila Cuervo S. A. to be the exclusive U.S. marketer of Jose Cuervo and Matador tequilas and a cordial based on the same spirit. Heublein planned to market these products on a nationwide basis through the liquor products division.

The liquor products division also marketed Harvey's sherries, ports, and table wines; Bell's Scotches; Gilbeys Canadian whiskeys; Byrrh aperitif wine; and the products of Vintage Wines, Inc.

The Arrow division accounted for about 10% of Heublein's sales in 1965. The division's principal products were Arrow cordials, liqueurs, and brandies, and McMaster's Scotch. Arrow's distribution system was particularly strong in the control states. In addition, Arrow's distribution in the open states was strengthened in 1965, when Heublein discontinued the production of its line of Heublein cordials and substituted the Arrow line.

Although the sales of the food division more than doubled between 1961 and 1965, it accounted for only 8% of the company's 1965 sales. Nevertheless, A-1 steak sauce was the company's number two profit producer in 1965, second only to Smirnoff vodka. Other food products included Cake-Mate icings and gels, Escoffier sauces, Grey-Poupon Mustard, and Maltex and Maypo cereals. In 1965, Heublein reached an agreement with the Costal Valley Canning Company of California to distribute and market Snap-E-Tom Tomato Cocktail. Snap-E-Tom was a tomato juice flavored with onion and chili pepper juices. It was designed for the pre-meal juice and the cocktail mixed markets, both of which had high profit margins.

Marketing. The case writer felt Heublein's unique advertising and promotion policies and campaigns set Heublein apart from the other liquor companies (see Exhibit 13 for the advertising expenditures of various liquor companies). Heublein considered liquor to be a branded consumer product, and viewed itself as a marketer of high-quality consumer products rather than as a liquor company. As a result, Heublein developed intensive advertising campaigns to sell its products for the growing, affluent young adult market, since it believed it was easier to get a new customer in this market than to get a 40-year-old Scotch drinker to switch to vodka. Because of the importance attached to advertising, Heublein spent 10.6% of sales for advertising in 1965, nearly double the 5.7% of Distillers Corporation.

In addition, Heublein was an aggressive innovator among liquor industry advertisers. In the 1950's, industry self-regulation prohibited depicting a woman in an advertisement for a liquor product. In 1958, Heublein advised the Distilled Spirits Institute that it believed this ban on the portrayal of women was "obsolete, hopelessly prudish, and downright bad business."

Exhibit 13

ADVERTISING EXPENDITURES OF MAJOR LIQUOR COMPANIES FOR 1965

Company	Advertising (Millions)	Sales (Millions)	Advertising as a Percent of Sales
Distillers Corp.-Seagram's Ltd.	$43,750	$762,520	5.7%
Schenley Industries	23,100	380,200	6.1
National Distillers & Chemical Corp. ...	19,669	810,900	2.4
Hiram Walker	17,750	498,174	3.6
Heublein, Inc.	17,495	165,522	10.6

Source: *Advertising Age* (January 3, 1966), p. 46.

Finally the DSI agreed and Heublein became the first liquor company to portray women in its ads under the new DSI self-regulation, an advertising practice later followed by nearly every major distiller. Heublein also pioneered a change in DSI regulations to permit liquor advertising in Sunday supplements. At the end of 1965, Heublein was pushing for the use of liquor advertisements on radio and TV similar to beer and wine advertisements.

Another unique feature of Heublein's marketing was the promotions it used. These were designed to appeal to the young adult group and used celebrities and offbeat approaches to gain attention (see Exhibit 14). An example of this approach was the Smirnoff Mule promotion launched in May, 1965. The promotion, Heublein's largest for a single drink, was designed to catch the discotheque popularity on the upswing. The total investment was about $2 million for advertising, merchandising, and sales promotion. *The New York Times* commented that:

> Included in the Smirnoff advertising mix are a drink, called the Smirnoff Mule; a song and dance, called simply The Mule; a recording called Skitch Plays "The Mule"; a copper-colored metal mug in which to drink the Smirnoff Mule; and a recent phenomenon called the discotheque . . . the Gumbinner-North Company [Heublein's advertising agency] has recruited such vodka salesmen as Skitch Henderson, Carmen McRae, and Killer Joe Piro to put it over. . . . In addition to Smirnoff ads, The Mule will be featured in local advertising by the 7-Up people.[10]

Distribution. Heublein sold its products directly to state liquor control boards in the 18 control states and to approximately 235 wholesale distributors in the 32 open states and the District of Columbia. Food products were sold through food brokers and wholesalers. It was Heublein's policy to strive to create mutually profitable relationships with its distributors. For example, one of the reasons for the creation of Popov vodka was to give Heublein's distributors a low-priced vodka brand to sell.

International operations. At the end of 1965, Heublein was involved in

[10]Walter Carlson, "Advertising: Smirnoff Harnesses the Mule," *The New York Times* (June 27, 1965).

Exhibit 14

SMIRNOFF MULE AD

THE SMIRNOFF MULE—SKITCH HENDERSON MADE IT A SONG. "KILLER JOE" PIRO MADE IT A DANCE.

NEW DRINK...SMIRNOFF® MULE
It swings!

Taste the new party favorite that's sweeping the country, the swingingest drink since Smirnoff invented vodka. It's the Smirnoff Mule, made with Smirnoff and 7-Up®. Just pour a jigger of Smirnoff over ice. Add juice of ¼ lime. Fill Mule mug or glass with 7-Up to your taste. *Delicious!* Only smooth, flawless Smirnoff, filtered through 14,000 pounds of activated charcoal, blends so perfectly with 7-Up. That's why the fuel for your Mule must be Smirnoff! *It leaves you breathless®*

SMIRNOFF VODKA 80 AND 100 PROOF. DISTILLED FROM GRAIN. STE. PIERRE SMIRNOFF FLS. (DIVISION OF HEUBLEIN). HARTFORD, CONN.

three types of overseas activities. The largest and most important was its licensing operation. Distillers in 32 foreign countries were licensed to manufacture and market Smirnoff vodka. Among the countries in which Heublein had such franchises were Austria, Denmark, Greece, Ireland, New Zealand, South Africa, and Spain. When selecting a franchise holder, Heublein looked for a local distiller who had good production facilities and who was a good marketer in his country. Heublein felt this policy allowed it to get established faster than if Heubein tried to set up its own plant. Heublein also felt it improved relations with the local government.

Under these franchise agreements, the distiller produced the neutral spirits in the best way possible in his country. To maintain quality control, however, Heublein installed and owned the copper filtration units and shipped the charcoal to these locations from Hartford. This was done at cost. The contracts called for a license fee (about 10% of sales) and also stipulated that certain amounts be spent by the franchisee for advertising. Usually, during the first three or four years, Heublein would add its 10% license fee to these advertising funds in order to help build up the business. Plans were under way at the end of 1965 to begin operations in six more countries, including Ecuador, India, and Nigeria.

Heublein also exported Smirnoff, primarily to military bases overseas. In addition, Heublein opened an operation in Freeport, Jamaica, in 1965, to produce Smirnoff and other Heublein liquor products, and to market these products to customers such as ships' chandlers and diplomatic agencies who could purchase tax-free liquor.

Between 1961 and 1965, Heublein's export sales increased 99%, royalties from licenses 145%, and profits from international operations 458%. In 1965, net export sales stood at $1.2 million, and profits before taxes from international operations, including license fees, were $880,000.

Production. At the end of 1965, Heublein owned and operated three plants throughout the United States, with an annual capacity of 20 million wine gallons for all product lines, and was building a plant in Detroit to replace the old Arrow plant. This plant was to cost $4.5 million and to have an annual capacity of 5.5 million wine gallons. When completed, this plant would give Heublein a total annual capacity of 25.5 million wine gallons. All these plants were highly automated.

Heublein had about 975 employees in 1965, of whom slightly less than half were hourly employees. In 1965, labor costs were only 3% of the total cost of sales.

Heublein did not produce the grain neutral spirits for its gin and vodka production, but rather purchased these requirements on contract and the open market from four distillers. Heublein maintained facilities in the Midwest for the storage of 8 million proof gallons, however, in case none of these suppliers could meet Heublein's stringent quality requirements. At 1965 consumption rates, this represented about a one-year supply.

According to Heublein, even the high-quality grain neutral spirits it received from its suppliers contained too many impurities for direct use in Smirnoff. The first step in Smirnoff production was, therefore, to redistill these grain neutral spirits. At the end of the redistillation, the alcohol was 192 proof. It was then blended with distilled water to reduce the mixture to 80 proof. This mixture was then filtered slowly through 10 copper tanks which contained over 14,000 pounds of activated charcoal. The filtering process required eight hours. According to company officials, it was during this process that the vodka became smooth and mellow and acquired its mild but distinctive taste. The only remaining step was to bottle the finished product, since vodka required no aging.

Heublein also redistilled the grain neutral spirits used in the production of its charcoal-filtered Milshire gin. However, the company did not redistill the liquors (purchased on the open market) used in the production of Heublein cocktails.

Most of the food products were manufactured at Hartford or at the plant in Burlington, Vermont. Heublein insisted on the same high-quality standards in the purchase of raw materials and production of its food products that it required in its liquor production.

HEUBLEIN, INC. (B)*

∧∧

Having acquired four companies during the past six years (both Timely Brands and Escoffier, Ltd., in 1960—manufacturers and marketers of specialty food products; Arrow Liquors Corporation in 1964; and Vintage Wines in 1965),[1] Heublein's management at the end of 1965 expressed continued interest in further acquisitions.

The kinds of companies being sought were not just profitable financial deals, but rather firms in which Heublein's management believed it could improve operations. Heublein's acquisition policies were explained more fully by Mr. Ralph Hart, Heublein's president, in a 1965 presentation before the Los Angeles Society of Security Analysts:

> Frankly, we take a long hard look at any potential acquisition. We ask ourselves: "Will the new product or company we acquire have a potential at least equal to existing Heublein products, in order not to dilute present equity? Will new products lend themselves to our channels of distribution and marketing techniques? Will these products have sufficient gross margin to allow for our type of distribution, advertising, and merchandising?"

The proposed Hamm acquisition

Early in the fall of 1965, Heublein's top management was seriously considering the possible acquisition of the Theo. Hamm Brewing Company. They were particularly interested because they felt Hamm's could profit immensely from what they felt was Heublein's major strength—the ability to market a consumer product extremely well. If the acquisition were consummated, Heublein would become the first company to engage in the production and sale of both beer and liquor.

Under the proposed agreement Heublein would acquire all of the outstanding shares of Hamm's common in exchange for 420,032 shares of Heublein's 5% preferred, and 200,031 shares of Heublein's 5% convertible preferred. Both preferreds had a par value of $100; the latter was convertible into three shares of Heublein common, subject to certain provisions against dilution of earnings. Although Hamm's stock was held by a family

---

[1]For further particulars, see Heublein, Inc. (A).

Exhibit 1

THEO. HAMM BREWING COMPANY CONSOLIDATED BALANCE SHEETS
(Dollars in Thousands)

	Nov. 30, 1964	Sept. 30, 1965
Current assets:		
Cash	$ 3,475	$ 3,153
Certificates of deposit	2,000	500
Commercial paper and marketable securities (at cost)*	26,560	24,044
Accounts receivable (net)	5,452	7,959
Inventories	5,352	6,479
Prepaid expenses	898	891
Total current assets	$43,737	$43,027
Investments and other assets	6,467	6,536
Property, plant, and equipment (net)	26,381	26,930
	$76,585	$76,493
Current liabilities:		
Trade accounts payable	$ 2,639	$ 2,926
Salaries and wages	1,207	1,304
Customers' deposits	932	1,151
Miscellaneous accounts payable and accrued expenses	470	1,301
Taxes other than taxes on income	2,038	2,299
Federal and state taxes on income	2,657	2,559
Dividends payable	1,538	660
Sinking fund deposits due in one year	100	100
Total current liabilities	$11,580	$12,302
Eight per cent debenture bonds	1,400	1,400
Stockholders' equity		
Capital stock	55,083	26,432
Capital surplus	...	26,273
Earned surplus	8,521	10,086
	$76,585	$76,493

*The market value of these securities was $28.1 million in 1964 and $25.7 million in 1965.
Source: Heublein acquisition study.

group and did not have a market price, Heublein's board estimated that the aggregate fair value was in excess of $62 million, or book value (see Exhibit 1). The proposed agreement stipulated that each class of preferred would have the right to elect one member to Heublein's board. In addition, it was provided that the $25 million of securities indicated on the Theo. Hamm Brewing Company consolidated balance sheet as of 9/30/65 would be liquidated and used to buy out dissident Hamm's stockholders prior to the acquisition by Heublein. This would have the effect of reducing Hamm's working capital and stockholder equity before the purchase by about $25 million.

Hamm's history and competitive position. Hamm's was a family-owned brewing company. During the five years preceding the proposed acquisition, sales and profits had remained relatively stable (see Exhibits 2 and 3). However, since industry sales had increased slightly more than 11% during this period, Hamm's market share had declined from 4.5% to 3.7%. In addition,

Exhibit 2

THEO. HAMM BREWING COMPANY CONSOLIDATED STATEMENT OF INCOME
(Dollars in Thousands)

| | Years Ended November 30 | | | | | Ten Months Ended September 30 (Unaudited) | |
	1960	1961	1962	1963	1964	1964	1965§
Revenues:							
Sales less allowances	$119,881	$115,874	$114,885	$119,584	$124,233	$106,109	$109,449
Interest	161	240	270	575	958	748	941
Dividends	81	62	50	51	61	58	42
Other	283	95	175	196	351	301	359
	$120,407	$116,272	$115,380	$120,405	$125,602	$107,217	$110,791
Costs and expenses:							
Cost of goods sold*	89,843	86,314	86,595	90,878	95,388	81,004	84,597
Selling, delivery, advertising, general and administrative expenses	16,263	17,065	16,200	18,534	21,423	18,196	19,026
Interest:							
Long-term debt	235	164	120	120	120	100	100
Other	8	159	2	16	13	12	...
	$106,349	$103,702	$102,918	$109,548	$116,945	$99,312	$103,723
Earnings before taxes on income	$ 14,057	$ 12,570	$ 12,462	$ 10,857	$ 8,657	$ 7,905	$ 7,068
Taxes on income:							
Federal	6,750	6,150	6,100	5,100	3,900	3,550	3,000
State	450	400	400	275	300	275	225
	$ 7,200	$ 6,550	$ 6,500	$ 5,375	$ 4,200	$ 3,825	$ 3,225
Net earnings (excluding the operations of the Eastern division and related distributing subsidiaries)	$ 6,857	$ 6,020	$ 5,962	$ 5,482	$ 4,457	$ 4,080	$ 3,843
Loss on operations of Eastern division and related distributing subsidiaries less applicable income tax benefits†	1,092	1,717	2,124	1,408			
Net earnings	$ 5,765	$ 4,303	$ 3,838	$ 4,074	$ 4,457	$ 4,080	$ 3,843
Preferred stock dividend requirements	210	210	210	210	210	175	142
Earnings applicable to common stock	$ 5,555	$ 4,093	$ 3,628	$ 3,864	$ 4,247	$ 3,905	$ 3,701
Per common share (dollars) earnings applicable to:							
Common stock‡	$2.14	$1.57	$1.40	$1.49	$1.63	$1.50	$1.40
Cash dividends declared	...	...	0.40	0.95	1.25	0.50	0.75

*Cost of goods sold includes federal and state excise taxes of between $32 and $38 million for each of the above periods.

†In 1960, the company acquired brewing facilities in Baltimore, Maryland, which were sold in 1963 for $6 million, the approximate net carrying amount of the facilities. Applicable income tax benefits ranging between $1.2 and $2.1 million have been netted against loss on operations of Eastern division and related distributing subsidiaries for the years 1960–63 inclusive.

‡Earnings applicable to common stock are based on the number of shares outstanding at the end of each period as adjusted for the recapitalization during the year ended November 30, 1961.

§Earnings for the 10 months ended September 30, 1965, were adversely affected by nonrecurring legal and centennial expenses aggregating approximately $400,000.

Source: Heublein acquisition study.

Exhibit 3

HEUBLEIN, INC., AND THEO. HAMM BREWING COMPANY
PRO FORMA COMBINED STATEMENT OF INCOME
(Dollars in Thousands)

	June 30, 1960 Nov. 30, 1960	June 30, 1961 Nov. 30, 1961	June 30, 1962 Nov. 30, 1962	June 30, 1963 Nov. 30, 1963	June 30, 1964 Nov. 30, 1964	Ten months to Sept. 30, 1965
	Heublein Hamm					
Net sales	$223,050	$224,156	$231,027	$241,579	$260,082	$249,056
Cost of sales	$167,872	$166,732	$172,389	$180,378	$194,963	$187,059
Selling, general and administrative expenses	33,323	36,359	36,755	40,515	45,385	43,164
Other income (deductions):						
Interest and dividend income	352	417	444	865	1,287	1,217
Interest expense	(560)	(595)	(363)	(344)	(342)	(215)
Miscellaneous—net	198	85	93	503	308	320
	$ (10)	$ (93)	$ 174	$ 1,024	$ 1,253	$ 1,322
Income before income taxes	$ 21,845	$ 20,972	$ 22,057	$ 21,710	$ 20,987	$ 20,155
Provision for income taxes	11,432	11,137	11,688	11,205	10,716	9,966
Net income before loss on discontinued operations of Hamm	$ 10,413	$ 9,835	$ 10,369	$ 10,505	$ 10,271	$ 10,189
Loss on discontinued operations of Hamm, less applicable income tax benefits	1,092	1,717	2,124	1,408	...	...
Net income	$ 9,321	$ 8,118	$ 8,245	$ 9,097	$ 10,271	$ 10,189
Deduct pro forma adjustments:						
Interest and dividend income	219	275	290	591	981	950
Interest expense	1,209	983	975	501	122	85
Income taxes	(738)	(638)	(652)	(549)	(496)	(418)
	$ 690	$ 620	$ 613	$ 543	$ 607	$ 617
Pro forma net income	$ 8,631	$ 7,498	$ 7,632	$ 8,554	$ 9,664	$ 9,572
Preferred dividend requirements:						
Heublein:						
5% preferred stock	$ 2,100	$ 2,100	$ 2,100	$ 2,100	$ 2,100	$ 1,750
5% convertible preferred stock	1,000	1,000	1,000	1,000	1,000	833
	$ 3,100	$ 3,100	$ 3,100	$ 3,100	$ 3,100	$ 2,583
Pro forma earnings applicable to common stock	$ 5,531	$ 4,398	$ 4,532	$ 5,454	$ 6,564	$ 6,989
Pro forma earnings per share (dollars):						
Assuming no conversion of convertible preferred stock	$ 1.15	$ .91	$ .93	$ 1.12	$ 1.37	$ 1.43
Assuming full conversion of convertible preferred stock	1.21	1.00	1.01	1.18	1.40	1.43
Actual Heublein earnings per share*	0.74	0.79	0.91	1.03	1.21	1.30

*Heublein shares outstanding in June of 1965, 4.9 million; approximate market price/share in 1965 (to September) $26-$27

Source: Heublein acquisition study.

Hamm's return on sales had lagged behind the industry leaders (see Exhibits 4, 5, and 6).

Exhibit 4

BEER: LARGER MARKETS, TOUGHER COMPETITION*

The bigger it gets, the rougher it gets. That sums up the brewing industry, which has just had its best year ever. But no one brewer had an easy time of it, and the competition will get even stiffer in the years ahead.

by Kenneth Ford, Managing Editor

No one in the brewing industry had anything but kind words last week for the nation's growing number of young adults.

Not only were they quaffing their share of brew and more besides, but even more significant, they appeared willing to cast aside some old-fashioned concepts about beer being a "blue-collar" drink.

For the nation's 190 brewers (four fewer than the year before) the moral was that patience pays off. All during the long, dry decade of the Fifties the industry watched total consumption lag behind population growth and per capita consumption remain static at a low level. Brewers pinned their hopes on the vast crop of war babies of the Forties, hoping that when they reached drinking age they would set off a beer boom, but also fearing they might move from the innocence of Coke to the decadence of Martinis in one easy step.

They didn't. When the 1963 figures were totaled up at this time last year, there were clear signs that the brewing industry was on the move at last. No one outside the industry realized how fast it was moving until the 1964 totals came in last month.

The results: total sales (consumption) climbed to 98.5-million barrels, up five per cent from 1963's 93.8-million barrels. Per capita consumption, the more meaningful measure of marketing effectiveness, jumped to 15.7 gallons, up 2.6 per cent from 1963's 15.3 gallons. Both gains were the best year-to-year increase posted by the industry since 1947.

It is a certainty that the industry will cross the 100-million barrel barrier in 1965. The only question is whether it will reach 101-million or 102-million barrels. No one will be unhappy if it doesn't go that high—the industry's most optimistic forecasters hadn't expected it to reach the 100-million barrel level until 1967.

But though the overall industry outlook is sudsy, neither leaders nor laggards are finding it easy selling.

Competition has never been fiercer. The nation's top ten brewers have staked out 57.7 per cent share of the total market, selling 56.6-million barrels of that 98.5 million total. The next 14 ranking brewers take 25.4 per cent of the total, or 25-million barrels. All together, the top 24 brewers, each doing better than one-million barrels apiece, account for 82.9 per cent of total sales, some 81.6-million barrels.

But even what would be a normally respectable gain was not enough to hold the previous year's position, much less advance, in the top 24 standings.

LOSSES AND GAINS

Carling dropped in 1964 from fourth to fifth; Hamm from seventh to eighth; Rheingold from tenth to 11th; Lucky Lager from 13th to 16th; Pearl from 17th to 18th; Narragansett from 19th to 21st and Jackson from 23rd to 24th. Yet five had made sales gains—Carling's posted a 1.7 per cent increase; Rheingold a 3.1 per cent increase; Pearl a 5.4 per cent increase; Narragansett a 2.8 per cent increase; and Jackson a 2.2 per cent increase.

The leading brewers had set such a blistering pace that merely running to keep up just wasn't fast enough.

First-place Anheuser-Busch (Budweiser–Busch Bavarian–Michelob) achieved a 10.1 per cent gain that carried it across the ten-million-barrel level, an industry

Printers' Ink (Feb. 12, 1965). Reproduced by permission.

Exhibit 4—Continued

record, and gave it a 10.5 per cent share of the total market. A–B phenomenal performance was the culmination of marketing programs set in motion as long as a decade ago. Basically, these concentrated on development of marketing executives, achieving the best possible communication with its 900 wholesalers throughout the country and expanding plants into growing markets. (Its new Houston brewery will be ready next year.)

Though A–B is one of the heaviest advertisers in the industry, it makes only evolutionary changes in its advertising program from year to year. "Where There's Life There's Bud" (1963) became "That Bud, that's beer" (1964) and now becomes "It's Worth It, It's Budweiser" (1965).

Expansion-minded Schlitz, eyeing the heavier-beer-drinking Canadian market (per capita consumption 16.4 gallons) tried to migrate north by buying control of Canada's Labatt Brewing, but found itself ensnarled in antitrust actions and other legal complications. The time and attention it had to devote to these were reflected in only a 5.3 per cent gain, in contrast to 1963's 13 per cent gain.

Another 11.6 per cent gain like the one Pabst made last year might well knock Schlitz out of second-place. And fast-rising Falstaff is a factor that Schlitz and Pabst marketing executives both must reckon with in the year ahead.

Falstaff surprised everyone by clipping Carling out of fourth place in the brewing industry. Carling had made sixteen consecutive sales gains that brought it up from 19th in the industry and was generally conceded to be the brewer to watch. Controlled by Canadian entrepreneur E. P. Taylor, its marketing strategy is based on two rules: build plants where the markets are growing (it now has nine in the U.S.) and advertise heavily.

But it was Falstaff's ambition and innovation that carried it ahead. It markets only one brand of beer, Falstaff, in 32 states westward from Indiana. These states have 45 per cent of the nation's population but consume less than 45 per cent of total beer production.

A COMPETITOR TO RESPECT

"If we were in the other 18 states, we'd be selling 10.5-million barrels instead of 5.8-million," says George Holtman, vice president, advertising. Holtman's boast is not idle. That Falstaff is a competitor to respect is attested to by Hamm's decline of 2.5 per cent. Both collided competitively in the Midwest generally and the Chicago market in particular. Falstaff began moving into Chicago three years ago and the 1964 figures reflect its arrival. Similarly, it began moving into the West Coast in recent years where traditional beer sales patterns are changing, too. Lucky Lager, long the leading West Coast brand, slumped 15.1 per cent, dropping below the two-million barrel level under the impact of competition from Falstaff and other interloping brewers. Among them: the Schlitz-Burgemeister brand team, Falstaff, Budweiser, and Carling. The latter is going to build its own brewery in the San Francisco area, which should make conditions in the important California market (it accounts for about 7.5 per cent of total consumption alone) even more competitive.

But the moral is not that the big bad national brands come in and knock off the poor little locals. Washington-based Olympia, strong in the Northwest, and Denver-based Coors both are making significant progress on the West Coast. Olympia scored a 22.1 per cent increase, and Coors, long the strong man of the Rocky Mountain empire, boosted advertising budgets by 11 per cent and barged into California. Result: a 12 per cent sales increase.

In the big New York market is was a locally-based brewer that led the pack— Brooklyn's F&M Schaefer Brewing. Schaefer soared to 4,250,000 barrels up 10.1 per cent, while Newark-based Ballantine dropped 3.9 per cent and Rheingold, up 3.1 per cent, slipped out of the top ten and found its claim to being top brand in the New York metropolitan area under severe pressure.

Ballantine, long handled by the Wm. Esty Co., is now looking for a new advertising agency. Rheingold, sold by the Liebmann family to Pepsi-Cola United Bottlers, switched agencies again. In recent years it has gone from Foote Cone &

Exhibit 4—Continued

Belding to J. Walter Thompson, back to FCB, and is now at Doyle Dane Bernbach. Rheingold, under the aegis of its new management, reportedly was moving ahead at year's end behind a barrage of television and radio spots.

COMPETITION KEEN IN EAST, TOO

Throughout the East, competition was similarly strong. Philadelphia-based Schmidt (Schmidt–Prior–Valley Forge) gained 13.3 per cent, Baltimore-based National climbed 21.5 per cent, and Manhattan-based Ruppert, strong in New England, moved ahead 22.5 per cent. Rochester-based Genessee (up 20.2 per cent) cemented its already strong position in upstate New York.

One result of this fierce competition was increased ad budgets. With most brewers offering what economists call "poorly differentiated products"—i.e., sameness—images were the most important function in marketing. Most brewers in *Printers' Ink's* annual marketing survey, of course, declined to give data on ad expenditures, though a few admitted increases ranging from four to six per cent. However, the industry operates on a so-much-per-barrel basis in its ad budgeting. *Printers' Ink's* study of beer advertising expenditures (October 2, 1964, page 25) found the industry average was 96-cents a barrel for the four measured media. This would put total spending in a 98.5-million barrel year at $94.4-million in those media. This, however, is only about one-third of total expenditures. Big chunks of money go for "rights" to broadcast sports events, a staple of beer marketing. For instance, Schlitz, now building a new brewery in Texas, paid out $5.3-million for rights to the Houston Colts games.

"It's all part of becoming a new resident of the area," a Schlitz spokesman explained. "We want to get known fast and this is how you do it."

So important are sports sponsorships that they significantly influence marketing strategy. For example, Schmidt's bought the old Standard Beverage plant in Cleveland from Schaefer (which then bought the old Gunther plant in Baltimore from Hamm). Schmidt originally intended to use the Cleveland brewery to supply its markets in Western Pennsylvania and Western New York state and had no immediate intention of entering the northeastern Ohio market. But the opportunity arose to buy a participation in radio-sponsorship of the Cleveland Browns' games. Schmidt's bought it and entered the market immediately.

CAN U.S. COMPETE ABROAD?

For the past few years, American brewers have enviously watched the success of imported European beers in the U.S. The European importers sell less than one per cent of the total sold in the U.S. but their profit margins are far better than the domestic brewers achieve on a unit basis. Would the same not hold true for U.S. and Canadian beers overseas? It is also a way to rise above the cannibalistic competition in the U.S. The other way is to increase the beer consumption of the American drinker. Though 1964's 3.3 per cent increase in per capita consumption was the best in recent years, the industry lags far behind the high of 18.7 gallons set in 1945 or even the postwar 18.4 gallons quaffed in 1947.

New products may help. Schlitz, Pabst and National are now strongly promoting malt liquor brands. A–B's Michelob and Hamm's Waldech in the super-premium class are upgrading beer's image and adding a new group of customers.

But it is a packaging development that may be of the most far-reaching significance. This is the home keg or draft beer that fits neatly into the family refrigerator. In the consumption battle, beer's increase in share must come from soft drinks, coffee, tea, and such—not merely from population growth or competitors' customers.

In the decade ending in 1963, beer consumption increased only 12 per cent while the population grew 19 per cent. Soft drinks shot up 49 per cent, soluble coffee 158, and tea 20 per cent.

The confirmed beer drinker guzzles about six quarts a week on a yearly averaged-out basis. That's about two and a half 12-ounce cans at a time.

What the industry must attract is the glass-at-a-time sipper. That's not much at a

Exhibit 4—Continued

time, but there are an awful lot of them and enough sips by enough people can boost beer back near the 20 gallons per capita consumption level of pre-World War I days.

It will take a revolution in American beer-drinking patterns to do it, but it could happen.

BEER: A REVOLUTION IN DRINKING?

Beer's flat consumption curve may get the upward kick it needs from the new refrigerator keg. . . .

Some brewers privately hail it as the most significant development in beer marketing in the postwar era. They think a keg of draft beer in the family refrigerator can't help but cause a gusty increase in per capita consumption.

Units like the one above have been in test markets for more than two years now, and indications are that a rush into this type of packaging is about to begin. Nine brewers now offer draft beer in one of three such packaging variations; more than a dozen others are negotiating with a leading supplier.

There are two basic types of kegs being used, the more elaborate, made by Reynolds Metals and Alcoa, utilize carbon dioxide to shoot the beer out; the other, made by National Can, utilizes squeeze-bulb-generated air pressure.

Falstaff, Hamm and National are using the Reynolds unit, called the "Tapper." Schlitz is now testing the Alcoa unit in eight markets. It's called the Home Keg.

Atlantic Lederbrau, Sterling Brew, Koch Brewing, Gettelman (owned by Miller's); Standard Rochester and National (using both) are marketing in National Can's Home Tap.

There are important differences in the units. Reynolds' Tapper holds 2¼ gallons, measures nine inches by 11½ inches so that it will fit in 98 per cent of existing refrigerators, weighs seven pounds empty and 26 pounds full, contains the equivalent of 24 12-ounce cans, and will keep draft beer flavor-fresh for three weeks under refrigeration.

The Alcoa unit, being tested by Schlitz, differs from the Reynolds unit in two ways—the carbon dioxide mechanism, and size. The Alcoa unit holds only 144 ounces but Schlitz is packing two to a carton so the consumer buys the same amount of beer as in the Reynolds unit. Because of quirks in state liquor laws, the Reynolds size is illegal in a few states. Falstaff is now testing a 3⅛-gallon size in Louisville that will meet such objections.

National Can's Home Tap, which holds one gallon, also fits snugly on the refrigerator shelf.

Because the Tapper carries a four-dollar deposit, Falstaff pioneered in extensive testing the Reynolds unit in Springfield, Ill.; Fort Wayne, Ind.; Tulsa, Okla.; Detroit; and Chicago. The beer itself is comparable in price to a case of 24 cans, making the initial outlay between eight and nine dollars, but the second-time cost is between four and five dollars.

Falstaff found that the average Tapper buyer was male and relatively prosperous. "These results tie in exactly with our predictions of what the beer drinker of coming years will be like," says Alvin Griesedieck, Jr., vice president, marketing. "Our projections show that although he will continue to be married, he will have a higher level of education, be a professional man or in the service industries, live in suburbia, and enjoy a higher income."

Griesedieck is enthusiastic about its potential. It should, he says, create "a revolution in beer-drinking habits." Others agree. Schlitz president Robert Uihlein, Jr., views the potential of draft beer in the home as "outstanding."

And that's what beer needs most.

Hamm's sold three brands of beer at the end of 1965: Waldech (premium price), Hamm's (premium and popular price), and Buckhorn (lower price).

Exhibit 5

HAMM AND INDUSTRY SALES
(In Millions of Barrels)

	Brewing Industry, Tax-Paid Only*	Hamm's Beer Sales, Tax-Paid Only	Tax-Paid Hamm's Sales as % of Tax-Paid Industry Sales
1955	85.0	3.1	3.6
1956	85.0	3.3	3.9
1957	84.4	3.4	4.0
1958	84.4	3.4	4.0
1959	87.6	3.5	4.0
1960	87.9	4.0	4.5
1961	89.0	3.7	4.1
1962	91.2	3.7	4.0
1963	93.8	3.8	4.1
1964	98.6	3.7	3.7

*The data given with respect to the brewing industry represent tax-paid withdrawals of malt beverages as reported by the Internal Revenue Service.
Source: U.S. Treasury Department data.

The 1964 sales breakdown among these brands had been 17,800 barrels[2] for Waldech, 3,624,700 barrels for Hamm's, and 57,800 barrels for Buckhorn, for a total of 3,700,300 barrels. In addition, Hamm's had produced some beer for sale to the F.&M. Schaefer Brewing Company under the Gunther brand in 1964.

In 1965, Hamm's beer was sold in 31 states and the District of Columbia. Most sales, however, were made in the midwestern, western, and southwestern parts of the United States. Hamm's relied exclusively on 479 independent wholesalers for its distribution, most of whom carried other brands of beer. Although any of these wholesalers could terminate his relationship with Hamm's at will, none of them accounted for more than 2.5% of Hamm's 1964 sales.

Exhibit 6

RETURNS ON 1964 SALES OF LEADING BREWERS

	Total Revenues (000)	Pretax Net (000)	Profit Margin (Per Cent)	Barrels Sold (000)	Pretax Returns/ Barrel
Anheuser-Busch	$491,384	$39,312	8.00%	10,235	$3.84
Schlitz	311,394	28,277	9.08	8,266	3.42
Pabst	227,610	20,421	8.97	7,444	2.74
Falstaff	211,943	13,604	6.42	5,815	2.33
Hamm	125,602	8,657	6.89	3,719	2.33

Source: Company annual reports.

---

[2] A barrel was equivalent to 31 U.S. gallons.

According to some industry observers, Hamm's four breweries were one of its principal assets. Three of these were owned outright, while the fourth was leased. The location and annual productive capacity of each of these plants was as follows:

Location	Annual Productive Capacity (barrels)
St. Paul, Minnesota	2,550,000
San Francisco, California	1,000,000
Los Angeles, California	500,000
Houston, Texas (leased)	450,000
	4,500,000

According to industry estimates, the cost of replacing Hamm's 1965 capacity would be about $135 million, or more than double the proposed purchase price. This estimate was based on the industry rule of thumb which set the costs of new plant construction at $30 to $35 per barrel at the end of 1965.

Like Heublein, Hamm's purchased most of the raw materials needed for its production—malt, barley, hops, and corn grits—from various independent suppliers. About one fourth of the malt and hops requirements were met by wholly owned subsidiaries, however.

The brewing industry. At the end of 1964, the beer market was approximately the same size as the distilled spirits market, or about $6.4 billion a year (see Exhibit 7). In addition, from 1960 to 1964, the beer market had grown at approximately the same annual rate as the liquor market, i.e., at about 2.5%. Per capita beer consumption had increased moderately during the period (see Exhibit 8).

Exhibit 7

ALCOHOLIC BEVERAGES, CONSUMER EXPENDITURES, 1942–64

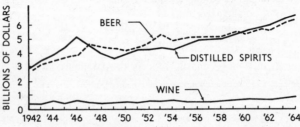

Source: *The Liquor Handbook, 1965*; cited by Glore Forgan, Wm. R. Staats Inc., in *Heublein, Inc.* (December, 1965).

Since people began consuming beer at a younger age than liquor, industry observers expected beer consumption to increase as much as, if not more than, liquor consumption through 1970. Most of this increase was expected to be

Exhibit 8

INDEXES OF PER CAPITA BEER CONSUMPTION, 1940–64

INDEX: 1940 = 100

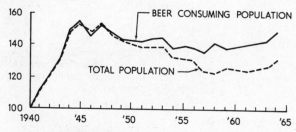

Source: United States Brewers Association; cited by Glore Forgan, Wm. R. Staats Inc., in *Heublein, Inc.* (December, 1965).

in the sale of packaged beer, since the sale of draught beer had decreased from 22% of total beer sales in 1955 to 19% in 1964.

The same observers felt that brand loyalty was not as strong for beer as for liquor. Nevertheless, the economies of high-volume production and the use of high dollar advertising seemed to be causing a gradual concentration of the beer industry, for the number of breweries operated in the United States decreased from 329 to 211 between 1953 and 1963. Moreover, the percentage of sales accounted for by the largest brewing companies had recently been increasing (see Exhibits 4, 9, and 10).

Exhibit 9

MARKET SHARE OF MAJOR BREWERS
(Per Cent)

	1951	1952	1953	1954	1955	1956	1957	1958	1959	1960	1961	1962	1963	1964
Top 25	57.5%	60.2%	61.3%	62.1%	64.3%	67.5%	69.2%	70.5%	73.8%	75.1%	77.4%	79.9%	82.2%	83.7%
Top 10	39.2	40.8	40.1	40.8	42.7	44.4	45.2	45.9	50.0	51.4	52.8	55.0	56.8	57.7

Source: Research Company of America.

Exhibit 10

ADVERTISING EXPENDITURES OF MAJOR BREWERS IN 1965

Company	Advertising (000)	Sales (000)	Advertising Per Cent of Sales
Jos. Schlitz Brewing Co.	$34,200	$311,375	11.0%
Anheuser-Busch, Inc.	32,500	491,384	6.6
Pabst Brewing Co.	15,900	227,610	7.0
Carling Brewing Co.	15,500	412,306	3.8
Falstaff Brewing Corp.	15,000	211,943	7.0

Source: *Advertising Age* (January 3, 1966), p. 46.

Exhibit 11

WIDE LINE SOFT DRINK COMPANY
1963 Balance Sheet for Year Ending December 31
(Dollars in Millions)

Current assets:			**Current liabilities:**	
Cash	$ 0.7		Bank notes	$ 1.3
Accounts receivable (net)	3.6		Notes payable	0.5
Inventories	3.3		Current portion long-term debt .	0.2
Short-term bonds	0.6		Accounts payable	2.6
Other	0.2		Federal and state income taxes ..	0.5
			Other taxes	0.1
Total current assets	$ 8.4			
Property, plant and equipment			Total current liabilities	$ 5.2
(net)	6.6		Long-term debt	2.4
Other assets	0.5		Customer deposit liability	1.2
			Deferred federal and state income	
Total assets	$15.5		taxes	0.4
			Stockholders' equity	
			Common stock	1.3
			Capital surplus	2.7
			Retained earnings	2.3
			Total liabilities and equity	$15.5

Source: 1963 Wide Line Soft Drink Company annual report.

The proposed Wide Line acquisition[3]

At the same time as the purchase of Hamm was being evaluated, several other possible acquisitions were being considered. One of these was the Wide Line Soft Drink Company, which in 1963 had total assets of $15.5 million (see Exhibit 11). Although Heublein's management felt that Wide Line could benefit from Heublein's ability to market consumer products, management nonetheless entertained some reservations. The most significant of these related to Wide Line's relatively weak competitive position. While Wide Line—with sales of $26 million in 1964—was among the top eight soft drink manufacturers in the country, its 2% to 3% market share was far below Coca-Cola's 31% and Pepsi-Cola's 23%. Also significant was the fact that Coca-Cola, Pepsi-Cola, and Seven-Up were three of the most experienced marketers of consumer goods in the country. In addition, while Wide Line's sales had increased 40% between 1959 and 1963, profits had remained relatively steady (see Exhibit 12). Moreover, profits represented only a 2% return on sales, even though Wide Line was spending only half of the industry average (as a percentage of sales) for advertising and promotion.

The Wide Line Company. Wide Line manufactured carbonated beverage concentrates which it sold to franchised bottlers in the United States and

---

[3]For purposes of security, the name, geographic location, and certain income statement figures of the company have been changed. The description of the industry and other aspects of the company's operations (e.g., market share, product line, etc.) are accurate.

Exhibit 12

WIDE LINE SOFT DRINK COMPANY
Income Statements for Year Ended December 31
(Dollars in Millions)

	1959	1960	1961	1962	1963
Net sales	$18.6	$21.7	$21.9	$24.4	$26.0
Cost of goods sold	13.5	15.3	15.2	17.0	18.9
Gross profit on sales	$ 5.1	$ 6.4	$ 6.7	$ 7.4	$ 7.1
Selling, general and administrative expenses	3.1	3.7	4.0	4.7	4.2
Advertising	1.4	1.6	1.6	1.7	2.0
	$ 4.5	$ 5.3	$ 5.7	$ 6.4	$ 6.2
Income from operations	0.6	1.2	1.0	1.0	0.9
Other income (charges)	0.0	0.1	0.0	0.0	0.0
Federal taxes	0.3	0.5	0.5	0.5	0.4
Net income	$ 0.3	$ 0.6	$ 0.5	$ 0.5	$ 0.5

Source: Various Wide Line Soft Drink Company annual reports.

foreign countries under its own brand names. During 1964, sales of Wide Line soft drinks by these franchise holders exceeded 45 million cases. Under these franchise agreements, Wide Line's franchise holders had to maintain certain quality conditions in their bottling operations, and were required to spend certain minimum amounts for advertising.[4] They were, however, allowed to produce carbonated beverages in addition to those sold under Wide Line's trademarks.

In addition to its sales to franchised bottlers, Wide Line also sold concentrates to private-label bottlers, to the dairy and ice cream industries, and to the fountain trade as syrups.

Wide Line also bottled and sold carbonated beverages under its own brand name in the south central region of the country. Wide Line entered the bottling business in 1962 when it acquired its largest franchise holder. This operation, now the bottling division, used about 20% of the Wide Line's concentrate production. The bottling division not only produced carbonated beverages under Wide Line's trademarks, which it sold to independent distributors who redistributed these beverages to various retail outlets such as chain stores, drug stores, and hotels, but also produced a lower cost beverage, which it sold directly to chain stores, independent supermarkets, and cooperative food stores. In addition, the bottling division produced beverages under private-label brands to meet the demand for a low-priced product.

Wide Line's product line was one of the most complete in the industry. The company produced 24 different flavors, including the basic four: cola, lemon-lime, orange, and root beer. Ten of these flavors were also produced in low-calorie form. Although no figures were available, it was the case

---

[4]Usually 30% of the cost of the concentrate. Half of the amount spent by the franchise holder, up to 50% of the concentrate cost, would be refunded by Wide Line.

Exhibit 13

SOFT-DRINK MARKET

Company	Cases (Millions)		Market Share (Per Cent)	
	1963	1964	1963	1964
Coca-Cola	560	600	31%	31%
Pepsi-Cola	420	440	23½	23
Royal Crown	185	200	10	10
Seven-Up	160	165	9	9
Canada Dry	145	155	8	8
Beverages Int'l.	55	60	3	3
Dr. Pepper	55	55	3	2½
Cott	35	35	2	2
Squirt	18	20	1	1
Shasta	15	20	1	1
No-Cal	10	10	½	½
No Grape	10	10	½	½
All others	133	160	7½	8½
Grand total	1,801	1,930	100%	100%

Source: *Printer's Ink* (April 9, 1965), p. 22.

writer's judgment that low-calorie flavors accounted for about 20% of Wide Line's total concentrate sales.

Wide Line maintained its executive offices and concentrate manufacturing facility in El Paso, Texas. It also maintained sales offices and cold storage facilities in California, New York, and Toronto, Canada. The bottling division owned or leased plants with a total of 20 bottling lines in seven cities spread throughout the south central region.

The soft drink industry. Soft drink sales increased 27% between 1955 and 1964, from 1.5 billion cases in the former year to over 1.9 billion in the latter (see Exhibit 13). Over one third of this increase resulted from the increase in per capita consumption from 218 bottles a person in 1955 to 240 bottles in 1964. The most important industry trend during this period was the increasing importance of low-calorie soft drinks. These beverages increased their market share from less than 2% in 1955 to 10% in 1964, and estimates of future growth ranged from a plateau of 10% (predicted by Coca-Cola) to a forecast of 35% by 1970 (predicted by Pepsi-Cola and Canada Dry). While the market positions of the four major soft drink manufacturers—Coca-Cola, Pepsi-Cola, Royal Crown, and Seven-Up—had not changed much between 1955 and 1964, Royal Crown had advanced slightly as its Diet-Rite Cola captured 40% of the low-calorie market (see Exhibit 14). There was some concern among the industry leaders that the private-label brands, which were sold primarily on a price basis, might try to use low-calorie drinks to increase their market share still further, since low-calorie drinks provided a greater opportunity for price cutting

Exhibit 14

SOFT-DRINK MARKET BY COMPANY AND FLAVORS (1964)

Company	Cola Market		Lemon-Lime		Diet Soft Drinks	
	Per Cent	Cases (Millions)	Per Cent	Cases (Millions)	Per Cent	Cases (Millions)
Coca-Cola	44%	530	21%	65	20%	38
Pepsi-Cola	33	400	11	35	20	38
Royal Crown	15	180	2	6	41	77
Seven-up	...	...	50	155	included in all others	
All others	8	100	16	50	19	37
Total	100%	1,210	100%	311	100%	190

Source: *Printer's Ink* (April 9, 1965), p. 23.

than regular soft drinks because of their lower cost. The increased volume of low-calorie soft drinks was also partially responsible for the growing importance of the two basic flavors: cola and lemon-lime (see Exhibit 15).

Exhibit 15

SOFT-DRINK MARKET BY FLAVORS

Flavor	1958	1963	1964
Cola	53%	60%	62%
Lemon-lime	10	15	16
Orange	5	9	8
Root beer	3	5	4
Other	29	11	10
Grand Total	100%	100%	100%

Source: *Printer's Ink* (April 9, 1965), p. 23.

Although adequate distribution was a crucial factor in soft drink sales, the primary selling tool used by most national carbonated beverage companies and their franchised bottlers was advertising. During 1964 these companies and their bottlers spent above $200 million on promotion. According to an industry rule of thumb, companies should spend about 10 cents per case on advertising. A comparison of actual and estimated advertising expenses for 1964 is as follows:

Company	Rule-of-Thumb Estimate (Millions)	Actual Expenditure (Millions)
Coca-Cola	$60.0	$59.0
Pepsi-Cola	44.0	35.0
Royal Crown	20.0	24.0
Seven-Up	16.5	12.0

In this advertising, most of the companies developed themes which they repeated for several years. For example, Coca-Cola developed, "Things Go Better with Coke." Soft drink companies also used special advertising and promotional campaigns to attract additional sales during the summer sales peak.

In 1964, industry sales were divided into four categories: the take-home business, 66%; the vending of soft drinks in cups, bottles, and cans, 15%; fountain sales, 10%; and bottles in nonvending coolers, which accounted for the remaining 9% of sales.

According to *Printer's Ink*, "Bold advertising strategies, new or revitalized products, new packages, and fast action characterize the carbonated-beverage industry. This decade and the next will see a continuation of changing consumer tastes and consequent changes in the soft-drink industry itself."[5]

---

[5]"Battle of the Brands: Soft Drinks," *Printers' Ink* (April 9, 1965), p. 26.

The company and its strategists: relating economic strategy and personal values

T hus far the situations we have examined have required us to decide whether a concept of purpose and a sense of direction would sufficiently strengthen a company's position in changing circumstances to be worth the effort. We have attempted to examine the concept of strategy in order to understand and use it in our appraisal of company situations and in our quasi-managerial decisions. We have seen the relationship between the obsolescence of strategy and the decline of company fortunes. We have also seen how results are affected by clear versus unclear conceptions of the nature of the company's product or its market segments, and by internally consistent versus inconsistent departmental policies and programs of action.

Strategy as projection of preference

Until now, our interest has been focused on an impersonal analysis of environmental information and decisions taken in response to it. True, we have noted in passing the contributions made to the formulation or execution of strategy by forceful personalities. But we have tried in the main to perfect a purely *economic* strategy—one that, in our judgment, constituted the most suitable combination of the company's strengths and its opportunities, no matter who might be the chief executive or what might be his aims in life.

We turn now to a series of cases which will provoke discussion of the relationship between a sensible economic strategy on the one hand and the personal values of those who design strategy on the other. We shall see at once that executives in charge of company destinies do not look exclusively at what a company might do and can do. Sometimes—in apparent disregard of at least the second of these considerations—they seem heavily influenced by what they personally *want* to do.

If we think back far enough, the strategies we recommended for the companies already considered probably reflect what *we* would have wanted to do had we been in charge of these companies. We tell ourselves (perhaps as part of the tendency to rationalize) that our personal inclinations harmonize with the optimum combination of economic opportunity and company strengths. For professional managers, especially in large companies, this convergence of what appears to be a sound economic strategy and personal desire is often likely to be quite genuine. But for certain entrepreneurial types, whose energy and personal drive far outweigh their formal training and self-awareness, the direction in which they want to go is not necessarily the direction which a logical appraisal suggests. Such disparity appears most frequently perhaps in small privately held concerns, or in companies built by successful and self-confident owner-managers. However, the phenomenon we are discussing may appear in any company.

Our problem now can be very simply stated. In examining the alternatives available to a company, we must henceforth take into consideration the preferences of the chief executive—and also those of other key managers—who must either contribute to or assent to the strategy if it is to be effective. Thus, besides trying to cope with the divergence between the chief executive's desire and the strategic choice which seems most defensible, we shall be confronted (as in Acoustic Research, Inc.) with the conflict among several sets of managerial personal values which must not only be reconciled with an economic strategy but also with each other.

The cases that follow were gathered and are presented to you as empirical evidence that the personal desires, aspirations, and needs of the senior managers of a company actually *do* play an influential role in the determination of strategy. We ourselves would argue also that they probably *should*—at least within the broad limits imposed by the managers' fiduciary responsibility to the owners and perhaps to other nonmanagement groups.[1] The conflict which often arises between what general managers want to do and what the dictates of economic strategy suggest they ought to do is best not denied or ruled out of order. It should be accepted as a matter of course. Then, to the extent practicable, the divergent implications of the elements of a strategic decision should be reconciled.

As you read the cases in this section of the book, apply to them the reasoning you have used thus far. In addition, note the impact of the personal desires of the chief executive upon the nature of the company and the principal characteristics of the strategy. Instead of rejecting such an intrusion of personal values into the formulation of strategy as unwarranted, try to recognize, in your recommendations for improved strategy, the need to meet the most important demands of the senior managers. In the study of human relations, you have no doubt recommended on occasion that the personal needs of the hourly worker be taken seriously and be at least partially satisfied as a means to securing the productive effort for which wages are paid. It should, then, come as no surprise that the president of the corporation also

[1] See p. 485, "The Company and Its Social Responsibilities: Relating Corporate Strategy and Moral Values."

arrives at his desk with his own needs and values—to say nothing of his relatively greater power to see that they are taken into account.

It becomes our mission now to attempt a reconciliation of economic strategy and the observed personal preferences of the executives of the company. The information in the cases will enable us to determine what these preferences are. After determining what strategies appear economically appropriate and what set of goals and policies we ourselves prefer, we must then examine this set to see how it might be amended to accommodate the values of the managers in the cases. This order of priority reflects the fact that it is not our *principal* function to conceive of strategies that will be *acceptable* to management. As students of Policy, we need to be able to design sound strategies more than we need to be able to sell these strategies door-to-door throughout the executive offices. The latter job, however, is not to be ignored. It is a part of the overall task for anyone who wants his ideas to be effective.

Knowing that personal values (often unexpressed and unclear) influence strategic choices and produce results different from what might be called the optimal economic strategy, we can now see why strategic proposals stemming from different unstated values come into conflict and why such conflict cannot be reconciled by talking in terms of environmental data and their match with corporate resources.

At first glance it seems futile to attempt to reconcile a strategic alternative dictated by personal preference with other alternatives oriented toward capitalizing on opportunity to the greatest possible extent. In actuality, however, the additional complication poses fewer difficulties than at first appear. The analysis of opportunity and the appraisal of resources themselves often lead in different directions. To compose three, rather than two, divergent sets of considerations into a single pattern may increase the complexity of the task, but the integrating process is still the same. We can look for the dominant or immovable consideration and treat the others as constraints; we can probe the elements in conflict for the possibility of reinterpretation or adjustment. We are not building a wall of irregular stones so much as balancing a mobile of elements, the motion of which is adjustable to the motion of the entire mobile. As we have seen, external developments can be affected by company action and company resources, and internal competence can be developed.

Modification of values

The question whether values can be changed is somewhat less clear. A value, for our purposes, is a "conception, explicit or implicit, distinctive of an individual or characteristic of a group, of the *desirable* which influences the selection of available modes, means, and ends of action."[2] Guth and

---

[2]William D. Guth and Renato Tagiuri, "Personal Values and Corporate Strategy." The definition is quoted from Florence R. Kluckhohn *et al.*, *Variations in Value Orientation* (Evanston, Ill.: Row, Peterson and Company, 1961).

Tagiuri emphasize that values are *concepts* of the desirable, not the "things, conditions, or ideas judged desirable as a result of applying the values to specific situations." Acquired early in life as the result of the "interplay of what he learned from those who reared him, and of his particular individuality and 'times,' "[3] a person's basic values are a relatively stable feature of his personality, although they may change somewhat with his level of knowledge and analytical skill.

Nonetheless, the preference attached to ends in concrete circumstances is not beyond influence. The physicist in a representative research company, who in his reflection of the values of pure science is opposed to commercial production, might withdraw his objection if he sees that his freedom to pursue his own projects can be better sustained by profits from operations than from government research contracts. Furthermore, his departure from the university and his present membership in the firm reflect some economic values and interest in profit for its own sake. He will retain the value orientation of the scientist, but may assent in this instance to the strategic alternative conceived in the value orientation of the businessman. At any rate, to presuppose that he would not do so is a common but futile approach to the value problem.

Guth and Tagiuri report some very interesting research which indicates that we may, in our use of stereotypes, ascribe much stronger value commitments to others than is justified. They report the results of a questionnaire regarding six basically different value orientations[4] that was administered to 178 R.&D. executives, 157 scientists, and 653 managers; despite differences among these groups that might be assumed to exist, all three showed relatively high theoretical, economic, and political value orientations, and relatively low aesthetic, religious, and social values. Indeed, all three groups put theoretical values first.

A second finding of this study indicates that R.&D. executives see the scientist and the manager as exhibiting greater value differences than is actually the case. Thus the scientist is viewed as much more dominantly theoretical than he actually is, the manager as much more dominantly economic and political. The latter's theoretical and religious orientation is seriously underestimated.

---

[3]Guth and Tagiuri, *op. cit.*, p. 4.
[4]These are the six types identified by Edward Spranger, who classifies all individuals as falling into one or another of the following:

1. *The Theoretical* (dominant intellectual interest in an empirical, critical, rational approach to systematic knowledge).
2. *The Economic* (orientation toward practical affairs, the production and consumption of goods, the uses and creation of wealth).
3. *The Aesthetic* (chief interest in the artistic, in form, symmetry, harmony, in experience for its own sake).
4. *The Social* (primary value the love of people and warmth of human relationships).
5. *The Political* (orientation toward power, influence, and recognition).
6. *The Religious* (mystical orientation toward unity and the creation of satisfying and meaningful relationship to the universe).

From these findings, two implications follow that merit particular emphasis at this point. First, the manager is much more "theoretically" oriented than the stereotype of the American businessman would indicate (but not, we would assert, more than his duties require). Second, values for these different groups may be easier to reconcile with each other and with requirements for a sound economic strategy than might at first be anticipated. Although one value orientation may be dominant in an individual and color his judgment of where opportunity lies and of what his company has power to achieve, other values are present, and effective appeal can be made to these by persons who want to influence the course of strategy. Sometimes, also, an appeal can be successful if it can show that a chosen strategy threatens the value it was designed to serve. For example, the extreme resistance of Mississippi and Alabama to integration, by evoking vigorous federal action, wound up pushing civil rights faster and further in these areas than would otherwise have been the case.

Awareness of values

Your interest in the role of value in strategic formulations should not be confined to assessing the influence of other people's values. Despite the well-known problems of introspection, we can probably do more to understand the relation of our own values to our choice of purpose than we can to change the values of others. Awareness that our own preference for an alternative opposed by another stems from values as much as from rational estimates of economic opportunity may have important consequences. First, it may make us more tolerant and less indignant when we perceive this relationship between recommendations and values in the formulations of others. Second, it will force us to consider how important it really is to us to maintain a particular value in making a particular decision. Third, it may give us insight to identify our bias and thus pave the way for a more objective assessment of all the strategic alternatives that are available. These consequences of self-examination will not end conflict, but they will at least prevent its unnecessary prolongation.

The object of this course of study is not to endow us with the ability to persuade others to accept the strategic recommendations we consider best: it is to acquire insight into the problems of determining purpose and skill in the process of resolving them. For students of Policy not yet in executive positions (as well as those who are), the chance presents itself now to assess their own personal opportunities, strengths and weaknesses, and basic values by means of the procedures outlined here. For a personal strategy, analytically considered and consciously developed, may be as useful to an individual as a corporate strategy is to a business institution. An effort, conducted by each individual, to formulate his personal purpose might well accompany the effort, made by the group within the classroom, to design purposes for various corporations. The problems encountered here may temper your criticism of the executives in the cases. If, more importantly, the encounter leads to a clarification of the purposes you seek, the values you hold, and alternatives available to you, the attempt to make personal use of the concept of strategy will prove extremely worthwhile.

As you consider the cases which follow, we have urged you, first, to complete the same kind of analysis you have previously undertaken to determine an economic strategy and to test it against the criteria which by now you habitually use. But look to see to what extent the strategy you have formulated corresponds to or comes into conflict with the values of the president or executives whose acceptance of the strategy is necessary to its implementation. So far as you can, try to identify the values that are implicit in your own decision. As you look at the gap between the strategy which follows from your values and that which would be appropriate to the values of the chief executive of the case, look to see whether the difference is fundamental or superficial. Then look to see how the strategy you believe best matches opportunity and resources can be adapted to accommodate the values of those who will implement it. Reconciliation of the three principal determinants of strategy which we have so far considered is often possible by adjustment of any or all of the determinants.

You should not warp your strategy to the detriment of the company's future in order to adjust it to personal values. On the other hand, you should not expect to be able to impose an unwelcome pattern of purposes and policies on the people in charge of a corporation. Strategy is a human construction; it must be responsive to human needs. It must ultimately inspire commitment. It must stir an organization to successful striving against competition. Somebody has to have his heart in it.

A NOTE ON THE METAL CONTAINER INDUSTRY*

∧∧

The metal container industry produces metal cans, crowns (bottle caps), and closures (screw caps, bottle lids) for over 135 industries that use these products to hold or seal an almost endless variety of consumer and industrial goods (see Exhibit 1). During the 1950's a number of metal container manufacturers experienced declining profit margins and loss of market share because of increasing competitive and technical pressures from within and outside the industry.

Two firms dominate the metal container industry: the American Can Company and the Continental Can Company. Of these 48 billion cans produced in 1963, 34 billion were manufactured by these giant corporations. Another 5 billion cans were manufactured by the Crown Cork and Seal Company and the National Can Company, both companies having an annual sales volume of over $100 million. In 1963 Crown Cork and the Bond Division of the Continental Can Company also produced approximately 70% of the 313·million gross of crowns used. In all, there are about 100 companies in the industry.

The 48 billion cans produced in 1963 had an estimated shipment value of $2.3 billion. The primary users of metal containers have been the food and beer industries, the two industries utilizing almost 80% of all metal cans produced (see Exhibit 2). In the five years from 1960 to 1964 the soft-drink bottler also became an important user. In addition to consuming annually approximately 70% of all metal crowns produced, bottlers used over 2 billion cans in 1963, an increase of 500% from 1958.

This note describes (1) new competitive pressures that have confronted the industry from 1955–64, (2) the effect of these pressures on the industry, and (3) the strategic responses of the major companies in the industry to these pressures. Additional information as to economic and technological characteristics of the industry is provided in an Appendix to this note.

PRESSURES ON THE METAL CONTAINER INDUSTRY

In 1961 Mr. Lucius D. Clay, at that time president of the Continental Can Company, stated: "The tin can is a fundamental part of the United

---

Exhibit 1

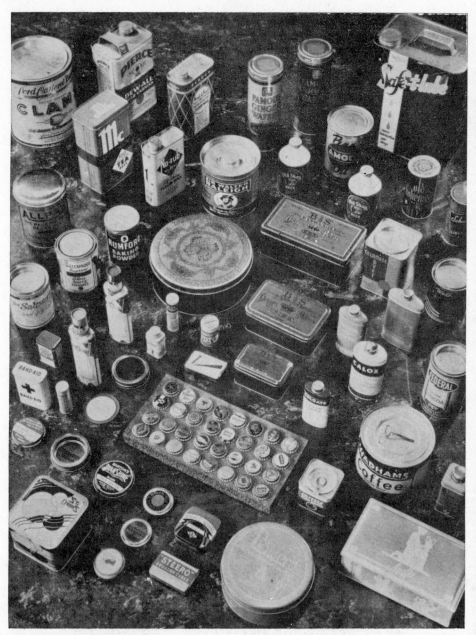

Source: Can Manufacturer's Institute.

Exhibit 2

SHIPMENTS OF METAL CANS BY PRODUCT PACKED EXPRESSED IN TERMS OF THOUSANDS OF BASE BOXES* OF METAL CONSUMED IN THEIR MANUFACTURE

	1955	1956	1957	1958	1959	1960	1961	1962	1963
Total shipments	98,024	105,107	101,702	103,818	108,162	105,166	109,358	114,956	109,707
For sale	85,477	89,928	87,667	89,180	93,993	89,917	89,656	93,764	88,739
For own use	12,547	15,179	14,035	14,638	14,169	15,249	19,702	21,192	20,968
Type of metal:									
Steel	...	...	...	...	...	...	n.a.	112,714	107,350
Aluminum	...	...	...	...	...	...	n.a.	1,792	2,356
Food cans, total	61,773	66,884	62,046	64,054	65,060	65,073	66,164	68,618	
Fruits and vegetables (including juice)	31,764	34,899	31,980	34,236	33,684	32,984	34,805	37,081	
Evaporated and condensed milk	6,138	6,150	5,425	5,175	5,085	4,883	4,737	4,393	n.a.
Other dairy products	1,034	1,083	889	728	636	510	519	582	
Fish and seafood	2,535	2,588	2,636	2,843	2,657	2,850	2,898	3,082	
Lard and shortening	2,580	2,394	2,248	2,383	2,324	1,986	2,256	2,356	
Meat (including poultry)	2,919	3,825	3,047	2,951	3,190	3,203	3,460	3,483	
Coffee	4,000	4,213	4,286	4,452	4,707	4,567	4,846	4,846	
All other food cans	10,803	11,732	11,584	11,286	12,777	14,090	12,643	12,795	
Nonfood cans, total	36,251	38,223	38,278	39,764	43,102	40,093	43,194	45,888	
Oil, open top—1 qt. and 5 qt.	6,778	6,778	6,230	6,338	6,811	5,715	6,026	6,304	
Beer cans	14,919	15,806	16,305	16,902	18,563	17,776	17,522	18,150	
Pet food	3,485	4,034	4,154	4,154	4,332	4,486	4,475	4,654	
All other nonfood cans	11,069	11,605	12,370	12,370	13,386	12,116	15,171	16,780	

*A base box is a measure of metal use.

n.a. Not available.

Source: U.S. Department of Commerce, Bureau of the Census.

States economy, and will never grow less than the economy grows."[1] (See Exhibit 3.) Because the industry grew up on a foundation of food and beverage preservation, another observer concluded: "The one certainty in the business is that the can will be around for as long as people like food and hate work."[2]

Exhibit 3

COMPARATIVE GROWTH OF POPULATION, GROSS NATIONAL PRODUCT, AND CAN SHIPMENTS
1953 = 100

	1953	1954	1955	1956	1957	1958	1959	1960	1961	1962
Population (millions) ..	100.0	101.8	102.9	103.9	105.0	106.1	107.22	108.36	109.5	110.7
Gross national product (billions)	100.0	99.5	108.7	114.2	120.9	121.1	131.9	137.4	141.9	151.8
Can shipments (000's of base boxes)	100.0	101.5	109.8	117.7	113.9	116.3	121.2	117.8	122.5	128.8

Source: Prepared by case writer.

Despite the optimism of these two observers, one speaker at the 32nd Annual American Management Association's Packaging Conference predicted that the metal can was doomed:

"The so-called tin can is on the way out," [claims] Michael M. Young, President of Philadelphia's Digit Machinery Works [manufacturers of equipment for] making composite [aluminum foil-paper combination] containers as he predicted that 85% of all cans used for packaging consumer products would be composites by 1970. . . .[3]

While industry executives are confident that the "tin can is not on its way out," major strategic questions have arisen during the last decade, questions that stem from efforts to assess the long-term effects on the industry of—

1. Changes in the basic concept of a container—termed by many the "packaging revolution."
2. The rapid acceleration in packaging technology.
3. The increased threat of self-manufacture.

The "packaging revolution"

Perhaps the trend of greatest long-run significance to the industry is the increasing number of functions the "container" is being asked to perform. Originally the container was designed solely to hold, protect, and preserve its contents. Then someone decided that a container, imaginatively labeled, could also provide a strong point-of-purchase reminder of the consumer's need for the "product inside." So the container was redesigned to add more

---

[1]Walter Guzzardi, Jr., "The Fight for 9/10 of a Cent," *Fortune*, April 1961, p. 224.
[2]*Ibid.*, p. 155.
[3]"Metals or Containers? Packaging Forecasts Differ," *Steel*, April 29, 1962, p. 25.

utility and appeal to the product by means of devices ranging from recipes printed on the outside to easy-dispensing spouts. The result has been that during the past ten years, this redesigning, in combination with advances in methods of product preservation and packaging technology, has reduced the importance of the preservation function of the container relative to its sales function. The container, or rather the "package," and the "product inside" have become increasingly one unit in their selective appeal to the consumer, and, to a lesser extent, in creating primary demand, e.g., aerosol dispensed whipped cream.

Some authorities have attributed the preoccupation with packaging in the United States to radical changes in merchandising patterns. With increasing emphasis upon self-service, the number of salesmen who promote one product over another has declined. Now the package must function as the salesman. Also, with the rapid advances in manufacturing technology, products tend to be of increasingly high quality and often little product differentiation can be achieved by "just more quality." In addition, there has been a rapid growth in the use of private labels, and this has tended to make brand names a somewhat less important influence on sales. All these factors, packaging experts argue, put a burden on products to speak for themselves. As one authority concluded: "These days you had better have an easier-to-open beer can [and] an easier-opening cereal carton or you are out of business."[4]

Accordingly, purchasers have been solicited by an array of new boxes, bottles, bags, and packaging gimmicks: "The industrial manufacturer and the supermarket packager alike today must give the customer an 'extra'; a package that enhances the value of the high-quality product by becoming an integral part of it, making it easier to carry or to use."[5]

"Extras" on consumer goods have taken many forms. For example, plastic bottles for hair preparations, aerosol containers which spurt products ranging from mustard to touch-up paint, miniature beer kegs that provide tap beer in the family refrigerator, self-opening or "pop-top" metal cans, "tin cans" made of paper, water-dissolving plastic bags for ready-to-eat foods, salt containers designed as table shakers, drinking glass containers for jam, self-igniting packages of charcoal briquets, porous plastic brewing bags for coffee, and flip-tox boxes for cigarettes. Extras on industrial packages have been added to increase the usability and convenience of handling, both for the distributor and the ultimate customer, e.g., color-coded packages to facilitate inventory maintenance and the use of polystyrene foam instead of shredded paper as packing material to obtain lighter and more compact containers.

The tremendous growth in the sale of packaging materials since 1940 reflects, in part, the increasing recognition given by manufacturers to the

---

[4]Carmon M. Elliot, Jr., manager of package design, Eastman Kodak Co., as quoted in Leon Morse, "The Swing to Service," *Dun's Review & Modern Industry*, November 1963, p. 133.

[5]*Ibid.*, p. 135.

role of packaging in selling their products. In 1940 shipments of packaging materials totaled slightly over $2 billion. By 1958 these shipments had grown to about $10 billion. In 1963 shipments of packaging materials amounted to $13 billion (55% of the total expenditure for packaging activity), an increase of 650% since 1940. During the same period two general economic indicators, Gross National Product and Consumer Expenditures for Non-durables, increased 550% and 234% respectively.

A major reason behind the growth of the packaging industry has been the shift to packaging for products previously sold in "containers." For example, starch in the aerosol dispensing form was introduced in 1960 and in 1963 accounted for over 25% of consumer starch purchases. Similar shifts were experienced with other household products such as room deodor-ants, car waxes, and furniture polishes. Estimated to be increasing at an annual rate of over 12%, sales of nonfood aerosol units in 1963 were over 1 billion units—18 times the number sold in the first year after the com-mercial aerosol container was introduced in 1948. Recent technological developments have also introduced food items to aerosol dispensing. Du Pont, a major supplier of aerosol propellants, made the following estimate of aerosol food sales for 1967:[6]

Aerosol Product	Merchandising Concept	1967 Sales (Estimated)
Cheese spread	Various flavored 6–8–ounce packages, small enough to allow the house-wife to have an assortment of dif-ferent types for different canapes, casseroles, or other dishes.	60 to 80 million units
Peanut butter	Smooth, even, quick application for sandwich making and other uses, packaged in economical 12- or 16-ounce containers.	60 to 80 million units
Cake frosting	An 8-ounce can allowing for the com-plete frosting of a standard 9-inch double layer cake easily and quickly without pans and beaters.	40 to 60 million units
Salad dressing	An economical 12-ounce "opened" container . . . never needing re-frigeration.	20 to 25 million units
Garlic butter	A gourmet treat in an 8-ounce pack-age suitable for two medium loaves of French bread.	10 to 12 million units
Popcorn seasoning	Flavorful, spray seasoning for appli-cation on hot popcorn from a handy, easily storable 3-ounce con-tainer.	5 to 7 million units

The aluminum top easy-opening can was heralded as the first significant innovation in the beer industry since the introduction of the can. This was quickly followed by the "pull-tab" top developed by Alcoa, providing still

[6]*Aerosol Market Report 1962*, "Freon" Products Division, Du Pont, p. 18.

another example of the impact of imaginative packaging. Pull-top cans, introduced in the spring of 1963, accounted for 40% of the beer cans sold in 1963. Beer company executives predicted this figure would climb to 75% by the fall of 1964.

One message of the packaging "revolution" seems to be clear: the container can no longer be thought of as just a means of product protection. It has a multiple function, not the least part of which is to serve as a prime marketing tool for its contents and the company that makes them. Product innovations, in fact, may come increasingly in the form of container-package designs rather than product designs per se. A case in point is the $117 million annual market in deodorants. These were first introduced in jars, but deodorant sticks, because of their ease of application, quickly replaced jars. Sticks gave way to squeeze bottles, which in turn were driven out of the market by the advent of the roll-on bottle. In 1964, in the latest innovation, deodorants were available in dry spray aerosol form. Yet according to experts, the deodorant itself has changed very little.

The evolution of the packaging concept has posed major strategic issues for the metal container industry. This is an industry that grew up converting steel into shapes designed to achieve a high level of product preservation (over 55% of the cans produced in 1963 packaged food) and one which has had little or no contact with the ultimate buyer generating and responding to the new trends.

The rapid acceleration in packaging technology

The original characteristics that promoted the use of the tin can and the crown in the early 1900's still make them well suited to certain food and beverage packaging jobs. These qualities are: (1) immunity to handling abuse; (2) ability to resist great heat and pressure, allowing pasteurization in the package; (3) preservation of a sterile condition for long periods; (4) lightness compared to the contents; (5) amenability to fabrication into differing sizes, and (6) low cost, allowing destruction after use.

However, recent advances in packaging technology have challenged the future competitive strength of these characteristics:

1. Increasing integration of packaging into the production process.
2. Reduction of the container requirements for products traditionally packed in tin cans.
3. Use of new methods of product preservation.
4. New packaging materials.

The integration of packaging into the production process. As the distinction between the product and its container has become increasingly blurred, product manufacturers, pushed by the machinery companies who design custom packaging systems, have moved toward carrying out a greater number of container conversion functions in their own plants. The development "that may ultimately prove to have the most far-reaching impact on the [package-supplying] industry is the production of the container by the customer himself, with only the basic packaging material being supplied by the 'container manufacturer.' Packaging Corporation of America has a system which allows carton making as well as filling by frozen food packers all at once; the company only delivers the rolled stock to the customer rather than the finished container as is the usual case now."[7]

Greater concentration of the packaging process in one location has been pretty much limited to packagers using flexible materials, i.e., cellophane, paper, and cloth. Flexible material suppliers, such as Union Bag–Camp Corporation and St. Regis Paper, have enlarged their machinery departments in order to provide the special-purpose machinery being demanded by packagers. Others have purchased packaging machinery companies. The forward integration occurring in the paper industry is in part an effort to ensure the industry of "captive" raw material customers by being able to provide the machinery service that product manufacturers need in order to perform a larger share of the conversion functions.

Reduced container requirements. The technical requirements of the can and crown have been, for the most part, a function of high-speed manufacturing and the *need* for a perfect seal to preserve (1) sanitation, (2) container strength, and (3) the flavoring or coloring of the contents. But for some products, these characteristics have been relatively unimportant, e.g., a container for wrapped candy in contrast to aerosol whipped cream. The packaging of the candy, termed an easy application by trade experts, has not required a coated or sealed container nor one able to withstand pressure, all in contrast to the whipped cream dispenser.

Packagers who have made heavy use of tin cans have been experimenting with new production processes and product designs that, among other things, reduce the structural demands placed on the container. The beer industry is a prime example of this trend. Brewers, who used 20% of the cans produced in 1963, have been experimenting with changes in the basic pasteurizing process. Traditionally, beer has been pasteurized in the bottle or can. But lately, brewers have been experimenting with pasteurization in bulk. Another process receiving considerable attention from the brewers is the sterilization of beer in its container by irradiation. Both techniques are expected to reduce the need for strong pressure and heat-resistant container properties.

New methods of food preservation. The development of better methods of product preservation has been a major goal of food processors. Since the early 1950's, despite the short shelf-life of frozen foods, their relatively high cost due to slow processing methods, and the sometimes poor quality, the fastest growth in food consumption has been in foods preserved by freezing rather than by canning (see Exhibit 4).

To overcome the problems of quality, shelf-life, and production time, a technique called freeze drying has been developed. Products processed by

---

[7]"Container Makers Grow with the Economy," *Financial World*, May 29, 1963, p. 7.

Exhibit 4

CONSUMPTION OF FRUITS AND VEGETABLES IN POUNDS PER CAPITA, 1953–62

Year	Vegetables			Fruit		
	Fresh	Canned	Frozen	Fresh	Canned	Frozen
1953	108.6	43.3	5.4	111.3	34.0	7.1
1955	104.6	43.5	6.6	101.6	35.5	8.7
1957	104.6	43.9	7.5	99.5	35.6	9.0
1959	102.9	44.8	8.9	100.9	33.9	8.8
1960	106.0	44.5	9.8	97.5	34.5	9.1
1961	104.3	44.6	10.0	92.1	35.3	8.9
1962	99.4	45.0	10.5	90.9	35.2	10.9

Source: U.S. Department of Commerce.

this method can be stored at room temperature for long periods. Reportedly the technique has been improved to the point where food quality closely approximates that of fresh items.

Although the commercial use of freeze drying has thus far been limited, trade experts anticipate that the improved quality combined with handling and transportation economies (in contrast to canned foods) will greatly increase the number of applications. According to one source, "The processing of surplus foods for distribution to foreign markets may widen the use of this method [freeze drying], particularly since transportation, refrigeration, storage and shelf-life are important considerations."[8]

An additional development, one in which the government has played a major role, has been preservation of food by nuclear irradiation. The process is still limited to the successful preservation of meat, but government authorities believe that a method of irradiation will be found to preserve effectively certain other kinds of food, supplanting preservation by canning and freezing.

New packaging materials. Expenditures for packaging materials (excluding value added by filling, labeling, and sealing) accounted for almost 35% of total U.S. expenditures for packaging during 1963. Of the estimated $13 billion spent on materials, $2.6 billion was spent on metal materials, 80% of which was used in the fabrication of metal cans. Steel has been virtually the sole metallic raw material used by the metal container industry. Next to automobiles and construction, the industry has been the third largest consumer of steel in the country. During the last decade, however, aluminum, and to a lesser extent fibre-foil and plastic, have increasingly entered traditional tinplate markets.

Discussing the growing competitive strength of aluminum, one author stated:

Steel has been the master of the can makers' fate for so long that both Amer-

[8]Standard & Poor's *Industry Surveys*, "Food Products: Basic Analysis," December 20, 1963.

ican and Continental seemed to find it [the competitive strength of aluminum] hard to recognize when it came along. In discussing aluminum, too many can executives had been tending to talk problems, not potential. Aluminum was commonly more costly than steel; it could not resist the same pressures. Changes would have to be made in production lines before aluminum could be run through. . . . The aluminum industry, led by Reynolds Metals Co., claims it had to shoulder its way directly to the can buyer to overcome can company inertia.[9]

Although still a relatively small factor in the metal container field in 1963 (see Exhibit 2), aluminum has made sizable inroads in the container market for motor oil and frozen concentrates, products that are shipped long distances and are not packed under pressure. Reflecting these inroads, the use of tinplate containers in 1963 dropped 5% from 1962, while the use of aluminum containers rose 20% despite a curtailed demand for citrus containers.

The use of aluminum beer can ends, spurred by the introduction of the self-opening can developed by Alcoa, has become another major market for this metal. Both Reynolds and Alcoa, furthermore, have built can plants to hasten the acceptance of an all-aluminum container in the beer industry. Reynolds also has built plants in Florida to supply aluminum cans to the citrus packers.

The principal appeal of aluminum has been its light weight, particularly when transportation costs have been an important factor in total cost. Aluminum experts argue, however, that the aluminum can is also (1) a better looking container than its tin counterpart, (2) cheaper to lithograph as the brushed aluminum plate serves as a base color, and (3) capable of sharper lithographing. In addition they point out that brewers have long agreed that aluminum is "more friendly to beer," reducing the problem of flavoring, a major concern of both the brewing and soft-drink industries. If the aluminum executives' confidence that the beer industry can be converted to use of aluminum is confirmed, domestic brewers would be the aluminum industry's biggest market. Exhibit 5 gives one company's estimate of the potential market for the aluminum can.

Aluminum has made further inroads in traditional tinplate markets as a component of the new fibre-foil containers (see Exhibit 6). Packaging experts point to the fibre-foil container as an example of the great potential of composite materials. Developed jointly by the R. C. Can Company and Anaconda Aluminum in 1962 for the motor oil market, the composite can accounted for an estimated 55% of the 2 billion motor oil cans sold in 1963 and 10% of total can production.

Cans made of fibre-foil are also making a strong bid for other metal container markets. Citrus juice may be next. Coca-Cola's Minute Maid Division reportedly has converted already to fibre-foil. . . . If, as it is believed, the can can be made strong enough for beer and vacuum packaged coffee, for example, their potential

---

[9]Guzzardi, op. cit., p. 157.

Exhibit 5

THE ALUMINUM CAN MARKET

	Total Potential Annual Market (Millions of Cans)	Aluminum Cans Produced (Millions of Cans)			Penetration % of Total		
		1961	1962	e-1963	1961	1962	e-1963
Frozen juice concentrate	1,750	900	1,000	1,400	51	57	80
Motor oil	1,700	300	350*	800*	18	21	47
Aerosol	1,000	25	30	45	2	3	5
Beer cans	9,000	40	60	120	0.5	0.7	1
Beer lids (on tinplate beer cans)	9,000	25	600	3,000	0.3	7	40

eEstimated.
*Includes fibre-foil cans.
Source: Reynolds Metals Company, as quoted in Standard and Poor's *Industry Surveys.*

market may be as large as 15 billion units, or a third of the 45 billion cans currently sold. . . .

The potential of the new type container is deemed so great that other major companies have invaded the market. These include Container Corporation, Crown Zellerbach, Seal-Right-Oswego Falls and Stone Container. . . .[10]

A strong appeal of the composite can, as with the aluminum can, has been its low weight. Generally the composite has run about 20% lighter than its "thin-tin" counterparts but slightly heavier than the all-aluminum container. But in addition to the advantages accruing from lighter weight, the composite can reportedly costs about 15% less to manufacture than either type of all-metal can.

Despite these advantages, many industry experts expect some of the recent gains of the composite can to be of short duration. The motor oil market is a case in point. In late 1963, blow-molded plastic containers, following developments that gave them significant economies over the metal and composite containers available, were introduced in one-quart sizes by major oil companies. In the last few years blow-molded plastic containers also packaged the major portion of liquid detergent sold, which as late as 1958 had been packaged solely in glass or metal. A recent article in *Printer's Ink* magazine reported that blow-molded plastic containers strong enough to serve as aerosol dispensers had been developed. While the plastic aerosol is more expensive than its metal aerosol counterpart, its proponents point out that the plastic aerosol can be fabricated into a variety of hitherto "impossible" can shapes.[11]

The versatility of the blow-molding process, first used by the glass industry and later adopted by plastic fabricators, has caused the aluminum industry to experiment with blow-molded metal containers.

[10]*Financial World*, May 29, 1963, p. 7.
[11]*Printers' Ink*, April 24, 1964, p. 19.

Exhibit 6

THE FIBRE-FOIL CAN

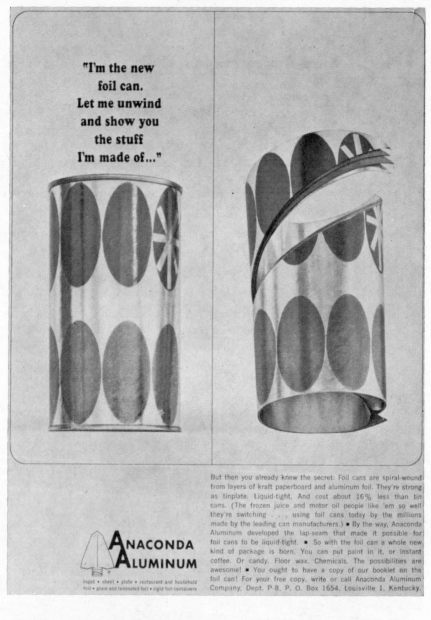

"I'm the new foil can. Let me unwind and show you the stuff I'm made of..."

But then you already knew the secret: Foil cans are spiral-wound from layers of kraft paperboard and aluminum foil. They're strong as tinplate. Liquid-tight. And cost about 16% less than tin cans. (The frozen juice and motor oil people like 'em so well they're switching . . . , using foil cans today by the millions made by the leading can manufacturers.) ■ By the way, Anaconda Aluminum developed the lap-seam that made it possible for foil cans to be liquid-tight. ■ So with the foil can a whole new kind of package is born. You can put paint in it, or instant coffee. Or candy. Floor wax. Chemicals. The possibilities are awesome! ■ You ought to have a copy of our booklet on the foil can! For your free copy, write or call Anaconda Aluminum Company, Dept. P-8, P. O. Box 1654, Louisville 1, Kentucky.

ANACONDA ALUMINUM

Ingot • sheet • plate • restaurant and household foil • plain and laminated foil • rigid foil containers

Cans are "blown" much like glass containers, from molten metal and may be produced in almost as great a variety of shapes. The one step can-making operation compares with 11 or 12 steps in conventional can-making [see Appendix]. Container cost is said to be no greater than standard tinplate and 20% lower than that of aluminum containers by present processes. American Can has purchased the development rights.[12]

Perhaps the greatest long-term significance of the influx of new materials will be that can companies will have to contend with the research and marketing strength of such giant, integrated companies as Du Pont, Dow Chemical, Weyerhaeuser Timber, Reynolds, and Alcoa. The forward integration of major material suppliers into the metal container industry has economic repercussions for the can manufacturer. In late 1963, for instance, Reynolds and Alcoa announced price increases in the sheet aluminum stock sold to can makers, but neither was reported to have increased the price of its own aluminum cans.

The threat of self-manufacture

The threat of customers manufacturing containers for their own use has hung over the metal container industry since World War II. For years the Campbell Soup Company has been the third largest manufacturer of cans in the country.

While only one large user of metal containers, Libby, McNeil & Libby, has converted to manufacturing its own cans since 1955, other packagers, smaller than the giant food packers but users of billions of cans annually, have been giving serious consideration to self-manufacture. The basis of their interest has been the belief that a firm with a large volume would inevitably benefit from manufacturing its own containers by making the packaging process a profit-making operation. However, the extensive machinery investment and technological skills needed for full self-manufacture, plus the increasingly rapid change in packaging technology during the last ten years, seem to have discouraged can users from making a major commitment to self-manufacture. While the threat of self-manufacture has been, for the most part, limited to the food packing industry, since 1960 two regional breweries have installed can lines to produce impact-extruded containers for their premium beer.

EFFECTS OF PRESSURES ON THE METAL CONTAINER INDUSTRY

The primary effects on the industry during the 1950's of the three principal pressures described in the first section of this note were:

1. The loss of minor market shares.
2. The narrowing of profit margins in traditional product lines.

Loss of market share

In 1957 the president of American Can estimated that his company was losing over $70 million annually in sales because of self-manufacture.

Department of Commerce figures indicate that from 1950 to 1960, self-

---

[12]*Modern Packaging*, April 1962.

manufacturers increased their share of the metal container market from 11% to 15%.

During this same period, packagers of motor oil and citrus concentrates, users of 4 billion cans a year moved rapidly away from the tin can, switching first to aluminum and then to fibre-foil containers. By 1960 the tin can's share of these markets had declined 50%.

Perhaps of greatest strategic concern to can companies was the declining share of tin cans in the growth of the packaging industry as a whole. Up until 1955 growth in metal-can consumption averaged 5.3% annually; by 1963 it was down to 2.1%. From 1947 to 1960 metal cans increased their share of the packaging market from 12% to 15%. In contrast, molded plastic containers, not even listed in 1947, had garnered 0.9% of the total volume of packaging materials by 1955; by 1960 plastics had grown to 1.5%. While statistics on the packaging industry are characterized by many gaps, Exhibits 7 and 8 illustrate the decline in the growth rate of tin cans in contrast to "newer" packaging materials (see also Exhibits 9 and 10).

Exhibit 7

GROWTH IN THE PRODUCTION OF PLASTIC AND METAL CONTAINERS
1957–59 = 100

	1953	1954	1955	1956	1957	1958	1959	1960	1961	1962	1965*	1970*	1975*
Plastic	50.1	49.0	64.6	74.4	82.9	91.9	125.8	134.7	156.0	189.5	263	437	720
Metal	100.3	90.2	98.3	98.8	101.5	92.9	105.3	107.6	106.5	117.1	128	150	175

*Projected.
Source: Federal Reserve Board Index of Industrial Production. Projections adapted from forecast of *Printer's Ink*, August 30, 1963, p. 315.

Narrowing of profit margins in traditional product lines

From 1956 to 1960 the average net income (before nonrecurring items) of the major producers of metal containers fell from 4.7% of net sales to 3.3%. One contributing factor was that steelmakers since 1954 had raised their prices five times, totaling a 15.2% increase. During this same period can makers raised their prices six times for a 19% increase, but in 1959 on the initiative of American Can the industry reduced its prices by 8%. In 1960 price increases had not offset rising raw material costs to the can makers, let alone increases in labor costs.

Reflecting the pressure of rising material and labor costs and the threat of self-manufacture, the margin on the typical packer's can (65% of independent can sales in 1960 were packer cans) declined to the point where in 1960 on a price of 2½¢ per can approximately 1.6¢ went to the tinplate producer. The remainder had to cover fabrication costs, the cost of coating and sealing compounds, and the cost of packing and shipping the can.

An executive of one can company, in summarizing his feelings about the difficulties his company was experiencing in adjusting to declining margins

Exhibit 8

GROWTH IN SHARE OF MARKET

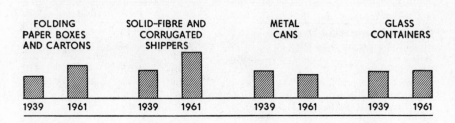

FOLDING PAPER BOXES AND CARTONS	SOLID-FIBRE AND CORRUGATED SHIPPERS	METAL CANS	GLASS CONTAINERS
1939 1961	1939 1961	1939 1961	1939 1961

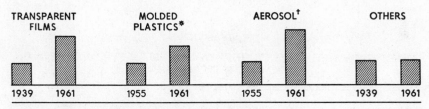

TRANSPARENT FILMS	MOLDED PLASTICS*	AEROSOL[†]	OTHERS
1939 1961	1955 1961	1955 1961	1939 1961

*1955 base includes cost of forming; 1961 includes materials only.
†Includes containers, valves, caps, and propellants.
Note: 100 equals share of market indexed as of 1939 or 1955 (molded plastics and aerosols).
Source: *Modern Packaging Encyclopedia*, 1962.

throughout the industry, commented: "Sometimes I think the only way out of this is to sell out to U.S. Steel, or to buy General Foods."[13]

THE RESPONSE OF THE METAL CONTAINER INDUSTRY

In responding to the events of the 1950's, the four major companies reacted in one or more of the following ways:

1. Product diversification.
2. Product specialization.
3. Increased customer service.
4. Heavy investment in research.
5. Closer cooperation with the steel industry.
6. Movement abroad.

Product diversification

During the last decade three of the four major companies in the industry have adopted some form of diversification. In each case the move to diversify was an effort (1) to gain opportunities in packaging areas growing more rapidly than the metal containers sector, and (2) to reduce vulnerability to competition from new packaging materials.

The American Can Company and the Continental Can Company moved

---

[13]Guzzardi, *op. cit.*, p. 157.

Exhibit 9

VALUE OF SHIPMENTS OF SELECTED PACKAGING MATERIALS, 1939–60
(In Millions of Dollars)

	1939	1947	1954	1960
Paper and paperboard containers	551.5	2,064.7	n.a.	4,704.1
Flexible packaging materials	103.1	256.2	n.a.	985.5
Metal cans	401.0	852.0	1,312	2,180.3
Glass containers	156.4	422.9	615	907.7
Closures	47.9	134.2	n.a.	254.1
Rigid-semirigid plastic containers	n.a.	n.a.	530	798.0
Total All Packaging Materials	1,721	5,178	n.a.	11,125

n.a. Not available.
Source: U.S. Department of Commerce, Census of Manufactures.

Exhibit 10

ESTIMATED PRODUCTION OR SHIPMENTS OF SELECTED CONTAINERS OR
PACKAGING MATERIALS, 1940–60

	1940	1950	1955	1960
Metal cans (1,000 tons steel)	2,192	3,893	4,485	4,801
Metal crowns (1,000 gross)	143,929	343,377	326,377	297,333
Aerosols (1,000 units)	...	30,000	n.a.	745,000
Glass containers (1,000 gross)	52,116	106,380	139,459	156,799
Aluminum foil converted (million lbs.) ..	n.a.	n.a.	144	227
Molded plastic containers (million lbs.) ..	n.a.	n.a.	139	145
Transparent packing films (million lbs.) ..	100	300	529	763

n.a. Not available.
Source: U.S. Department of Commerce, Census of Manufactures.

from being can manufacturers to become "diversified suppliers of pack-aging."[14] Both companies manufacture products to supply almost any form of packaging desired. Whereas metal containers used to account for over 75% of Continental's volume, they comprised only 50% in 1963. American's reliance on metal can sales dropped from 80% in 1955 to slightly over 60% in 1963.

These two firms have diversified to the point where they are important factors in papers, plastics, and glass products. . . . With their integrated papermaking facilities, they are in a good position to serve the needs of any customer who prefers foil-fibre containers. . . ."[15]

National Can, the third largest producer of metal containers, moved into the production of plastic containers, purchasing a small plastic firm in 1963. The company also invested heavily in fibre-foil machinery.

Both American and Continental, and to a lesser extent National, have strived to move away from their traditional roles as "tin" can producers

[14]"Price Trends Favor Can Makers," *Financial World*, August 22, 1962, p. 14.
[15]"Container Makers Grow with Economy," *Financial World*, May 29, 1963, p. 7.

by shifting into the use of new and varied materials. In a section of its 1962 Annual Report titled "Planned Progress—Rigid Containers," the American Can Company described this diversification:

Why Rigid Containers? Because the term more accurately describes [the] increasing use of a number of materials, plastics and paper composites, aluminum and extra-thin tinplate, and combinations of all these materials in the making of containers. While market studies indicate continuing modest growth for metal containers, . . . the increasing diversification of the company is aptly illustrated by the cover of this year's report [showing] some of the 125,000 acres of Alabama woodlands owned by the company.

Product specialization

The Crown Cork and Seal Company, nearly bankrupt in 1957, in large measure because of poor operating procedures, had not expanded outside the metal container field by the end of 1963. Instead, it specialized in the aerosol field, becoming the largest producer of steel aerosol containers. Following the strategy of concentrating upon the development of this container, while downgrading product lines (such as packer cans) most vulnerable to self-manufacture, Crown Cork enjoyed the highest profit margins of the four leaders in the industry (see Exhibit 11).

Increased customer service

As competition from new material suppliers and the interest of packagers in self-manufacture intensified, all four companies moved to expand the services they offered their customers. American Can, for example, provided customers with market studies of pet food consumption, and of seasonal and demographic influences on the consumption of citrus fruits, beer, and frozen bakery goods. Another service increasingly offered by the four companies has been help in new product planning and development, material handling advice, and assistance in production layout and design. American Can and Continental Can and to a lesser extent Crown Cork and National Can have established special service organizations to work with manufacturers on a large variety of technical and marketing problems. By broadening the scope of the peripheral services offered to their customers, the companies hoped to increase the economic reliance of the packager upon the industry.

Heavy investment in research

It is estimated that packaging suppliers, during the last few years, have been spending over $150 million annually on research to upgrade materials and machinery.[16] Both Continental Can and American Can spend an estimated 1.5% of their annual gross sales on research. According to Continental, "the constant changes in the packaging industry and the search for cheaper and better packages make research and development an even more important function today than in the past, and the company which does not maintain

---

[16]"Packaging: The Big Push Forward," *Dun's Review and Modern Industry*, November 1963, p. 164.

Exhibit 11

SUMMARY FINANCIAL FIGURES
Four Major Can Manufacturers

	1954	1955	1956	1957	1958	1959	1960	1961	1962	1963
American Can:										
Sales ($ millions)	652.4	714.8	771.6	1,000.6	1,037.0	1,107.4	1,059.0	1,093.3	1,180.5	1,149.4
Profit margin* (%)	11.5	12.2	11.7	12.7	12.9	11.8	11.8	13.6	13.0	12.3
Continental Can:										
Sales ($ millions)	616.2	666.3	1,010.3	1,046.3	1,080.4	1,146.5	1,117.0	1,153.3	1,182.9	1,154.0
Profit margin* (%)	8.4	9.5	11.4	10.5	10.7	9.8	8.7	10.6	11.4	11.5
Crown Cork and Seal:										
Sales ($ millions)	111.4	113.0	115.1	114.9	116.3	123.2	121.2	177.0†	190.2	205.4
Profit margin* (%)	6.1	5.7	3.5	3.7	5.5	6.7	8.1	12.8	13.4	13.2
National Can:										
Sales ($ millions)	41.1	70.9	81.5	88.4	100.7	101.8	109.5	114.8	121.8	126.6
Profit margin* (%)	4.4	6.7	9.1	7.2	6.9	5.0	5.6	7.5	7.1	7.6

*Operating profit margin before interest, taxes, and depreciation.
†Crown Cork and Seal merged with International subsidiary.
Source: Adapted from reports by *Value Line*.

adequate research and development facilities will soon find itself lagging behind. . . .[17]

In 1963 the Continental Technical Research Center in Chicago occupied several buildings, employed over 1,000 people, and was reported to be the largest and most comprehensive packaging research and development center in the United States. A principal focus of the center's efforts has been the testing and evaluation of all types of materials and production processes for the creation of new packages. In 1962 Continental reported that it had budgeted over $20 million for research during the 1963 fiscal year.

In 1963 American announced the start of construction on a research center at Princeton, New Jersey. The company's annual report of that year stated that the center would give major attention to "basic research in such areas as solid state physics and electrochemical phenomena, as a potential source of new products."

In addition to searching for new applications for existing containers and competitive uses of new materials, the can companies also have concentrated upon cutting their manufacturing costs. One way was to increase the speed at which cans were manufactured. As recently as 1958, typical production speeds rarely exceeded 400 cans per minute. In 1963 the most modern machinery produced certain types of cans as fast as 1,500 a minute. Indeed, production was so fast that available equipment to gather, handle, and transport the cans as they came off the can line was unable to keep up.

Other efforts have been made to reduce the amount of metal used in making a can, particularly important because tinplate and other raw materials have made up over 70% of the manufactured cost of the typical can. American has been experimenting with the use of ultrasonic welding of the can body, a process designed to eliminate the use of solder and to create a better seal. Another process under experiment, one developed by the aluminum industry to cut down on the amount of metal used and so bring its basic cost more in line with that of the tin can, is called "ironing." In effect, this technique allows use of a smaller amount of metal by spreading or distributing it so that the areas of the can subject to the greatest pressure are the strongest.

New methods of decorating the can have also appeared. "Electrostatic printing," a process designed to improve printing on irregular surfaces, is expected to make feasible the use of containers with more unusual shapes and surfaces. These types of containers have had limited use because of labeling difficulties. The process, unlike present methods, requires no contact with the material to be printed.[18]

Closer cooperation with the steel industry

Because the metal container industry has bought over $2 billion a year in

---

[17]Annual Report, 1960, p. 3.

[18]"American Can Acquires Rights to New Process for Printing on Packages," *Wall Street Journal,* November 7, 1963.

tinplate, the threat of the technological obsolescence of the tin can created a strong response from the steel industry. One such development has been a new lighter weight "skinny" tinplate, resulting from double rolling the conventional gauge of tinplate.

Until they [steelmakers] were faced with aluminum's claim based on lightness, the steelmakers had traditionally solved canners' problems by sheer bulk with heavier cans than need be. But . . . by cold-working the metal by a second pass through the rolling mill . . . they could cut the cost of freight for the material, the can, and the ultimate product.
. . . With all their new special equipment, tinplate makers can continue reducing the gauge of their material as far as can makers find it safe and convenient to go. . . .[19]

The economic stake of the steel industry in the future of the can companies, many can company executives believed, would be a significant factor in the ability, particularly of the nongiants, to adjust effectively to new competitive pressures. As an executive of one of the smaller companies put it: "A week doesn't go by that we are not working with some steel company on a new development . . . we won't lose this market to the aluminum and paper companies as they [the steel companies] have the resources to do fantastic things with steel."
Recently the United States Steel Corporation announced the introduction of a new steel foil designed to be used with composite containers. Steel manufacturers have also been testing an assortment of cans to be used as cooking utensils and serving dishes.

U.S. Steel [has] tested bulk cheese in a decorated reclosable tin can, which doubles both as an original container and as a table server. The company has no plans to enter the consumer packaging field; it devised the new containers as a stimulus for tinplate, a company spokesman says.[20]

Movement abroad

As margins in traditional markets narrowed in the United States under the increasing competitive pressures, some can companies established manufacturing facilities overseas, not only in Europe but also in Latin America, Africa, and the Far East. The purpose was to get into a position to profit from the rising standard of living of overseas countries. There was a need for inexpensive food preservation in many countries, and the demand for convenient food packaging was increasing in the more advanced foreign countries. Crown Cork and Seal, for example, established or expanded plants in 17 foreign countries from 1958 to 1964, becoming the largest potential overseas producer of tin cans in the short space of six years.

---

[19]"Thin Tin Gets Rolling," *Business Week*, May 11, 1963.
[20]"The Packaging Push, Aerosols to Flip Tops," *Wall Street Journal*, April 9, 1963, p. 23.

APPENDIX

In moving to adjust to the new environmental demands created by (1) the evolving concept of the package as an integral part of the product itself, and (2) the rapid advancement of packaging technology, for the most part initiated and sustained by companies outside the industry, the can companies, particularly the nongiants, were influenced by three major and long-standing industry characteristics:

1. The extensive facility investment required to compete effectively.
2. The traditional product orientation.
3. Marketing and distribution practices.

The extensive facility investment

The concentration of metal container production among a few large companies reflects the large-scale operations necessary for maximum efficiency and competitive costs. The production of the metal can is a highly mechanized and expensive operation, one in which direct labor costs have constituted a very small portion of total costs (see Exhibit 1).

The capital costs of installing a "line" (the equipment required for making cans) have been extensive. For example, a line to run beer cans costs from $750,000 to $1 million. The basic machinery or body forming equipment costs approximately $500,000 per can line, and lithography and coating equipment require an additional $300,000 and $225,000 respectively. One lithography and coating line typically feeds three or four forming lines, most can plants having a minimum of 12 to 15 forming lines. (Exhibit 2 illustrates the production process.) Nor are so-called incidentals inexpensive. A special forklift truck to transport tinplate coils costs $35,000. A device to turn these coils on end (they are delivered lying flat by the steel mills) can be purchased for $15,000. The coil shearing operation, recently adopted by all can manufacturers to reduce raw material expense, costs $300,000.

Because cans are made to physical tolerances often narrower than 1/5,000 of an inch, setup and tooling costs can run as much as $125,000 to $175,000. Nor can a tinplate line be converted to the production of aluminum cans without an additional expenditure of at least $175,000. Similarly, changes in can diameter or height have involved costs of $20,000 to $40,000, depending upon the type of can and the dimension being adjusted. Also, because cans are usually coated on the inside and have a gum sealant to make them vacuum-tight, running cans of similar size but for products with different chemical properties, and thus different coating requirements, involves costly cleaning and setup time.

The large capital investment coupled with high cost of changeover has placed can plants in the difficult position of trying to maintain a high level

Exhibit 1

1962 VALUE ADDED BY MANUFACTURE
(Dollars and Man-hours in Millions)

	No. Employees	Production Workers	Man-hours	Wages	Value Added	Cost of Materials	Value of Shipments
All manufacturing establishments	16,777,734	12,138,758	24,306.0	$59,176.0	$179,322	$221,404	$399,327
Fabricated metal product	1,085,000	834,090	1,724.0	4,287.0	11,115	11,217	22,298
Metal cans	53,069	46,018	99.0	305.4	772	1,339	2,112
Rubber and plastics	397,958	313,590	636.0	1,585.0	4,313	4,255	8,516
Stone, clay, glass	573,926	464,619	944.0	2,281.0	6,600	6,600	11,537

Source: U.S. Bureau of the Census.

Exhibit 2

METAL CAN PRODUCTION LINE

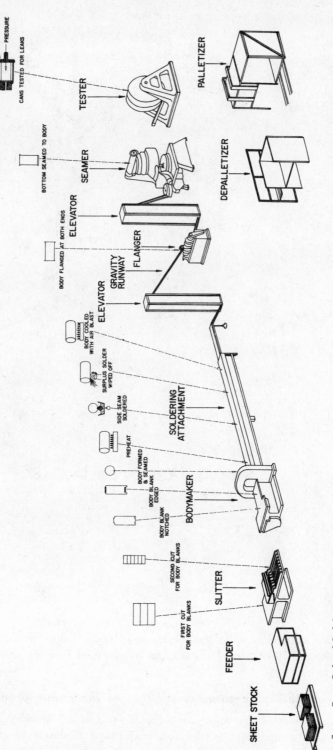

Source: Crown Cork and Seal Company.

Exhibit 3

of line utilization while minimizing setup costs. Consequently, volume discounts are often given for quantities in excess of 700,000 cans in order to
obtain long runs.

The traditional product orientation of the major producers

One result of the large economies of scale in the industry has been the
extensive commitment of the four major can producers to the beer and
food packing industries. Companies in both industries have (1) used very

large quantities of cans (over 75% of annual can production), (2) had very few changes in packaging style, and (3) used only a small number of different types (sizes, etc.) of containers. While these attributes have created packaging requirements most in line with the production capabilities of the large can manufacturer, the greatest threat of self-manufacture has also come from the packager with relatively stable, large-volume requirements.

The sales of beer and food cans have always accounted for the major part of the industry's production and that of its four largest companies. Sales of "general-line" (nonfood and nonbeer) containers, estimated to be about 7 billion cans annually, have been spread among a much larger portion of the approximately 100 companies in the industry. The relatively low level of concentration in the general-line segment of the industry has reflected (1) the greater diversity of products packaged, e.g., containers for the petroleum and automotive industry to hold motor oil, lighter fluid, antifreeze, gasoline additives; for the paint and varnish industry to hold turpentine, varnish remover, putty, paint, roofing cement; for other industries to hold liquid detergents, tobacco, hand cleaners, and so forth; and (2) the large number of small-volume manufacturers who use general-line containers. Although the "big four" have dominated the production of general-line containers, the smaller manufacturers have survived and prospered through specialization and concentration on low-volume, high-margin, often specially designed containers where cost advantage of volume production was not a factor. They have also specialized by localities, often taking advantage of the opportunities available because of the small lots they produce, to act as second or third suppliers to the large can users.

The four largest producers have tried to standardize the general-line can into a few basic shapes and sizes. Consequently, the cylindrical, rectangular or "F" style can and the cone top can have accounted for a majority of general-line containers. Cans within each basic type have been manufactured with different sizes of tops and special fittings to meet individual product requirements. The same basic can has been sold for a whole host of uses, e.g., what one customer uses as a paint can another may use to hold marshmallows, or motor oil, and so forth, new applications being limited only by the product's chemical and structural requirements.

Pricing and distribution practices

In the fall of 1963 Continental Can announced plans to raise prices on aluminum beer can ends, motor oil can ends, citrus cans, and miscellaneous other products. The company gave recent increases by aluminum companies in the price of aluminum sheet as the reason for the increases in keeping with its "policy of adjusting can prices to reflect changes in plate costs."[1] Because other can manufacturers, particularly American, did not announce similar increases, Continental was unable to maintain the new prices.

[1]"Continental Can Planning Some Increases," *Wall Street Journal*, October 17, 1963, p. 26.

Continental's inability to raise its prices in spite of the generally declining margins in the industry reflected the general reluctance of can manufacturers to pass on cost increases to their customers. According to one author:

> From 1946 to 1956 the costs of can companies' raw material and labor [have] more than doubled. Even in this inflationary era they could pass on only part of the increase to their customers. Some big packers found it economical to manufacture their own cans . . . Other customers . . . began to regard . . . "the glamor of self-manufacture as a more seductive prospective."[2]

The can manufacturers, although faced with rising costs, have not wanted to provide, by raising prices, further inducement for large can users to set up their own can plants. Also, rising prices would weaken the competitive position of tin cans in relation to plastics, aluminum, and glass containers. In addition, a 1950 court decision forbidding American Can to give long-term discounts to customers that bought on a seasonal or yearly basis encouraged large can users to buy from more than one supplier, thus increasing competitive pressures.

Rare is the client who buys all his cans from one company—most deal with two companies and play one off against the other. Anheuser-Busch, for example, splits the bulk of its $47.5 million worth of annual can purchases almost exactly between American and Continental. . . . A good example of a cagey buyer is [the] vice president in charge of purchasing for Rheingold's big New York brewery. . . . Using the leverage of hundreds of millions of cans a year, like many other buyers, he takes punitive action when one company slips in quality or fails to deliver. "At one point American started talking about a price rise," he recalls. "Continental kept its mouth shut. . . . American never did put the price rise into effect, but anyway, I punished them for talking about it." For a three-month period he cut the percentage of cans he bought from American.[3]

Because cans are relatively bulky items, transportation costs have been a major consideration in setting distribution policies. Various estimates have placed the radius of economical distribution for a plant at between 150 and 300 miles, depending upon the size and weight of the cans.

The high cost of transportation has led can companies to operate many plants (American and Continental manufacture cans in over 100 domestic locations). Usually a plant is located next door to or down the street from its major customer. Because of this, the manufacturer who has lost a large account has been in a difficult position.

A critical determinant of transportation costs is the weight/volume relationship, the cost climbing rapidly with an increase in can size and/or weight. A major advantage of aluminum and composite cans has been their low weight/volume ratio relative to the standard tinplate can.

---

[2]Walter Guzzardi, Jr., "The Fight for 9/10 of a Cent," *Fortune*, April 1961, p. 152.
[3]*Ibid.*, p. 152.

CROWN CORK AND SEAL COMPANY*

^^

The Crown Cork and Seal Company, a major producer of metal cans and crowns with sales of $205 million in 1963, had experienced the largest growth in sales and profitability since 1958 of any company in the metal container industry. Unlike most other can manufacturers, Crown had not diversified into packaging fields outside of metal containers in response to increasing competitive pressures.[1] Instead it narrowed its product line, concentrating upon supplying the fast-growing aerosol market and the expanding market for canned beer. Crown had also invested extensively in international facilities, particularly in underdeveloped countries, anticipating a tremendous growth in the overseas demand for metal containers.

Company executives believed the international markets, as living standards increased, would be the major source of future expansion. According to Mr. John F. Connelly, president and chairman of Crown Cork and Seal, "We have been moving as fast as we can into the international field, building plants in all underdeveloped countries. Presently we are only producing crowns in most of these facilities as nobody is canning in these areas as yet. But when they do start canning, we need only to add a body-maker and a seamer in order to produce cans."

Mr. Connelly planned for Crown's domestic operations to be the stable base from which the company would expand internationally.

The following pages describe the efforts to achieve such stability, discussing in turn the history of the organization, the domestic crisis of 1957, the pattern of operations and strategy which evolved from this crisis, the outlook for the future, and the situation as of February 1964.

The history of Crown Cork and Seal Company

The original Crown Cork and Seal Company was founded in 1892 by Mr. William Painter, the developer of the metal crown bottle seal. Mr. Painter's innovations revolutionized the beverage industry, introducing many bottle sealing and filling methods around which modern-day bottling lines are still being designed. But as the original patents expired, Crown's position declined

---

*Copyright © 1964 by the President and Fellows of Harvard College. Reprinted by permission.

[1]Described in "A Note on the Metal Container Industry."

under the increasing pressure of competition to the point where in 1927 the company was taken over and merged with the New Process Cork Company under the control of Mr. Charles McManus. The old name was retained, however.

The merger heralded a new era in Crown Cork's history. The company, investing heavily in research, diversified into new product areas, integrated backwards, and acquired and established several subsidiary companies domestically and overseas.

The first of several product developments of the McManus era was the "spot" aluminum crown used to seal beer bottles. Introduced right after the repeal of Prohibition, the spot crown increased company sales over 39% within one year. In 1935 the company purchased a steel mill, and developed the process of electrolytically coating strip steel with tin, a process first tried unsuccessfully by the English. Crown Cork's development made a tremendous impact upon the steel and can-making industries. Reasoning that a substantial market existed for canned beer, Mr. McManus purchased a can company and proceeded to develop, as a beer can, the first drawn, seamless metal container. The company experiencd little success with the can as a beer container, but when the idea of a pressurized container was popularized by the "GI Bug Bomb," the seamless can became the first civilian aerosol can. Another development was the introduction of the industry's first fibre-foil milk bottle cap.

By 1946 Crown was selling well over half the bottle caps used throughout the world and had introduced products that were still major components of the company's line in 1963.

Mr. McManus was described by company executives as a brilliant "tinkerer" and inventor but not as a president concerned with developing a strong management organization. His death in 1946 marked the beginning of another era in Crown history. No successor having been appointed, the company came under the control of Mr. McManus' personal secretary, Mr. John Nagle, whom McManus had named as trustee of the family's fortune. Under the leadership of Mr. Nagle, who named himself president, Crown experienced a decline in earnings, despite modest sales increases, which culminated in a net loss from domestic operations in 1956. Described by *Fortune* magazine as an effort to arrest this decline, Mr. Nagle and his followers took the following action during the early 1950's:

Through the late forties and into the fifties, Crown ran on the McManus momentum. . . . Dividends were maintained at the expense of investment in new plant . . . from a lordly 50% in 1940, Crown's share of United States bottlecap sales slipped to under 33%. In 1952 the chaotic can division had such substantial losses that the company was finally moved to act. The board omitted a quarterly dividend. . . .

The company needed "modernization," the board decided and the devices chosen were popular ones: Decentralization and expanded research and development. In 1953, Crown changed its corporate structure. The company was split into five divisions, each with its own sales force. . . . Under Charles McManus, Jr.'s, direction, some 50 high-salaried experts were hired to rev up R & D. The company got into plastics . . . Crown bought 141 acres outside of Baltimore for a research laboratory, with a planned staff of 300 and a budget of $5 million for salaries alone. . . .

A line-and-staff system was introduced. At headquarters and throughout the divisions, personnel were installed for engineering, manufacturing, technical operations, research, industrial relations, accounting and purchasing. Each plant manager received a complete staff. If a plant manufactured more than one product, there was a manager and staff for each product. To duplicate functions at every level of organization Crown, in 1953–1955, added 385 salaried employees. . . .[2]

The crisis of 1957

In 1956 Crown reported earnings of $381,000 on domestic sales of $115 million, not enough to cover payment of $550,000 in preferred dividends. The steady downward trend in operating profits during the early 1950's, in part a result of the elaborate line and staff organization and the increasing cost of research and development programs maintained, also stemmed from the company's very large and geographically concentrated production facilities (see Exhibits 1 and 2). For example, in 1954 Crown had built a plant in Leeds, Alabama, transferring a major portion of its crown portion there in order to be near the Birmingham steel mills. In Philadelphia the company operated one of the largest can plants in the world, concentrating over 80% of its can production under one roof on 55 can lines. (Although industry executives did not agree on the optimum number of lines for a can plant, most concluded that anything over 20 lines tended to be unwieldy and uneconomical.) In both cases the plants were located hundreds of miles from the markets needed to utilize the huge capacity of these facilities.

Except for the investment in the new Leeds plant in 1954, less than $1 million was invested in updating and replacing the machinery used in all locations between 1950 and 1957.

In the spring of 1957 Crown reported a loss of $600,000 in its first quarter of operations, the Bankers Trust Company of New York withdrew its line of credit and asked for repayment of the $2½ million currently being extended. At a special meeting of the board of directors, Mr. John F. Connelly, chairman and a substantial stockholder of the company (estimated at 24% of total shares in 1964), was named president.

Domestic operations since 1957

When Mr. Connelly assumed the presidency of Crown Cork, the company was on the verge of bankruptcy. In addition to the $2½ million loan called by Bankers Trust, there were $4½ million of short-term notes due by the end of 1957. In his first annual message to the stockholders, Mr. Connelly described his task as "halting, reversing and rebuilding [the company's]

[2]"The Unoriginal Ideas That Rebuilt Crown Cork," *Fortune*, October 1962, pp. 122–23.

Exhibit 1

ORGANIZATION

February 1957

Division	*Plant Locations*
Crown and Closure	Baltimore, Maryland
	Detroit, Michigan
	Leeds, Alabama
	St. Louis, Missouri
Can	Philadelphia, Pennsylvania
	Erie Avenue Plant
	Ashton Road Plant
	Baltimore, Maryland
	Chicago, Illinois
	Bartow, Florida
	Orlando, Florida
Machinery	Baltimore, Maryland
Western	San Francisco, California
	Los Angeles, California

Source: Company records.

status with the stockholder and customer alike," a task he saw as "appalling" in the spring of 1957.

Management was extremely discouraged. Sales were diminishing as reports were freely circulated among our customers that we were in difficulty. The complaints of stockholders were numerous and violent. . . . Six and one-half million dollars were owed to the banks and it was thought that an additional $7 million would be needed to get us through the seasonal peak of our business.

As a result of these conditions, Mr. Connelly instituted severe changes in the company's pattern of operations in an effort to survive the crisis of 1957 and rebuild the company into a stronger long-term competitor. These changes, initiated over a period of two or three years, were:

1. An extensive reorganization of the management and financial structures.
2. The modernization and geographical diversification of product facilities.
3. Product specialization.
4. Emphasis on customer service.

Management reorganization. Shortly after he became president, Mr. Connelly moved the company's headquarters from Baltimore to Philadelphia and started to eliminate the complicated divisional structure, an outgrowth of the previous management's efforts to improve the company's earnings position. The old structure had consisted of four major operating divisions: the Crown and Closure Division, the Can Division, the Machinery Division, and the Western Division (see Exhibit 1). A fifth division had existed, but in December of 1955 this (Specialty) division, whose main plant was in St. Louis, was merged with the Crown and Closure Division "in the interests of economy."

Exhibit 2

MANUFACTURING FACILITIES
Domestic Plants

1955

Location	Products
Baltimore, Maryland	Machinery, crowns, closures, cans
Bartow, Florida	Cans
Chicago, Illinois	Cans
Leeds, Alabama	Crowns and cans
Los Angeles, California	Cans
Orlando, Florida	Cans
Philadelphia	Cans
San Francisco, California	Cans
St. Louis, Missouri	Crowns, closures

1962

Atlanta, Georgia	Cans, crowns, and closures
Baltimore, Maryland	Machinery, crowns, closures
Bartow, Florida	Cans
Chicago, Illinois	Crowns and cans
Dallas, Texas	Cans
Ft. Worth, Texas	Cans
Orlando, Florida	Cans and crowns
Philadelphia	Cans and crowns
San Francisco, California	Cans, crowns, and closures
Spartanburg, North Carolina	Cans and crowns
St. Louis, Missouri	Cans, crowns, and closures
Winchester, Virginia	Cans and closures

Foreign Plants

Antwerp, Belgium	Crowns, closures, and machinery
Rio de Janeiro, Brazil	Crowns
Sao Paulo, Brazil	Crowns
Toronto, Canada	Cans and crowns
Montreal, Canada	Crowns
London, England	Crowns
Paris, France	Crowns
Tredegar, Wales	Crowns
Milan, Italy	Crowns
Mexico City, Mexico	Crowns
Casablanca, Morocco	Crowns
Rotterdam, The Netherlands	Crowns
Lima, Peru	Crowns
Lisbon, Portugal	Cork rods, discs, etc.
Salisbury, Southern Rhodesia	Crowns
Johannesburg, South Africa	Crowns
Port Elizabeth, South Africa	Crowns

Source: Company records.

The 1955 Annual Report commented on the rationale behind the institution of the divisional organization and the increased overhead it brought about:

In 1953 the company began to adapt a headquarters and operating division type of organization such as has been employed successfully by a larger number of American industrial corporations. The three former principal subsidiaries became divisions of the company and the Baltimore operations were established as two separate divisions in addition to the headquarters staff. General managers [were] appointed for each of the five divisions . . . the company recognizes the fact that during this period of change to a different type of organizational concept certain categories of administrative expenses would be higher than usual.

From 1957 to 1959 Mr. Connelly consolidated the management structure, reducing sharply the overhead. By 1959 Crown's employment was reduced by 1,647 people or 24% of its labor force. As one executive carefully put it: "We also lost the services of 11 or so vice presidents." In addition, the central research and development facility was disbanded. Within two years, overhead was reduced from over $11 million to $5 million. In the 1957 and 1958 Annual Reports, Mr. Connelly described these changes:

A few years ago, the company introduced an elaborate and costly line and staff type of organization. Aside from its cost and other disadvantages, it was incompatible with the size of our business. This type of organization has been largely eliminated and changed to one of greater simplicity, flexibility, and effectiveness. We consolidated three independent divisional product selling groups into one integrated sales organization. [In addition] a careful review of all classes of personnel accomplished by year end [1957] a reduction of 968 employees. These reductions were unrelated to business activity in that they largely comprised excess and nonessential personnel. In headquarters alone, which in the past has been severely criticized, there was a reduction of 80 people to approximately one-half of its original size. . . .

Elimination of this divisional staff-type of organization and the institution of straight-line operating management in our various manufacturing plants [have given] us better and more direct control over our operations.

While the company did not maintain an organization chart in 1963 ("we would spend all our time just trying to keep it up-to-date"), Exhibit 3 reflects how one might have looked.

In addition to the drastic reorganization and reduction of executive positions undergone since 1957, Crown also experienced a considerable turnover in top-level personnel. Mr. Siebert, Mr. Luviano, and the controller had been in their present positions less than two months as of February 1964. These gentlemen were the third group of executives to occupy the positions since 1958. The rapid turnover of top-level personnel reflected, in part, Mr. Connelly's strong belief in (1) the importance of an immediate and measurable contribution from his subordinates, and (2) the company not being a "training ground or retirement home" for executives.

As part of the company's reorganization, Mr. Connelly discarded divisional accounting practices at the same time he eliminated the divisional line and staff setup. Except for one accountant maintained at each plant location, all accounting and cost control was performed at the corporate level, the corporate accounting section occupying one half the space used by the headquarters group.

According to Mr. Connelly, "When we took over this place, it was com-

Exhibit 3

ORGANIZATION

February 1964

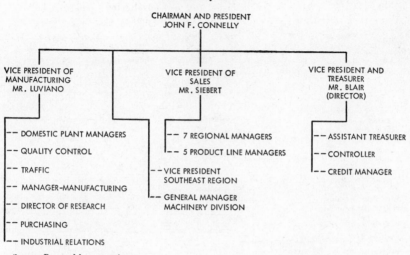

CHAIRMAN AND PRESIDENT
JOHN F. CONNELLY

VICE PRESIDENT OF
MANUFACTURING
MR. LUVIANO

VICE PRESIDENT OF
SALES
MR. SIEBERT

VICE PRESIDENT AND
TREASURER
MR. BLAIR
(DIRECTOR)

-- DOMESTIC PLANT MANAGERS

-- QUALITY CONTROL

-- TRAFFIC

-- MANAGER-MANUFACTURING

-- DIRECTOR OF RESEARCH

-- PURCHASING

-- INDUSTRIAL RELATIONS

-- 7 REGIONAL MANAGERS

-- 5 PRODUCT LINE MANAGERS

-- VICE PRESIDENT
SOUTHEAST REGION

-- GENERAL MANAGER
MACHINERY DIVISION

-- ASSISTANT TREASURER

-- CONTROLLER

-- CREDIT MANAGER

Source: Prepared by case writer.

pletely demoralized. So we started talking profits, a $10,000 saving would improve earnings 1 cent a share, a $1,000 saving ¹⁄₁₀ and so forth. We went to all our plants and did this, stressing that the company's future and that of the individual manager would depend solely on his profit performance, not on whether he was related to someone at corporate headquarters."

Whereas in 1956 each plant manager had his own accounting-control section and was responsible for all costs controllable at the plant level, in 1963 the control function was centralized in the home office; also, each plant manager had been made totally responsible for plant profitability, including any allocated costs (all company overhead, estimated at 5% of sales, was allocated to the plant level). As explained by Mr. Blair, vice president and treasurer, the cost- and profit-consciousness of the plant managers expanded to all aspects of company operations when they were made responsible for all costs. "The manager is even responsible for the profits on each product manufactured in his plant." The plant manager's compensation was not tied directly to profit performance. But as Mr. Blair pointed out, "He is certainly rewarded on the basis of that figure."

Financial reorganization. Reductions in personnel and inventory levels moved Crown past the 1957 crisis with the banks. Since that time the company had reduced the cash drain of its capital structure by purchasing or redeeming a major portion of the outstanding preferred and preference stock. By so doing, the company reduced required dividend payments by over $600,000. Crown also purchased and retired about 1.2 million shares of common stock (after giving effect to a four-to-one stock split in 1963). In addition the

Exhibit 4

CROWN CORK AND SEAL COMPANY

Comparative Statement of Profit and Loss for the Fiscal Years
1955–64, 1961–64 Consolidated
(Dollars in Thousands)

	1955		1956		1957		1958	
Products sold (sales)	$112,954	100.0%	$115,098	100.0%	$115,923	100.0%	$116,348	100.0%
Interest, royalties, and other income	499	0.4	188	0.1	237	0.2	559	0.5
Dividend from Crown International	400	0.4	400	0.4	500	0.4	500	0.4
	$113,583	100.8%	$115,736	100.5%	$116,660	100.6%	$117,407	100.9
Costs and expenses:								
Costs of products sold								
excluding depreciation	$ 92,430	81.8%	$ 95,803	83.2%	$ 98,278	84.8%	$ 96,922	83.3
Selling and administration	14,042	12.4	15,280	13.3	13,337	11.5	13,074	11.2
Depreciation	2,672	2.4	2,577	2.2	2,494	2.1	2,381	2.1
Interest	1,030	0.9	1,150	1.0	894	0.8	677	0.6
Nonrecurring expense covering relocation								
of operating facilities, etc.	448	0 4	440	0.4	637	0.5	1,203	1.0
	$110,622	97.9%	$115,250	100.1%	$115,640	99.7%	$114,257	98.2
Profits from operations	$ 3,230	2.9%	$ 486	0.4%	$ 1,020	0.9%	$ 3,150	2.7
Estimated taxes on income	1,406	1.3	105	0.1	266	0.2	1,213	1.0
Net Profit	$ 1,824	1.6%	$ 381	0.3%	$ 754	0.7%	$ 1,937	1.7
Pro forma combined summary of earnings								
reflecting terms of 1961 merger								
Net sales	n.a.		$153,578	100.0%	$158,668	100.0%	$161,733	100.0
Cost of products sold excluding depreciation .			123,541	80.4	129,260	81.5	130,183	80.6
Depreciation			3,669	2.4	3,787	2.4	3,706	2.4
Selling and administration expenses			19,001	12.3	17,597	11.2	17,694	10.9
Interest			1,342	0.9	1,115	0.7	896	0.7
Income tax			3,024	2.0	3,165	2.1	3,801	2.5
Net Income	n.a.		$ 3,173	2.0%	$ 3,232	2.0%	$ 4,739	2.9

*Crown Cork and Seal merged with Crown International in 1961.
n.a. Not available.
Note: Discrepancies may appear in totals as a result of rounding figures.
Source: Annual Reports.

company repurchased its plants, which had been sold on a leaseback arrangement during the late 1940's.

In 1963 Crown, through the sale of 400,000 shares of common stock and the issuance of $30 million in convertible debentures, raised $42 million. It used this cash to refund all existing long-term indebtedness, thereby substantially reducing its interest expense. Mr. Blair believed this last change in the company's capital structure corrected all the financial errors that had carried over from the pre-1958 period (see Exhibits 4 and 5).

Modernization and diversification of facilities. In 1957 the bulk of the company's products were produced in three locations (Baltimore, Leeds, and Philadelphia). Because of this concentration, high transportation costs had, in effect, eliminated Crown as a factor in many market areas. An additional limitation had been imposed by the fact that the company's 13 plants typically produced only one classification of products (see Exhibit 2). Consequently, the new management sought to introduce greater "flexibility" to their production capacity by expanding the number of geographical areas that could be served profitably. Crown, from 1958 to 1963, spent almost $82 million in

	1959		1960		1961*		1962		1963		1964	
	123,191	100.0%	121,211	100.0%	$176,992	100.0%	$190,178	100.0%	$205,396	100.0%	$218,209	100.0%
	339	0.3	804	0.6	874	0.5	505	0.3	908	0.4	1,185	0.5
	600	0.5	700	0.6								
	124,130	100.8%	$122,715	101.2%	$177,866	100.5%	$190,683	100.3%	$206,304	100.4%	$219,394	100.5%
	104,251	84.6%	$101,931	84.1%	$139,071	78.6%	$150,093	78.9%	$163,033	79.3%	$172,545	79.1%
	10,636	8.6	9,488	7.8	15,311	8.7	14,694	7.7	15,033	7.4	15,060	6.9
	2,087	1.7	2,513	2.1	4,627	2.6	4,908	2.6	6,039	3.0	7,362	3.4
	955	0.8	1,255	1.0	1,252	0.7	1,579	0.8	2,479	1.2	3,079	1.4
	2,033	1.7	1,826	1.5	2,517	1.4	1,820	1.0	1,505	0.7	985	0.4
	119,962	97.4%	$116,933	96.5%	$162,078	92.0%	$173,094	91.0%	$188,246	91.6%	$199,031	91.6%
	4,168	3.4%	$ 5,732	4.7%	$ 15,088	8.5%	$ 17,589	9.3%	$ 18,058	8.8%	$ 20,363	9.3%
	1,525	1.2	2,325	1.9	7,625	4.3	8,081	4.3	7,250	3.5	7,125	3.3
	2,643	2.2%	$ 3,407	2.8%	$ 7,463	4.2%	$ 9,508	5.0%	$ 10,808	5.3%	$ 13,238	6.0%
	171,012	100.0%	$168,366	100.0%								
	137,162	80.4	135,276	80.2								
	3,395	2.2	3,828	2.3								
	16,745	9.8	15,972	9.4								
	1,104	0.8	1,298	0.9								
	5,076	3.2	5,491	3.2								
	5,831	3.6%	$ 6,392	3.8%								

relocation expenses and on new facilities, a sum representing over one-half its total plant investment as of 1963.

In Baltimore, the company's crown and closure manufacturing facilities, occupying over 50 multistoried buildings, were vacated, much of the obsolete equipment being sold. New facilities occupying three single-storied buildings replaced the former plant. The company's electrolytic tin mill in Baltimore also was sold, in 1958.

The company's gigantic can plant in Philadelphia was vacated and set up as rental property. Its can lines were relocated in existing plants in order to expand their capacity and to convert them from single to multiproduct facilities. In 1959 the Leeds, Alabama, plant was vacated, its crown lines being transferred to a new plant constructed in Atlanta. In 1960 a plant was opened in Winchester, Virginia, to manufacture packer cans for the apple packing industry in the Shenandoah Valley region. A plant to manufacture cans and crowns was purchased in Dallas. This plant was to be a temporary facility until a new plant could be constructed in Texas. Crown manufacturing equipment was added to the Chicago can plant. Can lines

Exhibit 5

CROWN CORK AND SEAL COMPANY
Balance Sheets for Fiscal Years 1955–64, 1961–64 Consolidated
(Dollars in Thousands)

	1955*	1956	1957	1958	1959	1960	1961	1962	1963	1964
Current Assets										
Cash	$ 2,786	$ 3,030	$ 1,677	$ 1,905	$ 2,587	$ 2,204	$ 5,343	$ 5,831	$ 6,235	$ 7,637
Government securities			2,179†	...	...	...	527	913	1,735	49
Receivables	11,743	12,919	14,962	15,781	15,286	15,775	23,729	25,387	30,199	31,246
Inventories:										
Finished goods and work-in-process	17,845	19,319	16,582	13,417	16,013	16,251	25,011	27,206	33,349	32,498
Raw material and supplies	14,036	14,133	10,062	10,068	6,039	3,416	10,275	11,644	14,168	14,018
Prepaid expenses	776	817	610	479	593	513	1,463	2,397	3,539	3,475
Total Current Assets	$49,318‡	$50,218	$46,072	$41,650	$40,518	$38,159	$66,348	$73,378	$89,225	$88,923
Current Liabilities:										
Notes payable	$ 3,200	$ 7,700	...	...	$10,000	$ 1,875	$ 5,190	$21,635	$31,344	$16,887
Accounts payable	7,575	7,494	8,005	8,205	10,620	8,887	14,956	20,597	21,017	18,797
Customer deposits	213	212	268	160	291	213				
Provision for income tax	1,280	172	749	2,038	1,529	2,056	4,679	2,926	2,722	2,826
Total Current Liabilities	$12,268	$15,578	$ 9,022	$10,403	$22,440	$13,031	$24,825	$45,158	$55,083	$38,510
Working capital	$35,050	$34,640	$37,050	$31,247	$18,078	$25,128	$41,523	$28,220	$34,142	$50,413
Investment in Crown International Corporation	$ 1,460	$ 1,460	$ 1,460	$ 1,460	$ 1,460	$13,215	...	...	...	...
Investment in Crown Financial Corporation	...	...	...	...	...	...	...	$ 750	750	$ 1,452
Plant and equipment:										
Buildings	16,751	16,875	16,924	12,231	14,310	17,834	35,119	42,005	51,889	48,691
Machinery equipment	45,018	45,490	44,855	36,030	40,675	49,158	65,621	77,486	95,666	109,951
Construction in progress	1,306	1,111	1,007	3,744	7,372	1,446	3,387	5,102	7,667	4,368
Loss: Depreciation	(29,468)	(31,167)	(32,464)	(24,258)	(24,717)	(26,339)	(45,004)	(48,719)	(59,899)	(59,538)
Land	1,744	1,720	1,615	1,706	1,383	1,694	3,131	4,000	4,563	4,356
Patents, less amortization	393	536§	368	350	329	312	616	382	332	305
	$35,744	$34,582	$32,305	$29,803	$39,352	$44,105	$62,870	$80,256	$100,218	$108,133
Total Assets Less Current Liabilities	$72,293	$70,682	$70,815	$62,510	$58,890	$82,448	$104,393	$109,226	$135,110	$159,998
Preferred stock	$12,375	$12,375	$11,475	$ 7,875	$ 7,269	$ 7,269	$ 6,279	$ 5,624	$ 5,007	$ 4,485
Convertible preference stock							9,917			
Common stock	3,019	3,019	3,019	2,655	2,423	2,448	2,699	10,642	11,527	10,803
Paid-in surplus	10,705	10,705	11,059	10,420	9,656	9,793	2,036		11,274‖	11,424‖
Earned surplus	24,794	24,383	25,936	25,702	25,878	40,717	55,609	54,724	61,157	63,034
	$50,893	$50,482	$51,489	$46,652	$45,226	$60,229	$ 77,540	$70,990	$88,965	$89,746
Minority shareholders' equity in subsidiaries							7,629	7,871	8,320	8,920
Long-term debt	21,400	20,200	19,000	15,400	13,000	21,125	17,654	25,454	30,676	51,550
Deferred income taxes			326	458	664	1,094	1,560	4,911	7,149	9,782
	$72,293	$70,682	$70,815	$62,510	$58,890	$82,448	$104,393	$109,226	$135,110	$159,998

*Discrepancies in total figures due to rounding.
†Claims for prior years' federal income and excise profits taxes.
‡Adjusted to reflect cash surrender value of life insurance, $132,000 and $126,000 respectively.
§Listed as Other Assets in 1956 Annual Report.
‖Since January of 1963.

Source: Annual Reports.

were installed in the St. Louis crown and closure plant. In 1963 the company was constructing can plants in Fort Worth, Texas, and Spartanburg, South Carolina. Aerosol can lines were installed in the Atlanta, Chicago, and San Francisco plants and aerosol capacity was being expanded in Philadelphia and Baltimore.

Crown management believed that, because of the extensive investment in new facilities, its domestic equipment was the most technically advanced in the industry. Mr. Blair thought it was unlikely that any other major can producer could claim 60% of its total investment as being new within the last five years. To this factor, Mr. Blair attributed much of Crown's recent ability to maintain the highest operating margins in the industry.

In November 1963 Crown announced the purchase of the Mundet Corporation, a producer of polystyrene and specialty cork insulation materials and gaskets made of composition cork and rubber. The company also produced metal bottle caps and had a small plastics operation. By early 1964 Crown had sold the insulation and plastics portions of the business, recovering almost its entire initial investment. Crown also discontinued the manufacture of insulating materials. As explained by Mr. Connelly, "We were primarily interested in obtaining the Mundet crown plant which is ideally located to service the New York Metropolitan Area. The plant is being expanded to include can-forming lines." Previously New York customers had been serviced from the Philadelphia plant at a substantial transportation expense to the company. Mr. Connelly estimated that savings in trucking expense alone would exceed $300,000 a year.

Product specialization. In 1963 Crown derived about 50% of its sales from the production of cans and metal containers, about 43% from crowns, and the balance from bottling and packaging machinery. Domestically, cans accounted for over 65% of the total volume and almost 40% of profits. Although the profit margin on crowns was typically higher than those on cans and closures, the percentages were also generally representative of the importance of any one product group to net earnings.

The breakdown of total volume by the individual product groups has remained relatively constant since 1960. Within the container group, however, Crown concentrated upon producing cans for "hard-to-hold" products such as beer, soft drinks, and whipped cream that needed high strength or sensitivity protection from their containers and/or utilized convenience features such as aerosol dispensing or a "tear-top" lid. Specializing in these types of high-margin applications, the company had dropped over $20 million in low-margin or break-even applications since 1957; the percentage of "packer" cans in Crown's total volume declined greatly relative to the other three major manufacturers.

According to Mr. Siebert, sales vice president, the specialization in difficult applications, particularly beer and aerosol containers, had reduced the threat of self-manufacture to the company. Part of the reasoning behind the decision not to produce the fibre-foil container for the oil industry was a case in point. Despite its several million-dollar stake in the motor oil can business, Crown management, having captured 50% of this market by introducing the first aluminum one-quart oil can in 1958, decided not to produce the composite can. Their reasoning was:

1. There is a better and quicker return in the beer and carbonated beverage industries.
2. The economies of the paper can are such as to give the paper companies a significant cost advantage.
3. Because (a) the technology is simple, and (b) the petroleum industry is very standardized, the paper can lends itself to self-manufacture.
4. The company could not produce paper cans at a low-enough cost to prevent self-manufacture by the petroleum companies.
5. If necessary, the company could always make the container as it already made spiral paper tubing in which to ship can ends. In addition, the "Dacro" bottle cap utilizes a paper-foil composite material.
6. The composite can appeared to be only a stage as some oil companies were already experimenting wtih plastic containers.

By the end of 1963 the company had lost over $8 million in sales to the composite oil can.

One manager described the concentration on producing cans of high ability as "a result of the way we think the industry is going. Easy applications are already taken care of. To expand the use of the can, and particularly the aerosol, greater demands are being made of the 'can as a package.' "

One measure of the reliance upon difficult and demanding can applications was that aerosol sales, in 1963, accounted for 20% of total company sales, and sales to the beer industry, 50% of total volume. The emphasis on the beer can was also in part an outgrowth of a belief that the crown market was stagnating as beverages were being packed increasingly in cans.

Strong customer service. Believing that (1) there was little technical difference in product quality throughout the industry, all manufacturers having the ability to produce a high-quality can; and (2) the company with the strategically located and available line capacity would have a competitive advantage; Crown executives viewed their greatest competitive strength and challenge to be the provision of a very high level of customer service. Mr. Connelly and Mr. Blair believed this to be the advantage of "operating the company as a small business—we are only as big as our local plant." Messrs. Connelly, Luviano, and Siebert estimated they spent at least half of their time traveling in order "to stay close to the business and informed." Mr. Connelly explained that he gave a major portion of his time to sales, and handling accounts. "I insist on personally hearing about all complaints and problems. I may not know the answer but I will show concern and see that an answer is obtained very quickly." The deep involvement of the top corporate officers in the operations of the company reflected, according to Mr. Blair, "the key aspects of the can industry: the fact that nobody stores cans, and customers want them in a hurry and on time. As far as we are concerned, fast answers get customers."

As part of the policy of providing the fastest possible service, Crown tried to avoid the necessity of changeovers on its lines, preferring to invest in additional equipment. As explained by one manager:

> Our thinking has been to have the equipment and then go out and sell it. We believe the cost of 90% machine utilization and warehousing to be prohibitive. Also changing machine setups is a slow and inefficient process. Therefore we have had a heavy investment in additional lines which are maintained in a setup condition and can be gotten rolling in 15 or 20 minutes.

A major objective of the reorganization in 1957–59 had been to increase the service capacity of the sales force by consolidating the sales organization. Dividing the sales force geographically rather than by product, each salesman was given single account responsibility for all products. This consolidation was thought to provide customers with a service unique in the industry, a single contact for crowns, cans, closures, and machinery.

According to company executives, however, the most important aspect of Crown's emphasis on service was not its ability to deliver quickly, but rather the ability of the Crown sales force and its technical department to solve customer problems. For example, to the bottler this often meant a complete study of his markets, their growth potential, his distribution methods; for the food packer, a study of his most effective plant layout or technical help on a sanitation problem; for the aerosol packager, the redesign of a dust cap, or help with a production problem resulting from faulty valve mechanisms; and so forth.

Both the manufacturing engineering group and the research and development section devoted a large portion of their time to customers' production processes and product development problems respectively. Dr. Cliffcorn, director of Crown Research, estimated that over 60% of his section's time was spent on test-packing new products.

A heavy service orientation was reflected in all aspects of the company's research program. As explained by Dr. Cliffcorn:

> Our problem isn't basic research. Our research activities are directed primarily to technical problems. For example, the greatest problem facing the packaging industry is the determination of the true requirement of the container. We are using materials today that five years ago everybody said wouldn't do.
>
> Basically, we are looking for new uses for cans and new uses for existing shapes. For instance, I have been trying to interest the sales department in the extruded metal can—perhaps for dog food—so I have had some made up and sent to interested friends. As soon as we learn what they want we will make 1,000 of them within a week—timing is crucial around here.

Mr. Luviano, vice president of manufacturing, believed there was often a great deal of value in being second to implement a new idea, thereby learning from the mistakes of the first:

> There is a tremendous asset inherent in being second, especially in the face of the ever-changing state of flux you find in this industry. You try to let others take the risks and make the mistakes as the big discoveries often flop initially due

to something unforeseen in the original analysis. But somebody else, learning from the innovator's heartaches, prospers by refinement. For example, the "spot" insert used in a beer crown is 0.0018 inches thick. Now what determined that? Not brains, nobody envisioned that a 0.0018-inch thickness would be just what was needed, but rather experience; the trial and error of building upon, and learning from, your own and other people's mistakes and problems.

Mr. Blair felt that Crown's lack of interest in not "becoming enamored with all the frills of an R.&D. section of high-class, ivory-towered scientists getting little use out of such expenses," was a significant factor behind its recent success:

Certainly in the electronics industry high-class research is needed, but this is a much different "being" from the can industry. Too many people have been sucked in on this and have lost a great deal of money. In fact, at one time even Crown made this mistake, but we have recovered from these errors.

According to Mr. Connelly, Crown limited its pioneering:

We are not truly pioneers. Our philosophy is not to spend a great deal of money for basic research. However, we do have tremendous skills in die forming and metal fabrication, and we can move to adapt to the customer's needs faster than anyone else in the industry.

Mr. Luviano believed that Crown's introduction of the tear-drop lid reflected another aspect of the company's service policy. "When we developed our first tear-drop lids, we made them available to all our customers at the same time, rather than committing ourselves to giving preferential treatment to one of the large national brewers as did Continental."

With the exception of Mr. Blair, Mr. Connelly and all of his vice presidents were ex-sales executives. Mr. Connelly said this was indicative of the importance he attached to an "aggressive sales-minded" organization. Aggressiveness was emphasized by Mr. Siebert. While he admitted that personal relationships were important selling factors in the industry, Crown salesmen were evaluated on the basis of new business produced, all of the company's products being sold directly to customers by 100 technically trained salesmen.

In addition to the direct-line sales organization, five product sales managers also reported to Mr. Siebert. Their primary responsibility was the development of new product applications and the maintenance of customer service within their respective product lines or industries. These industries and lines were: (1) the brewing industry, (2) the soft-drink industry, (3) fabricated aerosol cans, (4) drawn aerosol cans, and (5) packer and general-line cans. The manager of fabricated aerosol containers described his job as:

. . . a combination of titles—sales and product development. On the development side—new applications, and ideas. Problem is to put more and different products into the can. If I see a future in any idea, I work it out with R.&D. and quality control to test its feasibility. If there is enough volume to justify tooling costs, I will go to the supplier and develop his interests. We don't do basic development, but we will work with the supplier to provide specs and answer technical questions. The basic thing is to sell him on an idea to increase his market and then to work with him to develop it.

To the soft-drink industry and to a lesser extent the brewing industry, Crown Cork was the only company in the country which could supply all of the packager's needs from the filling equipment to the cans and/or the crowns needed to seal the bottles. The machinery division supplied 60% of all the filling equipment used in the soft-drink industry and 90% in the brewing industry. The company's ability to offer a unique range of services, i.e., cans, crowns, machinery, to major beverage packers, had often provided an entry-way for new crown and can business.

March 1962

In his stockholder message of March 1962, Mr. Connelly concluded that the rebuilding and sharpening of Crown Cork's domestic operations had been more than accomplished:

In 1957, your present management accepted the challenge to rebuild your company. At that time we planned a very ambitious five-year program, the goal of which was to produce additional profits of $1 per share each year.

We have exceeded this goal so it is only natural to ask about the future.

We still feel that we have hardly scratched the surface of our potential. We have built a splendid organization full of enthusiasm—one that is now ready to take on a new challenge. We are confidently planning for the years 1962–67, expecting equal or even more dramatic performance than the past five years.

Admittedly long-range prognostication is risky but the groundwork has been laid so solidly that again we are setting goals to add a minimum of $1.00[3] per share profit in each of these years. We consider this goal very realistic and will determinedly do everything within our power to accomplish this objective.

The expansion of production capacity and its breaking up into smaller and more dispersed units, along with a strong service orientation, all introduced to correct conditions which had helped to precipitate the 1957 crisis, had become, according to company executives, the "solid groundwork" on which the effort to accomplish this objective would be based. International expansion was to be the principal means.

International expansion

Following its policy of selling in selected geographical markets, and locating plant facilities as near as possible to large customers, Crown, in 1960, had established a program to build plants in overseas locations. The objective was to be closer to what was anticipated would be the major growth areas for metal cans in the next 20 years. In 1928 Mr. McManus had organized an International Company as a subsidiary to manage the production and sale of crowns overseas. In 1961 the two companies were merged. The merger's proxy statement listed four primary objectives:

[3]In 1963 this goal was restated to read $0.25 per share owing to a four-to-one stock split.

1. Corporate structure will be simplified and a single management will be able to better coordinate and integrate the operation of the domestic and international business.
2. The foreign subsidiaries will become more closely identified with Seal and with each other by working directly with Seal rather than through an intermediary company.
3. Seal and International presently hope to eliminate the risk inherent in the substantial reliance of International's subsidiaries on a single product (crowns) by adding new products when market conditions are suitable in certain countries. The merger will simplify efforts to this end by enabling Seal to provide directly to the subsidiaries the necessary experience and management.
4. The merger will result in a reduction of administrative expense.

By the end of 1963 Crown was operating 21 plants outside the United States: seven in Europe, five in South America, two in Canada, one in Mexico, one in the Far East, and five in Africa. Several additional building sites had been selected in Africa for construction within the next five years.

Crown's policy was to create a wholly owned subsidiary operated by the nationals in each country. The corporate headquarters assisted but did not get directly involved in the development of the organization or the production facilities. For instance, in Nigeria the British subsidiary had played the major role in developing the facilities because they had a long-standing understanding of the key social, political, and educational aspects involved. "Then we don't get involved in the personnel problems of family moving, fringe benefits, local tax problems, tax laws, and so forth."

In the 1963 Annual Report Mr. Connelly commented on the development of the international side of the business:

Our associate companies are very well established locally and well guided by experienced, competent managements, nearly all being nationals of the countries where we are located.

It is impossible to place a value on our international business since the rights we have to operate in these countries, some on a pioneer basis, could not be obtained today.

Our profits and sales in the United States will continue to grow each year and growth in the international market is unlimited.

According to Mr. Blair, the company did not worry about expropriation as "our country diversification greatly reduces this risk. In addition, if we didn't believe in the people and their basic goodwill, we would not have any business being there at all."

The outlook for the future

Assessing the probable effect new materials would have on the company, both Mr. Luviano and Mr. Siebert stated that the company had no present plans to become involved in composite containers or to expand its use of aluminum beyond its current commitment to aluminum ends for beverage

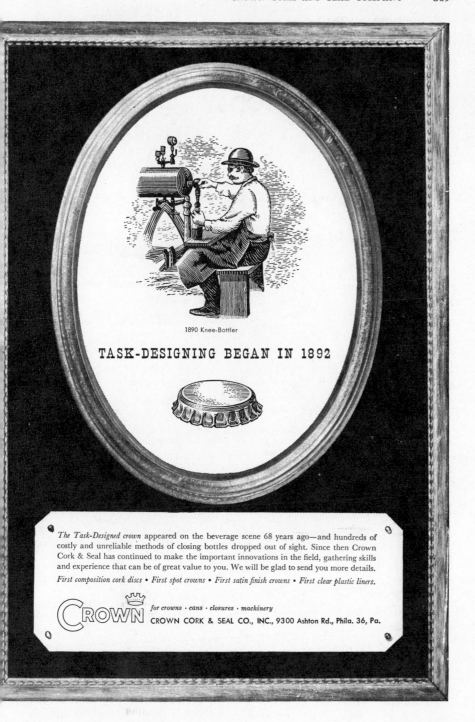

1890 Knee-Bottler

TASK-DESIGNING BEGAN IN 1892

The Task-Designed crown appeared on the beverage scene 68 years ago—and hundreds of costly and unreliable methods of closing bottles dropped out of sight. Since then Crown Cork & Seal has continued to make the important innovations in the field, gathering skills and experience that can be of great value to you. We will be glad to send you more details.

First composition cork discs • First spot crowns • First satin finish crowns • First clear plastic liners.

for crowns · cans · closures · machinery

CROWN CORK & SEAL CO., INC., 9300 Ashton Rd., Phila. 36, Pa.

cans and the production of aluminum cans for citrus packers at its Bartow, Florida, plant. As to plastics, both executives pointed out that the company was familiar with the technical problems of plastic fabrication, having been one of two developers of the plastic-lined crown, which in 1963 accounted for 20% of the industry's domestic crown sales. In addition, Crown recently

had acquired two small plastic moulding companies in England. Both men believed the company would probably become involved with new materials as their acceptance became "a fact." In the meantime Crown didn't plan "to pioneer."

Mr. Luviano questioned the wisdom of investing huge sums of money in a container "that next year may be obsolete. Our belief is that the aluminum and paper composite is still an interim package—one which just holds the product and costs less. We can't afford to work on the same thing. Ideally,

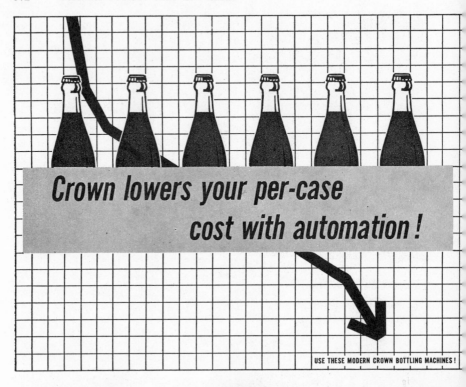

Crown lowers your per-case cost with automation!

USE THESE MODERN CROWN BOTTLING MACHINES!

Crown Uni-Blend Bottle and Can Fillers

The world's fastest—design-constructed for high-speed operation at a profit. Engineered to save maintenance. Known from coast to coast and abroad for precision and dependability—overall quality!

Crown Electronic Beverage Inspection Machines

The most effective means ever developed for safeguarding product purity. The machine is a combination of electronic, optical and mechanical elements which efficiently inspects and automatically rejects bottled liquids which contain any foreign particles.

Crown-von Gal Depalletizers

Handle 30 cases per minute or more—any b᷈ or package height without adjustment. Req᷈ minimum floor space and headroom. Pay for th᷈ selves in labor savings and extra production.

For filling, for inspection, for handling—savings come automatically with Crown! See your Crown representative.

CROWN
CORK & SEAL CO., INC.
9300 ASHTON RD. PHILADELPHIA 35, PA.

you would like to anticipate your competitors, but if you're caught off guard you try to come up with something better."

Commenting on the possibility of further integration by major suppliers and customers, Mr. Siebert, vice president of sales, thought the steel industry would not become involved in can manufacturing as "we [can manufacturers] are their biggest single profit factor right now." As to the possibility of major breweries producing their own cans, Mr. Siebert believed the beer can was "so far too technical" for self-manufacture to be a meaningful threat.

Mr. Blair, vice president and treasurer, believed that Crown's future sources of growth would be twofold: that which would come from (1) an increase in the general consumption of cans as consumer income rose, particularly in overseas markets; and (2) attacking the 75% market share held by Continental and American:

I think the basic tin can has been put to nearly every use there is so I don't feel new uses offer our greatest potential. Rather, if we can get 20% to 40% of all new (geographic) areas we enter, we have a great growth potential in contrast to American and Continental. This is where better service comes in, and if you're a customer with a gripe you will always be able to immediately reach John Connelly. (Crown maintained an open-phone policy for all its executives.)

According to Mr. Connelly, the important dimension of the company's future growth would be international development:

Right now we are premature, but this has been necessary in order for Crown to become established in these areas. In 20 years, I hope whoever is running this company will look back and comment on the vision of an early decision to introduce can-making in underdeveloped countries.

February of 1964. In 1963 Crown's operating margins declined for the second year in a row. In late 1963 and early 1964 Mr. Connelly made major personnel changes in the operations area of the company replacing (1) the manager of the company's largest can plant ($50 million in annual sales), and (2) the vice president of operations, the latter's job being filled by Mr. Luviano, the new vice president of manufacturing.

According to Mr. Connelly, inability of the ex-vice president of operations to control operating variances had brought about his replacement. Mr. Luviano's predecessor had sought to control manufacturing operations by maintaining strong functional responsibility at the corporate level. Discussing the changes he planned to institute, Mr. Luviano stated:

I'm a great believer in responsibility at the plant level. Consequently I plan to remove all authority from the corporate level people, making their function that of giving assistance to the plant managers. Then if the plant managers can't do the job, we will get someone who can.

As to the objective established in 1962 of adding $0.25 per share per year in earnings, 1963 fell short of this goal. In his 1963 message to the stockholders, Mr. Connelly commented: "While 1963 produced the highest sales and profits of our history, we in management are far from being satisfied with these results for we feel we could and should have done better."

Mr. Connelly, however, was able to report earnings of $2.03 per share compared with 1962's figure of $1.83, the latter being computed on the basis of 400,000 fewer shares of stock outstanding.

A NOTE ON THE PHONOGRAPH INDUSTRY*

The phonograph industry, a subdivision of the home entertainment field, produces equipment for the production of sound. Products include record players, turntables, amplifiers, speaker systems, tape recorders, and a variety of related equipment and accessories, as well as housings or furniture to contain the working parts. The industry may be subdivided into two broad categories—one that sells a complete sound system as a unit or package set, while the other sells the various major components as separate pieces. Industry products may also be divided into two broad classes—one that is made up of instruments of low or medium fidelity, while the other is composed of high-fidelity (hi-fi) equipment.

For an understanding of the industry and its products, some technical background is required. Accordingly this note starts with a brief discussion of sound, sound reproduction, fidelity, and the ways in which fidelity is measured. Subsequently the package set and component segments of the industry are discussed, attention being given to their postwar historical development, their relative market shares, the differences between the companies in these fields, their product lines, their marketing strategies, and their differing customer appeals. Special sections are devoted to the role of the dealer in selling the industry's products, and to component loudspeakers. The concluding portion of the note summarizes current industry developments.

The technical nature of industry problems, a divergence of opinion among even the well informed, popular misconceptions and misinformation, plus the scarcity of accurate statistical data are all factors that in various measure handicap not only the student but also the manufacturer and other members of the industry. As a result, many decisions have to be made on the basis of evidence that cannot be reliably verified. This note tries to give the student some of the same basic data a manufacturer might use in making estimates of the industry and its future.

Sound

Physically, sound consists of vibrations and is a form of energy. It begins at a source, such as a violin string which vibrates when played upon by a bow. The vibrating string alternately pushes against and draws away from adjacent molecules of air. Thus alternating impulses of compression and rarefaction move outward like a wave. Pictorially, sound can be represented by the familiar sine curve as shown in Exhibit 1.[1]

Exhibit 1

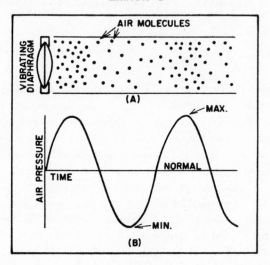

The loudness of the sound, its pitch, and its timbre all depend upon the varying features of the wave: (*a*) The greater the vertical distance between the peaks and trough of the wave, the louder the sound it represents. In more technical terms, this feature is referred to as *amplitude*. (*b*) The more often the wave is repeated in a given period of time, the higher the pitch of the sound. Technically, each repetition of the complete wave sequence is called a cycle, and the number of cycles per second (cps) is called the *frequency*. (*c*) The timbre of the sound depends on what is known as the *wave form*, e.g., the shape of the curve on the graph. The wave form of a musical sound is composed of fundamental vibrations plus additional vibrations which generally are harmonic overtones. For example, in the case of A below middle C, the fundamental vibration is 440 cps. The overtones include a second harmonic at 880 cps and a third at 1,320, as shown in Exhibit 2 below.

In addition to its physical definition, sound must be defined in physiological terms. In other words, a sound is not only a vibration with a characteristic amplitude, frequency, and wave form; it is also what we hear, a sensation physiologically perceived. Through faulty or incomplete perception, the physical sound and the sensation may differ widely. Individuals vary in their capacity to perceive sound accurately, and this is one of the fundamental facts that must be kept in mind in appraising the importance of

[1] All figures, unless otherwise indicated, are from E. M. Villchur's *Handbook of Sound Reproduction*. We wish to acknowledge permission by Radio Magazines, Inc., to use the figures, and also for permission to quote at length from the text.

high-quality sound reproduction in the phonograph and related industries. A "trained ear" will perceive sound more accurately than an untrained ear. In addition to hearing melody and rhythm, a trained ear will notice the clarity and accuracy of reproduced sounds. All ears are more or less trained, and the degree of training may be an important determinant of the quality

Exhibit 2

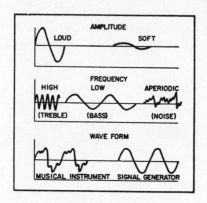 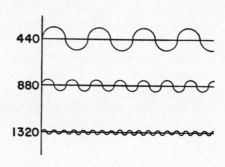

of sound reproduction equipment a purchaser will buy. Over the last 50 years the average ear has become more highly trained, and the average buyer today would regard a "talking machine" from 1900 as scratchy, tinny, and hopelessly inadequate, although at the time it was promoted with the following claims:

Beginning with the early tin foil machine, Mr. Edison has developed the phonograph step-by-step, until today the phonograph stands on the pinnacle of perfection. It perfectly reproduces the human voice; just as loud—just as clear —just as sweet. It duplicates instrumental music with pure toned brilliancy and satisfying intensity. Used with the Edison Concert Records, its reproductions are free from all mechanical noises; only the music or voice is heard. It is strong and vibrant enough to fill the largest concert hall. It is smooth and broad enough for the parlor.[2]

Clearly, standards for sound reproduction equipment were much higher in 1959 than in 1900. Listening to 78 rpm records today would produce a similar recognition of how much sound reproduction has improved just since 1948. One important question for the future might well be just how particular was the average ear likely to become?

Sound reproduction

Sound may be reproduced in a number of ways, but our discussion is confined to the reproduction of recorded sound. By means of recording equipment, the wave form produced by an instrument, an orchestra, a voice,

[2]Edgar M. Villchur, *Handbook of Sound Reproduction* (Radio Magazines, Inc., 1957), p. 53.

or other source, is represented by wavy grooves on a record or as magnetized particles on a tape. When the sounds so represented are to be reproduced, the process must be reversed.

Thus the first job of a sound reproduction system is to obtain an electrical impulse which varies in the same manner as the variations in the groove of the record. Several items of equipment are required, starting with a *needle* which follows the grooves precisely, and a *cartridge* which transforms the energy resulting from the needle movements into electrical impulses. The electrical signal or impulse is very weak as it leaves the cartridge, and it must be amplified before satisfactory sound can be obtained. An increase in the power of the signal is supplied by a *preamplifier* and an *amplifier*, or simply by one unit referred to as an amplifier. The electrical signal from the amplifier is then fed into a *loudspeaker* where it drives a mechanical oscillator, e.g., the *voice coil* and *cone* of the speaker. The speaker converts electrical energy into mechanical, and finally into acoustical energy—the alternating compression and rarefaction of air.

Fidelity

Fidelity, like sound, may be defined in two ways, one physical, the other physiological. In physical terms, perfect fidelity means that the reproduced sound has exactly the same wave characteristics as the source, i.e., the same frequency, amplitude, and wave form. No equipment reproduces sound with perfect fidelity, but the more nearly it approaches perfection the higher its fidelity. In physiological terms, perfect fidelity means sound reproduction so accurate that the ear is unable to distinguish between the reproduction and the source. This definition recognizes that the ear does not have perfect powers of discrimination. It may be unable, for instance, to hear any difference between a note at 1,000 cps and one at 1,001 cps. Neither definition, unfortunately, provides an absolute standard of what is or is not high fidelity since both definitions are in relative terms. They tell us that sound reproduction may approach perfect fidelity, and that some may approach perfection more nearly than others. They do not, however, define a lower limit for "high fidelity."

Besides these inherent difficulties in defining fidelity, another obstacle has been imposed by the industry that produces sound equipment. Some segments of the industry have opposed a precise definition because of the deterrent effect it might have on the use of the magic words "hi-fi" in product labeling and consumer advertising.

Measuring fidelity

Unfortunately there is no simple measure of fidelity; rather, there are numerous factors which interact to determine the fidelity of final sound output. Three of these factors are frequently mentioned in hi-fi advertisements, can be readily understood, and are of considerable value in appraising the fidelity of sound reproduction. These are *frequency response, flatness of response,* and relative freedom from *distortion*.

Frequency response. As commonly used, the term frequency response refers to the spectrum or range of frequencies which a system can reproduce. For example, a given system can be said to reproduce sounds from 40 cps to 15,000 cps. Since the best human ear can hear sounds ranging from 20 to 20,000 cps, this measure gives an idea of the range of sounds which will be reproduced and those which will be left out. In the example above, the listener would be deprived of the sounds from 20 to 40 cps and those from 15,000 to 20,000 cps.

Exhibit 3 indicates graphically the range of the human ear, the range of the 78 rpm record, and the ranges of selected musical instruments. Note particularly that the ear has a wider range than the 78 rpm record, which has been largely superseded. Regardless of the range that might be audible to a given listener or reproducible on a given record, it is significant that the vast majority of concert music falls between 50 cps and 10,000 cps. (One music instructor estimated that 90% of concert music fell within this range.) While the listener may realize that "a lot of frequencies are missing," he may not, in fact, be missing very much music.

Exhibit 3

APPROXIMATE FREQUENCY RANGES

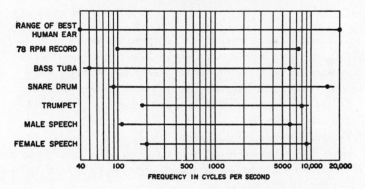

The range of frequency response has the advantage of being an easy measure to understand, and one that can be described in simple numerical terms. Hence it is widely advertised. By itself, however, it is completely inadequate as a measure of the response of a sound system because it tells little or nothing about the quality of the sound output within the indicated range. However, frequency response is sometimes thought to be, and is advertised as being, an indication of both range and quality.

Flatness of response. While a measurement of frequency response indicates the range of frequencies reproducible with certain equipment, flatness of response indicates the evenness of volume, relative to the original source, with which frequencies are reproduced. For example, in Exhibit 4, the broken line represents a response that is relatively flat for the whole range of indicated frequencies. The wavy line represents a response that is stronger than the original for some ranges, and weaker for others. Where the wavy line rises above the horizontal as in the 40 cps–100 cps range, the sound reproduced would be "boomy," that is, overemphasized in relation to other sounds. Where the wavy line dips below the horizontal axis, sounds would be underemphasized. For the listener to hear sounds at either end, where the wavy line drops sharply, he must turn the volume very loud.

Exhibit 4

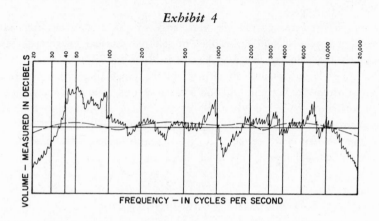

In the present state of product development, the broken line represents the type of response curve one could expect from a good amplifier, while the wavy line would roughly correspond to a good loudspeaker. Since a sound reproduction system will have a response curve roughly equivalent to the sum of the response curves of its various parts, present-day sets have response curves with even wider fluctuations than that represented by the wavy line. Thus, two sound reproduction systems that have a "response from 20 to 20,000 cycles" may sound very different owing to peaks and dips in acoustical output, and claims regarding frequency response, to be meaningful, must specify both *range* and *flatness*.

Distortion. A third important determinant of quality in sound reproduction is relative freedom from distortion. There are several types of distortion, but one form of distortion will suffice as an example: When the A below middle C is struck on the piano, as mentioned above, it produces vibrations in the fundamental frequency 440 cps, and harmonic overtones at 880 and 1,320 cps. One effect of distortion might be to produce harmonics of 885 or 1,311 cps instead. Such distortion, if perceived by the listener, is unpleasant and distracting.

The factor of distortion has not been greatly emphasized in advertising (except for amplifiers, where it is quite low), partly because of the difficulty of measuring it, and partly because test results were often unflattering to the product. The latter is particularly true for loudspeakers where distortion might be more than ten times that produced by an amplifier.

Historical developments

Package sets or factory-assembled phonographs were the traditional industry product. The industry which produced this equipment was dominated by large companies such as GE, RCA, Westinghouse, Philco, Emerson, Stromberg-Carlson, and Zenith. Prior to World War II, then, the situation could be characterized as one of large manufacturers selling ready-made units to the mass market.

The words "high-fidelity" and "hi-fi" came into common use after World War II to describe sound reproduction coming from equipment which purported to utilize wartime electronic advances to reproduce sound more faithfully. A limited group of hobbyists and "audiophiles" became interested in the possibilities of better sound reproduction, and went to considerable effort and expense to obtain the new types of equipment.

Because of the very limited market, existing phonograph makers did not manufacture the new products. Hi-fi fans resorted to homemade sets or sets made to order in a handful of radio shops which designed and built them. Thus a cleavage developed between the custom-made hi-fi rigs, or component sets, and the mass-produced home phonographs. The component sets were distinguishable by their superior sound reproduction (hence the name hi-fi), unique design, and much higher price. In fact, the prices of many were so high ($1,000 or more was not uncommon) that the market was limited to customers for whom cost was of little concern.

The market for high-fidelity products expanded as a result of three important developments: (1) The introduction of the long-playing record in 1948 increased the quality obtainable from recorded discs. In addition, it reduced surface noise and sharply reduced the cost per minute of recorded music. By increasing both the amount and the quality of sound which could be stored on a record, the long-play record in turn increased the difference between the quality of sound reproduction obtained from hi-fi and ordinary sets. (2) At about the same time, high-fidelity equipment prices began to come down as small manufacturers began to make component parts on a more standardized basis. (3) Sales of hi-fi equipment also benefited from an increase in demand for home entertainment. "The industry . . . attributes much of its growth, ironically enough, to television. TV, says the trade, accustomed Americans to the idea of home entertainment. Once surfeited with videofare, viewers turned into listeners."[3]

The next major development was the introduction of a high-fidelity product aimed at the mass market. This was a packaged hi-fi set, the Columbia "360," which came out in 1952. This event was later described by *Barron's* as follows:

About five years ago . . . [high fidelity] got its big boost in the mass market. Columbia introduced a low-priced table model phonograph made for it by Herold

---

[3]*Barron's*, May 13, 1957, p. 3.

Radio and Electronics, which gave a fidelity of reproduction unknown in inexpensive instruments at that time, RCA, Magnavox, Philco, Zenith, Ampex and others followed, with everything from $100 table models to $2,000 consoles.

Since these instruments reproduced well and many were cheaper than separate components, they seemed to offer a major threat to the latter. They proved, however, to be only a spur. [A] wider area of the public . . . began to hear and understand music for the first time, thus opening untapped markets for components.[4]

Industry size

Figures for overall sales of sound reproduction equipment are not generally available. Industry reporting services lump these sales figures together with other appliances, commercial equipment, and sometimes with television equipment. Published figures for a sector of the market, while easier to obtain, are difficult to evaluate and use because they appear to be developed from estimates rather than industry reporting services. The total market size and the respective shares in hi-fi, medium-fi, and low-fi, are not known with even rough accuracy. However, industry sales reporting by product-type is under way in high-fidelity components. Thus a component manufacturer may have a good idea of total component sales, but not much idea of the size of the overall market for phonographs.

There are, however, indications that the phonograph industry has expanded rapidly, especially since 1952. Sales of records (Exhibit 5) have grown steadily since the "battle of the speeds" in 1948 and 1949, when 78 rpm records were being challenged by both 45's and 33's. The growth in dollar sales is all the more significant when it is remembered that long-play (LP) records brought a substantial reduction in the cost per minute of recorded music.

Other indications of industry growth may be found in the figures for sales of phonographs retailing at $100 or over (Exhibit 6) and in two estimates covering dollar sales of components (Exhibit 7). Since prices of package set phonographs start at about $19.95, Exhibit 6 covers only a portion of the field.

Most of the products listed on Exhibits 6 and 7 are sold under a high-fidelity label, but, as previously indicated, this term has no precise meaning, and manufacturers are free to apply it to products of medium or low fidelity. In the case researcher's opinion, most of the products included in Exhibit 6 would not be classed as high fidelity under any strict definition of the term. In Exhibit 7, the very large figures for sales of components compiled by the Institute of High Fidelity Manufacturers are believed by the researcher to be inflated, while the lower figures offered by a components manufacturer are believed to be substantially accurate.

The package set manufacturers

In 1958 there were approximately 30 package set makers, and these could be subdivided into two groups according to whether their major corporate

[4]*Barron's*, September 28, 1958, p. 5.

Exhibit 5

SALES OF PHONOGRAPH RECORDS
MANUFACTURED IN UNITED STATES
(Dollars in Millions)

Year	Total Retail Phonograph Record Sales
1921	$105.6
1933	5.5
1940	48.4
1945	99.0
1946	190.0
1947	203.7
1948	172.2
1949	157.5
1950	172.2
1951	178.5
1952	189.0
1953	191.1
1954	182.7
1955	235.2
1956	314.0
1957	360.0

Note: Sales decline after 1921 associated with introduction of radio. Decline after 1948 associated with market battle between 33 rpm, 45 rpm, and 78 rpm speeds.

Source: *The New York Times*, March 17, 1958.

Exhibit 6

ESTIMATED RETAIL SALES OF PHONOGRAPHS SELLING AT $100 OR OVER

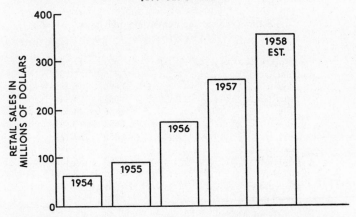

Source: Estimates by RCA and *Business Week*. See "Marketing, Everybody Gets in Hi-Fi Chorus," *Business Week*, September 21, 1957, p. 62.

activity lay in the field of electronics or home entertainment. Sales and profit figures for some major companies in each category are summarized as follows:

	1957 Sales (in Millions)	1957 Profit (in Millions)
Integrated Electronics Company:		
General Dynamics, Inc. (Stromberg-Carlson) ..	$1,562	$ 44.0
General Electric	4,298	247.0
RCA	1,170	38.5
Westinghouse	2,009	72.6
Home Entertainment Companies:		
CBS	385	22.0
Magnavox	87	3.7
Philco	372	4.3
Webcor	40	1.9
Zenith	160	8.1

Exhibit 7

ESTIMATED GROSS RETAIL SALES OF COMPONENTS

(Dollars in Thousands)

Estimates by Institute of High-Fidelity Manufacturers

1950	$ 12,000
1951	27,500
1952	47,000
1953	73,000
1954	96,000
1955	121,000
1956	166,000
1957	225,000
1958	280,000

Estimates by a Component Manufacturer

	1957*	1958*
January	$ 5,690	$5,954
February	5,176	5,930
March	5,694	5,184
April	6,051	5,145
May	5,356	4,534
June	4,693	3,381
July	3,246	3,721
August	4,537	4,386
September	6,387	6,481
October	6,110	8,519
November	6,484	
December	7,334	
Total 1957	$66,758	

10 months 1957—$53,940
10 months 1958—$53,235

*Estimates do not include turntables or record changers, and should be increased about 20% to compensate for same.

Source: Executive secretary, Institute of High Fidelity Manufacturers. A manufacturer of high-fidelity components.

For the integrated electronics companies, hi-fi was a sideline item, one of a multitude of products ranging from generators and refrigerators to vacuum tubes and portable radios. For the home entertainment group it occupied a more important place, and for companies like Webcor it was the major item of production. Among all makers of package sets, however, there were similarities in product line, marketing strategy, distribution channels, and advertising.

In 1959 most package set manufacturers produced a line ranging from portables and table models to expensive console sets and covering a wide price range from under $100 to over $1,000. Typically the products were mass produced and were advertised as having special quality features. For example, Columbia advertised controls for "balanced listening," and Stromberg-Carlson promoted "soundoramic true tone at low volume." Many sets were advertised as having three or four speakers, and some featured four-speed changers. While four speakers added glamour to the product, they did not necessarily signify quality sound reproduction. One consumer-testing magazine pointed out that "A single wide-range loudspeaker . . . will be likely to give far better performance than several small speakers," and also noted that "the speaker or speakers used in some [package sets] represent a retail value of not more than $5 to $10."[5]

The marketing strategy of the package set makers could be characterized as medium fidelity at moderate cost for the mass market. Following the lead of the Columbia 360, other package set makers put out multispeaker table-model sets which were superior in quality of sound output to previous models. Moderate cost, generally under $200, and convenient size were also characteristic of the new sets. While later development filled out the line up to very high-price brackets, both the researcher and two big-city dealers believed the bulk of package set sales were in the $100–$199.50 price range.

Another strategy was to make the hi-fi set visually attractive, an addition to the furniture in the home. Sets were offered in a variety of sizes and shapes, in various wood finishes, and in different furniture styles. Finally, consumer advertising was employed to create the mass-market acceptance which supported mass production of the sets. *Barron's* described the overall strategy as "trying to lure music lovers with packaged radio-phonograph combinations temptingly labeled 'High Fidelity.' "[6]

In marketing package sets, manufacturers could call upon extensive and well-developed resources including (1) nationwide two-step distribution organizations, (2) nationally known brand names, (3) heavy advertising budgets, and (4) the financial strength of a diversified and profitable corporation.

Advertising covered a wide range of mass media from newspapers and national magazines to radio and TV. "In fact, the heavy advertising budgets of such firms as RCA and Philco have made the entire country hi-fi con-

[5]*Consumers Research Bulletin*, November 1954, p. 22.
[6]*Barron's*, May 13, 1957, p. 24.

scious,"[7] and Columbia was reported to have an advertising budget of $1 million for the four months beginning in September 1957.[8] The message, in addition to noting quality, stressed style, appearance, and convenience. The message was aimed at the mass market, not the expert.

Distribution through distributors to dealers gave package sets coast-to-coast coverage through a large number of appliance and furniture stores, department stores, record shops, and discount houses. While some manufacturers had selective distribution, others tried for intensive coverage. The sets were generally given a full 40% markup.

Component manufacturers

In 1957 *Barron's* characterized the component manufacturers as "essentially a collection of small units—most do less than $5 million in sales annually. . . ."[9] While there were some larger companies (see Exhibit 8), there were more than 100 small independents. Many were privately held companies founded since World War II by a scientist or an engineer. Most were specialized, making one or a few components; none manufactured a full line (see Exhibit 9). While no detailed breakdown of sales by type of component was available, rough estimates are shown in Exhibit 10.

Component products. Components included a wide array of items which differed in many respects. They could be purchased as factory assembled units or unassembled in kit form. They were available in furniture, or as plain apparatus. Also, they came in a wide assortment of sizes, prices, designs, and quality ranges. Toward the modest end of the quality spectrum one might spend $138.50 for the following components as a group or $190.61 at list price:

> $59.95 Harman-Kardan A 12 12 watt amplifier
> 64.68 Electro-Voice 12 TRXB 12-inch speaker [speaker enclosure $70 extra]
> 42.62 Garrard 121 record changer
> 4.51 Wood base for Changer
> 18.95 G. E. diamond-sapphire pickup[10]

Toward the higher-quality end one might spend $1,000 or more for the following group, or $1,441.90 at list price.

> $ 109.00 Bogen PR 100A pre-amp and control unit
> 129.50 Bogen D070 power amplifier
> 1,038.80 Electro-Voice "Klipsch Type" Patrician IV D loudspeaker system
>   (shipping weight 400 pounds)
> 129.95 Reck-O-Kut (B-12H) "Rondine" deluxe turntable and tone arm
> 39.95 ESL "Soloist" cartridge[11]

Sets could be purchased outside the indicated price range ($138 to $1,000), but the researcher and several persons in the industry believed

[7]*Ibid.*
[8]*Newsweek,* July 29, 1957.
[9]*Barron's,* May 13, 1957, p. 3.
[10]The Radio Shack catalogue, 1958 edition.
[11]*Ibid.*

Exhibit 8

FINANCIAL AND PRODUCTION DATA FOR SELECTED COMPONENT MANUFACTURERS

(Dollars in Thousands)

		Financial Data				Date Founded or Incorporated	Product Data
		1954	1955	1956	1957		
Altec Lansing (Subsidiary of Altec Co., Ltd.)	Sales	$ 5,348	$ 4,289	$ 4,368	$ 4,659	1937	High-fidelity products include amplifiers, loudspeakers, and tuners. Other products include commercial sound reproduction equipment and transformers. Company also does some defense work.
	Net profit	450	325	415	193		
	Total assets	2,328	2,358	3,111	3,267		
David Bogen Co., Inc. (Subsidiary of Siegler Corp.)	Sales	4,508	4,583	5,200	37,719*		High-fidelity products include amplifiers, tape decks and tape recorders, and tuners. Other products include public address and inter-office communication systems, TV boosters, and UHF converters.
	Net profit	105	157	269	1,036		
	Total assets	1,565	1,552	1,941	34,956		
Daystrom, Inc. (High-fidelity products sold by Heath Co., a subsidiary)	Sales	62,472	73,816	63,192	74,402	1892	High-fidelity products marketed under "Heathkit" label and are primarily kits for home assembly. Kits include amplifiers, loudspeakers, and loudspeaker systems, record changers, tape recorders, and tuners. Other products available in kits include ham radio equipment, test equipment, and other electronic instruments. Business conducted by direct mail.
Harman-Kardon	Sales		1,000	2,000	3,000	1949	High-fidelity products include amplifiers and tuners.
	Total assets		300	400	750		
Marantz	Sales			170	400	1953	High-fidelity products include amplifiers and preamplifiers.
Muter Manufacturing Co. (High-fidelity products sold by Jensen Manufacturing Co., a subsidiary)	Sales	12,175	12,722	12,126	14,301	1959	High-fidelity products include loudspeakers and speaker systems Other products include radio components, transformers, and other acoustical equipment.
	Net profit	(280)	84	31	377		
	Total assets			5,200	5,880		

*Bogen became a subsidiary of Siegler in 1957 and 1957 figures are for Siegler.

Source: Altec, Bogen, Daystrom, and Muter figures are from published data. Harman-Kardon and Marantz figures are based upon estimates by a high-fidelity component manufacturer.

Exhibit 9

COMPONENT MANUFACTURERS

Name of Component	Number of Manufacturers*	Number of Manufacturers Making Only One Component
Amplifier and preamplifier	34	7
Loudspeaker and loudspeaker system	35	20
Phonograph cartridge	17	0
Record changer and record player	16	2
Tape deck and tape recorder	13	5
Tone arm	12	0
Tuner	17	1
Turntable	11	0

*Number belonging to the Institute of High Fidelity Manufacturers.
Source: The Institute of High Fidelity Manufacturers.

that sets ranging from $200 to $350 had a large share of the component market. While price was not a valid indication of quality, the popular-priced sets could be described as good hi-fi, but $500 or more was required to purchase the finest.

To a greater degree than package set makers, component manufacturers tended to compete on the basis of product features. While skills of mass production and mass advertising were important competitive tools for the package set maker, acoustical design, craftsmanship, and implementation of new technology were of primary importance to the component manufacturer. Of these features, the acoustical design of the product was generally thought to be the most important competitive asset.

Acoustical design varied widely, reflecting both an advancing technology and differing beliefs among designers on ways to achieve the best results. Product differences resulted primarily from differing engineering concepts regarding such elements as baffles, oscillators, or circuits. However, different designs might well use a substantial number of similar or identical parts. Amplifier tubes and condensers, turntable motors, and speaker cones were examples of such parts.

Exhibit 10

ESTIMATED BREAKDOWN OF COMPONENT SALES

Product	Per Cent of Total
Preamplifiers and amplifiers	25%
Tuners	15
Cartridges, record changes, and turntables	25
Speakers and speaker systems	25
Tape decks* and accessories	10

*Does not include home tape recorders. A tape deck only plays a prerecorded tape and requires connection to a sound reproduction system.
Source: Institute of High Fidelity Manufacturers.

Differing acoustical designs meant that quality was not necessarily a function of cost. One product might utilize a simple design which required less skill and effort in the manufacturing process than another, or it might use fewer or less costly materials, or a combination of the two. Of course, design was not the only reason for disparities in cost. Greater productive efficiency and economies of scale, especially in purchasing, might also account for disparities in the cost-quality relationship. In addition to such variations in manufacturing cost, there were also variations in markup. As a result, two pieces of equipment, while comparable in sound quality, might vary as much as 300% in price.

The importance of product features and product technology had several significant implications for the industry: (1) Changes in product features were frequent, and some component manufacturers appeared to make minor changes almost monthly. (2) The rapidity of change minimized the opportunity for savings through long production runs utilizing expensive machinery. (3) The importance of product design and the nominal machinery requirements meant that the industry was easy to enter. One Boston dealer noted, "With an idea, $20,000 in cash, and a pigeon loft you can be in the components business."

While the product line of a component manufacturer tended to be limited to one or a few components, a manufacturer might produce as many as 20 or more models of a single product. Most, however, manufactured only a few. For example, Rek-O-Kut, probably the leading turntable manufacturer, produced three basic models covering a price range from $59.95 to $129.95, with one model selling for $39.95 in kit form. A manufacturer's product line tended to utilize similar acoustical designs, with the different models varying in size, quality of materials, and in workmanship.

The products themselves were of two principal types: (1) completed components ready to be plugged into others for use as a set, and (2) kits which required the consumer to assemble and solder parts to build his own components. Some kits, such as "Heathkits" and "Dynakits," included illustrated instruction books and clearly marked parts. They could be assembled in a few hours by any amateur who could read and would follow the directions. These kits were nationally advertised, were available by direct mail, and were increasing in popularity. On the other hand, the true do-it-yourself fan could buy plans, select his own parts, and build a set from scratch.

Component marketing

The marketing strategy of component manufacturers was generally based on supplying high-quality equipment for a limited market which could both "hear the difference" and afford its advantages. Product price and outward appearance were of secondary importance. Promotional efforts were directed toward this limited market via selective media, and the advertising message was often of a technical nature.

The marketing practices of component and package set makers differed in many aspects, including distribution channels employed. Whereas package set makers used distributors who sold to retailers of various types, component manufacturers sold direct to the outlets that retailed their products. These outlets included radio parts jobbers, especially in the major cities, and an estimated 3,000 other dealers "in almost every city of any size."[12] The big-city jobbers had been first in the field, and originally they had sold not directly to the customer, but to radio repair men who made hi-fi installations in the home. These repair men bought at wholesale, and when consumers started to buy hi-fi equipment from the jobber, they, too, were given the wholesale price.

The practice of selling component equipment to consumers at wholesale prices, which originated as described above, was still in effect in 1959. According to *Barron's*, wholesale pricing "has been accomplished through the elimination of the distributor," that is, by direct selling to dealers. While a few manufacturers had tried the practice of using distributors, they had "dropped it in a hurry." However, most did supplement their one-step distribution with sales representatives or manufacturers' agents.[13]

Not all manufacturers tried for intensive distribution, as some franchised selected dealers and others granted exclusives. In general, selective dealerships were aimed at minimizing price cutting, which was widespread in larger cities.

Promotional efforts consisted mainly of consumer advertising, cooperative sales efforts with dealers, and exhibiting at industry fairs or hi-fi shows. In all three areas the approach differed from that of the package set makers. Consumer advertising media included such selective magazines as the half dozen or more catering to readers interested in high fidelity, as well as magazines believed to have an upper income readership such as *The Atlantic, Harpers, Saturday Review,* and *The New Yorker*. The advertising message often featured specifications of performance and results of laboratory tests. While component manufacturers did not generally make as much use of slogans as did package set makers, their claims were frequently optimistic. Numerous tests by consumer magazines, independent testing laboratories, and dealers with lab facilities were emphatic on this point. In addition, many ads overlooked major shortcomings while using statistics to emphasize less important, but more flattering aspects of the product.

A recent development in consumer advertising was the combined ad of two or more manufacturers which featured a component set made up of their respective products. The advertising copy contained general information rather than the more usual statistics on performance (see Exhibit 11).

Promotional efforts with dealers were of several types, including special deals and discounts, "push money" to salesmen, point-of-sale display material, and allowances for cooperative advertising. Dealer advertising was placed mainly in newspapers and on radio stations specializing in classical and semiclassical music.

---

[12]*Barron's*, September 28, 1958, p. 6.
[13]*Ibid.*

Exhibit 11

A TYPICAL COOPERATIVE ADVERTISEMENT

Many people have the impression that a room of auditorium proportions is required for proper stereophonic reproduction: On the contrary—a small or average size room has distinct advantages. In such a room the walls and ceiling actually function as part of the sound distribution system providing a happy balance between adequate separation and proper blending of the two speakers.

In the smaller room the effectiveness of stereo is never dissipated. Virtually wherever you sit you can enjoy the unique excitement of a room filled with music. In the very large room—the question of seating is much more critical.

The small room is ideal for stereo and high fidelity components are ideal for the small room:

• Components allow proper separation of speakers without requiring a mammoth enclosure for them and the other elements of a stereo system.

• Stereo high fidelity components are designed and produced by specialists, each of whom concentrates special skills on one of the vital elements of the system.

• Components add to the decor of a room. Use them in bookshelves, on tables, on cabinets, in room dividers. Because they are designed for all performance—with nothing spent on non-performing cabinetry—you get the most for your dollar.

• Components are remarkably easy to install and operate. If you can plug in and operate a TV set—you can install and operate a component system. And, incidentally, your standard LP records sound even better played over a stereo component system.

The components shown below provide one of the finest complete high fidelity systems you can own. To purchase it, simply take this ad to your dealer and tell him this is the system you want.

The Electro-Voice Marquis (enclosure) with SP12B 12″ Coaxial Speaker: Two of these fine speakers are used in a stereo system. Price is $98 for each in mahogany; slightly higher in walnut or blond limed oak. Use the new Electro-Voice Magneramic stereo cartridge for stereo or monaural records. Model 21 MD, $19.50 with .7—mil diamond stylus.

The Harman-Kardon Trio (Model A224) Stereo Amplifier: Stereo control center. Powerful 24 watt stereo amplifier. Dimensions are 13¹³⁄₁₆″ w. x 4⅜″ h. x 11½″ d. Price $99.95. Enclosure optional, $7.00.

The Harman-Kardon Duet (Model T224): AM/FM stereo tuner, matches the A224. Superb for stereo and standard reception. Includes exclusive Harman-Kardon stereo indexer. Price, $114.95.

The Rek-O-Kut Rondine, professional quality stereo and monaural turntable (Model N33H). Single-speed (33⅓ rpm). Dimensions for cabinet installation—17¾″ x 16⅜″. Styled by George Nelson. Feather-light Rek-O-Kut tonearm tracks perfectly, protects records against wear. Turntable and tonearm, $97.90.

Custom Stereo Components By

ELECTRO-VOICE · HARMAN-KARDON · REK-O-KUT
Buchanan, Mich.   Westbury, N.Y.   Long Island City, N.Y.

Electro-Voice Marquis   Harman-Kardon Duet   Rek-O-Kut Rondine Stereo Turntable & Tonearm   Electro-Voice Marquis

S YOUR LIVING ROOM SMALL ENOUGH FOR STEREO?

Stereo Components, Dept. A1
444 Madison Avenue
New York 22

Please send me your free brochure on stereo and stereo high fidelity component systems.

Name ....

Address ....

City ....Zone .... State ....

EHR-6

Source: Electro-Voice, Inc.

The hi-fi show was a form of promotion associated primarily with component manufacturers. Held annually in most major cities, the show featured equipment displays by leading component makers, and included displays by local radio stations and dealers. The shows, often held in large downtown hotels, lasted several days and the New York City fair lasted a full week. Shows drew large crowds of people who walked from room to room listening to demonstrations, meeting company executives, and picking up promotional literature.

Customer appeals

According to component manufacturers, components had four advantages over package sets: (1) The consumer could design his own set. He could choose parts by different manufacturers to build the set which sounded best to him. (2) Components were flexible. When a better component became available, the old one could be discarded; thus the consumer could improve his set part by part instead of scrapping it to buy a whole new one. (3) Components offered good sound reproduction, and if the consumer was willing to spend over $150, he could buy better sound reproduction with components than with a package set. The savings associated with components were due in large measure to savings in cabinet costs and in assembly labor. (4) Components avoided the inevitable distortion that comes from having loudspeakers and record player in the same cabinet.

Package set makers also claimed that their products had four advantages: (1) Package sets were convenient. They did not require wires strung around the room, there were a minimum number of controls and plugs, and the entire set was usually in one place. (2) They were available in fashionable furniture, a real consideration for the housewife. (3) A wide selection was available at prices below those of components, e.g., from $100 to $200. (4) The package set could be designed as an entire system by an expert; thus the various parts could be balanced in relation to one another. In contrast, when a consumer designed his own set, sound reproduction might suffer through imbalance, even with the finest components.

So far as price appeals were concerned, the only component sets available for under $100 came unassembled in kit form, whereas package sets started at $19.95. In the top price range—$1,200 to $2,000—components had little competition from package sets. In the price range between $100 and $1,200 both types were available. For many listeners price was a primary consideration, and many had a better idea of what they could afford to pay than of any other factor.

Some customers who wanted high fidelity might be motivated by its snob appeal, and this factor often made the customer inclined toward components. Spending more for a "co-axial" or "horn-loaded" speaker system gave the consumer something to display to his neighbors—something expensive yet "necessary for those who appreciate the best." The importance of hi-fi as a status symbol was widely recognized, but its significance for the industry could not be determined by the researcher.

Quality was also a major customer appeal, but, as previously noted, customers varied in their ability to perceive the quality of sound reproduction. Some differences in perceptive ability had their basis in individual physiology; others were age or sex determined. For example, an ear that could hear up to 20,000 cps at age 20 might well only hear up to 10,000 to 12,000 cps by age 65.[14] It was also widely believed that women were more sensitive than men to high frequency sounds, even though both sexes could hear them.

Of more importance was the fact that there were wide differences in what two physiologically equal ears might hear while listening to the same sound reproduction system at the same time. The listener with a trained ear would actually hear more than the casual listener, and be more sensitive to the quality of sound reproduction. The trained ear might notice, for instance, that the bass reproduction was weak, or missing, or quite distorted.

The ability of the ear to become increasingly sophisticated or trained might be crucial for the future development of the industry. If most ears became more highly trained, one could expect equipment to be made to more exacting standards. In addition, the training of the ear would tend to make the listener dissatisfied with his present equipment and a likely customer for an improved system.

For most customers, selection of sound reproduction equipment was rendered difficult by a variety of factors: indiscriminate use of the term hi-fi to describe almost any phonograph, conflicting advertising claims, and wide variations in price and products. Other sources of bewilderment included the customer's ignorance of engineering aspects, and his vague sense that the industry was in the throes of such rapid technological change that the item bought today might be obsolete tomorrow. Under these conditions, many customers placed a heavy reliance on help and advice obtained from the dealer.

The role of the dealer

Package and component dealers performed functions which were different in some respects. While many dealers carried both kinds of equipment, it is useful to separate the two for purposes of analysis.

Included among the package set dealers were department stores, music stores, and furniture and appliance outlets. One department store in a major city carried half-a-dozen brands, had three sound rooms for demonstration purposes, and carried a wide variety of sets from the table models to console stereo sets selling for $1,200 and up. High fidelity and TV shared a service department where customers could bring sets in need of repair. For this store, then, the major aspects of selling were display, demonstration, and willingness to provide service. A salesman at this department store said:

Our job here is to help. People who come in here are really in the dark. Many don't even know what high fidelity is. Up to a certain limit of knowledge, it's very easy to sell them, but beyond that point they just come in to look

---

[14]The loss of the frequencies from 10,000 to 20,000 was the equivalent of one octave.

around, they usually don't buy. When they start asking technical questions, you generally won't make a sale. It turns out they are looking for information. And when someone starts asking about amplifier circuits or magnet weights, it generally turns out they are building a component set.

But like I say, a lot of people come in here with only the advice of some relative who is an engineer. I had a woman here this morning who said her son told her to insist on three speakers. It's typical, and we could sell them junk if it had three speakers. We wouldn't do it of course. People have a lot of trust in the brands we sell here.

As far as stereo goes, way over half the people who come in here don't know what it is. I had a man buy a $450 stereo set today and then ask me how stereo worked. And when the wives come along, they are more interested in how it will look as furniture than what is in the box.

In a survey of 57 department stores, *The New Yorker* magazine found that department stores rated the brand names as the general package set characteristic of most interest to consumers, while the number of speakers was the *high-fidelity* characteristic package set customers thought was most important (see Exhibit 12).

Component dealers varied in size from small record shops with a component sideline to multistore component dealers selling nationwide via a mail-order catalogue. Most large department stores did not carry components. The most important component dealers were the large combination discount and mail-order catalogue dealers. Among the best known in the latter group were the Radio Shack in Boston, Sam Goody in New York City, and Allied Radio in Chicago. Allied Radio had over 500 employees, over 180,000 square feet of floor space, and several affiliated companies including one making its private "Knight" brand of components. In a 448-page catalogue, Allied listed over 32,000 stocked items. The Radio Shack had over 300 employees. Its private label "Realistic" brand was made in Japan. It had two multistory outlets in Boston and another store in New Haven.

The Radio Shack appeared to be representative of the discount mail-order dealers. One manufacturer described the role of the Radio Shack as having helped "open the New England hi-fi market through its newspaper advertisements, mail-order catalogue, and discount bargains." The Radio Shack's two Boston stores were both stocked with a wide line of component parts, records, and other small appliances. In addition, by 1958 one outlet had added a few package sets. At each location it had several demonstration studios of approximately living room size where a customer could compare the sound qualities of different combinations of equipment. Company salesmen assumed the role of an audio consultant; that is, a person familiar with the technical jargon and also able to point out strong and weak points in individual pieces of merchandise. Part of the salesmen's function was to recommend groups of components that could be combined into a suitable set. One salesman noted that he tried to "keep the customer from getting confused. We try to find their price range first and then show them three or four com-

Exhibit 12

HIGH-FIDELITY SURVEY RESULTS

	Department Stores	Music Stores	Both Types Combined
2. *a*) In making the sale is cabinet styling:			
Becoming more important	74.6%	74.1%	74.4%
Remaining the same	23.7	25.9	24.4
Becoming less important	1.7	...	1.2
	100.0%	100.0%	100.0%

3. In the list below, please number in order of importance the three strongest general sales influences on your customers:

	Department Stores	Music Stores	Both Types Combined
Performance of set.....................	3rd	1st	1st
Brand name	1st	2nd	2nd
Your sales staff	2nd	3rd	3rd
Advertisements	5th	4th	4th
Price	4th	5th	5th
Advice of audiophile friends	6th	6th	6th
High-fidelity shows	7th	7th (tie)	7th
Printed technical specifications	8th	7th (tie)	8th

4. What percentage of your total customers request a specific brand by name when looking at high-fidelity equipment: 48.0% (Department Stores), 45.1% (Music Stores), 47.1% (Both Types Combined)

7. Rank in order the high-fidelity features below that your customers consider most important:

	Department Stores	Music Stores	Both Types Combined
Number of speakers	1st	2nd	1st
Overall sound qualities	2nd	1st	2nd
Amplifier power	3rd	3rd	3rd
Diamond stylus	4th	4th	4th
Record changing operation	5th	5th	5th
Type of cartridge	6th	6th	6th

14. What percentage of your total high-fidelity console business would you estimate was done in sets selling:

	Department Stores	Music Stores	Both Types Combined
Under $300	66.9%	36.9%	57.7%
$300 to $499	24.3	38.5	28.6
$500 to $999	8.1	18.8	11.4
$1,000 and over	0.7	5.8	2.3
	100.0%	100.0%	100.0%

15. Are the salesmen in your present high-fidelity department:

	Department Stores	Music Stores	Both Types Combined
On a permanent basis?	96.6%	96.3%	96.5%
On a semipermanent basis?	1.7	...	1.2
Regularly rotated to other departments?	1.7	3.7	2.3
	100.0%	100.0%	100.0%

Note: These final few questions are about component parts of high fidelity (i.e., separate speakers, amplifiers, tuners, etc.) as distinct from preassembled consoles.

20. Do you carry components:

	Department Stores	Music Stores	Both Types Combined
Yes	6.8%	37.0%	16.3%
No	93.2	63.0	83.7
	100.0%	100.0%	100.0%

21. Please check the major reason or reasons below as to why you do not carry components (answered only by those not carrying components):

	Department Stores	Music Stores	Both Types Combined
Necessity of large and diversified inventory	1st	2nd	1st
Problem of meeting discount competition	6th	1st	2nd
Difficulty of demonstration and store installation	3rd	3rd	3rd

Exhibit 12—Continued

	Department Stores	Music Stores	Both Types Combined
Lack of adequate floor space in store ...	2nd	4th (tie)	4th
Lack of interest by your departments' customers	4th	8th	5th (tie)
Length of time to make a sale	5th	4th (tie)	5th (tie)
Problem of proper installation in the home	7th	6th (tie)	7th
Problem of giving salesmen proper technical training	8th	6th (tie)	8th
Problem of home servicing	9th	...	9th

Source: A survey made for *The New Yorker* magazine by its research staff. Data based upon answers to questionnaires returned by 86 leading department stores and music stores. Survey results published by *The New Yorker* in pamphlet form, copyright, 1958.

binations in that range. More than three or four and they seem to get too confused to buy."

The Radio Shack appealed to consumers on the basis of price as well as quality. It featured a wide array of "deals" whereby a customer received a discount for buying a specified set of components, and it had its own line of lower-priced "Realistic" components. The "Realistic II" set, for example, was listed in the 1958 catalogue as follows:

```
Realistic 10-watt Amplifier
Realistic 8″ Loudspeaker
Collaro TC-340GE Record Changer
Wood base for Collaro
New GE 4G-050 Dual Sapphire Pickup
Separate-Parts-Price ...................... $89.20
Net ...................................   69.95
```

The "deals" were made up of "quality-matched" components selected and balanced by the Radio Shack. The "preselected" sets were priced to save the consumer 25% of list without necessitating price cutting on any given piece of equipment. A Radio Shack executive noted, "We are basically selling packages of components, and price is becoming more important in these sales."

Typical of the discount, mail-order operations, the Radio Shack was larger than many component manufacturers. Partly as a result, it played a different role from that of a department store selling RCA or GE sets. It undertook extensive cooperative advertising campaigns with manufacturers, and had eight people in its own advertising department to handle layout, copy, and other aspects of promotion. The Radio Shack was able to take advantage of quantity discounts and to negotiate arrangements with manufacturers for special promotions.

In addition, as a result of its tests, the Radio Shack might return merchandise or merely stock an item without trying to sell it. Said one executive:

Some items we sell, others we just carry in stock. And that goes for the equipment of each manufacturer. If he has one or two good items, the salesmen will recommend them. Other items the customer will have to ask for. We'll carry it, but we won't try to sell it.

The most important criterion in our recommendations is quality. We want the product to stay sold. But we also consider profit margins and special commitments to manufacturers. Our salesmen generally don't know about different markups—so they generally sell on the basis of their own opinions. Of course, we try to keep them informed and well guided.

In increasing numbers, smaller dealers were carrying hi-fi components. Typically they, too, had demonstration facilities, though both the facilities and the selection of components were relatively limited. For some outlets, components were a specialty; for others they supplemented records, package sets, and appliances. In any case, the role of the dealer or salesman of components was still that of the "audio advisor" or consultant.

Component loudspeaker manufacturers

In 1958 the Institute of High Fidelity Manufacturers listed 35 component loudspeaker and speaker-system manufacturers among its members. Twenty of these companies made only the one component, although some of these were diversified outside of the components industry (see Exhibits 13 and 14). Product lines varied widely, with some small firms making only two or three models in a narrow price range while others, like Electro Voice, made over 20 speakers and speaker systems with prices ranging from $65 to $1,062.

There were three characteristics relating to loudspeakers which differentiated them from other components. First, they were the component where design and engineering concepts differed the most widely. Numerous different types were available, each with its strong and weak points, and each with loyal adherents. (A more technical discussion of some aspects of the most common type of loudspeaker may be found in the Appendix at the end of this case.)

Second, the loudspeaker was widely recognized as the weak link in the high-fidelity system. A hi-fi system was like a chain in that the quality of the final sound output was dependent on the weakest link. Since the perfection of the LP record, the loudspeaker had given the poorest relative performance. This situation was due mainly to the numerous compromises made when translating electrical energy from the amplifier into mechanical energy, and finally into acoustical energy. To help offset speaker deficiencies, progress had been made in amplifier design which helped compensate for shortcomings in the speaker.

Third, and largely as a result of the two factors discussed above, speaker manufacturers tended to be the most optimistic in their advertising claims.

Exhibit 13

COMPONENT LOUDSPEAKERS

Brand names of loudspeakers and loudspeaker systems produced by companies making no other components:

Acoustic Research	Janszen	Stentorian
Bozak	Kingdom Lounz	Tri-Channel
Bradford	KLH	University
Cabinart	Klipsch	Vitavox
Frazier	James B. Lansing	Wharfdale
Goodmans	R. J.	Wigo
Hartley	Racon	

Companies making loudspeakers and *one* other component:

A. M. I.—(amplifier)
National—(amplifier)
Stephens—(amplifier)
L. E. E.—tape recorders
Duotone—cartridges

Companies making loudspeakers and *two* other components:

E. I. C. O.—(amplifier + tuner)
Radio Craftsman—(amplifier + tuner)
Sherwood—(amplifier + tuner)
Taunoy—(amplifier + cartridge)

Companies making loudspeakers and *three* or more other components:

Altec Lansing—3
Electro-Voice—3
General Electric—3
Gray—4
Pilot—3
Weathers—4

Source: Institute of High-Fidelity Manufacturers.

Published statistics were often misleading, as the following quotations will illustrate:

The writer was once present at a demonstration of a loudspeaker whose bass response was supposed to extend to 20 cps. The demonstrator turned his audio signal generator on at 20 cps, and the loudspeaker "responded" vigorously, with a noise resembling machine-gun fire. Perhaps a tiny fraction of the sound was 20 cps energy; in any meaningful language this speaker could not have been described as having output at 20 cps. Its frequency range rating should have been restricted to that portion of the spectrum in which harmonic distortion was kept reasonably low.[15]

* * * * *

A 3-inch speaker for portable radios will "respond" when stimulated by a 30 cps signal—perhaps by having its cone tear loose and fly out into the air— and almost any speaker, even a woofer will make some kind of sound when stimulated by a high powered 15,000 cps signal. A frequency response rating must mean something more than that a signal of given frequency makes a

[15]"Loudspeakers," *Audio Magazine,* May 1956, p. 46.

Exhibit 14

DATA ON COMPONENT LOUDSPEAKER MANUFACTURERS

Name of Company	Estimated Sales and Profits		Total Assets 1957	Date Founded	Number of Employees 1957	Loudspeakers and Price Range	Loudspeaker Systems and Price Range
	1956	1957					
R. T. Bozak:			$ 150,000	1949	10	4 speakers, from $31 to $83	1 system, $78.75
Sales	$ 275,000	Over $ 300,000					
Profit	*	$ *					
Klipsch and Associates:			80,000	1945	7	"Approves" and uses speakers manufactured by Electro-Voice	4 systems, $350 to $820
Sales	117,000	101,000					
Gross profit	56,000	52,000					
Net profit	7,000	7,000					
KLH Research & Development:			*	1957	*	None	6 systems, $124 to $390
Sales	*	Under 100,000					
Profit	*	*					
James B. Lansing Sound:			450,000	1946	*	7 speakers, $29 to $125	8 systems, $166 to $855
Sales†	2,000,000	2,600,000					
Profit	*	*					
University Loudspeakers:			2,200,000	1938	*	24 speakers, $13 to $154	7 systems, $136 to $341
Sales	Over 2,500,000	Over 2,000,000					
Net profit	250,000	200,000					

*No estimate.

†Sales figures include some speakers for outdoor commercial use.

Source: Sales and profit estimates by a high-fidelity component manufacturer, except data on Klipsch, which is based on published figures. Speaker models and prices from 1958 catalogues of Allied Radio and the Radio Shack.

speaker move audibly, or that it makes an amplifier show an electrical output of some sort at its terminals. It must mean that within a stated frequency range, and for power devices within a stated range of power, the fundamental output of a given device is uniform to a stated degree.[16]

In addition to printing optimistic statistics, component-speaker manufacturers tended to withhold some data because it was not flattering. In a questionnaire sent by a group of Harvard Business School students to a dozen speaker manufacturers, every one refused to furnish a response curve for any model, generally because "the only valid response curve would be in the room where it was to be used. Besides, the best way to measure the quality of *our* speaker is to listen to it."

Current industry development

In the fall of 1958 three developments appeared to overshadow others in the rapidly changing sound reproduction industry. These developments were (1) a growing interest in stereophonic sound, (2) an increasing share of the market for components, and (3) a blurring of the distinction between components and package sets. In addition, there were indications of two possible future developments which might have a major impact on the industry: the growing popularity of tape recordings, and the concept of a single home entertainment center which would include TV and phonograph.

Stereo. Easily the most important change in the industry since the LP record was the introduction of stereophonic sound. "Stereo," as it was known in the industry, was the reproduction of sound through two separate systems, each of which produced slightly different sounds. To record a stereo disc or tape, sound was introduced through two (or more) microphones in different locations and *these sounds remained separate* even though they might use the same disc or tape for storage. The listener could mount one speaker to his left and hear it emphasize the violins, while the other, to his right, emphasized the violas and drums. The effect aimed at was one of "spaciousness" or "presence," with the listener having an illusion of an orchestra arrayed around his living room.

The demand for stereo was important for two major reasons. First, it probably would increase the new equipment market by attracting new music fans. Second, it would stimulate sales of additional equipment to people who already had "monophonic" sets. Conversion of a monophonic set to stereo required almost a 100% increase in equipment, while purchase of a stereo set from scratch would cost about 75% more than comparable quality in an ordinary hi-fi set.

The speed with which stereo would grow seemed to depend upon the speed with which a wide selection of stereo records could be produced and distributed. While stereo could be achieved on tapes and through tuners, it was not likely to stimulate much in the way of equipment sales until the new

---

[16]"High Fidelity Standards," *Audio Magazine*, November 1955, p. 42.

records were available. In the spring of 1959 stereophonic discs were being marketed in increasing quantities, although many were only of fair quality in the opinion of the researcher and others in the industry. In comparing the probable development of the stereo disc with that of the LP record, *The New York Times* noted:

The chances are that it will take a period of adjustment before the stereo disk achieves the perfection of the modern LP record. This is to be expected. It took about seven years for LP to iron out its bugs. It will not take stereo that long. The industry, for once, seems to have decided that there will be none of the mess that characterized the early days of LP—different speeds and an infinity of different recording curves.[17]

Some manufacturers were predicting a lift in sales late in 1958, while others looked to 1959 as the first real year of stereo. As to how extensive the ultimate demand for stereo might be, opinion varied widely.

While even an untrained ear could discern the special qualities of stereo, the researcher believed there were important limitations on its ability to produce an illusion of three-dimensional sound. In the first place, loudspeaker

Exhibit 15

Permission of the artist, copyright 1959, The New Yorker Magazine, Inc.

separation of from six to ten feet was necessary to achieve the stereophonic effect under ordinary living room conditions. Second, the stereophonic effect was not present in the entire room, but only along a path perpendicular to an imaginary line connecting the two speakers. One had to sit or stand in this path to "hear stereo" (see Exhibit 15).

The nature of the program material also affected the ability of stereo to produce a three-dimensional effect. With a train, bowling ball, or other special program material, the illusion was striking. With choral material it could also be impressive, for example, separating men's and women's

---

[17]*The New York Times*, March 16, 1958.

voices. But for orchestral material the effects were less noticeable. It should be noted, however, that the significance of the stereo illusion was the subject of wide debate, and the researcher was unable to obtain either a "consensus" of experts or a "feeling" for the long-term industry trend.

One factor that might help to prompt a widespread acceptance of stereo was the possibility that monophonic records might be displaced on dealers' shelves. *The New York Times* stated this point as follows:

First, several of the major record companies have been taking most of their original tapes in stereo for some years, and just about all are doing so now. There is a very good start, therefore, for an all-stereo disk repertory. Second, within a few short months there will be a flood of stereo record reproducing equipment at all price levels, from table model phonographs up. Third, record dealers are not going to react favorably to the idea of carrying dual lines in stock for any longer than is absolutely necessary. Dealers can and do exert pressure that would make an oil lobbyist grit his teeth in envy. Fourth, present investments in LP record collections need not be sacrificed when purchasing stereo because there is no question in anyone's mind that a stereo pickup will be able to play standard records very well: it will.[18]

On the other hand, the high cost of a stereophonic system was widely regarded as a factor that would impede widespread acceptance of stereo. "At a rough guess, the price for a minimum hi-fi stereo disk unit will be $550 for component parts. This assumes starting from scratch. The addition of an amplifier–preamplifier, speaker system, and cartridge to an already existing set should be near $200."[19] While so-called "stereo" sets were already on sale for $39.95, the researcher believed that they neither offered the stereo effect nor high-quality sound reproduction. Even higher-priced sets suffered the same shortcomings.

Increasing share of the market for components. Predicted for 1958 was a rise in the sales of components and a decline in package sets:

This prediction of a [component] sales pickup comes at a time when the larger package manufacturers . . . are looking for a dip in sales to about $400 million, down from last year's $453 million.

Ironically, the reason for the decline in packaged items and the increase in component sales is credited to the same cause—stereophonic sound.[20]

Stereo appeared likely to help the sale of components in two ways. First, it required a more complicated system, and in most cases a system with at least two separate parts. By accepting this feature, consumers were moving in the direction of accepting separate components. Second, stereo placed more emphasis on careful listening to the music and thus was expected to aid components which focused on high-quality sound.

Another factor that might contribute to an increasing share of the market

---

[18]*Ibid.*
[19]*Ibid.*
[20]*Wall Street Journal,* October 14, 1958.

for components was their widening national distribution. Well-known brands were available even in smaller cities, through a growing network of record shops and small dealers.

Growing similarity of component and package sets. A third trend was the blurring of the difference between package and component sets. There were at least three signs that the gap between the two was closing. First, some manufacturers were diversifying and producing both components and package sets. Among the component manufacturers, Fisher Radio and Pilot Radio had introduced high-quality package sets. Among package set makers, companies such as Stromberg-Carlson, GE, and RCA were producing and advertising a line of components. Second, the quality gap between components and package sets appeared to be narrowing. While still well below the performance of good components, package sets were improving. On the other hand, some components were entering the market more on the basis of price than quality. Among them were some of the private brands marketed by some of the discount houses. Third, some package sets were being manufactured in two or even more separated pieces. Such sets constituted a cross between single-package models and six- and seven-part component rigs.

Other trends. There were two additional possible trends for the more distant future: One was the increasing popularity of the tape recorder, and the other a growing acceptance of the idea of a single "home entertainment center," comprising both a phonograph and TV.

Tape recording, already in wide use professionally, offered several advantages. Tape eliminated surface noise, did not wear out as rapidly as discs, and offered fully comparable sound reproduction qualities. In 1958 tapes were superior to records for the reproduction of stereophonic sound.

Tape recorders and tape playback units (called tape "decks") usually could be played through a hi-fi system without any modifications to recorder or set. They had, however, two major drawbacks in 1958: a top-grade tape deck cost $500 to $600 or more, and this cost had to be added to that of the rest of the sound reproduction system. Second, studio recorded tapes were quite expensive. As stated by one source, "Stereo tape recordings . . . are available for those who can afford them (about $10–$20 for a single tape which will last half an hour) . . . some are really awe inspiring if played on the right equipment."[21]

A second possible long-run trend was the utilization of TV amplifier and speakers as the second part of the home sound reproduction system. In fact, it seemed possible that manufacturers would offer matched TV and phonograph sets. While most TV sets used sound equipment distinctly inferior to components (and even to many package sets), some advertisements were already appearing which called attention to the sound qualities of the TV set. It seemed probable that more emphasis on this aspect would soon appear, since a TV-phonograph combination offered the consumer a chance to save

[21]*Consumers Bulletin*, April 1958, p. 10.

money by utilizing his TV amplifier and loudspeaker instead of purchasing additional components to fill out for stereo. Unless the television sound system were roughly of equal quality to the phonograph, the stereo effect was apt to be compromised.

APPENDIX

This appendix is not an indispensable part of the industry note. It is intended to provide supplemental information for (1) those who are interested in hi-fi, and (2) other persons who may wish to read a little more about some of the technical aspects of speaker design and construction.

The loudspeaker is a mechanical system which oscillates in such a way

Exhibit 1

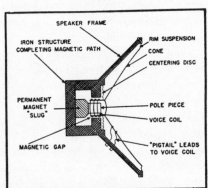

as to alternately push and pull nearby air—thus creating sound waves. However, to push and pull air satisfactorily, the speaker must have an enclosure; speaker and enclosure really form a single unit in a sound reproduction system. For purposes of convenience we will separate the two, considering first the speaker.

There are two principal types of speakers, the conventional moving coil speaker and the "electrostatic." The moving coil speaker, so-called because a coil oscillates in response to an alternating electric signal fed into it while it is immersed in a fixed magnetic field, is the more common. The alternating signal in the coil causes a second nonfixed magnetic field to form around the coil. The magnetic field of the coil alternates in polarity, and hence is alternately attracted and repelled by the fixed magnetic field. This alternating attraction and repulsion produces motion along the axis of the coil. Since the electric signals alternate in the same manner as the original sound source, the resulting oscillations of the coil are similar to those of the sound source (Exhibit 1).

The oscillations of a coil, however, are about as effective at producing sound as a motor-driven fan is with the blades removed. In both cases something must be added to give the movements a bite of the surrounding air. Hence a cone is attached to the coil to allow it to push and pull the air. The cone moves along the axis of the coil and is supported by elastic suspensions attached to a frame. The suspensions serve two functions. They allow the cone to move while staying on axis, which prevents the coil from rubbing against the magnet. In addition, they stretch (like a rubber band) when the cone moves forward, and exert a pull which helps bring back or "restore" the cone to its rest position.

Let us neglect the workings of the electrostatic speaker in favor of an exploration of some of the problems encountered in achieving high-fidelity performance from the dynamic loudspeaker. One of the major problems is caused by the elastic cone suspensions. With each lower octave the cone must quadruple its distance of travel to maintain constant power output (or to have a flat response with respect to input signals of varying frequencies). To reproduce very low frequencies, considerable stretch in the elastic suspensions is required. Beyond its "elastic limit" the suspension system becomes harder to stretch (try stretching a rubber band); thus cone movement is foreshortened at low frequencies, and declining sound output and distortion result.

In contrast, to produce high frequencies the cone travels a very short distance. Hence some of the construction problems for high and low frequency speakers are quite different. High-quality systems therefore use two or more separate speakers; one for low frequencies (called a woofer) and another for the high frequencies (called a "tweeter"). In loudspeaker construction, the signal from the amplifier is filtered so that only low frequency signals reach the woofer and only high frequency signals reach the tweeter. This filtering process is accomplished by a "crossover network."

Another important problem in loudspeaker design is the separation of the vibrations produced in front of the cone from those produced behind. As the cone moves forward building up air pressure in front of itself, it reduces the pressure behind, and the opposite happens as the cone reverses direction. The resulting compressions and rarefactions would tend to cancel out unless speaker enclosure construction prevented it (see Exhibit 2).

There are two principal ways of separating the vibrations produced at the front and back of the cone. One utilizes an infinite baffle for separation, and the other an enclosed cabinet. The infinite baffle is familiar to those who have seen speakers mounted in walls, closet doors, chimneys, and the like. To provide a complete separation at 40 cps the baffle must be 14 feet across, hence the use of walls instead of furniture. The enclosed cabinet surmounts this problem by killing vibrations in an acoustically absorbent sealed chamber. When sturdily constructed and lined with a material such as fiber glass, the cabinet is able to absorb or deaden the interior vibrations.

The enclosed cabinet has an important problem, however, in that the enclosed volume of air becomes a pneumatic spring. Thus, when the cone moves forward, it reduces the air pressure in the cabinet—or creates a partial vacuum. This partial vacuum affects movements of the cone unless the enclosure is large. Unless the enclosure is sufficiently large, or the pneumatic spring made a part of the speaker design [see Acoustic Research, Inc. (A)], the effect will be one of attenuated bass reproduction. (Adequate cabinet size for a 12-inch speaker is approximately seven to nine cubic feet; for a 15-inch speaker, nine to twelve cubic feet.) Enclosures of such size are obviously expensive to build (they require a considerable amount of furniture alone), and they occupy a considerable share of an ordinary-size room.

This discussion of speakers and enclosures is considerably simplified, overlooks many problems including those of resonant frequencies, and deals with only the most popular speaker and enclosures. Resonant (or bass-reflex) and horn-type enclosures are the other two major enclosure types. A discussion of their design problems would require further expansion of the complexities of acoustical design in loudspeaker-system construction.

Exhibit 2

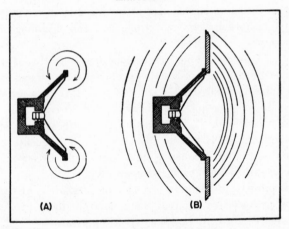

(A)   (B)

A final word, however, on the sound output of a system is in order. Sound, as heard by the listener, is also affected by the acoustics of the room environment in which the speaker system is located, and the location of the speaker within the room. These factors are sometimes overlooked but constitute an integral and important part of the design of the sound-reproduction system.

ACOUSTIC RESEARCH, INC. (A)*

∧∧

In the fall of 1958 the management of Acoustic Research was considering a major shift in corporate objectives. Instead of manufacturing a single product—high-fidelity loudspeaker systems—the company was considering production of a wider line of components with the eventual goal of introducing a component set for the home reproduction of recorded music. Management projected a two-stage expansion, with the first stage aimed at filling out its component line with a turntable and then an amplifier. The second stage would include the introduction of a two- or three-piece component set.

A speaker system, an amplifier, and a record player were the three basic units in a complete component set, although additional components could be incorporated. (See Exhibit 1.) In 1958 the speaker systems manufactured by Acoustic Research were being sold to the consumer for use with components made by other manufacturers.

According to company management, "AR" loudspeaker systems had three

Exhibit 1

COMPONENTS IN A HIGH-FIDELITY SYSTEM

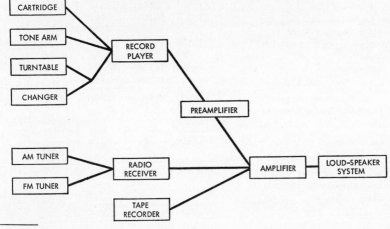

---

distinguishing characteristics—high quality, low price, and small overall size. This combination of qualities was made possible by a revolutionary change in loudspeaker design which had been patented by the company's founder. Management believed that with this radical improvement in design, AR was beginning to acquire a position of leadership in the industry.

Incorporated in 1954, Acoustic Research had begun production in the spring of 1955. In 1957 sales of approximately $1 million gave the company about 6% of the component speaker market, and placed it as about average in sales among component manufacturers. The results of four years of operations included continued sales growth, increased profits, and a strengthened financial position (see Exhibits 2 and 3). Sales volume in October 1958 was the largest in company history. To meet demand for increased production, AR had moved in 1956 from a "one-floor" loft to a four-story factory building in East Cambridge, Massachusetts. Employment had increased from six to fifty workers during the same period.

Exhibit 2

ACOUSTIC RESEARCH, INC.

Profit and Loss Statements for Years Ending December 31,
1954–57, and for Six Months Ending June 28, 1958

	1954	1955	1956	1957	First Six Months* 1958
Sales	$ 0	$56,773	$383,258	$973,262	$568,298
Less cost of sales:					
Direct labor	253	5,435	37,864	92,227	48,389
Net raw materials	...	29,997	182,689	528,112	242,502
Manufacturing overhead	35	400	11,100	98,794	72,269
R.&D. (not including labor)	908	56	7,568	6,940	4,497
Cost of sales	$1,196	$35,888	$239,231	$726,073	$367,657
Gross profit	(1,196)	20,885	144,027	247,189	200,642
Less operating expenses:					
Advertising and promotion	1,198	3,252	20,806	48,406	35,617
Shipping	9	1,188	4,548	10,553	5,106
Administrative	1,656	14,858	77,507	117,449	47,209
Total Operating Expenses	$2,863	$19,298	$102,861	$176,408	$ 87,932
Net profit from operations	(4,059)	1,587	41,166	70,781	112,710
Add purchase discounts and other income	...	...	...	4,285	5,070
Total Income	$(4,059)	$ 1,587	$ 41,166	$ 75,066	$117,780
Less other charges	...	...	...	3,920	11,405
Net profit before taxes	$(4,059)	$ 1,587	$ 41,166	$ 71,146	$106,375
Less federal and state income taxes	...	...	14,748	33,986	61,300
Net Income	$(4,059)	$ 1,587	$ 26,418	$ 37,160	$ 45,075

*Company accounting practices were modified during 1957. These modifications affected allocations in manufacturing overhead and administrative expenses particularly, since some supervisory help was shifted from the latter account to the former.

Source: Company records.

Exhibit 3

ACOUSTIC RESEARCH, INC.

Balance Sheets as of December 31, 1954–57, and June 28, 1958

	1954	1955	1956	1957	June 1958
Assets					
Current Assets:					
Cash	$ 1,443	$ 388	$ 10,703	$ 6,217	$ 3,097
Accounts receivable—assigned	...	...	...	125,604	80,055
Accounts receivable—unassigned	...	11,894	46,405	...	5,003
Inventories	2,264	5,760	43,127	69,297	183,864‡
Loans and exchanges	...	...	...	322	810
Total Current Assets	$3,707	$18,042	$100,235	$201,440	$272,829
Plant and equipment	$ 777	$ 1,466	$ 10,849	$ 34,017	$ 39,283
Less: Accumulated depreciation	35	396	1,754	9,389	17,574
Total Fixed Assets	$ 742	$ 1,070	$ 9,095	$ 24,628	$ 21,709
Patents, trademarks, and goodwill	10,000	10,000	10,000	1	1
Other assets	...	160	150	2,514	5,767
Total Assets	$14,449	$29,272	$119,480	$228,583	$300,306
Liabilities					
Current Liabilities:					
Notes payable—secured by accounts receivable	...	...	...	$ 43,921	$ 21,521
Notes payable—unsecured	...	...	...	...	25,000
Accounts payable—trade	$ 1,528	$10,060	$ 33,826	53,365	30,458
Miscellaneous accruals	730	434	21,119	13,876	21,236
Federal and state income taxes payable	...	...	14,749	34,770	15,635
Estimated income tax (current)	...	...	...	...	61,300
Total Current Liabilities	$ 2,258	$10,494	$ 69,694	$145,932	$175,150
Reserve for bad debts	...	...	...	5,767	6,537
Capital:					
Capital stock:					
Class A—no par value 1,300 shares authorized and issued	16,250	21,250	26,000	26,000	26,000
Class B—no par value 100 shares authorized—5 issued in 1958	...	...	...	...	560
Retained earnings	(4,059)	(2,472)	23,786*	50,844†	92,059
Total Liabilities and Capital	$14,449	$29,272	$119,480	$228,583	$300,306

*Retained earnings figure does not equal previous figure plus net income because of adjustments.

†Retained earnings figure includes write-down of patent from $10,000 to $1, and tax adjustment.

‡Of the total inventory, $78,854 represented finished goods, $105,000 represented raw materials and work in process.

Source: Company records.

Field research relationship and case design

The reception accorded to the university's field researcher by management and employees of AR was characterized by complete cooperation. The executives allowed the researcher unlimited freedom to interview personnel and to observe all phases of company operations and management behavior. They gave free access to all financial and operating records of the company. The attitude of the group, as expressed by one member, was, "We have no secrets. We want to share our knowledge. We hope that our experience may contribute to a better understanding of business organizations." In keeping with this point of view, management asked that the case be written using the company's real name.

Data about Acoustic Research are reported in a series of four cases. Acoustic Research, Inc. (A) contains pertinent technical data about the product line, and information on sales, finance, manufacturing, employee relations, and research and development.

Acoustic Research, Inc. (B) summarizes information about members of company management. First, data are reported about the individual members of management, their background, interests, and aspirations. Secondly, the case describes how the individual members of management worked with one another, and it reports several examples of group behavior.

Acoustic Research, Inc. (C) reports on the process by which major corporate objectives and policies were formulated by management. Specific data are given about key policies in regard to licensing, advertising, and products and pricing. In addition, data are presented on management's assessment of competitive conditions and on company strategy for the future.

Acoustic Research, Inc. (D) reports on developments occurring in the company up to and including 1964.

The product

In 1958 there were three loudspeaker systems in the AR line. Each was composed of three basic elements—a woofer, or low frequency speaker, a tweeter, or high frequency speaker, and a cabinet. These three elements, when properly combined, permitted the speaker system to reproduce the audible range of sound. Exhibit 4 summarizes data for AR's three models.

The most distinctive characteristic of an AR loudspeaker was its "acoustic suspension" woofer. Acoustic suspension was a revolutionary way of constructing low frequency loudspeakers which had been developed and patented by Mr. Edgar Villchur, founder and president of the company.

In simplest terms, acoustic suspension utilizes the principle of a vacuum. When the cone of the speaker moves forward to create sound vibrations, it reduces the air pressure in the sealed enclosure. The reduced air pressure in the cabinet then provides about 90% of the "restoring force" which pulls the speaker back to its original position (see Exhibit 5). Conventional speakers use an elastic material, which stretches like a rubber band, to provide this restoring force. Reproduction of low frequencies requires a particularly long "excursion" or movement of the speaker cone. These long excursions stretch the suspensions beyond their elastic limit, resulting in foreshortened movement of the speaker cone. Up to the elastic limit the stretch bears a linear relationship to the force applied, but beyond this point resistance to

Exhibit 4

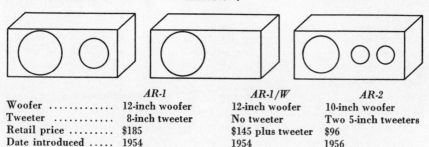

	AR-1	*AR-1/W*	*AR-2*
Woofer	12-inch woofer	12-inch woofer	10-inch woofer
Tweeter	8-inch tweeter	No tweeter	Two 5-inch tweeters
Retail price	$185	$145 plus tweeter	$96
Date introduced .	1954	1954	1956

stretching increases more than proportionally to the distance. (As an illustration, try stretching a rubber band beyond its elastic limit.) Beyond the elastic limit, the speaker cone is no longer able to follow a path corresponding to the signal, but follows a somewhat shorter path, causing distortion. Such foreshortened movement has been a major cause of the harmonic distortion present at low frequencies in even the best of speaker systems.

It was largely to overcome this difficulty that the acoustic suspension principle as used by AR was developed, and acoustic suspension has its greatest comparative strength in its ability to handle these long excursions with low distortion and good sound reproduction.

Exhibit 5

TOP VIEW OF AR-1 (CUT-AWAY)

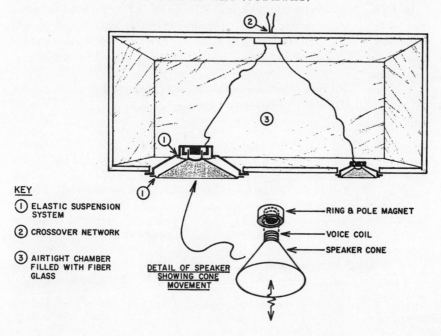

KEY

① ELASTIC SUSPENSION SYSTEM

② CROSSOVER NETWORK

③ AIRTIGHT CHAMBER FILLED WITH FIBER GLASS

RING & POLE MAGNET

VOICE COIL

SPEAKER CONE

DETAIL OF SPEAKER SHOWING CONE MOVEMENT

Management described the significance of the acoustic suspension principle as follows:

Acoustic Research has *replaced* the mechanical spring of the bass speaker suspensions with a pneumatic spring of near-perfect characteristics—the sealed-in air of the cabinet. The practical results of this fundamentally new approach to speaker design are:

1. Reduction of bass harmonic distortion, from values currently accepted as unavoidable in speakers, by a factor of four.

2. Uniform and extended low frequency response. We believe that the AR-1 established new industry standards in this respect.

3. Determination of optimum cabinet size as conveniently small—an extra dividend.

The size of the AR-1 speaker cabinet is dictated by acoustical considerations, and represents an advance in, rather than a compromise with quality. No allowances for size should be made in evaluating the performance of the system.[1]

The tweeters used in the AR-1 and AR-2 were purchased from other manufacturers. Management said that while the tweeters were of high quality they were in no way exceptional.

The AR-1 and AR-2 were complete loudspeaker systems ready for use, but the AR-1/W required the purchase of a tweeter by the consumer. The AR-1/W was designed to permit the consumer to select a high-quality tweeter of his own choice. One such high-quality tweeter was built in matching cabinet style by Neshaminy Electronics. Marketed under the brand name Janszen, the Neshaminy tweeter and its enclosure sold for about $180. Both companies had, in the past, displayed the combination system at audio fairs.

In trying to evaluate the technical quality of AR's three loudspeaker models, the field researcher studied numerous magazine reviews and several evaluations by independent testing companies. A representative selection of those reviews is given below, giving an idea of the specific characteristics of each model.

An evaluation of the AR-1 and AR-1/W published by the Audio League (an independent testing company) in 1956 contained the following summary of the findings:

The AR-1/W is one of the outstanding low frequency reproducers available today. It may well be the most outstanding. At any rate we do not specifically know of any other speaker system which is truly comparable to it from the standpoint of extended low frequency response, flatness of response, and most of all low distortion. The high frequency portion of the AR-1 system, while excellent by most standards, is not nearly so superlative a mechanism as the low frequency portion. For this reason there might be some argument as to whether the AR-1 system is the finest made today.

All of this is without regard to size or price. When it is considered that the AR-1 is truly small enough to sit on a table or be mounted in a bookshelf, or to

---

[1]From *A Revolution in Engineering Acoustics*, a pamphlet published by Acoustic Research, Inc.

fit unobtrusively in the smallest living room, and that the complete price is only $185, it becomes evident that the AR-1 has no competition in its price class or anywhere near it.

Paradoxically, we think it likely that the biggest drawbacks to the AR-1's overwhelming acceptance by the public are also its outstanding advantages, namely its low price and small size. There are many people who simply would not accept a speaker costing only $185 as being . . . one of the finest available to them. Many of these people will eventually settle for a [speaker] system with a substantially lower order of performance than the AR-1 but costing more and looking several times as impressive.[2]

The AR-2 was a loudspeaker system of slightly lower quality than the AR-1, but with the same basic design features. Since March 1957, when production of the AR-2 began, it had been the company's best selling model. Illustrative excerpts from magazine reviews appear in an AR advertisement reproduced as Exhibit 12 (p. 422).

The successful introduction of the AR-2 with its small size and low price had helped initiate, in the opinion of management and the field researcher, a new trend in the industry. Formerly many people had associated large size and high price with high quality (see AR-1 review given above). By 1958 small-size speaker systems were becoming commonplace, and advertising copy of several manufacturers featured the concept of "bookshelf size." In commenting on the trend, one dealer went so far as to state he expected to see very large "monsters" become "extinct in a few years."

In the fall of 1958 the company had exhibited a new loudspeaker model, the AR-3. With its radically new tweeter, management said the AR-3 was designed to compete with the best systems currently manufactured. Data on the AR-3 are given in Exhibit 6.

Exhibit 6

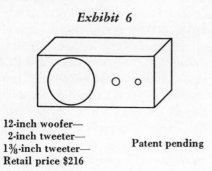

12-inch woofer—
2-inch tweeter—
1⅜-inch tweeter—   Patent pending
Retail price $216

The significant technical advance of the AR-3 was derived from its new tweeter design. This new tweeter produced highest-quality sound from a greatly simplified mechanism. The tweeter design completely eliminated the conventional speaker cone and required about one half as many parts as a conventional speaker. (Because the problems of reproducing high frequencies

---

[2]*Audio League Report*, Vol. 1, No. 11, January 1956.

were quite different from reproducing the lows, the new tweeter did not utilize the acoustic suspension principle.) The new tweeter was produced in two sizes, with the smaller size reproducing the very high notes and larger size reproducing the midrange.

According to management, the new tweeter had the following advantages:

1. The illusion of a wide source of sound.
2. Greatly improved flatness of response.
3. Reduced surface noise even at high-energy (volume) output levels.

The AR-3 was designed to offer the highest in speaker quality, and both management and the field researcher believed it superior to "any speaker system costing less than $1,000." While no independent evaluations were yet available, management described the AR-3 as the "hit of the 1958 New York hi-fi show," and "the only really new development this year in speakers." Management pointed out, however, that while the AR-3 was superior in quality and lower in price than other top-quality speaker systems, only a trained ear could detect the difference between the AR-3 and other speaker systems of fine quality. In addition, some listeners might prefer the sound qualities of another speaker system or might buy speakers on some basis other than quality of sound reproduction.

Marketing

Sales of Acoustic Research loudspeakers had continued their uptrend in 1958, showing a 24% increase for the first ten months over the like period of 1957. Management estimated that sales of the components industry for the corresponding period had increased by only 1%, as shown in Exhibit 7.

AR loudspeakers were sold primarily to consumers for use in home sound reproduction systems, and figures for the first half of 1958 indicated that over 95% of its unit sales were for home use. However, some units had found industrial and commercial applications. Management stated that at least seven recording companies, including Decca and RCA, used AR speakers for the important and exacting job of monitoring record production. Numerous FM radio stations used them for studio monitoring. Management also knew of an installation of ten AR-2's with an Aeolian Skinner organ in a church, an installation in a psychological laboratory for reproducing the sound of the human heart beat, and of the purchase of 30 AR-1/W's by the Air Force to reproduce the sound of jet engines. These sales were unsolicited, since the company had no commercial or industrial sales program.

Management had, on several occasions, stated two objectives. In the long run the company was aiming "to bring high fidelity to the mass market." More immediately it hoped "to expand the market for AR high-fidelity products." To accomplish these objectives, management had adopted a strategy of trying to provide the consumer with a product of the best-possible quality at the lowest-possible price. In the words of management, the plan was "to give the consumer the best buy possible."

AR's marketing program was based on management's belief that a superior product—once it became known—would sell on its own merits. Management believed that high quality at low prices would create its own market. Mr. A. J. Hoffman, vice president and treasurer, summarized the AR overall marketing approach as follows, "We aren't selling our speakers; we are offering them for sale. We depend upon the customer to beat the dealer's door down and insist on AR. We just open the mail in the morning and count the orders."

This point of view affected the company's marketing policies and, according to management, caused AR's policies to differ substantially from typical

Exhibit 7

ESTIMATED INDUSTRY AND COMPANY SALES AT FACTORY PRICES

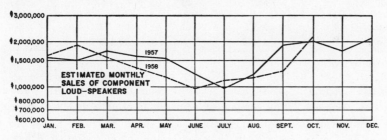

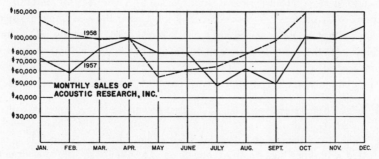

Source: Company records and company estimates.

industry practice in respect to four important factors. These were (1) prices and margins, (2) dealer relations, (3) channels of distribution, and (4) promotion.

Prices and margins. Prices and dealer margins were kept low in relation to those of competition in order to offer the consumer the best dollar value possible. Management said its own gross margin, about 35% in the first half of 1958, was on the low side for the industry. In addition, management noted, its suggested retail prices left the dealer a smaller margin (in both per cent and absolute terms) than other quality loudspeaker systems. AR allowed no quantity discounts for purchases in excess of three units. Its suggested retail prices left the purchaser of three units about a 33% markup

—less the transportation charge from Boston. Many competitors, in contrast, offered quantity discounts or special deals on large orders, or suggested an initial margin in excess of 33%. Management pointed out, for example, that the AR-2 gave the dealer a very thin profit. With its low price ($96 compared to speakers of comparable quality selling for as much as $200), the AR-2 gave the dealer a smaller absolute dollar sale, and a smaller margin on the smaller dollar amount.

Selected data on per product sales and gross margins for the first half of 1958 are shown in the following table:

	Unit Sales	% Unit Sales	% Dollar Sales	Gross Margin
AR-1	1,644	24%	37%	35%
AR-1/W	336	5	7	39
AR-2	4,863	71	56	34
Total	6,843	100%	100%	

Dealer relations.   AR's dealer relations could almost be characterized as a lack of relations. Many component manufacturers actively solicited dealers and maintained close working relations with them. In contrast, AR did not solicit new dealers. Instead, it depended mainly upon consumer demand to stimulate dealer interest in AR loudspeakers. AR did not maintain close relations with dealers, or favor particular dealers; the company granted all dealers—old and new, large and small—the same discounts. It permitted dealers to set their own prices, and to reduce prices below "suggested retail" if they wished.

The company made only four requirements of its dealers:

1. Initial purchase of at least three speakers, at least one of which had to be an AR-1.
2. Competent display and demonstration of an AR-1 at all times in conjunction with other high-quality components in a suitable acoustical environment.
3. Prompt payment of bills, or an explanation in advance for slow payments.
4. Dealers not to act as middlemen or transship speakers to unauthorized dealers.

Channels of distribution.   Like many other component manufacturers, AR used direct distribution—it shipped from the factory to the dealer. However, in contrast to industry practices, which included selective dealerships serviced by manufacturer's agents, AR distribution was not selective and did not utilize manufacturer's representatives. Subject to the four conditions mentioned above, any dealer could sell AR speakers.

In 1958 the company had about 350 dealers, and the list had been stable for about a year. Company records showed that sales were concentrated in a few large metropolitan areas, with the states of New York and California accounting for about 46% of the total. Ten large dealers, eight of them in New York, who published mail-order catalogues accounted for 24% of sales. Sales by state, as shown in company records, are given in Exhibit 8. Sales for selected cities, as compiled by the researcher, are given in Exhibit 9. In commenting on the effectiveness of its distribution coverage, Mr. Hoff-

Exhibit 8

SALES BY STATES—FIRST 26 WEEKS OF 1958

Area	Population in Millions	Unit Sales	Approximate Unit Sales per Million of Population
New England:			
Connecticut	2.243	79	35
Maine	0.933	16	17
Massachusetts	4.988	465	94
New Hampshire	0.533	15	28
Rhode Island	0.831	12	14
Vermont	0.389	10	26
	9.917	597	60
New York:			
New York City		1,698	
Brooklyn	7.892	67	246*
Queens—Jamaica		179	
Long Island	7.626	52	48
New York State (other)		319	
	15.518	2,315	149
Mid-Atlantic:			
Delaware	0.370	28	76
New Jersey	5.290	175	33
Pennsylvania	10.840	235	21.6
Washington, D.C.	0.860	123	143
	17.360	561	32
Dixie:			
Alabama	3.135	32	10
Arkansas	1.912	6	3.5
Florida	3.624	64	18
Georgia	3.677	14	4
Louisiana	2.975	14	4.8
Mississippi	2.200	14	6.4
North Carolina	4.283	37	8.8
Texas	8.582	164	19
Virginia	3.654	26	7.3
	34.042	371	11
Border South:			
Kentucky	2.995	3	1
Maryland	2.642	50	19
Tennessee	3.370	88	24
West Virginia	1.948	6	3
South Carolina	2.239	5	2.2
	13.194	152	12

*Includes a substantial volume of nationwide mail-order business.

Exhibit 8—Continued

Area	Population in Millions	Unit Sales	Approximate Unit Sales per Million of Population
Midwest:			
Illinois	9.230	504	55*
Indiana	4.274	36	8.4
Iowa	2.640	46	17
Kansas	2.030	12	6
Michigan	7.140	186	26
Minnesota	3.132	26	8.4
Missouri	4.175	62	15
Nebraska	1.365	13	9
Ohio	8.683	131	15
South Dakota	0.640	1	1.6
Wisconsin	3.623	57	16
	46.932	1,074	23
Southwest:			
Arizona	1.035	61	59
Colorado	1.480	70	47
New Mexico	0.799	43	54
Oklahoma	2.272	8	3.5
Utah	0.768	25	32.6
	6.354	207	33
Coast:			
San Francisco		417	
California (north)	12.877	54	66*
Los Angeles		339	
California (south)		36	
		846	
Oregon	1.649	29	17.5
Washington	2.556	111	43.5
Idaho	0.622	7	1.1
Montana	0.636	17	27
Wyoming	0.315	4	13
	5.778	168	29
Other:			
Hawaii		14	
Export		193	
Industrial, retail, and personal		345	
Total Number of Units Sold		6,843	

*Includes a substantial volume of nationwide mail-order business
Source: Company records.

man stated that "except for a few large cities like New Orleans and Miami, we have pretty good nationwide coverage. While about ten large dealers do account for a quarter of our business, that isn't especially high for our industry. We are spread out lots better than some of the components people— and there are some places where we are doing exceptionally well. In Ithaca a couple of Cornell students are really doing a job." (See Exhibit 9.)

Exhibit 9

UNIT SALES BY CITY, JANUARY–JUNE 1958

City	Population in Thousands	Unit Sales	Number of Active AR Dealers
Group I:			
Boston, Massachusetts	801	308	9
Ithaca, New York	29	50	1
Poughkeepsie, New York	41	52	2
Spokane, Washington	161	50	1
Group II:			
Cleveland, Ohio	914	30	5
Kansas City, Kansas	129	0	0
Kansas City, Missouri	956	14	1
Miami, Florida	249	1	1
Minneapolis and St. Paul, Minnesota	833	15	5
New Haven, Connecticut	164	3	1
New Orleans, Louisiana	570	9	2
Omaha, Nebraska	251	10	1

Source: Compiled by the field researcher from company records.

Promotion. Management stated that because of AR's strategy of providing top dollar value, its promotion budgets were quite limited. Management had chosen to concentrate expenditures primarily on consumer advertising. In contrast to industry practice, AR did not run special promotions with dealers, give dealer "push money," or advertise in trade papers to attract dealer interest. The company did, like other component manufacturers, display its speakers at trade fairs and occasionally at special gatherings such as professional engineering society meetings.

Consumer advertising was placed almost exclusively in magazines, and mainly in magazines that catered to readers interested in high fidelity. Occasionally ads were placed in magazines appealing to a wider readership such as *Playboy, Esquire, Saturday Review* and *Atlantic.* A small amount of advertising appeared in newspapers under a little used cooperative advertising plan available to dealers.

Advertising copy was factual and tended toward understatement in its claims. The message stressed advanced design and often included excerpts from magazine or other reviews. Management believed sales had been aided by these advertising policies, and by "a lot of free publicity about the AR products" in hi-fi magazines (see Exhibits 10–13).

A sales manager. In the summer of 1958 management had hired a sales manager, Mr. Maurice Rotstein, whose job included improving dealer relations and communications with the field. According to management, this move did not represent a major policy shift, but rather an attempt to explain company policies to dealers and improve relations by a more personal approach.

Exhibit 10
ADVERTISING COPY, AR-1

AR-1

PRESS COMMENT

"Your AR-1W speaker has been of inestimable value in the production of our recording series, *The King of Instruments*.' No other system I have ever heard does justice to the intent of our recordings. Your speaker, with its even bass line and lack of distortion, has so closely approached 'the truth' that it validates itself immediately to those who are concerned with musical values."

Joseph S. Whiteford, vice-pres.,
The Aeolian-Skinner Organ Co.

Atlantic   (John M. Conly)

"The AR-1W woofer gives the cleanest bass response I ever have heard."

AUDIO   (Edward Tatnall Canby)

"... the highs impressed me immediately as very lovely, smooth, unprepossessing, musical (for music) and unusually natural. No super-hi-fi screech and scratch ... As to the lows ... I was no end impressed, from the first time I ran my finger over a pickup stylus and got that hearty, wall-shaking thump that betokens real bottom bass to the time when I had played records and tapes on the speaker for some months on end."

The Audio League Report *

"Speaker systems that will develop much less than 30% distortion at 30 cycles are few and far between. Our standard reference speaker system,† the best we've ever seen, has about 5% distortion at 30 cycles."

*Vol. 1 No. 9, Oct., '55. Authorized quotation #30.
For the complete technical and subjective report on
the AR-1 consult Vol. 1 No. 11. The Audio League
Report, Pleasantville, N. Y.

†The AR-1W

The Saturday Review   (R. S. Lanier)

"... goes down into the low, low bass with exemplary smoothness and low distortion. It is startling to hear the fundamentals of low organ notes come out, pure and undefiled, from a box that is two feet long and about a foot high."

High Fidelity   (Roy Allison)

"... a woofer that works exceptionally well because of its small size, not in spite of it ... I have heard clean extended bass like this only from enclosures that were at least six or seven times its size."

The *Nation*   (B. H. Haggin)

"... achieves the seemingly impossible; a real and clearly defined bass in a cabinet only 14 by 11⅜ by 25 inches in size."

audiocraft

"The reproduced sound* so perfectly duplicated that of the organ that no one could be sure which was playing."

*At a demonstration of live vs. recorded pipe
organ, in which the reproducing system included
four AR-1's.

the AR-1 SPEAKER SYSTEM

A REVOLUTION IN ENGINEERING ACOUSTICS

AR-1 (2-way system in mahogany $185
AR-1 (2-way system in walnut or cherry) . $194
AR-1U (2-way system, unfinished fir) $172

AR-1W (woofer only, in mahogany $145
AR-1W (woofer only in cherry cabinet) ... $154
AR-1WU (woofer only, unfinished fir) $132

5% higher in the West and deep South

AR^{INC}

ACOUSTIC RESEARCH, INC.
24 Thorndike St., Cambridge 41, Mass.

Exhibit 11

ADVERTISING COPY—TECHNICAL RATING, AR-1

three reports on

SPEAKER DISTORTION

We believe that Acoustic Research speaker systems, by virtue of their patented **acoustic suspension** design, establish new industry standards in low distortion. This is a technical characteristic that can be directly interpreted in terms of musically natural reproduction.

Our opinion on the matter is shared by others:

1 **A** recent Master's thesis written at a leading engineering university (by George D. Ramig) involved distortion measurements on fifteen 12-in. and 15-in. loudspeakers,* including the AR-1. Here are some of the results:

PERCENT HARMONIC DISTORTION

	AR-1	Sphr 2	Sphr 3	Sphr 4	Sphr 5	Sphr 6	Sphr 7	Sphr 8	Sphr 9	Sphr 10	Sphr 11	Sphr 12	Sphr 13	Sphr 14	Sphr 15
50 cps (lowest used)	2.1	4.4	8.8	10.0	11.2	12.8	15.0	17.8	18.5	18.5	over-loads	23.2	31.0	31.0	43.0
55 cps	2.1	1.8	5.6	7.4	8.8	13.0	11.8	7.6	8.7	8.7	7.3	18.3	12.8	17.5	11.0
70 cps	1.9	1.9	2.7	4.4	5.3	5.9	7.1	2.2	5.4	5.4	9.6	7.2	3.0	4.4	6.3
80 cps	1.0	2.1	2.1	3.4	3.9	3.2	3.9	2.6	3.8	3.8	6.6	4.0	2.1	2.3	3.1

Measurements taken at 3 ft., 102 db on-axis signal level. Amplifier damping factor control "off", giving DF of 30. Data published with Mr. Ramig's permission.

*All speakers were directly baffled, a less than optimum mounting for some.

2 Joseph S. Whiteford, president of the Aeolian-Skinner Organ Co., has written us:

"No other system I have heard does justice to the intent of our recordings. Your speaker, with its even bass line and lack of distortion, has so closely approached the 'truth' that it validates itself immediately to those who are concerned with musical values."

3 The Audio League Report, in adopting the AR-1W as its bass reference standard, wrote:

"At 30 cycles, only 5% total harmonic distortion was measured, as compared to values of 30% to 100% of other speaker systems we have tested . . . we do not specifically know of any other speaker system which is truly comparable to it from the standpoint of extended low frequency response, flatness of response, and most of all, low distortion."

AR-1 and AR-2 speaker systems, complete with cabinets, are priced from $89 to $194. Literature is available on request.

ACOUSTIC RESEARCH, INC. 24 Thorndike St., Cambridge 41, Mass.,

Exhibit 12

ADVERTISING COPY, AR-2

Excerpts from PRESS COMMENT on the

High Fidelity (Tested in the Home)

"...With the (tweeter) control set to suit my taste (best described as row-M-oriented), oscillator tests indicated that bass was smooth and very clean to below 40 cycles, was audibly enfeebled but still there at 35, and dropped out somewhere around 30 cycles. No doubling was audible at any frequency.

From 1,000 to 4,000 cycles there was a slight, broad dip in the response (averaging perhaps 2 db down), a gradual rise to original level at 8,000 cycles, and some minor discontinuities from there out to 12,000 cycles. Then there was a slow droop to 14,000 cycles, with rapid cutoff above that.

Because of its slightly depressed 'presence' range, the AR-2 has what is to me a refreshingly sweet, smooth, and highly listenable sound. Music is reproduced transparently, and with very good detail. Its high end is unobtrusive, but its ability to reproduce the guttiness of string tone and the tearing transients of a trumpet indicate that it is, indeed, contributing highs when needed. This, I feel, is as it should be.

Its low end is remarkably clean and, like the AR-1, prompts disbelief that such deep bass could emanate from such a small box.

"...Like the AR-1, the AR-2 should be judged purely on its sonic merits...not on the theoretical basis of its 'restrictive' cabinet size. When so judged, it can stand comparison with many speakers of considerably greater dimension and price.—J.G.H."

AUDIO ETC.

"...I find the AR-2 remarkably like the AR-1 in over-all sound coloration. Its cone tweeter is not the same, but there isn't much difference in sound. (It costs less, but that doesn't prove much.) On direct comparison, given a signal with plenty of bass component in the very bottom, you can tell the difference between the two in bass response. Most of the time, in ordinary listening, I am not aware of it at all.

...I find AR-2, as with AR-1, remarkably clean and unobtrusive in its sound, easy on the ears for long-period listening, easy also to ignore in favor of the music itself. Either speaker has a way of simply fading into the surroundings (the size helps) leaving the music unattached and disembodied in the room. Excellent illusion!..."

Prices for Acoustic Research speaker systems, complete with cabinets, (AR-1 and AR-2) are $89.00 to $194.00. Size is "bookshelf." Literature is available from your local sound equipment dealer, or on request from:

ACOUSTIC RESEARCH, INC. 24 Thorndike St., Cambridge 41, Mass.

Exhibit 13

ADVERTISING COPY, AR-3

The terms "revolutionary" and "new" come easily to advertising copywriters. Such terms have been used to represent both substantial advances in the art and small changes in production technique, styling, or packaging.

Acoustic Research called the **acoustic suspension** woofer* of its AR-1 speaker system revolutionary. That judgment has since been supported by distinguished writers in both the engineering and musical fields, and by the two consumer organizations that have made special reports on the AR-1. (One of these organizations adopted the AR-1 woofer as its bass reference standard, and the other gave the AR-1 its highest and rarely used **AA** rating.)

Now Acoustic Research has developed a mid- and high-frequency speaker system** to match the quality of the AR woofer. We believe that this system establishes new industry standards in treble performance, and that it makes a contribution to treble reproduction similar in degree to that made by the acoustic suspension woofer to bass reproduction. Like the woofer, it does so by virtue of its simple yet revolutionary design.

The AR-3 three-way speaker system combines an acoustic suspension AR-1 woofer with the new tweeters. It has the most musically natural sound that we were able to create in a speaker, without compromise.

The AR-3, complete with the necessary "bookshelf" size enclosure, is $216 in mahogany or birch (5% higher in the West and Deep South.) Prices in other woods vary slightly.

U. S. Patent 2,775,309 was assigned to AR in December, 1956.
**Pat. applied for.*

ACOUSTIC RESEARCH INC., 24 Thorndike Street, Cambridge 41, Massachusetts

Finance

The financial condition of the company had improved during 1958 as a result of increased earnings retained in the business. Net profits were $45,000 for the first half of 1958 as compared with $37,000 for the full year 1957. The increased profitability was due partly to higher sales, but mainly to a higher per unit profit margin. The higher profit margin had been forecast by the president in the 1957 Annual Report, as follows:

Sales and production for 1957 exceeded our projections at the beginning of the year; on the other hand production efficiency was far behind expectations at least for the first two-thirds of the year. We know that the latter problem is solved, and a repetition of 1957 sales in 1958 would result in a far better earnings picture.

The treasurer's comments in the 1957 Annual Report illustrate other aspects of the company's financial condition:

There are many things that stand out on our financial report. Some of the more important items are:

1. Our company is undercapitalized. With a beginning working capital in 1957 of some $30,000, we had to find the means to turn over $985,000 gross business in a manufacturing and sales operation. We were able to accomplish this mainly because of a tight policy on the application of funds, and the working out of satisfactory banking arrangements which provided loan capital to compensate for the lack of equity capital in relation to our volume.

2. Our working capital ratio on December 28, 1957, was 1.34 to 1. This means that out of every $1.34 of current assets, $1 came from creditors in one form or another and $0.34 came from the corporation's net worth.

3. Of our net profit of some $37,000, $19,000 was applied to a net increase in working capital and $15,000 to a net increase in fixed assets.

4. A valuable asset which does not appear on our Statement of Financial Condition is the management group that we have developed in the past year. We have, through the combined efforts of management, developed a core of trained AR employees, which should have favorable effects upon future statements of financial condition.

I am pleased to announce that at the Annual Directors' Meeting held on January 28, 1958, immediately after the Annual Stockholders' meeting, it was voted to declare a dividend of $3 per share. A check for the dividend on your shares is enclosed.

Working capital needs were met by an accounts receivable loan from a local bank. Management described its relations with that bank as "most satisfactory." In the fall of 1958 the bank was granting credits of 80% of face value on AR's accounts receivable up to a maximum loan of $125,000. Originally the loan limit had been $75,000, but it had been increased on several occasions and management was certain it would be increased again if the need arose. AR turned most of its accounts receivable over to the bank and drew only as needed against the resulting line of credit. "When they granted us the original loan, they said we had undersold ourselves. Everything has gone smoothly since then," commented Mr. Hoffman. "They wish we would borrow more."

Acoustic Research's capital stock structure was an outgrowth of a financial and management reorganization which had taken place in February 1957. At that time Mr. Villchur, Mr. Hoffman and a group of associates raised funds and bought out the stock interest of Mr. Villchur's former partners. Among the others were three men who subsequently became members of AR's top management. The stock structure was as follows:

	No. Shares	Investment
Mr. Villchur	651	$ 5,000 and patent
Mr. Hoffman and others ...	649	$70,000

In 1958 the stockholders authorized 100 shares of a new Class B common stock. The Class B stock, which did not have voting power, was intended "primarily for sale to key employees. Five shares have been issued to the assistant plant manager, who was not previously a stockholder."[3]

It was company financial policy to retain almost all earnings in the business. The president explained this policy in the 1957 Annual Report:

> The enclosed Treasurer's Comments show why the earnings (1957) of $28.58 per share could not be used for a substantial dividend distribution. We are declaring a token dividend of $3 per share so that the stockholders' money will at least have earned normal bank interest.

Manufacturing

AR's manufacturing activity was basically an assembly and testing operation. Management, in reviewing progress made during 1958, stated, "We have progressed from doing things like a handicraft shop to using factory methods."

Manufacturing operations were located primarily on the second and third floors of a four-story building, with the first floor serving as office space and the fourth floor as a machine shop and testing area. The production area was partitioned into a number of rooms, with each room turning out one or more subassemblies. These moved either to the final assembly area on the third floor, or to another room to become part of a larger subassembly. On the third floor the three major subassemblies, the woofer, the tweeter, and the crossover (or internal wiring), were inserted into the cabinet. Prior to final assembly, the work flow was on a batch or job-lot basis, with final assembly on a line basis.

The final assembly line was a recent innovation, dating from the spring of 1958. Set up off the floor on metal legs, it was a track with rollers which permitted a cabinet to be pushed from one work station to the next. A worker would insert subassemblies which he took from nearby racks, fasten them (usually with the aid of power tools), and push the cabinet to the next station. In all, a man might perform 20 or more operations, and each man knew how to perform most of the operations performed at each station along the line.

The line employed from three to six workers depending on desired levels of production, and with four men could produce about 350 units a week. While the line was not strictly modern in the sense of a moving conveyor feeding work to operators doing highly specialized operations, management pointed out, "It is quite an improvement over assembling at benches the way we used to."

Aside from final assembly, most operations were done by hand. Work was performed at wooden benches, with a worker procuring his parts, performing several operations, and placing the finished pieces in racks or in reach of a worker who performed subsequent operations. Many operations utilized homemade jigs and fixtures, while others involved only pure manual

---

[3]Annual Report, 1957.

labor such as squeezing glue-like substances from tubes onto speaker parts.

AR did not use either expensive or complicated machinery in the production processes. Lathe and drill press work was performed on castings, and stamping and hydraulic pressing of parts was also done. More typical of company operations, however, was the use of power drills, power screwdrivers, and an assortment of hand tools such as pliers and screwdrivers.

Control of production operations was characterized by management as "control with a minimum of paper work." Mr. Hoffman kept the plant manager informed of desired levels of production and established weekly output needs. The plant manager, Mr. Harry Rubinstein, adjusted the plant schedule in accordance with Mr. Hoffman's estimates. Plant personnel maintained daily reports on production, rejects, and inventory. These reports were reviewed by Mr. Rubinstein and Mr. Hoffman. Actual scheduling of output, however, was still accomplished basically by word of mouth with the assistant plant manager telling each foreman how many of each part would be needed by what time. The foreman then apportioned work loads and, if necessary, modified job assignments. Time standards were not employed, but management found it possible to step up production substantially by setting higher goals or indicating a particular rush situation.

Quality control. Quality control was an important part of the manufacturing process, and was under the direct supervision of the plant manager. The company maintained two types of quality control—100% testing at certain critical stages in the manufacturing process, and sample tests of finished speakers. Most subassemblies were tested in at least one stage of manufacture prior to their arrival in the final assembly area. Management noted that the quality and uniformity of the final product depended upon the skill and care with which the inspection was accomplished. The acoustic suspension woofer was given particular attention.

A critical quality control problem with the woofer was the proper centering of its moving parts. Centering was first done visually. Then the woofer was plugged in so that it would oscillate approximately as it would in operation. While it was oscillating, an inspector would listen for possible rubbing sounds which indicated improper centering. In addition, the inspector would apply slight pressure with his fingers (changing the oscillation path slightly) and listen for the rubbing sound. The "finger test" was to insure that there was a margin of safety in the centering. By applying more pressure with his fingers the inspector could adjust the centering. These testing operations were done before a glue-like compound which held the speaker in place had hardened. Management stated that this testing operation was better suited to being done by hand rather than by instruments. Woofer testing was done in a room reserved for the operation, and was under the direct supervision of Mr. Rubinstein.

Management said that one reason for rigorous testing of subassemblies was the difficulty of determining causes of substandard performance in the final product. However, in addition to subassembly tests, each completed speaker system was tested with a stethoscope for air leaks (see Exhibit 14) and electronically for performance qualities. In addition, once or twice a day a sample speaker was taken to the fourth floor for exhaustive tests in the acoustical chamber. Mr. Rubinstein usually administered these tests himself, though in past years Mr. Villchur had also done testing.

Mr. Rubinstein stated that when performance of the final product was substandard, the unit usually had to be rebuilt. For example, during part of 1957 "something was haywire," and performance standards had required nearly 100% rebuilding of some batches of AR-2's. The reject rate at final assembly varied "from zero to about 10%," said Mr. Rubinstein, "with the average about 2%." As a result of exacting performance standards, management stated that customer returns for defective workmanship were infrequent.

Purchasing. Since manufacturing was primarily an assembly operation, purchased parts and materials accounted for an important part of the cost of the final product. In 1957, for example, purchases amounted to 72% of cost of goods sold. For the AR-2 the purchase price of the cabinet alone was 110% of the amount charged to the finished product for direct labor and manufacturing overhead. Opportunities for savings on purchases had occasioned the hiring of a materials manager, Mr. Emmanuel Maier, in the summer of 1957.

The principal duties of the materials manager were (1) systematizing purchasing, and (2) finding ways to reduce costs. In establishing more systematic purchasing, Mr. Maier had increased the number of suppliers of some items, had increased the number of products on which bids were solicited, and had established maximum and minimum inventory levels on some items. Important problems still existed, however, because certain products such as fiber glass could be purchased at considerable savings if bought in large quantities—a boxcar load at a time in the case of fiber glass. Such quantities in some cases constituted more than a year's supply. Difficulties were also encountered in scheduling purchases of specialized parts far enough in advance to give suppliers adequate lead time, and supplier lead-time problems still caused some purchasing to be done on an emergency basis.

Mr. Villchur had launched the cost-reduction program in 1957, and had devoted a considerable amount of his time over a nine-month period to these activities. Mr. Maier had joined the company during this period, and had continued the cost-reduction efforts under the direction of Mr. Villchur. Management pointed out that redesigning some parts had permitted savings in material without impairing quality but that "costs could be cut still more if we were willing to cheapen the product." Management stated that the results of the cost-reduction program, along with the improved quality control program, had changed the AR-2 from an unprofitable product to a profitable one during the second half of 1957.

Cost reduction had been accomplished in a number of ways. Savings were possible as increased output permitted the company to absorb higher tooling costs when necessary to achieve lower unit costs on parts. For example, the

Exhibit 14

ADVERTISING COPY—QUALITY CONTROL

Robert Bell, assembly foreman at AR

FACTORY INSPECTION
for AR SPEAKERS

A stethoscope is used in the production testing of every Acoustic Research speaker system, to detect possible air leaks in the cabinet. The speaker is driven by a twenty-cycle signal, and if there are any leaks a characteristic rushing sound can be picked up at the trouble spot.

This test procedure is necessary because the sealed-in air of an acoustic suspension enclosure is a basic working element of the speaker system. In conventional speakers the cone works against the springy stiffness of its mechanical suspensions; in AR speakers this stiffness is missing, and the cone works instead against the springiness of the enclosed air-cushion. Like the new air-suspension cars, the speaker literally rides on air.

The patented AR system requires a small cabinet, so that the enclosed air will be springy enough. And since the air-cushion does not bind or reach its elastic limit as do mechanical springs, the AR-1 has created new industry standards in the low-distortion reproduction of music. The "bookshelf" size of AR enclosures is associated with an absolute advance rather than a compromise in speaker bass performance.

AR speakers have been adopted as reference standards, as test instruments for acoustical laboratories, and as monitors in recording and broadcast studios. Their most important application, however, has been in the natural reproduction of music for the home.

The AR-1 and AR-2, two-way speaker systems complete with enclosures, are $185 and $96 respectively in either mahogany or birch. Walnut or cherry is slightly higher and unfinished fir is slightly lower in price.

Literature is available on request.

ACOUSTIC RESEARCH, INC. 24 Thorndike St., Cambridge 41, Mass.

expenditure of $3,000 for dies to produce die-cast speaker baskets for the AR-2 had reduced the woofer basket cost from $1.67 in materials and 42¢ in machining to 88¢ per unit. The tweeter basket had been reduced from $1.10 in sand-cast aluminum to 23¢ in molded plastic. Cost reductions had also been accomplished through locating new sources of supply, through locating army surplus stocks of standard items, and through modifications of material usage.

Employee relations

Management described its approach to employee relations as "trying to create employee dignity," "trying to make AR a good place to work," and "giving the employees a share in the rewards of the company's success." While no member of management had formal responsibility for employee relations, there were company-wide personnel policies on wages, employment, fringe benefits, and unionization.

It was company policy to pay above the going wage for comparable work. After a study of area wage rates by a professor from the Massachusetts Institute of Technology, management had set wages 10% above area rates as thus determined. In addition, the company paid a semiannual wage dividend based on corporate profits. While management used its discretion in establishing the amount of the dividend, it was company policy to pay a wage dividend before paying a dividend to the stockholders. The dividend was computed as a percentage of an employee's total income, including overtime, for the preceding six months. In July 1958 the dividend disbursement had been based upon the following schedule:

Production workers	6%
Foremen	7%
Salaried workers	8%
Supervisors	$500 each

Management received no wage dividend but had established a bonus based upon profits; 25% of pretax profits in excess of $90,000 were divided among the five executives.

It was company policy to provide continuous employment. Since sales had a seasonal dip in the summer, maintaining continuous employment meant the company built up a considerable inventory of finished goods during the summer months. Production schedules were reduced about 20% during the summer of 1958, and factory employees helped remodel the office area and parts of the plant. Management stated that even with these cutbacks, finished goods inventory was in excess of $100,000 in August 1958.

AR provided a number of fringe benefits for its employees. The company contributed toward tuition costs for employees taking night school courses, whether or not the course work related to an employee's job performance. Workers were given paid sick leave and group insurance. Free coffee was available in the plant area throughout the day.

While the plant was not unionized, management stated that it was not opposed to having a union "if the employees decided they wanted one." Management stated that if the employees wished to join, the company would invite representatives of several unions to the plant so the employees could choose. Mr. Villchur stated the company might modify some of its personnel policies if the plant were unionized, but he noted he "couldn't blame the employees for wanting the additional personal security that came with a good union."

While the policies described above applied to the entire company, each department was responsible for hiring and firing, training, raises, and promotions.

Research and development

Management described research as the key to AR's success. Company research activities had developed the acoustic suspension woofer and the new tweeter which, in the opinion of management, placed the company in the front ranks for the highest-quality speaker systems in the industry. The woofer and tweeter were inventions of Mr. Villchur who, even prior to the formation of Acoustic Research, had been studying and theorizing in both acoustics and engineering.

Mr. Villchur described the idea for his acoustic suspension principle as "a flash that came to me one day. I though about it and decided it wouldn't work. Some time later the idea came back, and I saw right away that it would work." Mr. Villchur designed a prototype model and constructed it at his home. He tested the model briefly and discovered that the enclosure was too small, so he enlarged it. "Then I plugged it in, and it was the best bass I had ever heard."

To measure the woofer's performance scientifically, Mr. Villchur used the field behind his home and some equipment borrowed from New York University. "I dug a hole in the ground, put the enclosed speaker in it, and plugged it in with an extension cord strung from the house. The surface of the earth became my infinite baffle and the flat, open field was my most valuable test facility." From the test and theoretical calculations, Mr. Villchur was able to approximate the optimum measurements for the speaker enclosure. "They turned out to be very close to our final production design," he recalled.

The work on the production model of the woofer was carried out by Mr. Villchur's former partner. "But with the tweeter it was different. I stayed with that right through the final development," he noted.

In contrast to Mr. Villchur's "flash idea" which had resulted in a workable woofer on the first try, the development of the tweeter was the result of a series of carefully controlled experiments. "It took over 250 models before we could design the final one. It emerged from a lot of considerations; we didn't suddenly have number 249 come out right. There were a lot of variables, so we held all but one constant in a new model, tested it, and varied something else on the next try. For about 50 tries we didn't even listen to it. Then we began adding subjective evaluation to the test results. We didn't have any blueprints or drawings. We had a serial number of each model and a piece of paper corresponding to each serial number. We recorded the specs of the model and the test results, then decided on modifications."

In contrast to the woofer, the tweeter was developed at the factory in Cambridge. "I did some subjective evaluation and some of the calculations at home, but about 80% of the work was done here. Now it's Harry's. He's been responsible for ironing out the bugs and getting the AR-3 into production."

Mr. Villchur stated that the research efforts on the turntable were of a different nature from those for either woofer or tweeter. "On the tunrtable we aren't working with something radically new; we are trying to eliminate some unsound practices which have crept into basically sound designs." Mr. Villchur also stated that his own role differed from what it had been in the previous cases. "I've worked out some general considerations, but not the details. We've been using outside consultants to perfect the details of the design. They bring their drawings to Harry, and he turns the drawings into parts, tries them out, and suggests revisions. Harry is coordinating the activities on the turntable."

Research facilities. "As far as laboratory equipment goes, I don't really know how much we have invested. I suppose an estimate of $4,000 for the sound chamber is in the ball park. And perhaps we have another $5,000 in the lab test equipment, $3,000 in general testing equipment, and some more in production testing equipment. Besides the plant equipment, I have a good hi-fi set at home."

Research expenditures. The company did not charge all research and development expenditures to the R.&D. account. Time spent by the company executives and employees was not allocated to this account, nor were the frequent long-distance phone calls, the raw materials, or the test equipment. "About the only things in the R.&D. account," said Mr. Hoffman, "are the consultant's fees. If we allocated other expenses the way a larger company would, our research and development for the first half of 1958 would probably be $25,000 instead of $4,497. It probably would have been at least $25,000 for 1957 also."

ACOUSTIC RESEARCH, INC. (B)*

^^

The top management of Acoustic Research, Inc., was composed of a five-man team. Mr. Edgar Villchur, founder and president, was responsible for overall direction of the company. Mr. Abraham Hoffman, the only other "official officer," was vice president and treasurer, responsible for operations. Mr. Harry Rubinstein was plant manager, Mr. Emmanuel Maier was materials manager, and Mr. Maurice Rotstein was sales manager. (For data on the education and experience of these men, see Exhibit 1.)

Exhibit 1

TABLE OF PERSONAL DATA

Name	Age	Education	Previous Experience	Years with AR
Mr. Ed Villchur	41	B.A., M.S.E., C.C.N.Y.*	Teaching, writing, and research	4 yrs.
Mr. Abe Hoffman	43	B.A., Pace College CPA	Public Accounting	1 yr. 9 mo's.
Mr. Harry Rubinstein	48	2 years C.C.N.Y. Dalcroze Certificate	Teaching (Music and Dancing)	1 yr. 4 mo's.
Mr. Manny Maier	42	B.A., M.S.E., Ph.D. C.C.N.Y.	Teaching (German)	1 yr. 2 mo's.
Mr. Maurice Rotstein	46	B.S., Ph.D. C.C.N.Y.	Teaching (History and Economics)	4 mo's.

*The City College of New York.
Source: Interviews with company personnel.

Mr. Villchur, president

After graduating from the City College of New York in 1933, Mr. Villchur received an M.S. in education in 1940. During the war he worked on aircraft electronics. This experience, plus some self-teaching and night school courses "in things like differential equations," provided the basis of Mr. Villchur's understanding of sound reproduction. After the war he opened a radio shop and built custom hi-fi sets, in addition to teaching courses in electronics and sound reproduction. He wrote numerous technical articles on sound reproduction, one series of which was revised and published as a 213-page *Handbook of Sound Reproduction*.[1]

"My ambition was to have an independent income so I could do research on my own. The breakthrough came when I moved to Woodstock, [New York] and began supporting myself by writing articles on hi-fi for *Saturday Review*, *Audio* and other magazines." While writing, Mr. Villchur was able to do research in his laboratory, and by 1953 he had constructed a prototype acoustic suspension speaker which he decided to patent. Unable to afford the services of a patent attorney, Mr. Villchur spent several months studying the complexities involved in filing an application and then completed it himself. Existing manufacturers scoffed at his patent saying, "You can't get good sound from such a small box!" As a result, Mr. Villchur decided to form his own company to produce the speaker.

Mr. Villchur did not want to go into business, but nonacceptance of his patent virtually forced him to do so. Under these circumstances he hoped to establish a company and then withdraw from active participation in its management. After four years of operations at Acoustic Research, Mr. Villchur believed his objective was on the verge of fulfillment. It had been delayed because some people initially brought into the company had turned out to be incompatible.

In 1954 Mr. Villchur was approached by a former student with a loft and some venture capital, and Acoustic Research was formed. Mr. Villchur was responsible for basic product development and promotion, and the student for production design and operations. This arrangement continued until a crisis in 1956. The situation was resolved in February 1957 when the company underwent a financial and management reorganization—Mr. Villchur and the student parting over "irreconcilable policy and personality issues." Mr. Hoffman and a group of associates bought out the former student, and Mr. Hoffman joined the company to take charge of operations.

In 1958 Mr. Villchur's job included overall direction of the company, product design and development, and advertising. "I used to handle dealer relations and also directly supervised the plant operations. Now I don't have any regular contact with dealers at all, and Harry has complete charge of the plant. We are building a management team I have confidence in, so I can withdraw from these things, and soon I hope to be able to concentrate even more on research."

Mr. Villchur described his goals for the company in terms of "making significant contributions in the audio field. The key to this is in our name, *Acoustic Research*; that's what we are doing. We want to develop real leaders, and we aren't going to market anything that isn't the leader in its class. Being one of the top three or four isn't our goal; we want to have *the* best buy for the money. And when better loudspeakers are built, we hope to be the one that builds them."

---

[1]Copyright 1957, Radio Magazines, Inc.

Speaking of his own satisfactions to date, Mr. Villchur said:

Nothing has compared to the first realization that the acoustic suspension speaker model would work. And the second biggest was hearing the new tweeter. I guess you could say my biggest satisfactions come from successful projects.

Next would be recognition of our projects in magazine write-ups. I'll have to admit that we like to have others recognize the merits of what we are doing.

And I suppose everyone likes to see things working and money flowing in, but this is very secondary. I thought I had given up the money side when I moved to Woodstock, so money is a weak satisfaction compared to pioneering in ideas.

In describing his personal goals for the future, Mr. Villchur stated that he would like to equip a fine laboratory at his home in Woodstock and have the freedom to work on projects of his own choosing. "I'd like to equip the lab myself so I wouldn't be obligated to the company or anyone else. I wouldn't want to feel obligated to work out things for commercial applications. I'd like real freedom to do basic research—and someday I think I'd like to do work on hearing aids."

Mr. Hoffman, vice president and treasurer

Mr. Hoffman graduated from the night school of Pace College in 1939, and passed his C.P.A. examination in 1940. He worked in public accounting from 1935 to 1955 and as a management accountant for a metal fabricating firm in 1956.

Mr. Hoffman said he had joined Acoustic Research as a result of the need to resolve the differences between Mr. Villchur and his former student:

I had known Ed since 1948 when he built a custom hi-fi set for my home. And when I heard that he was working for a way to solve this management problem, I was interested. We had a meeting in New York, and it was decided that each side should make the other an offer to resolve the problem. I raised money from friends, plus putting in all that I could lay my hands on, and our offer was accepted. All this was before I had even seen the company.

The financial statements showed a profit, but I figured the company's real asset was the acceptance of the speaker. I had a lot of confidence in Ed's judgment of the product and figured the business would be a mess. It was. The place was dirty and disorganized, and they didn't even have a set of books. I thought some business management would make a lot of difference, so I decided to leave accounting and come to work here. And that's been my job here, to be the businessman among the Ph.D.'s, the guy who keeps his eye on profits. It's still that way today.

Mr. Hoffman's direct responsibilities were in the areas of finance and control:

Enough information crosses the desk for me to keep track of what is going on. In addition to the daily reports on customer orders, backlog, inventory, and shipments, we keep a pro forma cash budget for the year. From these I can tell about how we are doing, how large our summer inventory build-up will be, and how much cash we will need from the bank.

As far as control goes, we could have a more formal system, but it would be expensive. Besides, friends have all the key jobs. I don't have to worry about the intentions of the plant manager or materials manager—no one is trying to pull anything for his own advantage, and I know we all have the same intentions for the company. If Manny [Maier] wants to buy something, we talk it over at lunch, and that's it.

I handle bank relations because I'm the only one that speaks the banker's language. We've had very good relations with the bank. We've been able to plan our needs and the bank has gone along.

We can get along in this business without a lot of money. The demand for our product is one reason; dealers have to pay or we stop shipping to them. Of course, if a dealer explains the situation, we will usually go along. But the point is that consumer demand causes him to want merchandise, and he has to pay up before he can get more. A second reason why we can get along without much money is that we don't have a lot of high-priced executives here. We do have enough executives to do four times as much business, but we only make a salary big enough to live on. If we get rich, it will be as stockholders.

We've followed Ed's philosophy in handling dealers. We treat everyone the same; no deals or discounts for big customers even though it sometimes costs us business. We don't believe in price fixing or limiting the number of dealers who can carry our speakers; we will sell to anyone with adequate demonstration facilities who will keep an Acoustic Research model on display. These policies go over well with the customer—but not the dealer. We're customer oriented—we think good sound will bring money.

At least this is the way it's been so far. It's Ed's philosophy, and it's worked. But we're just beginning to realize it may not be the best or most profitable way to run a business. Maybe one could sell more with greater promotion, and a more aggressive dealer organization, even though it would take a higher consumer price to pay the additional costs. Someone with a good product and a better sales effort might have done as well. We're not sure the customer knows or appreciates the way we are trying to operate . . . but I'll have to admit that this is more my idea than Ed's.

If we ever sold the business, I think I could convince the buyer of an un-tapped reservoir of sales through increased effort. We're going to try a little more sales effort, and that's why we have Maurice as our new sales manager. He's going to try to improve communications with our dealers and try to get us some new dealers in areas that are now blank spots. Up to now we have gone on the idea that good dealers would read about our product and order it, but we're realizing that this isn't always true. Some good dealers don't handle Acoustic Research, and some who do aren't so "good"—I mean they don't have adequate demonstration facilities or information. We really aren't sure what's needed, so we're playing it by ear.

Mr. Hoffman described his reason for joining Acoustic Research as follows:

I joined Acoustic Research for two main reasons. First, this place has real freedom. I can use my talents and abilities in an ethical atmosphere. There's no knifing or playing for special advantage, and we don't have to do a lot of un-ethical things as part of running the business. Second, this was a real opportunity financially. I was about as far as I could go in accounting, and the job didn't pay a lot. Here the pay is better, and there is real financial security. I had always been looking for a break, and this was it. Maybe you could add a third reason, one that isn't as important. I wanted to get away from New York City.

As far as job satisfaction goes, I think mine is mainly from showing others there is a good clean way to do business. We enjoy bringing quality to the consumer at low cost, and this is something that conventional practice in our industry can't do. Our position of relative strength lets us do this—we don't have to follow the rest.

Someday I would like to see Acoustic Research be like Lincoln Electric—paying high salaries to use up the increasing profits. I'd like to see all of our employees have a higher standard of living. Also I would like to develop a second string management to operate the company. I'd like more free time later on, so I could duck out when I wanted to. Right now I'm working harder than ever before and enjoying it, but I might want to retire at 50.

Mr. Rubinstein, plant manager

Mr. Rubinstein attended The City College of New York for two years, but left school in 1932 to do musical accompaniment. Subsequently he gave radio and concert performances, taught music and earned a certificate to teach dancing in New York State. During the war he was plant manager of a small factory making frames for meteorological balloons. He also studied industrial engineering at the night school of Pratt Institute. Following the war he held various jobs as a music and Dalcroze[2] instructor, including a job at the Stockbridge School in Interlaken, Massachusetts, where he met Mr. Maier.

Through Mr. Maier he met Mr. Villchur and the three became close friends. Both lent money to Mr. Villchur on a "friendship and confidence" basis in 1954, and this was later converted to stock. Mr. Villchur asked Mr. Rubinstein to become plant manager in January 1957, and six months later, when his contract commitments expired, he joined the company. In the interim, the company had hired and fired a plant manager who was technically competent, but who "didn't fit in."

Mr. Rubinstein noted that there were two major reasons why he accepted work at Acoustic Research—"money" and the "congenial atmosphere." He added:

I was building up what you could call a musical practice in western Massachusetts. I was a music consultant to a number of schools and also was working with several children's choruses. It was a seven-day-a-week schedule, and sometimes a little hectic, but it gave me more freedom than working for a single school.

In January when Ed asked me to come to work, I had no trouble turning him down. I had contract commitments through the end of the school year. But the second time he brought it up it made us think. My wife reminded me that I was getting older and that we could use more money. There wasn't much chance to earn more than $7,500 where I was because I was already going seven days a week. Ed made it financially very attractive to come here.

The second factor was the adult relationship here. I wasn't much interested

---

[2] A form of dancing emphasizing rhythm and movement.

in business, but this seemed like a humane way of getting into it. It was important to me to find a place that had a congenial atmosphere.

Probably the greatest satisfactions here are in the area of education. I'm working with Benny [George Benedetti, assistant plant manager] on personnel relations—trying to teach him not to be a pile driver. It's something I enjoy.

Another thing is that more money makes things easier. I can buy theater tickets, go to a concert, or take a trip when I want to. But it doesn't seem to matter, really. I think we were just as happy when we were scraping pennies.

Someday I'd like to train a second echelon of management to do the daily operating. With the AR-3, we are moving into problems that are new to everybody here, so I have to learn to do things myself. I learn to mix the chemicals, or listen for the acoustic values when we try out a new grille cloth. But after a while someone else should be able to take these things over, just as Benny and his helpers have been able to do in the production processes.

It won't work yet, because people here are still like young students—they miss the point of a lesson if they have too much freedom in what to study. They get absorbed in some small side issue unless you guide them. We have had this trouble here in quality control. There used to be times last year when we had almost a 100% reject rate on whole batches of speakers. We thought at first it was in the methods. But we found that when things went haywire we could move in, ask questions, check materials, focus attention on the problem, and the thing would be self-correcting. It cleared up when we focused attention on it. I would like to train younger management to see this the way I do, to keep their eyes on the things that are important.

I'd also like to have more free time someday. I'm not quite sure what for, but maybe to teach music literature or work with singing groups at my home.

As plant manager, Mr. Rubinstein's responsibilities included assembly operations, quality control, and personnel relations with the factory employees. Since he joined the company, plant layout had been modified to facilitate the flow of materials, production controls had been established, and final speaker assembly had been shifted from benches to an assembly line. Mr. Rubinstein said that drastic reduction in the number of rejects had been largely responsible for a doubling of output per worker. He also noted, "We're learning all the time. We have been trying to increase efficiency through better supervision and better methods and equipment, and not by making people work harder."

In the personnel area Mr. Rubinstein's comments turned to a discussion of wage rates:

We have a maximum rate for broad areas of jobs, of course, but some people will always go beyond it. Take a family man like our maintenance man. He's important to us. We just can't afford to lose him. He's getting more than $2.00 an hour right now, and he'll conceivably get more because he's got talents we need and we must pay it. Some people have been advised that their maximum is such and such an amount and that they're working close to it—that when they get there the chances are that they won't go further. But they also know that by doing a good job they can go further; they can get more money.

One way is through the wage dividend. It's a pretty widespread approach in industry. The basic philosophy is that the results of labor should accrue to both labor and management. The proportions are pretty much arbitrary, of course, who gets how much. In our case it all began with Ed Villchur. That was his philosophy—that the workers should get a dividend before we pay one to the management. And Manny and I and Abe, we all go along with it pretty well. We think that they should get a cut of the profits. I would expect that as we grow and make more money that we'll continue to give more and more to the workers. We think, in general, that the workers think this is a pretty important aspect of their earnings. They understand it.

One other policy we have here is that we try not to lay anybody off. When I came here, I inherited a couple of workers that didn't belong. You know, they had limited capacity for growth; some of them had pretty limited intelligence. A lot of them had bad attitudes. Well, if you inherit things like that when you come to work for a company, you don't want to make any quick change in personnel. I wanted to find out first what was going on in the company. After a while, I pretty well got on to everybody around here and I set up a list of people who might be eliminated from the scene after our real busy season. When the time came, I called them in one by one and discussed it with them. I tried to make it palatable and gave them their bonus as it had accrued up to that date and gave them their vacation pay. I guess there was a total of about seven people who were inherited that we got rid of this way after the busy season.

The office up front, of course, is always pushing in the spring for us to unload some of the employees. But Manny and Ed and I always say no. They didn't want to lay people off and I didn't want to lay them off, so we decided to keep them on. We used some of them to paint and clean up, do a lot of sweeping, fix the office area, and so on, until business picked up again. The employees know where we stand on this one. We tell them at our meetings.

I meet frequently, but not regularly, with Benny and the supervisors to discuss each man and to decide whether or not to give a raise. If we don't know the worker well, or haven't had a chance to see him in action, we call in the supervisor. Sometimes we call in the worker. I think it's important to be personal about this sort of thing. I'm not sure it's the best way, but it's the only way I know. I'm on a personal basis with everyone working here, right down to the sweepers. I walk around here a couple of times a day anyway, so I get to see everyone sooner or later.

Benny and I work closely, and, fortunately, we see a lot of things the same way. Of course, Benny has no academic background. He has a practical, in-service kind of background, but I work with him each day. For example, right now we're working on semantics. He wants very badly to do better, but he can't see the nuances in situations, and he murders the language. For example, I made a collection of his errors, here are a couple. . . . "Because of the eventuality of things. . . ." "Take the force of least resistance. . . ." and "we have been through real criterion."

*   *   *   *   *

Most of our backgrounds, you know, are academic. Abe is the only real businessman. I imagine he feels like an outsider when we gang up on him now and then.

Mr. Maier, materials manager

Mr. Maier studied five years at The City College of New York before graduating in 1936 with majors in education, German, and Latin. Subsequently he received his M.S. in education, a teaching license in German and Latin, and a Ph.D. in German literature in 1953. In 1954 he received a fellowship from Clark College to study Geography. He completed his preparatory work, took a one-year trip to France to do his research, and by 1958 had completed all requirements for the Ph.D. in Geography "except the last few chapters of the dissertation."

During these years Mr. Maier held a variety of industrial jobs, including truck driving, war work in an aircraft plant, work in a machine shop, in a button factory, and in city planning for Worcester, Massachusetts. He had also held teaching posts at New York University and the Stockbridge School at Interlaken.

Mr. Maier worked weekends at Acoustic Research starting in 1954, and on his return from France in 1957 he joined the company on a full-time basis. He said:

When I came back, Ed spoke to me about working here. He said the setup had improved and that the pay would be good. I took the job on a one-year basis—to see if I liked it and if I could do the work. After a year, it seems to be working out on both counts.

The main reason I came to work here was my dissatisfactions with staff relationships in teaching. A job with low pay and low status made for unsatisfactory relationships among the staff members. In addition, I was getting interested in city planning and geography, so I was already half way out of teaching.

I think the thing I enjoy most is the people I work with here. Another thing is the idea of a job well done. Business is still a mystery to me—how you turn nothing into money. But I enjoy seeing that it can be done on an honest basis. It's an interesting game and I enjoy it. If it ever got really serious, I don't think I would. Also there is a better income here than in teaching.

It is not my aim here to be a successful businessman, but to earn enough to buy freedom. I play the game according to my own philosophy, and not to make the most money. When I happen to write a sharp contract and have a supplier by the tail, if he shows me he is going to lose money on the deal I will usually let him off the hook. The boys know I do this and it's O.K. with them.

They leave me pretty much to run this job alone. On the big purchases, say $5,000 or so, I consult with Abe to see if it would upset the financial balance. Minor things I do alone. As for the price I pay, I pretty much make that decision myself. I do the negotiating with representatives of different suppliers. It's like a game of chess. If I goof up, and occasionally I do, and some of these sharpies get me, I tell the others and we all benefit from my mistakes. They poke fun at me and we all learn.

Another thing I do is wander around the plant, and if I see areas where materials are not being used right I suggest to Harry that we control this way or that so we don't waste so much.

As far as the personnel area goes, the way I reward people and check on them, for example, is interesting. I might go out into the stock room and say to the fellow out there, "How many cabinets of such and such a color do you have on your books?" He might tell me, say, "Thirty-five," and I say, "Are you sure that's right?" and I wait a little bit. And he might say, "You bet it's right; I counted them yesterday." Or he might say, "I'm not sure; I counted them two weeks ago." I say, "Why don't we count that color and see how far off your count is, if it *is* off?" and we go out and count them. If it doesn't come out right, I have him check another color and if that doesn't come out right, I have him count them all. This way I keep track on how accurate the records are and I also indicate to him that this is important and I want those records taken care of.

You see, we have this semiannual inventory here. We have to keep track and sometimes we need an inventory more often than that. The problem is to be able to figure out what we've got on hand whenever we have to have that information. Sometimes I tell the fellows to restack the stock so we can get an immediate count on it. The previous two men I had out there in the receiving room, I wanted them to figure out a way themselves that they could keep track of how much stock we had on hand. Well, the last two guys just couldn't do it. It just never got done and we never knew where we were. For example, once I thought I had 3,000 of a certain item when I had actually 5,000 of them. They were worth $1.25 each, and that's a lot of money sitting out there when we are having trouble getting money to expand. I do this pretty much constantly, going out there and checking on the inventory.

I'm out there every day trying to keep up on what we have and how the records line up with it, to get a general impression of the people who work for me. Every now and then I get impressions of other people, too, who associate with our men in their work but who report actually to Harry. If I think an employee is doing fine every day as I look at the way he keeps the place clean and the way he does the records and everything, well then when raises come up I don't have to evaluate him, I already know. For example, we have this one man out here who's taking care of our inventory now as a salaried man. He'd get a considerable raise because he's salaried and the other two men working there are hourly.

Of course I don't do it systematically or anything. When I get curious, I ask the girl how long the fellow has been here without a raise and we look in the book. If I decide to give him a raise, well I go to see him and tell him that I'm going to give him a raise, that I think he's been doing a good job. If I don't decide to give him a raise—if I don't like what he's been doing—well, I just do nothing. If he comes to see me in such a case, I tell him I'm not too happy but I'll consider it. And if he asks me why I'm not happy, well, I'll try, if I can, to point out specific illustrations of the things that he's doing that I don't like.

Mr. Rotstein, sales manager

Mr. Rotstein graduated from The City College of New York with an A.B. in mathematics in 1939. "That's where I met Ed and Manny—we've known each other well for over 25 years now." Following graduation he did odd jobs and worked a year as a junior textile buyer while continuing to take science courses. During World War II Mr. Rotstein was sent to radio school by the Signal Corps and, "like the Army, they put me in the Supply Corps."

After the war Mr. Rotstein returned to textile buying for a year and one half, and then went back to the academic life because he "didn't enjoy the crass commercial world." He taught history and economics while continuing his studies, and in 1956 he received his Ph.D. in history.

I was teaching in a high school and also at Queens College when Ed asked me if I wanted to handle the sales for Acoustic Research. I told him I was no salesman and he said that was exactly why he wanted me. This was in 1957, and the business wasn't ready for a sales manager at the time, but by this summer it was, so I took the job.

I guess there were two reasons why I came to work here. One was financial. I wanted my kids to have some real educational opportunities, and this was looming larger as they were growing up. On what I was making in teaching I wouldn't have been able to afford them those opportunities. Teaching is for rich men, and I may go back to it someday when I can afford it.

A second reason is that the manner of working here is congenial to me. It's Ed's way of doing things, and if he weren't here I wouldn't be either. Another consideration was that after the reorganization I had a financial and personal interest in the company.

I think there are several kinds of satisfactions here for me. For one thing, ours is a top product. It's the best of its kind, and there is a lot of satisfaction in that alone.

Another is that the job has challenge, it's not routine. We are a consumer-oriented company—and I'm basically a consumer myself—so I like this. But it means we are different from the others in our industry in this respect. This means my job is to make peace with our dealers—and let's face it, we do our business through dealers.

We sell by informing the public and letting them come to us, and we don't contemplate any change in this. We are offering our product for sale, not trying to sell it to people. To change this we would have to hire reps, pay commissions, and raise our prices.

Mr. Rotstein's major responsibility was dealer relations:

Not all dealers want to handle Acoustic Research. For example, I stopped in New Haven recently. It's a big town, big university population, and yet it isn't doing well for us at all. So I stopped in at one of the big hi-fi stores and introduced myself.

The salesman said, "Oh, yes, there's one of your speakers over there on the floor."

"But you're not a dealer of ours."

"No, but I use the Acoustic Research for demonstration purposes to help sell my own speakers."

He demonstrated one of his own speakers but wouldn't demonstrate the Acoustic Research for me. I think what he had done was doctor the Acoustic Research so that his own would then be favorable by comparison. And I think there may be others who carry our line for some such reasons. We aren't terribly distressed about it. But it does point up the fact that there are some dealers who don't want to handle Acoustic Research. And there are other dealers who haven't had enough calls for it. These are the two main reasons why we don't have more complete dealer coverage—and this won't be changed by trying to "sell" these dealers.

As far as company goals are concerned, I'd like to see us improve our dealer relations. I think a personal relationship will help a lot. And it also seems to help for us to give a frank explanation of our consumer orientation. Then they know it's a matter of policy and not malice when we let the discount house down the street sell Acoustic Research at cut-rate prices.

I think our biggest problem is going to be to get dealers to demonstrate our speakers properly. A lot of people buy it on reputation, despite the way it sounds at the dealer's. This is mainly because the dealer gets a lower margin on Acoustic Research and he tries to switch people away from it.

In fact we get letters all the time from people who complain that our dealers say they can't deliver. The customer waits for months while the dealer blames it on the factory. When I get one of these letters I write or call the person myself and tell them we have a thousand speakers in inventory. I mail them a list of dealers and suggest they try another one. Usually I see a "warranty card" from the person in a few days. But it reflects badly on the company, and I'm sure it costs us business.

Just then Mr. Villchur began testing equipment in his office, and the resulting music could be heard loud and clear in Mr. Rotstein's office.

It's a beautiful thing, but it's sometimes distracting. It's hard to think when that breaks in. That's Bach's *Magnificat in D*.

There are four policies that hurt us with most dealers:
1. No quantity discounts above 33⅓% no matter how many a dealer orders.
2. No prizes and no salesman "push money."
3. Low price, meaning low absolute profit.
4. No price fixing.

Fortunately, there is another side to this. Some dealers like Acoustic Research speakers and have one at home. They push Acoustic Research even though they make less per speaker—figuring they will have a higher volume all told.

Organization

Mr. Hoffman described the organization as "informal." The men had known each other for years before joining the company, called each other by first names, and wore sport shirts to work. Occasionally the management met in formal session, but most decisions were reached informally as the men rode to work together, ate lunch together, or visited each other socially in the evenings—"sometimes talking business." The company did not have an organization chart, and Mr. Hoffman did not want to draw up one. He said, "We try to discuss things rather than spell out formal levels of authority, and we pay attention to the person with the most experience. Of course, Ed's voice carries a majority of the stock, and he's also the genius of this organization. But we try for unanimity on major policy decisions, and to let the person with a responsibility have the authority. Maybe things are a little fuzzy, but it gets better cooperation. We're all friends here, and it's the way we like to work." (An organization chart representing the case writer's impressions is given in Exhibit 2.)

Exhibit 2
ORGANIZATION CHART

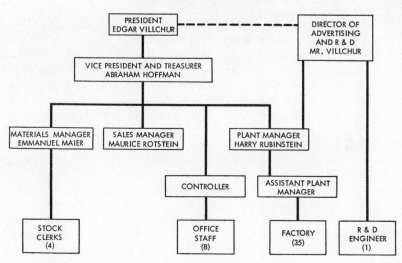

Mr. Villchur said, "Things are getting more formal as we grow. We are keeping written records of decisions, for one thing, but it doesn't have to change our personal relationships. We aren't formalizing levels of management."

*   *   *   *   *

The following incidents were recorded at various time during the six-month field research period.

The employee meeting

Mr. Villchur stopped Manny Maier in front of his office and began to run over the proposed agenda for the employee meeting to take place in the second-floor assembly area in a few minutes. Mr. Villchur said, "Well, I'll start off and introduce this guy from Harvard, and then I'll tell them about the dividend. Then I'll give the rest of you a chance to get into the act—okay?"

Manny smiled his agreement and said, "Wait a minute, Ed, I want to get a cigar before going up there."

ED: I thought you were the pipe-type, Manny.
MANNY: Well, maybe so—but a cigar is more impressive, eh?

The two men went upstairs into a large open room. At the far end the employees were gathered, waiting. As Mr. Villchur led the way toward the workers, he began to whistle a marching song. The employees began laughing and clapping hands in time to the music.

Mr. Villchur looked toward the door and said, "We'd better wait until Mr. Moneybags arrives." The smiles resulting from the remark greeted Mr. Hoffman who came through the door just then. A general call of recognition and welcome went up, and Mr. Hoffman took his place next to Ed Villchur, Manny Maier, and Harry Rubinstein.

ED: Before we get started here, let me introduce our guest. He's from Harvard, and is not merely a student but is a research associate. And for some reason he has taken an interest in us. Well, I just want to let you know that he represents Harvard and not us. Anything you want to say to him is all right with us. Go ahead. He'll keep it to himself. If you want to call the president a "son of a B——," that's up to you and it won't come back to us (*much protest and laughter*).

MANNY: God help you if it does! (*Another chorus of laughter*).

ED: We hope you will help him, but if you don't want to that's all right too. I just want you to know who he is before we begin.

Now this is our semiannual meeting to discuss the wage dividend. And that's what it is—a dividend, not a bonus. A bonus means we look around every once in a while and see things are going pretty well and so we decide to throw around some presents. But this is a dividend because you've earned it. It's earned by every one of you people. It depends on how many speakers go out and don't come back (*laughter*). Where's Ed (*quality control man*)? There he is.

Now the amount of dividend depends upon how well you do. The midyear dividend last year was 4%[3] because we found we were doing pretty well at midyear. But at the year-end we were doing much better and the dividend was 8%.

Now the midyear dividend in 1958 should not be compared to the year-end dividend of 1957, but rather to the 1957 midyear dividend. We are doing better this midyear than last year and so the dividend is going to be 6% this year.

The 4%–8% progress last year does not set any precedents, of course, for figuring what this year's year-end dividend will be. It all depends on how well we do. But we are doing much better this year than last year, and the year-end dividend will probably be something like last year's.

HARRY (*interrupting*): That's because most of our profits at this time of year are tied up in speakers and can't be paid out.

ED: Yes, that's right. Until we ship them, we can't pay more dividends . . . unless some of you want to take payments in speakers—or magnets.

MANY EMPLOYES: Oh, no! (*laughter*)

ED: The dividend checks will be given out tomorrow—before the bank closes (*laughter*).

* * * * *

HARRY: Our general operations are reasonably reasonable—except on the AR-1 woofers. We'll keep trying to improve them, and we'll just have to live with it until we work it out. We're making no promises for perfection now, Ed,

---

[3]Calculated on the previous six months' total earnings of each employee, including overtime pay.

we're just saying we're going to try to get better. You all know Ed's always demanding perfection, giving orders for perfect units. Well, we're trying, hum?

Ed's working on that new turntable now. One of these days it may even work (*laughter*).

A MIDDLE-AGED LADY: Will the new turntable be cheap enough for people like us to buy it on our pay? (*A long pause and, as Harry began to answer, Ed spoke up.*)

ED: Well, I'd like to say our whole goal here is to make the best equipment possible at a price way below the competition. We want Cadillac units at Ford prices. That's our goal.

Subsequently Mr. Rubinstein answered some questions on check-cashing policy and then the meeting broke up.

The table covering

Manny was standing by the counter in the office area rolling up a large piece of cloth when Ed came by.

ED: What's that?

MANNY: A table covering for the next display.

ED: That color?

MANNY: What's wrong with it?

ED: It's dead looking. There won't be any contrast with the walls. The place will look like a battleship. Everything will be gray.

MANNY: Oh.

ED: Didn't we have a neutral aqua color before? Say, why didn't we talk this thing over?

MANNY: I probably did.

ED: I don't remember it. I would never have voted for gray.

MANNY: We had gray before.

ED: I don't remember it.

MANNY: Well, I still have remnants of it.

ED: Well, I still think it will look like a battleship.

MANNY: I have to get some more anyway, because this won't be enough for the display. Shall I get aqua?

ED: Well, I think *some* other neutral color would be better.

MANNY: O.K., I'll check it.

ED: What do you mean this won't be enough? This should be enough for the show in Chicago,[4] shouldn't it?

MANNY: Well, I don't know.

ED: I'm pretty sure it will.

MANNY: O.K., we'll use this in Chicago.

A discussion of dealer relations

Mr. Hoffman and the researcher were discussing dealer relations in the former's office when the conversation turned to the possibility that many of the large dealers might "go sour."

---

[4] The company planned to participate in a Chicago show at a later date.

ABE: We have 10 or 12 very large dealers around the country, and they do about 25% of our business. There are some signs that a couple of them have gone a little sour on us this year. Some aren't selling as many as they did last year, while some of the smaller dealers have increased sales a lot. The big boys keep on selling Acoustic Research because they have customers that demand it, but they just don't display it the way they used to. If most of them were to go sour we might go direct—giving a 10% discount because we couldn't provide service.

Oh, come in Ed.

ED: Hi, Harvard.

ABE: Please join us, Ed. We were just talking about what would happen if most of our big dealers went sour. I was just discussing the possibilities of going direct. We could have our own dealers in the big cities and let anyone handle Acoustic Research in the smaller towns. There would be service problems and credit problems, and we would probably have to hire someone who is really good in the mail-order business. But Heath[5] is doing it, and we might have to some day.

ED: No, you don't want to mix direct and selective distribution. To do it right you would have to have fancy demonstration salons in the big cities. Besides, Heath is good. They have good specs, a good reputation, and you don't have to listen to the product before you buy it. You still have to listen to a loudspeaker, but you can no longer hear the amplifier.

Besides, Radio Craftsman tried it. They cut the price 20% and went direct. They went bust.

ABE: Does that mean we will?

ED: No, no. But we would have to do a lot better job.

ABE: We have a better product.

ED: Theirs was good.

ABE: But ours is premium.

ED: People still need to listen to it. If they hear it at a friend's home, we are O.K. Then we could go direct all the way. But if you are going to use dealers, you should get as many good ones as possible.

The main point is the speaker sells through the ears. Amplifiers can sell by the eyes—the specs.

ABE: Our biggest dealers sell a lot by mail now—so it's an idea. It's the ultimate logic of our position. Dealers say they don't get enough for handling our product, and if it's true, the ultimate thing is for the dealers to desert.

ED: No. Look at the history of other industries. For a while dealers tried to run the industry, now they just sell at the best price. They aren't trying to run things now!

ABE: But that was against GM and GE. Some manufacturers got knocked off in the process and we're no GE.

ED: Yes, but we are like GE in speakers. We have consumer pull.

*   *   *   *   *

ED: The first step should be our own demonstration salons (*in competition*

---

[5]Maker of "Heathkit" components. Heath products were sold by direct mail and through dealers, and the company was widely known for its amplifier kits.

with the existing outlets, not as exclusive outlets as Mr. Hoffman had suggested). This would be a lot less radical and a good way to begin direct distribution.

ABE: We might have to move pretty fast on this some day. We should have something like a general staff plan—some of these things thought out so we would know where we could move.

ACOUSTIC RESEARCH, INC. (C)*

∧∧

The field researcher, as part of his investigation, obtained data about the process by which major policy decisions were formulated at Acoustic Research, Inc. From his field notes he summarized information about three policies believed by management to be critical to the company's success: licensing policy, advertising policy, and product and pricing policy. In addition, the researcher interviewed the two officers of the company, Mr. Villchur and Mr. Hoffman, about possible changes in corporate objectives, future trends in the high-fidelity industry, and about company plans for responding to these trends.

Licensing policy

Mr. Hoffman explained the company's licensing policy as follows:

We will license other manufacturers to produce acoustic suspension speakers for a 2% royalty. This policy applies to anyone—big or small—so long as he is competent to make the speakers.

There are several reasons for this policy. For one thing, we think acoustic suspension is too big for us. We believe it's going to have a big impact on the industry, and that sooner or later a large percentage of the quality speakers will be made with acoustic suspension. To supply that demand, we either have to grow ourselves or to license others. Well, none of us here want to work in such a large company that things are run by reports and memoranda. We want to stay small, to run things on the basis of personal contact, and avoid the strain of managing a large company. With licensing we can stay small, collect some income, and have the kind of work atmosphere we want.

Second, we believe we owe it to the public to allow wide use of acoustic suspension. We don't want to keep it from the public just for our own benefit. Our success has been built on public acceptance, and we believe we owe this in return.

A third reason is that Ed doesn't want to be an inventor snarled up in patent litigation. Patent suits have a way of dragging on, and of getting the inventor all worked up at the ways other people will try to claim his ideas. Ed knows the history of these things, with the inventor jumping out the window. He doesn't want to get into that situation himself. He'd rather avoid the bitterness and keep his mind free to work on other things.

Besides, inventors are rarely sure of the patent. This is a philosophical patent, a patent on an idea and not on a process or gimmick. Ed knows these are the hardest to defend in court.

The reason we set the fee at 2% was to make it more attractive to license than to infringe on the patent or design around it.

So far we have only one licensee, the KLH Research and Development Corporation. That's the company formed by Eddie's former student and the group that left here at the time of the reorganization. From the royalties we can tell how they have been doing, and we also have the right to audit their books if we wish. They have given larger discounts, used "reps," and have produced more expensive models than we have. But just this summer they introduced a cheaper model to compete with the AR-2, selling at about $130. It is off to a good start, and we are watching to see how well it does.

But our policy isn't just for small companies. One of the very large companies [1957 sales over $1 billion] bought 30 AR-2's last year, and we wrote their management and offered them a license. We never heard from them, but just this week we got an order for another 40. The AR-2 would be great in one of their table model phonographs—it would put them way ahead of anyone else. Their engineers seem to know it. But when you write their management, it looks as though their right hand doesn't know what the left is doing.

*   *   *   *   *

We had another interesting problem come up the other day in connection with our licensing policy. Our largest dealer is having a loudspeaker system made for sale under his own brand name. We think its design may involve a patent infringement. We asked them about it in a conversation at one of the fairs recently. They said it wasn't an infringement, and we were ready to let it drop. But then Maurice dropped in to talk to them and they said, "Well, maybe it was. And what are you going to do about it?"

When Maurice got back and told me about it, I slept on it overnight and then told Ed about it. Then he, Maurice, and I discussed it, and we decided we wouldn't do business that way.

We made a policy decision based on this case. There was a legal question involved—either it was infringement or not. But more important, there was an ethical or moral question. We have a relationship with them; they are a customer. There is a responsibility for straight dealing on both sides. They seem to be kicking us in the teeth and believe they can get away with it because they are such an important customer. Well, we don't go along with that. We live up to our part of the responsibility. For example, we told them of our plans for the introduction of the AR-3 in advance so they could schedule their inventory requirements on the AR-1. We thought we owed a good customer a chance to know and plan ahead. We think that kind of relationship should go both ways, and if we don't get it we won't do business with them.

So right while Ed and Maurice were in the office, I called them. I got one of their executives on the phone and he hedged. He said he wasn't going to admit it was an infringement. I told him it wasn't so much a legal matter as one of ethics, but he didn't seem to understand.

Several days ago they sent us an order for $7,000 worth of stuff. So I sent them a note that the order was confirmed subject to their sending us in writing a statement that in their opinion it was not an infringement. This may be their way of asking us for a license—they just aren't used to asking manufacturers for much of anything because they are so powerful. But we don't play that way; we aren't going to be kicked around. We may charge them more than 2% for having tried it this way, too.

Advertising policy

Company policy on advertising, according to Mr. Villchur, was to portray simply and accurately the idea of advanced design. (See Exhibit 1. See also Exhibits 10–14 in Acoustic Research, Inc. (A).) The company's advertising was under the direction of Mr. Villchur who chose the media, planned the ads, and wrote the copy himself. An artist, described by Mr. Villchur as "one of the best in the business," did the artwork and advertising layout.

Mr. Villchur continued, "I cannot conceive of a conventional advertising agency writing AR copy, unless I consciously made a decision to abandon the ideals of scientific integrity. To use an analogy, it is probably true that courtesans can be trained for jobs requiring the maximum of feminine virtue and modesty, but I would consider it better judgment to start out with more appropriate candidates. While advertising agencies, like courtesans, have been at their jobs and gained wide experience and knowledge, they have not been at our kind of job."

Advertising was largely confined to magazines which were aimed at readers interested in high fidelity, although some ads were placed in magazines designed for a more general readership. A small amount of advertising appeared in newspapers under the company's cooperative advertising plan with dealers.

"Advertising in the more general type of magazine is on the AR program," Mr. Villchur continued, "but only when we have a product to offer the general public. We are presently in the position of selling propellers for outboard motors. When we get around to selling motor boats, we will broaden our advertising media and shift away from magazines which cater specifically to users of outboard motors."

Product and pricing policy

In regard to product and pricing policy, the field researcher obtained information about past decisions as well as management plans for the future. Information on past decisions is presented to give an idea of how product policy had been formulated and what factors had affected the company's decisions. The field researcher believed some insight into future decisions might be gained from considering those decisions already formulated.

The AR-2. Introduced in the fall of 1956, the AR-2, according to company management, was of slightly lower quality than the AR-1. At $96, it retailed at about half the price of the senior model.

According to Mr. Villchur, several factors had suggested delaying introduction of the AR-2 model: In the first place, sales of the AR-1 were at an all-time high of 350–400 units per month, and the AR-2 was expected to cut

Exhibit 1

ADVERTISEMENT FOR THE AR-3

The AR-3 is a three-way speaker system combining an AR-1 acoustic suspension woofer with two high-frequency units developed in AR's laboratory over the last year.

Like the AR woofer, the tweeters used in the AR-3 represent a radical departure from conventional speaker design, and patent application has been made.*

These new tweeters are neither cone-type nor horn devices—they could be described technically as hemispherical direct-radiators. We believe that their uniformity and range of frequency response, their low distortion, and their transient and dispersion characteristics establish new performance standards, and that the AR tweeters make a contribution to treble reproduction similar in degree to that made by AR's acoustic suspension woofer to bass reproduction.

The AR-3 has the most musically natural sound that we were able to create in a speaker, without compromise.

*Patent applied for by E. M. Villchur, assignor to Acoustic Research, Inc.

The AR-3 speaker system, complete with the necessary "bookshelf" size enclosure, is $216 in mahogany or birch—prices in other woods vary slightly. Literature on the AR-3 is available for the asking.

ACOUSTIC RESEARCH, INC. 24 Thorndike St., Cambridge 41, Mass.

into these sales. Second, the AR-2 was not expected to be as profitable as the AR-1. Finally, the company was still a handicraft shop and did not have facilities to produce the AR-2. Under these circumstances, Mr. Villchur noted that he had "seriously questioned the wisdom of introducing the AR-2 at this time." As he put it:

The AR-1 was selling great then, at $185, so why bring out a $96 item that is a helluva lot better than the price indicates, especially when it would cut into the sales of the AR-1? We were making a good gross margin on the AR-1, about 33%, and knew it would take many months of production before an equal margin could be made on the AR-2. But I decided to market the AR-2 at this time primarily because hi-fi has a future mass market and we're aiming for it now!

We priced it at $96 because I thought there was a market for a good speaker system that cost less than $100. Our prices leave little room for big margins by the dealer, middlemen, or for ourselves. But we have followed this policy for one main reason, to expand the market for AR high-fidelity products.

The AR-2 was introduced in the fall of 1956 and made what management described as a "big splash." Orders piled up during the winter, but it was March 1957 before the company could begin delivery in quantity. In the 1957 Annual Report, Mr. Villchur's letter to the stockholders contained the following comments:

The production, design and organization of procurement of supplies for the AR-2, for example, were such that the company lost money on at least the first 1,500 units shipped. The AR-1 was profitable at all times during the year, but to a lesser extent at the beginning than at the end of the year.

The management of AR decided, in March 1957, that the retail price of the AR-2 would be held, in spite of the high production cost, until the end of the year, at which time the costs would be examined again to determine whether it would be feasible to hold the prices. I am glad to say that labor and material costs on the AR-2 have been reduced so radically that the price need not be raised, under current conditions, for the unit to yield a reasonable profit. I am even more happy to point out that this reduction in producing costs has been achieved simultaneously with improvements in quality control, reliability and uniformity of materials, and appearance of the finished unit. Moreover, the reduction in labor costs has been achieved by rationalization of production methods, and has been accompanied by wage increases.

The AR-3. In the fall of 1958 management was considering the introduction of a top-quality speaker system, the AR-3. Management believed that the AR-3, with its newly designed tweeters, would compete with the best speakers available.

In August, prior to final decisions on tweeter design, cabinet design, and price, a prototype of the AR-3 was displayed at the hi-fi show in Chicago "to get public reactions." By the end of September the tweeter design had been finalized, a $216 price decided upon, and most of the cabinet design problems solved.

As October 3, the day for the year's biggest high-fidelity show, approached, there were several factors which suggested delaying the formal introduction of the new model. First, management pointed out that, at the $216 price, the superior quality of the AR-3 might displace much of the demand for the AR-1. Management stated that while this was all right in itself, the company still had a large inventory of parts (over a year's supply in some cases) for the AR-1. These parts might become obsolete inventory. Second, there were still some production problems to be solved before the AR-3 could be made in quantity. It might take only two or three weeks or as much as three months to get it into quantity production.

In discussing the decision to bring out the new line, Mr. Villchur stated, "We thought about those things. But you have to go along with progress— you can't delay it for inventory. The New York show is the big show of the year, and if we had a new product we wanted to have it ready. In fact, we put on a little pressure to get it ready."

Mr. Villchur, in discussing the pricing decision, noted:

Our decision to price it at $216 was based upon a fundamental strategy— marketing a "best buy" through progress in design. We priced it to be a best buy in the long run, not just when it came out. In other words, we didn't price it at what the market would bear. The AR-3 would have been a best buy this year at $316, leaving $66 more in profit. But we don't want to hold up a price umbrella for someone else to come in under. It's the same way we priced the AR-1 and the AR-2. Perhaps setting the lowest possible price on progress benefits only the consumer in the short run, but in the long run we think it is our best interest, too.

There is a second idea in our pricing. In pricing the AR-3 at $216 we were discounting future production savings. We don't know where the savings will come from, but we expect to find them. Abe and I always battle on this. He favors pricing for contingencies, and I'm for doing it on long-run economies. I want to bring it out at a price and keep it there—not reduce it later on.

The AR-3 was displayed at the New York show. In discussing its reception by dealers and the general public, Mr. Hoffman noted, "It was the hit of the show—the only real advance in speakers. We could have had a lot of orders if we had not discouraged them. As it was, we got about 50 orders." (By the end of November 1958 there were over 500 firm orders for the AR-3.)

Commenting in November on the results of exhibiting the model, Mr. Villchur noted, "As far as sales go, it was a good decision. But production-wise it wasn't. We still can't start filling those orders, and that isn't good."

Proposed change in corporate objectives

Mr. Villchur, in discussing proposed expansion into a wider line of components, noted that the possibilities included a turntable and an amplifier, with the eventual goal of introducing a two- or three-piece component set. He stated, however, that "any new products will have to meet our overall objective of significant contributions to the audio field. We won't bring out anything that isn't the leader in its class."

The turntable. The turntable was first on the list of possible new AR products. "Plans for the package set really rest on our ability to turn out a successful turntable," said Mr. Hoffman. "We will need a turntable before we can develop a full set."

A turntable is a component which plays only one record, requiring the listener to change the record after one side has been played. Turntables are generally preferred by persons who want the very finest in sound. The turntable's advantages include better sound reproduction through elimination of "rumble" and "flutter," and reduced "tracking error." In addition, records played on a turntable retain their original sound qualities longer than those played on a changer because they escape damage due to "dropping" and "slipping."

The turntable has the disadvantage of single play, with the listener being required to attend the record player after each record. (This means an interruption once in about 22 minutes when 12-inch $33\frac{1}{3}$ records are used.) A record changer, of course, has the advantage of convenience with some compromise of sound quality. Price is not significantly different between high-quality changers and turntables, though the changer would tend to be slightly higher.

Since highest-quality sound requires separation of the speaker system from the turntable, AR planned to design a set where the turntable and amplifier were together in one package, with the speaker in another. Management regarded development of a turntable as the necessary prerequisite to development of the amplifier-turntable package. It planned, however, to put the turntable on the market before developing the remainder of the component set.

The company expected to compete with existing high-quality turntables on the basis of equal or better quality at much lower prices. The best known quality turntables, complete with arm, cartridge, and diamond stylus, retailed for about $80. "We think we can bring one out for about 50% of what competition is getting, but we won't know until we get a full list of materials," said Mr. Hoffman. "It probably won't have any unique design characteristics, so it has to have a lot lower price to fit our policy of product leadership.

"While we've already put a lot of development time into the turntable, we really don't have a good guess on how soon we may have it ready. The AR-3 is getting our attention now. When we get the AR-3 running smoothly, we'll go back to working on the turntable, but I really can't give you an estimate on how soon we will be ready to introduce it."

Mr. Rubinstein, who was coordinating the development program on the turntable, noted that "a turntable is a delicate thing. We have built a prototype model which meets our standards of quality but is too sensitive to being bumped or jarred for use in the home. We are working to develop a model that is more practical for the mass market."

Management pointed out that a turntable was not a complicated product to manufacture. Mr. Villchur thought it might be simpler than speakers, since "you have some castings and an arm to assemble, and you buy the motor." Management also believed that space existed in the present plant to accommodate assembly of turntables. According to Mr. Rubinstein, the remaining development problems were primarily in design and materials, not company facilities and resources.

The amplifier. Management was also considering marketing an amplifier. "It might be our own," said Mr. Villchur, "or a good one made by someone else. Amplifiers are so damn good nowadays that the listener has a number of very fine ones to choose from. There aren't the improvements left in amplifiers and turntables that there are in tuners and speakers. If you want to pay enough, you can get quality that is better than the sense of hearing. So we aren't expecting to build something revolutionary. But we think a really good one at a low price has a market.

"We are considering marketing an amplifier already designed by another fellow. We would use his name on it, of course, and give him full credit. It is quite a unique amplifier, though, and we would have to build a special model loudspeaker to go with it. It would make a good combination for one part of a two-piece component set."

The component set. "We believe the future mass market is for people who like good music at reasonable prices, not for those who want to tinker with electronic apparatus," said Mr. Villchur. "The trend in this industry is toward product consolidation—like putting the speakers in a cabinet and selling them as one speaker system instead of selling three or four separate parts. And this means a trend toward sets—maybe two- or three-piece sets.

"Most component manufacturers are fighting the trend on this. They keep advertising that only individual components mean quality, but, from an engineering point of view, this is just nonsense. Your sound comes from a total set—and with separate components the listener selects the combination that makes up the set. He is the final designer. If he is an expert, okay. But otherwise you have an amateur doing the final design. With a set, the components can be matched and the final design done by engineering experts, which is as it should be.

"The package or component set—I don't know which it should be called— is an area where real contributions to progress can be made, but I'm not that interested in it right now. We would aim to build one for around $300 to compete with sets selling at $1,000 and up. Using a speaker like the AR-2, we think we can produce a good set for the average music lover."

Industry trends and corporate strategy

Mr. Villchur was asked to comment on industry trends and AR's strategy to keep its place in the industry. Speaking of the former, he said:

Technological change has come more rapidly in this industry since the war, but most of it has been based on prewar ideas. For instance, the basic change in amplifiers, negative feedback, was written up in the journals in 1931, but it wasn't in general use until 1947. In contrast, things are moving faster through immediate commercial application today. For example, GE came out with the variable reluctance magnetic pickup in 1946, and by the early 1950's, this was the generally accepted type of quality pickup.

Another thing, I think, is going to be a trend toward fine quality at lower prices. It's happening in speakers, largely as a result of the AR-2. But it's going to come in other products, too. Take amplifiers—the top four or five are already like transparent glass. When you can no longer see the glass, you can't improve on the quality. But you can make it cheaper. With turntables there is an opportunity to reduce the price, size, and weight. Speakers haven't yet achieved the same relative quality, but the AR-3 puts us a lot closer.

Probably another trend is toward "natural" sound. Some manufacturers have been making equipment that "colors" the sound by overemphasizing certain parts of the frequency spectrum—say 2,000 to 5,000 cycles. We think the trend is toward natural sound, and that is what we have been aiming for in our speakers.

Mr. Villchur also commented on the trend toward stereophonic sound. Rapid public acceptance of stereophonic sound, he stated, might enlarge his company's market without introducing new technical problems. He pointed out that AR speaker systems could be used, without modification, for either stereophonic or monaural sound:

Stereophonic sound doesn't affect speaker construction. But it may help AR in three important ways. First, stereophonic sound requires two speaker systems —so that increases the total market. Secondly, with the need for two systems instead of one, price becomes more important. Our policy of lowest possible prices gives us a competitive advantage here. And finally, since stereo requires more equipment and more furniture, speaker size becomes more important. If you tried to use two very large systems, the equipment could take up one whole side of a living room. Our speakers are definitely on the small side, and any living room can hold two of them. The AR-2 is ideal for stereo.

Mr. Villchur stated that he believed the future mass market would be in a two- or three-piece component set, with stereophonic sound encouraging the concept of a multiple-piece home entertainment center:

I think the question of whether TV is going to become part of the home music center is no longer debatable—it's a *fait accompli*. People are going to use the TV amplifier and speakers for their system. But whether anyone will build really good sound into TV, I can't say. We could design a smaller acoustic suspension speaker to fit TV sets that would improve the quality a lot. But it would also raise the cost of the set. I'm not sure that anyone will be interested in doing this.

After noting these trends in the industry, Mr. Villchur went on to point out the company's basic strategy:

Our strengths are in design and in our ability to promote the idea that we have made real progress in design. Our strategy is to make use of these two strengths.

As far as design goes, it isn't just a patent; it's an attitude. We are going to keep looking for ways to make significant contributions in the audio field. I always said the AR-1 would be superseded, and I'm glad we were the ones to do it. But we're not just looking in the speaker field. I suppose I know more about speakers now, but amplifiers used to be my area of greatest understanding. No company is going to have all the good ideas, and we don't expect it, but we are going to keep working on more than just speakers. We have sunk an awful lot of development time into a turntable already.

Of course, part of our strength is in the patent. We have no way of knowing just how strong the patent is until it comes up in a court test, but so far we don't know of any verified infringements. Thus far, all the infringements have been by advertising copy writers. They are trying to duplicate our claims and make it sound as if they have acoustic suspension. But we don't know of any manufacturer that is duplicating our speaker—and generally they miss the main point [e.g., the revolutionary construction of the acoustic suspension speaker.] When we test their product, it just doesn't measure up at all. This sidestepping indicates our patent is strong enough in its writing—no one has designed around it and ended up with equal quality. But only time will tell.

Prospect for growth

Mr. Hoffman commented on the future of the company as follows:

Over the next few years things probably will change quite a bit. I expect that we will see a lot of growth from several sources. First, I think the hi-fi business as a whole is going to grow, and so even if we just retain our percentage of the market, we'll probably grow quite a bit. Second, I expect that we'll secure a greater percentage of the market than we now have. Third, I think we're going to introduce new products and expand our line. And so, with this greater share of an increasing market, plus new products, I think that AR is due to see an awful lot of growth. I think our greatest growth will probably come when we get into a two-piece component set. Probably in three years, just roughly, we will be five times the size that we are at the present time.

Take the AR-3, for example: I've projected sales for it in 1959 at 7,000 units. That alone will add about $1 million to our volume. Of course, that could be off quite a bit, but with over 500 orders before we have run our first ad, I don't think it's too optimistic. And I expect the AR-2 to do considerably better—at least 20%.

*   *   *   *   *

Frankly the other members of management haven't thought much about the future growth of the firm—at least not in terms of what it will require of the company. They really haven't thought out where they want the company to go, or what will be required to get there. I guess it's something all five of us should consider—and something we should talk over as a group.

ACOUSTIC RESEARCH, INC. (D)*

In terms of sales, profits, and market acceptance of products, Acoustic Research had enjoyed considerable success in the 1958–1965 period. Sales, which had totaled $57,000 in 1955, the first full year of operation, had increased to $1.3 million for 1958 and $4.2 million for 1964. Profits after taxes for these same years had increased from $1,587 in 1955 to $117,000 in 1958 and $368,000 in 1964. As of November 1965, the company estimated that sales and profits for 1965 would be $5.3 million and $650,000, respectively. (An eight-year summary and detailed financial statements for 1963 and 1964 are shown in Exhibits 1–3.)

Mr. Villchur, who was still president and owner of 51% of the common stock of the company, said that everything had pretty much gone as they had planned at the time of the earlier case series. They had developed and introduced a turntable, had modified their speaker models slightly and introduced a new model, the AR-4, and were still working on an amplifier so that they could eventually offer a complete three-piece component set. Some of this had gone slower than management had expected, but the basic strategy had not changed. He added:

One thing I would like to emphasize is that some of my comments concerning growth in the earlier cases gave your students the wrong impression. I was never *against* growth; it was simply not an explicit goal. Growth is something which follows from your other goals and achievements, and that is the way it has worked out for us. *Not* growing has never been a goal of mine; that would be ridiculous.

Mr. Villchur and Mr. Hoffman[1] still held the same titles and performed about the same duties as in 1958, but there had been a number of other changes in management. Harry Rubinstein, who had been plant manager since 1957, left in the fall of 1961 to return to Stockbridge to resume teaching music. Roy Allison had taken his place, and George Benedetti had become production manager. Manny Maier, the materials manager, who had completed his thesis and received his Ph.D. in Geography, left the company in

---

[1]Mr. Hoffman, vice president and treasurer, owned about 8½% of the stock; no other members of the present management had any significant holdings or options.

Exhibit 1

ACOUSTIC RESEARCH, INC., AND WHOLLY OWNED SUBSIDIARIES

Financial and Operating Eight Year Summary, 1957–64

As at End of Year	1957	1958	1959*	1960	1961	1962	1963	1964*
Net Sales	$973,262	$1,334,478	$2,893,118	$2,495,868	$2,544,117	$2,389,836	$3,180,050	$4,188,621
Income Before Taxes	71,147	242,069	634,771	454,507	455,030	284,196	404,875	751,331
Net Earnings After Taxes	37,160	117,305	278,768	233,398	230,450	146,418	202,858	367,634
Shares Outstanding	1,300	1,305	1,305	1,292	1,292	1,292	1,284	1,270
Net Earnings per Share	28.58	89.89	213.62	180.65	178.37	113.33	157.99	289.48
Cash Dividends per Share	None	3.00	12.00	20.00	60.00	15.00	52.00	100.00
Current Assets	198,188	430,873	901,318	931,508	1,133,615	1,099,749	1,422,119	1,531,520
Current Liabilities	145,933	261,889	520,721	373,439	461,267	305,574	507,645	666,094
Working Capital	52,255	168,984	380,597	558,069	672,348	794,175	914,474	865,426
Shareholders' Equity	76,884	190,849	453,957	641,775	794,705	921,743	1,045,737	1,266,542
Equity per Share	59.14	146.24	347.86	496.73	615.10	713.42	814.44	997.28

*Fifty-three-week years.

Source: Company records.

Exhibit 2

ACOUSTIC RESEARCH, INC., AND WHOLLY OWNED SUBSIDIARIES
Comparative Consolidated Statement of Financial Condition
December 28, 1963 and January 2, 1965

	1963	1964
CURRENT ASSETS:		
Cash in Banks and on Hand	$ 296,129	$ 606,142
U. S. Treasury Bills	246,260	...
Accounts Receivable—Trade (less Allowance for Doubtful Accounts and Cash Discounts of $26,984 in 1964 and $26,054 in 1963)	309,977	359,826
Notes Receivable—Due within one year	2,667	3,500
Inventories	515,802	529,464
Loans to Employees, Claims and Advances Receivable	14,949	5,743
Prepaid Expenses	36,335	26,845
Total Current Assets	1,422,119	1,531,520
CURRENT LIABILITIES:		
Accounts Payable—Trade	113,741	91,942
Accrued Expenses, Payroll and Withheld Taxes	123,076	140,207
Dividends Payable in January 1965 and 1964	51,360	107,950
Customers' Credit Balances	4,138	3,232
Federal and State Income and Franchise Taxes Payable	149,382	311,634
Manufacturers' Excise Tax Accrued	65,948	11,129
Total Current Liabilities	507,645	666,094
WORKING CAPITAL	914,474	865,426
OTHER ASSETS:		
Plant and Equipment (less Accumulated Depreciation of $76,572 in 1964 and Accumulated Depreciation plus Investment Credit of $91,879 in 1963)	72,340	81,111
Patents, Trade-Marks and Goodwill	1	1
Cash Surrender Value of Life Insurance	58,305	71,352
Deposits and Unamortized Organization Expense	617	562
Notes Receivable due after one year	...	2,500
Plant Relocation Fund—U.S. Treasury Bills—June 10, 1965	...	245,590
TOTAL CAPITAL	$1,045,737	$1,266,542
CAPITAL CONSISTS OF:		
Capital Stock:		
Class A Common—No Par Value Authorized and Issued 1,300 shares	$ 351,000	$ 351,000
Class B Common—No Par Value Authorized 100 shares, Issued 5 shares	1,350	1,350
Retained Earnings	724,887	966,692
Total	1,077,237	1,319,042
Less—Treasury Stock—at cost		
Class A Common (30 shares 1964, 16 shares 1963)	24,000	45,000
Class B Common (5 shares 1964 and 1963)	7,500	7,500
TOTAL CAPITAL	$1,045,737	$1,266,542

Source: Company records.

Exhibit 3

ACOUSTIC RESEARCH, INC., AND WHOLLY OWNED SUBSIDIARIES
Comparative Consolidated Statement of Operations
for the Years 1963 and 1964

	Fifty-Two Weeks Ended December 28, 1963		Fifty-Three Weeks Ended January 2, 1965	
	Amount	%	Amount	%
Net Sales after Discounts	$3,180,050	100.0	$4,188,621	100.0
Less—Cost of Sales	2,092,181	65.8	2,660,400	63.5
Gross Profit before Manufacturers' Excise Tax	1,087,869	34.5	1,528,221	36.5
Less—Manufacturers' Excise Tax	64,442	2.0	77,132	1.8
Gross Profit	1,023,427	32.2	1,451,089	34.7
Less—Selling, Shipping, Administrative Expenses and Bad Debts	621,060	19.5	697,062	16.6
Net Profit from Operations	402,367	12.7	754,027	18.1
Add—Interest and Other Income	8,314	.2	11,526	.2
Total	410,681	12.9	765,553	18.3
Less—Premiums on Officers' Life Insurance and Other Charges	5,806	.2	14,222	.3
Net Income before Income Taxes	404,875	12.7	751,331	18.0
Less—Federal and State Income Taxes	202,017	6.3	383,697	9.2
Net Earnings for the Year	$ 202,858	6.4	$ 367,634	8.8

Source: Company records.

the summer of 1963 to begin teaching at the Bridgewater (Mass.) State Teachers College. His duties were assumed by George Benedetti. Maurice Rotstein, the sales manager, left in the summer of 1964, also to teach at Bridgewater. Gerald Landau became sales manager when Mr. Rotstein left.

Mr. Landau, who had started with AR in 1959 at the AR music room in Grand Central Station, had been assistant sales manager since 1960. Previous to joining AR, he had spent about eight years as a history teacher at the secondary school level in the New York City area. He had also spent about two years with a consulting firm doing systems and procedures work in "companies the size of AR," and had worked for RCA in their community relations department for about four years.

Mr. Allison, the new plant manager, had joined AR in 1959 as assistant to the president. He had studied electrical engineering in college, and at AR he had worked in the repair department and in production engineering before becoming plant manager in 1961. His experience before joining AR included several years in a publishing firm which specialized in trade magazines, where he had been editor of *Audiocraft Magazine* and audio editor of *High Fidelity*.

Mr. Hoffman said that both Mr. Landau and Mr. Allison had been brought into the organization in 1959 as understudies who could step into management when the appropriate time came. Mr. Hoffman felt that the principal reason for the management turnover in the past several years was as follows:

Effective work in business requires specialized training and interest in business, just like any other occupation or profession. Most of those who left had little of either, and as a result they were neither as happy nor as effective as they otherwise might have been.

In the fall of 1965 there were some strong differences of opinion within the company about their product policy, the role and importance of dealers, and the use of manufacturers' representatives. Some of the management felt the above issues were especially important in view of the changes that were taking place in the industry, the success and apparent ambitions of some of their principal competitors, the increasing "maturity" of the AR product line, and the larger size and longer history of AR as an organization compared to 1958. These issues, as well as industry trends and the development and introduction of the turntable and the new speaker, the AR-4, are discussed in the remainder of the case.

Industry trends

A number of developments had occurred in the "hi-fi components" industry during the 1958–1965 period. Some of the more important ones, in the case writer's judgment, are set forth below.

User convenience. The most noticeable trend from the standpoint of the hi-fi equipment buyer had been the increased attention on the part of manufacturers to user convenience. For example:

1. A high-quality stereo system (excluding speakers) which had consisted of seven separate electronic components as late as 1961 was now commonly available as a single electronic unit at about two-thirds of the price of the old system.
2. The practice of selling speakers and speaker cabinets separately, which had accounted for the largest portion of speaker sales in the industry in 1955, was virtually outdated. Mr. Villchur estimated that about 95% of all speaker sales were now represented by fully assembled systems.
3. The practice of selling turntables and turntable arms separately, which was almost universal in the 1950's and common until the early 1960's, had virtually disappeared.
4. "Music systems," a new category[2] of sound reproduction equipment, had become significant. The consumer could now choose from among three broad alternatives in his quest for a high fidelity sound system:
   a) The traditional package set.[3]

---

[2]Similar to the two- or three-piece "component set" referred to by Mr. Villchur on page 458 of this case and in the Acoustic Research, Inc. (C) case.

[3]A furniture-type console, completely self-contained and fully assembled at the factory, traditionally offered by the large consumer-electronics firms like GE, RCA, Westinghouse, etc.

b) Components[4] purchased separately and assembled by the consumer to form a complete system.

c) A "music system": generally, a pair of speakers (for stereo) plus a single unit which contained a record changer and the necessary electronic equipment, all of "component quality." Such music systems were designed by the manufacturer to be at least as convenient for the consumer to purchase, install, and operate as a package set.

Package sets and "music systems" are discussed in more detail below.

Package sets. Several company personnel felt that package sets were improving in quality and value and that the gap between components and package sets was continuing to narrow. They also felt that a system put together from separate components still offered the consumer the best value if he was willing to spend (for stereo) about $350 or more.

Consumer Reports, in a May 1965 article on radio-phonograph consoles, stated, "It's a rare listener who will get a full stereo effect from them." The problem of proper speaker separation for realistic stereo effect at normal listening distances had not been solved. With regard to the fidelity of the sound produced, the article continued as follows:[5]

. . . none of those [consoles] tested had the transparent, smooth sounds of a high-rated audio component system. . . . The majority were mediocre or worse in tone, the four lowest-rated Acceptable models sounding particularly distorted.

In summing up, however, CU made the following comments:

All in all, then, these "packaged" consoles aren't going to satisfy a demanding listener who wants the sound quality and stereo effect the ads promise. But, it should be added, neither will anything in the same price range. Top-grade sound from a system made up of components recently high-rated by CU would list at about $600—without a cabinet. So it is a straight case of paying more for more, less for less. On the other hand, if the buyer is "upgrading" his listening to one of these machines from a table model radio plus a portable phonograph—sources that currently furnish sound in millions of American homes—he's apt to consider the tone quality of the better consoles, by comparison, positively grand.

"Music systems." A number of manufacturers had entered the market with complete sound systems which were of good quality, but were neither package sets nor systems made up of individual components. Products in this classification lacked a descriptive or generally accepted name. KLH, which manufactured a wide range of audio equipment, had been a leader in the introduction of such products, and had used the terminology "music systems" to describe and distinguish its product.

As described previously, these systems were usually in three pieces: two

---

[4]The customary products of the components industry in the 1955–1965 period: turntable or record-changers, amplifiers, preamplifiers, FM tuners, speakers.

[5]Reprinted from *Consumer Reports* with permission. Copyright 1965, by Consumer's Union of the U.S., Inc., a nonprofit organization.

speakers, plus a record changer and electronic equipment in a third piece. AR personnel felt that the better music systems, as far as the average consumer was concerned, were approaching the quality of a component system made up of AR-4 speakers, the lower-priced Dynakit electronic equipment, and the AR turntable.[6] Music systems did not consist simply of separate components mounted in one box (with separate speakers); the best of these could more accurately be described as package sets without the single, large console, with quality approaching that of systems made up of the lower quality range of individual components, and with separate speakers.

"Portable music systems" were also becoming increasingly available and popular. Many large consumer electronics firms had marketed "portable hi-fi" sets for years, but these had generally been characterized by medium to low price (down to perhaps $20) and anything but "high" fidelity. In recent years prominent manufacturers of quality hi-fi components had entered this market with higher priced units.

Company personnel felt that these portable music systems were superior to previous models, but that the compromises necessary to achieve portability and low price placed them significantly below the quality level of acceptable high fidelity systems.

Speaker systems. The trend was clearly down the path that Acoustic Research had pioneered. In marked contrast to conditions in the middle and late 1950's, there were now dozens of models of speaker systems available which were similar to AR speakers in size, appearance, price, construction, and quality. These "compact" speaker systems, consisting of two or more separate speakers mounted in an enclosure, generally measured about 1 x 1 x 2 feet in overall size. Speaker systems of this type had largely displaced the much larger and more expensive systems of the middle and late 1950's, and the practice of selling speakers and cabinets separately had also declined greatly.

One major reason for the popularity of these compact speaker systems was their convenient size; the speaker could now fit more easily into the average living room or apartment. More important, perhaps, was the widespread recognition that smaller size no longer meant poorer quality: the use of the acoustic suspension principle had eliminated the need for large enclosures to achieve faithful bass response.

Consumer Reports, commenting in April 1965 on the results of an evaluation of 29 loudspeaker models, stated that the man about to shop for a speaker now had a wide choice. Nine of the speakers were judged to be fine performers, compatible with the best audio components that had been tested. The AR-2x was one of two speakers judged a "Best Buy" in this test.

The article went on to emphasize, however, that although neither the sound nor the laboratory measurements for any two speakers within broad quality groups were identical, these differences did not make it possible to rank speakers effectively within a group. All of the speakers "colored" the

---

[6]List price, with cartridge: $351.90 assembled; $299.90 in kit form.

sound to some extent, and it was not considered possible to state which of the particular colorations were "better" or "worse."

Mr. Villchur noted that all nine of the top-rated speakers employed woofers based on the acoustic suspension principle, and that four of them also used dome tweeters, a design introduced by AR on the AR-3 in 1959. AR did not receive any royalties from these products. The patent on the acoustic suspension principle had not survived an Indiana court test in 1961, and Mr. Villchur had decided not to appeal the case. No basic patents could be obtained on the dome tweeter because of previous literature on the subject.

Turntables. The design of turntables had also been influenced by Acoustic Research. The most significant change, as noted, was that the practice of selling turntables and arms separately had almost disappeared, at least in part because of the success of the AR turntable. In addition, Mr. Villchur pointed out that a special suspension system which had been refined by AR and used on its turntable had since been incorporated, in varying degrees, into five or six of the nine turntables tested by Consumer's Union in 1964.

Stereo. This continued to be popular, in spite of a cost of about 75% (if purchased originally as a stereo system) in excess of a similar monophonic component system. Of all new component sets purchased, stereo was estimated to account for well over 90%. For radio-phonograph consoles (package sets) selling in the $300 to $400 range, *Consumer Reports* indicated in May of 1965 that "monophonic-only and phonograph-only consoles have nearly disappeared from the market."

Broadening of line. Manufacturers who had been successful with an original line of components had tended to branch out into the manufacture or at least distribution of other components so that they would have either a full line of components and/or a complete "music system" to offer. Acoustic Research, for example, had introduced a turntable and was working on an amplifier; Fisher, prominent in electronics, had begun to manufacture separate speaker systems; and KLH, originally a speaker manufacturer, now offered complete music systems consisting of their own speakers with electronic equipment and Garrard changers. The trend, then, seemed to include both the addition of components and the marketing of complete music systems.

Private branding. There had been a major trend to private branding among large and medium mail-order or discount houses. A number of houses which accounted for a significant volume of speaker sales were pushing their own brands, either imported or manufactured for them by some of the five or so major speaker manufacturers.

Industry statistics. Industry statistics were no easier to come by than they had been 10 years ago, but Mr. Hoffman's best estimate was "about $100 million at retail" for the high fidelity components industry in 1965.

AR product summary

Although AR had not yet followed the lead of some competitors in bringing out a full line of components or a complete sound reproduction system, several speaker modifications, a new speaker system, and a turntable had been introduced since 1958.

Speaker systems. The AR-3, introduced at the New York Hi-Fi Show in the late fall of 1958, had received excellent reviews and was still the "top end" of the AR speaker line in 1965. Production of the AR-3 had not commenced until the late spring of 1959, and production had not caught up with demand until September of 1959. The original price of $216 had been maintained, and the model had been profitable from the beginning. The AR-3 had largely displaced the AR-1, although the company still manufactured a few AR-1 or AR-1W units in response to specific requests.

The AR-2a, a modification of the AR-2 which involved adding the 1⅜" dome super-tweeter developed for the AR-3 to the existing AR-2 speaker system to enhance the high end, was introduced in December 1959. According to management, acceptance of the new model had been immediate. Within a few weeks AR-2a volume equaled that of the AR-2, the previously best selling model, even though the AR-2a averaged $26 higher in price than the AR-2. Production had been sufficient to meet demand right from the beginning.

The AR-4, a new speaker system, which was half the size of other AR speakers, was introduced in September 1964 at the New York Hi-Fi Show. It was priced at $57, or about half the price of the popular AR-2a. The AR-4 incorporated a new 8" acoustic suspension woofer and a new 3½" broad dispersion tweeter. According to management, it was "immediately successful in terms of consumer acceptance, favorable press comment, and profitability for the company." (Descriptive literature on the new speaker is shown in Exhibit 4.)

Modifications of the AR-2 and the AR-2a were introduced in October 1964. The new models, designated the AR-2x and the AR-2ax, differed from the old only in the substitution of the 3½" cone tweeter (developed for the AR-4) for the two 5" cone tweeters which had been in use on both models previously. The prices of the new models were unchanged. Following the policy of not obsoleting their products in the field if at all possible, AR made the modifications available in kit form for existing owners of speakers.

Some indication of the market acceptance of speakers of various manufacturers can be obtained from Exhibit 5, which represents the results of a number of consumer surveys conducted by one of the leading hi-fi magazines. As may be seen for the past three years the percentage of respondents expressing a preference for AR speakers had been about three times as large as for their nearest competitor, KLH. An informal report from the same source expressing respondents' preferences for the first quarter of 1965 had just been received, in which it was apparent that the newly introduced AR-4 was doing very well indeed:

AR-2ax	12.1%
AR-4	10.9%
AR-3	5.9%
KLH 17	4.6%
KLH 6	3.5%

Exhibit 4

The AR-4 uses an 8-inch acoustic suspension woofer and a 3½-inch broad-dispersion cone tweeter.

The AR-4 does not have as wide a frequency range as our other speakers, but in smoothness and uncolored musical quality it holds its own even when compared to the AR-3.

Of all our speaker models the AR-4, by a wide margin, represents the highest quality per dollar.

SIZE: 19" x 10" x 9" depth

SUGGESTED AMPLIFIER POWER (RMS): 15 watts minimum per channel

TECHNICAL SPECIFICATIONS: Impedance 8 ohms. Frequency response and distortion curves are available on request.

PRICES: Oiled walnut $57.00
Unfinished pine (not suitable for staining) 51.00

5% higher in the West and Deep South

(shown without grille cloth)

5-YEAR GUARANTEE

AR speakers are sold under a five-year guarantee covering both materials and labor. Freight costs are reimbursed.

Source: Company records.

Mr. Villchur was highly pleased with these results, but pointed out that since the survey was drawn from the readers of a specialized magazine, the results were biased toward the more knowledgeable end of the market. He thought that about half of the above percentages would represent AR's total market share.

Exhibit 5

BRANDS MAGAZINE READERS WOULD BUY*

Speakers in Enclosures

(Per Cent)†

	1960	1961‡	1962	1963	1964
AR	16.3		27.2	28.3	29.6
Electro-Voice	10.7		9.3	7.1	8.4
J. B. Lansing	10.5		9.1	5.9	9.0
Jensen	7.6		2.4	4.7	4.7
University	7.4		5.3	6.4	4.1
KLH	4.4		10.1	10.1	10.3
Altec§	4.1		5.6	4.7	3.7
Bozak	4.0		6.7	8.9	6.4
Wharfdale			4.2	4.4	6.6

*Question: If you were to purchase components in each of the following categories, which brand would you buy in each category? (Question for 1960 *slightly* different).

†Per cent will not total to 100 because of "not stated" and "all others" categories.

‡No survey in 1961.

§Altec-Lansing after 1960.

Source: Company records, compiled from surveys by a leading hi-fi magazine.

Turntable. The new AR turntable was introduced to the industry at the September 1961 New York Hi-Fi Show. A single speed prototype with a price of $58 was shown, production quantities were promised for the end of the year, and orders were declined or discouraged at the show. Development and production difficulties and changes slowed deliveries considerably, but the turntable was very well received.

In his various annual letters to the stockholders, Mr. Villchur noted that the original estimate had been a sales volume of 10,000 units per year, and that the actual unit sales had been as follows:

1961	0
1962	2,019*
1963	16,976
1964	19,714

*Substantial order backlog.

No published surveys were available which would indicate what share of the market the AR turntable was achieving. Mr. Villchur, however, said that he would stake his reputation on at least a 50% share of the turntable (*not* record-changer) market. Mr. Landau indicated that dealers in many parts of the country had told him that AR turntables accounted for a minimum of 80% of turntable sales.

The new turntable was favorably reviewed by a number of high fidelity magazines. Some of these quotes are shown in Exhibit 6, which is a reproduction of a portion of a promotional pamphlet for the turntable. In addition, the AR turntable was designated the "Best Buy" by *Consumer Reports* in a September 1964 article. Nine turntable-arm combinations ranging in price from $50 to $170 and representing most of the widely sold offerings of leading audio manufacturers were tested, and the performance of the AR turntable was judged to be at least equal to that of the best separately sold turntables and arms which had been tested.

The quality level of all of the turntables was considered high, however. It was stated that all of the models tested were at least reasonably well-suited for use in top-grade audio systems, and that even the lowest ranked and lowest priced ($49.90 without base) machine should be considered by anyone with a tight audio budget.

Although turntables had traditionally been of significantly better quality than record changers, the quality differences between turntables and record changers also appeared to be decreasing. In an August 1965 article dealing with record changers, *Consumer Reports* noted that a "change of attitude is in order." Of the four changers tested one ($106.45 list price, with base, without cartridge) "was judged fully equivalent to that of the best single-play [i.e., turntable] machines."

The AR turntable was clearly a success in terms of technical performance and market acceptance, but unanticipated development costs and manufacturing expenses necessitated price increases. In April of 1964 the price of the introductory single-speed model was increased from $58 to $75, and the price of a two-speed model, introduced in the fall of 1963 at $68, was increased to $78.

Turntable development and introduction

Because the turntable represented an important element in AR's announced strategy of selling only products which "made significant contributions in the audio field," and in addition was intended to be an essential step toward management's goal of providing a complete audio system, an account of the development and introduction of the turntable is included here.

In December 1961, three months after the introduction of the turntable at the annual New York Hi-Fi Show, Mr. Villchur discussed with a case writer the development of the turntable and the reasoning behind the critical decisions concerning the introductory date and price:

We began development of the turntable by hiring some consultants. They had responsibility for the project for about two years. Well, after $25,000 and a couple of years' work, we scrapped their model and started in again. I took responsibility for the turntable in the summer of 1960. My lab in Woodstock was complete, and the AR-3 was on its way.

We showed it in New York in September of 1961 because that's the only big hi-fi show of the year. We thought production was closer at hand than it now

Exhibit 6

AR INC. turntable

(33⅓ & 45 RPM)

PROFESSIONAL quality. The AR turntable meets NAB specifications for broadcast equipment on wow, flutter, rumble, and speed accuracy. It is belt-driven and synchronous.

COMPLETE with arm, oiled walnut base, dust cover, and accessories including needle force gauge. Overall dimensions with the dust cover are 12¾" x 16¼" x 5¼".

FOR BUTTERFINGERS. This is a picture of the tone arm a second after it has been "accidentally" dropped. It floats down, but when the needle is in the groove the arm is free of restraint.

STABLE performance. The suspension design makes it insensitive to mechanical shocks from the floor or to acoustic feedback.

I-YEAR GUARANTEE

$78⁰⁰ LESS CARTRIDGE

5% higher in the West and Deep South

PRESS COMMENT on the AR TURNTABLE

quoted from **HiFi/Stereo** review *(Julian Hirsch)*

"The wow and flutter were the lowest I have ever measured on a turntable . . . The speed was exact . . . the only rumble that can be heard with the AR turntable, even with the tone controls set for heavy bass boost, is the rumble from the record itself.

"I found that records played on the AR turntable had an unusually clean, clear quality. The complete freedom from acoustic feedback (which can muddy the sound long before audible oscillations occur) was responsible for this."

quoted from **HI-FI** *(John Milder)*

". . . the best answer so far to the interrelated problems of rumble and acoustic feedback . . . the only time rumble is audible is when it has previously been engraved on a record by a noisy cutting lathe. Nor is feedback audible — even when the turntable, against customary warnings, is placed directly on top of a wide-range speaker system. There is simply silence."

quoted from **AUDIO**

"The AR turntable does run at exact speed (both speeds), and it introduces as little 'signal' of its own as any turntable we have had occasion to test."

quoted from **high fidelity**

". . . the lowest speed error USTC has encountered in *[fixed speed]* turntables . . . no hint of rumble . . . silent and accurate operation."

quoted from **INDUSTRIAL DESIGN**

". . . noteworthy for elegant simplicity."

Three magazines in 1963 have published descriptions of optimum stereo systems. *Gentlemen's Quarterly* selected the AR turntable for its top system ($3,824); *Popular Science* selected the AR turntable for its medium-cost and luxury systems; and *Bravo* selected the AR turntable for all three of its systems, economy, middle-class, and luxury.

The complete lists of components recommended by these magazines are available on request.

appears. I hoped we would be in production by the end of the year, but it now looks like it will be early 1962 before we are. My feeling was that there was a risk in making the announcement and having a long delay before we could ship, but that the risk was worth taking. By September 1962 the product would no longer be new and interesting, because other people were moving in the same direction already. Our chance to innovate in this sense had already passed, and we didn't want to lose any more time.

On price, I took a guess on what we could make it for, and on what we needed for impact in the market. My feeling was we should be under $60 retail, if possible. I think we can make it. I'm not sure, and Abe doesn't think we will make it. We are including the base and the dust cover in the price, and Abe doesn't think we can do all this, make our markup, and still be priced at $58.

Mr. Hoffman's views in December of 1961 were as follows:

We introduced it at the New York Trade Fair in September. This wasn't my idea of the way to do it, and Ed and I have discussed it a lot. The tentative price was set before we knew even within a close range what our production costs would be.

My philosophy on pricing any new product is this: Complete the design, get it going in production, and when you have the production prototypes, use them to develop a rational idea of cost, and when you have estimated cost, add a markup and then announce the product and start accepting orders.

The AR-2a[7] is the only one we have done this way. We made them, and we announced them shortly before we could deliver. By the time orders came in, we were ready to deliver. It worked out perfectly.

With the AR-1, AR-2, and AR-3 there was a lag of about six months between announcement and our first shipment. And we were not able to catch up with demand for several more months. This causes ill will among dealers and consumers, and put a lot of pressure on our whole organization to rush things up.

We discussed this throughout 1961, right up to the opening of the New York Show in September. My prediction was we wouldn't be able to meet orders until the middle of March 1962. I am still hoping we will be ready to go by mid-March, but even that is not a certainty.

I wanted it to retail at $66. Ed thinks $58 is a great price. It's his intuition, and he says we have to get the price down to $58 as long as our costs allow us to come in range of it. My attitude is, maybe he is right. I don't know, but I think we could sell as many turntables at $66 as at $58, and that gives us $4.67 more per unit. Maybe we won't need it, but maybe the contingencies will turn out to make it more costly than we now think. We can't tell yet. And Ed feels more strongly about $58 than I do about all these other things.

From the vantage point of 1965, it was clear that both Mr. Villchur and Mr. Hoffman had been optimistic in 1961 about the production costs and development time required for the turntable. Mr. Hoffman said:

By criteria of technical performance, market acceptance, and contribution to our company image, our new turntable has been an outstanding success. Financially, it has been a loss so far. We did not begin to break even on our turn-

---

[7]Case writer's note: The AR-4 was also introduced in 1964 in this manner.

table sales until the fall of 1964 and I estimate that we lost about $600,000 on it through 1964.

Mr. Allison, commenting in 1965, felt that their design and production problems had arisen from a lack of experience with that type of product. Very high performance standards and tight cost constraints meant that new materials and design approaches had to be found. Mr. Allison added:

We made some mistakes in judgment, and were also unlucky in that some of the new materials did not meet their manufacturers' claims of long-term stability. Things would have gone better if we had had more time to evaluate the design before going into production, but we still would have had lots of problems. A high-performance turntable has electrical and mechanical components of very high precision. None of us had much experience with a comparable product.

With regard to production problems, Mr. Allison indicated that redesign programs had complicated the usual routine of simplifying and working out the details of manufacture. He felt that these were now well under control, and that most of the potential cost savings in manufacture had probably been made by this time.

In looking back at the development of the turntable, Mr. Villchur said simply that they had badly misjudged development and production times and costs. Mr. Hoffman agreed, and added:

I have never been as enthusiastic about the turnable as Ed because the opportunities are so limited. Speakers cost more, we make more on them, everybody needs at least one speaker but not necessarily a turntable, and lots of people prefer a record changer anyway because of the added convenience.[8] It does add to our prestige and our company image, fills out our line, and probably results in some increased speaker sales, but I don't think it will ever be a big part of our business.

AR-4 development and introduction

The AR-4, introduced at the September 1964 New York Hi-Fi Show, was the most popular speaker (unit sales) in AR's line in the fall of 1965. It had presented far fewer development and manufacturing challenges or problems than the turntable, because it was essentially a major modification of the traditional speaker systems rather than a venture into a new type of product. Thus development time and costs were very much less than for the turntable.

Mr. Hoffman stated that the development of a low-cost small speaker system had been discussed back in about 1961, but was not undertaken at that time. He explained:

---

[8]Total market figures for changers or turntables were elusive, but, according to some company personnel, dealers estimated that of all record-playing devices sold, 90% were changers and 10% were turntables. Mr. Villchur pointed out, however, that since AR sales in 1964 were more than one turntable for every AR speaker sold, and since AR estimated that they had close to 20% of the speaker market, these estimates were not accurate. He thought the percentages of changer-turntable sales should be closer to 80%–20%.

Ed insisted that there was no tweeter which was cheap enough but good enough to put into such a "pygmy" speaker with an AR label on it, and that in addition there was no pressing need for such a speaker at that time. In the meantime we were busy with other things—mostly getting the turntable into production—and so nothing much was done.

As I reflect upon it now, the state of the art in 1961 would have permitted the development of an AR-4. I now regret that we did not undertake it at that time.

In late 1963, however, Ed got an idea for such a tweeter and started a project to develop a tweeter for the AR-4. The results were encouraging but not yet successful when, about six months later, Roy modified a purchased $3\frac{1}{2}''$ tweeter. The tweeter sounded good enough to Ed for him to stop work on his own development and let Roy go ahead—completing the tweeter work and developing an $8''$ woofer for the AR-4. We had a few prototypes made up, got some cost, price, and sales estimates together, and then we went ahead and began production. We agreed on a normal pricing formula, and we have made money right from the start.

Both the new $8''$ woofer and the $3\frac{1}{2}''$ tweeter were purchased from a high-volume original equipment manufacturer which sold speakers to many of the large set manufacturers. The woofer was made to AR's design, and was further modified by AR in their plant. The tweeter had been recently developed by the supplier, and AR had modified it for use in the AR-4 and the AR-2x and AR-2ax.

Both Mr. Hoffman and Mr. Landau felt that the AR-4 had not been promoted very much, and that it could make a lot more money if they would advertise it more. Mr. Landau stated:

Ed's concern here is not monetary. He believes that an ad must be built around a favorable comment. No comment, no ad. There are times when Ed departs from this, but not often, of course. Ed's approach is very effective but it contains a built-in restriction which in my opinion has worked against AR.

In response to a leading question from the case writer concerning the amount of promotion for the AR-4, Mr. Villchur said immediately, "I bet you've been listening to Abe and Jerry." Abe Hoffman appeared at that moment, and a lively discussion ensued concerning the amount of promotion other products had received and the proper basis for comparing promotional dollars. Mr. Villchur pointed out that there already had been three ads in 1965 dealing primarily with the AR-4, and that it had already had more promotion than the AR-2a had ever received. He added:

I have also given it the same attention as far as press releases are concerned, but I admit we haven't advertised it as much in the strictly hi-fi magazines as some of our other products because it really doesn't represent an advance in the sense the AR-3 and the turntable did. But it surely hasn't been slighted in terms of total promotion.

The discussion was terminated by an exodus to the usual excellent delicatessen-spread lunch, with each party even more convinced of the strength of his own position, and the case writer no wiser than before.

Major policies

Company policies and activities in the areas of manufacturing, employee relations, profit sharing, advertising, and promotion are discussed below very briefly. More extensive data on other selected areas, such as dealer relations and product plans, appear in the final section.

Manufacturing. The company was still in the same very old East Cambridge location, although it had expanded across the street into an old frame factory building. Speakers accounted for about 90% of the manufacturing space, and, according to Mr. Allison, production in this space could be expanded without much trouble to about a $7 million level in a wide range of product mixes.

Two moving speaker assembly lines were set up; any model could be run on either line. Subassemblies were made in various parts of the plant. Except for testing operations, there was a high degree of interchangeability among jobs on the assembly lines. Mr. Allison characterized the main trend of the past several years as in an increasing use of jigs and fixtures, the development of a formal quality control and process control section, and greatly expanded and improved incoming inspection procedures.

Manufacture of the turntable was principally an assembly operation. Inspection and testing accounted for about 50% of the total direct labor hours.

Purchasing, which amounted to about $2 million per year, was much more routine than it had ever been before. The paperwork and procedures had been set up with the help of Mr. Hoffman and an outside consultant, and the former felt they had good controls over purchasing activities.

Employee relations. In 1965 AR had about 150 employees, and was not unionized. Employee relations had become more formal than in the early years, however.

In 1964 a job-rating plan had been installed. Mr. Hoffman indicated that this had been a major effort, and had been done with the help of consulting engineers.

Mr. Hoffman was pleased with their more formal approach, and said that there now would be no more "playing it by ear" with regard to pay and promotions. He noted that several years ago they had discovered one man had been given six raises in five weeks, and that such a thing could not happen any more.

Profit sharing. The company had continued to pay employees bonuses based on profits, and all the employee benefits had been written up in a small handbook and distributed to the employees. Mr. Allison felt that AR's hourly rates were about the same as those at many places, but that the fringe benefits were significantly better. Mr. Villchur, who had written the handbook, emphasized that the bonus payments were in addition to a competitive wage, were earned by the employees, and were affected by the diligence with which every employee did his job, since the total amount depended upon the total company profits. He continued:

The bonus payments the first half of this year were the highest they have ever been. They amounted to 9% of total salary for hourly workers, 11% for supervisors, and 13% for management. Since in the past our first-half profits have usually been about 40% of the total for the year, the bonus payments for the full year may come out at about 11%, 13½%, and 16%.

In response to a question from the case writer as to the reasons for having such a bonus plan, Mr. Villchur replied:

I'm convinced that our bonus payments, which are based on total company profits, improve our profits. People know that their actions affect the total profits and their bonus, and they, therefore, have a stake in the business. Even if you could prove to my satisfaction that the bonus scheme ultimately costs us money, though, I would want to retain it anyway. I think the profits should be shared.

Mr. Hoffman had a somewhat different philosophy concerning bonus payments:

I would not want to pay a bonus which costs us money. I only want to pay a bonus if it makes us money.

Advertising. Mr. Villchur continued to control advertising on a company level, and it had not changed greatly. The emphasis had remained, in Mr. Villchur's words, on advertising which "was believable, had something new to say, and was both interesting to the reader and relevant to his buying decisions." Most of the advertising was placed in magazines that catered to readers interested in high fidelity rather than in mass media magazines.[9] Relatively little newspaper advertising, available to dealers under a cooperative plan, had appeared in the past; in 1965, such ads were increasing as the sales department took the initiative in approaching dealers. Most of the advertising continued to emphasize either the editorial comments of others about AR products, or "prestige" applications, such as recording studio monitoring equipment. In discussing the value of editorial comment, Mr. Villchur stated:

The AR-3 and the turntable represent the most significant advances, and are clearly tops in their field. There have been more editorial comments about those that we can use in our advertising than for our other products, and I think the leadership they have established carried our other products along as well.

Editorial comment is infinitely more valuable than your own pleadings, and we have usually had five times as much editorial comment as others have had on their products. The main reason is that we have had some products worthy of comment. People often think that buying advertising space will get you favorable editorial comments, but I don't think that is true to any great extent. We received a great deal of editorial comment when were were just starting out and did very little advertising, and the only reason is that we had a notable product.

[9] Both KLH and Fisher, in contrast, were frequent advertisers in *The New York Times* magazine section.

Promotion.   Two new types of promotion had been undertaken in recent years. The first of these, inaugurated in 1959, was a permanent demonstration and display room in Grand Central Terminal in New York City. A variety of program material was played continuously through AR speakers and turntables, but no sales were initiated. In his letter to the stockholders for the year 1959, Mr. Villchur stated:

Our preliminary studies indicate that the expense of this display is more than covered by its benefits in increased sales. We are now considering the possibility of establishing similar demonstrations in other cities.

A similar demonstration room was opened in Cambridge, Massachusetts, in late 1960.

The exact impact of the music rooms was difficult to ascertain because no sales were made at them. A study by the company in 1961, however, indicated that in comparing the four quarters immediately preceding the establishment of the music room to the six quarters immediately after, the percentage of AR's sales in the city area to their total national sales had increased from about 43% to 58%, beginning rather abruptly at the date of the music room opening. Mr. Villchur added that no other major factors had influenced their sales at that time, and that these results were particularly encouraging in view of the importance of the New York City market size.

The second form of promotion consisted of the sponsorship of a number of "live vs. recorded" concerts. In its early advertising, AR had emphasized objective measures of speaker performances as relevant, but not complete, evidence of speaker quality. The new promotion had been undertaken partly in response to the arguments of those who insisted that objective measurements were irrelevant and that the only true test of a speaker was "how it sounds in your home."

The basic format was to have the live performers alternate their playing with a reproduction of the same selection by the same group played through AR-3 speakers. The first, involving the Fine Arts Quartet, took place in January of 1959, and subsequent performances included this same group as well as a number of other groups appearing in series of three to five days in a number of major cities. In some cities several series were performed; three series took place in New York, and 10 days of concerts were given in Chicago. Mr. Villchur felt that this was an exceedingly reliable and convincing test of the quality of a sound reproducing system, and that the concerts, which had been attended by an estimated 15,000 people in total, had been highly useful.

Future

A number of issues which seemed to the case writer to be the most actively discussed in the company are included in this final section.

Dealer relations.   Both Mr. Hoffman and Mr. Landau, the new sales manager, felt that the attitude and practices of the company concerning dealer relations were changing and should continue to change. Mr. Hoffman characterized the new approach as "not turning down orders any more," and Mr. Landau felt that the basic trend was to view the relationships with dealers as important and as one of "selling" rather than merely "informing." He added:

You can sum up the changes in our dealer relations by saying that we now have a more realistic awareness of the role of the dealers. I think they are extremely important, and that they can make you or break you over the long run.

One example of the changed emphasis, Mr. Landau felt, concerned the company's first use of a manufacturers' representative. In July of 1964, at Mr. Landau's urging, very shortly before he became sales manager, the company engaged a representative for Southern California. This particular area had been chosen because it was a large but well-defined marketing area in which both interest in hi-fi and incomes were high. AR sales in Southern California had not been growing, and Mr. Landau had found out informally from other firms' sales managers that AR's share was a lower portion of its national total than several other companies were getting. Because of this, he decided to try using a manufacturers' representative in that area. He added:

I think our rep in California is one of the best in the country, and he has been doing a good job for us. He has increased sales to old dealers, opened up new ones, and gotten us into some large outlets that we were not in before. Within a period of about a year, he increased our unit sales of the big speakers alone by about 40%. He represents Dynaco and Scott also. The only possible conflicting item he might have is Scott speakers, but they are not an important speaker line. He has several people working for him, and carries some inventory for the other companies. Establishing warehouse facilities out there might be the next step for us.

I think some form of sales force in the field is inevitable over the long run. Other manufacturers have it. Our previous dealer policies were based on the firm belief that we had a superior product, good enough to bring in customers in spite of the dealers, and that we could therefore bring antagonistic dealers to heel. Even if that was the case at one time, I would have preferred to have done a more active job of accentuating AR's virtues for the dealer rather than treating him in a high-handed, patronizing manner.

Aside from the issue of the usefulness of manufacturers' representatives with regard to dealer relationships, Mr. Landau felt that AR continued to have a number of additional economic disadvantages in competing with other manufacturers for dealer loyalty and support:

1. Average dealer markup of about 33% rather than the more common 40%.
2. No attempt to maintain retail prices whereas most other manufacturers did everything possible "by law or otherwise" to maintain prices.
3. Limit of 2% of dealer's purchases for cooperative advertising allowance, closely supervised, compared with up to 5% by others, "loosely supervised."
4. No "spiffs" (payments to salesman by *manufacturer* for selling manufac-

turer's model, usually done without knowledge of dealer), whereas "the standard spiff for selling an X speaker [a major brand] in New York used to be $5, and maybe still is."

5. No absorption of freight costs, as some others did.
6. To all intents and purposes no volume discounts, whereas others gave these.
7. Tighter credit policies than most competitors.

Mr. Landau continued:

As a result, a lot of our dealers try to switch customers away from AR. By switching I mean trying to influence a serious buyer who comes in and asks for AR by name to buy some other brand of speaker, not simply recommending a speaker other than AR to someone who asks the dealer's advice. I can easily see why dealers do this, and I don't get mad at them for it. Instead, I try to explain the economic loss to themselves when they do switch. It is an economic issue, not a moral one. I see it as something I have to work with and try to overcome so we can sell more AR products. If we cut out all the dealers who sometimes try to switch people to other speakers, as we tried to do at one time, we wouldn't have any dealers left.

I wouldn't mind changing our policies on any of these items if I thought it would mean higher profits for us, but the effects are awfully hard to predict. I would rather at this time place more reliance on some form of sales organization, and perhaps the use of a topflight advertising agency which specializes in all kinds of promotion on the retail level. In this way I would hope to convert a hostile dealer to a neutral one and a neutral one to a friendly one rather than cut the dealer off.

According to Mr. Landau, the company now had a more realistic approach with regard to enforcing specific requirements on dealers. Display and demonstration requirements had originally been quite rigid, and two professional shopping services had been employed to run periodical checks to see that the standards were maintained. He felt that the program had resulted in too many letters of complaint, arguments, misunderstandings, and hard feelings, with occasional dealer resignations or suspensions because of inaccurate shopping reports.

One large prestige dealer in Detroit, for example, who had been suspended in 1959 for allegedly "doctoring" an AR speaker so that other speakers being demonstrated would sound better, still refused to deal directly with AR. Mr. Landau was aware that this outlet was obtaining AR speakers from other dealers in the area, however, and kept track of its sales by asking the other dealers to state, "Three for me and six for Gregory," on their orders. He noted that any such transshipments in the past would have resulted in one warning and then suspension of the dealer. He added that he had Gregory's on his "unofficial" dealer mailing list, so that it could be just as well informed as "official" dealers.

In summing up, Mr. Landau stated:

I still think we provide the best value, but differences in speaker quality are decreasing all the time. A reduction of quality and product differences over time happens in most industries, and then you have to build your position around marketing skills, not just product quality. There is no continuing payoff for having been first. In the business world, who remembers, or cares, who pioneered in radio or TV or automatic dishwashers?

Maurice [Rotstein] used to look upon his role as one of communication—to inform the dealers of what the company was doing and what we had available to sell. Ed did the selling by establishing product leadership and doing the advertising, and in addition he set up the structure of dealer relationships and policies. Maurice saw his role as essentially a passive one, whereas I see mine as an active one. I call on dealers, not only to keep them posted, but also to explore ways of increasing their sales; I try to open new accounts; and I do everything I can to push our products through the dealers.

Another important difference is that Maurice conducted himself in an almost painfully honest manner. I believe Maurice was constitutionally incapable of doing anything which he felt was dishonest in the slightest way. Of course, everyone prefers to function on the highest moral plane possible, and Acoustic Research is a firm which makes this possible for its employees, but I am not as much a stickler for absolute and full disclosure every time I talk to any dealer.

The basic difference between some of the people in the company and myself is that I have no illusions about the operation of ethics in business. Indeed, I think that in most business operations as they occur today the issue is irrelevant.

My goal is to make as much money as soon as possible, within the limits of legality and running a continuing business. As a sample of a difference in viewpoint: If in my best business judgment it were profitable for AR to bring out products which were merely competitive, I would do so. I don't want to leave any stones unturned in an effort to increase sales. I would be delighted if we could drive the other speaker manufacturers out of business and thereby have the field all to ourselves.

Mr. Villchur did not share Mr. Landau's views on either the desirable course for AR to follow with regard to dealer relations or the amount of change which had in fact occurred. However, he was highly pleased with the recent sales performance.

Looking to the future, Mr. Villchur stated:

I will not run a dealer-oriented company. I was against the move to sign on a rep for Southern California, and I don't think we should acquire any more reps. I don't think it is a wise course for us to follow in the long run, and I don't think it is necessary in the short run either. It is true that the product differences among speakers and turntables are declining, but they are still significant and we still have a decided edge. We will simply have to stay ahead as the battle moves on to new products—speakers of the AR-4 size, for example, or component systems. I don't think being dealer-oriented is smart for any company, and wooing dealers is definitely not the answer for AR. We wouldn't be any good at it, because that takes a distinctive set of skills and attitudes, just as our approach does.

I don't like the morality of capitalism in the first place, but in spite of that I think I am being more capitalistic than the capitalists who claim to like the morality. If the system consists of rewards based on the free competition of your products in the marketplace, how do you rationalize trying to maintain high prices under the guise of "Fair Trade"—a misnomer if ever there was one— and bribing your dealer network with exorbitant margins? How can you justify your existence as a company if you have no product superiority? All you are then doing is trying to convince the people, by whatever means possible, to part with some of their money so that you can stay in business.

If anyone were to convince me that we would positively have to become a dealer-oriented company in order to survive, I simply wouldn't steer any more. I wouldn't block the transition, because I have obligations to other stockholders and to our employees. But that kind of game is not for me.

"More opportunistic selling." Mr. Hoffman and Mr. Landau both felt that AR was gradually moving toward more opportunistic selling techniques in addition to modifying their basic dealer relationships. Mr. Hoffman noted that the company was "far from aggressive in comparison with most other competitors," but that some problems had been handled differently in the recent past than they would have been in the early days.

Mr. Landau recalled that one example of a changing approach to selling had occurred in 1964, at the time of a price increase on the turntable. It had been decided that the retail price increase from $68 to $78 would be announced as of a certain date. Dealers who had turntables in stock which they had acquired at the lower (discounted) old dealer price could then make an extra profit on each unit that they sold at the new retail figure. He continued:

> Before our decision to increase the price was known outside the company, I called our larger dealers and told them that they would be wise to place an order now for *speakers* and turntables—in any proportion—which could be cancelled *in total* at any time, but not in part. I suppose they knew the game I was playing, but a number of them gave us extra orders.

Mr. Hoffman pointed out that another indication of a change in attitude toward selling speakers had occurred recently.

A 10% federal excise tax, imposed at the manufacturer's level, had been in effect for many years on speakers of the type commonly used in radio and TV sets. "High fidelity" speakers had generally not been subject to this tax. In the spring of 1965, however, the government announced some changes which made it seem certain that speakers previously exempted would now become subject to the tax as of April 1. Mr. Hoffman checked into the provisions of the tax more carefully, however, and found that completely enclosed speakers (which included most "high fidelity" speakers) would still not be taxed.[10] This was not then generally realized, he indicated, either by any other manufacturers that he knew of or by the trade associations and their legal counsel.

Dealers and manufacturers, of course, encouraged the public to buy equip-

---

[10]Imposition of any tax was delayed at the last minute, and it was uncertain whether it would be imposed at a future date.

ment before the new tax and higher prices would go into effect. Like other firms, AR benefited and orders poured in.

Mr. Villchur had been against filling these orders because people were buying under a misapprehension. Mr. Hoffman and others prevailed on him to go ahead and sell, however, on the grounds that if they did not fill the orders, people would just buy some other kind of speakers anyway. Mr. Hoffman added:

This decision might have gone differently before. If Maurice had been here, I think he might have sided with Ed in not shipping speakers to dealers or consumers who didn't "really" want them at that time; that consensus would have prevailed. Jerry [Landau] was strongly in favor of selling, however, since he felt we were not misleading anybody and people would just buy some other brand of speaker if they couldn't get AR speakers.

We worked a lot of overtime filling the orders, and we had the best first quarter we have ever had. We probably sold an extra $500,000 worth of speakers, made an extra $250,000, and no third party suffered in the process.

Industry structure and competition. Mr. Landau was sure that the shakeout of manufacturers and expansion of product line of the remaining manufacturers which had taken place in the last several years would continue.

Last year for the first time that I can remember there were empty display booths at the New York Hi-Fi Show. This year there are even more, although six companies have each taken on three booths.

I think that quality differences will diminish as the industry matures, and there will be a greater reliance on product differentiation by marketing and promotion. This has been true in lots of other industries—radio, TV, and automobiles, to name a few. Styling, price, advertising, and your dealer organization are bound to become more important. We have been running parallel to the early stages of most American industry, when a great technical man or inventor founded a company with a new product and dominated it through the early stages, often with his own unique approaches to marketing.

KLH, which was acquired by Singer Sewing Machine Company last year,[11] is obviously our major competitor at present, but they may not be our most serious threat in the long run. We have been battling them for a long time, and we have remained first in quality speakers with about twice the market share they have for years.

Fisher is going into speakers, however, and in the long run they may be our major problem. They are easily No. 1 in the quality electronic components field, not because of any major quality differences or product characteristics, but be-

---

[11]KLH was formed in 1957 by three former associates of Mr. Villchur's who left Acoustic Research to form their own company. KLH became a licensee under the acoustic suspension patent; in 1958 their estimated sales were "under $100,000." KLH had differed from AR in producing more expensive speaker models, giving higher dealer discounts, and using dealer reps. They also became a leader in bringing out "music systems," as described previously. Industry sources estimated KLH sales at about $10–$12 million in 1965, of which less than 25% was thought to represent sales of individual components. KLH was acquired by the Singer Sewing Machine Company in 1964 (1964 sales: $896 million) for a reported $3.6 million of Singer stock.

cause they have a good product and very good marketing and advertising. Their dominance in electronics is greater than ours is in speakers, and I would guess that they are several times our size. They have a low-priced model competing with our AR-4 and the KLH 17. *Popular Science* judged them all qualitatively equal, and therefore chose Fisher as the best buy because of a slightly lower price at the time.

In a peculiar way, however, AR faces another and perhaps still more powerful rival: the house-brand speaker. At Allied Radio, Knight Speakers are first, AR is second; at Radio Shack, Realistic Speakers are first, AR is second; etc. We are second in these major chains by a substantial amount—perhaps five to one.

New products. The major new product on which the company was working was a transistorized, integrated amplifier.[12] The plans in 1958 had been to develop a vacuum tube amplifier, but as it became apparent that transistorized units would eventually displace vacuum tube units, the company decided not to develop a component which was rapidly becoming obsolete. There were at present a number of transistorized units on the market, but Mr. Hoffman indicated that almost all of the makers had had reliability problems in the field, and that most of them had been forced to make numerous changes and repairs. Dynakit and Marantz, two high-quality manufacturers of conventional (i.e., vacuum tube) amplifiers, had not yet introduced a transistorized model.

Mr. Hoffman felt that a transistorized amplifier would give AR a very good package of components, and said they would bring one out as soon as they thought they had the reliability problems solved. Mr. Allison indicated that they would be ready to go in the production of this when the time came, and would use people with experience in this kind of manufacturing process to help them get set up. He explained:

Speaker and turntable products don't give us much background for electronics manufacture and there are only two ways to get the experience you need. Either you make your own mistakes and learn, or you hire somebody who has already acquired the experience. Both cost money, but hiring somebody is cheaper.

Mr. Villchur indicated that the amplifier would have the simplest possible set of controls, in contrast to many existing models. In addition, the terminals and connecting wires between the amplifier, speakers, and turntable would be color-coded so that it would be virtually impossible for anyone to connect them improperly. He added:

Another way to simplify the system for the average purchaser would be to manufacture, or have made for us, a cartridge that we would install in the turntable arm right at the factory. There are one or two available now which I think are perfectly satisfactory for almost all of the purchasers of our turntables, and there is no point to making them choose and buy one separately and go through the bother of trying to mount it properly. We succeeded in changing the pattern of having turntables and arms sold separately, and it should not be any

---

[12]A single unit serving the purpose of the amplifier and preamplifier of earlier systems.

more difficult to eliminate the confusion and mystique surrounding the selection and installation of a suitable cartridge.

We have also considered offering people an attractive walnut shelf designed specifically for our turntable and the new amplifier, but I doubt that we will go ahead with it. We can't get the price down below $50, even with a smaller margin for us, and that price tag on a wooden shelf just doesn't fit the Acoustic Research image. We could distribute plans for the shelf and suggest that people have it made locally, or make it themselves, if they want to. But it doesn't seem like a very attractive proposition for us.

We will never manufacture a single console. That is too big and expensive a piece of furniture, speakers don't sound best on the floor, and there is no practical way that I know of to solve the problem of inadequate speaker separation for good stereo effect in the average room.

We might, however, go to a three-piece system, with the turntable and amplifier in one piece of furniture and the speakers separate, although we have no definite plans to do so at present.

Mr. Villchur also made some comments on the product development process at AR:

The normal relationship between development and the executive staff is for the executive to assign a job to the development staff, and they do the best they can with it. The executives make their decisions on the basis of what they think the market needs are.

In this case, I am president, product planner, and director of research and development. While I in general have to follow that method in my own mind, the difference in my case is this: since I am only interested in bringing out superior products, rather than products which are merely competitive, I therefore give unusual emphasis to ideas which will give me an edge.

I tend not to get such ideas about products which aren't needed, or wouldn't fit into the AR line. If I do, I discard them. I do tend to get ideas that will fit the AR line, because I think about those problems more. But the basic difference is that you can produce *competitive* products on demand from an executive staff, but you cannot produce *superior* products—inventions, so to speak—on demand.

Company atmosphere. In commenting on the important but intangible attitudes and policies within the company as these related to company operations and future growth, Mr. Hoffman stated:

We are now a business entity, not just a few people experimenting with a new product in a loft somewhere. We have over 150 employees, many of whom have been here for eight years or more, and many of whom are over 40 years old. This is now their career and their job, and I think the company has some responsibility to them. They're not just casual labor. As a result, company growth, profits, and stability have to be important to us.

This means the conflict between basing policies on profit considerations and basing them on personal values is stronger than ever. We have done some things just because Ed or some of the others in the organization wanted to do them that way, or to prove a point to "society," and not necessarily because it would make the most money for us. It is one thing to do that when you are small and new, have few obligations to your employees, and are taking the risks with your own money. I think it is different now.

The conflicts do not concern policies like trying to make the best possible product at the lowest possible price, or being consumer-oriented, because I think that is the way to profits in the long run. There are more basic problems. The first objective has to be to make money, not to operate in a certain style, unless it also contributes to making money. You have *got* to be profit-oriented if you are in a society which rewards profits, and the more profits you make, the better. since that will help you get stronger and bigger.

Ed and I agree on most things on running a business. We both want to operate within legal limits, and at the upper end of the range of general business ethics. We disagree on "operating with taste." This is a highly subjective term which Ed uses to apply to pricing, advertising, dealer relations, product policy, employee policies—the "image" of the company. I'm all for operating with taste if it is good business, but I don't believe in foregoing profitable opportunities for reasons of taste, providing the actions are legal and ethical. We might want to sell someday and our profit record will certainly have an influence on the price we can get.

I really don't know why this company has made so much money. We have had very good products, which came from Ed, and we also now are good at manufacturing and distribution. We are thorough and careful by industry standards, and have our everyday administration down to a fairly simple routine. We are confident enough of the future, and have enough money to keep inventories on hand throughout the year and can deliver any of our products in New York the day after we receive the order. Maybe that is all there is to it.

Looking back over the past 10 years of Acoustic Research's activities, Mr. Villchur responded as follows to the question of what had been most satisfying to him personally:

Nothing compares with the thrill of finding out in 1954 that the woofer I designed and made actually worked as I thought it would. Second, I think, would be the satisfaction of developing the dome tweeter, although that was a much slower process. Third would be the development of the turntable, which was also a slow process.

The real satisfactions for me have come from analyzing a practical problem with the aid of the physical sciences, working out a solution, and finding out that you are right. I have thought a lot about what to do next, and in my own mind I have become committed to doing something about hearing aids. I want to define the problem much more broadly than I did when building a better woofer, and it will take a lot of time. But that is what I want to do.

The company and its social responsibilities: relating corporate strategy and moral values

We come at last to the fourth and final component of strategy—the moral aspects of choice. In our consideration of strategic alternatives, we have so far moved from what the strategist *might* and *can* do to what he *wants* to do; we now move to what he *ought* to do—from the point of view of society and his own inner standards of right and wrong. Ethics, like preference, may be considered a question of value. To some the suggestion that an orderly and analytical process of strategy determination must find its way through the tangle of ethics is repugnant. Proponents of this view find it sufficient if business lives up to its legal obligations: obeys the antitrust acts, keeps honest expense accounts, and pays its bills and taxes. Beyond this point, they argue, we cannot and should not prescribe codes of conduct or standards of responsibility. Nor should we imply that the choice among alternatives should be influenced by the judgment that one is morally superior to another.

The moral aspect of strategic choice

While fully aware of the problems involved, we contend that the business-man must examine the impact on the public good of the policy alternatives he is free to elect and implement. We are not impressed by the argument that it is difficult to distinguish in what way one strategic choice is morally superior to another. The study of comparative ethics reveals that every known human society has been governed by codes of conduct. Despite numerous tragic interruptions, these codes have progressively tended to embody a more comprehensive concept of the public good and a fuller recognition of social rights and duties. This progress—which presumably continues, at least in slow motion, within most democratic societies today—has not been achieved in the absence of any consensus as to what, in the confrontation of responsibility with self-aggrandizement, separates right from wrong.

Thus in the professional sector of the business community, away from the back alleys of self-interest and used car lots, it is quite often possible to distinguish legal but shabby behavior from that of a higher ethical quality. One who manipulates the letter of an agreement to his own advantage can be told from the person willing to observe its spirit. The exploiter of human relationships for narrow ends reveals himself, and the quality of an individual's personal purposes can be readily deduced from his behavior.

We are concerned here, however, with the ethics of strategic choice, not with the morality of personal behavior. The ethics of strategy often involves a conflict of obligations. For example, the cigarette industry has an obligation to tobacco farmers, workers, and stockholders on the one hand, and to the consuming public on the other. Similarly, the pharmaceutical manufacturer is caught between the need for safety and the need for speed in exploiting a new drug. Anyone in genuine doubt about the ethical quality of a strategic alternative will find plenty of advice available as to which is on the side of the angels (although advice may differ from different quarters when legitimate claims are in competition). Formal and informal associations of businessmen and corporations themselves develop observable norms of conduct which influence the behavior of their members in matters where law and regulation do not apply. On the average these norms are rising in response to the expectations of the total society that men free to choose between meaner and better purposes will choose the better. It may, even so, be hard to get a good decision, but it is not difficult to locate in any range of alternatives the issues to ponder.

Relevance of the public good

Explicit attention to questions of the responsibility of business to society is criticized by those who argue that uninhibited pursuit of self-interest is in the long-range interest of society. Classical economic theory postulates that in atomized markets, perfect competition produces not only the optimum allocation of economic resources but also optimum satisfaction of the general interest. But classical economic theory is only partially applicable in practice. Instead of transitory small firms in perfect competition, we have permanent organizations of great size, power, and influence. Instead of a free market, we have a mixed economy, with different industries operating under varying degrees of public regulation and control.

The alternative to still greater intervention by the state in the economic sphere is for businessmen to exhibit a clear and lively sense of public obligation. Indeed, the emergence of the doctrine of social responsibility is the principal justification for leaving corporation power unchecked.[1] And large segments of our society—government, organized labor, organized religion,

---

[1]The argument for limiting corporate power by new controls is stated by Carl Kaysen, "The Corporation: How Much Power? What Scope?" In Edward S. Mason, *The Corporation in Modern Society* (Cambridge, Mass.: Harvard University Press, 1960).

and educational institutions—are gradually raising the standards of performance which they expect business to meet. The expectation that business will behave not only legally but with due regard for the rights of competitors, customers, and the general public grows daily more determined. Supposed as well as real abuses are sufficient to put businessmen on the defensive. Their critics are an articulate group, with easy access to the ears of legislators. In the press and in congressional hearings, some critics will inflate alleged instances of business irregularities with an unscrupulousness that would put the Robber Barons to shame.

The strategist who is sensitive to these aspects of the business environment soon concludes that there are two reasons for examining the impact of his policy choices upon the public good. The first is his professional concern for legality, fairness, and decency—his professional contempt for returns improperly or unfairly secured. The second is the threat of regulation that will be forthcoming if business behavior does not meet the standards applied to it by society. Men of conscience will be concerned with their public responsibilities because they choose to be. Other men will be concerned because they must be.

With confidence men and embezzlers, we have no problem of policy. When their alleged fraud is proved, they go to jail. But if the Stock Exchange ignores the association, however innocent, of one of its members with a scandal, the Securities and Exchange Commission would be quick to apply both its regulatory and its persuasive powers. Similarly, if the cigarette industry had not adopted a code to regulate its own behavior in persuading young people to smoke, the Federal Trade Commission would probably have brought pressure to bear to achieve the same ends. If the National Association of Broadcasters did not have its so-called Voluntary Code to govern programming, the recurrent aspirations of the Federal Communications Commission to impose new restrictions on telecasters would long since have had more tangible effects. Though to many observers the broadcasting code seems more honored in the breach than the observance, its inadequacy does not alter the conclusion that voluntary industry-wide agreements to restrain competitive practices in the public interest are a potent deterrent to additional legislation and could be an impetus to more responsible practice. This code might usefully be broadened, in response to newly evident needs, to check dramatized violence.

You will find that most instructors in Business Policy will not presume to prescribe what is right in detailed codes. They will ask, however, that you take into account the impact on society of your strategic choices and plans. They will remind you that the business firm, as an organic entity meaningfully related to its environment, must be as adaptive to demands for responsible behavior as for economic service. At the same time the opportunity remains to shape public attitudes and expectations in much more effective presentations of the inherent difficulty in business of satisfying all the conflicting claims made upon it.

Conflict of responsibilities

Once it is established that the firm must take into account the legitimate interests of other segments of society, the problem is far from solved. Rather, the already complex process of formulating a strategy capable of balancing economic opportunity, corporate resources, and personal and organizational aspirations is complicated now by an additional dimension. Furthermore, though right and wrong may be easy to determine in cases where all good lies on one side and all harm on the other, in other cases obligation to society may lead in several different directions. In some of these instances, determination of the proper course of action from the point of view of contribution to the public good is virtually impossible. The basic problem is the variety of interests which must be harmonized, the range of insistent and sometimes shrill definitions of right and justice, and the conflict among legitimate claims.

The professional manager of a large, publicly held corporation is clearly in some sense responsible to the owners of his business, to its employees, to its suppliers and customers, and even to his competitors—since he owes it to them to compete "fairly." He is also responsible in some ways to certain institutions, including the local government and community, the national government and community, and the fraternity of businessmen with which he identifies himself. It is clear at once that if the interests of any one of these groups are pursued exclusively, the interests of the others will suffer. It is clear also that the stockholder interest, which was once thought to be dominant, is no longer of unchallenged primacy. Indeed, in the publicly held corporation, it is not even particularly insistent. Conventions as to what constitutes a fair dividend in relation to market price are fairly well observed. When return does not meet the individual needs of an investor, his recourse is to make other investment choices. Conventions governing the extent to which other interests must be considered exist but are less clearly defined. Often the executive finds himself in situations in which it is impossible to reconcile the legitimate claims of everyone concerned. For example, there is frequently a need to move an obsolescent plant from a town that is economically dependent upon its payroll. Once such a problem has been allowed to arise, it is almost impossible to solve it without damage to some interests.

You will find, therefore, that the cases and issues presented in this section—and the similar issues which you will encounter in your business life—are even less susceptible to predetermined answers than some of the other problems we have encountered. But wrestling with the problem and debating the solutions proffered by your associates can have a result that will be of immense value to each individual. That is, it can help you to develop your own values and personal philosophy and to clarify the standards of moral and ethical behavior which you yourself will elect to live by. The consideration of strategic alternatives will thenceforth be simplified for you, since you will very quickly rule out alternatives which require action that you consider improper. Similarly, within the corporation, the range of strategic alternatives ✓ that must be evaluated is reduced to more manageable scope if the chief executive will make a clear pronouncement indicating what broad limits are imposed by social and ethical considerations. Acting responsibly thus becomes one of the shared goals of the corporation.

The philosophy that you develop must be a personal achievement, reflecting personal goals and purposes, the level of culture to which heredity and education have brought you, and the degree to which your personal purposes are other than self-centered. Breadth of perception must be allied to breadth of purpose before either is effective. The increasing professionalization of business management, which is in part consequent upon the recognition of obligations that go beyond the short-run financial interests of the corporation and the individual, provides stronger and stronger support to those who look beyond their own goals to those of the society of which they are important and influential members.

But events of 1966–1968 have greatly accelerated the participation by business in the social problems of our time. Corporate involvement in public ✓ issues is increasing on two fronts—educational activities as contribution to community development and entrepreneurial ventures in undeveloped areas or needed services that are expected to produce some profit for the service rendered. The Job Corps centers of many companies, the entry of firms like General Electric, Time, Inc., Raytheon, Litton Industries, and Xerox into education, the efforts of U.S. Gypsum, Aerojet, Lockheed, Ford, and of innumerable individual business leaders in the National Alliance of Businessmen to rehabilitate housing, establish factories and training facilities in the ghettos, and to provide training and jobs for hard core unemployed reflect a genuine and widespread recognition of obligation. The profits which may ultimately attend this enterprise will be neither large nor immediate. In any case they are clearly less the likely reward than the satisfaction that accompanies effective contribution to problems hitherto intractable to individual or governmental attention.

Under an acceptance of responsibility to society accelerated by the idealism ✓ of our youth, public inquiry into racism and injustice, and violence in the cities, business and society are redefining the proper role of industry. It is now expected that corporate power and management skill should be applied in areas like education, social justice, and the rehabilitation of cities and regions. These are the problems left unattended by medicine, law, the church, and the schools. They are complex enough to be worthy of the highest technical, professional, and organizational skills that business executives can muster.

Corporate responsibility and individual self-expression

We have thus far been concerned with the question of the firm's responsibility to those segments of society which its activity affects. An increasingly important problem is the firm's responsibility to insiders. This problem concerns the relative freedom of members of the firm to express views on public issues, even though these views may bring criticism upon the organization. It is at best difficult to balance the freedom of the individual and the consequences of his participation in public affairs against the interests of the corporation. The difficulty is increased if the attitudes of management, which instinctively are overprotective of the corporation, are harsh and restrictive. Short-run embarrassments and limited criticism from offended groups—even perhaps a threatened boycott—may be a small price to pay for the continued productivity within the corporation of men whose interests are deep enough and broad enough to cause them to take stands on public issues. The degree to which an organization is efficient, productive, creative, and capable of development is dependent in large part on the maintenance of a climate in which the individual does not feel suppressed, and in which a kind of freedom (analogous to that which the corporation enjoys in a free-enterprise society) is permitted as a matter of course. Overregulation of the individual by corporate policy is no more appropriate internally than overregulation of the corporation by government. On the other hand, personal responsibility is as appropriate to individual liberty as corporate responsibility is to corporate freedom.

The complexities of successfully integrating public responsibility into corporate strategy are great, but not insuperable. Conflicting responsibilities can be ordered in the same way as conflicting personal values, never perfectly, but often workably. Just as no one individual can achieve all he wants, so no corporation can satisfy all the demands made upon it by the special interest groups of society. If his concept of what constitutes the greatest good is clear, the executive who chooses his course accordingly can in good conscience withstand the abuses of those who demand a different course. So long as he does not make his decision in deliberate disregard of his responsibilities to the system which gives him power, he may not be much hurt.

The scandals of price fixing in the electrical equipment industry, conflicts of interest in Washington, and the personal interests of some corporation presidents in companies serving their firms as suppliers have all suggested that a code of conduct for executives should be formalized. It would alert insensitive men who thought they were doing no real wrong to their responsibilities. To supplement the negative and sometimes contradictory prohibitions of the law and to cover borderline cases of conflict of interest, our colleague, Robert W. Austin, has suggested a simple code as follows:

1. The professional business manager affirms that he will place the interest of the business for which he works before his own private business.
2. The professional business manager affirms that he will place his duty to society above his duty to his company and above his private interest.
3. The professional business manager affirms that he has a duty to reveal the

facts in any situation where (a) his private interests are involved with those of his company, or (b) where the interests of his company are involved with those of the society in which it operates.

4. The professional business manager affirms that when business managers follow this code of conduct, the profit motive is the best incentive for the development of a sound, expanding, and dynamic economy.[2]

This code is intended to govern behavior rather than strategic choice, but the first two affirmations it calls for are unequivocal guides to policy. Such a code would have considerable impact on the scope of businessmen's effort to achieve a reconciliation or combination among economic strategy, their personal values, and their social responsibilities. Clarification of personal, corporate, and national purpose is essential before the relevant interests are known and the proper priority of duty determined. Explicit, perhaps sequential, attention to all these categories of purpose will disentangle many an otherwise hopeless confusion.

The problem of final choice

We have now before us the major determinants of strategy. The cases studied so far have required consideration of what the strategy of the firm is and what, in your judgment, it ought to be. Concerned so far with the problem of formulating a viable strategy rather than implementing it, you have become familiar with the principal aspects of formulation—namely, (1) appraisal of present and foreseeable opportunity and risk in the company's environment, (2) assessment of the firm's unique combination of present and potential corporate resources or competences, (3) determination of the noneconomic personal and organizational preferences to be satisfied, (4) identification and acceptance of the social responsibilities of the firm. The strategic decision is one than can be reached only after all these factors have been considered and the action implications of each assessed.

In your efforts to analyze the cases, you have experienced much more of the problem of the strategist than can be described on paper. When you have relinquished your original idea as to what a company's strategy should be in favor of a more imaginative one, you have seen that the formulation process has an essential creative aspect. In your effort to differentiate your thinking about an individual firm from the conventional thinking of its industry, you have looked for new opportunities and for new applications of corporate competence. You have learned how to define a product in terms of its present and potential functions rather than of its physical properties. You have probably learned a good deal about how to assess the special competence of a firm from its past accomplishments, and how to identify management's values and aspirations. You may have gained some ability to rank preferences in order of their strength—your own among others.

---

[2]Robert W. Austin, "Code of Conduct for Executives," *Harvard Business Review*, September–October 1961, pp. 53–61.

The problem implicit in striking a balance between the company's apparent opportunity and its evident competence, between your own personal values and concepts of responsibility and those of the company's actual management, is not an easy one. It is not solved either by your familiarity with the basic concepts expounded in this text or by the practice which your case discussions have so far provided. The concepts we have been discussing will help you to prepare to make a decision, but they will not determine your decision for you. Whenever choice is compounded of rational analysis which can have more than one outcome, of aspiration and desire which can run the whole range of human ambition, and of a sense of responsibility which changes the appeal of alternatives, it cannot be reduced to quantitative approaches or to the exactness which management science can apply to narrower questions. A man contemplating strategic decision must be willing to make it without the guidance of decision rules. He must have confidence in his own judgment, which will have been deepened and seasoned by repeated analysis of similar questions. He must be aware that more than one decision is possible and that he is not seeking the single right answer. He can take encouragement from the fact that the manner in which an organization implements the chosen program can help to validate the original decision. For example, the wisdom of deciding to expand from national to international operations may depend on the quality of the implementing action taken.

Some of the most difficult choices confronting a company are those which must be made among several alternatives that appear equally attractive and also equally desirable. Thus a large land-development company with a very large income could move cash into virtually any activity it wished. But since its special competence was essentially nontransferable to other activities requiring large amounts of capital, and since the expansion of land development seemed unwise, the company was faced by an embarrassment of riches. Once the analysis of opportunity has produced an inconveniently large number of possibilities, any firm has difficulty in deciding what it wants to do and how the new activities will be related to the old.

In situations where opportunity is approximately equal and economic promise is offered by a wide range of activities, the problem of making a choice can perhaps be resolved if reference is made to the essential character of the company and to the kind of company the executives wish to run. The study of alternatives from this point of view will sooner or later reveal the greater attractiveness of some choices over others. Economic analysis and calculations of return on investment, though of course essential, may not crucially determine the outcome. Rather, the log-jam of decision can only be broken by a frank exploration of executive aspirations regarding future development, including perhaps the president's own wishes with respect to the kind of institution he prefers to head, carried on as part of a free and untrammeled investigation of what human needs in what parts of the world the organization would find satisfaction in serving. The fiction that return on investment alone will point the way ignores the values implicit in the calculations and the contribution which an enthusiastic commitment to new projects can make. The rational examination of alternatives and the determination of purpose are among the most important and most neglected of all human activities. The final decision, which should be made as deliberately as possible after a deliberate consideration of the issues we have attempted to separate, is an act of will and desire as much as of intellect.

A NOTE ON THE UNITED STATES
DRUG INDUSTRY*

∧∧

Classified by the U.S. Bureau of the Census under "chemicals and allied products," the U.S. drug industry comprises three segments which to some extent overlap. These are (1) biological products, (2) medicinal chemicals and botanical products, and (3) pharmaceutical preparations.

Characterizing the biological products segment, the Census Bureau states: "This industry comprises establishments[1] primarily engaged in the production of bacterial and virus vaccines, toxoids and analogous products . . . serums, plasmas, and other blood derivatives for human or veterinary use. Excluded are the activities of the American Red Cross, hospitals and other institutions which are important collectors of blood products."[2]

Characterizing the medicinal chemicals and botanical products segment, the Census Bureau states: "This industry comprises establishments primarily engaged in (1) manufacturing bulk organic and inorganic chemicals and their derivatives, and (2) processing (grading, grinding, and milling) bulk botanical drugs and herbs."[3] Among the important synthetic medicinal chemicals are the following: vitamins, sulfa drugs, antibiotics, hormones, and aspirin—the last a long-time leader in terms of pounds produced.[4]

Characterizing the pharmaceutical preparations segment, the Census Bureau says: "This industry comprises establishments primarily engaged in manufacturing, fabricating, or processing drugs in pharmaceutical preparations for human or veterinary use. The greater part of the products of these establishments are finished in the form intended for final consumption, such as ampoules, tablets, capsules, ointments, medicinal powders, solutions, and

---

[1]The term "establishment" denotes a single plant or factory in which manufacturing operations are performed.

[2]U.S. Bureau of the Census, *1958 Census of Manufactures*, Vol. II, Part I, p. 28C–1.

[3]*Ibid.*

[4]For these medicinal chemicals and selected subproducts, statistics covering production and sales in pounds, total sales value, and per pound unit value are maintained by the U.S. Tariff Commission in its annual report, *Synthetic Organic Chemicals, U.S. Production and Sales*. These data are not comparable, however, with Bureau of the Census data on the medicinal chemical segment.

suspensions."[5] Pharmaceuticals for human use are grouped by the Bureau under the following classifications: antibiotics including penicillin; cough and cold preparations; laxatives and stomach ulcer preparations; vitamins; analgesics including narcotics; tranquilizers, sedatives, and hypnotics; hormones including insulin; and other pharmaceutical preparations including anesthetics, antiseptics, etc.

The three segments comprising the drug industry are said to overlap for two reasons. First, some duplication exists because products of one segment (particularly medicinal chemicals and botanical products) are incorporated into another (particularly pharmaceutical preparations). Second, establishments classified in one segment frequently also manufacture products classified in another. For example, in 1958 establishments classified in the pharmaceutical segment actually shipped a higher dollar volume of biological products than did establishments classified in the biological products segment ($59.4 million to $23.7 million). While there is a relatively large overlap in the shipments of products primary to each segment, the "specialization" and "concentration" ratios for establishments in the industry as a whole are high; in 1958, for example, shipments by plants in the three drug-industry segments "consisted of 94% drugs and medicines and only 6% other chemical products. These plants also accounted for approximately 94% of the drugs and medicines produced in all manufacturing industries."[6]

Some indication of the purely economic importance of the drug industry in the economy as a whole may be gained from the comparative sales and shipment figures shown below:

SALES AND SHIPMENTS
(Dollars in Millions)

	Sales	Shipments
All manufacturing*	$356,424	
Chemicals and allied products	27,824	
Drugs	4,165	
Biological products		$ 100.6
Medicinal chemicals and botanical products ...		293.3
Pharmaceutical preparations		2,919.6

*Except newspapers.

Note: Sales figures are for corporations only. Shipments are for all establishments classified in the industry. Shipments are not totaled for all manufacturing, chemicals, and drugs "due to the extensive duplication arising from shipments from one establishment to another in the same industry classification."

Source: Sales figures from Federal Trade Commission–Securities and Exchange Commission, *Quarterly Financial Report for Manufacturing Corporations, 1961*; shipments figures from U.S. Bureau of the Census, *Annual Survey of Manufactures, 1961*.

As indicated by the $2.9 billion figure for shipments of pharmaceuticals, this is by far the largest segment classified under drugs; it in turn breaks down into two quite different subdivisions: (1) ethical, and (2) proprietary.

[5]U.S. Bureau of the Census, *op. cit.*, Vol. II, Part I, p. 28C–1.
[6]*Ibid.*

The essential difference between these two lies in the way their products are promoted: ethical pharmaceuticals are promoted primarily to the medical, dental, and veterinary professions; proprietary preparations, primarily to the public. Concomitantly, ethicals are nearly always sold by prescription, proprietaries over the counter. This difference in method of selling, however, does not obtain in every case. Nor is there any essential difference in the nature of the product itself. Vitamins, for example, can be either ethical or proprietary, depending on how they are promoted.

As the largest, fastest growing, and most controversial subdivision of the whole drug industry, ethical pharmaceuticals will receive the lion's share of attention in the following pages. These will be devoted to industry trends rather than focused on the status quo, and will review major shifts or changes occurring in the following areas: (1) products, (2) sales, (3) profits, (4) industry structure, (5) R.&D., (6) marketing, (7) public regulation, and (8) future challenges and opportunities.[7] In the course of the discussion, the therapeutic properties of certain specific drugs may be mentioned, but in no sense can any statement in this report be taken as authoritative on scientific matters.

Product trends

Among product trends in the drug industry, three very general ones stand out. (1) Organic and inorganic chemicals have come to play increasingly prominent roles, with biologicals and botanicals correspondingly less important. Lending impetus to this change has been the fact that products similar to natural remedies can be synthesized by the chemist and in their artificial form are generally both easier to control and cheaper to manufacture. (2) Medicinal products have increasingly reached the hands of the consumer as packaged and put up by the manufacturer rather than by the corner druggist. In other words, more and more of the industry's products are being retailed as pharmaceuticals. (3) A very fast rate of new product introductions and reportedly also of old product obsolescence has been characteristic of the largest industry segment, i.e., ethical pharmaceuticals. For example, according to one analyst, no fewer than 4,562 new pharmaceuticals were introduced from 1952 through 1961 inclusive. (These include as separate categories new single chemicals, duplicate single products put out by various manufacturers, compound products having more than one active ingredient, and new dosage forms.)[8]

Further highlighting the rapid pace of change in ethical drugs are the following data cited by Standard & Poor's:

---

[7]See also "The United States Drug Industry: Competitive Strategies and Policies," BP 778.

[8]Figures assembled by Paul de Haen, a consultant to the pharmaceuticals industry, and cited by Standard & Poor's "Drugs, Cosmetics, Basic Analysis," *Industry Surveys*, December 13, 1962, p. D-10.

Nearly 70% of ethical sales in 1960 came from products introduced in 1951 or later; about 20% of 1960 sales came from products launched after 1957. . . . Antibiotic discoveries during the period [between 1949 and 1960] more than doubled this group's share of the market, while two new categories of drugs, tranquilizers and diuretics,[9] garnered nearly 11% of prescription sales in 1960.[10]

In contrast to ethical drugs, proprietaries are more stable. According to Standard & Poor's, ". . . vitamins, cold remedies (including proprietary antihistamines), analgesics and laxatives and cathartics are the most important proprietary products. These items for the most part are standard and their ingredients change little from year to year."[11]

The fast pace of new product introduction has important consequences, especially for ethical pharmaceuticals where the pace—though recently slowing down—is fastest. It helps to bring about shifts in sales and profit standing among the various companies, depending on discoveries and product obsolescence. It also helps to explain some outstanding features of the industry, such as (1) a faster than normal rate of sales growth; (2) a higher rate of pretax profits than is normal in other industries; (3) a paucity of successful new entrants into pharmaceuticals from outside that helps confine 90% of sales to only 28 well-established companies;[12] (4) the use of high-cost marketing methods to get technical information on prescription drugs to doctors; (5) concentration on R.&D. as a key functional activity; and (6) partly consequent upon some of the foregoing factors—intense scrutiny of industry affairs by agencies of government.

Sales trends

For the drug industry as a whole, sales have moved rapidly upward. Although the pace has recently slowed, corporations in this industry have grown much faster than those in other chemicals and allied products and faster than the all-manufacturing average:

CORPORATE SALES, 1957–62

	Sales (Dollars in Millions)		Per Cent Change
	1957	1962	
All manufacturing*	$320,039	$389,304	+21.6
Chemicals and allied products	23,427	30,254	+29.1
Drugs	3,165	4,548	+43.7

*Except newspapers.
Source: Federal Trade Commission–Securities and Exchange Commission, *Quarterly Financial Report for Manufacturing Corporations.*

---

[9] A class of drug used in cases of edema.
[10] Standard & Poor's, *op. cit.*, December 13, 1962, p. D–10.
[11] *Ibid.*, December 8, 1960, p. D–15.
[12] *Business Week*, December 10, 1960, p. 141.

But generalizations that apply to the industry group as a whole do not necessarily apply with equal force to all its segments. From the following figures on shipments, it may be observed that most of the growth has been contributed by pharmaceuticals:

SHIPMENTS BY INDUSTRY SEGMENT, 1954–61

	Shipments (Dollars in Millions)		Per Cent Change
	1954	1961	1954–61
Biological products	$ 66.6	$ 100.6	+51.1
Medicinal chemicals and botanical products	281.0	293.3	+ 4.4
Pharmaceutical preparations	1,700.5	2,919.6	+71.7

Source: U.S. Bureau of the Census, *1958 Census of Manufactures* and *Annual Survey of Manufactures, 1961.*

Again, what is true for the pharmaceutical segment as a whole does not necessarily hold good for each of its major product categories. How widely sales trends have varied for different types of pharmaceuticals over a relatively short span of time is suggested by the following figures:

PHARMACEUTICAL SHIPMENTS BY MAJOR CATEGORIES

Pharmaceuticals	Shipments, 1961 (Dollars in Millions)	Per Cent Change, 1958–61
For human use:		
Tranquilizers, sedatives, and hypnotics	$314.4	+32.8
Laxatives and stomach ulcer preparations	202.5	+27.5
Cough and cold preparations	212.6	+23.9
Analgesics, narcotics	306.6	+19.6
Other pharmaceutical preparations	668.4	+17.3
Antibiotics	360.8	− 0.3
Hormones	144.3	− 4.7
Vitamins	271.9	− 9.6
For veterinary use	97.9	+11.6

Source: Figures compiled by U.S. Bureau of the Census, cited by Business and Defense Services Administration, "Chemicals & Rubber," *Industry Report,* November–December 1962, pp. 3, 4.

Within pharmaceuticals, as might be expected from the rapid pace of new product introductions, most of the expansion has reportedly been in the ethical division, which by 1962 was estimated to account for about 70% of all pharmaceutical sales as against 30% for proprietaries. Proprietary drugs have not stood still, however, as attested by statistics on their retail sales: under $1.1 billion in 1953; over $1.7 billion in 1961.[13]

---

[13]*Drug Topics* figures, cited Standard & Poor's, *op. cit.,* December 13, 1962, p. D–16.

To dramatize the effect that sales trends in a single drug or family of drugs can have on the fortunes of the maker or seller, one may cite the experience of Merck & Company, Inc., with corticosteroids for treating arthritis; of Parke, Davis & Company with Chloromycetin, the first broad-spectrum antibiotic; and of Eli Lilly & Company with Salk polio vaccine:

In 1950, because a research gamble paid off, Merck captured the entire market for [corticosteroids]; sales jumped from $94-million in 1950 to $160-million in 1953. But in 1954, competitive steroid drugs entered the market, and Merck's sales dipped to $145 million. By 1958, Merck's share of the steroid market was down to 17%, and only the advent of other new drugs kept the sales curve rising.

In 1950, too, Parke, Davis introduced the first broad-spectrum antibiotic under the trade name Chloromycetin; in one year, sales climbed $32-million. However, before the company could recover its development costs, patients began reporting unfavorable reactions to the new drug and doctors turned away from it. In two years, sales fell $28-million and profits nearly $10-million before confidence in the drug was restored.

In a different field, Lilly had put a heap of money into research on tissue culture. When the Salk polio vaccine came along, Lilly was in the best position to fill demand. Sales went from $141-million in 1955 to $200-million in 1957, profits from $16-million to $32-million. Then the rush demand evaporated; in 1958, sales dropped to $180-million and profits to $23.7 million.[14]

Profit trends

Sparked by patent-protected new inventions and swiftly climbing sales, the profits of drug corporations have been high, as indicated in the following graphs. Out of 20 major industry groups and 9 major industry subdivisions, drugs have led the field in pretax profit on sales and investment except in a few quarters, as shown on page 500.

Drug profits have not, however, expanded quite so steadily as drug sales. For example, a significant dip was experienced by ethicals in 1952, when the price of penicillin dropped 40% following a buildup of production facilities and supply in the unpatented "narrow-spectrum antibiotics."[15] This disequilibrium in a major product category hit just at a time when U.S. drug firms were also losing lucrative foreign sales owing to currency restrictions and the revival of European industry.

As might be expected from the impact of new product developments on sales, profits for the ethical division of the pharmaceutical segment have generally been higher than those for the proprietary division. On the other hand, owing to a steady demand for proprietary products, especially among the growing numbers of oldsters (who compose that portion of the population most likely to engage in self-medication), profits for proprietary companies

---

[14]*Business Week*, December 10, 1960, p. 150.

[15]Penicillin and streptomycin are known as narrow-spectrum antibiotics owing to their relatively limited range of usefulness. Between 1950 and 1951, production of penicillin increased from 412 to 430 thousand pounds; of streptomycin from 160 to 315 thousand. See Standard & Poor's, *op. cit.*, October 10, 1952, p. D–13.

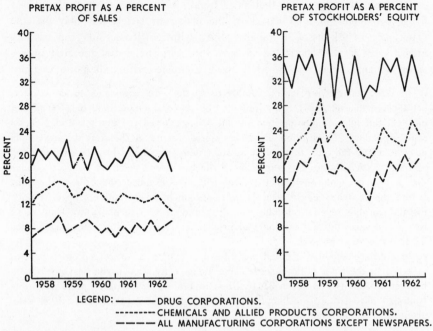

PRETAX PROFIT AS A PERCENT OF SALES

PRETAX PROFIT AS A PERCENT OF STOCKHOLDERS' EQUITY

LEGEND: ——————— DRUG CORPORATIONS.
---------- CHEMICALS AND ALLIED PRODUCTS CORPORATIONS.
— — — — ALL MANUFACTURING CORPORATIONS EXCEPT NEWSPAPERS.

Source: Federal Trade Commission–Securities and Exchange Commission, *Quarterly Financial Report for Manufacturing Corporations.*

have been relatively steady. This situation has provided impetus for companies specializing in one division of pharmaceuticals to acquire an interest in the other, and thus has helped to bring about changes in the industry's traditional structure.

Industry structure

According to Bureau of the Census statistics for 1958, the three segments of the drug industry included over 1,300 establishments, but most of them were small, as indicated by the following figures:

DRUG INDUSTRY ESTABLISHMENTS BY SIZE-CLASS, 1958

	No. of Establish- ments	Under 20 Em- ployees	20–249 Em- ployees	250–999 Em- ployees	1,000 Employees and over
Biological products	116	81	33	2	0
Medicinal chemicals, etc.	129	79	42	6	2
Pharmaceutical preparations ..	1,114	796	260	44	14
Total	1,359	956	335	52	16

Source: U.S. Bureau of the Census, *1958 Census of Manufactures.*

Of the small companies, a large number tend to be unprofitable not only in a relatively poor year like 1953–54, but also in a relatively prosperous year like 1959–60. Data for drug corporations with and without net income are shown in the following figures:

CORPORATE RECEIPTS, PROFITS, AND LOSSES IN THE DRUGS AND MEDICINES INDUSTRY
(Dollars in Millions)

	July 1953– June 1954	July 1959– June 1960
Total number of returns	1,323	1,307
Returns with net income:		
Number	750	896
Total receipts ($)	1,796	2,867
Net income ($)	253	538
Returns with no net income:		
Number	573	411
Total receipts ($)	81	53
Deficit ($)	6	2

Source: U.S. Internal Revenue Service, *Statistics of Income: Corporation Income Tax Returns.*

Even more important for understanding the structure of the industry is the fact that relatively few companies account for a large proportion of the sales. For pharmaceuticals, the largest drug segment, the Census Bureau reported the following:

CONCENTRATION OF SALES, PHARMACEUTICALS

No. of Companies	Per Cent of Total Shipments		
	1947	1954	1958
4 largest	28	25	27
8 largest	44	44	45
20 largest	64	68	73

Source: U.S. Bureau of the Census figures, cited *Statistical Abstract of the United States.*

In keeping with these findings is the often cited fact that only 28 or 29 companies account for roughly 90% of both profits and sales in drugs. However, concentration of profit within this group appears to be declining slightly:

In 1957, the 29 largest drug companies accounted for 89.8% of total industry sales, as measured by joint studies of the FTC and the SEC. In 1961, they accounted for 90.1%. However, in the same period, their share of industry profits fell from 93.8% to 90.9%.[16]

Commenting on sales concentration in the ethical and proprietary divisions of the pharmaceutical segment, Standard & Poor's added the following details:

Of . . . ethical drug sales in 1961, about 45% was accounted for by the 15 largest companies. Another 12.5% came from ethical divisions of primarily non-drug companies. . . . Four Swiss firms . . . provided about 7%, and the ethical divisions of proprietary firms some 22%.

*   *   *   *   *

The proprietary field is dominated by 14 companies that accounted for about 90% of total 1961 sales. . . .[17]

Despite the high level of sales concentration, industry analysts point out that "no single company accounts for as much as 10% of total drug sales, and relative standings of the largest firms change frequently."[18]

In spite of its high profits, the drug industry attracted few additional entrants between 1954 and 1958 and actually lost numbers in the pharmaceutical segment:

NUMBER OF DRUG INDUSTRY
ESTABLISHMENTS AND COMPANIES

	1954	1958
Biological products:		
Establishments	93	116
Companies	86	110
Medicinals and botanicals:		
Establishments	115	129
Companies	107	114
Pharmaceutical preparations:		
Establishments	1,163	1,114
Companies	1,128	1,064

Source: U.S. Bureau of the Census, *1958 Census of Manufactures*, and *Statistical Abstract of the United States*.

Deterring the founding of new ethical companies by outsiders is the need for having established marketing and research organizations and the difficulty of creating these from scratch. As pointed out by Standard & Poor's:

It is extremely difficult and time consuming for an outside firm to build up a drug research and marketing organization. A research team would probably take 8–10 years to pay its way through new product development. Most doctors are already seeing as many detail men [drug company representatives] each day as they care to. For these reasons, most outside firms attempting to diversify into pharmaceuticals have done so via the acquisition route.[19]

[16]Standard & Poor's, *op. cit.*, December 13, 1962, p. D–9.
[17]*Ibid.*, p. D–8.
[18]*Ibid.*
[19]*Ibid.*, December 8, 1960, p. D–13.

While some outsiders have bought into drugs, trends affecting industry structure more profoundly have been (a) movement toward international operation through setting up or acquiring manufacturing subsidiaries abroad, (b) vertical integration among segments, and (c) diversification of proprietary firms into ethical drugs and vice versa.

As to vertical integration, there have been several instances of firms in the medicinal chemicals segment integrating forward into pharmaceuticals. Some have done so through purchase or merger, others by setting up a new division. For example, both Olin Mathieson Chemical Corporation and American Cyanamid Company (who entered medicinal chemicals with bulk penicillin during World War II) later acquired pharmaceutical businesses by purchasing respectively E. R. Squibb & Sons and Lederle Laboratories, Inc. Similarly, Merck & Company, Inc., a very much longer established factor in the fine and medicinal chemicals field, merged in 1953 with Sharp & Dohme, an ethical pharmaceutical company. In contrast, Chas. Pfizer & Company, also originally in fine chemicals, set up an ethical pharmaceutical division from within in 1950.

Examples of diversification within pharmaceuticals are even easier to find, with the result that many of the larger companies now have both ethical and proprietary interests.[20] Indeed, a recent survey showed 20 companies to be thus diversified, of which those listed on the following page were major examples.

Classifying the major companies in pharmaceuticals according to background, size, and activities, *Business Week* divided them into the following groups: (1) very large companies, either with interests other than drugs or vertically integrated within the drug industry; (2) large companies with no outside interests that produce a full—or relatively full—line of pharmaceuticals; (3) somewhat smaller companies dealing strictly in pharmaceuticals but not in a full line; (4) foreign-owned companies, difficult to compare with their U.S. competitors in the absence of data on their purely U.S. operations; and (5) hundreds of small companies known as compounders because they "buy chemicals in bulk and mix common medicines such as vitamins, cold tablets, aspirin, and antacids, plus a few ethical drugs for packaging and sale under their own labels."[21]

To these domestic suppliers might be added foreign competitors, whose sales in the U.S. market, though still small, grew rapidly through 1961, as attested by the import-export figures at the bottom of the following page.

Still another classification of domestic pharmaceutical companies was that offered by the president of Merck, who told a congressional subcommittee that the industry broke down into three classes: the "creators," the "molecule manipulators," and the "coat-tail riders."[22] This classification, of course, was based on the type and amount of research carried on by each group, and

---

[20]*Business Week*, December 10, 1960, p. 146.

[21]*Ibid.*, p. 145.

[22]*Ibid.*

COMPANIES IN BOTH PHARMACEUTICAL AND
PROPRIETARY BRANCHES OF DRUG INDUSTRY

Parent Company	Ethical Branches	Proprietary Branches
Abbott	Abbott	Lake
Amer. Home Prod.	Wyeth	Whitehall
	Ayerst	
	Ives-Cameron	
	Fort Dodge	
Bristol Labs.	Bristol Labs.	Grove Labs.
Carter Products	Wallace	Carter Products
Chemway	Crookes-Barnes	Dunbar Labs.
Colgate-Palmolive	Lakeside Labs.	S. M. Edison
Hoffman-La Roche	Roche Labs.	Downing Co.
Johnson & Johnson	McNeil	Johnson & Johnson
	Ortho	
	Ethicon	
McKesson and Robbins	McKesson and Robbins	Norclift
Mead Johnson	Mead Johnson Labs.	Edward Dalton
Miles	Ames	Miles
	Dome	
Norwich	Eaton	Norwich Pharmacal
Pfizer	Pfizer Labs.	Family Prods. Dept.
	Roerig	Labaron
	Globe Labs.	
Plough	Plough Labs.	Plough
Rexall Drug & Chem.	Riker Labs.	Rexall
Richardson-Merrell	Merrell	Vick Products
	National Drug	
	Walker	
	Hess & Clark	
Schering	Schering	Pharmaco
	White Labs.	
Smith, Kline & French	S K F Labs.	Menley & James
	Norden Labs.	
	Julian Labs.	
Sterling	Winthrop	Glenbrook Labs.
	Breon	Sterling Products
Warner-Lambert	Warner-Chilcott	Warner-Lambert
		Standard Labs.

Source: *American Druggist*, cited Standard & Poor's *Industry Surveys*, December 13, 1962, p. D-8. After compilation of this table, Merck & Co., Inc., also diversified into proprietaries by setting up its Quinton Co. Division in 1962.

EXPORTS AND IMPORTS OF MEDICINES
AND DRUGS
(Dollars in Millions)

Year	Exports	Imports
1952	$221.2	$ 6.1
1955	226.5	6.9
1958	277.7	14.9
1961	275.3	35.1
1962	269.9	37.2

Source: U.S. Bureau of the Census, *United States Exports . . .* and *United States Imports . . .*

reflects the key importance of the research activity to firms in the ethical division of drugs.

Research and development

In the drug industry, research and development is interpreted somewhat broadly to include not only the search for new compounds with medicinal effects, but also elaborate testing procedures designed to determine the safety and efficacy of the drug, and elaborate quality control procedures designed to secure purity and uniformity in manufacture.

Describing its own procedures, one maker, Merck, reported that discovery and testing on one new product—a hypertensive—involved completing the following steps before application was made to put the new drug on the market: (1) use of a background of discoveries that blood pressure was affected by the body's output of two specific hormones; (2) formulation of an hypothesis that production of a hormone might be blocked by its a-methyl analog, based on Merck discoveries of a blocking property in the a-methyl analog of another amino acid; (3) demonstration of such blocking action in the test tube; (4) after years of refinement in techniques necessary to prove biochemical reactions in animals, demonstration of such blocking action in animals by two of some fifteen outside researchers to whom Merck had furnished samples of the drug; (5) further tests of efficacy and also of safety in animals, conducted respectively by researchers at one of the U.S. National Institutes of Health and by Merck; (6) safety in animals having been demonstrated by Merck, exploratory clinical trial of the drug conducted on ten human patients by the NIH researchers; (7) long-term study initiated with several species of animals to demonstrate safety for chronic administration of the drug; (8) preclinical report issued, based on known information, to interest clinicians in testing the drug on humans; (9) clinical trials initiated in leading medical centers in Europe as well as in the United States; (10) following initial encouraging tests, clinical trials expanded to involve more than 200 physicians in 32 countries and nearly 2,000 patients; (11) continuation of clinical trials and application for clearance of the drug by the U.S. Food and Drug Administration.[23]

How elaborate R.&D.'s quality control procedures can be in some firms on some products is indicated by the following description, also from Merck, of controls used in manufacturing the company's new live vaccine for measles:

. . . tests are the principal reason that the vaccine takes 20 weeks to make—the testing alone takes nearly 14 weeks.

The vaccine is checked for many qualities—including potency, identity, sterility, moisture content, and safety. The safety testing alone includes tests in tissue cultures of chick embryo, chick embryo liver, chick embryo kidney, and human cells. Specific tests for the presence of fowl leukosis are made in chick embryo cell culture. The vaccine is tested in embryonated eggs and by several innoculation methods in animals, including adult mice, suckling mice, rhesus mon-

---

[23]*The Merck Review*, special issue, "Testing New Drugs," Spring 1963.

keys, and grivet monkeys. Tests are also performed for bacterial contamination and specifically for the presence of tuberculosis and pleuro-pneumonia-like organisms.[24]

In terms of research costs, the relatively few research-performing companies in ethical drugs claim to lead all other industry groups in the per cent of sales spent on R.&D.[25] Moreover, this percentage has been rapidly growing; according to estimates by Standard & Poor's, it increased from 5.7% in 1951 to 9.1% a decade later.[26]

In terms of dollars as well as percentages, pharmaceutical industry research has grown significantly—up to $268 million in 1962, or five times what it was ten years ago, according to trade association sources.[27] Official statistics (which exclude quality control and routine testing from the definition of research and cover only R.&D. in industry facilities) provide the following comparative figures (dollars in millions).

COMPANY AND FEDERAL FUNDS FOR R.&D. IN INDUSTRY FACILITIES
(Dollars in Millions)

	Funds 1956	Funds 1961	Per Cent Change 1956–61
All industry	$6,583	$10,891	+65.3
Chemicals and allied products	651	1,092	+67.7
Drugs and medicines	94	181	+92.6

Source: U.S. National Science Foundation, *Review of Data on Research and Development*, September 1962.

Excluded from the figure of $181 million is a substantial but unspecified amount spent by the drug industry on research performed outside its own facilities (in hospitals, etc.). Included is a relatively small amount (estimated at about $7 million or under 4%)[28] spent on drug research in industry facilities by the federal government. In contrast to this relatively small percentage are federal expenditures for 1961 research in the facilities of such defense-connected industries as aircraft and missiles (94% of a $3,964 million total) or electrical equipment and communications (65% of $2,377 million). Partly as a consequence of doing so much in a few defense-connected categories, the federal share of all research conducted in industry facilities was 59% in 1961.[29]

[24]*Ibid.*

[25]Business and Defense Services Administration, *The Pharmaceutical Industry Outlook for 1962 and Review of 1961.*

[26]Standard & Poor's, *op. cit.*, December 13, 1962, p. D–10.

[27]Pharmaceutical Manufacturers' Association figures, cited *The New York Times.* September 30, 1962.

[28]Business and Defense Services Administration, *op. cit.*

[29]U.S. National Science Foundation, *Review of Data on Research and Development,* September 1962.

To say that the federal government spends but little on medical research within drug-industry facilities is not to say that its expenditures are small in total. On the contrary, federal funds support by far the largest and fastest growing share of medical research performed by all agencies: $442.4 million in 1961, or 40% of the total, up almost eightfold from only $59.2 million as recently as 1956.[30] These federal funds are spent through eight National Institutes of Health (for allergies, arthritis, cancer, heart, etc.) which make various grants and awards (mainly for research projects, fellowships, training projects, and traineeships). Most of the money has been used on an extra-mural basis to support approved projects carried on by outside institutions, mainly hospitals, medical schools, and university departments.[31]

Despite increased expenditures on R.&D. by government and private industry, the pace of new discoveries in drugs has slowed, owing to a variety of factors. Among these might be mentioned (1) the stubborn nature of remaining research problems; (2) the relatively small amount of "basic" research being carried on in industry facilities (only $30 million out of $181 million in 1961);[32] and (3) caution induced by a rising number of drug suspensions (20—including those for veterinary use—reported as suspended or contested in 1959–61, versus only one reported in 1955–58).[33]

Operating also to slow the pace of new introductions if not of new discoveries has been the mounting backlog of new drugs awaiting clearance by the federal agency charged with this function, i.e., the Food and Drug Administration (FDA). Indicating the trend toward a slowdown in new drug discoveries and introductions are the following official figures:

Year	Total New Drug Applications	Applications Passed			Supplemental Applications* Passed
		Human	Veterinary	Total	
1955	606	343	90	433	2,277
1956	520	346	61	407	2,492
1957	530	334	59	393	1,400
1958	435	280	68	348	1,494
1959	448	230	43	273	1,067
1960	480	222	46	268	819
1961	463	155	68	223	931

*Providing for changes in applications in effect.
Source: U.S. Department of Health, Education and Welfare, *Annual Reports, 1955–61.*

A related statistic also worth noting is the declining number of new single chemicals (entities not previously known, and developed by one manufacturer) appearing among pharmaceutical introductions since 1959:

[30]U.S. Department of Health, Education and Welfare, *Annual Report*, 1956, p. 175; 1961, pp. 208, 237.

[31]*Ibid.*

[32]U.S. National Science Foundation, *op. cit.*

[33]U.S. Department of Health, Education and Welfare, *Annual Reports*, 1955–61.

Year	New Single Chemicals
1959	63
1960	45
1961	41
1962	28

Source: Figures developed by Paul de Haen, industry consultant, cited by Standard & Poor's "Drugs, Cosmetics, Basic Analysis," *Industry Surveys*, December 13, 1962, p. D-10; and "Current Analysis and Outlook," *Industry Surveys*, April 11, 1963.

According to Standard & Poor's, "The decline in new products has given emphasis to combinations of existing drugs in new dosage forms and quantities. It has also led to greater cross licensing of pharmaceuticals by full-line companies."[34]

Though the pace of major breakthroughs may be slowing down, research and development remains a key activity, especially in ethical drugs, for both social and profit reasons. Socially, research is all-important for its impact on health and on the size and makeup of the population. Profitwise, research is important because major new discoveries lead to ballooning sales at premium prices.

Ability to capture the market, however, before competitors step in with a like product, depends on possession of a strong marketing organization and aggressive marketing policies.

Marketing

For selling pharmaceuticals (the form in which most drugs reach the ultimate consumer) most, but not all, marketing techniques are by now well established. On ethicals, these include: (1) promoting particular products to the medical professions only; (2) limiting media to advertisements in professional journals, sample distribution, and direct mail; (3) placing heaviest reliance on sales representatives known as "detail men" (of whom there are about 15,000) to carry the company's highly technical message to doctors; (4) pushing the patented trademarked name of the individual company's product in order to pull sales away from similar or substitute products of other manufacturers or from identical products sold under their generic names at lower prices; (5) pricing new drugs high in order to assure, so far as possible, earning back more than development costs before the new product is outmoded; (6) selective cross licensing of competitors, with the result that there may be more than one supplier even of a patented drug; (7) selling by some vertically integrated companies of bulk drugs to compounders, with the result that the number of sellers for many end products is greater than the number of drug producers; and (8) serving foreign

---

[34]Standard & Poor's, *op. cit.*, December 13, 1962, p. D-10.

markets not only through exports (6.7% of drug industry sales in 1961), but to an even larger extent through manufacturing abroad (17.3% of sales in 1961 accounted for by foreign subsidiaries).[35]

Besides these common policies which the major companies carry out individually, there are other common policies carried out through trade associations such as the National Pharmaceutical Council or the Pharmaceutical Manufacturers' Association. These include (1) seeking legislation (on the books in 44 states by 1959)[36] to prohibit druggists from substituting another trade name of the identical drug in place of the particular trade name prescribed; (2) combatting practices deemed hostile to the general industry interest—for example, the practice of the federal government in buying drugs from foreign countries (at a reported three-year saving of $12 million),[37] including one country (Italy) that recognizes no patent protection on drugs; and (3) running a series of institutional ads in the mass media to help build a good public image for the industry by associating it with life-giving, health-restoring product advances. This last policy marks a recent innovation, and is part of the industry's response to the criticisms of its prices and products given wide publicity in the majority report of the U.S. Senate's Kefauver Committee.

While many policies in marketing are common to most major members of the ethical pharmaceutical industry, some other policies in this area differ significantly among makers. For one thing, according to *Business Week*, some of the companies that entered the field relatively recently from outside have failed to observe the old-line "code" that forbids one competitor to publicize the difficulties of another, to make exaggerated claims about "absolute" safety or "no" side effects, or to offer elaborate and expensive entertainment to doctors. "A few of the old-line leaders are having quiet talks with their newer competitors to try to persuade them to be more restrained in their promotion and entertaining. . . . They are also talking to medical groups, cautioning doctors to be less receptive to—and, in some instances, less demanding of—favors from drug houses."[38]

Another important and more tangible marketing issue on which company practice varies is choice of distribution channels. Thus independent merchant wholesalers and manufacturers' sales branches are both used widely to distribute drugs and allied products. Sales in 1958 were about evenly divided between them (see page 510).

In 1962 some major pharmaceutical companies such as Lilly, SKF, and Mead-Johnson sold almost exclusively through drug wholesalers. On the other hand, according to Standard & Poor's, Upjohn sold almost entirely direct to retailers, while smaller companies used both methods.[39] As a result,

[35]*Ibid.*, p. D–12.

[36]Up from only four states in 1953. See U.S. Senate Subcommittee on Antitrust and Monopoly, *Administered Prices, Drugs* (Report No. 448; 87th Cong., 1st. sess.). (Washington, D.C.: U.S. Government Printing Office), p. 236.

[37]*Boston Globe*, April 7, 1963.

[38]*Business Week*, December 10, 1960, p. 153.

[39]Standard & Poor's, *op. cit.*, December 13, 1962, pp. D–11, D–12.

WHOLESALE TRADE, DRUGS, DRUG PROPRIETARIES, AND DRUGGISTS' SUNDRIES, 1958

Establishments	Number	Sales (Millions)
Merchant wholesalers	3,042	$2,827
Manufacturers' sales branches	518	2,840
Agents, brokers	209	289
Total	3,769	$5,955

Note: Comparable figures for 1954 on merchant wholesalers showed 2,801 establishments with sales of $2,174 million. Comparable figures for manufacturers' sales branches are not available.
Source: U.S. Bureau of the Census, *Census of Business, 1958*.

independent pharmacists reportedly obtained about 60% of their prescription drugs from wholesalers.[40]

As to trends on channels, Standard & Poor's has the following to say: "Many companies have taken steps to increase their direct sales of drugs to retailers.[41] However, in view of the large number of small items which must be readily available, it is expected that drug wholesalers will continue to play an important role in the drug industry."[42]

In this connection, it is interesting to note that only one drug wholesaler— McKesson and Robbins—blankets the whole country, and that this potent entity (sales $708 million in 1962, profits $9.4 million, with drugs reportedly accounting for 62% of volume and 74% of net income)[43] recently decided to compete with some of its own customers by making nonpatented prescription drugs and selling them under their generic names at prices up to 90% lower than those of comparable brand-name products.[44] This decision achieved wide publicity when it was announced in October 1961, but little information is available on the company's experience to date. The Annual Report for 1962 merely states that the new line of ethicals has been "well received." According to *Value Line*, most early sales were in South America rather than in the United States. Two reasons were advanced to account for this circumstance, (1) that "less affluent, less brand-conscious" areas may offer the "most ready market for this less expensive medication"; and (2) that McKesson and Robbins, as a wholesale distributor for the brand-name drugs of competing companies, is in a "touchy position" in the domestic market.[45]

---

[40]*Business Week*, December 10, 1960, p. 148.

[41]These included Abbott, Pfizer, and American Cyanamid in 1960.

[42]Standard & Poor's, *op. cit.*, December 13, 1962, p. D–11. Further evidence that drug wholesalers are adversely affected by competition from manufacturers' branches may be found in statements of The National Wholesale Drug Association. Their *Yearbook, 1961* provides the following statistics:

	1956	1960
Sales index (1950 = 100)	153	178
Per cent profit on sales	2.21	1.76

[43]Annual Report, 1962; *The Value Line Investment Survey*, August 20, 1962, p. 456.

[44]*The New York Times*, December 14, 1961, p. 27.

[45]*The Value Line Investment Survey*, August 20, 1962, p. 456.

Passing out of wholesale into retail channels, ethical drugs reach the ultimate consumer at the instance of physicians, through drugstores, hospital dispensaries, and doctors. According to Standard & Poor's, these three outlets account, respectively for 60%, 21%, and 19% of total ethical drug distribution.[46] According to another source that cites figures only for retail outlets, drugstores currently account for 98% of all civilian spending on prescriptions and for 66% of spending on packaged medicines:

1961 CIVILIAN SPENDING ON PRESCRIPTIONS AND PACKAGED MEDICINES
(Dollars in Millions)

	All Outlets	Drugstores
Prescriptions	$2,261	$2,209
Packaged medicines	1,747	1,156

Source: *Drug Topics*, July 16, 1962, p. 2.

As to trends in the number of drug outlets, the most notable change, as indicated in the following figures, is the rising importance of the chain drugstore:

NUMBER OF DRUG OUTLETS

	1957	1960
Physicians	226,625	255,972
Hospitals*	6,818	6,876
Drugstores:		
Independent	48,715	49,074
Chain of four or more	4,585	5,052
Total Drugstores	53,300	54,126

*Accepted for listing by the American Hospital Association.
Source: Physicians and hospitals: American Medical Association and American Hospital Association figures, cited *Statistical Abstract of the United States*; drugstores: *Drug Topics*.

In keeping with this evidence, another source has stated that recent prescription volume growth has been accounted for entirely by drug chains, large independent drugstores, and Rx specialty stores, with small- and medium-sized drugstores actually declining in importance.[47]

---

[46]Standard & Poor's, *op. cit.*, December 13, 1962, p. D–11. Included in the percentage for doctors would be, presumably, some of the free samples given to the profession by drug companies. Some of these samples, however, find their way back into channels of trade. Repackaged and sometimes carelessly relabeled, such drugs constitute a problem for the FDA in enforcing the Pure Food and Drug legislation.

[47]A. C. Nielsen Co., *Twenty-eighth Annual Survey of Retail Drug and Proprietary Store Trends*, 1962, p. 16.

The ultimate purchasers of drugs are of course the people who buy medication and drugs for themselves, for animals, and even increasingly for plants. Encouraging from the point of view of future volume—although threatening, perhaps, from the point of view of prospects for eventual price controls on drugs—is the increase in the number of potential human consumers, especially in the number aged 65 and over. Since these have the greatest incidence of chronic illness, they also have the greatest need for medication. According to Standard & Poor's, "Average drug charges for the over-65 group were $22 annually in 1960 compared with $11 for the 35–54 group."[48] Persons in the 65+ category are expected to increase in number by more than 50% in the 20 years ending 1975:

U.S. POPULATION TRENDS

	1955	1960	1965*	1970*	1975*
Total (millions)	165.3	180.0	195.7	213.8	235.2
Age 65+ (millions)	14.1	16.6	17.6	19.5	21.9
Age 65+ (% of total)	8.5	9.2	9.0	9.1	9.3

*Assumes 1955–57 level of fertility will continue.

Source: U.S. Bureau of the Census figures (*Current Population Reports*), cited in U.S. Department of Health, Education and Welfare, *Health, Education and Welfare Trends, 1961*.

In the light of many factors so far described, it is not surprising that the wholesale price index for drugs and pharmaceuticals was relatively high after World War II. What may be surprising, however, is the leveling off and recent decline:

WHOLESALE PRICE INDEX (1957–59 = 100)

Year	All Commodities	Drugs and Pharmaceuticals
1954	92.9	100.4
1958	100.4	100.5
1961	100.3	98.3

Source: U.S. Bureau of Labor Statistics, *Prices: A Chartbook, 1953–62.*

Running counter to wholesale price trends, however, the retail price index for drugs continued to advance through the later 1950's. And an even faster rise in medical services contributed to mounting consumer concern with the costs of medical care:

CONSUMER PRICE INDEX (1957–59 = 100)

Year	All Items	Prescriptions and Drugs	Prescriptions	Medical Care Services	Medical Care
1954	93.6	91.7	89.2	85.5	86.6
1958	100.7	100.6	100.7	100.0	100.1
1961	104.2	101.1	99.2	113.1	111.3

Source: U.S. Bureau of Labor Statistics, *Prices: A Chartbook, 1953–62.*

[48]Standard & Poor's, *op. cit.*, December 13, 1962, p. D–9.

Adding to consumer awareness of the high price of drugs have been such factors as the higher prices of the newer medicines and the increased use of medicines for treating greater numbers of diseases. These factors are reflected in the increased average price per prescription and the increased number of prescriptions per person:

AVERAGE ANNUAL RX EXPENDITURES IN THE UNITED STATES

	1957	1961
Average expenditure per Rx	$ 2.64	$ 2.97
Number of Rx per person*	3.8	4.1
Rx expenditures per person†	$10.03	$12.17

*Calculated by dividing the total number of prescriptions filled by drug stores by the total population.
†Calculated by multiplying line 1 by line 2.
Source: *Drug Topics*, March issues.

Reflecting such factors, official figures show high percentage gains in private expenditures for medical care including drugs and drug sundries, 1954–61. Moreover, during the same period those expenditures have taken a rising share of disposable private income:

PRIVATE EXPENDITURES FOR MEDICAL CARE

	1954	1961	Per Cent Change 1954–61
Total expenditures ($ million):			
Drugs and drug sundries	$ 2,163	$ 4,014	+85.6
Total care	11,895	21,120	+77.6
Per capita expenditures ($):			
Drugs and drug sundries	13.60	22.16	+62.9
Total care	74.77	116.60	+55.9
Medical care as a per cent of private disposable income	4.6%	5.8%	

Source: U.S. Social Security Administration, *Social Security Bulletin*, December 1962.

Although prices for drugs have risen less than those for service elements in medical care, price resistance has broken out among public and institutional buyers as well as among individuals. For example, the federal government has purchased low-priced drugs abroad and has claimed savings of over $12 million in the three years ending 1962.[49] Some local welfare agencies have refused to reimburse for trade-name drugs bought at relatively high prices in cases where generic-name products are cheaper.[50] Hospitals have also favored generic-name dispensing. In some places single unions (including the United Automobile Workers) or groups of unions (including nine major

[49]*Boston Globe*, April 7, 1963.
[50]*The New York Times*, October 7, 1960.

ones in New York City) have established their own drugstores or drug chains to fill prescriptions on a cut-rate basis.[51]

Reflecting in part the demand for cheaper drugs, changes have occurred in the distribution system. The switch of McKesson & Robbins from whole-saling only to both wholesaling and making ethical drugs might be regarded as one facet of this story. Another would be the advent of additional types of retail outlets. These have long included grocery chains (for proprietaries) and mail-order houses (for both proprietaries and ethicals). More recently, discounters have entered the field. As might be expected, these show a greater readiness to sacrifice margins and undermine fair-trade prices than their predecessors. According to estimates by the A. C. Nielsen Company, there were 792 "genuine full-line mass merchandisers in operation by 1962, of which 91% handled drug items, while 22% had Rx departments."[52]

Commenting on some of these changes in the distribution pattern, Standard & Poor's indicated that they "put pressure on prices right back to the pro-ducer," and added up to a "marketing revolution."[53]

If trends in drug expenditures have helped to create a demand for cheaper drugs, data on drug company margins have helped to bring about some of the pressure on prices. For an understanding of the wide gross margins characteristic of this industry, one must turn to information on production processes.

Production

Helping to explain relatively low cost-of-goods-sold and high gross-margin figures for drugs are various factors in the production area, i.e., a relatively small expense for direct labor and materials, and a relatively low investment in depreciable fixed assets, as suggested by the tables below and on page 515:

COMPARATIVE LABOR COSTS, 1961

	All Manufacturing	Chemicals and Allied Products	Drugs
Total payroll ($ million)	88,164	4,528	633
Total wages ($ million)	54,803	2,516	272
Wages/payroll (%)	62.2	55.6	43.0
Value added by manufacture ($ million) ..	163,801	14,768	2,440
Wages/value added (%)	33.5	17.0	11.1

Source: U.S. Bureau of the Census, *Annual Survey of Manufactures, 1961.*

Another important reason for the relatively low percentage cost of goods sold in drugs is that quality control—often a costly production function—is frequently classified under R.&D. by manufacturers of drugs, and R.&D. is entered "below the line" like general and administrative expenses. How

---

[51]*Ibid.*, June 22 and 27, 1960.
[52]A. C. Nielsen Co., *op. cit.*, p. 14.
[53]Standard & Poor's, *op. cit.*, December 13, 1962, p. D–12.

COMPARATIVE MATERIALS COSTS, 1961

(Dollars in Millions)

	Cost of Materials	Value of Shipments	Materials/ Shipments (Per Cent)
Drugs*			
Biological products	$ 37	$ 101	36.6
Medicinals, botanicals	147	293	50.2
Pharmaceutical preparations	696	2,920	23.8
Other chemical products*			
Organic chemicals	1,817	3,944	46.1
Inorganic chemicals	1,427	3,108	45.9
Plastic materials	1,163	2,124	54.8
Synthetic rubber	406	696	58.3
Soap, detergents	894	1,898	47.1
Paints, varnishes	1,142	2,033	56.2
Fertilizers	887	1,234	71.9

*The total value of shipments and cost of materials for industry groups are not published due to extensive duplication arising from shipments between establishments in the same industry classification.
  Source: U.S. Bureau of the Census, *Annual Survey of Manufactures, 1961*. (In April 1963, value of shipments figures were revised, but these most recent figures have not been used owing to the fact that revision for other data in the Bureau's general statistics have not yet been published.)

COMPARATIVE INVESTMENT DATA, 1962*

(Dollars in Millions)

	Net Fixed Assets	Total Assets	Fixed Assets/ Total Assets (Per Cent)	Sales	Fixed Assets/ Sales (Per Cent)
All manufacturing† ..	$110,848	$286,625	38.7	$389,304	28.5
Chemicals and allied products	11,365	27,111	41.9	30,254	37.6
Drugs	1,165	3,840	30.3	4,548	25.6

*Fourth-quarter figures for assets; January–December figures for sales.
  †Except newspapers.
  Source: Federal Trade Commission–Securities and Exchange Commission, *Quarterly Financial Report for Manufacturing Corporations, 1961.*

costly quality control can be on some products is at least suggested by the following quotation from testimony presented to the Kefauver Committee by Merck:

This process of testing is pursued endlessly through the manufacturing process. Thus in making one of our ophthalmic solutions no less than 121 separate tests are made before [the company] is ready to assign its trade name. Subsequent to manufacture, 750 more separate tests are made to check stability. . . . Incidentally, these tests require at least several hundred man-hours of skilled conscientious labor, not to mention the most advanced equipment.[54]

In terms of trends, it is significant that the drug industry has achieved

---

[54]Report of the Senate Subcommittee on Antitrust and Monopoly, *Administered Prices, Drugs*, p. 294.

its phenomenal growth without commensurate increases in variable direct costs, although total investment has risen even more rapidly than sales:

GROWTH AND COST INCREASES FOR DRUGS
(Dollars in Millions)

	1958	1961	Per Cent Change
Measure of growth:			
Sales	$3,350	$4,165	+24.3
Value added by manufacture	2,096	2,440	+16.4
Shipments:			
Biological products	64	101	+57.8
Medicinals, botanicals	322	293	− 9.0
Pharmaceutical preparations	2,592	2,920	+12.7
Cost factors:			
Total payroll	546	633	+15.9
Wages	251	272	+ 8.4
Cost of materials:			
Biological products	25	37	+48.0
Medicinals, botanicals	149	147	− 1.3
Pharmaceutical preparations	701	696	− 0.7
Investment:			
Total assets	2,742	3,554	+29.6
Net fixed assets	828	1,094	+32.1

Source: U.S. Bureau of the Census, *1958 Census of Manufactures*, and *Annual Survey of Manufactures, 1961*; Federal Trade Commission–Securities and Exchange Commission, *Quarterly Financial Report for Manufacturing Corporations*.

This rising productivity of most of the factors of production appears due less to using more effective production controls than to finding more efficient processes and cheaper, more readily available materials. The history of penicillin or of corticosteroids indicates how dramatically costs can be affected by breakthroughs that arise from R.&D. rather than from improved production management per se.

From what has been said about production and cost/profit factors, one might also expect a trend toward an increase in the number of drug firms. As previously noted, however, factors in the marketing and research areas have operated to inhibit this development. Nonetheless, as pointed out by the Bureau of the Census, production considerations do affect the structure of the industry as follows:

Since specialized equipment or relatively large investments in capital are not prerequisites for many products primary to the industry [pharmaceuticals], the industry is characterized by the presence of a relatively large number of small firms. In 1954, approximately 62% of the 1,163 establishments classified in this industry had fewer than 10 employees, and in 1958 the comparable percentage [was] 59%.[55]

The fact that production considerations help to create large numbers of

[55]U.S. Bureau of the Census, *op. cit.*, p. 28C–2.

drug firms while marketing and research considerations help to keep most of them small is part of the background of industry data needed for an understanding of the recent investigation of the industry by the Senate Subcommittee on Antitrust and Monopoly (the Kefauver Committee). Senator Kefauver hoped to prove a need for increased regulation of the industry in ways that would affect its prices, not just help assure safety of its products. The latter goal, however, was the traditional objective of Pure Food and Drug legislation up to 1962.

Government regulation

Early legislation. The first Federal Pure Food and Drug Act was passed in 1906; it prohibited sale in interstate commerce of adulterated or misbranded products. This law was tightened in 1938, after a sulfa elixir distributed by a small Tennessee manufacturer proved to contain a poisonous solvent which resulted in nearly 100 deaths.

Commenting on the changes effected in 1938, an official release of the U.S. Department of Agriculture (USDA)[56] stated, "The new act goes much farther than the old law in that it contains positive requirements for informative labeling in the interest of consumers in addition to the negative prohibitions against mislabeling contained in the old statute.[57] The new act amplifies and strengthens the provisions designed to safeguard the public health, and extends the scope of the law to include cosmetics [except soap], therapeutic devices, and certain drugs that now escape regulation."[58] These were "drugs intended for diagnosing illness or for remedying underweight or overweight, or otherwise affecting bodily structure or function."[59]

Besides extending the scope of the law and making labeling more informative, other major changes included (1) elimination of the "fraud joker" in the old law under which the government had to prove that false claims of curative effects on the labels of patent medicines were made with willful intent to deceive; (2) the prohibition of traffic in drugs and devices which are dangerous to health under the conditions of use prescribed on the label; and (3) a prohibition of traffic in new drugs—except drugs intended solely for investigational use by qualified scientific experts—unless such drugs have

[56] In 1938 the Food and Drug Administration (FDA) was part of the Department of Agriculture. Subsequently, FDA was transferred to the Department of Health, Education and Welfare (HEW).

[57] Major labeling changes were those requiring (1) a warning on specified habit-forming drugs for human use; (2) precautionary labeling on drugs liable to deterioration; (3) revelation of any difference from official standards in the strength, quality, or purity of "official" drugs (i.e., those recognized by the U.S. Pharmacopoeia, National Formulary, or Homeopathic Pharmacopoeia of the U.S.); (4) revelation of active ingredients on the labels of nonofficial drugs, including the quantity or proportion of certain specified ingredients; (5) a declaration that nonofficial drugs were illegal if the strength thereof differed from the standard claimed; and (6) a warning on the labels of drugs and devices against probable misuse which might be dangerous to health.

[58] Cited by Commerce Clearing House, Inc., *Food Drug Cosmetic Law Service*, 1938, p. 126.

[59] *Ibid.*

been adequately tested to show that they are safe for use under the conditions prescribed in their labels.[60] Under this section (No. 505) of the law, persons wishing to introduce a new drug into interstate commerce had to file an application that included (a) full reports of investigations made to show whether the drug was safe;[61] (b) a full statement of the composition of the drug; (c) a full description of methods and facilities used in manufacturing, processing, and packing; (d) samples of the drug; and (3) specimens of labeling proposed. Applications—processed by the FDA—became effective after 60 days unless challenged. If applications were denied, the makers' recourse was to the courts.[62]

Except for laws that (1) postponed the effective date of certain provisions of the 1938 act to 1940, and (2) brought specified antibiotics under a compulsory public testing program, no important drug legislation was passed until 1962. Then, under the influences of the "thalidomide disaster"[63] and the recent Kefauver investigation, further sweeping changes were enacted.

Drug act amendment of 1962. Reflecting the mixed influences that led to its enactment, the Drug Act Amendment of 1962 contained provisions aimed primarily at strengthening health safeguards, but also at increasing price competition through provisions designed to gain a wider acceptance for nontrademarked products marketed under their generic or scientific names by smaller, less well-known manufacturers. Major changes in health safeguards were outlined as follows by *Time*, which headed its list with a radical new clause that had failed of passage in 1938:

No new drug can be marketed until the manufacturer has satisfied the FDA that it is both safe and effective. Under the old law, only safety had to be proved, and approval was automatic after 60 days unless FDA took negative action. . . . Even after a drug is on the market, FDA can summarily order it withdrawn if evidence appears that the medicine is unsafe or ineffective. The old law prescribed a long legal procedure to obtain withdrawal, and then only when danger had been proved.

Before any drug is even tested in human beings, the manufacturer must give FDA evidence that it has had adequate testing in animals—this will include pregnant animals—and appears safe.

. . . Package inserts and ads to doctors must contain a warning of undesirable effects.

Every batch of every antibiotic for use in man must be tested by government laboratories. Under the old law, some antibiotics were so tested, but not all.

Every plant in which a drug is manufactured or processed in any way will

---

[60]*Ibid.*, p. 124.

[61]For a company description of steps involved in development and testing of one of its new drugs, see the section on R.&D. above.

[62]Commerce Clearing House, Inc., *op. cit.*, pp. 521, 522.

[63]Thalidomide, used abroad in various brands of sleeping pills, was blamed for serious malformation of several thousand infants whose mothers had taken the drug during pregnancy. At the time this result was traced to its cause, U.S. introduction of the drug was being held up by Dr. Frances Kelsey of the FDA under Section 505 of the 1938 Act.

now have to be registered with FDA, inspected at least every two years, and open to inspection at any time.[64]

Changes designed to enhance acceptance of lower-priced drugs included (1) the provision cited above regarding plant inspection, which would, it was hoped, increase doctors' confidence in the output of small makers; and (2) a provision that "every drug container, package, leaflet and advertisement to doctors must show the general or 'established' name of the drug in type at least half as big as that of the trade name."[65] This, it was hoped, would help break the hold on the market of the trademarked products of large manufacturers.

Commenting on the probable effects of these new provisions, Standard & Poor's indicated that some of the provisions, specifically the certification of all antibiotics (which is done at the manufacturer's expense) and the compulsory inspection of all producers, would be likely to raise costs. Also, the longer time allotted for drug clearance was expected to "reduce the number of applications and lengthen evaluation time." Moreover, "some drug firms claim the lengthened time will give competitors a chance to develop comparable products prior to FDA certification, thus limiting profits for new product introduction." On the other hand, the provisions regarding generic names and plant inspections were "expected to cost manufacturers more money, but not increase generic sales appreciably."[66]

Commenting on the impact that the new act may have on industry structure, the same source offered the following prediction:

In particular, conditions will be more difficult for smaller companies, some of which will be unable to meet the added expenses, and a number of intraindustry acquisitions may result. Most sought after will be small firms with a unique market niche or potential products that have not received adequate marketing effort. However, drug companies should become less attractive to diversification-minded firms in other industries.[67]

Not only the new law, but new regulations made by the FDA to implement the law will have an important effect on the industry. A proposal, stemming from the thalidomide disaster, that regulations forbid doctors from giving an investigational drug to a patient without his knowledge would have hampered testing and was not adopted.[68] On the other hand, shortly after the new regulations drawn up in February 1963 became effective (as amended) in June of the same year, industry spokesmen declared that the Pharmaceutical Manufacturers' Association would file a request "to ensure their 'enlightened administration.'" At the same time, the PMA's president, Dr.

---

[64]Time, October 19, 1962, p. 40. See also Federal Code Annotated, Title 21, Par. 357, and 1962, pp. 878 ff.

[65]Ibid.

[66]Standard & Poor's, op. cit., December 13, 1962, p. D–11.

[67]Ibid.

[68]Time, October 19, 1962, p. 40.

Austin Smith, indicated that the requirements for establishing drug effectiveness and safety were hampering research. " 'One company, which tested 67 agents before the regulations, is now testing 17,' he said. . . . Another manufacturer reportedly dropped 30% of its projects. 'There is no question that drug research and development is being inhibited,' said Dr. Smith."[69]

Future challenges and opportunities

The drug industry faces major challenges and opportunities. Among these are (1) serving an expanding world market with a population growing at the annual rate of 1.7% or by about 46 million persons a year;[70] (2) improving present remedies; and (3) seeking—along with public and institutional researchers backed by an even larger total budget—cures for the outstanding unsolved problems in arthritis, cancer, nerve diseases, and the common cold. "It is expected that such developments will be slow in coming."[71]

---

[69]*The New York Times,* July 6, 1963.
[70]United Nations, *Demographic Yearbook,* 1960.
[71]Standard & Poor's, *op. cit.,* December 13, 1962, p. D–10.

XEROX CORPORATION*

∧∧

In 1959, the Xerox Corporation employed 1,900 people, and its profits were approximately $2 million on sales of slightly over $33 million. In mid-1964 it was estimated that 1964 sales would be in the neighborhood of $270 million and yield profits of nearly $38 million; by that time the company employed 11,300 people. It was believed that by year's end Xerox would be the 225th largest industrial company in the United States and that, on *Fortune* magazine's list of the largest 500 industrial firms, it might rank among the first dozen in return on investment and in sales-profit ratio. Other aspects of Xerox progress are reflected in the statistical comparisons furnished in Exhibit 1.

Almost all of Xerox' growth had come from its accomplishments in the office-copying field. Although estimates of the office-copy market's size were rough, the company was generally believed to have at least 50% of it— attained after its 1960 introduction of a xerographic copy machine. Office copying is defined as the service (machines and/or ancillary equipment) supplied to users who make from 1 to 20 copies of documents. It is differentiated in this way from duplicating and other processes where larger numbers of copies are customarily made. The lines of distinction seemed to be blurring in 1964 as office-copier manufacturers were designing machines that showed promise of moving more directly into the duplicating and other high volume fields.

Xerox history

Xerox (originally known as the Haloid Company) was founded in Rochester, New York, in 1906 as a sensitizer of photographic papers. Haloid, the original name, was derived from the word "halogen," a salt used in emulsion for coating photographic paper. During the next three decades the company enjoyed a modest degree of prosperity. In the early 1930's a new photocopy paper was introduced and a manufacturer of photocopy machines was acquired, making Xerox the first company to offer a complete line of photocopy products including machines, supplies, equipment, and service. By the end of World War II, sales were approximately $7,000,000, and both wages and material prices were rising more rapidly than the prices of the

Exhibit 1

XEROX CORPORATION
Nine-Year Statistical Comparison

	1955	1956	1957	1958	1959	1960	1961	1962	1963
Yardsticks of Progress									
Total operating revenues (thousands of dollars)	$21,390	$23,560	$25,807	$27,576	$33,309	$40,182	$66,236	$115,220	$176,036
Net income per common share	$ .08	$ .08	$ .09	$ .10	$ .12	$ .13	$ .28	$ .71	$ 1.13
Income before taxes to total operating revenues	12.35%	12.46%	13.17%	13.54%	14.28%	15.05%	19.44%	26.71%	28.64%
Operations (Thousands of Dollars)									
Total operating revenues	$21,390	$23,560	$25,807	$27,576	$33,309	$40,182	$66,236	$115,220	$176,036
Rentals, service and royalties	2,724	3,746	4,929	6,070	7,955	10,841	30,909	65,847	114,077
Net sales	18,666	19,814	20,878	21,506	25,354	29,341	35,327	49,373	61,959
Payroll (excluding benefits)	6,880	7,797	8,889	9,798	12,725	17,659	25,526	36,653	55,112
Depreciation of plant and equipment	883	1,181	1,459	1,768	2,266	3,389	7,799	15,721	24,574
Amortization of patents and patent licenses	...	1,070	1,049	1,039	962	708	1,425	1,570	3,070
Income before taxes	2,642	2,936	3,399	3,734	4,757	6,049	12,875	30,779	50,423
Estimated taxes on income	1,480	1,634	1,905	2,107	2,645	3,432	7,445	16,801	27,850
Net income before equity in net earnings of 50% owned companies	1,162	1,302	1,494	1,627	2,112	2,617	5,430	13,978	22,573
Equity in net earnings of 50% owned companies	...	...	...	...	(34)	(7)	46	(84)	428
Net income	1,162	1,302	1,494	1,627	2,078	2,610	5,476	13,894	23,001
Total dividends declared	450	637	645	658	793	1,002	1,118	2,688	4,895
Financial (Thousands of Dollars)									
Cash and marketable securities	$ 1,971	$ 1,609	$ 1,443	$ 1,535	$ 1,651	$ 2,129	$ 5,801	$ 6,322	$ 6,933
Inventories	3,911	4,540	5,087	5,483	5,730	5,999	6,643	8,672	14,300
Current assets	8,670	9,285	10,195	10,982	12,501	15,738	25,867	37,412	59,327
Current liabilities	3,474	3,256	3,608	3,770	6,683	11,394	25,290	29,310	41,982
Working capital	5,196	6,029	6,587	7,212	5,818	4,344	577	8,102	17,345
Cash flow*	2,045	3,553	4,002	4,434	5,340	6,714	14,654	31,269	50,217
Property, plant and equipment at cost†	8,594	10,551	12,946	15,877	24,182	38,724	68,285	106,666	162,736
Accumulated depreciation and amortization†	2,729	3,553	4,667	5,849	7,360	9,272	15,743	29,982	52,545
Net property, plant and equipment†	5,865	6,998	8,279	10,028	16,822	29,452	52,542	76,684	110,191
Additions to property, plant and equipment†	1,911	2,314	2,740	3,710	9,242	16,960	31,902	40,092	58,229
Patents, patent licenses and patent applications, at cost	1	3,857	3,805	3,854	6,459	11,815	21,671	23,177	39,789
Accumulated amortization of patents and patent licenses	...	1,072	2,078	3,117	464	1,172	2,596	4,167	7,237
Long-term debt (including current installments)	3,008	3,002	3,000	2,900	4,800	4,799	19,810	41,258	54,029
Shareholders' equity (net worth)	7,959	11,056	12,600	14,715	17,685	29,424	34,589	48,686	85,235

General and Ratios

	1955	1956	1957	1958	1959	1960	1961	1962	1963
Preferred shares outstanding at year end	...	...	...	4,500	20,000	19,400	...	...	...
Common shares outstanding at year end	15,424,440	16,124,440	16,324,440	16,524,940	16,775,065	18,905,500	19,343,060	19,463,049	20,341,430
Net income per common share	$ .08	$ .08	$ .09	$ .10	$ .12	$ .13	$ .28	$ .71	$ 1.13
Cash flow per common share	$ .13	$ .22	$ .25	$ .27	$ .32	$ .36	$ .76	$ 1.61	$ 2.47
Common dividends declared per share	$ .03	$ .04	$ .04	$ .04	$ .04¼	$ .05	$ .053¾	$ .14	$ .25
Book value per common share	$ .52	$ .69	$ .77	$ .89	$ 1.05	$ 1.56	$ 1.79	$ 2.50	$ 4.19
Shareholders at year end	2,195	2,806	3,121	3,359	4,647	9,002	12,167	14,925	26,375
Employees at year end	1,251	1,359	1,530	1,650	2,068	2,973	3,778	5,297	7,918
Working capital turnover	4.12	3.91	3.92	3.82	5.73	9.25	114.79	14.22	10.15
Current ratio	2.50	2.85	2.83	2.91	1.87	1.38	1.02	1.28	1.41
Net worth to net property, plant and equipment†	1.36	1.58	1.52	1.47	1.05	1.00	.66	.63	.77
Total operating revenues to net receivables	7.86	7.68	7.26	7.13	7.23	6.37	6.23	7.08	6.98
Net income to net worth	14.61%	11.77%	11.86%	11.05%	11.75%	8.87%	15.83%	28.54%	26.99%
Net income to net operating investment (total assets)	7.84%	6.75%	7.27%	7.34%	5.72%	4.52%	5.37%	9.96%	10.66%
Cash flow to net worth*	25.69%	32.15%	31.77%	30.13%	30.20%	22.82%	42.37%	64.23%	58.92%
Cash flow to net operating investment (total assets)*	13.80%	18.42%	19.48%	20.01%	14.69%	11.62%	14.37%	22.41%	23.27%

*Cash flow defined as net income before equity in net earnings of 50% owned companies plus depreciation of plant and equipment, and amortization of patents and patent licenses.

†Includes rental equipment and parts.

NOTE: Per share data adjusted to reflect change of each common share into three common shares effective April 20, 1955, into four common shares effective December 1, 1959, and into five common shares effective December 17, 1963.

company's machines and papers. In 1946, profits of $101,000 were realized on sales of $6,750,000.

Mr. Joseph C. Wilson became president of Xerox in 1946. The company had not been markedly successful, and the cost-price squeeze seemed likely to continue. Under Mr. Wilson's direction, Xerox set to work to improve its current product line. In addition, according to Mr. Wilson, "we were desperate for new products, but we had no resources for a significant research effort of our own." Dr. John Dessauer, research and engineering director (in 1964 Dr. Dessauer was executive vice president for research and engineering), had read an article about an electrostatic-photographic copying process invented in the 1930's by Chester Carlson. Beginning in 1940, Mr. Carlson accumulated a net of patents on his process, which later became known as "xerography" after the Greek word *xeros*, meaning "dry." For several years Mr. Carlson tried to interest a number of firms, among them IBM, in his process, but without success. The Battelle Memorial Institute became interested in 1944, however, and worked out a development arrangement with Mr. Carlson. Battelle was a nonprofit industrial research organization, and it too made efforts to interest industrial firms in the Carlson process.

In January 1947, Xerox, Battelle, and Mr. Carlson made an agreement whereby Xerox acquired some of the rights to xerography in return for royalty payments.[1] At the time, there was no assurance that xerography would be a commercial success. Although executives were certain that the office-copying market would grow tremendously, xerography was only a process, no xerographic machines had yet been produced, and bigger companies had already rejected opportunities to invest.

Between 1947 and 1952 Xerox made a total profit of $2,315,000 on its regular product line, and spent $4,300,000 on xerographic development. During this same period $3,500,000 was raised through borrowing and the issuance of common stock.[2] The first Xerox machine was produced in 1950—it was run manually, and proved useful only for making master sheets for use in offset printing. This in itself opened a new market for Xerox, but an effective office-copying machine had not yet been produced. Further research produced other xerographic products, among them the Copyflo Printer, a machine that printed from microfilm in continuous rolls. By 1956, nearly 40% of the company's sales were made up of xerographic products; meanwhile, millions were being poured into research and developmental work on a xerographic office copier. Between 1953 and 1960, for example, nearly $70 million was expended in the development of xerographic products. Operations supplied slightly under 50% of the funds needed.

In the spring of 1960, what some people have called Xerox' "thirteen year gamble" on xerography began to pay off with the introduction of the 914

---

[1] In 1948, Xerox acquired exclusive rights to everything connected with xerography. *Fortune* magazine (July 1962) estimated that by mid-1966 Battelle will have received over $5,000,000 in cash and 355,000 shares of Xerox stock. Mr. Carlson was said to be entitled to 40% of Battelle's share.

[2] *Fortune*, July 1962, pp. 3–8.

Office Copier. In brief, the 914 had a rotating aluminum drum coated with a film of selenium. The surface of the drum was given a positive electrostatic charge. The document to be copied was scanned by a moving light source, and the positive charge on the drum was retained only on those areas that corresponded to the black or printed portions of the document being copied. The drum thus bore a latent image of the document itself. A negatively charged powdered ink was then cascaded over the drum, and formed a visible image by adhering to the positively charged areas of the drum surface. The ink particles were then transferred to the copy paper by an electric charge against the paper, and fused in image form by a heat process. Clean dry copies were thereby produced in a matter of seconds.

The 914 was the first fully automatic dry copier to be introduced by the office equipment industry. As indicated, it could produce highly faithful copies, on ordinary paper, of any flat or bulky object fed into the machine. By pressing a button, copies could be produced at the rate of one every eight seconds, and no chemicals or special papers were necessary. A picture of the Xerox 914 (the name refers to the size of paper that the machine can handle), together with a description of some of its major characteristics, is furnished in Exhibit 2. It will be noted from Exhibit 2 that the 914 was a desk-sized machine. As such, it required a central location in a user's office or plant, and ran contrary to the trend toward smaller, desk-top copiers. The size, cost, and technical complexity of the 914 were such that it was made available on a rental basis. Initially the machine itself rented for $95 per month, and copies were priced at $3\frac{1}{2}\cent$ each after the first 2,000, which were free; in 1964, the 914 could be purchased outright for $29,500.

The 914 was a success. Although Xerox' published statements did not carry data on the performance of individual items in the company's product line, the 914's impact on the office-copy market was so great that a number of financial analysts made their own estimates of the 914's results. Samples of such estimates are shown below:

KIDDER PEABODY ESTIMATE

	1961	1962	1963	1964 (est.)
% revenues derived from 914 installations	51%	70%	75%	70%

LAIDLOW & CO. ESTIMATE

	Aggregate Unit Year-end Installations	Average Number in Use	Annual Revenue per Unit	Approx. Total Revenue (in Millions)
1960	2,000	1,000	$5,000	$ 5
1961	9,000	5,500	5,000	28
1962	19,000	14,000	4,950	69
1963	32,000	25,500	4,900	125
1964 (est.)	47,000	39,500	4,850	192

Exhibit 2

Don't buy an office copying machine.

The Xerox 914 Copier   The new Xerox 813 Copier

Borrow ours—either one.

If you make lots of copies—more than 2,000 a month—you'll want the Xerox 914. The perfect copying machine. It makes dry copies in seconds, automatically, for about a nickel a copy. It makes copies on ordinary paper. It copies from colors, pencil writing, ball point pen signatures, rubber stamps, rigid three-dimensional objects.

If you make less than 2,000 copies a month, you'll probably want the new Xerox 813. It does everything the 914 does except copy rigid three-dimensional objects. (But then the 914 can't fit on a desk.)

When you borrow the 914 or the 813, you pay only for the copies you make. No capital investment. Including all charges, it costs you about 5¢ per copy plus a penny for supplies, based on a minimum number of copies made per month. And there are no maintenance contracts to buy. Xerox takes care of both machines.

Xerox Corporation, Rochester 3, N.Y. Branch offices in principal U.S. and Canadian cities. Overseas: Rank Xerox Ltd., London; Fuji-Xerox Co., Ltd., Tokyo.

Now everybody can have xerocopies.

XEROX

In mid-1963, Xerox introduced the 813 Copier. The 813 was a desk-top machine, could not reproduce from three-dimensional objects, and was slightly slower in copy time than the 914. In all other technical respects it was similar to the 914. Although exact markets could not be pinpointed, it was generally believed that the 914 best suited those customers who had need of about 100 copies per day, and that the 813 best served the 40-100 copy per day customer. Xerox officials indicated that neither of its machines was planned for customers whose daily copying requirements were less than 30 or 40. The 813 was also furnished on a rental basis, and was an immediate success. Outsiders estimated that 3-4,000 units were installed in 1963, and that an additional 30,000 would be rented during 1964. Rental charges were substantially lower on the 813 than on the 914, and the per copy charge was also different. Xerox executives did not believe that the 914 and 813 conflicted to any great extent with one another in the market place, and that any conflict was more than offset by the likelihood that each machine might help open up new markets for the other.

By mid-1964, therefore, both the 914 and 813 were well-established, and Xerox was profiting handsomely (see Exhibit 1). Another xerographic machine, to be known as the Xerox 2400, was shortly to be introduced to the market. The 2400 was intended to invade a new market through its ability to "eliminate the arbitrary division that has existed between copying and short-run duplicating." The 2400 was designed to be six times faster than the 914 and able to produce—without master or other intermediate sheets—from 1 to 499 faithful copies with a single dial setting. It was expected that the 2400 would produce copies at a cost directly comparable to those of various short-run duplicating processes while continuing to offer the unique advantages of the company's other xerographic machines.

The Xerox product line was not confined to the 914, the 813, and the prospective 2400. It also included several Copyflo Continuous Printers for microfilm reproduction; the 1824 Printer for the reproduction of engineering prints from microfilm; LDX Systems (Long Distance Xerography) for facsimile reproductions over distances ranging from "a room to a continent"; photocopy and offset master machines; and several products related to its traditional haloid product line. The great bulk of sales, of course, came from xerographic machines, and it seemed probable that increasing proportions of future sales would come from that source. The company also had a number of joint ventures with other firms, most of which had to do with specialized applications of xerography. Finally, Xerox had acquired Electro-Optical Systems (EOS), a research and development company, in 1963. EOS was engaged in advanced technological work, much of it for the federal government in such areas as space vehicle subsystems.

In addition to its success in the U.S. market, Xerox was beginning to enjoy what it hoped would be a comparable boom in other countries. The foundation for Xerox' overseas activities had been laid in 1956 and was described by Mr. Wilson:

In the middle fifties, it seemed to us that Xerox could never attain its full potential unless it became a worldwide enterprise. With the surging growth of the economies overseas, with the flow of new technology in Europe and Japan, as well as North America, it was our belief that for us to become a great corporation would require that Xerox become international in scope, that all its personnel and policies acquire world view. On the other hand, we then did not have the people nor the money to build an international organization of our own. After months of investigation and negotiations, we formed the partnership with The Rank Organization which has resulted in Rank Xerox of London and Fuji-Xerox

of Tokyo, two of the world's fastest growing enterprises. Here, too, appears another cornerstone of our philosphy. Rather than delay a decade or more while
an opportunity perhaps withers away, we decided then, as we will in the future,
that it is better to share a situation with people of integrity and resolution than
to await a whole position of our own. Thus there has grown in a very short time
a global marketing and service organization, and we have reinforced our position with the help of people of very great power indeed.

Rank Xerox did no developmental or engineering work, but was responsible
for all manufacturing and marketing outside North and South America. It
was estimated that Rank Xerox sales in 1964 would total almost $42 million,
an increase of over 130% above the previous year. The 813 was not to be
introduced to European or United Kingdom markets until the summer and
fall of 1964, and one financial house estimated that the continued growth of
Xerox' overseas activity might raise the share of earnings contributed by
overseas profits from about 2¢ per share in 1963 to as much as 20¢ per share
by 1965.

Despite the success of its current machines and its hopes for the other
xerographic products currently in the research or pre-introduction stages,
management was not complacent about the future. Though Xerox had maintained Mr. Carlson's original policy of securing as many patents as possible
on products and processes related to xerography and had a strong patent
position in 1964, executives knew that other companies were devoting substantial resources to research and development in the office-copy and duplicating fields.[3] Mr. Wilson commented:

By far the most important event of 1964 has been the advent of serious, vigorous competition, particularly in electrostatic copying. You may think it strange
that I do not look upon this as an unmixed evil. Of course, there must be some
adverse impact upon volume or profit. The gloomy side is there for all to grasp;
it takes no sage interpreter quickly to conclude that the attraction of Xerox'
almost unmatched—yet still unseasoned—reputation for profit making may soon
be blemished by its old adversaries like Kodak, 3M or Apeco; or by the newer
ones, such as Addressograph-Multigraph, SCM, or Dennison; or by those to
come, as recently indicated by IBM. Some of the old ones like 3M are entering
new horses in the race such as their maturing new process of fast, high quality,
inexpensive document reproduction called Adherography. Some of the newer ones
who follow the xerographic technology, in its Electrofax form, are using lower
prices to compete, as we predicted in February, 1963. Some are innovating in an
old technology, diazo, and by making strides toward more mechanization, convenience; and new master papers are gaining away from us some important
applications. I would be the last to deprecate these changes; the last, I hope,
to underestimate them; the last, I know, to be complacent about them.

---

[3]A major deterrent to Xerox' competitors was their inability, as of mid-1964, to
produce a machine that could make copies on ordinary paper. All other current machines
required either sensitized papers or some type of specially prepared master sheets. Xerox
recognized, however, that competitors were making rapid strides in the improvement of
both their papers and their machines, and that many of them had the research capability
to undertake new or modified copying processes.

Xerox strategy

Xerox' publicly stated goal was to achieve "continuous growth at a rate averaging not less than 20% a year" in order that it might "achieve a billion dollars in sales in the not-too-distant future." The goal was to be achieved through the effective implementation of policies in a number of major areas, each of which will be described briefly below.

Innovation and research and development. Xerox management planned to continue to stress innovation and creativity. Mr. Wilson stated:

A stress on imaginative analysis of the future is a basic part of Xerox management, one which continues to be a hallmark. . . . We believe first in innovation—throughout the company. We want to create new services that have not been rendered before and secure a profit from them. Our best rewards have come from things of this sort, like the 914—unheard of at the time it was introduced, but now one of the most successful products in America. This is the first principle. . . . It is self-evident that our future growth must come from products and services which are far more complex than these which are our present heartland. Therefore, we must learn to be different people than we have been. But we have transformed ourselves in the past decade from a small chemically based company to a medium-sized one based on physics and marketing.

Xerox was an organization four years ago which could not look much farther ahead than the introduction of the 914, because that task was straining its every resource. In contrast, now it is an organization whose higher echelons are constantly nagged by consciousness of the need to have specific plans for 1968, 1969, 1970, 1971, 1972, 1973, 1974 and 1975. These men are worried that we do not yet have specific plans for new products and services to be introduced in 1972, let us say, and perhaps this is the most important part of the whole strategy. Just as it was important to make this whole organization dissatisfied with results in any year which projected a profit increase of less than 20%, so it is important now to make it dissatisfied that we do not have a specific plan for the tenth year ahead.

Financial analysts estimated that Xerox had spent about $5 million (7.5% of sales) on research and development in 1961. The amount had risen each year, and it was believed that the company would spend nearly $24 million (8.9% of sales) in 1964. Xerox had recently established a separate laboratory for fundamental research and planned to devote approximately 10% of its research dollars to that activity. Xerox' research efforts were believed to be substantially higher than those of other office-copy machine producers. The company's research was not confined to xerographic products; intensive work was being done, and more was planned for the future, in other aspects of graphic communications.

Patents. Xerox had continued to pursue the aggressive patent policies adopted by xerography's inventor. Although most of Mr. Carlson's basic patents had expired, Xerox diligence in patent filing had resulted, by 1964, in a complex of more than 400 U.S. and 200 Canadian patents. In addition, the company owned patents in Latin America, and Rank Xerox owned over

600 patents in 30 other countries. The patents, plus the company's continuing research efforts, made Xerox management confident that competition would not be able to surprise it with superior products in the field of electrostatic copying.

Marketing and customer services. Top management had always placed heavy emphasis on aggressive marketing directly to existing or potential customers. In 1958, 386 sales and service people serviced the United States and Canada through 17 branches. By 1964, there were 118 sales and service outlets in 86 cities, and the marketing organization had grown to more than 4,500 people. The problems presented by such rapid growth had not led the company to reduce its high standards of selection and training, or its emphasis on customer service. Mr. Wilson commented:

As we moved into the business equipment field, largely through leasing and servicing our own devices, that half century of experience in managing our own direct sales force was a source of strength; that deep rooted tradition of allowing no barrier between us and our customers has been a treasured asset.

Our marketing force at the end of 1964 had more people than the entire company employed in 1961 and the average age of our sales and service people is less than 28. There is no figure on the balance sheet to reflect this value but we assert that no item on the balance sheet, probably not even the aggregate of all the assets, has greater value than this force of Xerox people.

International and other ventures. Xerox was deeply committed to the further expansion and development of its international operations. It was expected that Rank Xerox and the latter's Japanese affiliation would continue to grow, and Xerox itself planned to continue its studies—both short- and long-range—of the social, economic, and technological developments and needs of other parts of the world.

In addition, the company intended to continue its program of joint ventures with other firms in areas of interest to Xerox. The company had recently formed a company, together with Technical Operations, Inc., to develop and exploit new photographic processes using vacuum coated silver halide emulsions. A joint venture with Scionics was investigating the possibilities of combining microfilm with cards used in tabulating systems. These were typical of some of Xerox' newer joint ventures, which were in addition to those of long duration with other firms such as Bell & Howell.

Diversification. As implied earlier, Xerox did not plan to rest on its office-copy laurels. Although management was reluctant to divulge detailed information, there was no question but what diversification possibilities were being actively investigated. In a speech to a group of security analysts, Mr. Wilson made the following comments on diversification:

We aim, during the next five years, to diversify, while at the same time we protect our core of office copying by introducing new generations of graphic systems. We have identified several major fields into which we plan to enter.

The key word is "diversify" but for us it is an enormously complex and difficult task. We must identify—at least ten years ahead—where there are markets, each of which has the potential of several hundred million dollars. Then we must conceive and develop simultaneously several sets of innovative products and services which will gain a high, profitable, appropriate share of these fields. At the same time we must nurture, through research, fertile technologies from which applications, not now identified, may be developed into profitable products and services. Obviously, there is frequent, continuous interaction between these two extremes: of devising inventions from needs to devising needs from inventions. We also must constantly watch for proper, compatible acquisitions to support these broad objectives.

Our program now is this: to grow in our chosen field of graphic communications for the office as the fundamental task of Xerox, but also to enter several already identified fields, which are unrelated to office work, or, in some cases, even to the technology of xerography. In every case the selection of these new ventures has been based upon many criteria, but in each case, one of them has been the determination that they promise realistic, potential, profitable sales to Xerox of several hundred million dollars annually.

Esprit. Another factor of importance in Xerox' past successes, and one that management emphasized as equally important to the company's future, was what various members of the management group defined as the company's "esprit." Xerox personnel were proud of the company's creative talents and its willingness to take risks, and executives emphasized that the Xerox spirit was not a means to an end but, rather, a matter of emphasizing human values for their own sake. The enthusiasm and spirit of the organization were effectively described in the informal comments of one of the junior members of management who had worked for Xerox for less than two years:

This is a *gung ho* company, and everybody in it is *gung ho.* It's partly the atmosphere of success, but it's a lot more than that. The company isn't full of geniuses, but it is full of people who work like hell, enjoy what they're doing, and want to make a contribution.

Young people get a chance to carry the ball here, and our senior people give them plenty of opportunity. Xerox is run on progressive principles, based on a belief in human beings. The average age of Xerox employees is 33, and each person is given a clear field to operate in. There's a challenge for the company and for all of us, and we love it.

I've been here two years, and I know this intangible thing runs all through the company. It starts at the top, and goes all the way down. Joe Wilson [Mr. Joseph Wilson, president of Xerox] has always picked his people carefully. They're tough, hardworking people who believe in what they're doing and in the people who work for them.

It may be hard to keep this as we get bigger. We may get over-organized like other companies do when they grow rapidly. I'd predict, though, that we'll keep this *gung ho* spirit. I know one thing, we'll all work like hell to keep it.

Xerox and social responsibility

Xerox management believed that the company had responsibilities that extended beyond economic performance. The company's attitude was set forth in a speech by Mr. Wilson in 1964, portions of which follow:

It seems beyond belief that anyone could contest the view that the businessman . . . must expand his vision beyond the limits of making maximum profit . . . to encompass many of society's harassing problems which wash the edges of his island.

Today, civic endeavor is a safe, indeed, an essential, corporate path. It is apparent that businessmen make the decisions, in an important degree, which will affect one-half of the national income in the form of wages and salaries, interest and dividend payments, and retained earnings; they greatly influence jobs for more than 30 million people, almost as many as all other types of employment combined.

The corporation cannot refuse to take a stand on public issues of major concern; failure to act is to throw its weight on the side of the status quo, and the public interprets it that way.

Inevitably the corporation is involved in economic, social and political dynamics whether it wills or not, and to ignore the noneconomic consequences of business decisions is to invite outside intervention. . . .

Profit, after all, becomes machines, factories, food, shelter, security for the future . . . fellowship, freedom, peace.

The company attempted to give practical expression to this attitude toward Xerox' responsibilities. At the management level, executives were encouraged to play active roles in community and social affairs, and Xerox itself, through both management and employees, took an active part in the communities in which company plants and offices were located.

Xerox also made substantial financial contributions to educational and welfare institutions. In 1964, for example, it was estimated that Xerox' gifts for these purposes would total over $1.1 million. When criticized by a stockholder who asked that such contributions be stopped "in view of the low dividend yield on the common stock," Xerox took the view that the stoppage of such contributions would be in direct opposition to the longer range interests of Xerox stockholders. In brief, management maintained that Xerox itself could attain its own goals only if the society in which it operated continued vigorous and healthy, and that its attitude toward "education and other matters a little removed from the obvious and shorter range aspects of business has helped the company immeasurably in attracting and holding the people of brains and principle in whose hands are the attainment of your company's high objectives."

The United Nations television series

In 1964, Xerox decided to spend its entire television advertising budget (see Exhibit 3 for Xerox' advertising and sales promotion budgets for 1960–

1964) to underwrite a series of programs on the United Nations. Although the decision provoked a storm of protest, Xerox officials believed that it represented a natural extension of the philosophy that had been the basis of the company's advertising for several years. Donald Clark, vice president for corporate advertising, explained that philosophy:

We're in business to sell our products and services at a profit. Our advertising must carry our message to the right people at the right time at the most economical cost. People wonder, therefore, why we use a mass medium like television, and why we select controversial program subjects. It may seem like a paradox, but the reasons tie naturally to our entire advertising philosophy.

Innovation has been a requirement for everything we have done during recent years. Prior to 1960, I doubt if many people had ever heard of us. If they had, they probably thought we made antifreeze or some sort of mouthwash. Our total

Exhibit 3

XEROX CORPORATION
Advertising and Sales Promotion Budgets 1960–64

Items	1960	1961	1962	1963	1964
Advertising:					
Print media	$395,000	$ 838,584	$ 730,300	$1,220,000	$1,024,000
TV media	...	...	516,000	1,344,700	4,192,000
Production	39,000	150,000	118,000	303,000	351,000
Miscellaneous	...	...	...	...	35,000
Sales promotion	$135,000	$ 236,800	$ 365,000	$ 586,000	$ 884,300
Approximate Total	$569,000	$1,225,384	$1,729,300	$3,453,700	$6,486,300

1959 operating revenues were a little over thirty million dollars, and we were selling in a highly specialized market. The advent of the 914 Copier in early 1960 gave us our first opportunity to expand sales rapidly and move into the general office equipment market.

In planning the 1960 introductory advertising and sales promotion program for the 914, we recognized that our success would depend to a great extent upon our ability to set ourselves apart from all of our competitors. Our company was unknown, our advertising budget too small, our product too good, and our goals too high to become entangled and lost in the jungle of claims being used to describe the advantages of competitive copying devices.

A quick analysis revealed that our 1960 advertising budget was completely inadequate to enter into a space battle with our major copying competitors. So, we decided to limit our campaigns to major business publications and to use only those ads having the unique and fresh approach giving us the something different we desired.

The first ad appeared in *Fortune* and was a six-page, four-color gatefold with an unusual die-cut aperture to arouse interest. This was the first time *Fortune* had ever allowed such an insert, and it proved to be the different idea we were after. The ensuing ads followed a definite format—each one emphasizing a particular feature of the 914. We used color for color's sake and repeated the same basic ad construction from one to another in order to build association and recognition.

As our sales program progressed, and our advertising budgets expanded, we began to look for other unusual and interesting ways to tell the story.

Results of our space advertising were most satisfying. These ads created discussion within the advertising fraternity and proved to be most effective in telling our product story in a provocative and interesting way.

But, something was still lacking. Our early sales experience showed it is very difficult, if not impossible, to describe the 914 Copier and its operation adequately. It simply had to be seen to be appreciated. Our salesmen quickly came to learn that demonstration is the key to sales success, and it was this need to demonstrate which led to our use of television.

Television makes it possible for us to demonstrate the 914 Copier in a way that can be surpassed only by a personal, live demonstration at a trade show or in one of our branch offices. Right in his own home, the business executive or government official can see the machine doing the things we claim. Therefore, we decided to take the leap into mass market TV in the fall of 1961. But we did it on a very special basis.

For our initial efforts, we selected documentary-type public service programs. Research studies had shown that the audiences of such programs have a high percentage of well-informed, higher income viewers who are most likely to be in responsible positions within business and government—people who can influence the selection and purchase of a copier. Also statistics showed that we could reach this influential leadership group most economically through documentary-type television. Therefore, what appeared to be mass-market television really was very selective because of the types of programs we chose.

As we gained experience, we actually began to look for the unusual, controversial, provocative subjects which provide us a unique opportunity to set ourselves apart from the usual television fare. Some of the programs we have sponsored in recent years have dealt with subjects such as birth control, East Germany, integration, boxing, as well as such award winners as "The Kremlin," "The Making of the President—1960," and the "Cuba Missile Crisis."

Our commercials are planned to be interesting and provocative. Each tells its own story via actual on-the-air demonstrations of the product in an entertaining manner. Most notable of these have been the little girl making a picture of her doll on her daddy's office copier, a chimpanzee making copies, and a little boy copying his arithmetic test paper and his pet turtle. We believe these commercials help sell our product and simultaneously achieve the fringe benefits of entertaining while upholding our reputation for innovation—something different.

We are as interested in ratings as the next advertiser, but not just in overall audience size. One program might give us a 40 per cent share of an audience, but upon analysis, only 10 per cent of that 40 share are people interested in Xerox and its products. To us it makes much better sense to select another program which may get only a 10 per cent share of the audience, but have that entire 10 per cent be potential customers. In other words, our primary interest is in the quality of a quantity audience.

The idea for the United Nations (UN) television series came from Mr. Paul Hoffman, managing director of the UN Special Fund, and his wife, the president of a public relations firm in New York City. In late 1963, they were seeking ways of publicizing the UN in preparation for its twentieth anniversary in 1965. Together with friends from the entertainment industry, they considered the idea of a series of television programs that would publicize the nonpolitical activities of several of the UN's subagencies. Each program was to deal with an aspect of subagency work, and would be produced, directed, written, and acted by prominent figures from the entertainment industry. A basic part of the original idea was that all participants would either donate their services or work at the minimum rates permitted by their professional organization. To illustrate, the British actor Peter Sellers customarily received approximately $750,000 for a movie; it was hoped that Mr. Sellers might make his services available for one of the UN programs at "scale" of roughly $350 per week.

The Hoffmans' idea was discussed with UN Ambassador Adlai Stevenson and several leaders from the motion picture industry, and was greeted with enthusiasm. Within a very short time, such entertainment figures as the following indicated a desire to be associated with the project: Peter Glenville, Stanley Kubrick, Joseph Mankiewicz, Otto Preminger, Robert Rosen, Sam Spiegel, Fred Zinneman (producers and directors); Reginald Rose, Tad Mosel, and Peter Stone (writers); Henry Mancini, Richard Rodgers, Andre Previn, and Elmer Bernstein (composers); Frank Sinatra, Paul Newman, Gregory Peck, Marlon Brando, Henry Fonda, and Glenn Ford (actors). The original discussions concerned a series of eight one-hour shows. Later, because of costs and other reasons, it was decided that six 90-minute shows would be offered and that each would be an original undertaking developed jointly by the entertainment industry and the UN.[4] It seemed probable that production costs might total approximately $2.5 million and network time an additional $1.5 million. The total cost would thus run in the neighborhood of $4 million, although that figure was only an estimate. It was also decided that both the purpose and dignity of the project and the fact that those who would work on the programs would be doing so for nothing or for minimum rates would make it necessary that the programs carry no commercial messages.

Although the series was still only in the idea stage, a search began for financial backing. Mr. Frederic Papert, a partner in Xerox' advertising agency, heard about the undertaking, discussed it with the Hoffmans, and described it to Mr. Wilson and other Xerox executives. A series of meetings ensued. Xerox' initial reaction was lukewarm because of the absence of commercial messages and because the possible cost would equal or exceed the amount the company planned to spend on television advertising. After further discussions, however, Xerox officials began to modify their original views. Finally, in a meeting that lasted less than an hour, Mr. Wilson, Mr. Linowitz (chairman of the board), Mr. McColough (executive vice president), Mr. Rutledge

---

[4]The planned number of shows was later reduced to five. Among the initial story ideas were a modern version of the "Christmas Carol" involving the UN and the problems of language translation.

(group vice president), and Mr. Clark decided unanimously that Xerox would underwrite the series. Mr. Clark described the meeting:

It was like a Quaker meeting in a way. We didn't say very much. We all wanted to do it, but we knew it was a gamble. All we had was an idea of the costs, some ideas for stories, and a lot of verbal commitments from a lot of people. There were no contracts, no scripts, no network deals. I thought it might turn out to be like trying to nail a four-foot slab of jello to a wall. But Joe [Mr. Wilson] wanted to do it, and so did the rest of us, so we all voted for it.

A nonprofit foundation (Telsun) was set up to administer the UN television series. Three Xerox officials (Messrs. Wilson, Linowitz, and Clark) were joined on Telsun's board by a number of prominent people, among them the Hoffmans, Mr. Eugene Black, and General Alfred Gruenther. Mr. Clark was one of the four people given decision-making and administrative responsibility for Telsun activities. Xerox agreed to put up $4 million to cover all costs of the series; any surplus was to go to the United Nations. It was agreed that the programs would be put on the air beginning in late 1964 or early 1965. Xerox was to have first rights for subsequent international television, domestic television reruns, and theatrical rights, but any income from such sources was to go to the UN or its agencies via Telsun. The same restrictions on commercials would apply to any other uses of the programs. Xerox' only identification would be the company logo at the beginning and end of each program accompanied by a voice saying, respectively, "Xerox Corporation is privileged to bring you the following major television event" and "This program has been one of a series produced and telecast as a public service through funds provided by Xerox Corporation."

It was also agreed that Xerox would have no casting or script control, and that its only stipulation could be that the programs be in good taste and that no country could be shown as "good" or "bad." It was obvious to Xerox officials, however, that any and all arrangements would be fairly loose in terms of any influence that the company might exert. This was particularly true because of the financial arrangements with the artists, the speed with which at least the initial programs had to be prepared, and the fact that all or most of the programs might be produced outside the United States. As Mr. Clark put it, "We had a check list of 20 things in our initial negotiations, and got agreement on most of them. But we had to get committed mostly on the basis of faith in all those people doing what they said they'd do."

Xerox' decision to underwrite the UN series was announced in April 1964. In a luncheon speech at the United Nations, Mr. Wilson stressed that the company's decision had been a "cold and calculated" one taken in Xerox' best interests. In addition, he said, ". . . it is a part of our philosophy that the highest interests of a corporation are involved in the health of the earth's society. . . . We are proud to be part of this enterprise which, as we all know, is making history." In his speech Mr. Wilson acknowledged that he and other Xerox officials anticipated some criticism of their decision.

In order to offset such criticism and to get as much publicity as possible for its UN venture, Xerox had already prepared a major promotional and public relations campaign to be carried out jointly with Telsun. The campaign was successful and both Xerox and the UN series received immediate favorable publicity from many parts of the world (see Exhibit 4). Adverse reaction was minimal and at first the company received only a few letters from people who disliked the United Nations or thought that Xerox was spending too much money on the television series. Between April and June the company received about 300 letters on the UN series, most of which were favorable.

Exhibit 4

THE IRISH TIMES
(Dublin)
April 11, 1964
U.S. Firm "Sponsors" the U.N.

The decision of the Xerox Corporation to sink about $4 million into a television series about the United Nations may emerge as the most controversial U.S. advertising investment of the year.

The series will consist of six 90-minute film dramas based on U.N. activities to be shown on network television at peak viewing hours starting next January. Xerox's $4 million commitment is equivalent to its entire advertising budget for 1964.

Advertisers have sponsored shows on controversial subjects before, of course, but the U.N. project is unusual in several ways. The company, in effect, is buying a show sight-unseen without even a glimpse at a pilot film or script.

The widespread organized opposition to the U.N. in the United States has long inhibited Madison Avenue support for the organization.

Corporate Angel

Moreover, because of the nature of the U.N., Xerox will not really be a "sponsor" at all but will be a sort of corporate angel. For its $4 million Xerox will not put on a single commercial, but will simply be identified at the start of the shows.

Mr. Joseph C. Wilson, president of Xerox, has acknowledged that the U.N. represented a controversial issue, but said: "We are willing to accept that risk. In supporting this project we may create some enemies, but we also hope to win many more powerful friends."

Mr. Wilson said that more than half of the cost of the series will come out of Xerox's advertising budget with much of the remainder emanating from the company's public relations budget. Xerox plans to expand its total advertising budget next year, he said, so it will have funds to do some additional television advertising beyond the U.N. series.

Mr. Wilson said that his company firmly endorsed the work of the U.N. but said that its motivations in supporting the series went beyond simple "idealism." It is important for Xerox to be favourably known throughout the world as an institution that is willing to take a risk in order to improve understanding, that will accept a challenge of its short-run position in order to buttress the long years ahead," he said.

He added: "How ridiculous it would be for us to build a showroom in New York without simultaneously trying to build a peaceful world."

Xerox owns first international TV, rerun and theatrical rights to the six dramas, he said, and some bidding already has begun on the series. Proceeds from foreign distribution will be turned over to the U.N.

Xerox's agency, Papert, Koenig, Lois, Inc., which originally brought its client into the series, stands to lose billings as a result of its initiative. The company will pick up its commission on only about $1.3 million of the total outlay.

Exhibit 5

PROTEST LETTER

(address omitted)

Mr. Joseph C. Wilson
President
XEROX CORPORATION
6 Haloid Street
Rochester, New York

Dear Sir:

Newspapers all across the country—and we read several out-of-state papers—carried the facts that Communists led the rioting which hit Rochester a few days ago. One paper quoted a reliable source that Jewish business establishments were hit more heavily than non-Jewish businesses; that there was a plan and the plan was followed in the rioting; that a Jewish business located between two non-Jewish business establishments would be completely demolished and looted while the others were not.

In view of facts that cannot be denied, it does seem strange that Xerox Corporation would suddenly announce the expenditure of $4 million in advertising to improve the image of the United Nations during the lifetime of which a billion people around the world have been enslaved by Communist animals. What is the interest of Xerox Corporation in the UN? I know that no business would deliberately set out to destroy the hand—in this case the U.S.—that was feeding it and that is why I question the judgment of Xerox as relates to its sudden interest in UN? UN is a total and abysmal failure. Under its banner more Communists and fellow-travelers have been allowed to infiltrate our country, its people, and its institutions than in any other way.

I also know that every dime Xerox spends on this type of advertising may be deducted on income tax. $4 million is a vast amount of money and a flat deduction of this much—or more—could mean a sizeable difference in what Xerox would be required to pay the government while advertising the Xerox unit.

On May 11, 1964, the National *Observer* carried a small news item to the effect that your Mr. Sol M. Linowitz, Chairman of the Xerox Board, had been "appointed" to head up a committee of citizens to increase the interest of Americans in the Foreign Aid program. Why? Beginning with Lenin and Marx, the Communist plan has been to tax U.S. citizens to their knees, thus making comparatively easy the complete and final takeover. We have reached our knees and yet there apparently is no letup in what our government is willing to spend on Foreign Aid, in many instances making direct payments to outright Communist nations.

Why is Xerox interested in Foreign Aid? I checked with several people at TVA today to determine how many Xerox machines they have in use. Nobody seemed to know the exact number, which are being paid for out of taxpayer pockets. This might be a good place to start to find out just how well Xerox is doing at the expense of the U.S. taxpayers. You have a fine machine, completely revolutionizing the reproductive process. Surely America has been kind (and charitable) to your company in helping it to attain such fabulous success. Only in America could such success become a reality. Is it necessary to sell America short by undermining the intelligence of the American people? I honestly question your interest in improving the UN image and in continued Foreign Aid, the two weakest links in our national safety, both of which could eventually lead to our complete capitulation. Please read the attached thoughtfully and seriously. It is available to you for the asking and such an effort is worthy of your $4 million.

(name omitted)

Beginning early in July, however, Xerox received almost 15,000 letters in a month's time. The letters, four examples of which are reproduced in Exhibits 5–8, were for the most part critical of Xerox' UN television venture. They

Exhibit 6

PROTEST LETTER

(address omitted)

Dear Sir:

We wish to commend you on the proposed plan to use four million dollars belonging to your company for the purpose of furthering world peace. It is truly a wonderful thing to believe that some day we may work and live side by side with our fellowman without prejudice, envy or greed. We agree with you wholeheartedly.

However, we do not agree with the method you have chosen. You have only to read the United Nations charter to find that it was not written with the best interests of the free countries in mind. Two well-known Communists, Alger Hiss and Harry Dexter White, aided in writing the charter.

Under the United Nations, we made a mess out of the Korean War and committed atrocities in Katanga unbelievable to the civilized mind.

The ultimate goal of this world peace shrine is to abolish the rational defenses, armies and police, of each country and replace them with the United Nations police. Each nation would have policemen from another country. This would make the countries helpless under the thumb of the United Nations masters.

The basic idea of the U.N. is good, however, it has become a tool in the Communist machinery with which to bury us.

Many of us seem to have lost sight of the basic goodnesses we have provided to us by the Bill of Rights and the Constitution. If you would use your funds for refreshing the minds of American citizens to these facts, we are certain that more Americans would hold their heads higher with pride in America. Also creeping Socialism and Communism wouldn't stand a chance.

Sincerely,
(name omitted)

ranged in tone from intelligent inquiry to strident and emotion-laden criticism. Some, as indicated by Exhibit 8, were from business firms whose principals indicated a willingness to forego the use or purchase of the company's copying machines. Nearly 50% of the writers of critical letters enclosed pamphlets and documents bearing such titles as *The Fearful Master; A Second Look at The United Nations; The UN Today, Dream Becomes a Nightmare; How TV Is Brainwashing the People;* and *The Communist Attack on the John Birch Society.*[5] The company noted that in many instances a critical individual had written several letters, each addressed to a different member of management or the Xerox board of directors; an analysis indicated that approximately 4,000 people had written the 15,000 letters. Twenty-five per cent of the critical letters came from California, and an additional 8.0% and 6.6% came from New York and Texas, respectively. An additional seven states accounted for 25.5%. No letters came from five states (Alaska, Hawaii, Vermont, Iowa, and South Dakota).

Half the critical letters were in longhand. The remainder were typed, either in original or copy form.[6] Although most people signed their names, a few did not, and several did not include return addresses. A small fraction of

---

[5] A conservative political organization.
[6] A few of the letters were xerographed.

Exhibit 7

PROTEST LETTER

(address omitted)

Mr. Peter D. Chabris
Vice President
Xerox Corporation
6 Haloid Street
Rochester 3, New York

Dear Mr. Chabris:

I recently learned that the Xerox Corporation was planning to advertise and glorify the United Nations and to incorporate its advertising in a campaign to praise the United Nations.

As a lawyer, and in particular a lawyer who has studied constitutional law and the United Nations I believe that this is a very serious mistake on the part of your company for the following reasons:

1. The United Nations is an instrument by which Americans will be deprived of their constitutional rights and in particular their property rights.
2. It has been used and will continue to be used to further communist objectives.
3. The great majority of knowing Americans recognize the United Nations for what it is, and will express their hatred of the United Nations against your company if it promotes it.

It is my firm conviction that if you study those few, brief, points which I have mentioned above you will want to study more about what the United Nations really stands for and will not want to involve your fine, outstanding company in such an advertising program.

Very truly yours,
(name omitted)

P.S. Incidently, my associates and myself are considering switching to the Xerox system to avoid the unnecessary use of carbon copies and we would feel much better about it if your firm was not promoting the United Nations.

the letters mentioned the name of a prominent conservative political organization, but none of these identified their writers as members of that organization.

Although Xerox officials did not know whether the 15,000 letters had been prompted by any direct cause or causes, the company had been sent a copy of one of the conservative organization's recent publications. The organization had suggested that its members write to Xerox concerning the latter's underwriting of the UN series, and try to convince Xerox officials about the true nature of the UN. It pointed out that the letters should be friendly and persuasive in view of the fact that many Xerox officials might really believe that the UN was basically a desirable organization. The publication also pointed out that as many as 100,000 letters might convince Xerox that its sponsorship of the UN television series was not a good business move. Prospective letter writers were admonished not to suggest that Xerox products might suffer a boycott, and mentioned that a major airline had been persuaded by a torrent of letters to remove the United Nations insignia from its airplanes.

Exhibit 8

PROTEST LETTER

(company name omitted)

(address omitted)

Mr. Sol M. Linowitz
Chairman of the Board
XEROX CORPORATION
1250 Midtown Tower
Rochester 3, New York

Dear Mr. Linowitz:

It has come to my attention that the Xerox Corporation plans to sponsor several television programs eulogizing the United Nations. While it is certainly your right to reinvest your company's profits according to your view of its best interests, it is hard to see how promoting a world Socialistic government could be so viewed.

As Dr. Watts points out in the enclosed booklet, the United Nations can never realize its goal of providing world peace, since it follows the policy of "perpetual war for perpetual peace." Aren't we, in fact, falling into the reactionary fallacy of assuming that big government will protect our freedom and prevent war? Has big government ever accomplished this? Doesn't big government (especially World Government) in reality destroy freedom by exerting more control over individuals (or nations) thereby forcing increasing uniformity? Doesn't big government (especially World Government) also cause violence or war by using coercion to insure that each individual (or nation) adheres to whatever policy the government currently believes to be right?

In any case, it is also our right to reinvest income according to how we view our best interests, and the promotion of World Socialism is not viewed as being in our best interests. At present, our company, together with an affiliate, is renting three Xerox copiers. In addition, other associated companies have Xerox machines. If the UN programs are put on, we will do everything in our power to replace these, as well as encouraging other businesses to do likewise.

Trusting that you will reconsider, I am

Very truly yours
(name omitted)

EAST-WEST TRADE*

∧∧

Introduction

During 1964 the U.S. government reviewed its policy of placing strict limitations on U.S. trade with the Soviet Union and the Communist countries of Eastern Europe. In his January 4, 1965, State of the Union Message, President Johnson indicated that his administration desired to follow a more liberal trade policy in Eastern Europe when he stated:

In Eastern Europe restless nations are slowly beginning to assert their identity. Your government, assisted by leaders in labor and business, is now exploring ways to increase peaceful trade with these countries and with the Soviet Union.

The intended liberalization of trade with Communist countries had significant implications for American businesses, particularly in those industries where the Communists desired to secure advanced or specialized types of machinery, industrial plants, and industrial processes and technology from the West.

Background: East-West trade

Trade between the European Communist countries and free world industrial countries was close to $3.5 billion each way in 1964. It had grown at an average rate of nearly 10 per cent a year during the previous decade, or somewhat more than the rate of growth in the overall trade of Western industrial countries. There were significant variations, however, in the relative importance of East-West trade to the countries of the West. The U.S. share in this trade was particularly small—about one-tenth of total Western exports in 1964—and even this figure was abnormally high because it included large wheat sales which were not considered to be a normal feature of this trade. For Western Europe, trade with Eastern Europe has ranged between three and four per cent of total trade. For the United States, the proportion, even in 1964, was barely one per cent.

The total economic significance of this trade was small for all the countries concerned. For Communist Europe, total imports from the West represented only one-half of one per cent of the Soviet Union's gross national product in 1964 and only two per cent of the combined national product of the other

Eastern European countries. For Western Europe, the significance was even less, and for the United States it was negligible. Estimated 1965 U.S. exports to all European Communist countries were only $200 million, less than forecasted exports from the United States to Switzerland.

The trade was of somewhat greater significance for particular industries in the Eastern European countries. The Soviet Union and the East European countries were interested primarily in buying advanced or specialized types of machinery, industrial plants, and industrial processes and technology from the West to meet specific economic planning goals or to become self-sufficient in certain industrial sectors. To finance their purchases they sold to the West mainly industrial raw materials, minerals including gold, foodstuffs, steel products and particularly oil. They sold relatively small quantities of manufactured goods.

U.S. policy

During the period immediately following World War II, the United States treated trade with the Soviet Union and its Eastern European allies no differently from trade with other countries. Security controls on this trade were not imposed until 1948 and only then in response to what was considered to be aggressive Soviet expansion in Eastern Europe. In the period of the Berlin blockade and the Korean War, these controls were expanded and the United States was able to gain the cooperation of the other principal trading nations in an international embargo of strategic commodities.

In the early years of these controls, the United States was the predominant source of capital, of advanced industrial technology, and of exportable resources in the West. Thus, the United States possessed a considerable unilateral capacity to insure that Western resources would not contribute to the growth of Soviet military power.

In recent years, however, the underlying situation has changed markedly. The ability of the Western Europeans to trade grew rapidly as a result of their dramatic economic recovery. Furthermore, they saw the death of Stalin and the end of the Korean War as marking sufficient change in the political climate to justify a resumption of their historic trade with Eastern Europe. The capacity of the Communist countries to trade also increased, following the growth in the strength of their economies.

These developments created pressure on the part of the Western Europeans to reduce the internationally agreed upon Western restrictions on exports to the East. As a result, the International Embargo List was gradually shortened. The West European countries reduced their controls accordingly; the United States did not do so to the same degree. Although total exports to the East by members of the Organization for Economic Cooperation and Development (OECD)[1] were almost three times as high in 1963 as in 1948, U.S. exports were 60 per cent lower.

[1] OECD members are: Austria, Belgium, Canada, Denmark, France, Federal Republic of Germany, Greece, Iceland, Ireland, Italy, Japan, Luxembourg, Netherlands, Norway, Portugal, Spain, Sweden, Switzerland, Turkey, United Kingdom, United States.

1964–1965 developments

Western European policies toward East-West trade continued to diverge from U.S. policies in the 1964–1965 period. During 1964 both Great Britain and France extended long-term credits to the Soviet Union for capital equipment purchases. These credits, to be repaid over periods between 5 and 15 years, represented the first break in the "credit barrier" created by earlier refusals on the part of all Western industrial nations to allow more than five years for the repayment of credits to finance Soviet purchases.

During this period there were increasing signs that a number of the Eastern European countries desired and, in fact, were achieving a greater degree of independence from the Soviet Union, particularly in economic matters, and were interested in establishing increasingly friendly relations with the United States. In a speech in the Senate, Senator James W. Fulbright, chairman of the Senate Foreign Relations Committee, remarked that Eastern Europe was "one of the few areas of the world, perhaps the only one, where American prestige is rising rather than declining."[2]

As a result of the changing environment, an increasing number of individuals and organizations began to call for a review of U.S. policy toward East-West trade. On April 29, 1964, the U.S. Chamber of Commerce, in a major policy innovation, urged the government to cut back the list of items barred from sale to the Soviet Union and other European Communist countries. The Chamber called for a level of trade in that area equal to that of the Western European nations. This resolution was described as "the first on East-West trade by a major business organization that moved beyond generalities to a specific policy recommendation."[3]

The Chamber of Commerce resolution and other statements were based on arguments that went beyond the "if we don't sell to them the Europeans will" attitude that was frequently expressed. It was argued that the United States could use trade to influence the internal evolution and external behavior of Communist countries. Specifically, trade would be used as a policy instrument to encourage the trend toward greater national independence in Eastern Europe and the trend toward greater concern for consumer needs in all the European Communist countries. By refusing to trade, the United States would put itself in a posture of hostility that could be at odds with these developments as well as with other elements of overall U.S. strategy toward these countries. A willingness to trade, on the other hand, was seen as concrete evidence of the U.S. belief in constructive and peaceful relations.

Strong arguments against East-West trade were also presented. In general, these arguments were based on the conviction that trade with the Communists merely served to strengthen nations hostile to the United States. By selling them goods and services of any nature, whether wheat or technologically ad-

---

[2]*Congressional Record*, July 26, 1965, p. 18227.
[3]*New York Times*, April 30, 1964.

vanced machinery and equipment, it was argued that they would be helped to solve some of their pressing internal problems, and that it would be easier for them to use their limited resources for building up their military power and strengthening their potential for subversion abroad. Moreover, this argument held that by expanding trade with these countries the West would bestow upon them a kind of respectability and prestige which would enhance their position in the developing countries and which they would use to the ultimate disadvantage of the West.

By early 1965, however, discussions revolved more around the question of what political concessions, if any, should be extracted from the Communists as a precondition for trade, rather than whether the United States should refuse to trade at all. In a statement on East-West trade issued in early March, for example, the Executive Council of the AFL/CIO proposed that, "No trade or credit concessions should be accorded to . . . any Communist government without an adequate political *quid pro quo* like ceasing subversion and invasion of Vietnam, dismantling the Berlin Wall, and calling off their military infiltration of the Congo."[4] George Meany, the president of the AFL/CIO, said that American labor does not support the idea that anything is to be gained by a straight business deal with the Communists. "It would be utterly unrealistic," he said, "for American industrialists and traders to think that they can do 'business as usual' with Communist governments."[5]

The Johnson administration favored increased trade as beneficial in itself, without requiring that it be directly related to political concessions. On February 16, the President created The Special Committee on U.S. Trade Relations with East European Countries and the Soviet Union. This 12-man committee, composed primarily of business leaders, was charged "with exploring all aspects of expanding peaceful trade in support of the President's policy of widening constructive relations with the countries of Eastern Europe and the U.S.S.R." The Appendix contains the statement of the committee which introduced its report to the President, the recommendations of the committee, and a Statement of Comment submitted by one of the members.

In its report, submitted on April 29, the special committee stated its belief that a relaxation of restrictions on trade between the United States and the Communists of Eastern Europe would help promote American foreign policy objectives. The report emphasized that East-West trade was a political rather than an economic issue and that ordinary motivations, such as economic or financial gain, had no place in trade relations with the Communist countries. In general, the committee recommended that the President be given broad discretionary powers to use trade as an instrument of national policy, including the freedom to grant "most favored nation" tariff treatment to any Eastern European country. The committee recommended that the federal government should decide and provide in bilateral agreements "the permitted scope of

---

[4]*New York Times*, March 2, 1965.
[5]*Ibid.*

the trade in terms of security considerations," but that, within such limits, the amount of trade that took place should be left to U.S. business and the U.S. consumer to decide.

After receiving the committee's report, the President restated his administration's desire to expand East-West trade, when he remarked at a press conference on May 7:

We must hasten the slow erosion of the Iron Curtain. By building bridges between the nations of Eastern Europe and the West, we bring closer the day when Europe can be reconstituted within its wide historic boundaries. For our part, after taking counsel with our European allies, I intend to recommend measures to the U.S. Congress to increase the flow of peaceful trade between Eastern Europe and the United States.[6]

In May 1965, the Research and Policy Committee of the Committee for Economic Development (CED) issued a report on East-West trade which also recommended that East-West trade be expanded on a selective basis. In its report the CED stated:

We believe that, subject to [certain] conditions, the interests of the West would be served in present circumstances by an expansion of East-West trade brought about by mutual East-West reduction of the obstacles to trade. Restrictions on the trade are necessary for strategic reasons, to guard against injury, and to obtain for the West a reasonable share of the gains from trade. But these limitations would still leave scope for significant expansion of trade. Moreover, the West should be in a position to respond more affirmatively to tendencies of some Eastern countries to trade more freely with the West and to follow more market-oriented practices.[7]

The Rumanian request for synthetic rubber plants

As part of its policy of improving relations, on a discriminating basis, with those Communist countries which demonstrated relative degrees of national independence, the United States agreed in 1964 to a Rumanian proposal for talks between the two countries on trade and other matters. Discussions were held by U.S. government officials with a Rumanian delegation in Washington from May 18 to June 1, 1964. At the end of the talks a joint communique was issued setting forth certain specific agreements between the two countries.

The United States agreed to establish a general export licensing procedure under which most commodities might be exported to Rumania without the necessity for individual export licenses. In addition, the United States agreed to grant export licenses for a number of particular industrial facilities in the fields of chemicals, petrochemicals, electric power, the production and processing of petroleum, and glass manufacturing. Included in the petrochemical sector were two synthetic rubber plants.

[6]*New York Times*, May 8, 1965.

[7]Committee for Economic Development, *East-West Trade—A Common Policy for the West* (New York, May, 1965), p. 19.

Also included in the communique was an agreement that products, designs and technology exported to Rumania from the United States would not be transshipped or re-exported without the prior consent of the U.S. government. In addition, the two governments agreed on arrangements for the mutual protection of industrial property rights and processes, including a provision for third country or international tribunal arbitration of disputes arising out of a contract violation.

In a statement placed in the *Congressional Record*, Senator Fulbright said that "the Rumanian government attached particular importance to the willingness of the United States to issue export licenses for the construction of two synthetic rubber plants in Rumania." In explaining the reasons for their position, he said:

The Rumanians are undertaking to strengthen their economic independence of the Soviet bloc by broadening their industrial base with advanced industrial equipment. The major foundation of Rumanian industry is petroleum and the two projected rubber plants were to have an important part in expanding the country's petrochemical industry. Rumanian officials stressed the importance of the two plants to their economic development—and, therefore, to their growing independence of the Soviet bloc. It is clear that the agreement to allow the sale of two synthetic rubber plants was not a marginal or incidental arrangement in relations between the United States and Rumania. According to the Department of State, the ability of Rumania to purchase the two plants from the United States became a fundamental element in our new policy toward that country.[8]

During the following months, with the encouragement of the U.S. government, a number of American firms discussed the possible sale of rubber plants with the Rumanians.[9] In October 1964, a representative of the Goodyear Tire & Rubber Co. wrote to Secretary of State Dean Rusk, informing him that Goodyear had decided against accepting the contract. The Goodyear position was explained in an article titled "An Order Goodyear Didn't Take" which appeared in the company's house organ, *The Wingfoot Clan*, on December 3. Although published primarily for Goodyear employees, *The Wingfoot Clan* was widely read throughout the American rubber industry. Some excerpts from this article appear below:

Even to a dedicated profitmaking organization, some things are more important than dollars. Take the best interests of the United States and the free world, for example. You can't put a price tag on freedom.

And when you believe in something you may be called upon to back up your belief with action. That goes for a company such as Goodyear, just as it does an individual.

Recently, Goodyear did just that—it stood firmly on the side of freedom, as a foe of aggression. Goodyear did this even though the company stood to lose financially.

---

[8]*Congressional Record*, July 26, 1965, p. 18228.

[9]The project, estimated to be worth $40 million, was to be the first major contact between American enterprise and the Rumanians since World War II.

The company's refusal to sell a modern synthetic rubber plant to Communist Rumania has made news throughout the nation.

The Associated Press and United Press International duly reported Goodyear's decision and their stories appeared in hundreds of newspapers from coast to coast. . . .

* * * * *

Goodyear feels that the dangers far outweigh the possible benefits in the proposed deal. . . .

Why is Goodyear so opposed to the transaction?

Because we foresee the knowledge that Rumania seeks to purchase from the United States in the potential role of an international agitator, we don't believe that the United States should allow any Communist nation to acquire the knowhow to produce a synthetic rubber which competes head-on with natural rubber.

* * * * *

While synthetic and natural rubber are now competitively priced, Goodyear believes the Communists could—if they wished—disrupt natural rubber markets in Malaysia, Liberia and other so-called underdeveloped countries. The Communists are not governed by marketing conditions in setting their prices and in the past have, in fact, used cut-rate prices as an economic club.

The State Department, in commenting on the situation, has said that the Rumanians have assured the United States that they won't divulge the polyisoprene secrets they purchase from us to other Communist nations. With due respect for the State Department's belief in the Rumanians' promise, Goodyear would prefer not to entrust its production secrets to the Communists.

* * * * *

The *Daily News* [*New York Daily News*, with a 2.4 million circulation] ran an editorial entitled "Ten Cents from Russia, Maybe" in which it castigated U.S. businessmen for believing Soviet Premier Kosygin's hint that Russia might repay its World War II debts to the United States if U.S. firms would sell Russia anything it wanted to buy, on long-term credits. The editorial also stated:

"Meanwhile, there is one honorable exception—and there may well be many more that we haven't heard of—to the list of U.S. firms now yearning to do business with the Communists.

"The Goodyear Tire & Rubber Co. recently refused point blank to sell a synthetic rubber plant to Red Rumania, despite a Commerce Department OK on such sales and the administration's desire to cozy up to Rumania.

"Goodyear considers such deals unpatriotic and injurious to our side, and how about fixing the patriotism of this company in your memory?"[10]

By late November, the Rumanian trade representatives were reported to be engaged in extensive negotiations with officials of the Firestone Tire & Rubber Co., and on January 5, 1965, an announcement was made that the Firestone and Rumanian officials had initialed a preliminary contract. It was also reported that the final contract would probably be signed in the early spring.

---

[10]*The Wingfoot Clan*, December 3, 1964, as cited in the *Congressional Record*, July 26, 1965, p. 18230.

On April 20, however, Firestone issued the following public statement:

The Firestone Tire & Rubber Co. has terminated negotiations for a contract to design and equip a synthetic rubber plant in Rumania.

Later, in a speech to the Senate on July 26, 1965, Senator Fulbright made the following comments on the events which led to Firestone's announcement:

In the months that followed Firestone found itself subjected to unusual competitive pressures and to a nuisance boycott campaign conducted by an extremist political organization.

* * * * *

Prior to issuing this public statement, Firestone executives conferred with Department of State officials on April 16 in order to advise the Department of the company's intention to terminate the Rumanian negotiations because of the unexpected extent and intensity of competitive pressures and because of the rightwing agitation against Firestone's proposed transaction with Rumania. The events leading up to the abrupt termination of the negotiations are a case study in the defeat of an important and carefully considered policy of the U.S. Government by irresponsible private interests, aided and abetted by the failure of Government officials actively to support the President's established policy.[11]

The Young Americans for Freedom

The organization referred to by Senator Fulbright was the Young Americans for Freedom (YAF), a college-age conservative group which claimed 25,000 members in 1965. The YAF had been organized in 1960 to support conservative political candidates and programs. Four U.S. Senators and 34 members of the House of Representatives served on the National Advisory Board of the YAF.

The Philadelphia chapter of the YAF was the first to take action against the Firestone project. The treasurer of the chapter, quoted in the May 8 issue of *Human Events*,[12] described the involvement of his organization as follows:

"After reading in *Human Events* about the Firestone Tire & Rubber Co.'s plan to build a synthetic rubber plant in Communist Rumania," writes Philadelphia YAF treasurer David K. Walter, "the Philadelphia County Chapter of Young Americans for Freedom launched a drive to force Firestone to reconsider and withdraw these plans."

"Letters sent to the office of the president produced unsatisfactory replies. Philadelphia YAF then organized picketing of Firestone stores in the Philadelphia area." Picket signs appeared paraphrasing Firestone's slogan: "When Red wheels are rolling, the name is known as Firestone?"

The Philadelphia campaign soon became national, with YAF demonstrations in Los Angeles, Cleveland and cities on the east coast.[13]

---

[11] *Congressional Record*, July 26, 1965, p. 18228.

[12] *Human Events* was a journal of conservative opinion.

[13] *Human Events*, May 8, 1965, "Big Conservative Win," as cited in the *Congressional Record*, July 26, 1965, p. 18231.

The chairman of the Philadelphia YAF chapter was later quoted as saying:

We immediately started getting a response from all over the country. Once it was put on a national basis, they really rallied to the cause. I understand that where the pressure really hurt was when a couple of dealers dropped their franchises.[14]

Senator Fulbright quoted from a letter sent to all YAF chapter chairmen by the Philadelphia chairman of that group:

It is up to YAF members from coast to coast to organize these protests and voice our dissent. Please join with us. Arrange for your chapter to picket local Firestone stores. Distribute handbills urging the public to write the Firestone Tire & Rubber Co. and local newspapers expressing their disapproval of this action.[15]

Senator Fulbright also introduced into the record the text of a handbill distributed to passing cars and pedestrians, as follows:

We are at war with the Communists. In South Vietnam, Americans are being killed daily by Communist bullets. It would be disastrous for American companies to supply the atheistic Communist governments with valuable materials, especially rubber, which the Reds must have to wage their war on free nations.

In the past month, Communist Rumania shipped 500 heavy-duty trucks of military value to Red China, the principal supplier of the North Viet Communists.

The Reds must have rubber to wage war. The synthetic rubber plant which Firestone plans to build in Communist Rumania parallels the steel which the United States sold to Japan prior to World War II. Americans got the steel back —at Pearl Harbor. No nation can wage war without large quantities of synthetic rubber.

Goodyear refuses to trade with the Communists. Among the companies which refuse to trade with Communist governments are Goodyear Tire & Rubber Co., Standard Oil of New Jersey, and the du Pont Co. of Delaware.

A Goodyear statement tells us: "Even to a dedicated profitmaking organization, some things are more important than dollars. Take the best interests of the United States and the free world for example. You cannot put a price tag on freedom."

What you can do. Firestone's plans to build a synthetic rubber plant in Communist Rumania can only strengthen the Communists and throw away American jobs. Express your opinion by writing Firestone Tire & Rubber Co., 1245 Firestone Parkway, Akron, Ohio.

Time is short. Write today before you lose the address.[16]

Firestone's reaction

It was reported in the press that "The campaign apparently caught Firestone officials off guard. Many franchised dealers whose concern is strictly

---

[14]*Akron Beacon Journal,* May 14, 1965.
[15]*Congressional Record,* July 26, 1965, p. 18229.
[16]Reprinted in *Congressional Record,* July 26, 1965, p. 18229.

with selling tires asked Firestone to get the conservatives off their back, since they were losing business to Goodyear."[17]

"Firestone sent its Eastern region public relations man, Bernard Frazier, to speak to YAF leaders in different cities. Frazier was described by those who listened to him as a sincere individual who believed Firestone was acting in the national interest by 'building bridges' to Eastern Europe, as President Johnson has urged."[18] In an interview with a reporter, Frazier was quoted as saying that he took the position "that this was a policy established by the Government and the State Department, and if they (the YAF) had a quarrel with the policy, the proper course of action was to get the policy changed."[19]

It was further reported that "Firestone also spread the word that some Rumanian trucks and tractors, photographed in Red China, had Goodyear tires on them, and that Goodyear, with Commerce Department approval, had been selling synthetic rubber (but not plants) to Rumania."[20] Goodyear officials replied that, while they had received a license to export synthetic rubber to Rumania some time after the authorization of such licenses by the government in June 1964, no shipments had actually been made. "Goodyear has denied it knowingly sold such tires to Red China and says Peiping might have purchased them somewhere on the black market."[21]

In a further effort to ameliorate the situation, Firestone asked the assistance of William Ayres, a Republican congressman from Akron.[22] In describing his talks with YAF leaders in which he defended Firestone's action, Representative Ayres was quoted as saying:

All I told those kids was, "Look, you're just making fools of yourselves, damaging the free enterprise system with your picket signs." They ought to take their signs up to the State Department.[23]

In spite of the Firestone efforts, the YAF continued its campaign. YAF leaders planned a major demonstration at the Indianapolis 500-mile race on May 31, 1965.[24] Thousands of people from all over the country usually attended this event, and Firestone usually timed a major promotional effort to coincide with it. As part of the demonstration, the YAF planned on establishing an Indianapolis office called "The Committee Against Slave Labor" to call attention to their claim that forced labor would be used to help build the Firestone plant. The YAF also planned to hire a plane to carry a banner over the Indianapolis speedway stadium denouncing the deal and to saturate the stadium with a half-million pamphlets sharply criticizing Firestone.

---

[17]*Washington Evening Star*, May 8, 1965, "United States Embarrassed: Firm Facing Boycott Drops Rumania Deal" by Bernard Gwertzman, as quoted in *Congressional Record*, July 26, 1965, pp. 18228-29.
[18]*Ibid.*
[19]*Akron Beacon Journal*, May 14, 1965.
[20]*Washington Evening Star*, op. cit.
[21]*Ibid.*
[22]*Akron Beacon Journal*, May 14, 1965.
[23]*Ibid.*
[24]*Washington Evening Star, op. cit.*

Some aspects of competition in the tire and rubber industry

In attempting to measure the impact of the YAF campaign, it is necessary to consider Firestone's competitive position, particularly in the tire industry. Like its major competitors, Firestone had diversified interests outside the tire industry, but tires produced for the original equipment and replacement markets still formed the company's principal source of income.

For many years Firestone had maintained its position as the second largest producer of tires, in both the original equipment and replacement markets. One executive close to the tire industry estimated that Goodyear and Firestone accounted for about 20 per cent and 15 per cent of replacement tire sales respectively and said that these market share data had remained relatively constant during the last five years.

In general, the major manufacturers utilized similar distribution systems. In recent years there has been a trend toward the use of company-owned stores. In October 1963, Firestone announced that its stores numbered 820, and that a major program of modernization and relocation was under way. In 1965 it was reported that Firestone operated 850 stores and Goodyear 900.[25] The tire companies had moved into the company-owned store business to maintain distribution which would otherwise have been lost through the decline in the number of independent dealers. Government figures showed a decrease of 2,000 dealers between 1958 and 1960, the last year for which data were available. Company-owned stores had been diversified into large-scale retail operations, selling such items as home appliances as well as tires, batteries, and accessories (TBA) and automotive services. The most universal diversification had been toward the offering of automotive services, which involved the addition of service "bays" to tire stores. The motivation behind the expansion of products and services was the desire to attract more customers and to have the opportunity to sell more to each one. As a result, the total number of different products sold through company-owned stores had reached an estimated figure of 6,000 items.

In spite of the trend toward company-owned stores, most tires continued to be sold through independent dealers and service stations. Firestone's 1964 Annual Report announced that the company's tires were sold in more than 60,000 outlets in the United States and Canada, and in an additional 90,000 outlets abroad.

Tire prices were typically competitive among the major brands for each grade level. However, the "list" selling price of a tire was typically modified by a trade-in allowance for the consumer's old tires. Discounting was an accepted way of meeting price competition, and the president of one tire company estimated that less than five per cent of total tire sales took place at the list price. In addition, heavily advertised price promotions on third line, popular-sized tires were common and resulted in intense price competition on these lines.

---

[25] *Advertising Age*, July 26, 1965, p. 76.

Purchasing arrangements and discounts received by dealers varied considerably. Many dealers carried more than one brand and played off one rubber company against another. Dealer discounts ranged from a low of 25 per cent off list to as much as 40 per cent, after taking advantage of volume discounts, cash discounts, and end-of-year volume rebates. The tire manufacturers had relatively little control over their independent customers, and many dealers could easily switch to competitive brands of other major producers.

As a result of the intensive competition characteristic of the industry, Firestone had not been able to maintain a consistent growth in its earnings, although its 1964 sales of $1.5 billion and earnings of almost $80 million were the highest in the company's history. Selected financial data on the major tire producers for the 1955–1964 period are presented in Exhibit 1.

Reactions to the Firestone decision

The reaction of the conservative elements to Firestone's decision to terminate its negotiations with the Rumanians was expressed as follows in *Human Events*:

Lyndon Johnson is in the White House, the Americans for Democratic Action have a vice president and liberals outnumber conservatives in Congress by a good majority. But conservatives throughout the country have just scored a stunning upset victory over the liberal elements who have been pushing America into selling its technical know-how to Communist countries.

*   *   *   *   *

Letters sent to Firestone showed the American people boiling mad over this plan to increase trade with a Communist country while American soldiers were dying in Vietnam. In addition, the public realized the synthetic rubber was of obvious military value.

*   *   *   *   *

The Firestone story is bound to have national impact. It shows what can be accomplished by conservatives in the face of strong counter-pressure. And it most certainly will have an effect on American businesses that desire to do business-as-usual behind the Iron Curtain. There are reportedly some 40 American firms dickering with Communist countries at the present time over deals similar to the Firestone-Rumanian one. But they had better be on their guard. YAF is planning to call attention to every one of them.[26]

The Department of State maintained a position of noninvolvement in this matter. "In a press and radio briefing on April 21, 1965, [a State Department press officer] replied as follows to a question on how the negotiations began and who broke them off":

On the first part of it, the issuance of the export licenses to go ahead on the negotiations was a result of the interest of the Rumanian Government in that type of plant. As to circumstances surrounding the break-off, I would address

---

[26]*Human Events, op. cit.*

Exhibit 1

SELECTED FINANCIAL DATA ON MAJOR TIRE PRODUCERS, 1955-64

Year	1955	1956	1957	1958	1959	1960	1961	1962	1963	1964
Net Sales (in millions of $)										
Goodyear	$1,372	$1,359	$1,422	$1,368	$1,579	$1,551	$1,473	$1,592	$1,731	$2,011
Firestone	1,115	1,115	1,159	1,062	1,188	1,207	1,183	1,278	1,382	1,449
U.S. Rubber	926	901	874	871	977	967	940	1,007	980	1,087
B. F. Goodrich	755	724	735	697	772	765	758	812	829	872
Net Income (in millions of $)										
Goodyear	$ 59.7	$ 62.5	$ 64.8	$ 65.7	$ 76.0	$ 71.0	$ 76.2	$ 71.1	$ 81.2	$100.2
Firestone	55.4	60.5	61.7	53.8	64.6	65.0	63.6	60.0	63.4	79.0
U.S. Rubber	33.6	31.9	29.7	22.7	35.6	30.7	27.1	25.7	22.1	30.1
B. F. Goodrich	46.7	43.8	39.4	35.5	37.6	30.0	31.0	26.3	27.1	34.0
Per Cent of Net Income to Net Sales										
Goodyear	4.3%	4.6%	4.6%	4.8%	4.8%	4.6%	5.2%	4.5%	4.7%	5.0%
Firestone	4.9	5.4	5.3	5.1	5.4	5.4	5.4	4.7	4.6	5.5
U.S. Rubber	3.6	3.5	3.4	2.6	3.6	3.2	2.9	2.6	2.3	2.8
B. F. Goodrich	6.2	6.0	5.4	5.1	4.9	3.9	4.1	3.2	3.3	3.9
Net Income per Share of Common Stock										
Goodyear	$ 1.68	$ 1.75	$ 1.82	$ 1.85	$ 2.13	$ 1.99	$ 2.44	$ 2.00	$ 2.28	$ 2.81
Firestone	1.99	2.17	2.18	1.89	2.26	2.27	2.22	2.09	2.21	2.75
U.S. Rubber	5.04	4.74	4.31	3.05	5.30	4.45	3.80	3.50	2.90	4.27
B. F. Goodrich	5.26	4.90	4.40	3.95	4.18	3.33	3.39	2.87	2.95	3.71

Source: Company Annual Reports.

you either to the Rumanian Government or the Firestone company. It's a matter between the two.[27]

Further information on the reaction of the Department of State was set forth in an article in the *Washington Evening Star* on May 8:

The State Department was told about the collapse of the negotiations about two days before it was publicly announced. This was about the same time Rumania heard about it.

On April 19, Under Secretary of State George W. Ball called in Rumanian Ambassador Petre Balaceanu to repeat that the U.S. Government still approved sale of the synthetic rubber plants and had nothing to do with Firestone's decision.

Because of great State Department sensitivity over the issue, Ball's meeting with Balaceanu was not announced to the press. The State Department did not want to appear as having a direct interest in the Firestone-Rumania deal, since it already had been attacked by conservative groups for "ordering" Firestone to sell to the Communists.[28]

Congressional reaction could perhaps best be described as "vigorous." In a speech in the Senate on May 17, Senator Young of Ohio made the following comments:

Here is a dastardly wrong perpetrated by narrowminded, bigoted, self-appointed vigilantes who consider themselves superduper patriots. They did a disservice to their Nation. Their action not only injured the Firestone Tire & Rubber Co. but was to the prejudice of every businessman and of every working man and woman in the great Akron area.

*   *   *   *   *

Our officials regret that Rumania is now negotiating with West German and English plants for this same contract which would have brought additional employment to Akron workers and additional money deposited in Akron banks.

*   *   *   *   *

It seems unbelievable and unconscionable that a group playing God with other people's patriotism can intimidate and browbeat officials of a nationally known and respected company with threats of a boycott.[29]

And in his speech in the Senate on July 26, Senator Fulbright made the following additional comments:

It is disturbing, however—very disturbing indeed and very mischievous— when private groups or businesses or individuals take it on themselves, by act or omission, to alter or dictate or defeat official policies of the U.S. Government directly and not through our duly constituted governmental agencies such as the Congress. This amateur policymaking—or policy-breaking—can be accomplished by almost any group or organization endowed with the conviction that it knows more about some aspect of foreign policy than anybody else and with the will to intimidate officials or other organizations that are not very hard to intimidate.

---

[27]Quoted by Senator Fulbright, *Congressional Record*, July 26, 1965, p. 18232.

[28]*Washington Evening Star, op. cit.*

[29]*Congressional Record*, May 17, 1965, p. 10680.

It has been done by business interests seeking a competitive advantage, by organized labor, and by those sterling patriots whose self-designated task it is to keep the rest of us in line, loyal and true to the red, white, and blue.

*   *   *   *   *

If our Government has not always honored its responsibilities in connection with the foreign business activities of private organizations, it has at least acknowledged them. In a statement to the Senate Committee on Foreign Relations on March 13, 1964, Secretary of State Rusk said:

"The use of trade with Communist countries for national purposes is a matter for national decisions. The volunteer efforts of individuals or organizations to impose their private notions on our overall trade policy can only frustrate the effective use of this essential national instrument."[30]

Senator Fulbright was quite critical of the actions taken by Goodyear, and he said:

The Goodyear Company at first showed an apparent interest of its own in the possibility of doing business with Rumania. . . . Then, for reasons which are not entirely clear, Goodyear suddenly "got religion" and grandly refused to traffic with the Red heathen.

Having defeated temptation, the Goodyear Tire & Rubber Co., for reasons no doubt of pure idealism, decided to publicize its profit-sacrificing patriotism. The Goodyear house organ, the *Wingfoot Clan*, on December 3, 1964, expressed the cloying sentiment that

"Even to a dedicated profit-making organization, some things are more important than dollars. Take the best interests of the United States and the free world, for example. You can't put a price tag on freedom."

Who can argue with this? But so profound is Goodyear's patriotism that it was not satisfied with mere patriotic generalizations. No indeed, Goodyear was willing to make financial sacrifices in the fight against aggression. Standing resolute against Firestone's greed and the shocking lack of patriotism of the President and the Department of State, Goodyear acted on its own superior knowledge of foreign policy by proclaiming its refusal to do business with Communist Rumania.[31]

Nor did Senator Fulbright withhold his criticism from the Department of State:

The role of the Department of State in this memorable affair is, to say the least, equivocal. Having determined that the building of bridges to the East was important for the advancement of American national interests, . . . the State Department now seems to be taking the disingenuous position that all this, after all, was a private affair involving an American private company and a foreign government.

*   *   *   *   *

When important policies of the Government are threatened by irresponsible,

---

[30]*Congressional Record*, July 26, 1965, p. 18226.
[31]*Ibid.*, p. 18230.

selfish interests, it is not adequate for the executive branch to accept the defeat of these policies with nothing more than expressions of regret. Had the State Department officials with whom Firestone executives conferred on April 16 indicated that a strong public statement of support for the Rumanian transaction might be provided by the Secretary of State or by the White House, it is possible that Firestone could have been persuaded to carry out the sale of the two synthetic rubber plants. As it turned out, Firestone was told in effect it was on its own.[32]

Goodyear executives made no immediate response to the termination of the Firestone-Rumanian negotiations. On June 11, however, almost two months after the Firestone announcement, the marketing manager of Goodyear's tire division issued the following "Sales Department Instructions" to Goodyear salesmen:

SALES DEPARTMENT INSTRUCTIONS
Akron, Ohio
June 11, 1965

I am sure that every Goodyear employee will enjoy reading the attached reprint of page 4 from the *Human Events* magazine of May 8, 1965.

Surely every Goodyear salesman will proudly show this article to commercial accounts, competitive dealers—especially Firestone and Goodyear dealers.

We are sending a small supply to your district office and I am sure if you would like additional copies to mail to some of your friends—especially those in the tire business—that you will be able to get the number you need from your district manager.

I am also attaching a photostat of page 21 from the May 1965 issue of the *New Guard* magazine. There will not be an extra supply of these sent to your district because we have only a limited number.

Tire Division[33]

It was reported that on April 22, the executive director of the YAF received a letter from Mr. Frazier, Firestone's eastern region public relations director.[34] The letter reportedly announced the termination of the negotiations and asked the YAF to bring public attention to it. Firestone executives, it was believed, made no additional public statements after the announcement of April 20.

Senator Fulbright's critical remarks in his speech in the Senate on July 26 prompted a second editorial in the Goodyear house organ on August 5, 1965. This editorial, entitled "Facts for a Senator's Consideration," is reproduced below.

Your company's role in the controversy surrounding the possible construction

---

[32]*Ibid.*, p. 18232.

[33]Letter as quoted by Senator Fulbright in the *Congressional Record*, July 26, 1965, p. 18231.

[34]*Human Events, op. cit.*

of a synthetic rubber plant in Communist Romania is the reason for this report of facts significant to every employe.

Senator William Fulbright (Dem.-Ark.) did not have all the facts in his possession in a recent speech on the Senate floor, and his charges now have made it possible for Goodyear to set the record straight for the first time, an opportunity the company welcomes.

Fortunately, the nation's press and news magazines plus quite a few columnists are now digging into the background and some very objective reporting is taking place.

To make certain that all employes are aware of Goodyear's actions, The Clan is presenting a chronological report of events to date and an explanation of the reasons for company policy in the matter.

On June 9, 1964, a trade delegation from Communist Romania visited the Goodyear plant at Beaumont, Texas. This was one of several U.S. manufacturing facilities in various industries visited by the Romanians, at the request of our Government.

Although the company was reluctant to approve this visit, it was decided to do so in an effort to cooperate with our Government.

While in Beaumont, the Romanian delegation got a casual look at activities but was not permitted to observe detailed manufacturing processes involved in the creation of polyisoprene rubber, the product which exactly duplicates natural rubber and is considered one of the Free World's important manufacturing secrets. There are only two known commercial producers of polyisoprene rubber in the world—Goodyear and Shell Oil Company. It is the basic product used in the manufacture of critical military vehicle tires and high speed airplane tires.

During the tour, the Romanians requested samples of the synthetic polyisoprene rubber and Goodyear applied in June 1964 to the Government for an export license to comply with this request, again cooperating with our Government. The license was actually granted by our Government in December of 1964 but was never used by Goodyear.

Goodyear never applied for a license to build a plant or to export know-how.

But even before the granting of the license to send the rubber samples, the company had declined to participate in the development of a polyisoprene rubber plant behind the Iron Curtain. On October 1, 1964, Goodyear had advised the State Department by letter that the company did not desire to build such a plant because the company did not believe such information should be sent behind the Iron Curtain because of its strategic value and because we felt the Communists could use this synthetic natural rubber to disrupt natural rubber prices, if they so desired. This action would seriously affect the economies of such countries as Malaysia and Liberia, who are friendly to the United States, and who depend on natural rubber for export.

No public statements were made of the decision since all activity in the area was considered confidential and no definite action had progressed beyond the discussion state.

On October 22, 1964, however, Washington newsmen reported that Goodyear had declined an invitation to build the plant. This they learned from news sources inside the Government, not from Goodyear. The news stories appeared in hundreds of publications across the nation, with most reporting that Goodyear felt this highly prized technical know-how could become available to other Communist nations.

The first company statement on the subject came on the pages of this paper December 3, 1964, when a report similar to this one was prepared to inform employes of the facts—there was no public release. *The Wingfoot Clan* is printed solely for the purpose of keeping our employes informed and is not an external publication.

Many of you will recall the article—it was a no-nonsense statement of fact in which Goodyear, a private enterprise organization, said that it was passing up a substantial profit because it believed that such action was in the interest of national security. The shortage of natural rubber in World War II seriously handicapped our nation's military effort.

The article also reported that leading Americans, a number of respected publications and our customers had expressed their approval of the company's refusal to build a plant for the Communists.

Then on January 5, 1965, it was revealed in Washington that the Firestone Tire & Rubber Company had signed a preliminary agreement with the Romanians to build a synthetic rubber plant behind the Iron Curtain. Although this revelation prompted many Americans to write letters to Goodyear praising the company's refusal to build the plant, none of these letters was ever released, not even within our own organization.

On April 20, Firestone announced that it was terminating negotiations with the Romanians and would not build a synthetic rubber plant in that country. No reason was given for the action.

During the period when it appeared that Firestone was going to build the plant in Communist territory, Goodyear received many letters and queries from customers, our dealers and competitive dealers asking for the background on Goodyear's decision.

In an effort to explain Goodyear's reason for refusing to build the plant in Romania, reproductions of articles in *Human Events* and *New Guard*, publications which reported the facts in detail, were distributed June 11, 1965—SIX WEEKS AFTER Firestone's termination of negotiations—to Company representatives in the field to enable them to answer queries from customers, Goodyear dealers and competitive dealers.

On July 26, 1965, Arkansas's Senator Fulbright questioned Goodyear's refusal to build the plant for the Communists; questioned State Department action in not making certain that Firestone negotiations were successful, and questioned what he described as "the nuisance activities of a minor vigilante group . . . which calls itself Young Americans for Freedom."

The State Department has already denied Senator Fulbright's charges that it did not support Firestone and your company's reasons have been released and distributed to the press.

They are: "Our decision not to build a synthetic rubber plant for Communist Romania was based solely on the fact that we did not believe such technical know-how should be sent behind the Iron Curtain where it could become available to Communist nations. The current situation in Viet Nam reinforces that decision in a manner that is far too convincing for all Americans."

Goodyear acted in good faith in declining to build the plant in Communist territory. This decision was made without fanfare and obviously was not calculated to provide a competitive advantage. The activities of a competitor in this area were never the subject of public discussion and even Goodyearites were not aware of the extent of the repercussions in the public marketplace against Firestone until reading about it in the American press.

It is also interesting to note that Senator Fulbright has pinned the extremist label on the Young Americans for Freedom, an organization that numbers 50 members of the U.S. Congress (both Republicans and Democrats) on its advisory board, and has the vocal and financial support of leading educators and public officials throughout the nation.

The chronology of two events in this entire affair provides the most convincing evidence in refuting any charges made against this company by Senator Fulbright:

1. *The Wingfoot Clan* article intended only for INTERNAL consumption appeared on December 3, 1964, almost six weeks AFTER the story had received nation-wide press attention and more than a month before Firestone announced on January 5 it was building a plant in Communist Romania.
2. The second event to be noted is that Firestone announced on April 20, 1965 it was terminating negotiations to build a synthetic rubber plant in Communist Romania. No reason was given.

Goodyear's INTERNAL letter to its own field organization (in response to inquiries from Goodyear dealers and competitive dealers) was not sent until June 11, 1965, more than six weeks AFTER Firestone announced publicly it was not going to build a synthetic rubber plant behind the Iron Curtain.

The facts do not support the Senator's contention that Goodyear applied competitive pressure to prevent Firestone from building the plant and the follow-up stories in the American press represent some very objective reporting on that subject.

Senator Dodd replies to Senator Fulbright

In a speech to the Senate on October 15, Senator Thomas J. Dodd, Democrat of Connecticut, expressed his disagreement with the position taken by Senator Fulbright. Included in his remarks were the following:

The question raised by the senior Senator from Arkansas in this case involved more than a determination of the propriety of decisions taken by two American business firms.

I hope that I have misread the Senator's intent, but it seemed to me that his remarks carried the strong inference that the question of developing trade with the Communist-ruled states of Europe is no longer open to controversy.

Actually, as the President's Special Committee on U.S. Trade Relations with East European Countries pointed out in summarizing the case for and against such an expansion, "there are persuasive elements" in the arguments on each side.

"No one policy is wholly right or wholly wrong," said the committee, "and any course chosen has its own risks."

And just as it would be wrong to take the stand that all those who favor increased trade with the Communist countries are pro-Communist or "soft on communism," it is completely contrary to the facts to suggest that those who oppose such expansion are rightwing extremists whose activities merit investigation.

Even within the liberal political community there are sharply divergent views on the advisability of increased East-West trade. The executive council of the AFL-CIO has come out strongly against expanded trade with the Communist countries.

In addition, liberal scholars of national reputation, like Dr. Hans Morgenthau and Dr. Zbigniew Brzeszinski, have taken the stand that any expansion of East-West trade should be made conditional on political concessions from the Communist side.

Finally, in addition to myself, the senior Senator from Illinois, the senior Senator from Wisconsin, and the senior Senator from Kentucky, have all warned against an unconditional expansion of East-West trade.

The President's special committee made this point: "The committee does not believe that many U.S. firms would be interested in selling their most advanced technology. They bargain hard for satisfactory terms for such technology as they are willing to sell. These practices would hold all the more for trade with Communist countries."

Further on the report pointed out that: "The President should use his authority to permit the sale of nonstrategic technology in support of U.S. trade negotiations with individual Communist countries. The decision to permit the sale is a Government decision to be made on foreign policy grounds. The decision to sell and the terms of sale of such machinery and equipment should be left to the individual U.S. business firms."

This view is restated in recommendation 12 of the committee: "Trade with Communist countries should not be subsidized, nor should it receive official encouragement. The U.S. Government should decide the permitted scope of the trade in terms of security considerations. Within these limits, the amount of trade that takes place should be left to U.S. business and the U.S. consumer to decide."

*   *   *   *   *

Judged in the light of these wise ground rules, the action of both the Goodyear Co. and the Firestone Co. in refusing to sell a synthetic rubber plant to Rumania was unchallengeably proper.

*   *   *   *   *

I have many differences on questions of domestic policy with the Young Americans for Freedom. But they were acting completely within their rights as citizens in opposing the Firestone rubber deal and in bringing pressure to bear on the Firestone Co. in support of their views.

We have accorded every freedom of action to critics of our Vietnam policy, because this is the American tradition.

It is my hope that those who may disagree with the administration in other areas will not, in future, be denigrated as vigilantes, but will instead be granted the same freedom of criticism and the same liberty of action that we grant the critics of administration policy in Vietnam.[35]

*   *   *   *   *

---

[35]*Congressional Record*, October 15, 1965, pp. 27111, 27112, and 27113.

APPENDIX

INTRODUCTORY STATEMENT FROM THE REPORT TO THE PRESIDENT OF THE SPECIAL COMMITTEE ON U.S. TRADE RELATIONS WITH EASTERN EUROPEAN COUNTRIES AND THE SOVIET UNION

The White House
Washington, D. C., April 29, 1965

The President
of the United States

DEAR MR. PRESIDENT:

You have asked us "to explore all aspects of the question of expanding peaceful trade" in support of your policy of "widening our relations" with the countries of Eastern Europe and the Soviet Union.[1]

Any useful consideration of the desirable degree and pattern of peaceful trade relations between ourselves and these countries must begin with the Soviet Union itself.

The Government of the Soviet Union has steadily, over many years, by words and deeds, declared its hostility to our own country. The U.S. Government and the American people support the most powerful defense system the world has even seen in recognition of this fact.

Without this preponderant military power, it would be idle and even dangerous to explore the possibilities of expanding peaceful trade, or for that matter, of any peaceful relations with the Soviet Union. For the same reason, we rule out from these considerations any kind of strategic trade that could significantly enhance Soviet military capabilities and weaken our own position of comparative military strength.

With a secure defense, on the other hand, we can prudently seek practical means of reducing areas of conflict between ourselves and the U.S.S.R. Indeed, we assume the United States has an obligation in today's nuclear world to pursue such possibilities as part of its long-term commitment to strengthen the prospects for peace in the world.

While the Communist threat remains, its nature constantly changes, because the conditions of men and nations everywhere are changing. Thus, our Government must be forever reexamining its policies, programs, and methods to make certain that they are appropriate to the times and to the national purpose.

It is now clear that the ties between the East European nations and the Soviet Union are neither quite so numerous nor so strong as they have been in the past; the forces of nationalism are growing. Between the Soviet Union and Communist China, sharp differences have arisen. There is also a ferment in all of the European Communist countries as they try to cope with the awakening demands of

---

[1]It is understood that policies with respect to trade with Communist China, North Korea, North Vietnam, and Cuba are outside the terms of reference of this Committee. Our findings and recommendations do not apply to trade with these countries. The terms "Communist countries" and "European Communist countries" as used in this report refer to the nations of Eastern Europe and the U.S.S.R.

their people for a better life within the confines of a system geared more for military power than for human welfare.

It is an essential part of U.S. strategy to resist Communist efforts to expand through aggression. At the same time, we know that the danger of aggression will never be overcome until the Communists change their view of the world and the goals they ought to seek. Through our attitudes and actions, therefore, we must aim to influence these countries toward decisions that stress the attainment of prosperity through peaceful means. To appear hostile toward all of their objectives deprives us of the opportunity to influence the choices they make as to kinds of objectives or as to means of achieving them.

The possibilities of "peaceful coexistence" and mutually advantageous trade do not sound convincing coming from those who speak of "burying us." We know very well that coexistence means something different to Soviet leaders from what it means to us. Within the framework of a policy so labeled, they believe they can still pursue hostile actions against the free world so long as major war does not result. But they have found it necessary to change their view of coexistence over the past decade and the conditions of the modern world will cause it to change further over the next decade. Much the same may be said of Soviet motivation and desire, and that of most of the East European nations, for increased trade with the United States. This Committee, therefore, has come to believe that in a longer time perspective the possibilities of "peaceful coexistence" —in the genuine meaning of that expression—can be made to grow. We conclude this in spite of Soviet professions and not because of them.

We are aware that the Communists have their conviction as to how the forces of history will operate and that they profess to be convinced that time is on their side. We also have our own conviction. We believe that men and nations function best in an open society. There are signs that pressures for greater openness within Soviet society are mounting. The reasons may be pragmatic rather than ideological, but they are nonetheless real. The Soviets want a modern and technically advanced society. Their own experience shows that the building of such a society can be severely handicapped by a closed and tyrannical political order and a rigid, centrally directed economic system.

We desire to encourage the growth of forces in the European Communist countries that will improve the prospects for peace. Within these countries we seek to encourage independence from Soviet domination and a rebuilding of historical ties with the West. In each of these countries, including the U.S.S.R., we seek an opening up of the society and a continuing decentralization of power. It is in our interest to promote a concern with internal standards of living rather than with external adventure.

We must look at our trade policies toward European Communist countries in that broad context. Trade is a tactical tool to be used with other policy instruments for pursuing our national objectives.

Trade cannot settle the major outstanding issues between ourselves and the Communists, nor can it, by itself, accomplish a basic change in the Communist system. Over time, however, trade negotiations and trade relations can provide us with useful opportunities to influence attitudes in these countries in directions favorable to our national interest. Trade involves contact of peoples and exchange of ideas and customs as well as of goods and services. It requires the building of mutual trust, and good faith, and confidence. An expansion of trade would require from the Communists a growing commitment to international rules and adherence to international standards for responsible behavior; it cannot be based on Soviet-imposed conditions or usual Communist trading practices.

Trade and government-to-government negotiations which set the framework for trade can be means of reducing animosities between ourselves and individual Communist countries and can provide a basis for working out mutually acceptable solutions to common problems. A constructive attitude toward trade can serve as a counterpart to our national determination to convince these countries through our deterrent military power that they cannot gain their objectives through aggression. Properly conceived and wisely administered, a growing trade with East European nations and the Soviet Union could become a significant and useful device in the pursuit of our national security and welfare and of world peace.

In sum, trade with the European Communist countries is politics in the broadest sense—holding open the possibility of careful negotiation, firm bargaining, and constructive competition. In this intimate engagement men and nations will in time be altered by the engagement itself. We do not fear this. We welcome it. We believe we are more nearly right than they about how to achieve the welfare of nations in this century. If we do our part, time and change will work for us and not against us.

These are the general propositions which underlie the specific findings and recommendations which we now submit. They are based on excellent briefings and supporting papers prepared by government agencies in answer to questions the Committee raised, on materials submitted to the Committee by interested private organizations, and on a careful review of some of the most pertinent published material on this subject. The members of the Committee have found that exposure to this source material and thorough discussion of the issues brought new perspectives and fresh judgments. We would emphasize, on the basis of our experience, that public understanding of how trade can best fit into our national strategy is essential to the effective use of trade as an instrument of national policy.

The members of the Committee are:

J. Irwin Miller (Chairman)
Chairman of the Board,
Cummins Engine Co., Inc.;
Member, Executive Committee,
World Council of Churches

Eugene R. Black
Chairman, Brookings Institution;
Past President, International Bank
for Reconstruction and Development

William Blackie
President, Caterpillar Tractor Co.;
Director and Chairman of the
Foreign Commerce Committee,
U.S. Chamber of Commerce

George R. Brown
Chairman of the Board, Brown &
Root, Inc.; Chairman, Board of
Trustees, Rice University

Charles W. Engelhard, Jr.
Chairman, Engelhard Industries;
Director, Foreign Policy Association

James B. Fisk
President, Bell Telephone Laboratories; Past Member, President's
Science Advisory Committee

Nathaniel Goldfinger
Director of Research, AFL-CIO;
Trustee, Joint Council on
Economic Education

RECOMMENDATIONS

1. The Committee believes that peaceful trade in nonstrategic items can be an important instrument of national policy in our country's relations with individual Communist nations of Europe. Political, not commercial or economic considerations, should determine the formulation and execution of our trade policies.

2. The United States should in no case drop its controls on strategic items that could significantly enhance Communist military capabilities.

3. In respect to nonstrategic trade, the United States should use trade negotiations with individual Communist countries more actively, aggressively, and confidently in the pursuit of our national welfare and world peace.

4. We should not, however, remove our present restrictions on this trade either automatically or across the board. Communist countries are changing, in varying degrees and in different ways. We should adapt our trade policies to the political circumstances and opportunities that present themselves from time to time in the individual countries. At present significantly greater trade opportunities exist in certain East European countries than in the Soviet Union.

5. Negotiations with each of these countries should involve hard bargaining, from which the U.S. Government should expect to receive satisfactory assurances regarding the removal of commercial obstacles arising from differences in our economic systems. We should bargain for agreements on matters related to trade, such as reasonable settlements of outstanding financial claims and procedures to avoid dumping, and, as appropriate, understandings on a variety of cultural, informational, and other matters at issue between us.

6. Provision should be made in trade agreements with Communist countries for frequent review at specific intervals. This would provide the opportunity to negotiate for new gains and to settle additional matters of disagreement.

7. An aim of American policy in trade negotiations with Communist countries should be to bring their trade practices into line with normal world trade practices.

8. To accomplish these purposes, we must be able to use our trade policies flexibly and purposefully in support of such negotiations. The President should have the authority to remove or, if necessary, impose trade restrictions as required for the achievement of our foreign policy objectives.

9. In administering export controls, the determination of what is strategic should be made primarily by the Department of Defense. The power to withhold or release nonstrategic goods or advanced technology for trade should be exercised by the President as an instrument for accomplishing foreign policy objectives.

10. The President should be given discretionary authority to grant or withdraw most-favored-nation tariff treatment to and from individual Communist countries when he determines it to be in the national interest. There should be a distinction between this MFN tariff treatment and the MFN tariff treatment we grant by statute to free world countries. It should be granted to Communist countries only for the duration of the trade agreement of which it is a part, and it should be subject to periodic review.

11. The President should continue to exercise his authority to allow Government-guaranteed commercial credits up to 5 years' duration, if such terms are normal to the trade and if they are considered to further the national interest.

12. Trade with Communist countries should not be subsidized, nor should it receive artificial encouragement. The U.S. Government should decide the permitted scope of the trade in terms of security considerations. Within these limits, the amount of trade that takes place should be left to U.S. business and the U.S. consumer to decide. In terms of foreign policy considerations, however, it should be recognized that trade with European Communist nations can be as much in the national interest as any other trade.

13. In view of the changes now taking place and of changes that will continue to take place in the Communist societies, the United States should, at regular intervals, review its total trade policies toward the whole Communist world to ensure that they remain consistent with, and effective in support of, foreign policy objectives.

14. If trade with Communist countries is to be used for these objectives, the U.S. public, the Congress and the executive branch must have a thorough understanding of the problem, the opportunities that trade affords, and U.S. national objectives in this field. The U.S. Government should take every opportunity to make explicit what it intends to do and what it seeks to accomplish. It should act to remove any stigma from trade with Communist countries where such trade is determined to be in the national interest. The foreign policy advantages of such trade to the United States are not widely enough appreciated. With greater public awareness of both facts and objectives, the United States will be in a stronger position to use this trade as it must be used—for national purposes and to support national policy.

*   *   *   *   *

In conclusion, we emphasize that these findings and recommendations constitute a long-term strategy.

The intimate engagement of trade, over a considerable period of time, when taken with the process of change already under way, can influence the internal development and the external policies of European Communist societies along paths favorable to our purpose and to world peace. Trade is one of the few channels available to us for constructive contacts with nations with whom we find frequent hostility. In the long run, selected trade, intelligently negotiated and wisely administered, may turn out to have been one of our most powerful tools of national policy.

The members of your Committee have found this assignment difficult, challenging, and important. We hope this report will be useful to you and to the Nation.

Respectfully submitted,   (signed)

J. Irwin Miller, Chairman
Eugene R. Black
William Blackie
George R. Brown
Charles W. Engelhard, Jr.
James B. Fisk
Nathaniel Goldfinger
Crawford H. Greenewalt
William A. Hewitt
Max F. Millikan
Charles G. Mortimer
Herman B. Wells

Statement of comment by Mr. Goldfinger

I have reservations about several issues in the Report and respectfully submit the following comments.

At the outset I wish to make it clear that I am not opposed to the expansion of economic and financial relations with the Soviet bloc under all conditions. However, I am concerned about the conditions.

Trade relations with the Soviet Union and its European satellites should be viewed as a tool of our Nation's foreign policy. Therefore, the Report should have placed greater emphasis on the political aspect of this issue.

There is also inadequate caution in the Report about the risk of exporting American technology—particularly advanced technology—to those countries. In centrally planned, totalitarian states, military and economic factors are closely related. There is no reason to believe that the export of American machinery and equipment to those countries will necessarily redound to the benefit of their peoples.

Moreover, in our readiness to engage in bilateral trade negotiations with individual countries of the Soviet bloc, we should have no illusions about the ability of trade, in itself, to alter Communist attitudes and policies. Neither is trade, as such, a sure force for peace, as indicated by the two World Wars between trading nations.

Recognition of these realities should result in greater emphasis on the principle of *quid pro quo* concessions than is contained in the Report. In my opinion, there should be no expansion of trade, extension of Government-guaranteed credit or most-favored-nation tariff treatment without political *quid pro quo* concessions from them.

The Report's discussion of most-favored-nation tariff treatment omits or only briefly deals with several thorny problems concerning potential imports from those countries—such as goods produced by slave labor, dumping, market disruption, international fair labor standards and the need for an adequate trade adjustment assistance mechanism at home.

In conclusion, I believe considerations of national security and international policy objectives should have top priority in evaluating trade relations with the Soviet bloc—over any temporary or marginal commercial advantages that may exist.

Book Two

implementing corporate strategy

The accomplishment of purpose:
organizational structure
and relationships

W e must now turn our attention to the concepts and skills essential to the implementation of strategy. The life of action requires more than analytical intelligence. It is not enough to have an idea and be able to evaluate its worth. Men with responsibility for the achievement of goals, the accomplishment of results, and the solution of problems, finally know the worth of a strategy when its utility is demonstrated. Furthermore, a unique corporate strategy determined in relation to a concrete situation is never complete, even as a formulation, until it is embodied in the organizational activities which reveal its soundness and begin to affect its nature.

Interdependence of formulation and implementation

It is convenient from the point of view of orderly study to divide a consideration of corporate strategy, as we have divided it, into aspects of formulation and implementation and to note, for example, the requirement of the former for analytical and conceptual ability and of the latter for administrative skill. But in real life the processes of formulation and implementation are intertwined. Feedback from operations gives notice of changing ✓ environmental factors to which strategy should be adjusted. The formulation of strategy is not finished when implementation begins. A business organization is always changing in response to its own makeup and past development. Similarly, it should be changing in response to changes in the larger systems in which it moves, and in response to its success or failure in affecting its enviroment. For the sake of orderly presentation, we have arranged the cases so that henceforth the data will require us to focus less on what the strategy should be than on ways to make it effective in action and to alter it as required. We are taking forward with us, however, all our previous interests. We shall continue to examine each firm's strategy against the criteria we have developed in order to practice the skills we have gained and to verify the decisions made by the executives of the company.

We have already seen that the determination of strategy has four sub-activities: the examination of the environment for opportunity and risk, the systematic assessment of corporate strengths and weaknesses, the identification and weighting of personal values, and the clarification of public responsibilities. Implementation may also be thought of as having important subactivities. In very broad terms, these are the design of organizational structure and relationships, the effective administration of organizational processes affecting behavior, and the development of effective personal leadership.

In deciding on strategy, the general manager must force his mind to range over the whole vast territory of the technological, social, economic, and political systems which provide opportunity for his company or threaten its continued existence. When he turns his attention to carrying out the strategy tentatively determined, he addresses himself, within the limitations of his knowledge, to all the techniques and skills of administration. To deal with so wide a range of activity, he needs a simple and flexible approach to the aspects of organized activity which he must take into account. By considering the relaitonships between strategy and organizational structure, strategy and organizational processes, and strategy and personal leadership styles, the student should be able to span a territory crowded with ideas without losing sight of the purpose which he seeks in crossing it.

Each of the implementing subactivities constitutes in itself a special world in which many people are doing research, developing knowledge, and asserting the importance of their work over that of other specialists. Thus the nature of organization, about which every general manager must make some assumptions, is the subject of a richly entangled array of ideas upon which one could spend a lifetime. The design of information systems—particularly at a time when the speed and capacity of the computer fascinates the processors of information—appears to require long study, an esoteric language, and even rearrangement of organizational activities for the sake of information processing. Similarly, performance appraisal, motivation and incentive systems, control systems, and systems of executive recruitment and development all have their armies of theoretical and empirical proponents, each one fully equipped with manuals, code books, rules, and techniques. Leadership itself has been approached less formally, but its nature has been estimated from every point of view ever applied to the interpretation of organized human affairs.

It will, of course, be impossible for us to consider in detail the knowledge and theory which have been developed during the course of a half century of researches in administration. It will be assumed that your own experience has introduced you to the major schools of thought contending in the developing administrative disciplines, and that where necessary, the knowledge you have will be supplemented by further study. Just as the general manager must be able to draw upon the skills of special staffs in leading his company, so he must be able to draw upon these special studies in effecting his own combination of organizational design and organizational practices. The simple prescription we wish to add here is that the nature of the corporate strategy must be made to dominate the design of organizational structure and processes. That is, the principal criterion for all decisions on organizational structure and behavior should be their relevance to the achievement of the organizational purpose, not their conformity to the dictates of special disciplines.

Thus the theses we suggest for your consideration are first that conscious strategy can be consciously implemented through skills primarily administrative in nature. Second, the chief determinant of organizational structure and the processes by which tasks are assigned and performance motivated, rewarded, and controlled should be *the strategy of the firm*, not the history of the company, its position in its industry, the specialized background of its executives, the principles of organization as developed in textbooks, the recommendations of consultants, or the conviction that one form of organization is intrinsically better than another.

The successful implementation of strategy requires that the general manager shape to the peculiar needs of his strategy the formal structure of his organization, its informal relationships, and the processes of motivation and control which provide incentives and measure results. He must bring about the commitment to organizational aims and policies of properly qualified individuals and groups to whom portions of the total task have been assigned. He must insure not only that goals are clear and purposes are understood, but also that individuals are developing in terms of capacity and achievement and are reaping proper rewards in terms of compensation and personal satisfactions. Above all, he must do what he can to insure that departmental interests, interdepartmental rivalries, and the machinery of measurement and evaluation do not deflect energy from organizational purpose into harmful or irrelevant activity.

To clarify our approach to the problem of adapting the concepts and findings of special disciplines to the requirements of policy, we list here 12 aspects of implementation which may serve as a convenient map of the territory to be traversed. It should be remembered that cases you will analyze have not been researched or written to prove these propositions. The list is designed only to make it possible for you to use your own specialized knowledge and adapt it, within limits imposed by your own characteristic attitudes toward risk and responsibility, to strategic requirements.

1. Once strategy is tentatively or finally set, the key tasks to be performed and kinds of decisions required must be identified.

2. Once the size of operations exceeds the capacity of one man, responsibility for accomplishing key tasks and making decisions must be assigned to individuals or groups. The division of labor must permit efficient performance of subtasks and must be accompanied by some hierarchical allocation of authority to insure achievement.

3. Formal provisions for the coordination of activities thus separated must be made in various ways, e.g., through a hierarchy of supervision,

project and committee organizations, task forces, and other *ad hoc* units. The prescribed activities of these formally constituted bodies are not intended to preclude spontaneous voluntary coordination.

4. Information systems adequate for coordinating divided functions (i.e., for letting those performing part of the task know what they must know of the rest, and for letting those in supervisory positions know what is happening so that next steps may be taken) must be designed and installed.

5. The tasks to be performed should be arranged in a time sequence comprising a program of action or a schedule of targets. So that long-range planning may not be neglected, this activity should probably be entrusted to a special staff unit. Its influence may be enhanced by attaching it to the president's office, its usefulness by having it work in close cooperation with the line. While long-range plans may be couched in relatively general terms, shorter range plans will often take the form of relatively detailed budgets. These can meet the need for the establishment of standards against which future performance can be judged.

6. Actual performance, as quantitatively reported in information systems and qualitatively estimated through observation by supervisors and the judgment of customers, should be compared to budgeted performance and to standards in order to test achievement, budgeting processes, and the adequacy of the standards themselves.

7. Individuals and groups of individuals must be recruited and assigned to essential tasks in accordance with the specialized or supervisory skills which they possess or can develop. At the same time, the assignment of tasks may well be adjusted to the nature of available skills.

8. Individual performance, evaluated both quantitatively and qualitatively, should be subjected to influences (constituting a pattern of incentives) which will help to make it effective in accomplishing organizational goals.

9. Since individual motives are complex and multiple, incentives for achievement should range from those that are universally appealing—such as adequate compensation and an organizational climate favorable to the simultaneous satisfaction of individual and organizational purposes—to specialized forms of recognition, financial or nonfinancial, designed to fit individual needs and unusual accomplishments.

10. In addition to financial and nonfinancial incentives and rewards to motivate individuals to voluntary achievement, a system of constraints, controls, and penalties must be devised to contain nonfunctional activity and to enforce standards. Controls, like incentives, are both formal and informal. Effective control requires both quantitative and nonquantitative information which must always be used together.

11. Provision for the continuing development of requisite technical and managerial skills is a high-priority requirement. The development of individuals must take place chiefly within the milieu of their assigned responsibilities. This on-the-job development should be supplemented by intermittent formal instruction and study.

12. Dynamic personal leadership is necessary for continued growth and improved achievement in any organization. Leadership may be expressed in many styles, but it must be expressed in some perceptible style. This style must be natural and also consistent with the requirements imposed upon the organization by its strategy and membership.

The general manager is principally concerned with determining and monitoring the adequacy of strategy, with adapting the firm to changes in its environment, and with securing and developing the people needed to carry out the strategy or to help with its constructive revision. The manager must also insure that the processes which encourage and constrain individual performance and personal development are consistent with human and strategic needs. In large part, therefore, his leadership consists of achieving commitment to strategy via clarification and dramatization of its requirements and value.

We shall return to each of these considerations, looking first at some general relationships between strategy and organizational structure. We shall look also at the need for specialization of tasks, the coordination of divided responsibility, and design of effective information systems.

Strategy and organizational structure

It is at once apparent that the accomplishment of strategic purpose requires ✓ organization. If a consciously formulated strategy is to be effective, organizational development should be planned rather than left to evolve by itself. So long as a company is small enough for a single individual to direct both planning for the future and current operations, questions of organizational structure remain unimportant. Thus the one-man organization encounters no real organizational problem until the proprietor's quick walks through the plant, his wife's bookkeeping, and his sales agent's marketing activities are no longer adequate to growing volume. When the magnitude of operations increases, then departmentalization—usually into such clusters of activities as manufacturing, production, and finance—begins to appear. Most functional organizations ultimately encounter size problems again. With geographical dispersion, product complexity, and increased volume of sales, coordination must be accomplished somewhere besides at the top. We then find multiunit organizations with coordinating responsibility delegated to divisions, subsidiaries, profit centers, and the like. The difficulty of designing an organizational structure is basically consequent upon and proportionate to the *diversity* and *size* of the undertaking.[1]

The subject of organization is the most extensive and complex of all the subtopics of implementation. It has at various times attracted the interest of economists, sociologists, psychologists, political scientists, philosophers, and, in a curiously restricted way, of creative writers as well. These have

---

[1]A model of corporate development has been described by Professor Bruce R. Scott of the Harvard Business School faculty in his unpublished paper, "A Stages Model of Corporate Development," January 1968.

contributed to the field a variety of theoretical formulations and empirical investigations. The policy maker will probably find himself unable to subscribe wholeheartedly to the precepts of any one school of thought or to the particulars of any one model of the firm. Indeed, established theories of the firm are inadequate for general management purposes. The impact of most organizational studies, from the point of view of the eclectic practitioner looking for counsel rather than confusion, has been to undermine confidence in other studies. The activities of present-day social science have in particular badly damaged the precepts of classical scientific management. Progress in the reconciliation of divergent insights into the nature of organization, however, can be expected in due course.

Regardless of disputes about theory among scholars, the executive in, say, a company that has reached some complexity, knows three things. The tasks essential to accomplishing his purposes must in some way be subdivided; they must be assigned, if possible, to individuals whose skills are appropriately specialized; and tasks that have been subdivided must ultimately be reintegrated into a unified whole. The manager knows also that once he lets performance out of his own hands, and once no one in the organization is performing the total task, information about what the left hand is doing must be made available to the right. Otherwise problems and risks cannot be detected and dealt with.

Subdivision of task responsibility

In every industry conventional ways of dividing task by function have developed to the extent that the training of individuals skilled in these functions perpetuates organizational arrangements. But identification of the tasks *should* be made in terms of a company's distinctive purposes and unique strategy, not by following industry convention. True, the fact that every manufacturing firm procures and processes raw materials and sells and delivers finished products means that at least production and sales and probably procurement and distribution will always be critical functional areas which must be assigned to specialized organizational units. But these basic uniformities which cut across company and industry lines provide the individual firm with little useful guidance on the issues it finds so perplexing, namely, how much weight to assign to which function, or how to adapt nearly universal structural arrangements to its own particular needs.

A manufacturer who plans to perform services for the government under cost-plus-fixed-fee contracts, to cite a very limited example, feels less need for a fully developed cost control system and cost-related incentives than one whose contracts are governed by a fixed price. To illustrate more broadly the way in which strategic choice determines the relative importance of tasks, consider the manufacturer of a line of industrial products who decides to diversify in view of declining opportunity in his original field. Product improvement and the engineering organization responsible for it become less vital than the search for new products, either internally or through acquisition. But if the latter task is not recognized as crucial, then it is unlikely to be assigned to any individual or unit, but will rather be considered as an additional duty for many. Under the latter circumstances, accomplishment may well be impaired.

Once the key tasks have been identified (or the identification customary in the industry has been ratified as proper for the individual firm), then responsibility for accomplishing these tasks must be assigned to individuals and groups. In addition to a rational principle for separating tasks from one another, the need will soon become apparent for some scale of relative importance among activities to be established.

Distribution of formal authority among those to whom tasks have been assigned is essential for the effective control of operations, the development of individual skills, the distribution of rewards, and for other organizational processes to which we shall soon give attention. The extent to which individuals, once assigned a task, need to be supervised and controlled is the subject of voluminous argument which, temporarily at least, must leave the general practitioner aware that too much control and too little are equally ineffective and that, as usual, he is the man who must strike the balance.

The division of labor is thus accompanied by the specialization of task and the distribution of authority, with the relative importance of tasks as defined by strategy marked by status. The rational principle by which tasks are specialized and authority delegated may be separation by functions, by product or product lines, by geographical or regional subdivision, by customer and market, or by type of production equipment or processes. The intermixture of these principles in multiunit organizations has resulted in many hybrid types of formal structure which we need not investigate. The principal requirement is that the basis for division should be relatively consistent, easily understood, and conducive to the grouping of like activities. Above all, the formal pattern should have visible relationship to corporate purpose, should fix responsibility in such a way as not to preclude teamwork, and should provide for the solution of problems as close to the point of action as possible. Structure should not be any more restrictive than necessary of the satisfaction of individual needs or of the inevitable emergence of informal organization. The design should also allow for more complex structure as the organization grows in size.

As you consider the need to create, build, and develop an organizational structure for the firms in the cases you will study shortly, you will wish to avoid choosing a *typical* pattern of organization on the grounds that it is "typical" or "generally sound." And preference you may have for divisional versus functional organizations, for decentralized rather than centralized questions, for a "flat" rather than a "steep" or many-stepped hierarchy, should be set aside until you have identified the activities made essential by the strategy, the skills available for their performance, and the needs and values of the individuals involved. The plan you devise should ignore neither the history of the company nor that of its industry, for in ongoing organizations formal structure may not be abruptly changed without great cost. Any new plan that you devise for gradual implementation should be as economical as is consistent with the requirements for technical skill, proper support for principal functions, and reserve capacity for further growth. The degree of centralization and decentralization that you prescribe should not turn on your personal preference, and presumably will vary from one activity to another. Strategic requirements as well as the abilities and experience of company executives should determine the extent to which responsibility for decisions should tend toward the center or toward the field. In a consumer credit company, for example, freedom to extend credit to doubtful risks can really be allowed only to relatively experienced branch managers though company strategy may prescribe it for all.

That so little need be said about the nature of the formal organization, and so much must be determined by the particulars of each individual situation, should not be taken as evidence that formal organization does not matter—a conclusion implied by some students of organizational behavior. On the contrary, progress in a growing organization is impossible without substrategies for organizational development. Restructuring the organization becomes a goal in itself to be worked toward over a period of years—perhaps without the interim publication of the ultimate design.

But though it is impractical, except in cases of harsh emergency, to make sweeping organizational changes with little preparation and upon short notice, this is not to say that no major role is played by structure, by clear and logical subdivisions of task, or by an openly acknowledged hierarchy of authority, status, and prestige—all serving as the conscious embodiment of strategy and the harbinger of growth to come. As you check the relation between strategy and structure, whether in your study of cases or in your business experience, ask yourself always the policy questions: Is the strategy sound and clear? If goals are clear, have the tasks required been clearly identified and assessed for their relative importance? If key activities are known, have they been assigned to people with the requisite training, experience, and staff support they will need? The answers to these questions do not carry one very far along the road toward successful strategy implementation, but they provide a convenient starting point from which the rest of the trip can be made.

Coordination of divided responsibility

As soon as a task is divided, some formal provision must be made for coordination. In baseball, the park outside the diamond is subdivided into left, center, and right fields, and a man is assigned to each. But if there is no procedure for handling a ball hit halfway between any two areas, the formal division of labor will help only the opposing team. Most important work of organizations requires cooperation among the departmental specialists to whom a portion of the total task has been allocated. Many forces are at work to make coordination so essential that it cannot be left to chance.

For example, the flow of work from one station to another and from one administrative jurisdiction to another creates problems of scheduling and timing, of accommodating departmental needs, and of overall supervision lest departmental needs become more influential than organizational goals.

As soon as a second individual joins the first one in an organization, he brings with him his own goals, and these must be served, at least to a minimal degree, by the activity required of him in service to the organization. As soon as a group of such individuals, different in personal needs but similar in technical competence and point of view is established to perform a given function, then departmental goals may attract more loyalty than the overall goals of the organization. To keep individual purposes and needs as well as departmental substrategies consistent with corporate strategy is a considerable undertaking. It is a major top-management responsibility in all organizations, regardless of the apparent degree of commitment and willingness to co-operate in the common cause.

The different needs of individuals and the distinctive goals of functional specialties mean that, at best, the organization's total strategy is understood differently and valued for different reasons by different parts of the organization. Some formal or informal means for resolving these differences is important. Where the climate is right, specialists will be aware of the relative validity of organizational and departmental needs and of the bias inevitable in any loyalty to expertise.

Formal organization provides for the coordination of divided responsibility through the hierarchy of supervision, through the establishment and use of committees, and through the project form of organization (which, like temporary task forces, can be superimposed upon a functional or divisional organization). The wider the sphere of any supervisor's jurisdiction, the more time he is likely to need to bring into balance aspects of organized life which would otherwise influence performance toward the wrong goals. The true function of a committee—and were this role more widely understood and effectively played, committees would be less frequently maligned—is to bring to the exploration and solution of interdepartmental problems both the specialist and generalist abilities of its members. The need for formal committees would be largely obviated in an ideal organization, where each member was conscious of the impact of his own proposals, plans, and decisions upon the interests of others. To the extent that an individual manager seeks out advice and approval from those whose interests must be balanced with his, he performs in man-to-man and face-to-face encounters the essential coordination which is sometimes formalized in a committee structure.

Coordination can play a more creative role than merely composing differences. It is the quality of the way in which subdivided functions and interests are resynthesized that often distinguishes one organization from another in terms of results. The reintegration of the parts into the whole, when what is at stake is the execution of corporate strategy, is what creates a whole that is greater than the sum of its parts. Rivalry between competing subunits or individuals—if monitored to keep it *constructive* rivalry—can exhibit creative characteristics. It can be the source of a new solution to a problem, one that transcends earlier proposals that reflected only the rival unit's parochial concerns. The ability to handle the coordinating function in a way that brings about a new synthesis among competing interests, a synthesis in harmony with the special competence of the total organization, is the administrator's most subtle and creative contribution to the successful functioning of an organization.

Effective design of information systems

If corporate strategy is to be effectively implemented, there must be organizational arrangements to provide members with the information they will need to perform their tasks and relate their work to that of others. Information flows inward from the environment to all organizational levels; within the company it should move both down and up. In view of the bulk of information moving upward, it must be reduced to manageable compass as it nears the top. This condensation can be accomplished only by having data synthesized at lower levels, so that part of what moves upward is interpretation rather than fact. To achieve synthesis without introducing distortion or bias or serious omission is a formidable problem to which management must remain alert. Well handled, the information system brings to the attention of those who have authority to act not the vast mass of routine data processed by the total system, but the significant red-flag items that warn of outcomes contrary to expectations. A well-designed information system is thus the key to "management by exception." This in turn is one key to the prevailing problem of the overburdened executive.

In the gathering and transmitting of information, accounting and control departments play a major task. One obstacle to effective performance here is devotion to specialty and procedure for its own sake, as accountants look more to their forms than to larger purposes. The Internal Revenue Service, the Securities and Exchange Commission, the Census Bureau, and the Justice Department, all with requirements which must be met, impose uniformities on the ways in which information is collected and analyzed. But nothing in the conventions of accounting, the regulations of the government, or the rapidly advancing mathematical approaches to problem solving in any way prevents the generation and distribution within an organization of the kind of information management finds most useful.

Now, with the speed of the computer, data can be made available early enough to do some good. We shall have much more to say about the uses of information when we turn to the organizational processes that determine individual behavior. It is important to note that the generation of data is not an end in itself. Its function should be to permit individuals who necessarily perform only one of the many tasks required by the organizational mission to know what they need to know in order to perform their functions in balance with all others, and to gain that overview of total operations which will inform and guide the decisions they have discretion to make. Designing the flow of information is just as important as choosing a principle of subdivision in outlining organizational structure. Information is often the starting point in trying to determine how the organization should be changed. It is a way to monitor the continuing adequacy of strategy and to warn when change is necessary.

THE SOLARTRON ELECTRONIC
GROUP LTD. (A)*

∧∧∧

ORGANIZATION, OBJECTIVES, AND PRODUCT PLANNING

"I do not think we could have expanded as we have if it had not been for
forward planning" said Mr. John Bolton, chairman and managing director of
The Solartron Electronic Group Limited, in November 1958. "Nor would
I have the same degree of confidence in our future as I do if we were not
continuing to plan ahead."

The Solartron Electronic Group and its subsidiary companies, with headquarters in Thames Ditton, Surrey, England, designed and manufactured
two main types of electronic equipment: (1) A range of approximately 80
laboratory and other precision test instruments ranging in price from £50
to £700, such as oscilloscopes, power supplies, amplifiers, and servo test
equipment. In the year ending June 30, 1958, such instruments comprised
66% of total company sales and 69.9% of total company deliveries. (2)
A variety of "systems engineered" products with higher unit prices, which were
broadly defined as electronic systems designed to perform a series of operations comprising a definable task. In a majority of cases these systems were
designed, constructed, installed, and serviced by Solartron for customers
relatively unfamiliar with electronic equipment. They comprised single products or families of products, each one of which was so chosen that it could
constitute an important field of activity for companies in the Solartron group.
They included:

a) An electronic reading machine designed to read digits 0 to 9, eight alpha-
betical letters, and four accounting symbols at speeds up to 300 characters per
second. The first production model of this machine had been sold to Boots
Chemists (a chain of pharmacies) at a price of £223,000 and was scheduled
for delivery in November 1959. It was to be used in connection with a digital
computer to analyse daily the sales registered on tapes from approximately 2,000
cash registers. During the 1958–59 year, six additional orders from large firms
were expected to bring total sales to seven.

---

b) *Radar simulator devices* designed to reproduce the radar image of aircraft or missiles, operating singly or in formation, for defense planning and training purposes. By November 1958, £400,000 of orders, varying from £60,-000 to £180,000 per system, had been received from defense and military authorities of European countries including Germany, Italy, and Sweden.

c) *High-speed electronic checkweighers* designed to checkweigh packaged products at an accuracy of ±0.2% as the filled packages moved on a production line at a speed of up to 120 per minute; to deflect and count underweight and overweight packages; and to signal continuously to the packing mechanism any correction required to keep the delivered weight constantly correct. Thirty-two production units at £1,500 each were planned for 1958–59, for sale largely to food and other consumer goods manufacturers.

d) *An X-ray spectrometer* designed to provide an automatic, nondestructive method for the quantitative analysis of crystalline materials, such as metals and chemicals. Six units at approximately £10,000 each were planned for 1958–59, for sale to scientific and engineering organizations.

e) *Cybernetic teaching machines* designed to teach punch-card operators the manual skills needed for punch-card preparation by giving a series of exercises, evaluating progress and mistakes, and automatically varying the speed of the exercise while concentrating on those parts in which errors were made. This machine was the first of a planned series of inductive logic computing devices. Ten to 12 units at £500 each were planned for 1958–59, for sale to companies employing punch-card equipment.

f) *A range of analogue computer "building blocks"* from which a custom-built analogue computer could be assembled, designed chiefly for use in solving complex mathematical problems.

Solartron also performed precision engineering and design and development work on a contract basis, and sold electronic equipment made by other firms through its domestic and foreign sales organizations.

Exhibit 1 shows actual and forecast sales by product group and company. Exhibit 2 shows the companies of the Solartron group, their dates of incorporation, deliveries in the fiscal year ending June 30, 1958, and principal products or functions. Exhibits 3 and 4 present the Group's consolidated balance sheets and profit and loss statements for recent years, with forecasts through June 1963. Exhibit 5 shows operating profits and losses of the various subsidiary companies for the nine months ended March 31, 1958. The table at the bottom of page 584 indicates the rate of Solartron's growth from 1950 through mid-1958.

Organization

In November 1958 Solartron included The Solartron Electronic Group Ltd. (the parent company), eight domestic, and three overseas subsidiaries. The parent company was owned largely by members of management and their families. A number of employees were also shareholders. From 1951 to 1958 a majority of the common shares had been held by Mr. Bolton. After December 1958, holdings were distributed as follows:

Per Cent

Mr. Bolton 40
Other managers, employees, and families 40
Outside shareholders 20

Solartron's senior executive group was the eight-man Group board of directors which met monthly and included two men for each of the following major functions: general management (including personnel administration), production, and finance, and one each for marketing and research and development. The average age of these men in November 1958 was 38 years. As indicated in the company letterhead, they held the degrees shown below, and most of them held executive positions in Solartron's subsidiary companies:

J. E. Bolton, D.S.C.,[1] M.A. (Cantab.), M.B.A. (Harvard), Member British Institute of Management (M.B.I.M.), chairman and Group managing director, and temporarily chairman of Solartron Industrial Controls Ltd., and Solartron Radar Simulators Ltd.

L. B. Copestick, Associate Member Institute of Electronics (A.M. Inst. E.), Associate Member British Institute of Radio Engineers (A.M. Brit. I.R.E.), chairman and managing director, Solartron Research and Development Ltd.

J. E. Crosse, chairman and managing director, Solartron Engineering Ltd.

R. A. Henderson, director of Robert Benson Lonsdale, Merchant Bankers.[2]

Eric E. Jones, Member Sales Managers Association (M.S.M.A.), Group marketing director, managing director of Solartron-Rheem Ltd.

E. R. T. Ponsford, chairman and managing director, Solartron Laboratory Instruments Ltd.

STATISTICS INDICATIVE OF SOLARTRON GROWTH
(Years Ending June 30)

	1950	1951	1952	1953	1954	1955	1956	1957	1958
Personnel	18	22	66	110	240	400	550	600	830
Floor space (sq. ft. 000)	4	4	6	8	30	35	65	70	85
Assets (£000)	8	12	34	74	226	420	654	902	1,344
Deliveries (£000)	13	20	34	90	152	399	758	1,005	1,434
Exports (£000)					10	20	80	186	335
Development write-off (£000) (specific products)						24	38	76	72
Net profits after taxes and development write-off (£000)*		1	1	3	5	4	12	6	23
Nonspecific development expenditure (£000)†					10	25	50	75	120

*Includes retained profit plus sundry appropriations (see Exhibit 3).
†Written off in overheads—e.g., market research, planning new factories, etc.

---

[1]Distinguished Service Cross (war decoration).
[2]An investment banking firm.

Exhibit 1

SCHEDULE OF DELIVERIES 1954-55 TO 1957-58 AND TARGETS THROUGH 1962-63*
(In £000's)

Product Group	Actual				Possible Targets for Next Five Years				
	1954-55	1955-56	1956-57	1957-58	1958-59	1959-60	1960-61	1961-62	1962-63
Solartron Laboratory Instruments Ltd.:									
Standard instruments	£300	£589	£741	£945	£1,400	£2,000	£2,750	£3,500	£4,500
Government and outside contracts	42	63	37	57	60	100	150	250	250
Solartron Engineering Ltd.:									
Government and outside contracts	35	87	115	96	60	100	125	150	200
Solartron Research & Development Ltd.:									
Government and outside contracts	5	10	44	75	100	100	125	125	150
Data processing	...	...	...	32	130	250	300	400	500
Radar Simulators Ltd.	...	...	6	111	250	400	500	600	750
Solartron Industrial Controls Ltd.	...	...	6	12	60	150	250	300	350
Solartron Electronic Business Machines Ltd.	...	...	2	10	50	200	300	400	500
Solartron Electronic Group Ltd.:									
Merchanting and sundries	16	9	54	96	140	200	250	275	300
Total Deliveries	£398	£758	£1,005	£1,434	£2,250	£3,500	£4,750	£6,000	£7,500
Export content included in above figures	£ 20	£ 80	£ 186	£ 335	£ 600	£1,000	£1,500	£2,250	£3,500
Total orders	400	800	1,250	1,900	2,750	4,000	5,500	7,000	8,500
Total personnel at year-end	400	550	600	830	1,250	1,750	2,250	2,750	3,500

*It was apparent in March 1959 that it would probably be necessary to extend the 1962-63 targets to 1963-64, that is, to spread the five-year program over six years. Figures for 1959-60 through 1962-63 are "maximum" targets.

Source: Company records.

Exhibit 2

COMPANIES OF THE SOLARTRON ELECTRONIC GROUP LTD.

(Subsidiaries Wholly Owned Except Otherwise Indicated)

Companies in United Kingdom	Date of Incorporation	Personnel Strength in Nov. 1958	External Deliveries in Year Ending June 30, 1958 (000)	1957–58 Deliveries as a Percentage of Total	Functions
Solartron Laboratory Instruments Ltd. (SLI)	1948	375	£1,002	69.9	Manufactured approximately 80 standard laboratory and precision instruments at Thames Ditton plant in production lots of batch size (0–50 per month). Sales were made largely to scientific and engineering organizations in the U.K. through a sales force of approximately 20 technical service representatives.
Solartron Engineering Ltd. (SE)	1951	194	£96	6.7	Supplied the mechanical engineering requirements of the individual companies within the Group. Also undertook a selected amount of outside work to ensure competitiveness and to utilize fully its capacity. Located at recently built Farnborough plant.
Solartron Electronic Group Ltd. (parent company)	1954	280	£96	6.7	General management and staff activities, merchanting, and sundries.
Solartron Research and Development Ltd. (SR.&D.)	1954	144	£107	7.5	Performed outside contract R.&D. work; all research and development on standard electronic instruments; plus a portion of the work on "systems engineered" products (chiefly data handling and analogue computers). Also produced prototypes and initial production runs of instruments and other equipment (such as magnetic data tape recorder). Located in Dorking, Surrey.

Company	Year		£	%	Description
Solartron Electronic Business Machines Ltd. (SEBM)	1955	20	£10	0.7	One of three "development" companies at the Farnborough plant. Responsible for developing, manufacturing, and marketing (in cooperation with Group commercial department) electronic business machines primarily for office use. Principal product in 1958 was the reading machine.
Industrial Automation Developments Ltd. (jointly owned with Scribbans-Kemp Ltd.)	1956	...	...	...	Responsible for developing under contract hydraulic programmed actuator for industrial packaging use. Work actually being carried out by SIC.
Solartron Industrial Controls Ltd. (SIC) ..	1956	29	£12	0.8	Responsible for developing, manufacturing, and marketing industrial controls* under "quasi-consulting assignments." Principal products checkweigher, X-ray spectrometer, and punch-card teaching machine.
Solartron Radar Simulators Ltd. (RS)	1957	58	£111	7.7	Responsible for developing, manufacturing, and marketing radar simulator devices for defense and training purposes. Principal product aircraft simulator sold to NATO countries.
Solartron Rheem Ltd. (jointly owned with Rheem Co. of New York)	1958	...	...	...	Responsible for developing products of joint interest to Solartron and Rheem.
Total		1,100	£1,434†	100†	

Overseas Subsidiaries:

Solartron Inc. (Associated Company in U.S.A.)	1956	6
Solartron SRL (Italy)	1957	3
Solartron GMBH (West Germany)	1958	12

Associated companies in India, France, and Sweden, and a subsidiary in Holland were in process of formation.

*An industrial control was broadly defined as a device to improve the quality of an industrial process by sensing some property of the product, processing the data thus obtained, and actuating the controls of the plant or machine involved to achieve a desired end. The variety of sensing effects that might be used ranged from simple weighing to spectroscopic examination by X-ray.

†Includes £335 or 23.4% exports.

Source: Company records.

Exhibit 3

OUTLINE PROFIT AND LOSS ACCOUNTS FOR THE YEARS ENDED JUNE 30, 1955-58 AND TARGETS THROUGH 1962-63

(In £000's)

	Actual				Possible Targets for Next Five Years				
	1954-55	1955-56	1956-57	1957-58	1958-59	1959-60	1960-61*	1961-62*	1962-63*
Deliveries	£398	£758	£1,005	£1,434	£2,250	£3,500	£4,750	£6,000	£7,500
Less: Direct labor	75	119	141	192	270	420	560	720	900
Materials	134	226	289	468	750	1,180	1,590	2,000	2,500
Gross margin on deliveries	£189	£413	£575	£774	£1,230	£1,900	£2,600	£3,280	£4,100
Add: Overheads in development and W.I.P. increase	30	60	60	48	70	100	100	100	100
Gross margin on trading	£219	£473	£635	£822	£1,300	£2,200	£2,700	£3,380	£4,200
Less: Manufacturing overheads	105	214	258	356	480	730	950	1,150	1,400
Administration overheads	20	50	63	66	90	120	160	200	250
Commercial overheads	53	123	197	226	320	480	620	720	900
	£178	£387	£518	£648	£ 890	£1,330	£1,730	£2,070	£2,550
Net profit before development write-off	41	86	117	174	410	670	970	1,310	1,650
Development write-off (specific products)	24	38	76	72	125	175	225	300	400
Net profit before appropriations	£ 17	£ 48	£ 41	£ 102	£ 285	£ 495	£ 745	£1,010	£1,250
Loan interest	5	6	16	29	30	32	32	32	32
Preferred dividends (gross)	4	15	15	16	18	18	18	18	18
Ordinary dividends (gross)	...	...	...	...	22	44	88	132	220
Sundry appropriations	4	...	...	2	...	...	...	...	...
Taxation	4	15	4	34	120	220	320	433	517
Retained profits	...	£ 12	£ 6	£ 21	£ 95	£ 181	£ 287	£ 395	£ 463

*See note, Exhibit 1.
Source: Company records.

Exhibit 4

THE SOLARTRON ELECTRONIC GROUP LTD.

Balance Sheets as of June 30

(In £000's)

	Actual					Forecast			
	1955	1956	1957	1958	1959	1960	1961	1962	1963
Assets									
Cash at bank	£ 77	£ 1	£ 3	£ 7	£ 5	...	...	£ 175	£ 283
Trade and sundry debtors	99	154	259	400	475	£ 750	£1,000	1,200	1,500
Stock-in-hand and materials, etc.	85	89	121	158	200	270	350	450	560
Finished instruments	29	96	105	118	150	180	200	225	250
W.I.P. production	59	62	72	233	270	350	440	540	650
W.I.P. development	40	72	103	90	75	50	25	...	...
Associated companies	...	...	...	109	150	150	175	200	225
Total Current Assets	£389	£474	£663	£1,115	£1,325	£1,750	£2,190	£2,790	£3,468
Freehold land and buildings	40	74	118	88	96	100	110	120	130
Improvements to leasehold factories	2	3	5	7	75	100	125	150	175
Equipment, plant, and machinery	22	36	35	46	125	175	225	275	325
Furniture, fixtures, and fittings	11	26	31	34	80	110	130	160	200
Motor vehicles	13	23	33	37	17	15	20	20	25
Goodwill	18	18	17	17	17	...	...	...	...
Total Fixed Assets	£106	£180	£239	£ 229	£ 410	£ 500	£ 610	£ 725	£ 855
Total Assets	495	654	902	1,344	1,735	2,250	2,800	3,515	4,323
Liabilities									
Bank overdraft	£ 75	£139	£173	£ 58	£ 118	£ 77	£ 20	...	...
Progress payments	...	...	21	109	75	...	...	...	...
Trade and sundry creditors	104	117	166	410	410	600	700	800	900
Higher purchase commitments	10	18	18	18	40	75	70	65	60
Current taxation	8	18	21	30	20	150	260	375	505
Total Current Liabilities	£197	£292	£399	£ 625	£ 663	£ 902	£1,050	£1,240	£1,465

Exhibit 4—Continued

Liabilities—Continued	Actual				Forecast				
	1955	1956	1957	1958	1959	1960	1961	1962	1963
Future tax	£ 6	£ 18	£ 20	£ 51	£ 150	£ 260	£ 375	£ 505	£ 625
Unsecured loans	53	85	218	364	365	350	350	350	350
6% preferred shares (£1 each)	97	100	100	100	100	100	100	100	100
7½% preferred shares (£1 each) ..	95	100	100	100	100	100	100	100	100
Ordinary shares (10/each)	47	47	47	47	220	220	220	220	220
Retained profit and reserves	...	12	18	57	137	318	605	1,000	1,463
Total Liabilities	£495	£654	£902	£1,344	£1,735	£2,250	£2,800	£3,515	£4,323
Note: Monthly sales volume	£ 55	£ 70	£125	£ 200	£ 250	£ 400	£ 500	£ 600	£ 750

Source: Company records.

Exhibit 5

SUBSIDIARIES AND GROUP ABRIDGED MANUFACTURING, TRADING, AND PROFIT
AND LOSS ACCOUNTS FOR THE NINE MONTHS ENDED MARCH 31, 1958

Subsidiaries	*SLI*	*SE*	*SR.&D.*	*SEBM*	*SIC*	*RS*	*Total*
Sales	£365,996	£221,473	£114,389	£ 9,798	....	£15,226	£726,882
Increase/decrease in W.I.P.	64,775	(5,850)	30,589	4,667	£30,874	....	125,055
Net output	£430,771	£215,623	£144,978	£14,465	£30,874	£15,226	£851,937
Materials consumed	272,995	75,189	60,977	2,596	16,964	4,069	432,790
Direct wages	47,318	38,507	29,213	5,275	6,182	4,959	131,454
Manufacturing overheads	99,145	79,302	39,028	10,713	13,326	6,157	247,671
Works cost	£419,458	£192,998	£129,218	£18,584	£36,472	£15,185	£811,915
Net profit (loss) of subsidiaries	£ 11,313	£ 22,625	£ 15,760	£(4,119)	£(5,598)	£ 41	£ 40,022

Holding Company.

	SEG		
Sales	£917,756		
Cost of sales	636,742		
Gross profit	£281,014		
Commercial overheads	£157,779		
Administration overheads	46,412		
Net profit of holding company	£ 76,823		76,823
Combined net profit			£116,845
Appropriations:			
Interest (gross)			21,734
Preferred dividend (gross)			10,103
Total			£ 31,837
Profit before development write-off, taxation, and participating dividend			£ 85,008

Source: Company records.

Bowman Scott, M.B.E.,[3] M.B.A. (Harvard), B.Sc. (Eng.), Associate City and Guilds Institute (A.C.G.I.), Associate Member Institute of Electrical Engineers (A.M.I.E.E.), Group personnel director, and managing director of Solartron Electronic Business Machines Ltd.

J. L. E. Smith, M.A., director of Coutts & Co., Bankers,[4] and chairman of Solartron Industrial Automation Developments Ltd.

The purpose of board meetings was described as follows in a memorandum written by Mr. Bolton to explain and defend his practice (once criticized by the outside members) of allowing board meetings to "wander away" from a strict interpretation of the agenda:

. . . they are not, in these days, intended for transmission of information because this can be done effectively via detailed management data in the form of monthly reports. . . .

It seems to me that [their] main purpose lies in the area of creative discussion in order to achieve not only a better understanding of each other but also of the human and technical factors which govern the job we are doing. These factors of course change almost continuously. This in my view is how an effective and flexible policy (whether it be at board level or at research level) is rough hewn from the range of opinions which a balanced team should have. As you may have seen, I usually endeavour to bring out something controversial so that at least one member of the board will get hot under the collar about it. If we can each of us do this without fear then I think we are creating a very powerful team relationship which will ensure that we are approaching the various new problems which we shall continuously face in a coordinated and constructive way. . . .

In addition to the general management functions performed by the board, the parent company also provided a number of services to the Solartron companies, including purchasing, personnel, commercial activity (such as overseas selling), publicity, secretarial, accounting, and internal consulting (Group productivity services department).

The boards of directors of some of the subsidiary companies did not actually meet; management responsibility rested with the managing directors and other senior executives concerned.

Company objectives

A number of Solartron's objectives had been stated explicitly in recent years, either in the firm's Annual Reports, in other written documents, or orally by company executives. These statements have been quoted or paraphrased below:

For the long run. Expansion into rapidly growing sections of the electronics industry as fast as "balanced attention" to the various factors of production would allow, taking into consideration (1) rate of development of the existing staff; (2) rate of integration of new personnel; (3) rate of

---

[3]Member of Order of British Empire (war decoration).
[4]A commercial bank.

development of the company's markets; (4) pace of R.&D. activity, as influenced by human and financial considerations.

For the next five to ten years. (1) Achieving more intensive effort in the major fields already chosen, in order to build "strong, viable, subsidiary units in those areas." There were to be fewer radically new products developed than in recent years, and emphasis was to be placed instead on perfecting and increasing the applications of equipment already developed. (2) Increasing export sales of Solartron products in order to broaden the company's customer base and spread development costs over an increased number of production units. (3) Making more effective use of the relatively large organizational structure created for the purpose of preparing for future expansion.

With respect to people. "Our emergent philosophy of life lays great stress not only on the importance of the individual as a person, but on the essential need to devise a 'permissive' system in which individual initiative is nurtured and encouraged to make its maximum possible contribution to the whole. . . . We recognize that in selecting a team of potentially outstanding young men and women at all levels and in training them to carry increasing responsibility, the natural corollary is that they should want to make a personal contribution to decisions affecting their particular working group or company's future, in an atmosphere which is as free as possible of status barriers and prejudice. Furthermore, that they should want to know that those who demonstrate outstanding qualities of leadership and judgment can progress to Board level." In line with this objective the following policies had been adopted:

a) Whenever possible, promotions to senior positions were made from within the organization. The principal exceptions to this rule were senior specialists such as Mr. Christopher Bailey, designer of the reading machine, and Mr. George Sanders, head of the Group productivity services department.

b) To the extent possible, managers at all levels of the company were given the opportunity to discharge their responsibilities as they thought best within the broad framework of agreed-upon objectives. In this regard, Mr. Gordon Bates, who was leaving Solartron to do management consulting in the consumer marketing field, said that he and many of his colleagues felt themselves to be "part of an experiment in British industry." He contrasted Solartron with a number of older, larger firms that he and his friends had worked for, saying, "The standard form in many of these firms is to treat the younger men like useless appendages during the first 15 years or so, and then gradually let them in on one aspect of operations. Here the form is to give man a little more than he thinks he can handle as soon as possible."

c) To encourage personnel to increase their potential, fees for suitable training courses and conferences were paid by the company, while "Training within Industry" classes were held during working hours. There was also a library of technical and management books.

d) An attempt was made to keep executives throughout the company informed on current developments. In this regard, Mr. P. B. H. Cuff, Group purchasing director, said that in his early years with the company Mr. Bolton had on several occasions stopped him to tell him of recent events that had no immediate bearing on his work but were of great interest to him in understanding the company's position. By 1958, annual management conferences were being held for all senior and junior executives, at which board members described the current state of affairs and plans for the future in their areas.

e) To avoid unnecessary status barriers, reserved spaces in the parking lot had been eliminated. On most memoranda the names of executives were alphabetized; the use of first names was encouraged; and all personnel, regardless of position and function, were expected to "clock in" at the same time.

f) Since 1954, the personnel selection and training functions had been entrusted to a director, Mr. Bowman Scott.

g) To assure attractive working conditions, a pension scheme had been established, as well as an employee restaurant, a health centre, a sports and cricket club, and a trend toward yearly or longer term employment contracts.

With respect to formal organization. "Our policy is to develop a number of virtually independent company units within the Group, each concentrating on either a specialized function such as research, or a logically grouped sales and production activity such as test instrumentation. . . . We envisage each individual company unit growing to a size of perhaps 500–700 personnel— a size which we believe will meet, on the one hand, the need to maximise personal satisfactions, and, on the other, to operate near to the optimum unit size for the technical requirements of our particular industry. The dangers of growing apart are apparent, but we are confident that through our group structure and because of the experience our senior executives have gained in working as a very closely knit team, we shall be able to achieve the principal benefits of centralized policy-making and the economics of joint services, without hampering the exercise of individual initiative in the separate companies."

Mr. Bolton was particularly desirous of avoiding what he termed a "peaky" organization, in which management thinking would be dominated by his personal views. In this regard he said he had found that people in an organization tended to create a pinnacle, even when the managing director was anxious not to become an all-powerful father-figure. People had come to him, for example, and suggested that he ought to buy a new car, since his Jaguar was not as new as it might be and therefore not fully appropriate to his position. He said that one of a number of problems that could arise in a peaky organization was the difficulty of hiring "number-two" men who were intimidated by the individual brilliance of their prospective bosses and feared being completely submerged by them.

In contrast with the "peaky" organization, "great-man" approach to management, Mr. Bolton expressed the opinion that managerial needs were, like vacuums, abhorred by nature, and that they would ultimately be filled of their own accord. For example, he indicated that if he and Mr. Eric Jones, Group commercial director, had not pushed product diversification, "two other chaps would have, and the result would have been the same." Similarly, he believed that if Solartron had not developed the reading machine or the radar simulator, some other firm would have done so.

With respect to finance. Objectives in finance were (1) to increase borrowed in relation to equity and preference funds on a 2:1 ratio; (2) to use company funds principally for working capital; and to use other sources, such as lease-back arrangements, for plant and fixed assets; (3) starting in 1958–59, to establish a progressive common stock dividend record against the possibility that in three to five years there might be opportunities for greater expansion than were visualized in 1958 (although profits had been sacrificed for balanced and rapid growth in the first ten years, increasing dividend payments were believed to be important ultimately because company executives considered that English companies were judged on a dividend rather than earnings-yield basis) ; (4) to achieve gross margins[5] on products in full production (beyond the initial progress-payment or pilot-production stage) of 60% or more; (5) to reduce overhead spending progressively, until it declined to approximately 33% of projected gross sales.

With respect to R.&D. (1) ". . . We have established a prime objective of achieving entirely new developments which show substantial improvements in contemporary design practice. As a rough rule of thumb, we have endeavoured to produce new designs which will be some three to five years ahead of the existing state of the art in other countries, and in this way we hope to achieve a breathing space in which our new products can become fully established before the pressure of competition might catch up with them." (2) "In contrast with many military organizations, where research funds are all too often taken as a symbol of power, and prevailing sentiment is to get as much as you can and to hell with the whole, we are attempting to build the feeling instead that R.&D. funds are a means by which a subsidiary or research team can make a contribution to the Group, and that this contribution, rather than the power involved, is the important thing." (3) "Eventually we are aiming for more and more new projects at SR.&D.[6]— tending more toward research and away from development—and we intend to have the development work done by the individual manufacturing subsidiaries."

Product planning

Early product history. The initial development of Solartron's product line was described by a company executive as follows:[7]

The start and growth of the enterprise has followed a familiar pattern; at first a handful of men in a shed, and then a leap-frogging into larger and larger premises as the work prospered. In 1947 two young engineers, Mr. E. R. Ponsford and Mr. L. B. Copestick, scraped together a few hundred pounds, hired a disused stable, and set up as makers of electronic test instruments. Both had been appren-

[5]Sales price less "bought-out" materiels and direct wages.
[6]Solartron Research and Development Ltd., a subsidiary.
[7]Solartron Research and Development Ltd., a subsidiary.

ticed in the electronic industry and were aware of shortcomings in the available equipment. In 1948 they registered the name Solartron, but eighteen months were to pass before they were in a position to produce an electronic instrument of their own—the first proprietary laboratory amplifier on the British market. The main activity of the two directors and their three employees at first was the development, manufacture, and repair of equipment under government contract. This steady work enabled them to lease a small factory in Kingston, and additions to the board brought enough working capital to proceed with more ambitious plans. Two years after the introduction of their first instrument the company was invited to exhibit at the Physical Society's Exhibition, and this they regarded as a mark of acceptance in the sphere of electronics.

The early years were hard but rewarding in every sense except the material. Many of the founders' old associates and trainees were anxious to join the company, even at reduced wages, for the sake of opportunities to come.

Ploughing back of all profits was never adequate to finance the rapidly growing production and development, and substantial additional capital was introduced when Mr. John Bolton and Mr. John Crosse joined the company in 1951 and 1952, respectively.

Thus, by the 30th June 1953, at the end of the first five years of its corporate life, Solartron had become established with 110 personnel, 7,500 square feet of factory space, and a turnover of approximately £100,000 per annum. There were then two companies, Solartron Laboratory Instruments Ltd., with a growing product line of electronic test instruments, and Solartron Engineering Limited, which was responsible for the precision mechanical engineering and metalwork aspects of Solartron products. The stage was set for the broadening of the organizational and products base and substantial increase in sales volume during the second five years, 1953–58.[8]

Diversification. During its second five years, Solartron diversified into "systems engineered" products. The initial decision to do so was made in 1952–53 as a result of what were considered to be the limitations of laboratory instruments as a product line on which to base future growth. The reasoning of the company's board, as reported in 1958, was as follows (paraphrased):

On the one hand, delivery periods must be kept short. For, once a customer has ordered an instrument, he expects rapid delivery (a month or less) or will seek an alternative source of supply. On the other hand, inventories must be kept at a minimum, because as a rapidly growing company our finances will be limited. Operations will therefore be continuously balanced between the risk of an inventory buildup if sales decrease and a scramble to increase production if sales increase.

Solartron could safely base its expansion on laboratory instruments only if it specializes intensely in one type of instrument, as certain firms have done in the United States. Because of the size of the United Kingdom market, however,

Our wisest move would be to seek additional "systems engineered" products this will not be feasible.

[8]From a paper presented May 27, 1958, before a meeting of the Seminar on Problems in Industrial Administration at the London School of Economics and Political Science.

with higher unit prices and longer delivery requirements. Such products would broaden our customer base and reduce the complexity of current operations. Because they would lengthen our order book, it would also be easier to obtain outside finance.

In order that we can make the maximum contribution and utilize our resources to the fullest, these new products should be in rapidly expanding sectors of the electronics industry where it will not be necessary to design somebody else out of the market.

Choosing new-product areas. In connection with this analysis, Mr. Bolton prepared a rough evaluation of the industry's future growth along the lines of Exhibit 6. This was based on the assumption that already developed sectors of the industry would remain a constant or decreasing proportion of the total, while undeveloped and as yet unknown sectors would become larger. Overall, a fivefold increase over 20 years was estimated, with particular segments changing in relative importance roughly as indicated in Exhibit 6.

Entering new fields. As a consequence of this analysis, Solartron began slowly to diversify during its second five years. Impetus to enter new fields came from various sources: In 1953–54 a study was made of the business machine field, and it was concluded that the most important undeveloped requirements were (1) fast input devices for computers; (2) memories with large storage capacity and quick access; (3) equipment for sorting information. Of these, the first was selected for development and work was started on the reading machine (see Exhibit 7). In 1954 a decision to develop the checkweigher was made, based on the belief that accurate control of weight was a fundamental future need in automated processes—especially where packaged articles such as food were concerned, since such items are sold by weight. The choice of this field was also related to development and engineering skills already possessed by Solartron. With this product, work was started in the field of industrial controls. In 1955 evidence of strong interest by the Swedish Air Ministry touched off development of the company's radar simulator device. In 1957 "Anglicization" (adaptation to British components) of an American-designed "data-tape" recording machine was begun under license from the Consolidated Electrodynamics Corporation. During this same period the Group sponsored research and development in the field of data processing (chiefly analogue computers).

In speaking of the company's diversification, Mr. Eric Jones, Group commercial director, said: "Not everyone was agreed that we should go into systems, perhaps partly because when you look two or three years ahead in a new field, it looks more like science fiction than commercial reality. I think even J. B. [Mr. Bolton] thought that diversification might be premature. But I pushed radar simulators, he pushed business machines, we got agreement to develop the checkweigher, and here we are today."

Allocating R.&D. funds. "We are compromising between forward research and spending on present products," said Mr. Bolton, "and we are doing it by eye." Mr. Bolton stated that this compromise involved making

Exhibit 6

SOLARTRON ESTIMATES OF FUTURE GROWTH
OF ELECTRONICS INDUSTRY

Market Sector	Solartron Rough Estimates of Sales of Sector as a Per Cent of the Total Electronics Industry	
	1953	1973
1. *Domestic Radio and TV* Comments: Few export sales; domestic market will probably reach a plateau as in the U.S. Would have to compete with large, well-established firms. Not for us	25	10
2. *Communications* Comments: Major European networks already installed. Sales will be for improvement and replacement purposes. Industry cartelized; suppliers often affiliated with communications firms. Not our cup of tea	20	8
3. *Radar and Navigational Aids* Comments: A growing field which should have possibilities for us. Assume market percentage will remain the same. Total increase will thus be fivefold.	5	5
4. *Military Requirements* Comments: Assume total static even though electronic share will increase, therefore ultimate percentage of the market down. Not so interesting as some other sectors	35	15
5. *Data Processing* (including business machines and industrial data processing equipment) Comments: Increasing use for computation as well as to reduce paper work. Digital computers have already been extensively developed by several large firms but analogue techniques and a number of other problems remain. An interesting field for us.	*	20
6. *Industrial Controls* Comments: Ultimately will be larger than data processing. Since automation of production operations will come after the automation of paper work, however, this sector will develop more slowly. This deserves our attention	*	15
7. *Scientific Education* Comments: May never loom too large but relatively untouched. Has possibilities	*	5
8. *Atomic Energy* Comments: Insignificant at present but will grow.	*	5
9. *Miscellaneous*	15	17

*Negligible.
Source: Company's records.

Exhibit 7

COMPUTERS OR CLERKS

The electronic computer is ten years old, a teenager among industrial machinery with a teenager's problems of adjustment to society. During its first decade, when it

Exhibit 7—Continued

was being used largely as a research tool for resolving equations beyond the capacity of mathematicians, the decision to buy a computer or not depended on the straightforward point whether a company or a Government research department had enough work of this kind to justify the investment of upwards of £150,000 in a single computer. There was no question of doing the work by other means. Such abstruse scientific, aerodynamic and even economic calculations were either done on a computer or not done at all. But now computers are being offered to a wider market as machines that will mechanise clerical work and control production processes, and they are being judged by different standards. Here a company does have a choice between two alternatives—it can choose between electronic computers and human clerks, or labourers.

The saving of labour by a computer can be exaggerated. The real gift it brings to management is the opportunity to cut through the red tape and the paper work that assumes alarming proportions once a company's operations reach a certain size. Much of this routine could now be transferred to computers, inside which it would be promptly assimilated, sorted, added to, subtracted from, pigeonholed, filed for future reference, while a neat printed record appeared at the other end. But is this worth doing?

The answer varies from company to company, depending on how vital it is to the sound management of the business to have quick access to day-to-day information. Boots, which is making a big change-over to electronic accounting, obviously sets great store by prompt reports on the changing level of sales and stocks for the 60,000 different items sold by the company's retail shops. Bibby's, manufacturing animal feeding stuffs, uses a computer to keep watch on rapidly changing raw material prices, so that the feeding-stuff formula can be varied to make allowance for them— a job that requires an unexpectedly large number of weekly calculations. Tube investments, selling products that vary from order to order, uses a computer to sort the orders, stipulate the most economical raw material, give manufacturing instructions and prepare cost figures, spending 30 seconds on planning and printing instructions about each order, against 35 minutes by ordinary methods. The Banco di Roma has just installed a computer to handle all the accounts of its 200–300 branches. Many other examples can be found among the 100–odd computers now in use in this country where resort to a fast-thinking computer has probably improved a company's efficiency. But users are noticeably reluctant to quote any estimate of the amount of money saved by electronic accounting. Boots calculate that the company's change to electronic book-keeping will stop the annual 10 per cent rise in clerical staff that has gone on now for several years. But even this type of saving is difficult to assess.

Computers still have obvious limitations; skillful handling is needed to make them earn their keep. Initial cost is the biggest single factor. At the first exhibition in the world devoted entirely to electronic computers, which has been open in London during the past ten days, the price of the 27 different models on sale ranged all the way from £20,000 to £800,000, the cheapest being made by Elliott and the dearest by IBM. A computer consists of two basic parts; one which does the arithmetic and is relatively cheap to make, and the other which acts as a "memory" and stores all the relevant data and instructions upon which the computer operates. There are several ways of building a "memory"; some of them are cheaper than others but unfortunately they are also slower-working. If the "memory" is slow, this tends to hold up the rate at which the computer works.

As a rough rule of thumb, the cheaper computers have small "memories"; the more expensive the machine, the bigger its memory and the faster it can get at the facts. In scientific calculations, calculating ability is frequenty more important than capacious memory, so the small computers, many of which are only just on the market, are ideally suited for research purposes, providing the maximum computing ability for the minimum cost. For business accounting, however, a big "memory" is more important than calculating ability; the machine is required to hold data about stocks, or invoices, or temperature levels, or railway schedules, or insurance policies,

Exhibit 7—Continued

and carry out one or two simple calculations on them when the need arises. The ideal computer for business accounting therefore tends to come in the £100,000 to £300,000 range.

It would be unfair, however, to blame the high cost of computers entirely on the electronics engineer. The computer itself frequently costs less than the mechanical equipment that goes with it. The second big limitation on the use of computers is in the design of this equipment. A computer cannot read—yet. Data have to be fed into it in a form it can understand, from punched cards, punched tape or magnetic tape, and fed out again in a form that the operator can understand. This requires tape readers, mechanical feeds and printing equipment, all of which operate at unnaturally high speeds. The purely mechanical difficulties created by these high speeds make all this ancillary equipment extremely expensive, considering the basic simplicity of its design. Some steps have been taken towards the development of electronic "readers" that could read type faces and transmit the results direct to the computer; the specification put out by the banks for a machine that would "read" magnetic characters printed on cheques has given a marked fillip to this type of research.

The first two "reading" machines of their kind were exhibited at the computer exhibition, one of them being Solartron's complex reader, which is now said to be able to decipher not only carbon copies but even handwritten characters. The cost is £25,000 for a machine "reading" three reasonably similar type faces; the much simpler apparatus developed by Electric and Musical Industries solely for "reading" a specially designed type printed in magnetic ink, and intended primarily for cheque sorting, might cost one-tenth of this amount when in production. These figures give some indication of the cost of the trimmings that go with a computer. Ferranti, the first company to make computers in this country, designing machines used mainly by laboratories for vast calculations, sells one basic computer for £50,000, but the full installation costs £160,000.

The third big limitation on the use of computers lies with the customer rather than the machine. Production engineering must be fairly well understood in industry by now, but the application of the same technique to office work is not. In most cases, wholesale changes in routine are needed to fit the job to the computer and it is doubtful whether this is always appreciated by the buyer. Commercial computers have a vast appetite for work, but they are not the "thinking machines" that scientists were discussing at the National Physical Laboratory a week ago. They cannot plan the way a job ought to be done; they can act only on data and instructions fed to them by human operators and if the work is badly planned, the computer can do nothing to correct it.

Some experts have a shrewd suspicion that managements have found it more difficult to adjust their methods to computers than they had expected, rather in the way of those housewives whose pressure cookers sit unused on the top shelf. Their evidence is the large number of commercial computers used—on the admission of the owners—mainly for calculating wage packets. To put a computer to this work is like taking a steam-roller to crack a nut—a useful way of filling odd moments but a sad under-employment of the machine's great capabilities. But wage calculations happens to be one of the easiest jobs to tailor for a computer—this is why manufacturers frequently use it for demonstrations purposes—and it gives both computer operators and management a breathing space to learn how to use their new toy.

Although manufacturers can supply computers with a plan of work built into them, this is essentially a job that can be carried out only by men who know and have worked in the company buying the machine and who understand its business. The planning of work for a computer goes far beyond the mere mathematics of working out a code of instructions telling the machine how to do the job. It calls for a certain amount of imagination to grasp the computer's potentialities for helping the company, and although the manufacturer's staff can give advice on what is or is not technically possible they cannot be expected to understand how each business works or the best way that it should be run. Management must be prepared to spend some

Exhibit 7—Continued

time learning to do the job itself. It may take months, or even years, to learn how to get maximum value from a computer. In some cases, it is still going to be cheaper and less troublesome to do the job with clerks.

SOURCE: *The Economist*, December 6, 1958, pp. 915–16. Reproduced by permission.

choices between "picking up basic principles at an early stage, or applying more intensive effort to remaining problems in already developed areas— such as increasing the reliability of a particular kind of oscilloscope." He explained that in the most recent operating year (1957–58) this choice had been made by allocating Group R.&D. funds to the various product groups in proportion to their estimated growth in sales over the subsequent five-year period. Mr. Bolton added: "To some extent we are still a little paternalistic in this regard, in that I am still doling the money out as from a family kitty, basing individual allocations on the individual family members' estimates of their needs, scaled down to fit the total budget."

Picking individual projects. According to Mr. James Rothman, administrative assistant for SR.&D., the principal sources of ideas for new projects were as follows: (1) Company staff, which was the principal source of ideas involving logical extensions of existing products, either by simple adaptation (such as redesigning a machine to read in polar as well as X and Y coordinates), or by using new principles or components. These were the source of the largest number of new projects. (2) Outsiders who joined Solartron and brought new ideas with them. This was the main source of radically new developments. (3) Outside requests of the "we need help badly" variety. In this respect, senior engineers were encouraged to visit with customers and discuss their problems. The company's technical service engineers also turned in as many as 2,000 visit reports each month, in which they reported on unresolved difficulties they had encountered in the field.

Over 100 possibilities for new projects were generated by these various sources in the course of a year. Of these, approximately 10% were chosen to be worked on, and the remainder were either rejected or held in abeyance. In the case of SR.&D., decisions were made by Mr. L. Copestick, managing director, and Mr. R. Catherall, research director. In the case of SEBM, SIC, and Radar Simulators, decisions were made by the senior executives involved. Decisions were made on a basis of these criteria: the estimated sales and gross profits that would result from making a given investment, and the interest of the engineers involved in carrying out the project.

Although formal calculations were not always prepared in selecting projects, a work order stating the estimated completion date and cost was issued at the time a project was begun. During the course of the project, monthly comparisons of work-in-progress (labor, materials, and overhead) were made with the budgeted cost by the senior executives and project engineers involved.

In late 1957 Mr. Rothman had been asked to devise a formula so that the decision whether a proposed project should be financed with Group funds could be made by a representative committee on the basis of the project's profitability ratio (the ratio of present value of profits over three years to the initial investment). Efforts to formalize the research and development program had been under way for over five years. This formula was enthusiastically received by Mr. Bolton, but it had not been implemented because it had been viewed more coolly by senior SR.&D. executives, on the grounds that the present system worked well, and that the estimates needed to calculate the profitability ratio would be too sketchy to be of real value. Excerpts from the summary of Mr. Rothman's proposal follow:

NEW PRODUCTS ASSESSMENT SUMMARY

It is suggested that the decision whether a proposed development project should be financed by Group should be based very largely on its profitability ratio. . . .

In order to obtain a fair assessment of the profitability ratios, a representative committee would be formed to collate and agree upon the individual forecasts from which the profitability ratios would be calculated. . . . This committee would also draw attention to other intangible factors that might affect a decision on a particular product.

The Managing Directors of the development companies concerned could start development on any project approved by the Committee. However, in order to ensure that the Group's financial resources are not overstrained at any one time, a subcommittee of the Group Board will decide at three-monthly intervals the amount to be spent on development by each company in the next but two three-monthly period. This decision would be based on a consideration of projects under way and of projects approved by the New Products Committee.

It would then be the responsibility of the Managing Directors concerned to ensure that they did not overspend their budgeted allocation.

The aim has been to provide an agreed selection process and while providing short-term stability in development budgets, it is designed to give long-term flexibility in allocation of funds for SEG sponsored development.

BASIC INDUSTRIES*

^^

In May, 1966, Pete Adams, plant manager of Basic Industries' Chicago plant, was worried about the new facilities proposal for toranium. His division, metal products, was asking for $1 million to build facilities which would be at full capacity in less than a year and a half (if forecasted sales were realized). Yet the divisional vice president for production seemed more interested in where the new facility was to go than in how big it should be. Adams wondered how, as plant manager, his salary and performance review would look in 1968 with the new facility short of capacity.

Basic Industries, metal products division

Basic Industries engaged in a number of activities ranging from shipbuilding to the manufacture of electronic components. The corporation was organized into five autonomous divisions (see Exhibit 1). In 1965 these divisions had sales totaling $500 million. Of the five, the metal products division was the most profitable. In 1965, this division realized an after-tax income of $16 million on sales of $110 million and an investment of $63.7 million.

This position of profit leadership within the company had not always been held by metal products. In fact, in the early 1950's, Basic's top management had considered dropping the division. At that time, the division's market share was declining owing to a lack of manufacturing facilities, high costs, and depressed prices.

A change in divisional management resulted in a marked improvement. Between 1960 and 1965, for example, the division's sales grew at 8% a year and profits at 20% a year. The division's ROI during this period rose from 12% in 1960 to 25% in 1965.

Ronald Brewer, president of metal products division since 1955, explained how this growth had been achieved:

Planning goes on in many places in the Metal Products Division, but we do go through a formal planning process to establish goals. We establish very specific goals for products and departments in every phase of the business. This

---

*Copyright © 1968 by the President and Fellows of Harvard College. Reprinted with permission.

Exhibit 1

ORGANIZATION CHART FOR BASIC INDUSTRIES

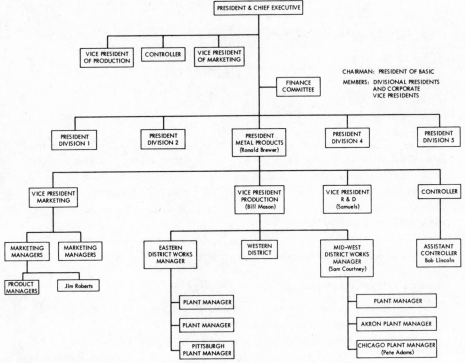

Source: Case writer's notes.

formal and detailed planning is worked out on a yearly basis. We start at the end of the second quarter to begin to plan for the following year.

We plan on the basis of our expectations as to the market. If it's not there, we live a little harder. We cut back to assure ourselves of a good cash flow. Our record has been good, but it might not always be. Some of our products are 30 years old. We've just invested $5 million, which is a lot of money for our division, in expanding capacity for a 25-year-old product. But we're making money out of it and it's growing.

Along with detailed planning for the year to come, we ask for plans for years three and four. Our goal is to make sure that we can satisfy demand. Any time we approach 85% of capacity at one of our plants, our engineers get busy.

They will give the plant manager the information as to what he needs in the way of new equipment. The plant manager will then fit the engineer's recommendation into his expansion plans. The plant manager's plan then goes to our control manager. The marketing people then add their forecasts, and by that time we have built up the new facilities proposal. On the other hand, the marketing people may have spearheaded the project. Sometimes they alert the plant manager to a rapid growth in his product and he goes to the engineers. In this division, everyone is marketing minded.

*   *   *   *   *

We measure plants, and they measure their departments against plan. For example, we have a rule of thumb that a plant must meet its cost reduction goals. So if one idea doesn't work out, a plant must find another one to get costs to the planned level. We make damned sure that we make our goals as a division. Our objective is to have the best product in the market at the lowest cost. It's a simple concept, but the simpler the concept, the better it's understood.

Well, on the basis of his performance against plan, a man is looked at by his superior at least once a year, maybe more. We take a pretty hardnosed position with a guy. We tell him what we think his potential is, where he is going to go, what he is going to be able to do. We have run guys up *and* down the ladder. In this division, it's performance and fact that count. We have no formal incentive plan but we do recognize performance with salary increases and with promotions.

You know, we have divisions in this company which are volume happy. We here are profit conscious. We had to be to survive. What I'd like to see is interest allocated on a pro rata basis according to total investment. I grant you that this would hurt some of the other divisions more than us, but I think that treating interest as a corporate expense, as we do, changes your marketing philosophy and your pricing philosophy.

For example, most new facilities proposals are wrong with respect to their estimates of market size—volume attainable at a given price—and timing. You can second-guess a forecast though, in several ways, and hedge to protect yourself. There is a feeling at Basic Industries that there is a stigma attached to coming back for more money. That means that if you propose a project at the bare minimum requirement and then come back for more, some people feel that you've done something wrong. Generally, this leads to an overestimate of the amount of capital required. It turns out that if you have the money you do spend it, so that this stigma leads to overspending on capital projects. We at metal products are trying to correct this. First, we screen projects closely. We go over them with a fine tooth comb. Second, internally, we set a goal to spend less than we ask for where there is a contingency.

Also, when a project comes in at an estimated 50% return, we cut the estimate down. Everyone does. The figure might go out at 30%. But this practice works the other way too. For example, in 1958 Bill Mason [metal products' vice president of production] and I worked like hell to get a project through. Although it looked like 8% on paper, we knew that we could get the costs way down once it got going, so we put it through at 12%. We're making double that on it today. We haven't had a capital request rejected by the finance committee [see Exhibit 1] in 8 years.

Of course, every once in a while we shoot some craps, but not too often. We are committed to a specific growth rate in net income and ROI. Therefore, we are selective in what we do and how we spend our money. It's seldom that we spend $500,000 to develop something until we know it's got real market potential. You just don't send 100 samples out and then forecast a flood of orders. New products grow slowly. It takes six or seven years. And given that it takes this long, it doesn't take a lot of capital to develop and test out new ideas. Before you really invest, you've done your homework. Over the years we've done a good job in our new products, getting away from the aircraft industry. In 1945, 70% of our business was based on aircraft. Today it's 40%. The way we do things protects us. We have to have a very strong sense of the technical idea and the scope of the market before we invest heavily.

The metal products division's main business was producing a variety of basic and rare nonferrous metals and alloys such as nickel, nickel-beryllium, and titanium in a myriad of sizes and shapes for electrical, mechanical, and structural uses in industry. One of the division's major strengths was its leadership in high-performance material technology. Through patents and a great deal of proprietary experience, metal products had a substantial technological lead on its competitors.

Toranium

In the late 1950's metal products decided to follow its technological knowledge and proprietary production skills into the high-performance materials market. One of metal products' most promising new materials was toranium, for which Jim Roberts was product manager (see Exhibit 1).

Roberts was 33 years old and had a Ph.D. in chemical engineering. Prior to becoming a product manager, he had worked in one of metal products' research laboratories. Roberts explained some of toranium's history:

Developing toranium was a trial-and-error process. The lab knew that the properties of the class of high performance materials to which toranium belonged were unusually flexible, and, therefore, felt such materials had to be useful. So it was an act of faith that led R.&D. to experiment with different combinations of these materials. They had no particular application in mind.

In 1957 we developed the first usable toranium. Our next problem was finding applications for it. It cost $50 a pound. However, since a chemist in the lab thought we could make it for less, we began to look for applications.

In 1962, I entered the picture.

I discovered it was an aerospace business. When the characteristics of our material were announced to the aerospace people, they committed themselves to it. Our competitors were asleep. They weren't going to the customer. I went out and called on the customers and developed sales.

In 1963, we decided to shift the pilot plant from the lab and give it to the production people at Akron. We decided that we simply were not getting a good production-oriented consideration of the process problems. The people at Akron cut the costs by two-thirds and the price stayed the same.

In 1963, I also chose to shut off R.&D. on toranium because it couldn't help in the market place. We had to learn more in the market place before we could use and direct R.&D.

I ought to mention that under the management system used by Mr. Samuels [vice president of R.&D.], the product manager, along with R.&D. and production, shares in the responsibility for monitoring and directing an R.&D. program. This arrangement is part of an attempt to keep everyone market-oriented.

From 1962 to 1965, sales of toranium increased from $250,000 a year to $1 million a year just by seeking them, and in 1965 we put R.&D. back in.

This material can't miss. It has a great combination of properties: excellent machinability, thermal shock resistance and heat insulation. Moreover, it is an excellent electrical conductor.

We can sell all that we can produce. Customers are coming to us with their needs. They have found that toranium's properties and our technical capabilities are superior to anything or anyone in the market.

Moreover, pricing has not been a factor in the development of markets to date. In fact, sales have been generated by the introduction of improved grades of toranium at premium prices. Presently, General Electric represents our only competition, but we expect that Union Carbide will be in the market place with competitive materials during the next few years. However, I don't expect anyone to be significantly competitive before 1968. Anyway, competition might actually help a little bit in expanding the market and stimulating the customers as well as in educating our own R.&D.

Now, if one assumes that no other corporation will offer significant competition to toranium until 1968, the only real uncertainty in our forecasts for toranium is related to metal products' technical and marketing abilities. R.&D. must develop the applications it is currently working on, and production will have to make them efficiently.

This production area can be a real headache. For example, R.&D. developed a toranium part for one of our fighter bombers. However, two out of three castings cracked. On the other hand, we've got the best skills in the industry with respect to high pressure casting. If we can't do it, no one can.

The final uncertainty is new demand. I've got to bring in new applications, but that shouldn't be a problem. You know, I've placed toranium samples with over 17 major customers. Can you imagine what will happen if even two or three of them pay off? As far as I'm concerned, if the forecasts for toranium are inaccurate, they're underestimates of future sales.

New facilities proposal

Sam Courtney, district works manager (to whom the plant managers of the Chicago, Akron, and Indianapolis plants reported) explained the origin of the new toranium facilities proposal:

The product manager makes a forecast once a year, and when it comes time to make major decisions, he makes long-range forecasts. In January 1965, we were at 35% of the toranium pilot-plant capacity. At that time we said, "We have to know beyond 1966, we need a long-range forecast. Volume is beginning to move up."

The production control manager usually collects the forecasts. Each year it is his responsibility to see where we are approaching 85% or 90% of capacity. When that is the case in some product line, he warns the production vice president. However, in this instance, toranium was a transition product and Akron (where the pilot plant was located) picked up the problem and told the manager of product forecasting that we were in trouble.

The long-range forecast that Courtney requested arrived at his office about March 1, 1965, and clearly indicated a need for new capacity. Moreover, Roberts' 1966 regular forecast, which was sent to production in October 1965, was 28% higher than the March long-range projection. It called for additional capacity by October 1966.

Courtney's first response was to request a new long-range forecast. He also authorized the Akron plant to order certain equipment on which there would be a long lead time. The district works manager explained, "It is obvious we are going to need additional capacity in a hurry, and the unique properties of toranium require special, made-to-order, equipment. We can't afford to lose sales. Producing toranium is like coining money."

At the same time, Courtney began discussions on the problem with Bill Mason, vice president of production for metal products. They decided that the Akron plant was probably the wrong location in which to expand the toranium business. Courtney commented, "There are 20 products being produced in Akron, and that plant cannot possibly give toranium the kind of attention it deserves. The business is a new one, and it needs to be cared for like a young child. They won't do that in a plant with many important large-volume products. We have decided over a period of years that Akron is too complex, and this seems like a good time to do something about it."

The two locations proposed as new sites for the toranium facilities were Pittsburgh and Chicago. Each was a one-product plant which "could use product diversification." While Pittsburgh seemed to be favored initially, Mason and Courtney were concerned that the toranium would be contaminated if it came in contact with the rather dirty products produced at Pittsburgh. Therefore, Courtney asked engineering to make studies of both locations.

The results of these initial studies were inconclusive. The Pittsburgh plant felt that the problem of contamination was not severe, and the economic differential between the locations was not substantial.

After the initial studies were completed, Roberts' new long-range forecast arrived. The following table compares this forecast with Roberts' previous long-range forecasts:

ACTUAL AND PROJECTED SALES

Date of Forecast	1965	1966	1967	1968	1969	1970	1971
			(Dollars in Millions)				
March 1964	1.08	1.30	...	...	2.20	...	...
March 1965	1.17	1.40	1.60	...	...	2.80	...
March 1966	...	1.80	2.50	3.40	...	...	5.60
Actual	1.00	...	...	...	...	...	...

In response to this accelerating market situation, Courtney and Mason asked Adams (plant manager at Chicago) to make a "full-fledged study of the three locations" (Akron, Pittsburgh, and Chicago). At the same time, Mason told Brewer (president of metal products), "We're now about 90% certain that Chicago will be the choice. Associated with the newness of the material is a rapidly changing technology. . . . The metal products R.&D. center at Evanston is only ten minutes away. . . . Another important factor is Adams. Titanium honeycomb at Chicago was in real trouble. We couldn't even cover our direct costs. Adams turned it around by giving it careful attention. That's the kind of job toranium needs."

Peter Adams was 35 years old. He had worked for Basic since he graduated from college with a B.S. in engineering. After spending a year in the corporate college training program, Adams was assigned to the metal products division. There he worked as an assistant to the midwestern district manager for production. Before becoming Chicago plant manager in 1963, Adams had been the assistant manager at the same plant for two years.

In working through the financial data on the toranium project, Adams chose to compare the three sites with respect to internal rates of return. He made this comparison for the case where capacity was expanded to meet forecasted sales for 1967 ($2.5 million), the case where capacity was expanded to met forecasted sales for 1971 ($5.6 million) and the case where capacity was expanded from $2.5 to $5.6 million. The results of Adams' analysis are summarized in the following table:

	Chicago	Pittsburgh	Akron
	(Dollars in Thousands)		
1. Incremental capital investment for capacity through 1967	$ 980	$1,092	$ 765
Internal rate of return	34%	37%	45%
2. Incremental capital investment for capacity through 1971	$1,342	$1,412	$1,272
Internal rate of return	52%	54%	55%
3. Incremental capital investment to raise capacity from $2.5 to $5.6 million	$ 710	$ 735	$ 740
Internal rate of return	45%	47%	46%

While the economics favored Akron, Adams was aware that Mason favored Chicago. This feeling resulted from conversations with Courtney about the toranium project. Courtney pointed out the importance of quality, service to customers, liaison with R.&D., and production flexibility to a new product like toranium. Furthermore, Courtney expressed the view that Chicago looked good in these respects, despite its cost disadvantage. Courtney also suggested that a proposal which asked for enough capacity to meet 1967 forecasted demand would have the best prospects for divisional acceptance.

By the end of April 1966, Adams' work had progressed far enough to permit preparation of a draft of a new facilities proposal recommending a Chicago facility. Except for the marketing story which he obtained from Roberts, he had written the entire text. On May 3, Adams brought the completed draft to New York for a discussion with Mason and Courtney. The meeting, which was quite informal, began with Adams reading his draft proposal aloud to the group. Mason and Courtney commented on the draft as he went along. Some of the more substantial comments are included in the following excerpts from the meeting.

Meeting on the draft proposal

ADAMS: We expect that production inefficiencies and quality problems will be encountered upon start-up of the new facility in Chicago. In order to prevent these problems from interfering with the growth of toranium, the new facilities for producing toranium powder, pressing ingots, and casting finished products will be installed in Chicago and operated until normal production efficiency is attained. At that time, existing Akron equipment will be transferred to the Chicago location. Assuming early approval of the project, Chicago will be in production in the first quarter of 1967, and joint Akron and Chicago operations will continue through September 1967. The Akron equipment will be transferred in October and November 1967, and Chicago will be in full operation in December 1967.

MASON: Wait a minute! You're not in production until the first quarter of 1967, and the forecasts say we are going to be short in 1966!

ADAMS: There is a problem in machinery order lag.

MASON: Have you ordered a press?

ADAMS: Yes, and we'll be moving by October.

MASON: Well, then, say you'll be in business in the last quarter of 1966. Look, Pete, this document has to be approved by Brewer and then the finance committee. If Chicago's our choice, we've got to *sell* Chicago. Let's put our best foot forward! The problem is to make it clear that on economics alone we would go to Akron . . . but you have to bring out the flaw in the economics: that managing 20 product lines, especially when you've got fancy products, just isn't possible.

COURTNEY: And you have a better building.

MASON: All of this should be in a table in the text. It ought to cover incremental cost, incremental investment, incremental expense, incremental ROI, and the building space. And Sam's right. Akron is a poor building; it's a warehouse. Pittsburgh is better for something like high-pressure materials. But out in Chicago you've got a multi-story building with more than enough space that is perfect for this sort of project.

COURTNEY: Pete, are we getting this compact enough for you?

MASON: Hey, why don't we put some sexy looking graphs in the thing? I don't know, but maybe we could plot incremental investment vs. incremental return for each location. See what you can do, Pete.

COURTNEY: Yes, that's a good idea.

*   *   *   *   *

MASON: Now, Pete, one other thing. You'll have to include discounted cash flow on the other two locations. Some of those guys [division and corporate top management] are going to look at just the numbers. You'll show them they're not too different.

*   *   *   *   *

MASON: The biggest discussion will be, "Why the hell move to Chicago?"

COURTNEY: You know, Pete, you should discuss the labor content in the product.

MASON: Good. We have to weave in the idea that it's a product with a low labor content and explain that this means the high Chicago labor cost will not hurt us.

ADAMS: One last item: Shouldn't we be asking for more capacity? Two-and-one-half million dollars only carries us through 1967.

MASON: Pete, we certainly wouldn't do this for one of our established products. Where our main business is involved, we build capacity in five- and ten-year chunks. But we have to treat toranium a little differently. The problem here is to take a position in the market. Competition isn't going to clobber us if we don't have the capacity to satisfy everyone. If the market develops, we can move quickly.

After the meeting, Courtney explained that he and Mason had been disappointed with Adams' draft and were trying to help him improve it without really "clobbering" him. "Adams' draft was weak. His numbers were incomplete and his argument sloppy. I've asked him to meet with Bob Lincoln [assistant controller for metal products] to discuss the proposal."

The result of Adams' five meetings with Lincoln was three more drafts of the toranium proposal. The numerical exhibits were revised for greater clarity. The text was revised to lessen the number of technical terms.

Adams, however, was still very much concerned with the appropriate size of the new facility. "Mason is only interested in justifying the location of the new facility!" Adams exclaimed. "We plan to sell $5.6 million worth of toranium in 1971. Yet we're asking for only $2.5 million worth of capacity. It's crazy! But, you know, I think Mason doesn't really care what capacity we propose. He just wants 'sexy looking graphs.' That's o.k. for him, because I'm the one who's going to get it in the neck in 1968. So far as I can see, Brewer has built his reputation by bringing this division from chronic undercapacity to a full-capacity, high ROI position."

The next step in the toranium facilities proposal was a formal presentation to the top management of metal products on June 2, 1966. There were two capital projects on the agenda. Brewer began the meeting by announcing that its purpose was to "discuss the proposals and decide if they were any good." He turned the meeting over to Mason, who, in turn, asked Adams to "take over and direct the meeting."

Adams proceeded by reading the draft proposal, after first asking for comments. He got halfway down the first page before Brewer interrupted.

BREWER: Let me stop you right here. You have told them [the proposal was aimed at Basic Industries' finance committee] the name, and you have told them how much money you want, but you haven't told them what the name means, and you haven't told them what the products are.

At this point a discussion began as to what the name of the project was going to be. The meeting then continued with Adams reading and people occasionally making comments on his English and on the text.

BREWER: Look, let's get this straight. What we are doing in this proposal is trying to tell them what it is we are spending their money on. That's what they want to know. Tell me about the electronic applications in that table you have there. I have to be able to explain them to the finance committee. I understand "steel" and "aerospace" but I don't understand "electronic applications" and I don't understand "electronic industry." I need some more specific words.

SAMUELS [vice president of R.&D.]: Let me ask you a question which some-one in the finance committee might ask. It's a nasty one. You forecast here that the industry sales in 1971 are going to be about $7 million, or maybe a little less. You think we are going to have 75% or 85% of this business. You also think we are going to get competition from G.E. and others. Do you think com-panies of that stature are going to be satisfied with sharing $1.5 million of the business? Don't you think that we may lose some of our market share?

This question was answered by Roberts and pursued by a few others. Essentially Roberts argued that the proprietary technology of the metal products division was going to be strong enough to defend its market share.

BREWER: Let me tell you about an item which is much discussed in the fi-nance committee. They are concerned, and basically this involves other divisions, with underestimating the cost of investment projects. I think, in fact, that there was a request for additional funds on a project recently which was as large as our entire annual capital budget.[1] Second of all, as a result of the capital ex-penditure cutback, there was a tendency, and again it has been in other divisions, to cut back on or delay facilities. Now it's not really just the capital expenditure cutback that is the reason for their behavior. If they had been doing their plan-ning, they should have been thinking about these expenditures five or six years ago, not two years ago. But they didn't do the estimates, or their estimates weren't correct, and now they are sold out on a lot of items and are buying products from other people and reselling them and not making any money. It's affecting the corporate earnings, so the environment in the finance committee today is very much (1) "Tell us how much you want, and tell us *all* that you want," and (2) "Give us a damned good return." Now I don't want us to get *sloppy*, but, Bill, if you need something, ask for it. And then make Pete meet his numbers.

ADAMS: Well, on this one, as I think you know, the machinery is already on order and we are sure that our market estimates are correct.

BREWER: Yes, I know that. I just mean that if you want something, then plan it right and tell them what you are going to need so you don't come back asking for more money six months later.

*   *   *   *   *

BREWER: I am going to need some words on competition. I am also going to need some words on why we are ready so soon on this project. We are asking for money now, and we say we are going to be in operation in the fourth quarter.

SAMUELS: Foresight (*followed by general laughter*).

MASON: Well, it's really quite understandable. This began last October when we thought we were going to expand at Akron. At that time, it was obvious that we needed capacity so we ordered some machines. Then as the thing developed,

---

[1] Metal products division's capital budget in 1965 was $7.9 million.

it was clear that there would be some other things we needed, and because of the timing lag we had to order them.

BREWER: OK . . . now another thing. Numerical control is hot as a fire-cracker in the finance committee. I am not saying that we should have it on this project, but you should be aware that the corporation is thinking a lot about it.

* * * * *

BREWER: [Much later on in the discussion.] There are really three reasons for moving. Why not state them?

1. You want to free up some space at Akron which you need.
2. There are 20 products at Akron, and toranium can't get the attention it needs.
3. You can get operating efficiencies if you move.

If you set it out, you can cut out all of this crap. You know, it would do you people some good if you read a facilities proposal[2] on something you didn't know beforehand. You really have to think about the guy who doesn't know what you're talking about. I read a proposal yesterday that was absolutely ridiculous. It had pounds per hour and tons per year and tons per month and tons per day and—except for the simplest numbers, which were in a table—all the rest were spread out through the story.

* * * * *

Adams indicated that he was disappointed with the meeting. Brewer seemed to him to be preoccupied with "words," and the topic of additional capacity never really came up. The only encouraging sign was Brewer's statement, "Tell us all that you want." But it seemed that all Mason "wanted" was $2.5 million worth of capacity.

Adams saw three possibilities open to him. First, he could ask for additional capacity.

This alternative meant that Adams would have to speak with Courtney and Mason. The Chicago plant manager viewed the prospect of such a conversation with mixed feelings. In the past, his relations with Courtney and Mason had been excellent. He had been able to deal with these men on an informal and relaxed level. However, the experience of drafting the toranium proposal left Adams a little uneasy. Courtney and Mason had been quite critical of his draft and had made him meet with Bob Lincoln in order to revise it. What would their reaction be if he were to request a reconsideration of the proposal at this late date? Moreover, what new data or arguments could he offer in support of a request for additional capacity?

On the other hand, Adams saw a formal request for additional capacity as a way of getting his feelings on the record. Even if his superiors refused his request, he would be in a better position with respect to the 1968 performance review. However, Adams wondered how his performance review would go if he formally requested and received additional capacity and the market did not develop as forecasted.

---

[2]The finance committee reviewed approximately 190 capital requests in 1965.

As his second alternative, Adams believed he could ask that the new facili-ties proposal specify that metal products would be needing more money for toranium facilities in the future.

This alternative did not pose the same problems as the first with respect to Courtney and Mason. Adams felt that saying more funds might be needed would be acceptable to Courtney and Mason, whereas asking for more might not be. However, the alternative introduced a new problem. Brewer had been quite explicit in insisting that the division ask for all that was needed so that it would not have to come back and ask for more in six months. To admit a possible need for additional funds, therefore, might jeopardize the entire project.

In spite of this problem, Adams felt that this alternative was the best one available. It was a compromise between his point of view and Mason's. If top management felt that the future of toranium was too uncertain, then why not ask for contingent funds? This would get Adams off the hook and still not actually increase metal products' real investment.

As his third alternative, Adams decided he could drop the issue and hope to be transferred or promoted before 1968.

ASSOCIATED PETROLEUM*

^^

In September 1966, Jim Robbins was getting increasingly worried about the new capital request for iso-chlorathane. As manager of the industrial chemicals division's functional chemicals product group, Robbins was responsible for providing adequate quantities of iso-chlorathane at competitive quality and cost. Normally, providing such capacity presented few problems. In this instance, however, everything seemed to be going wrong.

The forecasted market for iso-chlorathane was exploding. Whereas the October 1965 forecast showed no capacity problem until 1969, the June 1966 forecast showed sales capacity constrained by middle 1967. Moreover, the process technology of iso-chlorathane was changing. A new low-cost process was being developed but would not be "on line" before 1969. Finally, there were shortages of the raw material on which the current process was based.

"I think I could handle this mess," Robbins explained, "if it weren't for all my other products. You know that our new facility for plexon is running 60%–80% over the planned cost of $10 million. Given the atmosphere in the golden tower [the general manager's office], that's not too good."

Associated Petroleum was an international firm engaged in all aspects of the oil industry. The company's operations were organized into six areas: exploration and production, transportation, refining, marketing, chemicals, and research. The chemicals area, whose operations were principally domestic, was divided into three divisions: petrochemicals, industrial chemicals, and synthetic fibers and resins. In 1965, the chemicals area contributed $452 million in sales revenue which represented 13% of the corporate total.

Each division in the chemicals area was self-supporting and contained its own research and staff groups. Division executives were held responsible for planning the future of their divisions and for operating them successfully. Although plans and problems were discussed regularly with headquarters personnel, central management's greatest influence arose through performance appraisal based on such measures as ROI (return on investment).

Industrial chemicals

Industrial chemicals was the largest chemicals division with market sales of $212 million in 1965. Basically, industrial chemicals was organized into the traditional functional areas of marketing, production, engineering, and R.&D. (see Exhibit 1). However, in 1964, the division added a fifth area called operations. The operations area was designed to serve a central, coordinating function for the division's activities. The other two chemicals divisions did not have operations areas, nor did they plan to adopt them at the time of the case.

Exhibit 1

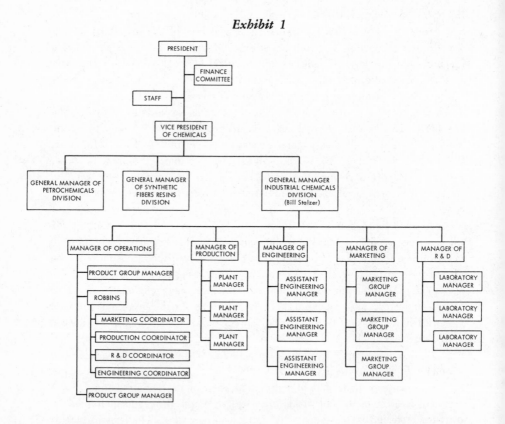

The reason for the creation of the operations function sheds light on the nature of its task. Industrial chemicals sold its products to other Associated divisions as well as to outside industries. Moreover, these products served as raw materials in some cases and as end products in other. For example, one chemical compound might have been sold to 20 outside customers in six different industries and to two other Associated divisions for use as raw material in four instances and as complementary end products in three others.

Since this variety of application and use was multiplied by the thousands of products that industrial chemicals produced, the need for a formal planning and coordinating function was apparent.

It was this function that the operations department was to perform. To do this, the area was divided into product groups, each of which was responsible for coordinating the production, engineering, and sale of a group of products. Product groups were created around different stages in the production process: that is, one product group was responsible for a group of basic "first-stage" chemicals while another had more complex, intermediate products. One of a group's most critical tasks was planning capacity requirements. Thus the group played a key role in the capital planning process.

Product groups were responsible for perceiving the need for additional capacity and developing a detailed proposal asking for this capacity. This proposal, which specified volume, kind of process, capital needed, and timing, was submitted to the divisional management. If they approved the proposal, it was submitted to the corporate finance committee for final approval. Projects that satisfied cost of capital requirements and were consistent with corporate strategy were usually accepted.

The relationship between the product groups and the functional departments in industrial chemicals was not that of "staff" vs. "line." For example, both product group managers and plant managers were held responsible for satisfactory output and cost. Both marketing managers and product group managers were held responsible for achieving budgeted sales levels.

However, this joint responsibility was not always accompanied by joint authority. The product group manager could "hire and fire" only four men: the functional coordinators reporting to him. Any other personnel that worked for the product group had to be obtained from a functional area on a project basis. For example, the engineering department decided on the number and allocation of engineers in industrial chemicals.

Rewards and punishments

Bill Stalzer, general manager of industrial chemicals, explained how men were measured and rewarded in the division.

We certainly have the data to measure a man against present and past performance, but we don't have an automatic or mechanical examination. There are just too many interrelationships in this company to put the finger on someone on the basis of one set of numbers.

Performance against plan is only a starting point. Did a man meet his planned market share, net income, and ROI? If not, why not? Every man is bound to have some bad luck. We want to know how he dealt with the adverse conditions. Did he cut back or take a gamble? Does he see the broad, corporate issues, or is he myopically fixed on the details of the problem? These are the important questions. We're interested in future performance, not past glories or mishaps.

In this regard, we also place great emphasis on what one might call interpersonal skills. For example, we feel that a key part of a manager's job is developing and training his subordinates. You can't measure whether or not a man has adequately performed this key task in terms of dollars, but nevertheless, it is a critical aspect of a manager's overall evaluation.

However, let me make one point perfectly clear. While we place emphasis on subjective criteria for evaluation, we do not ignore actual performance against plan. We'd be poor managers if we forgot to make profits. It is always a natural assumption that a man who makes plan consistently is doing the rest of his job well also. I know this may not be the case, but if a man makes plan, examination of other aspects of his performance tends to be less intense. On the other hand, if a man doesn't perform well against plan, we will most likely look into his total performance in greater depth. However, not making plan is not a personal disaster for a good manager.

Functional chemicals

Jim Robbins was the manager of the functional chemicals product group. Robbins was 42 and had been an assistant manager of industrial chemicals engineering before becoming group manager in January 1965. Four men reported directly to Robbins: Lee Fifer, production coordinator; Ralph Miller, marketing coordinator; Bob Scott, R.&D. coordinator; and Sam West, engineering coordinator (see Exhibit 1). The functional chemicals group operated from a set of offices in the corporate headquarters building in Houston, Texas.

In 1965, the group's 10 products accounted for 424 million pounds (total output) of production valued at over $50 million (including internal product shipments transferred at market price).

Iso-chlorathane

In April 1966, Jim Robbins, manager for functional chemicals, explained that one of his products, iso-chlorathane, was "taking off" (see Exhibit 2):

There are 12 firms producing and selling iso-chlorathane in the United States. Six of these account for over 75% of industry sales, which are currently at the rate of 1,280 million pounds a year. We're selling at the rate of 265 million pounds a year, which is our capacity level. In fact, we are turning down outside sales. While our anticipated need in 1969 is 300 million pounds, I think we can get the additional 35 million pounds by using our expense budget.[1]

The problem, however, is that 300 million pounds in 1969 is a low forecast. That forecast came out last October, and now the market is going wild. I expect that in his June forecast Ralph Miller [marketing coordinator for functional chemicals] will predict a considerably greater need.

In the past, they have built the iso-chlorathane capacity in bits and pieces because this division seems to have a great fear of overexpansion. In 1950, Associated built a plant at Baton Rouge. In 1953, the plant was up to 134 million pounds and they put in 16 million more. In 1954, there was a report proposing

[1] Capital expenditures under $100,000 did not require corporate management's approval. Such expenditures were included on an expense budget which was approved by divisional management.

expansion of the plant by 40 million pounds. The proposal was refused by division officers on the basis of a weak marketing story. A 60 million pound expansion was finally carried out in 1957 and brought the plant up to 210 million pounds. In 1962 they built a second plant at Philadelphia which was rated at 35 million pounds. Since then, they have gradually brought its theoretical capacity up to 55 million pounds.

Today, however, we see a tremendous market for iso-chlorathane and we are determined to build a facility that will meet our *long-term* needs. It's just good economics to do it.

Exhibit 2

ISO-CHLORATHANE
DEMAND/CAPACITY RELATIONSHIPS
(Millions of Pounds per Year)

	Forecast						
	1965	*1966*	*1967*	*1968*	*1969*	*1970*	*1971*
U.S. market October 1965							
Forecasted demand	940	1,040	1,124	1,214	1,312	1,416	1,630
Existing or planned capacity as of April 1966	1,340	1,220	1,240	1,330	1,350	1,350	1,350
Balance	400	180	116	116	38	(66)	(280)
Associated's position							
Forecasted demand as of June 1966							
Market sales	150	164	210	270	310	352	
Internal use	104	120	130	155	178	192	
Total*	254	284	340	425	488	544	
Theoretical capacity existing or planned as of April 1966	265	300	300	300	300	300	
Balance	11	16	(40)	(125)	(188)	(244)	

*Total sales used to determine ROI. All internal sales valued at market price.
Source: Case writer's notes.

Sam West, engineering coordinator for functional chemicals, pointed out that the iso-chlorathane capacity problem had another important dimension: the process for making the product was in transition. The process by which Associated made iso-chlorathane was based on a raw material called prime gas. However, in 1962 a new type of technology was developed that used another raw material, feed gas, to make the product. West explained the situation as follows:

Feed gas sells for 2 to 4 cents per pound, which means an iso-chlorathane cost of 5.5 to 7 cents per pound. Prime gas costs 6 to 8 cents per pound, which yields an iso-chlorathane costing 7.5 to 9 cents per pound. Furthermore, since investment per pound is about the same for both processes, the ROI picture is even more dramatic.

I think this article sums up the situation. [Excerpts from the article follow.]
The demand for iso-chlorathane with its broad market base has flourished in
the U.S. economy. Its end products are incorporated in a wide variety of plastics
and foam products.

However, slowing the expansion of industry capacity is the producers' indecision about whether iso-chlorathane process technology is sufficiently developed
to permit a switch from prime gas to feed gas raw material. Feed gas's compelling attractiveness can be summed up succinctly: manufacturing costs of feed
gas are 2c to 4c per lb. vs. 6c to 8c per lb. for prime gas.

But feed gas technology is new and untried and a choice of processes is limited.

*   *   *   *   *

There seems to be little argument that the future, be it sooner or later, does
belong to feed gas-based iso-chlorathane production. Vested interest in prime gas
and untested technology appear to be only short-term deterrents.

In April 1966, the R.&D. department of industrial chemicals was still
unable to transfer its feed gas-based process from the laboratory to a pilot
plant. Therefore, the functional chemicals group arranged to meet with representatives of R.&D. to discuss the situation. A transcript of part of that
meeting follows:

R.&D.: The problem facing us is that of basically inappropriate pilot plant
equipment. During the first phase, the instrumentation broke down under the
high pressure. We are now experimenting with a different kind of sensing device
and coupling.

WEST: But as far as you know, high pressure is going to be a problem regardless of what you do?

R.&D.: That's right.

ROBBINS: Now wait a minute! Let's not leave the problem with the sensors.
What kind of material do you want?

R.&D.: It has to be a special bonded metal. We've been told that it will take
six weeks to get it.

ROBBINS: What! Can't we get that for you in the shop?

WEST: Sure. What are the specifications? [He obtained them, went out and
returned with confirmation of the fact that the plant had the metal and the appropriate sensors could be constructed that afternoon.]

ROBBINS: OK. Now what about the other equipment you need? You want a
four-gallon container. That is what are you going to use when you're scaling
up, isn't it?

R.&D.: Yes. That's right—four gallons. But it has to be made from super-
strength steel. We've been told that it takes 14 weeks to get it.

ROBBINS: Can't we make that also? [West, Fifer, and Robbins decided that
the plant could make it.]

R.&D.: But aren't bonded metals on allocation? [When a material was on
allocation, the government had deemed it to be scarce and was controlling its
use.]

WEST: I told them it was in the national interest. [At this point in the meeting the men from R.&D. left.]

ROBBINS: Don't they know that we are in a *hurry*? How can they contemplate
14 weeks?

WEST: Well, it's the way they think about this kind of thing. Whenever someone says that something will take 10 weeks they wait 10 weeks. That is the way they have been trained.

ROBBINS: But they sounded like business as usual.

FIFER: Well, they don't know about things like this. I didn't know that we had that steel in the shop.

ROBBINS: Sure, I didn't either, but on a thing like this we'll move heaven and earth. If a corporation like Associated really wants something, we can get anything we want in a month.

After R.&.D.'s discouraging report, Robbins started negotiations with certain U.S. chemical firms (not in the iso-chlorathane business) in an attempt to secure licenses on their feed gas-based processes. Associated's major competitor in the iso-chlorathane market had already purchased exclusive rights to one of the new processes from a Japanese firm. However, this competitor was having problems with quality and was rumored to have lost over $2 million in equipment and materials.

Robbins' negotiations resulted in more frustration and little accomplishment. Most of the processes were still in the laboratory stage. Moreover, those firms with the most promising results seemed interested in entering the iso-chlorathane market themselves.

From May to September, Jim Robbins' life as manager of the functional chemicals groups was chaotic.

May

Sam West, Robbins' engineering coordinator, reported that he desperately needed engineering help. "I've got seven major projects on the fire, and I need 100 man months of engineering more than I've got, and I can't get that damn engineering department to move," he said.

At the end of April 1966, year-to-date sales for functional chemicals were only 70% of plan. (Year-to-date sales for industrial chemicals were 82% of plan.) However, Robbins was philosophical about the situation: "The important thing around here is to update your plan and have a reasonable explanation for why you are under. You have to be able to put on a good dog and pony show for divisional management."

June

In June, Miller's forecast for iso-chlorathane came out.

	1966	1967	1968	1969	1970
		(Millions of Pounds)			
Market sales	164	210	270	310	352
Internal use					
Industrial	60	60	75	80	90
Fibers	50	60	65	75	80
Other	10	10	15	23	22
Total	284	340	425	488	544

Robbins explained the implications of rising sales as follows:

The June forecast really puts the pressure on. As a basic chemical, iso-chlorathane faces strong price competition. Price cutting has already resulted in a price decline from 13c per pound in 1963 to 10c per pound this year. Moreover, I see no letup in this slide. In fact, we project a price of 7c per pound for 1971.

Now, the problem is that these sales forecasts are based on our meeting these price cuts. Given current prices on raw materials, a new plant with the prime gas-based process means a decline in iso-chlorathane ROI from last year's 14% to 10% in 1971. However, if we get a new feed gas-based process plant to replace Baton Rouge, ROI should jump to about 21% in 1971.

Yet all I hear from R.&D. is that the feed gas process is great but it is far from being commercial. You know, it's OK for a little guy not to have the leading technology. But for Associated, it's impossible. Our strategy is to compete with the largest oil and chemical companies by staying ahead of their laboratories and being first with low-cost plants.

Moreover, how the hell am I going to plan ahead when I get forecasts like Miller's? Look at the synthetic fibers division. They're one of our biggest customers. Yet we can never tell how much they will need. Last October, they told us they wanted 40 million pounds in 1966 and saw a need for 50 million pounds in 1970.

Sales for the functional chemicals group as of June were 81% of plan for the year to date. (Divisional sales were 85% of year to date plan.) Robbins indicated he was pleased.

July

R.&D. came up with a "promising" breakthrough on the feed gas process. However, their best estimate for getting a plant "on line" (if things worked out) was late 1969.

The iso-chlorathane problem was further complicated by a shortage of prime gas, the raw material for the present process. Prime gas was produced by Associated's petrochemicals division. In addition to its use as a raw material for making iso-chlorathane, prime gas was the basic input in making nylostyrene, a product produced by the synthetic fibers division (see Exhibit 3).

However, fibers' need for prime gas would be reduced considerably in 1968. In that year, the division was scheduled to open a large nylostyrene plant using a new process based on a new raw material. A representative of the petrochemicals division commented on the situation.

Long term we are going to have prime gas coming out of our ears (see Exhibit 4). Everyone wants to switch from prime gas to feed gas, and prime gas is a by-product of the process for making feed gas. However, today we're short because we don't have enough stills, and the ones we have are running into technical problems. Right now we're doing our best to work with fibers and industrial chemicals to allocate what we've got.

Purchasing offered no help. A representative of Associated's corporate pur-

Exhibit 3

PRODUCT FLOW

PETROCHEMICAL DIVISION	INDUSTRIAL CHEMICALS DIVISION	SYNTHETIC FIBERS AND RESINS DIVISION

Key: The dotted line indicates that R.&D. was working on feed gas-based processes for iso-chlorathane.
Source: Case writer's notes.

chasing department explained that "the world is short of prime gas. There is some capacity at Monsanto but they won't sell to a competitor like Associated. And the problem is that no one will build new capacity in the face of feed gas. Everyone's afraid of the new feed gas technologies."

On July 11, the functional chemicals group met to discuss the alternatives open to them with respect to iso-chlorathane:

ROBBINS: Let's see. Long term we're looking for a plant that will replace Baton Rouge. How big shall we build this thing, or study it anyway?

WEST: For what year do you want it?

ROBBINS: 1973 or '76? What is our forecast? We have one for 1976, don't we?

MILLER: Yea, '76. I figure about 750 million pounds.

ROBBINS: OK. If we keep Philadelphia that means about 700 million pounds. So why don't we study 700 million and half of that? The marketing people have been telling us 500 isn't big enough. Let's throw 700 at them and see what they do.

FIFER: I think we should put out a white paper on iso-chlorathane which states all the problems we are facing, and send it to engineering. I just don't think they know what our problems are.

MILLER: You might also send it to R.&D.

ROBBINS: OK, Sam, when can you do it? While you are on vacation?

WEST: Yes.

*   *   *   *   *

WEST: In the short term, we have a prime gas shortage at Baton Rouge and Philadelphia. There is competition between iso-chlorathane and nylostyrene. Lee [Fifer] and Tom McWilliams [production manager for nylostyrene] get together periodically to negotiate priorities.

ROBBINS: Who is the stumbling block to making modifications needed to get additional output?

Exhibit 4

PRIME GAS SUPPLY AND USAGE FOR NYLOSTYRENE AND
ISO-CHLORATHANE PRODUCTION FOR PERIOD FROM
JANUARY 1, 1967, THROUGH 1970

(Thousands of Pounds per Day—Average)

	1967 (1st Half)	1967 (2nd Half)	1968 (1st Half)	1968 (3rd Qtr)	1968 (4th Qtr)	1969	1970
Philadelphia							
Supply	108	108	108	108	108	108	108
Desired usage							
Nylostyrene	62	69	75	50*	45*	0	0
Iso-chlorathane	58	58	58	58	58	58	46†
Total	120	127	133	108*	103	58	46
Baton Rouge							
Supply	213	213	213	213	213	213	213
Desired usage							
Nylostyrene	126	126	126	90*	74*	65	55
Iso-chlorathane	105	102	89	85	115	115	0†
Total	231	228	215	175*	189	180	55

*Fibers division expected its new nylostyrene process on line in late 1968.
†Feed gas-based process for iso-chlorathane scheduled to be on line in late 1969.
Source: Case writer's notes.

FIFER: Nobody.

ROBBINS: Well, who is going to do this?

FIFER: We are hoping to get McWilliams to.

WEST: They are as anxious to get it going as we are, and we hope we can use their engineering time to do it.

* * * * *

ROBBINS: Another alternative is to buy iso-chlorathane from Grace. Also, Ralph [Miller], you were going to look overseas. Did you find anything?

MILLER: No, I started, but then this thing with fibers started and you went on vacation and everything else went on vacation.

ROBBINS: Another thing is that Japanese company. Purchasing swears they have 100 million pounds of iso-chlorathane capacity. My calculations indicate that if this is true, they may have 15 million pounds to sell.

FIFER: But we can't make any money if we buy iso-chlorathane at their prices.

ROBBINS: Hell, short term our problem is to meet our commitments. I don't give a damn about the economics.

* * * * *

ROBBINS: I think we've had enough on this damned iso-chlorathane. We've got to worry about that $2–$2.5 million overrun on the plexon facility.

FIFER: Want to hear about real short-term problems?

ROBBINS: Can we do anything?

FIFER: No, but maybe you should be informed. Because of the strike at the Houston plant and the war in Viet Nam, there is now a shortage of the chemicals which we need to run at low pressures. However, running at higher pressures means we are using 10,000 more pounds of prime gas per day to get the same output.

ROBBINS: Well, one thing we know is that fibers is a source of a great deal of trouble. They're taking a great deal more iso-chlorathane than their commitment. [Fibers division was able to draw on whatever iso-chlorathane it wanted from the storage tanks. There were accounting records but no control numbers.]

MILLER: I think we're heading for real trouble. Our inventories of iso-chlorathane are at the danger level, and with Baton Rouge running at 60% of capacity because of the prime gas shortage, things look bad.

ROBBINS: Look, I agree, but the problem is the process. Our current process based on prime gas yields a low cost iso-chlorathane. In fact, I think we're the lowest in the industry. So we could expand using prime gas and still show a pretty good return, particularly since prime gas is going to be an almost "free" commodity after nylostyrene stops using it. But Stalzer is "hooked" on feed gas and it's not very easy to change his thinking. And you can't use equipment designed for the prime gas process for the feed gas process.

MILLER: But the damn feed gas process is at best years away, and given R.&D.'s speed, perhaps we'll never see it. What's this going to do to our plan?

ROBBINS: Ralph, I don't want to go through the plan because it will scare us. If we look at what we said we were going to do and compare it with where we are, we'll be so upset we won't be able to operate.

August

Not much progress was made on the iso-chlorathane problem. Vacation schedule and problems with other products left little time for iso-chlorathane.

Associated was contemplating a major acquisition and Robbins was giving a great deal of his time to an evaluatory task force to which he had been assigned.

In other areas, industrial chemicals had acquired a small chemical manufacturer, and the iso-chlorathane group was working on the problems of assimilation. Moreover, it was becoming apparent that the new facility for plexon would overrun its planned cost of $10 million by much more than 20%–25%.

On the other hand, year-to-date sales for functional chemicals were now 83% of plan (year-to-date sales for industrial chemicals were now 87% of plan), and West finally obtained an engineer for the group to work specifically on iso-chlorathane.

September

The overrun on the new facility for plexon was now approaching 60%–80% and was occupying most of Robbins' time.

R.&D. work on the feed gas process proceeded with some success. However, because of equipment problems and critical material shortages, the estimate for getting a plant "on line" was still late 1969.

The new engineer for iso-chlorathane had studied the possibility of an "interim" expansion of iso-chlorathane facilities. His figures showed that a $5.2 million addition to Baton Rouge could provide needed product capacity through 1968. (Existing facilities could not be expanded beyond the 425 million pound level. Additional capacity would necessitate a new plant to replace Baton Rouge.) However, the project ROI depended on the cost of prime gas.

While the prime gas shortage was relieved (due to improved efficiency of the stills) to the point where the functional chemicals group could meet its 1966 iso-chlorathane commitments, there was not going to be enough prime gas to satisfy projected iso-chlorathane needs for 1967. Since other companies were not selling the raw material, Robbins saw only two ways of getting additional prime gas: (1) to increase output of current prime gas facilities (by improving the stills, etc.), or (2) to build an incremental new prime gas facility. However, according to the new engineer, existing equipment was already being overworked and, therefore, the first alternative would result in expensive prime gas (7 cents per pound). The engineer's analysis is included as Exhibit 5.

Robbins was perplexed. Obviously, Associated's management would not accept a project with a 6% ROI, but it was equally clear to Robbins that, with the uncertainty surrounding the new feed gas technology and the behavior of competitors, the management climate was not conducive to expenditures for additional prime gas facilities or new plants. Moreover, the decision to build new prime gas facilities belonged to the petrochemicals division, not to industrial chemicals.

Exhibit 5

ENGINEER'S ANALYSIS

Alternatives	Cost of Raw Material to Industrial Chemicals	Cost of Iso-chlorathane	Average Selling Price of Iso-chlorathane 1967–1971	Incremental Investment and ROI ($ Millions)		Total Investment and ROI ($ Millions)	
1. "Interim" expansion							
a). New prime gas facility	6¢	7.50¢	8.5¢	$5.2	23.0%	$40.5	10.3%
b). Squeeze existing facility	7¢	8.25¢	8.5¢	$5.2	6.0%	$40.5	8.1%
2. New 500 million lb. plant to replace Baton Rouge—prime gas process (ROI based on 425 million lb. sales)	6¢	7.00¢	8.5¢	$40.0	13.2%	$40.0	13.2%
3. New 500 million lb. plant to replace Baton Rouge—feed gas process (ROI based on 425 million lb. sales)	2¢	6.00¢	8.5¢	$40.0	25.0%	$40.0	25.0%

Source: Case writer's notes.

Robbins saw three alternative courses of action:

1. Put more pressure on his group and other interested organizations within Associated Petroleum to settle the iso-chlorathane issue. While there were many specific actions that could be taken along these lines, the following came to Robbins' mind:

   a) Have the new engineer write up an official proposal for the incremental investment in new prime gas facilities. This action was certain to meet opposition given top management commitments to the feed gas technology. However, it made the most economic sense.

   b) Meet with people outside the product group and get some help on the long-term process problem. Over six months had passed since Robbins realized that iso-chlorathane capacity was going to be a problem. Yet he had not even begun to draft a new capital proposal. Robbins considered meeting with some people from other divisions or from R.&D. But the problem was whom to meet and what to ask. Meetings with R.&D. didn't seem to get anywhere at all. Moreover, Robbins was concerned about developing his subordinates. He was used to letting a man learn by doing, even if it took a long time. If he assumed the task of coordinating R.&D., for example, Robbins felt he would impede Scott's [coordinator for R.&D.] development as a manager. Besides, if he gave his men a little more time, he was hopeful they would resolve the problem themselves, an occurrence that would put two feathers in Robbins' cap.

In any event, the product group manager was sure that a great many of his and his group's problems were due to the nature of Associated's organization and he certainly couldn't change that.

2. Shift the emphasis of the group's activity from iso-chlorathane to the group's other nine products. Iso-chlorathane had already diverted the group's attention and effort to the point that the plexon facility was going to run more than 100% over its planned cost. If the group couldn't show a few bright spots, better than planned performance, its 1967 plan review in November was going to be a nightmare. At any rate, being out of capacity on iso-chlorathane wouldn't be that big a tragedy. The product's market share would not be hurt because competitors were also out of capacity and uncertain about the new feed gas process.

3. Get assigned to manage the new acquisition that was being studied by the task force of which he was a member. Barring a minor miracle, Robbins saw a rather grim performance for his group in 1966, and future prospects did not look much better. Given such a record, he felt that his chances for advancement would not be particularly good. However, the task force was going to recommend acquisition, and assignment to the new operation would provide a graceful exit from a messy situation.

The accomplishment of purpose:

organizational processes and

behavior

Our study of strategy has brought us to the prescription that organizational structure must follow strategy if implementation is to be effective. We have seen that structural design involves inevitably (1) a suitable specialization ✓ of task, (2) a parallel provision for coordination, and (3) information systems for meeting the requirement that specialists be well informed and their work coordinated. We have seen that a variety of structures may be suitable to a strategy so long as the performance influenced by structural characteristics is not diverted from strategic ends.

We turn now from structural considerations to other influences upon organizational behavior. A logical structure does not insure effective organized effort any more than a high degree of technical skill in individual members insures achievements of organizational purposes. We suggest the following proposition for testing in your analysis of cases: *Organizational performance* ✓ *is effective to the extent that (in an atmosphere deliberately created to encourage the development of required skills and to provide the satisfactions of personal progress) individual energy is successfully directed toward organizational goals.* Convergence of energy upon purpose is made effective by individual and group commitment to purpose.

Man-made and natural organizational *systems* and *processes* are available to influence individual development and performance. In any organization the system which relates specific influences upon behavior to each other (so ✓ as to constitute an ultimate impact upon behavior) is made up of some six elements: (1) standards, (2) measures, (3) incentives, (4) rewards, (5) penalties, and (6) controls. The distinguishing characteristic of a system, of course, is the interaction of its elements. This interdependence will vary from organization to organization and from situation to situation and cannot always be observed, controlled, or completely analyzed.

The familiar processes which bear on performance are (1) measurement, ✓ (2) evaluation, (3) motivation, (4) control, and (5) individual development.

√The most important aspect of a process is the speed and direction of its forward motion and the nature of its side effects. So far as the uniqueness of each company situation allows, we shall look at combinations of these organizational systems and processes in the following order:

1. The establishment of standards and measurement of performance.
2. The administration of motivation and incentive systems.
3. The operation of systems of restraint and control.
4. The recruitment and development of management.

These processes have been studied in detail by specialists of several kinds. We shall not attempt to extract all the wisdom or expose all the folly which, over the years, has accumulated in the study of human relations and organizational behavior. We are now concerned, as always, with the limited but important ways in which specialized bodies of knowledge can be put to use in the implementation of strategy. The idea of strategy will dominate our approach to the internal organizational systems which animate structure, just as it dominated our discussion of the factors that determine structure itself. It may be desirable to point out that our aim is not to coerce and manipulate unwilling individuals. It is instead to support and direct individuals who are at least assenting to or, more desirably, committed to organizational goals. Commitment to purpose remains in our scheme of things the overriding necessary condition of effective accomplishment.

Establishment of standards and measurement of performance

If progress toward goals is to be supervised at all, it will have to be observed and measured. If it is to be measured, whether quantitatively or qualitatively, there must be some idea of where an organization is compared to where it ought to be. To state where an organization ought to be is to set a standard. A standard takes shape as a projection of hoped-for or budgeted performance. As time passes, positive and negative variances between budgeted and actual performance are recorded. This comparison makes possible, although it does not necessarily justify, relating incentives and controls to performance as measured against standards. For example, managers in the Hilton Hotels group prepare detailed forecasts of their anticipated revenues, costs, and operating profits, all based on past records and future projections that take growth targets into account. The reward system recognizes not only good results but accuracy of forecasting.

It is virtually impossible to make meaningful generalizations about how proper standards might be set in particular companies. It can be said, however, that in any organization the overall strategy can be translated into more or less detailed future plans (the detail becoming less predictable as the time span grows longer), which permit comparison of actual with predicted performance. Whether standards are being set at exactly the proper level is less significant than the fact that an effort is being made to raise them steadily as organizational power and resources increase. External events may, however, invalidate predictions. It must be recognized that for good reasons as well as bad, standards are not always attainable. Hence the need for skill in variable budgeting.

By far the most important problem of measurement is that increased ✓ interest in the measurement of performance against standards brings increased danger that the executive evaluation program may encourage performance which detracts from rather than supports the overall strategy.

The temptation to use measurement primarily for the purpose of judging executive performance is acute. The desire to put management responsibility in the ablest hands leads to comparing managers in terms of results. Failure to meet a standard leads naturally to the assignment of blame to persons. The general manager's most urgent duty is to see that planned results are indeed accomplished. Such pressure, unfortunately, may lead to exaggerated respect for specific measures and for the short-run results they quantify, and thus to ultimate misevaluation of performance.

The problems of measurement cluster about the fallacy of the single cri- ✓ terion.[1] When any single measure like return on investment, for example, is used to determine the compensation, promotion, or reassignment of a manager, the resultant behavior will often lead to unplanned and undesired outcomes. No single measure can encompass the total contribution of an individual either to immediate and longer term results or to the efforts of others. The sensitivity of individuals to evaluation leads them to produce the performance that will measure up in terms of the criterion rather than in terms of more important purposes. Since managers respond to the measures management actually takes to reward performance, mere verbal exhortations to behave in the manner required by long-range strategy carry no weight, and cannot be relied upon to preclude undesirable actions encouraged by a poorly designed measurement and reward system.

Faith in the efficacy of a standard measure like return on investment can reach extreme proportions, especially among men to whom the idea of strategy is apparently unfamiliar. Thus a visiting top manager from a major automobile manufacturer told a class that the company being discussed could solve its apparently bothersome problem of designing an effective relationship between the home office and the branches by giving the branch managers a great deal of autonomy and then judging their performance solely on the basis of return on the capital employed by each. A student who was not convinced answered this argument as follows:

Although this solution to the branch-home office relations problem had merit, it overlooked the fact that the company was dependent for a great deal of its capital on bankers who evaluated the company on bases other than return on investment. If the proposed solution was accepted, the branch manager might in-

---

[1]See John Dearden's "Limits on Decentralized Profit Responsibility" and "Mirage of Profit Decentralization" in E. P. Learned, F. J. Aguilar, and R. C. K. Valtz, *European Problems in General Management*, pp. 570–97. These articles first appeared in the *Harvard Business Review*, July–August 1962, pp. 81–89; and November–December 1962, pp. 140–54.

crease his return on investment by allowing his delinquency percentage to rise. Rising delinquency percentages might cause the bankers to withhold new credit from the company. The condition could therefore arise in which the branch manager, though carrying out policies which make his performance appear good under the evaluation system being used, would actually be acting in a manner destructive to the welfare of the company as a whole.[2]

Instances in which performance is measured in terms of just one figure or ratio are so numerous as to suggest that the pursuit of quantification and measurement as such has overshadowed the real goal of management evaluation. If we return to our original hypothesis that profit and return on investment are terms that can be usefully employed to denote the results to be sought by business, but are too general to characterize its distinctive mission or purpose, then we must say that short-term profitability is not by itself an adequate measure of managerial performance. Return on investment, when used alone, is another dangerous criterion, since it can lead businessmen to postpone needed product research or the modernization of facilities in the interest of keeping down the investment on the basis of which their performance is measured. Certainly we must conclude that evaluation of performance must not be focused exclusively upon the criterion of short-run profitability or any other single standard which may cause managers to act contrary to the long-range interests of the company as a whole.

As you discuss the cases that follow, you will be concerned with developing more adequate criteria. Our concern for strategy naturally leads us to suggest that the management evaluation system which plays so great a part in influencing management performance must employ a number of criteria, some of which are subjective and thus difficult to quantify. It is easy to argue that subjective judgments are unfair. But use of a harmful or irrelevant criterion just because it leads itself to quantification is a poor exchange for alleged objectivity.

Against multiple criteria, it may be argued that they restrict the freedom of the profit-center manager to produce the results required through any means he elects. This may of course be true, but the manager who does not want his methods to be subject to scrutiny does not want to be judged. Accountants, sometimes indifferent to the imperfections of their figures and the artificiality of their conventions, do not always make clear the true meaning of an annual profit figure or the extent to which a sharp rise from one year to the next may reflect the failure to make investments needed to sustain the future of a product line.

If multiple criteria are to be used, it is not enough for top management simply to announce that short-term profitability and return on investment are only two measures among many—including responsibility to society—by which executives are going to be judged. Such an announcement did not prevent violation of the antitrust laws by managers in the electrical industry,

---

[2]David J. Dunn, "Evaluation of Performance" (unpublished student paper). Reproduced by permission.

who believed it was more important for them to produce the expected profit than to inform their superiors that the basis for conducting business both honestly and profitably had disappeared. To give subordinates freedom to exercise judgment and simultaneously to demand profitability produces an enormous pressure which cannot be effectively controlled by endless talk about tying rewards to factors other than profit.

The tragedy of men, honorable in other ways, working for seniors who were apparently unaware of price-fixing practices, should dramatize one serious predicament of the profit-center form of organization, where, characteristically, management expects to solve the problems of evaluation by decentralizing freedom of decision to subordinates, so long as profit objectives are met. Decentralization seems sometimes to serve as a cloak for nonsupervision, except for the control implicit in the superficial measure of profitability. It would appear to preclude accurate evaluation, and the use of multiple criteria may indeed make a full measure of decentralization inappropriate.

To delegate authority to profit centers and to base evaluation upon proper performance must not mean that the profit center's strategic decisions are left unsupervised. *Even under decentralization, top management must remain familiar with divisional substrategy, with the fortunes—good and bad—that attend implementation, and with the problems involved in attempting to achieve budgeted performance.* The true function of measurement is to increase perceptions of the problems limiting achievement. If an individual sees where he stands in meeting a schedule, he may be led to inquire why he is not somewhere else. If this kind of question is not asked, the answer is not proffered. An effective system of evaluation must include information which will allow top management to understand the problems faced by subordinates in achieving the results for which they are held responsible. And certainly if evaluation is to be comprehensive enough to avoid the distortions cited thus far, immediate results will not be the only object of evaluation. The effectiveness with which problems are handled along the way will be evaluated, even though this judgment, like most of the important decisions of management, must remain subjective.

To quote Dunn once more:

In effect then, subordinates will not only be judged on the results, but on the effectiveness with which they overcome problems of known magnitude. This involves subjective judgment that raises the question of fairness. I submit the responsibility of top management is to *be fair*, not to evolve a system that proves its fairness beyond the question of a doubt. It is nice to be nice and to establish evaluation systems by which everyone is relieved of fears of personal prejudice and favoritism. It is much more important, however, that an evaluation system contribute to the long-range welfare of the company. If this need necessitates management's requiring subordinates to accept subjective judgment in good faith, then this is what has to be done. If making these judgments requires management's time, then the time will have to be spent.[3]

---

[3]*Ibid.*

The process of formulating and implementing strategy, which is supervised directly by the chief executive in a single-unit company, can be shared widely in a multiunit company. Preoccupation with final results need not be so exclusive as to prevent top management from working with divisional management in establishing objectives and policies or in formulating plans to meet objectives. Such joint endeavor helps to insure that divisional performance will not be evaluated without full knowledge of the problems encountered in implementation.

When the diversified company becomes so large that this process is impracticable, then new means must be devised. *Implicit in accurate evaluation is familiarity with performance on a basis other than through accounting figures.*

The formula of evaluation most consistent with the concept of strategy that is outlined in these notes is what is called "management by objectives." Instead of simply evaluating "traits," like some of the older appraisal systems, this process entails at all levels of management a meeting between subordinate and superior to agree on the achievements which the subordinate will try to accomplish during the forthcoming period. The subordinate's suggested objectives are modified if, after discussion, they appear either impractical or understated. They are checked for the contribution they will make to the larger strategy of which they must be a part. They are designed to include quantitatively nonmeasurable items as well as items budgeted in the formal short-term and long-range plans. The problems of successfully designing such a system are easier to see than to solve. Nonetheless, an acceptance of the imperfections and inexactness of such a system, plus a shared interest in the problems to be overcome in serving strategy, make possible a kind of communication which cannot be replaced by the application of a single criterion. Certainly, it is the quality of his objectives and of his attempts to overcome obstacles posed by circumstance and by competition that is the most important thing to measure about a manager's performance.

Motivation and incentive systems

The influences upon behavior in any organization are visible and invisible, planned and unplanned, formal and not formal. The intent to measure affects the performance which is the object of measurement; cause and effect obscure each other. The executive who refuses to leave the implementation of strategy to chance has available diverse means of encouraging behavior which advances strategy and deterring behavior which does not. The positive elements, always organized in patterns which make them influential in given situations, may be designated as motivation and incentive systems. The negative elements, similarly patterned, can be grouped as systems of restraint and control. Organization studies have led their authors variously to prefer positive or negative signals and to conclude that one or the other is preferable. The general manager will do well to conclude that each is indispensable.

Whatever the necessity for and the difficulties of performance evaluation, the effort to encourage and reward takes precedence over the effort to deter and restrain. Thus, properly directed, motivation may have more positive effects than control. Certainly, the general manager-strategist, whose own prior experience is likely to have made him intensely interested in the subject of executive compensation, should welcome whatever guidance he can get from researchers or staff assistants working in the field of job evaluation and compensation. Unfortunately, here also the prevailing thinking is often oriented less toward the goals to be sought than toward the requirements of the systems adopted.

The human relations movement has developed convincing evidence that executives, like workers, are influenced by nonmonetary as well as financial incentives. At the same time, it is no longer argued that financial rewards are even relatively unimportant, and much thought has been given to equitable compensation of executives.

Unfortunately for the analyst of executive performance, it is harder to describe for the executive than for the man at the machine what he does and how he spends his time. The terminology of his job description is full of phrases like "has responsibility for," "maintains relationships with," and "supervises the operation of." The activities of planning, problem solving, and directing or administering are virtually invisible. And the activities of recruiting, training, and developing subordinates are hardly more concretely identifiable.

In any case, it is fallacious to assume that quality of performance is the only basis for the compensation of executives. Many other factors must be taken into account. The job itself has certain characteristics that help to determine the pay schedules. These include complexity of the work, the general education required, and the knowledge or technical training needed. Compensation should also reflect the responsibility of the job-incumbent for people and property, the nature and number of decisions he must make, and the effect of his activities and decisions upon profits.

In addition to reflecting the quality of performance and the nature of the job, an executive's compensation must also have some logical relationship to rewards paid to others in the same organization. That is, the compensation system must reflect in some way a man's position in the hierarchy. On any one ladder there must be suitable steps between levels from top to bottom, if incentive is to be provided and increased scope recognized. At the same time, adjustments must be made to reflect the varying contributions that can be expected from individuals in the hierarchy of the staff versus that of the line.

Furthermore, in a compensation system, factors pertaining to the individual are almost as important as those pertaining to performance, the job, or the structure of the organization. A man's age and length of service, the state of his health, some notion of his future potential, some idea of his material needs, and some insight into his views about all of these should influence either the amount of total pay or the distribution of total pay among base salary, bonuses, stock options, and other incentive measures.

Besides the many factors already listed, still another set of influences—this time coming from the external part of the environment—ordinarily affects the level of executive compensation. Included here are regional differences in the cost of living, the increments allowed for overseas assignment, the market price of given qualifications and experience, the level of local taxation, the desire for tax avoidance or delay, and the effect of high business salaries on other professions.

Just as multiple criteria are appropriate for the evaluation of performance, so many considerations must be taken into account in the compensation of executives. The company which says it pays only for results does not know what it is doing.

In addition to the problem of deciding what factors to reward, there is the equally complex issue of deciding what forms compensation should take. We would emphasize that financial rewards are especially important in business, and no matter how great the enthusiasm of a man for his work, attention to the level of executive salary is an important ingredient in the achievement of strategy. Money, it is said, cannot buy happiness. On the other hand, happiness, valuable as it is, cannot buy food, shelter, access to culture, travel, or college educations for one's children. Even after the desired standard of living is attained, money is still an effective incentive. Businessmen used to the struggle for profit find satisfaction in their own growing net worth. Even though taxes may limit asset growth severely, the income is still important. As Crawford Greenewalt says in his *Uncommon Man,* the salary figure provides satisfaction by indicating the worth of the contribution made, even if most of it is paid out in taxes.[4]

There is no question about the desirability of paying high salaries for work of great value. Yet until recently, it was clearly social policy in the United States, as elsewhere, that executive take-home pay be kept at a modest ceiling. As a consequence, profit sharing, executive bonuses, stock options, stock purchase plans, deferred compensation contracts, split-dollar insurance, pension, group term insurance, savings plans, and other fringe benefits have multiplied enormously, and they have been directed not so much toward providing incentive as toward enabling executives to avoid high taxes on current income. It is as incentives, however, that these various devices should be judged. Regarded as incentives to reward *individual* performance, many of these devices encounter two immediate objections, quite aside from the ethics of their tax-avoidance features. First, how compatible are the assumptions back of such rewards with the aspirations of the businessman to be viewed as a professional person? The student who begins to think of business as a profession will wonder what kind of executive will perform better with a profit-sharing bonus than he would with an equivalent salary. He may ask whether a doctor should be paid according to the longevity of his patients and whether a surgeon would try harder if given a bonus when his patient

[4]C. H. Greenewalt, *The Uncommon Man; the Individual in the Organization* (New York: McGraw-Hill), 1959.

survived an operation. Second, how feasible is it to distinguish any one individual's contribution to the total accomplishment of the company? And even if contribution could be distinguished and correctly measured, what about the implications of the fact that the funds available for added incentive payments are a function of total rather than of individual performance? In view of these considerations, it can at least be argued that incentives for individual performance reflect dubious assumptions.

If, then, incentives are ruled out as an inappropriate or impractical means of rewarding individual effort, should they be cast out altogether? We believe not. There is certainly some merit in giving stock options to the group of executives most responsible for strategy decisions, if the purpose is to assure reward for attention to the middle and longer run future. There is some rationale for giving the same group current or even deferred bonuses, the amount of which is tied to annual profit, if the purpose is to motivate better cost control—something surprisingly difficult to do in a business environment marked by booming sales and high income taxes. Certainly, too, incentive payments to the key executive group must be condoned where needed to attract and hold the scarce managerial talent without which any strategy will suffer.

In any case, as you examine the effort made by companies to provide adequate rewards, to stimulate effective executive performance, and to inspire commitment to organizational purposes, you will wish to look closely at the relation between the incentive offered and the kind of performance needed. This observation holds as true, of course, for nonmonetary as it does for financial rewards.

The area of nonmonetary incentive systems is even more difficult to traverse quickly than that of financial objectives. Executives are as much members of the human race as other employees; they are thus as much affected as anyone else by pride in accomplishment, the climate for free expression, pleasure in able and honest associates, and satisfaction in work worth doing.

They are said to be moved also by status symbols like office carpets, thermos sets, or office location and size. The trappings of rank and small symbols of authority are too widely cultivated to be regarded as unimportant, but little is known of their real influence. If individual contribution to organized effort is abundantly clear, little attention is likely to be given to status symbols. For example, the R.&D. executive with the greatest contributions to the product line may favor the "reverse status symbol" of the lab technician's cotton jacket. This is not to say that symbols have no potentially useful role to play. Office decor, for example, can be used to symbolize strategy, as when a company introduces abstract art into its central office to help dramatize its breaks with the past.

Very little systematic work has been done to determine what incentives or company climate might be most conducive to executive creativity, executive commitment to forward planning, executive dedication to the training of subordinates, or executive striving for personal development and growth. All these are of utmost value, but their impact is long-run and peculiarly intangible. It is well known, however, that the climate most commonly extolled by men in upper management positions is one where they have freedom to experiment and apply their own ideas without unnecessary constraints. This type of positive incentive is particularly suited for use in combination with the "management-by-objectives" approach to the problem of executive evaluation. Given clear objectives and a broad consensus, then latitude can be safely granted to executives to choose their own course—so long as they do not conceal the problems they encounter. In other words, the executive can be presumed to respond to the conditions likely to encourage the goal-oriented behavior expected of him.

We may not always know the influence exerted by evaluation, compensation, and advancement, but if we keep purpose clear and incentive systems simple, we may keep unintended distractions to a minimum. Above all, we should be able to see the relevance to desired outcomes of the rewards offered. The harder it is to relate achievement to motives, the more cautious we should be in proposing an incentives program.

Systems of restraint and control

Like the system of incentives, the system of restraints and controls should be designed with the requirements of strategy in mind, rather than the niceties of complex techniques and procedures. It is the function of penalties and controls to enforce rather than to encourage—to inhibit strategically undesirable behavior rather than to create new patterns. Motivation, as we have said, is a complex of both positive and negative influences. Working in conjunction, these induce desired performance and inhibit undesirable behavior.

The need for controls—even at the executive level—is rooted in the central facts of organization itself. The inevitable consequence of divided activity is the emergence of substrategies, which are at least slightly deflected from the true course by the needs of individuals and the concepts and procedures of specialized groups, each with its own quasi-professional precepts and ideals. We must have controls, therefore, even in healthy and competent organizations manned by men of goodwill who are aware of organization purpose.

Like other aspects of organizational structure and processes, controls may be both formal and informal, that is, both prescribed and emergent. Both types are needed, and both are important. It is, however, in the nature of things that management is more likely to give explicit attention to the formal controls that it has itself prescribed than to the informal controls emergent within particular groups or subgroups.

Formal and informal controls differ in nature as well as in their genesis. The former have to do with data that are quantifiable, the latter with subjective values and behavior. Formal control derives from accounting; it reflects the conventions and assumptions of that discipline and implies the superior importance of what can be quantified over what cannot. Its influence arises from the responsiveness of individuals—if subject to supervision and appraisal —to information that reveals variances between what is recorded as being expected of them and what is recorded as being achieved. If the information depicts variances from strategically desirable behavior, then it tends to direct attention toward strategic goals and to support goal-oriented policy. But if, as is more often the case, the information simply focuses on those short-run results which the state of the art can measure, then it directs effort toward performance which, if not undesirable, is at least biased toward short-run objectives.

To emphasize the probable shortcomings of formal or quantifiable controls is not to assert that they have no value. Numbers do influence behavior— especially when pressures are applied to subordinates by superiors contemplating the same numbers. Numbers are essential in complex organizations, since personal acquaintance with what is being accomplished and personal surveillance over it by an owner-manager is no longer possible. As we have seen, the performance of individuals and subunits cannot be left to chance, even when acceptance and understanding of policy have been indicated and adequate competence and judgment are assured. Whether for surveillance from above or for self-control and self-guidance, numbers have a meaningful role to play, and well-selected numbers have a very meaningful role. We in no way mean to diminish the importance of figures, but only to emphasize that figures must be supplemented by informal or social controls.

Just as the idea of formal control is derived from accounting, the idea of informal control is derived from the inquiries of the behavioral sciences into the nature of organizational behavior. In all functioning groups, norms develop to which individuals are responsive if not obedient. These norms constitute the accepted way of doing things; they define the limits of proper behavior, and the type of action that will meet with approval from the group. In view of the way they operate, the control we have in mind is better described as *social* rather than *informal*. It is embedded in the activities, interactions, and sentiments characterizing group behavior. Sentiments take the form of likes and dislikes among men and evaluative judgments exercised upon each other. Negative sentiments, of great importance to their objects, may be activated by individual departure from a norm; such sentiments can either constitute a punishment in themselves, or can lead to some other form of punishment.

The shortcomings of formal control based on quantitative measurements of performance can be largely obviated by designing and implementing a system in which formal and social controls are integrated. For example, meetings of groups of managers to discuss control reports can facilitate inquiry into the significance of problems lying behind variances, can widen the range of solutions considered, and can bring pressure to bear from peers as well as from superiors. All these features can in turn contribute to finding a new course of action which addresses the problem rather than the figures.

One of the most vexing problems in attempting to establish a functional system of formal and social controls lies in the area of ethical standards. In difficult competitive situations, the pressure for results can lead individuals into illegal and unethical practices. Instead of countering this tendency, group norms may encourage yielding to these pressures. For example, knowing that others were doing the same thing undoubtedly influenced some electrical industry division managers to flout the antitrust laws when they could not otherwise meet the sales and profit expectations of the home office. On a lesser scale, group norms can be supportive to suppliers making expensive gifts to purchasing agents, or to salesmen offering extravagant entertainment to customers.

Where top management refuses to condone pursuit of company goals by unethical methods, it must resort to penalties like dismissal that are severe enough to dramatize its opposition. If a division sales manager, who is caught having arranged call-girl attentions for an important customer, against both the standards of expected behavior and the policy of the company, is not penalized at all, or only mildly, because of the volume of his sales and the profit he generates, ethical standards will not long be of great importance. If he is fired, then his successor is likely to think twice about the means he employs to achieve the organizational purposes that are assigned to him.

But there are limits to the effectiveness of punishment, in companies as well as in families and in society. If violations are not detected, the fear of punishment tends to weaken. A system of inspection is therefore implicit in formal control. But besides its expense and complexity, such policing of behavior has the drawback of adversely affecting the attitudes of an individual toward his organization. His commitment to creative accomplishment is likely to be shaken, especially if he is the kind of person who is not likely to cut corners in the performance of his duties. To undermine the motivation of the ethically inclined is a high price to pay for detection of the weak.

The student of general management is thus confronted by a dilemma: if an organization is sufficiently decentralized to permit individuals to develop new solutions to problems and new avenues to corporate achievement, then the opportunity for wrongdoing cannot be eliminated. This being so, a system of controls must be supplemented by a selective system of executive recruitment and training. No system of control, no program of rewards and penalties, no procedures of measuring and evaluating performance can take the place of the individual who has a clear idea of right and wrong, a consistent policy for himself, and the strength to stand the gaff when results suffer because he stands firm. This kind of person is different from the human animal who grasps at every proferred reward and flinches at every punishment. His development is greatly assisted by the systems, standards, rewards, incentives, penalties, and controls which permit the application of qualitative criteria and avoid the oversimplification of numerical measures. It is always the way systems are administered which determines their ultimate usefulness and impact.

Recruitment and development of management

Organizational behavior, in the view we have just taken of it, is the product of interacting *systems* of measures, motives, standards, incentives, rewards, penalties, and controls. Put another way, behavior is the outcome of *processes* ✓ of measurement, evaluation, motivation, and control. These systems and processes affect and shape the development of all individuals, most crucially those in management positions. Management development is therefore an ongoing process in all organizations, whether planned or not. As you examine cases which permit a wide-angled view of organizational activities, it is appropriate to inquire into the need to plan this development, rather than to let it occur as it will.

In days gone by, before it was generally realized that relying on a consciously designed corporate strategy was far safer and more productive than simply trusting to good luck, a widely shared set of assumptions operated to inhibit the emergence of management development programs. These assumptions have been described as follows:

1. Good management is instinct in action. A number of men are born with the qualities of energy, shrewdness of judgment, ambition, and capacity for responsibility. These men become the leaders of business.
2. A man prepares himself for advancement by performing well in his present job. The man who does best in competition with his fellows is best qualified to lead them.
3. If an organization does not happen to have adequate numbers of men with innate qualities of leadership who are equal to higher responsibilities, it may bring in such persons from other companies.
4. Men with the proper amount of ambition do not need to be "motivated" to demonstrate the personal qualities which qualify them for advancement.
5. Management cannot be taught formally—in school or anywhere else.[5]

The ideas that we have been examining here suggest that these assumptions are obsolescent. Men are, of course, born with different innate characteristics, but none of these precludes acquiring knowledge, attitudes, and skills which fill the gap between an identifiable personality trait and executive action. Good performance in lesser jobs is expected of men considered for bigger jobs, but different and additional qualifications are required for higher responsibility. Thus the most scholarly professor, the most dexterous machine operator, and the most persuasive salesman do not necessarily make a good college president, foreman, and sales manager. The abilities that make the difference can be learned from experience or to some extent from formal education. As a substitute for training and supplying the requisite experience internally, companies can import managers trained by competitors, but this approach, though sometimes unavoidable, is risky and expensive. The risk

---

[5]K. R. Andrews, *The Effectiveness of University Management Development Programs* (Division of Research, the Harvard Graduate School of Business Administration, Boston, 1966), p. 232.

lies in the relative difficulty of appraising the quality of outsiders and estimating their ability to transfer their technical effectiveness to a new organization. The cost lies chiefly in the disruption of natural internal incentive systems.

The supply of men who, of their own volition, can or will arrange for their own development is smaller than required. Advances in technology, the internationalization of markets, and the progress of research on information processing and organizational behavior all make it absurd to suppose that a man can learn all he will need to know from what he is currently doing. In particular, the activities of the general manager differ so much in kind from those of other management that special preparation for the top job should be considered, unless it is demonstrably impossible.

The multiplication of company-sponsored and university management training programs is evidence that the old idea that managers are born not made has been displaced by the proposition that managers are born with capacities which can be developed. In the process of seeing to it that the company is adequately manned to implement its strategy, we can identify training requirements. In other words, strategy can be our guide to (1) the skills which will be required to perform the critical tasks; (2) the number of persons with specific skill, age, and experience characteristics who will be required in the light of planned growth and predicted attrition; and (3) the number of new individuals of requisite potential who must be recruited to ensure the availability, at the appropriate time, of skills that require years to develop.

No matter what the outcome of these calculations, it can safely be said that every organization must actively recruit new talent if it aims to maintain its position and to grow. These recruits should have adequate ability not only for filling the junior positions to which they are initially called, but also for learning the management skills needed to advance to higher positions. Like planning of all kinds, recruiting must be done well ahead of the actual need.

Men with the ultimate capacity to become general managers should be sought out in their twenties, for able men today in a society in which the level of education as well as economic means is rising rapidly are looking for careers, not jobs. In this same spirit companies should recruit—not meeting the needs for clerk, field salesman, or laboratory technician alone but making an investment in the caliber of executive who in 25 years will be overseeing an activity not even contemplated today.[6]

One of the principal impediments to effective execution of plans is shortage of management manpower of the breadth required at the time required. This shortage is the result of faulty planning, not of a natural scarcity of good raw material. Consider the bank which wishes to open 50 branches overseas as part of its international expansion. It will not be able to export and replace 50 branch managers unless, years earlier, deliberate attention has been given to securing and to training banker-administrators. These are not technicians

---

[6]*Ibid.*, p. 240.

who know only credit, for example; they must know how to preside over an entire if small bank, learn and speak a foreign language, establish and maintain relationships with a foreign government, and provide banking services not for an exclusively American but for a different group of individual and corporate customers.

After successful recruitment of candidates with high potential, speeding the course of management development is usually the only way to keep manpower planning in phase with the requirements of strategy. Thus the recruit should be put to work at a job which uses the abilities he has and challenges him to acquire the knowledge he lacks about the company and industry:

> For men educated in this generation sweeping out the stockroom or carrying samples to the quality control laboratory are inappropriate unless these activities demand their level of education or will teach them something besides humility. To introduce the school-trained men of high promise to everyday affairs may mean the devising of jobs which have not existed hitherto. Expansion of analytical sections and accounting and financial departments, projects in market research, rudimentary exploratory investigations in new products departments, process control or data processing projects are all work which will use school-taught techniques and yet require practical and essential exposure to the company and solutions to the problem of establishing working relationships with old hands. Any recruit, no matter how brilliant his academic achievement, has of course much to learn that schools cannot teach him. His seasoning should be accomplished while he works with the power that he has, not doing a sentence of indeterminate length in clerical work of no difficulty.[7]

The manpower requirements imposed by commitment to a strategy of growth mean quite simply that men overqualified for conventional beginning assignments must be sought out and carefully cultivated thereafter. Individuals who respond well to the opportunities devised for them should be assigned to established organization positions and given responsibility as fast as capacity to absorb it is indicated. To promote rapidly is not the point so much as to maintain the initial momentum and to provide work to highly qualified individuals which is both essential and challenging.

The rise of professional business education and the development of advanced management programs make formal training available to men not only at the beginning of their careers but also at appropriate intervals thereafter. Short courses for executives are almost always stimulating and often of permanent value. But management development as such is predominantly an organizational process which must be supported, not thwarted, by the incentive and control systems to which we have already alluded. Distribution of rewards and penalties will effectively determine how much attention executives will give to the training of their subordinates. No amount of lip service will take the place of action in establishing effective management development as an important management activity. To evaluate a manager in part on his effort and effectiveness in bringing along his juniors requires subjective

---

[7] *Ibid.*, pp. 240–41.

measures and a time span longer than one fiscal year. These limitations do not seriously impede judgment, especially when both strategy and the urgency of its implications for manpower development are clearly known.

In designing on-the-job training, a focus on strategy makes possible a substantial economy of effort, in that management development and management evaluation can be carried on together. Thus a "management-by-objectives" program, already characterized as a most appropriate approach to evaluation of performance, can be simultaneously administered as an instrument of development. For example, in Texas Instruments, Inc., Mr. Pringle could use his conference with his superiors not only to discuss variances from budgeted departmental performance, but also to discover how far his suggested solutions are appropriate or inappropriate and why. In all such cases, discussion of objectives proposed, problems encountered, and results obtained provide opportunities for inquiry, for instruction and counsel, for learning what needs to be done and at what level of effectiveness.

Besides providing an ideal opportunity for learning, concentration on objectives permits delegation to juniors of choice of means and other decision-making responsibilities otherwise hard to come by. Throughout the top levels of the corporation, if senior management is spending adequate time on the surveillance of the environment and on the study of strategic alternatives, then the responsibility for day-to-day operations must necessarily be delegated. Since juniors cannot learn how to bear responsibility without having it, this necessity is of itself conducive to learning. If, within limits, responsibility for the choice of means to obtain objectives is also delegated, opportunity is presented for innovation, experimentation, and creative approaches to problem solving. Where ends rather than means are the object of attention and agreement exists on what ends are and should be, means may be allowed to vary at the discretion of the developing junior manager. The clearer the company's goals, the smaller the emphasis that must be placed on uniformity, and the greater the opportunity for initiative. Freedom to make mistakes and achieve success is more productive in developing executive skills than practice in following detailed how-to-do-it instructions designed by superiors or staff specialists. Commitment to purpose rather than to procedures appears to energize initiative.

A stress on purpose rather than on procedures suggests that organizational climate, though intangible, is more important to individual growth than the mechanisms of personnel administration. The development of each individual in the direction best suited both to his own powers and to organizational needs is most likely to take place in the company where everybody is encouraged to work at the height of his ability and is rewarded for doing so. Such a company must have a clear idea of what it is and what it intends to become. With this idea sufficiently institutionalized so that organization members grow committed to it, the effort required for achievement will be forthcoming without elaborate incentives and coercive controls. Purpose, especially if considered worth accomplishing, is the most powerful incentive to accomplishment.

If goals are not set high enough, they must be reset—as high as developing creativity and accelerating momentum suggest.

In short, from the point of view of general management, management development is not a combination of staff activities and formal training designed to provide neophites with a common body of knowledge, or to produce a generalized good manager. Rather, development is inextricably linked to organizational purpose, which shapes to its own requirements the kind, rate, and amount of development which takes place. It is a process by which men are professionally equipped to be—as far as possible in advance of the need —what the evolving strategy of the firm requires them to be, at the required level of excellence.

Although the processes of recruiting, training, and providing successive job opportunities and challenges are less formal than systems of compensation, control, and performance measurement, they have their own canons and precepts. Their claims to attention and to deference for their own sake must also be subordinated to the requirements of strategy.

The chief executive will have a special interest of his own in the process of management development. For standards of performance, measures for accurate evaluation, incentives, and controls will have a lower priority in his eyes than a committed organization, manned by people who know what they are supposed to do and committed to the overall ends to which their particular activities contribute. The general manager is not blind to the needs of his subordinates to serve their own purposes as well as those of the organization, any more than he is blind to the need, under the rules of accounting, for total assets to equal total liabilities. Wherever conflicting claims are made upon his attention, he requires that they be reconciled in a way which does not obscure organizational objectives or slow down the action being taken to attain them.

*   *   *   *   *

In examining the cases that follow, try to identify the strategy of the company and the structure of relationships established to implement it. Note the standards that have been established for measurement purposes. Are they appropriate for measuring the progress of the organization toward its goals? Is the way performance is measured likely to assist or impede constructive behavior? What pattern of possible incentives encouraging appropriate behavior can be identified? Do they converge on desired outcomes? What restraints and controls discouraging inappropriate behavior are in force? What changes in measurement, incentive, and control systems would you recommend to facilitate achievement of goals? If your analysis of the company's situation suggests that strategy and structure should be changed, these recommendations should, of course, precede your suggested plans for effective implementation.

NEFCO (AR)*

^^^

Background

In the summer of 1960 the Northeastern Food Company was a large regional chain of retail food stores with further prospects of profitable growth. The company was founded shortly after World War I by Edward Norfield, an uncle of the current executive vice president. The business prospered during the period of food chain expansion of the 1920's and blossomed into eminence with the development of the supermarket in the late 1930's and early postwar years. From 1940 to 1950 sales increased almost two and one-half times, from $34 million to $81 million. Sales grew at an even faster rate during the last decade and profits kept pace (see Exhibits 1 and 2). In 1960 there were NEFCO stores in northeastern states from Massachusetts to Maryland.

The rapid growth of NEFCO was attributed by students of the industry at the Harvard Business School and elsewhere primarily to the quality of its management, considered nationally to be among the most competent in food retailing. The company's top management group prided itself not only on its technical ability, but on its analytical approach to policy and operations and on its encouragement of new ideas and executive talent.

Top management. The senior officers of NEFCO, William Shae (president) and Harold Norfield (executive vice president) in particular, took time, whenever they felt the need, to reexamine their situation and determine NEFCO's place in its changing industry. One such study resulted in an orderly decentralization of the company over a period of five years beginning in 1954. The role of the store manager, to cite one consequence, was greatly increased.

Each line and staff vice president at the home office was encouraged to set general objectives five and ten years ahead. Detailed plans for the opening of new stores and the entry into new markets were made three years in advance. In addition, an estimate of the personnel requirements which the future would impose and training programs geared to filling projected needs were included in the plans.

The keystone of NEFCO policy was said to be William Shae's oft-quoted

Exhibit 1

NEFCO CONSOLIDATED BALANCE SHEET, JUNE 1, 1959
(In Thousands)

Current Assets:

Cash	$ 5,661
Accounts receivable	1,973
Inventories	23,242
Prepayals	813
Total Current Assets	$ 31,689
Net fixed assets	74,675
Other assets	1,063
Total Assets	$107,427

Current Liabilities:

Accounts payable	$ 9,221
Accrued expenses	4,508
Other accruals	3,122
Total Current Liabilities	$ 16,851
Deferred taxes	818
Long-term debt	54,345
Capital stock and surplus:	
2,018,072 of 6,500,000 shares authorized are outstanding	11,894
Retained earnings	23,519
Total Liabilities	$107,427

Source: Company records.

statement that "the most important asset in a business is people." Decentralization, planning, and training were the means by which NEFCO leaders said they sought to create an environment in which "interested, able, productive, and dedicated people" would operate to produce a growing, profitable, ethical, and flexible business. One professional student of the industry noted that "working at NEFCO seemed to mold any man into a professional manager."

A great deal of effort was exerted to make certain that NEFCO's approach to business was reflected in its stores. The image of the NEFCO store in the community was kept under close scrutiny. Competitive prices, quality merchandise, and "friendliness" were the objectives toward which operating policy was oriented. A frank and smooth-working relationship with the Union of Retail Clerks was carefully nurtured in a further attempt to administer company policy through cooperative people. Training programs and annual personnel reviews structured towards development and promotion within the NEFCO organization reinforced the efforts of management at store level. Decentralization had made the store manager a key man in translating the company's objectives into satisfied customers.

The store manager. The NEFCO store manager was expected to (1) make good local merchandising decisions, (2) foster more storewide spirit among employees, (3) develop the supervisory potentials of store personnel by

Exhibit 2

NEFCO CONSOLIDATED STATEMENT OF EARNINGS
FOR 52 WEEKS ENDING JUNE 1, 1959
(In Thousands)

Retail sales	$387,308
Costs and expenses:	
Cost of sales, etc.	$370,711
Depreciation and amortization	4,146
Total Costs and Expenses	$374,857
Earnings before taxes	$ 12,451
Estimated federal taxes	5,751
Net earnings	$ 6,700

Other Information
(In Thousands)

	Sales	Earnings	Earnings per Share
1930	$ 22,400	$ 544	$0.28
1940	33,858	418	0.21
1950	81,000	1,409	0.70
1954	133,537	1,626	0.81
1955	159,066	2,185	1.09
1956	199,432	2,790	1.38
1957	246,872	3,677	1.81
1958	314,285	5,017	2.48
1959	387,308	6,700	3.32

Source: Company records.

better on-the-job training, and (4) carry out smoothly the transfer of employees from one department to another. To accomplish these objectives, an organization was developed which attempted to give the store manager the local merchandising advantage of the independent as well as the purchasing power of the big chain.

The store manager was given responsibility (1) for all personnel in his store, (2) for control and conservation of all property in his store, and was held accountable for (3) control of operating expenditures, and (4) for the conduct of store operation and sales programs. In a number of areas, security, maintenance, store layout, and store organization, the central office provided help for the manager in the form of policy guidelines and staff organizations. The place of the store manager in the formal organization is presented in Exhibit 3.

Entry into soft goods market

It was with this background that NEFCO approached its entry into soft goods, a field in which the soft goods discount house had brought about a change described by some as comparable to that occasioned in food retailing

Exhibit 3

TYPICAL ORGANIZATION CHART

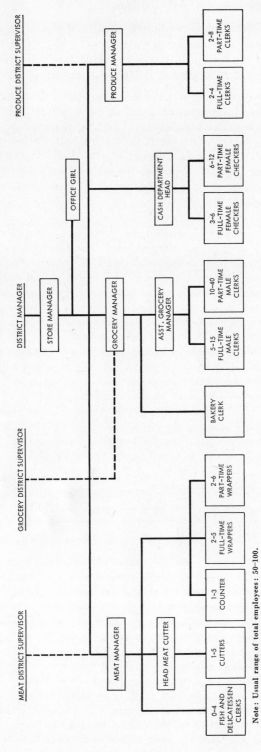

Note: Usual range of total employees: 50–100.
Source: Store opening manual.

by the development of supermarkets. (See Appendix at the end of this case for "Soft Goods Join the Retail Revolution.") Mr. William Shae expressed his views on this development and its import for food retailers in a speech given in the fall of 1959, parts of which are excerpted below:

Ours is a very dynamic business. Innovations of all kinds face us all the time. We believe in experimentation, in trying out new ideas, new equipment, new methods, and new products. We don't think it is healthy for us to wait until others have found out how good these innovations are before we put them into use ourselves. On the contrary, we want to be in the vanguard, and are always scouting on the frontiers. We encourage our people to innovate. But we try not to go all out on anything in a big hurry. It is better to experiment on a small scale—the mistakes cost less.

*   *   *   *   *

Over the years, and especially recently, we have been watching other retailing business. The general-merchandise field has lured some supermarket operators into big experimental undertakings. We have gone along on a modest scale in our own stores. On the other hand, we have felt that in certain strategic locations it was advantageous to us to have a discount house next to our supermarket or almost adjacent to it. We have encouraged and sought to attract discounters. We have had satisfactory sales results in our supermarkets from this neighborly relationship. We like it. So do others.

Today the discount house as a neighbor is being sought by many supermarkets. The discount houses are now asking for special real estate inducements. NEFCO is not interested in holding umbrellas for anyone. Therefore, we are seriously considering operating discount houses ourselves so that we can have such stores where we would otherwise have to pay a premium for neighborly relations. We are also currently studying the closed-door discount stores, because we believe in being prepared to meet changing conditions and to take advantage of new opportunities which may present themselves to us.

In whatever course we follow, we are interested in doing only those things which will help *our* supermarkets.

Other executives reported the development of NEFCO's decision to enter soft goods as follows:

Mr. Harold Norfield, executive vice president and general manager, said:

For the past several years the discount business has been mushrooming. As part of an industry group we discovered that from a location point of view when we were next to discounters our volume was increased by some 15%. We began our experience with discounters with an (A Company) store in southern Massachusetts. Later we were in a very nice center next to a (B Company) store and we had very good experience there. Thus, we began our connection with the discount business by locating next to them in various centers.

Now in western Massachusetts we had a store next to a (C Company) store in a center. Within the same trading area an (A Company) store opened next to a store which was part of a small independent chain of supermarkets. Because the A Company store was extremely well managed, relative to the C Company's, we discovered that we were losing business. It became apparent that the strength of our neighbor was going to have a lot to do with our own volume.

It also seemed to us that the discount house was part of a revolution, perhaps a small one, which was changing the face of retailing.

Noting that the discount house was a permanent revolution Mr. Harmon Stoddard, vice president, finance, went on to say:

The average discount department store is a hard thing to finance. The lease umbrella given by the supermarket as financial support to the discounter is basically a guarantee of the discounters. That means that if the discounter goes under we are in the discount business anyway. If we had this liability (and we did), it seemed as if we might as well be in the discount business ourselves and do it the proper way.

Another reason is diversification out of the food business. If our food business ever comes under pressure, if our markets in this area become saturated, if we cannot grow in food, then our discount houses offer an outlet for expansion. Thus, the potential for horizontal expansion is extended by entry into the nonfood business. There is a single criterion as to where we will expand—return on investment.

Mr. Goldman, vice president of sales, said:

It all began around 1955–56 when we were thinking seriously about what we now call general merchandise, and used to call nonfood items. We were trying to decide how to get into the area properly. The first Grand Union Grandway store opened that year so that we had their idea (all under the same roof, in the same store) to consider. We wanted nonfoods because they make money for us and also give our customers a larger variety of goods to choose from in our stores. In 1956 William Shae was asked to make a speech to United Department Stores, his subject: his attitude and NEFCO's to nonfoods. He set what is still our policy. "One, we are not going to go into the nonfood business in our supermarkets any more than we already have. It doesn't seem right for us. Basically, it's not our business. Two, department stores with more foresight would have beat the discounters. We would like an Altman's or an Orbach's as a neighbor but it didn't work out that way."

We began to get evidence on the various ways of handling the problem. The problems arising from being under one roof seem to outweigh the possible savings. The answer for us was having discounters as neighbors, and we proceeded to move into centers and experienced good volume.

Around 1957 and 1958 a lot of food chains began to do the same. The discounter became the key tenant in the center. He began to use some of his bargaining power to shift part of the rent burden on to the supers. The center developer would bargain with five or six food chains.

However, all this time we never closed our eyes to the *acquisition* of an existing discount chain if it was available at the right price. We were looking for a small chain (so that the price wouldn't be out of our range) which was reasonably successful. If it was a smash, nobody would want to sell it.

Selection of Sadler's

At the time William Shae was making his speech, NEFCO was already involved in serious negotiations with Sadler's, a Connecticut chain of ten department stores. Each store was an attractive well-built structure in a shopping center outside a principal city or town. The stores had 14 departments including hardware, men's and women's clothes and furnishings, children's and teen-age clothes, shoes, domestics, cosmetics and drugs, toys, and automotive equipment. All but the women's department were leased[1] to concessionaires who specialized in retailing a specific line of merchandise.

Sadler's had been started in 1955 as a family enterprise. Sol Feinman, the chief operating executive, was the only member of management with extensive experience in soft goods. NEFCO management later reported that, as the number of stores and sales volume grew, Mr. Feinman's merchandising acumen and the capital resources of his relatives were gradually being stretched to the breaking point. The management of the stores was theoretically delegated to store managers, but Mr. Feinman himself took part in virtually all operating decisions. In addition to running the stores, he controlled buying and merchandising for Sadler's women's department, planned the layout of new stores, and took a major part in negotiations with shopping center owners and Sadler's lessees.

Mr. Norfield described the Sadler situation as follows:

Over the past three or four years we have ended up being neighbors of Zayre's, J. M. Fields, Korvette, Virginia Dare, and others. We were considering an acquisition, and Harmon Stoddard came to us with a proposal to buy Sadler's. Sadler's was near us in seven centers and was going to be next to use in five more. Their company had been run by a family group. Feinman, I think, was a cousin. In fact there was only one active manager, Feinman.

While this had been all right as long as the company was running a few stores, as soon as they began to expand Feinman found himself out of his depth. He simply had too much to do. As far as we saw it, it appeared that he began to want a change from the situation where his partners were milking the business and acting as a drain and a source of confusion while he did all the work.

As the company grew, it also ran out of cash. Thus, apparently they began to think of sale. Now, Feinman came in contact with Harmon Stoddard in some location negotiations and it seems that they talked together and the idea came up. Harmon presented it to a group of us and the first time around, we said no. The next time we got one of our directors who has a broad background in nonfood retailing to go out and look at the stores and make a careful study. This time we decided it was O.K.

After 1957 NEFCO had received invitations-to-buy from several discount houses. Not until 1960, however, after considerable discussion and study among the executives of NEFCO, primarily Messrs. Norfield, Stoddard

---

[1]Historically, the owner of the soft goods discount house has been a specialist in the retailing of clothing only. Rather than extending his own capital and merchandising experience to such diverse lines as hardware, millinery, shoes, or even food, he usually leased space and fixtures to specialists in those lines. The lessee usually provided his own stock, promotion, department manager, and paid through rent for services provided by the store. The store owner's control over the operations of leased departments varied according to the terms of the individually negotiated leases.

Exhibit 4

SADLER'S INC. *ET AL.* CONSOLIDATED BALANCE SHEET, DECEMBER 31, 1959

(In Thousands)

Current Assets:

Cash	$1,040
Accounts receivable (net)	1,281
Inventory (cost or market "retail method")	2,422
Prepayals	340
Total Current Assets	$5,083

Fixed Assets (Net):

Furniture and fixtures	$1,333
Automobiles	42
Leasehold improvements	287
	$1,662
Other assets (including $80,000 in U.S. government bonds)	227
Total Assets	$6,972

Current Liabilities:

Accounts payable	$2,024
Accrued expenses	476
Other accruals	2,093
Total Current Liabilities	$4,593
Long-term debt	1,163

Capital:

Common stock	170
Preferred stock	81
Capital surplus	115
Earned surplus	850
Total Liabilities	$6,972

Source: Company records.

(financial vice president), Goldman (vice president of sales), and Shae, was the decision reached to proceed. In the spring of 1960 Messrs. Stoddard and Feinman negotiated Sadler's purchase by NEFCO. According to Mr. Stoddard, "the price was right. . . ." (See Exhibits 4, 5, and 6.)

The deal was closed in December but the number of shares wasn't set until February. During that time the price of our stock went up. At the time of our first negotiation the stock was selling in the low 50's. When the number of shares was set, we were selling in the 80's. So each day the number of shares came down.

As an outcome of the acquisition, certain plans, described by Mr. Goldman, were developed:

Our plan is fairly clear in that I think I know what we want. We just don't know the time schedule. The job is, first, building an organization. Then, once

Exhibit 5

SADLER'S INC. *ET AL.* CONSOLIDATED INCOME STATEMENT FOR CALENDAR YEAR 1959

(In Thousands)

Net sales (Sadler's owned departments)	$7,653
Cost of goods sold	5,223
	$2,430
Rental income	1,685
Gross profit	$4,115
Operating expenses (see Schedule 1)	3,984
Operating profit	$ 131
Depreciation and amortization	96
Net operating profit	$ 35
Other income	18
Net profit before taxes	$ 53

Schedule 1

Operating Expenses

Direct salaries (including officers' salaries of $135,000)	$1,719
Rent, electricity, and water	841
Taxes	117
Insurance	97
Repairs	58
Advertising	632
Interest	96
Other	424
Total	$3,984

Source: Company records.

that's done we can step out and build new stores. One problem, though, which really complicates this is that before we purchased them Sadler's had made commitments in five new locations. I really feel this hurt. It meant we had to contend with expansion before they had worked out their organization. If these turn out to be really live people, we may be able to handle it anyway.

Our long-range plan is not to use Sadler's as a neighbor until they are organized and running. I would guess that by the end of this year they'll be organized. Then give them a year to break in and they'll be ready to go. We'll do what they are able to take. If they learn fast, we may be able to expand sooner than I expect. We don't know whether or when we'll be doing these things but we know what has to come first.

*   *   *   *   *

You know, decisions here don't get made in an authoritarian way. We think you can't operate with any effectiveness in that way. We may plant a seed and if nothing happens in six months may make a decision. There are 12 or so men here who constitute a top echelon. Each of us operates as if nobody owns the company but himself. Then if I believe something, I will get others to recognize the issue and we will have a meeting. Then when we reach a consensus, we move.

Exhibit 6

MR. GORMAN'S PRO FORMA OPERATING
STATEMENT FOR SADLER'S;*
CALENDAR YEAR 1960
Rental Operations Only
(In Thousands)

Total income	$3,588
Total direct expenses (see Schedule 1)	3,314
	$ 274
Managerial salaries	72
	$ 202
Taxes at 40%	81
Estimated net after taxes	$ 121

Schedule 1
Operating Expenses

Direct salaries	$ 825
Rent, electricity, and water	1,040
Taxes†	19
Insurance‡	50
Repairs	62
Advertising	787
Interest§	19
Other	512
Total	$3,314

*The opening of three Sadler stores was planned for calendar 1960.
†Real estate taxes not payable until second year.
‡$700,000 of life insurance on officers with cash surrender value of $130,000
was surrendered on purchase.
§The greater part of Sadler's debt to be retired or renegotiated by the parent.
Source: Company records.

You see, no one of us has that power and we won't make a decision unless there
is compatibility. That is the key thing—we all operate together.

Building an organization

The acquisition of Sadler's created new responsibilities and problems for
NEFCO management. In early April, Mr. Norfield indicated the most important of these were the need to establish policies and create a store image:

We are building an organization from scratch. We have to establish policies,
the image which we want our stores to have, and so on. Everything has to be
done. We don't know how to run this kind of a store and we will have to learn.
We are now in the process of deciding what we want.

The organization will be built on my yellow pad. Building the framework of
our company, providing order for our activities, is one of my principal responsibilities.

. . . We took over from the sellers only one man *really*, their general manager [Sol Feinman]. He is a good merchant and will be the only man among

us with real soft goods experience. Under him we plan to build an organization something like this:

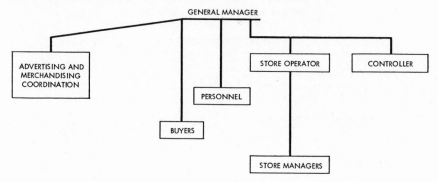

We will put two of our men in, one as the store operator and the other as the controller. Results will come out of this group, and we will just have to learn what is right. Our management group will work together on settling policy matters, such as what we should stand for, what relations Sadler's should have to NEFCO, and what type of concessionaires we should have. They will be:

William Shae, president and chairman.
Harold Norfield, executive vice president and general manager.
Robert Fitz, vice president of development.
Richard Goldman, vice president of sales.
Harmon Stoddard, financial vice president.
John Gorman, vice president of mergers and acquisition.
[See Organization Chart, Exhibit 7.]

Appointment of a stores superintendent. In April 1960 Mr. Daniel Kraft, 30, a graduate of New York University, was assigned the position of stores superintendent within the Sadler organization. (See Exhibit 8 for the formal organization under which he was to function.) Before joining NEFCO four years earlier, Mr. Kraft had worked for a leading New York department store as a department manager. At NEFCO he was originally hired as a nonfoods buyer and was later promoted to nonfoods sales manager. In the fall of 1959 he was detached from sales activities for training in store operations. During the month of March he visited the stores to acquaint himself with Sadler's discount operations.

Approach of the stores superintendent. In determining his own responsibilities, as well as where Sadler's should fit into the NEFCO organization, Daniel Kraft attempted to identify areas in which policy was needed. (See Exhibit 9 for the list Kraft prepared in March.) He believed that there were two major requirements: (1) the need for NEFCO management to learn the discount business, and (2) the necessity to teach Sadler personnel how to operate in an organized and effective manner. Mr. Kraft said:

The NEFCO organization provides a number of arms—real estate, construc-

Exhibit 7

PARTIAL ORGANIZATION CHART OF THE
NORTHEASTERN FOOD COMPANY

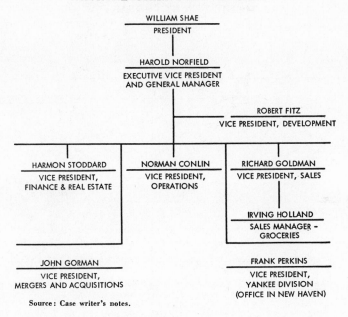

Source: Case writer's notes.

tion, maintenance, security, personnel, promotion, and so forth—each of which is offering a helping hand to Sadler's group. . . . [Ordinarily] when NEFCO takes over a small chain of retail stores, there are no great problems involved. The people put in charge of integrating the new chain with NEFCO know how to use what NEFCO has to offer. . . .

There were other circumstances, Mr. Kraft noted, complicating the conversion of Sadler's to NEFCO policies. Only three Sadler executives (except for store managers) were available after the merger. Information with which to plan policy was wholly lacking. "There was actually no body of data collected in one place describing Sadler's employees," he said.

The limited Sadler organization comprised Mr. Feinman, the general manager; Mr. Parnas, in charge of advertising and promotion; and Mr. Levy, the controller. Mr. Levy was later replaced by Ronald Arnold from the NEFCO organization. Mr. Kraft did not think the lack of data or lack of organization was a real fault of Sadler's.

These men have been part of a revolution and they didn't have time. This very revolution which is going on in the retailing field led me to ask to be involved in the Sadler's reorganization. So far, Ron and I, working with Sol Feinman, have set up a tentative organization. We have also established a holiday pay policy and a vacation policy.

Establishing policy.   Mr. Kraft stated that policy making at NEFCO

Exhibit 8

PARTIAL ORGANIZATION OF SADLER'S DIVISION, INCLUDING WORKING RELATIONSHIPS OF SADLER'S, MAY 6, 1960, TO THE PARENT COMPANY*

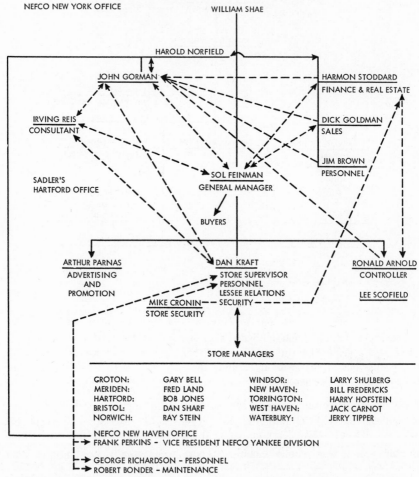

*Dotted lines denote working rather than formal relationships. These relationships evolved during the month of April, 1960.

Source: Case writer's notes.

involved a discussion of diverse ideas until the group agreed upon a common view. He said:

I do not set the objectives when planning policy. That is for Mr. Harold Norfield to decide. I don't really have a policy of my own. My only objective is that I want Sadler's to be to the discount business what NEFCO is to food marketing. This means aggressiveness, flexibility, competitiveness.

Mr. Kraft acknowledged that top management was faced with a number

Exhibit 9

MEMORANDUM FROM MESSRS. KRAFT AND ARNOLD TO MR. GORMAN BASED UPON THEIR FIRST EXPOSURE TO THE SADLER'S ORGANIZATION, MARCH 28, 1960

Outlined below is a brief summary of points which we are presently in the process of scheduling and studying:

1. Issuance of weekly merchandising reports, i.e., "Open to Buy" and Sales Reports showing actual versus planned.
2. Preparation of quarterly merchandising and expense budgets.
3. Reporting on a four-week basis plus periodic profit and loss by stores.
4. Write up of a uniform, standardized set of instructions and procedures for merchandising, accounting, security, operations, personnel, etc.
5. Preparation of a predetermined checklist of what is to be accomplished in a store visit by merchandising personnel.
6. Schedule of meetings of buyers and store managers—generally once a month.
7. Evaluation of advertising controls and the necessary follow-through.

of unresolved policy questions, one of which was how Sadler's and NEFCO should work together. He said, however, that he himself was really concerned only with his immediate objective, "to increase the responsibility and authority of Sadler's store management. These men work long hours and don't have the help we can offer them, but on the other hand, they aren't handling the problems that we think store managers ought to handle. I want to upgrade the operating effectiveness of the store managers."

Developing store managers. Mr. Kraft began his task of developing store managers by attempting two forms of action: (1) to relieve managers of some of the operating detail through the use of NEFCO staff divisions, and (2) to broaden their perspective and widen their opportunity for taking initiative and assuming responsibility.

Store managers' meetings

Mr. Kraft early instituted regular store managers' meetings. The first of these was held June 5 at the Hartford Sadler offices. The meeting was attended by all ten Sadler's store managers and by Mr. Feinman, Mr. Parnas, Mr. Cronin (Sadler's security officer), Mr. Smith (NEFCO New York office, construction and maintenance department), Mr. Bonder (NEFCO Yankee division, maintenance), Mr. Arnold (Sadler's controller), and Mr. Richardson (NEFCO Yankee division, personnel). Mr. Kraft announced at the opening of the meeting that its purpose was to gain understanding. Future meetings were to be scheduled on a monthly basis with a planned agenda, and it was hoped that the store managers would be active participants who determined the agenda. Continuing, Kraft stated, "We are trying to feel our way through what is a very complicated situation. In particular, [we want to learn] how we can help you. We feel we can help you today by setting a few policies."

Maintenance. Mr. Kraft introduced Mr. Pete Smith who first described the organizational structure of the NEFCO construction and engineering division and then presented Mr. Robert Bonder from the maintenance supervision office in New Haven. Bonder passed out a copy of maintenance policy procedures and read from it.

BONDER: One thing I didn't write in this policy statement was about preventive maintenance. Once a month we have a maintenance mechanic come to check up on each store. We want to be sure that maintenance is not being handled by the store manager. Sometimes when you will ask us to do something via the communications form, we are going to be slow—we have to be. We have to see what the landlord's responsibility is in the leases. I hope, I know, we'll get your cooperation.

KRAFT: Thanks, Bob. Just to get our thinking straight on this, let me explain. Our service arm is a truly magnificent organization. If you work with them, they'll break their back for you. However, their services *are not free*, and sometime in July you will be on a store profit and loss basis. Let me clarify this. We don't want you bringing in what may be perfectly O.K. outside construction or maintenance people. You don't have to. For the time being everything that has anything to do with store maintenance should go on the store's communication form to Pete Smith. If none of these procedures seems to work, use your own best judgment. Store service is a nerve center, and literally any problem you have should go through this.

Very specific questions were raised by the store managers about their relationship with NEFCO maintenance personnel. In answer to one, Mr. Bonder said:

If the maintenance man is in the store and you have other things, one or two little minor things to do, sure, ask him without bothering to use the forms. I spoke with the vice president, construction and engineering, and he had these two things to say: (1) Use forms whenever appropriate, but not for personal messages, and (2) store service in New Haven is to be used for maintenance only; everything else should go through the home office.

Other questions and answers followed:

BELL [Groton]: What is the procedure going to be with vendors? A man came into my store the other day with a mop and he said that this was the authorized mop in the stores.

BONDER: We have tried to test all mops and find which are the best mops for you to have in your store. We'd like to use the one we have for a few more weeks.

FEINMAN: The question is not answered. The fact is, we will do the buying at the home office. But if we're going to get into detail, we're not going to get anywhere.

KRAFT: Let me clarify this. Nothing is authorized for store managers until you get it in writing in this area of purchasing. Another point—there are to be no interviews or pictures unless Sol approves. This is a tested policy by which we live happily.

SHULBERG [Windsor]: What is going to be your policy on window washers?

When are we going to have to get rid of our people, or are you going to approve special people, or what?

BONDER: We never throw people out. If you are happy with the man you have, O.K. We will look at their price; if it is too high, they are notified and given a chance to meet what we consider a competitive price.

KRAFT (*breaking into the conversation*): On this point of windows, I want to say something. We at NEFCO keep our floors and windows clean and I think maybe it is a fetish with us. Larry, can you say something in this area about cleanliness?

SHULBERG [Windsor]: Well, the porter service is inadequate as it stands now. If the major problems are going to be handled by you, then I think everything will be O.K.

FEINMAN (*breaking into conversation*): The details will be handled, we don't have time to talk about them. Until such time as people get to you, keep things reasonably O.K.

SMITH: We have to learn your type of operation in order to get our service organization functioning in a useful way to help you.

Discussion continued, covering floor washing, broken fixtures, rest rooms, and other areas of maintenance. Feinman repeatedly asked the store managers to stay out of details. Kraft offered the following generalization:

Maintenance leads to good store appearance, and as you all know this is very important for sales. In particular, the register makes the last customer impression; keep it clean, get the junk out from under the register, and dust off things.

Your people have some idle time up front—stress with them the importance of neatness, keep your front end shining. Also, in the area of the front end, my own thinking is—Sol, check me out on this—that one major display of a fast-moving timely item will be very important.

FEINMAN: This makes very good sense. We're not giving that area of the store proper attention. But this requires your thinking, your judgment. The registers are just a matter of housekeeping.

Personnel policy. Dan Kraft brought up the matter of personnel policy. He mentioned that trouble had arisen with the State of Connecticut over certain hours and hiring details.

A general discussion of personnel followed. Problems considered, other than violations of the labor laws, included (1) lack of customer service and suggestive selling, and (2) the inadequate number of people filling stock. Mr. Feinman stressed the importance of personal appearance. At one point he said heatedly:

We have to control the personnel of the departments. Their appearance and the appearance of help in general is very important. We run fairly decent stores; our personnel have to look right.

What kind of people are we letting into our stores to work there? What kind of impression are we giving? (*There was a deadly quiet in the room.*) We can write all the bulletins in the world and it won't help. You have got to look at your employees. Every time I come into the store I see dreadful things. I see some boys in dungarees. I was in one store the other day and I saw a woman clerk who had terrycloth bedroom slippers on. Maybe the girl with the apron on behind the snack bar changes it every day. Maybe she ought to be changing it twice. We can't have employees in this store wearing terrycloth bedroom slippers! Part of the problem is that your employees don't know what to do. You have to tell them. We can't be your eyes!

Mr. Hofstein, of the Torrington store, observed that "representatives of the leased department [were] the chief offenders," to which Feinman replied: "If they argue with you, you have the authority. If you tell them what you want to do—to run a store right—and they argue with you, I want to know about it."

During the coffee break which followed Mr. Feinman's speech, Mr. Kraft spent most of his time chatting with store managers. At one point one of them expressed to Mr. Kraft his annoyance with Mr. Feinman's behavior at the meeting. He said, "Christ, Feinman's a tough nut." Kraft said, "You've got to admire him. He is certainly going to get more out of this operation than you or I ever will. He started as a poor boy with a candy stand and look where he is today!"

Security practices. Upon resumption of the meeting, Dan Kraft introduced the subject of security practices, noting that security was a very broad and very crucial area for reasons both economic and emotional. He then introduced the security officer for the Sadler's organization, Mike Cronin.

Mr. Cronin discussed the "concept of security" and a variety of specific subjects—professional shopping to check security aspects of store operations (Merit Shopping), guard policy, locks and keys, pilferage and procedures for making an arrest, and employee purchases. His comments ranged from noting the apprehension of two cashiers in the test shopping of three stores to a discussion of NEFCO policy in the event of armed robbery.

Labor laws. After lunch Mr. Kraft introduced Mr. George Richardson of the New Haven personnel office to discuss the labor laws of Connecticut. Mr. Richardson stated the company's policy to obey the law and described what the law required. Problem areas then taken up were the laws relating to working hours for minors and women, the use of time clocks, the classification of office girls and supervisory help, breaks, lunch hours, and general hiring policy.

In closing, Mr. Richardson said that he thought "all NEFCO policies could be summarized by the Golden Rule and by Mr. William Shae's statement that 'Our most important asset is people.' You can buy a lawn mower at the Topp's store but it's the people who bring the customers into Sadler's."

At this juncture Mr. Kraft turned the meeting over to Mr. Feinman, who said:

Well, boys, we've got to do more business. Last week nobody made plan. Some of you came so close that if you had just put in a little more effort I'm sure you could have made it. It's just terrible that you can come that close to plan and not make it. I don't know what the answer is but I think we're going to have to do a lot more in-store promotion. It's necessary! We've got to get the concessionaires to cooperate. You've got that speaker in the store and you've got to use it.

He noted that Mr. Jones of the Hartford store was very successful at selling over the loudspeaker. Referring to the concessionaires, Feinman went on, "We don't make enough use of the people in the stores, the values they can offer."

Promotion. General discussion followed among Mr. Feinman, Mr. Parnas, Mr. Kraft, and the store managers concerning effective types of promotion. Noting the diversity of ideas brought up, Mr. Feinman said, "We can do some of it. It's apparent to me that you fellows know what will or what won't work. You've got to do it. The extent to which we request these things from our concessionaires is the extent to which we get values." Arguments ensued over specific promotional points; for example, the number of items to be broadcast over the speaker each day, the kind of items, and the number of times the same item could be promoted.

SHARF [Bristol]: Would it be possible for us to see the numbers on other stores? I don't really mean numbers, specific numbers, but perhaps our ranking. I want to know where things are better, and then maybe we can find out which approaches are working and why.

Mr. Parnas picked up Sharf's suggestion and went further, proposing contests and rankings which might produce competition among stores and prod the store managers to find out why certain things sold better somewhere else. He gave as an example the fact that although Waterbury's total sales were far higher than Torrington's, its millinery sales were lower.

Neither Mr. Feinman nor Mr. Kraft nor the store managers liked the naming of specific stores. Mr. Feinman went on to say:

We don't want specific numbers. Some stores should be low and we can't criticize them because they are. It's natural that because of size and location one store outsells another consistently.

But let's have six specials six days a week. It will work. You can use the same item more than once during the week. On Saturday and after five o'clock you can break the fair-trade laws. I don't think they're enforced except by complaint, and those inspectors aren't in the stores after five. They don't work the same kind of week that we do.

Mr. Kraft summarized the discussion concerning promotion and stated that if the store managers wanted to see a departmental ranking within stores for all the stores this could be arranged. He then introduced Ronald Arnold who was to be responsible for accounting in the new organization.

Mr. Arnold began by remarking, "It is the intent of a report to convey understanding and not just be a mass of figures." He said that there was nothing worse than to send out a report to the store managers with 100 figures on it and expect them to get something out of it. "We want to give you meaningful and interpretable data. If you have ideas as to what will help you, let us know. The rank of store departments by stores will be on the report as of next week."

Summation of meetings. Mr. Kraft then noted that the official agenda had been completed and threw the floor open for questions. A variety of subjects were brought up. The following excerpt is taken from over an hour of discussion:

KRAFT: I hope that next time there will be more feedback. We just mentioned the profit and loss statement briefly and we'll tell you more about it in the future. I am trying to give you an idea of what's coming up that will affect you, but until policies are really firm, I can't give you any more information.

The next meeting will be three weeks from today at the same place. At that time I would like to hear the results from the two groups that I want you store managers to set up. The first will have as its subject the problem of the reduction of store managers' hours. I want to know all the ways in which you think we can set about reducing the number worked by a store manager. (Currently this runs to around 60–70 hours per week.) The other group will discuss the problem of a central warehouse. It may be that there will be a warehouse for Sadler's in the relatively near future. This idea is under discussion at the central office, and to help me, because I have to make a report to Mr. Gorman, I'd like you to give me your ideas on the subject. You can handle this over the phone, I would imagine.

FEINMAN: You don't have to get together; you can do it over the phone. But I think you ought to get together. You store managers are fairly close to each other and you ought to know what's going on in your stores. You ought to meet with each other occasionally, have lunch together once a week as a regular thing. We must get more sales; that's the thing which bothers me. There I'd like your advice.

HOFSTEIN: Do we know what our best selling price lines are? Are we selling some goods at too low a price? Would it be possible for us to make some sort of survey and find out in this area what's going to be important? It may be we are selling a dress at $1.98 which is just a magnificent value but that our customers don't want to pay this kind of price. Perhaps they think that if the price is that low the quality is terrible.

FEINMAN: An excellent idea! We may be advertising merchandise at too low a price; in fact, I'm sure we are. I think it's an excellent subject for a study.

CARNOT: Is this sort of thing universal? Would such a survey in one area apply to another? Aren't there differences between store trading areas?

FEINMAN: Yes, it's universal.

LAND: I think our biggest loss in sales comes from poor service. I'd like to forget about the word "self-service."

HOFSTEIN: We are not in the self-service business. We are self-selection.

FEINMAN: Not until sizes are right and always available and clearly marked are we in the self-selection business. And at this point that just isn't the case. As far as getting customer service, I'd like you store managers to work on it and then tell us what you did at the next meeting.

At 4:30 P.M. the meeting closed. Afterwards, Mr. Kraft said that he thought the meeting had gone reasonably well, although it had been an hour and a half too long. He was of the opinion that Mr. Feinman's urge to make specific decisions made his task of encouraging feedback from the store managers more difficult.

Solutions to specific problems

On June 6 Mr. Kraft attended a series of meetings at NEFCO head-quarters in New York scheduled to work out solutions to specific problems, functional and organizational, involving a variety of NEFCO staff divisions. During the course of the day Kraft spoke with John Gorman, Jim Brown (personnel), Irving Holland (grocery sales manager), Dick Goldman, and the key men controlling store supplies and store security.

Discussion covered the organization of Sadler's personnel operation, personnel policy for Sadler's, the possible unionization of Sadler's store employees, liaison between NEFCO's and Sadler's merchandising operations, central purchasing of store supplies, and the conflict between store security and customer convenience as criteria for new store layout. In each case the result of discussion was a decision to handle a specific problem in a given way, or the establishment of a policy or procedure to cover future questions arising in a given area.

The discussions of merchandising liaison with Irving Holland and Dick Goldman (vice president of sales) illustrate the day's activities. The subject was policy on the place of food in Sadler's stores.[2] NEFCO's grocery buyer took part in Kraft's and Holland's conversations.. The three discussed current warehousing arrangements, the introduction of candy into the Sadler's stores, the place of food items as fliers in Sadler's promotion, and finally areas in which Sadler's and NEFCO could help each other.

In the discussion of food items as fliers, it was clear that Kraft wanted to use food more intensively than did Holland. Kraft asked for a clear-cut policy, and it was decided that 20 items a year would be the maximum number of food items used for promotion. In the areas of possible coopera-tion between the two groups, Kraft suggested three possible points at which he thought Sadler's might help NEFCO: (1) in the testing of ideas or gim-micks in the stores where NEFCO might not want to experiment in its own stores; (2) reciprocal couponing, such as was being planned for West Haven in order to trade traffic; and (3) the possibility that Sadler's buyers could help NEFCO in the nonfood area. Holland suggested that a fourth area existed: On occasion NEFCO stores were stuck with merchandise which they could not move, and perhaps Sadler's with its own peculiar market could help in unloading the NEFCO stores.

Later in the morning Kraft met with Mr. Richard Goldman. Mr. Goldman was eating lunch in his office. Kraft inquired about the progress which had

---

[2] While food was not one of the standard lines of merchandise carried in a soft goods discount house, the experience of Sadler's had been that a well-promoted food item, a "flier" such as a seven-cent hot dog or a "cost"-priced quart of pickles was a tremendous traffic builder.

been made in locating various men needed to fill out the Sadler's organization. Mr. Goldman reported that progress had been made and noted which NEFCO people were responsible for follow-up.

The discussion then shifted to food items. Kraft explained that the policy worked out with Holland was 20 food items a year.

GOLDMAN: I think 20 is too high. What are you building?

KRAFT: Excitement.

GOLDMAN: You shouldn't have a number on a policy. It is not a policy if you do. Here is a policy: (1) You can't sell below cost; you have got to be legal. (2) You can use food items only to build *traffic*. (3) Naturally, there will be no NEFCO brands. Stay away from all our private brands. (4) As of now you can't use our trucks. The problem is that the union may object when they are asked to deliver merchandise to a nonunion store.

KRAFT: But you guys aren't talking to each other. As I understand it, we are going to be inviting the union in.

GOLDMAN: Have we?

KRAFT: Not yet.

GOLDMAN: Until we do, this is policy. Look, Dan, you are in the discount business; you don't need a union. (*Goldman went on to discuss food policy.*) Look, Dan, why is X Company outselling Sadler's in Torrington? I hear it's because X Company has better values. You have to run Sadler's like it is your own business. Forget that you are with NEFCO. You don't build a business on food gimmicks. Build your business on value. You make up your mind how you are going to do business and then do it that way. Use your judgment and look at yourself as a manager of a discount chain, not as a liaison with NEFCO and Sadler's.

Following the meeting with Dick Goldman, Mr. Kraft described what he conceived his role to be. He explained that as he saw it his task was to get the Sadler's organization *moving*.

Mr. Norfield told me that there is no doubt that I will not be able to get perfect policies set up everywhere. If I am able to set things up so that there is a 5% savings in supplies, it is very possible that a 10% savings will eventually be realized. But my job is to get things organized and going immediately while still building towards long-range NEFCO goals. In fact, if it turns out that we have to take a loss in supplies in the short run, two to six months, we will do this as long as it is expected that by centralizing in the long run we will save 5% or 7%. So that in each area I feel that I am making compromises and just coming out with a working solution that approaches what I expect NEFCO will be doing in the future. You know an awful lot of nice pretty policy decisions are being made in the home office, but the messy condition that the Sadler's organization is in makes this job—well, I am working regularly 10 to 15 hours a day and I still can't get everything done. There is just so far that one can overextend one's self.

APPENDIX

SOFT GOODS JOIN THE RETAIL REVOLUTION[1]

By Gerald B. Tallman and Bruce Blomstrom

*   *   *   *   *

During the last five years, a group of New England merchants in intense competition wtih one another have hammered out a fundamentally new type of retail institution that seems destined to spread across the country—the self-service soft-goods supermarket, often, but inappropriately, called a "discount department store."

In the perspective of changing retail competition, self-service soft-goods supermarkets represent the latest surge in a long history of efforts to feature lower prices and better values. If the full promise of their recent growth is developed, they may well have an impact on retailing comparable to that caused by (1) the founding of the variety chains in the latter part of the nineteenth century, (2) the growth of mail-order houses prior to World War I, (3) the founding of the economy apparel chains before and after World War I, (4) the explosive development of food chains prior to 1933, (5) the innovation of the food supermarkets during the early 1930's, and (6) the growth of discounting in appliances following World War II.

FAST GROWTH

The store which many operators credit with having set the precedent for this new type of operation (although not actually the first soft-goods supermarket) was established in 1954 near Providence, Rhode Island. By late 1958 there were, in New England, over 85 stores fitting the definition of self-service soft-goods supermarkets doing business at an aggregate rate of at least $200 million per year. Toward the close of 1959 over 110 such stores were in operation in New England with aggregate sales estimated to be at the rate of $300 million per year. Of the sales growth during 1959, approximately two thirds is believed attributable to the opening of new stores during the year, and the balance to growth in the sales rate of previously established stores.

Though the earliest soft-goods supermarkets we know of were established in New England, they are no longer limited to this one area. By mid-1959 Sam Gottesfeld, writing in the *Women's Wear Daily*, identified a "partial list" of 59 cities outside New England having such stores in existence or about to be established.[2] The rapid growth of stores outside New England is being accomplished in part by the expansion of New England companies and in part by new entries into the field. In New England the three largest groups operate under the names of Zayre, J. M. Fields, and King's Department Store. Among the store groups with principal activities outside New England are the Atlantic Mills stores of the Virginia Dare Stores Company, the Shoppers' Fair stores of Mangel Stores Corporation, and the Clark stores of the M. N. Landau Company.

These self-service soft-goods supermarkets already have achieved in New Eng-

[1]*Harvard Business Review*, September–October 1960, pp. 133 ff.

[2]Sam Gottesfeld, "Self-Service Discounters Mushrooming over Nation," *Women's Wear Daily*, June 29, 1959.

land a position which neither their retail competitors nor their manufacturers can afford to ignore. Their national significance is increasing rapidly—especially when combined with that of the "closed door" or "membership" discount houses which during the same period of time have been spreading from the West Coast into the Midwest. These latter stores serve only holders of membership cards which, with gradually diminishing selectivity, have been available primarily to government employees, union members, and other groups. The total volume of their business, though spread over a larger area, is similar to the New England volume of the stores which are discussed in this article. With the exception of promotional methods, the basis of their low operating costs is also similar.[3]

*   *   *   *   *

SOMETHING OLD, SOMETHING NEW

The bits and pieces of retail operating methods that have been brought together to build this new type of store are all old, but the resulting combination is unique and will have a profound effect on the retail merchandising of lower priced soft goods. The two main characteristics which in combination differentiate these stores from other large retailers are as follows:

1. Their emphasis is on soft goods, especially apparel for women and children—The product mix varies substantially from store to store, but most of the stores carry hard goods including appliances; it is estimated, however, that for the stores in New England hard goods account for no more than 30% of total sales, with appliances accounting for about one third of this hard-goods volume.

2. They are operated on a completely self-service basis with check-out stands —Most of the stores have one or more individual department check-outs in order to minimize pilferage, but the stores typically have a single checkout location for over 90% of their merchandise. Most stores provide shopping carts, such as those used in grocery supermarkets, for the convenience of customers in carrying merchandise within the store.

*   *   *   *   *

Facilities and practices

Certain other characteristics of these supermarkets should also be borne in mind:

With the exception of a few firms operating in old mill buildings, the stores have all their selling space on a single level. Individually, they are large in size, with areas ranging from 25,000 to over 100,000 square feet. Most new stores are built specifically for use as soft-goods supermarkets and are over 50,000 square feet large, with at least 80% of this area utilized as selling space and available for customer circulation.

An annual sales volume of $1.0 million is probably minimal for the stores which are 25,000 square feet in area, and the volume for the average store is somewhat over $2.5 million per year. One of the well-established stores with about 140,000 square feet of space is operating at an annual sales rate of $12.0 million.

With few exceptions, the supermarket buildings have been located away from downtown shopping areas. In the past many were located in isolation from other

---

[3]See Sam Gottesfeld, "Membership Discount Stores," *Women's Wear Daily*, a series of articles in the March 28 to April 5, 1960, issues.

stores; but more recently managements have tended to locate in suburban shopping centers, or to become the focus for development of new centers. The essential factors determining location have been—

1. Reasonable accessibility (by automobile) for large low-to-middle income groups.
2. Adequate parking space (usually equal to three or four times the store area).
3. Relatively inexpensive land and buildings.

The stores are open long hours, usually 12 hours a day, 6 days a week.

They typically carry many different kinds of merchandise. Although they are highly selective in regard to the price range carried in each category, they generally carry a wide assortment in the types and prices of merchandise handled. Average turnover is 10 to 15 times a year.

With gross margins in the range of 20% to 30%, these stores have margins approximately three quarters the size of those longer established stores with which they are in competition. We estimate that their selling prices for comparable soft-goods merchandise are around 15% lower, on the average, than those of competing stores.

All of the stores used leased departments which, in some instances, account for as much as 50% of total sales and, in other instances, as little as 10%. In almost all stores, shoe and millinery departments are leased. Other products commonly sold under leasing arrangements are . . . cosmetics, domestics, housewares, and hardware. But the stores retain direct merchandising responsibility for most clothing lines.

The stores have substantially fewer personnel in relation to sales than do other soft-goods stores. Wage costs are only 5% to 8% of sales, approximately one third of the equivalent cost in department stores. Self-service reduces the number of employees in the store and simplifies the training problem.

The companies do not handle close-out or distress merchandise or seconds to any significant extent, in contrast with some older operations in the New England area that emphasize price.

Discount houses compared

Certain differences between self-service soft-goods supermarkets and discount houses have already been mentioned. People compare the two so often, however, that the distinction needs to be stressed, particularly since many supermarkets actually bill themselves as "discount department stores."

Some of the differences are basic and important. Through 20 years of development, a common element in discount house operation has been the concentration on products which are so identifiable that consumers can make direct price comparisons between the offerings by various retailers of identical merchandise (as in the case of a particular model of refrigerator, TV set, fountain pen, or coffee percolator). Most of these truly discountable items would fall in the hard-goods category.

In soft goods, however, widely recognized brand names are less common, and even in the case of a specific brand, direct price comparisons between identical products are less feasible. Many items in soft-goods lines are characterized by more rapid style change and obsolescence than is typical of hard goods. Thus confusion results as to whether a difference in price tags reflects (a) "discounts,"

(b) markdowns of obsolescent merchandise, or (c) normal price variances indicating distinctions in style and quality.

Another difference is that there is little uniformity in the size, layout, and
methods of operation among discount houses. And, while various services may
be held to a minimum, discount houses seldom have adopted full self-service.
No precise tabulations are available, but we believe that the average value of a
unit of merchandise sold in discount houses is substantially higher than in the
soft-goods supermarkets.

Trend toward "face lifting"

The brief history of soft-goods supermarkets has shown a significant evolution
from the old mill buildings to the attractive though simple special-purpose premises on which they are now being established. In this connection it is interesting
to draw a parallel between the development of the food supermarkets and the
changes now taking place in the soft-goods stores. The early food supermarkets
occupied low-cost space in old garages, warehouses, and empty factory buildings.
Management gave maximum attention to low prices and minimum attention to
quality of environment and of store fixtures. It frequently maintained the operating expenses at 7% to 10%. However, as competition between supermarkets
increased, the quality of buildings, of fixtures, and of service was increased—
but at the expense of crude economy, so that supermarkets now have expenses
roughly twice those of the early period.

The shift from "cheap" environments has been taking place at a very rapid
rate in the soft-goods outlets. They have been turning to modern buildings and
specially designed fixtures which, though strictly utilitarian, are far more attractive than the unpainted tables and pipe racks of the early stores. This upgrading
of facilities has been accompanied by gradually increased expenses and gross
margins.

Will management stop—or be able to stop—the trend toward improved facilities while its cost and price position is still significantly lower than that of
conventional competitors? The question is crucial to the future of soft-goods
supermarkets. We believe that the answer is yes.

* * * * *

Demise of the shoestring

In 1954 and 1955 square footage ranged from 20,000 to 35,000 per store. In
1956 some stores were as large as 50,000 square feet. By 1958 several stores
contained 75,000 square feet, and by the end of 1959 the largest store in New
England was about 150,000 square feet in size.

In New England, at least, opportunities for shoestring openings of soft-goods
supermarkets by individuals seem to be disappearing. Consider these facts:

The amount of capital investment required has increased enormously. At the
same time, store operations have become increasingly stable, so that manufacturers have found it possible to cut back on the amount of credit they extend
to retailers.

The investment in buildings has increased from a minimal rental of $0.75 to
$1.00 per square foot to close to $2.00 per square foot for new buildings, with

mill building rentals now close to $1.25 per square foot. In mid-1958, one individual planning to operate in a slightly remodeled rented plant and anticipating a gross investment of $70,000 actually required over $130,000 to achieve operations at a $1,500,000 annual sales level.

Even with the use of large mortgages and leaseback arrangements, the cost of new buildings is much greater than that for rental in the early days of soft-goods supermarkets. The fixed capital investment in a new one-story building with adequate parking is probably $10.00 to $15.00 per square foot plus the cost of fixtures, or approximately $620,000 for a 50,000-square-foot store.

It is interesting to note that the founders of the early soft-goods supermarkets in New England were in close communication with each other. With few exceptions, they were either former employees or employers of each other or relatives, friends, or fraternity brothers. These interwoven lines of communication do not seem to have reduced the aggressive spirit with which managements competed, but they may explain, in part, why the New England development has proceeded so much faster than in other areas.

*   *   *   *   *

CONSUMER APPEAL

An examination of the self-service soft-goods stores in the perspective of their products, operations, and competition indicates that two of the principal appeals to consumers are (a) lower price and (b) convenience and freedom in shopping. Compared with most stores carrying the same type of merchandise, self-service outlets provide a price saving of from 10% to 20% of retail price. The majority of customers patronizing such stores belong to an economic class to which this saving is important.

Conveniences that count

Most of the self-service stores require customers to change travel patterns; shoppers must make special trips or go farther. However, the development of food supermarkets and of suburban shopping centers has already demonstrated that convenience is defined by factors other than proximity and availability to accustomed travel paths and public transportation. While these other factors are not new in the long history of retailing, some of them have been exploited more fully by the soft-goods supermarket than by any of its competitors:

Shopping hours.   The long hours that the stores are open (including evenings) afford the customer a generous degree of flexibility. This is a major consideration for the housewife whose only baby sitter is her husband. The stores also offers adequate parking and a general aura of informality which make it easy for the housewife to shop, either alone or with her family. An unpublished survey of two stores by two graduate students at the Harvard Business School reported that 50% of the shopping groups included children and 30% included men.[4]

Variety of merchandise.   Another attraction is the choice of products and price ranges carried. As noted earlier, the majority of self-service soft-goods stores are highly selective as to kind of merchandise sold; they do not attempt to meet the

---

[4]"Zayre Corporation" unpublished report written for the Marketing Research Course (Harvard Business School, Spring 1959).

needs of the whole socio-economic spectrum. For the types of products handled, however, they frequently have a broader selection than is available in any but the largest department stores.

Browsing around.   Many people like to feel free to examine merchandise without any sense of responsibility to retail salespeople, or to rush in and pick up a desired piece of merchandise without waiting for a salesperson.

Satisfaction guaranteed.   Most of the self-service soft-goods retailers have followed a policy of absolute rights for returns and adjustments. The mail-order houses have long demonstrated the effectiveness of such a policy in overcoming consumer doubts about the quality of unseen merchandise not supported by the reputation of a manufacturer's advertised brand. This policy has apparently gone a long way toward establishing in the minds of consumers a confidence in the quality of goods handled by these stores.

Well-defined market.   Operators of many of the soft-goods supermarkets have focused their attention on a relatively narrow band in the socio-economic spectrum. The owner of one soft-goods supermarket in the metropolitan Boston area justifies his location as the one which, within a three-mile radius, includes the largest number of families in the $3,000 to $5,000 yearly income bracket. He considers it an advantage that this area contains relatively few families having substantially different incomes, for he can concentrate on stocking only goods of the price and quality desired by his primary market.

NEFCO (BR)*

~~~~~~

Between June 7 and the second week in July, Mr. Kraft, newly appointed stores superintendent of Sadler's, a recently acquired chain of soft goods stores, was actively engaged in a succession of meetings and conferences. The purpose of this action, Kraft said, was "getting things organized and going immediately while still building towards long-range NEFCO goals."

According to Mr. Harold Norfield, executive vice president, NEFCO had to assemble information about Sadler's before policy could be set. As a consequence, Mr. Kraft often found himself developing a system of NEFCO–Sadler relations without benefit of policy guidelines. At the store level, Kraft felt it necessary to learn the discount business and the job of stores superintendent while decentralizing store management in the NEFCO pattern. In addition, he had responsibility for coordinating the merchandising of toys, hardware, and cosmetics.

Driving from store to store in itself consumed many hours. Kraft lived in Yonkers, New York. He tried to spend some evenings with his wife and two children. Whether he spent the night at his home or on the road, his work day began at 9:00 A.M. and seldom ended before 9:00 P.M. His work with the store managers required one or two days in the stores each week.

Weekly division management meeting

On Wednesday, June 7, Mr. Kraft attended for the first time the weekly division meetings run by Frank Perkins, vice president of the NEFCO Yankee division at its New Haven offices. Both Mr. Feinman and Mr. Parnas were present. The agenda comprised (1) experiments in trading traffic between neighboring NEFCO and Sadler's stores, and (2) NEFCO advertising.

En route to New Haven Mr. Kraft spoke of the customer's view of Sadler's and NEFCO and of the relationship between the two:

The image of NEFCO is one of quality, value and a friendly store. Competitive price, however, is a keystone of NEFCO policy. Even so, it is clear that NEFCO will never be low price on an areawide basis.

Sadler's image has still to be worked out, but even before the formal acquisition it was a certainty and quite obvious to anyone familiar with NEFCO that certain policies would be followed in building the new Sadler's organization. It was a certainty, for example, that the stores would be law-abiding, that they would never price below cost and never violate any of the labor laws. It was also clear that quality and value would be part of the Sadler's image.

I feel that there is a real place for food items in the stores, but it was very clear from what Dick Goldman [vice president of sales] said what the policy on food items is going to be [see NEFCO (AR)]. Food items are not going to be important. I think this makes sense from NEFCO's point of view. You've got to think of the long-run implications of bringing food into a discount house. Through our magnificent canning operation we might be able to cut retail price on some staple items 50%. But what would be the implication of this for the supermarket business? The kind of thing which we do now may set some very important precedents that might be very difficult to live with in the future if we are not careful. Thus in addition to being law-abiding and running a quality store, one of the policies which Sadler's will follow is not to emphasize food items.

At the division meeting it was decided that reciprocal couponing could be worked out to the profit of both organizations. The main part of the meeting, however, was devoted to discussing the development of an advertising format which would be consistent with that of NEFCO, as well as strengthen the quality image of the NEFCO stores in the consumer's mind. Later Mr. Kraft noted that for his purposes the meeting had been a "waste of time."

Following the meeting, Mr. Feinman, Mr. Parnas, and Mr. Kraft lunched together. At one point Mr. Feinman observed:

Sadler's has to improve its promotional technique in order to increase sales. At the moment our promotion program is in a state of chaos. I am upset because I feel that the stores, the newspapers, and all those in contact with Sadler's think we're being foolish.

Mr. Parnas spread an advertisement of a competitor out on the table. It showed a number of items which were being sold as part of a sale. The striking fact was that the competitor was selling items such as Kodak film, Cannon sheets, and Kotex below cost, a practice illegal in Connecticut.

PARNAS: What do you think of that?

FEINMAN: I'm upset. I feel that hard-hitting promotion is the only answer to this kind of competition. In each ad we need several specific items that are hot. Why don't we have franks at seven cents in the circular for next week? They worked last time. I asked you to get them (to Parnas) and you didn't. I'm just not very happy about that circular.

You know, Dan, I'm also upset because I think you're not devoting enough time to *sales.*

KRAFT: Have you ever been told by NEFCO exactly what my job is in the organization? Do you know what my job is? Did you see the letter which was sent out announcing my move to Sadler's division?

FEINMAN: No, Dan, I never saw such a letter. I don't know what you're supposed to be doing although I know they call you store superintendent. Do you think that that's an adequate title, or that my title of general manager is adequate? I know that we're both doing more than our titles imply.

KRAFT: You know, Sol, there are just so many things which I can do at one time.

FEINMAN: Look, Dan, I know that you have a lot to do, but some things come first. You've got to give more time to *sales*. I'm not knocking personnel or security; those things are important. But we've got to have *sales*, and I wish that we could get some of your help in this area.

KRAFT: Sol, weren't you in on the discussion which determined my place in the organization? No? I really assumed that you were.

Later the three returned to the division offices where they looked over plans for the new Stamford store. At the same time they discussed Mr. Kraft's plan to hire a new man to manage the West Haven store in order to replace Jack Carnot who (all three felt) was doing a poor job. Mr. Kraft was due back in Hartford for an afternoon meeting with Mr. Gorman, NEFCO vice president of mergers and acquisitions, but delayed his return 45 minutes in order to interview a candidate for the West Haven position. As a result, he returned to Hartford too late to find Mr. Gorman.

Driving back to Hartford, Kraft reflected aloud upon his new position:

You know, Sol is too narrow-minded in his approach to increasing sales. By emphasizing one tool, gimmick promotion, he is ignoring all the other factors which make a success in the long run. He is trying to make decisions without looking at the total picture.

Look, what's my place in this organization? I am store superintendent. Now, if you took an uneducated person from Kentucky and told him you were a doctor, and I told him that I was in retailing, he would know what we meant, wouldn't he? But if you told him you were a neurologist and I told him I was a store superintendent, he wouldn't know what we were talking about. Well, Feinman doesn't know what we mean at NEFCO by "store superintendent," although it's a very well-defined position. It means you are responsible for the entire success of the stores, sales *and* profits, personnel, security, and all other areas which affect the stores' long-run success. Feinman is constantly asking me to look at sales and to help him out in this area, but that's not really my job. I have to see that it gets done, but I can't get involved in doing it.

I have been asked to make this organization run, to get it going in all areas. I have to set this organization on the right road and build the foundation for a long-run profitable future.

My next step is to build up someone to operate as a field supervisor so that he can relieve me of some of the leg work my job requires. Some time ago I asked Frank Perkins if he had someone available in his organization and he suggested Ed Roth. Roth was a NEFCO store manager for many years and then moved up to field supervisor. I plan to give him some experience in the discount business by having him take over the management of the Hartford store and then help me to open the Stamford store. I am very happy to get someone as able as Ed for the job.

The following three days, Thursday, Friday, and Monday, June 8, 9, and

12, Mr. Kraft concentrated on organization and planning. In addition, he helped James Little, of NEFCO's New York office personnel staff, formalize Sadler's personnel procedures and review the security improvement program. On June 13 Mr. Kraft directed his attention to merchandising problems.

The Hartford store

During the week of June 12 Sadler's held its Sixth Anniversary Sale. One million copies of a 24-page circular had been mailed to the population in the vicinity of Sadler's stores. The bargains listed in the circular were intended to highlight values available throughout the store. Increased traffic and sales were expected as a result of this mailing. Mr. Feinman had little confidence in the Hartford store manager's ability to exploit the expected increase in traffic. A visit to the store on the first day of the sale confirmed his suspicions. He called Mr. Kraft on June 13 and ordered him to the store.

Mr. Kraft went directly to the Hartford store, briefly greeted Mr. Jones, the manager, and then methodically went through the store with a copy of the circular in hand. At each department he asked the department manager to show him where the circular items were. Mr. Kraft looked in every case to ascertain if the merchandise in question had been marked properly, if there was a specific "as advertised" sign on it. He mentioned general merchandising tips. To the women's department manager for example, he said, "Nylons should be arranged by sizes in clear plastic boxes. Why don't you get some from the hardware department? You can borrow them. It makes it easier for the customer to buy, and when it is easier, she buys more."

At each department he asked which items listed in the circular were moving, which were not, what was in stock, and why some were not in stock. He checked the floor, the back rooms, and the stock rooms for cleanliness. He looked for price tags and register tapes on the floor (a security hazard) and counted 56 carriages in use for storing or displaying stock.

After a check of the entire store, Kraft suggested lunch to the manager. In the privacy of Jones's cash office, Kraft combined lunch with a summary of his observations. He covered general store appearance, service, security, and the carriage problem. Only "50% of your carriages are available for use," he said at one point. "Now how can we lick this? What are *you* going to do about it?"

Mr. Kraft then discussed with Jones the results of the circular, item by item. He noted that some department managers had allowed themselves to run out of stock on advertised items by the second day of the seven-day circular week. He urged Mr. Jones to check closely on their promises to get more merchandise.

Following lunch Mr. Kraft returned to his office. Within an hour Mr. Feinman called again. Kraft summarized his morning's activities for Feinman. Not satisfied with Kraft's reliance on the store manager to resolve the problems Kraft had observed, Mr. Feinman asked Kraft to return to the Hartford store at once.

Back at the store, Kraft looked for trouble spots in the store's appearance and operation. At the hardware department he found what he considered an entirely unsatisfactory situation and said to the hardware department manager:

You are not merchandising. You are not doing the job that has to be done to sell. Why are you out of stock on this? . . . This is advertised and is good value; why hide it? Where is the sign? . . . What the hell does DWW mean? You have got to make the advertising dollars produce what *you* paid for it. It is your money [lessee pays for the advertisement of his items] not mine. . . . We can't be your eyes. This aisle looks like an outhouse.

The department manager agreed. Mr. Kraft pointed out other faults—bad signs, out-of-season items displayed together, e.g., storm windows and radiators. "Bird seed doesn't sell. Why give it three feet? Why only two and one-half feet available in a five-foot aisle? . . . Get this crap off the floor. . . . I don't know what to tell you. Can I help you? Can I call your boss to get you some support?" Now, obviously upset, the department manager explained that he knew he was in the wrong but was getting neither support nor money from his boss. Mr. Kraft left without further comment.

The shoe department was still using carriages for stock. In one of the stock rooms Kraft took some rubbish out of a large cardboard box and dumped into it the contents of one of the carriages. He pushed the empty carriage onto the floor.

Walking through the store, he spoke of the hardware department manager's problems. "How much can you do with a guy who is working 77 hours a week and then Sunday? How mad can you get?" Later in the day Kraft made peace with the department manager. He did not relinquish his position, but said he understood that the department manager had not been operating under ideal conditions. The department manager promised to have the department shipshape by the next day.

*   *   *   *   *

Kraft stopped at the employee's rest room. Inside he began singing, "I got trouble" to the tune of "I've got music." He interrupted his singing to say, "And tomorrow we talk about image!"

The advertising meeting

On Wednesday, June 14, Mr. Kraft began the day with a nine o'clock visit to the Hartford store. A quick check showed that the hardware department was now clean and orderly. The principal purpose of Mr. Kraft's visit, however, was to introduce Mr. Edward Roth to the store manager. Roth was to assist in managing the store before taking on the job of field supervisor for Sadler's. At ten o'clock Mr. Kraft returned to the Hartford office for a meeting to discuss advertising policy. Messrs. Feinman, Kraft, Parnas, and Roth, as well as John Gorman (NEFCO vice president of mergers and acquisitions) and John Shalleck (director of the advertising agency used by NEFCO), were in attendance.

The meeting began with a discussion of the store image Sadler's advertising created in the consumer's mind. The decision arrived at was that Sadler's weekly newspaper advertising should convey a *value* image so that the words "Sadler's" and "value" become synonymous in the minds of the public. One or two items per ad were to be highlighted to focus on a specific department.

In a typical exchange, Dick Goldman responded as follows to a remark of Mr. Feinman:

But you are talking about merchandising, not advertising policy.

FEINMAN: Aren't they intertwined?

GORMAN: The purpose of this meeting today is to hammer out concepts. You have got to do this before you can get to the details of the coordination of store merchandising.

ROTH: You have a reliable store, you can back your goods.

GORMAN: You have a convenient beautiful store.

GOLDMAN: These are themes which make up *you.* Use them and repeat them.

Later Feinman said:

Let's summarize. We've decided that we need more planning and an institutional approach.

GORMAN: Sol, that's not strong enough. If I were Art Parnas, I wouldn't know what to do. You should say, "This is the format; this is what we are going to do."

KRAFT: But you've got to tie the merchandising into the ad, you have to be in stock.

GORMAN: Absolutely, otherwise it's unethical. We decided at management meetings on Saturday and Monday that we are going to adopt the following policy: We are going to be a true discount department store built upon the principles of fair merchandising. We're going to strive to have values in each concessionaire's department comparable to the rest of the store.

*   *   *   *   *

GOLDMAN: In the future your key man will have to be a well-paid and well-motivated manager.

ROTH: You have to feed the manager information.

KRAFT: On this point let me say that we are trying to improve our managers by giving them information.

GOLDMAN: But we have to have the right people; there is just so much you can do if the talent isn't there.

GORMAN: You're absolutely right, Dick, but these men have to be given a chance. They had been operating under really bad conditions previously, and as far as we can see at this point I think it's generally accepted that there is only one man who won't make the grade. Nine will.

FEINMAN: Well, we have outlined where we want to go.

GORMAN: We need an advertising manager and some source of continuity in our consideration of problems requiring creativity and imagination.

SHALLECK: There is no doubt that a man inside is worth more than an agency. But getting the right man may be hard.

*   *   *   *   *

GOLDMAN: These guys are all overworked. How can we get this done fast? They need help. Maybe an agency isn't ideally the thing to get first, but we have to get it to them.

GORMAN: We cannot have a man who will try to operate with the goal of pleasing Sol Feinman. He's got to have his own ideas and fight for them. That's the sort of man we need in this organization.

The conclusions of the group, arising from the above interchange of ideas are summarized below:

The women's departments in our stores are as good as any in the country. If we can get the customer to come to Sadler's for routine staple items, we will have loyal customers. Then we might study the layout of the stores and consider the place of gimmicks. The very carnival atmosphere which is so good for promotion may contradict the image of value.

FEINMAN: Gimmicks work and build traffic.

GOLDMAN: The gimmick *idea* is right and O.K., but you have to be careful how you do it.

SHALLECK: You want as an objective to build your customer count. To do this, you ought to get a little sophisticated and break down your market, then aim your advertising at segments of the market. For example, you can put a little thing in an ad that really gets the teen-age girl going, that says the store is for her.

FEINMAN: We can do this, but these clever little things that you're talking about, we just don't know how to do. Can we get an agent?

GORMAN: It's our philosophy at NEFCO that you own the mechanic but that you hire the special talent.

A general discussion of organization followed, considerable attention being given to the store manager's problems:

GORMAN: Part of the problem here is that we would not give anybody a straight answer until last week because we didn't know until last week what policy would be. We really didn't know what the nature of the animal we bought was and what sort of thing we wanted from it. Now that a policy has been set, we can get going on how to build. At times during this building process, Dan is going to have to do more than his assigned work.

FEINMAN: I've been trying to say this. Sometimes Dan is going to have to be more than store superintendent.

GOLDMAN: Yes, but Dan will be the only man who answers questions about the stores.

FEINMAN: You know, I will have to learn how to run this way and so will Art Parnas. I am not used to this.

As conversation proceeded, Mr. Gorman drew on his pad a chart, as shown below, of the organization which had been planned during discussions with the NEFCO management group the previous Sunday and Monday:

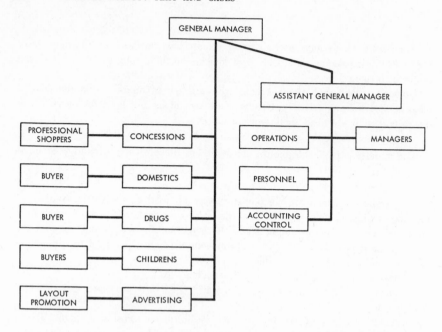

GORMAN: Let me give you my ideas on organization and the thoughts of those who were at the meeting Monday. Since the store manager is going to be God Almighty in his store, a supervisor may remind and suggest but not give him orders. Art's total responsibility, therefore, will be coordination at the store level of all concessionaire's operations. He will be doing merchandising, not worrying about cleanliness and so on. The store operating superintendent, Kraft, is going to take care of all the operating details. Then the advertising manager will handle that area.

Mr. Gorman then laid out on the table the organization chart which he had prepared:

This is the organization as it was set up Monday. (1) There will be a very competent general manager in this organization. We have one but he needs a backer-upper. You know how we believe in backing up at NEFCO. We believe that you can't depend upon just one man. An assistant manager must be available to relieve Sol of the operating detail. That will leave him free for the area in which he is superb, merchandising. Immediately we are going to get a drug man and then once there is an advertising man, Art will move in and handle the concessionaires. We don't even know whether the assistant general manager exists or not. He may simply be a combination of Art and Dan.

*   *   *   *   *

You see, we're not sure that "operations" here at Sadler's are the same thing we think of at NEFCO.

FEINMAN: Maybe operations means more than at NEFCO and it seems to me, Dan, that this is what John is trying to tell you.

GORMAN: Operations in a discount department store such as Sadler's may mean more than the purely technical detail of "operations." In particular it requires a flair for sales and a willingness to shape activities so that they are directed toward producing sales through proper use of operations techniques.

KRAFT: Yes, this is what I've been trying to do all along. I've been trying to tell you this.

FEINMAN: Dan, I know you've been trying to help me and I make a lot of noise now and then, but I hope you can ignore it.

KRAFT: You know, John, I love sales, this is what I love to do.

GORMAN: Sure, Dan. The operations man with the store managers has to have a sales flair to keep Art's suggestions going and to implement Sol's ideas.

*   *   *   *   *

Other discussion included Mr. Kraft's reference to the need to develop a promotional plan for the Fourth of July. Accordingly the focus of the meeting was directed to this subject.

The Fourth of July, and other major national holidays, posed a major problem for the Sadler's management. It was their belief that stores should observe these holidays and remain closed. It was a problem requiring a management decision because there were no holiday-closing laws in the State of Connecticut. The question was complicated by the fact that Sadler's major competitors planned to stay open on the Fourth.

FEINMAN (*to Mr. Gorman*): What should we do?

GORMAN: I'll tell you what we are doing in *food*. If our competition stays open, we *hate* to do it, but we're going to. We stay open. It's a real problem. Here we are trying to upgrade the manager's job, in the rest of the food industry a stinking job, and we don't want him to work. And, you know, the Fourth of July is a truly major holiday.

FEINMAN: I think the answer is to see what could happen Tuesday if we did stay open. What kind of sales do you think we could make during that period if we stayed open all day? (*Kraft and Parnas estimate $15,000 for each of the stores.*) O.K., then we will get something like 10% of that from each of the departments, that's $1,500. In addition, we get 25% margin on 20% of that $15,000, or $800. For that $2,300 the cost would be advertising, a double-page spread in the newspaper (*Art suggests $1,400*), and then another $900 for labor and overhead. Well, there's our answer.

GORMAN: Then let's beat hell out of Monday, and give the people—customers and employees—an institutional ad showing the reason why we are closing on Tuesday. Let's really slap our competitors in the puss.

The group then planned a Salathon for July 3 and a pre-July 4 sale to begin Thursday, June 29. The meeting was interrupted for dinner and then continued until 10:00 P.M. Mr. Gorman distributed what he called an improved version of the organization chart (see Exhibit 1) prior to adjournment.

On Thursday and Friday, June 15 and 16, Dan Kraft worked with the managers of the Windsor, Torrington, New Haven, and West Haven stores. Succeeding days were taken up with paper work as well as a sales plan for the next quarter, part of NEFCO's program for decentralized store management.

Exhibit 1

TENTATIVE ORGANIZATION FOR SADLER'S

(Neat Draft)

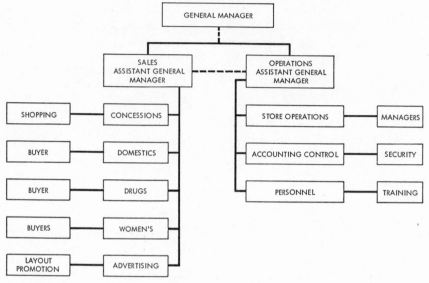

Source: Company official.

Kraft's second weekly division management meeting

Wednesday, June 21, Mr. Kraft along with Mr. Parnas, Sadler's acting advertising director, attended Frank Perkins' weekly management meeting. The agenda included NEFCO–Sadler relations.

Following a review of divisional sales, Mr. Perkins stated it was his policy to have each store manager sit in on a weekly meeting in order to gain experience from presenting a particular problem to a higher level management group and perspective from hearing problems discussed at the division level. He then introduced the Darien store manager who explained to the group he was not reaching the upper income group in his market. He noted that although NEFCO traditionally did not aim for the upper end of the market, in his area the upper income group constituted 25% of the population.

After a general discussion of the problem, it was decided that the store manager should send a personal form letter to the "rich shore people," as an invitation to try Sadler's.

During the break that followed, Kraft showed Frank Perkins the increase in Sadler's sales which had resulted from distribution of the anniversary circular. Perkins noted the sales performance which the neighboring NEFCO store had experienced in each area. When he saw the striking contrast, he decided it was worthy of the attention of the meeting and put the comparative results on the blackboard in the meeting room:

City	Sadler's ($)	NEFCO ($)
Torrington	+35,000	+1,100
Waterbury	+40,000	−1,300
Norwich	+50,000	−100
Hartford	+50,000	−800
Windsor	+30,000	+1,300
Meriden	+40,000	−200
West Haven	+45,000	+300

Upon resumption of the meeting, Dan Kraft discussed the effect of the circular. Perkins then told the group he thought the results were striking and pertinent. He noted the increase in Sadler's sales was so dramatic that NEFCO would be doing itself a disservice if it did not study how to take advantage of the increased traffic stimulated by future circulars.

Subsequent discussion touched on methods of trading Sadler's and NEFCO traffic, including reciprocal couponing.

Following the meeting, Messrs. Kraft, Parnas, and Burke (the latter a member of NEFCO's training department sent down to help Mr. Kraft determine policy and prepare procedures manuals) chatted about specific points developed at the meeting which had confused Mr. Parnas. In one instance Mr. Parnas questioned the advice given to the young Darien store manager.

PARNAS: I'm just a bit amazed as to what is expected of a manager. Wouldn't it be better if the division advertising office wrote the letter? Wouldn't they have a better idea of how to write it?

KRAFT: Who is closer to the market? Who knows exactly how the people ought to be addressed? And don't forget his home office will give him all the help he asks for. But he is going to have to write that letter.

PARNAS: I'm still just a little amazed.

KRAFT: I think Frank Perkins put his finger on it when he said that Sears Roebuck has the right idea. They pay a man a $20,000 salary and then make him one billion per cent responsible for everything under him.

PARNAS: But he has to be a master of detail in order to run a store properly.

KRAFT: No, he has to *control* the details.

Shortly thereafter Mr. Feinman arrived. After lunch Feinman, Parnas, and Kraft, with the floor plan of the West Haven store in hand, discussed the planned rearrangement of the store's fixtures. For one and one-half hours the three argued about a solution to the various problems raised by the reset. Feinman dominated the proceedings. With a draftman's rule and colored pencil he went about changing the floor plan. He worked on three copies of the plan, making changes on each of them.

En route with the case writer to the West Haven store following the conference, Kraft said heatedly:

We have been trying to reset that store for at least seven months. This afternoon was just one of the several conferences. Do you think he would ask the store manager what he thought the new layout ought to be? Do you think that he would ask any of the lessees what their feelings were? Do you think he would ask the fixture people to come and sit in on the meetings so that they could express their opinions and so that they would know what we were trying to do and what we had decided? Or do you think that he would ask one of the construction people in New York, who was going to have to draw the final plans, to come up?

This is just typical of the way Feinman operates. As far as I am concerned, I will be surprised if this plan isn't changed another ten times before we get the store reset. Feinman expects me to go in and talk to the lessees with these three plans in order to explain what he wants. If I showed these plans in this state to Harold Norfield, he would tell me to pick up my paycheck.

Feinman insists on operating by making decisions on the spur of the moment, without taking the time to get the people involved sitting around to discuss what has to be done. He is always running off on a hundred things. I am going to get an ulcer working with that man.

I have been trained to operate in an organized and deliberate manner, and Feinman's approach to problems is driving me frantic. In the areas which I control I'll be damned if I'm going to let Feinman get his fingers in. In those areas which I can control myself, which are my responsibility, I am able to get things done in an organized and rational way and am coming along nicely.

The second store managers' meeting

Monday, June 26, was the occasion of the second store managers' meeting. Present at the meeting were Daniel Kraft, James Little and Ned Hammond (both of NEFCO New York personnel department), George Richardson (Yankee division personnel department), Fritz Hansmann (Sadler's women's clothes buyer), nine Sadler's store managers, and Joe Rooney. Harry Hofstein, manager of the Torrington store, and Mr. Feinman were absent.

Early in the meeting Dan Kraft announced the transfer of Jack Carnot to the Waterbury store as manager, the appointment of Joe Rooney as manager of the West Haven store, and that of Jerry Tipper as field supervisor. With respect to Tipper's assignment Kraft stated: "I hope that in the future this time on the road will be a regular rotating position among the managers. It may also be that Jerry will be involved in the opening of the Stamford store."

Kraft then covered a number of specific problems. One of these, lessee relations, was a great source of friction between Sadler store managers and the managers of the leased departments. In essence the trouble was that their respective responsibilities were detailed in the leases and these were all being renegotiated. Kraft described this problem and attempted a temporary resolution. "We have the responsibility and authority," he noted, "to make the lessees perform as a representative part of the store."

ROTH [Hartford—Jones did not attend]: Top management is not using enough teeth to impress this upon the lessees. They have to keep their eyes on their merchandise and make sure that they do not run out. They are always doing this, always running out of stock and they say that they can't get any more.

KRAFT: Anyone else?

LAND [Meriden]: There is a natural tendency for the department manager to cover up for the lessee for whom he is working, to protect him as best he can He is doing the natural thing when he does this.

KRAFT: You know, I think you really put your finger on it. That is very true.

SHULBERG [Windsor]: Yes, it is perfectly true. We are an intrusion upon them in their operation. When I tell them to do something, they always think of it as Sadler's trying to get something out of them.

CARNOT [West Haven]: They tell me this is their department, and that I should stay out of their business.

ROTH [Hartford]: But you know you can do something about this. When I got into my store, I called all my department managers together and had coffee with them and we had a discussion. They really didn't cooperate and get into the spirit of things, however; they were pretty close mouthed. When I told them that I thought it was all one store, that I didn't see any barriers between departments, and that I was managing and considering problems from the customer's point of view, then they really opened up and I heard something. They had some gripes. They didn't like all the food in the stores.

KRAFT: Really? (*He smiled broadly.*)

ROTH [Hartford]: They don't like the fact that we are taking their tables from the front end. As a matter of fact when they told me this, I thought the situation over and began to give them back some of their tables. Even though I am not sure it is best for the sales in the short run, it may be better from the overall long-run store picture. I wanted to show them that I was going to work with them wherever I could. Then another thing, they say that they are getting our fury on problems like messy stock rooms and cluttered aisles but that we don't give this kind of criticism to our own people. They say that the women's department people are as guilty as anyone else.

KRAFT: Anybody else?

LAND [Meriden]: We have to be the shining example. I think Ed is absolutely right. Once we are the best in the store, it will be easier to keep the rest of the store running right.

*   *   *   *   *

NED HAMMOND [NEFCO personnel]: It seems to me that this relationship of you and the department manager and of the department manager and his boss is a long-range fundamental problem and that you are not going to solve it overnight. It is a basic problem which you are going to have to think about and attack in an organized way.

KRAFT: Well, we can't say anything about this yet until Harmon finishes his renegotiation of the leases with the concessionaires.

ROTH [Hartford]: I think one of the reasons I am getting friendly response from my department managers recently is that I show them, whenever I can, that I am genuinely interested in their problems. Whenever they come to me with a gripe, which I have encouraged them to do, I do my best to solve their problems quickly and fairly.

KRAFT: O.K., let me say that this is an important, a make-or-break question, and it is our intention to exert all efforts possible to be fair and firm.

Kraft next introduced Jim Little of NEFCO personnel who spent ten minutes describing NEFCO personnel procedures.

Hammond: May I interrupt for a second? (*To the store managers.*) NEFCO has acquired many companies over the years, and we have always gone through this same sort of breaking-in period, getting to know each other and each other's problems. We have certain procedures and certain standard ways of doing things which we have worked out over the years and found to be very effective ways of handling ·problems. I am sure that, so far, all you are seeing is a confusing mass of paper and policies and statements, which seems to make your job harder, more confusing, and not any easier. I recognize that this transition period must be a pain in the neck. New ways of doing things, the procedures, always give problems. I would like to tell you about a meeting we had with the executives of a food company we recently acquired. Our vice president, Norm Conlin, explained to them the way NEFCO feels about certain things: (1) NEFCO likes people who have the guts to stand up and say what they think when they think they are right. We don't like "yes" men, and (2) NEFCO has been made by the people we have acquired. Conlin pointed out at that meeting that every man there representing NEFCO had come in through an acquisition. So, we can only try to help you. We are here to serve you. You have to tell us what you think.

For the next hour Jim Little led the group in a discussion of personnel policy and procedures. Immediately following, Fritz Hansmann, the women's sportswear buyer for Sadler's, discussed plans for the approaching fall season and problems of merchandising control. At the end of that section of the meeting Mr. Kraft asked Fred Land, as manager of the top-volume store, to lead a discussion on the subject of new promotional gimmicks.

At one point in this discussion when the legality of a proposed promotion was questioned, Mr. Kraft had the following to say:

We are a chain of discount houses. As far as NEFCO is concerned there are two kinds of laws: there are those laws regarding morality, labor, and payroll policies, and these we follow to the letter and bend over backwards one thousand per cent to follow in spirit. Then there are laws relating to prices and promotional gimmicks and other things like that. These we recognize that we are going to break on occasion, and it will be management's decision to decide when. I think I am the only executive at NEFCO who has one file in his drawer which is called "lawsuits."

Mr. Hammond, breaking in, said:

I think what you mean, Dan, is that there are laws relating to operating procedure and those relating to merchandising practices, and as a discount house we must distinguish between them.

Later in the discussion of promotion, the problem of lessee relations was brought up again:

Land [Meriden]: I think that while we are talking about promotions we ought to recognize that promotions can be fine but that it is pitiful when you look at the amount of merchandise which the lessees are out of in *staple* lines. You know, the ranking of departments across all the stores which you gave us recently gave me an ability to go through the store and pick out what the departments were doing. I was then able to talk with my department manager and ask him why he was not doing as well as the rest of the store.

KRAFT: O.K., let's talk about staples. Whenever I'm in the store, they always tell me, "It's coming in." They never say "we goofed," or "we're out of stock," or "we're having trouble getting this item."

The store managers explained to Mr. Kraft that they were constantly asking the lessees, the department manager, and the department owners for action and that they were getting absolutely nothing in response.

KRAFT: You know I'm going to be frank with you. I get no answer, and with all due respect to Mr. Feinman he often gets no answer from the lessees. Part of the problem is that two of the men involved are short of working capital.

BELL [Groton]: Domestics?

KRAFT: We will either buy him or kick him out. Now, what can we do to help you handle this problem with the lessees?

SHULBERG [Windsor]: I think that the department manager personnel are part of the problem. I had a department in which I was having an awful lot of trouble and I made them give me three different managers before I finally found one that could do the job. But when he got in there, the department began to function well and I had no more problems.

ROTH [Hartford] (to Kraft): I think you and the owners ought to get together and visit each store and decide what is going to be accepted, what arrangements are acceptable to both of you, and let the owner [the concessionaire] tell the department manager what the arrangement is.

KRAFT: This is really the crux of the problem. It seems to me that this gets back to our problem which Fred brought up.

SHULBERG [Windsor]: Yes, the department manager is the man in the middle. He really has nobody to talk to and he may want to work for me, but then he thinks, "What will my boss think?"

Following a luncheon intermission, Kraft reconvened the meeting:

O.K., it is decided that Jerry Tipper and I will create a short checklist of common problems which come up with the lessees. We will try and work these out. If you get recurring problems with your department managers after you have done everything you can, you call me up and I will back you up 100%.

O.K., what can we do to build customer consciousness? Ray?

STEIN [Norwich]: I suggest that the only thing to do is the sort of thing I do in my own store, that I have weekly meetings to make sure that they [the salesclerks] treat the customer the way they would like to be treated when they are customers. The only thing I can think of is repetition. If you keep at it long enough, they are bound to learn. I know, for example, that in my store I try to get the girls to walk up to a customer and say something other than "may I help you?" When a customer is browsing around, she doesn't want to be disturbed, and the one thing you don't want her to be able to do is to refuse your help. I tell them to say "hello," or "how are you," or "that dress comes in red," or "that blouse comes in size six to nine," and so on. On the other hand, the girls just don't seem to pick this up unless you keep repeating it.

KRAFT: Jack?

CARNOT [West Haven]: Yes, I think repetition is the right thing; that is what I am trying to do.

LAND [Meriden]: If we make the employees feel good, feel that they are part of a wonderful organization, then I think that it will be an easy thing to get them customer conscious. If we say hello to all the employees and make a point of commenting on the new hairdo of that neglected girl in the store, I think it makes all the difference.

KRAFT: Fred, I think you have hit it on the nail again. It is getting to the point where I think you should be sitting up here and not me. You know one thing you can do is use the mike in the store to say hello. If you want to, you can comment about that girl's hairdo over the mike. It will make her blush like hell, but she will love you for it. Another thing is that just before opening you can turn the music up and make sure you have a good bright march on when you do. It really brightens things up.

TIPPER [Waterbury]: I tell our employees all the time that when a customer comes in she is the one who pays our salary and that it's our business to pay attention to her. She is always right. And you know I have gotten feedback from our guard that this policy really pays off. He hears people saying, "Oh, I can return this, I can always return things here." "We don't have to worry about buying it. If it is not right, they will always take it back. I know that." The customers love our policy on returns.

KRAFT: Ed?

ROTH [Hartford]: There are two things that we are talking about here: the employees, and the customer. On the first, the employees, the store manager has to be able to pay personal attention to his employees. That means freeing up some of his time so that he can be able to do this. The employees working in our stores have to have the basis for loyalty and this comes from the store manager.

KRAFT: O.K., Fred said it. The manager sets the tone. You can be tough and fair but set the right atmosphere.

The discussion of customer consciousness continued for five minutes and then after a few brief announcements Mr. Kraft called for the managers' report on the warehousing problem. Dan Sharf made the presentation, the gist of which was that the managers agreed that central warehousing should be introduced as soon as possible. "There is no doubt that we will achieve greater efficiencies." The managers did not support their recommendations with any dollar estimates of savings, and Mr. Kraft spent the next few minutes eliciting such estimates from them. He summarized the discussion of central warehousing as follows:

O.K., as it stands, let me tell you this. We, as far as I know, are going to go central. The geographers will find a location. I am going to have to sell the cost savings you presented to NEFCO management.

How about the other subject you worked on. Let me tell you what I plan to do. I will take your suggestions, work out my own recommendations based upon yours, and then send it in to top management.

Well, who is reporting on store managers' hours?

SHULBERG [Windsor]: We had a lot of discussion about this, and there was general consensus on what I am about to propose. There was one dissent. We would like one day off, three nights a week off, and on late nights, to come in early the next morning. We have two schedules but I don't have them here. Harry had them down.

ROTH [Hartford]: I am that dissenter, but I also have the notes on the schedules. Here they are, we will alternate I and II with our assistant managers:

I		II	
Monday	9–6	Monday	1–10
Tuesday	1–10	Tuesday	9–6
Wednesday	9–6	Wednesday	1–10
Thursday	1–10	Thursday	9–6
Friday	9–6	Friday	1–10
Saturday	1–10	Saturday	9–6

We want the day off on Monday or on Wednesday, again alternating with our assistant.

KRAFT: Right now, what are your schedules?

	Shulberg and Sharf	Tipper, Bell, and Stein	Fredericks, Land, and Carnot	Ed Roth
Monday	9–6	8:30–6	9–10	9–6
Tuesday	9–10:30	11–10:30	9–6	9–6
Wednesday	9–6	8:30–6	9–10	9–6
Thursday	9–10:30	11–10:30	9–6	9–10:30
Friday	9–6	8:30–6	9–10	9–10:30
Saturday	9–10:30	11–10:30	9–6	9–6

KRAFT: That's roughly 60 hours a week for all of you, right? (*The store managers agreed.*)

Well, we have to cut that. Of course, since we are crazy enough to go into retailing, you realize that what we are working on isn't going to go for the period Thanksgiving to Christmas.

STEIN [Norwich]: What about the day off? Who is going to cover the store then? What will be the schedule?

SHULBERG [Windsor]: On the day that I am off, my assistant will work 9 to 10:30. That's going to be standard. It has to be that way.

KRAFT: Well, I wonder if you can tell us how things were at the chains where you were working. What sort of schedules did the managers work there?

TIPPER [Waterbury]: At Fields we worked three 9:00 to 6:00 days alternating with three 1:00 to 10:00 days.

KRAFT: Are you serious? Whatever made you come to Sadler's? (*Kraft's remark followed by further bantering around the table.*)

LAND [Meriden]: At Woolworth we worked five 9:00 to 5:00 days and one night.

CARNOT [West Haven]: At Kresge we worked four 9:00 to 5:30 days and two nights until 9:00. Those days were 9:00 to 9:00. (*The meeting broke up in general laughter.*)

FREDERICKS [New Haven]: At Klines the executives worked one day 9:00 to 9:00, one other night on a 10:00 to 9:00 day and three 9:00 to 6:00 days.

KRAFT: Zayre's works the same schedule we do.

SHULBERG [Windsor]: Now, Mr. Kraft, when we were talking about days off, we obviously didn't consider Saturday. I want you to realize that. We recognize that that is the day when we have to be in the store.

KRAFT: You know, we don't know yet whether you shouldn't be taking Saturdays. It may turn out that you ought to be in the store in the early part of the week, building, rather than Saturday when things are rolling.

ROTH [Hartford]: And what are you doing for the guy underneath you? The only way you can build the guy underneath you is to give him responsibility for the store on big days.

KRAFT: Absolutely right, but at the moment, and I am saying this in all confidence to you at this meeting and it shouldn't go further, it doesn't look as if many of the assistant general managers are going to make it. They are just not good enough people.

LAND [Meriden]: Are we in the future going to be able to expect that our assistant store manager is going to be grooming for a store manager's job?

KRAFT: Absolutely, in the future we won't hire a man for an assistant manager unless we think he can make it.

Well, I don't know whether I am going to be able to get this whole package from top management. I expect that in two years we will be able to get better than what you have asked for, but right now I want to be able to sell a package without haggling.

SHULBERG [Windsor]: Well, if we can't get the whole package, then we have agreed that we want the day off. The way it will work out when we get the Monday off is we will get a two-day weekend every other week, and then we can do something with the family and it will really be something. We will be working a lot of those late evenings and early mornings which we asked for anyway.

KRAFT: That's what I thought would be right. Look, I am staking my and my family's future on Sadler's and NEFCO's Sadler's division. In the future we are going to be the best discount house in the business. So I think that you are betting your time and your effort on a good thing.

Following the store manager's reports, Mike Cronin led a discussion of security problems, at the end of which Mr. Kraft closed the meeting:

I want to thank you for the cooperation you have shown to me and all the NEFCO people who have been besieging you. With all the things we are putting in, procedures and so on, it is still our basic job to run the store. I have one job here, given to me by NEFCO's executive vice president and general manager, to build up the store manager until he runs that store. If you give me the cooperation you have been giving, I am sure we will finish my job soon. The store manager's job is 100% the man. Some 90% is the correct attitude and 10% pure technical competence. I know you have got the competence and the attitude, and we'll just concentrate on our funneling your attitudes in the right directions.

If you stick with Sadler's, we are going to make it the best run discount house in the country, and you can be happy betting your and your family's future on it. Fair enough? Meeting adjourned.

On Tuesday and Wednesday, June 27 and 28, Mr. Kraft and Mr. Robert Fitz, vice president of development, made a swing of the Sadler's stores, and some of those of Sadler's competitors, in order to evaluate the merchandising aspects of the Sadler's operations. Kraft described the trip tersely by noting that "Mr. Fitz was not happy with what he saw." On Thursday Mr. Fitz reported his findings to a meeting of the NEFCO top management. On Friday Mr. Gorman remarked that "in two days Robert saw all the problems with which we have been dealing these past months and he was not very happy about them. This sort of thing occasionally happens, and although yesterday people were all excited today it has already died down."

Friday, June 30, Mr. Kraft spent the first two hours of the morning working out solutions to a variety of operating problems in the stores. Mr. Gorman talked privately with Mr. Feinman about the latter's adjustment to the integration of Sadler's into NEFCO. When Mr. Reis (a consultant) arrived, discussion shifted to technical matters related to inventory control and warehousing, two problems which were to take up most of the day.

At 11:00 A.M. Kraft was called into Mr. Feinman's office to meet Mr. Cantor. Mr. Feinman introduced Cantor as an old friend and neighbor and the "doughnut king" in New England. Kraft was informed that Feinman had arranged for Cantor to lease space in the new Stamford store for a doughnut stand. Outlining the terms of the arrangement, Mr. Feinman explained that he had found a space for the doughnut man on the floor. The discussion concerned details, and Kraft closed by saying that he was delighted to have Mr. Cantor come in but that he, Mr. Cantor, would understand if Kraft checked with the NEFCO bakery organization to see if they considered his operating acceptable. Mr. Cantor accepted this reservation to the agreement.

After Cantor left Feinman's office, Mr. Feinman explained to Mr. Kraft that he thought the introduction of the doughnut stand involved pushing the cash registers to the left side of the store. Cantor was to get 28×14 feet and pay 10% rent on sales of $150 a week. Feinman estimated it would cost $2,000 to put Cantor's fixture in, but beyond that there would be no investment. Mr. Kraft noted that the doughnut stand would replace the registers at the natural exit point. In addition, after Kraft and Feinman took a scale to the Stamford floor plan, it appeared that one register would be lost. Mr. Kraft questioned whether they could afford to lose one register because if store sales increased a tie-up would occur at peak traffic periods.

Mr. Feinman explained that the discussion worked out in such a way that he had found himself in a bad bargaining position. He observed that an offer to let the doughnut man into future stores and all existing ones might prove to be a strong enough inducement to make Cantor shift his position on the floor.

Mr. Kraft was clearly unhappy about the decision but chose not to dispute it. He did, however, tell Feinman that NEFCO surveys had shown customers were irked by having to wait in line. They had also indicated that while shoppers might like to dawdle through the store, once they arrived at the check-out line they wanted to move quickly out of the store, even if they had nowhere else to go. In reply Mr. Feinman said he believed "instinctively that a customer in a discount house might feel a little different." She would want to feel that she was buying at a place where there was traffic, where everybody came for bargains.

Later in the morning conversation with John Gorman and Irving Reis shifted to Raymond Hoffman, who was under consideration for the position of assistant general manager in charge of merchandising. Mr. Hoffman was expected in Hartford that morning for a final interview.

FEINMAN: I think the idea is a very good one. What are your opinions of Hoffman?

REIS: He has a very fine reputation, a tremendous potential for growth, and, for his age, a marvelous merchandising background.

GORMAN: You know a problem we face is that before we hire him we are going to have to spell out clearly his responsibilities and his future. It is one thing to ask one of our own people to come down to a rather undefined situation and quite another thing to *hire* a good man on this basis.

With Mr. Gorman leading, it was decided that the new man would be called "assistant to the general manager." He would be in control of the buyers and their operations and work as an assistant to Mr. Feinman.

GORMAN (*to Feinman*): You are the merchant, and he will be your assistant. This will push you upstairs away from the details which you dislike. You just have to recognize, Sol, that details aren't your cup of tea. You set policy, decide what you want, and then it's up to him to see that it gets done. Is that all right with you?

FEINMAN: That's precisely what I want.

GORMAN: Then you have to do the same thing with this man here (*pointing to Kraft*), who will be your operations assistant. You will tell him how you want those stores to look and he'll have to get it done. The same thing with Art and the concessionaires. You tell him what arrangements you have made, what the formal agreements are, and what promotions are coming, and it will be up to Art to get things done.

Now what I'd like to do is set up a framework of time within which I can come down here regularly and help clear out the pipeline. I have time freed up now and I'm going to schedule things so that I can get down here on a regular basis. If I can handle some of the detail and some of the leg work and just follow up on things, then it will free you so that you can start looking ahead and building.

I'll make some decisions and some of them will be wrong, but if you tell me what to do, I'll try to clear it up and give you time to get out in the field (*to Kraft*) and work with the store managers to plan. Some of my decisions are going to be wrong, but it seems to me that this way we would be able to get going faster towards planning. Is there a place for me?

FEINMAN: Yes. I'll tell you what we can do. We have to be sales-minded. Personnel is very important; so is security and maintenance and so on. But they are number two, and sales is number one. Let me give you an example. Dan, you were in the store the other day in West Haven. You saw some towels there which you thought were priced badly. You know much more about domestics than I ever will. You know what you should have done, you should have changed the price right then while you were in the store.

KRAFT: Before I left the store, I called Art and told him about the situation. Domestics is one of his assigned departments. He promised me that he would follow up on it but I know that he's been over his head with work.

FEINMAN: He doesn't have the *time*. When you see something wrong when you're in a store, whether it's my department or Art's, you have to handle it right there and then.

GORMAN: Dan, I don't agree with Sol in principle, or for the long run, but in the short run we can't be as straight-laced about organization as we might like. We're going to have to cross lines. You'll have to let each other know about it, but until we get set up, when you see a fire put it out whether or not it's in your bailiwick.

KRAFT: O.K., this is perfectly fine with me. I'd like to make one request though, that you relieve me of all my specific duties involving the coordination of advertising in my assigned departments and I'll take as my responsibility trouble shooting in all departments.

FEINMAN (*laughing*): I can't relieve you of that responsibility. Who else will do it? I don't have the time. What I'm trying to do is give you this job in addition to what you're doing.

GORMAN: What we're saying, Dan, is this. You came out of a very highly and well-structured organization. If you had crossed lines back there, you'd have gotten spanked unless you had a very constructive contribution to make. In this organization you're going to have to be a jack-of-all-trades, at least for a while. Maybe in a few months you can firm up lines, after we get the new men with their feet on the ground. I know that you people have too many things to do, but all we can do at this point is give you more. You people have to have some time to get the bees out of your bonnet, but that's going to have to wait for a while.

Soon after this discussion Messrs. Feinman and Gorman left the room to interview Raymond Hoffman. Mr. Kraft spent the rest of the morning (1) discussing the sales presentation made the previous day by the Sweda representatives (who sold cash registers which would produce data for inventory and merchandising control) with Irving Reis; (2) talking over the telephone with several of his store managers about their problems; (3) interviewing an applicant for a job; and (4) planning sales for the next quarter.

At about 1:30 P.M. Dan Kraft and Ron Arnold stopped their work for a few minutes to chat. Kraft appeared very depressed. He said, "As far as I am concerned this was a *terrible* week; everybody is jumping on me, and I'll be glad when it's all over." Telling Arnold of his experience in Mr. Feinman's office, he said, "You know, I've been working at 190% of my capacity. Well, if they want me to work 200%, I guess I'll have to."

Arnold was in a correspondingly unhappy mood. He had been encountering all sorts of difficulties in the transfer of the Sadler's books to the New York accounting office methods. "You know," he said, "I've got so many problems that I can't even figure out what I've got to do next. It all seems so big and unsolvable that I don't know what I'm going to do. The way things are working out I am having to do every single thing myself. I am getting no cooperation from the home office." Kraft agreed. Conversation continued with the two discussing the difficulties they were having in eliciting cooperation from New York.

At 2:00 P.M., Messrs. Gorman, Feinman, Kraft, and Arnold had a meeting in Mr. Feinman's office. Areas covered were payroll control; problems with some of the NEFCO divisions which were, as Mr. Gorman put it, "holding themselves back as if you fellows have the plague instead of pitching in and helping wherever they can"; lessee cooperation on circulars; other methods of promotion, particularly reciprocal couponing; the possibility of a central warehouse and Dan Kraft's warehouse expense report; and, finally, the presentation of Kraft's sales forecast for the quarter.

Everybody seemed happy at this meeting. The sales plan was revised with all involved in the best of spirits. Mr. Feinman tactfully explained his objections; Mr. Gorman entered the discussion only on those occasions when he felt that technical advice was needed. There was much joking and no friction. Mr. Kraft believed Mr. Feinman had eagerly awaited the institution of a sales plan. He thought that one reason for the success of the meeting was the fact that his and Feinman's goals had "finally" coincided.

After the meeting, and in private, Mr. Arnold noted:

It was a great meeting. Everybody was relaxed. It just had to come. Everything has been gloomy for so long that this meeting was a godsend.

Why was it so good? Gorman exercised a stabilizing influence on Sol. Mostly, at long last, we took up one problem at a time, made deliberate decisions, and even decided on occasion not to do anything until more information was available. That is the only way you can ever get anything done so that it's finished once and for all.

The fact that Sol is going to go on vacation for three weeks on Monday . . . probably helped. So does the fact that it's Friday. . . .

Monday, July 3, was occupied with the shifting of Mr. Feinman's responsibilities to Mr. Kraft for the duration of the former's absence. By the end of the day the Salathon was reported an outstanding success. In addition to successful pre-4th days on Thursday, Friday, and Saturday, the average Sadler store did $40,000 on Monday, a 12-hour day, as opposed to the usual $6,000 day.

On Wednesday, July 5, Mr. Kraft spent the better part of his morning working out plans for the formalization of personnel procedures with Jim Little. The rest of the day was consumed handling voluminous memoranda and letters left by Mr. Feinman. He came across a group of problems which were to be prime trouble spots during the next weeks. They were all in the area of lessee relations. Previously he had had contact with lessees through his store managers, but now, because of Mr. Feinman's absence, he had to handle several problems at top management level. Two typical examples are as follows:

1. The hardware delivery problem in West Haven:

From the day the store opened the hardware concessionaire found it totally impractical to use the loading dock at the Sadler's store in West Haven. It was therefore necessary for merchandise to be unloaded at one of the front doors before store opening. According to the terms under which the store was leased from the owners of the West Haven Shopping Center, this procedure was illegal. Various attempts had been made to work out a compromise solution, but, Mr. Kraft noted, the issue had reached the stage where the driver of the hardware man's truck had been threatened with arrest by the night watchman at the West Haven Center. Harmon Stoddard finally worked out a solution with the center owner. Mr. Kraft remarked:

Here is a perfect example of the type of small problem which can blow up if it is handled by snap decisions which supposedly solve it. Now, Gorman, Stoddard, Feinman, the center owner, the night watchman, and myself are all involved. If it had been handled right, it could have been settled in 15 minutes once and for all.

2. Shoes in West Haven:

a) On June 28, when Kraft visited the West Haven store, he found the shoe department in a state which appalled him. The merchandise was dirty, worn, and consisted of unappealing styles. He rebuked the department manager and notified Mr. Feinman of the matter.

b) Negotiations by Messrs. Shae, Norfield, and Stoddard with Mr. Hirsch, the owner of American Footware (the concessionaire in West Haven), resulted in an agreement which gave American the shoe concession in the new Stamford store and the right to prove themselves in all their present locations over the following 365 days. In return, NEFCO had a unilateral right to cancel all American's leases at the end of that time.

c) On Monday, July 10, Kraft received a call from Joe Rooney complaining about the intolerable state of the shoe department in his store. Kraft called Mr. Hirsch and told him that the shoes were dirty, old, out of style, and a detriment to the store. He elicited from Mr. Hirsch a promise to get all the inferior goods out of the store by markdowns.

d) On July 14, Joe Rooney called Mr. Kraft at Hartford to say that American had fulfilled its promise and that he thanked Mr. Kraft for getting such prompt action. But he noted that at the same time that the markdown goods went out of the store in came an assortment that made the original merchandise look beautiful.

e) Kraft then called Hirsch. Hirsch at first protested that the situation could not exist but then admitted that he had closed one of his stores in the Midwest and was "scattering the merchandise around the country."

f) Kraft then noted to Parnas, who had listened to the conversation on a second wire, that "as the agreement stands, Hirsch has the occasion and the incentive to give Sadler's a real screwing, which he can do as long as he does not break the lease. This can continue for 365 days."

g) Kraft called New York and described the situation to Mr. Gorman, including problems with the hardware and domestics concessionaires.

h) Within an hour Kraft got a call from American Footware. Gorman had brought Harmon Stoddard into the picture and Stoddard had called Hirsch. The result was that the new goods which were inferior were going to be marked down that day and there would be no more dumping.

i) Kraft hung up the phone. In a slightly incredulous voice he said, "Boy, when I call New York, I get results. I find it strange to be working regularly with the vice presidents, but the problems I am facing are such that it seems to be the only effective way of getting them resolved." He then noted that he had been getting increasingly involved with the relationship of NEFCO to the concessionaires at the top management level, "not by my own design, but seemingly by accident. I guess that it is mostly because I am the only figure down here all the time who is a liaison with NEFCO."

TEXAS INSTRUMENTS INCORPORATED (A)
(CONDENSED)*

On April 17, 1959, Texas Instruments Incorporated (TI) of Dallas, Texas, merged with the Metals and Controls Corporation (M & C) of Attleboro, Massachusetts. One of the fastest growing large corporations in the country, TI had achieved a compound annual growth from 1946 through 1958 of 38% in sales and 42% in net income. The president had publicly predicted that volume would more than double in 1959 to a sales level near $200 million. Almost half this growth, he added, might come through mergers, with M & C contributing $42 million to $45 million. To date TI's principal business had been in electronic and electromechanical equipment and systems, semiconductors and other components, and exploration services for oil, gas, and minerals.

So highly was TI regarded by the market that in May 1960 its common was selling at about 70 times the 1959 earnings of $3.59 a share.

M & C activities

Itself the product of a 1932 merger and a postwar diversification, M & C had three major groups of products: clad metals, control instruments, and nuclear fuel components and instrumented cores. The company had grown steadily, and in 1959 had plants in two U.S. locations and five foreign countries. Reflecting predecessor corporation names, the clad metal lines were known as General Plate (GP) products, and the control instrument lines were known as Spencer products. Included in the former were industrial, precious, and thermostat metals; fancy wire; and wire and tubing. Included in the latter were motor protectors, circuit breakers, thermostats, and precision switches. Among these Spencer lines there were some that utilized GP products as raw materials; i.e., GP thermostat bimetals and GP clad electrical contacts.

Apart from a portion of GP's precious metal products which went to the jewelry trade (where appearance and fast delivery from stock were key considerations), most GP and Spencer products had to be designed to specific customer requirements and produced to customer order. Thus engineering

---

know-how and close coordination between the sales and production departments on delivery dates were important. Owing to the technical nature of the products and also to their fast-changing applications, a company sales force with a high degree of engineering competence was essential. To serve its several thousand customers, many of whom purchased both Spencer and GP products, the company maintained a force of 50 men in the field, divided into Spencer and GP units.

With Spencer products facing important competition from four other firms in the $10 million to $40 million annual sales bracket, tight control of costs was important for securing the large orders generally placed by the kinds of customers to whom these products were sold. Buyers included manufacturers of fractional horsepower motors, household appliances, air conditioning, and aircraft and missiles. In contrast, GP industrial metals met no direct competition, although clad metals for industrial uses met with competition from alloys.

M & C's premerger organization

At the time TI took over M & C, a task force of four junior executives had just completed, at the acting president's request, a critical study of M & C's organizational structure. So far its nuclear activities had been conducted by an entirely separate subsidiary, and the GP and Spencer activities had been organized as shown on Exhibit 1.

Under the acting president at the top level came a tier of predominantly functional executives (the vice presidents for marketing, engineering, and finance, the treasurer, and the controller). At the third and fourth levels of command, the structure increasingly showed a breakdown by product lines. For example, at the fourth level in manufacturing there were four separate groups corresponding to the major Spencer lines, and six separate groups corresponding to the major GP lines. Approximately the same breakdown appeared among the fourth-level product specialists in marketing. Although there was no profit responsibility at this level, the controller had been sending marketing's product specialists a monthly P & L by product line, in the hope of encouraging informal meetings among the people in marketing, engineering, and production who were working on the same lines.

Even at the second level, the predominantly functional division of responsibilities was neither complete nor unalloyed. Thus the vice president for marketing was also the vice president of Spencer Products, and in this capacity he had reporting to him the Spencer engineers. As a result, the company's vice president of engineering was, in effect, the vice president only of GP engineering, although he also served in an other-than-functional role by acting as the vice president of M & C International. (In 1958 exports and other foreign sales totaled about $2 million.)

After confidential interviews with 140 people, members of the M & C task force reportedly concluded that this organizational structure was causing or contributing to a number of company problems. Accordingly the task force

Exhibit 1

PREMERGER METALS AND CONTROLS ORGANIZATION

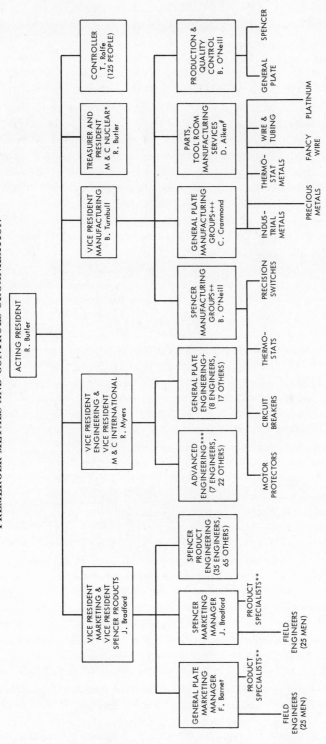

*Detail on M & C Nuclear not disclosed.

**Responsible for factory-customer coordination on specifications, prices, delivery, and new applications on different product lines (broken down about as shown in the manufacturing department).

***Responsible for long-range product development for GP lines.

+Worked on new applications and process designs for GP lines.

++Principal operations in Spencer production departments were parts-making and assembly.

+++Principal operations in GP industrial, precious, and thermostat metal departments were bonding and rolling; in GP wire and fancy wire departments, drawing; and in GP platinum department, melting and refining. Some GP facilities were shared, and roughly 5% of direct labor hours for each GP department were devoted to work for other departments.

#Reporting to Aiken were units were making two GP and three Spencer parts.

Source: Interviews and company records.

recommended sweeping changes, first to the acting president by whom they had been appointed, then to his successor, Mr. Edward O. Vetter, a 39-year-old TI vice president brought in following the merger.

Mr. Vetter's review and appraisal

As soon as he arrived at M & C, Mr. Vetter spent most of four days in closed meetings with task force members. At the same time he scheduled public meetings with all executives; these sessions he devoted to general discussions of his aims for the organization and to reassurances that drastic changes would not be made.

From these discussions Vetter learned that a great many people at M & C felt that the three major functional departments were not cooperating well enough in the exploitation of new product opportunities based on existing markets and skills. Although in a few isolated instances, marketing, engineering, and production personnel concerned with a particular product had formed small informal groups to work on common problems, the three departments had not been seen as working together with maximum effectiveness, particularly in new product development. To blame, besides top management's inattention and the absence of a comprehensive plan, was a lack of clear-cut responsibility and authority.

Other problems, too, provided additional evidence of the failure of functional groups to work together harmoniously and effectively. Thus there was continued squabbling between process engineers and production supervisors, with neither group being willing to accept the other's suggestions for improvements in manufacturing methods. With both groups reporting to different vice presidents, conflicts too often came up for resolution at top levels. Here many times decisions were postponed and issues left unresolved.

Vetter was also told by many members of the organization that the personal influence of marketing's product specialists played too large a role in company decisions. Formally assigned to coordinate certain aspects of factory-customer relations (see notes to Exhibit 1), these specialists were said to determine the amount of R.&D. time given to particular lines, with the result that some lines had grown quite strong while promising opportunities elsewhere were neglected. Similarly personal relationships between product specialists and production personnel largely determined scheduling priorities.

After becoming familiar with these problems, Mr. Vetter decided that M & C provided a golden opportunity for applying TI's philosophy of organization by what TI called "product-customer centered groups." Basically this plan involved putting a single manager in charge of sales, manufacturing, and engineering on a particular product line, and making this manager responsible for profits. This type of structure, Mr. Vetter noted, was what had been proposed by M & C's own task force on organization. According to TI's president, it offered advantages not only in managing existing lines but also in finding new opportunities for discerning and serving new customer needs.

As he was collecting information on M & C's organizational arrangements, Mr. Vetter had dictated the following set of notes for his own use:

It appears as if natural product groups already exist here. General Plate, Spencer and Nuclear have always been separate, and International sales are set apart under Richard Myers. Within these major groupings there is also a somewhat parallel division of the manufacturing and marketing facilities along product lines. There are ten production departments that are each organized to produce a particular product line, while there is an almost parallel organization of marketing product specialists under James Bradford.

Bringing together product managers and production supervisors for similar product lines would seem to be the logical implementation of TI's management philosophy. Of course, one problem would be the rearrangement of some of the production facilities in order to locate all the equipment under a product manager's control in one area. While we do have ten product-manufacturing departments, some of these share facilities and perform work for one another. In addition, the parts department performs fabrication operations for several production departments. In spite of this, there are no major pieces of equipment that would have to be physically relocated. We estimated that some duplicate equipment will have to be purchased if we go ahead with product-centered decentralization; in order to accomplish this about $1.5 million will have to be spent almost three years before it would otherwise have been committed.

I believe that the "inside" product specialist—the man at the factory who lives with both the manufacturing and the marketing problems for his line—is a key man. Our products are mainly engineered to customer order and, as such, require a great deal of coordination on delivery dates, specifications, and special applications. In addition to performing this liaison, the product managers could be the men who sense ideas for new product applications from their marketing contacts and then transmit these to the product engineering personnel at the factory.

These men would not be salesmen. A field sales force would still be needed to make regular calls on all of our clients and to cultivate the associations with our customers' engineering staffs. One significant question here is how to organize the sales force. These men are highly skilled and quite expensive to employ—each salesman should enter commitments of at least $1 million yearly in order to justify his expenses. Since our customers are spread all over the country, it would appear economical to assign field salesmen by geographical areas, each to sell all, or at least a number of, our products. Unfortunately, this system might take a good measure of the responsibility for the sales supervision. Our problem here is to leave sales responsibility at the product group level without having an undue duplication of field sales personnel.

The filtering down of responsibility and authority would mean that we would need more "management skill" in order for the product managers to be able to manage the little companies of which each would be in charge. The product manager must be capable of making sales, manufacturing, financial, and engineering decisions. He is no longer judged against a budget but becomes responsible for profits. We would need talented men to fill these positions—a shift in the organizational structure would undoubtedly force us to hire some new people. Nevertheless, there are tremendous benefits to be gained in terms of giving more people the chance to display their talents and in just plain better functioning of the M & C division.

The organization of engineering personnel brings up a whole hornets' nest of questions. First of all, there are two distinct engineering functions: product engineers, those concerned with current product designs and new applications for existing products; and advanced engineers, those who work on long-term product development. There is little doubt that the new applications sales effort would benefit from placing the product engineering personnel in close organizational contact with the marketers. This would mean splitting engineering up among all the product groups and would probably make for a less efficient overall operation. Decentralization of the advanced engineering groups is easily as ticklish a problem. Again, it would probably receive a more marketing-oriented stimulus if it were placed under the supervision of the product manager. I wonder, however, if he might not be motivated to cut long-term development more drastically than top management normally would in times of business recession. Furthermore, I wonder if the economies of centralized advanced engineering and research in terms of combined effort and personnel selection are not so great as to make decentralization of this function an extremely poor choice. The basic question we have to answer here is to what degree should we sacrifice operating economy in order to give our engineering personnel a greater marketing orientation.

*   *   *   *   *

Scheduling has long been a bone of contention here wherever facilities are shared. Conflicts for priorities between product specialists are always occurring. If we decentralize, however, the amount of facilities that are shared will decrease substantially and this problem should be alleviated. Again we have the basic choice of retaining the centralized scheduling groups or splitting the function up among the various product groups.

In addition to the above issues, Mr. Vetter was considering the proper timing for an organizational change. He was debating whether a change should be made by gradual steps or whether the transfer in corporate ownership provided a convenient opportunity for making radical changes with a minimum of employee resentment. In general, the M & C personnel expressed some regrets because the family that had founded the company was no longer associated with it. They recognized, however, that the continual top management conflict of recent years necessitated a change and were pleased by the fact that a recognized leader in the industry had taken over the company.

TEXAS INSTRUMENTS INCORPORATED (B)*

In May 1960 Tom Pringle, the manager of the Industrial Metals product department at Texas Instrument's Metals & Controls division, was considering several courses of action in the face of his department's failure to meet forecasted sales and profits during the first four months of 1960. The rebuilding of inventories by M & C's customers, which had been expected as an aftermath of the settlement of the 1959 steel strike, had not materialized and shipments from Pringle's product department were running about 12% below forecast. Furthermore, incoming sales commitments during these four months were 15% below expectations. The product department's direct profit, according to preliminary statements, was 19% below plan.

In light of these adverse developments, Pringle was studying the advisability of three specific moves which would improve his profit performance: (1) eliminating his $30,000 advertising budget for the latter half of 1960, (2) postponing the addition of two engineers to his engineering group until 1961, and (3) reducing further purchases of raw materials in order to improve his department's return on assets ratio. Until now, Pringle had been reluctant to make any concessions in his department's scale of operations since there was a very strong accent on rapid growth throughout the Texas Instruments organization. This attitude toward expansion also appeared to prevail in the new top management group in the Metals & Controls division. The enthusiasm of the Texas Instrument's management had caught on at Metals & Controls with the formation of the product-centered decentralized organization.

THE 1959 REORGANIZATION

In June 1959, just three months after Metals & Controls Corporation had become a division of Texas Instruments Incorporated, Mr. Edward O. Vetter, the division vice president, instituted a product-centered organization. This decentralization was carried out in accordance with Texas Instruments' policy of placing ultimate responsibility for profitable operation at the product level. The framework that emerged was similar to that which existed elsewhere in the company.

Mr. Vetter organized four major product groups at Metals & Controls: General Plate, Spencer Controls, Nuclear Products, and International Operations. To augment these groups, six centralized staff units were organized at the division level: Research and Development, Legal, Industrial Engineering, Control, Marketing, and Personnel (Exhibit 1). The four managers of the product groups and the six managers of these staff departments, along with Mr. Vetter, comprised the management committee for the Metals & Controls division. This committee was a sounding board for helping each responsible manager make the proper decision as required by his job responsibility. In the case of profit performance, the ultimate responsibility for the division was Vetter's.

Exhibit 1

ORGANIZATION CHART, METALS & CONTROLS DIVISION

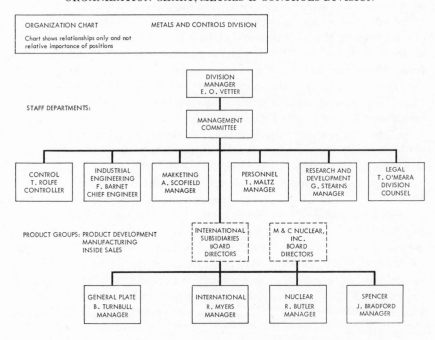

Within each product group, several product departments were established. The General Plate products group, for example, included the Industrial Metals, Electrical Contacts, Industrial Wire, and Precious Metals departments (Exhibit 2). The manager of each of these departments was responsible for its "profit performance." He was supported by staff units such as Industrial Engineering and Administration which reported directly to the group manager (Burt Turnbull for General Plate products). The expense of these staff units was charged to the individual product departments proportionally to the volume of activity in the various departments as measured by direct labor hours or by sales dollars less raw materials cost. The product departments were also charged with those expenses over which the manager and his supervisory group were able to exercise direct control, such as labor and materials.

Exhibit 2

ORGANIZATION CHART, GENERAL PLATE PRODUCTS GROUP

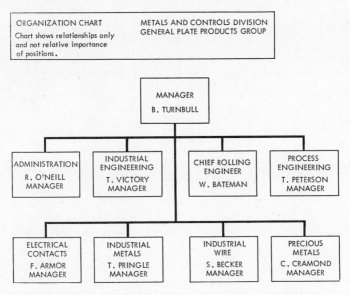

The field sales force of 50 men was centralized under the manager for marketing, Al Scofield (Exhibit 1). These men were divided about evenly into two major selling groups: one for General Plate products, and the other for Spencer products. The 25 salesmen assigned to General Plate and the 25 salesmen assigned to Spencer were shared by the four General Plate and four Spencer product departments. Each individual product department also maintained "inside" marketing personnel who performed such functions as pricing, developing marketing strategy, order follow-up and providing the field sales engineers with information on new applications, designs, and product specifications for its particular line.

The Industrial Metals department

Tom Pringle was manager of the Industrial Metals department of the General Plate products group. Sales of this department in 1959 were approximately $4 million.[1] Pringle was responsible for the profitability of two product lines: (1) industrial metals and (2) thermostat metals. His department's sales were split about evenly between these lines, although industrial metals had the greater growth potential because of the almost infinite number of possible clad metals for which an ever increasing number of applications was

---

[1] All figures have been disguised.

being found. He was in charge of the marketing, engineering, and manufacturing activities for both these lines and had six key subordinates:

INDUSTRIAL METALS DEPARTMENT
Years of Service with the Metals & Controls Organization

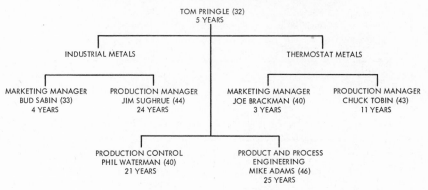

TOM PRINGLE (32)
5 YEARS

INDUSTRIAL METALS

THERMOSTAT METALS

MARKETING MANAGER
BUD SABIN (33)
4 YEARS

PRODUCTION MANAGER
JIM SUGHRUE (44)
24 YEARS

MARKETING MANAGER
JOE BRACKMAN (40)
3 YEARS

PRODUCTION MANAGER
CHUCK TOBIN (43)
11 YEARS

PRODUCTION CONTROL
PHIL WATERMAN (40)
21 YEARS

PRODUCT AND PROCESS
ENGINEERING
MIKE ADAMS (46)
25 YEARS

The function of the marketing managers in the Industrial Metals department (Bud Sabin and Joe Brackman) was to supervise the "inside selling units." These units were responsible for developing marketing strategy, pricing, contacting customers on special requests and factory problems, for promotional activities, and for coordinating product development and sales. In May 1960, in addition to its regular work, the Industrial Metals inside selling unit was developing a manual of special applications for its products which it hoped would improve the ability of the field sales force to envision new uses. The production managers had line responsibility for the efficient use of manufacturing facilities, for meeting delivery promises to customers, and for expenses incurred in producing the department's products. The product and process engineering group had responsibility for designing new products and devising new production processes. The production control manager formulated guidelines to aid the foremen in scheduling work through the plant, supervised the expediters and clerks who served as a clearinghouse for information on delivery dates, and was responsible for ordering raw material and maintaining a balanced inventory.

In accordance with Texas Instruments' policy of placing ultimate responsibility for profitable operation at the product level, Tom Pringle's performance was measured, to a large extent, by the actual profits earned by the Industrial Metals department. The old M & C system of evaluating performance according to fixed and variable department budgets had been supplemented by the establishment of these "profit centers." Although the system passed actual profit responsibility to the product department manager level, the Texas Instruments' top management had always retained some control over the profit centers by requiring each manager to formulate a one-year plan which was subject to review by higher management. As a result, profit planning was instituted whereby each manager set forth a detailed plan for the year's operations under the direction of the management committee. His actual performance was continually being evaluated against the plan.

Formulation of the profit plan. In October 1959, Tom Pringle began to prepare his department's profit plan for 1960. This was part of a company-wide effort in which all department managers participated. The first step in the process was to prepare a detailed estimate of expected sales for the year. These estimates were gathered from two sources: the inside selling units and the field sales force. Management felt that one would serve as a good check on the other, and, furthermore, believed that widespread participation in preparing the plan was one way to insure its effectiveness. Bud Sabin and Joe Brackman, then, began to prepare estimates of 1960 sales by product lines with the help of the individual product specialists within the inside marketing group. Sabin and Brackman were also aided by the Texas Instruments central marketing group which prepared a report which estimated normal growth for their product lines. Pringle suggested that they prepare their estimates by subdividing the market into three parts: sales resulting from normal industry growth at current levels of market penetration; increased sales resulting from further penetration of the market with existing products; and increased sales from new products detailed by specific customers. At the same time, Herb Skinner, the manager of the General Plate field sales force, asked the field engineers to predict the volume of orders that each Industrial Metals customer would place in 1960, without referring to the reports being readied by the product marketing groups. In this way, the marketing managers made forecasts by product line and the field force made forecasts by customer.

The field selling force came up with estimated thermostat metal sales of $2,350,000 for 1960, and the inside group estimated sales of $2,420,000. Pringle felt that these two estimates were in reasonably good agreement. On the other hand, Bud Sabin, the Industrial Metals marketing manager, estimated sales of $3,050,000, while Skinner's group predicted only $2,500,000. Sabin predicted that 20% of the increase would come from normal growth, 50% from increased market penetration with existing products, and 30% from new products. Sales for Sabin's group had been $1,400,000 in 1958 and $2,100,000 in 1959. Pringle felt that the disparity between the two estimates was significant and he discussed the matter with both men. All three men finally decided that the sales force had submitted a conservative estimate and agreed that Sabin's figure was the most realistic goal.

Once the sales estimate of $5,470,000 was agreed upon by Pringle and his marketing managers, the process of estimating manufacturing costs began. The manufacturing superintendents, Chuck Tobin and Jim Sughrue, were furnished the thermostat and industrial metals sales estimates and were instructed to forecast direct labor costs, supervisory salaries, and overhead expenses. These forecasts were to be made for each manufacturing area, or cost center, under their supervision. Sughrue was responsible for five cost

centers and Tobin for four, each of which was directly supervised by a foreman. These expenses were to be forecast monthly and were to be used as a
yardstick by which the actual expense performance of the manufacturing
personnel could later be measured.

Jim Sughrue had previously calculated the hourly labor cost and the output
per hour for each of his cost centers for 1959. To estimate 1960 salaries and
wages, he then increased 1959 expenses proportionately to the expected sales
increase. He followed the same procedure in determining 1960 overhead
expenses, such as expendable tools, travel, telephone, process supplies, and
general supplies. Chuck Tobin's task was somewhat simpler since the sales
projection for his cost centers required a level of output that exactly matched
the current production level. For salaries and wages, he merely used as his
1960 estimate the actual cost experience that had been reported on the
most recent monthly income statement he received. For overhead, he applied
a historical per-cent-of-sales ratio and then reduced his estimate by 3% to
account for increased efficiency. In discussing the overhead estimate with his
foremen, Tobin informed them that he had allowed for an 8% efficiency
increase.

Since this was the first time any attempt at such detailed planning had
been made at M & C, and since the M & C accounting system had recently
been changed to match Texas Instruments', very little historical information
was available. For this reason, Pringle did not completely delegate the responsibility for the various marketing and manufacturing estimates to his subordinates. Instead he worked in conjunction with them to develop the forecasts. He hoped that his participation in this process would insure a more
accurate forecast for the year. Furthermore, he hoped to develop the ability
of his supervision to plan ahead.

Pringle estimated direct materials cost and consumption factors himself.
Since it was impossible to predict what all the various strip metal prices would
be, he calculated the ratio of materials expense to sales for 1959 and applied
it to the 1960 sales projections for each of the product lines in his department.

The marketing, administration, and engineering groups that serviced Pringle's Industrial Metals group forecast their expenses by detailing their personnel requirements and then applying historical ratios of expenses to
personnel to estimate their other expenses. From these dollar figures, Pringle
was able to estimate what proportions of these amounts would be charged to
his department.

With the various forecasts in hand, Pringle estimated a direct profit of
$1,392,000 on a sales volume of $5,470,000. Once this plan had been drawn
up, it was reviewed by the division management committee in relationship
to the specific profit and sales goals which it had established for the division.
In reviewing the plans for each product department in terms of the specific
group goals, it became obvious that the combined plans of the General Plate
product departments were not sufficient to meet the overall goal, and that
based on market penetration, new product developments, and other factors,

the planned sales volume for Industrial Metals should be revised upward to $6,050,000 and direct profit to $1,587,000 (Exhibit 3). This was discussed among Vetter, Turnbull, Scofield, and Pringle and they agreed that it was a difficult but achievable plan.

Exhibit 3

INDUSTRIAL METALS DEPARTMENT
Initial and Revised Profit Statements for 1960*

	Initial	Revised
Sales	$5,470,000	$6,050,000
Direct labor	435,000	480,000
Direct material	1,920,000	2,115,000
Overhead	875,000	968,000
Marketing	305,000	346,000
Administration	161,000	161,000
Engineering	382,000	393,000
DIRECT PROFIT	1,392,000	1,587,000

*All figures have been disguised.

Actual performance, 1960. On May 10 Tom Pringle received a detailed statement comparing the actual performance of his department for January through April with his budget (Exhibit 4). Sales were 12% below plan, and direct profit was 19% below plan.

In addition to these figures, manufacturing expenses by cost centers were accumulated for Pringle. He passed these along to the production superintendents after he had made adjustments in the budgeted expense figures to allow for the sales decline. Pringle had devised a variable budget system whereby he applied factors to the forecast expenses to indicate what an acceptable expense performance was at sales levels other than the planned volume. Chuck Tobin and Jim Sughrue then analyzed the actual expenses and, one week later, held meetings with their foremen to discuss the causes

Exhibit 4

COMPARISON OF ACTUAL AND
BUDGETED PERFORMANCE,
JANUARY–APRIL 1960*

	Budgeted	Actual
Sales	$2,020,000	$1,780,000
Direct labor	160,000	142,400
Direct material	704,000	593,000
Overhead	322,000	287,000
Marketing	100,000	116,400
Administration	54,000	55,800
Engineering	126,000	136,600
DIRECT PROFIT	554,000	448,800

*All figures have been disguised.

of both favorable and unfavorable variances. The most common explanation of favorable manufacturing variances was either extremely efficient utilization of labor or close control over overhead. Unfavorable variances most frequently resulted from machine delays which necessitated overtime labor payments.

Specific problems. Pringle was currently faced with three specific problems. In light of his department's poor performance these past months, he was considering the effects of eliminating his $30,000 advertising budget for the remainder of 1960, postponing the addition of two new engineers to his staff for six months, and reducing raw materials purchases in order to decrease inventory and thus improve his department's return on assets performance.

He had discussed the possibility of eliminating the advertising budget with Bud Sabin and Joe Brackman but had not yet reached a conclusion. Advertising expenditures had been budgeted at $30,000 for the final six months of 1960. The Industrial Metals department ads were generally placed in trade journals read by design engineers in the electrical, automobile, and appliance industries. Pringle did not know for certain how important an aid these advertisements were to his sales force. He did know that all of his major competitors allocated about the same proportion of sales revenue for advertising expenditures and that Industrial Metals ads were occasionally mentioned by customers.

In late 1959, Pringle had made plans to increase his engineering staff from eight men to ten men in mid-1960. He felt that the two new men could begin functioning productively by early 1961 and could help to revise certain processes which were yielding excessive scrap, to develop new products, and to assist the field engineers in discovering new applications for existing products. Pringle estimated that postponing the hiring of these men for six months would save $20,000 in engineering salaries and supporting expenses.

Pringle also knew that one of the important indicators of his performance was the department's ratio of direct profit to assets used. This figure had been budgeted at 40% for 1960, but actual results to date were 31%. Pringle was considering reductions in raw materials purchases in order to decrease inventories and thus improve performance. He had discussed this possibility with Phil Waterman, the production control manager for Industrial Metals. Pringle knew that significant improvements in the overall ratio could be made in this way since raw materials inventories accounted for almost 20% of total assets and were at a level of ten months' usage at present consumption ratios. He recognized, however, that this course of action required accepting a greater risk of running out. This risk was important to assess since most customers required rapid delivery and Pringle's suppliers usually required four months' lead time to manufacture the nonstandard size metals in relatively small lots required for the Industrial Metals' cladding operation.

The purpose of the profit plan. The degree to which the plan was used as a method for evaluating performance and fixing compensation was not completely clear to Pringle. Everyone seemed to recognize that this first effort was imperfect and had errors built in because of inadequate historical data. He had never been explicitly informed of the extent to which top management desired product department decision making to be motivated by short-run effects on planned performance. Pringle stated that during the months immediately following the initiation of the plan he had concluded that short-term performance was much less significant than long-run growth and that he had preferred to concentrate on the longer run development of new products and markets.

Pringle knew that the Metals & Controls operating committee met every Monday to review the performance of each product department from preliminary reports. Customarily Burt Turnbull, the manager of the General Plate group, discussed both Pringle's incoming sales commitments and actual manufacturing expenses with him before each meeting. Pringle also knew that each manager was given a formal appraisal review every six months by his superior. It was common knowledge that the department's performance in relation to its plan was evaluated at both these sessions. Furthermore, Pringle was aware of the fact that Turnbull's performance as product group manager would be affected by his own performance with Industrial Metals. Over a period of months, Pringle had learned that the management committee utilized the comparison of actual and planned performance to pinpoint trouble spots. On occasion Vetter had called him in to explain any significant deviations from plan but normally he was represented at these meetings by Burt Turnbull. It was Pringle's impression that Vetter had been satisfied with the explanation he had given.

In their day-to-day decisions, Pringle's subordinates seemed to be influenced only in a very general way by the profit plan. They reviewed their monthly performance against plan with interest, but generally tended to bias their decisions in favor of long-run development at the expense of short-run deviations from the plan. More recently, however, Pringle realized that top management was not satisfied with his explanations of failure to meet plans. The message, though not stated explicitly, seemed to be that he was expected to take whatever remedial and alternate courses of action were needed in order to meet the one-year goals. He was certain that real pleasure was building up for each department manager to meet his one-year plan.

In commenting on the use of planning at M & C, Mr. Vetter, the division vice president, stated four major purposes of the program:

To set a par for the course. Vetter believed that performance was always improved if the manager proposed a realistic objective for his performance and was informed in advance of what was expected of him.

To grow management ability. Vetter believed that the job of manager was to coordinate all the areas for which he was given responsibility. He saw the planning process as a tool for improving these managerial skills.

To anticipate problems and look ahead. Vetter felt that the planning process

gave the department managers a convenient tool for planning personnel requirements and sales strategy. It also set guideposts so that shifts in business conditions could be detected quickly and plans could be altered.

To weld Texas Instruments into one unit. The basic goals for each division
were formulated by Vetter in recognition of overall company goals as dissemi-
nated by Haggerty, the company president. These were passed down to the
product department level by the product group manager at each Texas Instruments division. Profit planning was thus being carried out by the same process
by every department manager in the corporation.

Vetter recognized, however, that many reasons could exist for performance
being either better or worse than planned. He stated that in his experience
extremely rigid profit plans often motivated managers to budget low in order
to provide themselves with a safety cushion. In his view, this made the entire
profit planning process worthless.

DENNISON MANUFACTURING COMPANY (A)*

A recent magazine article introduced the Dennison Manufacturing Company as follows:

> Only a few years ago, Dennison Manufacturing Company of Framingham, Massachusetts, looked the very model of the sleepily staid old New England company. Its rambling red brick plant was picturesque, but little else. . . . About all it had to show for 120 years of corporate existence was $2 million a year in profits and a clutter of thousands of paper products—boxes, tags, labels, ribbons, wrappings, coated papers and stationery items—along with labeling and punching machines. (To generations of school children Dennison was best known for its gummed rings for reinforcing looseleaf notebook pages.) . . .
>
> Yet in 1964, Dennison suddenly jumped into the modern world, and with gusto. Knowing that something needed to be done for its growth, and believing that the answer was to get some new products, Dennison management went all the way. It came up with a machine for the red-hot office copier market based on electrostatic technology it had licensed a few years before from Radio Corp. of America. . . .
>
> At the same time, Dennison's basic business has been booming thanks to a strong economy and President [Phillip] Hamilton's reorganization of the business along modern lines. For all of its small size and complex product line, Dennison has a strong position in its specialty field. . . .[1]

The change which had occurred in the decade 1957–67 had been dramatic. Instead of a "paternalistic, sleepy firm," Dennison was regarded as a growth company. The investment community backed up this analysis by trading Dennison common stock at 29 times its previous year's earnings.

Dennison was one of the oldest converters of paper products in the United States. Founded in 1844 to manufacture quality paper boxes for the jewelry trade, it had expanded its product line to include a wide variety of paper products (4,000 made for stock, plus made-to-order items), numerous gummed and coated papers, and several machines to facilitate efficient use of paper products. Included among the latter were pinning machines, and machines for high-speed printing of price and inventory data on tags. The

---

*Copyright © 1968 by the President and Fellows of Harvard College. Reprinted by permission.

[1]*Forbes*, February 15, 1967, p. 64.

latest addition to this line was the Dennison high-speed electrostatic copier, with a capability of 1,800 copies an hour.

Dennison's corporate goals, as stated in internal publications and by members of management, could be summarized as follows:

1. Growth through invention and acquisition, and through obtaining exclusive distributorships in the paper-product field.
2. Development of useful paper products and machines which give those products their full meaning.

One top manager described the distinctive competence of the company as being its ability to obtain a "product edge." Cited as examples were the development of a paper patch tag (around the turn of the century), the more recent development of the thermiage process[2] for labeling plastic bottles (1958), and the low-cost, high-speed copier (1967).

As of 1966, Dennison revenues were divided as follows:

Dennison brand-name products sold to resale outlets	33%
Made-to-order tags, tickets, labels, industrial crepe paper, and setup boxes	31
Plain and coated or gummed paper	21
Machinery and equipment sales and rental	15
	100%

Total revenues had expanded from $41 million in 1957 to $87.4 million in 1966. Net earnings had gone from 5.1% of sales or $2.1 million to 6% of sales or $5.3 million in the same period. Return on equity improved from 10.8% in 1957 to 17.8% in 1967. The expansion had resulted from both internal growth and acquisitions. Three new divisions—thermiage, copier, and holiday (paper specialties)—had been formed during this 10-year period. In 1966 the copier division alone accounted for over $13 million in sales. (See Exhibit 1 for financial details.)

There was an explicit commitment among members of top management to internal growth and profits. The president, Mr. Phillip Hamilton, said, "I believe that earnings is the best measurement of how you are doing." This sentiment was amplified by Mr. Frank Swisher, the treasurer, who stated, "I think one of the key values here is that we as managers should be making a fair return on the stockholders' investment. Of course this is within the framework of not milking the consumer. I know that Dennison has always been very socially-conscious. I just don't think that social responsibility is incompatible with profit. Wages and fringes, profits, and a good return on investment are not incompatible. In fact, for long-run success they must exist together."

In addition to growing from within, Dennison had been actively acquiring other companies. Its acquisitions had all been oriented toward paper prod-

[2] A heat sensitive dye which allowed four-color printing in a single pass on most types of plastic and cellophane.

Exhibit 1

DENNISON MANUFACTURING COMPANY

Ten-Year Financial Summary, 1957–1966

(Dollars in Thousands)

	1957	1958	1959	1960	1961	1962	1963	1964	1965	1966
Sales and equipment rentals ...	$40,992	$40,545	$43,391	$45,523	$47,501	$52,366	$53,795	$57,173	$69,835	$87,410
Taxes on income	1,999	1,784	2,170	1,875	1,760	2,096	2,523	2,036	2,505	4,502
Net earnings	2,103	1,839	2,219	1,983	1,829	1,982	2,354	2,193	2,913	5,252
As a per cent of sales	5.1%	4.5%	5.1%	4.4%	3.9%	3.8%	4.4%	3.8%	4.1%	6.0%
Per share of common stock* ..	$ .82	$ .70	$ .87	$ .77	$ .70	$ .77	$ .94	$ .87	$ 1.18	$ 2.20
Cash dividends	1,324	1,152	1,325	1,379	1,373	1,371	1,366	1,367	1,371	1,545
Debenture stock	235	235	235	235	235	235	235	235	235	235
Common stocks	1,089	917	1,090	1,144	1,137	1,136	1,131	1,132	1,136	1,310
Per share*	0.48	0.40	0.48	0.50	0.50	0.50	0.50	0.50	0.50	0.575
Stock dividend—common				100%						100%
Settlement of prior years' tax claims		$ 282		$ 320						$ 244
Earnings reinvested:										
This year	$ 779	$ 969	$ 894	$ 924	$ 456	$ 611	$ 988	$ 826	$ 1,542	$ 3,706
Total to date†	$13,975	$14,943	$15,837	$16,004	$16,460	$17,071	$18,058	$18,884	$20,426	$18,347

Exhibit 1—Continued

	1957	1958	1959	1960	1961	1962	1963	1964	1965	1966
Current assets	$16,875	$17,969	$19,007	$18,758	$20,334	$19,973	$21,570	$22,677	$27,854	$35,949
Current liabilities	2,606	2,595	3,166	3,785	7,974	6,802	6,344	7,945	12,598	17,546
Working capital	14,269	15,374	15,841	14,973	12,360	13,170	15,226	14,732	15,256	18,403
Working capital ratio	6.5 to 1	6.9 to 1	6.0 to 1	5.0 to 1	2.5 to 1	2.9 to 1	3.4 to 1	2.9 to 1	2.2 to 1	2.0 to 1
Plant and equipment—net	$ 7,137	$ 7,017	$ 7,423	$ 9,045	$11,926	$11,953	$11,611	$12,635	$17,192	$20,787
Added this year—gross	1,931	1,055	1,613	2,799	4,388‡	2,068	1,658	2,580	7,942§	7,500
Provision for depreciation	1,045	1,151	1,142	1,123	1,301	1,845	1,831	1,780	2,685	3,568
Long-term debt	....	....	....	....	....	....	....	....	3,515	6,334
Stockholders' equity	21,914	22,883	23,788	24,536	24,911	25,430	26,426	27,386	28,884	32,860
Equity per common share*	7.50	7.93	8.32	8.73	8.89	9.17	9.60	10.00	10.61	12.36
Shares of stock outstanding										
Debenture stock	29,420	29,420	29,420	29,420	29,420	29,420	29,420	29,420	29,420	29,420
Common stocks	573,238	573,238	573,608	1,139,086	1,136,226	1,130,666	1,131,041	1,134,261	1,138,886	2,278,552
Market price range*										
"A" common stock { high	$ 10	$ 8	$ 9⅝	$ 14¼	$ 20½	$ 14¾	$ 27¼	$ 42	$ 25¼	$ 43
low	5⅜	5¾	7¼	8⅜	13¼	7½	9½	15¼	13⅞	23¼

*Based on number of shares outstanding at end of each year and adjusted for stock splits in 1960 and 1966.
†Reflects $757,000 in 1960 and $6,029,000 in 1966 transferred to "Common Stock" in connection with stock splits.
‡Includes net value of plant and equipment of Dennison Eastman Company.
§Includes net value of plant and equipment of Dunn Paper Company.
Source: 1966 Annual Report

Exhibit 1—Continued

DENNISON MANUFACTURING COMPANY AND WHOLLY OWNED SUBSIDIARIES

(Years Ended December 31, 1965 and 1966)

ASSETS

Current Assets	December 31, 1965	December 31, 1966
Cash	$ 1,958,338	$ 1,374,145
Trade accounts receivable, less allowances of $594,000 ($326,000 in 1965) for discounts, etc.	12,368,287	15,926,869
Merchandise, materials and supplies		
Finished merchandise	$ 3,547,741	$ 5,613,901
In process	5,457,951	7,853,738
Raw materials	3,451,541	3,836,947
Supplies	627,142	710,129
	$13,084,375	$18,014,715
Prepaid expenses	442,805	633,337
Total Current Assets	$27,853,805	$35,949,066
Other Assets		
Investment in British subsidiary, not consolidated— at cost	$ 169,775	$ 169,775
Miscellaneous receivables, investments, etc., less allowances of $133,723 ($97,120 in 1965)	514,673	563,997
Goodwill	1	1
	$ 684,449	$ 733,773
Property, Plant and Equipment—on the basis of cost		
Land	$ 397,252	$ 401,421
Buildings and building equipment	7,068,411	7,688,087
Machinery, equipment, etc.	31,851,381	35,744,490
Construction in progress (estimated cost to complete $2,348,000)	...	1,544,353
	$39,317,044	$45,378,351
Less allowances for depreciation	22,125,427	24,591,044
	$17,191,617	$20,787,307
Total Assets	$45,729,871	$57,470,146

ucts. In 1960 the company acquired a manufacturer of ribbons. In 1961 it acquired Eastman Tag and Label Manufacturing Company and thus effectively expanded its made-to-order business to the West Coast market. This acquisition, which added $3.5 million sales in its first year, had grown substantially since. Dunn Paper Company, acquired in 1965, was the first entry by Dennison into the manufacture of paper. Less than 10% of Dunn's output was sold to other Dennison divisions, but the acquisition added to Dennison's sales and profits.

In 1967 a merger was consummated between Dennison and National Blank Book. National's 1966 sales were $24.6 million. This merger added a broad

Exhibit 1—Continued

LIABILITIES AND STOCKHOLDERS' EQUITY

	December 31, 1965	December 31, 1966
Current Liabilities		
Notes payable	$ 4,430,000	$ 6,700,000
Accounts payable	2,898,987	4,996,250
Accrued compensation and related taxes	3,562,964	3,007,911
United States and Canadian income taxes	1,576,888	2,329,463
Current maturities on long-term debt	128,700	512,637
Total Current Liabilities	$12,597,539	$17,546,261
Deferred Federal Income Taxes	$ 734,000	$ 730,000
Long-Term Debt (less current maturities)		
4½% Notes to bank	$ 3,000,000	$ 2,700,000
4¾% Notes to bank	...	3,000,000
4½% Notes payable to former stockholders of acquired subsidiary in equal annual installments to 1970	514,800	386,100
6½% equipment notes due in equal monthly installments to 1971	...	247,607
	$ 3,514,800	$ 6,333,707
Stockholders' Equity		
Debenture stock, $8 cumulative, par value $100 per share (entitled in liquidation to and callable at $4,707,200):		
Authorized and issued 29,420 shares	$ 2,942,000	$ 2,942,000
"A" common stock, par value $5 per share: Authorized 3,000,000 shares (1,200,000 in 1965); issued 2,335,127 shares (1,145,470 in 1965)	5,727,350	11,675,635
Voting common stock, par value $5 per share: Authorized 200,000 shares (80,000 in 1965); issued 106,449 shares (75,318 in 1965)	376,590	532,245
Capital in excess of par value	74,646	22,330
Earnings reinvested	20,425,688	18,346,813
	$29,546,274	$33,519,023
Less treasury stock at cost—146,642 shares (51,081 in 1965) of "A" common stock; 16,382 shares (30,821 in 1965) of voting common stock	662,742	658,845
Total Stockholders' Equity	$28,883,532	$32,860,178
Total Liabilities and Stockholders' Equity	$45,729,871	$57,470,146

line of commercial and school supplies to Dennison's product list. National produced over 3,500 stock items, including loose-leaf ring and post binders, data processing binders, indexes and fillers, spiral-bound notebooks, bound blank ledger and columnar journal books, analysis and worksheet pads, diaries, and other personal books. In 1966 National's sales by end use were 68% to commercial users, 25% for schools, and 7% for personal use.

Dennison's strategy had remained relatively constant from 1957 to 1967. The main variations in the operation of the company which had led to rapid development were thought by management to be the changes in organizational

Exhibit 1—Continued

STATEMENT OF CONSOLIDATED EARNINGS AND EARNINGS REINVESTED
(Years Ended December 31, 1965 and 1966)

CONSOLIDATED EARNINGS

	1965	1966
Sales and equipment rentals	$69,835,241	$87,410,324
Costs and expenses:		
Cost of products sold	$40,987,198	$48,886,888
Selling, administrative, and general expenses	23,152,523	28,225,822
Interest expense:		
Long-term debt	108,596	278,498
Other	168,587	265,595
United States and Canadian income taxes	2,505,000	4,502,000
	$66,921,904	$82,158,803
Net Earnings (per share: $2.20, 1966; $1.18, 1965)	$ 2,913,337	$ 5,251,521

Provision for depreciation of property, plant and equipment included above amounted to $2,684,767 in 1965 and $3,568,057 in 1966.

CONSOLIDATED EARNINGS REINVESTED

	1965	1966
Balance at beginning of year	$18,883,833	$20,425,688
Add:		
Federal income tax refunds relating to prior years		244,334
Net earnings	2,913,337	5,251,521
	$21,797,170	$25,921,543
Less:		
Excess of par value of "A" Common and Voting Common shares issued in connection with 100% stock distribution over available amount of capital in excess of par value	...	$ 6,029,294
Cash dividends paid:		
Debenture stock—$8 per share	$ 235,360	235,360
Common stocks—$.575 per share in 1966; $.50 per share in 1965	1,136,122	1,310,076
	$ 1,371,482	$ 7,574,730
Earnings reinvested at end of year	$20,425,688	$18,346,813

structure and the change in the bonus system. Mr. Dana Huntington, the chairman of the board, said, "I am convinced that the biggest single factor in our recent success was the assignment of profit responsibility for a product line to a well-trained group of managers in a single operating unit. The second biggest factor was that we began paying management based on results."

Organizational structure

Pre-1955. Until 1955, Dennison was organized along functional lines. Except in merchandising, there were no managers whose responsibility related to particular product lines. Thus a single sales department was responsible for selling the whole range of products, and the same held true for each salesman in a territory. The difficulties of this arrangement were described by an executive who had been in the field at this time:

We just couldn't keep abreast of the various lines. The salesmen were scattered too thin. Just the problems of keeping the price book up-to-date, making changes as products were introduced or became obsolete, were horrendous. As a district sales manager at the time, I couldn't possibly direct my men intelligently. There was no rhyme or reason to the associations which we had between salesman, markets, and customers.

Mr. Huntington, then executive vice president of the company, put the problem as seen from his level more succinctly: "It seemed to be the general opinion that God was responsible for profits or at least that somebody up There was looking out for us. Obviously we want Him on our side, but it takes more than that to do the job." Based on his experience as manager of Dennison's box division, where he had been responsible for both production and sales, Mr. Huntington decided to move in the direction of decentralized product line division. Prior to the first step taken at this time, the organization chart had been as shown below:

PARTIAL ORGANIZATION CHART PRE-1955

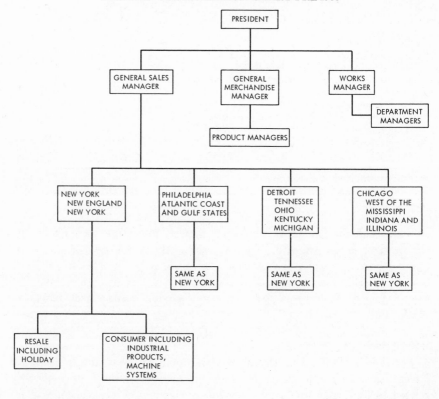

The 1955 reorganization.   Mr. Huntington described as follows the changes which he and Mr. Hamilton, then sales manager, effected in 1955:

In 1955 Phil Hamilton and I started to rearrange the sales organization so that we were organized by markets served and geographically within markets served. We started the process of selecting salesmen who would be capable of handling the burden of a professional approach to selling. This was accomplished largely through transferring and upgrading the existing sales force.

We established national sales managers here at Framingham for each product. We were convinced that the key to future success was marketing. We then got the sales manager and the merchandising manager for each product line to work together as a team.

Much later, after this step was well understood, we did away with the general works manager (production manager) and set up production units which corresponded to the marketing units. It was a big job teaching new techniques and new ways of thinking. Not all of the people we had in managerial positions were capable of making the switch.

The change to profit consciousness and a growth orientation required a difficult educational effort. Many of the people within the company at all levels commented on the past orientation of the Dennison organization. Typical of such comments was the following:

The orientation of the old management was to high principles, proper treatment of employees, and to making Dennison a nice place to work. The thought of making money beyond a certain regular profit was not important.

PARTIAL ORGANIZATION CHART 1955-59

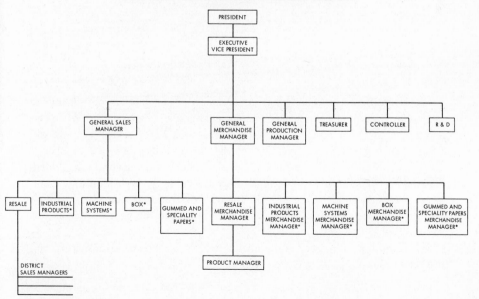

*Similar to resale division.

Another man further down in the organization said:

Our biggest problem in Dennison was convincing ourselves that we were as good as the best and better than most. This change in management philosophy has made us more forceful and aggressive. The monkey has been put on our backs at all levels to get results. . . .

While the process of reorientation to profit consciousness was being carried out, the company structure for 1955–59 was organized along the lines shown in the chart on page 721.

The 1960 organization. After the initial process of reorienting managers to think like general managers was under way, it was decided to introduce a product-group form of organization. The company's seven product lines were divided into three groups of two to three lines each, and three vice presidents were appointed to supervise each group. To these vice presidents there reported separate sales, merchandise, and production managers for each line:

PARTIAL ORGANIZATION CHART 1960–63
(Production, Sales, and Merchandising Managers)

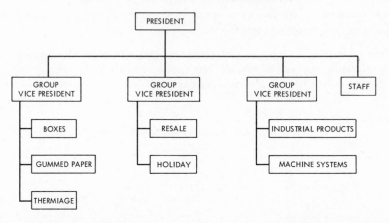

Mr. Huntington recalled that assignment of project responsibility to particular individuals had necessitated changes in personnel. "When we found that the idea of group vice presidents was not working out, we did a lot of shifting of personnel. One of the major difficulties was to change the way of thinking." One member of a divisional management group added, "There has really been a change. The message came through loud and clear: 'What has been good in the past is not necessarily good now. If you don't like the way things are, change them. This is a time for growth and a time for building.' "

Mr. Hamilton talked about the change which he and Mr. Huntington had originated in the following terms:

People continued to work here because it was a low-pressure organization. It was a pleasant place to work, and they were satisfied. There weren't many ambitious, driving men in positions of power in the company. There were always a few people who thought we could be doing better, but the type of organization we had tended to attract people who were satisfied with the climate.

Our changes were evolutionary. It had to be. We had a shortage of qualified people and we had a complicated task in disentangling the production process. Of the top 40 people here 10 years ago about one-third have become motivated, and the rest have given no great resistance or assistance to the changes which we were trying to accomplish.

A division manager talked of the old Dennison as follows:

I guess we were smug and inclined to produce and create at our own convenience. We were fortunate—or unfortunate—in having a marketing position which would allow us to do that. We had never really had a purge, nor was the management inclined to be a hard pusher of people. We were steady, and anything but aggressive. We just weren't keeping up with progress in management techniques.

We had to become aggressive, but there were many sacred cows in the organization. When Phil Hamilton came in, we got a driver. He acted as a whip, and started to slowly put more direct pressure on people. Many in the organization responded. They knew that we weren't as efficient as we should be. He instilled a sense of urgency that had been lacking before. Many of the people had to unlearn a lot, but a lot of progress had been made.

Mr. Huntington commented on the evolutionary nature of the changes by saying:

We had to change some personnel. Three years ago we set a policy of compulsory retirement at 68. Previous to that time we had many people working into their 70's and even some into their 80's. Now, at management's option, people can be required to retire anytime after they are 65.

We have been slow in making changes. I think that out of the whole company we have not gotten rid of more than 25 or 30. We forced out four or five so far this year, six or eight last year and six the year before that. I can remember back in 1939 when one of the former presidents fired 32 people in one day to "make a clean sweep in the organization." That isn't the way it should be done. The fear, disruption, and self-protection that result are too harmful. Since I have had anything to say in the matter, we only take a few at a time. In each case we try to remember our responsibility. For long-service employees, we attempt to make adjustments in their jobs, get them to retire early, or at the very worst give them six months to find a new position. I think more and more executives are thinking this way.

The 1963 organization structure. In 1963 it was decided to make a general manager responsible for each product line. This move was implemented gradually, and by 1967 Dennison's formal organization had evolved into a profit-center divisional organization. There were profit-center divisions in the following businesses:

Resale products   Paper products sold through distributors and
                           retailers, stock tags, labels, crepe paper and
                           streamers, notebook fillers, diaper liners.

Copier	The Dennison line of copiers, including a large office copier, a desk-top office copier, a coin-operated rental machine, a high-speed copier and several specialized electrostatic copiers. Sold direct.
Industrial products	Made-to-order tags and labels sold directly to the end user.
Marking systems	Machines, tags, and attaching devices which formed a complete system allowing the user to print variable information on a tag near its point of use, and mechanically to attach the tag or label to an object. Distributed mainly to soft goods manufacturers and to retailers.
Thermiage	Machines and supplies for a Dennison-developed process for labeling plastic bottles. Sold direct mainly to manufacturers of branded consumer items and to contract packaging firms.
Holiday	Decorated wrapping paper and ribbons sold through distributors and retail outlets. In smaller markets, holiday division products were sold by resale division salesmen.
Box	Setup and folding specialty boxes, sold mainly to the jewelry and high-priced novelty trade.
Gummed and coated paper	All types of coatings applied to paper purchased outside the company. About 45% of this division's sales were made to other Dennison divisions.

In addition to these divisions, Dennison had three active subsidiaries which it treated as separate profit centers. Their activities were paralleled to the mainstream of Dennison's business:

Dennison Eastman	A West Coast manufacturer of made-to-order tags and labels. This company merchandised the products of Dennison's marking systems division as well as its own line of products.
Dunn Paper	A specialty paper manufacturer. Of the production of its three paper machines, about 10% was sold to Dennison divisions.
National Blank Book	Manufacturer of loose-leaf ring and post binders, data processing form binders, indexes and fillers, spiral-bound notebooks, bound blank ledgers and columnar journal books, analysis and worksheet pads, and diaries and other personal record books.

Besides the divisions and subsidiaries, there were three other main cost centers. These were the financial office, including the treasurer's and controller's staff; the service department including industrial engineering, facilities, mechanical maintenance, warehousing, and facilities planning; and the R.&D. center. The 1967 Dennison organization chart appears below:

PARTIAL ORGANIZATION CHART MAY 1967

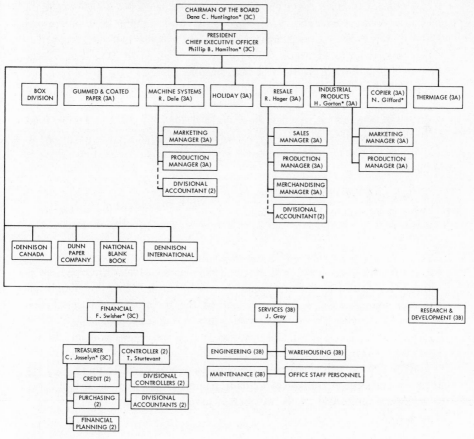

*Inside director.

Note: The numbers in parentheses refer to the bonus plan to which the individual belongs.

The bonus system

Until 1956, the Dennison Company had a history of paying year-end bonuses at the discretion of the board of directors. These bonuses had generally been thought of as relating most closely to salary level and seniority with normal payment based on a percentage of salary, but the exact determination was not fixed.

In 1956, the executive committee decided to develop a formula to determine bonus payments for each of three levels of employees: wage and weekly salaried personnel (Plan 1), middle management (Plan 2), and top management (Plan 3). For the Plan 1 group, the formula was such that payments went up and down slowly as company profits changed. Thus, beyond a certain minimum corporate profit level ($3 million), the Plan 1 bonus would increase 0.7% for each 1% increase in company profit. (For example if the bonus one year was 5% of annual salary, doubling the company's profits would bring the bonus to 8.5% of annual salary.) For the middle management group (Plan 2) there was a one-to-one correspondence between changes in overall company profit and the group bonus (for example, doubling profits would double this group's bonus). At the top management level (a group which had grown to 41 people from the group [Plan 3] of 31 people who in 1960 held line or staff positions at both headquarters and the divisions), the bonus plan had gone through an adjustment designed to make it peak, and peak sharply, only as earnings were increased.

In 1956, the executive committee decided that the Plan 3 bonus fund (1)[3] should be tied to return on investment, and that bonus payments to individuals would be proportionate to salary. The formula for the fund was as follows:

$$\left(\begin{array}{l}\text{Plan 3}\\\text{bonus}\\\text{fund}(1)\end{array}\right)=\left(\dfrac{\text{Pretax prebonus earnings}(2)}{\begin{array}{l}\text{Stockholders' beginning}\\\text{equity}(3)\end{array}}-0.11\right)\times 0.13(5)\times\left(\begin{array}{l}\text{Pretax}\\\text{prebonus}\\\text{earnings}(2)\end{array}\right)$$

Within this formula, the 11% reduction (4) in the earnings/equity percentage reflected the belief that stockholders should earn a "normal" 11% return before any bonus at all would be paid. The 0.13(5) was simply an arbitrary figure, inserted because it served the function of relating bonus levels under the new plan to levels under preexisting arrangements.

With the fund computed, the next step was to see how many months of salary it would cover for all members of the Plan 3 group. Subject to the limitation that no one could receive bonus payments equal to more than six months' salary, each individual's bonus payment then became his monthly salary figure multiplied by the number of months that the bonus fund could support:

$$\left(\begin{array}{l}\text{Individual}\\\text{corporate bonus}\\\text{payment}\end{array}\right)=\left(\dfrac{\text{Fund }(1)}{\begin{array}{l}\text{Participants' aggregate}\\\text{monthly salary }(6)\end{array}}\right)\times\left(\begin{array}{l}\text{Individual's}\\\text{monthly}\\\text{salary}\end{array}\right)$$

Although by 1966, this original plan had been supplemented by other arrangements, it was still used to compute at least a portion of the bonus payable to all Plan 3 executives. When applied to the year's adjusted return on investment (ROI) for the 41 persons covered at that time, the formulas detailed above yielded the following results:

---

[3] The numbers in parentheses are keyed to statements in the text explaining their origin and to the sample calculation shown on page 727.

CORPORATE BONUS CALCULATION, 1966

Pretax earnings as reported	$ 9,754,000
Plus bonuses under Plans 1, 2, 3	$ 1,484,000
Pretax prebonus earnings (2)	$11,238,000
Stockholders' beginning equity (3)	$28,884,000
Rate of return on investment (ROI) (2)÷(3)	38.9%
Less normal return (4)	−11.0%
Adjusted ROI	27.9%
Bonus rate (adjusted ROI times 0.13) (5)	3.627%
Bonus fund Plan 3 (earnings x rate) (1)	$ 407,600
Participants' aggregate monthly salaries (6)	$ 80,000
Individual's bonus—corporate (7)=(1)÷(6) ($407,600/$80,000)	5.01 months' salary

Source: Company records.

Graphical representations of these calculations are shown in Exhibit 2.
Under the original corporate bonus plan, all Plan 3 executives, whether
headquarters or divisional and whether line or staff, had their bonuses computed alike. Subsequently, in 1964 the executive committee decided that this
formula alone did not sufficiently tie incentive payments to profit improvement, or to individual performance in the area for which each executive
was especially responsible. To overcome these difficulties, it was decided that

Exhibit 2

DENNISON BONUS PLANS COMPARED

(Basis: Size of Bonus Fund)

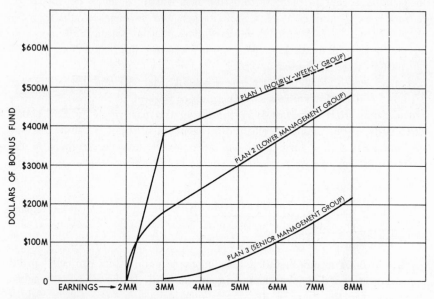

Note: Plan 2 shown after Plan 3 members deleted.
Source: Company records.

Exhibit 2—Continued

(Basis: Months of Bonus to Participants)

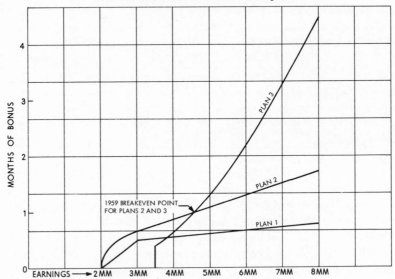

Note: (*a*) Plan 1 curve based on average participant.
    (*b*) Plan 3 curve based on 1960 opening capital ($23,788M).
    (*c*) All curves based on November 1959 participants and pay levels.
Source: Company records.

only part of each executive's bonus should henceforth be computed under the general corporate plan. Getting the rest would be made dependent on moving toward attainment of a profit target, and payments would be made on a different basis for divisional executives, the corporate staff men who advised them in their work, and the top headquarters line. Plan 1 and Plan 2 calculations were unaffected.

Plan 3 was divided into 3 parts; Plan 3A, Plan 3B and Plan 3C. Plan 3A was for division executives. This group comprised 24 men in 1966. (See organization chart for May 1967 for those who participate in this plan.) Two-thirds of the bonus payment for members of Plan 3A now became dependent on a new formula shown below—still, however, subject to the limitation that bonus from whatever source would not go above six months' salary:

$$\begin{pmatrix} \text{Divisional} \\ \text{bonus} \\ \text{calculation (8)} \end{pmatrix} = \frac{\text{Actual divisional profit improvement}}{\text{Budgeted divisional profit improvement}} \times 0.3 \times \begin{pmatrix} \text{Participant's} \\ \text{annual salary} \end{pmatrix}$$

This formula meant that if a division made none of its projected profit improvement, no divisional bonus would be paid. If the division reached its target, then the Plan 3A divisional bonus calculation (8) would yield a figure of 30% of the combined yearly salary payments to participating executives. Since, however, the divisional bonus was weighted by multiplying by two-thirds, reaching target would yield a bonus payment of only 20% of salary (equivalent to 2.4 months). Thus, in a year when no corporate bonus was paid, a division would have to earn its target 2.5 times over for its Plan 3 executives to earn their six months' salary limit. On the other hand, the larger the corporate bonus was, the sooner divisional executives would reach this six months' salary cutoff point, beyond which extra performance resulted in no higher bonus payment. (In 1966, for example, when all divisional executives would attain 1.67 months' salary from their one-third of the 5.01 months' corporate figure, (1) divisional executives could increase their bonus no further by reaching more than 173% of target.) The formula for the total payment to an individual was as follows: Payment to an individual = $\frac{1}{3}$ (individual's bonus-corporate [7]) + $\frac{2}{3}$ (individual's bonus division [8]).

The new Plan 3B was for staff executives. (Twelve participants in 1967—see organization chart for some of their positions.) One-third of the Plan 3B bonus was computed under the original Plan 3. The rest was then based on the average divisional figure (i.e., an average of the number of months of salary paid out to the managers of each of Dennison's eight divisions as calculated in Plan 3A). For corporate executives and inside directors who were not division managers, Plan 3C was developed (five men in 1966). As with Plan 3A and Plan 3B, Plan 3C provided that one-third of a man's bonus would be based on the old Plan 3 calculations while the remaining two-thirds (9) was dependent on how much was realized of a budgeted increment in consolidated corporate earnings. The formula under which this two-thirds portion was computed was the same as the formula for the divisional bonus:

$$\text{Individual's bonus} = \frac{\text{Actual profit improvement}}{\text{Budget profit improvement}} \times 0.3 \times \left(\begin{array}{c} \text{Individual's} \\ \text{annual salary} \end{array} \right)$$

According to Dennison's treasurer, more managers had been hurt than helped by tying bonus payments so closely to individual achievements. Thus, in 1966, of the 41 executives included in Plan 3, only 11 earned as much as or more than the corporate bonus alone would have permitted. Of these 11, 7 earned the maximum of 50% of annual salary and 4 earned 44%. For the rest, four earned a relatively low 14%; the rest lay between 28% and 36%.

Mr. Hamilton commented on some aspects of this bonus plan as follows:

There is always a question about the division between base pay and bonus. How much of a man's total compensation should be left to bonus? My view is that we should hold the base salary level even with the market. A bonus is payment for the accomplishment of a reasonably hard task. If a man has been successful in the past, this should be reflected in his base pay. The bonus should be the payment for current extra effort.

One trouble Dennison had in the past was that bonuses came to be regarded by some people as a part of the base pay. The fact that there can be broad swings from year to year now tends to discourage thoughts like that.

We are paying for profit improvement. With the bonus system as currently formulated, we direct our general managers at that goal. I have told the fellows that the principal ways to get profit improvements are first through increasing sales volume, second through improving our gross margins, and third through cost reduction. I expect them to get results in all of these areas.

Mr. Huntington commented that he believed the bonus system gave a new freedom to top management. He said, "Whereas once the major advantage of working for Dennison was working conditions and security, we are now able to say, 'If you are not up to the job, we will have to get someone who can handle it!' Of course this is true only with the younger men. With some of the older men, we have to have compassion. We in top management are more responsible than they are for what they are now."

Bonus determinants

With bonus payments to each participant dependent on such factors as salary, departmental profit, and realization of profit targets, Dennison operated under clearly defined policies regarding salary levels, allocation of shared costs, transfer pricing, and forward budgeting.

Salary levels. Several members of management commented that in the past Dennison's salaries had been low in comparison to other firms in the area. It was observed at all levels in the organization that Dennison had made a conscientious effort to catch up and become competitive in the salary structure.

At the divisional level, the general manager requested a pool of funds for salary increases during the following year when budgets were made up. The division manager then divided up this pool among the employees, subject to review by the salary committee composed of Messrs. Hamilton, Huntington, and Swisher. The managers interviewed said that in general all specific requests for salary increases had been granted. One manager stated that he believed requests were granted because they were well documented. For each job, the standard procedure manual set a salary range. (See Exhibit 3.) The division general manager then determined where in the range a particular manager should fall.

Exhibit 3

DENNISON SALARY RANGES, 1967

	Low	High
Foreman	$ 7,200	$10,000
Salesman	7,200	18,000
District sales manager	13,000	20,000
Division marketing manager	13,000	22,000
Division production manager	13,000	22,000
Division manager	17,500	35,000
Corporate staff manager	17,500	35,000

Source: Company records.

Shared costs. One of the most constantly troublesome problems in the accounting system was the problem of joint costs. According to the controller, almost every cost category for which the divisional general manager was held responsible included some joint costs. Only cash discounts, wage increases, travel and expense, advertising samples, and selling were unaffected by the performance of other departments; 21 other lines on the profit and loss statement all represented shared costs. The system of cost allocation within manufacturing was described as follows:

Overhead costs and other shared costs are allocated to the various production departments based on some standard, such as number of orders processed, orders received, square feet of floor space, number of employees or historical usage of a particular service department. These estimated allocations are then built into the standard cost rate for the department.

Transfer prices. Besides being affected by shared costs including overhead charges, divisional profits reflected the prices at which materials or services were transferred from division to division. The company's practice in respect to transfer prices was described as follows:

Each department . . . makes goods and transfers them to other divisions at the standard industrial engineering cost. Any variances for a department are then automatically allocated by the computer to the divisions which use the output from that particular department. This allocation is made on the basis of the percentage of total hours used in the previous year. In other words, if department 22 worked 1,500 hours for division X and 7,500 hours for division Y and 1,000 hours for division Z, 15% of any variances would be absorbed by division X, 75% by division Y and 10% by division Z.

Exact figures on transfers among divisions were not readily available, but the controller gave the following estimate for each division as to what percentage of its work was done for others and whether it was, on balance, a buyer from or maker for other divisions:

Division	Per Cent of Work Done for Other Divisions	Net Buyer — Net Maker + Equal Balance =
Box	25%	+
Copier	0	0
Gummed paper	45	+
Industrial products	25	=
Holiday	0	0
Marking systems	2–3	—
Resale	10	=
Thermiage	15	+

One staff manager noted the possibility that destructive competition could result from the prevalence of transfers among divisions, but he believed this problem was not, in actual practice, important:

Although there is some possibility for improving your own picture at the expense of someone else, we have not seen much of that here. Most of our managers are not playing things that close to the vest. I would say that there are two causes: first, the managers are not that good with numbers; besides, the relationships are not really that direct. Second, the faster the managers are running, the less time they have to argue, and they have been kept running pretty fast.

Everyone seems to be totally involved in the positive side. If any negative effects show up, they are soon drowned in the tremendous work load. Another important reason is Mr. Hamilton. He is a strong needler, an expert "follow upper," and a good coordinator. He is easily dissatisfied with anything less than the best. He is always right at the manager's shoulders keeping him performing well.

A division manager indicated that people at his level wanted to be judged on the basis of performance only within areas over which they had complete control. He therefore looked forward to having each division become self-sufficient over time:

They want to have the managers assume a corporate outlook. This is why one-third of the bonus is based on corporate profits. This new system, however, makes the manager want to split up the skills and make certain that he is judged only on what he controls. I think that more and more we shall see each division pull into itself and become self-sufficient. The further this process goes, the less of a problem we will have.

Budgets. The profit targets used in calculating bonus payments at Dennison were established through the operation of the company's budgeting system. This system, of course, also set targets for sales and costs, and in effect provided a plan for each upcoming year. The budgeting process was described as follows by Mr. Swisher:

In September each year, I issue a letter to all general managers forecasting the general business climate by quarters. Wherever this information is relevant, they use this letter as the basis for their forecasts of activity. They follow the pattern of economic activity predicted in order to make a breakdown of sales by months. The divisional accountants and controllers prepare facts and figures regarding the historical seasonal patterns and trends. These are then given to the product managers who make the actual forecasts. Although we don't do our forecasts by items, we do look at the differentiation between the old, staid item, the new dynamic ones with proven potential, and the new items with unknown potential.

All of our forecasting is based on customer charges and not on orders received.[4]

Once these steps are carried out, the results are consolidated and submitted to the policy committee which approves the sales budget.

Since we change our standard costs every two years, it is easy to prepare a profit figure in the years when the standard costs don't change.

Once the sales and profit figures are set, we go after the marketing and ad-

---

[4]Because a high percentage of business in some divisions was made to order, there could be a considerable time lag between receipt of an order and billing the customer. Hence the distinction between "charges" and "orders."

ministrative budgets. We determine an expense budget for each group in the company. Once a budget for R.&D., maintenance, or advertising had been determined, the manager is charged that figure. He can't improve his bonus by cutting down these areas which could have had long-run effects.

The budget for each year is worked out as precisely as possible. The improved budgetary process which has been worked out over the past few years has made the targets we set more realistic. The fact that the budget is prepared in exactly the same format as the monthly profit and loss statement aids the manager in understanding both the need for and use of the budgets.

When Phil Hamilton and I review the budgets, we want them to be realistic as possible and to be firm plans. This system will work only if the very top management is extremely committed to making it work.

Mr. Hamilton indicated that one of the most difficult problems in this process lay in assigning to each division a task that would be both fair and challenging:

It's difficult to make sure that the tasks for each of the divisions are equally hard. This is really the purpose of setting the budget. We try to set goals which will be difficult to achieve but well within the potential of the division.

One of the most difficult problems is to set a stiff enough task. We have tried to make it so that the divisions don't compete with each other, and are just competing with themselves and their own past performance. Of course we do let the managers know which divisions have done well. We recognize that money isn't the only motivation among our managers. In many cases, pride is as important a motivator as money.

Mr. Hamilton further indicated that the major role in setting targets was played by himself and Mr. Swisher:

The targets for each division are set by Swisher and me. We make up the budget based on projections and estimates furnished by the individual divisions. These estimates are placed within the context of the guidelines established by the executive committee and adjusted to give the overall company its required growth.

A divisional manager gave the following account of the budget-setting process as it appeared to him:

By and large the budgets come up from the bottom of the organization. On the sales side, the marketing manager and his product managers are well equipped with data on past sales, market activity, the economy, and new product introductions. They make predictions for one year in advance, broken into major product categories. In this way they arrive at their expected volume. Meanwhile, production, accounting, engineering services, etc., attempt to determine our production costs. From there we go into a little wilder speculation on the variances which we might get in such areas as primary material costs, labor and overhead charges, and warehousing costs. These are all put together to get the forecasting for the division.

I would say that the figures are generally accepted if they are reasonably in line with the economic projections made by Mr. Swisher, the expected new product growth, and with realistic profit improvement possibilities within the division. I would say that top management people have a very good seat-of-the-pants understanding of the business we are in.

Impact of the bonus system on managers

Among managers working under the bonus system, there was some disagreement as to whether the bonus or other factors were directly responsible for Dennison's improved performance. Typical of some comments was the following statement by one division manager:

I don't believe I work any harder because of the bonus. I feel the additional responsibility which the organizational change has placed upon me, and it is nice to be rewarded, but at this level in the company, we have to think about the long run as well. I have to maintain a corporate point of view.

Another division manager talked about the incentive pay as follows:

The first year we made our minimum target and got a 30% bonus. This past year we got 50%. Once you get a taste of a bonus like that [in this man's case roughly $12,500] it is one hell of an incentive. Of course they raise the targets on you after a big year like that, but it is worth shooting for.

Another member of the divisional management who was not a general manager echoed this statement. He added, however, that he was looking more toward his own future career than to the immediate payment of the bonus. He was frank in his desire to be a general manager. The most satisfying thing to him was the fact that he felt his progress and accomplishments were being carefully measured.

Among some of the lower echelons, the group receiving the highly leveraged bonus payments was known as "the forty thieves." For the most part, however, this appellation was used by the middle managers less in derision than with envy. One product manager (a position just one step below the Plan 3 bonus program) said:

Our division is a sleeping giant which we are trying to get to awaken. I know that most of the important everyday decisions are made at my level or one level above. At the division and corporate level, the decisions are made with regard to profit requirements, credit policies and other more general guidelines. The duty of applying these guidelines is placed at my level.

We now have effective communication of what is expected right from the directors' level on down. I'm sure that the directors put in the bonus system so that other people could share in the responsibility and in the reward for success. If I am good, lucky, and successful, I know that a share of this pot awaits me.

Exhibit 4 shows the management profile of Dennison.

Exhibit 4

DENNISON MANAGEMENT PROFILE

Name	Position	Years with Dennison	Years in Present Position	Age	Education	Functional Background
Dana C. Huntington	Chairman of the Board	48	6	68	BS	Marketing
Phillip B. Hamilton	President	33	1	56	MBA	Marketing
Francis Swisher	V. P. Finance	42	9	68	BS	Control
Calvin Josselyn	Treasurer	26	2	48	BS	Control
Thomas Sturtevant	Assistant Controller	3	2	32	MBA	Control
John Gray	General Manager Service	16	1	39	MBA	Production
Howard Weeks	V. P. International Business	39	7	62	BA	Marketing
Howard Gorton	General Manager Industrial Products	36	6	65	MBA	Marketing
Robert Dale	General Manager Marking Systems	7	3	49	MS	R&D
Ray Hager	General Manager Resale	30	3	52	BS	Sales
Nelson Gifford	Operations V. P.	10	1	37	BS	Control

DENNISON MANUFACTURING COMPANY (B)*

The major changes introduced in Dennison Manufacturing Company during the previous decade from 1957 to 1967 had been a new organizational structure, a new plan of executive compensation, and a new budgeting system to set profit targets. The effectiveness of these changes was thought by many in the company to be related to the way in which the information and control systems of the company were used by top management. As early as the turn of the century, Dennison had begun an extensive development of time standards and standard costs.

Over the years the company developed a sophisticated standard cost accounting system. Due to the long history of a functional organization pattern and the physical setup of the plant, the practice of allocating costs to the department was well established and accepted. As the organization structure was changed, the control system evolved into a profit-centered form. In addition to the formal accounting system top management made extensive use of informal tools for communicating expectations and obtaining information.

Organization of accounting and control

Commenting on the organization of Dennison's control and accounting function, Mr. Swisher, the chief financial officer of the company, indicated that all accounting at Dennison was handled centrally through seven divisional accountants and three divisional controllers, all of whom reported to the corporate assistant controller. Although they were physically located in the divisions, these men's salaries and promotions were determined by the accounting department. The accountants and their staffs, he said, recorded divisional sales and costs, examined the latter to "make certain their division does not get overcharged," set up standard costs, "made up the price book based on standard costs," and analyzed and interpreted control figures for management. The controllers' functions were, Mr. Swisher added, "more managerial." Their responsibilities included plans and budgets, inventory control, return on investment (ROI) analysis, internal auditing, and comparative studies of divisional performance.

Mr. Swisher added the following comments on relationships between the accountants and controllers and the divisional executives with whom they worked:

There has to be a feeling of joint responsibility of selling, merchandising, production, research, service and accounting for the results of the division. Instead of taking pot shots at one another and being destructively critical, each area is forced to cooperate by being constructive in its analysis and selling its programs for the improvement of the whole.

Centralized accounting has been the system in this company for 40 years. In the early days there was some conflict of interest between divisional loyalty and corporate loyalty. I think now that the situation is accepted by everyone.

There is still a slight tendency to be loyal to the operating people in the area in which you are working. This is only natural. At times we find minor areas where the accountants and controllers are able to give a break to the operating area. For example, with our standard cost system, items are credited at standard with a variance and charges are made at actual. We have an excess cost category which is for occurrences beyond the control of the manager. We keep a pretty careful watch on this account, and I am sure that it is not abused.

Distribution of control reports

Control reports at Dennison were distributed to both corporate and divisional managers, with copies being readily available to all managers at or near the level of the executives for whom the reports were prepared. A partial list of such reports was as follows:

Report	Periodicity	Lowest Level at Which Received
Corporate profit and loss	Monthly	Corporate
Divisional profit and loss	Monthly	Division
Gross margin report by commodity—300 categories	Monthly	Product Manager
Orders received report	3 times per month	Product Manager
Orders charged	4 times per month	Product Manager
Budget variances by operation within department	Monthly	Department Manager
Efficiency of direct labor by burden center	Weekly	Foreman
Efficiency of direct labor by employee	Monthly	Foreman
Indirect labor, repairs payroll against budget	Weekly	Foreman
Errors, machine repairs, miscellaneous expenses	Monthly	Foreman
Sales by districts, by salesmen	Monthly	District Sales Manager
Sales expenses, advertising	Monthly	Division Marketing Manager

Mr. Sturtevant, the assistant corporate controller, said by far the most eagerly awaited report of all was the monthly divisional P&L statement. Distributed on the ninth of the month, this was analyzed at once by a group composed of the divisional general manager, his major functional executives, and the divisional accountant. Next day, or as soon as schedules permitted, Mr. Hamilton met with the group to review their analysis.

Several management people believed that there was still some room for improvement in the way the numbers were analyzed. One limitation on the usefulness of this procedure, an executive stated, was the varying background and skill that division managers brought to their interpretive task:

Our system has given us standardized information, but we find that there is uneven capability for using that information among our various managers.

The divisional accountants played an important role in helping to interpret the information received. As one divisional manager put it, "The accountant is my financial watchdog. He is very important in that he calls things to my attention and suggests improvements." Other division managers also explicitly alluded to the useful contribution of the divisional accountant to the smooth functioning of their divisions. One manager, however, added that he wished he had more voice in choosing the particular accountant to serve with his division.

A divisional accountant had the following to say of his relationships with divisional and corporate executives:

I identify with the division. I have to do everything possible to help the management keep professionally oriented and to give them the advice that I feel will benefit the division most.

Information in Dennison goes all the way to the top. Mr. Hamilton likes to get all the information that he can. Any piece of data gets good exposure. His favorite question is "Where are the wild ones?" I have made it a point, however, never to say anything to the president that I hadn't said to the general manager of my division. However, I will make the same strong arguments for a position in Mr. Hamilton's office that I will in the division manager's office.

Although Mr. Hamilton did not have a background in finance, he was known among members of management for his determined use of the numbers generated by the control system. He said:

The control function is one of closing loopholes. In the past we had some problems such as payment of invoices without checking on delivery of goods, slow claims adjustment, and poor internal control on work-in-process and finished goods inventory. I think that this is in the process of being corrected. We have just hired an internal auditor, a policeman to see that the practices set down are observed.

The general manager of a division is at the mercy of his accounting information. Cost reduction takes a positive attitude. You have to keep at it. The whole process of improving profits is one of re-energizing and restimulating the manager. Proper information allows the corporate management to do this. If I have any complaint about our present accounting system, it is that not all of the accountants and controllers are as bold as they should be. They tend to keep quiet rather than give the independent analysis needed by management.

Exhibit 1

DENNISON MANUFACTURING COMPANY
Resale Line
(March—Three-Month Report Final 1967)

	Mo. Budget	%	Mo. Actual	%	YTD Budget	%	YTD Actual	%	Previous Year	%
01 Gross sales	$1,431,000		$1,192,431		$3,950,000		$3,380,197		$3,323,971	
02 Returns and allowances	27,000—		29,752—		81,000—		82,341—		70,532—	
04 Net sales	1,404,000	100.0	1,162,679	100.0	3,869,000	100.0	3,297,856	100.0	3,253,439	100.0
05 Primary cost	733,400—	52.2	616,231—	53.0	2,039,200—	52.7	1,757,635—	53.3	1,660,327—	51.0
06 Secondary cost	153,600—	11.0	116,470—	10.0	420,000—	10.9	381,179—	11.5	342,311—	10.5
07 Transportation	51,900—	3.7	42,193—	3.6	139,700—	3.6	101,743—	3.1	116,733—	3.6
08 Total 05–07	938,900—	66.9	774,894—	66.6	2,598,900—	67.2	2,240,557—	67.9	2,119,371—	65.1
09 Secondary revenues	465,100	33.1	387,785	33.4	1,270,100	32.8	1,057,299	32.1	1,134,068	34.9
10 Cash discounts	30,000—	2.1	24,766—	2.1	81,700—	2.1	70,112—	2.1	64,721—	2.0
11 Wage increases	5,736—	0.4	6,532—	0.6	16,850—	0.4	16,431—	0.5	20,033—	0.6
12 Soc. Sec. dep. var.	200—	0.0	74—	0.0	500—	0.0	102—	0.0	3,103—	0.1
13 Commodity var.	1,650—	0.1	1,403—	0.1	1,650—	0.1	823—	0.0	310—	0.0
14 Service var.	805	0.1	80	0.0	3,200—	0.1	160	0.0	17,795—	0.5
15 Secondary var.	26,821—	1.9	30,363—	2.6	71,563—	1.9	86,417—	2.6	432—	0.0
16 Trans. var.	27,034—	1.9	44,921—	3.9	70,491—	1.8	84,319—	2.6	64,491—	1.9
17 Price var.	3,240—	0.2	15,346	1.3	9,000—	0.2	29,421—	0.9	7,296—	0.2
18 Volume var.	20,000—	1.4	15,211	1.3	50,000—	1.3	17,117—	0.5	37,087—	1.1
19 Mfg. P&L	12,000—	0.9	18,379—	1.6	36,000—	0.9	41,223—	1.3	48,253—	1.5
20 Acc. year end diff.	4,800—	0.4	3,582	0.3	12,450—	0.3	10,002—	0.3	21,821—	0.7
21 Profit improvement	8,000—	0.6	6,349	0.6	20,000—	0.5	13,995	0.4	13,005	0.4
28 Total 10–21	72,496—	5.2	86,030—	7.4	208,004—	5.4	249,056—	7.6	182,087—	5.6

Researcher's Note: The figures on this and the following page have been disguised and as such are not placed here for detailed analysis. It is important to note the detail available to Mr. Hamilton before the meeting and the tone of the meeting in light of the fact that Line 49 profit was 35% below budget.

Exhibit 1—Continued

	Mo. Budget	%	Mo. Actual	%	YTD Budget	%	YTD Actual	%	Previous Year	%
29 Net before mkting.	$392,604	27.9	$301,755	26.0	$1,062,096	27.4	$808,243	24.5	$951,981	29.3
30 Admin. salaries	10,900—	0.8—	10,950—	0.9—	32,800—	0.8—	31,743—	1.0—	30,321—	0.9—
31 Travel and expense	3,200—	0.2—	6,593—	0.6—	23,500—	0.6—	17,137—	0.5—	19,593—	0.6—
32 Miscellaneous	100—	0.0—	1,700—	0.1—	2,200—	0.1—	4,053—	0.1—	5,737—	0.2—
33 Estimating	12,000—	0.8—	8,354—	0.7—	4,000—	0.1—	3,011—	0.1—	4,978—	0.2—
34 Trade associations	1,500—	0.1—	4,533—	0.4—	7,500—	0.2—	5,191—	0.1—	5,130—	0.2—
35 Advertising samples	38,000—	2.7—	35,791—	3.1—	120,000—	3.1—	90,311—	2.7—	111,131—	3.4—
36 General and mkting. overhead	15,000—	1.1—	15,000—	1.3—	45,000—	1.2—	45,000—	1.4—	42,371—	1.3—
37 Selling	102,000—	7.3—	100,193—	8.6—	306,125—	7.9—	294,312—	8.9—	263,321—	8.1—
38 Sketches and orig.	8,000—	0.6—	12,341—	1.1—	24,000—	0.6—	25,112—	0.8—	25,677—	0.8—
39 Excess and dropped	5,500—	0.4—	6,331—	0.6—	16,241—	0.4—	12,219—	0.4—	17,833—	0.5—
40 Research and eng.	16,700—	1.2—	8,294—	0.7—	51,350—	1.3—	29,227—	0.9—	48,117—	1.5—
41 Accruals	11,500—	0.8—	11,500—	1.0—	34,500—	0.9—	34,500—	1.0—	20,100—	0.6—
48 Total 30-40	224,400—	16.0—	221,580—	19.1—	667,216—	17.2—	591,816—	17.9—	594,309—	18.3—
49 Revenue after mkting. ...	168,204	11.9	80,175	6.9	394,880	10.2	216,427	6.6	357,672	11.0
50 Ind. research	5,750—	0.4—	2,831—	0.2—	16,500—	0.4—	16,325—	0.5—	13,073—	0.4—
51 General and admin.	21,000—	1.5—	20,752—	1.8—	63,000—	1.6—	62,243—	1.9—	53,138—	1.6—
52 Interest	10,971—	0.8—	11,947—	1.0—	33,127—	0.9—	37,100—	1.1—	23,192—	0.7—
53 Year-end bonus	12,000—	0.8—	10,001—	0.9—	36,000—	0.9—	30,419—	0.9—	24,497—	0.8—
58 Total 50-53	49,721—	3.5—	45,531—	3.9—	148,627—	3.8—	146,087—	4.4—	113,900—	3.5—
59 Earn. before tax	118,483	8.4	34,644	3.0	246,253	6.4	70,340	2.2	243,772	7.5
60 Income taxes	59,241—	4.2—	17,322—	1.5—	123,126—	3.2—	35,170—	1.1—	121,886—	3.7—
69 Profit after taxes	59,242	4.2	17,322	1.5	123,127	3.2	35,170	1.1	121,886	3.8

The monthly profit review

At all levels, executives at Dennison manifested keen interest in what the top officers were thinking. Many talked in personal terms about requests made by Mr. Hamilton, opinions expressed by Mr. Swisher, or other clues which the individual felt he had to the workings of the Dennison corporate mind.

Perhaps the chief source of this vertical communication was the monthly profit review sessions held by Mr. Hamilton with the managers of each division. Generally the division general manager, the marketing, production, and sales managers, the divisional accountant, divisional controller, and company controller would attend these sessions. It was only when a special question of fact existed that other members of the divisional staff were brought in.

Mr. Hamilton spoke of these meetings as being one of his most important management tools. Before each meeting, he received the monthly profit and loss statement for all divisions. (See Exhibit 1 for a sample monthly P&L statement and examples of supporting data.) He generally spent a weekend reviewing both the overall figures and supporting data before holding the meetings. He said of these meetings:

The monthly P&L offers me a timely tool for management. In addition to the divisional figures, I get a lot of supporting data. In addition to reviewing the figures, we talk about problems and planning. I found that my questions have caused some of the managers to have group meetings beforehand to go over their own results and prepare. I now make the general managers make statements and lay out the problems at the beginning of the meeting. They should welcome the opportunity to discuss the problems and not to sweep them under the table.

I am apt to be rough on people whose skin is a little tender. I tend to lean heavily on those areas that I feel need emphasis.

The profit review sessions lasted between one-and-a-half and two-and-a-half hours. The following Appendix provides an excerpt from the March profit review meeting for the resale products division.

APPENDIX

EXCERPTS FROM A MONTHLY PROJECT REVIEW MEETING, RESALE PRODUCTS DIVISION

Those present were:

Phillip Hamilton—President Dennison
Thomas Sturtevant—Corporate Controller
Ray Hager—General Manager, Resale Products Division
John Redmond—Sales Manager, Resale Products Division
Robert Hawkins—Production Manager, Resale Products Division
Spurgeon Condo—Merchandise Manager, Resale Products Division

Selected excerpts from the meeting.[1]

---

[1] All internal numbers have been disguised in order to preserve confidences.

HAMILTON: Well, Ray, will you please start out the quarterly profit review, emphasizing particularly the March results?

HAGER: As you can see, the results were not good. Sales are not meeting budgets. Customer charges are not as high as orders received, and generally the results are down. Of course we all know the budget did not follow our normal seasonal pattern, and the sales are not as healthy as they were forecast to be when we made our budget considerations. John, do you want to say why?

REDMOND: Well, we lost at least $60,000 volume on the diaper liner deal which wasn't introduced as it normally is in the last part of March. This volume will be made up when we run the promotion in April.

HAGER: How is that volume coming in now?

REDMOND: It's a little late; there are some problems in bringing it in. International Paper Company and P&G are both promoting their disposable diaper liners heavily.

HAGER: Is Johnson & Johnson still pushing disposable diaper liners?

REDMOND: I never hear about them—not in the market place, but I think Curity is taking as much as before.

Our government business is off $30,000 in orders received. This is due to some GSA bids we didn't get. We got a new bid in, though, on $40,000 to $80,000 worth of polyethylene envelopes.

CONDO: We got the order!

REDMOND: Oh, I didn't know that! It hadn't come in yesterday . . . .

General business conditions have really been off. We have been suffering, along with Detroit. Also, if you remember, we had the budget adjustment so we took $250,000 from the normal seasonal pattern, and moved it forward. The expectation was for a good first quarter with a poorer last quarter.

HAGER: Do you think we are getting a more healthy picture now?

REDMOND: Yes, the "Polyethylene" envelopes are coming in strong. We have got an $11,000 new account and a lot more attention. Our reports are indicating that we have been a lot more aggressive and a lot more successful in holding on to distribution.

HAGER: Another cause for alarm is our credit problem.

REDMOND: Yes, that cost us $48,000 in sales. If credit problems continue the way they have, we are going to be in a real bind.

HAMILTON: Let me ask a question that has me disturbed. Even if the sales budget was deliberately increased $250,000, it only produced a slightly greater profit than last year. Unless we increase our sales more substantially, we are going to have a decrease in overall profit.

STURTEVANT: We had two objectives in changing that $250,000 from the last quarter to the third. First, we thought that the first half was going to have a greater percentage gain over 1966 than the second half. Second, we want to reflect in Line 49 earnings what they should be at that time of the year.[2]

HAMILTON: We were wrong when we increased the budget for that reason. We had to stretch to get a volume-profit relationship which would get us an 8% increase in overall profit. We had to get the $600,000 increase in sales just to get hold even in profits. . . .

*   *   *   *   *

[2]"Line 49 earnings" refers to line 49 of the divisional profit report shown in Exhibit 1. The bonus for divisional personnel was determined by "Line 49 earnings" improvement.

HAMILTON: O.K., Ray, go on with your discussion.

HAGER: We have to make a certain percentage increase in each line. If we reach our budget in orders received, we will not be doing too badly. If we had had the promised volume, we would have had $690,000 increase in Line 49. Our basic problem is sales.

STURTEVANT: Right. But you realize one rather shocking fact is that to make our sales budget, we will have to bill over $2 million a month for the rest of the year.

HAGER: We will have the new West Coast warehouse on-stream.

STURTEVANT: How will that help?

HAMILTON: Yes, we want an orderly opening of the warehouse—we don't want to push it if it is going to create problems later.

HAGER: Incidentally, how is the warehouse going to be charged to me? Nobody has told me.

STURTEVANT: You're being charged as a parent company is being charged.

HAGER: Who is controlling the cost there?

HAMILTON: This isn't the place to go into this. Tom, explain it to Ray later. If he doesn't like it, he can write me a letter, and we will adjudicate the matter later.

We are not going to worry about this monthly figure right now. . . . [Discussion proceeded on several items such as changes in transportation terms, and cash discounts.]

*   *   *   *   *

HAMILTON: I notice there are some commodity variations.

HAGER: Before you get down there, how about the wage cost? [There was then some discussion of the wage costs.]

HAMILTON: Well, really, in the whole scheme of things, that is rather insignificant. I am adverse to any further monkeying with the second variation. I am not sure that the philosophy of allocation is completely right. But this way, at least, we maintain comparability. You are charged according to the budget. The budget was set on this basis so that you should be willing to accept the result.

STURTEVANT: Ray [Hager] would be interested. We are now trying to get standard costing for the warehouse. We could then get it so that you could plan on what your actual costs would be, and not have to worry about things hidden under the rug at the end of the year.

HAGER: This would be great. This is perhaps the area I feel most hazy on. . . . [Discussion proceeded on the warehouse costs and other allocated costs.]

HAMILTON: Let's look at this volume variation account. Why don't we have more here now than last year? Last year we had a $15,000 volume gain. I don't think it's been less busy. It must be the change in standards that now shows above the line.

HAGER: In two areas outside of the division, in Department 3, Industrial Products, and Department 25, we are working only 40 hours a week. Our new color presses are down to 40 hours as well. We have been trying to work them the 45 hours. We are having to absorb their negative variances.

HAMILTON: To what extent has the inventory and build-up in the West Coast warehouse helped to absorb the hourly rate?

STURTEVANT: That was last year.

HAWKINS: Department 5 has a $2,020 loss in efficiency and a $1,000 gain in wages. It doesn't take into account the problem of the incentive bonus, and getting production back up to standard.

HAMILTON: I noticed you had $366 loss due to off-standard work[3] in the corner-cut and double-scoring machine. Why? I thought these were good. [See Exhibit 1.]

Exhibit 1

DENNISON MANUFACTURING COMPANY

To: Mr. R. C. Hawkins

From: P. J. Mahoney

Subject: March 1967 Departmental Variations

Date: April 13, 1967

Page 2 of a six-page report sent to Mr. Hamilton before the meeting

4. Department 4

Efficiency—$463 Gain

Only problems are on the Kluge Dieout and 9 x 12. Delays are very heavy on the Kluge and low efficiency is the problem on the 9 x 12.

Indirect—Stock—Ship—Jog—Continue to operate at more hours than budgeted.

Adjustor—Same story.

Misc. Expense—$451 Loss
  Die Sharpening $1,275.
  Misc. Small Exps. 36.

5. Department 5

Efficiency Loss	$2,020	
Label Pkg.	$286	Low efficiency
Wire Pkg.	178	Low efficiency
Quad Run	130	Off-Std. work and delay
2H Ace	79	Off-Std. work and delay
Roc Die	148	Off-Std. work and delay
150 Ct.	70	Delay
2H 150	141	Delay
*Corn Cutting Machinery	169	Delay and Off-Std. work
*Double Scoring Machine	198	Delay and Off-Std. work
S. H. Machine	94	Delay and Off-Std. work
410 Env.	173	Off-Std. work

Misc. Expense—$466 Loss	
Manpower	$516
CH Bus Stab	70
	$586

*These items discussed during monthly profit review.

---

[3]Off-standard work was seconds or discards which were produced as the result of machine difficulties.

HAGER: It is always better to make an efficiency gain. But we can't with the rates in those machines. The standards from Department 42 [not under the control of the division] really don't apply to Resale. We can't get the same production rate.

HAMILTON: What about 21B? This department always had a gain. It has now got a substantial loss.

*   *   *   *   *

HAMILTON: You fellows have a sizable profit improvement plan going. How is it coming along?

HAGER: We are not getting the factory engineering we expected. If I don't get the service I think we should be getting from the engineering department, can I cut my engineering expense?

HAMILTON: If it is clear-cut that you are not getting what you should get, you can hire outside. The fact is that we have so many bodies with a salary that we have a million dollars budgeted in that department. So either they deliver some results or we are going to have to cut back on the number of bodies. Let's say it's clear that they are unable to deliver the results to your division; then I would say that you will have to hire outside, but they will have to drop one, two, three, or more people. Of course factory engineering is now in new hands and we will have to see the results. I want to make this judgment in terms of factual reports. Can you do this for me? What have they been doing—time, date, number, etc.?

HAGER: The place we are getting results from in factory engineering is in installation. Of course if I had an engineer in my department, we could do it ourselves. We don't need the high-priced talent in the factory engineering department. What we really need is their help in the area where originality is required. . . .

HAMILTON: All right. Let's move on to the expenses. We have some special work to do.

HAGER: Before we move on, I think we should take another look at having an engineer assigned to our department.

HAMILTON: It is entirely possible to assign an engineer. Hawkins, you call a meeting with you and me, Hager, and Gray. . . . [Two engineers and a methods man were later assigned.]

*   *   *   *   *

HAMILTON: Having gone through all this, it is as clear as crystal that we need billings. We can't make the dollar profit if we don't get the sales. Let's see now. Have we covered all the soft spots and special situations? [General agreement.]

HAGER: As we get a clearer picture of the economy, we can lay plans, and move forward in both the engineering efforts and in cleaning up the product line.

HAMILTON: John [Redmond], you should figure which areas you could get the mileage out of in your sales program. It is that sort of thing that I am willing to pay for. Not only should you provide some incentive for the salesmen to push, but you have got to develop some incentive for the customers to buy. . . .

CONDO: This might call for a dealer-jobber type promotion. Also, I think we need some incentive for the salesmen. We have just put out a promotion on Color

Brite crepe paper which seems to be going well. With a six-carton order we will give a rack free. I think this is what will get the customer to buy.

HAMILTON: No question, business has softened. We have to get an answer and figure a way to make the customers move the product off our shelves. We mustn't wait for government programs to take hold. We must do far better than average if we are going to equal our past performance. [At this point, Mr. Hamilton made some statements about some of the economic measures which President Johnson was taking to improve the economic situation in the United States. He listed several factors, enumerating the cut in the discount rate, releasing of the highway funds, etc.]

HAMILTON: When they want to suppress business, they can push it down easily. But it takes the public time to respond to a stimulus. We as a company have to build up the stimulus for our own customers. We can't rely on the government to do it. Too, we can't just put pressure on the men. Neither Ray nor I just sit out here and say "Get more sales" and expect that we will have more sales. We have got to find ways to make the customer want our products and make our salesmen want to sell them. We have to be constantly on the look-out for other small businesses, and some way of reviving interest. Also another way is through judicious acquisition. . . .

*   *   *   *   *

HAMILTON: This line from time to time needs new items. We should be looking. There are over 700 members in the National Stationery Manufacturers Association. Maybe one of them would provide us with an opportunity for an acquisition which would "beef up" our line. We are not alone in this area, and we must keep looking. . . .

*   *   *   *   *

HAMILTON: John [Redmond] I am glad to see the monkey is on your back, and you, Condo, as merchandising man, you must give him the meat to cook in the kitchen. Are there any vacancies or problems that you have in your salesmen line-up? What about the "weak sisters"?

REDMOND: Well, basically, I don't think a "strong sister" up there in _____ would do us any good.

HAMILTON: What about in _____?

REDMOND: I don't think we are weak there.

HAMILTON: Are you satisfied with your line managers?

REDMOND: Yes.

HAMILTON: What about your capital equipment program? Can you use up your budget?

HAWKINS: Why, sure, I could use up all the budget even before you took 40% away.

*   *   *   *   *

HAMILTON: How's the MacAdams press doing? O.K.? We have the follow-up on our expenditures. . . . About this inventory problem, it says here that we have $4,200,000 compared to $2,955,000 last year. Where did this come from?

STURTEVANT: Well, crepe and dealer labels and some of the other products have been produced according to budget, not according to sales.

HAMILTON: Well, what control have we got to prevent this going merrily on? Can I rely on you to control this?

ALL: Yes, sir, yes, yes, yes.

HAGER: I disagree partially with what you said. I think a lot of the inventory that we have now is just simply necessary inventory versus the inadequate inventory that we had last year.

HAMILTON: Well, on the other hand, this division has its own controls on inventory. But the inventory committee is advisory—you have got to take the responsibility for the results. So, when you are long on inventory, just don't let Hawkins, your production manager, make any more of it. Right?

HAGER: Right.

HAWKINS: I never thought I'd hear it. We have got too much inventory in our finished goods.

HAMILTON: Tom, do you have anything to add? Ray, John, . . . Phil?

Well, thank you, gentlemen, for a good report. I think the answer is obvious —just get the sales.

In reviewing this meeting with the case writer, Mr. Hamilton said:

As you saw, I was trying to make certain that the soft spots were recognized and explained. Of course the obvious thing is sales, but, as I said, we can't just ask for more sales, we have got to get new products and new plans.

I think that the expenses are generally well contained. If we are going to get profit improvement, we are just going to have to blast it out. In that one place where I talked about the $300-plus expense variation, I was trying to make them all aware of the fact that it is the small variation which makes the difference between great performance and mediocrity. . . .

We worked hard with this division to get a budget which would absorb the increased costs. They have got to meet the budget, but I recognize that they need the help of the staff groups. In at least one case they haven't been getting what they have been paying for. I'll have a status report tomorrow on that problem. We've got to get support for the divisions.

DENNISON MANUFACTURING COMPANY (C)*

^^

In May 1967, Mr. Phillip Hamilton, president of Dennison Manufacturing Company, was faced with a recurrence of the question of a transfer price between divisions on a new product. By the time the issue was presented to him, it was clear that no settlement could be reached through direct negotiations among the division managers involved. Although at the time the issue arose only two divisions were involved, the nature of the product made it clear that this decision would affect a third division and could potentially set a precedent for handling other questions of this type.

The product. The new product had been developed through research and design efforts on attaching devices. Called Secur-A-Tach, it was a substitute for string or wire in tying items together. Secur-A-Tach was a piece of molded nylon with specially molded end-pieces which locked together. Once joined the Secur-A-Tach ends could not be separated without destroying them, thus making the attachment tamperproof. Secur-A-Tach was designed to withstand a strain of 20 lbs. pressure. It could be made in a variety of lengths and colors. (See Exhibit 1 for an illustration of the Secur-A-Tach device.)

Priced to sell for $2.40 per thousand with a 50% gross margin[1] Secur-A-Tach was thought to have a very large potential market. Total realizable potential was believed to be between $1 million and $3 million sales per year. Retail stores could use them to attach price tags and stock tags to high-ticket items such as purses, jewelry, etc., without fear of customer switching. Also, items in pairs, such as shoes, could be securely and easily joined for display. Another major use was thought to be with shipping tags and stock tags used by manufacturers. Ease of attachment, tamperproof design, strength, and appearance were thought to be the major advantages which Secur-A-Tach enjoyed. It was also believed that the fact that tags could be bought without being prestrung would eliminate one of the major problems faced by the purchasers of tags. Tangled strings were often a nuisance.

History of the product. Secur-A-Tach had been developed by Mr. Gerry Merser, a product manager in the marking systems division in cooperation

---

[1]All internal cost, sales and expense data are disguised; however, essential relationships have been preserved.

Exhibit 1

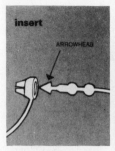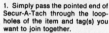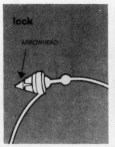

1. Simply pass the pointed end of Secur-A-Tach through the loopholes of the item and tag(s) you want to join together.

2. Insert arrowhead firmly into socket. You can *feel* it snap into place.

3. When Secur-A-Tach bond is pulled apart, the arrowhead breaks off and hooking-holding power is lost forever. Can't be used again!
Two lengths (5" and 9") meet most attaching needs.

Dennison secur-a-tach

Secur-A-Tach is available in several lengths and assorted colors. Special lengths can be made available on request.

Dennison
MANUFACTURING COMPANY
INDUSTRIAL PRODUCTS DIVISION
Framingham, Mass., Drummondville, Quebec, Watford Herts., England

with one of Dennison's outside suppliers. The idea for the product and its subsequent development had resulted from the success enjoyed by the Dennison Swiftach system, also developed by Mr. Merser. Swiftach was a device for attaching tags to soft goods by putting a molded nylon fastener through the garments with the aid of an attaching gun. The marking systems division had achieved 85% saturation in the major retail chains with Swiftach. Sales

Exhibit 1—Continued

of guns and fasteners approached $1.2 million per year. (See Exhibit 2 for pictures and literature on the Swiftach system.)

Mr. Merser and others in the marking systems division believed that the Secur-A-Tach market was potentially even greater. They thought that the wider appeal of Secur-A-Tach would be an opening wedge to customers who were unacquainted with Dennison's tags and marking machines. Initially it was believed that the marking systems, industrial products, and resale divisions

Exhibit 2

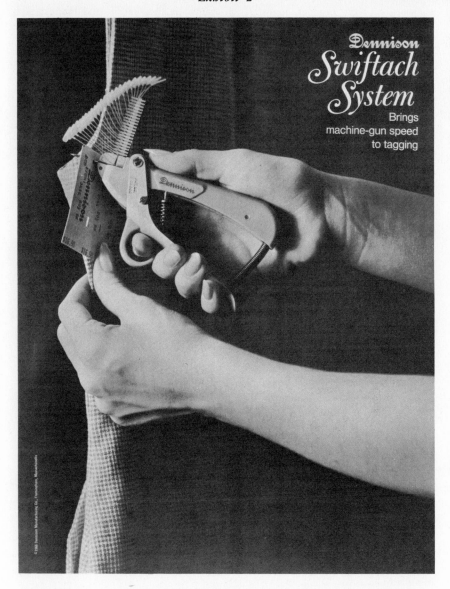

had the greatest potential for selling Secur-A-Tach. The question which had been sent to Mr. Hamilton was an issue raised between the industrial products division and the marking systems division.

The divisions' proposals. Mr. Howard Gorton, manager of the industrial products division, wrote the following letter to Mr. Hamilton:

Industrial Products Needs for Secur-A-Tach

The proprietary aspects of Secur-A-Tach by the marking systems division are

well understood and appreciated by industrial products personnel. However, by
the nature of the product, industrial products division has a vital interest and
must be given completely parallel consideration in all regards for the industrial
products markets.

Delineation of the industrial products needs are:

1. Simultaneous launching date.

    a) Secur-A-Tach is even more suited to industrial products than Swiftach.
Hence industrial products sales force must not be denied the product
until marking systems has made market coverage.

    b) Lead time of even 30 days would be a serious disadvantage to indus-
trial products.

    c) Aside from any or all of the above reasons, a lead time for market
coverage by marking systems division would cut into industrial products division tag sales volume by the cost of strings or wires if nothing else.

2. Orders to be accepted and filled according to date of receipt.

3. Market coverage must be along normal lines as between marking systems
and industrial products.

    a) "Raiding" of customers by selling the attachment only to the customers
of the other division must not be permitted in either the retail or industrial markets.

    b) Sale of the attachment for use on competitors' tags to be permitted
and encouraged by both divisions.

4. Secur-A-Tach must be transferred from marking systems to industrial products according to normal procedures, i.e., without profit or discount arrangement just as pressure sensitive labels and dial-set tags are transferred
in reverse. Credit for production and thereby contribution to the corporation to be shown statistically on the records of the marking systems division.

In reply, Mr. Robert Dale, manager of the marking systems division, wrote
this letter to Mr. Hamilton:

I have been in a discussion with Mr. Gorton on this subject. As we are at
opposite points and have not reached agreement, he felt he would like to refer
it to you for a decision. In view of my heavy travel schedule I wanted to put
the following in writing.

As you know, this product fits the product line of marking systems, industrial
products and resale. It should be spread across as broad a distribution front as
possible. Industrial products, less than resale, can probably do much with it.
However, two questions concerning this product and the interdivisional handling are:

1. Time of launching.

2. Cost to industrial products or resale.

My feelings on this matter are as follows:

1. It is not practical to contemplate simultaneous launching as requested by
industrial products. There is only one mold on order, due July 15. It would
be foolhardy to order additional molds until the first is proven out. The
capacity of the one mold is insufficient to handle the business we see on
demand from marking systems division customers alone, let alone that from
other divisions.

The earliest that sufficient capacity would be available for industrial products is probably September, at which time additional molds would be delivered. During this interval I see no major problem as most of what marking systems division sells will be in retail channels.

2. Cost: As we have handled Swiftach successfully by allowing 35% secondary revenue, so I would suggest Secur-A-Tach be handled. Transferring at cost does not provide means of recovering mold cost, development expense, and other miscellaneous expenses incurred. Transferring at sell less 35% provides for recovering of expenses to the producing division and also gives a higher than normal return to the selling division.

The divisions

Industrial products. The industrial products division was the second oldest division in Dennison. Its basic charter was to sell paper products to manufacturers. Based on this charter, it made tags and labels to order for large customers. Its activities included designing, printing, collating, stringing or wiring, and in many cases storing the tags or labels which would serve to identify the products of the manufacturer. In addition to this business the industrial products division produced and sold industrial crepe for electrical insulation purposes. (See Exhibit 3 for disguised financial data on the industrial products and marking systems divisions, and Exhibit 4 for a partial organization chart.)

Exhibit 3

DISGUISED DIVISIONAL FINANCIAL DATA
(Dollars in Thousands)

	Marking Systems Division		Industrial Products Division	
	1966 Actual	1967 Budget	1966 Actual	1967 Budget
Sales	$9,500	$11,100	$6,010	$6,900
Cost of goods sold	5,800	6,600	4,420	4,950
Secondary revenue...........	$3,700	$ 4,500	$1,590	$1,950
Marketing, G&A	1,800	2,100	1,140	1,350
"Line 49" profit (profit after marketing)	$1,900	$ 2,400	$ 450	$ 600

Source: Company records.

Mr. Gorton described his division's basic strength as the ability to put together almost any combination of paper with printed information in an attractive way. The major sales strategy of the division was to go into a customer's operation, to analyze his needs for tags and labels, and to design a final product which would eliminate insofar as possible the need for hand inscribing data and multiple handling of the tags.

Mr. Gorton's division had to rely on its ability to do complicated things to paper such as multiple color printing of both sides, production of manifold tags, special wiring or stringing, or special paper combinations. Simple tags were often sold on a basis of low price and rapid service. In these cases, the

Exhibit 4

PARTIAL ORGANIZATION CHART

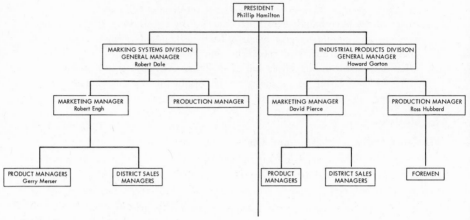

Source: Company records.

division was competing against small one-man shops which could produce simple tags on a $2,000 Heidelberg press. It was deemed almost impossible for a large company to compete for the smallest low-price end of the business. Dennison tended to specialize in the more complicated tag and label products, produced on machines which cost up to $100,000 each. It was in the area of solving complicated problems or delivering large quantities that Dennison had an advantage.

This division had not made any breakthroughs with totally new products. Mr. Gorton said that a new product for the industrial products division meant an adaptation or minor adjustment in an existing product idea to make it solve customers' problems. He believed that much of the division's ingenuity had been aimed at the development of the complicated devices which produced the tags and labels more cheaply, rather than at new consumer applications. He also added, "Although some might think that we didn't keep up with progress, it has to be remembered that two of the most glamorous and profitable divisions of the company are offshoots of the industrial products division. Both marking systems and thermiage were spawned from this group." Another member of the division management echoed these feelings and said, "For many years the money which might have gone to developing a couple of divisions which are now the senior citizens has gone to promoting the more glamorous machine-oriented divisions. From a corporate point of view this is probably right, but now as these new developments pay off, I hope we get a chance to enjoy some of the benefits."

The targeted increase in profits for the industrial products division in 1967 was roughly $150,000. Mr. Gorton and his managers believed that they had a difficult task to accomplish if they were to meet that goal and obtain their 30% divisional bonus. Mr. Gorton said of this goal:

Phil Hamilton thinks there is a great deal of room for profit improvement through cost reduction. I am less sure. There is quite a difference in obtaining a reduction in stock goods line versus obtaining a cost reduction when the products are made in short and medium production runs on general purpose machines. With some of the changes which we have made to get increased volume, with the constant attention to our estimating procedures, and with the help of new products, I think we have a fighting chance.

A major cost reduction program in the past had reduced indirect labor from 22 people to 15 in a three-year period, while sales had increased by $2 million.

The industrial products division was organized into two separate parts, marketing and production. Marketing, under Mr. David Pierce, was then divided into six regions, each with a district sales manager. In addition, three product groups, industrial crepe, tags, and labels, reported to Mr. Pierce. The salesmen were given a quota and received a commission on sales. Salesmen were guaranteed 90% of the commissions which they would receive if they reached quota. In addition, they were guaranteed 90% of their previous year's earnings. Owing to an 8% commission rate after the quota was reached, this provision frequently caused their base salaries to rise.

The bonus paid to district managers was equal to the average of the commissions paid to his salesmen on sales in excess of quota. As a percentage of total compensation, the bonuses received by the district managers were the lowest in the sales line.

Secur-A-Tach was thought of by the personnel in the industrial products division as being of great potential value to their division. By eliminating prestringing and wiring of tags, it would simplify the made-to-order production process. At the same time it would be a great convenience for the customer. Unless the industrial products division could sell Secur-A-Tach, the division's revenues would be cut by the cost of wiring. As one man said, "Although attachment isn't an end in itself, Secur-A-Tach should give us an important plus over competition. We can offer something that no one else can." Another man said, "This product is really a natural for our division. We should eventually be able to sell as much as, if not more than, the marking systems division."

The whole question of divisionalization was raised during discussion of Secur-A-Tach. One man said: "Dennison is so divisionalized that sometimes we get into problems. I have seen very few transfers of personnel among the divisions. I personally think it would be hard to get anyone to transfer out of our division. The division managers are somewhat jealous of the experience developed in the people under them. I really don't think that divisionalization has meant greater opportunity for the people in the company. The opportunity comes through growing in your own division. There is a lot less cooperation here across division lines than there used to be. I think the sense of responsibility which managers have developed precludes them asking for help."

Another man echoed these feelings, but less strongly, in saying, "The tendency is for divisions to draw into themselves. If our division were moved across the street, given control over all its own production and services, we would do better." One middle manager said, "If we are going to have profit responsibility, I think we should have it at each level. I don't think it should stop at the division level."

A final factor that Mr. Gorton saw as relevant to the disputed transfer-price issue was the fact that materials as well as finished products were to some extent transferred between divisions. Industrial products made about $1.25 million for the resale division and about $500,000 for marking systems. On a dollar basis, trade with the resale division about balanced out, but Mr. Gorton believed that currently a substantial amount more was produced for the marking systems divisions than was purchased from it. He believed that the percentage of industrial products' output sent to other divisions had been relatively constant for the past five years.

Marking systems division. The marking systems division's basic charter was the development, production, and marketing of machines which could print variable information on tags or labels at a customer's site, and machines which could attach tags or labels to the end products. The development of Swiftach and Secur-A-Tach had simplified the customer's task of attaching tags and labels considerably. Before Swiftach, tags and labels had to be hand-sewn to garments, or hand-tied or wired to hard goods. These new developments speeded up the process considerably.

The marking systems division had been split off from the industrial products division in 1955. It grew quickly until 1959 when its growth tapered off. One member of the division's management said:

We were a sleeping giant. We had lots of technology that was not being used. For years this division wasn't marketing oriented. Marketing was looked at as an expense rather than an investment. Our salesmen were selling 50% more per man than our competitors which meant they were so busy with their current customers they couldn't make cold calls and find new customers.

Mr. Robert Dale, the current general manager of the division, took over in January 1965. Since that time he had increased the sales force from 38 men to 56. In the two years of his management, profits were up 38%.

Mr. Dale believed that with the new product introductions which had been made since 1965, the marking systems division was at least equal to and in most cases better than any of his competitors.

In raising the issue of pricing transferred products at a figure other than cost, Mr. Dale recognized that he was going against past practice. He felt, however, that this was justified because the product development costs had cut into his division's profits, and his division was buying the molds and paying for the sales promotion literature. The industrial engineering costs did not provide for recovery of these expenditures. He furthermore believed that the lead time in introduction which he requested for his division was the most fair solution. Until the first mold had proven itself at production rates, there would be a capacity constraint on the production of the Secur-A-Tach and he did not believe his division should suffer.

The marking people in the marking systems division felt strongly on the issue as well. One man said:

We realize that this new product has a very broad market which certainly is over and above this division's charter. It will give us and the other divisions a powerful lever to open new doors for Dennison.

We were frankly disappointed in the way Swiftach was handled by the other divisions. We achieved 85% penetration, but it was by hard door-to-door sales effort. If we handled Secur-A-Tach exclusively for a few months, I am sure that we could make a large impact. I worry about two divisions calling on the same customers with the same product. In the case of some large department stores and chains, our two sales forces overlap. Industrial products makes all their tags and labels while we supply their marking and pinning machines. Although this won't occur often, it has been a serious source of friction in the past.

Another worry was expressed about the transfer at cost. "Without giving the division any profit, what incentive is there for our product manager to work with the other division's salesmen."

At the very least, marking systems was anxious to assure that there be a clear-cut division of customers between the industrial products division and the marking systems division.

Further complications. In addition to the question of the transfer price between marking systems and industrial products, there was the problem of the discount structure. Marking systems would be selling directly to the end user, and therefore wished to establish as high a price as possible, allowing full markup. The industrial products division would also be selling to end users, but when the resale division started to sell the product, it would be through its normal channels of distributors and wholesalers. Included among their customers would be small printing shops. These channels would expect their normal discounts. Some within the marking systems division were worried that allowing the Secur-A-Tach to be sold through all of these channels would enable their own customers to buy through third parties at a lower price than would be charged by marking systems. It was believed that small printing houses often passed material on at cost in order to keep their presses full. A typical discount structure was as follows:

> Printing shops .... 10% off list
> Wholesalers .... 35% off list
> Distributors .... 40% off list

It was believed that different packaging would help mitigate the problem of parallel sourcing, but marking systems personnel could not see why they should be placed at any disadvantage in selling their own product. Others within the company discounted the possibility of any difficulties arising in this fashion.

Another potential problem was the question of special packaging, colors, or sizes. If the other divisions wanted Secur-A-Tach packaged in lots of less than 1,000 or with the other division's own label, the marking systems division personnel felt that special charges would have to be made.

Corporate viewpoints. Mr. Frank Swisher, financial vice president of Dennison, said:

I see no valid substitute for transfer at cost. We have operated on this basis successfully and although we have had many discussions in the past, no argument for change has seemed compelling. Cost is a definite figure upon which we can get agreement. We don't spend our energy arguing about market value, etc. Transferring at cost has the added advantage of putting the emphasis on marketing. The selling division gets measured by its results.

Mr. Thomas Sturtevant, the assistant corporate controller, said:

I believe that we must maintain our policy of transferring goods at cost. If we change that, we will devote far too much energy to arguing about the rules of the game rather than playing it.

I do believe, however, that the division which develops a product should have first crack at the production capacity. They should be allowed to sell all they can; they spent the time and money to develop the product. Once they have sold all they can to their own market, I believe the products should be transferred to the other divisions at cost without a statistical measure of what the profit might have been. Our system is set up to measure the selling force. Production is simply a cost center for the divisions.

I can't see that the divisions should have a valid complaint if they are measured and paid on the basis of the rules set down at the beginning of the year. They will be judged on the basis that they were told they would be.

The individual product manager shouldn't really worry about his success being recognized. The commodity report will show both sales and gross margin received throughout the company on the sales of his product. When corporate officers want to know how much he has contributed to the company, they can easily find out.

Effect on managers' bonuses. Regardless of the decision reached on the transfer-price dispute, it appeared unlikely bonus payments to managers below the division level, including the product manager, would be noticeably affected. However, changes in profit distribution between the divisions did have a slight impact on the bonus of the divisional general managers, the divisional marketing managers, and the divisional production managers. In the case of industrial products, each $7,500 profit after marketing but before corporate expense ("Line 49" profit on Exhibit 3) meant an increment in bonus of 1% of their annual salary. In the case of marking systems, a $25,000 change would have the same effect. If for example, the industrial products division sold as little as $200,000 worth of Secur-A-Tach, the difference between transfer at cost and transfer at 35% off list as suggested by marking systems division would amount to 4% of the division management's annual salary. This would be from $600 to $1,000 per man.

The role of leadership in the
achievement of purpose

So far, we have discussed the formulation and execution of organizational mission without giving much emphasis to the role of the chief executive as a leader in these activities. We have made room, to be sure, for the general manager's personal values, aspirations, and sense of social responsibility, and in this respect we have gone beyond traditional organizational theory. But the personality of the chief executive has to this point been a shadow on our model rather than a part of it.

Review of the cases so far examined in the course of our study will, however, underscore the fact that individual personality leaves a vivid imprint on company affairs. While the mere projection of personal genius or desire, as in the case of Villchur of Acoustic Research, does not represent, in our opinion, the most effective relationship of personal leadership to corporate strategy, yet we know that without it there would be no company.

The choice of corporate purpose and the design and administration of organizational processes for accomplishing purpose are by no means impersonal procedures, unaffected by the characteristics of the leader. The study of leadership may be approached from many vantage points. Our concept of strategy can be used once again to give order and perspective to the multiple functions and roles of the general manager and to illumine the range of leadership styles which may either assist or impede organizational performance.

If we look back at the roles and activities of the general managers we have studied, we can identify three main aspects of leadership. First, we have seen the general manager as the architect of strategy. The requirements of this role are analytical ability, creativity, self-awareness, and sensitivity to society's expectations regarding the businessman's broader social responsibilities. Second, we have seen the general manager as an implementer of strategy, that is, as one who supplies organizational leadership. In this area, opportunities for choice are limited. Thus, if strategy is to be maintained, the organizational leader must promote and defend it; he must integrate the conflicting interests which necessarily arise around it; he must see to it that the organization's essential needs are met; and he must be the judge of results. Third, we have seen—but so far have not focused upon—the general manager as *personal leader*.

In the area of personal leadership, our lens narrows to the general manager as a person different from all other persons. Within the range of choice permitted by his own knowledge and command of himself he achieves a leadership style. This pattern of personal behavior reflects his individuality as much as his office; it does not follow inevitably from the organizational responsibilities he has assumed. The contribution made to company performance, character, and tone by the personal style of the leader and by his concept of his responsibilities will be our final area of inquiry. Thus we shall proceed in these notes from the impersonal and general to the highly personal and individual aspects of leadership.

The general manager as architect of strategy

From our assumption that strategy can and should be deliberately determined and specifically articulated, it follows that the general manager must play several roles. These carry with them stringent requirements, even though they imply no specific prescriptions as to what he should do. Thus, to be a leader in the activities of searching out and analyzing strategic alternatives and finally making or ratifying decisions among competing choices, the general manager must be an analyst. His need for intellectual ability equal to this requirement is fundamental; it becomes more compelling as alternatives become more difficult to evaluate and choices become harder to make. The rough-and-ready opportunist is not our preferred prototype, valuable as are his energy and ingenuity.

To find strategic choices that are not routine and to determine a strategy uniquely adapted to external opportunity and internal strengths requires the policy-making executive to be an innovator. The entrepreneurial or risk-taking element in strategy formulation often requires the strength to defy the apparent implications of industry trends and to deviate from conventional industry decisions. In folklore psychology, the personalities of the critical analyst and the energetic and creative innovator-entrepreneur are supposed to be antithetical. The strategist, however, must span these opposites. Fortunately, their irreconcilability has been greatly exaggerated.

In addition to powers of analysis and innovation, the strategist must have a sense of personal purpose and an awareness of personal needs. No general prescription can be offered as to what these purposes should be—only the need to bring personal goals into harmony with those suggested by external opportunity and corporate competence. Similarly, awareness of society's expectations requires the analyst-innovator to determine the extent to which he intends to take these expectations into account. In short, in his role as an architect of strategy the general manager examines and becomes informed about the environment external to his company, he examines his own organization, he examines himself, and he determines his own responsiveness to the multiple demands being made upon his company by elements of the community at large. In his role as strategist, he must often think and decide for himself. His role as organization leader is, however, a much less solitary one. As executive in charge of implementation, he is much less the lone planner than the doer embroiled on the field with the troops.

The general manager as organization leader

Since strategy does not become either acceptable or effective by virtue of being well designed and clearly announced, the successful implementation of strategy requires that the organization leader act as its promoter and defender. You will recall George Romney's efforts in American Motors to persuade long-time industry executives that the big car was not the key to company success, and that American could survive only by departing from the uniform practices of the three automotive "majors." Seven years and the departure of a number of top officials were required to effect this change.

The tendency of organizations to veer off course in response to circumstances, special interest, and sudden opportunity means that the general manager must be the defender of strategy. When in a recession year the American consumer turned to the compact car, Mr. Romney probably had little difficulty in promoting his strategy. But when the market changed again, his successor would have the problem of holding the line against those who wanted to follow the market. As Selznick points out in *Leadership and Administration*,[1] a given strategy is subject to being undermined until it has been institutionalized. A neutral body of men does not become a committed organization until goals have been "infused with value." It is the role of the general manager, therefore, not only to make the fundamental analytical-entrepreneurial decisions which are to determine the character of the organization, but also to present these to his organization in a way that appeals to the imagination and engages the support of members whose efforts are essential to success. An organization has to *prove* a strategic decision good or bad, quite apart from its intrinsic merit.

Like any administrator, the chief executive finds himself in the role of mediator and integrator. That is, he must deal with conflict among special interests and among organizational tendencies leading in different directions. For example, in his quest for results, he must become skilled at balancing the need for present profitability against the need to invest in future success. With financial analysts seizing on every quarterly report, he must look beyond the pressures they exert to the less insistent demands of long-term development. Similarly, in the administration of organizational systems, he must balance the desirability of uniformity against the requirement for flexibility, the needs of the individual against the needs of the organization, and

---

[1] P. Selznick, *Leadership and Administration* (Evanston, Ill.: Row, Peterson and Company, 1957).

the interests of special subgroups against the interests of the organization as a whole. The impossibility of resolving such conflicts to the complete satisfaction of all is a fact of life which he must accept. But this inevitability does not permit him to rely upon his own personal identification with one interest or another in place of seeking out the optimum adjustment as dictated by strategic rather than political or expedient considerations. Conflict in organization is inevitable and virtually necessary. Its occurrence, identification, and reconciliation is a daily affair in a healthy, striving association of competent and independent individuals. But progress against competition ultimately requires cooperation of a high order. Commitment to common purpose is ultimately the best assurance that the integration of differences can be achieved.

The general manager cannot effectively lead an organized advance toward chosen goals unless he is aware that his organization has certain needs that are not fulfilled simply by the pursuit of strategy itself. Individuals and departments demand recognition of the validity of their personal and organizational subgoals; individuals further require incentives for performance and a climate conducive to satisfying interpersonal associations and personal development. These things must be given attention for their own sake. Otherwise the intermeshed relationships and processes which are intended to enhance organizational performance will decline into unconstructive conflict and irrelevant activity. The management of NEFCO placed such considerations ahead of the need even to determine the combined mission of the merged organization.

Whether he is conscious of it or not, the general manager is responsible for what is often called the climate of his organization. Intangible as it may be, climate is readily felt. The term "climate" is used to designate the quality of the internal environment which conditions in turn the quality of cooperation, the development of individuals, the extent of members' dedication or commitment to organizational purpose, and the efficiency with which that purpose becomes translated into results. Climate is the atmosphere in which individuals help, judge, reward, constrain, and find out about each other. It influences morale—the attitude of the individual toward his work and his environment.

At the risk of being overprescriptive, but in the hope of suggesting the kind of climate most consistent with successful implementation of strategy, we offer the following description, which is shaped by the requirements of management development:

The most important characteristics of favorable climate from the point of view of management development appear to be these:

1. Absence of political maneuvering for position, with penalties for unfair personal competition and petty conspiracy.
2. Rejection of preferment on grounds other than approval of performance—i.e., blood relationships, friendship, and ethnic, educational, or social background.

3. High standards of excellence explicit in instructions for work as well as in its evaluation; expectations of continuous improvement and competence with increasing experience; disciplined attention to meeting detailed commitments.
4. High value assigned to interpersonal amity and tolerance of individual differences.
5. Willingness to take risks (and acceptance of the inevitability of occasional failure) in delegating responsibility to the relatively inexperienced.
6. Acceptance and encouragement of innovation with consequent freedom to act upon ideas. Disapproval in cases of failure attached to results and causes rather than to departure from conventional practice as such.
7. High standards of moral integrity, including rejection of expediency even at the cost of windfall profits.

The patient establishment and stubborn defense of these values is a practicable undertaking for the leader of an organization. No other duty of his office except perhaps the decision about objectives and strategy is as important.[2]

What is said here about executive development appears to us to apply equally well to a climate generally suitable for the successful accomplishment of strategic purposes. The general manager need not strive to create exactly the climate thus described, but he should determine, rather than leave to chance, the net effect upon people and purposes of the organizational processes over which he presides.

Important as climate is, the general manager must to some extent subordinate sensitivity to climate and members' personal needs to the dominant and inescapable requirements of his role as judge and critic of results. As persistently as Sir Halford Reddish, he must *insist upon* the accomplishment which has been projected and must apply the measures, rewards, and penalties available to this end. In this role he is not the supportive figure who listens sympathetically to all the reasons why something cannot be done. Rather, he holds fast to his conclusion that it will be done—unless prevented by external developments. When a decision is finally taken that reasonable accomplishment can and must take place according to plan, individuals who fail must, if necessary, be replaced. At some point, to preserve commitment and to remain on course, the needs of the organization must be asserted as primary. Commitment to strategy must be tested under adversity before it can be known to be effective. The range of the leadership role—from sensitivity to human needs to insistence upon required performance—has eluded many of the leaders whom we have seen at work. The instinctive, unschooled leader is likely to adopt one role—for example, the role of listener or the role of judge—and to stay in it regardless of circumstances.

The manager must play multiple roles to adapt his leadership to the changing requirements of the situation. He can keep from becoming confused only by steadfastly maintaining his own attention and directing that of others toward the purposes to be achieved. Though he knows that purposes must

[2]K. R. Andrews, *The Effectiveness of University Management Development Programs* (Boston: Division of Research, Harvard Graduate School of Business Administration, 1966), pp. 247–48.

change and that rigidity is harmful, he does not abandon course at the first sign of trouble. He avoids becoming overpreoccupied by internal conflict. Since executives in departmental positions are much more organizational leaders than architects of strategy, the general manager should expect that solving conflict and satisfying organizational needs should be much less his customary preoccupation than promoting and defending organizational purpose and harvesting organizational results.

The general manager as personal leader

A wide variety of leadership styles characterizes the behavior of the executive. Under the requirement that he press for planned results, the general manager may behave like a petty tyrant and use his power to abuse those whom he considers offenders. At the other extreme, he may inquire objectively into reasons for failure to achieve results expected, and without raising his voice he may establish a new schedule to match new conditions. He may turn to daily detailed reports to find some discrepancy with which to needle a subordinate, or he may work entirely through intermediaries in calling attention to lapses from standards. It is not appropriate here to review the classifications which have been applied to patterns of leadership. Thus, personalities have been said to range from dominant to inconspicuous; behavior from self-oriented to organization-oriented to people-oriented, or from task-centered to relationship-centered, or from autocratic to democratic to laissez-faire; and approaches from "classical" to "human relations" to "revisionist."[3]

Different kinds of personal leadership may be characterized in various ways, *ad infinitum.* The classification is less important than the possibility that *leadership style is not necessarily innate or entirely dominated by personality.* Even if the roles which the general manager must play are many, and if he must shift from one to another in response to need, yet it may be possible for him to create for himself a distinctive style which will characterize his performance in all his roles—a style which will be both satisfactory to him and functional in its effect upon his followers.

Men in leadership positions are not required to have a personality of any given mold. The effort to relate personality traits to executive effectiveness is no longer pursued as naïvely as once it was. Business leaders generally are likely to be characterized by such qualities as drive, intellectual ability, initiative, creativeness, social ability, and flexibility. These qualities permit a fairly wide range of style so long as it is dynamic and energetic. Obviously, our prescriptions regarding effective leadership would be faulty if they required an individual to do violence to his own personal needs or to convert his natural powers to artifice. Awareness of the impact of his natural force-

---

[3]See, for example, R. Tannenbaum and W. H. Schmidt, "How to Choose a Leadership Pattern," *Harvard Business Review,* March-April 1958, p. 95; and W. G. Bemis, "Revisionist Theory of Leadership," *Harvard Business Review,* January-February 1961, pp. 26 ff.

fulness upon his organization is likely to be adequate for tempering the leader's distinctive behavior to organizational needs.

The general manager will, therefore, examine his own characteristic behavior to try to see whether it meets or complicates the needs of his own organization and whether it directs or distracts the attention given by his followers to organizational goals. To some extent, depending on his powers of self-control, he can modify his behavior in the direction of the need he sees.

The charismatic leader, who, by virtue of his personal magnetism, energy, and force, influences his followers to efforts they would not otherwise make is providing a personal contribution to the implementation of strategy which the less conspicuous administrator cannot effect. Sir Halford Reddish is a dramatic personality who, no doubt, has inspired his followers on occasion with admiration, fear, gratitude, and affection. At the same time he has succeeded in dramatizing organizational strategy. He personifies purpose rather than personal power. Although it is not necessary to be flamboyant or eccentric, strategy is well served if the leader is a man whose personal purposes are known and whose commitment to organizational purposes is conspicuous. The sheep in sheep's clothing may be quietly effective, but he does not inspire. When adversity obscures the prospects of success and organizational morale falters, dynamic and articulate leadership—centered upon achievement rather than personality—can make the difference between success and failure.

It must, of course, be admitted that charisma may be more conspicuous than effective. It may evoke in subordinates indignation and amused tolerance rather than heightened accomplishment. The more important danger is that the genuinely strong leader will produce weakness in his organization. Personal strength leads to organizational weakness when fear replaces initiative or awe obscures independent judgment.

Evaluating the contribution that dynamic personal leadership can make to organizational performance, we look for its effects in the dramatization of goals and in the motivation of membership to more than mediocre effort. Strategy is once again the criterion against which we evaluate the effectiveness of the phenomenon under study.

For those who are themselves currently engaged in developing personal values and objectives, it is vitally important to consider the extent to which the role of personal leadership is shaped by personal goals. Harmony between leadership style and the ends sought is essential to effectiveness. It is possible that it can be cultivated.

The quality of leadership

We should like therefore to suggest, at the risk of appearing unrealistic, that the principal contribution that personal leadership can make to organizational performance is the projection of the leader's own quality as a person. The depth and durability of his personal values, his personal inner standards of excellence, and the clarity of his integrity can be influential. Corporate purposes are by definition a projection in part of the leader's own personal goals and a reflection of his character. Though the spotlight of fashion today falls upon the business applications of advanced research in the social sciences and in mathematical decision making, we can borrow from Emerson and say that a corporation is essentially the lengthened shadow of a man. It is the mission of the business leader to instill into the organization a tone and quality which, though it may elude measurement, is not unimportant on that account. In the company in which one executive says to another, "Let's have no hanky panky on expense accounts until this stock issue has been completed," it is not hard to project the ethical level of the total enterprise. At the other extreme, the expectations of responsible behavior in The Rugby Portland Cement Company must be as clear as day.

We come to the point where the influence of the leader takes effect through *the person he is* rather than the roles he fills. The character of the leader may be decisive in creating organizational commitment of the depth and quality required by bold purposes or by adverse competitive circumstances. Disagreements about the extent to which ethical behavior can be prescribed do not obscure the plain fact that, for men of goodwill, ethical leadership is more inspiring than that which is not. Few people have problems in distinguishing the difference. The general manager as a personal leader is finally significant not so much because he is the dramatist of organizational progress and performance as because he is the exemplar of the most durable of human aspirations—the desire to devote one's powers to causes worth serving. Purpose attracts commitment when it deserves to do so. Leadership is finally most effective when it clarifies the quality of purpose.

A NOTE ON THE MANUFACTURE AND DISTRIBUTION OF PORTLAND CEMENT IN THE UNITED KINGDOM*

Cement manufacture

Portland cement was developed from an invention of a laborer in Leeds, England, in 1824. It was called "portland" cement because the concrete made from it resembled the well-known Portland building stone in color and texture. Its manufacture is today a major world industry. World consumption has risen from 81 million tons in 1938 to 315 million in 1960 and is still rising.

Cement itself is manufactured from a closely controlled mixture of calcium carbonate, alumina, and silica. Calcium carbonate is found in various forms of limestone fairly liberally throughout the world. To be suitable for the manufacture of cement, the calcium carbonate content of the limestone must be relatively free from impurity. Soft chalk, which is very high in calcium carbonate, is found uniquely on either side of the English Channel toward the southern part of the North Sea. Chalk is easier to process than hard limestone, and its availability accounts, in part, for the fact that nearly half of British production is located in southeastern England.

Alumina is found in some forms of clay or shale. A relatively small amount of sand supplies the silica requirements.

From 3,000 to 3,600 pounds of raw materials are required to make a ton of cement. These are quarried with large diesel or electric-power shovels and conveyed to the works, which is normally placed nearby. There they are crushed and ground to a fine powder, and—in what is known as the "wet process"—mixed in strictly controlled proportions with water to form cement slurry. (Slurry normally contains about 40% water by weight.) The liquid state of the mixture is necessary to facilitate a perfectly homogeneous mixture of the raw materials and to permit rapid adjustment of the proportions by

---

*Much of the material included in this description was taken, with permission, from a paper, "The Manufacture and Distribution of Cement," prepared by the Chairman of The Rugby Portland Cement Company Ltd., Rugby, England.

Copyright 1964 by l'Institut pour l'Etude des Méthodes de Direction l'Entreprise (IMEDE), Lausanne, Switzerland. Reprinted by permission.

merely adding materials which quickly become uniformly dispersed through-out the liquid.

The slurry, when chemically correct, is fed to the kiln, which in a modern works is a large steel cylinder from 300 to 500 feet in length and 9 to 14 feet in diameter. It rotates at the rate of approximately once every 45 seconds, on a slightly inclined axis. The slurry is fed in at the higher end.

Near the lower end of the kiln is the burning zone, where fuel is injected into the kiln and fired to produce a temperature of about 2,500°F. Pulverized coal is the usual fuel in Britain, but oil and natural gas are used in other countries where these fuels are readily available. The water in the slurry is driven off as steam, together with the carbon dioxide content of the calcium carbonate and minor quantities of other gases. The remaining materials are fluxed in the intense heat and leave the kiln in the form of pea-sized nodules called "cement clinker." The chemical part of the process, completed at this point, is closely controlled throughout by chemists who test the raw materials, the coal, and the slurry every hour, day and night.

Thereafter, the process is largely mechanical. The cement clinker is ground in large water-cooled mills to a predetermined fineness, and a small amount of calcium sulphate, or gypsum, is added, in order to control the "setting time" of the resultant powder, now finished cement.

As it leaves the mills, the cement is weighed automatically and then pumped through pipes by compressed air to the large concrete silos in which it is stored. It remains in storage until it is withdrawn by mechanical means to the packing plant, where it is packed into paper sacks, which are auto-matically filled, sealed, weighed, and delivered by means of conveyors to the truck, the rail car, or the ship. It may be withdrawn from the silos into special bulk trucks which deliver it unpacked.

The uses of cement

Cement is used as the binding agent in concrete and in mortar. Concrete, one of the world's primary construction materials, is composed of cement, sand, aggregate (clean gravel and stones), and water. Cement reacts chem-ically with the water and hardens, within a few hours after mixing, binding the sand and gravel particles in a solid mass. Concrete can be used without reinforcing (as in highway pavements, which contain only wire matting for temperature stresses), or it can be used with steel reinforcement, as in build-ings and bridges.

The structure of the industry in the United Kingdom, 1960

The cement industry in the United Kingdom consists of six financially independent groups, all of which have been members of the Cement Makers' Federation since its establishment in 1934.

The three largest interests held, in 1960, about 88% of the home market and have provided much of the leadership within the Federation. Associated Portland Cement Manufacturers Limited is considerably the largest company, with about 62% of the United Kingdom market. The Tunnel Group and The Rugby Portland Cement Company Limited have each about 14% of the United Kingdom market. Practically all the United Kingdom export trade is conducted by these three makers, which are also the only companies having manufacturing subsidiaries abroad.

The Federation regulates the internal affairs of the industry and arranges an interchange of technical information and industry-wide statistics. By far its most important function, however, is establishing the basis of selling prices and conditions of sale, in order, it is asserted, that the costs of distribution —which average nearly 20% of delivered cost of cement—can be controlled. Membership is voluntary, and voting power is proportionate, although not directly, to the previous year's home deliveries. Approval of any proposal, however, requires the concurrence of at least four of the nine members. The Federation has no control over the production of any manufacturer, nor is it concerned with the export trade.

The British cement industry also maintains a large research and promotional organization, the Cement and Concrete Association, part of whose function is to increase the use and uses of concrete. Cement itself has no substitute; however, it is used only to form concrete, which is in competition with steel, brick, stone, tile, timber, and many other materials.

The industry also organizes its conduct of labor relations. For more than 35 years it has operated a National Joint Industrial Council at which industry-wide wage rates and working conditions are set. The industry has never had a national strike or lockout. Holidays with pay and profit-sharing plans were features of the industry for many years before World War II.

Postwar growth of the industry

The postwar progress made by the industry is shown in Exhibit 1.

Exhibit 1

U.K. CEMENT DELIVERIES
(000 Tons)

	Home	Export	Total
1939	7,587	665	8,252
1946	5,479	1,095	6,574
1951	8,144	1,974	10,119
1952	9,147	2,055	11,202
1953	9,335	1,917	11,253
1954	10,079	1,769	11,848
1955	10,759	1,766	12,526
1956	11,275	1,600	12,875
1957	10,709	1,382	12,091
1958	10,675	1,145	11,820
1959	11,683	1,088	12,771
1960	12,463	1,000	13,463
1961	13,800	800	14,600
1962	13,768	315	14,083
1963	13,715	251	13,966
1964	16,545	258	16,803

The economics of the industry

Siting of the plant. It is considered a matter of prime importance that cement plants be located as close as possible to raw material deposits. Adequate water supplies, fuel, and electricity and access to road, rail, and water transport must also be available. Thorough technical investigation is required, since both the physical and chemical properties of the raw materials will influence the design of many of the factory components.

Costs of production. The manufacture of cement is a highly mechanized process and employs comparatively little labor. The capital investment is among the highest for any industry; it equals almost £20,000 per man employed, which is over six times what it was before the War. Depreciation is therefore a heavy charge, and will become progressively heavier as prewar plants are replaced.

Coal is the largest individual item in the cost of production. It takes approximately 800 pounds of coal, including the coal used to generate electricity, to make a ton of cement.

In general, industry production costs are distributed as follows:

	Per Cent
Coal and power	45–50
Direct labor	10–15
Consumable equipment	9–12
Depreciation (installed cost)	9–12
Indirect factory labor and other overheads (supervision, testing, maintenance, cost accounting, etc.)	15–20
Manufacture cost	100
Average haulage	20–30 of M.C.
Sales expense	5– 8 of M.C.
General administrative overhead	10–15 of M.C.

Profit margins are not disclosed. It has been asserted that current prices allow profits only because the manufacturers are still using, in part, equipment installed in the late 1930's. As greater proportions of new, more expensive plant installations are brought into use, prices may rise to cover increased depreciation charges.

Leaders of the British cement industry have repeatedly stated that manufacture of cement in the United Kingdom has for years been conducted with the highest efficiency and one of the lowest unit costs of any producing country in the world.

Distribution. The distribution of cement to the site where it will be used is a more technical and complicated problem than at first sight appears, for it is not the cost of production at the place where the cement is made but the cost at the site where it will be used that is important. The geographical distribution of demand, which in itself varies quite considerably from year to year (and can be materially distorted at different times by large airport programs, road works, reservoirs, and similar forms of construction using large quantities of cement), is not coincident with the geographical distribution of the works.

Many companies in the industry maintain a fleet of trucks for road delivery. Little bagged cement goes by rail, owing to the costs of double-handling. Delivery in bulk (in special vehicles both by road and rail) has rapidly increased in recent years and now accounts for nearly 60% of the home trade.

Pricing and the role of the cement makers federation

The manufacturers feel that a joint policy of distribution and price can avoid the severe price competition which, in the early 1930's, created difficulties for both producers and users. For example, a works near to a large consuming area might be able to supply only one third of the demand in that area, leaving the remaining two thirds to come from a much greater distance. If there were not a coordinated price policy, it has been said, a builder taking his supplies from the nearer works would pay one price, while his competitor would have to pay a higher price for cement coming from a more distant works. This would assertedly lead to endless complications in bidding for construction projects.

The Federation's price arrangements, therefore, have the following objectives:[1]

1. To sell and distribute cement throughout the country in the most efficient and economical manner commensurate with the interests of the country as a whole, of the users of cement, and of the manufacturers—in particular by:
   a) Encouraging the delivery in any particular area from the nearest works, with the object of avoiding unnecessary and wasteful haulage.
   b) Eliminating depots (except where these perform useful functions) and delivering straight from works to construction sites.
   c) Providing a stable system of prices which takes into account the high proportion of the cost of transport in the price of cement and avoids disproportionate price differentials which would otherwise arise between various parts of the U.K.
2. To provide a price system giving sufficient stability to enable manufacturers individually and collectively to plan production in advance efficiently and economically, and individually to undertake the heavy expenditure required to meet increasing demand for cement.
3. To ensure during any temporary shortage of cement that prices remain at a reasonable level.
4. To eliminate unnecessary and expensive advertising.
5. To provide for standard forms of packages, bulk delivery, and the like.
6. To arrange, for the convenience of both manufacturers and buyers, standard conditions of supply and forms of quotation and contract.
7. To facilitate joint research and exchange of information to improve the standard and the potential utility of cement.

To achieve these aims, the Federation's present system provides for the

---

[1]Summarized from a policy statement of the Federation.

same delivered price at the same point of delivery for all brands of cement, irrespective of the works from which the cement may come.

There are 48 cement works in the U.K. (Cement works very near one another usually have the same base price.) There are 37 base prices, one for each location where cement is manufactured. These base prices are nearly the same at every factory, although there are slight variations made for the type of raw materials used and the delivered price of fuel to the works. For the former, for instance, plants using chalk as their source of calcium carbonate have base prices about 5 per cent lower than those using limestone, since all limestone crushing and grinding expenses are eliminated. In 1961, the base factory price (delivered within five miles of plant) of ordinary portland cement ranged from 111/6d. to 127/6d. per ton.

Radiating from each works is a series of concentric circles at four- or five-mile intervals, the circles from any particular works continuing until they meet the circles radiating from another works. The delivered price within each of these circles increases by 1/6d. for each of the first six circles and by 1/- for each subsequent circle (see Exhibit 2).

These price increments do not, in fact, cover actual transportation costs; therefore, manufacturers allow 10–15% of the base price plus the zone price increments for covering haulage costs. As a result, between 20 and 30 miles from a producing unit is considered the "break-even" haulage distance, below which haulage costs are less than the allowance in the base price plus the incremental price increases, and above which the converse is true. The more efficiently a producer can operate his truck fleet, the greater will be his break-even haulage distance.

The pricing scheme means that every buyer at a particular point will pay exactly the same price for his cement. It also means that there is every inducement for a manufacturer to save transport costs by selling as much of his production as possible within the circles controlled by his own works. The further he delivers cement from his own works, the more likely he is to run into the circles controlled by another works, where the price he will receive will begin to decrease. The Federation asserts that the effect of this arrangement is to save as much as possible of the heavy transport costs and so maintain throughout the country, on the average, a lower level of prices than would otherwise be the case.

There exist standard merchant discounts. Retail building material suppliers are entitled to a merchant's discount, but they in turn must sell cement at the same prices, in the particular zones, which apply to the manufacturers. Thus a buyer pays the same price whether he buys from a manufacturer or a merchant. Merchants play a major role in supplying small orders, since the minimum order normally accepted by a manufacturer is six tons. A relatively small percentage of industry sales is made directly to merchants for their own accounts, but much more cement is delivered to the customer "on site" at a merchant's order.

Exhibit 2

ILLUSTRATION OF THE FEDERATION'S PRICING AGREEMENT

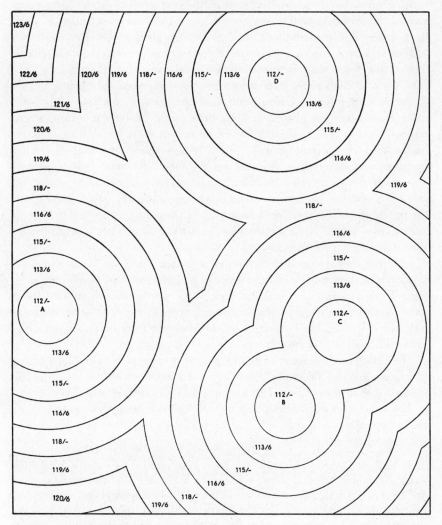

Sales price in shillings and pence per ton shown for each four- or five-mile zone.

The Restrictive Trade Practices Act

In 1956 England passed the Restrictive Trade Practices Act, which required that all trade agreements be registered with the Registrar of the Restrictive Practices Court. These agreements subsequently had to be justified before the court, which would decide whether they were contrary to the public interest. On March 16, 1961, the Restrictive Practices Court handed down its decision: it upheld the Federation's price agreements with only minor modifications.

In essence, the Federation argued that, because of its price-fixing agreement, U.K. cement manufacturers could operate with more certainty of profit than under free competition. Because of this greater security, they were willing to accept a lower return on investment and thus could sell cement appreciably lower than if prices had not been fixed.

Experts on both sides agreed that, in order to attract new capital into the industry, a net return on investment of at least 15% would have to be available. The Federation proved that, in order to yield such a return, a new cement plant would have to price its cement at least 25 shillings per ton higher than the current average price. It also established that Federation members were earning, on the average, less than 10% return on investment. The court therefore concluded that, had the price-fixing arrangement not existed, the price of cement would have been "significantly" higher, and the public would have suffered accordingly. Thus the court upheld the main price-fixing clause. It found that the industry was efficient and had acted with a sense of responsibility.

The presiding judge was concerned only that the price-fixing agreement should be as honorably administered in the future as had been true in the past. Thus he requested, and the Federation agreed, that if at any future date the Registrar should wish to determine whether prices were still being kept at a fair level, the Federation would cooperate fully by making cost and price data available for inspection.

The Federation's practice of giving quantity discounts based on total annual purchases from *all* Federation members was disallowed by the judge, on the grounds that it did not reflect true economies from volume sales.

The court also scrutinized, and upheld with one exception, minor agreements regarding terms of sale. In summing up his decision, Mr. Justice Diplock remarked:

> In the result, therefore, the Respondents have satisfied us that the main price-fixing conditions, other than those providing for general rebates to large users and large merchants, are not contrary to the public interest, and that the ancillary restrictions, other than that relating to the prohibition upon the quotations and contracts for the supply of cement for periods exceeding twelve months, are also not contrary to the public interest.[2]

In commenting on the court's decision, Sir Halford Reddish observed:

> I am not being wise after the event if I say that the judgement accorded closely with our expectations, for we were confident throughout that a detailed examination of our arrangements would show conclusively that they were in the public interest, and the cement makers were not alone in their satisfaction with

---

[2]*Judgment in the Restrictive Practices Court on an agreement between Members of the Cement Makers' Federation,* printed by the Cement and Concrete Association, 1961.

the outcome of the case. Over four thousand buyers of cement sent us replies to a questionnaire before the hearing: something like 97 per cent of them were strongly in favour of a continuation of the present system."[3]

---

[3]*Investors Chronicle*, March 24, 1961.

THE RUGBY PORTLAND CEMENT COMPANY LIMITED (A)*

^^^

History and growth

The forerunner of the present Rugby Company began producing lime in the early nineteenth century at a works near Rugby, England. Cement manufacture began at the works in the late 1820's, and thereafter became its principal business. Its "Crown Cement" trademark was registered a few years later. In 1925, the then existing partnership became a private limited company with a share capital of £100,000 owned by descendants of the previous partners. In 1929, Mr. (now Sir[1]) Halford Reddish, a chartered accountant with a consulting practice, joined the board which previously had comprised only representatives of the two descendant branches of the original owners. Four years later, upon the death of the general manager, Sir Halford became managing director, and shortly afterwards, chairman.

At that time, the cement industry was in the middle of a deep depression. Prices were at a very unprofitable level. In spite of this crisis, Sir Halford decided to expand and modernize the company's production facilities. Contrary to previous industry tradition, he also decided to operate the plant 52 weeks in the year, thus ensuring steady employment for all the employees. Despite the depression and difficulties of selling the increased output, a profit was realized at the end of the first year of the new management. In 1934 a second manufacturing site was obtained when a nearby company went into receivership. Erection of a new factory at the second site plus the modernization and expansion of the Rugby works required substantial fresh capital. In 1935, the company became a public company with its shares quoted on the London Stock Exchange, and additional capital of £140,000 was introduced. Since that time, additional equity capital has been raised by occasional "rights" issues.

Rugby also acquired substantial chalk-bearing lands near Dunstable (about 48 miles to the south of its Warwickshire plants) from which high calcium carbonate chalk was railed daily to its Warwickshire plants.

[1]In early 1958, Her Majesty Queen Elizabeth II knighted Mr. Halford Reddish for his public services.

In 1936, Rugby acquired a third site and erected its Rochester works. In 1939, another company was purchased and its facilities were combined with those at Rochester. In 1945, Rugby acquired another company, and although its production facilities were closed, Rugby used its brand name and distribution organization.

Rugby made major additions to its three plants in Great Britain after 1946.

In 1962 Rugby acquired the entire share capital of Eastwoods Cement Limited (owning three cement plants in the United Kingdom) and in 1963 the entire share capital of Chinnor Industries Limited (owning one cement plant in the United Kingdom). Both are now wholly owned subsidiaries.

During 1964, the Stock Exchange value of the company's shares fluctuated between £45 million and £50 million.

During the immediate postwar years, export trade was very profitable, with unit margins several times those of the home market sales. The proportion of Rugby's deliveries accounted for by exports reached a maximum in 1951 and 1952 at about 43%. In 1961, however, Sir Halford said that in recent years export sales had become almost marginal because of the increased competition (much of it subsidized) from non-British manufacturers and the growth of cement industries in areas formerly importing cement. Rugby had itself established overseas subsidiaries and built manufacturing plants in Trinidad and western Australia. The former started production in 1954, and the latter in 1955. Both units were able to supply cement at substantially lower prices than existing imported cement and made useful contributions to Rugby's consolidated profits.

With a rapidly developing local market plus export trade in the eastern Caribbean, the Trinidad factory had to be extended within less than five years of starting its operation. In 1963 the capacity of the Australian plant had to be doubled.

In highlighting Rugby's growth, Sir Halford said in 1964:

In 1933 we had the one not very modern works at Rugby and total net assets with a book value of £109,250. At the end of 1963 the total net assets of the company at book value amounted to £23,965,537. (The real value today is substantially higher.) Additional capital introduced from 1st January 1933 to 31st December 1963 amounted to £23,856,287.

Shareholders have subscribed for shares (including premiums)	£ 9,200,000
by leaving profits in the company	13,262,287
And others (by minority interests in, or loans to, subsidiary companies)	1,394,000
	£23,856,287

Net profit before taxes rose from less than £4,000 in 1933 to almost £2.7 million in 1963. Postwar growth produced 18 years of successive record group profits, 1945–63 (see Exhibits 1–3). Early in 1965 Sir Halford stated that 1964 would be the nineteenth.

By the end of 1964 the nine company works and their annual capacities in tons were:

UNITED KINGDOM

Southam	500,000	Barrington	500,000
Rochester	400,000	Ferriby	125,000
Rugby	320,000	Lewes	75,000
Chinnor			280,000

OVERSEAS

Trinidad	185,000	Western Australia	250,000

The organization, 1965

It is understood that the company is planning to increase its annual productive capacity by some 1¼ million tons in the near future.

The company also operates extensive chalk quarries near Dunstable, some 48 miles from Rugby.

At the end of 1964, Rugby had about 2,400 employees in its seven U.K. factories, other U.K. subsidiaries, overseas operation, and headquarters in Rugby, England.

The board of directors (January 1965) consists of four executive directors and four "outside" (i.e., nonexecutive) directors.

The executive directors are Sir Halford Reddish, chairman and managing director; Mr. R. L. Evans, for many years deputy managing director, now a managing director; Mr. M. K. Smith, head of the legal department; and Mr. Maurice Jenkins, assistant managing director.

Sir Halford plays a leading role in all major policy decisions, and is particularly concerned with financial management, public relations, and the general "leadership" of the company.

Mr. Evans (also a chartered accountant) joined the company in 1934, and he and Sir Halford have worked closely together in the development of the business. As second in command he in effect heads the administration department, a small control and coordination group consisting of assistants to the managing directors, whose main work is to coordinate the activities of the functional and service departments and the subsidiary companies.

Sir Halford, who is director of four other major companies in the U.K. and a member of several semipublic councils, spends the greater part of each week in London; but he and Mr. Evans normally meet in Rugby on Sunday mornings to discuss current problems and to do forward planning for "two or three balance sheets ahead."

Mr. Smith generally confines himself to the legal aspects of the company's affairs.

Mr. Jenkins, who was for some time personal assistant to the chairman,

Exhibit 1. THE RUGBY PORTLAND CEMENT COMPANY LIMITED

Consolidated Balance Sheet Statements, 1946 and 1951–63

(1,000's of £)

ASSETS	1946	1951	1952	1953	1954	1955	1956	1957	1958	1959	1960	1961	1962	1963
Current assets	576	1,847	1,982	2,616	3,836	4,211	4,521	4,195	4,692	6,744	7,597	8,226	14,293	14,736
Fixed assets (1937 valuation or cost if subsequently acquired)	1,673	3,271	3,591	3,876	6,171	7,861	8,613	9,309	9,487	9,809	10,627	11,258	12,060	21,905
Less: Accumulated depreciation	436	987	1,125	1,261	1,562	1,635	1,969	2,306	2,601	3,008	3,456	3,930	4,414	5,240
Net fixed assets	1,237	2,285	2,466	2,616	4,609	6,226	6,644	7,003	6,886	6,801	7,171	7,328	7,646	16,665
Investment in subsidiary companies (not consolidated)	209	33	393	793	760	…	…	…	…	…	…	…	2,603	…
Total Assets	2,022	4,165	4,841	6,025	9,205	10,437	11,165	11,198	11,578	13,545	14,768	15,554	24,542	31,401
LIABILITIES AND NET WORTH														
Current liabilities	367	1,355	814	776	1,327	1,498	1,759	1,292	1,190	1,191	1,364	1,328	1,931	7,436
Debt capital:														
4% debenture	420	…	…	…	…	…	…	…	…	…	…	…	…	…
Mortgage loans 5/par	…	…	…	…	…	400	480	560	640	720	800	768	736	704
4½% unsecured loan 1957-62	…	…	1,000	1,500	1,500	1,500	1,500	1,500	1,500	1,500	1,500	1,500	…	…
Total Debt	420	…	1,000	1,500	1,500	1,900	1,980	2,060	2,140	2,220	2,300	2,268	736	704
Share capital:														
4% and 6% preference shares	325	825	825	825	825	825	825	825	825	825	825	825	1,000	1,000
Ordinary shares 5/par	325	500	500	750	1,250	1,500	1,500	1,500	1,500	1,750	2,000	2,000	3,000	7,500
"A" shares 1/par	…	…	…	…	…	50	50	50	50	50	50	50	50	300
Capital reserve	325	610	563	810	1,265	1,300	1,358	1,415	1,275	2,133	1,950	2,002	9,818	5,330
Revenue reserves:														
General reserve	100	500	500	750	1,125	1,500	1,750	2,000	…*	…	…	…	…	…
Reserve for future taxation	…	249	408	504	352†	390	320	303	350	1,000‡	1,217	1,373	1,364	1,404
Reserve for ordinary and "A" share dividend payment (Net)	161	52	55	55	115	201	230	230	276	329	383	383	544	689
Undistributed profit	…	73	175	56	120	106	275	451	2,947	3,067‡	3,741	4,520	5,352	6,348
Total Capital and Reserves	1,236	2,809	3,026	3,750	5,102	5,873	6,308	6,774	7,223	9,154	10,166	11,153	21,128	22,571
Interest of outside shareholders in a subsidiary company	…	…	…	…	1,277	1,165	1,117	1,072	1,025	980	938	805	747	690
Total Liabilities and Net Worth	2,022	4,165	4,841	6,025	9,205	10,437	11,165	11,198	11,578	13,545	14,768	15,554	24,542	31,401
Net working capital	210	491	1,168	1,841	2,510	2,712	2,762	2,903	3,502	5,553	6,233	6,898	12,362	7,300
Equity/debt ratio	2.9/1	3.0/1	3.0/1	2.5/1	3.4/1	3.1/1	3.2/1	3.3/1	3.4/1	4.1/1	4.4/1	4.9/1	28.7/1	32.1/1

*In 1958 the general reserve was merged with undistributed profit.

†During 1954, £125,000 was transferred from reserve for taxation into general reserve. With reductions in profits tax rate, the tax reserve established by the company in the two previous years exceeded its new liability.

‡In 1959, £440,000 was transferred from undistributed profit to capital reserve for future taxation, against the contingency of overseas profits being brought to the U.K. at some future date.

Exhibit 2

CONSOLIDATED PROFIT AND LOSS ACCOUNT, 1946 AND 1951–63
(1,000's of £)

	1946		1951		1952		1953		1954	
Consolidated trading profits	213		522		656		744		904	
Other income	...		19		20		24		27	
Less: Depreciation	79		124		142		136		210	
	£	%	£	%	£	%	£	%	£	%
Net profit before taxes	134	100	417	100	534	100	633	100	721	1†
Taxation—profits tax*	} 39		100		102		125		62	
Income tax			150		255		300		313	
Total Taxes	39	29	250	60	357	67	425	67	375	§
Net profit after taxes	95		167		177		208		346	
Preference dividends	12	9	21	5	21	4	22	3	22	
Ordinary dividends (net)	22	16	52	12	55	10	55	9	115	
"A" share dividends (net)	...		...		...		...		...	
Retained in business	61	46	94	23	101	19	131	21	209	
Ordinary dividend per share (gross)	7½d		1/–d		1/–d		1/–d		1/–d	
Capital distribution per share (gross)	3d		3d		3d		3d		...	
"A" share dividend per share (gross)										
Net profit before taxes as return on total capital and reserves	10.85%		14.87%		17.65%		19.50%‡		17.65%	
Gross ordinary dividend as return on capital equity employed, i.e., ordinary shares plus disclosed reserves (less reserves credited to "A" shares)	4.36%		5.04%		4.54%		4.12%‡		6.20%	

Profits tax was the estimated liability for the year ending with the statement. *Income tax* was the estimated liabi‖ on the profits of the year. This procedure gives rise to the reserve for future income tax in the balance sh‖ The estimated income tax for the future period is put into this reserve; and at the end of each year, the actual liability for the year is withdrawn from the reserve and put into current liabilities, from which the actual remitta‖ is made.

†In December 1963 scrip issues were made: ordinary shares, 3 for 2; "A" shares, 5 for 1. The equivalent divide‖ on the previous capital would therefore be as follows: ordinary is 6¾d; "A" 3/9d.

‡Excluding the £500,000 of additional capital introduced at end of 1953.

§Excluding the £1,000,000 of additional capital introduced at end of 1954.

was appointed assistant managing director on January 1, 1965. He works closely with Sir Halford and Mr. Evans in the general administration of the company.

Apart from the administration department already mentioned, the head office is organized into seven main departments:

Functional:	Service:
Engineering	Accounting
Production	Legal
Sales	Secretarial
Transport	

The sales department under a general sales manager is further subdivided under five sales managers: the northern area, the midland area, the eastern area, the London and southern area, and export respectively.

The secretarial department also embraces property management and insurance departments.

Each head of a department or subdepartment has a trained deputy.

Exhibit 2—Continued

1955	1956	1957	1958	1959	1960	1961	1962	1963
1,256	1,369	1,397	1,500	1,877	2,183	2,465	2,691	3,415
39	65	51	52	57	99	105	105	102
—270	340	342	381	443	506	550	535	861
%	£ %	£ %	£ %	£ %	£ %	£ %	£ %	
5 100	1,093 100	1,106 100	1,171 100	1,491 100	1,777 100	2,020 100	2,260 100	2,656
5	109	135	60	45	88	174	125	77
5	255	235	260	475	550	602	675	556
0 43	364 33	370 34	320 27	520 35	638 36	776 38	800 36	633
5	729	736	851	971	1,139	1,244	1,460	2,023
23 2	23 2	23 2	23 2	24 2	24 1	24 1	27 1	31
72 17	194 18	194 18	230 20	268 18	306 17	306 15	460 20	574
29 3	36 3	36 3	46 4	61 4	77 4	77 4	84 4	115
51 35	477 44	484 44	553 47	618 41	732 41	837 42	889 39	1,303
1/-d	1/1½d	1/1½d	1/3d	1/3d	1/3d	1/3d	1/3d	7½d†
...	...	...	...	...	...	...	...	...
1/-d	1/3d	1/3d	1/6d	2/_d	2/6d	2/6d	2/9d	7½d†
7.42%	17.30%	16.30%	16.20%	16.29%	17.48%	18.11%	10.69%	11.77%
6.09%	6.36%	5.84%	6.06%	5.43%	5.56%	5.06%	3.82%	4.47%

Each plant is in charge of a works manager (who is a fully qualified engineer) reporting to the chief engineer and the production manager at head office. Immediately under him is an assistant works manager, a chief chemist, a works engineer, and a works electrician. Then come foremen in charge respectively of the quarry, the yard (loco shunting operations and the yard gang of general laborers), engineering maintenance, electrical maintenance, and packing plant, with charge-hands in each case. Shift supervisors are on duty for the process plant which is a continuous operation. The chief tester (under the chief chemist) is in control of all the laboratory testers. The storekeeper, works clerk, sales-order clerk, and despatch clerk come under the assistant works manager.

Reasons for growth

Sir Halford feels that the company's growth and profitability are attributable to several interrelated activities. But overriding them all, he insists, is the human element—good human relations, which he defines simply as a recognition of the essential human dignity of the individual.

"The efficiency, the good name, the prestige, the progress of any business," he says, "depend in the final analysis, not on the magnificence of its plant, not on the splendour of its offices, but on the spirit of the human beings who

Exhibit 3

INDICES OF DELIVERIES, PROFIT, AND NET WORTH

1946–64

(Base: 1946 = 100)

Year	Deliveries[a]	Capital[b]	Profits
1946	100	100	100
1947	105	184[c]	140
1948	138	203	195
1949	139	208	214
1950	155	219	262
1951	168	227	311
1952	208	245	398
1953	214	303[d]	473
1954	238	413[e]	538
1955	302	475	765
1956	307	510	816
1957	294	548	825
1958	296	584	874
1959	319	741[f]	1,113
1960	357	822	1,326
1961	388	902	1,507
1962	395	1,709[g]	1,686
1963	562	1,826[h]	1,982
1964	714	n.a.	n.a.

[a]These are total group deliveries, in tons, used as an index basing point.

[b]"Capital" here equals total equity capital, including reserves.

[c]In 1947, £1,000,000 of new capital was raised: £500,000 from new preference shares sold, and £500,000 from new common shares. Without this sale of shares, the index would have remained at 100.

[d]In 1953, £500,000 of new common shares were sold. Without this sale, the index at the end of 1953 would have been 265.

[e]In 1954, £1,050,000 of new capital was raised, £50,000 by the sale of "A" shares, £1,000,000 by the sale of new common shares. Without this new capital, the index would have been 330 at the end of 1954.

[f]In 1959, £1,075,000 of new capital was raised through sale of common shares. Without this sale, the index would have been 655 at the end of 1959.

[g]In 1962, the capital was increased—first, by a rights issue of 2,000,000 ordinary shares at 45/6d. each: and later by the issue to the stockholders of Eastwoods Ltd. of 2,000,000 ordinary shares fully paid and 175,000 6% cumulative preference shares fully paid.

[h]In December 1963, £4,500,000 of the Share Premium account was capitalized and used to make a scrip issue of Ordinary shares to the holders of Ordinary shares on the basis of three new for every two old. The issued Ordinary share capital was thus raised to £7,500,000.

n.a. Not available.

are working together in that business and whose lives are bound up with its success.

"The most valuable asset in any company's balance sheet is one written in invisible ink. It reads something like this: 'The loyalty, the efficiency, the capacity for work of all employed by the company, their pride in the job and in the company's achievements and their joy in having a part in those achievements.'"

1. *Emphasis on operating efficiency* was considered one of the most important of these activities. Sir Halford said that the key to lower unit costs when producing with expensive, continuous-process equipment was keeping the plant operating as close to full capacity as possible and minimizing every

element of operating and overhead costs. Therefore, avoiding downtime, improving efficiency of men and machines, and fuel and power economies were all important. To accomplish these ends, Rugby employs an elaborate monthly cost reporting system which facilitates pinpointing any items of excessive costs. The factory managers are held responsible for costs under their control, and the chief engineer and production manager are continually watching fuel and power costs and working on means of increasing machine efficiency. Excess overtime, costly repairs, stores usage, and factory staff costs are other items which attract the attention of the central cost control department.

The company's research on improvement of its manufacturing process has produced several cost savings. One major outcome of such research was the development of a "wetting" agent for the slurry. Without affecting the chemical properties of the finished product, this agent produced the same "liquidity" and thus the same mixing and handling properties in a slurry containing only 35% water contrasted with 41% previously required. The smaller amount of water to vaporize meant appreciable fuel savings.

Another recent development was the installation of a pipeline from the chalk quarries near Dunstable to the two Warwickshire plants, through which a chalk slurry is pumped a total distance of some 57 miles. This became a possibility when a Pipeline Act came into force in the U.K. in 1962. The Rugby company received the first authorization granted under this act.

Currently, the company is installing experimentally computer control of the manufacturing process at its Rochester works.

Worker efficiency is also a matter of continuous attention. Because of the expensive equipment and need to operate without stoppages, misconduct on the job, unexcused absences, and excessive tardiness are considered grounds for release. Such strictness is necessary because, for example, a kiln burner[2] could, through ten minutes' neglect, permit many thousands of pounds' worth of damage to the equipment. Sir Halford said that his insistence that all employees "play the game according to the rules of the organization" was not only necessary for efficiency but was also a matter of loyalty. "But," he added, "I hold firmly to the view that loyalty should be a two-way traffic. If the head of a business expects a man to be loyal to him, then I say that the man has every right to expect the same loyalty from the head of the business."

Finally, emphasis was placed on clerical and procedural efficiency. Sir Halford said that greater use of mechanized accounting and invoicing, and continuous analysis and improvement of office procedures was essential. Periodic evaluation of the forms and paper work systems is conducted to eliminate unnecessary ones. "Forms are apt to breed like rabbits," he said. "They must be kept under constant review."

2. *An effective sales organization* is the second contributing factor to growth and profits. Manufacturing savings effected by maintaining peak production are attainable only as long as the output can be sold. The general

[2]The kiln burner is the man in charge of operating one or more kilns—a highly skilled job.

sales manager said, "Since the industry sells on a common price arrangement, you don't sell cement by selling cheaper than the next man. You sell on delivery service, goodwill, product quality, and on contact with the customer. Competition is severe and exacting for this reason." Under the general sales manager are the area sales managers, each of whom has under him a number of salesmen. The salesmen are paid entirely by salary.

3. *Overseas manufacture and other subsidiary activities* have accounted for much of the company's growth and its increased profits in the past five years. Rugby is continually conducting site investigations and negotiations in search of new overseas opportunities for expansion.

4. *Transportation* of the U.K. cement sales is another reason for RPC's growth and profitability. Rugby's fleet has grown from 52 trucks in 1946 to 345 in 1964 (106 flatbed trucks, 35 bulk tippers, and 204 pressurized bulk wagons)[3] plus extra trucks hired in the peak construction season. Rugby is proud of the efficiency of its fleet, the operating costs of which remain below the transportation allowance in the delivered price. The fleet averages less than 7% delays for repair, less than 10% nonoperating idleness, and 6% on-the-job delays. Company officials believe that their truck fleet is one of the most efficient in the industry. The major reason for this efficiency, the directors believe, is the highly centralized scheduling of truck dispatches. Each day the central transportation department, working with the sales department, prepares schedules of the following day's dispatches of all trucks from each of the works. Scheduling attempts to maximize the number of deliveries by each truck and to make as uniform as possible the work load at the packing and loading plants.

5. *A philosophy of teamwork:* Sir Halford and the other directors of Rugby believe that the most important reason for the company's success has been the achievement of company-wide teamwork through the chairman's human relations philosophy and application of profit-sharing and employee-shareholding plans. Rugby has no "personnel" department; development of teamwork is the job of managers at all levels within the company. The impersonal term "personnel" and the word "welfare," with its slight connotation of something akin to charity, are banned from the Rugby vocabulary.

During the course of his career, Sir Halford has developed a philosophy of business as a team effort. A concrete expression of this philosophy was his introduction at Rugby of employee-shareholding and profit-sharing plans. Commenting on the relationship between his philosophy and these plans, he said:

I am convinced that no scheme of profit-sharing or employee-shareholding can succeed unless it is built on a firm foundation of confidence within the business and of real *esprit de corps*, of a strong feeling on the part of all employees of pride in the company and its achievements. The goodwill of those working together in an industrial enterprise cannot be purchased for cash—of that I am

---

[3]Flatbed trucks carry cement in bags; pressurized bulk wagons carry loose cement in large tanks which are slightly pressurized to remove the cement at the delivery site; bulk tippers are fully enclosed dump trucks which carry loose cement.

sure. A scheme which is put in with the primary object of buying goodwill is almost certainly doomed to failure from the start. It may indeed not only do no good but may even do positive harm by creating suspicion, however ill-founded.[4]

Teamwork, commendable in any organization, is held to be doubly important in the cement industry where production in large units of continuous-process plant makes it impossible to associate individual effort with specific product output. Mutual confidence is felt to be the basic ingredient of teamwork: the board's confidence that all employees will put forth a fair day's work, operate and maintain the plant intelligently, and follow the leadership of the company; the employees' confidence in the capability and integrity of the directors and that discipline "which is as fair as it is firm" will be maintained.

Esprit de corps and company policies

The following paragraphs summarize the most important company policies which Sir Halford felt had established *esprit de corps* within Rugby.

1. Personal contact between top executives and operating people all over the world is relatively frequent. Sir Halford visits the Trinidad and Australian plants at least once a year, and someone from the central headquarters staff visits them, on an average, every three months. At home, Sir Halford not only delivers his annual "message to his fellow workers," but he always personally makes presentations which are given to men with 25 years' service and again after 50 years' service. Such presentations are made in the presence of the recipients' colleagues, and Sir Halford usually gives a brief review of the current progress of the company.

2. In his annual messages to the other employees, he describes recent developments within the company, emphasizing the cooperative roles played by employees and shareholders. He frequently discusses the importance of profits. The following is part of his message following the 1951 operations:

I want now to say something about profits, because a lot of nonsense has been talked about profits in the last few years, often by politicians of all parties who have never been in industry and have no practical knowledge of industry.

You and I know that profits are the reward and the measure of economy and efficiency, and are essential to the maintenance and expansion of a business. They are, in fact, the real and only bulwark behind our wages and salaries, for if this company ceases to make profits it can only be a comparatively short time before you and I are out.

Let us recognize that it is up to every one of us in this team to go all out all the time, to give of our best, to maintain and increase our production with economy and efficiency, and, in turn, the profits of the company: first—and note that I put this first—because it is the job we are paid to do, and it is only common honesty to our shareholders to do it; and secondly in our own interest to safeguard our jobs for the future.

3. Another aspect of the teamwork is the "works committee" at each plant.

---

[4]Quotation from *This Is Industrial Partnership,* a pamphlet written by Sir Halford in 1955 explaining his philosophy and the profit-sharing and employee-shareholding schemes of Rugby.

Composed of the works manager, the works engineer, the safety officer, and five representatives elected from the factory work force, the committee meets without exception each month with a senior member of the headquarters staff in attendance. The committee discusses matters of particular interest to the works concerned, and suggestions for operational improvements. The head office staff take this opportunity to clarify and discuss newly announced changes in policy and other company developments such as the annual financial statements.

Late in 1961, an IMEDE researcher had the opportunity to attend a works committee meeting at the Rochester works. Mr. R. L. Evans was the head office representative in attendance. The committee chiefly discussed matters of plant safety and of amenities for the workers, such as a sink and hand towels for workers at a remote plant location. The Rochester works manager said that this meeting was typical, especially insofar as it was primarily concerned with safety and working conditions. The researcher was impressed at the free and easy manner in which the workers entered into the discussions. Mr. Evans explained in great detail some minor points of company policy on tardiness and vacation time. The works manager commented that the worker representatives occasionally brought up very minor points in the committee. "I think," he added, "that some men do this just to show that they are on their toes and doing a good job for their fellow workers. The result is that the committee functions very well, and in a very good spirit."

4. Another policy is that no one but Sir Halford has the authority to release people during slack periods. He has in fact never authorized a layoff. For instance, the rail strike in 1955 almost closed the Rochester factory as coal reserves ran low. As the shutdown date approached, Sir Halford announced that no one would be laid off, but that

   a) Some men would have to take their vacations during the shutdown; and
   b) Everyone would have to agree to do any job given him (at his usual pay rate) during the shutdown.

(Last-minute settlement of the rail strike saved Rugby Cement from its contemplated shutdown.)

5. Since 1954, the company has offered its weekly paid employees the option of having their contract of employment terminable not by the usual one week's notice but by one month's notice by either side for employees having ten years' service, two months for those having 15 years, and three months for those having 20 years. Of those to whom the offer has applied, over 85% have opted for the longer notice.

In 1964 the options were amended. Now an employee with five years' unbroken service may opt for six weeks' notice on either side; after ten years for two months' notice; and after fifteen years for three months' notice.

The company has no long-term agreements with senior staff, all of whose service is subject to termination by three months' notice on either side. "We don't want anyone working with us unless that's where he wants to be," said Sir Halford, who is firmly opposed to long-term service contracts.

6. The final key policy of the company was summarized by Sir Halford:

If there is to be a lively interest and pride in the company and its doings, then it is necessary that all employees be kept informed as far as possible about what is going on.[5]

A carefully thought-out system of communication is of prime importance. But to us "communication" is not just a matter of issuing directives or disseminating information on policy changes. Rather I would describe it as an attitude of mind.

To give one small example: we should regard it as an affront to a man's dignity if he read first in the press something about the company which he could properly have learned from inside the company. We therefore do everything we can to ensure that all releases issued to the press appear on all our notice-boards a few hours before they appear in the newspapers.

Apart from the various aspects of teamwork within an organization, two other features of any profit-sharing or employee-shareholding plan were felt necessary by Sir Halford. The first was that any such scheme must be tailored to suit the circumstances of the company and the outlook, philosophy, and intention of its leader. The second feature was simplicity.

The profit-sharing scheme

Sir Halford said that the Rugby profit-sharing scheme, inaugurated in 1935, was designed to emphasize two things:[6]

a) That the efforts of the employees are the efforts of a team—that we are all working to one end; and

b) The essential partnership which exists between the Ordinary shareholders and the employees.

In speeches both to shareholders and workers, Sir Halford referred to the partnership between capital and employees. He said that capital was nothing more than the "labor of yesterday—the production of yesterday which was surplus to the consumption of yesterday."

Fundamental to the partnership was the following bargain:[7]

. . . the labour of today is guaranteed payment for its services and the profit is calculated only after the remuneration of that labour has been paid. Capital, therefore, takes the risk and in return takes such profit (or loss) as arises *after* the labour of today has been paid in full.

But to my mind this difference in the basis of their respective remuneration in no way destroys the conception of industrial enterprise as essentially a partnership between the labour of yesterday (capital) and the labour of today. Nor is it destroyed if the "bargain" is varied slightly by guaranteeing the greater part of labour's remuneration irrespective of profit or loss and by making an additional but smaller part of it dependent on the results of the enterprise as a whole.

The employees' profit-sharing scheme provided for an annual bonus in excess of industry-negotiated wages (wage earners) or contracted salary

[5] Quotation from *This Is Industrial Partnership.*
[6] *Ibid.*
[7] *Ibid.*

(staff) for all Rugby workers. Basic points of the scheme are summarized below:[8]

1. To qualify for the profit-sharing bonus, an hourly-paid or salaried employee must have completed, on December 31, twelve months' unbroken service to the satisfaction of the Directors.
2. For the purpose of calculating the bonus, each qualified employee is treated as if he held a certain number of Ordinary shares in the company. A staff employee's "notional shares" are related to his annual salary. An hourly-paid worker's shares vary in proportion to his length of service up to forty years.
3. The bonus is calculated at the full rate per share of the gross dividend declared and paid to the Ordinary shareholders for the financial year in question and is paid immediately after the Annual General Meeting. For example, for 1963 the Ordinary dividend declared was 7½d. per share. Thus an hourly paid worker with five years' service, holding 900 notional shares, would receive a bonus of (900 × 7½d.) or £28. 2. 6.
4. Certified sickness or compulsory National Service are ignored in calculating the number of years of unbroken service.
5. Any employee who leaves or is under notice to leave prior to the date of payment forfeits his bonus.
6. The scheme confers no rights in respect of any capital distribution, or distributions other than those declared as dividends on the Ordinary shares of the company out of revenue profits.
7. The scheme is subject to modification or withdrawal at any time at the discretion of the Directors.

Sir Halford emphasized that the bonus was not automatic. In a very small number of cases each year, bonuses were withheld completely or in part because service was not "to the satisfaction of the directors." If a man's record for the year was questionable, including several unexplained tardinesses, for instance, it was submitted, without name, to the works committee of the factory. In all cases, the directors had abided by the committee's recommendations. Sir Halford said that withholding the bonus was not so much a penalty to the slack worker, but was necessary in fairness—in loyalty—to those who gave 100% service during the year.

Summarizing, Sir Halford said:

I believe that this is important: the bonus must be something that is earned—not something which becomes a right. I also feel that the link with the Ordinary shareholders' dividend is fundamental: if the dividend per share goes up, so does the bonus; if the dividend is reduced, the bonus falls too—which is as it should be.

The "A" share scheme

After the war, Sir Halford saw two factors that made the profit-sharing scheme inadequate in emphasizing the partnership between capital and labor. He felt that the twin virtues of hard work and thrift no longer assured

---

[8]This explanation of the profit-sharing scheme contains only the major aspects. Full details are available in Sir Halford Reddish's booklet: *This Is Industrial Partnership.*

a man of personal savings for his old age—taxation *restricted* savings and inflation *devalued* them. Unlike the Ordinary shareholder's income which flowed from an asset whose market value reflected both the company's prosperity and inflationary pressures, the employees' profit-sharing bonus was not reflected in a realizable capital asset. Thus he did not have a "hedge" against inflation.

To supply this need, Sir Halford presented his "A" share plan, in late 1954, for approval by the Ordinary shareholders. He said that the scheme was designed to do three things:[9]

To give practical form to the unity of interest which I have always held to exist between the Ordinary shareholders and the employees; to give a return to the Ordinary shareholders on profits "ploughed back" in the past; and to give to every full-time employee the opportunity to have in his hands a capital asset readily realizable on death or retirement. It was received enthusiastically by shareholders and employees alike.

One million "A" shares of 1s. each were created with the following conditions attached to them:[10]

1. For any financial year after 31st December 1954 for which (*a*) the net profits before tax are not less than £900,000, and (*b*) the gross amount distributed as dividend to the Ordinary shareholders is not less than £300,000, the holders of the "A" shares shall be entitled to an amount of £70,000 plus 20% of any excess of the said net profits over £900,000 [see Exhibit 4]. However, (i) the amount attributable to the "A" shares shall not exceed 12½% of the net profits; and (ii) in the event of the issue of additional Ordinary share capital by the company after 31st December 1954, otherwise than by the way of a capitalization of reserves or undistributed profits, the said figure of £900,000 shall be increased by a sum equal to 6% of the proceeds or other consideration received by the company.[11]

2. Any amount attributable to the "A" shares as ascertained under (1) above may be distributed as dividend or carried forward in the books of the company to the credit of the "A" shares for subsequent distribution, as the Directors may decide.

3. The holders of "A" shares have no voting rights.

4. In a winding-up, the "A" shares participate only insofar as the amount of their paid-in capital value and the "A" share credit carried forward on the company books, but have no further participation in assets.

5. No further "A" shares can be created without the sanction of an Extraordinary Resolution passed by the holders of the "A" shares. [But see later.]

Half of the "A" shares were offered to the Ordinary shareholders at par and half to the employees.

---

[9]Explanation of "A" share plan summarized from *This Is Industrial Partnership.*
[10]*Ibid.*
[11]Because additional equity had been introduced since 1954, the 20% now applies to profits in excess of £1,568,190.

Exhibit 4

PROFIT PARTICIPATION OF THE "A" SHARES

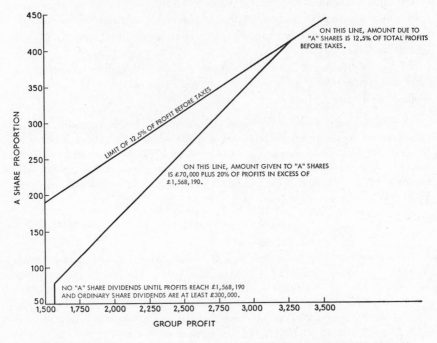

GROUP PROFIT

SUMMARY OF EARNINGS AND GROSS DIVIDEND PAYMENTS, 1954–63
(1,000's of £)

Year	1954	1955	1956	1957	1958	1959	1960	1961	1962	1963
Profit before tax	721	1,025	1,093	1,106	1,171	1,491	1,777	2,020	2,260	2,656
Gross ordinary dividend ..	200	300	338	338	375	437	500	500	750	938
Gross attributed to "A" shares	..	95	109	111	124	179	222	252	269	287
Actual "A" share dividend ..		50	63	63	75	100	125	125	137	187
Difference carried forward as "A" share credit	..	45	46	48	49	79	97	127	132	100
Cumulative "A" share credit*	..	45	91	140	189	268	365	493	624	316†

*The "A" share credit was contained in the Undistributed Profit account in the balance sheet. The directors considered this credit as a "dividend equalization reserve" to supply "A" dividends if they were not earned according to the formula (i.e., if pretax profits were below £1,568,190 from 1963 onwards).
†After deduction of £408,163, the gross equivalent of the scrip issue of £250,000.

"*All* full-time employees of the company were included: this was not a get-rich-quick exercise for the favored few," said Sir Halford.

Allocation to the employees was done by dividing all employees into groups according to remuneration, responsibility, and status within the company (length of service was not a factor). Those in the first group were offered 250 shares, followed by groups of 500, 750, 1,000, 1,500, and so on.

(Most factory production workers were in the first group.) After some years, when these 1/-d. "A" shares were quoted at over £6 on the Stock Exchange, the allocation of shares to newcomers was proportionately reduced. Over 95% of Rugby's employees had exercised their option and purchased the "A" shares.

Sir Halford was particularly concerned about two aspects of the scheme. About the first, he said:[12]

> I was anxious that there should be no element of a "gift" from one partner (the holders of the Ordinary shares) to the other (the employees); and that the equity owned by the Ordinary shares should be unimpaired. I was convinced that the holders of the Ordinary shares could have no legitimate cause for complaint if the profits were so substantially increased in the future and some comparatively small part of the increase went to the employees as a reward for their efforts.
>
> The "A" shares should be worth no more than was paid for them when issued, so that the employees could feel that whatever increased value accrued thereafter was due to their teamwork, with, I do not forget, nor do I allow them to forget, the capital provided by their partners in the enterprise.

This reason, and tax considerations (discussed later) dictated that the minimum profit level at which the "A" shares would start participating (£900,000) should be well above the profit levels when the "A" shares were issued.

The second aspect was that the main object of the scheme was to ensure to employees a capital sum on death or retirement. Sir Halford foresaw that the "A" shares might have some speculative attraction to the general public and he did not want the employees to be tempted into selling and thus depriving themselves of retirement or death benefits from the plan. He also felt that anyone leaving the firm should be required to sell his shares back at par and thus enable newcomers to participate. To accomplish these ends, Sir Halford arranged that the shares allocated to the employees were to be held on their behalf by Staff Nominees Limited (a company brought into being for the purpose), which was accountable to the employees for dividends declared and was authorized to act on their behalf in all matters relating to the "A" shares.

The following conditions applied:

1. Initially and whenever an employee moves upward to a new group, he is given the opportunity to buy his allocation of shares at par. A new employee is offered his allocation after a year's service. If an employee fails to take his shares when offered he is not given a subsequent opportunity.
2. "A" shares may be sold by the employee at any time *at par* to Staff Nominees Limited and *must* be sold at par if for any reason he leaves the company.
3. An employee's shares are realized at market value (market price is established by quotation on the London Stock Exchange of the "A" shares

---

[12]Quotation from *This Is Industrial Partnership.*

allotted originally at par to the Ordinary shareholders) *only* in the event of the employee's death while in the service of the company, or upon his reaching the age of 65 (55 for women).

4. Any dividend declared on the "A" shares is paid immediately to the employee.

Fifty thousand shares remained unallocated to the employees after the initial distribution. They were held by RPC Benevolent Fund Ltd. (a company which exists for the purpose indicated by its title) pending their issue to newcomers. The directors felt that this block of shares and those shares which Staff Nominees Limited bought back, at par, from employees who left, would be sufficient to offer shares to new and promoted employees for the foreseeable future.

In December 1963, the company's Articles of Association were amended giving power to the "A" shareholders to capitalize from time to time any part of the profits allocated to the "A" shares in the past but remaining undistributed, and therefore to increase the number of "A" shares for this purpose. The "A" shareholders agreed to capitalize £250,000 of the net amount standing to the credit of the "A" shares by a scrip issue of five new for each one held. The effect was to amend the market price of the "A" shares to around 30/-d. and so increase their marketability.

In his message to his fellow workers in the company following the 1958 operations, Sir Halford said the following about the "A" share plan:

. . . Quite often a man will say to me: "This 'A' share scheme of yours—tell me, has it increased production?" And I reply: "I haven't the slightest idea, but I shouldn't think so." So he says: "But surely that was the object. It's an incentive scheme, isn't it?" "On the contrary," I tell him, "I have always insisted that it should *not* be called an incentive scheme, because that to my mind would imply that we in Rugby Cement were not already doing our best, were not doing our duty in return for our wages and salaries. And that I will not have."

What our "A" share scheme does is to give to the employees the opportunity to build up capital available on retirement or on earlier death, and to promote the feeling that we are all one team working to the same end in partnership with our shareholders. The value of the "A" shares depends in the long run on the success of our efforts in making profits. And don't overlook the fact that half the "A" shares were issued, also at par, to the holders of our Ordinary shares. They very rightly benefit too, as they have seen these 1/-d. shares change hands on the Stock Exchange at prices up to 42/-d.[13]

Apart from the capital aspect, the holding of "A" shares by the employees of the company, and also, of course, our "profit-sharing" schemes, give some reward for successful endeavour—which is surely right.

The taxation aspect. For the company, the profit-sharing bonus was considered a wage bonus and therefore a before-tax expense. The "A" share dividends, however, were similar to Ordinary dividends, being paid out of after-tax profits.

---

[13]In January 1964, the "A" shares were quoted on the Stock Exchange at the equivalent of 186 shillings per original share.

For the employees, the profit-sharing bonus was taxed as ordinary wage or salary income. Taxation of the employees in connection with "A" share distribution was a most difficult problem and one on which Sir Halford spent many hours in consultation with the Board of Inland Revenue.

The law held that if at the time of issue the value of the shares was greater than the amount the employees paid for them, the difference was taxable as a "benefit" arising from employment. The Rugby "A" share sale to its employees, however, had two characteristics which affected any ruling under this law:

1. "A" shares were not quoted on the market until two months after issue; thus it was a matter of discussion whether at time of issue they were worth more than the par value paid for them.
2. Employees were not free to sell their shares at market price except on retirement or death.

Final agreement with the Inland Revenue was reached which assessed the value of the "A" shares at time of issue slightly above par.

Tax assessment for shares issued subsequently to newcomers or to promoted employees required a different arrangement with the Inland Revenue, since by that time a market value was established. Final agreement resulted in considering a variable fraction of the difference between current market value and par value as taxable income. The fraction varied inversely with the length of time between the recipient's age and 65 when he could realize the market price of the "A" shares. For instance, a 25-year-old newcomer receiving 500 "A" shares would have to consider as income, for income tax purposes, only 10% of the difference between market value and the price paid (one shilling per share), because he could not realize the market value for 40 years. On the other hand, a 50-year-old man receiving 500 "A" shares would have to consider 60% of the difference as taxable income, because he was much closer to realizing the gain. (All dividends received by employees on their "A" shares up to retirement age are treated, for tax purposes, as "earned" income and therefore attract the earned income allowance.)

THE RUGBY PORTLAND CEMENT COMPANY LIMITED (B)*

^^

Late in 1961, an IMEDE research team decided to attempt to expand the Rugby Portland Cement case by adding information on the ways in which various employees of the company viewed their jobs. To this purpose, an IMEDE researcher toured each of the company's three cement works in England; he also conducted interviews with a number of hourly paid workers and with a substantial number of middle- and top-management executives. This case includes excerpts from some of these interviews, as well as some of the researcher's impressions of what he saw.

VIEWS OF SOME RUGBY WORKMEN

Rugby's management was very cooperative in helping the researcher to interview some of the workmen. Although, in theory, it would have been useful to interview a rather large number of workers selected at random, this was not practicable for certain reasons:

1. There were limitations on the research time available for these interviews.
2. There was a chance that some men, if chosen at random, might:
    a) Not be able to articulate their views;
    b) Be less than wholly frank;
    c) Be unable to leave their work posts at the desired time.

Accordingly, Mr. R. L. Evans, deputy managing director, and Mr. Baker, works manager of the Rugby works, selected from the Rugby work force four workers who, they thought, would be articulate, honest, and as representative as possible of the general sentiments of the entire Rugby worker group. The researcher interviewed the four men separately, in an office at the Rugby plant; nobody else was present during the interviews. The names of the four men interviewed have been disguised.

Interview with Mr. Ryan

Mr. Evans and Mr. Baker, in arranging the interviews, mentioned that Mr. Ryan should provide a highly entertaining and useful interview, that he

---

was outspoken and highly articulate. Mr. Ryan, who had been working for the company since 1956, was an Irishman; he appeared to be about 40 years old. He worked in the transport department of the company as a truck driver and had been a member of the Rugby works committee for some time. The researcher asked each of the four men only one question to begin: What did the man think about working for the company, what were the bad points and the good points? Mr. Ryan began:

Well, I might tell you I'm an old union man, been a sort of union agitator all my working life. Before I came here I never held a job longer than eighteen months. I've been here almost six years now, and I can tell you this, I'm going to stay here the rest of my life. And, mind you, I got a lot less to gain by staying here than most of the men. I have no A-shares, because you know you only get one chance to buy them A-shares, and when I had to buy them, I didn't have the money because my wife just had to have an operation. So now for the rest of my life I got to work here knowing that I'll never have no A-shares, and I think this is unfair, and I keep fighting to get me shares, and maybe I will and maybe I won't, but I'll stay on here no matter what.

And another thing is I'm a very bad timekeeper—sometimes it's my fault, and sometimes it was because I had to take my wife to the doctor and so I'd come in late, and so for three straight years I lost my profit-sharing bonus on account of being late so much. [Mr. Ryan had actually lost his bonus in two nonconsecutive years, management reported.] So you can see what I mean when I tell you that I got much less to gain by working here than the other men.

But even though there's lots of little things could be done, this is a wonderful place to work, and that's the Lord's own truth. I'm not saying anything to you I wouldn't say right to the Chairman's face if he asked me—I'm not a man to say what he doesn't mean.

You got to remember this: It's no good coming down to a cement works if you don't want to work hard. But they pay you good, and the main thing is, you always get treated fair. If you got a complaint, you can take it as high as you want, right up to the Chairman himself, but it's no good complaining unless you give 'em the facts. That's what they want to see: facts.

Another thing you ought to write down is this: In this company, I'm just as good as anybody, as good as the Chairman or Mr. Evans—that's what you won't get anywhere else. We all know this here, and we know you've got to work as a team. And I'll tell you this, I know the Chairman would let me buy my A-shares if he could, but you see he's got to be fair to the other workers too. But I do think that you get punished awful hard for being late. [Mr. Ryan's profit-sharing bonus would have amounted, in those years when he lost it, to about £30. His weekly wages were about £15.]

Over in Coventry, you know [about 15 miles away], in the car and airplane factories a man can make £30 a week, while here he'll only make about £15, but we get the £15 for 52 weeks of the year, plus the profit-sharing, the A-shares, and lots of other benefits. The company buys up lots of clothes for us, so we can get them cheaper. I once compared what I earned in a year with a friend of mine who works in Coventry for £29 a week, and you know what? I came out £48 ahead of him for the year, because those fellows are always getting laid off.

And let me tell you this: You'd never get a better firm to work for, no matter where you went; there isn't another company like this, at least none I've ever heard about.

You know, when I tell you we work hard here, you've got to remember that the Chairman doesn't ask us to do anything he doesn't do himself. You know, he works 18 hours a day, and when he come down sick recently and had to have that operation, his doctors told him to take it easy, and so he did—he only worked ten hours a day.

[Mr. Ryan then gave the researcher a very detailed description of what was involved in his truck driving. He stressed that the equipment was the best obtainable, that the company paid much more attention to driver safety than to delivering a maximum daily tonnage of cement, that scrupulous care was taken, at great expense, to be certain that the customer received all the cement he had been billed for.]

You see my truck out there? That truck, it's brand new, and it cost £10,000, and they expect me take care of it like if it was my own, and I do. [The truck in fact cost slightly over £3,500.] And I know I've got 42 hours a week guaranteed, and more hours on weekends if I want to make extra money, and that's a hell of a nice thing for a truck driver. And as soon as I've driven 11 hours in a single day, even if I didn't get home with the truck by the time my 11 hours was up, the company would send out another lorry with two drivers to drive me and my truck home, that's how careful they are about the 11-hour rule. And you see them fine overalls we drivers got, and them jackets? Mr. Reddish, I believe, bought them for us out of his own pocket. That's just the kind of man he is. [In fact he didn't; they are provided by the company.]

I told you I used to be a union man, but I tell you this, if a union came in here now, it would hurt the workers—they'd get less pay, they couldn't touch anything they weren't supposed to. That's the kind of a union man I am today.

In summing up, and this is God's own truth, I think Sir Halford Reddish ought to be England's Prime Minister, and Mr. Evans ought to be the Secretary for Foreign Affairs.

Interview with Mr. Mason

Mr. Mason was a foreman in the "raw plant," where the slurry was made. He had been working for the company about 14 years and appeared to be about 50. He began:

Well, wherever I went, I don't think I could better myself, that's what I'd say. The Chairman puts us in the picture about what's going on; he has more of a fatherly concern for us, I think. I've known the Chairman 30 years, and if he says a thing he means it. He's put in some wonderful plans for the men, he has. For example, when my father died, we got about £1,000 for his A-shares, and this was a big help, because I've got a sister who isn't very well, and this money pays for her. From the workman's point of view, if you want it, I find that they're very, very satisfied. I've got 30-odd men working for me, and I get all the points of view, so to speak, and I think I can say that they're all happy to be working here. Now, of course, there's some men as will always find something to complain about, you're going to have that anywhere, but in the main I think that the men like working here very much.

You're an American, so I'll put it in American: Damn it all, we're on to a good thing here and we know it.

I've got a brother, a son, and two brothers-in-law working here, and my father before he died. They all came to work here before I did. Now do you think they'd have come if this wasn't a good place to work?

I do believe honestly, and I'm not handing you any bull, that we couldn't better ourselves. And you've got to remember this: Sir Halford will give any of his men a proper hearing any time. And what's astonishing is that as the firm gets larger, the company seems to give us more attention, when you'd think it'd be the other way around.

Now you take your average Englishman, he's the biggest grumbler in the world, about anything at all. But you won't find much grumbling here. You'd have to kick them out to get the men here to leave.

Interview with Mr. Toot

Mr. Toot, who appeared to be about 50, had been with Rugby about seven years. The researcher received the distinct impression that Mr. Toot was temperamentally a sort of cynic who only grudgingly would admit that a workman's life could be decent, although this impression was formed on the basis of very little evidence. Mr. Toot began:

Taken all around, I should say that this is a very good place to work. A workman here knows that he can go as high as he likes, if he has the ability. You get fair treatment here. I suppose that work here is 80% satisfactory. For the other 20%, it's hard to say what the objections might be. But one thing is, when a man first came to work here, he didn't get enough participation in the bonus system [the profit-sharing scheme], but they've changed that now.

If a man's willing to do an honest day's work, he'll generally be satisfied here. I suppose I could say this: The longer a man's been here, the more he wants to stay.

Now, you get some fellows, especially young ones, come in and they can't stick the work; it's too heavy or too hard for them. They usually leave, if they're this type, in 12–18 months. If a man sticks it a year or a year and a half, he'll probably stay here until he's through working.

This is a long-term policy job, so to say. It's good if you're thinking about your old age, because the company really takes care of you after you retire. I don't suppose you know this, but all the company's pensioners [retired workers] get a ton of coal from the Chairman at Christmas. There's a Christmas party for the pensioners. And men like Mr. Evans and Mr. Baker visit the pensioners very regularly. The company doesn't just forget you when you've stopped working for them—they take care of you.

I suppose when I think of it, it's hard to say what kind of objections, you might say, a man could have to working here, if he's not just a casual laborer who doesn't care about doing an honest day's work, if he doesn't care about doing a good job. This is a good place to work.

Interview with Mr. Forster

Mr. Forster had been working for Rugby for 48 years, and he worked in the quarry. He talked rather little, much less than the previous three men.

Well, I've been working here all my life, and that's a fact. It's hard work, and no doubt about it, but it's a wonderful company to work for. I was here, you know, when Sir Halford took over, and it was wonderful when he did. He promised us steady work, and we've had it ever since. Some of your casual lads, now, who come here looking for an easy day's work and high pay, they don't stay; but a real man, a man who doesn't mind work, he'll be happier here than anywhere else I've ever heard of.

RANDOM IMPRESSIONS OF THE RESEARCHER

In the course of his tour of the three different works, the researcher spent a great deal of time with Mr. R. L. Evans, who toured each plant with him, and with the works managers. The researcher was especially struck by two facts. First, Mr. Evans and the works managers appeared to know a great deal about the background of every company employee. The researcher was, while walking through the plant, introduced to one worker who had been a chef in Wyoming some years ago. Another worker was pointed out as having been (he was now 72) a good rugby player in his youth. These and similar details were forthcoming quite frequently from Mr. Evans or the works managers. Second, the workers all said "Hello" to Mr. Evans as he passed through the plant, and Mr. Evans would chat with them about their families and how things were going.

Another impression, although a difficult one to justify with explicit evidence, was that the various managers were more than superficially concerned with their workers and their lives. Words and phrases which often recurred in the four days of conversation included: "fair treatment," "decent work for a man," "take care of our men," "expect them to work as part of a team." All individuals interviewed referred to themselves as being part of a single team; they did so either implicitly or explicitly.

MULTI-PRODUCTS, INC.*

"The average young fellow today has no concept of how to beat a competitor and how to squeeze money out of every dollar," Richard B. Haws, president of Multi-Products, Inc., of Los Angeles, California, said in February 1959 to Bertram Stace, an old friend and stockholder. "It's not really their fault —they've just had lousy training over the past 20–30 years, as far as the acceptance of responsibility and of being held accountable for the stewardship of a job is concerned. If we ever begin to have a depression as we did back in 1929 to 1931, God knows how the industries of this country would suffer. Just look at the way they waste money. . . ."

Mr. Haws's career, 1902–56

"I was born in 1902, the son of poor parents," Mr. Haws continued. "One day when I was a small boy I was sitting in our hometown drugstore and the wealthy owner of a pottery (his son lost all of it) came in and sat down beside me. He talked to the druggist and then he turned to me and said, 'No use talking to you, you'll never have any money.' I will never forget those words. I don't resent them—they were the greatest driving force in my life. If they've been before my eyes once, they've been before them five million times."

Picking up his office copy of *Who's Who,* Mr. Haws showed Mr. Stace that he had attended college for three years, worked as a salesman in a local business for another five, and then moved to New York in 1929 to sell for the Lawton Machinery Company. "We were living in a nice apartment and had all our money in the market when the crash came. I went to our landlord and asked him to let me break the lease, but he pointed out that he needed money more than ever now and refused. I went home to think about it and then returned and pleaded with him to let us move to one of his cheaper apartments. Finally he agreed. He moved us the next day and that night brought up a new lease for me to sign. I looked him in the eye and said, 'Oh no. When you moved us out of that first apartment, you broke the lease. We're moving out of here tomorrow.' That's the sort of sharp thinking—in that case born out of financial necessity—that young fellows don't seem to use today. They certainly don't learn it in business schools."

Mr. Haws thought his Lawton Machine Company days had been an invaluable experience. "Young fellows today are soft—they don't believe me when I tell them that my wife often would wait for my phone call in the late afternoon to see if I'd sold a machine. If so, I'd have enough money for her to buy food for supper! Those were the days when we were ashamed to admit we had lost an order. We were paid straight commission; anyone could ask for a raise but all you got was 'Go out and sell some more machines.' I remember the sales manager used to say, 'Any salesman can come in, push the desk in my lap and call me a S.O.B. as long as he produces—but he'd better keep on producing.'

"When I was with Lawton, I met a young statistician whose head was full of ideals and up in the clouds, but he was dead broke. I suggested he sell machines until he found another job. I showed him the sales pitch and sent him off with a machine under his arm. The next day he was back saying he couldn't take it. I told him anybody could sell machines and if he couldn't he had no guts. He stuck with it two months until he got another statistical job. You've got to have guts and imagination to get someplace. A friend of mine who was president of a large company put it this way, 'If I have a guy around me who hasn't been in jail, I have a weak man!'

"It was during my time with Lawton that I realized I wanted a nice house, expensive car, fine clothes—the things that money can buy. I decided then and there I had the ants in my pants to want excitement and to get all or nothing. If you know what you want and what you can afford, it's pretty easy to set up a program for yourself. I've tried to get others to do the same, but they don't. It's pretty difficult for a young man or a student because he's not had the business experience to see what you can get out of life, and what money will buy. But then, even older men don't do it. Take my associate Joel Dennis. He's happy to earn about $15 an hour, save up for a new expensive camera, throw on a $47 suit of clothes that doesn't fit properly, and just lead that sort of life. Maybe he's happy, but he doesn't have the ants in his pants I do. .. . ."

Mr. Haws told his friend that he decided he didn't aspire to be a Lawton sales manager, but rather wanted a "show of my own" and was willing to pay for the necessary experience. He had left his $18,000 Lawton job to work first for a large company as a $6,000-a-year procedures man and later for a medium-sized company as a financial officer. During his stay with the second company he was given warrants and stock. When he left he had about 27,500 shares which had cost him some $12,000; by 1959 these shares were worth over $1 million. In 1953 he became president of a small manufacturing company, and four years later he was asked to head Multi-Products, Inc.

Multi-Products, Inc., 1946–56

Mr. Haws's friend, Mr. Stace, was a stockholder in Multi-Products, Inc., and knew something about its early history from published records. The company was founded by Earle M. Cave in January 1946 to make a consumer item. By 1951 the company had lost some $500,000 on five years' sales of

$625,000 and Mr. Cave started a new line. During the next two years Multi-Products expanded into two related and one unrelated lines through acquiring three small companies. The company's 1954 statements showed a net profit of about $290,000 on $5.7 million sales, a net worth of $3.3 million, and an accumulated deficit of $80,000; however, the auditors "were unable to form an opinion as to the overall results of operation" because management had decided to defer certain expenses totaling $375,000.

The next year, Mr. Stace recalled, the company ran into difficulties. The June 1955 quarterly report showed a six months' profit of about $60,000 on about $2.7 million sales, but when the annual report came out there were losses of about $3.6 million on $6 million sales.

Early in 1956 the company underwent litigation. Mr. Stace recalled the basic issues were whether the net income for the period ending June 30, 1955, were overstated and both income statement and balance sheet invalid and whether at the time the quarterly report was issued management knew the company was operating at a loss. The testimony showed that four entries, labeled "management adjustments" by the disapproving controller, had turned a $300,000 March quarter loss into a $60,000 profit before the statement was forwarded to the company's banks. The court ruled that the June profit had been overstated by almost $1 million owing to improper deferment of certain expenses, calculation of the cost of goods sold on the basis of cost formulae rather than by using the cost system, and failure to establish reserves for anticipated losses.

In court Mr. Cave said that accounting, especially details such as divisional operating data or cost entries, was beyond his "purview of operation," interest, or knowledge. He stated that he relied completely on the judgment of Mr. Bangs, vice president of finance, on all accounting matters, and on the auditors on all financial questions pertaining to the company statements. He said that in general "it was not my custom to have any contact whatsoever with the people at the working level, such as Mr. Land or Mr. Heyden (assistant controllers). If I had identified myself at any time with the minutiae between the juniors below any of the vice presidents, then I would have been totally unable to have kept my proper purview of the overall operation of the company and longer term planning of the company. I stayed expressly away from all matters which fell totally below the vice presidential levels." He said the first time he had "any conception" of the losses was when the new auditors showed him the 1955 financial statements in February 1956 after his return from a vacation. Besides, over $2 million was due to auditors' adjustments.

Both Mr. Cave and the Multi-Products, Inc., counsel stressed that investors bought the company's stock on the basis of its potential long-term growth, not the statements, and so it would not have materially mattered one iota if the six months' statement ending March had shown a profit or a small loss. According to published reports, Mr. Cave never owned over 2% of Multi-Products, Inc., stock and did not speculate.

After losing $4 million on $5.9 million sales in 1956, the firm faced financial disaster. Only selling a large block of shares at $2 a share to an investment fund in January 1957 avoided bankruptcy. (Mr. Stace ruefully recalled that the stock back in 1952 had sold for $42 a share.) New directors and a new management, including Mr. Haws, were brought in, and the division making products unrelated to the other lines was sold.

Multi-Products, Inc., under Mr. Haws's management, 1957–59

Mr. Haws explained to Mr. Stace that since coming to Multi-Products, Inc., he had concentrated on three areas: organization, acquisitions, and employee motivation and compensation.

Organization. "For about the first month after I joined Multi-Products, Inc., I just watched operations and got the feel of the situation," Mr. Haws said. "Then I went to work on our organization. There were 51 people in the accounting department. I called in the head of the department and told him to move the people into another room. He protested there was only room for 12 there and I said, 'That's right, by tomorrow you'll only have 12 people in your department.' I also called in the head of the merchandising department and showed him a new room with space for three people and the secretary. He had to reduce his staff from 11. Quality control had seven people and a secretary. I told the superintendent he would have two people including himself to do all the scheduling, the expediting and control. The department heads said this was impossible. I said, 'All right. I will stay after five o'clock tonight and want you to come in and tell me if you're man enough for the job or else resign.'

"Actually, volume has grown much better than I anticipated, and we still have only 12 people in the accounting department. Goes to show there were a lot of people sitting around on their hands doing nothing. You know, a partially employed person is the most ineffectual person in the business; he is inaccurate, lazy, and—worst of all—keeps other people from working.

"About March I took the department heads to dinner at the hotel. I told them what I was trying to do, put up a sales and profit chart, and said, "We'll start work at 8:15 in the morning, and not 8:45 or whenever you seem to feel like wandering in.' The treasurer broke in with, 'Let's take a vote on it.' I said, 'Fine, but if anyone votes against the proposal, I'll accept his resignation.' There was no vote.

"After the meeting the treasurer said, 'You certainly got off easy.' I replied, 'No, I had to listen to you. That's enough anguish for one evening. I don't have enough cash on me, so come in tomorrow morning and you can get your check.' I fired him right there; he was 45 years old but as yet he had not learned that organization conduct was more important than personal convenience."

In reorganizing the company, Mr. Haws said he decided whom to let go almost on a replacement basis. "Who cares about accountants, salesmen, shop foremen, or treasurers? But purchasing agents, merchandisers, and engineers are rather important to you. You have to know where to start a fight and where not to. You must move slowly because you have not possession of all the facts. . . ."

Acquisitions and new business. The company needed to generate sufficient new business to utilize the large loss carry-forward generated since December 31, 1955. "The fundamental reason for our being in business is to utilize the tax losses," Mr. Haws explained. During 1957 he revamped the product line, acquired two small companies making similar products, and reduced the size of the loss to about $470,000 on sales of $3.7 million. By June 1958 the company showed earnings of $75,000 on sales of about $2 million, but much faster profit generation was needed. Mr. Haws started to diversify.

The first acquisition was the Seward Company which was obtained through an exchange of stock in July 1958. Shortly before, Seward had invested in a relatively large amount of new fixed assets. By changing the write-off period from three years to ten, Multi-Products maximized the immediate profit and thus effectively deferred the tax loss carry-forward beyond its normal expiration date. The extra profit was recorded as deferred income on the statements and was included in income for tax purposes only. By February 1959 Multi-Products had protected almost $1 million of its tax loss.

The other two unrelated businesses were bought in October 1958 and January 1959 on an "incentive" basis. Mr. Haws explained, "The man who owned the first one foresaw estate problems and wanted to sell the business for $1.5 million, its asset value. I said I would offer him $2 million if I could have it my own way with less than 30% down. I paid him $500,000 and picked up $400,000 of the company's cash the next day. In order to make up the $1 million balance of his original $1.5 million asking price, he will receive two thirds of the after-tax profit without limit of time. Obviously, if there are never any profits, he will never get any more than the down payment already made. Over the next five years, if his two-thirds share of the profits generate more than the $1.5 million asking price, he gets his excess up to the full $2 million offer. The business is currently producing after tax profits of $40,000 a month. I was talking to the seller the other day about cutting out his fancy profit-sharing ideas, Cadillacs, hotel suites, and other perquisites, and he said he wouldn't work so hard without them. I replied, 'You scare me to death! You've only got $500,000 for your company so far and that's *all* you get if you don't produce profits.' I paid $25,000 down for the second business, which had $280,000 in cash, and made a similar incentive arrangement for the rest of the sales price.

"In other words, I am giving these men an incentive to continue to produce profits and thus am much more sophisticated than others using similar formulas. Some are good at this sort of thing. They pay an inflated cost above the company's net worth as a *contractual* obligation, which puts ether on the balance sheet as goodwill or some other evasive term, and they have to amortize the ether over a stipulated period on their operating statement, which adversely affects profits and gives their stockholders an untrue picture of earnings. On the other hand, I give the seller the full purchase price above asset value *only* if he earns it.

"I can't understand acquiring a company to add to your losses. Men who contractually overpay must be either awfully young or look too far into the future. Look at this article in today's *Wall Street Journal*[1] about Mr. Zeckendorf's company. Real estate is the safest investment in an inflationary economy and Webb & Knapp's assets have grown from $7 million in 1945 to $210 million in 1957, yet it lost money last year; the common stockholders have never received a dividend, and the preferred is $60 in arrears. When that happens, something is really wrong! Anytime you increase assets, your return on investment should increase proportionately. There's no point in getting big just for bigness' sake. Under my incentive system, we know the management of the purchased company will work hard to show a profit and not allow earnings to show a decreased return on investment."

Employee motivation and compensation. "The problem that really concerns me the most is turning young men into cost- and profit-conscious executives, who are worried about getting sales, controlling costs, setting profitable prices, and spending the company's money. I put a young man in charge of a division. He'd go out and buy some steel. If it were too brittle, would he tell the purchasing department to send it back? Heavens no! He'd just put it in inventory! Same with capital equipment. He'd buy some machinery, and if it didn't work, he'd put it to one side and forget about it, and not even try to get salvage value out of it. Another division head was losing $120,000 but was very indignant when I called him into the office to hear what he was going to do about it because he thought we could just borrow money from a bank. I said, 'You've got 60 days to turn this situation around. I've got no place in the company for a loser.'

"I've got another fellow who came in and said, 'It has been just 14 months since my last raise.' I said, 'What do you want to talk about?' He replied, 'my raise.' And I said, 'The length of time has no relation as to whether you get a raise or not.' I added that he was reviewed a few months ago, at which time he told me about how many letters he wrote but didn't tell me what business he had brought into the house and the profit that he had earned. He replied, 'I worked hard,' and I said, 'I don't know about that. We've got working rules that you start work at 8:15; you're here at 8:30 or 8:45, and during the baseball season you're at the ball park. Sure, I know that you tell the secretaries that you are calling on a customer, but I just happen to know that you were at the baseball game. You come back tomorrow and tell me how much business you have brought in, and how much profit you have made for the company, and whether you are earning the salary you have.'

"Engineers are far too loyal to what they call their 'professional ethics.' A company may have a contract to do something, but the engineer will see that he could do it just that much better. The customer didn't ask for it, the specifications didn't ask for it, and if we do it, we won't be able to make

---

[1] *The Wall Street Journal*, February 9, 1959, p. 1.

a profit or deliver on time. But because of this professional idealism, the engineer goes ahead and does it anyway, with the result that we lose money, the customer is mad because we are late, and perhaps it doesn't work any better than it would have anyway.

"All the other professions—doctors, lawyers, teachers—except the engineer have to collect their bills. Ninety-nine per cent of the latter are living off somebody else's money. If you ask them what have they contributed to earn their money, they get insulted. And if I suggested I wasn't going to pay them unless they contributed to the company, they'd quit. It's never seemed to dawn on some of them that they have to earn their keep.

"Dr. Collins is an example. I noticed that he had more and more unexcused absences and was coming in at 9:00 or 10:00 A.M. and leaving at 3:00 P.M. so I inquired around and learned he was discussing setting up his own company. I called him in the next day and said, 'Let's let our hair down. I'm not going to have this sloppy behavior.' He said, 'You never said anything about my working Saturdays and Sundays when we set up that new division,' to which I replied, 'No, I didn't say anything about my doing it either, but that's why we pay you a good salary. When are you going to leave?' He asked me when I wanted him to and got the reply, 'Tomorrow.' He said, 'I'd hoped you'd let me stay around until I get my company going. Anyway, my time ought to be my own.' And I said, 'O.K. fine, I'll give you a check tomorrow and you'll have all the free time you want.' You know, he's got a wife, two kids, is buying a home, but doesn't recognize the security he owes his family judging by the way he treated his job. His company never got off the ground and now he's broke and looking for a job. I'd like to help him, but my responsibility ended when he transferred his loyalties.

"Expense accounts and perquisites are another problem. Some fellows never put a limit on their hotel bill, so of course they get the most expensive room in the house. I just stopped three executives from leaving in the company plane at 3:00 P.M. instead of 5:00 P.M. They just wanted to get to their destination in time for supper; they hadn't thought that their salaries cost the company $55 an hour, or $110. Another young fellow came in here and said the company should give him a country club membership for entertaining customers. I said, 'No. You may be entertaining five customers now, but soon it will be fifteen people because in fact the company would be paying for your wife's and kids' weekends at the club.'

"You find this lack of cost-consciousness at all levels of the organization. Take those three girls out there, who are executive secretaries and assistants and are paid from $450 to $550 per month. I told them, 'I have a fetish against coffee breaks, which I think are the doom of American industry. Just get a few people around a coffee machine, and I'll bet three out of five of them will have something to gripe about. You are being paid enough money to know that this really does cost money. I don't want coffee drunk at the desk, but if you want to drink coffee, you can check in and out on a time clock and be paid an ordinary clerical salary.' I also asked them to exert their influence on the other girls to try and stop this coffee break business.

"About a week later I went past the coffee machine and found one of the three girls there talking to another secretary. She asked me if I would like a cup of coffee and I said I couldn't afford it. She said, 'Oh, I would be glad to spend the 10 cents.' And I said, 'That's not the point. The company can't afford the time.' So I put in an order to cut her salary $50 per month. That brought all three girls into my office, saying it was a very unfair thing to do. I said, 'I wasn't unfair. Here's a girl who violated an order that I had given. . . .' I then pointed out that I am not running a charitable organization, but running a business, and I can't allow any individuals to destroy the organization. So she has $50 less a month.

"In short I guess people don't realize—and perhaps I didn't either when I was an employee—that you buy manpower the same way you buy productive machinery. You must get a return for your investment.

"We have constant reviews and checks to be sure we're getting a return. Those with an annual salary of $6,000 or less get a semiannual review, while those over $6,000 get an annual one. If the supervisor doesn't recommend a raise, the man has 90 days to correct the faults found. If he does not correct them, he is out. Of course, when I let a man go, the supervisors often come in and really squawk; however, they are more careful the next time when writing their appraisals.

"There are several ways I check on the supervisors' evaluations. I sometimes call in a supervisor and make up fictitious stories about how I never saw so-and-so at work, or how I always see him coming in at 9:00 o'clock in the morning. Then I ask him if he is afraid to put a complete evaluation on somebody. Then I start in on another man. I make him defend all his recommendations. Sometimes they just plain collapse—the supervisors can't really defend their recommendations. They have to have a really good look at what each man does and not just say the whole department has done well. Also, I'll pick out three or four cards sent to me by the personnel department on people coming up for review, and I'll walk around their departments in the morning and at 4:45 in the evening. You can really get an idea of how hard a person works by doing that a couple of times for three or four days. You pick up enough information to justify your comments, and my objections to the supervisors often hit near enough home."

Future plans. Mr. Haws's long-term objective for the company was to utilize the tax loss carry-forward through more diversification, but he told Mr. Stace that his personal objective was to leave Multi-Products, Inc., after another year or so. "I've really worked myself out of a job; I don't do a darn thing except read *The Wall Street Journal* and look for new acquisitions." His contract, which he—but not the company—could cancel, was up in 1961; his salary was about $35,000 with a $17,500 a year consulting fee guarantee for five years after leaving the company, and he had 60,000 of the 113,000 outstanding warrants at $2 a share. The stock was selling for $9 a share in February 1959.

In summing up his career, Mr. Haws felt he had learned to take calculated risks and win, but that young men with whom he worked did not do so. "If I ever had $5,000 in the bank, I'd be mad because it is not earning me a penny. When I am 60 or 65, I don't want to be a total dependent on somebody else, as nine-tenths of these people are destined to be. I offered 5,000 shares of the company at $2 apiece to one young man, and he said, 'I'll let you know in a while. I've got to think it over.' I said, 'I'll give you ten seconds to decide and those ten seconds have just passed, and the offer is off.' Heavens, a young man should have jumped at a chance like that!"

LITTON INDUSTRIES, INC. (AR)*[1]

^^

Litton Industries, a company with headquarters in Beverly Hills, California, had a 1967 sales volume of $1.6 billion, while its 1966 sales of $1.2 billion had placed it 57th on *Fortune's* list of the country's 500 largest industrials. This position had been reached after spectacular growth that had commenced in 1953 with the founding of a company named Electro Dynamics Corporation. In July 1954 after its first nine months of operation, the company had total sales of $3 million and earnings of $154 thousand. The company later changed its name to Litton Industries, Inc., and since that time had grown to its present size through a combination of mergers, acquisitions and internal growth. It should be noted that, contrary to popular opinion, almost 50% of Litton's annual growth was regularly achieved from internal expansion within the company. This fact was often overlooked by observers of the company, in their haste to report on the more glamorous aspects of Litton's merger and acquisition activity.

In 1967, because of its spectacular performance, and the manner in which the acquisition portion of its growth had been achieved, Litton was classified as a conglomerate company.[2] The "popular" definition of the word conglomerate, however, was anything but clear, although general usage had lent it the connotation of encompassing corporations that had grown spectacularly through the acquisition of operating units from a wide range of different industries. Arguments concerning the viability of the conglomerate organizational form ran from the wildly enthusiastic to the highly skeptical. Barton M. Biggs, in an article entitled *Day of Reckoning? Conglomerates Can't Keep Making Two Plus Two Equal Five Forever*, sounded a note of caution:

Stock markets have always had their fads or manias (to use the more impolite term), and the diverse range of the last 40 years runs the gamut of everything from investment trusts in 1929 to small, unseasoned growth companies in 1961–1962. These days the rage on Wall Street is the so-called conglomerate, otherwise known as the "free form" or the "multi-market" company, run by the

---

[1]Data for this case were collected largely from published sources.
[2]For example, see Barton M. Biggs, "Day of Reckoning?" *Barron's*, April 3, 1967.

new breed of wheeler-dealer entrepreneurs who, according to their advocates, personify the highest form of creative capitalism.

"Castro Pesos"

Basically the attraction of a conglomerate is synergistic, i.e., the earnings of the whole are worth more to the market than those of the various parts. The emphasis is on growth by acquisition, either by trading the high multiple stock of the conglomerate for the low multiple shares of the acquisition (otherwise known as Litton's "chain letter operation"),[3] or by swapping a convertible security ("Castro pesos" in the trade lingo of Meshulam Riklis[4]).

* * * * *

This article does not suggest the imminent collapse of conglomerates. Instead, it questions the validity of certain assumptions espoused by their supporters, discusses some rather aggressive accounting practices[5] and cites some developing problems. It concedes that many conglomerates will continue to prosper, but cautions that in spite of synergism, two and two cannot indefinitely continue to make five.

Any discussion of conglomerates must begin with management. Litton, as the first of the really swinging conglomerates, has been the fountainhead of managers for its progeny; as far as Wall Street is concerned, past association with Litton implies that a manager has learned how to successfully practice synergism. Actually, the experts agree that the management of a conglomerate is probably the most demanding of all managerial skills. Thus, *Fortune* quotes Lammont du Pont Copeland, president of Du Pont, as saying that: "Running a conglomerate is a job for management geniuses, not for ordinary mortals like us at Du Pont."

The manager of a conglomerate must be not only an entrepreneur, wise in the ways of deals, but he also must be a renaissance man with the experience and diversity to manage four or five different businesses. In addition, since it is absolutely essential to his plans that the price of his stock keep rising, he must be Wall Street-oriented and a skilled promoter readily accessible to analysts.[6]

The (AR) case describes the growth of Litton from a fledgling electronics company to one of the country's major corporations, the (BR) case contains data on the day-to-day operating procedures of the company, while the (C) case describes Litton's management philosophies.

If Litton could maintain its annual compounded growth rate of 36.6% until 1971, sales would reach $5.5 billion, a figure which at that time would place the company among the top 10 industrial corporations in the United States[7] —a rank that would have taken only 18 years to achieve. In contrast, however, one leading investment advisory service—Value Line—predicted that 1970–1972 sales would only reach $2.8 billion. From the case data, an attempt can be made to settle this question by asking: What is Litton's

---

[3]Case writer's note. In fairness to Litton it should be noted that on several occasions Litton had acquired companies with a higher P/E ratio than their own.

[4]Chairman and president of Rapid-American Corporation.

[5]Case writer's note. Litton was known, however, for its conservative accounting methods as is noted in a later, but unquoted, portion of Mr. Bigg's article.

[6]Biggs, *op. cit.,* p. 3.

[7]Ranked according to sales volume.

strategy? Why has it been so successful? Can this success and growth be maintained in the future?

Company history, 1953–57

In November 1953, a new company was incorporated in Delaware under the name of Electro Dynamics Corporation. In the same month this corporation acquired the ownership of Litton Industries, Incorporated, a small manufacturer of high-quality magnetron tubes[8] located in San Carlos, California. Reporting on this event, *Fortune* magazine commented:

In the late summer of 1953 three young men quit their high-paying jobs with Hughes Aircraft (where they had helped push sales from $2 million to $200 million in just five years) to strike out on their own in the electronics business. Charles B. Thornton had been vice president and assistant general manager at Hughes; Hugh W. Jamieson, a research scientist turned engineer and businessman, had been one of the two chiefs of Hughes's large radar-development group. Roy L. Ash had been Hughes's assistant controller. The oldest, Thornton, was forty. All three were fairly well off. Counting in their wives' jewelry, their houses, securities, and cash, they were probably worth $200,000—about enough money to go into business in a loft.

But Thornton, Ash and Jamieson had larger ideas. They were pioneers in advanced electronics, a business hardly heard of before Hughes Aircraft was pushed into it, largely by Thornton, in 1948. . . . Thornton, Ash, and Jamieson were determined to start a company that would not only rival Hughes in advanced government electronics work but compete in all important commercial electronics markets. On the West Coast these ambitious aims were considered then to be pretty much of a joke.

By late November 1953, however, Thornton had talked hardboiled Lehman Brothers into raising $1,500,000, with which the three bought a small microwave-tube company in San Carlos, California, owned by an engineer named Charles Litton.[9]

Recalling the founding of Litton, *Forbes* magazine quoted Thornton as saying:

"We started this business with a plan," said he [Thornton] last month, "and that plan is nowhere near completion."

The "plan" Thornton talks about, and he does so all the time, sometimes seems little more than a vague generality. In his first annual report to Litton stockholders—scarcely more than a band of insiders in those days—he simply said that his goal was to become "a major company in military, industrial and commercial electronics."[10]

Fortune also mentioned that Litton started with a definite purpose in the form of a defined plan.

---

[8]A magnetron tube is a diode vacuum tube in which the flow of electrons is controlled by an externally applied magnetic field to generate power at microwave frequencies. It is one of the principal components of radar equipment.

[9]William B. Harris, "Litton Shoots for the Moon," *Fortune*, April 1958, p. 114.

[10]"Man on the Move," *Forbes*, July 15, 1961, p. 15.

The plan, broadly stated, is to make Litton competitive with any company in the U.S., no matter what its size, in the most difficult fields of advanced electronics.[11]

Armed with this "plan" and some finance, Electro Dynamics Corporation initially embarked on a program of research and development in three distinct areas: computers and control systems, radar systems, and navigational systems. This R.&D. program was, to a large extent, made possible because of the high rate of cash generation that was forthcoming from the San Carlos tube plant. The emphasis on research work was soon followed by a program of acquiring companies that were engaged in one phase or another of electronics. At about this time, the name of the original magnetron tube plant was changed from Litton Industries to Litton Industries of California, while the corporate name of Electro Dynamics was changed to become Litton Industries.

In 1954 the new Litton identity acquired Digital Control Systems of La Jolla, California—a small firm that specialized in new and advanced techniques relating to digital computers. It also held several important patents in this area. This purchase was closely followed by: West Coast Electronics, a company that produced communication and navigation equipment and specialized in electronic devices; Ahrendt Instrument Co., a designer and manufacturer of electronic and electromechanical servomechanism equipment; U.S. Engineering Co., a major producer of electronic hardware and etched (printed) circuitry; and the Automatic Seriograph Company which held the proprietary rights to an automatic film magazine for taking a series of X-ray pictures. With the added revenue provided by these acquisitions, coupled with internal growth of the existing operations, 1955 revenue totalled $8.9 million and net earnings reached $436,000.

Commenting on the year's performance, in the 1955 Annual Report, Thornton stated, "Litton Industries has successfully continued its planned growth; effective expansion of product bases and rewarding research and development accomplishments have typified the year." He continued later in the report,

The significance of your company's past year's operations is the progress made toward accomplishing our objective—that of becoming a major company in military, industrial and commercial electronics, today one of the most dynamic and growing industries in our national economy.

As the acquisitions were accomplished many of the units were left as relatively autonomous divisions. Exhibit 1 shows the organization as it appeared in September 1955.

The fiscal years of 1956 and 1957 saw further rapid expansion into an increasing range of electronic industries. Exhibit 2 contains a summary listing of the acquisitions and mergers for this period and indicates the type of business that the acquired companies were engaged in prior to their acquisi-

[11]Harris, *op. cit.*, p. 116.

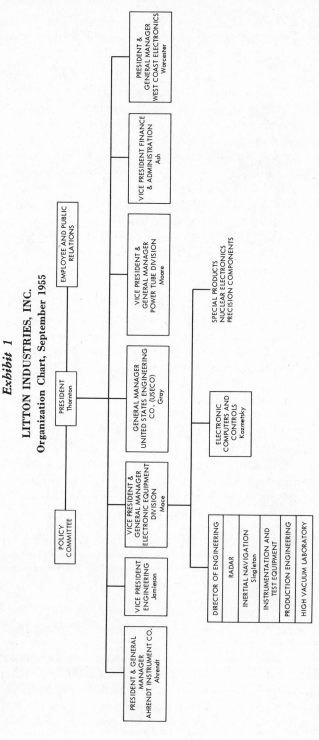

Exhibit 1

LITTON INDUSTRIES, INC.

Organization Chart, September 1955

POLICY COMMITTEE

PRESIDENT
Thornton

EMPLOYEE AND PUBLIC RELATIONS

PRESIDENT & GENERAL MANAGER AHRENDT INSTRUMENT CO.
Ahrendt

VICE PRESIDENT ENGINEERING
Jamieson

VICE PRESIDENT & GENERAL MANAGER ELECTRONIC EQUIPMENT DIVISION
Mace

GENERAL MANAGER UNITED STATES ENGINEERING CO. (USECO)
Gray

VICE PRESIDENT & GENERAL MANAGER POWER TUBE DIVISION
Moore

VICE PRESIDENT FINANCE & ADMINISTRATION
Ash

PRESIDENT & GENERAL MANAGER WEST COAST ELECTRONICS
Worcester

SPECIAL PRODUCTS
NUCLEAR ELECTRONICS
PRECISION COMPONENTS

ELECTRONIC COMPUTERS AND CONTROLS
Kozmetsky

DIRECTOR OF ENGINEERING

RADAR

INERTIAL NAVIGATION
Singleton

INSTRUMENTATION AND TEST EQUIPMENT

PRODUCTION ENGINEERING

HIGH VACUUM LABORATORY

Source: Company records.

Exhibit 2

LITTON INDUSTRIES, INC.

Summary of Acquisitions and Mergers

Date Acquired	Company	Nature of Business
1953		
November 1953	Electro Dynamics Corp.	Parent company—formed to enter electronics industry. Set up by Thornton, Ash, and Jamieson.
November 1953	Litton Industries, Inc.	Manufactured magnetrons and klystrons used in ultrahigh frequency electronic applications.
1954		
— 1954	Digital Control Systems	Specialized in new and advanced techniques relating to electronic digital computers. Held several important patents.
August 1954	West Coast Electronics	Communication and navigation equipment and specialized electronic devices. Acquired, in particular, for two R.&D. programs with production potential.
1955		
January 1955	Ahrendt Instrument Co.	Designs and manufactures electronic and electromechanical servo-mechanism equipment.
January 1955	U.S. Engineering Co. (USECO)	One of the largest producers of electronic hardware and etched (printed) circuitry in the United States.
June 1955	The Automatic Seriograph Co.	Held proprietary rights to an automatic film magazine which provided a series of X-ray pictures. The device was called the automatic seriograph and is manufactured by the Ahrendt Instrument division.
1956		
July 1956	Triad Transformer Corp.	Transformers, wave filters, magnetic component products. 1956 Sales: $3,518,609.

Exhibit 2—Continued

Date Acquired	Company	Nature of Business
1956 Continued July 1956	Utrad Corporation	Product line of pulse transformers. Complementary products to Triad. Also manufactured and distributed certain of Triad's products in the East.
1957 January 1957	Chromatic TV Labs.	Acquired part of their assets only. These related to the development of a new type of color television tube later named as the Chromatron. Useful in radar displays. Acquired from Paramount Pictures, Inc.
August 1957	Digital Control Systems Inc.	Research and development on digital computers. Held several patents. Prior to acquisition, Litton was a licensee of several of the patents. 1956 Sales: $5,714.
November 1957	Maryland Electronic Manufacturing Corp. (MEMCO)	Research, development and manufacture of electronic devices including air navigation aids, radar microwave antennas and telemetering equipment.
1958 January 1958	Monroe Calculating Machine Co.	Business machines, calculators, etc. The acquisition provided for the application of Litton's developments in electronic computing to the business machine field. 1956 Sales: $45 million.
April 1958	Roger White Electron Devices	Research, development and manufacture of electronic devices including microwave sweep generators, traveling wave tube amplifiers and gas tubes. Sales: $436,000.
August 1958	Airtron, Inc.	A manufacturer of specialized microwave components and equipment for radar and other microwave communication. Products are used in a majority of the nation's most advanced missile, aircraft and ground installations. Sales: $7,281,000.

Exhibit 2—Continued

Date Acquired	Company	Nature of Business
1958 Continued		
— 1958	Westex Corporation	Formerly a division of Western Electric. Specializes in sound recording. Westex had an international sales and service organization of 35 foreign offices that could be used to market other Litton products.
1959		
March 1959	Times Facsimile Corporation	Diversified line of facsimile and photo transmission and receiving equipment.
— 1959	Svenska Dataregister, A.B.	Manufactures cash registers and other point of sale systems. Products sold by Sweda in both United States and overseas. The Sweda sales companies were also bought at this time.
1960		
February 1960	Western Geophysical Co.	Operates in the field of geophysical research and exploration. Also engaged in the manufacture, research and development of electronic, optical and electromechanical instruments. Has a fleet of small ships.
— 1960	Servomechanisms (Canada)	Not purchased as an operating concern. Purchased only for its building and 50 staff.
— 1960	Integrated Data Processing, Inc.	
— 1960	Fritz Hellige & Co., G.m.b.H. (Germany)	Manufactures medical and optical instruments. Able to produce parts of inertial guidance systems for use in planes used by European air forces.
1961		
April 1961	Applied Communications Systems	Produced audio-visual devices. A division of Science Research Associates.
April 1961	A. Kimball Co.	Punch tag marking and punch tag reading equipment and related supplies. Products can be sold with Monroe/Sweda cash register systems.

Exhibit 2—Continued

Date Acquired	Company	Nature of Business
1961 Continued		
June 1961	London Office Machines Ltd.	Largest distributor of office machines in London.
June 1961	Simon Adhesive Products Corp.	Pressure sensitive adhesive products used in point of sale and punched tag equipment field.
July 1961	C. Plath K.G. (West Germany)	Manufacturers and worldwide distributors of marine navigation instruments. Potential manufacturers of inertial guidance equipment.
July 1961	Cole Steel Equipment Co., Inc.	Manufactures and sells office equipment and furniture. This acquisition included nine other companies that were affiliated with Cole. Also brings a catalog dealer organization 22,000 strong.
October 1961	Ingalls Shipbuilding Corp.	Produces nuclear-powered submarines, surface vessels and develops and installs marine electronics.
November 1961	Aero Service Corp.	Aerial survey work, photographic analyses, geophysical surveys, etc.
1962		
July 1962	Poly-Scientific Corp.	Design, development and manufacture of electromechanical devices for rotary components, slip rings, brush assemblies, etc.—used in guidance systems.
August 1962	McKiernan-Terry Corp.	Manufactures radar antennas, sonar equipment, ship stabilizers and similar hydraulic and heavy precision mechanical equipment.
October 1962	Emertron, Inc.	Production of high-precision electronic systems and components for missiles and aircraft—radar, beacons, altimeters, etc.
— 1962	Aerospace Research & Engineering Department of General Mills	Builds vehicles to examine the atmosphere including meteorological studies and collection of nuclear weapon debris.
1963		
February 1963	{ Winchester Electronics, Inc. { Pyne Molding Corp.	Manufacture high-quality connectors and terminals for missiles, aircraft, communications systems and test and power equipment.

Exhibit 2—Continued

Date Acquired	Company	Nature of Business
1963 Continued		
September 1963	Adler Electronics Inc.	Development and manufacture of advanced telecommunications equipment.
November 1963	Clifton Precision Products	Research, design and manufacture of synchros, instrument servomotors and navigational computers.
1964		
— 1964	Advanced Data Systems	Produces automatic revenue control systems.
February 1964	Fitchburg Paper Co.	Broad line of specialty type papers, including reproduction papers for office commercial and general use, plastic saturating base papers for plastic laminates, standard and special offset papers.
— 1964	Bruder & Co., Inc.	Manufactured infrared food heating equipment.
June 1964	Streater Industries Inc.	A broad line of display equipment for retail stores including merchandise control centers, check out and sales register related equipment. Planning and design services for merchandising enterprises.
August 1964	Profexray, Inc.	Manufacture and sale of medical, diagnostic and X-ray equipment.
— 1964	Mellonics Systems Development	Design and implementation command and control systems, and data processing systems for satellites and other space vehicles.
October 1964	Royal McBee	Manufacture of typewriters and other office equipment.
November 1964	Hewitt-Robins Inc.	Entered into a technical assistance agreement plan to conduct joint research and development based on complementary nature of materials handling and processing systems of Hewitt-Robins and control capabilities of Litton, especially for bulk material handling.

Exhibit 2—Continued

Date Acquired	Company	Nature of Business
1965		
— 1965	A. Carlisle & Co.	Producer of package and product identification materials. Linked with Eureka division.
January 1965	Magnuson X-ray Co.	Distribution and sale of medical, diagnostic and X-ray equipment and films and related supplies.
— 1965	Microwave Devices (Division of Sylvania Electric)	Capability in microwave tubes for airborne radar systems; reflex klystrons receivers; and rocket tubes and planar triodes for signal generators, transponders and beacons.
— 1965	George A. Henke G.m.b.H.	Medical instruments.
June 1965	The Leopold Company	Manufacture and sale of office furniture.
December 1965	Everett Waddey Co.	Stationery, office supply and printing business.
1966		
January 1966	Alvey-Ferguson Co.	Computer-controlled warehousewide unit handling systems.
July 1966	Sturgis Newport Business Forms	Manufacture and sale of business forms, including sales books, guest checks, snap out forms, continuous data processing forms, checks and register forms.
October 1966	Imperial Typewriters (UK)	Manufacture of typewriters.
November 1966	Apollo Industries	An option to purchase is held on this company. Apollo produces vehicular revenue control systems and is a subsidiary of Taller and Cooper, Inc.

Exhibit 2—Continued

Date Acquired	Company	Nature of Business
1967		
February 1967	Jefferson Electric Co.	
February 1967	Division of Wilson Marine Transit Co.	Great Lakes water transportation.
February 1967	Rust Engineering Co.	Engineering and construction.
	Louis Allis Co.	
March 1967	American Book Co.	Educational Publishing.
April 1967	Stouffer Foods	Engaged in food preparation and service.
May 1967	Kester Solder Co.	Manufacture of solder.
June 1967	Business Equipment Holding Ltd. (Australia)	Sales 1965: $11,052,956.

Source: Company records.

tion by Litton. This exhibit also summarizes, and can be used as a reference for, all acquisitions up to mid-1967.

During these early years the company became heavily engaged in the design and manufacture of inertial-guidance equipment. This device was felt to have important applications in missile and aircraft navigation. Litton was the pioneer in the field of inertial-guidance as applied to airplanes which, in later years, proved to be one of the company's major sources of sales revenue. One description of this important phase of Litton's development read:

> The best example [of the potential electronic equipment and systems market] is the project Litton started in 1954, inertial-guidance devices. The project was under the direction of Dr. Henry Singleton, formerly on the faculty of MIT, who was lured to Litton from North American where he had been in the same kind of work. The perfection of an inertial-guidance system (or call it a non-magnetic automatic compass) is of paramount importance to the military: it is the only kind of directional equipment that can't be jammed. Missiles would approach a target "silently" in the sense that there would be no radiation from directional radar systems to disclose their whereabouts. . . . Singleton, working at Beverly Hills with a team of only six scientists and engineers, designed in just three years the equipment for a practical inertial-guidance system. . . . Litton's inertial-guidance development bears out Thornton's contention that a company need not be big to win business in electronic markets where the basis of competition is brains.[12]

In 1957–58, the price of one inertial-guidance system was nearly $300,000 which meant that the incorporation of the equipment into a series of missiles or aircraft designs would provide the company with a highly desirable large-scale source of revenues.

Litton's entry into another major electronic field took place, in what appeared to be typical Thornton fashion, at about the same time,

> Litton got into digital development in early 1954 for the good reason that a corporation in advanced electronics must have high competence in computer techniques. The way Thornton & Co. entered this field was typical of the way they operate—they simply chose a man to head the effort and told him to get together the best digital computer group he could find.
>
> The man they chose was George Kozmetsky, . . . a thirty-six-year-old Harvard Business graduate and D.C.S. They chose Kozmetsky instead of a physicist or mathematician because Litton's hopeful ultimate objective was to enter all computer markets.[13]

It was these early days of Litton's development that, in large part, set the tone and pattern for the growth which later carried the company over the $1 billion sales mark.

By the end of fiscal 1957, sales volume had reached $28 million and net earnings had climbed to $1.8 million. The total number of employees reached 2,700 and in July, after being listed for a year on the American Stock Ex-

---

[12]*Ibid.*, p. 208.
[13]*Ibid.*

change, the company's common stock was listed on the New York Stock Exchange.

1958–60

Perhaps the first really large acquisition that Litton consummated took place in early 1958. This was the purchase of the $40-million-sales Monroe Calculating Machine Company, a company that was primarily engaged in the manufacture and sale of commercial business machines. The 1958 Annual Report stated the rationale behind this move.

The addition of Monroe Calculating Machine Company during the year, with its excellent product group and extensive sales and service branches across the nation, provides the marketing capability for the application of the company's developments in electronic computing to the business machine field.

The same report also hinted at an additional reason for an acquisition of this type.

The long-range plan of Litton Industries, first stated in our 1954 report to shareholders, said in part, ". . . This plan is designed to establish strong proprietary product values and a broad base on which to grow—a profitable balance between commercial and military electronic products." This report and those of the intervening years reflect the progress which has been made toward the fulfillment of the company's longer range objectives.

Forbes magazine commented about the Monroe acquisition as follows:

Without Monroe, Litton would be dependent upon government contracts for roughly 70% of its sale volume. With it, defense contracts account for little more than half. . . . "Some people were disappointed when we first bought Monroe," Thornton recalled last month. "We got calls from people saying, 'We thought you were in the electronics business. What are you doing with an office machine company?' You wanted to say, 'What the hell do you think electronics *is*? We don't sell electrons. We sell products.' "[14]

The Monroe acquisition helped boost fiscal 1958 revenues to $83 million, up from $28 million in 1957.

Litton continued to acquire companies throughout the 1958–1960 period. Apart from Monroe, the more notable additions included Westrex Corporation, Svenska Dataregister, A.B., the manufacturer of Sweda cash registers, and Western Geophysical Co., an organization which operated in the field of geophysical research and explorations.

The Westrex Corporation, formerly a subsidiary of Western Electric Company, brought to Litton Industries, in the terms of the 1958 Annual Report, "a worldwide sales and service organization covering more than fifty countries. Westrex also supplements the company's knowledge and techniques in the expanding field of electronic communications."

The Svenska acquisition provided the base with which the Monroe division

---

[14]"Man on the Move," *Forbes*, July 15, 1961, p. 18.

could expand its range of business machines into the area of point-of-sale recording. The 1960 Annual Report commented on the acquisition of Western Geophysical as follows:

The application of Litton technology to Western's instrumentation developments, and the addition of Western's seismic knowledge and field experience and capability to Litton technology, offer interesting potential for the furtherance of the corporation's penetration into such advanced fields as antisubmarine warfare, oceanography, and earth currents, as well as for further advancement in the field of oil exploration.

By the end of fiscal 1960, sales had risen to $187 million and earnings to $7.5 million. The number of employees had also increased markedly and stood at an all-time high of 17,400. *Forbes* magazine reported some doubts expressed by the financial community concerning Litton's rapid growth, as follows:

In a cynical world, such fast-climbing success gives some people vertigo. The very sharpness of Litton's growth—in sales, in earnings and, most of all, in stock market value—has inclined some disbelievers to look upon Litton as a brilliantly conceived stock market promotion.[15]

Exhibit 3 presents a simplified organization chart which shows the basic form of the company as of April 1960.

1961–63

Far from being simply a stock market promotion, however, Litton continued to grow, acquiring approximately 16 new companies in this three-year period.

Fortune magazine, in an attempt to illustrate why Litton had continued to be successful, said in 1963:

What sticks out all over the company is not just diversification—everybody does that—but a superb sense of timing. Litton's secret is that it has made a practice of doing what other companies are not doing, and of *not* doing what everybody else is doing. From its very beginning, when almost all industry was scrambling after contracts for military systems, Litton walked the other way and concentrated on electronic components, the profitable hardware of the advanced sciences. When other makers of inertial navigation and guidance equipment went after the glamorous missile market, Litton shot for manned military planes, which turned out to be a far bigger market than anybody supposed. When semiconductors were the rage, Litton stayed out of the business, figuring that the market would shortly be overproduced and would go the way of the receiving-tube business. (It did.) Other companies were lured into marketing big general purpose computers; Litton fortunately stayed out of that, too, and instead developed a promising business in small inexpensive computers. And now, while everybody else is going hopefully at space, Litton has turned its gaze downward

---

[15]*Ibid.*, p. 16.

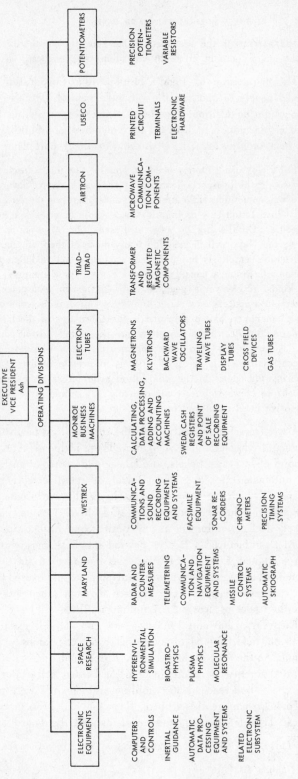

Exhibit 3

LITTON INDUSTRIES, INC.

Partial Organization Chart, April 1960

Source: Company records.

to the bottom of the sea through its recently purchased Ingalls Shipbuilding which has a foothold in the atomic-submarine business.[16]

The acquisition of Ingalls Shipbuilding Corporation, in October 1961, caused people to question the rationale behind Litton's growth plan. At the time of its acquisition, Ingalls' sales were approaching $60 million, it had been losing money, and, in the eyes of many, shipbuilding was a tired industry in a highly competitive world. *Fortune* reported:

But the more Litton looked at Ingalls the more fascinated it became with the wonderful prospects looming in the vasty deep. Says Ash: "We saw that here was something right under our noses that we should have been in before." . . . What Litton saw in Ingalls was a whole new market for its already proved capacities. On the Ingalls ways at Pascagoula, Mississippi, were attack submarines; the Navy will be needing many more of them in the future as an answer to Russia's emphasis on undersea warfare. Such a submarine costs some $70 million, of which a considerable share goes for computers, controls, sonar, and all kinds of electronic gear, and for navigation equipment, including inertial systems. As matters now stand, the Navy's Buships is essentially its own weapon-system manager, and a shipyard is the fabricator of the hull and the assembler of parts. But drawing a long bow into the future, Litton could be confident that within—how long?—ten years perhaps, the Navy would begin to think in terms of contracting entire weapons systems to private industry, and Litton would be superbly placed to do the job. Litton even foresaw the gradual replacement of submarine crews by electronic controls. "A submarine," says Ash, "is the most expensive hotel in the world."[17]

Apart from Litton's entry into the shipbuilding business, the Monroe division acquired several new companies. These included: A. Kimball Co., a maker of point-of-sale tags, tickets, and labels, and owner of an important system for the automated ticketing and control of retail inventory; Simon Adhesive Products, which made pressure sensitive adhesive products used in point-of-sale and punched tag equipment; Cole Steel Equipment Company, Inc., a maker of office equipment and furniture; and Eureka Specialty Printing Co., which manufactured a line of printed supplies—mostly trading stamps. One source quoted Fred R. Sullivan, the manager of the Monroe division, as saying, "We now make everything at point-of-sale except the money that goes into the cash register." The Monroe division alone was estimated to have generated sales of nearly $157 million in 1963.

The years 1962 and 1963 also saw considerable expansion in the purely electronic field. A total of seven electronic companies were acquired in this period. At the end of fiscal 1963, Litton had amassed 36 divisions, which operated seventy-one plants in both the United States and nine foreign countries. Sales had reached $553 million and earnings were up to $23.3 million.

To help manage this empire, Roy Ash had been named president, while "Tex" Thornton remained as chairman of the board and chief executive

---

[16]Carl Rieser, "When the Crowd Goes One Way Litton Goes the Other," *Fortune*, May 1963, p. 117.

[17]*Ibid.*, p. 220.

officer, though in actual practice this change was more nominal than substantive. The organization had also been divided into groups that exercised control over divisions engaged in similar activities. As of 1963 there were five such groups: the business-machine group with sales of approximately $160 million (29% of total sales); shipbuilding with a contribution of $85 million (15%); electronic components with sales of $49 million (9%); the commercial electronic equipment and services group with sales of $49 million (about 9%); and the electronic systems group with sales of nearly $210 million (38%). The last-mentioned group, electronic systems, had been the fastest growing, a performance which was largely a result of the rapidly increasing sales of inertial-guidance systems.

In 1963, as had happened several times in prior years, observers continued to question the probability of Litton continuing to achieve its historical rate of growth. A typical report commented:

But quite naturally, too, the dazzling nature of Litton's rise has produced skeptics. In Wall Street there are a considerable number of bears who find Litton overpriced at a thirty-to-one earnings ratio and the stock at times has been heavily short-traded. The skeptics argue that no company, when it has become as big as Litton, can keep sales growing at 30 to 50 per cent per year and that when growth slows up the glitter of Litton will be gone. Others point out that while Litton recently has managed to turn a 4.1 per cent after-tax profit on sales —fair enough in the electronics field—still this is nothing spectacular. And finally there are those who wonder whether a company that has grown and diversified so fast won't someday get out of hand, organizationally speaking.[18]

1964–67

Once again the skeptics were proven wrong. At the end of fiscal 1967, some four years after the above report was written, Litton's sales had reached $1.6 billion and earnings had kept step at $70.1 million. During this period another 26 companies had been acquired, among which were the Fitchburg Paper Co.; Royal McBee Corporation; Hewitt-Robins Inc., a manufacturer of materials handling and processing systems; and Stouffer Foods, a restaurant operator and producer of frozen foods.

Commenting on the first two of these acquisitions, the 1964 Annual Report stated:

Litton complemented its rapidly growing line of papers and paper products by adding the operations of Fitchburg Paper Co., producer of reproduction papers for office commercial and general use and other quality papers for a variety of applications.

*   *   *   *   *

After the close of fiscal 1964 we reached a preliminary agreement with Royal McBee Corp., to bring together its operations with Litton. . . . If approved, the merger will have far reaching significance for both Litton and Royal McBee. In addition to Litton's extensive line of business machines, office supplies and related equipment, we will be able to offer the Royal line of manual and electric typewriters and electromechanical data processing systems.

---

[18]*Ibid.*, p. 115.

The 1965 Annual Report commented on the addition of Hewitt-Robins, Inc., to Litton as follows:

Additional areas of industrial interest unfolded when Hewitt-Robins, Inc., joined Litton Industries, bringing with it outstanding skills in materials conveying, processing, and control. Among its accomplishments during the year, the Hewitt-Robins Division completed a new facility for the Duquesne Light Company of Pittsburgh. The conveyance system for this Pennsylvania public utility transports thousands of tons of coal daily from the mine to a preparation plant six and one-half miles away.

Hewitt-Robins people are active in many other fields too—a few of which include production of mobile plants for raw material processing in road construction, flexible flow lines for liquids and gases, mobile conveyance systems for mining, vibrating equipment, and precision gears and speed reduction for power transmission.

The addition of Hewitt-Robins appeared to be difficult to explain in terms of Litton's prior pattern of operations. *Business Week* commented:

Litton has shown it can shape big opportunities quickly.

A case in point is its latest group, newly formed Transportation Systems, which encompasses Ingalls Shipbuilding Corp. (acquired in 1961), Hewitt-Robins (1965), and Alvey-Ferguson Co. (January 1966), which builds computer-controlled, warehouse-wide unit handling systems complementary to the equipment built by Hewitt-Robins.

"Our first big project," says John B. Cogan, group vice-president, "is to apply a systems engineering approach to the problems of transporting ore in the Great Lakes area. We intend to link ships and conveying systems into one carrying system." With this in mind, Litton last January set up Litton Great Lakes Corp., to study the feasibility of constructing a $25 million shipyard on the lakes near Cleveland. The study is expected to be completed in May.[19]

The Stouffer Foods acquisition was explained in the 1967 Annual Report's letter to shareholders as follows:

Shortly after the close of the fiscal year, Stouffer Foods Corporation joined Litton. Stouffer's experience in the processing, packaging and marketing of food, coupled closely with Litton's capabilities in electronic cooking technology, should produce major advances in the fast-growing markets of home, commercial and institutional food preparation.

The company was organized in 1967 into seven reclassified groups: Business Equipment which accounted for $480 million sales; Industrial Systems and Equipment with around $230 million in sales; Defense and Space Systems with approximately $375 million; Components with close to $110 million; Marine with a sales volume of $165 million; Professional Services and Equipment with $140 million; and Educational Systems with $25 million. (See Exhibit 4 for a detailed organization chart.) Of the yearly growth in sales volume almost 50% was reported to come from internal growth and the remainder from acquisitions.

---

[19]"What Puts the Whiz in Litton's Fast Growth," *Business Week*, April 16, 1966, p. 179.

Exhibit 4

LITTON INDUSTRIES, INC.

Partial Organization Chart, November 1967

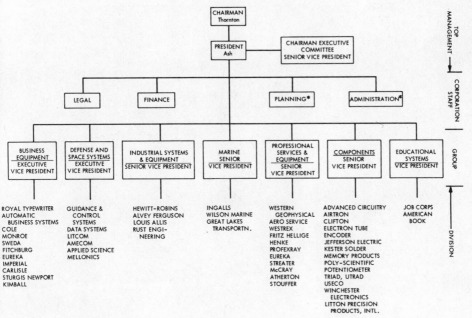

*Titles not finally determined.
Source: Company interviews.

Commenting on how Litton had changed over the years, *Business Week* said:

Litton has . . . abandoned all pretense of being an electronics company. Today it is a giant conglomerate in technology.

* * * * *

Increasingly, . . . it is performing a myriad of professional and business services—store design, computer preparation of income tax forms, design of educational curriculums. It even conducts broad economic studies, such as one it is currently making for the Greek government, on how best to develop the island of Crete and the Peloponnesus peninsula.

* * * * *

A former Litton officer describes the scene today: "Litton now is something like a Fourth of July skyrocket. First, 10 stars burst. Then each of them burst into 10 others."[20]

Financial

Litton's financial performance had caused the company's common stock to be considered by the stock market as one of the leaders in the growth field. Exhibit 5 illustrates the company's growth in graphical form by depicting sales, net earnings, and net earnings per share for the years 1957–1967. Over

[20] *Ibid.*, p. 175.

Exhibit 5

LITTON INDUSTRIES, INC.

Sales, Net Earnings, Earnings per Share, 1957–1967

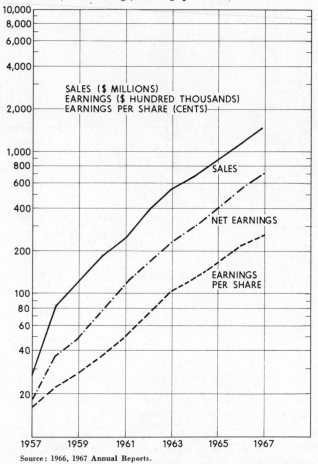

Source: 1966, 1967 Annual Reports.

this period, the growth in all three factors had been at virtually a constant rate, with sales averaging an annual compounded growth of 36.6% between 1961 and 1967.

A summary of financial operations for the 10-year period 1958–1967 is contained in Exhibit 6.

Because Litton, especially in its early years, aimed to grow in the electronics market, Exhibit 7 is included to show the change in factory sales of electronic products between 1950 and 1967. This exhibit also shows the growth in four segments of the total electronics market; namely, government, industrial, consumer products, and replacement components.

The original financing of Litton was arranged in 1953 with Lehman Brothers, a New York investment banking house. Commenting on this original attempt to raise capital, *Forbes* magazine reported:

Exhibit 6

LITTON INDUSTRIES, INC.
Summary of Operations, 1958–67

	1958	1959	1960	1961	1962	1963	1964	1965	1966	1967
Operating Results										
Sales and service revenues	$83,155,473	$125,525,561	$187,761,242	$250,114,456	$393,807,709	$553,146,239	$686,135,497	$915,573,929	$1,172,233,328	$1,561,510,340
Earnings before taxes on income	7,004,437	10,805,756	15,365,182	19,687,457	30,849,499	43,796,403	56,151,444	71,539,247	96,212,024	120,061,135
Federal and foreign taxes on income	3,342,234	5,851,725	7,910,328	9,529,134	14,533,547	20,500,296	26,384,123	31,787,234	40,597,821	49,991,008
Net earnings	3,702,203	4,954,031	7,454,854	10,158,323	16,315,952	23,296,107	29,767,321	39,752,013	55,614,203	70,070,127
Per share*										
Per pro forma share outstanding at year end†	...	...	...	...	...	...	...	...	2.19	2.60
Per common share outstanding at year end	.22	.28	.37	.50	.74	1.04	1.28	1.64	...	...
Depreciation	2,090,083	2,235,128	3,213,720	5,131,267	8,527,000	11,467,000	16,780,000	22,998,000	26,577,000	33,778,000
Financial Position (Year-End)										
Net working capital	$23,117,831	$38,741,071	$53,846,309	$73,631,064	$113,478,440	$151,350,137	$198,260,860	$235,752,097	$320,364,523	$401,424,847
Property, plant and equipment—at cost	22,781,070	29,633,695	41,545,708	60,860,252	106,787,138	140,975,286	175,228,276	246,306,480	278,666,273	364,685,240
Accumulated depreciation	7,915,605	11,850,224	17,563,971	22,987,124	43,820,326	55,085,040	70,560,357	89,427,211	110,438,942	144,001,824
Net property, plant and equipment	$14,865,465	$17,783,471	$23,981,737	$37,873,128	$62,966,812	$85,890,246	$104,667,919	$156,879,269	$168,227,331	$220,683,416
Total assets	57,750,861	83,254,170	119,004,373	172,771,125	269,491,286	354,945,287	423,697,443	630,023,274	742,535,485	945,024,472
Shareholders' investment	27,994,799	34,546,600	50,568,249	63,730,972	102,934,058	121,967,925	154,749,892	231,998,008	308,879,441	426,986,538
General Statistics (Year-End)										
Shares of common stock outstanding*	16,486,346	17,080,977	19,773,084	20,263,430	21,876,263	22,396,812	22,632,720	22,980,730	20,982,316	21,536,644
Shares of preferred stock outstanding	...	...	...	...	...	...	463,681	868,905	169,292	128,257
Shares of preference stock outstanding	...	...	...	...	...	...	...	...	3,989,239	5,125,338
Stock dividends on common stock	2½%	2½%	...	2½%	2½%	2½%	2½%	2½%	2½%	2½%
Stock splits of common stock	...	...	Two for one	...	...	Two for one	...	...	Two for one	...
Number of shareholders of record:										
Common	5,801	8,589	16,322	21,936	32,755	43,417	57,323	59,009	78,744	90,455
Preferred	...	...	...	...	...	...	10,203	16,175	4,346	4,153
Preference	...	...	...	...	...	...	...	...	35,703	37,272
Number of employees	8,600	12,400	17,400	23,000	37,700	43,000	46,900	65,500	75,900	95,500

The above tabulations summarize the company's financial statements as contained in its annual reports for each of the years 1958 through 1967 which include the operations of businesses acquired under the pooling of interests concept from the beginning of the year in which the acquisition occurs. On the basis of including operations of pooled businesses prior to their years of acquisition, operating results would have been as follows:

	Sales and Service Revenues	Net Earnings	Earnings Per Share
1963	$ 723,800,000	$26,263,000	1.04
1964	832,377,000	33,085,000	1.31
1965	1,069,422,000	43,264,000	1.65
1966	1,340,964,000	60,928,000	2.28

*Adjusted for stock dividends and stock splits.

†Litton's convertible preference stock was first issued in March 1966. The earnings per share have been computed on the basis of the number of common shares that would have been outstanding, assuming full conversion of the preference stock, at July 31, 1967, and July 31, 1966, respectively.

Source: 1967 Annual Report.

Exhibit 7

FACTORY SALES OF ELECTRONIC PRODUCTS
BY MARKETS, 1950–67

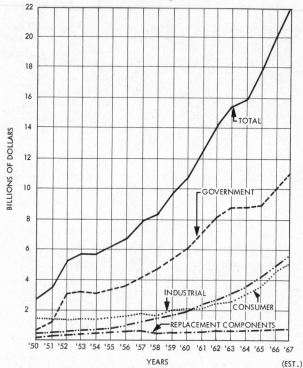

Source: *Electronic Industries Yearbook* (Washington, D.C.: Electronics
Industries Association, 1967), p. 4.

The way to sell that market [government electronics], Thornton thought, was
to build a company loaded with brainy men who could come up with new weapons.
"The concept," he now says, "would have been evident to any nine-year-old child
willing to think about it."

Thornton's concept was evident to many others besides nine-year-olds. Lehman
Brothers, by one insider's count, had "dozens" of similar propositions to choose
among at the time Thornton made his pitch. What made Lehman back Thornton
and reject so many others? "We were impressed by Thornton himself," says
Thomas. "He spoke our language."[21]

The original financing consisted of the following securities:

525,000 shares of $0.10 par value common stock	$ 52,500
2,500 shares of $100 par value preferred stock	250,000
$1,200,000 of five year 5% sub. income debentures	$1,200,000
	$1,502,500
Less expenses, etc. (approx.)	2,500
Net capital raised	$1,500,000

---

[21]"Man on the Move," *Forbes*, July 15, 1961, p. 15.

Exhibit 8

LITTON'S AND STANDARD & POOR'S "425"
ANNUAL AVERAGE P-E RATIO, 1955–66

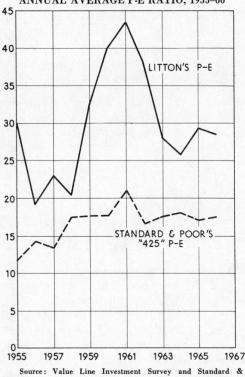

Source: Value Line Investment Survey and Standard & Poor's.

Also sold at the same time, for 1¢ per share, were options to purchase 300,000 shares of common stock for $1 up until January 31, 1960. Lehman bought 25,000 of these options while Thorton, Ash, and Jamieson purchased the remainder.

The company later chose to convert these initial securities into common stock, and subsequently converted one share of preferred for 100 shares of common as well as exchanging the debentures for common at $10.75 per share, issuing 111,611 shares in the exchange. The initial capitalization was thus equivalent from the purchasers' point of view to 886,611 shares of common stock. Over the years Litton, in lieu of cash dividends, had paid seven 2½% stock dividends and split the stock 2-for-1 on three separate occasions. Thus for an average initial investment per common share of $1.70, the investor would have seen his holding appreciate (at mid-1967 market prices) to approximately $900—an average annual compounded appreciation rate of 69%.

This tremendous appreciation in market value was, over the years, a factor that kept the stock market pricing the share at a high price/earnings multiple. Exhibit 8 shows the company's average price/earnings range for the years

1955–1967 coupled with the same variable for Standard & Poor's "425" industrials. The lowest multiple of 19 was recorded in 1956, while the highest value of 43.5 occurred in 1961. This high average level of price/earnings ratio had been one of the key factors in allowing Litton to acquire companies on advantageous terms.

A further example of the importance of stock market reaction to Litton's growth—and Litton's attempt to ensure the reaction was favorable—is contained in this extract from *Business Week*.

Besides beating the bushes for likely companies, and stalking them when they are found, corporate acquisition men devote much ingenuity to baiting each deal with just the right mixture of cash, stock and other securities.

It's a bit like designing a breakfast food box. The idea is to put together a package that seems to offer the selling stockholders a lot—while costing the buyer as little as possible. . . .

To cope with this, a new kind of convertible stock has been invented—or rather revived from the 1920's. . . .

The new stock is called by the tongue-twisting name of convertible *participating* preferred.

*   *   *   *   *

Litton solved the problem [of their old convertible preferred selling at parity with the common stock thus preventing Litton from giving out preferred at a premium for acquisitions] by creating the convertible participating preferred. . . . The new shares carry no dividend, but are rigged in other ways so that they should retain some premium over Litton common until 1989. This is accomplished mainly through a rising conversion privilege, which really amounts to a stock dividend, but which gets capital gains treatment.

Share-for-share. A holder of Litton's new preferred can convert it into common this year on a share-for-share basis. Next year, though, he will get 1.0309 shares of common stock per share of preferred. . . . The same thing will be possible each year until 1989, when the rate reaches 1-for-2.0145.

*   *   *   *   *

As added protection, Litton has set a floor under the new preferred with a rising scale of redemption prices and a proviso that holders may at Litton's option, sell 3% of their preferred back to the company each year. . . .

The inventor. Most Wall Streeters credit the idea for the new stock to young (42) Seymour M. Rosenburg, Litton vice-president for long-range planning and development, though the company line is that it was brainstormed by a group of executives.[22]

---

[22]"A Relic of the 1920's Returns," *Business Week*, August 13, 1966, p. 80 ff.

LITTON INDUSTRIES, INC. (BR)*

^^

Litton Industries, Inc., a company with 1967 sales of $1.6 billion, had shown spectacular growth since its formation in 1953. The history and financial performance leading to this growth have been described in Litton Industries, Inc. (AR).

The present case describes some of the organizational policies and internal structure that characterized the company's operation in 1967. The information is presented under five headings, namely, "Opportunity Planning," "Public Relations," "Organization," "the Control System," and "Internal Communications."

Opportunity planning

In order to gain an understanding of how a multi-industry company with some 6,000 products set its stance and identified its growth potential, there follows a detailed description of the Litton opportunity-formulation process.

Planning at Litton was considered to be a line and not a staff activity. The division manager, the group vice president, and the president himself were all actively concerned with planning for their appropriate level. This is not to say that each line officer had to be an economist or be skilled in the techniques of trend forecasting. Rather he was charged with the responsibility of initiating, understanding, finalizing, and presenting his plans at the appropriate time and place. The genesis of the majority of Litton's plans took place at the division level. At least once a year, and possibly more frequently[1] with some of the larger divisions, the division manager was required to submit to his group vice president a description of what he wanted his division to do during the coming 12-month period. Basically he was required, as Mr. Ash put it:

. . . to firstly assess the strengths and weaknesses of his division in detail. Then he must look at the world around him. He knows his own industry best and he is expected to determine niches, opportunities or whatever you like to call them that his division could possibly exploit. In addition, he must examine each of his existing products to see where he could do better, what he could per-

---

*Copyright © 1968 by the President and Fellows of Harvard College. Reprinted by permission.

[1]The frequency was determined by need rather than by formal schedules.

haps dispense with and how he plans to take the appropriate action. In effect, he progressively narrows in on a match between the world around him and his own division's capabilities.

I should tell you that we dislike the word planning here because it tends to suggest staff activities, and also implies a sense of rigidity and neatness of approach. Because of this, we have substituted the word "opportunity." This has more of the flavor we want—it suggests innovation and new ways of doing things. We want, wherever possible, major steps forward—not just successive refinements. It's with this in mind that we push our division managers very hard to really identify the opportunities and to be creative in doing so.

Using this basic approach, the division manager created his opportunity or business plan. At this stage there was no great emphasis on financial data, although in broad terms the projected revenue, profit, and capital required for the various opportunities had to be identified. The emphasis was on the logic of the proposals and how well thought-out the various alternatives were. In addition a missed or unidentified opportunity was as catastrophic as a poorly supported or overly ambitious proposal.

At the group level, the division opportunity plans were evaluated, discussed, and modified as appropriate. A group vice president stated that he did not so much view his position as one of telling the division manager what to do, but rather he acted as a sounding board which allowed the division manager to test and try out new ideas and suggestions. In the final analysis, however, the group vice president felt that he had to reach some agreement with the division manager's proposals and to check them for consistency with the other divisions of his group. The relationship was one of cooperation, with both the group and division managers trying to arrive at the most advantageous final solution. The process at this stage was described by another group vice president as follows:

The development of an opportunity plan is not a financial rigamarole. Basically, I try to look at what assets we have, what are the opportunities that exist and what are the risks and rewards that could result. Each opportunity is tried as a complete package, considering what we can get out of it and whether we can make a go of it. If we think the best route to exploiting the opportunity is the acquisition of another company, then we will recommend which one and why.

The third and final major step in the opportunity planning process was the presentation of the division plans to the company's president, Mr. Ash. Each division had a separate opportunity session which was attended by approximately five people: the division manager and probably one divisional marketing and one divisional technical expert, the appropriate group vice president and Mr. Ash. At this session the *division manager* presented his opportunity plan for the coming year. Mr. Ash commented on these sessions as follows:

Our evaluation of opportunities is systematized, not formalized. We try to emphasize the analysis aspect of the opportunity session rather than the formal presentation side of things. *Everybody digs in.* I bring to the meeting the companywide perspective yet the least detailed knowledge, while the division manager brings the most intimate knowledge with his special perspective and, of course, the group vice president is somewhere in between with both perspective and knowledge. We attempt to hammer out strategies as distinct from tactics. If the proposals seem a bit weak or data is missing we will send them back to the drawing board and have the division manager try again. There is no satisfactory technique that suits all divisions. We don't set goals that they have to meet. Some divisions, by the nature of their business, will grow faster than the corporation as a whole, while others will be slower or perhaps even temporarily static. The real question we ask ourselves is, have we made the very most of the opportunities that are available to us in each environment as the division or group managers and myself see it. Of course, the group vice president has done most of his own soul-searching before he comes to these sessions.

One group vice president commented on the meetings:

The essence of the opportunity session is that a whole variety of talents is brought to bear on the new opportunities that exist. However, you must remember that this is not a democratic institution—Mr. Ash has the final say on any proposal.

As you mentioned earlier, it is in these meetings that the allocation of company resources is effectively made—although in actual practice this is something of a misnomer, because to my knowledge there has never been an occasion when a good project or opportunity has been held up for lack of funds. It is not really a matter of having a certain size pie and trying to equitably share this out among all the competing claims. That's just a textbook notion of how things *should* go.

Once the opportunity session had been successfully completed, the division manager then generated a set of detailed and interlocking financial plans that reflected the decisions taken in the meetings. These plans contained profit and loss statements, balance sheets and supporting data for the coming 12-month period on a month-by-month basis. Financial data were also included for a 24-month period on a quarterly basis and for a 36-month period on a yearly basis. The financial plans were developed on a "running-year" system and were submitted ultimately to the corporate financial vice president. Once checked for accuracy they were returned to the divisions as a "charter" for the coming year's operations. The details of the financial plan and its use as a reporting and control device will be discussed later in the case. It is important to note here, however, that the opportunity planning and review was completely independent of the financial planning and review, and that it was the opportunity sessions that formed the basis upon which the financial plans were developed.

In considering the role of Mr. Ash in the opportunity review sessions, it is important to note that he relied upon at least two other "inputs" to help him relate each division's activities to those of the corporation as a whole. These two inputs were: (1) an overall plan for Litton as a corporation, and (2) the identification of opportunities outside existing corporate group activities. These latter were developed by a corporate staff planning function[2] at company headquarters.

Litton's overall plan was something about which very little was publicly said. As Mr. Thornton told the researcher, "We do not disclose the details of our plan because we feel that this could be viewed as a promotion. We are more interested in replacing words and pseudo-promises with results."

Exhibit 1

A REPRESENTATION OF LITTON'S OVERALL OPPORTUNITY PLAN*

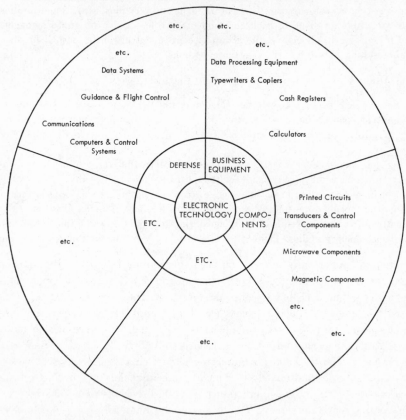

*The above diagram is representative of the structure of Litton's plan. As was explained in the text, the actual details were not released by the company.
Source: Company records.

Although it was clear that the plan involved financial considerations, the opportunity aspects of it were embodied in a chart of the form shown in Exhibit 1. This figure is a representation of the plan drawn up in 1955 and which was still in use in 1967. It can be seen that the "relative" environment

[2] In November 1967, this staff activity was being reformed and attempts were being made to dispense with the word "planning."

has been divided into basic areas which are then further subdivided into more specific product groupings. The format was highly flexible and the completion of any one part could occur at any time.

An example of the company's opportunity orientation can be seen in the acquisition of Stouffer Foods. The Professional Service and Equipment Group's Atherton division had developed the technology of electronic microwave cooking and was marketing an electronic oven for commercial use. Litton came to see that an essential adjunct to the widespread use of electronic ovens was the need to develop a food technology which could make the best use of the new technique. The opportunity was there, because the labor involved in food preparation for hotels, hospitals, company cafeterias, and similar institutional food outlets was becoming prohibitively expensive. To take advantage of this opportunity, Litton decided to save time by acquiring the requisite food technology rather than developing its own capabilities. The result was the purchase of Stouffer Foods. Thus a completely new area of endeavor, or an opportunity, was opened up.

It seemed clear that the existence of an overall plan was in no way a limiting factor in the company's operations. A case in point was the purchase of Ingall's shipyard. A move into the shipbuilding business was not envisaged in the original plan, but was an opportunity that arose unexpectedly and, as it turned out, was one which suited Litton's strengths. The shipbuilding industry had great potential, but it was old and inefficient and needed a big shot of technology and systems management. Litton could provide these skills as well as the electronic parts that went to make up a large portion of a modern ship's fittings. Thus what initially seemed to be an unattractive proposition (and was, in fact, at first rejected) was destined to become an important part of Litton's 1967 operations. Litton's approach to opportunities thus remained flexible, although at the same time the overall plan continued to provide a certain cohesiveness and direction. This factor distinguishes Litton from many of the more financially oriented multi-industry corporations.

The second input to the role played by Mr. Ash in the opportunity review sessions came from his knowledge of the activities and leads being generated by the corporate planning group. This staff group identified opportunities and sifted acquisition possibilities that would normally fall outside the domain of the operating groups and divisions. They also played an advisory role, together with a division, in exploring opportunities, although they would never assume a dictatorial position. They were also active in the actual mechanics of completing an acquisition and integrating it into Litton.

It is appropriate to make mention here of the company's acquisition procedure, as this was a direct outgrowth of the opportunity-evaluation process. Potential acquisition possibilities could enter the Litton organization from any one of three sources: (1) From the division manager or group vice president as a part of their opportunity planning; (2) from the corporate planning staff or some other member of top management; or (3) from outside the company, such as when people came forward with suggestions or requests

for Litton to consider a potential candidate. Generally speaking, the responsibility for consummating an acquisition was placed on the source that recommended it. In the case of the group or division managers, negotiations and
details were their responsibility after it had been determined with corporate
management that such an acquisition was desirable, and that the range of
terms and conditions were agreed on by Ash or Thornton. They were expected to be the driving force behind the acquisition, although they were
also expected to call upon headquarters for professional and technical assistance in legal and financial matters. It should be noted that although these
line managers might have initiated a possible acquisition, they could not
commence proceedings until Mr. Ash, by way of the opportunity sessions, had
given corporate approval. Possible acquisitions that came from the other two
sources were usually handled by the corporate planning staff. In most instances, however, Mr. Ash and/or Mr. Thornton would approve the final
price and perhaps enter the negotiations as they reached their climax. All legal
work connected with the activity, including antitrust considerations, was the
domain of the corporate legal staff, while the postnegotiation merging of the
acquired company into Litton was also handled at the corporate level. In
late 1967, the scope of this latter function was being expanded by the
enlargement of the corporate "planning" function. The idea was to actually
transfer a man from corporate "planning" to the acquired company for a
period of several months where he was responsible for ensuring that the
opportunities that gave rise to that particular acquisition did, in fact, become
a reality. In short, the aim was to "digest" the new acquisition into Litton as
quickly and painlessly as possible.

The company did not have a single set of specific acquisition criteria
except with regard to the overall opportunity plan shown in Exhibit 1 and
in relation to antitrust considerations, where great care was taken to ensure
that no antitrust regulations were violated. Each acquisition was examined, of
course, in the light of its ability to fulfill an opportunity potential. Mr. Thornton spoke of the acquisition process as follows:

> We have not restricted our vision. We have an overall objective that the company
> is working towards and this is broken down into some general *guidelines* which
> help us decide which companies we should acquire, although we do not have a
> specific checklist that evaluates the candidates for us.

Mr. Ash elaborated on some of the guidelines which influenced the company's
search for acquisition candidates:

> Our acquisition criteria are not explicitly listed, but generally speaking there
> are certain attributes against which we evaluate each potential acquisition. For
> instance, we do not want to become involved with companies or industries that
> are dependent for their future growth upon the growth of the economy as a
> whole or, put in another way, each opportunity must have a growth potential in
> its own right. Most suitable acquisitions will ideally be greater than a certain
> critical mass, that is, the acquisition shouldn't be of such a size that it has be-

come dependent on the economy for growth, neither should it be so small that it has to struggle for survival. Apart from these factors, we also try to avoid getting into situations where we are just selling brainpower. We want to obtain some leverage on our skills by selling an end product and not just the skill itself. In addition to these guidelines there are certain industries which have characteristics that we feel are not suited to our particular business philosophy. As an example we are not interested in acquiring financial companies or in becoming involved with retailing.

These sorts of guidelines, coupled with our overall plan for the company, shape the nature and type of acquisitions that we consummate.

One group vice president commented in a slightly different way:

There are three categories of what I suppose you might call acquisition criteria. Firstly, we are looking for products that have an inherent growth in them —you have to acquire a potential. Secondly, we are looking for places where Litton's management skills can be helpful. These first two criteria are considered together, not separately. Then, having lined up some candidates, we apply the usual mathematical skills to see how the financial aspects will work out. These results are not measured against a list of requirements, but are viewed in the context of the overall opportunity. An essential part of this, of course, is projecting out what an acquisition will do for us in the future. In a lot of cases we are buying time, not *just* particular product skills.

Public relations

The term public relations encompasses a wide range of activities such as relations with the financial community, speeches by top corporate executives, relationships with the press, relationships with government agencies and local authorities, as well as corporate advertising policy and, of course, stockholder relationships. At the corporate level in Litton, most of these activities came under the jurisdiction of a staff group headed by a vice president. His responsibility was, in reality, concerned with Litton's "image" to the outside world and one of his tasks was to ensure that the image presented was a *consistent* image.

We shall deal firstly with the area of relations with the financial community. For a company that was pursuing a rapid course of growth, good relationships with the country's "sources of capital" was a particularly important consideration. For instance, it was well-known that the higher a company's price-earnings ratio became, the more likely it was to have an advantage in acquiring, by an exchange of stock, other companies whose price-earnings ratios were probably at a lower level. Litton had always been particularly well placed in this respect.[3]

The reasons for a company's command of a high price-earnings ratio are difficult to determine, but one important contributing factor is undoubtedly the degree of its exposure to both the financial analysts and to the investing public. At corporate headquarters there were two people solely engaged in

---

[3]See Exhibit 8, Litton Industries, Inc. (AR), for relative levels of P-E ratios.

providing financial analysts with access to the company, as well as supplying them with data and statistics concerning Litton's operations. Another vehicle for telling the investing public about the activities of Litton was the company's annual report. This was more than just a financial statement. It was carefully planned as a means both of conveying an image and of reducing the public's confusion concerning Litton's multi-industry approach to business. Each year the report took a different theme to dramatize its message. In 1965 the report was graced with many full color reproductions of classical works of art. In 1966 the report commenced with an essay on "Managing Ideas" by Allan Nevins, an American scholar who had twice received a Pulitzer prize for his biographical works. There was also a photographic interpretation of the same theme by one of the country's leading photographers. The 1967 report dramatically built its theme around the artistry and techniques of stained glass, with many full-plate color illustrations incorporated into the text. In addition to distributing these annual reports to the American financial community, Litton also had them printed in the languages of those countries where it had overseas divisions. The reports were then distributed to members of the government, industry and other public figures in those countries. One notable extension of this practice was the publication of a Russian edition, although the company had no business relationships with the U.S.S.R. The Russian language version was regularly sent to high-ranking officials in the Soviet government and clearly were read by somebody, as on two separate occasions they were given very "poor reviews" in *Pravda*. In a recent discussion with *Fortune* magazine, Ash stated Litton's reasons for placing such emphasis on their annual report:

We've been undertaking a lot of new and different activities in fairly rapid order, and so we can use the annual reports to tell the public about them in great detail. Now the public believes it understands the products and work of most billion-dollar companies. It may not really know them, but it thinks it does. With Litton they don't even *think* they know—so we like to help them get acquainted. That's the first reason. The second reason, and I guess your advertising people don't like this, is that we don't do much institutional advertising. We've been spending only about $50,000 a year on institutional advertising, and you'll have to agree that's very little for a billion-dollar company. So our annual report serves some of the same functions. Our salesmen use it. Of course, we do product advertising.[4]

Investigating the advertising policies further, it was clear that at the corporate level, as indicated by Mr. Ash above, there was little or no institutional advertising. The small amount of advertising that was done at the corporate level, however, was aimed at the engineers and technical people. The form of this advertising was somewhat unique. It consisted of a series entitled "Problematical Recreations" which was based on a collection of mathematical and logic puzzles that would appeal to the engineer. They ap-

---

[4]"How Litton Keeps It Up—The View from Inside," *Fortune*, September 1966, p. 152.

peared in certain technical journals under the Litton name and had proved so popular that they had been republished in both pamphlet and book form. There were enthusiastic puzzle fans following this Litton series in most major countries of the world.

Apart from this limited corporate advertising, the divisions were free to advertise as they saw fit, the only restriction being that they were required to identify themselves as a division of Litton Industries. Most divisional advertising was product oriented.

Another important part of Litton's public relations was in the area of speechmaking. The main speakers for the company were Mr. Thornton and Mr. Ash although several other top executives were also active in this regard. Most of the speeches were either directly about Litton's approach to doing business or else were on subjects where Litton's activities could be used as an illustration. The speeches were primarily made to various management groups, business schools, and occasionally to national or regional civic and industry groups. There were also a number presented to the security analysts. Mr. Ash commented:

I spoke to the New York analysts this year, and Tex did about two years ago, but those are the only two times in our history we've been there. Anyway, there's no need for us to go looking for interested investors—the security analysts keep coming to us.[5]

As for the press and other public relationships, most of these activities were at least "cleared" by headquarters although as the public relations director put it, "We don't try and tell division people what to do. We have certain facilities here and we hope they will make use of them. We do like to know when the Litton name is going to be put before the public eye, such as in a press release or magazine article. It's a matter of cooperating to our mutual advantage."

Organization

One basic tenet upon which the Litton organization was built was the importance attached to the line as distinct from the staff organization. This is not to say that the company "looked down" on the staff, but rather that it took great pains to avoid building up an excessive body of staff personnel which might have obscured the delegation of authority in the line.

In the Litton system, the key role was played by the division manager. He was responsible for the day-to-day operations of the company and for the generation of revenue within the organization. Because he was such an important link in the chain, the company provided him with a great deal of autonomy and freedom to operate his own division.[6] As one division manager put it:

---

[5] *Ibid.*, p. 154. Mr. Ash commented that, contrary to the impression conveyed by this quotation, the company was considered (by the analysts) to have made *relatively* frequent presentations to the New York Security Analysts.

[6] See Exhibit 3, Litton Industries, Inc. (AR), for a partial organization chart.

We ultimately have only three responsibilities. Firstly, we are checked that our return on gross assets[7] is reasonable and that it does in fact represent a worthwhile use of the capital employed. Secondly, we are expected to make an operating profit[8] that is in line with the nature of the opportunities in our particular business. Both of these measures, of course, are expected to show improvement over time, that is, we have to grow. The only other requirement they place upon us is that we stay out of jail. Very simple really!

In actual practice the division managers were not quite as free as the above quotation would suggest. Although the aim was to keep the organization decentralized at the division level and to have each of these operate as true profit centers, there were several activities over which the division manager had little control. The following table, in Exhibit 2, lists the responsibilities reserved for corporate headquarters. These responsibilities were not listed anywhere in the company, nor was there any one person who could (or perhaps would) quote more than a few of those included. The list was compiled by the researcher from information supplied by nine separate executives at various levels within the organization.

Most of these activities were centralized for reasons of control, although the pension fund, insurance, real estate, and cash control were centralized in large part because of the operating efficiencies that could be obtained. It must be emphasized here that the twenty activities listed in Exhibit 2 were not hard and fast rules that were laid down by corporate headquarters. Rather they were areas in which it seemed clearly advantageous to maintain the responsibility at the corporate level. Both the group vice presidents and the corporate staff saw themselves in the role of facilitators with regard to the divisions. There was very little sense of imposition by the headquarters on the division's freedoms. The feeling was more one of how do we (at corporate) let the divisions make the most of their opportunities? This feeling of a freedom from interference was also shared by the division managers who were interviewed. One division manager commented:

There are no objectives—it's purely profit planning. As a division manager you are certainly master of your own show.

Another, when discussing the staff-line relationships, said:

Take public relations for example. This needs to be handled at the corporate level as far as coordination is concerned. However, in actual practice we almost have more freedom than if we owned the show ourselves. In effect, I feel I make all the important decisions here—sure we have to check some things with corporate and we have certain financial targets we aim to meet—but what business doesn't? In fact, it's better running this business now than it was as an inde-

---

[7]Return on gross assets was defined as the ratio of operating profits to gross assets, expressed as a percentage, where gross assets was the total left-hand side of the balance sheet at cost, i.e. with depreciation and amortization added back in and all rents capitalized at a 10-year rate.

[8]Operating profit was defined as the profit before interest, taxes and management fees, where the management fee was a fixed sum charged for corporate overhead.

Exhibit 2

LITTON INDUSTRIES, INC.

Activities Outside the Control of the Division Managers

1. Pension fund.
2. Most insurance work had become centralized at corporate headquarters.
3. Legal work. Although divisions could and did have legal groups, these were under the control of the corporate level. Items specifically reserved for the corporate legal staff were: acquisition legal work, tax planning, SEC, antitrust and litigation.
4. Every year division managers had to report conflicts of interest, private dealings with customers or suppliers, equity transactions and dealings.
5. All real estate was handled at headquarters.
6. The raising of capital.
7. Each division had to meet the performance requirements of their financial plan. This was checked by headquarters.
8. The payment of an annual management fee.
9. Reporting on a monthly basis.
10. Cash control was at corporate headquarters.
11. Salary or wage changes had to be approved by the supervisor and the supervisor's supervisor. Salaries greater than $30,000 were approved by Ash.
12. There were 17 basic accounting policies that the divisions were required to follow.
13. The divisions were subjected to an internal audit.
14. The division managers could not go outside the company for management consulting help without concurrence.
15. Some aspects of the acquisition procedure, notably legal, final price, and integration of the acquired company were corporate responsibilities.
16. Opportunities were subject to review and acceptance in the opportunity sessions.
17. Indiscriminate use of the Litton name was not permitted.
18. The divisions did not report independently to financial and credit services.
19. Stockholder relations were reserved for corporate.
20. Loss pricing, or unusual risk-taking, such as fixed price research and development bids.

Source: Company interviews.

pendent. I have a really skilled staff I can call on for help and yet, thank goodness, they are never down here poking around. Because we pay a fixed management fee, I have no hestitation in calling them in, as they are essentially free.

Thus the aim at Litton was to build an organization with the division as the fundamental building block. These divisions were decentralized and acted as individual profit centers. The corporate organization was purely a means of "knitting" the diverse units together by such linking threads as the opportunity review. All the mandatory interaction in the organization was vertical, the horizontal interaction developed on the mutual self-interest of each division. There had never been a general corporate get-together of executive personnel although such meetings had occurred frequently on a group basis in recent years. The division managers had no requirement placed on them to purchase or buy from other divisions. The prerogative was purely in their own hands. In short, there was *no* attempt to interfere with the divisions on the basis of any ideas of centralized planning efficiencies. The increase in individual motivation provided by this delegation of responsibility and autonomy was felt to outweigh any advantages that could be gained by imposing centralized "slide-rule" efficiencies from the corporate office. Although there was no direction from headquarters, divisions were normally internally structured on a functional, as distinct from a decentralized, basis. This was possible because Litton's divisions were of such a size that they usually operated in only one or two locations and on a limited range of products.

As mentioned earlier, the company possessed no organization chart, nor did it possess any policy manuals at the corporate level,[9] although the company employed a total of 94,000 people in 1967. This was probably a result of top management's wish not to give any impression of rigidity, and of the fact that the organization was changing so rapidly that any chart would have been quickly outdated. In addition, the lines of reporting and communication were vertical and the division manager had to know only the relatively few people with whom he would be in contact. The flexibility and lack of formalized procedures in the organization are reflected in this comment by one officer:

When I joined the company, I was shown the office I could use and then left to it. Of course I had had the normal introductory conversations with key people —as one does upon joining an organization—and we had discussed the general reasons behind my having been hired. I then waited for several weeks for the orders to come down—they never did. I soon realized that I had to create my own area, find out what needed to be done, and get to it. I can tell you it took a bit of getting used to, but now I wouldn't have it any other way. I would say that's a typical example of how things operate here.

The group vice presidents were, in effect, extensions of the chairman and the president. As one group vice president said,

We aim to be Ash's alter ego, and to be his representative to the divisions. It's simply a matter that Mr. Ash can't be in close contact with every division head all the time. We try to make his reach extend further. In fact we are really trying to do ourselves out of a job because we want to minimize our role, not maximize it.

A measure of the enthusiasm provided by the "organization" can be gained from the fact that the company as a whole had no single *direct* incentive plan in operation. There were, however, two stock option plans. The first plan had been started when the company was formed and consisted of a pool of issued and outstanding common stock from which key executives were offered options at 25% of market value. These options were issued equally over a five-year period from the stock in this pool which was held in a charitable trust called the Foundation of the Litton Industries. In early 1968 there were between 300 and 400 executives who were optionees under this plan. In December 1966, a second "qualified stock option plan" was introduced to complement and supplement the original plan. The purpose of the qualified plan was stated as being "to aid the corporation in retaining its key employees and the key employees of companies acquired by the corporation and to assist the

---

[9]Except for a manual detailing the company's accounting policies.

corporation in attracting additional key employees." Although these stock option plans were not directly tied to performance in the sense that an executive had to meet certain criteria, such as return on investment in order to qualify, they nonetheless did provide a form of incentive because a manager's performance was subjectively evaluated in determining whether he was eligible to participate. Of course, the divisions were free to develop their own incentive plans if they so desired, and several of the divisions had developed cash bonus plans for their top management. The main incentive in the total organization, however, appeared to be the opportunities for advancement provided by the continuous growth of Litton, as well as by the fact that many top executives over the years had moved out of Litton to assume high-ranking positions in other companies. Commenting on this movement of executives, Ash said:

> We aim to keep a continuous upward spiraling of our best talent. We will move people across the organization from say, a controllership of a large division to the managership of a smaller one. Staff people will move into line positions[10] and line people may move into staff roles at headquarters. But in all our moves, the aim is to take the person up, not just across. We are also finding that many of our top men leave us after a period of years. This is mainly because they are dynamic people who want to be at the top of the tree—when they meet a block here, their inclination is to move to areas where they can go higher. We feel this is probably a good thing. It helps us continue to keep moving people up and thus the organization stays young.

Although Litton's organization was highly flexible and lacking the normal and somewhat rigid structure of companies of similar size, the company had developed an effective control system that was quick to highlight deviations from expected performance. A description of this system is the subject of the next section.

The control system

The crux of the control system was the financial plan generated by each division once a year and updated as required. As was described earlier, under the heading of opportunity planning, each division was required to develop a financial plan that included the results of the opportunity session coupled with the performance expected from existing product lines. The plan was on a running year basis and included projections for 12 months on a monthly basis, for 24 months on a quarterly basis, and for 36 months on a yearly basis. Each plan consisted of a full balance sheet and a profit and loss statement for the appropriate period coupled with complete surrounding data. The original plans were approved by headquarters and were then updated quarterly.

In addition to the plan, divisions returned to headquarters a monthly report showing actual performance. This was compared to the plan and signifi-

---

[10]For example, the officer in charge of the corporate treasurer's and controller's offices was recently made executive vice president in charge of the Business Equipment Group.

cant deviations noted and explanations sought. The corporate controller, in explaining this procedure, noted:

Although this type of reporting system is common procedure in many companies, we realize here that when we receive the report, it is past history. We expect divisions to call up if anything is out of line and not wait to send in the report. We probably make as many mistakes in this company as in any other company, but our reaction is fast enough to catch them before they get out of control.

With regard to performance, we don't have any standard objectives that each division is expected to meet. As a planning guide we have set a return on gross assets of 20% as the bogey—and it's surprising how many divisions meet it. What we try to do is to see the financial plans in the context of the operations they describe. To help us in this regard, we travel to many of the divisions and try to get a feeling for what they are up to. I would guess that I spend about a third of my time keeping up with the products we make and the types of market we sell to.

Another form of control was that exercised over cash. The treasurer's office at corporate headquarters acted as the company's banker, and all cash generated by the divisions, apart from any local compensating balances, was wire transferred to headquarters on a daily basis. Similarly, requests for cash from divisions were attended to on a daily basis.[11] In this way Litton could minimize the amount of cash held in the total corporation and ensure that it was gaining the maximum return with its short-term investments. However, the control of cash by headquarters also served another useful function. The controller stated:

Cash control is a very sensitive system. It's a magnifying glass and the way we operate is a real time system. If something is going wrong at one of the divisions it shows up immediately in the comparison of their actual cash position with the projected cash position shown in their financial plan. If the cash starts getting out of line we immediately ask for an explanation.

Apart from these more traditional methods of control, Litton had several mechanisms in operation which, although not primarily designed as control devices, did feed back information on the division's operations. One of these was the real estate function performed by the corporate treasurer's office. The real estate staff was attached to headquarters and was responsible, once a capital expenditure had been approved in the opportunity sessions, for activities such as new site selection, lease negotiations, a review of the economic analyses made on major expenditures, design criteria, land purchase, construction, and disposals. There were real estate staffs at Beverly Hills, Chicago, New York, and Zurich, Switzerland. Apart from the above activities, the office also conducted a postcompletion audit of a capital expenditure project to see whether the original projections were being met. It was in this audit that an important control function was exercised.

---

[11]This procedure did not apply to foreign subsidiaries. However, there was at headquarters a foreign currency specialist who was responsible for hedging soft currencies, moving money between foreign divisions, and the borrowing of capital outside of the United States.

Another area of indirect control was the corporate consulting services. These were available in three major areas: financial, data processing for business applications, and help on factory operations. Offices were located at Beverly Hills, Chicago, and Orange, New Jersey. The actual consulting work in itself was not a control, but the fact that corporate personnel were closely examining a division's operations did mean that a certain feedback of information was inevitable. Thus areas of gross negligence would be highlighted.

A third area of indirect control was in the legal staff. As almost all legal work was under the guidance of corporate headquarters, this provided yet another information channel.

In using these various corporate services—for which he was charged a fixed management fee regardless—the division managers appeared to recognize that although these services of necessity exercised certain indirect controls, this was not their prime function.

Any discussion of control would be incomplete without a mention of the internal audit function. Litton had a *highly* developed internal auditing staff which, as well as being responsible for auditing, was also available to division managers for special surveys. It was another of the many lines of communication that extended between the corporate headquarters and the divisions. Consequently, although a great deal of authority was invested in the division managers, there were also many techniques of surveillance that ensured that any dangerous deviations from normal were quickly detected. The relatively formal devices discussed above were ancillary to yet another form of control which was derived from the company's emphasis on "face-to-face" communications throughout the organization. This is the subject of the next section.

Internal communications

One particularly distinguishing feature of Litton was their emphasis on direct communication between personnel. This can be illustrated by this extract from an analyst's report on the company:

The most effective means of contact which provides both communication and understanding is personal conversation. Litton's corporate management has recognized that the improved technology of today's communication industry allows a company to be controlled through extensive personal contact. Therefore, Litton's main tool of communication and understanding, i.e., control, is personal contact within its management, made possible by the extensive utilization of the telephone and the jet aircraft.[12]

Another publication somewhat dramatically described the communication process as follows:

At the company's cozy, rambling, two-story early-American headquarters in Beverly Hills, the staff makes liberal use of squawk boxes (intercoms), often in

---

[12]T. L. Stebbins, "Litton Industries, Incorporated," *Estabrook & Co.*, July 25, 1967, p. 5.

20-second bursts, using their own form of oral shorthand. Says Ash: "We exchange information so we can work together and so we can face the outside world prepared with one consistent set of facts."

Litton executives hate memos. They substitute personal visits and long-distance phone calls. "We spend millions,"[13] concedes Ash. "It's our lifeblood." Doors are nearly always open, and men move in and out with a bustle that sometimes makes Litton on Monday morning resemble a war room. If a big deal arises, the wheels really spin, often far into the night. But the company can move fast; it decided to buy Hewitt-Robins Inc.—which has a line of bulk materials handling equipment—2½ hours after the chance arose.[14]

This aversion to the delays involved in memos and the written word was typical of the real-time approach used in the company. The emphasis was on a continuing personal contact for all levels of discussion. Telephone meetings were a common method of discussing a mutual problem and providing information. Apart from these meetings, the company had only two other committees. One was the executive committee of the board, which never met in scheduled formal sessions but had the authority to act as needed between board meetings. The other was the committee of trustees that supervised the pension fund. Decision making was thus assigned to individuals and not to groups, with the result that the normal transferral of information which takes place in group meetings was absent.

In summary, then, the communication system at Litton was based firstly on need, secondly on flexibility, and thirdly on immediacy. It was indeed an efficient real-time system of control and information gathering.

The overall effect of Litton's unique style of internal organization was summarized by Mr. Thornton as follows:

Our organizational purpose is to motivate the individual manager. We believe in placing responsibility on people and not on groups, and, having given a person responsibility, we like to provide an environment in which he can truly exercise his own judgment. We think that the increase in motivation or "individual efficiency" that results from this approach enhances the overall organization's effectiveness. We may not have the most efficient organization, but we certainly have a very effective one. In fact I am sure it is more effective than one that would be designed by the so-called expert who would probably show that a lot of the things we do are too expensive and wasteful. However, it's something you can't prove because there are too many intangibles involved.

---

[13]One source in the company placed the annual telephone bill for corporate headquarters at $7 million.

[14]"What Puts the Whiz in Litton's Fast Growth," *Business Week*, April 16, 1966, p. 176.

LITTON INDUSTRIES, INC. (C)*[1]

^^^

Litton Industries, Inc., a company with 1967 sales of $1.6 billion, had shown an average annual sales growth rate since 1961 of 36.6%. The history and financial performance leading to this growth rate have been described in Litton Industries, Inc., (AR).

With a view to gaining additional insights into the reasons for Litton's success and into its potential for future growth, this case describes the background of the top management in addition to presenting comments on Litton's operations made by people both inside and outside of the organization.

Management background

As an aid to understanding Litton's performance, it is necessary to have an appreciation of the background surrounding the two men who were largely responsible for the company's conception and for its growth. These two were the chairman "Tex" Thornton and the president Roy Ash.

Thornton, Litton's chief executive officer, went to Texas Tech., where he found himself more interested in business than in engineering studies, and as a consequence changed to business administration for a B.C.S. degree. He worked in Washington for a while as a civilian. At twenty-eight he became a full colonel in the Air Force, in charge of putting modern business planning and control systems into the Air Force. At one time he had 2,800 officers working for him all over the world. After the war he went into the Ford Motor Co., taking with him nine very bright young Air Force officers. They hired out as a group, and became known in Ford as the "Whiz Kids." Thornton left Ford in 1948, figuring his chances for a top management job there had dimmed considerably when Henry Ford II put Ernest Breech in the top spot, and Breech, quite understandably, brought in people trained in car business to assist him. Hughes Aircraft offered Thornton the job of building up Hughes Aircraft, the only company Howard Hughes ever started from scratch, and he took it.

*   *   *   *·   *

Ash, now thirty-nine [1958], vice president and chief financial officer, was first brought to Hughes by Thornton from the Bank of America in 1949. Ash had been one of the 2,800 Air Force officers under Thornton, but not one of

[1]Data for this case were collected largely from published sources.

Thornton's Whiz Kids. "Tex took all the bright guys in the Air Force to Ford," Ash says modestly, "and when he went to Hughes, scraped around the bottom of the barrel and found me." Ash is probably the only graduate of Harvard Business School who never went to college. He had been picked from a batch of Air Force officer-training-school graduates to go to Harvard Business School and work on an economics study for the Air Force. The Business School's officials, impressed with Ash's handling of the Air Force study, suggested that he come back after the war and get his graduate degree. When told that Ash didn't have an undergraduate degree, they waived the requirement. He got out of Harvard Business in 1947 and went to the Bank of America as a top statistician.[2]

Company philosophy

The following quotations concerning the company's corporate philosophy have been obtained, in the main, from a series of speeches made by Roy Ash to business and educational groups. They serve to illustrate some of the premises upon which Litton's operational performance has been based.

We at Litton have formed a certain set of basic philosophical notions that form the framework, the foundation, for Litton management actions. We tend to look at them as kind of a four-legged platform on which we base our own attitudes, our own points of view, and our own actions in the business world.

First, we are absolutely convinced that there is a good and honorable meaning and purpose of being in business, being in business management, and being businessmen.

*   *   *   *   *

. . . The efficiency and the efficacy with which he [the businessman] performs this job is, in our system, measured by the profit which the businessman achieves for his enterprise. Profit is the measure of his responsiveness to the marketplace, as the customers which make it up go about determining the highest and best use of their resources.

*   *   *   *   *

The second cornerstone of Litton's philosophy relates to our observations and perceptions of the world around us and what they mean to us. . . .

As we see it, we are in the midst of a boiling revolution—a revolution in many ways and in many places all at once. . . .

*   *   *   *   *

The key notion, then, in our second philosophical cornerstone is that change is not to be feared—even though that is a natural human emotion—but instead, change presents golden opportunities.

*   *   *   *   *

So, at Litton the management job is to build upon the opportunities represented by our changing world. Our corporate goal is to convert to practicable and marketable uses the cascading technological developments of the second industrial revolution that we are now in, and out of that to build a commercial suc-

---

[2]William B. Harris, "Litton Shoots for the Moon," *Fortune*, April 1958, p. 119.

cess by converting the technology of the day into new and useful products and services to improve this changing world.

* * * * *

. . . Our third philosophical notion is to build and create. To do so, we need builders and we need creators—people who create change, who fit our observations of the world around us and our plans to succeed and to survive in that world. We need people who are problem creators as much as problem solvers, who do not spend a great portion of their effort resisting change and trying to restore the past. We clearly need to build a company around men of creativity, men of initiative, of individual responsibility and energy.

This kind of man adds up to a man of enterprise. We call him an entrepreneur. . . .

* * * * *

The fourth cornerstone of our philosophical notions is just as important to us as it is to any sort of four-legged stool, automobile, or other device that must rest squarely on the ground. It is the environment that has to be created for this kind of person to operate effectively.[3]

In defining the nature of Litton's business Ash said:

The business of Litton Industries is the fusion of the technical revolution of this era with society's increasingly demanding needs. . . .

The function of our business, and thus of the many entrepreneurs that make up its management, is to translate the cascading technology of the era into a continuing flow of useful products and services that will enrich the day-to-day lives of all of us of this generation, and will add another step of progress for future generations. By successfully doing so, we intend to create, in our time, a new major lasting corporate member of our industrial society.[4]

Ash has also indicated that one of the key concepts of Litton's management was the "systems" approach. In a speech given before the Minnesota Society of Certified Public Accountants on November 18, 1965, Ash said:

During this whole process of gearing industry to meeting this vital public sector need, a new and valuable dimension has been developed and added to our industrial capability—that is "systems management," a new level of industrial ability to organize and direct toward an integrated common goal a multiplicity of expert skills from a large number of professional and technical disciplines.

The systems management concept is new, not old. Systems analysis is not merely a matter of better cooperation, or more astute planning of known variables. History is peppered with examples of fruitful analysis applied to difficult problems. In the modern era, the concept of systems analysis grew out of the more basic "operations analysis" that received its impetus during World War II.

Yet another aspect of Litton's corporate philosophy is embodied in this

[3]Roy L. Ash, "An Address before the Young Presidents' Organization," Phoenix, Arizona, April 29, 1966, p. 2 ff.

[4]Roy L. Ash, "Entrepreneurship Is Leadership," an address at the Krannert Graduate School of Industrial Administration, May 7, 1965, p. 1.

extract from an address to the Financial Analysts Federation in San Francisco on May 17, 1967.

. . . For, just as all economists have come to realize that economies of scale, whether of mass production or mass selling, are the keys to much of our society's industrial success to date, so do "economies" of scale of technology offer equally dramatic promise for the years ahead. I do not at all mean the economy that results from cost saving in doing research and development work more efficiently, or of eliminating duplicate research and development, but the even more productive economies that derive from whole new technical solutions and innovations that come from true multidisciplinary endeavors across multi-industry fields.

Single product or industry companies tend naturally to be technologically narrow; not only because they are size limited—by the market for their narrower product line—but also because only limited technical fields relate to their existing products. On the other hand, more and more of the technologies pertinent to the future of society are inherently of such scale, that is, of both size and multidisciplinary scope, that only a multi-industry company containing a breadth of technical competence can be fully responsive to the opportunities. . . . As we see it, the firm built upon the economies of technological scale is organized to create, develop, and offer to the markets of the present and future a flow of new and innovative products that can never be expected from the classical conglomerate of only financially related elements.

In fact, a striking parallel exists for your analysis. Where a number of the present industrial giants of U.S. and world industry were formed in earlier years under an impetus to capitalize on the economies of production and marketing scale so important in the industrial revolution, so Litton is being formed to capitalize on the "economies" of technological scale for this era.

Company organization

In the very early days of Litton's history when the company was still known as the Electro Dynamics Corporation, Thornton detailed some of the factors around which he hoped to build the Litton organization. He said, in 1954:

. . . We believe that the scientific advancement of the arts in this field of advanced electronics is way ahead now of the usefulness of arts in products which are now being designed and produced.

We do have and want to have a research organization but expect to control the size of that so that it is in balance with the sales and profit base of our organization. Except for the research organization, the type of engineers who are attractive to us are those whom we feel have their "feet on the ground"; those who realize the necessity—as nearly as any engineering organization can—of designing on a schedule and within a cost budget. We are building a close working relationship between our engineering department and our manufacturing organization similar to that which we had the first few years at Hughes, and as nearly as possible like that which exists at Litton Industries [a reference to the original Litton magnetron plant] now.

Not only is Litton one of the finest facilities I have seen any place, but the organization has that enviable compatibility between engineering and production people which is so important in producing a highly complex product. As you know, the magnetron power transmitters are the most precise products produced in America and Litton has the highest quality and lowest cost of any manufacturer in that field.

* * * * *

. . . , in summary, we are trying to build our new company on the same basis that we built Hughes Aircraft Company. This is a working organization from myself on down. We want smart, able, intelligent people who in their professions have not "arrived" and are still working hard to get there. I believe the strengths at Hughes Aircraft that helped us [Hughes' top management and key scientific personnel] overcome some serious limitations was that each person we had and brought in was relatively unknown but had outstanding capabilities.[5, 6]

In an address to the Associated Business Publications Seminar on May 27, 1963, Roy Ash spoke in a similar view.

But these characteristics—of creativity, of enterprise—are not ones of organizations, or groups, of people; they are uniquely characteristics of individuals— one at a time. Organizations can carry out ideas, plans, grand designs. Machines and modern managerial techniques can add efficiency and productivity in carrying out these plans. But only an individual human can have that spark of insight, that creative thought, that motivation to accomplish, which makes the efforts of organization useful.

In fact, my own company, Litton Industries, was deliberately conceived and is organized to achieve the efficiencies of modern scientific management methods, but also to give even more emphasis to the "art" of business—inspiration, imagination, innovation, initiative.

The structure of Litton and its deliberately nurtured atmosphere are all geared to encourage individual initiative and creativity—both technical and managerial— to assume the maximum of personal responsibility, and to inspire the output of high personal energy, all at many points throughout the organization, not just at the nominal top.

Another speech, this time to the Stanford Business School Alumni Association on February 12, 1963, elaborated on the delegation of responsibility in the Litton organization.

The preamble to the Litton Constitution begins the definition of these responsibilities of the entrepreneurial managers of our divisions as (1) the operational management of the personnel, facilities, funds, and other resources of the division to achieve maximum operating results in established product fields and under

---

[5]Personal correspondence from Charles B. Thornton to Professors Edmund P. Learned and Myles L. Mace dated April 7, 1954.

[6]Case writer's note: Professor Learned, in making this letter available, cautioned the case writer to ensure that the tightness of style used in the letter did not lead the reader to misunderstand its true meaning. Professor Learned noted that on many occasions Mr. Thornton had told him that the success of Hughes in attracting capable men had depended on the combination of an aggressive, farsighted, top management group, the scientific reputation and leadership of Si Ramo and Dean Wooldridge and a few other key leaders they attracted, and other factors, such as the California climate, possible pay advantages, and the opportunity to work with scientific pioneers.

current company policy, and (2) the initiation and presentation to corporate management of ideas, proposals and plans for research programs, new product lines, major facilities improvements and changes in policy and planning to build and improve further the future strength, value and profitability of the division and of Litton. And the third responsibility assigned in somewhat euphemistic terms, since it refers to the light reins held on the spirited thoroughbreds, begins "the furnishing of appropriate information to corporate management for its continued understanding of the division's operations."

On May 17, 1967, at the Financial Analysts Federation in San Francisco, Ash said:

To quote the president of a major industrial company, who very successfully practices a different form of management, "Their's, that is, Litton's, is a job for management geniuses, not for ordinary mortals like us at _____ [$3-billion-a-year company]." We in Litton are clearly not management geniuses, as you know.

The misconception is the commonly held belief that the higher one goes in an organization the greater the expertness he will find—a popular picture of a single all-wise executive, with corporate functional specialists at his side, rendering sixth-sense decisions across all facets of operations. But, as we see it, an opposite concept is a more valid one. For, the multiproduct line company both requires, and makes possible, the multimanagerial concept of organization— where the basic management strength is at the lowest level of business viability, not the highest. In this way single purpose specialized management concentration is brought to bear directly on each product, its technology, production, marketing, and the integration of these at the product line level of profitability, not removed to a higher, less knowledgeable, and more remote level.

* * * * *

In the monolithic company, the individual general management candidate moves directly into the total managerial job from a functional responsibility that he presumably performed with excellence over the years. In a multimanagerial company—one attribute of free-form management—the potential managerial candidate moves from functional to general management responsibilities at a low level relative to the total of the company. He begins developing his own experiences early, at less risk to the total company, and subject to early evaluation as divisional general managers and potential corporate managers as a sound basis for orderly succession.

* * * * *

. . . , since the criticism is that our concept of management is particularly susceptible to business adversity, it is interesting to note that even in our short life span we have gone through two specific periods that NICB called major business recessions, as well as countless single industry rolling adjustments. And it's been our experience during these periods of adversity that have convinced us of the validity of our "control" system. I won't discuss in detail our particular system of information and understanding and this control except to say that it uses the new tools extensively. It basically consists of:

1. An intensive and continual effort—involving top to bottom management— given to opportunity identification and evaluation, and establishment of product by product strategies.

2. A conversion of our strategies to their expected future results, a detailed following for variances and their meaning, and a continual iteration of the process.

3. A reservation of specific areas for joint corporate division management action, and

4. An extensive, but informal use of on-site dialogue where the information flow is least filtered; . . .

Out of such information and understanding, systems, we're convinced, have more rather than less "control" than most.

A summing up of the major organizational concepts practiced at Litton was contained in an address before the Young Presidents' Organization on April 29, 1966:

Our form of organization, the way in which we distribute authority and responsibility, the communication and control, the techniques and systems we feel are all geared to the kind of environment that we are attempting to create.

* * * * *

We have a modus operandi at Litton, a fetish in some ways, of single individual responsibility rather than group responsibility, of maximum emphasis on a line organization, rather than a staff organization, of very little shared responsibility. We have no executive committees, as an example. In a company of 70,000 people, you find most of them tend to form themselves into committees one way or another. But we don't have committees.

* * * * *

Our pace of operation in the Litton environment is deliberately geared to the times we are in. It is the pace that is equal to the rate of a revolution. . . . And, as a result, we depend again on the highly expensive—and I suppose that would be measured as inefficient—use of airplanes and telephones. Again, we can't prove that it is more efficient to spend all the money we do for airplanes and telephones. But, we are absolutely convinced that this is one of the most inexpensive ways of communication within an organization in contrast to the much slower pace of paper. . . . We deliberately attempt to de-emphasize paper as a media of communication, even though we try to sell a lot to others who are using paper for such a purpose.

* * * * *

I think I am coming near the end of the time that I have. I just want to indicate one additional element of our environment that bears upon our point of view. That is the de-emphasis at Litton on the trappings of an institution. Organization charts! You wonder when you have a company of over 70,000 people, without an organizational chart? Well, I must say that I don't think you can find one on any bulletin board or in any notebook of any of our corporate offices. Our organizational charts are in our heads. We know what they are, but they are highly flexible.

We have one policy that seems to be very useful and almost says everything that you could possibly write into any other policy. So, we don't need a whole policy manual because with one sentence we can define our policy and that is: WHEN IN DOUBT, DO THE RIGHT THING.

Under the heading *"The Obsolete World of Alfred P. Sloan"* one investment research group applauded Litton's approach to company organization and management.

Until recent years, when Roy Ash and Tex Thornton of Litton Industries began to articulate a new philosophy of management, General Motors Corporation was credited with having "written the book" of modern management. Alfred P. Sloan, president and later chairman of G.M. from the early 1920's to the mid-1950's, was (and still is in some circles) credited with being the "Grand Old Master" of modern management and his book, *My Years with General Motors*, published in 1964, is probably the only management book ever to become a best seller.

*   *   *   *   *

While Sloan's book was a recent best seller, we are encouraged to find that corporate managers today tend far more to quote from the speeches and writings of "Tex" Thornton ("Mr. Outside") and Roy Ash ("Mr. Inside") of *Litton Industries* when engaging in conversation about the philosophy of management.[7]

In contrast to this optimistic note, *Fortune* magazine reported in an analysis conducted amongst conglomerate companies that their performance was not perhaps all that had been expected.

What is the relationship between diversification and growth in earnings per share? To get at this question we did a correlation analysis in which companies [from *Fortune's* 500] were assigned two variables: one was the number of industry categories; the other was the company's average annual growth (compounded) in earnings per share between 1956 and 1966. . . . The answer to this question is surprisingly negative: the coefficient of correlation turns out to be 0.086, a figure that is not statistically significant. In short, there isn't any relationship between diversification and earnings growth.[8]

---

[7]John Westergaard, Richard R. Fields, "Investing in Modern Management: The 'Free-Form' Corporation," Equity Research Associates, New York, September 20, 1966, p. 4 ff.

[8]Thomas O'Hanlon, "The Odd News about Conglomerates," *Fortune*, June 15, 1967, p. 176.

Effecting major changes in
strategy and organization

The final set of cases in this book may be viewed as presenting an opportunity to reexamine the full range of concepts and subconcepts involved in the formulation and implementation of corporate strategy. Analysis of the Olivetti cases, stimulating and challenging as it will prove, provides opportunity for review as well as advance. Such company histories provide an opportunity to determine the need for change, to decide the adequacy of the plan for change, and to determine the extent to which the company's own plans should be extended or amended and further action taken. In studying the Olivetti series, which begins with a history of the company and concludes with the managing director's philosophy of management, you will be able to apply your criteria for evaluating the soundness of strategy, use your insights into implementation, and exercise all your innovative powers in devising recommendations for the strategic and organization problems which the company still faces.

In addition to reviewing the concepts and skills of the Policy course and applying them to more complex situations, you will find opportunity as well to concentrate on the problem of transition, which is the usual state of all growing companies. During transitional periods case data reveal the processes of strategic formulation and implementation proceeding simultaneously, intermixed as in real life and interacting one upon the other. The model presented in this text, which for analytical purposes presents strategy formulation as being reasonably complete before implementation begins, may nonetheless serve as an effective instrument of analysis and as an aid to recommendation.

To study a firm in transition between strategies and organization forms will mature expectations about the extent to which the practices we have recommended in these notes are being followed or can be followed in the world of business. Some of the strategic questions which our point of view designates as fundamental are literally unanswerable in some instances, either because information is inadequate or because there are no organiza-

857

tional means for addressing the questions. The president of a firm cannot, for example, actually assess its powers simply because he decides to do so. Besides knowledge and judgment, accurate analysis of organizational capacity requires some vision of the opportunity to which it might be applied. The perception to determine the true significance of nascent weaknesses and strengths is not easily come by. When some men spend a lifetime without becoming aware of their own personal goals and of what it is that they most wish to do, it is not reasonable to suppose that corporate goals are easily determined or changed. The need to make strategic responses to non-economic considerations is not always strongly felt.

Thus, choosing a strategic course and deciding on first steps to implement it in an ongoing organization is very different from attacking the same problem in a classroom. Attempting in a few hours to combine inadequate experience and highly selective case data to determine a strategy and course of action for a total firm is artificial. In spite of this artificiality classroom activity is highly useful in developing concepts, self-confidence, and an appetite for responsibility—but it should not be confused with literal reality. Discussions which examine the problems of transition come closer to real life but are still somewhat removed from it. Just as the general manager—as architect of strategy, organization leader, and personal leader—may have to play these roles simultaneously, so he may have to preside over formulation and implementation at once. So long as ultimate clarification of purpose emerges, or is in the making, he need not become confused.

In these final days, then, we aim to furnish you with further practice in the situational use of a prescriptive model. We would reestablish the primary reality of the developing situation of a unique firm in its own changing environment over the remoter reality of the conceptual framework we have attempted to provide. We have no apologies for the latter; indeed, we think it has great power. This power lies not in elaboration of its own elegance or in rigorous deduction from its own definitions. Its strength is to be found in its utility for understanding and devising meaningful action in situations involving an entire firm. The firm is in itself a congeries of systems in changing relationships to all the forces having influence upon it or being influenced by it. The complexities implicit in the Olivetti company series provide a test of your ability to comprehend these systems well enough to decide the issues which are still in doubt. You will have opportunity to see an executive of high intelligence moving to transform his company from personal to professional management. You will be able to evaluate his deliberate decision regarding the kind of leadership his situation required, and to decide whether your choice would have been the same and—if not—whether the probable consequences would have been more or less favorable.

We arrive finally at the point where only the case material and your own insights into it can tell you more. Your own ideas about the nature of general management and the tasks of the general manager should by now be quite far advanced. Nearing the conclusion of the formal study of management, you have by now been introduced to many subject matters, many techniques, and much information. These have sometimes come to you shaped by the points of view of research—research governed by the requirements of a specialized discipline. Sometimes, in the interest of presenting material that is usefully detailed, you have been presented with only a partial view of the policy problems of business.

Allying himself to no one school or doctrine, the practitioner-generalist, unlike the staff specialist or researcher in the special disciplines, must at a minimum develop a set of simple ideas and concepts with which to deal with the fundamental policy problems encountered in his professional experience and personal development. The flexibility and comprehensiveness of these ideas are more important than their genealogy in theory. Unmoved by the fads of the moment, the generalist does not become successively a devotee of "engineering" scientific management, or of "behavioral" scientific management, or "mathematical" scientific management. At the same time he does not discount the possibility that these studies may help him. If he takes responsibility for the future development as well as the present success of his firm, he cannot be content to be an intuitive manager, unaware of the criteria he applies in making his decisions. He will attempt to analyze himself and the roles and responsibilities of leadership. Knowing that all schools of thought and systems of special expertise have concepts of value, he will choose the insights and concepts which make sense to him. In the uniqueness of his own management experience and personal and moral values, he will attempt to create a new unity appropriate to his own purposes. It is our hope that the prescriptive framework offered here will provide at least an introductory way to conceive of the universe of general management and the range of business policy decisions. This framework provides standards and tests against which the experienced practitioner or the aspirant to general management alike can test the quality and scope of his own policy concepts.

ING. C. OLIVETTI & C., S.p.A. (A–1)*

∧∧∧∧∧∧∧∧∧ ∧∧

THE OLIVETTI STORY: TOCCO OLIVETTI

In 1966, Ing. C. Olivetti & C., S.p.A., was one of the world's leading producers of typewriters, calculators, and other business machines. Olivetti was listed by official Italian government sources as the sixth largest industrial company in Italy. Olivetti was number 103 on *Fortune's* list of 200 largest industrial companies outside of the United States. Olivetti's U.S. subsidiary, Olivetti Underwood, ranked as number 483 on *Fortune's* list of the 500 largest industrial companies in the United States.

The Olivetti Company in 1965 comprised 28 associated companies, in as many countries, each with its own commercial distribution network; 108 general agents operating in 117 countries; 18 industrial plants, of which 9 were in Italy and 9 abroad; and 54,000 employees, of which 25,000 were in Italy and 29,000 abroad.

Olivetti's consolidated sales of 281 billion lire in 1965 (approximately $450 million) were divided 20% in Italy and 80% abroad, while manufac· turing output was divided 75% in Italy and 25% abroad.

Financial statements for 1965 showed Olivetti earning net profits after taxes equal to 4.0% of sales, and equal to 8.2% of shareholders' capital stock.

The worldwide Olivetti organization was managed from headquarters in Ivrea, a small town in the foothills of the Alps in northern Italy. It was here that Camillo Olivetti founded the company in 1908. Under Camillo Olivetti, and later his son Adriano, the company broadened its line of products from typewriters into office furniture and filing cabinets in 1931, teleprinters for teletype communication in 1937, adding machines in 1940, calculators in 1946, bookkeeping machines in 1951, and electronic computers in 1960.

Exhibit 1 contains summary information on Olivetti earnings, assets, and liabilities, for the years 1957–65. Exhibit 2 presents a detailed income statement and balance sheet taken from Olivetti's annual report for 1965.

Exhibit 3 shows pictures of several Olivetti products: the Lettera 32, the Praxis 48, the Tekne 3, the Electrosumma 20, the Divisumma 24, and the Programma 101. (See pages 876–78.)

---

*Copyright © 1967 by the President and Fellows of Harvard College. Reprinted by permission. This case was made possible by the cooperation of the Olivetti Company.

Exhibit 1

ING. C. OLIVETTI & C., S.p.A.

Statement of Financial Situation

(The table below shows the financial position from the year ended March 31, 1957, to the year ended December 31, 1965.)

Assets

	31-III-57	31-III-58	31-III-59	31-XII-59	31-XII-60	31-XII-61	31-XII-62	31-XII-63	31-XII-64	31-XII-65
	(Million Lire)						(Million Lire)			
Buildings	6.419,5	7.149,5	7.789,3	8.199,4	9.081,7	10.777,9	15.741,8	19.889,0	20.931,9	20.669,5
Plant and equipment	7.197,6	9.099,8	10.637,2	11.401,5	12.726,8	15.212,7	20.518,3	24.524,8	25.406,6	24.530,7
EDP equipment	...	...	...	...	...	1.430,0	3.282,4	7.132,4	10.512,4	820,0
Inventories	4.935,5	5.324,2	4.453,6	5.290,8	7.066,9	10.867,8	14.919,4	21.781,1	20.865,2	13.326,0
Cash, Banks, Securities	1.789,1	1.957,2	1.486,5	1.797,9	1.859,7	2.114,1	3.707,3	3.757,3	2.270,9	3.760,7
Investments in subsidiaries	3.187,9	4.555,9	7.029,7	11.888,4	26.740,8	33.228,3	38.034,8	25.615,8	45.422,6	50.257,4
Accounts receivable, notes receivable	9.270,9	10.437,5	10.988,1	11.497,0	14.447,9	24.293,0	32.344,2	39.508,5	37.365,9	38.715,9
Due from subsidiaries	6.585,7	9.217,5	10.034,0	14.440,8	24.159,1	33.037,2	50.845,9	56.387,3	41.901,3	46.321,3
Uncalled capital, unpaid share premiums	...	...	...	...	...	...	7.079,6	...	...	...
Unamortized expenses	...	...	...	114,2	79,7	169,4	1.995,6	1.560,9	1.145,0	729,1
Total	**39.386,2**	**47.741,6**	**53.018,4**	**64.630,0**	**96.162,6**	**131.130,4**	**188.469,3**	**200.157,1**	**205.821,8**	**199.151,6**

Liabilities

	31-III-57	31-III-58	31-III-59	31-XII-59	31-XII-60	31-XII-61	31-XII-62	31-XII-63	31-XII-64	31-XII-65
	(Million Lire)						(Million Lire)			
Capital stock	7.800,0	10.800,0	13.500,0	13.500,0	25.000,0	40.000,0	60.000,0	60.000,0	60.000,0	60.000,0
Reserves: Ordinary	126,9	152,2	181,7	216,9	260,0	460,6	8.000,0	873,2	873,2	876,8
Reserves: Extraordinary	2.531,1	1.726,1	1.133,1	2.272,5	1.624,6	799,7	1.074,8	1.000,0	1.000,0	1.066,8
Reserves: Premiums on shares	...	...	...	...	...	12.500,0	17.962,3	...	...	...
Accumulated depreciation: Industrial buildings	498,8	665,8	863,6	1.373,0	1.945,9	2.581,7	2.944,0	3.537,9	5.951,2	7.877,7
Accumulated depreciation: Machinery and special equipment	4.013,0	5.654,5	7.370,8	8.467,7	9.656,1	10.965,6	11.760,2	13.395,3	17.063,7	19.435,5
Accumulated depreciation: EDP equipment	...	...	...	...	...	314,6	644,5	1.519,3	4.578,3	568,5
Retirement fund	3.094,4	3.690,3	4.439,2	5.246,5	6.807,1	9.069,6	12.446,0	16.263,5	19.455,9	21.127,9
Social activities and welfare fund	...	...	...	...	...	140,8	193,2	300,9	300,9	200,9
Debentures	5.246,5	8.188,0	8.125,3	11.010,6	10.887,9	10.637,2	35.368,9	35.081,8	34.655,3	34.074,9
Swiss loan	2.190,0	2.190,0	2.190,0	2.190,0	2.190,0	2.190,0	2.190,0	2.190,0	2.190,0	2.190,0
Accrued liabilities	1.588,9	1.813,6	2.062,6	2.012,6	2.373,8	2.589,3	3.232,4	4.316,7	4.540,6	6.588,9
Due to subsidiaries	13,9	60,0	...	...	223,7	163,0	160,5	5.335,5	2.436,2	359,0
Accounts payable	1.297,2	966,9	1.324,6	2.428,1	4.285,2	2.777,9	6.188,5	12.989,9	7.216,3	6.688,0
Due to banks	4.799,3	4.624,1	4.560,6	6.063,8	12.544,6	15.517,6	7.396,5	20.258,5	16.629,6	5.848,0
Mortgage loans	1.947,4	2.930,4	2.407,4	2.152,1	1.802,0	1.967,8	1.596,7	1.318,0	1.099,5	864,9
Notes payable	...	...	...	2.200,0	2.300,0	...	...	...	4.000,0	...
Miscellaneous liabilities	3.733,5	3.689,3	4.155,8	4.633,6	10.249,1	13.651,5	12.109,4	21.776,6	23.759,4	26.459,3
Net profit	505,3	590,4	703,7	862,6	4.012,6	4.803,5	5.201,4	...	71,7	4.924,5
Total	**39.386,2**	**47.741,6**	**53.018,4**	**64.630,0**	**96.162,6**	**131.130,4**	**188.469,3**	**200.157,1**	**205.821,8**	**199.151,6**

Exhibit 1—Continued

Income Statement

(The table below shows the income statement from the year ended March 31, 1957, to the year ended December 31, 1965.)

	31-III-57	31-III-58	31-III-59	31-XII-59	31-XII-60	31-XII-61	31-XII-62	31-XII-63	31-XII-64	31-XII-65
		(Million Lire)					(Million Lire)			
Expenses										
General expenses	6.986,9	9.428,2	11.565,4	9.156,8	15.222,8	19.474,9	24.049,6	32.400,9	30.658,7	28.343,3
Taxes	1.362,0	1.112,1	1.262,9	879,8	1.584,2	2.362,7	3.068,3	4.643,4	2.028,4	3.014,2
Depreciation	1.445,5	1.865,6	2.073,1	1.735,5	2.042,2	2.497,0	1.887,6	3.350,3	9.543,8	6.016,4
Retirement fund	718,2	702,2	748,9	806,2	1.560,6	2.262,6	3.373,5	3.678,2	3.192,4	4.124,4
Extraordinary reserves	750,0	1.100,0	520,0	700,0	...	...	5.201,4	...	...	...
Net profit	505,3	590,4	703,7	862,6	4.012,6	4.803,5	...	...	71,7	4.924,5
Total	11.767,9	14.798,5	16.874,0	14.140,9	24.422,4	31.400,7	37.580,4	44.072,8	45.495,0	46.422,8
Revenue										
Gross profit	11.692,5	14.733,4	16.800,4	14.063,8	24.282,1	31.283,5	37.422,3	43.921,4	45.270,6	46.188,5
Other income	75,4	65,1	73,6	77,1	140,3	117,2	158,1	151,4	224,4	234,3
Total	11.767,9	14.798,5	16.874,0	14.140,9	24.422,4	31.400,7	37.580,4	44.072,8	45.495,0	46.422,8

Source: Company records.

Exhibit 2

ING. C. OLIVETTI & C., S.p.A.

Income Statement for the Year Ended December 31, 1965

Expenditure

Beginning inventory 31-12-1964	Lit.	20,865,231,783
Transfer to Olivetti Bull	Lit.	— 3,868,674,449
Net beginning inventory	Lit.	16,996,557,334
Purchases	Lit.	26,034,091,817
Work done and related costs	Lit.	60,415,342,031
Cost of production and administration	Lit.	13,658,227,175

Financial liabilities:

Interest, costs, and bank charges	Lit.	2,269,309,821	
Interest on loans	Lit.	141,325,011	
Interest on debentures	Lit.	2,010,723,385	
		Lit.	4,421,358,217
Tax liabilities		Lit.	3,014,247,876

Depreciation of fixed assets:

Ordinary	Lit.	2,728,441,335	
Extraordinary	Lit.	3,287,944,077	
		Lit.	6,016,385,412

Less:

Ending inventory	Lit.	13,325,991,919
Net profit	Lit.	4,924,543,712
Total	Lit.	122,154,761,655

Income

Sales	Lit.	121,920,483,423
Miscellaneous income	Lit.	234,278,232
Total	Lit.	122,154,761,655

Exhibit 2—Continued

Balance Sheet for the Year Ended December 31, 1965

Assets

		31-12-1965
1. Fixed assets:		
Residential buildings	Lit.	1,344,884,948
Industrial buildings	Lit.	19,345,589,007
Machinery and specific equipment	Lit.	15,340,680,072
General plant	Lit.	8,163,452,211
Electronic equipment	Lit.	820,000,000
Furnaces	Lit.	468,609,405
Motor vehicles	Lit.	557,954,815
Patents and furniture	Lit.	1
	Lit.	46,041,170,459
2. Inventories	Lit.	13,325,991,919
3. Current bank a/cs and cash:		
Cash	Lit.	637,726,552
Banks	Lit.	2,186,569,029
	Lit.	2,824,295,581
4. Other current assets:		
Government bonds and security deposits	Lit.	936,464,014
Investments in subsidiaries	Lit.	50,257,426,367
	Lit.	51,193,890,381
5. Accounts receivable:		
Customers	Lit.	32,007,231,823
Subsidiaries	Lit.	46,321,293,777
Notes outstanding	Lit.	6,708,628,417
	Lit.	85,037,154,017
6. Unamortised expenses	Lit.	729,129,312
Total assets	Lit.	199,151,631,669
7. Contra items:		
Director's deposits	Lit.	2,600,000
Securities	Lit.	455,088,772
Guarantees	Lit.	27,601,022,343
	Lit.	28,058,711,115
Total	Lit.	227,210,342,784

Liabilities

		31-12-1965
1. Capital stock:		
Common stock	Lit.	36,000,000,000
Preferred stock	Lit.	24,000,000,000
	Lit.	60,000,000,000
2. Reserves:		
Ordinary	Lit.	876,823,416
Extraordinary	Lit.	600,000,000
Reinvestment in South Italy	Lit.	400,000,000
	Lit.	1,876,823,416
3. Accumulated depreciation:		
Ordinary depreciation	Lit.	16,705,056,290
Extraordinary depreciation	Lit.	11,176,697,285
	Lit.	27,881,753,575
4. Retirement fund	Lit.	21,127,944,115
5. Social services and activities fund	Lit.	200,843,573
6. Accrued liabilities	Lit.	6,588,894,395
7. Funded liabilities:		
Debentures	Lit.	34,074,865,000
Swiss loan	Lit.	2,190,000,000
	Lit.	36,264,865,000
8. Debts:		
To banks	Lit.	5,847,966,870
Guaranteed	Lit.	864,951,428
Notes receivable guaranteed	Lit.	—
To suppliers	Lit.	6,688,007,855
To subsidiaries	Lit.	358,958,843
Miscellaneous	Lit.	26,459,321,155
	Lit.	40,219,206,151
9. Net profit	Lit.	4,924,543,712
10. Profits brought down	Lit.	66,757,732
Total liabilities	Lit.	199,151,631,669
11. Contra items:		
Directors' deposits	Lit.	2,600,000
Securities	Lit.	455,088,772
Guarantees	Lit.	27,601,022,343
	Lit.	28,058,711,115
Total	Lit.	227,210,342,784

Source: Company records.

Exhibit 4 shows pictures of the Olivetti home office building and two factories in Italy. (See pages 882–83.)

Exhibit 5 shows pictures of the Olivetti employee health center, employee housing and employee cafeteria in Ivrea. (See pages 886–87.)

In 1962, Olivetti published a booklet titled: *Olivetti, a Contemporary Image of Style and Industry,* which contained a history of the company, emphasizing the evolution of its philosophy of management. Excerpts from this booklet follow:

A small factory at the foot of the Alps

The Olivetti typewriter factory, later incorporated as Ing. C. Olivetti & C., S.p.A., began operations in 1908 at Ivrea, a pleasant little town in Piedmont, at the foot of the Alps. The social climate in which the firm was born had scarcely felt the impact of the Industrial Revolution, but the idea of Progress and a general belief that hard work and practical enterprise would produce a radiant future were in the air. In Italy, professional technicians were growing in number, and in public esteem were beginning to rank with philosophers, scientists and artists. Prominent among them were the new captains of industry. In this group, the name of Olivetti has a particular resonance, for Camillo Olivetti, the founder of the company, stood out among other industrial pioneers in background, original character and in the conscious ideals that gave his enterprise a special significance.

Camillo Olivetti did not exactly fit the old romantic stereotype of the self-made man who works his way up from the bottom. He came from a moderately prosperous small-town family. His father farmed and dealt in real estate in the Canavese district of northern Piedmont, which lies between the Valle d'Aosta and the Po River. Camillo took his degree in electrical engineering under the celebrated scientist, Galileo Ferraris, at the Turin Polytechnic, and then spent two years in California as assistant to Ferraris when he held the chair of electrical engineering at Stanford University. Subsequently Camillo established the first plant in Italy for electrical measurement instruments, the C.G.S. factory. When he was almost 40, he decided to leave C.G.S., which had been set up in Milan, to return to his native region.

By history and geography, the Canavese district has a distinct regional character. In 1907 its center, Ivrea, was like an overgrown village, living mainly by handicrafts and trade with the farmers of the fertile surrounding countryside. The sleepy small town, agreeably situated between the River Dora and the foothills, was dominated by its ancient past and its great four-towered medieval castle. Certainly it did not seem to be the most suitable setting for the revolutionary ventures of an engineer who had been living in the great world of the United States and Milan, and who now intended to start making a machine for which nobody appeared to feel the need.

While in other countries typewriters were already coming into general use, in Italy they were still regarded with distrust. Little had changed in the half century since the Novara lawyer, Giuseppe Ravizza, invented the "clerk's clavichord." The first practical example of a device for mechanical writing, the invention met with a general indifference that embittered Ravizza's life. But Camillo Olivetti set about carrying out his own project in a spirit very different from that of Ravizza's visionary and essentially dilettante approach. His experience in the United States had shown him that it was inevitable for mass production to replace artisan ingenuity in the field he was entering.

In Turin, the nearest big city, the largest Italian automobile plant—Fiat—had been operating for ten years and employed fifty workers. Camillo Olivetti started industrial production of typewriters with some 20 men, headed by Domenico Burzio, a former blacksmith who had worked with him for many years. The factory was a plain red-brick building covering about 500 square yards. It still stands in Ivrea, dwarfed by the huge Olivetti plants that have since grown up beside it.

The modest factory, which housed the firm's first Browne and Sharpe automatic lathes and its first milling machines, also served as a school for the largely untrained staff. Two years went into training and experiment before the first typewriter, the model M1, could be put into production, and it was only in 1911 after being shown to the public at the Turin Exhibition, that the M1 started on its way to success. In the same year it received official sanction, winning the Ministry of the Navy's competition for an order of 100 machines, and a little more than a year later another official order was received from the government postal system. "From that moment," Camillo Olivetti later wrote, "began the truly marvelous progress of our industry." Between that moment and today, more than half a century after Olivetti started as an unlikely challenge to the giants of the industry established in America and abroad, the company has earned an international position of the first rank. Ivrea is still the headquarters and home of the company, but it would now be hard to find much trace of the old home's original handicraft atmosphere. The antiquated Piedmontese town has become part of the history of modern industry, and the Ivrea of today has grown along with the company, whose presence has influenced the environment materially and morally.

Camillo Olivetti's democratic ideals were dramatically put to the test right after the First World War when throughout Italy the relations between labor and capital were violently strained. To back up their demands the workers occupied the factories, and it was then that the unusual relations between management and labor that had been established with the founding of the company proved to be based on farsighted moral views and not on mere paternalistic makeshifts. Camillo's evident good faith convinced the union leaders that the workers' interests would be met, without the need for agitation, by a man whose expressed ideal in operating the plant was "a state of things in which the greater share of the fruits of labor go to those who have labored usefully."

Camillo Olivetti owed his forcefulness as an industrialist to moral attitudes of this sort, which had a particular allure at a time when such views were considered highly unconventional. As an ethical capitalist, he felt it his duty to criticize the inadequacies that weakened the system. He never had any doubts about the worker's right to share in the profits, and it was on this basis that he understood cooperation between the classes, a conciliation whose ethical premise he found in religious inspiration. He wrote: " 'Forgive us our debts as we forgive our debtors,' goes an ancient prayer to which all believers can subscribe. We do not ask for total forgiveness, for this would require that all men have the Christian spirit one hundred per cent—and this is too much to ask. But if men had fifty per cent of this spirit, it might then be possible to insist that the interest rate on capital be low enough so that even the working man can develop his capacities. As is often the case, following moral law in this instance would also have an immediate practical value."

New approaches to techniques and organization

For the Ivrea factory the period between the two World Wars marked the end of the handwork and pioneering phase. To survive in a market dominated by experienced foreign competitors, Olivetti had to face problems which more firmly established concerns in other fields had already solved. A new typewriter, the M20, was brought out in Italy in 1920 and immediately afterward was shown at the Brussels International Fair. In 1922 a new corporation, the Olivetti Foundry, was established; in 1924, the O.M.O. (Officina Meccanica Olivetti) machine-tools plant. In that year the company employed 400 workers and typewriter production reached the rate of 4,000 a year. By 1926 the number of workers had risen to 500 and production to 8,000. The rhythm of expansion, reflecting the inner dynamics of the firm, was intense and continuous. The growing number of employees made the old, almost patriarchal, type of management obsolete. The first industrial revolution of the pioneers like Camillo Olivetti was about to be superseded by the second, that of the managers. In 1925 and 1926 Adriano Olivetti, at the request of his father, Camillo, traveled in the United States to study American production methods. On his return to Ivrea he applied the ideas acquired on his visits to American factories to the reorganization of the Olivetti plants and the creation of new cadres of trained young personnel. Thanks to these systematic innovations, by 1929 production soared to 13,000 annually, without any increase in the labor force.

The company was accordingly in a good position to face the great depression of 1930 and 1931. The lowered costs of production made it possible to initiate a bold expansion campaign by building up the Italian sales organization, opening new branches in the main cities and staffing them with additional sales personnel. The first associated company abroad, the S.A. Hispano Olivetti was established at Barcelona in 1929, and the next year Olivetti Belge, the Belgian associate, was founded. A new product, the M40 typewriter, was brought out and subsequently held the market successfully for many years. Other products were planned, such as the Olivetti portable and the Synthesis horizontal card files. Along with production and sales, human relations within the company were transformed. Social insurance and assistance provisions were broadened; new work-time study methods were adopted; and new psychological and esthetic criteria were applied in advertising.

Adriano's innovations added impetus to the heritage of Camillo's experience and moral force, and he was gradually given full responsibility for running the firm. By 1933, the year in which Adriano Olivetti became director general of the company, the battle to survive the world depression had been won.

A specific meaning underlying the Olivetti story was becoming apparent. The replacement of manual by mechanical writing and calculating, and the creation of machines for rationalizing office work in business and industry were the motive force of an enterprise inspired by a responsible view of the economic, social and cultural implications of labor and industrial life. In this respect, the impress of Adriano Olivetti's personality was tangibly evident in the company's achievements, whether in organizing the social services, planning a new factory in terms

of economic and social development, opening another line of production, studying the design of a new product, balancing form and function in an industrial
building, or in drafting effective advertising copy.

The Olivetti style

When Olivetti celebrated its 25th anniversary, in 1933, the reorganization
begun in 1927 had revamped every aspect of the company's life. Production
amounted to 15,000 office machines and 9,000 portables. The company employed
870 people. In Italy, the sales network included 13 branches and 79 conces-
sionaries, and abroad Olivetti was actively represented in dozens of countries.

In succeeding years, the line of products was extended and elaborated. Studies
for the construction of adding machines began in 1934. The semistandard Studio
44 was brought out in 1935. Plans for a teleprinter got under way in 1936 and
the year following, it went into production. The first planer milling machine,
designed by Camillo Olivetti, was produced by the O.M.O. plant in 1938.

The years between 1938 and 1942 saw the construction of the group of buildings for the new I.C.O. plant, whose long facade in reinforced concrete and glass
still stands out among successive enlargements as a bold and functional architectural solution. At Massa, in Tuscany, the Olivetti Synthesis company began
production of filing cabinets, card files and metal office furniture. The first permanent summer camp for employees' children was inaugurated at Champoluc, a
mountain area near Ivrea. In 1938 Adriano Olivetti succeeded his father as president of the company, a position he held, except for brief interruptions, until his
death in 1960. For 22 years the history of the Ivrea plant and the biography of
its president make a single story. Adriano Olivetti set a perhaps unique example
of how full and coherent a part industry can play in the social and cultural life
of the community.

A personal religious inclination, which he owed in part to his father's influence, was fused in him with a responsible sensitivity to contemporary values.
Adriano Olivetti was aware of the spiritual impoverishment and the moral cor-
ruption that the superficial acquisition of the means of "civilization" visit on
society and the standards proper to Western culture, but he considered them
errors in the system which could be corrected. This was his outstanding trait as
a modern industrialist, thinker and reformer. He considered material progress
as an essential factor in human redemption. He did not view science as a destroyer
of tradition, fundamental values and the feeling for the absolute that goes with
religious morality. On the contrary, he identified the course of science with that
of truth, its conquests with a continuous verging toward freedom from suffering.
The background for his philosophy lies in various sources, ranging from his personal interpretation of the contemporary French Catholic trend represented by
Mounier, Weil and Maritain, to his familiarity with American developments in
the social sciences. But they are united in a single theme running through everything he accomplished: the reconciliation of material and spiritual values. It is
a motivating idea which he formulated in a book published just after the War,
L'Ordine politico delle communita (*The Political Order of the Communities*),
and which recurs in his most disparate activities. Thus it underlies his work in
industrial organization, town planning, social services, political campaigning,
adult education, sociology, technical and scientific research, the visual arts, publishing and public administration. His interest was centered not so much on the

industrial enterprise considered as an end in itself, as on the human and physical environment in which it operates. Even the most specifically technical and organizational problems were studied by him from this point of view. Whatever he gave his attention to achieved a firm balance between the growing industrial power of his company and the world around it. This approach led him to an intense interest in town planning, considered not merely as a means of pragmatic and esthetic improvement, but as a positive factor in group living and social progress. The idea of organically reconstructing city and territory by planning at local and regional levels was in his view of the world innate and necessary. He saw everything in terms of how best the individual could live with his neighbors in a given environment, and of democratic social organization "on the scale of man." His enthusiasm for town planning was an integral part of his interest in social assistance methods, the use of free time, and the administration of community life to permit the most effective individual expression.

The future historian of 20th-century Italian life will find that at the beginning of all the studies and work in town planning during the last several decades is Adriano Olivetti's master plan for the Valle d'Aosta, which was published in 1937. Going beyond municipal limits, it was the first attempt at regional planning. Moreover it was the first time, at least in Italy, that a public leader considered town and regional planning an essential field of study in building a modern country. The creation of the social services and housing settlements in Ivrea and the model village of La Martella, near Matera, in one of the worst of southern Italy's depressed areas, are only two of the important examples of Adriano Olivetti's work as a social thinker and organizer. Town planning, understood as the science of community living, is necessarily also concerned with architecture. Adriano's passion for industrial architecture was closely connected with his philosophy, hence with the need he acutely felt to improve living conditions by means of specific programs and actual constructions. The form of a building interested him, but he was even more concerned with its purpose. Radically different in approach from the pure esthete, he aimed to promote the construction of buildings, whether for habitation, work, study, research or recreation, that would correspond to people's needs, be satisfying esthetically and above all embody the feeling of community life. This particular concept is one of the most salient traits in his personality as a modern humanist. His outstanding merit, as George Friedmann recently put it, is that of "having succeeded in bringing together mechanized industry and the new form of beauty that has appeared on our horizon—the beauty of technical civilization."

In his vision, factories built "on the scale of man" would produce a continual stream of products designed for man. The desirability of devoting special attention to product design had been emphasized by Camillo Olivetti from the very beginning of the Ivrea factory. At that time he wrote, "A machine should not be a gewgaw for the living room, ornate and in questionable taste. It should have an appearance that is serious and elegant at the same time."

His son echoed these words in more contemporary terms when he summed up the principles of Olivetti design: "The design of every product stands out for its clarity, unity and logic. The office machine designs are pleasing but not oversmooth, rational but not inhuman, discreet but not banal."

With respect to Olivetti design, a few years ago an American writer quoted an observation by Schiller which might well apply to the achievements promoted by Adriano Olivetti: "One of culture's most important tasks is that of subjecting man to the influence of form even in his merely physical life, and to make his life esthetic by introducing the norm of the beautiful wherever possible, for only from esthetic conditions and not from physical conditions can moral life develop." If the "norm of the beautiful" is an essential condition for a fuller life, this same norm is an indispensable influence on man's will and psychology, making him aware of his powers of mind, imagination and fantasy. In the light of this reasoning, advertising must be seen as a means of stimulating and developing the moral and esthetic values inherent in human nature. Believing this, Adriano Olivetti contributed to his company's advertising the standards determined by his close involvement with current cultural developments and his lively feeling for the forms of contemporary art. He had no faith in the hard sell. The company produced quality products and its advertising would have to meet the same high standards. Planned and maintained on the level of art, Olivetti advertising does not aim at quick impact, but at fresh and personal expression having a long-term effect in depth. These principles have themselves become "the company's true hallmark, standing for a firm founded on modern technology, efficiency, honesty, elegance and human welfare."

The close bond between technology and the forms of publicity, and the influence of functional architecture and modern geometric design on the company's products, graphic work and printing, have created a unified image embracing numerous activities that complement each other. Each achievement is identifiable as expressing the company's "style," in the broadest sense of the term.

Olivetti, a world enterprise

This complex but unified corporate image is the creation of Adriano Olivetti and the many technicians, industrial designers, graphic artists, architects, painters, writers and social scientists he enlisted to work closely with him. The image took its present form mainly during the last several decades, in step with Olivetti's development on a world scale. Before the war the company had already begun to attract intellectuals and artists. The war years created a hiatus. Camillo Olivetti died toward the end of the sinister period when the triumph of extremist nationalism, racism, and the forces of destruction saw the wreck of the values and ideals for which he had worked, and in which he believed religiously. Adriano Olivetti, obliged to go into exile in Switzerland, was able there to develop and then publish his political and social ideas, in his book *L'Ordine politico delle communita*, which served as a point of departure for his activities on his return to Italy after the liberation. By 1945, the factory was employing more than 4,000 people. Besides typewriters, the company was producing adding machines, calculators and teleprinters. A new plant was built in Turin to supplement the production capacity of those in Ivrea. The factory at Massa, which had been partially destroyed during the hostilities, was rebuilt. Between 1948 and 1954 the entire range of products was redesigned. Four new typewriter models and three calculators were produced. Increased production called for the reorganization of the distribution network not only in Italy and the few countries where the company was represented before the war, but all over the world. The last ten years were marked by the unprecedented growth of what today is the largest manufacturer of office machines in Europe.

Adriano Olivetti's theories in politics, social service, town planning and esthetics presupposed a forward-looking policy of expansion in production and sales, for only the physical expansion of the enterprise could provide daily proof of the validity of his "revolutionary" approach.

In his personality, thinker and reformer, farsighted organizer and dynamic promoter complemented each other without conflict. Underlying his thought was the conviction that organized production is part and parcel of contemporary culture. He refused to follow what he called "the tragic march toward efficiency and profit," in the materialist sense, but was dominated by the idea of directing every effort toward ideal ends. In 1958 he wrote: "Labor has to participate in the aims of the factory, I realized when I started working. This realization implied the answer to some of the fundamental questions of my life, questions dramatically repeated in moments of doubt and uncertainty, questions profoundly decisive for the faith they presuppose and the obligations they denote: Can industry have aims? Are these aims simply to be found in the index of profits, or is there not also an ideal, a destiny and vocation in the life of the factory?"

The program of technical and organizational improvements initiated some 30 years ago in the Ivrea plants has been continuously carried forward, with the same objectives, up to the present day. At the end of 1951, after completion of the postwar reorganization, the labor force numbered 5,000 and clerical and managerial personnel, 1,000. By 1956 the total number of employees, including those in the Italian and foreign sales organizations, was 16,000. In 1959 there were 25,000 employees, while production reached 735,000 unit equivalents of a standard typewriter. The year following, production rose to 1,035,000, and in 1961 to 1,390,000 units. The number of Olivetti employees in 1961 was about 39,000. In the same year the Underwood Corporation (whose connections with Olivetti will be discussed below) had about 12,000 employees. New divisions had been added in recent years to the Ivrea plant constructed between 1938 and 1942. In line with the main building and connected with it by an overhead passage, a series of new plants houses various production facilities. Behind these, a large building for the company school and cafeteria has been erected. Nearby, the Study and Experiment Center, inaugurated in 1955, is used by specialists engaged in designing new machines and working out new production methods. Opposite, on the same street, stand the social services and cultural center and the library, which are the concrete expression of the particular human climate that distinguishes the organization.

The development of the company and its increasingly broad economic influence on the region centering on Ivrea, suggested the desirability of a progressive decentralization program. Accordingly, a teleprinter plant was set up at San Lorenzo; the new machine-tools factory was constructed at S. Bernardo; and other small plants and workshops for the production of accessory equipment were similarly decentralized. Also in Piedmont, the Aglié plant was purchased in 1955 for the mass production of portables; and in Lombardy the more recent electronic research laboratory was constructed at Borgolombardo, near Milan. Finally, there is the Pozzuoli factory, near Naples, which not only raises Olivetti's production capacity, but also contributes to the needed industrialization of southern Italy and has helped to raise the living standard of a depressed area. Other factories were constructed abroad. Most extensive of the foreign plants is that of the Hispano Olivetti company, in Barcelona, where production and assembly shops are laid out around an office building, dining hall, sports fields and swimming pool. Also in operation abroad are the factories of British Olivetti in Glasgow, Olivetti Argentina in Buenos Aires, Olivetti Industrial in Sao Paulo, Brazil (the last two recently constructed), and of Olivetti Africa in Johannesburg.

The list of Olivetti products today ranges from typewriters to office furniture, from teleprinters to machine tools, from calculators to accounting machines, and from data-processing equipment to electronic computers. Sales have been developed as dynamically as production. Thirty-nine branches and two hundred and fifty exclusive distributors make up the commercial network in Italy. Abroad, a group of 22 companies associated with Olivetti have created their own sales organizations, either patterned on the Italian system or based, where more suitable, on local conditions. The Olivetti associated companies are located in Argentina, Australia, Austria, Belgium, Brazil, Canada, Colombia, Denmark, France, Germany, Great Britain, Japan, Mexico, Peru, Portugal, Spain, the United States, Sweden, Switzerland, South Africa, and Venezuela.

The last years of Adriano Olivetti's life saw the achievement of projects that had been on the company's program for some time, as well as the opening of highly interesting new prospects. In 1958 when Olivetti celebrated its 50th anniversary, new products, new factories, new sales organizations were carrying the image of a vital contemporary enterprise all over the globe. Olivetti's advanced level of technology and organization allowed it to compete successfully in all the main foreign markets, and production was now predominantly devoted to export. Consequently, every move to reduce tariff barriers and customs obstacles created new possibilities for Olivetti sales abroad. In fact, the measures already adopted toward trade liberalization and European economic integration have confirmed this by stepping up the rhythm of exports, and justify particularly favorable prospects for the future as the common market treaties are progressively implemented.

Another factor promising further notable development for Olivetti is the agreement that was signed at the end of 1959 with Underwood, the famous American office machine company. Under the terms of this agreement for close cooperation, Olivetti became the majority shareholder in the American company. Mr. Ugo Galassi of Olivetti, still in charge of the Italian Sales Organization, took over as President of the new American Allied Company. Underwood, operating an extensive sales network in the United States, needed other competitive products to offer along with models produced in its American factories. Following the merger, Underwood filled this need with machines constructed by Olivetti, especially in the calculator and accounting machine line. Similar relations were established between Olivetti and Underwood Ltd. of Toronto to cover distribution in Canada.

The Underwood deal was the last large-scale operation conceived and carried out by Adriano Olivetti. On February 27, 1960, he died on a train traveling near Aglié. He was at the height of his dynamic career at the service of his company and the country, and the many-sided enterprise he summed up and represented was progressing as he had intended. A few months before his death he wrote: "Time is flying. Things are on the move. We cannot stop to rummage among the old formulas and institutions of the past. We now stand before the new. In easier times we may and should improve the social institutions of the past, but we would still be looking backward if these improvements were to be only technical. It is necessary to go beyond that, to see whether within the limits of a given economy and a changing society these forms and institutions can be modified or replaced by new solutions inspired by new principles."

The secret of the achievement connected with the name of Olivetti lies in this moral impetus which has vitalized the company from its pioneering period to the present day. The company's world importance was not achieved fortuitously. Besides the ability of its labor staff and management, it owes a great part of its success to the broad ideas of Adriano Olivetti, and of those who are continuing his work. In 1960, Giuseppe Pero, who entered the firm in 1920 as one of the first associates of Camillo Olivetti, became president of the company. In the present as in the past, his dedication to the company has been a central factor in its development.

In little more than half a century, the Italian, then the European public, and now the whole world have seen this company project a constantly varied but fundamentally unified series of ideas, forms and colors which make up its theme and visual image. If the result has been the creation of a distinctive style, a recognizable "face," it is thanks to what lies behind this face: a spirit whose aim is to unify this variety for a specific objective. And the objective has been to make a moral and cultural as well as a practical contribution to the life of our times.[1]

Tocco Olivetti: the Olivetti touch

From the time Adriano Olivetti joined Olivetti he had concerned himself with the development of a unified approach to both the internal and external world of his company. Ricardo Musatti, who was director of the advertising and press department for Olivetti in 1962, expressed Adriano Olivetti's underlying philosophy.

Two fundamental ideas inspired the thought and action of Adriano Olivetti. First, the conviction that industry in view of its great influence in the contemporary world, ought to have a code of ethics and a system of objectives going beyond the purely economic sphere which in any case it has long overlapped. Second, the conviction that present-day mass civilization, more dynamic and richer in technical and scientific resources than any period in the past, should make every effort to achieve the "kingdom of Vocations," a human society organized so that every man may give the best in him by expressing himself most fully and constructively.[2]

Horizon wrote of the roots of the Olivetti style.

In the late twenties, the Olivetti Company reflected the state of Italian industrial design, which had got off to a lively start and then fallen back into eclectic, perfunctory and sentimental habits. But by 1930, the philosophy of the Weimer Bauhaus group began to filter into Italy, just at the time when its influence in Germany was being undermined by the Nazis. The philosophy of this school was congenial to Olivetti's temper. It combined high technical skill with the purest aesthetic ideas. Besides, as one of his assistants has put it, "Olivetti's force is that he has always wanted to be in the vanguard." The Weimer school

---

[1]*Olivetti, a Contemporary Image of Style and Industry* (published by the Olivetti Company, 1962).

[2]*Ibid.*

brought together workers in all the arts: the architects Mies van der Rohe and Gropius; the painters Klee and Kandinsky; designers such as Herbert Bayer and Moholy-Nagy. In the early thirties, the painter Xanty Schawinsky, who had spent four fruitful years at the Bauhaus, came to work for Olivetti. Soon one could sense the direction the new Olivetti style was taking. The stern austerity of the Bauhaus was somewhat softened and made more poetic by the Italian atmosphere, but here was the same formidable use of photography, the brilliant play of type, and the disdain for irrelevant frippery which marked the Bauhaus style. By 1938, Olivetti had recruited an extraordinary team of designers who were to transform his wishes into reality in a series of startling posters, striking exhibition displays, and subtly conceived booklets.

Discussing the role which [Adriano] Olivetti himself played in creating the company style, Pintori [one of the designers who played an important role in developing Olivetti advertising] recently remarked: "At the beginning, he was intimately involved with everything we did, . . . He not only chose the men who did the work, but he gave suggestions and criticisms of the finished work down to the last detail. Particularly with the architects, he was constantly involved in the job—but with us too. He is a man teeming with intuition. He has a style and although he may not be able to fabricate it in any special way he knows how to communicate its sense and then to judge its results.[3]

The Olivetti style became known inside and outside the company as the *"Tocco Olivetti,"* or the "Olivetti Touch." While the Olivetti touch, according to company executives, had influenced virtually every aspect of the company's operations, it was most visible in the areas of advertising, product design, company architecture, and social services.

Advertising

Advertising was the first area in which *tocco Olivetti* came to be expressed. Adriano Olivetti's first job in 1928 with the Olivetti Company was advertising director, and he continued to supervise this area actively until his death in 1960.

The approach which Adriano Olivetti took to advertising set the company apart radically from its competition.

The innovation it [the Olivetti Company] introduced in Italian advertising was based on the refusal to conform to the so-called public taste. The refusal did not stem from the desire to be in the vanguard at any cost, but from the conviction that public taste does not exist: like fashions it is not created by masses of people but by individual personalities whose example is accepted and then becomes general habit. To convey the idea of special quality requires stimulating the average taste by means of unconventional forms and language. In this connection Olivetti advertising put less emphasis on the product than on the service it offered and its message of modernity and progress.[4]

The underlying philosophy was, "We do not stupefy the customer with the

---

[3]"Olivetti: A Man and a Style," by Kermit Lansner (November 1959, HORIZON). © 1959 by American Heritage Publishing Co., Inc. Reprinted by permission.
[4]*Ibid.*

sound of our advertising voice, or use it as an instrument of aggression against him. We do not evoke vast materialistic instincts or sexual urges. We are not tied to the salesman's fleeting problems." Another early member of the advertising staff is quoted as saying, "We know the rules of advertising so that we can disobey them. For us advertising is like soap for the spirit, clean and virtuous." Dr. Musatti put it this way:

Olivetti has always insisted that we must present the ideal of a mechanical culture, that we must give the idea that the machine, the typewriter, is the last word in modern culture. Do you remember one of Pintori's most famous posters? On the left was an inkwell with an old fashioned pen. In the inkwell was a beautiful rose. To the right there was nothing but the words Olivetti Studio 42. The pen belongs to the romantic past, the typewriter is of the world today.[5]

Industrial design

Camillo Olivetti had had an appreciation for the importance of the aesthetic in machine design, but his tastes had called for a revolution against the traditional "ornate gewgaws." He had approached design from the functionalist point of view, arguing that anything which did not have a place in the mechanical functioning of a machine was unnecessary. This approach had been contrary to the standards of his contemporaries who still reflected the love for "gingerbread," of the early 1900's. Dr. Musatti said of this period:

The problem of the relations between useful object and aesthetic form has existed from the earliest times, and has always found a contemporary solution. The triumph of the Machine Age and the somewhat misunderstood principle of functionalism led to the debasement of the aesthetic value of tools and utensils, which at other times had been the object of elaborate handworks.[6]

Adriano Olivetti, however, approached the problem differently from his father. He said: "The design of every product stands out for its clarity, unity and logic. The office machine designs are pleasing, but not over-smooth, rational but not inhuman, discreet but not banal." Starting in 1930, Adriano Olivetti had tried to make this concept of industrial design a reality in the Olivetti products. He had met some resistance from his father who still could not see the reasoning behind the great concern and expense for the aesthetic. It was reported that there had been some heated discussions about the necessity of redesign for aesthetic reasons but Adriano Olivetti persisted.

The height of Olivetti advances in product design stemmed from the work of Marcello Nizzoli. Marcello Nizzolo, when a young painter and advertising artist, had been encouraged by Adriano Olivetti to become a product designer and then an architect. Destined to become world-famous as an industrial designer Nizzolo over the years had been responsible for the industrial design of many Olivetti machines including the Lexikon 80, Lettera 22, the Studio 44, the 82 Diaspron typewriters and the Divisumma, Tetractys and Audit calculating and accounting machines. Olivetti won several international prizes

---

[5]"Olivetti: Elegant and Tough," *Fortune*, September 1960, pp. 137 ff.

[6]*Notes Towards the History of a Factory* (published by the Olivetti Company, 1958).

Exhibit 3

PICTURES OF OLIVETTI PRODUCTS
Lettera 32—Portable Typewriter

Praxis 48—Compact Electric Typewriter

Exhibit 3—Continued

Tekne 3—Electric Typewriter

Electrosumma 20—Electric Adding Machine

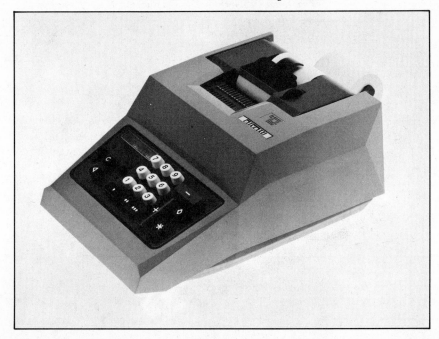

Exhibit 3—Continued

Divisumma 24—Printing Calculator

Programma 101—Desk Top Computer

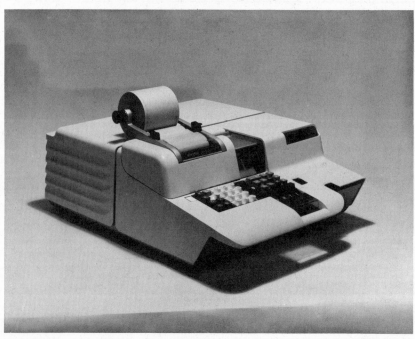

for the design of these products. The Lettera 22 was selected in a worldwide poll conducted by Illinois Institute of Technology as first among the ten best examples of contemporary industrial design. It has been exhibited at the Metropolitan Museum of Art.

The evolution in product design has proceeded around two basic themes since 1940. The first theme, expressed in the calculating machines, was that of a six-sided solid parallelogram with rounded corners. The second major theme was the "fluid ovoid" form expressed in the typewriters. Variety in relation to these themes was introduced through keyboard design, which was directed at relating the required key positions to cubic, cylindrical and rectangular overtones. Color, too, was a tool which was widely employed.

In later typewriters, Olivetti exhibited a trend away from the fluidity for which it had become stylistically famous. As other manufacturers followed by rounding corners and making graceful sweeps of metallic form, the Olivetti style turned to intersecting planes, oblique angles, and sharply contrasting colors. The Praxis 48 and the Olivetti Tekne epitomize the concept of sharp linearity in both form and color.

The importance of design in Olivetti's history can perhaps be measured by one executive's comment: "With Adriano, you always knew when you had to consult him. Any question of product design had to be personally approved." Even in 1966, the men in research and development admit that they made compromises to get the required product characteristics within an aesthetically pleasing package. One executive, looking toward the future said, "Clearly, Olivetti no longer has a position as a leader. Others have become aware of the importance of that which Olivetti pioneered." Olivetti executives often attested to the fact that in 1966, Thomas J. Watson, Jr., president of IBM Corporation, paid tribute to Olivetti's pioneering understanding of the importance of industrial design. While accepting the Tiffany Award for "Encouragement of American Design," he said:

> I'd like to take credit for all of the things you've seen as coming out of my own head . . . actually they came from a company called Olivetti, which hasn't had the success in the business field lately that it really deserves, but Adriano Olivetti, an Italian, many, many years ago decided that it was with a theme of excellence, through color, through interiors, through design and through products, and particularly through buildings, that he could establish his company as a worldwide symbol. And he did. . . . And some of us in IBM thought perhaps we could do it too, so I wanted to pay my respects to his leadership. He's now gone.

Architecture

Architecture was another important concern of Adriano Olivetti. The earliest Olivetti factory built in Ivrea had been patterned after the original Underwood plant in Hartford, Connecticut. It was done in the red brick style common in New England. Planning expansion of facilities immediately preceding and following World War II, however, Adriano Olivetti decided to apply principles of modern functional design when enlarging the factory building. His idea was the creation of a unified environment which would allow the buildings and the workers to fit harmoniously with the environment. In this regard, Dr. Zorzi, director of advertising, in 1966 said, "Architecture and the role of man in an urban society were the two great passions of Adriano Olivetti, and in building his factories he was able to serve them both. He disliked the idea that work should be solely a source of income for the worker, a necessary evil which should be endured in order to gain material recompense. He hoped that by introducing 'the norm of the beautiful' into the workers' surroundings, some of the drudgery might be eliminated."

In making his selection of architects, Adriano Olivetti reportedly did not rely upon a single school of design. Again according to Dr. Zorzi, "He believed in intelligence. He chose young men, 25 to 30 years old, in whom he had confidence and gave them the commission." By the time of his death he knew most of the great architects of Europe, some of whom were in his debt for having been given their first chance.

The example which was often cited as the culmination of the effect of *tocco Olivetti* on the company's architecture was the factory at Pozzuoli (see Exhibit 4). This factory allowed Olivetti to show his concern for both architecture and social responsibility. In 1952, when Olivetti decided to build the plant in Pozzuoli, in the economically underdeveloped South, the town was very poor. It was located about 20 kilometers north of Naples on the Gulf of Baia. The inhabitants had never done factory work, and were largely dependent upon agriculture and tourism. Adriano Olivetti decided to build the factory, without particular government encouragement, except for a limited fiscal advantage.[7] "He was making a pilot experiment in a depressed area. . . . He chose a poor town with little employment, yet not so poor as to be crushed. His aim was to found a productive enterprise in the presumably inefficient South and to lure other industry into the area if it were successful."[8]

Adriano Olivetti appointed Mr. Cosenza, an avowed communist, as his architect for the Pozzuoli factory. Both men felt that there would have to be a transition from the unfettered agrarian life which the people of Pozzuoli were used to leading to the regimented existence of a factory population. The architect described his concept as follows: "I wanted to make the factory less like a prison. You can't change the fact that it is a prison, but I wanted to make it as different from the old-fashioned factory as I could. I know Olivetti feels the same way." *Horizon* described the factory as follows:

From Via Domitiana, which passes the main facade, the building might be taken for an elegant resort hotel or a sanatorium in the modern style. For there in the background are the heights of Mount Campiglione, and stretching before the factory is the Gulf of Baia with Capri and Ischia visible in the distance when the day is clear. Cosenza has created a plant which is unique in its sense of freedom and elegance. From every bench and point of the assembly line there is a view of the outdoors. Light pours in with all its Mediterranean clarity and

[7]There was some tax advantage; for ten years no tax on income was required.
[8]K. Lansner, *op. cit.*

abundance. Spotted here and there among the low buildings which are joined together in a coherent whole are ponds caught in free form concrete walls. Landscaping encloses the entire industrial bulk and reunites it with nature. . . .

So splendid is the whole establishment that there is a wry truth to the remark which the director of the plant made as he summed up the effect of the factory on the people of Pozzuoli: "For those who haven't found employment here, the factory is like Kafka's castle. It is a kind of Paradise where the lucky ones have gained entrance."[9] (See Exhibit 4.)

As *Fortune*[10] declared, "the *tocco Olivetti* included turning aesthetics into profit." The Pozzuoli plant was a good example. Judged on an output per man-hour basis, productivity in the plant was as good as, if not better than, in the plants in the more industrial North, according to company executives.

The architectural design of the most recent building, a large structure erected in Ivrea to house the firm's headquarters, has been a matter of controversy. (For a photograph of this building see Exhibit 4.) One executive spoke somewhat disparagingly about it saying that it was a "$5,000,000 hostage to the Canavese region." Another made the comment: "If Adriano saw this, he would go to Tanganyika and start over. It is so out of place in the Canavese countryside." Several executives pointed out that the new building disrupted many of the more informal patterns of communication which had existed prior to 1963. With its long corridors and enclosed offices, these executives reported that informal contact with other executives was less frequent than it had been previously. Also some executives wondered about the appropriateness of having the headquarters of a large international corporation in a remote provincial town like Ivrea.

Social services

From the beginning of the Olivetti Company, there has been a strong concern for the well-being of the workers. Camillo Olivetti had been a humanist as well as an industrialist. Adriano Olivetti in *Notes Towards the History of a Factory*, described the social services of the early period.

My father before me guided the workshop with an eye to intelligence, but listening also to the wisdom of the heart. In those days they took on at the plant all the youths who had a reputation in the parish of being capable, hard workers. They used to set aside at least one hour a day for the employee who wanted a job for his wife or sister-in-law, or who needed a loan to buy furniture or pay off a debt; the employee who felt underrated by his section chief or wanted a transfer for reasons of health or a leave for a period of convalescence. For all of them, whenever possible, a remedy or a solution was found.

This personal touch, introduced by men of heart, was inevitably lost as the factory became larger. My father understood this long before I did. . . . My father created a fund. This fund served to guarantee social security to the employee above and beyond the limited amount provided by Italian law. Thus, no one was forced to go into debt in order to pay for his father's or sister's funeral.

---

[9] *Ibid.*

[10] *Fortune, op. cit.*, September 1960.

Exhibit 4

PICTURES OF OLIVETTI COMPANY HEADQUARTERS AND TWO FACTORIES
IN ITALY

Company Headquarters in Ivrea, Italy

Typewriter Factory in Scarmagno, Italy

No one had to forego a last farewell to his mother who might be dying in a distant place. Mothers were furnished with beds, mattresses, coats, shoes for their children; and no one remained without wood in the winter. Orphans and widows received ample assistance; and no convalescent was ever forced to return to work before he was able.

In the process of reorganizing these services, I came to understand the inti-

Exhibit 4—Continued

Adding Machine Factory in Pozzuoli, Italy

mate relationship between health assistance and social assistance. I realized how insensitive to such problems are those who have never had to face them, or those concerned only with the objectives of efficiency or profit.[11]

In order to "establish a responsible administration with some guarantee of stability and to develop higher standards of scientific objectivity" Olivetti set up the Labor Management Council to run the Olivetti social services. The charter of that group said: "The Olivetti Social Services place joint responsibility on workers and management. Each employee, by his work, contributes to the life of the company and so to the life of the organizations created within it, and is therefore entitled to assistance without any question of charity arising. Likewise, all workers have an equal right to social service benefits; each case is judged on its merits and by criteria as objective as possible which are subject to constant study and revision."

Adriano Olivetti said of the work in social services: "If the material and moral aims of our work are upheld, one day this factory will be an integral part of a new and authentic civilization directed toward a freer, happier and more conscious development of the human individual." In 1966 the company estimated it spent 2,700 million lire for social services. In addition the by-laws of the company state: "Once 8.5% [of the par value of the shares] has been

[11]*Notes Towards the History of a Factory.*

assigned to both preferred and common shares and before any other appro-
priation that may be resolved by the general meeting, a sum equal to 4%
of the net profit of the financial year shall, provided there are sufficient funds,
be deducted from the residue and placed at the disposal of the board of
directors, which with a view to supplementing the company's ordinary expenditure on social services and activities shall assign said sum to boards, institutions or organizations situated in the areas where the company's main
factories are located and having as their object the development of education
and technical and scientific research."

Dr. Volponi, the director of social services at Olivetti, explained: "We
consider the social services as an important part of the system. Everyone
working in the company has a right to these services, and the process of determining who gets what is public knowledge. At present we have a cafeteria;
a complete health clinic, including medical services for dependents; library
facilities with over 150,000 volumes; vacation houses in the mountains and
on the seashore; recreational facilities of varied natures; employee housing
(see Exhibit 5); transport facilities to get workers from their homes to work;
and a cultural center.

One executive explained the reasoning behind the extensive social services:
"The Italian government was far behind in accepting its responsibilities toward its citizens. The money which it took in was used inefficiently and the
recipients of state largess often got too little too late. Perhaps this explains
some of the traditional Italian attitude towards taxes." Illustrating the early
concern of the Olivetti Company for employee welfare were the maternity
benefits. Long before paid maternity leaves were required by law, Olivetti
was granting time off with pay. In 1966 an expectant mother was given
nine and a half months off with full pay—three months before the baby was
born, and six and a half months after. This contrasted with the national
allowance of five and a half months at 80% pay. All medical care for both
mother and child were taken care of by the company.

The company had long advocated an enriched cultural life for its employees. It sponsored concerts, plays, debates, and any other form of activity
which the employee council requested, with the objective of "making life to the
measure of man."

Dr. Volponi explained how the programs were controlled:

The Consiglio di Gestione is structured in such a way to secure a balanced
representation of the interests of both employees and management. It includes:

A president, who is nominated by the company's chairman of the board;

Ten elected members (four are elected by factory employees and four by office
employees through a two-stage election process; one by both factory and
office employees, one by executives);

Eight appointed members, nominated by the company's chairman of the board
(chosen among experts in the field of health, recreation, dietetics, sociology,
etc.).

Elected members are entitled to be away from the job for the time required in performing their functions within the Consiglio di Gestione without any loss of pay.

This committee is a survivor of many which were set up in Italy after the war. The others died out because of pressure from managements and from Communist unions which preferred to have a complete split between management and the workers. I think that our committee at Olivetti survived because we gave it practical day-to-day problems to deal with. They had weekly meetings to apply the more general schemes which they developed to the particular case.

When asked about the future direction in which the social services of Olivetti might go, Dr. Volponi replied:

The main reason that Olivetti social services are so large is that the gap between public social services and those which were required was so large. Now there is a trend to control the general amount of special services which we offer since the public services are improving. We will no longer duplicate that which the country is doing. For example, there is now a national kindergarten, so the meaning of our kindergarten is reduced. We hope we can remain advanced over the other companies and over the state services. Certainly I don't see a rapid expansion, but as the state takes over functions which we served previously, we will be using our ingenuity to give better service. The amount we spend is practically a part of an unwritten contract. It is my job to help make sure the money is wisely spent.

The most important feature for the workers is the participation in and free discussion of the content of the social services. They get to work with the whole picture. It is a process of civic education. Olivetti social services have kept alive some important social awareness. In this sense we have helped to preserve some of the traditional features of the environment so as not to have just a uniform Olivetti suburb.

The effect of *tocco Olivetti* had been profound in years past. An article in *Fortune* magazine, September 1960, characterized the Olivetti spirit as being "elegant but tough." Most members of management felt a deep commitment to an attempt to continue with this distinctive corporate style. They recognized the large role which Adriano Olivetti had in formulating and spreading the style, and the knowledge of its existence was valuable to them. As one young executive said: "*Tocco Olivetti* meant that I was working for something which was more than an economic institution. As an Italian I am proud of our cultural heritage, and the spirit of Olivetti, *tocco Olivetti*, is a form of its expression. It is the humanist approach to capitalism."

Exhibit 5

PICTURES OF OLIVETTI EMPLOYEE HEALTH CENTER, EMPLOYEE CAFETERIA, AND EMPLOYEE HOUSING, IN IVREA, ITALY

Employee Health Center, Ivrea, Italy

Employee Cafeteria, Ivrea, Italy

Exhibit 5—Continued

Employee Housing, Ivrea, Italy

ING. C. OLIVETTI & C., S.p.A. (A–2)*

^^^

During the period 1958–1963 unconsolidated sales of the Olivetti Company rose from 40,045.5 million lire to 121,687.7 million lire, or by about 204%. Personnel increased from 24,974 in 1958 to 56,536 in 1963. The book value of property, plant, and equipment, net of depreciation, rose from 9,105.3 million lire to 33,093.7 million during the same period.

The extraordinary growth experienced by the company during the late 1950's and early 1960's was financed through retained earnings and through debt. Debentures amounting to 33,190 million lire were issued during the period 1958–1963 and bank overdrafts were increased by more than 15 billion lire.

Among the reasons for the company's extraordinary growth was the acquisition of working control of the Underwood Corporation in the autumn of 1959. The Underwood Corporation, a U.S. typewriter manufacturer long-established but on the verge of bankruptcy in the late 1950's, proved to be the key to the large opening up of the U.S. market to Olivetti. During the early 1950's, Olivetti's representation in the United States (through the Olivetti Corporation of America) had been restricted to exclusive sales agents in the principal cities. In 1950, only 1.7% of company sales volume was achieved in the United States; by 1966, 21.5% was realized in the American market.

The Underwood acquisition, however, had a serious impact on the financial structure of the Olivetti Company. An investment of almost $100 million—an amount far in excess of anticipations—was required before Underwood was placed on a firm, profitable footing. In addition, substantial increases in the Olivetti Company's inventories took place, partly as a result of overoptimistic predictions about the immediate achievement of sales results in the United States, and partly as a natural result of providing stocks of Olivetti products to the former Underwood dealers. Compounding these difficulties was the Italian recession which in the early 1960's, cut substantially into the company's sales at home. (See the Appendix for a description of the Italian environment.)

At about the time that the Underwood acquisition was being undertaken, the Olivetti Company was becoming seriously involved in first developing and then distributing a line of computers and peripheral equipment. Even by 1963, computers did not represent a large part of Olivetti's sales—about 5%—but the computer program provided a substantial drain on company funds.

Extraordinary growth in sales of the company's basic product lines, acquisition of the Underwood Corporation, and the attempt to enter the computer field all contributed to a difficult financial situation clearly in evidence by mid-1963.

These events were described in an article in the September 12, 1964, issue of *Business Week* as follows:

Business Abroad: "Why GE is joining Olivetti"

It took a long time. Since last February, Olivetti has been dickering with General Electric about control of its capital-draining computer division. But not until last week were the final details ironed out and the deal signed.

The two companies plan to form a jointly owned subsidiary to be called Olivetti-General Electric, in which GE will hold controlling interest, reportedly 60%. [It actually turned out to be 75%.] GE will pay an unspecified amount of cash—estimated to run well over $20 million—to Olivetti for its computer operations. GE also will supply the bulk of the capital over the next few years for expansion of the new company. . . .

New life. For Olivetti, the present deal with GE is very important. It lops off an operation that helped put the company into a tight financial squeeze. GE's cash payment, plus the fact that Olivetti's subsidiary—Underwood—has gone into the black for the first time since the Italian company took it over, will pump new life into Olivetti's shaky finances.

Instead of cash, Olivetti will throw the bulk of its electronics division into the new Olivetti-GE. This includes three plants, a spanking new electronics research laboratory at Rho (near Milan), its three basic computer models—the Elea series—with most of their peripheral equipment, and the company's electronics sales organization.

Olivetti still is keeping one foot in electronics, however. It will continue producing its electronic accounting and billing machines, along with the rest of its equipment for mechanical integration. It also hangs on to its automatic production data collector, and numerical control equipment for machine tools. It plans to bring out additional products, including a desk computer.

I. *Luxury product*

Computers never did represent a large part of Olivetti's sales. Last year they probably accounted for no more than 5% of total consolidated sales of $422.7 million (but perhaps 25% if important peripheral equipment is included). The computer operation absorbed a disproportionate amount of money. According to one company source, Olivetti has invested "not less than $30 million to $50 million" in the electronics field. The total sum is probably a great deal more, and most of it went into the computer operation.

"Sales," as in most computer operations, were actually almost entirely rentals, so that each computer sold meant more capital tied up. At the end of last year, Olivetti listed on its balance sheet $11.4 million as the value of the computers rented out. The computer business was a luxury Olivetti couldn't afford.

Three models. Olivetti's venture into computers goes back to 1954, when it launched a computer research project. In 1959—about two years after IBM entered the Italian computer market—Olivetti brought out its first computer, the Elea 9003, which falls into the range of the IBM 7070. Two years later, Olivetti introduced its second model, the 6001, which was designed primarily for scientific work, then modified for commercial use. Finally, late last year, Olivetti added the smaller 4001, a relatively low-cost machine.

To complement its computers, Olivetti had to sell peripheral equipment made by other companies until it could develop its own, which took it until 1962. It never did manage to make its own punch-card system; instead it acted as exclusive sales agent in Italy for a system developed by Machines Bull.

Stiff competition for the Italian market also complicated Olivetti's computer efforts. Today, nine companies vie for a share of the Italian market, and this number could double in the next four years.

Limited range. Olivetti's basic problem was that it simply wasn't big enough to play the computer game. While the money it poured into research and development was a heavy stake for Olivetti, it was peanuts compared to the sums laid out by the American giants.

As a result, the company's technology was weak. While its competitors were bringing out third-generation computers, Olivetti's whole line was limited in range and basically a modification of the computer it first developed.

In the eyes of Milan financial men, the GE deal marks a turning point in Olivetti's fortunes. With world competition on the upswing and Italy's economy anything but healthy, Olivetti's rehabilitation won't be easy, even after the computer amputation. But at least the operation has staunched the flow of capital away from further development of its basic lines, which have made Olivetti the biggest European office machine producer and one of the world's largest makers of calculating machines.

II. *Family affair*

The late Adriano Olivetti was the man largely responsible both for building Olivetti up to its glittering stature and, ironically, for pushing it into its financial crisis. . . .

Adriano was the eldest of Camillo's six children, each of whom got an equal share of the 60% of the company's stock that Camillo had held.

Despite the fact that he controlled no more stock than any of his five brothers and sisters, Adriano held full command of the company because of his age and personality.

Buildup. Under Adriano's hand, Olivetti flourished. The company already had branched out from its original typewriter business when it brought out a line of office furniture in 1930. In 1937, it started making teleprinter equipment that, since it has a monopoly in Italy, still provides a comfortable source of profit. Three years later, Olivetti sold its first adding machine.

Then came a series of achievements that helped bring Olivetti to the head of its field. In 1948, the company brought out its Lexikon 80 and Divisumma 14, the world's first printing-calculating machines and, in 1956, the first automatic printing calculators, the Divisumma 24 and then Tetractys. Along the way, Olivetti moved into electric typewriters, bookkeeping and billing machines, office filing systems, machine tools, and the variety of by-products of its electronics work.

Even today Olivetti accounts for more than a fifth of world typewriter production, almost a third of world calculator output, over 40% of world calculator exports.

Last straw. To reach this position, Adriano set Olivetti spinning through a period of almost feverish growth, especially after World War II. For the Italian operation alone, sales shot up from $64.1 million to $194.7 million from the fiscal year ending Mar. 31, 1958, to Dec. 31, 1963.

Abroad, Olivetti complemented its massive export growth with heavy investments, building or buying plants in Scotland, Spain, Argentina, Brazil, Mexico, Colombia, South Africa, the United States, and Canada. This expansion, along with the heavy development costs and—above all—Adriano's plunge into computers, blotted up an enormous amount of black ink.

Adriano's last big move—buying control of Underwood Corporation in 1959—pushed the company and the Olivetti family to the wall. Underwood was old and sick. Olivetti had to replace its machinery almost entirely and revamp its sales organization. It took more than four years to put Underwood into the black. For the record, Olivetti claims the Underwood venture has cost it a total of about $48 million. Actually, insiders say, it cost a good deal more.

Hard times. Under the strain of these investments, Olivetti's debts snowballed. Between 1958 and the end of 1963, long-term debt rose from $21.3 million to $66.6 million. More ominously, bank debts shot up from $7.6 million to $32.5 million.

Even in the best of times, Olivetti would have been hard pressed to finance its investments out of its own coffers. As it was, times were getting harder. Rising labor costs bit into profits; competition on the home market increased, while the market itself grew less buoyant as the Italian economic miracle faded.

More important, the situation grew bleaker in Olivetti's export market, which accounts for about 70% of the sales of its Italian plants. Olivetti had based a good deal of its expansion on the expectation that the Common Market would absorb its increased output. But sales didn't rise as fast as expected. Economic crises in Argentina and Brazil in 1962 also hurt badly.

The company entered 1964 with substantial overcapacity and warehouses full of unsold products.

Setting the stage. As if these problems weren't enough, the Olivetti company was afflicted with the squabbling of the Olivetti family. When Adriano died in 1960, the family named long-time company man Giuseppe Pero to run it.

Pero's death last November finally set the stage for the deal that has now been made. The family was unable to agree on a successor. Adriano's son, Roberto, was its most active member in the company, but he couldn't influence his older relatives. Olivetti lurched into its financial crisis with no one at the helm.

With money tight and the company headless, the banks balked at extending Olivetti's loans. Moreover, the family had cornered itself into its own financial crisis. The company's mounting debts and reinvested profits had not been enough to finance expansion, so its capitalization had been increased from $17.2 million in 1958 to $96 million in 1962.

Unwilling to give up control of the company to outsiders, and afraid to let one branch of the family get more shares than another, the six family branches subscribed most of the capitalization increases themselves, and boosted their total control of voting stock from 60% to 72%. To raise the money, they borrowed from banks, putting up their stock as security. But as the value of Olivetti's stock plummeted with the whole Italian stock market, the banks began pressing the family to put its financial house in order.

III. *Band of angels*

This spring, the family finally faced the inevitable. In May, it agreed to sell almost half of its stock (at well below market value) to a group that is providing the money and management to put Olivetti back on the track. This group consists of the government-controlled bank Mediobanca (government-controlled medium-term credit institution), Istituto Mobiliare Italiano (IMI), the government-controlled credit institution, Fiat, Pirelli, and LaCentrale, a Milan *holding company*.[1] (private)

The consortium has put up the money to consolidate Olivetti's short-term debts. It also has overhauled the company's management. The prestigious Bruno Visentini, long-time adviser to the Olivetti family, vice-president of IRI, the powerful government holding company that controls Mediobanca, and the man who engineered the family sell-off, moved into the presidency. . . .

Although a sell-off of the computer division was brewing for a long time, it was the new controlling group that pushed through the GE deal. With the computer business lopped off, glutted warehouses cleared by cuts in work hours and a sell-off of inventory, and with Underwood finally in the black, Olivetti's prospects are much brighter now than a few months ago.[2]

EVENTS AS REPORTED IN OLIVETTI ANNUAL REPORTS

The 1964 Olivetti Annual Report described the agreement with General Electric Company as follows:

Activities in the electronic sector. In the electronic sector, we have to place on record before all else the agreement we have reached with the General Electric Company of New York. On the basis of this agreement, the Olivetti Electronics Division and the Olivetti Bull Company are to continue their activities in design, production and distribution of electronic computers and of other equipment for data processing, and associated research activities, in a company in which General Electric will have a 75% stock holding and to which it will contribute the financial means required for subsequent development.

The agreement, ensuring full employment for workers and the future workers and technicians brought together and trained by Olivetti, foresees further gradual increases in activities in the sector with matching development of research, production and distribution. In addition the opportunity will be presented to offer products in all Common Market countries, the rest of Europe and in the world as a whole, and will offer Italian users, on the other hand, an increasingly wide and complementary range of equipment of high technical and functional quality.

It must be remembered that right from the beginning this activity—initially pioneered by nature and later established in the industrial and commercial fields

---

[1]The respective shares of the deal amounted to approximately 50% each for the government-controlled institutions (Mediobanca and IMI) and the private companies (Fiat, Pirelli, LaCentrale).

[2]Quoted from p. 140 of the September 12, 1964, issue of *Business Week* by special permission. Copyrighted © 1964 by McGraw-Hill, Inc.

—was deliberately confined to the Italian market. In fact, the huge financial commitment, arising necessarily from the system of establishing computer centers rather than that of selling outright, rapidly came to such an amount in this field as to necessitate a limitation on installations, with a consequent ceiling to the volume of output, and hence ever greater difficulties in amortizing the costs of overheads and research. To this had to be added the huge burden of scientific and technical research and the expense of the organization of sales and technical assistance to cover which, apart from any other consideration, expansion abroad would have been essential while being impossible from the point of view of finance and organization by ourselves alone.

The agreement with General Electric permits our company to reappraise what it has accomplished in this field, to remain in the field of large and medium computers, even if with no more than a minority interest, and at the same time— since our company will continue to produce independently machines which are based increasingly on the use of electronic techniques and components—to benefit from a wider scientific and technical experience for those products which it is our task to develop.

Contrary to the rumors which had circulated, it was found that the basic structure of the company was sound. Olivetti used only one-fifth of the line of credit which had been established for it by the intervening consortium. In terms of dollars this amounted to a little more than 6 millions on an asset base of over 300 millions. The Underwood operation, which had been cited as one of the major financial drains on the company, began to earn a profit in March 1964, only 10 months after the new management group moved in.

By the end of 1965, the crisis had passed. It was clear to all in management that there was no danger of imminent collapse. The 1965 Annual Report opened with the following statement concerning the improvement in Olivetti's position:

To the Stockholders:

In our last report, we described to you the comparatively difficult circumstances of 1964. In that year, at the lowest point of a recession which involved the whole Italian economy, and which, following a period of exceptional expansion, afflicted in particular the capital goods market, our Company had to give effect to a series of measures aimed at:

a) relieving itself of the heavy financial burden represented by research and production in the field of medium and large electronic computers;

b) allowing a process of financial and business reorganization of our subsidiaries in Italy and abroad and, in particular, undertaking the thorough consolidation of Underwood's position;

c) intensifying our efforts to contain production costs as necessitated by the continuous increase in the cost of labor on the one hand, and by the sharpened competition on world markets on the other;

d) laying the foundations for bringing our products up to date as demanded by the increasingly rapid evolution of the office equipment market. In this market a number of our competitors have strengthened their structure or have been merged into larger groups. Likewise in this market the pace of technical progress imposes an increasingly rapid rate of renewal of traditional products. In this setting, our company had to prepare the instruments in its traditional policy of technical excellence, to anticipate the future evolution in the development of demand in new and complex fields requiring increasingly refined technology.

A year ago we explained the agreements reached and the measures taken for these purposes, and noted the practical beginning during 1964 of the work of reorganization which, as we announced, was to be developed and extended over successive years. We cannot yet say that we have covered the greater part of the course we set for ourselves. Above all with respect to the development of products for new and future fields, we have to face up to growing efforts in research, experimentation and design. But we have certainly taken several important steps forward in the process of renewal and diversification of our traditional product ranges (typewriters and calculating machines).

The first favorable evidence of our efforts is represented by business and financial results. To be explicit, in 1965 there was definitely an improvement in our company's financial position. Also, in spite of further pressure on the costs of many of the factors of production and distribution and the contraction of turnover in Italy due to the persistence of general economic difficulties in the country, the accounts show favorable developments in our business. Consequently, after two years of sacrifices suffered by the stockholders, it is with satisfaction that we propose to resume payment of a dividend. We also inform you that the liquidity position of our company (and in general terms of the group as a whole) permits us to look forward with sufficient peace of mind to the demands imposed by forthcoming burdensome corporate plans.

APPENDIX

SOME NOTES ON ITALY

In 1966 Olivetti was the sixth largest company in Italy. The five larger companies were Fiat, a producer of automobiles, tractors, aircraft and engines with sales in 1965 of $1.5 billion; Finsider, producer of iron and steel with sales of $979 million; ENI, a government-owned producer of petroleum products, engines, textiles and machinery with sales of $938 million; Pirelli Group, a producer of rubber products with sales of $739 million; and Edison Group, a producer of chemicals and synthetic fibers with sales of $732 million, which—with government encouragement—merged with Montecatini, a producer of chemicals and minerals with sales of $581 million in mid-1966.

Postwar economic achievements and problems

During 1948–1961, Italy achieved one of the highest and best sustained economic growth rates in the world and became a strong and solvent international competitor. Starting in 1962, however, the country suffered from a reduction in the rate of expansion from which it began visibly emerging in late 1964. Rates of yearly increase in gross national product at 1963 prices were as follows for the period from 1952–1965:

1952 .... +4.3%		1959 .... +6.4%
1953 .... +7.6		1960 .... +6.2
1954 .... +3.9		1961 .... +7.8
1955 .... +6.4		1962 .... +6.2
1956 .... +4.5		1963 .... +5.5
1957 .... +5.3		1964 .... +2.7
1958 .... +4.9		1965 .... +3.4

Source: *Main Statistical Data of Italy*, Istituto per gli Studi di Economia (ISE), Milan, 24-26 May, 1966.

In 1965 the country's population of 52 million attained a per capita income of $802. The comparable figure for 1938 was $365; for 1951, $467; and for 1959, $645.

This economic achievement, however, was not equally shared throughout the country. The part of Italy north of Rome was very prosperous and technically advanced, while the southern part, called the Mezzogiorno, was impoverished and still largely agrarian. This dualism in the Italian economy contributed significantly to the problem of unemployment and underemployment which had long plagued Italy, even during its boom years. With a total labor force of approximately 21.5 million, unemployment was estimated by one source at 721,000, and underemployment (workers who were working less than 33 hours a week) at 520,000, or in total about 6%.

Mostly as a result of the great boom of the late 1950's, the country faced an inflation in the early 1960's. Wholesale price indices, on a base of 1953, increased from 99 in 1951 to 110.4 in 1965; retail prices took an even sharper rise from 117.8 in 1951 to 145.8 in 1965. In consequence, the current balance of payments turned more sharply negative, and the net short-term reserve position deteriorated. Beginning in 1963, government action was initiated to bring the rapid expansion of money and credit under control. By mid-1964 the balance-of-payments deficit had been abolished, and the economy showed signs of stabilizing. Whether or not the government had overreacted, thus causing a greater than necessary decrease in the growth rate was a subject still being debated by some Italian executives.

Foreign trade in 1938, 1951, and 1965 in millions of lire at 1965 prices was as follows:

	1938	1951	1965
Import of goods	737,968	1,559,691	4,592,000
Export of goods	575,675	1,336,879	4,492,500
Trade balance	−162,293	−222,812	−99,500

Source: *Main Statistical Data of Italy*, ISE, Milan, 24-26 May, 1966.

Gross national product in billions of lire at 1963 prices in 1951 was 15,370; in 1965, it was 32,084.

The mixed economy

In 1966 the Italian government had direct and complete control over tobacco manufacture, matches, salt processing, iodine, railroads, telephones, electric power, and hydrocarbon exploration and development. In addition, it controlled several large holding companies, which in turn controlled a broad variety of enterprises.

Istituto per la Ricostruzione Industriale (IRI), the largest of the holding companies, controlled, according to one estimate, approximately one-fourth of total national industrial investment in 1965. The IRI, established in 1933, controlled more than 140 companies in industry and public utility.

IRI companies produce 94% of the nation's pig iron and 58% of its steel, and are represented in nearly all branches of engineering; IRI shipyards account for 80% of the nation's shipbuilding capacity, and IRI ships account for 65% of Italian mixed passenger-and-cargo tonnage and for 8% of dry cargo tonnage; IRI's airline stands in the front rank of the world's air companies in international services. IRI is responsible for all Italy's urban telephone services and for the bulk of short-distance trunk lines, for Italian broadcasting and television, and for the construction and management, during 30 years, of a network of more than 2,200 km. of toll motorways, of which some 1,000 km. were in service at the end of 1964.[1]

Other state-owned and operated activities were described by a February 1966 *Business International* report on Italy as follows:

Ente Nazionale Idrocarburi (ENI), created in 1953, operates worldwide in oil, natural gas and petroleum products, and pipelines. ENI's corporate structure controls 100% of the country's oil output, 15% of oil refining, and 97% of methane gas output. In three 50-50 ventures in the South with the state financing company Breda, ENI manufactures plate glass, railroad equipment, and electro-technical apparatus—in some cases in direct competition with private Italian and foreign firms. . . .

Ente Nazionale per l'Energia Elettrica (ENEL) was formed in 1962 to take over 80% of power production and all distribution. Private power companies are compensated with obligations which will be redeemed over a 10-year period. Private power production is only allowed for use within a company, not for outside sale.

Ente Minerario Siciliano (EMS) was created in 1962 for the promotion of mineral development and manufacturing deriving from minerals in Sicily. It was to be captitalized at $35 million, with authority for five-fold expansion. EMS will have first option on exploration permits. If a private firm gets a license and makes a strike, EMS has an option to acquire 25% of the exploiting firm. If firms that held permits at the beginning of 1963 make strikes, EMS has first claim on 51% of any companies set up for exploitation, except in the case of firms such as ENI, Montecatini, and Edison, which are already exploiting their funds.

Most commercial banks (in addition to those owned by IRI) and the majority

---

[1] IRI, *Salient Aspects of Business in 1964*, p. 3.

of medium- and long-term credit banks are owned and controlled in part by the Government. About 80% of Italy's credit activities are under direct or indirect control of the Government.[2]

The government

In 1966 Italy was governed by a "center-left" coalition of Christian Democrats, Democratic Socialists, Nenni Socialists, and Republicans, which together represented 60.3% of the popular vote. The remaining percentage of the popular vote went to the Communists (about 25%), and to two very small extreme right-wing groups, the Liberals and Neo-Fascists.

In the postwar years, it had been the Christian Democrats who were the leaders of the coalition. This group comprised big-business conservatives, moderate reformers and welfarists, and some leftist planners favoring government control and private operation of industry. (It had the support of the Roman Catholic Church, which at certain times had threatened excommunication to Catholics who voted for the Communists.) The Democratic Socialists, as their name implied, favored the mixed economy, with state intervention through ownership. The Republicans also favored the mixed economy but did not claim Marxist heritage. The Nenni, or old-line Socialists, favored state ownership of industry, but in addition had traditionally leaned toward the Marxist concepts of proletarian revolution. Until 1957 the Nenni Socialists had formed a coalition with the Communists. In 1963 they joined the existing coalition of Christian Democrats, Democratic Socialists, and Republicans. Efforts were under way to merge the Democratic Socialists and the Nenni Socialists, a move which would further strengthen the coalition, but which would increase the relative power of the Christian Democrats.[3]

The private business community reportedly was shaken by the nationalization of the electric power industry in 1962, the introduction of a withholding tax on dividends in 1962, and the imposition of tight monetary and credit moves to check inflation in 1963–64. To some big-business conservatives, these moves illustrated the growing power of the Socialists in the management of the affairs of the country. On the other hand, some analysts pointed out that an even greater problem was the fact that a coalition government was inherently unstable and therefore incapable of providing any firm and consistent direction.

The five-year economic development program, 1965–69

On January 29, 1965, the Italian Cabinet approved an economic development program for the five years 1965–69. This program, the first of its kind in postwar Italian history, was developed on the basis of an evaluation of the present situation, which led to the identification of the problems to be solved, to the establishment of objectives or targets to be achieved, to the development

---

[2]Reprinted from the chapter on Italy, dated February 1966, *Investing, Licensing & Trading Conditions Abroad*, a monthly updated reference service, published by Business International Corporation, New York.

[3]The Nenni Socialists and the Democratic Socialists merged on October 31, 1966.

of policies to be pursued and the instruments to be used, and to identification of the cost of the action planned. The objectives of the program and the policies to be pursued in the industrial sector of the country are presented below:

The targets of the scheme approved by the Italian Cabinet on January 29th of this year may be compared with the general objects of the government's economic policy announced by Prime Minister Moro in his programmatic declarations to Parliament on December 12, 1963.

These objects, to which the present Moro government made explicit reference when presenting itself to Parliament on July 30, 1964, were at that time expressed by the Prime Minister in the following words:

It is our common conviction that the problems connected with government action cannot be tackled singly and occasionally, but must be viewed within the general framework and in compliance with definite priorities regarding importance and urgence; in relation, that is to say, to a policy of economic planning making it possible, provided there is an adequate expansion of income—and this is an indispensable condition—to redress the existing area, branch and distributional imbalances and remove the major shortcomings in our country's social facilities.

The scheme for the 1965–69 five-year plan submitted to CNEL[4] translates these general objects into the following terms:

(1) Full employment of the labour forces (by 1969 open unemployment should be reduced to a level not exceeding 1.5%–1.6% of the labour forces, as compared with 2.7% in 1964);

(2) Narrowing of the gap between agricultural and non-agricultural incomes to be achieved essentially by increasing the gross product of agriculture (at an average annual rate of 2.8%–2.9%) and by reducing agricultural underemployment by 750,000 units over the five-year period considered;

(3) Localization in Southern Italy of 40–45% of the new jobs in non-agricultural branches, as compared with 25% in the five years 1959–63;

(4) Raising the level of social uses of income (housing, education, social security, scientific research, transportation, etc.) to 27%–27.5% of the available domestic resources as compared with 24% in the five years 1959–63.

An essential feature of development, as described in the scheme, is the rate of growth of the national income, assumed to be equal to a yearly average of 5% taking into account on the one hand prospective increases in employment and productivity, and on the other hand the volume of resources to be allocated to various uses—investments, social objectives and consumption—during the five years considered.

Policies in Industry—In laying down the general lines of industrial policy the programme is based on the following development assumptions:

increase of the added value in industry at the average annual rate of 7%, this being the mean between 6%–6.1% for Central and Northern Italy and 11.5%–12% for Southern Italy;

development of employment at an average annual rate of 2.4% (Center North 2.0%; South 4.2%);

---

[4]Consiglio Nazionale dell'Economia e del Lavoro.

expansion of productivity at the rate of 4.3% a year (Center North 4.0%; South 7%–7.5%).

The above-mentioned developments should be made possible by a volume of gross investments amounting to about 11,300 billion lire, of which 4,000 billions in Southern Italy.

In the field of industry, the intervention policy aims at creating the conditions required for the attainment of these targets. The scheme does not make forecasts or fix production targets for each branch of industry, but supplies lines of guidance for the development of the three basic branches: power sources, steel and chemistry.

The scheme also considers the general lines of intervention by public and government-controlled enterprises in the coming five years. All together these enterprises should absorb 4,700–4,900 billions of lire of investments, of which 3,400–3,500 in industrial branches.

The scheme also establishes the priorities to be respected by public action for the purpose of improving the efficiency of industry: improvement of external economies through the attainment of targets in the field of social expenditure and territorial readjustments; the financing of technological research and development; the reorganization and strengthening of financial and fiscal incentives for the purpose of reorganizing and rationalizing the less efficient branches (giving priority to investments in the textile industry, the machine tool industry, the agricultural food industry and shipbuilding). Fiscal and financial incentives and forms of technical aid should also be provided for the rationalization and development of small industries and handicraft concerns.

As far as the financing of industry is concerned, the requirements of the planning policy are essentially those of ensuring an adequate flow of funds in forms providing greater stability as regards the financial management of enterprises. In this connection a better organization of medium-term industrial credit is expected as well as an expansion of the financing of small and medium enterprises through the acquisition of minority shareholdings not involving entrepreneurial responsibilities.

The scheme provides, moreover, for the protection of free competition as well as for the adoption of policies designed to prevent dumping by foreign enterprises.

Lastly, public action will aim at promoting exports, particularly by strengthening the system of credit facilities and export credit insurance.

This policy is linked with the necessity of maintaining a high rate of increase for exports in order that a balance of current items may be achieved before the end of the five years.[5]

---

[5]"The Five-Year Economic Programme (1965–1969)," Giovanni Pieraccini, Budget Minister, *Review of Economic Conditions in Italy*, Banco di Roma, Vol. XIX, No. 2, March 1965, Rome.

A NOTE ON THE OFFICE MACHINE INDUSTRY*

∧∧∧

The basic functions of office machines are recording, manipulating, and disseminating data. These operations have been necessary since the beginning of commerce. For thousands of years, a man with a pen performed all of these functions. With the development of the typewriter and mechanical adding machines in the latter part of the nineteenth century, the functions of record keeping and logical manipulation became separated.

The period following 1950 saw a revolution in data handling, which seems to have arisen from two causes: technological advancement and the development of the systems concept of information handling. With the advent of electronic data processing equipment, there was a recognition that the end product of the industry was not machines, but rather useful information. This concept helped to motivate the development of multifunctional machines: writing devices with logical capabilities and logical figuring devices with writing capabilities.

This note provides background information for the study of the Olivetti Company. It is divided into four sections:

1. A description of office machine products and their uses.
2. A description of companies in the industry, their financial strength and their product commitments.
3. A review of marketing problems in the industry.
4. A description of recent developments in office machine products.

1. THE PRODUCTS

In order to examine the office machine industry, it may be useful to divide the equipment produced into two groups: (1) logical figuring machines and (2) data transmission devices.

The figuring machines included:

Adding machines, which performed addition, subtraction, and multiplication through repeated addition. They could be either hand or electrically powered. For most applications they were purchased with printing capability so that a written record of both input data and results was obtained.

Calculating machines, which performed the same functions as adding machines, but also provided automatic multiplication and, in most cases, automatic division. Currently they were available in three basic types: the rotary calculator, which provided no written record; the printing calculator, which provided a written record; and the electronic calculator which provided a written record with greater speed and in some cases had provision for programming.

Accounting machines, which did the same basic jobs as either the adding machines or the calculating machines. Their advantage was that they provided additional capabilities for format setting by which data could be set into columns on a ledger card or statement. At the upper end of the price spectrum, accounting machines also had alphanumeric printing units and some programming and memory capabilities.

Punched card unit record equipment, which used the familiar punched card as its unit of data memory. The speed with which cards could be sorted, collated, and printed enabled the user of this equipment to process readily large amounts of data. The nature of the punched card also allowed multiple use of the same data. For example, a single card which listed a transaction could be used in generating accounts receivable records, inventory records, sales reports, and profit-center accounting reports.

Digital program computers, which were the most complex of the products of the office machine industry. In them, data could be manipulated with all the normal arithmetic operations, could be compared logically for equality or high and low conditions, and could be shifted rapidly from one "storage" area to another, or to a computation program. Basic advantages of these machines were high operating speed, almost complete accuracy, logical decision capability, minimal operator intervention, and rapid input and output.

Among the data transmission devices were:

Dictating machines, which recorded verbal communication for later replay. They were used as part of an office information system and in applications when only temporary records were required, such as preliminary inventory counts, etc.

Typewriters, which produced a more permanent written record of desired communication. These machines were differentiated on the basis of portability, quality of printing, and hand-powered or electric typebars.

Teleprinters (or teletypers), which were basically electric typewriters so connected that pushing a key on one machine generated impulses which were received by a similar unit and translated into a written communication at the receiving unit. Thus, they allowed immediate transmission of written communications over long distances.

Copying machines, which were designed to produce copies from an original document. The invention of Xerography and direct electrostatic copying made the cost of reproduction low enough and the quality of copy high enough to induce wide use of these machines.

Duplicating machines, which made multiple copies more rapidly and less expensively than did copying machines on long runs of identical material. With the invention of high-speed copying machines the line between copying and duplicating had become less distinct. On a product basis, the chief remaining distinction was that duplicating machines required the preparation of a special master sheet from which the copies were produced.

Figure 1

THE FAMILY TREE OF THE OFFICE MACHINE INDUSTRY

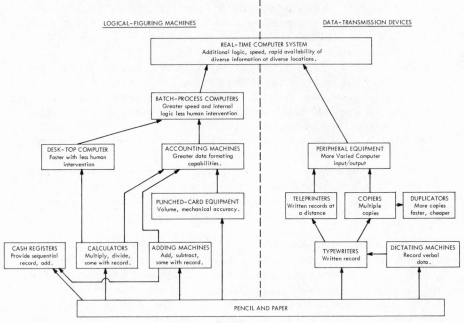

Figure 1 illustrates one view of the functional relationships among some of the major categories of machines which were produced by companies in the office machine industry. The relationship between products connected by arrows was one of increased capacity for performing the stated functions by reason of (1) increased speed of operation, (2) decreased human intervention, (3) additional storage or memory capacity, or (4) potential for multiple use.

Exhibit 1 considers in detail the types of machines included in the categories listed above, with brief descriptions of their important features, and current information on prices, estimated sales volume, and projected trends of sales. Estimates have been gathered from industry sources. In dealing with estimates for the office equipment industry, however, caution is required. As late as 1953, it was estimated that fewer than 100 computer systems would ever be installed in the United States. As of 1966 over 27,000 had been installed. Most current predictions called for a rapidly expanding demand in all areas of the office equipment field. Differences were a matter of degree. Still the uncertainty in estimates must be noted. Most analysts agreed, however, that any large marginal demand would come through new and currently unforeseen applications rather than through population growth and business expansion.

Exhibit 1

TYPES OF MACHINES, PRICE, SALES POTENTIAL, AND SPECIAL FEATURES

Type of Machine	Price Range	Total Annual Market (1966—Estimated)	Growth Potentials (Estimated)	Important Features
Adding machines	$60–$350	$250 to $500 million	10% to 15% annually (through 1972)	Hand or electrical operation. Speed of calculation. Special keys, multiple printing colors.
Calculators (total)	$300–$2,500	$150 to $200 million	7% to 13% annually	See Exhibit 2 for comparative features of electromechanical calculators.
Rotary calculators	$775–$1,150	N.A.	Small decline	Speed and price—1,300 cycles per minute present top speed.
Printing calculators	$595–$1,200	N.A.	Almost all growth in calculators has been in this segment in recent years (Olivetti Divisumma 24 introduced in 1952)	Multiple accumulators for running check balances; "memories" of previous calculations.
Electronic calculators	$1,650–$5,000	N.A.	Very new segment of industry—growth potential probably good	Programmable and nonprogrammable models, with substantial obvious advantages to the programmable models.
Accounting machines	$360–$25,000	$400 million to $700 million	0–12% annually	Automation of both typing and computation in wide variety of report or statement formats.
Unit record equipment ...	Leases cost $300 per month and up	$700 million to $1 billion	–2% to +7% annually	Classification and tabulation of large quantities of data at low unit cost.
Digital computers	$50,000 and up Rentals $500 per month and up	$3 billion to $5 billion	7% to 16% per year over next ten years	Input/output capabilities. Speed of calculations.
Dictating machines	$300 and up	$40–$65 million	Although steady now, could "take off" at growth rates up to 20% per year	Plastic disc recording versus magnetic tape recording. Latter fully erasable and reusable.

Exbibit 1—Continued

Type of Machine	Price Range	Total Annual Market (1966—Estimated)	Growth Potentials (Estimated)	Important Features
Typewriters, mechanical: portable	$30–$100	3,000,000 units	6% per year over period 1965–70	Low cost, low weight, straightness of type, aesthetic appeal.
Typewriters, mechanical: standard manual	$180–$300	1,300,000 units	Stable	Price, stability, length of usable life.
Typewriters, electric	$119–$700	750,000 units	10.2% increase 1966–1970	Constant character impression; typing ease; automatic repeat keys, carriage return, spacing.
Typewriters, tape-oriented	$2,500–$7,500 (paper tape-oriented) $7,500–$21,000 (magnetic tape-oriented)	5,000 units (total installed machines)	N.A.	Complete accuracy of multiple typings; ease of insertion of nonprogrammable material.
Copying Machines		$1 billion	—	
Thermographic	$200 average	25,000 units	3% per year	Low initial cost and low cost per copy; insensitive to some colors; useful when quality requirements of reproduction are low.
Diffusion dye transfer reversal	$300 average	14,000 units	4% decline	Low cost with good quality reproduction. Process slow and "wet."
Dye transfer copying machine	$300 up	10,000 units	5% decline	Process slow and wet, but image good and can make multiple copies from single matrix.
Xerography	Leased Xerox 914 $25 per month + 3.5¢ per copy with $95 per month minimum Sale Price $29,500 + 0.9¢ per copy additional payment. Supplies are extra.	25,000 new machines per year	37% increase to 1970	Low cost per copy, uses ordinary paper, automatic multiple copying, book copying and built-in exposure control.

Exhibit 1—Continued

Type of Machine	Price Range	Total Annual Market (1966—Estimated)	Growth Potentials (Estimated)	Important Features
Direct electrostatic copier	N.A.	40,000 new machines per year	44% increase to 1970—then levels off	A "dry" process. Cost per copy lower than Xerography on comparable machines. (See Exhibit 4 for comparison of features and cost of machines.)
Other processes				
Stabilization	N.A.	$2 million	Remain steady	Long storage life of materials and simple mechanical operation make this process suited to coin-operated machine applications.
Diazo	Lamps cost from $150 to $20,000	$5 million–$63 million (includes supplies)	N.A.	Lowest cost copying method. Technology makes direct copying of letters difficult.
Duplicators	—	$2–$3 billion (includes supplies)	—	
Spirit duplicators	$200–$350	50,000 units	–5% per year	Low cost of machines and supplies. Poor image quality and rapid fading in sunlight.
Mimeograph	$750 and up	50,000 units	–2% per year	Time required for and cost of master preparation are chief limitations of this process, though image quality superior to spirit.
Offset duplication	$750–$5,000	14,000 machines	5%–12%	Low cost on long runs, excellent image quality and speed.
Teleprinters	N.A.	N.A.	N.A.	Typically used as part of communication infrastructure of a nation. Latest application is as input-output device for real-time computer systems.

Source: Case writer's estimates and conclusions from search of industry and company literature.

Exhibit 2

COMPARATIVE FEATURES OF ELECTROMECHANICAL CALCULATORS

Characteristic	Printing				Nonprinting			
	Olivetti Divisumma 24GT	Olivetti Logos 27	Marchant 416S	Monroe 1421	Facit CA-2-16	Friden SBT	Marchant TR	Monroe IQ213
Price	$575	$1,100	$1,235	$1,175	$785	$950	$945	$755–$1,085
Speed	240 c.p.m.	600 c.p.m.	500 c.p.m.	800 c.p.m.	400 c.p.m.	500 c.p.m.	1300 c.p.m.	600 c.p.m.
Short-cut multiplication	Yes	Yes	Yes	No	Yes	No	No	No
Keyboard	10-key	10-key	10-key	10-key	10-key	full	full	full
Accumulators	2	1	2	1	1	2	1	1
Constant memories	2	2	1	1	1	1	1	1
Input data capacity	12 digit	15	12	12	11	10	10	10
Product register capacity	13 digit	20	16	21	16	21	20	21
Quotient capacity	13	15	8	10	9	11	11	11
Credit balance	Yes	Yes	Yes	Yes	No	No	No	No
Automatic re-entry of product	Yes	Yes	Yes	Yes less than 12 digits	Yes	Yes by hand	No	Yes by hand
Automatic use of quotient	Yes	Yes	Yes	Yes	Yes	No	No	No
Automatic placement of decimal quotient	No	Yes	Yes	Yes	No	No	No	No
Automatic cancellation of registers	Yes	Yes	Yes	Yes	No	No	No	No

Source: Company Repair Manual.

Commenting on the expanding amount of information processed each year by consumers of office machines, one report stated: "The proportions of the [information] explosion are huge. Paper records are multiplying at the rate of 1 million new documents per minute, 250 billion pages per year, 62 million file cabinets per year at a cost of $39 billion annually or over 5% of the G.N.P." Another report continues, "Based on similar years' estimate of total business investment in plant and equipment, the percentage of plant and equipment investment that is spent on information systems will go from 4% in 1961 to 13% in 1970."[1]

Exhibit 2 presents a comparison of features built in to various models of electromechanical calculators.

Exhibit 3 gives a comparative list of small computers and their monthly rental costs with the names of manufacturers of larger computers also.

Exhibit 4 compares the features and costs of various models of electrostatic copying machines.

2. THE OFFICE MACHINE INDUSTRY

Office machine manufacturers could be classified, according to the nature of their products, into three separate categories.

Category I: Firms specializing in the manufacture of a wide range of electro-mechanical or simple electronic equipment such as typewriters, calculators, and accounting machines.

Category II: Companies specializing in duplicating and/or copying machines.

Category III: Firms specializing in the manufacture and sale of sophisticated equipment such as computers and associated peripheral devices.

There had been a trend, however, toward companies expanding their product lines to cover more than one category. For example, Olivetti's major competition in 1964 was with firms in Category I, but it began producing the Copia II copying machine and Programma 101 in the United States in 1965, which put it into competition with firms in Categories I and II.

The major competitors in each product category were as follows:

Category I	Category II	Category III
Burroughs	Addressograph-Multigraph	Burroughs
Facit-Odhner	Bell & Howell	Control Data
Friden	Dennison	GE
IBM	A. B. Dick	Honeywell
Litton-Monroe	Kodak-IBM	IBM
NCR	Olivetti	International Computers
Olivetti	Minnesota Mining & Mfg.	and Tabulators
Olympia	SCM	NCR
Remington	Xerox	RCA
Litton-Royal McBee		Scientific Data Systems
SCM		Sperry Rand

[1]"Surviving the Information Explosion," *Iron Age*, April 14, 1966, p. 30.

Exhibit 3. GUIDE TO SMALL COMPUTERS

MANUFACTURER	MODEL	DATE FIRST INSTALLED	TYPICAL MONTHLY RENTAL	LINE PRINTER	MAGNETIC TAPE	PUNCHED PAPER TAPE	PUNCHED CARDS	MICR	OPTICAL SCANNING	VISUAL DISPLAY	MAGNETIC LEDGER CARD	TYPEWRITER I/O	MAGNETIC CARDS	DISC FILE	DRUM FILE	ESTIMATED NUMBER IN USE ON ORDER
ADV. SCIENTIFIC INSTR.	210	3/62	$ 2,000	•	•	•	•					•				28
ADV. SCIENTIFIC INSTR.	2100	7/63	2,000	•	•	•	•					•				7
ADV. SCIENTIFIC INSTR.	6020	5/65	3,000	•	•	•	•				•		•			15
ADV. SCIENTIFIC INSTR.	6040	6/65	6,000	•	•	•	•				•		•			8
ADV. SCIENTIFIC INSTR.	6130	7/66	1,000	•	•	•	•				•		•			4
BURROUGHS CORP.	B260	6/63	1,500	•			•					•				230
BURROUGHS CORP.	B270	6/62	1,650	•	•		•	•				•				170
BURROUGHS CORP.	B280	6/62	1,585	•	•	•	•					•				140
BURROUGHS CORP.	B5500	7/64	7,400	•	•	•	•					•		•	•	70
BURROUGHS CORP.	B300	2/65	1,645	•	•	•	•	•				•		•		200
BURROUGHS CORP.	B2500	1/67	4,195	•	•	•	•	•				•		•		30
BURROUGHS CORP.	B3500	5/67	7,500	•	•	•	•	•				•		•		20
BURROUGHS CORP.	E4000	1/66	550 to 1,200			•	•				•					
BURROUGHS CORP.	E2190	5/65	780			•					•					
CLARY CORP.	DE-60	2/60	251			•						•				350
CLARY CORP.	DE-600	5/66	335			•						•				7
COMPUTER CONTROL CO.	DDP-224	12/64	2,800	•	•	•	•			•			•	•		40
COMPUTER CONTROL CO.	DDP-116	1/65	1,600	•	•	•	•			•			•	•		135
COMPUTER CONTROL CO.	DDP-124	2/66	2,400	•	•	•	•			•			•	•		44
CONTROL DATA CORP.	3300	12/65	11,600	•	•	•	•		•	•	•	•		•	•	60
CONTROL DATA CORP.	3200	5/64	10,900	•	•	•	•		•	•	•	•		•	•	90
CONTROL DATA CORP.	3100	2/65	8,170	•	•	•	•		•	•	•	•		•	•	114
CONTROL DATA CORP.	1700	3/66	6,800	•	•	•	•		•	•	•	•		•	•	95
FRIDEN	6010	6/63	600			•	•					•				350
GENERAL ELECTRIC	115	4/66	1,375	•			•					•				610
GENERAL ELECTRIC	215	9/63	6,000	•	•	•	•			•		•		•		x
GENERAL ELECTRIC	225	4/61	8,000	•	•	•	•			•		•		•		x
GENERAL ELECTRIC	235	4/64	10,900	•	•	•	•			•		•		•		700
GENERAL ELECTRIC	415	5/64	7,300	•	•	•	•			•		•		•		240
GENERAL ELECTRIC	425	6/64	9,600	•	•	•	•			•		•		•		105
HONEYWELL	120	3/66	3,175	•	•	•	•			•		•	•	•	•	250
HONEYWELL	200	7/64	5,300	•	•	•	•			•		•	•	•	•	960
HONEYWELL	1200	1/66	7,500	•	•	•	•			•		•	•	•	•	85
HONEYWELL	2200	12/65	11,500	•	•	•	•			•		•	•	•	•	60
IBM	360/Model 20	9/65	1,565	•	•		•			•			•			6,720
IBM	360/Model 30	9/65	6,600	•	•	•	•	•		•		•		•		6,100
IBM	1130	11/65	695	•		•	•					•				360
IBM	1401	9/60	1,600–8,200	•	•	•	•	•		•			•			6,950
IBM	1440	11/63	3,000	•	•		•	•		•			•			3,400
IBM	1460	4/63	8,900	•	•		•	•		•			•			2,300
IBM	1620	9/60	2,050–2,825		•	•	•					•				1,730
IBM	1800	9/66	2,455–5,100	•	•	•	•					•				300
MATHATRONICS	848	6/63	5,000*	•												500
MONROE INTERNATIONAL	Monrobot XI	1961	700				•					•	•			600
NATIONAL CASH REGISTER	315 RMC	7/65	9,800	•	•	•	•	•	•		•	•	•			50
NATIONAL CASH REGISTER	315-100	11/64	4,000	•	•	•	•	•	•		•	•	•			200
NATIONAL CASH REGISTER	315	1/62	8,500	•	•	•	•	•	•		•	•	•			200
NATIONAL CASH REGISTER	310	4/61	2,500				•	•	•		•	•				46
NATIONAL CASH REGISTER	500	9/65	1,200	•			•				•	•				510
NATIONAL CASH REGISTER	390	5/61	1,800				•	•			•	•				1,070
PHILCO CORP.	1000	1962	7,000	•	•		•									30
RADIO CORP. OF AMERICA	301	1960	7,000	•	•	•	•			•		•	•	•		651
RADIO CORP. OF AMERICA	70/15	1965	2,900	•	•	•	•			•		•				160
RADIO CORP. OF AMERICA	70/25	1965	8,200	•	•	•	•			•		•				88
RADIO CORP. OF AMERICA	70/35	1966	8,800	•	•	•	•			•		•	•	•	•	75
SCIENTIFIC DATA SYSTEMS	92	2/65	1,500	•	•	•	•					•		•	•	90
SCIENTIFIC DATA SYSTEMS	910	8/62	2,200	•	•	•	•					•		•	•	185
SCIENTIFIC DATA SYSTEMS	920	9/62	2,400	•	•	•	•					•		•	•	137
SCIENTIFIC DATA SYSTEMS	925	2/65	2,500	•	•	•	•					•		•	•	41
SCIENTIFIC DATA SYSTEMS	930	6/64	2,700	•	•	•	•					•		•	•	145
SCIENTIFIC DATA SYSTEMS	9300	12/64	4,875	•	•	•	•			•		•		•	•	17
SCM	7816	1964	400			•	•					•				500
UNIVAC	1004-1-01/02	2/63	1,450	•		•	•							•		3,400
UNIVAC	1004-2	7/64	1,575	•		•	•							•		
UNIVAC	1005	4/66	1,750	•	•	•	•							•		280
UNIVAC	1050	9/63	5,500	•	•	•	•					•			•	330
UNIVAC	418	8/63		•	•	•	•					•		•		120

This chart is compiled from data in *Administrative Management*, July 1966, and *Computers and Automation*, September 1966. The column headed Typical Monthly Rental is open for interpretation. *Computers and Automation* estimated average rentals to be considerably higher than did *Administrative Management*. For example, the Burroughs 270 was estimated by the former to rent at $7,000 per month in comparison to the $1,650 shown above. The difference in average rentals can probably be traced to the difference in computation methods. *Administrative Management* was giving the average cost of the central processing unit, whereas *Computers and Automation* listed the average rental for the total system. *Computers and Automation* figures are compiled from user surveys rather than from company data. The variation between the two sets of data is indicative of the complication of the systems in use. John Diebold has estimated that by 1975 over one-half of the hardware cost of a computer will come from the peripheral equipment attached. Beyond the systems listed in the chart above, there are many larger systems. These larger systems are made by the following companies:

Advanced Scientific Instruments
Burroughs
Control Data Corporation—CDC
Digital Equipment Corporation—DEC
Electronic Associates, Inc.
General Electric—GE
Honeywell Electronic Data Processing
International Business Machines—IBM
National Cash Register—NCR
Radio Corporation of America—RCA
Scientific Data Systems—SDS
Univac—Sperry Rand

Rental costs on some of these systems exceed $200,000 per month.

Source: Sales literature of various companies.

Exhibit 4

COMPARISON OF ELECTROSTATIC COPIERS

Model	Xerox			Bruning		SCM		Olivetti
	2400 Console	914 Console	813 Table	2000 Console	3000 Table	55 Console	33-44 Table	Copia II Console
Book copier	Yes	Yes	No	No	Yes	Yes	No	Yes
Development	Dry	Dry	Dry	Dry	Neutral Solvent	Neutral Solvent	Neutral Solvent	Neutral Solvent
Copy feed	Sheet	Sheet	Sheet	Sheet	Sheet	Sheet	Sheet	Roll
Original size	0" to 8 7/8" x 14 7/16"	0" to 9" x 14"	5 1/2" to 9" x 14"	11" x 14"	0" to 8 1/2" x 14"	0" to 9" x 14"	5 1/2" to 11" x 14"	8 1/2" x 6" to 14"
Copy size	8" to 8 1/2" x 13"	7" to 10" x 15 1/2"	10" to 8 1/2" x 14"	11" x 14"	4" x 7 1/2" to 8 1/2" x 11"	6" to 10" x 15 1/2"	5 1/2" to 11" x 14"	8 1/2" x 6" to 14"
Speed: 1 Copy 1 Original	12 sec.	52 sec.	25 sec.	17 sec.	22 sec.	12 sec.	17 sec.	17 sec.
5 Copies 1 Original	2,400/hr.	130 sec.	70 sec.	40 sec.	90 sec.	44 sec.	55 sec.	49 sec.
Cost per Copy (1,500 per month)	*	$0.0733	$0.0617	$0.0815	$0.0575	$0.0867	$0.0626	
Cost per Copy (10,000 per month)	$0.0014–$0.0035†	$0.0475	$0.0475	$0.0395	$0.0405	$0.0340	$0.0413	

*NOT recommended in this small an application.

†Depends on copies per original mix.

Figures, courtesy Charles Bruning Company, Division of Addressograph-Multigraph.

On page 911 are the 1965 company sales figures for major firms in the industry and the components of each company's product line, as well as estimates of the 1965 dollar volume for worldwide sales of major types of office equipment. While these figures are estimates only, they do indicate a total world market for office equipment, exclusive of supplies, totaling over $7.1 billion. Figure 2 shows relative sales growth since 1960 for selected companies in Categories I and II.

Between 1950 and 1966, the office machine industry experienced both rapid expansion and consolidation. Many of the former well-known firms of the

Figure 2

SALES GROWTH OF SELECTED COMPANIES 1960–65

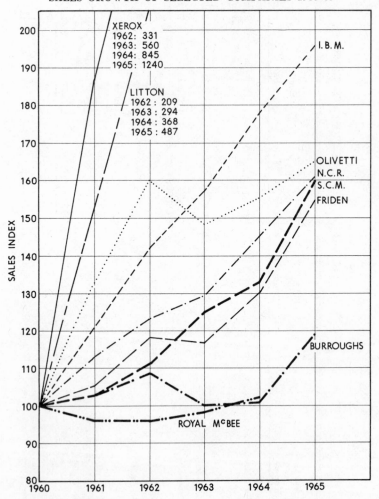

Source: *Moody's Industrials* and annual reports of companies for the particular years.

1965 SALES AND PRODUCTS OF MAJOR MANUFACTURERS OF OFFICE MACHINES

	1965 Sales All Products ($000,000)	Type-writers	Calculating Machines	Accounting Machines	Cash Registers	Desk-Top Computers	Digital Computers	Copying and Duplicating Equipment	Tape Controlled Typewriter
1965 World Sales (office machine) ($000,000)*		700	750	600	650	40	3,500	900	
Addressograph-Multigraph	269.1							X	
Bell & Howell	185.7							X	X
Burroughs	456.7		X	X	X		X		
Control Data	160.5						X		
Dennison	69.8							X	
A. B. Dick	N.A.							X	
Facit-Odhner	N.A.	X	X					X	
Friden division of Singer	96.5		X	X		X	X		X
GE	6,213.6						X		
Honeywell	700.4						X		
IBM	3,572.8	X	X	X			X	X	X
International Computers and Tabulators (ICT)	150.0						X		
Kodak	1,463.5							X	
Monroe†	N.A.		X		X	X			
NCR	736.8			X	X	X	X	X	
Olivetti	450.0	X	X	X					
Olympia	75.0	X	X						
RCA	2,042.0						X		
Remington‡	195	X							
Royal McBee†	N.A.	X						X	
Scientific Data Systems	43.9						X		
SCM	149.7	X	X	X		X		X	X
Sperry Rand‡	1,247.6						X	X	
3M Co.‡	1,000.3							X	
Xerox	392.6							X	X

*Figures estimated by the case writer do not include supplies or computer software.
†Monroe and Royal McBee are divisions of Litton Industries.
‡Remington and Sperry Rand are divisions of Sperry Rand.
X = Company competes in this particular line.

industry were no longer separate companies, having merged or been acquired. Among the more important of these combinations were:

1954 .... Royal Typewriter acquired McBee Company forming Royal McBee.
1955 .... Sperry Corporation merged with Remington Rand to form Sperry Rand.
1958 .... Smith Corona merged with Marchant Calculators to form Smith Corona Marchant, later called SCM Corporation.
1958 .... Litton Industries acquired Monroe Calculators.
1959 .... Olivetti acquired Underwood Corporation.
1960 .... Litton Industries acquired Sweda Cash Registers.
1961 .... Litton Industries acquired London Office Machines.
1963 .... Singer Company acquired Friden Calculator.
1965 .... Litton Industries acquired Royal McBee.
1965 .... Olivetti acquired Federal Division of Victoreen.
1966 .... Litton Industries acquired Imperial Typewriters, Ltd.

By 1966, Litton Industries, a broadly diversified firm, had over one-third of its sales in the office equipment industry. Approximately one-eighth of the Singer Company's 1966 sales were from office equipment.

Following is a list of the trade names by which some of the more important companies in the field were represented:

COMPANY OWNERSHIP

Parent Company	Country	Trade Name	Country
Advidaberga Ind. A.B.	Sweden	Facit	Sweden
		Odhner	Sweden
AEG–Telefunken	Germany	Olympia	Germany
		Fichner	Germany
		Brunswiga	Germany
Grundig	Germany	Adler	Germany
		Triumph	Germany
Litton Industries	U.S.	Royal McBee	U.S.
		Monroe	U.S.
		Sweda	Sweden
		Imperial	U.K.
Machines Bull	France	Wanderer	Germany
Olivetti	Italy	Underwood	U.S.
		Everest	Italy
Paillard, S.A.	Switzerland	Hermes	Switzerland
		Precision	Switzerland
Rheinstahl	Germany	Zuse	Germany
Singer Company	U.S.	Friden	U.S.
SCM Corporation	U.S.	Marchant	U.S.
		Hamann	Germany
Sperry Rand Corporation	U.S.	Remington	U.S.
		Torpedo	Germany

The magnitude of the total assets of some of the companies which were operating in the office machine market, at the end of 1965, were:

	($000's)
IBM	3,774,918*
Sperry Rand	915,417
Singer	890,980
AEG–Telefunken	767,214
Litton	630,023
Olivetti	550,000†
National Cash Register	494,117
Xerox	468,462
Burroughs	443,514
SCM	96,931
Advidaberga	N.A.
Grundig	N.A.
Paillard	N.A.

*Cash and marketable securities, $665,747,000.
†Estimated consolidated assets from available published figures.
Sources: "The Fortune Directory of the 500 Largest U.S. Industrial Corporations," *Fortune*, July 15, 1966, pp. 232–48. "The Fortune Directory of the 200 Largest Industrials Outside the U.S.," *Fortune*, August 1966, pp. 148–52.

One company's estimates of unit sales for selected categories of office machines for the principal manufacturers of office machines are shown below:

1963 WORLDWIDE MARKET SHARES FOR SELECTED CATEGORIES OF OFFICE EQUIPMENT

	Typewriters		Calculators		Accounting Machines	
	No. of Units	%	No. of Units	%	No. of Units	%
Olivetti	1,175,000	23.0	716,000	34.1	23,000	17.5
Remington	900,000	17.6				
Royal McBee	650,000	12.7				
Olympia	500,000	9.8	75,000	3.6		
IBM	400,000	7.8				
SCM	300,000	5.9				
Adler-Triumph	250,000	4.9				
Hermes	150,000	2.9				
Facit-Odhner			200,000	9.5		
Victor			140,000	6.7		
National Cash Register			115,000	5.5	27,000	20.5
Burroughs			100,000	4.8	27,000	20.5
Friden			60,000	2.9		
Total	4,325,000	84.6	1,406,000	67.1	77,000	58.5
Others	785,000	15.4	694,000	32.9	55,000	41.5
World total	5,110,000	100.0	2,100,000	100.0	132,000	100.0

Source: Estimates by the Olivetti Company.

3. A REVIEW OF MARKETING PROBLEMS

Although much of the growth which was predicted for the information revolution was expected to be taken up in massive integrated data processing systems, most people in the industry expected the more mundane office records to grow as well. Two industry executives spoke on this question as follows:

> We find that as office equipment becomes more and more sophisticated and centralized, there is just that much more demand for unsophisticated, easy-to-use items that can be operated in decentralized locations, branch offices, warehouses and the like.
>
> CHARLES W. DOULTON,
> President, Elliot Business Machines

"Far from undercutting the traditional office equipment," says Scott Cass, Friden's public relations director and a chairman of the office machines group of the Business Equipment Manufacturers' Association, "the advent of the electronic computer systems has actually increased the demand for the workhorse business machines, as improved to meet today's needs for increased speed and versatility and compatibility with integrated systems. In our segment of the industry we have been witnessing an average yearly 15% sales increase for most of the past decade of automation."[2]

All three categories of firms within the office machine industry had reacted similarly to the marketing challenges of the information explosion. Each group had been attempting to secure new business through increased consciousness of customer data processing requirements, and through giving increased value for the customer's dollar. This section will describe current practices and apparent trends in four topics related to marketing: pricing, channels of distribution, customer service, and the "systems approach."

Pricing. Prices in the office equipment industry had been relatively stable, worldwide. Among firms in Category III, makers of computers and peripheral equipment, this practice seemed to be related to a price umbrella which IBM had established and to that company's practice of price maintenance. In this category, comparison of one machine with another on a total cost basis was difficult, which made it easier to maintain prices. While prices had been maintained on individual models of equipment, however, the development of new generations of computers and computer peripherals had led to cost reductions per unit of performance. IBM estimated that in 1956 it cost $1.38 to make 100,000 calculations with its first generation vacuum tube computer. Upon the introduction of the System 360, IBM estimated that this cost had fallen to 3.5¢ per 100,000 calculations.

In Category II, the copying field, there also had been general stability in world prices. This may be traced to the dominating presence of Xerox and Rank-Xerox[3] throughout the world. As of 1966, however, there were increasing evidences of price competition and consumer cost consciousness. In October 1966, both Xerox and Charles Bruning announced price reductions on their

---

[2]"General Office Machines," *Dun's Review,* September 1965, p. 140.

[3]Rank-Xerox was a joint venture between the Rank organization in Britain and Xerox with sales rights for Xerox machines throughout the world except for the United States and Japan.

copying equipment. Also, at the 1966 Business Equipment Manufacturers' Association show, several new low-cost models of convenience copiers were announced. Electrostatic copiers became available at prices as low at $545.

In Category I, the electromechanical equipment field, there had been price parity and stability, with little evidence of significant change in sight. Products were highly substitutable among manufacturers which tended to keep prices in line.

As of 1966, prices had been stable for many years, but, when valued in constant dollar prices, had actually declined in many countries of the world. For example, in Germany, Olivetti had reduced the price of its Divisumma 24 printing calculator by 10% since its introduction in 1955. This represented a constant dollar reduction of almost 25% due to inflation of other prices.

New products in the electromechanical field constantly brought lower cost per unit of performance. Increased operating speed or additional operating features had been added without proportional increases in selling prices.

Channels of distribution. During the period preceding World War II, the office machine industry distributed its products largely through independent dealers. There was subsequently a trend away from this.

Office Appliances, a magazine for office equipment dealers, reported in 1963:

Dealers are well aware of the new forces at work in their field. Some have already selected to confine their efforts to comparatively narrow lines. Others are making an attempt at carrying and servicing all general categories of machines. Not too many of them are satisfied that this is practical, unless their business is departmentalized into several specialized areas of sales and service.

Office machine dealers are generally enjoying a good business volume. Over the past decade the trend has been steadily upward. However the increase in dealer volume throughout the entire range of office machines has not kept pace with the overall ratio.

The reason is, obviously, that more and more office machines are being sold through other types of outlets. . . . In the area of legitimate office machines, the direct seller is the dealer's biggest competitor. There are no indications that this competitive pressure will diminish in the future.

The typewriter is still the most important product in the office machine dealer's picture, followed closely by adding machines and small calculators. Beyond this there is no unanimity. Some dealers handle duplicators, cash registers, dictating machines and other items in the machine category; but only in isolated cases do these products contribute heavily to the dealer's overall volume and profits.

The typewriter is rapidly becoming an electronic device. . . . If the distribution pattern for this equipment follows that of present [electronic] equipment, the dealer will find it difficult to find a product to sell. Most manufacturers will try to meet the market with a direct organization.

*   *   *   *   *

In the years ahead the gap between accounting machines and less sophisticated data processing equipment will become narrower. Some of this equipment will be manufactured by firms long associated with dealers. Whether this continues to hold or not depends on the sales and service facilities which dealers offer the manufacturer.

*   *   *   *   *

The next five years will witness some interesting progress in the data processing field. Leading manufacturers of such equipment are admittedly turning their attention to equipment that may be used by small and medium sized business organizations. Its installation will be in connection with complete systems, probably involving all of the accessory equipment too.[4]

It was becoming apparent that the dealer was having trouble reaching the giant corporation and large governmental agencies where over 40% of the sales of small office machines were made. The average office product dealer had less than four outside salesmen.

Although exact figures on sales forces are not readily available, 1966 estimates in the industry indicate the following number of salesmen in the United States for selected companies.

IBM—electric typewriter division	5,000
Olivetti	3,000
Xerox	1,500
Bruning-Addressograph-Multigraph	800

Each of Litton's divisions—Monroe, Sweda, Royal McBee, et cetera—had a separate sales force specialized by product type. Salesmen for SCM, Friden, Olivetti, and NCR also were specialized by divisions or product category.

These patterns of operations and distribution channels were also used in countries other than the United States. One executive in the industry said: "If anything, our distribution pattern in the less industrialized countries must include more intensive sales and educational efforts." Abroad Olivetti had over 3,000 salesmen, and Xerox through Rank-Xerox over 800.

Customer service and the systems approach. One of the basic differentiations which could be made among the categories of firms in the office machine industry occurs along the dimension of customer service. Customer service included applications engineering which facilitated the sale of a machine, and it included repairs, supplies, customer education, and leasing.

Among firms in the electromechanical-equipment Category I, the basic approach of the salesmen of many companies continued to be that of the hard-selling peddler. Many of the companies for many years had been trying to get salesmen to consider what applications the customers might have for the machines in order to advise the most useful products, but the low dollar volume per sale usually resulted in a fast in-and-out approach. There was a long life expectancy for most machines in this category, so new sales quite often came about through appeals based on styling or relatively marginal new features. According to a spokesman for one company in the field, the basic

---

[4]"The Changing Scene in Office Machines," *Office Appliances*, July 1963, pp. 37, 41.

sales process was getting the customer to accept a demonstration and a trial use of the machine. Once the customer's resistance has been lowered to the point of accepting a demonstrator for a few days' trial, this company's executives believed that the probability of a sale was at least 50%.

As the number of machines purchased by an individual client became larger, the requirement for salesman knowledge became greater. When a company was trying to sell to an insurance company or other large user, the salesman had to be prepared to work with a time-study analyst and give full and accurate cost data, and the company may even have had to provide a full-time service man. In the United States such sales accounted for 20%–30% of the unit sales of office equipment in Category I.

In Category II, the copying field, customer service and the systems approach assumed an even more vital role, according to industry spokesmen. The first reason for this was the necessity of educating business organizations to their need for copying equipment and the saving which a well-organized copying system could bring. The second reason was that a high percentage of the revenue and profit in the copying field came from service contracts and supplies.

In the direct electrostatic copying process such as the SCM, Olivetti, Royal, and Bruning machines used, over 70% of the revenue came from the sale of paper and supplies. Xerox sold only about one-quarter of the supplies used by its customers, emphasizing the convenience of using uncoated paper. The Charles Bruning division of Addressograph-Multigraph made some inroads into Xerox's competitive position by emphasizing the "copying systems" approach. The main sales theme was "Let us analyze your total copying and duplicating requirements and save you money." Xerox retaliated with a "copy consultant" concept of promotion. These efforts all represented attempts to organize the customer's work flow around a proliferation of the company's products. As of 1966 it was estimated that Xerox had 76% of the market, SCM had 10%, and Addressograph-Multigraph 7.6%, with the remainder among many competitors.

In Category III, the field of sophisticated computers, service and the systems approach were considered by many industry spokesmen as indispensable. Frank Cary, when he was vice president of an IBM Data Processing Division, said: "We sell solutions to problems, that's why IBM sells so many machines." The machines of this category were often thought of as integral to the proper functioning of the company which uses them. To be successful over any lengthy period of time, a manufacturer of such machines had to ensure that service was available and that it was available at a reasonable price. To this end, many manufacturers offered service contracts as part of the leasing price of their machines. In the case of large computer installations or multiple installations of smaller machines, they often provided full-time service men to ensure immediate attention to problems.

It was estimated that IBM spent over $60 million per year on educating its employees and customers. Development of the programming which enabled a customer to use the equipment which he purchased was an expensive and continuing process. In 1964 *Fortune* estimated that the programming and software market amounted to $1.5 billion annually. Of this market, computer manufacturers provided $1.1 billion as a part of the service which came with the purchase or lease of a machine. It was estimated that by 1971, the cost of the software for systems would be equal to the cost of the hardware. Even for a small machine such as Olivetti's Programma 101, elaborate support efforts had to be maintained. Olivetti had developed over 500 programs which would be of general interest and were available free to the purchaser of the Programma 101.

4. A DESCRIPTION OF RECENT DEVELOPMENTS IN OFFICE MACHINE PRODUCTS

Until 1950, the office machine industry was noted for its stability. Many of the product designs had been successfully sold for as long as 20 years and product lives of from 10 to 15 years were common. As of 1966 new developments were coming more rapidly. In electromechanical equipment many in the industry were talking of a five-to-seven-year product life. In the copying field, Xerox rapidly changed its 2400 copier after only two selling years. The Xerox 914 was changed after seven years. In the computer business, too, life cycles were becoming shorter. IBM had chosen a four-to-five-year sum-of-the-digits depreciation schedule for the equipment which it leased. Honeywell maintained an eight-year straight-line depreciation schedule.[5]

The expense of product development had been considerable. "Research expenditures as a percentage of sales are 8%–9% in the case of Xerox, 6% for IBM, 4% for SCM and 3%–4% for Burroughs and National Cash."[6] *Fortune* estimated that IBM budgeted $4.5 billion for financing rental of machines and for plant and equipment for the development of the System 360. Univac (Sperry Rand) had losses of over $200 million during its attempt to enter the computer market. Only in 1966 did this division become profitable after 12 years of losses.

These expenditures yielded some important new developments in products. This section will describe some of these developments under the general headings of:

A. Improvements in Basic Office Equipment.
B. The Boom in Data Transmission.
C. Developments in Peripheral Equipment.

A. Improvements in basic office equipment

Three detectable trends had emerged in the small-machine segment of the office equipment market: An increase in the speed of operation of many ma-

---

[5]"Forecasting Office Equipment Earnings," *Financial Analysts Journal*, March-April 1966, p. 39.
[6]*Ibid.*

chines; a trend toward greater ease of operation; and the evolutionary rather than revolutionary development of new product concepts.

Increase in speed. Increases in operational speeds had been particularly noticeable among calculating machines. A typical mid-1950 calculator would operate at 200 to 250 cycles per minute while the new breed of electronic desktop calculators performed internal calculations at speeds measured in milliseconds.[7] The increase was apparent, however, in both electromechanical and electronic machines. The fastest electromechanical printing calculators were working at 800 cycles per minute, a rate considered by some manufacturers to be the upper limit for such equipment.

The high speeds of the electronic calculators had been achieved through the use of the latest technology, as is illustrated by this description from *Iron Age* of one of the most advanced machines built by the Victor Company.

Heart of the Victor electronic calculator is a $\frac{1}{8}''$ square of metal that is paper thin.[8]

An equivalent solid-state circuit would require 250 transistors, diodes and other components. It allows Victor to pack a research calculator into a 25-lb. package of typewriter size.

The unit will operate to 20 digit answers, develop the square root of a six digit number in six seconds. . . .[9]

Greater ease of operation. The trend toward greater operator convenience was apparent in all product types. Many of the newer electric typewriters have been designed to avoid operator fatigue and the chance of errors. Olivetti's latest machines incorporated mechanisms which prevented jammed typebars by automatically locking the keyboard should the operator depress two keys at once. The keyboard was readily freed by pressing the backspace key. Similarly, the Olivetti machines prevented "flying capitals," which sometimes occurred with earlier models if a character key was depressed while the machine was shifting from upper to lower case.

On a different level, the advent of the tape typewriter had removed the operator's fear of making mistakes. Originally introduced in the Friden Flexoriter during the middle 1950's and later followed by the IBM magnetic tape machines, the tape typewriter produced both a typed page and a coded magnetic or paper tape. Any errors were corrected, or additions readily included, by retyping the appropriate portion. A perfect final copy was then automatically obtained by running the corrected tape through the machine. The operator was thus freed from completely retyping copy in order to obtain an error-free result.

In the case of calculators, improvements had been introduced that added

---

[7] Typical electronic speeds are: Multiplication 1/3 second; division 1/4 second; addition and subtraction 1/125 second; square root, 1/2 second.

[8] The circuit referred to here is made by use of the metal-oxide-silicon process as distinct from using discrete component parts.

[9] "Computers, calculators count on electronic advances," *Iron Age*, October 21, 1965, p. 30.

to the ease of operation. Many of the electronic machines, for instance, included function keys that eliminated routine calculations on a step-by-step basis. An example was the provision of a square-root key or, at a more advanced level, the possibility of programming the machine for specific problems. Machines such as the Monroe Epic 2000 could be programmed to perform a sequence of complicated calculations which could then be repeated as often as desired by simply entering new sets of variables. This equipment had the added ability to store one such program in its memory while another program was being used. The Olivetti Programma 101 went a step further and allowed a library of programs to be stored on magnetic cards. Thus any program could be quickly entered into the machine with a minimum of operator downtime. In addition to these improvements, most recently designed calculators provided larger registers, more accumulators, and other technical improvements that allowed the operator to tackle a wider range of problems than was previously possible.

Absence of radically new machines. In spite of the many advances in small business machines cited above, the customer had been provided with very little additional capability, apart from speed and convenience, than that which he had traditionally expected from his office equipment. One exception was the ability to change type styles rapidly on a typewriter—a feature that was provided by the introduction of the IBM Selectric typewriter in 1961. At the time of this note, however, the trend of gradual improvement rather than radical innovation was expected to be a characteristic feature of the small-machine segment of the office equipment market for at least the foreseeable future.

B. The boom in data transmission

The transmission of data between machines had traditionally been accomplished by the use of punched cards or punched paper tape. In the past, few physically separated machines had communicated with each other, in machine language. Russell W. McFall, president of Western Union, believed, however, that this situation would change. He said in 1965:

> We estimate that less than 1% of the computers now in service are tied to communication channels. . . . But by 1975, when the industry estimates an annual computer market of more than $12 billion compared to today's $3 billion, we expect a whopping 60% to be linked to communications.[10]

Perhaps one of the more glamorous commercial uses of large-scale data transmission was the American Airlines Sabre System of seat reservations which had been fully operational since late 1964. This $30 million computer operation allowed travel agents from all over the United States to communicate with an electronic reservations center that quickly checked loadings and, if seats were available, reserved one for the agent's customer on the desired flight. An inquiry received a reply in 2½ seconds, accomplished by transmit-

---

[10]"General Office Machines," *Dun's Review,* September 1965, p. 159.

ting the data over high-speed leased lines between the agent and the reservations center. This application has been so successful that other airlines were
adopting the same technique.

At the other end of the scale, too, data transmission was finding applications in the problems of small business operations. A case in point was the
growing availability of billing services for the physician in private practice.
Such services relieved the physician of the need to do any bookkeeping or
customer billing. The system comprised a simple desk-top punched card
reader, ordinary telephone lines, and a specially modified receiving key
punch. The company providing the service, which was usually a bank or a
hospital's accounting department, had one or two receiving key punches tied
to telephone lines. The doctors who subscribed to the service received prepunched IBM cards that contained all the basic information such as doctor's
code and patient's name and address. When a patient came to the doctor's
office the receptionist took one of the prepunched cards and noted the variable
information relating to the type of treatment and cost. Near the end of the
day the secretary called the service company and, with the use of a telephone
company data set and the simple IBM card reader, transmitted the patient
information to the receiving key punch. Any variable information was quickly
keyed in by the use of digit buttons on the reader. In this way the service
organization obtained a deck of punched cards, one for every visiting patient,
and then, with the use of central-unit-record equipment, billed the patient at
the end of the month and also provided the physician with both an income
statement and a report showing the age of accounts receivable outstanding.

Between the provision of simple billing services for physicians and the
elaborate reservations procedure of the American Airline's Sabre System lay
a tremendous area of potential applications for transmitting data between machines of all types—machines that could handle routine matters with a minimum of human intervention.

In the field of data transmission by computers, the single most important
innovation was the concept of the "computer utility." The computer utility
concept may be likened to the country's telephone system, a large central
computer being analogous to the present telephone exchange. Any subscriber
requiring computer service could simply dial a number to have his input/output
device connected to a computer. He would be charged only for the actual
amount of time that he used the central processing unit, and through the
medium of time sharing could be only one of many subscribers using the
equipment at the same point in time. The grandest visions foresaw such a
system spanning the entire nation, so that most information processing would
be accomplished by an integrated network of supercomputers.

Although no such large-scale system was currently available, many smaller
more limited uses of this concept were in operation. Keydata Corporation of
Boston provided such facilities in the field of inventory-record accounting and
customer billing for a range of subscribers. Western Union and General Electric also maintained central computers from which it was possible to lease

time. For communicating with the central location remote terminals were used to send and receive the necessary information.

The process that allowed one central processor to be used by many subscribers simultaneously was known as time sharing. Much of the original work on this technique was performed at MIT under the auspices of Project MAC. The basic functioning of the process was described by John Pfeiffer, one of the editors of *Fortune*, as follows:

> Forty investigators or research teams have access to the Q 32 [computer] by remote control, through communication lines hooked to the computer from their own laboratories which are fitted with teletypewriters and other equipment. The forty laboratories are like subscribers to a central telephone exchange. They get service merely by "dialing" the computer which switches automatically from station to station and devotes a period or "quantum" of lightning fast calculating time to each investigator in turn.
>
> This idea is fairly simple, but working it out calls for some fancy traffic control. As a hypothetical example suppose twenty users go "on the air" at once. The Q 32 turns its attention to user No. 1, transferring his program from an external and relatively slow memory unit, a kind of circulating library, to its fast, built-in working memory in about a fortieth of a second. The machine devotes another fortieth of a second to the problem—the quantum, which on the Q 32 represents about a month of human computing time—and still another fortieth of a second is consumed in shifting user No. 1's program back to external memory and bringing in user No. 2's program.
>
> On this schedule the machine takes a twentieth of a second to serve each user (about the time required to wink an eye), or a total of one second for all twenty users. . . .
>
> Although the Q 32's time is being shared, each user feels he is getting full attention. The machine comes around to him every second or so, and it may take ten or more passes to handle his problem. But typing his instructions and the machine's responses take appreciably longer than that, so the user often begins receiving an answer as soon as he finishes asking his question.[11]

Such a system had obvious advantages to both the small and the large user. Moreover, it seemed clear that the technology of time sharing and the concept of the computer utility would ultimately bring the power of the computer within the reach of the smallest company.

In 1966 it was estimated that the United States had installed computer systems which cost $7.5 billion, and the figure was predicted to climb to $15 billion by 1970. The 1966 dollar figures represented some 27,000 general purpose computers actually installed while another 10,000 were slated as being on order. Of all the systems actually functioning one source estimated that nearly 80% were leased.

These figures for the United States compare to a world total of 35,000 installed computer systems. Of these, 6,000 were located in Europe, 1,900 in Japan and about 900 in Canada. A measure of the number of computers per capita

---

[11]Gilbert Burck and the Editors of *Fortune*, *Computer Age* (New York: Harper and Row, 1965), pp. 65–67.

can be obtained from the following figures. In the United States there were 386 computers for every million nonagricultural workers. In Switzerland the figure is 125, in Sweden it is 95, while in France the number is 60 and in Spain it drops down to 7.[12]

C. Developments in peripheral equipment

The peripheral equipment market included all the computer hardware that was ancillary to the central processor itself. Examples were card readers, output printers, typewriters terminals, character readers, visual or graphic input and output devices, communication links, tape units and so on. The devices in this field normally were provided by the mainline computer manufacturers, but there were indications that specialist companies were beginning to compete in the peripheral equipment market. An upsurge of demand for such equipment followed directly from the concept of time sharing, because as one central computer served more customers, the number of peripheral terminal devices increased proportionately. An appreciation of the growing role of peripheral functions compared to the main frame and operating memory (central processor) functions may be gained from Figure 3.

Figure 3

COMPARISON OF ROLE OF PERIPHERAL AND CENTRAL PROCESSOR FUNCTIONS, 1963–73

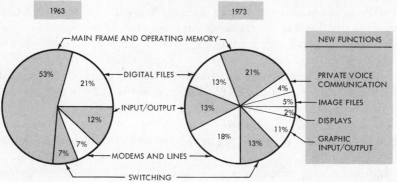

Source: John Diebold, "What's Ahead in Information Technology," *Harvard Business Review,* September–October, 1965, p. 77.

In recent years there had been considerable discussion concerning the nature of the man-machine interface between the operator and the computer. Until 1966 the only practical means of communicating with the computer had been through the use of a keyboard. Recent advances made it possible to communicate directly by means of graphical representations and also by handwriting. The next logical step would be voice communication, but some

[12]Quoted from the February 19, 1966, issue of *Business Week* by special permission. Copyrighted © 1966 by McGraw-Hill, Inc.

observers believed that such a capability was technically so far away that the keyboard would be the only practical means of communication in the fore-seeable future. One noted authority after extensive research into the question of practical voice communication with the computer, believed that such a capability was possibly 50 years away. Exhibit 5 shows one writer's projec-tions of information-processing developments until 1974.

Three new techniques for communicating directly with computers were graphical input/output devices, optical character recognition units, and hand-writing scanners.

Graphical input/output devices. The following passage gives some idea of the potential of this technique.

A major breakthrough in the art of communicating with computers is Sketch-pad, developed by Ivan Sutherland at MIT's Lincoln Laboratory. Sketchpad makes it possible to use the face of a TV-type display tube like a sheet of paper on which sketches can be drawn with a light-sensitive pen or electronic stylus. An operator draws on a Sketchpad display tube mounted on the console of the laboratory's TX2 computer. The pen contains an electric eye that responds to bright spots which appear on the tube in the form of tiny tracking crosses. When the pen is moved along just above the tube's surface, a glowing fluorescent line forms. Freehand sloppiness is automatically transformed into neat lines.[13]

From this simple beginning in 1961, graphical displays had advanced to the stage where their application to business was both practical and desirable, especially in the area of engineering design.[14] Costs, however, were high, and simple systems that had their own central processor (as distinct from a time-shared system) would rent for between $20,000 and $30,000 a month.

Optical Character Recognition units. Optical Character Recognition was the process of directly reading printed characters by a machine. Although de-vices which could do this had been available since the early 1960's, the early machines were limited in the type and style of character they could recognize. Newer machines could read a wide range of fonts at up to 2,000 characters per second, but there were only one or two accepted types of font which mini-mized reading errors.

Machines were specifically designed for a variety of purposes such as read-ing cash-register tapes, reading typewritten pages and recognizing special characters or symbols. Depending on the application, speeds ranged up to a high of about 2,000 characters a second. Machine rentals covered a range from around $400 per month to $16,000 per month. It would appear that the machines held great potential for getting information into the computer with extremely high efficiency. In most cases it seemed clear that a "keyboard" would still be required to prepare the documents that the machines would read; that is, unless handwriting scanners improved to the point where they could read complete character sets.

---

[13]Gilbert Burck and the Editors of *Fortune, op. cit.,* p. 53.
[14]R. A. Siders and others, *Computer Graphics: A Revolution in Design* (New York: American Management Association, Inc., 1966), p. 24.

Exhibit 5

INFORMATION-PROCESSING DEVELOPMENTS—SELECTED TECHNICAL PROJECTIONS

AREA	DEVELOPMENT	WILL BECOME AVAILABLE IN— (1965–1974)	USER PRICE (IN $ THOUSANDS) MINIMUM	MAXIMUM	CAPABILITY
DIGITAL FILE STORAGE	LOW-COST EXPENDABLE DISK	bar ≈1967–1970	$10	$20	100-200 millisecond access, 5-10 thousand bits
	REUSABLE THERMOPLASTIC FILM	bar ≈1967–1970	10	50	10-100 millisecond access, 500 thousand bits
	HIGH DENSITY, PHOTOCHROMIC MICROIMAGE	bar ≈1969–1972	80	120	200-500 microsecond access, 400 pages per square inch
CHARACTER READERS	LIMITED FONT-PAGE READER	bar ≈1966–1969	100	250	2-3 documents per second, 2-3 fonts
	MULTIPLE FONT-PAGE READER	bar ≈1966–1967 / bar ≈1967–1969	200 / 100	500 / 200	8-15 documents per second, 6-10 fonts
	HANDWRITTEN DOCUMENT READER —FULL CHARACTER SET	bar ≈1968–1972 / bar ≈1968–1971	120 / 80	250 / 150	30 characters per second, limited capacity / 50 characters per second
IMAGE STORAGE AND RETRIEVAL	CHIP OR DISCRETE FILM	bar ≈1965–1968 / bar ≈1966–1969	500 / 10	800 / 50	60 second access, 2-4 thousand pages / 30 second access, 1 thousand pages
	CONTINUOUS– ROLL FILM, MAGNETIC SCANNING, SEARCH LOGIC	bar ≈1967–1970 / bar ≈1968–1971	400 / 100	800 / 200	120 second access, 5 thousand pages / 120 second access, 500 thousand pages
	CONTINUOUS-ROLL ERASABLE FILM, MAGNETIC SCANNING	bar ≈1969–1972 / bar ≈1969–1972	400 / 100	600 / 200	120 second access, 4 thousand pages / 180 second access, 1 thousand pages
COMMUNICATIONS	DIAL-UP FACSIMILE	bar ≈1967–1969	Line: $100-$500 per month / Terminal: $25,000		2 pages per minute
	DIAL-UP DATA TRANSMISSION	bar ≈1968–1971	Line: $50-$150 per 3 minutes / Terminal: $300		200 thousand bits per second
MULTIPROCESS SYSTEMS	CENTRAL SWITCHING MATRIX	bar ≈1965–1967 / bar ≈1966–1968	150 / 50	250 / 150	Magnetic or mechanical / Microelectronic semiconductor
	SUPERVISORY CONTROL PROGRAM	bar ≈1965–1969 / bar ≈1966–1970 / bar ≈1968–1972	100 / 200 / 300	250 / 400 / 750	Priority and switching / Optimum job scheduling / Adaptive control

Source: John Diebold, "What's Ahead in Information Technology," *Harvard Business Review*, September–October, 1965, p. 81.

The forerunner of Optical Character Recognition (OCR) was Magnetic Ink Character Recognition or MICR. The relative merits of the two systems were described by one author as follows:

The success that has been enjoyed by the MICR (Magnetic Ink Character Recognition) in the banking industry has raised some question about the relative merits of reading magnetic characters as compared to conventional optical scanning. I believe that, except for some very special cases, optical reading can do anything that magnetic reading can do and do it better, and it can do many things that magnetics cannot do.

The present MICR equipment cannot be extended to read the alphabet. This is not, strictly speaking, correct for all such equipment but the simple form of scanning that uses a single vertical line does not give enough resolution for reading the alphabet. This type of simple scanning means that the quality of printing must be superb and, incidentally, expensive. Magnetic reading also requires that there be intimate contact between the paper and magnetic head—a very difficult thing to do under some circumstances. Imagine trying to use a magnetic head to read a sheet of paper with multiple lines, or a book, or a document with creases, staples, tears, tape and other attachments. The great argument for magnetic reading is that the equipment can read through overprinting. This argument is certainly valid but by using infrared sensitive photocells, it is also possible to read pigment inks even though they are overprinted by dye inks.

Magnetic reading logic is somewhat less expensive than most present-day optical recognition equipment. If, however, one were to design OCR machines for the style and quality of printing used by MICR machines, then the OCR equipment would be no more expensive.

The new CM7 European Magnetic Readers look very promising in that they can read alphanumerics and do it inexpensively. The quality of printing must be of the highest, as in the American system, and the problems of contact between paper and magnetic heads remain.[15]

Handwriting scanners. The current state of the development in handwriting scanners was described by one source as follows:

International Business Machines Corporation introduced its first commercial model of a machine that reads 15 hand-printed characters—the ten digits and the letters C, S, T, X, and Z.

IBM and others have been working for several years on experimental optical scanners that can accept hand-printed characters for processing by a computer. IBM tried out one version of the machine last year in its pavilion at the New York World's Fair.

Now, after field-testing by a department store and a utility, IBM is offering the commercial model for delivery in the first quarter of 1968. The new IBM 1287, which also reads machine-printed and credit-card printed numbers, is priced at $162,000 and up, or may be leased for $3,600 a month and up, not including the computer.

IBM and others make optical scanners that recognize a wide variety of machine-printed characters. IBM's top model of this type, the 1428, can be leased for about $3,200 a month.

The new machine is aimed at processing sales checks, meter readings, and other documents without having a clerk translate them into punched cards or

---

[15]Jacob Rabinow, "Optical Character Recognition," *Data Processing Magazine*, January 1966, pp. 18, 19.

some other "machine-language" form. The IBM 1287-II, priced at $180,000, accepts cash-register and adding-machine rolls, as well as individual documents.

The new machine uses a curve following beam that traces around the outline of a character in order to identify it.[16]

---

[16]*The Wall Street Journal*, October 5, 1966.

ING. C. OLIVETTI & C., S.p.A. (A–3)*

PRODUCT DEVELOPMENT STRATEGY

In the summer of 1966, Olivetti executives were giving considerable thought to the competitive strength of the existing Olivetti product line and the future direction of Olivetti's product development activities. The Olivetti 1965 Annual Report stated:

. . . in this market, the pace of technical progress imposes an increasingly rapid rate of renewal of traditional products. In this setting our company has to prepare the instruments in its traditional policy of technical excellence, to anticipate the future evolution in the development of demand in new and complex fields requiring increasingly refined technology. . . .

The structure of our manufacturing (and sales) activity has continued on the road of diversification, extending to increasingly complex and differentiated product groups. . . .

Evolution of the product line, 1910–65

From 1910 until 1937, Olivetti continued to make only typewriters for sale in the basic office-machine market. During this period several large improvements were made in the standard office typewriter, and new models, semistandard and portable machines were introduced. Although it took until 1913 for Olivetti to produce the first 1,000 typewriters, by 1937 the company was producing 21,575 office machines and 15,694 portables in a year. In 1937 the company entered into the field of telecommunication with the introduction of the T1 teleprinter. Three years later Olivetti entered the calculating field with the MC4S adding machine. Later modifications of this machine made it possible to multiply automatically as well as add. An important breakthrough for the company came in 1948 when it introduced two new pieces of equipment, the Divisumma 14, a four-operation printing calculator, and the Lexikon 80 typewriter. These two machines represented new departures in their fields. The Divisumma 14 was the first *printing* four-operation calculator. The Lexikon 80 broke away from the traditional linearity of typewriters to set a new standard of aesthetic appeal in office machinery.

The 1950's saw Olivetti entering the data processing field with tabulating machines through an alliance with the French company Machines Bull. The alliance with Machines Bull produced a joint venture, Olivetti Bull S.p.A., which sold Bull's punched card equipment in the Italian market.

In 1955 Olivetti introduced the first model of a series of small bookkeeping machines (Audit Class) derived from the printing calculator experience. In the same year Olivetti started development of an electronic computer which appeared on the market in 1960, taking advantage of the existing sales organization of Olivetti Bull. (IBM had begun to sell its computers in Italy in 1957.) Olivetti also commenced the development of a proprietary line of peripheral equipment to complement the computers. The entrenched position of IBM, the proliferation of other central-processing-unit manufacturers, and the increasing financial burden of research and development and computer leasing eventually proved to be too much for Olivetti. In 1964, Olivetti entered the joint computer venture with General Electric Company, as described in Ing. C. Olivetti & C., S.p.A. (A–2).

Olivetti did not vacate the electronic computer field entirely. It remained in the peripheral equipment business, and continued in the field of electro-mechanical accounting machines with electronic memories and small desk-top electronic calculators with programming capability.

Olivetti's main products have remained manual typewriters, electric type-writers, calculating machines, and accounting machines. In 1965, sales of these product lines constituted 81.08% of the group's volume.

The product line in 1966

Olivetti's product mix had changed radically during the postwar period. The following chart, derived from annual reports of the period, illustrates this shifting product mix.

OLIVETTI COMPANY PRODUCT MIX

(Sales in Lire = 100%)

Year	Typewriters Manual	Elec-tric	Total	Calcu-lators	Book-keeping Machines	Furn-iture	Other†	Total
1942*		...	96.1%	3.9%	...	...	...	100.0%
1950*		...	57.3	42.7	...	...	...	100.0
1956*		...	40.2	37.2	6.6%	3.1%	12.9%	100.0
1958*		...	37.0	54.0	9.0	...	...	100.0
1959*		...	34.9	54.2	10.9	...	...	100.0
1960		...	25.9	46.0	13.5	4.6	10.0	100.0
1961		...	24.4	42.8	16.9	4.9	11.0	100.0
1962		...	23.0	39.9	20.5	5.3	11.3	100.0
1963 .... 17.2%		6.1%	23.3	40.5	17.6	6.2	12.4	100.0
1964 .... 17.8		5.9	23.7	40.1	15.5	5.9	14.8	100.0
1965 .... 16.3		11.8	28.1	38.0	15.0	5.3	13.6	100.0

*Not strictly comparable, included only as a rough measure.

†Teleprinters, copying machines, machine tools, numerical control devices and peripheral equipment for computers.

As late as 1963, Olivetti had manufactured only one model of an electric typewriter; by 1965, it had four electric typewriter models. There had been a similar profusion of models within the other product lines. Thus, while the basic product line appeared deceptively simple (there were 5 typewriter lines, 4 adding machine and calculator lines, and 3 accounting machine lines), in reality there was an abundance of types and sizes.

Traditional products

The five basic typewriter lines included:

1. A lightweight portable from which three models were derived—the basic model was the Lettera 32.
2. A semistandard portable—the Studio 44.
3. A manual standard—the Diaspron 82.
4. A compact electric—the Praxis 48.
5. A full-size office electric—the Tekne 3—from which three different models were fabricated.

The four adding machine and calculator lines included:

1. A basic hand-operated adding machine—the Prima 20.
2. A small-capacity adding and multiplying machine—the Electrosumma 20.
3. A fully automatic printing calculator—the Divisumma 24.
4. The superautomatic printing calculator—the Logos 27.

The three accounting machine lines included:

1. An all-numeric accounting machine—the Audit 402 series.
2. An alphanumeric accounting machine—the Audit 413 series.
3. An electronic billing machine—the Mercator 5000.

Exhibit 1 provides a detailed description of the various models which constituted Olivetti's worldwide product line in the summer of 1966. For examples of basic product line see Ing. C. Olivetti & C., S.p.A. (A-1), Exhibit 3.

New products

Programma 101. The Programma 101 was a completely self-contained desk-top computer which combined the operating characteristics of a calculator with the programming capability of a computer. Programma 101 created, recorded, and stored programs within its memory to direct its calculations. It had logical choice capabilities utilizing, in addition to new inputs, stored results of previous calculations. It thus had the capability to do addition, subtraction, multiplication, division, and square roots and make choices between alternate routines. Once a program was created, it could be stored on a magnetic card for later use within the machine which created it, or in any other Programma 101. The use of these magnetic cards enabled routine operations to be performed by a relatively unskilled operator. It also enabled the purchaser to take advantage of a library of over 500 programs developed by Olivetti Underwood. These programs covered many of the more common applications of the machine.

Exhibit 1

THE WORLDWIDE OLIVETTI PRODUCT LINE

Typewriters

Model	Description	Price	Weight	Writing Line	Sales Features
Lettera 31 Dora	Portable	$49.95	9¼ lbs.	8.9"	Low price
Lettera 32	Portable	$69.50	9¼ lbs.	8.9"	43 keys. Paragraph indent key. Touch control. Paper support. Light weight. Vertical and horizontal half-space. Front tabulator set and clear.
Lettera 33 "Deluxe"	Portable	$74.50	10¼ lbs.	9.2"	Same as above plus more stylish design. Leathered metal case.
Studio 44	Semistandard	$99.50	15 lbs.	10.0"	Touch control. Four-line spacing positions. 43 keys. Heavy-duty construction. Transparent card holder. Erasing table.
Diaspron 82	Manual, standard	$245.00	31 lbs.	10.7" 13.9" 17.2" / 27.5" 26.6"	Single bar or 8-key decimal tabulator. Quiet. Automatic margin. Graduated margin scale. Lateral paper guide scale. Touch control.
Praxis 48	Compact, electric	$295.00	23 lbs.	11.0"	45 keys; 4 repeating keys. Fully electric carriage return. Tabulators. Repeating electric backspace key. Vertical and horizontal half-space. Automatic paragraph key. Touch control. Automatic title centering. Prevents flying caps, ghosting, piling, blurring, by locking keyboard if two characters struck together. 840 strokes per minute.
Tekne 3	Standard, electric	$450.00†	52.4 lbs.	12.8" 17.2" 26.8" / 14.0" 18.0" 27.6"	Same as above plus 46 keys. Adjustable platen. Decimal or single-bar tabulation. Pressure adjustment. Same error preventing features as the Praxis. 840 strokes per minute capacity with memory to capture 2 consecutive strokes at 1,780 per minute.

Exhibit 1—Continued

		Typewriters			
Model	Description	Price	Weight	Writing Line	Sales Features
Tekne 4	Standard, electric	$500.00†	53 lbs.	12.8" 14.0" 17.2" 18.0"	Same as Tekne 3 plus fitted with carbon coated polyethylene ribbon.
Editor	Proportional spacing, electric	$725.00†		12.8" 14.0" 17.2"	Same basic unit as Tekne 4 plus proportional spacing with 2, 3, 4, or 5 basic units of space used according to the letter. Automatic increase in typing pressure for uppercase letters. Skip tabulation. Reverse tabulation. Interchangeable use of 2 left-hand margins by a keyboard control. Right-hand margin justifying through typing point indicator.
Other models produced:*					
Underwood 18	Portable	$59.95	12 lbs.		10.0"
Underwood 21	Semistandard	$114.50	14 lbs.		10.0"
Touchmaster 5	Manual, standard	$245.00	31 lbs.	10.0"	14.0"
				12.0"	26.0"
Typemaster 6	Deluxe manual, standard	$260.00	32 lbs.	10.0"	12.0"
				14.0"	
Underwood Scriptor	Standard, electric	$410.00	48 lbs.	12.0"	20.0"
				14.0"	26.0"
Underwood Forum	Standard, electric with carbon or fabric ribbon	$460.00	49 lbs.	12.0"	20.0"
				14.0"	26.0"
Underwood Raphael	Variable spacing, electric with polyethylene ribbon	$590.00	49 lbs.	12.0" 14.0"	

*U.S. produced. Sold overseas through agents, not through Olivetti.
†Not available in the United States.

Exhibit 1—Continued

		Figuring Machines			
Model	Description	Price	Weight	Operations	Registers	Sales Features

Model	Description	Price	Weight	Operations	Registers	Sales Features
Prima 20	Hand-operated adding machine	$99.50	8½ lbs.	+ −	1 register, 11-digits capacity	Standard 10-key keyboard with single (0) double (00) and triple (000) zero. Direct subtraction. Automatic credit balance. Red printing totals, subtotals, and negative balances. Repeat key. Control switch for total subtotal. Addition and subtraction operated without having to release operating handle. Column indicator.
Quanta 20	Electric adding machine	$168.50	10 lbs.	+ − multiply by repetition	1 register, 11-digits capacity	Same as above, except electrified. No triple zero (000) key, 160 cycles per minute.
Electrosumma 20	Electric adding machine	$229.00	11½ lbs.	+ − multiply by repetition	1 register, 9-, 10-, or 11-digit capacity	Standard 10-key keyboard, single zero (0) and double zero (00), 215 cycles per minute. Electric. Clearing, repeat, and backspace keys. Credit balance, totals, subtotals are listed in red. Correction key.
Electrosumma 22	Electric adding machine	$260.00	22 lbs.	+ − multiply by repetition	1 register, 10-, 11-, or 12-digit capacity	220 cycles per minute. Electrified clearing, backspace, nonadd, repeat nonprint, and dater code keys. Red print for totals and credit balance.
Electrosumma 22 Duplex, E-24	Two-register electric adding machine	$385.00	27½ lbs.	+ − multiply by repetition	2 registers, 13-digit capacity available	240 cycles per minute. Same as Electrosumma 22 plus second register which allows intermediate totals and accumulation for grand total. Separate add, subtract, subtotal, and total key for each register.

Exhibit 1—Continued

			Figuring Machines			
Model	Description	Price	Weight	Operations	Registers	Sales Features
Multisumma 20	Automatic printing, adding, multiplying machine	$346.00	11½ lbs.	+ − × automatic	1 register, 11-digit capacity available	Same as Electrosumma 20 plus accumulation of multiplication products, negative multiplication, fully automatic multiplication.
Multisumma 24	Automatic printing, adding, multiplying machine	$425.00	32 lbs.	+ − × automatic	1 register, 13-digit capacity	Same as Multisumma 24 GT without grand total accumulation.
Multisumma 22	Semi-automatic printing, adding, multiplying machine	$310.00	22 lbs.	+ −	13-digit capacity	Similar to Electrosumma 22 with semi-automatic multiplication, i.e., multiplier entered from right to left. No need to manually enter zero.
Multisumma 24 GT	Automatic printing, adding, multiplying machine	$560.00	32 lbs.	+ − automatic	2 registers, 13-digit capacity	Direct positive and negative multiplication. Dynamic memory of constant multipliers or results of intermediate calculations. Automatic date printing. Whole or partial clearance of amounts in keyboard. Wide platen (5⅛"). Grand total accumulates products and totals which can be returned from the accumulator to the register with controlled algebraic sign. Totals, subtotals, and credit balances printed in red.

Model	Type	Price	Weight	Operations	Registers	Features
Divisumma 24	Automatic printing, calculator	$625.00	33 lbs.	$+ - \times \div$	1 register, 13-digit capacity available	240 cycles per minute. Short-cut multiplication. Automatic superseding constant multiplier (memory). Automatic totals in multiplication and division. One step product usability. Immediate quotient usability. Credit balance indication. Rotary printing. Movable decimal indicators. Column indicators. Printing of date or key. Automatic double spacing after totals.
Divisumma 24-GT	Automatic printing calculator	$725.00	33 lbs.	$+ - \times \div$	2 registers, 13-digit capacity	All features of the Divisumma 24 plus the following additional features: True "memory device" within second register. Automatic re-entry of products for successive multiplication. Automatic accumulation of products and sums with printed record of individual extensions. Products, Grand Total. Automatic squaring with no re-entry.
Tetractys	Automatic printing calculator	$875.00	33½ lbs.	$+ - \times \div$	2 registers, 13-digit capacity	All standard features of the Divisumma 24 plus two registers. Black register for all calculations and green register for accumulation. Automatic credit balance in both registers with credit balance indicators. Automatic accumulation of products, quotients and sums. Automatic re-entry of product for consecutive multiplication. Automatic re-entry of quotients, accumulated products, sums, or totals. Automatic squaring with no re-entry, and elevation of a number to any power within the capacity of the machine.

Exhibit 1—Continued

Figuring Machines

Model	Description	Price	Weight	Operations	Registers	Sales Features
Logos 27	Super-automatic printing calculator	$1,100.00	59 lbs.	+ − × ÷	1 register plus 3 memories, 20-digit capacity	600 cycles per minute, standard 10 keyboard, multiplication by nine's complement, 1 accumulator, 2 operative memories, 15-digit capacity which receives all results of operations and first and second terms. 1 independent memory which can store any number at the option of the operator without additional keyboard entry. Programmed rounding or discarding of terminal digits. Automatic calculations of percentages. Automatic scaling in multiplication. Automatic placement of decimal point in quotient. Division by divisors larger than dividend. Uniform capacity in all calculating registers printing. Simplified operation.
Programma 101	Desk-top computer	$3,800.00	65 lbs.	+ − × ÷ ∨	10 registers, 22 digits	See description on pages 930 and 941.

Exhibit 1—Continued

Accounting Machines

Model	Description	Price	Sales Features
Electrosumma 22-CR	Electric adding machine with automatic shuttle carriage	$450.00	Similar to Electrosumma 22 plus the additional features as follows: Automatic shuttle carriage with interchangeable programming device to control carriage movements and automatic functions. Calculates and prints on either the advance or return motion of the carriage. Carriage has front and rear feed with a split platen. Used separately with different line spacing, the smaller section carries the tape for an adding listing operation. Totals and subtotals without idle strokes.
Electrosumma 4-CR Duplex	Two-register adding machine with automatic shuttle carriage	$685.00	Similar to Electrosumma 24 Duplex plus the additional features as follows: Interchangeable carriage programming device. Calculates and prints on either the advance or return motion of the carriage. Split platen for use in adding listing operations.
Multisumma 2-CR	Electric adding-listing machine with multiplication	‡	Similar to Electrosumma 22 plus the additional features as follows: Direct multiplication. Automatic carriage tabulation. Split platen (12″ − 3″).
Tetractys-CR	Two-register automatic printing calculator with automatic tabulating carriage	$1,250.00	Similar to Tetractys plus the additional features as follows: Automatic carriage with split 15″ platen. Interchangeable program drum to control carriage movement and automatic functions. Full date control to print month, day and year. Convertible to function as a duplex adding machine or two-register printing calculator.

‡Not sold in the United States.

Exhibit 1—Continued

Accounting Machines

Model	Description	Price		Sales Features
Audit 402	Numeric super-automatic accounting machine	$1,225.00	*Keyboard:*	Numeric—12 keys—0 to 9 plus double and triple zero.
			Controls:	Program selection lever, 2 motor bars for selective functions, control keys for the two registers.
				Clear entry key, entry indicator, credit balance indicators for the two registers.
			Carriage and printing group:	Split platen divided in two sections; total length mm 437.
				Parallel printing, capacity 13 digits.
				Variable alphanumeric date device.
				4-position line spacing; spacing multiple of mm 2.5 or 2.125 (1/12″).
				Paper controls: rear feed, front feed, adjustable tally-roll holders, optionals for the transport of continuous stationery, double front feed, extra ribbon.
			Registers and memory:	2 registers with credit balance, capacity 12 x 13.
				Numeric entry memory, capacity 12 digits.
			Programming:	Mechanical programming by means of a bar designed to contain instructions for 4 programs allowing for 32 stop selections.

Functions:
    Addition.
    Subtraction.
    Transfers between registers.
    Printing and clearing of registers.
    Carriage movement direction and stop position of the carriage.

Carriage movement selective according to:
    Selection (one out of four).
    Two motor bars selection (black and red).
    Negative or positive content of the 1st register.
    Zero sensing selection for registers and entry keyboard.

Automatic branching from one selection to another.
Automatic opening and closing of the front feed.
Date print.
Interline.
Nonprint.
Interlocks from program or keyboard keylock.

Audit 413	Superautomatic numeric accounting machine	$2,100.00

Similar to 402, but with: 3 registers, capacity 12 x 13; two of the three registers have credit balance. 1 algebraic memory, capacity 12 digits, to be used for accumulation controls or constant information.

Audit 1502	Superautomatic alphanumeric accounting machine	$3,200.00

Similar to 402, but with: Alphabetic keyboard—47 keys, space bar, function keys. Program instructions allow 64 selective stop conditions. The machine is incorporated into a desk with two shelves and one drawer.

Audit 1513	Superautomatic alphanumeric accounting machine

Similar to Audit 413, but with: Alphabetic keyboard—47 keys, space bar, function keys. Program instructions allow 64 selective stop conditions. The machine is incorporated into a desk with two shelves and one drawer.

Exhibit 1—Continued

Accounting Machines

Model	Description	Price	Sales Features
Mercator 4100	Superautomatic numeric accounting machine with electronic computing unit		Similar to Audit 413, but with: 3 registers (two with credit balance), capacity 12 x 13. Electronic unit for multiplication up to 19 digits product and print up to 12 digits. Computing speed—40 milliseconds. Program functions: addition, subtraction, multiplication, multiplication and division per 10 or powers of 10, discard of decimals and rounding-off, constant factor, recall of data from electronic unit into entry keyboard memory. The machine is incorporated into a desk with two shelves and one drawer.
Mercator 5100	Superautomatic alphanumeric accounting machine with electronic computing unit	$5,850.00	Similar to Mercator 4100, but with: Alphabetic keyboard—47 keys, space bar, function keys. Program instructions allow 64 selective stop conditions.

The Programma 101 printed at the rate of 30 characters per second. Printout was automatic, eliminating the need for complicated format control and speeding the programming effort. Programma used ten registers to record programs, perform arithmetical operations, and store data and results. Each register was capable of storing 22 digits plus decimal point and sign. Five of the registers could be subdivided into registers having a capacity of up to 11 digits plus point and sign. Programma handled decimals automatically. Figures were entered exactly as they were read. Programma printed the decimal point automatically and automatically calculated algebraically correct results taking into account the sign of the data.

Operating the Programma was relatively simple. It required only normal 115 volts 60 cycle A.C. No air conditioning or specialized wiring was required. Programma could be operated in program mode as an electronic computer, in manual mode as an electronic calculator, or a combination of the two. In program mode, the operator inserted a magnetic program card, then entered the variables. Programma automatically performed the desired operations in the correct sequence, printing out the desired answers as well as the input data. Computations could be repeated as often as required with a single insertion of the program card. To change to another type of computation, it was necessary only to insert another program card. In manual mode without a program card, numbers were entered and function keys were depressed to produce and print almost instantaneously the desired results. To create a program, the same keyboard was used. In this instance, only the function keys were depressed, and no numbers were entered. A magnetic card was then inserted into the machine and the program permanently recorded.

Copia II. The Copia II copying machine was the first product which Olivetti had made for worldwide distribution in the growing copying market. It was a console model electrostatic copier comparable in performance to the Xerox 914. The Copia II permitted the operator to select the size of copy from the smallest dimensions, $8\frac{1}{2}'' \times 6''$ to the largest, $8\frac{1}{2}'' \times 14\frac{1}{2}''$, by setting a single pointer. The paper was fed from a coated roll which was sufficient to produce 2,000 letter-size documents.

The Copia II produced from 1 to 25 copies, 7 seconds apart from single sheets, rigid materials, or bound books. Originals were not fed through the machine so that even three-dimensional objects might be reproduced. The copying surface extended to the edge of the top working surface, eliminating possible damage to book bindings and eliminating the distortion which is often found near the edge in other copiers.

The Copia II had been acquired through Olivetti Underwood's purchase of an American firm, the Federal Division of Victoreen, in 1965. Previously Olivetti had produced gelatin-master duplicating machines, mimeograph machines, and a desk-top electrostatic copier in its SADA subsidiary in Turin. These machines had been marketed only in Italy and the effort had been successful. The new Copia Manufacturing Company, a subsidiary of Olivetti Underwood, planned to market the new machine throughout the world through the Olivetti branches and agents.

Teleprinters. Olivetti had been traditionally relatively strong in the teleprinter field. Since the company's initial entry in 1937, Olivetti had dominated its home market and had been very successful in some selected export markets. In 1966 there were four basic models of teleprinters in production. These models were:

1. Sending-receiving page teleprinter—output and input typed out. Standard continuous form. (There was also a receiving-only page teleprinter.)
2. Sending-receiving page teleprinter with sliding type basket. (There was also a receiving-only model.)
3. Sending-receiving printing reperforator—output on continuous forms and serially printed on tape. (There was also a receiving-only model.)
4. Sending-receiving tape teleprinter.

With these four models, the Olivetti Company spanned the input-output methods for long-distance message transmission. Each of the basic units could be fitted with accessories for conversion to more sophisticated uses, such as punched tape transmission. Olivetti planned to exploit the growing market for remote computer terminals and data collection equipment, building on the combination of several different experiences: (1) the communication through teleprinter experience, (2) small accounting systems experience, and (3) large system software through the data processing experience gained with Olivetti Bull and the recent sold computer business.

Miscellaneous. Other products which had been introduced into the line during the company's six years in the data processing field included:

1. RP-60 Production Reporting Terminal.
2. MZ On-Line Printer.
3. CMC 7-7004 Magnetic Ink Printer for MICR (Magnetic Ink Character Recognition) encoding.

Olivetti also produced metal office furniture. Because of high shipping cost, sale of this product was restricted to Italy. The furniture was notable for its modern design and flexibility of arrangement. It was constructed in modular units which could be fitted together in many ways to provide a customized appearance with a single theme.

The other major product line which Olivetti manufactured was machine tools. Although the initial production had been for in-plant use, Olivetti had expanded production to serve outside customers as well. In 1966 over 50% of the production was exported. With the expertise which had been developed in electronics, the line had been extended to include numerically controlled devices as well. In 1966 Olivetti manufactured:

1. Drilling machines.
2. External and internal grinders.
3. Planer-type milling machines.
4. Special-purpose machines for mass production, e.g., a numerical control machine tool for Skoda tractor which manufactured a complete tractor axle without human intervention. This machine was over 210 feet long.

Planning for future growth

Programma 101 was the product which offered immediate stimulus for growth in 1966; the Copia II was expected to have the same effect for 1967. Beyond those products which were already announced and in production, the researchers from the Harvard Business School sought further information about the direction which future growth would take.

Dr. Peccei, managing director of Olivetti, declared one of his goals to be: "a renewal of the product line within three years with new products in each of our lines." He believed most of Olivetti's growth would have to be internally generated. He also said: "I personally don't think we should combine with another company in our same business."

Dr. Peccei believed the main hope for accomplishing the company's product-line-renewal objectives lay in research and development. He declared that strengthening the research and development group was one of his major goals for the next three years.

Dr. Roberto Olivetti (son of Adriano Olivetti) was in charge of the research and development division of the company. This group was organized as one of the line departments of the company.

Dr. Roberto Olivetti outlined the philosophical approach to research and development which the company had followed since 1952. He said:

As early as 1955, we became interested in developing new electronic technology for our product line. At that time the notion of using electronics in the size of machine which was our bread and butter was out of the question. The technology was not available to miniaturize to a point where we could use electronic circuitry for our calculating machines. We saw, however, that electronics was the wave of the future. We had to move ahead in our basic product line. We felt that the only way we could develop the strength and experience to work in the area which was important to us was to work on the larger machines. In many ways we succeeded. The idea was to take the technology, build a group, then use the group on products which are our daily bread. We got some rather important fallout from that effort. Much of our strength in numerical control and data transmission comes from the knowledge which we gained working with the larger electronic machines. Also the Mercator series of accounting machines and the new Programma 101 have resulted from this background; it is very difficult to conceive that our company could come out with such product without the experience of the larger computer, both from the hardware and software point of view.

Ing. Montalenti, who had worked closely with Dr. Peccei at Fiat-Argentina, was the only member of Olivetti's top management who had come from outside the company with Dr. Peccei. He now reported directly to him as assistant to the managing director.

Ing. Montalenti estimated that from the inception of a new idea to its appearance in the market, there was approximately four years' work. He said that this estimate assumed the company was making an application of substantially known technology to the business machines field.

Ing. Montalenti said: "We have felt required to institute a scheme of milestones and check points. It is just that some have gotten lost when asked to predict items like time required for development, cost of development, production cost, et cetera." The company was starting to use PERT charts and PERT-COM to schedule product development. The use of these aids was complemented by an internally developed system of scheduling.

He said that the possibility of using research organizations both in Italy and abroad gave the company great leverage in the use of its in-house capacities. For example, the company had not committed itself to a large permanent staff in Italy starting the operation in the reprography field. It was able to rely on the small laboratory which Olivetti Underwood had established in the state of New York and on the development work which the company was able to contract out to development organizations.

Under Roberto Olivetti there were two major branches in the research effort. Ing. Jarach was responsible for engineering of new products while Roberto Olivetti took direct responsibility for the new product development activity. When products were ready to be tooled and the production process was planned, they fell under the responsibility of Ing. Jarach.

The researchers asked Ing. Jarach about the company's plans for the near term. He replied that by 1969 his group hoped to have 18 new products in production and ready for sale. Ten of the products would be derivatives of the present product line and the remaining eight would be either totally new concepts in the old line of machines or else extensions of the product line into new areas. These eight products would be mainly in the area of teleprinters and accounting machines and hopefully would supply the building blocks for a new generation of peripheral equipment. He felt that given the size of his group, meeting the objective of 18 new products would be difficult but feasible.

Discussing the ten new products which would be derived from the present product line, Ing. Jarach said that the effort was to "perfect the machines." He said: "I am not sure that we can go much farther with the purely mechanical devices. Our goal in that area is cost reduction. We do a value analysis of the machines and features. Sometimes it has been possible to get cost savings and make major advances in machine performance, but usually we must content ourselves with savings." The search for savings by the research and development group was focused on a two-pronged attack. First there was a conscious attempt to increase the number of interchangeable pieces among the various products. The hope was for the eventual use of modular units such as keyboards, printing units, memories, etc., which could be used in a large number of machines in varying combinations. The second approach to cost reduction was to try to lower the number of pieces. He said this was especially important in the typewriter market. Assembly and adjustment were becoming increasingly costly. The company had made a major advance when it introduced the Lettera 32. This machine required only about 30% the number of pieces in the Lettera 22, yet it had improved durability and performance.

In the area of totally new products, the discussion centered on the Olivetti company's capacity in electronics. Ing. Jarach said that the problems in this area were mostly to gain experience at all levels. "The important thing is for Olivetti to become known in the market and earn a worldwide reputation for electronics." He hoped that within three years Olivetti would be able to introduce micrologic devices in some equipment. He noted that there were difficulties in accomplishing this in Italy. "It is impossible to purchase such capabilities here. We have very few subsidiary industries. Even today there is no manufacturer in Italy with the capacity to produce printed circuits consistently in line with the quality level required by Olivetti."

He said: "We believe that the items we are working on now will be capable of being extended and kept up to date through 1975. The teleprinters, accounting machines, and the Programma 101 can all be used as separate machines or else connected as part of a system. We are maintaining contact with some of the major computer manufacturers in order to assure compatibility of our new products with theirs."

Keeping in close touch with the present market, new developments, and future trends was Signor Piol, Olivetti's director of product planning and of marketing. He worked closely with the commercial organization and with research and development personnel in order to arrive at realistic appraisals of market potential and product needs. The marketing division, while giving attention to maintaining the firm's share of market for traditional products, was giving special emphasis to developing new products including electronic desk computers, electronic accounting machines, and particularly terminals. In addition to staff functions, the marketing division performed line functions for products still being developed. Signor Piol was familiar with or actually participated in the Olivetti Company's exploration of markets for possible new products.

Commenting on the situation as he saw it, Signor Piol said:

In a sense we already are in the peripheral equipment field. We have communication terminals. Our teleprinters and paper-tape readers are already in service. We consider that in many cases we will be able to use these same devices for adaptation to the on-line applications. Besides the present developments in the use of existing equipment, a new line of terminals specifically designed for on-line applications is under study. This makes sense to us since to meet this market it is only necessary to make an effort to educate the marketing and sales organization on the new applications.

He was concerned about the problem of timing:

In this area many applications have already been realized by various companies and we have participated in a more or less active capacity in a significant number of negotiations and actual applications. An activity of this type has for our organization the meaning of a very important experience; hence the importance of being there actively right from the beginning.

At the present time we are able to take advantage of the contacts of our well-established traditional sales organization, utilizing small qualified task forces in a staff capacity for the purpose of developing our sales. The job of such task forces is twofold; to help the customer to solve his problems, and to give to our sales organization the possibility of an active participation in this market. It will also help the sales organization to prepare more readily to stand on its own feet in order to meet the future needs of the customer.

Signor Piol talked of the sales emphasis which Olivetti would be making. He said:

We will have to specialize in applications. To give you an example, if we design our accounting machines so that they can be used both as separate machines and as input terminals, we will gain a lot. First, we will be able to afford to give excellent service, we will be able to train the necessary number of people. Second, we will be able to have volume production. Third, we will be able to help our customers to grow. We shall be able to give them software at all stages of their development. I see Olivetti as *the* expert in equipment and software in a field, such as banking *or* department stores, and staffed with people who are able to offer a complete solution in problems of the human-machine interface. In Europe we already have the connections and the sales experience which will make banks and insurance companies receptive to our approach. Our products are well known. The same, of course, applies to other lines of products.

Signor Piol doubted if anyone could make a realistic estimate of the market potential for peripheral equipment. He said the whole area was too fluid to allow confident estimates to be made. Diebold Co., however, had estimated that by 1975 around 50% of the total computer market would be in terminal and data input-output devices. Signor Piol summed up by saying:

. . . Competition will be very keen. I cannot be sure that Olivetti can obtain a big share of the market. Companies like IBM do not concede a market. Still, we have great marketing strengths in some areas of the world, and a small percentage of the total market would be enough to justify the entry. Besides, since much of the equipment which we propose to use is near our current product line our major investment would involve little risk.

ING. C. OLIVETTI & C., S.p.A. (A–4)*

^^^

In 1965 almost 80% of the Olivetti Company's sales were made outside of its home market, Italy. Sales by major market area in 1965 broke down as follows:

	Sales (In Billions of Lire)	% of Sales
United States	60.6	21.5
Italy	56.6	20.1
France	28.5	10.1
Other EEC countries	21.9	7.8
Other European countries	41.2	14.6
Latin America	40.4	14.4
Canada	11.9	4.2
Asia—Oceania	11.4	4.1
Africa	8.9	3.2
Total	281.4	100.0%

This may be compared with the distribution of Olivetti sales in 1960:

	% of Sales
Italy	44.6
United States	15.1
France	6.6
Germany	7.4
All other countries	26.3
Total	100.0%

In 1950, comparable figures were:

	% of Sales
Italy	70.0
France	3.1
United States	1.7
Germany	1.5
All other countries	23.7
Total	100.0%

Sales in standard units[1] had expanded from 128,416 in 1950 to 1,693,153 in 1965.

According to the 1964 Olivetti Annual Report, Olivetti's share-of-market by region was as shown below:

OLIVETTI MARKET SHARE BY REGION
(Units Basis)

Product	World	EEC	North America	Latin America
Standard typewriters	27%	31%	21%	} 44%
Portable typewriters	20	25	20	
Adding machines	33	42	27	} 49
Calculating machines	40	49	32	
Accounting machines	18	N.A.	N.A.	N.A.

In 26 countries abroad the products were distributed through a direct sales organization made up of 28 associated companies operating more than 400 branches and direct sales centers. The associated companies also employed agents and dealers in secondary market areas.

In 117 countries, mostly those classified as developing countries, Olivetti was represented by 108 independent general agents, most of which distributed noncompeting lines of equipment. These companies bought directly from Olivetti and resold either directly to the public or else through dealers and other agents.

Olivetti had plants in nine countries outside of Italy. These plants produced approximately 34% of Olivetti's total output in 1965. The comparable figure for 1950 was 16%. The location and activity of each of the company's foreign plants in 1965 was as follows:

Glasgow (Great Britain)	Production of typewriters.
Barcelona (Spain)	Production of typewriters and calculating machines.
Hartford, Conn. (United States)	Production of typewriters.
Toronto (Canada)	Partial production and assembly of typewriters.
Mexico City (Mexico)	Production of typewriters and assembly of calculating machines.
Buenos Aires (Argentina)	Production of typewriters and assembly of calculating machines.
São Paulo (Brazil)	Production of typewriters and assembly of calculating machines.
Bogotá (Colombia)	Assembly of typewriters and calculating machines.
Johannesburg (South Africa)	Assembly of typewriters and calculating machines.

---

[1]For comparison purpose a standard unit is a Diaspron manual typewriter with 26 cm. carriage and tabulator. All other models are related to the Diaspron by coefficients of comparison based on list price.

Evolution toward multinationality

In the fifteen years from 1950 to 1965, the importance of the company's foreign activities increased significantly. The groundwork for this advance, however, had been laid early in the company's history. In 1920, only 12 years after the company was founded, two foreign sales branches were formed to distribute Olivetti products in Argentina and Holland. In 1929 the first foreign subsidiary was founded in Spain. By 1933 Olivetti was distributing its products in Egypt, Tunisia, Brazil, Bolivia, Chile, Ecuador, Syria, Albania, Austria, Belgium, Czechoslovakia, Denmark, France, Yugoslavia, Holland, Spain, Sweden, Turkey, and Hungary. France, Brazil, and Mexico were added to this list prior to the outbreak of hostilities in World War II.

The company's first manufacturing activity abroad began in 1930 in Barcelona, Spain. No new additions to the company's overseas production capacity were made until 1947 when the plant in Glasgow, Scotland, was built. The remaining plants abroad began operation as part of the Olivetti Company in 1949 (Johannesburg, South Africa), 1951 (Buenos Aires, Argentina), 1957 (São Paulo, Brazil), and 1959 (Mexico City, Mexico; Hartford, Conn., United States; Toronto, Canada; and Bogotá, Colombia).

Management views on company multinationality

Developing the Olivetti Company into a "truly multinational firm" was among Dr. Peccei's principal concerns in 1966. He stated, "We must change from an Ivrea-based company with a Canavese mentality to a company with a truly multinational outlook if we are to take full advantage of our resources wherever they may be."

Dr. Paolo Rogers, director of the office of international relations, a formal department added to the company's structure by Adriano Olivetti in 1954, described a "truly multinational" company as follows:

If we are to be a truly multinational company we must have more than factories in many parts of the world, multinational management, and multinational ownership. We must have something more, of an undefinable character, which I call a global outlook. We must be alert and sensitive to national and international developments, and able to seize opportunites, turning the dynamic evolution of markets to our own profit. While doing this we must have a constant preoccupation with preserving the corporate image, respecting the laws and mores of the host countries, and influencing their political and economic development. We must do this if we are to be citizens in good standing of the world as well as of individual countries. This is a big order, perhaps even an ordeal, but there is no escape or alternative.

The mere traditional export approach to multinationality clearly will no longer work. If we want to market our products in many countries of the world, we must be concerned about making a real contribution to their industrial development. This does not mean that we should be willing to establish a manufacturing facility in every country where we market our products. It means, however, that we will be faced with the challenge of reconciling the imperative need to pursue large scale production at home with a genuine consideration with regard to the trend toward industrialization in developing countries.

In 1959, when the Olivetti Company purchased a controlling interest in Underwood Corporation, Adriano Olivetti expressed the following view of the responsibilities of a multinational company.

You cannot be a business "visitor" over a certain size. It isn't fair to just take all that money out of the economy—any economy, even as strong and as rich an economy as the United States. You also have to make a contribution to the economy. Moreover, quite beyond such ethical considerations, if you ignore the responsibility of contributing to an economy, something will happen to stop you. National economies have various ways of protecting this fairness.

Multinational market economics

In assessing opportunity for the company in the present world market, one key company executive noted:

Right now, we are primarily interested in the major markets and those which will emerge within the next few years. It takes a reasonably sophisticated economic system to use an important number of our machines. Presently this condition exists only in Europe and in the United States. Latin America is close to the takeoff point, hence our interest there. The Soviet Bloc is ready, too, but we will have to develop new techniques for meeting that market.

For now we can see little rationale for additional major commitments, especially in Asia, Africa, and the Near East. We have the eighth largest investment of any non-American company in the United States. We have our plants in Italy, the United Kingdom, and Spain to protect our stake in Europe, and we have four plants in South America. These are the areas in which we see rapid future development of our sales potential over the next 12 to 15 years.

Total industry unit sales of typewriters, adding machines, and calculating machines by market area were estimated each year by the company's office of economic studies and planning. These estimates, developed from published national data, were used as the basis for five-year projections of market growth, using multiple correlation and regression analysis. Dr. Franco Momigliano, director of economic studies and planning, stated that his office's projections of market growth were used in the process of preparing local budgets. "When a local manager's market projections differ significantly from those of my department, I would say that about 50% of the time the budget will be prepared with the manager's projections in mind and 50% of the time with my office's projections. I would also say that about 50% of those times when my office's projections are used, they turn out to be correct."

Company executives were naturally reluctant to release their country-by-country total market and company market share data for publication. They allowed the researchers to study these data, however, with the objective in mind of developing some method of presenting them which would protect the company, while at the same time provide the reader with data useful in addressing the problem of determining potential market opportunity. An approach to disguise of the data was developed by the researchers which, in their view, met these conflicting considerations. Exhibits 1 through 5 present disguised company estimates of total unit sales and company market share, by product and by major market area of the world.

In making market projections for the future, Dr. Momigliano noted that his office had discovered the following statistical relationships:

1. In developed countries, the replacement demand for office typewriters can range from 50% to 60% of the total annual demand. In the field of calculating machines (excluding hand adding machines), for the present time it remains relatively lower. We believe the replacement demand will tend in the coming years to catch up with the percentages already reached by office typewriters.

2. Demand for portable and semiportable typewriters has a high correlation with all indices on consumer goods (income, gross national product, production consumer goods, etc.) except in certain less developed areas, where semistandard typewriters (intermediate types between the portable and the office models) are frequently used as substitutes for larger typewriters.

3. The most important variables according to which we can explain the past and forecast future trends in office-machine demand and specifically in demand for Olivetti products (hence in our share of the market) can be divided into two categories: variables under total or partial company control (endogenous) and variables outside company control (exogenous).

Among the variables outside company control (exogenous) we could mention gross and net national capital investments, gross and net national product, industrial production index, production investment goods, consumer goods, and population growth by age groups, by education levels, by skills, and so forth. Generally the coefficient of elasticity of demand for office machines relative to national capital investments, minus replacement sales, is quite near 1 and tends to exceed the value of 1 in countries with less developed economies. It stays under 1 in more economically mature countries. Demand for substitution of machines is generally governed by the average life of the machine, and by the type of sales trend in new products in the previous years.

Among the endogenous variables, those under company control, we could specifically mention the number of salesmen (compounded by their salaries) and the prices.

As a general rule, in situations where the market is scarcely saturated and where there is a highly dynamic potential demand, the elasticity of our products sales to the change in number and in wages of the salesmen can be about 1, tending to go under 1 in situations of particularly saturated markets or in recessive trade cycles (in which sales increase occurs at highly climbing marginal costs).

It is quite difficult to estimate the elasticity of demand to the price of our products because list prices of office machines have maintained a relatively stable trend now for many years.

Nevertheless we can state (on the basis of several research findings) that:

a) In general the elasticity of sales to list price variations is less than that noticeable through variations in discounts or used machine trade-in values;

b) The elasticity of sales to price variations tends to be quite high in our

Exhibit 1

DISGUISED ESTIMATES OF UNIT SALES OF STANDARD MANUAL TYPEWRITERS, BY COUNTRY, 1956 THROUGH 1964, AND COMPANY MARKET SHARE, 1964

Country	Unit Sales of Manual Typewriters									Market Share
	1956	1957	1958	1959	1960	1961	1962	1963	1964	1964
Italy					110,521	131,952	130,765	118,483	90,055	75.6%
Austria			20,021	16,743	22,829	20,830	15,530	14,026	15,992	5.2
Belgium-Luxembourg	24,097	16,124	17,645	21,894	23,155	21,139	24,121	23,100	25,238	24.2
Denmark	6,209	7,688	8,439	13,913	15,308	16,100	15,963	10,531	15,007	3.6
France				99,900	109,236	130,640	123,437	114,889	113,286	16.3
West Germany				222,835	288,207	282,934	165,197	143,181	138,381	1.4
Great Britain	127,765	143,118	122,393	140,997	179,692	173,369	149,266	143,889	165,757	12.6
Holland				43,366	43,754	50,434	40,017	40,314	41,586	11.2
Portugal					8,247	7,160	7,498	7,395	9,034	11.1
Spain				32,080	33,196	39,601	47,863	56,997	63,096	78.4
Sweden				18,762	22,558	33,128	23,998	21,096	18,823	4.3
Switzerland			23,594	23,459	28,765	27,101	24,407	24,481	21,510	5.9
Canada			45,521	51,577	57,379	58,078	63,806	51,605	50,907	42.2
United States	737,793	698,120	574,311	624,917	574,696	566,738	587,526	550,418	563,562	22.3
Argentina					66,252	64,989	52,929	36,247	50,190	61.1
Brazil					67,613	81,164	100,954	82,885	80,017	55.2
Colombia					21,434	22,819	18,665	14,697	13,850	40.2
Mexico					37,417	37,635	40,430	34,962	23,234	72.3
Peru					6,093	10,726	11,646	11,934	12,808	20.7
Uruguay					2,445	6,275	4,777	1,800	3,112	65.6
Venezuela					14,217	9,593	8,846	11,254	12,375	40.1
South Africa					18,973	16,168	15,522	19,772	22,448	38.6
Australia			38,076	35,892	43,112	36,117	40,341	37,515	43,020	19.0
Japan				14,037	16,700	19,274	21,438	38,804	25,812	4.0
Hong Kong					9,067	6,895	8,005	8,363	11,270	5.1
Malaysia					8,604	9,895	9,178	8,403	11,654	11.2
Other countries (Asia, Central Africa, Latin America)					215,100	239,478	220,836	232,308	239,478	17.0

Source: Company records.

Exhibit 2

DISGUISED ESTIMATES OF UNIT SALES OF STANDARD ELECTRIC TYPEWRITERS, BY COUNTRY,
1956 THROUGH 1964, AND COMPANY MARKET SHARE, 1964

| Country | Unit Sales of Electric Typewriters | | | | | | | | | Market Share |
	1956	1957	1958	1959	1960	1961	1962	1963	1964	1964
Italy					10,883	14,774	20,244	25,330	28,704	81.0%
Austria		1,742	696	1,355	1,711	2,480	3,060	3,137	2,990	45.6
Belgium-Luxembourg	1,838		2,003	2,322	3,466	4,622	5,424	6,234	6,773	38.6
Denmark	968	744	1,258	1,645	2,166	2,912	4,270	3,399	4,773	18.5
France				5,806	9,676	18,384	21,287	25,158	22,255	32.2
West Germany				27,632	31,589	42,399	54,000	66,488	75,279	14.3
Great Britain	6,376	5,209	4,704	6,893	12,700	12,318	15,008	15,888	27,005	23.0
Holland				3,387	4,354	6,289	8,708	9,192	9,676	10.2
Portugal					126	310	484	532	677	50.1
Spain				97	484	1,935	3,870	5,322	6,289	74.2
Sweden				3,998	8,377	6,342	10,051	10,308	9,778	19.1
Switzerland			2,903	3,387	5,806	8,708	14,514	14,514	12,579	6.1
Canada			9,447	13,053	16,927	19,375	21,072	28,702	29,512	24.2
United States	204,704	208,277	190,789	252,025	269,705	305,078	381,836	405,473	450,096	9.3
Argentina					174	2,225	2,613	919	1,742	70.9
Brazil					968	1,838	3,096	2,129	2,129	20.2
Colombia					774	968	855	1,084	1,422	26.4
Mexico					1,055	1,055	1,132	1,142	1,345	61.7
Peru					48	242	339	581	1,161	19.1
Uruguay					19	213	252	106	174	41.0
Venezuela					484	774	1,161	1,838	2,129	27.1
South Africa					435	793	1,597	2,903	4,354	25.6
Australia			1,306	1,306	3,048	2,371	3,677	3,290	3,870	3.1
Japan				1,935	2,903	4,838	5,806	7,741	8,708	8.8
Hong Kong					194	290	532	629	726	3.2
Malaysia					36	124	213	387	387	17.2
Other countries (Asia, Central Africa, Latin America)					4,838	9,676	13,546	15,482	17,417	18.5

Source: Company records.

Exhibit 3

DISGUISED ESTIMATES OF UNIT SALES OF PORTABLE AND SEMISTANDARD TYPEWRITERS, BY COUNTRY, 1956 THROUGH 1964, AND COMPANY MARKET SHARE, 1964

Country	Unit Sales of Portable and Semistandard Typewriters									Market Share
	1956	1957	1958	1959	1960	1961	1962	1963	1964	1964
Italy	121,345	114,216	139,168	157,594	160,132	186,342	189,582	204,671	193,545	63.4%
Austria	23,568	28,560	29,690	35,473	40,216	44,682	46,192	42,975	43,743	7.9
Belgium-Luxembourg	31,466	25,275	25,589	28,884	34,907	31,281	37,815	44,555	63,602	14.7
Denmark	9,330	12,293	13,868	19,518	26,181	29,176	39,823	28,489	52,452	4.3
France	61,033	67,910	68,747	66,413	77,506	107,532	123,563	144,736	175,230	13.1
West Germany	323,565	346,788	421,599	373,250	451,664	468,974	560,941	505,815	551,650	1.7
Great Britain	105,446	137,684	144,708	180,795	187,805	187,031	185,096	223,714	273,878	14.3
Holland	51,237	53,901	52,696	51,666	49,526	55,120	58,488	79,758	83,721	3.2
Portugal	6,920	5,954	6,794	6,926	6,786	7,371	6,791	6,822	7,788	14.1
Spain	26,660	38,522	45,721	51,414	51,797	60,251	67,705	81,398	98,648	53.2
Sweden	26,726	34,079	35,274	37,590	45,905	50,269	62,532	65,423	68,432	5.2
Switzerland	34,028	34,150	43,388	43,875	55,599	56,145	59,391	65,810	62,823	5.6
Canada	75,919	92,799	89,110	75,176	84,788	78,712	88,274	92,383	81,774	12.7
United States (1,000's)	1,174	1,540	1,257	1,291	1,394	1,484	1,717	1,629	1,787	7.1
Argentina	1,136	3,218	3,629	1,625	2,510	22,823	18,630	5,119	7,399	97.2
Brazil	14,278	20,119	22,715	23,364	24,013	29,854	32,450	32,450	32,450	44.2
Colombia	6,175	2,801	5,831	9,200	15,244	16,864	11,496	12,339	11,267	42.5
Mexico	27,707	40,113	40,180	40,433	48,984	55,088	43,654	29,222	24,803	77.2
Peru	14,287	21,286	15,989	12,508	13,745	24,070	25,695	25,639	40,575	6.0
Uruguay	1,874	3,694	305	221	1,299	5,646	4,534	2,274	3,894	23.3
Venezuela	11,508	18,007	19,221	26,264	17,970	24,336	17,066	24,495	32,359	25.1
South Africa	10,437	11,884	12,062	9,355	11,823	12,280	12,710	18,473	21,287	53.4
Australia	16,060	21,743	34,307	30,541	51,320	27,065	55,400	47,082	53,218	14.7
Japan	5,549	7,926	6,879	14,077	18,215	16,613	38,065	51,002	54,516	7.4
Hong Kong	6,140	8,163	8,481	13,517	22,241	22,298	24,466	28,944	29,889	6.3
Malaysia	6,294	12,709	8,608	11,496	17,475	9,372	15,324	21,575	35,525	7.9
Other countries (Asia, Central Africa, Latin America)	103,840	129,800	153,164	176,528	199,892	223,256	211,574	223,256	231,044	15.6

Source: Company records.

Exhibit 4

DISGUISED ESTIMATES OF UNIT SALES OF ADDING MACHINES, BY COUNTRY, 1956 THROUGH 1964, AND COMPANY MARKET SHARE, 1964

Country	Unit Sales of Adding Machines									Market Share
	1956	1957	1958	1959	1960	1961	1962	1963	1964	1964
Italy	38,542	41,605	53,807	56,946	63,672	70,423	75,328	57,425	44,711	79.4%
Austria	4,618	5,764	6,111	6,643	7,756	9,674	7,597	9,259	9,311	24.6
Belgium-Luxembourg	4,728	5,218	5,455	5,743	7,073	11,122	11,592	11,718	13,721	39.2
Denmark	5,175	7,137	7,499	11,500	14,686	14,873	10,082	15,699	18,480	20.8
France	23,386	22,561	19,876	38,485	44,366	52,960	62,639	69,976	68,607	25.6
West Germany	97,879	98,532	120,970	86,397	89,776	108,999	113,908	71,837	80,108	17.9
Great Britain	21,965	22,454	33,728	32,335	39,488	55,069	52,951	52,417	58,856	53.0
Holland	11,310	11,867	9,229	12,704	14,056	18,941	17,375	16,977	20,582	11.8
Portugal	1,164	1,424	1,870	1,690	1,648	2,385	1,925	2,018	2,009	41.4
Spain	7,925	8,589	10,716	9,681	9,826	10,658	17,635	19,848	20,582	58.3
Sweden	11,766	13,700	14,746	16,891	12,162	21,923	20,336	20,150	19,488	9.2
Switzerland	14,484	15,792	16,785	18,207	19,365	22,627	24,151	22,696	21,562	5.3
Canada	27,669	29,069	25,280	28,275	25,191	32,619	33,093	37,853	40,184	36.0
United States	348,592	341,784	333,296	413,502	391,654	414,671	449,869	475,443	460,647	16.0
Argentina	544	1,528	5,054	2,410	13,416	24,863	21,294	15,184	29,207	91.9
Brazil	13,917	21,562	22,542	30,383	33,323	36,264	45,085	45,085	49,005	58.0
Colombia	4,031	2,948	2,137	2,346	7,143	10,210	9,465	9,866	9,425	36.5
Mexico	10,810	9,542	11,609	11,892	13,554	27,674	16,971	13,007	16,519	42.8
Peru	2,037	2,468	1,825	2,282	2,771	5,168	6,028	5,121	5,611	52.7
Uruguay	901	1,868	250	120	1,666	3,563	2,403	2,220	1,705	95.2
Venezuela	3,802	5,764	6,308	6,946	3,632	4,605	3,323	5,713	5,602	43.3
South Africa	3,588	5,142	6,041	4,757	11,196	18,641	4,162	7,557	10,056	47.6
Australia	6,481	7,078	9,637	7,507	13,011	11,957	14,440	17,638	18,132	14.0
Japan	1,508	2,111	2,466	5,067	15,070	34,365	34,881	41,552	56,846	6.5
Hong Kong	244	364	261	359	859	1,275	1,370	1,930	2,332	46.4
Malaysia	1,196	979	1,174	815	1,437	2,378	1,096	3,532	3,723	47.3
Other countries (Asia, Central Africa, Latin America)	19,602	24,503	30,383	48,025	65,667	84,289	74,488	73,508	88,209	27.9

Source: Company records.

Exhibit 5

DISGUISED ESTIMATES OF UNIT SALES OF CALCULATING MACHINES, BY COUNTRY, 1956 THROUGH 1964, AND COMPANY MARKET SHARE, 1964

Country	Unit Sales of Calculating Machines									Market Share 1964
	1956	1957	1958	1959	1960	1961	1962	1963	1964	1964
Italy	28,530	33,133	36,944	45,224	53,315	64,888	70,165	93,939	87,980	81.6%
Austria	6,209	6,420	6,407	8,660	9,073	9,491	9,833	9,055	9,704	42.4
Belgium-Luxembourg	5,559	5,296	4,618	7,131	7,900	8,474	9,660	8,914	11,524	47.0
Denmark	3,389	3,971	4,176	4,600	4,358	6,325	6,509	5,997	6,099	33.4
France	39,233	30,904	37,246	42,614	53,554	58,421	64,237	61,509	66,715	40.6
West Germany	52,946	63,309	67,518	72,375	78,254	84,327	80,913	84,290	96,260	16.2
Great Britain	17,595	16,635	15,432	16,365	18,734	20,804	22,245	19,973	25,384	6.2
Holland	7,541	5,307	12,046	10,004	11,386	10,320	11,743	14,050	16,376	25.9
Portugal	1,978	1,898	1,795	2,390	2,461	2,401	3,643	2,746	3,882	44.0
Spain	7,693	8,673	9,909	6,981	8,214	8,017	15,657	21,892	20,621	44.0
Sweden	13,890	15,135	14,807	14,094	12,607	12,572	20,654	21,396	22,772	15.6
Switzerland	22,726	27,181	22,063	18,639	23,235	25,764	23,573	23,503	23,047	12.4
Canada	12,946	15,247	10,160	13,776	11,540	14,539	18,731	19,311	23,047	47.6
United States	161,790	164,232	144,679	175,621	197,740	196,312	227,935	224,567	218,340	19.8
Argentina	342	2,407	1,879	3,393	7,510	16,982	12,556	10,854	13,100	46.1
Brazil	3,639	10,553	8,491	12,130	20,015	26,686	27,899	30,325	24,260	32.2
Colombia	2,461	2,837	2,336	2,170	3,867	4,979	4,688	3,917	3,777	27.0
Mexico	7,766	6,414	8,019	6,447	9,511	12,972	11,901	9,024	11,815	56.0
Peru	1,716	1,988	1,243	1,998	2,085	3,179	3,604	4,289	3,486	35.0
Uruguay	1,326	1,685	228	239	1,070	2,558	1,263	543	522	62.1
Venezuela	2,696	4,702	5,564	6,453	3,707	4,087	3,987	5,005	7,441	69.6
South Africa	3,614	3,335	2,231	2,067	3,621	4,749	3,309	5,059	6,191	41.6
Australia	5,474	6,658	6,590	5,323	5,542	3,809	4,939	5,546	7,885	15.3
Japan	5,038	5,036	5,245	9,101	28,877	29,550	58,992	44,010	41,242	20.3
Hong Kong	564	634	855	710	1,412	1,188	1,228	1,929	1,437	12.1
Malaysia	1,287	1,047	827	993	1,561	815	878	2,580	1,984	12.1
Other countries (Asia, Central Africa, Latin America)	33,964	36,390	41,242	48,520	57,011	65,502	63,076	72,780	76,419	25.6

Source: Company records.

products (values of near 2.50–3.00) only for the simpler products (portable typewriters, small hand adding machines) and tends to progressively lower in value (in certain cases even under 1) in passing to the more sophisticated products with more typical use as production goods;

c) Finally one can state that in general, *ceteris paribus*, the elasticity of demand to prices tends to decrease in passing from a clientele which is more generic, less qualified or skilled, to one which is more sophisticated (which tends to take into consideration more numerous factors, such as performance, technical assistance, etc.).

4. The average physical life of an office typewriter (that is, its survival, even after several switches in ownership, until its destruction) can be estimated at about 21 years. (The modal life of a typewriter is 18 years.)

These averages are very different from market to market and from one category of consumers to another (in relation to the different intensity of machine use and to the varying attention clients pay to technical obsolescence). Especially the more advanced and mature clientele is accustomed to substituting new typewriters for used ones every five years. (The *average* general time lapse between initial sale and the first trade-in of every machine runs from 8–9 years.)

To aid in the development of some quantitatively supportable projections of market opportunity for the company's basic product lines, readers are referred to the country-by-country data in the *United Nations Statistical Yearbook, 1965*. Of particular relevance are the estimates of national income and gross domestic product for 1956 through 1964, pp. 542–46; average annual rates of growth of real gross domestic product at market prices for the periods 1950–60, and 1960–64, pp. 562–65; estimated population and rate of population increase, area and density for the world by regions for the years 1930, 1940, 1950, and 1964, pp. 80–98; a breakdown by sector of expenditures on gross national product at market prices for selected years, pp. 546–54; and a breakdown of the industrial origin of gross domestic product at factor costs, pp. 554–62.

Multinational market "politics"

In discussing the company's multinational posture from his viewpoint as director of international relations, a position which could be described as company "secretary of state," Dr. Rogers stated:

All markets today are accessible to the enterprising corporation, but before going in, the peculiarities of each market must be carefully studied. As a rule, policies and attitudes of a corporation do not apply to a given market without adjustment.

We must aim at a continuous expansion of our exports, but it is clear that in the future we will also have to take more and more industrial commitments abroad. The hope for a continuing expansion of our exports, therefore, lies in our ability to produce ever more sophisticated and technologically advanced products, which will represent the backbone of exports from Italy throughout the world. In other words, we are going to be involved in a dynamic and well balanced distribution of production worldwide and with a concentration of efforts centered on invention and innovation at our base in Italy.

A company the size of ours cannot operate purely on the basis of the conditions which exist today. We have to become involved in predicting the political future.

The European Economic Community has become an important reality. We are convinced that the trend towards European integration is irreversible. Long before the community came into existence we had planned for it. We feel, too, that the Latin American integration will inevitably be successful and we are planning accordingly. Of course, there are going to be some rough moments ahead within and without these emergent blocs. This is why our policies must be flexible in order to allow our operations to meet successfully changing intermediate operations.

The future of the West, we believe, is dependent on the development of free economic exchange. We have always supported free trade between nations, and we will continue to do so. Athough the Kennedy Round negotiations have currently bogged down, we believe that they will ultimately bring about a further significant reduction in trade barriers.

When asked to comment specifically on the relationship between some world political trends and the Olivetti Company multinational pattern of operations, Dr. Rogers replied:

Two current problems are the Glasgow plant and our plants in South America. In Britain, the plant is presently justified by the EFTA tariff wall, a reasonably strong home market, and what remains of commonwealth tariff preferences. If we eventually have a United Europe, or if EFTA fades away as a force, the British plant would be justified only by its impact on and usefulness to the British domestic market or by its usefulness in the context of a worldwide distribution of production.

In South America, we have to work with unstable political conditions in many of the individual countries, and with the uncertainties of LAFTA. We have to be constantly aware of developments and exert whatever influence at our command, in order to encourage tariff reduction particularly in the field of our interest. The eventual establishment of a custom union in the area will affect seriously the pattern of our exports. These emergent trends call for a continuous review of our policies and for an accurate preparation of the whole organization to meet adjustments as they become necessary.

Entry into the Soviet market

In December 1965, Olivetti signed an agreement called the *accordo quadro* or "framework agreement" with the Russian authorities, whereby Olivetti was retained as consultant for the creation and the introduction in the U.S.S.R. of office equipment and data processing equipment providing at the same time technical assistance for the training of personnel. In its capacity as consultant, Olivetti was ready to implement the *accordo quadro* by the creation of manufacturing facilities for producing standard office equipment, and to design a program of instruction to train Russian citizens in the use and maintenance of such equipment. The first step in implementing these broad guidelines took place in the spring of 1966 when the company conducted a several months' training course in equipment operation and maintenance in Italy and Russia for approximately 100 Russian technicians. A second step was taken when the company participated with a large exhibit of its own machines in the Moscow International Exhibit of Office Equipment in September 1966. This exhibit was subsequently sold to the Russian government to be used as a training center.

Olivetti executives believed that the Russian market would provide considerable opportunity to the company within the next five- to ten-year period. Although the Russians had developed a "huge computer for some of their government planning needs," they had virtually no basic office equipment in use. "Most of the office work is done by pen rather than by typewriter, and by abacus rather than by adding machine or calculator," reported the company executive responsible for administering the *accordo quadro*. "The addition of basic office equipment to the Russian economy will have an enormous impact on its efficiency."

We had tried for years to enter the Russian market, but we always ran into the problem that office equipment was not in the plan. It got to be a vicious circle. First, they would tell us that they were interested but that there was no allocation of resources to office equipment in the current plan. When the new plans were being developed, they would tell us that no interest in office equipment was in evidence in the country.

When Russian planners decided that resources would be allocated to the development of an office equipment industry, they came to the Olivetti Company to develop some type of working relationship. In explaining why they came to Olivetti, one company executive commented: "First of all, they knew us from our previous efforts to penetrate the market. Then, who else could they go to? The very poor trade relations between Russia and the United States prevented them from going to U.S. companies, and the history of conflict between the U.S.S.R. and Germany prevented them from going to the German manufacturers. There is no company outside these two countries that comes even close to matching Olivetti in the breadth of its experience in office equipment."

Company executives believed that there was no real alternative to agreeing to help the Russians to develop their own manufacturing capability in office equipment through giving manufacturing licenses and know-how. "It is our view that a country as large and economically powerful as Russia will inevitably develop its own office equipment capability," stated one company executive. "Even though this means that we will in the long run be developing a competitor to ourselves, we will probably be getting much more out of the Russian market than we would have gotten otherwise. Until they develop their own capability, for example, we believe we will have an opportunity to supply them with many of our products produced here. A rough estimate of what this could amount to over the next five-year period is about 100,000 basic office machines. In addition, given the current state of affairs in the world, it is very difficult to imagine the Russians as competitors outside of their market area."

As of mid-1966, negotiations for the implementation of the *accordo quadro* were under way on a wide range of prospective cooperation projects. No firm agreement was reached as yet. In view of the wide scope of these projects, the limitation of financial resources on the part of the Russians coupled with certain limitations entailed in the financing policy of the Italian government was likely to require an accurate assessment of priority needs and a selective process of decision. The Italian government provides guarantees for loans to Italian companies to finance transactions with foreign governments which involve extended payment periods. Such a financial arrangement might be developed for the *accordo quadro*. However, the amount to be allocated to the Olivetti-Russian venture is conditioned by actual availability of funds as well as by policy determination as to geographical distribution of the same.

ING. C. OLIVETTI & C., S.p.A. (B–2)*

^^

In June 1966, the management of the Olivetti Company was concerned with the problem of rapidly rising labor costs in its Italian factories. Apart from attempting to offset these increases by improving the efficiency of local manufacture, executives were giving serious thought to the desirability of specializing production on a worldwide basis in order to help reduce the cost of direct labor as well as to diversify risk and improve production flexibility. This problem had been faced before on a somewhat different scale when, in 1955, the decision had been made to decentralize from Ivrea. One historical report of the company stated it like this:

> The development of the company and its increasingly broad economic influence on the region centering on Ivrea suggested the desirability of a progressive decentralization program. Accordingly a teleprinter plant was set up at San Lorenzo; the new machine tool factory was constructed at San Bernado;[1] and other small plants and workshops for the production of accessory equipment were similarly decentralized.[2]

The 1966 concept of decentralization, however, was to specialize on a worldwide basis, particular factories concentrating on the production of one or perhaps two items of the product line. Thus, for instance, the Spanish factory in Barcelona might produce all the Lettera portables for distribution around the world including Italy. The advantages of this specialization philosophy were felt to have both political and economic ramifications. Among the many arguments in favor of such a move, the most frequently mentioned were:

> Olivetti would gain the benefit of having larger production runs in one factory;
> The company would be insured against the effects of an economic slump in one particular country adversely affecting the entire worldwide operation;
> The present problems of personnel shortages in Ivrea would be offset;
> There would be a reduction in the duplication of production resources;
> Because Italy was responsible for 70% of world manufacture, the placement of manufacturing units closer to markets should reduce costs and/or improve delivery times.

[1]It should be remembered that these new plant locations were respectively 2 km. and 3 km. from Ivrea.

[2]*Olivetti, A Contemporary Image of Style and Industry* (published by the Olivetti Company, 1962), p. 18.

These advantages had at their core the need to ensure the optimal utilization of foreign plant capacity consistent with minimizing political and economic risks. Basically the problem was which country should produce what and where it should go?

Tentative steps had already been taken toward answering this question. Growth forecasts for the large economic areas (EEC, EFTA, and LAFTA) had been made and the interrelationship of these areas with the U.S. market considered. Olivetti executives were conscious of the need to construct a plan that was flexible enough to meet the changing world political scene and had predicated recent tactical decisions on this strategic requirement.

The proposed plan to produce the Lettera 32 in Spain

The Lettera 32, production of which was being reviewed from the standpoint of possible cost savings, was the first machine that Olivetti executives had actively considered as suitable for production specialization. At the time of the case no decision had been reached on the matter, mainly because the Lettera 32 production question was but a part of the whole issue of how to specialize products on a plant by plant basis. Thus it was impossible to consider the question in isolation.

At the time of the case the main contenders for producing this portable were the Aglié plant just south of Ivrea, the Spanish factory in Barcelona, and, running a poor third, the Latin American factories. The researchers believed that the general sentiment favored Spain but there was still some diversity of opinion.

Dr. Momigliano, Olivetti's director of economic studies, put it like this:

I don't know whether the decision has been taken yet, but my observations favor the move to Spain. As always, however, there are two sides to the coin. Some managers feel that the Lettera 32 is already too expensive owing to our high labor rates. Consequently they argue that we should either delete the product completely or else manufacture it in a low labor cost area. It is perhaps possible that some of them are simplifying the problem too much or are not making adequate distinction between direct cost and full cost. If we load the present cost structure with full overhead we would make a loss even now in Italy manufacturing portable typewriters. But this is not true if we consider only the direct costs. In 1969 we predict that even the direct costs will not be covered if we keep the same selling price, as a result of the foreseeable increase in manpower costs. By 1969 then, the problem must be resolved.

The most obvious solution would be that of transferring this production, before 1969, to another country where the cost of manpower is considerably lower than in Italy and where the rate of growth of that cost would not be likely, for at least another 10 years, to reach Italian manpower costs.

Nevertheless, one should keep in mind that right now in Italy, portables, even in limited quantities, still contribute to coverage of part of the company's overhead expenses (in large part fixed). For this reason, a premature transferral of portable production to another country should be regarded as opportune only if, after stopping production in Italy, other more remunerative production could be substituted.

Now, if we consider some of the other factors, the issue begins to get even more complicated. For instance there are three possible overseas countries, namely, Argentina, Mexico, and Spain. Some economic considerations and existing factory sizes, in my opinion, argue against the first two. Spain, on the other hand, has a large factory and a manpower force, the efficiency of which could be increased if it were applied to a large-scale uniform production, designed for a worldwide market—a production such as that of portable typewriters. At present perhaps the most important motive encouraging our examination of the problem of transferring Lettera 32 is we would like to expand the production of more sophisticated products in the Canavese region, while at the same time avoiding an increase of our investments in the plants and manpower in this area.

Ideally, then, we should effect a progressive transfer of the portable production to Spain and progressively utilize the plants and manpower thereby freed for the newer, more sophisticated Canavese production (especially the electronic calculator, Programma 101).

Unfortunately a number of technical reasons makes a progressive transferral of this type quite difficult. What is called for is a progressive transferral which would avoid situations that result in either a momentary lack of manpower in the Canavese region (and hence would necessitate hiring) or a surplus of labor with the consequent need for dismissals.

The maximum need for personnel and plants for Programma 101 will come in the next few months. That is, in the startup production phase in which productive efficiency is relatively low and when, in addition, we need to form inventory for our associates around the world. Meanwhile, the Spanish factory, for technical reasons, would not be able to reach full production of portables for another 18 months to 2 years.

Thus we have an example of a problem which perhaps could, in part, have been avoided had opportune planning and estimates regarding the utilization of all our productive resources around the world, and regarding the dynamics and the location question for these two specific products, been made way in advance.

In any event with everything considered I feel the balance tips in favor of the move to Spain. Such a move must be made, however, within the context of an overall policy of production specialization.

Another opinion on this proposed move came from Ing. Tufarelli, the director of foreign industrial subsidiaries.

The Spanish plant employs 3,400 people of whom nearly 700 produce sewing machines while the plant itself has over 600,000 square feet of floor space. This is quite a sizable operation and consequently we have to plan how best to utilize its resources in the future. There are two changes that we predict will occur over the next few years in Spain and it is our job to prepare for them. Firstly, the political and economic future of the country will approach the average of the other European countries. Consequently we believe that over the long haul the large differences in labor costs will begin to get smaller. Unfortunately, unlike the United States and the United Kingdom, Spain does not have good statistics, but we have assumed that Spain will grow and develop at a rate equal to the median of Western European countries. Secondly, we know that as a country improves its standard of living, sewing machine production and usage start to show a decline. Just for these two factors alone we feel it is wise to act now by adding better production in an attempt to solidify the operation. Olivetti is fairly powerful in Spain and if there are no changes in tariff barriers then we could probably weather most storms. However, we predict that barriers will fall even further and consequently we want to be stronger and more flexible to meet this challenge.

The general manager of the Spanish subsidiary, Ing. Berla, stated his position as follows:

I have put forward my proposals to headquarters and some people have been out to visit us. As yet I have heard no word although I expect a decision will be forthcoming within the next week or so. I might add that I am awaiting this decision with more than a little anxiety! It is a particularly important decision for Hispano Olivetti because if we make all the Letteras here we will be able to greatly expand our exports and, as the Spanish government pays a subsidy on exports, this means we could expect a sizable addition to our cash inflow from this source. [See Exhibit 1 for details of the subsidy.]

In fact the whole question of exports is vitally important to the company here. The Spanish government is very favorably inclined toward exporters and, in addition to the subsidy I have just mentioned, there are many tangible and intangible benefits that accrue from being a serious exporter.

A long-range manufacturing plan

Although the Lettera 32 was the only specific product actively under consideration for decentralization in 1966, there was a definite attempt to establish a long-range manufacturing plan that would encompass all products and all countries. This was a formidable task and obviously one of key importance to the company if it was to remain competitive in the years ahead. The task was largely being handled by Ing. Tufarelli and various "staff" personnel who were called in on specific aspects of the problem (see Exhibit 2 for a partial organization chart). It was clear that the formulation of any plan was still in the very early stages. Ing. Tufarelli's comments on the plan were as follows:

The Lettera 32 problem is only part of a long-range plan to better utilize our manufacturing subsidiaries. This plan is taking shape but has not yet been clearly defined. Basically our objectives are fourfold. First, to specialize production facilities so that we can achieve a concentration of production in certain classes of product. Second, we want to take best advantage of labor costs and existing plant facilities. Third, our current thinking is to keep the technologically more complex products closer to Ivrea, and lastly we want to ensure that all factors such as political considerations, shipping costs, tariff barriers, export incentives, transfer prices and so on are fully taken account of.

In Latin America our immediate aim is to obtain complete integration of our facilities. We are really doing the "pioneering" work among these countries. The second phase in this area is to integrate the operations with European Olivetti. This is still some time away, however.

The trend to specialization has a mixed origin. In Italy we have to maintain

Exhibit 1

IMPORT TARIFFS AND EXPORT INCENTIVES

	Import Tariffs		*Export Incentives*
Argentina	Typewriters: electric (excluding portables) manual	50%* 175%*	18% on invoice price + fixed amount per machine varying from $5.55 to $11.46.
Brazil	Typewriters: electric and portables manual	40%* 80%*	N.A.
Colombia	N.A.		N.A.
Italy	Typewriters Calculators	13%† 11%†	Tax on export of 3% invoice price. When paid, government credits firm with 6%. Credit not collectible with any predictability.‡
Mexico	Electric typewriters Calculating machines	15% 30% (only tariff ad valorem)	N.A.
Spain	Typewriters: electric 11% manual 43% } f.o.b. invoice price		11% f.o.b. invoice price + tariff in country of destination. Payable in Cash.
United Kingdom	Typewriters: electric 30% manual 15% } f.o.b. invoice price		Some export financing.
United States	Typewriters 0% Calculators 12.5% ad valorem		

*From non-LAFTA countries.
†From non-E.E.C. GATT countries.
‡As of December 31, 1965, Olivetti had a 10 billion lire credit outstanding.
Source: Company records.

full employment which is highly inflexible. The acceleration of our program is largely a bid to gain flexibility. However, the company has to identify, in a geographical and organizational context, the specialization that production centers should have in relation to the worldwide market. In other words, it would not be technically possible for the company to respond promptly and satisfactorily to market needs if production facilities, planning staff, engineering staff and so on catered to a variety of markets at the same time. For instance, the light consumer market (portable typewriters) and the electronic data processing market require very different technical and managerial skills. A proper consideration of the geographical set-up may help us in solving the problem of developing the precise skills we need for each part of our product line.

Someone asked what the Italian government would think if we planned to diversify away from Italy. I don't think we would change any trend as we would still have exports from here. Although worldwide, we also have local obligations and because of the predicted market expansion our plan would not drastically reduce exports from Italy.

Exhibit 2

PARTIAL ORGANIZATION CHART, JULY 1966

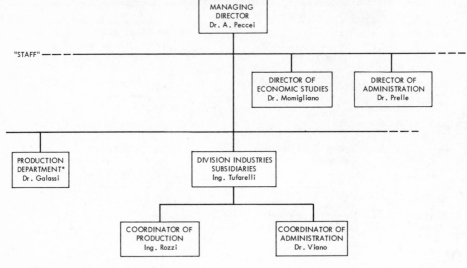

*Italian factories.
Source: Company records.

The whole thing can be viewed as a type of insurance plan because with our present setup if there is an economic depression in Italy we would hurt the worldwide organization. On the other hand the Italian government is also insured because if things got really difficult we could reduce production elsewhere and maintain it in Italy. I hope we will never have to do that!

Dr. Momigliano had conducted several economic surveys for Olivetti on trends in the Italian economy and industry. Appendix A summarizes a technique that he used to compare various proposed plant locations within Italy. He thought this technique would be applicable, with minor modifications, to rationalizing production on a worldwide basis. He summarized the problems as follows:

Specialization of production on a country-by-country basis seems to be the way to go. Spain is the most logical first move, but the real, and to my knowledge as yet unanswered, question is: Given our existing production subsidiaries, how do we plan a logical step-by-step program of decentralization?

In further defining this problem the remainder of this case will describe the existing non-Italian production facilities of Olivetti with a special emphasis on some of the larger foreign operations.

Olivetti's overseas industrial subsidiaries

Olivetti's overseas factories could be classified into two basic types: assembling and manufacturing. Those with assembly operations acquired nearly all their component parts from one of the Italian or foreign factories and then simply assembled and tested the final machine. The manufacturing subsidiaries, however, had their own workshops and fabricating facilities that converted the raw material into component parts and then assembled these "home-produced" parts into the required products. In such operations, the factories were almost entirely self-contained and had very little dependence on Ivrea for their production requirements.

In 1966, there were nine overseas industrial subsidiaries. The tabulation below shows the location of each plant and the type of product manufactured or assembled.

City	Country	Date of Establishment	Operation and Production
Barcelona	Spain	1929	Manufacturing typewriters and calculators
Bogotá	Colombia	1959	Assembling typewriters and calculators
Buenos Aires ..	Argentina	1932	Manufacturing typewriters and calculators
Glasgow	Great Britain	1947	Manufacturing typewriters
Hartford, Conn.	United States	1959	Manufacturing typewriters and adding machines
Johannesburg ..	South Africa	1949	Assembling typewriters and calculators
Mexico City ...	Mexico	1959	Manufacturing typewriters and assembling calculators
São Paulo	Brazil	1957	Manufacturing typewriters and assembling calculators
Toronto	Canada	1959	Partial manufacture and assembly of typewriters

Exhibit 3 illustrates the location of these plants. Exhibit 4 contains a summary of the important labor statistics for each plant, while Exhibit 5 details selected corporate taxes rates by country. Exhibit 6 shows sample transportation costs between representative major markets and manufacturing centers.

There was a loose management liaison between each of these factories and headquarters in Ivrea with the local plant manager seemingly having almost complete autonomy over his own operation. He was allowed to make some changes in the design of the machine as long as it did not affect the final performance or exterior appearance. Usually such modifications would relate to the availability or otherwise of local materials and, although the plant manager normally would inform Ivrea of any change, he was not formally required to do so. Ing. Rozzi, the headquarter's coordinator of production, gave as an illustration Argentina's use of a plastic material as a sound absorber in typewriters. This material replaced the special very soft cardboard material called for in the original product specifications. The substitute was not considered to be as good but it did do the job adequately and overcame the problem of Argentinian import restrictions on the original material. The change was put into effect by the local plant manager.

The industrial subsidiaries reported to Dr. Viano on all nontechnical matters and to Ing. Rozzi on technical questions. Dr. Viano and Ing. Rozzi who were in adjoining offices on the top floor of the new administration center in Ivrea

Exhibit 3

FACTORY LOCATIONS AND WORLD MARKETS

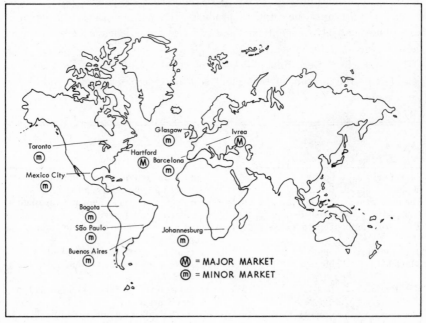

Source: Prepared by case writer.

reported to Ing. Tufarelli who had overall responsibility for all overseas industrial subsidiaries. This group (see Exhibit 2) effectively acted as "filters"
through which the overseas factories' correspondence and information was
channeled to the appropriate staff and operational people in the central
organization. No correspondence was entered into directly between industrial
subsidiaries and production personnel in Ivrea without the knowledge of this
headquarters group. However, the responsibility for all day-by-day production
was effectively in the hands of the foreign manager. Once the product to be
manufactured had been decided upon he could change methods, assembly
techniques, and even, as stated earlier, some specifications, should he deem
it necessary. Ing. Tufarelli described the degree of local responsibility as
follows:

Regarding some specific instances of local responsibility I would say the main
areas are as follows: The manager can decide anything related to the operation
of the company once the company has stabilized. He has to develop the budget,
have it approved, and then meet or improve upon budgeted results. He has local
responsibility for production; periodically there will be a review and he must
give good reasons for any major deviation. He must consult headquarters fully
on any increases in indebtedness, major swings in the cash position of the company, and also on matters that affect overall corporate planning. The reporting
of financial fluctuations is especially important where the currency is weak such

Exhibit 4

LABOR STATISTICS FOR THE FIRM'S PLANTS*

	Average Wage (Including Any Fringe Benefits) (Lire per Hour)	Size of Olivetti Work Force	Turnover (% of All Employees)	Absenteeism (% of Total Work Force)
Barcelona	550	3,400	3–4	8
Bogotá	N.A.	25	5	9
Buenos Aires	850	950 (approx.)	6	10
Glasgow	800	400	N.A.	N.A.
Hartford, Conn. ..	1,930	2,214	25–30	4
Italy	1,150	15,600	2–3	12–14
Mexico City	400	526	10	11
São Paulo	400	920	12	9

*Data for the assembly plants in Johannesburg and Toronto have been excluded from this exhibit.
Source: Company records.

as in Latin America. He has only limited control on production that he makes for export; home office has a big interest in this.

Almost all the overseas factories had originally been established to allow Olivetti products to be sold behind high tariff barriers or within closed markets. The South American factories were examples of this policy, as was the British plant which had been established in 1947 to gain a foothold within the British Commonwealth. However, as times and situations changed, some of the original placements were no longer considered to be ideal, and management believed that any long-range plan of production specialization should not necessarily be constrained by 1966 plant siting. It was deemed possible that,

Exhibit 5

SELECTED CORPORATE TAX RATES BY COUNTRY

	Corporate Income Taxes	Turnover Tax (Basically a Sales Tax Imposed at All Levels of Distribution)
Argentina*	38%	—
Brazil*	31	15% (as of July 1, 1967)
Colombia*†	12–36	—
Italy‡	30–35	3.3
Mexico*	5–42	1.8
Spain	32.7	2.4
United Kingdom§	38.75	—
United States	48	—

*Also has dividend tax.
†Also has an excess profits tax of 20%–50% on excess of 12%–36% on assets.
‡Italy has additional taxes of 0.825% of net worth and 16.5% on that part of each year's income which, after deduction of income tax assessed, is in excess of 6% of net worth.
§Also has a profit tax of 15% that can be waived in the case of overseas trade corporation.
Source: Company records.

Exhibit 6

REPRESENTATIVE TRANSPORTATION COSTS
BETWEEN MAJOR MARKETS AND MANUFACTURING CENTERS*

A. Shipping by trailer trucks from Italy—capacity 600 units.

Ivrea to Barcelona   *Lire*

Loading cost: 2 hrs. x 4 men x 2,000 lire/hr.	16,000
Transport from Ivrea to Barcelona (1,000 km.)	450,000
Total cost	466,000
Unit cost	777
Ivrea to Frankfurt	780

B. Transoceanic Shipping—600 units or 70 cubic meters.

Ivrea to New York (or Mexico)

Loading cost for trailer truck	16,000
Transport from Ivrea to Genoa	45,000
Freight from Genoa to New York (19,200 lire/cubic meter)	1,345,400
Total cost	1,406,400
Unit cost	2,344

Freight from Genoa to Vera Cruz 21,850 lire per cubic meter
Genoa to Buenos Aires 26,820 lire per cubic meter
Genoa to Santos   30,600 lire per cubic meter

*All costs relate to the Diaspron 82 standard typewriter with 26-cm. carriage.
Source: Company records.

over a period of time, one plant could be slowly phased out in favor of another, should a clearly reasoned economic or political rationale emerge.

The most important subsidiaries were those in Spain, the United Kingdom, the United States and Latin America. The resources and capabilities of each of these factories will be described in more detail in the sections which follow.

THE SPANISH FACTORY

Products

The Spanish product lines and production volume in 1965 were as follows:

Model	*Yearly Production Volume (Units)*
Lettera 22	30,000
Studio 44	50,000*
Underwood 21	60,000†
Lexikon 80	40,000
Summa Prima Electrosumma 20 Multisumma 20	12,000 total
Sewing machines:	
Singer—cheap straight line	5,000
Singer—straight line	10,000
Singer—zig zag	10,000
Wertheim (all models)	15,000

*Some of this quantity were exported to Olivetti Underwood.
†Exported to Olivetti Underwood.

Plant

Olivetti's Spanish operations were carried out by three companies which, although separated legally, were operated for all intents and purposes as one unit. The three companies were Hispano Olivetti S.A., which manufactured office equipment, Rapida S.A., which manufactured sewing machines for Singer and Rapida,[3] and Commercial Meccanografica S.A., which formed the selling organization. Only the first two companies will be considered in this case.

The original plant had been built before the war and, although the working facilities appeared to be modern and well-run, the design of the factory buildings did not allow the most efficient work flow to be achieved. The factory produced many of its own tools in a tool room that was equipped with several Societé Genevoise jig borers, the latest spark eroding equipment and many other modern machine tools. The company had completely tooled in 1965 the Multisumma 20 and in 1966 was engaged in tooling the new model MS 60 standard manual typewriter. The workshop was equipped with a wide variety of screw machines, punch presses, and special-purpose production equipment. The production engineers had recently completed a study of screw machine operation and, by the use of queuing theory, had established that one operator could handle 4–5 screw machines simultaneously. The factory was almost entirely self-contained except for the production of electric motors which were purchased items. There was, however, a move to divest some of the processes that could be more satisfactorily subcontracted in the Barcelona area. The most notable possibility was to close down the iron foundry, the castings from which formed a major item in sewing machine production, and to concentrate only on the die casting of aluminum alloy parts which were used almost exclusively for office equipment.

The typewriter assembly lines were situated on the top floor of a multistoried building and they used mainly roller conveyors for transportation between work stations. A wide use was made of power-driven hand tools to ease the assembly. Production control was exercised through the use of production recorders and punched card equipment to produce the daily control reports.

Production efficiency

The Spanish factory measured its production efficiency on a similar basis to that used in Ivrea, i.e., by means of the P/T concept. The June 1966 P/T ratio was 3.50 which compared with the Italian ICO plant's ratio of 2.10. The ratios, however, were not strictly comparable because Spain had high indirect costs related to maintenance and services. Ing. Berla, the general manager of Hispano Olivetti, expressed the opinion that a Spanish P/T ratio of 3 was equivalent to a ratio of 2.4 in Italy. Ing. Tufarelli stated that with everything included, Spain could be only about 10% less efficient than Ivrea should the transfer of Lettera 32 production take place.

Labor

As shown in Exhibit 5, production units in Barcelona employed a total of 3,400 people. Of these, 2,700 were employed by Hispano Olivetti and 700 by

---

[3]The sewing machines sold by Rapida carried the trademark "Wertheim."

Rapida. The work force was approximately 20% female. The guaranteed work-week (by law) was 48 hours and, in addition, the plants normally worked considerable overtime. In 1966 there were only 10 Italian nationals in the entire organization.

Labor costs in Spain were among the lowest of any of Olivetti's industrial subsidiaries, being higher only than those in Brazil and Mexico. The average total labor cost was 550 lire per hour with the actual take-home pay being around 495 lire per hour. Berla predicted that labor costs would rise at about 15% a year till 1968. From 1969 on he believed this trend would flatten off somewhat and follow recent European experience with a 5–6 year lag. In 1966 absenteeism was 8% of the total work force and annual labor turnover was in the range of 3%–4% of all employees.

Hispano Olivetti provided similar social services to those available in Ivrea. These included a nursery school, a canteen, summer camps, and—unusual for many factories—a large employee swimming pool.

The situation in Spain regarding labor unions was somewhat different from that obtaining in many countries. Because of the political regime in Spain, the official political view was that the aims of the employer and employee should be the same. Consequently there was only one union known as the "Sindacato" to which both labor and management belonged. This union was split into differ-ent trade groups. In Olivetti's case the workers elected 12 men who represented the workers' point of view. In most practical situations, however, the president of the factory union dealt directly with the personnel manager. If the two were unable to negotiate a settlement, an independent arbitrator could be called. The workers theoretically had little power of retaliation against unfair manage-ment treatment because no such institution as the strike was officially recog-nized. In spite of this doctrine, strikes did occur and, although the police might be called, there were so many workers that little could be done. In 1963 Hispano Olivetti sustained a two-month strike when the workers pegged the production output at 65% of normal. The strike was against management's attempts to curtail overtime—a lucrative source of income for the workers as they received nearly 75% more pay per hour. Olivetti's last labor contract, negotiated in 1965, was due for renewal in 1967 and every two years thereafter.

Spanish law decreed that a worker could not be fired or made to resign unless he was caught fighting or stealing or otherwise breaking the law. At the age of 65 the worker had the choice of retiring on a somewhat meager pension or staying on and working until his death. The majority of workers chose the latter course and consequently there was never any shortage of door-openers, attendants and general hangers-on.

The future

In 1966 Ing. Berla had proposed to corporate headquarters in Ivrea that Spain take over the worldwide manufacture of both the Lettera 32 typewriter and the new semiportable model. These two machines had approximately 70% of their parts in common.

He had several reasons for promoting this point of view. First, he wanted to increase the productivity of his 3,400 workers. He felt this would be possible by means of high-quantity production runs—predictions estimated the 1969 market would require a total of 600,000 machines. Secondly, by exporting heavily Hispano Olivetti would be able to take advantage of Spanish export incentives which gave an 11% rebate on the landed cost in the country of destination. This was payable semiannually in cash by the Spanish government. Thirdly, Ing. Berla thought that as the Spanish cost of labor was only about 50% of that in Italy, there would be a worthwhile cost saving to the company. In addition, he was confident that if the Lettera 32 were exclusively produced in Spain, the factory's P/T ratio could be reduced to 3 in the first year of operation and to 2.8 in the second year. Fourthly, he argued that even though Spain was currently outside the European Common Market, the savings in manufacturing costs would more than offset the 13% tariff barrier (EEC) applicable to GATT countries. He did admit, however, that the political situation might be a cause for concern. On the other hand he pointed out that the portable was the least important product in Olivetti's product line and thus exposure to political risk would be minimal.

Expansion of the existing plant in Barcelona was almost impossible because of the shortage of available land. Nevertheless, the belief was expressed that production in the existing facilities could be increased considerably before serious overcrowding occurred. If new buildings should be needed, the cost of building in Spain was about 30% less than in Italy (about 75,000 lire per square meter). There were several exemptions and fiscal advantages if factories were built or expanded in designated areas of the country.

THE BRITISH FACTORY

Products

In 1965 the British factory produced only the Diaspron standard manual typewriter, at a rate of 27,000 units a year. Of these, 8,500 were exported to a select number of markets determined by Ivrea (mainly Australia and New Zealand) while another 6,000 units were sold to the British government. The 1966 production rate was substantially similar to 1965's. Prior to October 1963, the plant had also produced the Lettera 22 at a rate of 160 machines a day, but in October the product was dropped and the work force reduced from a total of 1,050 to the current level of 400 workers. On May 23, 1966, another change occurred when Dr. Giovanni Fei returned to headquarters in Ivrea after 12 years of managing the United Kingdom subsidiary. He was replaced by Mr. G. Sacco. Mr. Sacco had just completed setting up Olivetti Nederland N.V. in Holland before coming to the British company.

Plant

British Olivetti Ltd.'s factory was located in Glasgow, Scotland, while the company's head office was located in Berkeley Square, London. The subsidiary was established in 1947 as a means of entering both the British and the British

Commonwealth markets, but neither of those markets had been closed for the 12 years prior to 1966 and there seemed to be little likelihood of their closing again in the near future. Thus, the original *raison d'être* for the plant's existence had been lost. This fact, coupled with Britain's uncertain relationship with the European Common Market, was cause for considerable debate among Olivetti's top management regarding the future of the Glasgow plant.

During 1966 the company was preparing for a changeover to the new standard typewriter model MS 60. Somewhat in contrast to any idea of a specialization policy, however, this new model was being simultaneously tooled and introduced at three different localities, in Spain, Italy, and Great Britain. The cost of tools in the United Kingdom was estimated at £415,000 and the cost of required new machinery at £400,000. It was planned to depreciate these items fully in five years and four years respectively.

Production efficiency

Although British Olivetti produced the Diaspron 82 at the rate of only 115 a day, the total cost of production was estimated to be 12%–13% below the cost of producing the same unit in Ivrea. This was largely due to the low cost for direct labor at the Scottish plant (800 lire/hr.) and the fact that all the machine tools used for production had been completely written off. Another factor that could potentially improve both the efficiency and flexibility of this operation was the availability of competent subcontractors in the area. The Glasgow facility provided the possibility of producing considerably greater outputs without added capital investment. The British company's management considered that this aspect of production in Scotland was frequently overlooked by top management of the company in Italy.

Labor

The Glasgow plant maintained no social services for its workers apart from the normal fringe benefits such as holiday pay and so forth. This was in marked contrast to the Spanish and Italian factories where libraries, health services, and summer camps were part of the Olivetti tradition.

The attitude toward layoffs in the United Kingdom was very similar to that obtaining in the United States. Although such practice was frowned upon, it was quite possible, if an emergency demanded, to tailor the work force to meet the needs of the moment. Consequently there was a degree of flexibility that was not available in either of the Spanish or Italian companies. On the other hand, the hiring of new labor, although not difficult, was considered to be a slow process if a sizable increase in the work force was required. The workmanship of the Scottish employee was described by Mr. Sacco as being of very high quality.

The future

Owing to the discontinuation of Lettera 22 production during October 1963, the factory building was considerably underutilized. Mr. Sacco believed that it would be quite possible to double production within the existing facilities without any major renovations. The present building was rented from the British government at a cost of £30,000 a year, and the lease was not due for renewal for another 10 years. However, there was no land readily available on the present site for any sizable building extension, if such were needed.

In January 1966, the British government had revised the investment incentives that it made available to new or expanding industries. Basically the country was divided into development and nondevelopment districts, and Glasgow was in a development district. In such an area the government would make a cash grant of 40% toward the cost of new plant machinery which in their opinion qualified as a new investment. Qualification was largely a matter of satisfying the Board of Trade that such equipment was being used to increase the manufacturing capability of the purchasing organization and that it held forth the prospect of providing increased employment. The grants were payable within about six months of the presentation of claims and were treated for tax purposes as reducing the cost of assets—in effect a depreciation tax credit. In addition the grants were nontaxable. For equipment that for some reason did not qualify for grants, an "initial allowance" of 30% was permitted. The "initial allowance" was an accelerated "wear and tear" allowance. In the case of new industrial buildings and structures the grants could be either 25% or 35%, depending on certain detailed requirements, while the "initial allowance" was 15%. Similar provisions had been made for computers in which case 20% of the cost of the equipment was paid for by the government.[4]

Among several top Olivetti people there was a growing feeling that a decision regarding the future of the Glasgow factory should be made in the near future. Basically, the problem was to decide whether to close the plant down completely or to expand its output by specializing in the production of one particular model.

When the researchers questioned Mr. Sacco on possible products that British Olivetti could manufacture if the production capacity of the plant were expanded, he replied:

With the skilled workmen we have available in Scotland—workmen who are used to an industrial society—I feel we should look at making items like the Praxis 48. Here we can subcontract parts such as the electric motor. This would be extremely cheap to purchase. There is a growing trend toward the use of electrics all over Europe. The British home market is currently only making about 18% of its sales in electric typewriters. I've only been here about six weeks but already I feel that the decision regarding the future of Glasgow is important. It should be decided one way or the other—the present operation is not making the best use of the resources we have.

THE UNITED STATES FACTORY
Products

Most of the products manufactured by the Hartford, Connecticut, factory had their origin with the Underwood Corporation. In one instance only—the

---

[4]Extracted from *Investment Incentives* (London: Her Majesty's Stationery Office, 1966).

Divisumma 24—was an Olivetti product being assembled at Hartford. The various models and their production rates in mid-1966 were as follows:

Model	Feature	Production Units per Day
Touchmaster Five and Typemaster Six ..	Standard	608
Scripto	Electric (fabric ribbon)	⎫
Forum	Electric (polyethylene ribbon)	⎬ 210
Raphael	Proportional electric	⎭
Add-Mate	Adding machine	250
Divisumma 24	Calculating machine	15

Three other products were being produced in the United States in localities other than at Hartford. The Copia II copying machine was being manufactured on Long Island, office supplies were produced at Burlington, New Jersey, while the Programma 101 was scheduled for production at a fourth locality.

Plant

The Olivetti Underwood factory, located in Hartford, Connecticut, was still referred to by the locals as the "Underwood plant." The factory was a six-story, old brick building dominated by two large chimneys, both of which had the word "Underwood" set into the surface with multicolored stone. As one walked alongside the factory building past the open first-floor windows one could see a great variety of machine tools in operation. The average age of the machine tools in the factory was around 18 years.

The building was large by any standards with a total floor area of 22 acres (i.e., 967,000 square feet). It was estimated that there was sufficient excess floor space to double at least the production of electric typewriters.

Production efficiency

The exterior appearance of the factory belied the operating efficiency of the manufacturing operation. The researchers were especially impressed by the automatic paint-spraying line, by the advanced "type" manufacturing department, and by the intricate system of overhead conveyors used in the assembly shops. These conveyors had been installed at a cost of nearly $400,000. These and other methods had served to bring the direct labor efficiency to a level that was basically comparable with Ivrea as measured by the number of hours required for a given output. However, the direct labor cost was 70%–80% higher than in Ivrea. In order to improve the overall efficiency as much as possible, a great deal of attention was being paid to reducing the overhead. Mr. Gandi, vice president in charge of coordinating engineering and production at the Olivetti Underwood plant, summarized the reasons why overall efficiency was high:

We worked hard to make the Hartford plant as efficient as possible. The main improvements can be summarized as follows:

We now have a much tighter control on indirect labor than in the past.

I think we are generally more conscious of cost in the United States than they are in Italy.

We have little R.&D. expenditure to support here.

We gave the old Underwood a chance to survive rather than to die. The workers realized this and consequently there is quite an incentive to produce.

In the United States the workers are used to producing at a steady pace throughout the day. However, in Italy the Latin temperament favors very high output in the first hours of the morning and the afternoon followed by a considerable slackening in the rate once the quota has been achieved. On incentive jobs here, the assembly workers achieve an average of 125% of standard while those in manufacturing usually achieve at least 135%–140% of their standard. Thus our overall *costs* are only running 25%–30% higher than would be the case in Italy for the manufacture of a similar product.

Labor

The work force in August 1966 stood at a level of 2,214 people of whom 1,867 were paid by the hour and 347 were on a salary. Women employees accounted for 850 of the total. The average wage paid in the factory was $2.58 per hour, but the cost to Olivetti Underwood after including all fringe benefits was $3.09 per hour [1,930 lire]. The average length of service for all employees was somewhere between 12–15 years while their average age was 50 years. Over 120 people qualified for a four-week vacation in 1966—a privilege accorded only to employees with more than 25 years of service.

The availability of labor in the area was a most serious and acute problem. Underwood had difficulty in obtaining the type and quality of labor that it required and this was reflected in the labor turnover figures which were running as high as 25%–30% a year. At the time the researchers visited the plant, the company was short of 69 hourly and 32 salaried personnel. This dearth of labor was largely accounted for by the expansion plans of a local aircraft engine manufacturer which was following a policy of hiring 1,500 new people a month. This firm had been somewhat successful in its efforts owing to the higher wage rates it was able to offer. (Olivetti Underwood's rates were considered as about average for the areas.) Another large local employer was the Royal typewriter plant which had a work force of 3,900. This plant was situated about two miles from Olivetti Underwood's factory and there was a considerable interchange of personnel between the two companies. Absenteeism at Olivetti Underwood was very low, being in the vicinity of only 4% per year.

The workers were represented by two unions and the labor contract was renegotiated every two years. Although Olivetti Underwood provided fringe benefits that were comparable with those for the majority of employers in the area, nothing similar to the social services provided in Ivrea was required in Hartford.

Olivetti Underwood had discontinued the old Underwood policy of increasing and reducing the production work force as sales requirements fluctuated. After an initial reduction in work force from 2,400 to 1,800 following the Olivetti takeover, the policy had been to maintain a stable production rate with no, or an absolute minimum of, layoffs. This policy had reportedly gone a long way in cementing employer-employee relations.

Olivetti Underwood was fulfilling an important role for the parent company by serving as the latter's eyes and ears in the American industrial scene. Because the United States was at the forefront of industrial technology, it was very common for engineers from Ivrea to visit Hartford and spend weeks or months investigating a new process or method of manufacture. Upward of 15 engineers a year had come from Ivrea to spend between three months to three years on a specialized problem. Mr. Gandi saw this exchange of personnel assuming even greater importance in the future. In fact the "Olivetti Technical Center in the U.S.A.," had recently been set up under Mr. Gandi's leadership to further this aspect of Olivetti's move toward multinationality.

When questioned about the major problems facing him, the factory manager replied:

Undoubtedly our major problem is a shortage of labor. It is almost impossible to get the type of labor we require and consequently we have to spend a good deal of our waking hours trying to ensure that the work force is maintained. A second problem is to update our aging machine tools. And I suppose a third problem would be to keep our sights realistically set on the life of the product we manufacture. The average life of a business electric typewriter runs around eight years, mainly because of style changes and the secretary getting tired of using the same machine. Most typewriters, however, will last for over 30 years and consequently we are probably engineering in too much life that will never be used. This is one area that might, over the long term, provide some really worthwhile cost savings.

THE LATIN AMERICAN FACTORIES

The four Latin American factories were located in Bogotá, Colombia; Buenos Aires, Argentina; Mexico City, Mexico; and São Paulo, Brazil. The table on page 979 shows some relevant product line and production data for each operation.

Olivetti's problem in Latin America was to allocate production between the factories so that, as the tariff barriers between LAFTA countries (see Appendix B) disappeared, the company would be in an advantageous position to derive the benefits of large-scale manufacture. In 1966 the company still made the standard manual typewriter in all countries and, although in the past this had been an older model than that produced in Ivrea, there was now a growing tendency for all subsidiaries to produce the latest model machine.

The need to keep the standard typewriter as the backbone of production was largely dictated by the local governmental authorities. This machine was the most popular for use in government offices. Further, if it were made within

LATIN AMERICAN FACTORIES

Factory	Products	Work-shop	Assem-bly	Number of Personnel	Cost Per Sq. Meter of Floor Space (Lire)	Absenteeism	Personnel Turnover	Year Factory Started
Bogotá	Diaspron		x					
	Lettera		x					
	Studio		x					
	Quanta		x	25	rented	9%	5%	1960
	Prima		x					
	Electro-summa		x					
Buenos Aires	Lexikon	x	x					
	Divisumma	x	x					
	Prima	x	x					
	Quanta	x	x	950	50.000	10%	6%	1951
	Electro-summa	x	x					
	Multisumma	x	x					
São Paulo	Lexikon	x	x					
	Studio	x*	x					
	Lettera	x	x	920	45.000	9%	12%	1955
	Prima		x					
	Quanta		x					
	Tekne	x*						
Mexico City	Diaspron	x*	x					
	Lettera	x*	x	526	rented	11%	10%	1963
	Studio	x*	x					
	Prima		x					

*Workshop production is only partial.
Source: Company records.

the country then a large portion of foreign exchange that would otherwise be used on typewriter imports could be saved. Olivetti executives believed the manufacture of this basic model in each area was necessary for the successful negotiation of any complementation agreement. (See Appendix B for an explanation of this term.)

A quotation from *Business International* regarding Olivetti's manufacturing plans in Latin America read as follows:

> Italy's Olivetti has also organized its production in the light of regional integration. It has manufacturing operations in São Paulo, Buenos Aires, and to lesser degree Mexico, plus assembly operations in Chile. Components for the Mexican and Chilean facilities are mainly sourced in Brazil and Argentina for some products, and from the parent in Italy for others. Specializing its plant in Buenos Aires to produce adding machines and the one in São Paulo to make electric and portable typewriters in order to interchange components allows Olivetti to achieve 100% LAFTA content and rationalize production in pace with LAFTA's goals. Both of these factories produce manual typewriters, too, and together they supply the Uruguayan market.[5]

In many ways the problems of specializing production in South America were similar to the problems the company faced on a worldwide basis. Although in this case the plan had to be internally consistent with both LAFTA's goals and with the overall pattern of Olivetti's decentralization policy.

One executive of the company believed that Latin America was the key to Olivetti's production problem. He reasoned that the real nature of the cost-price squeeze being experienced in Italy was simply a repetition of the disease that had struck the U.S. typewriter companies in the late 1950's, i.e., that at some stage in the development of a country, wages rise to the point where particular industries are no longer able to compete with producers in the less developed countries on a worldwide basis. Manufacturers of typewriters and office machines, being heavily dependent on labor, were particularly vulnerable to this sort of development. Thus, he argued, to gain the maximum long-term benefit from any production specialization plan the company should look well into the future and select the country or countries where labor costs would remain lower, on an absolute basis, than in most others. This criterion, plus an allowance for the costs incurred in transporting finished products to the market, would decide the optimum strategy that Olivetti should pursue to ensure the maximum long-run advantage over its competitors. He believed that the Latin American countries might prove to be such an area of long-run advantage.

APPENDIX A

A TECHNIQUE FOR LOCATING NEW PRODUCTION FACILITIES

The following notes describe a technique that Dr. Momigliano, who was in charge of Olivetti's economic studies, used for choosing a new factory site in

---

[5]Business International Research Report, "LAFTA Key to Latin America's 200 Million Consumers," *Business International*, 1966 (New York), p. 52.

Italy. He felt, however, that with minor modifications it might be a suitable approach to determining how to specialize production on a worldwide basis.

The main differences between this study and what we would do for foreign subsidiaries is to include factors relating to governmental policies in other countries, tariffs, customs regulations, and export incentives. What we try to do in all cases is to have the most efficient production possible, make the best utilization of the available work force, and ensure a reasonable profit. The minimum profit we accept is a little greater than the percentage interest on the capital invested. With these criteria in mind we consider the following variables:

1. *a*) Distances from the main factories and from the major markets. In Italy we measure the distance of the factory from the geographical center of the country to establish the market distance. For the rest of Europe the distance is from the factory to the border of entry of the appropriate country. For overseas countries the market distance is from the Italian port to the port of entry.

 b) The distance that the average worker has to travel to the factory. This should not be more than one hour when public transport is used.

 c) Distance from Ivrea.

 d) Distance from the administrative center of Italy, i.e., Rome.

2. The cost of money for the potential plant sites. This is important in Italy because the government gives special interest rates in different areas.

3. Land cost.

4. The availability of land.

5. The transfer cost, i.e., the cost of moving from one factory to another and the cost of lost production if any.

6. The availability of electricity and/or gas.

7. The availability of workers. We construct a demographic survey which predicts movements over the next 20 years.

8. The local wage scale for skilled and common workers.

9. The cost of transferring skilled workers (if necessary).

10. The availability of local public facilities, such as hospitals, public offices, communication facilities, etc.

11. Fiscal advantages, such as tax concessions, export incentives, etc.

12. The feeling of people in the area toward the establishment of a new factory—political and social implications.

For each of these variables we determine a weighting factor either directly, or, in the case of qualitative factors, by estimation. We then form a matrix with the possible localities running horizontally and variables running vertically.

In one study we had 44 variables and 7 regions with 3 to 4 subdivisions in each region. We did the survey for 3 products and made a comparison with Ivrea as a base. The best region had the following advantages over Ivrea by product type.

Portable typewriter 3%
Standard typewriter 6%
Adding and multiplying machines 11%

These results show that the type of machine to be transferred is a critical factor. This is because the fiscal advantages (item 11 above) usually favor the product requiring the greatest capital investment. Of course we take great care to ensure we allow for the percentage advantage over time. For instance, after, say, 10 years any fiscal advantages or protection could disappear thus entirely reversing the original advantages. This must be allowed for.

APPENDIX B

LATIN AMERICAN FREE TRADE ASSOCIATION (LAFTA)

The Latin American Free Trade Association (LAFTA) was formed by nine countries—Argentina, Brazil, Chile, Colombia, Ecuador, Mexico, Paraguay, Peru and Uruguay—which signed and ratified the Treaty of Montevideo on February 18, 1960. The treaty became effective on June 1, 1961. In 1965 Venezuela announced its intention to join the association and actually ratified the treaty in 1966.

The original treaty was not aimed at providing a fully integrated market; rather its objective was to provide free intra-LAFTA trade on "substantially all" goods by 1973. The wording "substantially all" was generally felt to mean about 80% of the internal LAFTA trade. In December 1964, an unofficial conference of Latin American parliamentarians from thirteen countries resolved to "create a unicameral organ to be called Latin American Parliament, which will be established in the city of Lima, Peru, on July 2, 1965." Along with the attempts at economic integration there was a growing feeling that some form of political integration could also prove to be both realizable and worthwhile.

The Montevideo Treaty provided a complex set of measures aimed at reducing tariffs, but basically there were three different techniques that formed the nucleus of tariff cutting.

1. The first method included all the reductions in tariffs or taxes on a list of products that were made by a member country each year. These cuts were added to the concessions previously granted to make up each member's *national list*.
2. The second approach was by way of the *common list*. This list included the goods that all members agreed to include in their national lists by 1973. The consensus on which goods to include was determined by negotiation every three years. Over the 12-year period to 1973 there was time for four such meetings, so each meeting was bent on adding to the *common list* 25% of the products that make up intra-LAFTA trade. The first meeting in 1964 satisfied this requirement.
3. The third and final means used for tariff reduction was by means of *complementation* agreements. In this instance, two or more countries got together to give equal concessions to each other on a product or industry basis.

Two examples had been accomplished and many more were in the formulation stage. The first example was pioneered by IBM World Trade and involved the elimination of duties on data processing machines using punched cards. The countries involved were Argentina, Brazil, Chile, and Uruguay. The firm suggested to the respective governments that if such duties were mutually eliminated, IBM would build plants in Brazil and Argentina and arrange for another U.S. firm to license a Chilean paper producer to manufacture the card stock needed by the machines. By this means IBM was able to ensure that a large enough sales market was established to make manufacturing worthwhile. The other example of a complementation agreement was arranged with Argentina, Brazil, Chile, Mexico, and Uruguay and involved electric tubes used in radio and TV equipment. This agreement provided sizable markets for companies like RCA and Philips of Holland. Meetings aimed at exploring the possibility of complementation agreements for office equipment were held in 1964.

Some selected statistics regarding the growth of LAFTA and the 1966 tariffs on office equipment follow:

1. General Statistics (LAFTA).

	Population (Millions)	Increase %	GNP ($ Billions)	Increase over Preceding 5 years %
1962	176	—	46	+28
1964	187	+6	69	+64

2. Trade *between* LAFTA countries.

	1960	1961	1962 ($ Millions)	1963	1964
Imports	375	359	420	525	646
Exports	340	299	354	425	558

3. Representative office equipment tariffs (1966) per cents.

	Internal LAFTA Tariff %*	Tariff from Sources External to LAFTA — %
Argentina:		
Electric typewriters	30.0	50.0
Manual typewriters	42.0	175.0
Electric adding machines	25.0	175.0
Brazil:		
Electric typewriters	30.0	40.0
Manual typewriters	38.0	80.0
Electric adding machines	10.0	30.0
Chile:		
Electric typewriters	45.0	200.0†
Manual typewriters	45.0	200.0†
Electric adding machines	40.0	200.0†
Paraguay:		
Manual typewriters	25.5	66.5†
Electric adding machines	30.5	66.0†
Peru:		
Electric accounting machines	20.0	30.0
Uruguay:		
Electric typewriters	90.0†	105.0†
Manual typewriters	16.0†	105.0†
Electric adding machines	26.0†	105.0†
Electric calculators	26.0†	105.0†
Electric accounting machines	46.0†	105.0†

*These percentages do not include port improvement duties, consular fees, or taxes based on gross weight (where applicable).

†These tariff percentages are in addition to certain nontariff charges such as prior deposits. Prior deposits may range up to 200% depending on the country and the product category.

Source: Company records.

ING. C. OLIVETTI & C., S.p.A. (D)*

On February 16, 1966, the executives of Olivetti received copies of a memo announcing a change in the organization structure. This was the second major change in organizational structure since Dr. Aurelio Peccei had assumed the managing director's post in May 1964. The previous organization, instituted in November 1964, had been on the basis of product divisions. This latest reorganization brought the company back to a functionally organized pattern.

The problem of organizational structure was one of the most difficult which the Olivetti Company had to face. Dr. Peccei had declared, "We must rationalize our organizational structure. . . . Olivetti grew rapidly during the '50s and early '60s. It was haphazard growth which affected our structure and our personnel. Now we must develop a structure which will aid us in meeting our commitments."

Dr. Roberto Olivetti made a comment appropriate to this problem. "Our rate of expansion was perhaps too great. The organization grew while it was using procedures which were based on the requirements of a much smaller company and in many ways it was unprepared to shoulder the weight of the problems which it has to face." As of July 1966, no further changes had been made in the organization, but Dr. Peccei made it clear in interviews that he was interested in innovations which would make more effective use of the managerial talent. He said, "When I arrived I found that we had good men who were being poorly used."

The history of the organizational structure was a difficult factor which Dr. Peccei had to consider in his reorganization plans. *Business Week* said of that history:

For nearly three decades, the office machine producer grew almost as an extension of his [Adriano Olivetti's] personality. It was organized along vague functional lines, all running to the boss. He managed Olivetti on a face-to-face basis. Every product color, every advertisement bore the stamp of his personal approval.

"An unpredictable genius" is the way one company veteran remembers the ex-chief. But it was a genius that won a following. His staff was charged with a loyalty amounting almost to reverence.

This created an exhilarating atmosphere to work in, but more important, the atmosphere was effective. Situated in a country whose industrialization lagged behind most of Western Europe, Olivetti was a world leader.[1]

Adriano Olivetti stressed mobility of the executives. He expected the executives he hired to be able to assume many functional roles. He also placed a great deal of emphasis on getting intelligent young men and giving them wide latitude within a framework of broad guidelines and careful supervision. One of the positions most important in the training of these men was director of personnel. Seven of the executives who reported directly to Dr. Peccei or who were presidents of important subsidiaries had occupied that position. Although Adriano Olivetti "let you know which decisions had to be brought to him and which you could make yourself," there was never a clear and permanent organizational structure under his leadership.

Roberto Olivetti, Adriano's son, spoke of his father's business goals and organizational methods as follows:

He was totally committed to this company and the growth of this company. When my father took power in the company he started to apply Taylor's concepts of scientific management to our manufacturing process. He started to experiment in various ways. My grandfather did not particularly want to make the company grow. While he was away for his health, Adriano and some of the other young men in the company built a new plant with their own money. It was hard for Adriano to bring change to the company, but he succeeded.

He was a manager of great energy, capability, and talent. As a leader of the organization he used basically two tools: his personnel policy and the informality of his communication and organization methods. His great personal concern was the problem of hiring the right people. He personally interviewed the majority of the people who are now executives.

He felt that if something was going wrong in the organization, the man responsible should be able to deal successfully with it or else he should be replaced. He felt that it was men, not organizations and structure which solved problems. He therefore relied heavily on his ability to judge character and to inspire people to do their best.

His organization was informal. There were no regular meetings. Whenever an important decision was to be made, he called the people in whom he had faith. He surrounded himself with very intelligent people and listened to their judgment. He was constantly concerned with the development of managers. He was constantly involved in helping the younger executives to prepare for future positions. The top two levels of the organization were in constant contact with him. Everyone knew his ideas and goals. He had a strong, forceful personality which helped him to sell the others on his goals.

He never really understood or cared for the accounting system. He had a sense for profit and his ideas made money, but he didn't rely on the formal accounting system to help him make his judgments. He left the finance and control work to Dr. Pero.

When Adriano Olivetti died in 1960, Dr. Giuseppe Pero became both

---

[1]Quoted from the November 20, 1965, issue of *Business Week* by special permission. Copyrighted © 1965 by McGraw-Hill, Inc.

president and managing director. Under Adriano, Dr. Pero had served as a mediator regarding finances between Adriano and the other members of the family. While Dr. Pero was managing director, the company retained a functional organization. All of the functional units reported directly to him. (See Exhibit 1 for a partial organization chart for 1960–1963.) From early 1963 until his death, Dr. Pero retained the presidency but there was a triple managing directorship in which Roberto Olivetti and Camillo Olivetti (his cousin) shared the position with Dr. Pero. The operating organization beneath the top level remained relatively unaffected. (See Exhibit 2 for a partial organization chart for 1963.)

Exhibit 1

PARTIAL ORGANIZATION CHART, 1960–1963

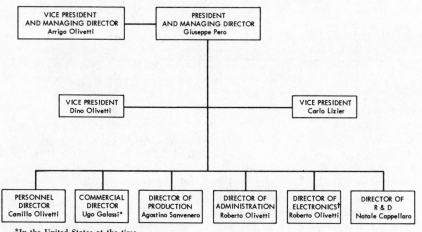

*In the United States at the time.
†After November 9, 1961.
Source: Company records.

After the crisis following Dr. Pero's death, Dr. Peccei came to the company as managing director in May of 1964. He set as his first goal the gaining of an understanding of the organization. By November he was ready to act. He said, "I detected a crystallization of old patterns. Too much thought was given to the questions of how to present the facts and to whom they should be presented. I thought that new emphasis had to be given to the facts themselves." He went on to say, "New ideas were being held down by old habits which had to be broken. Too many people were living with the experiences of the past, assuming that the old solutions could be put to use on our current problems. . . . Of course, many of the ideas and relationships which were cherished were still good and applicable, but not for long."

The reorganization was announced on November 11, 1964. (A copy of the memo concerning the change is included as Exhibit 3.) The new organization had two basic sections: operating divisions and staff groups.

Exhibit 2

PARTIAL ORGANIZATION CHART, 1963

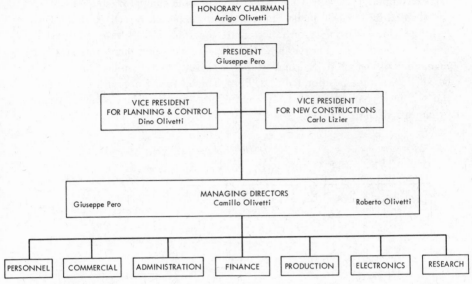

Source: Company records.

The operating divisions were:

1. The office machine group (Dr. Ugo Galassi)—This group had responsibility for all research and development, production, and selling in Italy of typewriters, mechanical-calculating machines and office furniture. In addition, this group was responsible for the sales of accounting machines which were not linked into a system. Under this office was included responsibility for export sales and for certain administrative functions.

2. The Systems Division (Dr. Roberto Olivetti)—This group was responsible for research and development, production, and sales of accounting machines, teleprinters, data transmission systems, and any other new electronic device which was developed.

3. The Division of Foreign Industrial Subsidiaries (Dr. Aurelio Peccei)—This group was held responsible for the operations of the six subsidiaries outside of Italy which had production facilities. These were the subsidiaries in Britain, Spain, Argentina, Brazil, Mexico, and the United States.

4. The Machine-Tool Division (Ing. Ezio Testore)—This division assumed responsibility for the development, manufacture, and sale of machine tools and associated numerical-control devices.

5. Italian noncommercial subsidiaries—This division was responsible for the management of units such as the employee housing and other nonbusiness ventures into which the company had entered under Adriano Olivetti.

The staff functions which reported to Dr. Peccei were:

1. Research and Development   (Natale Cappellaro)
2. Administration   (Camillo Prelle)
3. Finance   (Gian Antonio Brioschi)
4. Industrial Relations   (Rigo Innocenti)
5. Advertising and Press   (Ricardo Musatti)
6. Office of International Relations   (Paolo Rogers)
7. Service and Technical Assistance
   to Customers   (Giovanni Giovannozzi)
8. Purchasing   (Bruno Jarach)
9. Plant Construction   (Massimo Castellani Longo)
10. Central Research Laboratory   (Oddino Mavitano)
11. Product Planning   (Elserino Piol)
12. Economic and Planning Studies   (Franco Momigliano)

As in the past the new organization included a management committee composed of the director of research and development, the director of the office machines division, the director of industrial relations, the director of the systems division, the administrative director, the director of production (office machines division), the director of export sales, the assistant to the managing director and the director of finance. (See Exhibit 4 for an organization chart.)

Between November 1964 and February 1966 several changes took place in top management personnel assignments. Among these were the appointment of Dr. Gabetti as president of Olivetti Underwood, the appointment of Ing. Berla as general manager of Hispano Olivetti, and the initiation of a marketing function under Sig. Elserino Piol.

Looking back on the divisional organization, one company executive stated:

We started to implement the new structure at the operating level in Italy by creating separate systems-oriented branches. But we realized that in most markets we did not have the volume potential to justify creating separate branches. In these markets, the idea was to have a local specialist in systems reporting to the branch manager and also reporting to the systems division in Ivrea. This meant he would have two bosses, which would make things difficult. We didn't get far in implementing the new structure due to this difficulty. Also, we didn't want to limit the opportunities of our regular salesmen to progress to selling the more sophisticated equipment. A wide and clean separation of systems salesmen from regular salesmen would have done this.

The divisional organization lasted for 15 months. According to Dr. Peccei, it accomplished its primary goal of breaking up the old patterns which existed in the organization. However, as a whole, it was not judged to be successful. Dr. Peccei gave his views of the reasons for its lack of success as follows:

After the old patterns were broken, new problems became apparent. First, our policy of constant employment made it difficult to give the desired degree of autonomy to the two divisions (Systems and Office Machine). We couldn't change the work forces independently, and the divisions had to depend on each other for centralized services. Second, management had not yet learned to assume responsibility. There was still a tendency towards allowing decisions to be made centrally. The third basic reason for lack of success in a divisional operation was that we could not make a complete change. We could not organize divisionally in all of the countries in which we operate. And if we cannot organize on a divisional basis throughout our organization, then having that pattern in the home office has lost some of its meaning. Fourth, there was a gross imbalance between the Systems and Office Machine Divisions in terms of revenue. The Systems Division couldn't produce the current revenue to support a massive research program, yet it was from the Systems group of products that we expected our future growth to come. This imbalance made it difficult for the Systems Division personnel to make a claim for present resources which would be representative of their future importance.

With all of these factors facing us, we felt it was better to return to the functional organization structure.

On February 16, 1966, a new organizational structure was announced. This structure brought about a partial return to the functional departments which had existed prior to the 1964 reorganization. (A copy of the memo announcing the change is included as Exhibit 5 at the end of the case.) Among the reasons given in the text of the memo for the change were the problems of new product introduction, the need for better information systems, and the need for developing better budgets and operating plans.

The organization was again divided into operating divisions and staff functions. Under the new plan, the operating divisions were:

1. Research and Development Division (Roberto Olivetti)—This division had responsibility for initiating work on new products and for coordinating the information flow dealing with new technology and new products and production techniques. Under this division were separate groups responsible for each of the general types of products manufactured by the company. For example there were separate R.&D. project offices for electric typewriters and for manual typewriters, et cetera.
2. Production Division (Ugo Galassi)—This division was responsible for all production in Italy and for aiding the Division of Industrial Subsidiaries in the accomplishment of production programs which were interdependent with the Italian factories. Under the director of this division were some functional staff members such as a director of methods study, a director of production engineering, a director of industrial administration, et cetera. Also reporting to the director of the division were plant managers who were independently responsible for a budgeted production program.
3. Commercial Division (Aurelio Peccei)—This group had responsibility for commercial policy, for the sale of products, and for technical assistance. Under this division were staff functions such as marketing services, personnel service, and service and technical assistance to customers. Also in this group were the Italian commercial subsidiary, the export sales group, and the Secretary for Collaboration and International Development.
4. Foreign Industrial Subsidiaries Division (Nicola Tufarelli)—This group was responsible for coordinating the activities of those subsidiaries which have manufacturing facilities.

5. Machine Tool Division (Ezio Testore).

The corporate staff functions reporting to Dr. Peccei were:

1. Economic Studies and Planning	(Franco Momigliano)
2. Product Planning	(Elserino Piol)
3. Administrative Office	(Camillo Prelle)
4. Financial Office	(Gian Antonio Brioschi)
5. Office of Industrial Relations	(Rigo Innocenti)
6. Noncommercial Italian Subsidiaries	(Mario Caglieris)
7. Office of Advertising and Press	(Renzo Zorzi)
8. Office for International Relations	(Paolo Rogers)
9. Legal Office	(Piera Rosiello)

In addition there were various special consultants to the managing director dealing with such areas as copying machines and related products, industrial properties, and product quality. Also the coordinating committees which had been established under the previous organization continued in existence. (The organization chart as of June 1966 is shown in Exhibit 6 at the end of the case.)

Dr. Peccei commented on his current views on the problem of organization as follows:

I believe that a company having the characteristics of Olivetti (international, diversified, in a highly dynamic sector, with a strong sales organization) should set itself an organization pattern along these lines:

A number of Technical Divisions, responsible for Research and Development and manufacturing (in Italy and other countries) for each fairly homogeneous family of products (e.g., portable typewriters, professional typewriters, electro-mechanical calculators, electronic calculators and related products, accounting machines, teleprinters, copying and duplicating machines, peripheral equipment, and numerical control machine toools) ;

A worldwide marketing and sales organization;

A central nucleus of corporate functions, such as Long-Range Planning, Product Planning, Treasurer, Comptroller, Personnel Policy (including top personnel recruiting and administration and some of the information functions), International Relations.

An attempt towards this setup was made in 1964 but it was premature, as already stated.

A much deeper preparation was necessary *within the existing system* in order, before changing it, to achieve:

A better definition of the entire product line (especially with regard to new products) ;

A rationalization of manufacturing activities among the various industrial centers in Italy and abroad;

A more efficient accounting and data-processing system, and financial budgeting system;

A more complete preparation of the entire management in these new concepts.

Therefore a more conventional organization setup was decided upon again in February 1966, as an interim measure for the expected duration of the intermediate three-year period 1966–68 during which time reorganization studies and all other necessary preparations will be completed.

Exhibit 3

ING. C. OLIVETTI & C., S.p.A.
Memo Concerning Organizational Changes, 1964

November 11, 1964

To All Executives:

At the request of the managing director, the executive committee* has decided to effect a transformation of the organizationl structure of the company, to bring about a definite assignment of responsibility, and to arrange the necessary coordination of the management of the firm.

To that end, starting November 1, 1964, the various management activities will be regrouped and articulated in central staff functions and in operating divisions reporting directly to the managing director. The divisions and services are as follows:

I. Management Committee

This group will be called together periodically by the managing director in order to obtain its assistance in examining problems which are of general management interest.

It will include:

Ing. Natale Cappellaro in his position as general consultant on new Research and Development.

Dr. Ugo Galassi, in his position as Director of the Office Machine Division.

Sig. Rigo Innocenti in his position as Director of Industrial Relations.

Dr. Roberto Olivetti in his position as Director of the Systems Division.

Dr. Camillo Prelle in his position as Administrative Director.

Ing. Agostino Sanvenero, in his position as Assistant to the Managing Director for Production.

Sig. Guido Treves, in his position as Director of Export Sales.

Ing. Nicola Tufarelli in his position as Assistant to the Managing Director.

Avv. Gian Antonio Brioschi will function as secretary of this committee.

II. Operating Divisions

1. Office Machine Division, reporting to Dr. Ugo Galassi with responsibility for the planning, producing and selling of typewriters, mechanical calculating machines, and office furniture. Also, the commercial organization which is directly responsible to this division will be responsible for the sales of accounting machines which are not part of an integrated system.

The division will have the following organizational structure:

a) Research & Development Project group under the supervision of Ing. Natale Capellaro composed of:

R.&.D. Project office for calculating machines and writing apparatus under the direction of Sig. Teresio Gassino on whom also depends the project office for accounting machines and special apparatus which are a part of the Systems Division.

R.&D. Project office for electric typewriters.

R.&D. Project office for manual typewriters.

b) Director of Production—Ing. Agostino Sanvenero with responsibility for the management of the factories which make typewriters, adding machines, calculating machines and office furniture, as well as machine tools and special products. Foundries, sintering and technical service are the responsibility of the director of production of typewriters and calculating machines.

---

*Committee representing the Board of Directors, composed of Prof. Visentini, Dr. Peccei, Dr. Roberto Olivetti, and Dr. Silvio Borris.

Exhibit 3—Continued

c) Italian commercial sales will be the interim responsibility of Dr. Ugo Galassi.

d) Export sales under Guido Treves will be responsible for the commercial subsidiaries, the concessionaires abroad, the office of special affairs as well as the commercial activities of the industrial subsidiaries relative to the products fabricated by the Office Machine Division.

Also a part of this division are the following services:

Administrative service.

Personnel service.

2. Systems Division under Dr. Roberto Olivetti has the responsibility for planning, producing and selling accounting machines, teleprinters, systems for data transmission and all other apparatus both mechanical and electromechanical which are not a part of the Office Machine Division. The sales of these products, with the exception of those indicated in 1 for which the Office Machine Division will assume responsibility, will be the direct responsibility of this division. The Systems Division will organize these sales through an appropriate structure with the collaboration of the other divisions.

The division will assume the following organizational structure:

a) R.&D. Project group, with the supervision of Ing. Natale Cappellaro, composed of:

R.&D. Project office for teleprinters.

R.&D. Project office for telecommunication.

R.&D. Project office for electronic-mechanical devices.

R.&D. Project office for accounting machines and other special products.

b) Production group under Mario Merighi, with the responsibility for the factories producing accounting machines and teleprinters and for launching into production new products of this division.

c) Commercial group under Dr. Marcello Ceccoli, with the responsibility for the sale of products of the division with the exception of those products handled by other divisions as indicated beforehand. He will coordinate in all questions regarding these activities.

d) Center for Collaboration with Olivetti-General Electric under Ing. Fernando Grignolo will assume the responsibility of strengthening and supervising the operation of the technical and commercial accords with Olivetti-General Electric and with General Electric.

Ing. Adriano Sarti will assume the function of assistant to the director of the division.

Under the auspices of the division will be constituted the following services:

Administrative Service.

Personnel Service.

3. Division of Foreign Industrial Subsidiaries, held in the interim by Dr. Aurelio Peccei, to whom will report the following subsidiaries:

British Olivetti Ltd.

Hispano Olivetti S.A.

Olivetti Argentina S.A.

Olivetti Industrial S.A.

Olivetti Mexicana S.A.

Olivetti Underwood Corporation.

Under the auspices of this division will be constituted the following services:

Production Coordination.

Sales Coordination.

Administrative Control.

4. Machine Tool Division, under Ing. Ezio Testore, with the responsibility for planning, producing and selling machine tools and numerical controlled devices. The organizational structure of the division will be defined by a supplementary memo from the managing director.

Exhibit 3—Continued

   5. Italian noncommercial subsidiaries.

III. Central Staff

   1. R.&D. Planning Staff under Ing. Natale Cappellaro will be responsible for all projects related to new product planning and development.
   2. Administarative Department under Camillo Prelle will set standards and coordinate in matters of cost accounting and administration and with responsibility to arrange preparation of budgets, and other internal control documents and for the data processing center.
   3. Financial Department under Avv. Gian Antonio Brioschi.
   4. Personnel Management Relations Department under Rigo Innocenti, with the function of coordinating and standard setting for all which concerns personnel, internal relations and social services and with the responsibility for the management of the corresponding central services.
   5. Department of Advertising and Press under Ricardo Musatti will be responsible for coordinating the activities of publicity and industrial design.
   6. Department of International Relations—Dr. Paolo Rogers.
   7. Service and Technical Assistance to Customers—Ing. Giovannozzi.
   8. Purchasing Department under Bruno Jarach will be responsible for all inventories, warehouses, and purchasing.
   9. Director of Plant Construction.
   10. Central Research Laboratory.
   11. Department for Product Planning under Elserino Piol is responsible for studying the objectives and the optimal specifications for new products.
   12. Central Economic and Planning Studies under Dr. Franco Momigliano will be concerned with economic-commercial forecasts, market studies, and long- and medium-term corporate plans and coordination of annual operating plans.

Other features of the present organization structure which have not been specifically modified will remain unchanged.

The managing director will define as necessary, through internal memoranda, the development of the organization structure, operating procedures and the relationships between the operating divisions and the staff functions and the corresponding groups within divisions. Further memoranda will also define a regular schedule of coordinating meetings among various executives to control the execution of any particular program.

The executive committee trusts in the collaboration of all executives in helping to achieve efficient functioning of the new organizational structure.

Exhibit 4

ORGANIZATION CHART, NOVEMBER 11, 1964

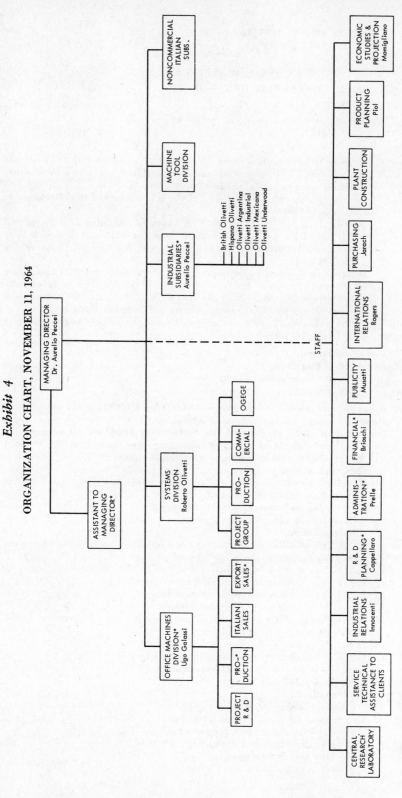

*Member of the Management Committee.
Source: Company records.

Exhibit 5

ING. C. OLIVETTI & C., S.p.A.
MEMO CONCERNING ORGANIZATIONAL CHANGES, 1966

Ivrea, February 16, 1966

From: The President
To: All Executives
Purpose:

> In order to advance in a rapid and coordinated fashion with the programs of developing and integrating new products into our line and in order to obtain more successful product introduction;
> In order to increase the efficiency of our production and to insure that our costs remain competitive;
> In order to attain tighter control over expenses and more effective annual and triennial budgets, correlating the pertinent summary data with their explanations by means of a study which will organize an integrated information system;
> In order to coordinate and improve our commercial activities responding to the requirements of the new products and at this time to bring forth a new perspective on work, it has been decided to change the organization structure announced in the memorandum of November 1964.

To this end, after February 21, 1966, the organization which reports to the managing director will be divided as follows:

I. Operating Divisions.
II. Corporate Staff Functions.
III. Consultative and Coordinating Committees.

I. Operating Divisions

1. Research and Development group—under the direction and entrusted to Roberto Olivetti, has the responsibility for research, for special projects, for the initiation of all products of this company in Italy and for coordinating these projects with all of our associated companies throughout the world.
The group will have the following organizational structure:
a) Personnel service.
b) Management control.
     Programming and related control.
     Formation and internal control of budgets.
     Organization and internal procedure.
     Normalization.
c) R.&D. Project office for calculating machines and other printing apparatus.
d) R.&D. Project office for electric typewriters.
e) R.&D. Project office for manual typewriters.
f) R.&D. Project office for mechanical teleprinters.
g) R.&D. Project office for telecommunication.
h) R.&D. Project office for electronic devices.
i) R.&D. Project office for accounting machines and special apparatus.
j) R.&D. Project office for furniture.
k) R.&D. Project office for metal furniture.
l) Office of technical projects for industrial design.
m) Department of Testing and Experimentation.
     Research laboratory service.
     Testing.
     Prototype and preproduction testing.
n) Direction of developmental coordination.
     Systems Division product development.
     Production engineering group.
     Machine tool development.
     Technical acquisitions.

Exhibit 5—Continued

In order to assure the successful launching of products coming from the Systems Division product development group, the factory at San Bernardo which is a part of the production group will suitably inform that office of progress. Insofar as that group is responsible for established programs of production, it will report to the production group under Ugo Galassi. Ing. Grignolo will assume the post of assistant to the director of the group, in particular to concern himself with tying in the efforts of this office with the associated companies abroad and with Olivetti-GE.

2. Production group, whose direction is the responsibility of Dr. Ugo Galassi. This group has the responsibility for production of the products in Italy and for assisting the Division of Industrial Subsidiaries in that which concerns the interdependent programs of production for the Italian factories and the foreign factories.

The group assumes the following organizational structure:

a) Personnel office.

b) Industrial Administration Service—has the duty of planning and accomplishing internal administrative control of the production operation and the formulation of budgets and the attendant consequences of that operation. Under this office is also the cost study service.

c) Organizational Procedures—has the task of developing, in coordination with the director of budgets and information, research and studies to balance the existing procedures with the requirements of the new structure and to determine optimal solution to some of the related organizational problems.

d) Director of Technical Acquisitions—concerns himself with acquiring that which others have produced which might be important to the production function.

e) Director of Planning, Methods and Testing has the task of programming and controlling production, of developing efficient productivity, of establishing standards and coordinating centrally the analogous activities of the other factories. This job includes the following activities:

Time and method studies.

Technical study of incentives and related problems in collaboration with the industrial relations director.

Control of advanced production.

Quality control.

Study of internal logistics and of industrial planning.

Reporting to this office is the raw materials and semifinished goods inventory director. This office shall prepare a study on the policies regarding raw material and semifinished goods.

f) Director of Production Engineering—has the task of developing and improving the technology and means of production, of improving machine tools and automated devices for improving efficiency, of establishing standards and achieving centralized coordination of analogous activities of the other factories. This position includes the following activities:

Updating and improving the work cycle.

Planning and construction of machines and apparatus for the optimization of production efficiency.

Planning and construction of electric and electronic apparatus for inclusion in the production process.

Maintenance and revision of production machinery.

g) Director of Plant Service.

h) Plant manager—calculators.

i) Plant manager—general parts.

j) Plant manager—special parts.

k) Plant manager—Scarmagno.

l) Plant manager—Aglie.

Exhibit 5—Continued

m) Plant manager—Massa.

n) Plant manager—Pozzuoli.

o) Plant manager—accounting machines.

3. Commercial Division—under the direction of the managing director, Dr. Aurelio Peccei. This group has the responsibility for commercial policy, for the sale of products and relevant technical assistance. This group will work in close collaboration with the Division of Foreign Industrial Subsidiaries.

The group will assume the following organizational structure:

a) Personnel service.

b) Marketing services—this group under Elserino Piol has the task of studying and recommending the commercial policy of the company in collaboration with the directors of other interested groups. Temporarily this will include the function of product planning. In particular this will include:

Defining the optimal specifications of products in relation to the company's objectives and the market conditions.

Studying the methods of sale in relation to the evolution of the commercial structure and the requirements for the introduction of new products into the market.

Strengthening the marketing activity by preparing sales material by class of product and by end application.

Strengthening the preparation of commercial personnel for new products and new sales techniques.

Strengthening the preparation of the clientele for new products.

This office will also have responsibility for sales of products which have not yet been released to our normal channels of distribution.

c) Service and Technical Assistance to Customers (STAC) has the task of studying and elaborating the policies of assistance to our customers in collaborating with other interested groups. In particular this group is responsible for:

Standards.

Technical and management training of the cadre of STAC.

Coordination of all training schools of STAC.

Study and development of operating techniques for our machines.

Assembly and timely distribution of technical bulletins to all who may be concerned.

Compilation of technical publications.

Management of spare parts inventories.

This group is functionally coordinated with STAC in the Division of Industrial Subsidiaries.

d) Italian commercial subsidiary—under the direction of Avv. Guido Lorenzotti, will function as an example of a commercial subsidiary engaged in sales in Italy. Except for functions and services offered at a corporate level, it will have its own administrative organization.

e) Foreign commercial subsidiaries—under Sig. Guido Treves will be responsible for sales subsidiaries and for relations with concessionaires. This office will have its own administrative service. It is charged with coordination with the Division of Foreign Industrial Subsidiaries in order to assure a coherent commercial policy for the entire organization abroad and particularly to insure the optimal employment of Italian production by the foreign industrial and commercial subsidiaries.

f) Secretary for Collaboration and International Development. This office is responsible for administering the implementation of the international agreements of which we are signers.

Administrative services for this group with the exception of the subsidiaries will be handled by the administrative secretary of the company.

4. Foreign Industrial Subsidiaries, under the direction of Nicola Tufarelli, to which will report the following subsidiaries:

Exhibit 5—Continued

British Olivetti Ltd.
Hispano Olivetti S.A. (Barcelona)
Olivetti Argentina S.A.
Olivetti Industrial S.A.
Olivetti Mexicana S.A.
Olivetti Underwood Corporation.

Under this division are constituted the following services:
a) Production Coordination Service.
b) Administration.
5. Machine Tool Division.

II. Corporate Staff

1. Economic study and planning, under Franco Momigliano with responsibility for:
   Economic studies.
   Prediction of market trends and quantitative analysis relative to our products.
   Market research.
   Elaboration of corporate programs for medium and long term.
   Supplying predictions for annual and triennial plans.
   Indications for optimum selection among corporate alternatives.
   This department is to assure coherence among the annual operating plans, the chosen alternatives and the approved medium- and long-term plans.

2. Department of Product Planning—see Marketing.

3. Administrative Department—this department retains its functions announced previously with the following additions:
   a) Administrative secretariat—which includes for the moment accounting and auditing.
   b) Director of Budgets and Information, under Dr. Giovanni Fei, with the responsibility for budgets and associated items, except for the subsidiaries; for setting standards; for collaborating in setting budgets; and for coordinating and controlling them. In this effort he is functionally responsible to the aforementioned administrative service.
   Also this director has the task of developing, availing himself of the collaborative efforts of other interested services, research and study of material on organizational structure and on the assembly and dissemination of information which is available within the organization.
   To this group report the central service for organization and the Data Processing Center.
   c) Director of Consolidation. This unit has the task of furnishing and formulating the balance sheet of ICO and of the other subsidiaries in order to arrive at a consolidated statement. It is responsible for providing the relevant standards.
   d) General Accounting Service, concerns itself with the actual operating accounts.
   On the administrative director depends functionally the administrative responsibility for the technical commercial group, the division of industrial subsidiaries and the Italian commercial subsidiary.

4. Financial Department, under the direction of Avv. Gian Antonio Brioschi.

5. Department of Industrial Relations, under Rigo Innocenti, has particular concern for the personnel services of the various groups and divisions and for the social services of the corporation.
   For the study of technical problems of standards for personnel, the department of corporate relations shall consult with the production group. [Also included in this office is the negotiation of labor contracts.]

6. Direction of noncommercial Italian subsidiaries.

7. Department of Advertising and Press, under Renzo Zorzi, is responsible for

Exhibit 5—Continued

coordination of publicity, printed matter and industrial design of the associated companies.

8. Department for International Relations, under Dr. Paolo Rogers.
9. Legal Department, under Piera Rosiello, supervised by Gian Antonio Brioschi.
   Special consultants to the managing director:

   Natale Cappellaro—special consultant to the managing director for new products.

   [Researcher's note: Ing. Cappellaro is the inventor of the Divisumma family of calculating machines.]

   Agostino Sanvenero—technical consultant on new factories and industrial properties.

   Umberto Montalenti—assistant to the managing director, president of S.A.D.A. [manufacturer of duplicating equipment] and coordinator of R.&D. purchase.

   Adriano Sarti has overall responsibility for developing Olivetti's position in the copying-machine market.

   Director of plant construction.

   Service for analysis of product quality.

III. Consulting and Coordinating Committees.

1. Management committee.
2. Other committees as defined by the managing director.

Exhibit 6

ORGANIZATION CHART, JUNE 1966

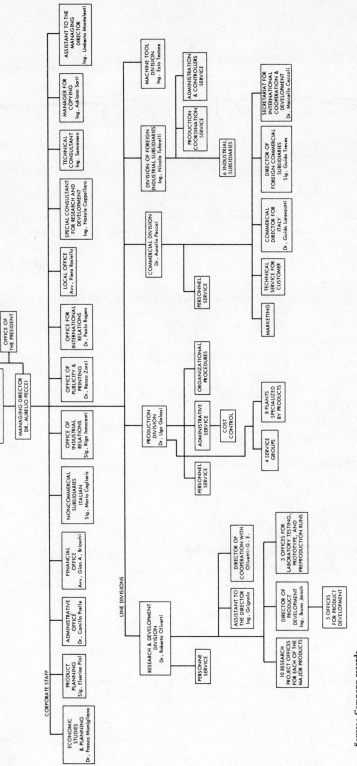

Source : **Company records.**

ING. C. OLIVETTI & C., S.p.A. (E–1)*

∧∧∧

"We must reshape our whole information and control system to provide more forceful management tools," stated Dr. Peccei in mid-1966. This case describes the company's management control policies, organization, and techniques, particularly those involving accounting and financial personnel.

ORGANIZATION FOR CONTROL

The responsibility for preparing the company's overall budget and analyzing its total performance rested with Dr. Prelle, director of administration. Dr. Prelle reported directly to Dr. Peccei, the company's managing director.

Each major department of the company had an administrative manager who prepared the budgets for his department as well as analyzed the results of operations. These administrative managers reported directly to their respective department heads. On budgetary and accounting matters, however, they had a functional responsibility to Dr. Prelle.

Administrative department

Dr. Prelle's accounting and control activities were divided into three areas: budgets and information under Dr. Giovanni Fei; general accounting under Dr. Dante Seta; and consolidations under Sig. Mario Caglieris.

The data processing department reported to Dr. Fei. This department, which worked three shifts, prepared, among other things, the daily production schedules, the purchase requisitions, the payroll, and various production and accounting records. Dr. Prelle's department included about 240 people distributed among the following activities: data processing and systems, 100 people; balance sheet accounts, 40 people; and, general accounting, 100 people.

Dr. Giovanni Fei prepared the Italian budget and analyzed the results of operations. In contrast, Sig. Caglieris was responsible for the preparation of the company's financial statements for tax, legal, and stockholder purposes. In addition, Sig. Caglieris was responsible for developing the consolidated financial statement, and, for that purpose, was developing accounting procedures to be followed by all the Italian and foreign subsidiaries. (See the Appendix for a discussion of changes which were occurring in internal and external reporting.)

Sig. Caglieris described the relationship between his and Dr. Fei's function as follows:

Dr. Giovanni Fei and I both report to Dr. Prelle. Dr. Fei is responsible for the analysis of and accounting for cost centers, which gets him involved in cost accounting and internal reporting problems. He talks to managers in terms of their function. Typically, these discussions are about procedures involving technical or economic considerations.

In contrast, I am concerned with external accounting reports. These especially involve tax and legal considerations. When I talk to a manager it is usually in reference to a particular account. Depreciation is a good example. I'll talk to the manager about depreciation on a piece of equipment for tax or public reporting purposes, whereas Dr. Fei will discuss depreciation in terms of making an economic appraisal of a cost center. . . . This is a typical structure for an Italian company.

Dr. Seta was responsible for general accounting services for the Italian company. Such services were highly centralized, including, for example, invoicing for the small- and medium-sized Italian branches. Complete centralization was not possible, however, because of the unreliability of the mail service and the data-phone transmission facilities. "Clearly, the trend in the company," stated Dr. Prelle, "is to centralize services, like accounting and data processing, and to decentralize decision making at the operating level."

Department directors and administrative managers

The director of each major department was responsible for controlling his own operations. To assist the directors in this work, each of the directors' staffs included an administrative manager responsible for the preparation of budgets and financial plans, and the analysis of operating results. Typically, the administrative manager's staff included no more than two people, himself and an assistant. According to one administrative manager:

The directors of the major departments—Export Sales, R.&D., etc.—all report directly to Dr. Peccei. Dr. Peccei holds each director responsible for his own operations. As a result, Dr. Prelle does not act directly as the controller of, say, Export Sales or any of the other major departments. . . .

Each subsidiary company had a controller. While nearly all the managers of the domestic and foreign subsidiaries were Italian, typically, the controllers of the overseas subsidiaries were natives of the local country. These controllers reported directly to the local manager of the subsidiary and functionally to Dr. Prelle.

Auditing and internal controls

As was the custom in Italy, the company did not use an independent accounting firm to audit its books. Under Italian law the company's stockholders appointed a three-man board of auditors. These men examined a copy of all the company's legally required books every three months, paying particular attention to the adequacy of the company's cash position. The board of auditors did not concern itself with internal controls and auditing.

The auditing of subsidiary companies was the responsibility of the respective administrative managers. According to one administrative manager:

Because of the limited size of my staff, I can not really audit on a continuing or even random basis the operations under my jurisdiction. Fortunately, at least in the past, the company doesn't seem to have required "heavy" auditing of its operations.

Whenever I visit a subsidiary I do my auditing mostly by selecting sample transactions in such areas as accounts receivable, stock records, and general procedures. This is generally a very quick review, however.

In the future I think the company will have an internal auditing staff working out of Ivrea. Dr. Prelle, of course, has always kept an eye on things personally. Now, he is starting to develop an audit program based on an internal auditing staff.

Overseas, our subsidiaries have public auditors who perform the standard audits required by local law or custom. Of course, whenever the administrative managers involved in overseas operations are overseas, they meet with these auditors and discuss the audit results.

BUDGET PREPARATION AND TIMETABLE

Between July and December 31 the budgets for the next operating year beginning January 1 were established. Depending on the nature of its operations, each department budgeted by month at least some of the following items: revenues, expenses, assets, liabilities, capital expenditures, cash receipts, cash disbursements, and sources of funds. The directors of the major departments prepared the budgets for their respective departments according to general guidelines set by Dr. Peccei. Dr. Prelle then took these budgets and prepared the overall company budget, which was submitted to Dr. Peccei and the board of directors.

In July, when preparation of the budgets began, Dr. Peccei communicated to all managers through their respective directors the general goals he hoped operations would achieve during the following year. During August, while on their vacations, managers were expected to consider how they could achieve these goals. Next, in September, a companywide sales budget was drawn up by the directors of sales. In addition, several alternative production budgets were prepared independently to the sales budget by the director of production. These budgets were then reviewed by Dr. Peccei, who selected the alternative production budget which, in his judgment, optimized the company's production and sales plans. Then, if necessary, the sales budget was revised and the directors of the other departments (R.&D., etc.) were informed as to whether or not their budgets were appropriate, given the selected production plan. It was anticipated that by October the overall company budget would be completed. By December 31 each department was expected to have established the details of its operating budget.

The budgets for the major subsidiaries were presented personally by each subsidiary's chief executive officer to the director at Ivrea who was responsible for the subsidiary. Unlike other subsidiary budgets, the Olivetti Underwood budget, because of the size of the subsidiary, was presented to Dr. Peccei in much the same fashion as were the department budgets.

All of the budgets were submitted in terms of local currency on standard forms with Italian captions. However, for the purpose of presenting consolidated budgets to Dr. Peccei, the individual budgets of the foreign-based companies were translated into lire.

The projected official rate of exchange during the budget period was used for translation purposes. This rate was applied to *all* income statement and balance sheet items, including beginning balances. Consequently, translation gains and losses were not calculated. Since Olivetti measured the overseas managers' performance in local currency and did not prepare consolidated statements, this particular translation procedure was considered adequate for budget presentation purposes.

Production budgets

Dr. Galassi, director of production, described the procedures followed by the production group in preparing their budget as follows:

Dr. Peccei has given me certain guidelines to follow. These include such directives as: increase productivity 30 per cent in the next three years. Then, there are some social constraints I must observe such as: it is not the policy of Italian companies—particularly Olivetti—to lay off workers. In addition, there are some operating facts I must accept. For example, it is impossible to improve efficiency in each plant at the same rate.

With these considerations in mind, in June, I ask the various plant managers to submit to me by mid-July their programs for improving output without increasing the work force.

From the plant managers' reports—plus my staff's thinking—we put together a number of alternative production plans. While I'm preparing my plans, the director of commercial sales in Italy, Dr. Lorenzotti, the director of export sales, Sig. Treves, and Ing. Tufarelli, the director of foreign industrial subsidiaries, are preparing their sales forecasts.

Then, in September, we have a meeting with Dr. Peccei at which the production and sales directors negotiate the production situation machine by machine. Dr. Peccei listens to our discussions and after studying the proposals he selects one of our alternative production budgets.

Fortunately, in recent years the production requests from the commercial group have matched our production plans very closely.

Once Dr. Peccei decides on the production plan, we then establish our production schedule purchases and shipments in detail for the next year by days and individual production centers. We also set up our detailed manning tables and maintenance schedules for the year. All of this planning is done by computer. By October 4 these detailed plans for the next year are completed.

Once we start producing according to this plan on January 1, we would generally need a lead time of about 6 months before we could make any significant changes in it. As a result, if sales dip below forecast, we are compelled to produce on plan with the output going to inventory.

Commercial budgets

Typically sales budgets were based on the sales estimates submitted by the various field managers. These estimates were influenced by general guidelines previously established by the directors of Italian sales, export sales, and foreign industrial subsidiaries.

The sales budgets submitted by the field managers were divided into two parts—projected sales revenues and the projected costs required to achieve this volume. The sales forecast was broken down by machines and by several types of customers, such as government, etc. The cost estimates were broken down by similar categories.

The reasonableness of the field managers' sales projection was tested against economic forecasts prepared by Dr. Momigliano, director of economic forecasting. Dr. Momigliano, through correlation and multiple regression analysis involving external and internal factors, had established demand models for Olivetti-type products for various countries and regions throughout the world.

OPERATING BUDGETS AND PERFORMANCE MEASUREMENT

For budgetary control purposes the Olivetti Company could be thought of as being divided into six major organizational groups: administrative, research and development, commercial sales (Italy), commercial sales (export), production (Italy), and industrial subsidiaries (overseas production subsidiaries). In general the performance of these groups was evaluated against their ability to meet budgeted results in the local currency. More specifically, the administrative and the research and development groups were evaluated as expense centers, that is, their performance was evaluated in terms of their ability to deliver their budgeted services at budgeted cost. Accomplishments of commercial sales groups, both Italian and overseas which bought from the Italian plants, were measured against budgeted sales and certain key operating ratios, such as the inventory-to-sales ratio. To the extent the overseas industrial subsidiaries imported products from Italy, they were judged in the same way as the commercial subsidiaries. However, since the production output of these particular subsidiaries created profits at the local level, the industrial subsidiaries were being increasingly regarded as profit centers.

Each month, Dr. Prelle prepared reports for Dr. Peccei comparing the total company's operating results to date with the budget and its various budget units. The format of these reports was the same as the budget format. Next, the various department directors met with Dr. Peccei to discuss their department's performance to date and their plans for the future. According to one department director:

Dr. Peccei looks closely at variances from budget. He regards meeting the budget as being very important.

Measurement of performance—production

The key measures of performance for the production group were number of workers, total output by machine-type, quality level achieved, and the so-called P/T efficiency ratio which measured labor efficiency. This efficiency ratio compared the actual time spent performing an operation with the established theoretical time for the job based on engineering studies. Dr. Galassi, director of the production department, described his method of evaluation as follows:

Every Friday at 5 p.m.—one hour after the last shift ends at 4 p.m.—I get a computer printout showing how production did during the week compared to the plan.

My production managers get similar printouts for their operations on Friday afternoon also. Then, after they have had the weekend to think things over, I discuss the prior week's results with them on Monday morning. . . . If I'm to achieve the goals Dr. Peccei has set for me—maintain quality, reduce costs and increase output—I've got to keep the pressure on my managers in the areas that are critical to success.

I look at three figures in particular—output by machines, number of workers, and the efficiency ratio. In trying to improve these factors we must be careful not to let our quality slip, so I pay close attention to quality levels also. If these are in line with the budget, then everything else is going to be all right. . . . Every worker knows the standard time for his job, whether he be a direct employee, an indirect employee, or a service employee making small tools, et cetera.

Looking to the future, Dr. Galassi planned to install a standard cost system. He said:

We have been very successful using the theoretical time measures in the past. However, we must now tie a cost in lire to these standards. Such economic data would be very useful for decision-making purposes.

However, we have a problem implementing this objective since we use 24,000 different parts, some of which involve four or five operations to make.

Despite these problems, we are moving ahead on preparing standard costs.

Measurement of performance—commercial

Commercial managers were judged principally in terms of their ability to increase their share of the markets they served while at the same time maintaining a certain level of local profit. The performance of the commercial operations was also measured against certain key target ratios established by the budget which varied from one situation to another according to the nature of the particular selling job to be done. These target ratios included discounts to list price, inventory to sales at list, accounts receivable to sales at list, and selling expenses to project sales at list price.

Measurement of performance—foreign industrial subsidiaries

It was difficult to compare production efficiency of the foreign industrial subsidiaries. The product mix was highly variable, the labor cost varied from about 75 cents (U.S.) per hour in Brazil to about $3 (U.S.) per hour in the United States and the production techniques differed slightly.

Given this situation, Ing. Tufarelli, Ivrea manager of foreign industrial subsidiaries, commented:

We haven't defined expected performance very scientifically. Also, we don't yet use standard reports and measurements. However, there are three main factors I look at: First, profitability related to investment; second, market share; and, third, the ability of managers to develop management among their subordinates. These are different objectives from those for the foreign commercial subsidiaries. They should seek sales volume at a minimum distribution cost.

The fact that foreign industrial subsidiaries also sell products imported from Ivrea complicates any attempt to use a return on investment measure because the total cost of goods sold is a combination of local manufacturing cost and cost of imports based on a transfer price.

Dr. Gabetti, manager of Olivetti Underwood, indicated that 40 per cent of his total sales came from U.S. production and the rest was imported at a transfer price. He explained, "We are dealing with a conglomerate profit, part based on transfer prices and part based on production cost. We estimate the two kinds of profit, but cost separation is difficult because the same salesman handles sales of both kinds of products."

Questioned about using rate-of-return analysis in economic studies, Dr. Momigliano, director of economic forecasting, replied:

We didn't use until recently a rate of return on projects. Up to now, as a matter of fact, the cost organization of our company did not allow a sufficiently precise method of allocating most expenses for research, development, design, engineering to the various models. By stimulation of Dr. Peccei, in the next months, special studies shall be made to achieve a more precise method of allocation, at least in the phase of planning and forecasting, of those expenses which were previously considered as general and indivisible and allocated as capital to the various models. The introduction of this methodology might also correspond in my opinion to the development of a new philosophy in the company somewhat superseding the old one, according to which the optimal criteria were directed above all to maximizing sales, revenues, and market shares, even if under the condition of a minimum rate of global return.

Asked if there was much variation—after adjustment—in return on investment between the six foreign industrial subsidiaries, Ing. Tufarelli answered:

For a number of years we had heavy investments in Brazil and Argentina in anticipation of the Latin American Free Trade Association (LAFTA) and we did not produce at capacity, which meant a low rate of return. Now we are near capacity and differences in return on investment between subsidiaries is due only to local conditions. Over the long run we expect the rate of return to level off everywhere at about the same figure.

Ing. Tufarelli explained which decisions were made locally and which in Ivrea. He said:

Local management decides anything related to presenting, receiving approval for, and carrying out the annual budget. This includes local borrowing, advertising, and sales campaigns. Within overall company guidelines local management determines its volume of production and the means of carrying this out. Local management consults Ivrea on increasing both short- and long-term debt and financial arrangements where the local currency is weak.

There was close communication between the industrial subsidiaries and Ing. Tufarelli particularly concerning the development of middle managers. According to Ing. Tufarelli, there was not very much interchange of non-Italian personnel between subsidiaries. Also, according to Ing. Tufarelli, none of the countries where the industrial subsidiaries operated had, as yet, sufficient management talent to send to other subsidiaries. In the future Ing. Tufarelli believed there might be more interchange, but so far the only two attempts made had failed because the managers' families had been unhappy with the move to a foreign country.

Foreign industrial subsidiary manager's point of view

The viewpoint of a foreign manager who dealt with Sig. Treves on questions of transfer price and Ing. Tufarelli on matters related to production outside of Italy was expressed by Dr. Gabetti, manager of Olivetti Underwood. Dr. Gabetti explained that in his view Olivetti followed a centralized financial strategy. For example, the parent company set the payment terms for products purchased from Ivrea. As a result, as Olivetti Underwood gained financial strength through the years of its development, its repayment period was reduced from 27 months to 6 months. On the other hand, Olivetti Underwood set its own inventory and accounts receivable levels.

The researcher stated to Dr. Gabetti that in Italy he had observed a philosophy of fixing the production schedule for the year and then mostly adhering to it even though the market might falter, and asked whether the U.S. production policy was the same. Dr. Gabetti explained, "Our orders to Italy are firm commitments. Any weakening of our market results in us having higher inventories, or we increase the discount to keep the inventory down. In the United States, production is more flexible. As the need arises, we switch from one product to another or, in extreme cases, we have the possibility of cutting back by laying off production personnel."

When Dr. Gabetti was asked how he felt the parent company should measure the foreign subsidiaries' financial performance, he answered, "We should be measured by relating current equity and net profit on sales, taking into account the transfer prices we have been assigned by Ivrea."

Return on investment as criterion for performance measurement

Avv. Brioschi, director of finance, was asked by the researcher if the company had ever considered using some form of return on investment as a criterion to measure the performance of managers. He replied:

In the past it was not a strict policy to make profits on our commercial subsidiaries. Forcing them to make a profit might have been considered an obstacle to growth.

A new policy is being developed to have the commercial subsidiaries make higher profits and to relate these profits to their capital. We must adopt a criterion of return on investment so that we can see when it is worthwhile to stop growth because of low marginal returns. This is particularly true in the case of the industrial subsidiaries, where we are increasing our investment in production facilities.

The old philosophy was that it was to our advantage to sell as much as possible. While higher sales increased distribution costs, it was assumed the greater volume would lead to more than proportional production economies. The argument ran that even if the commercial subsidiaries might at times lose money, we made profits in Ivrea, where our production facilities were located.

Unfortunately, this was not entirely true. Of course, we got economies of mass production, but only up to a point. We made many model changes and our product line proliferated. This cut down the length of production runs. Then, mass production also required more investment in production facilities. As a result, the old philosophy was based on assumptions which were not fully realized.

Financing sales growth in the office machine business is always a problem. Our method of distribution through hundreds and hundreds of branches in Italy and overseas ties up a tremendous amount of capital in inventories and accounts receivable. For every typewriter we sell we have to put four or five in customer hands for trial periods. Then, our subsidiaries did—and still do—buy from us on liberal credit terms. As a result, at certain times every lira of sales increase required a lira of additional investment. By pushing sales at almost any cost we exaggerated our capital problems.

APPENDIX

CHANGES IN INTERNAL AND EXTERNAL FINANCIAL REPORTING

In June 1966, the Ing. C. Olivetti & C., S.p.A. was in the process of preparing its first consolidated balance sheet and income statement. Previously, the parent company's investment in subsidiaries had been recorded on the parent's financial statements according to the cost method (i.e., all investments in subsidiaries were shown as assets on the parent's statements at their original costs, and income from subsidiaries was only recognized to the extent that dividends were received by the parent.

Typically, Italian companies reported their subsidiaries on a cost basis. Neither the tax nor stock exchange rules required full consolidation. Currently, the government was considering a law which would require parent companies to add to their annual reports the basic data about the balance sheets of their subsidiaries. The same law set up the possibility for the official Control Commission (Organo di Vigilanza) to require consolidated statements.

In February 1966, the consolidation department was established under the direction of Sig. Caglieris, who reported to Dr. Prelle, director of administration. According to Sig. Caglieris:

Prior to this year, the company had prepared consolidated sales and inventory figures only. The foreign figures were translated into lire using the exchange rate at the end of the accounting period. These consolidated figures were principally used internally, although the consolidated sales figure was included in our report to stockholders. Now we are planning to get the mechanism to prepare fully consolidated financial statements established by January 1967. Hopefully, we will be able to have our first fully consolidated statements in January 1968.

The main reason for preparing consolidated statements is that the Managing Director needs a uniform, reliable overall view of the company so that he can better appraise the contribution of each activity to the whole company. That is particularly important today because, as you know, our overseas production and sales are increasing.

Historically, each of our subsidiaries has maintained its books according to local tax or accounting practices. As you might well imagine, this has led to a great diversity of accounting practices. As a result, my first task has been to establish a set of uniform accounting definitions for consolidation purposes only. Now I will have to check these accounts with the headquarters and field people to see if they are feasible. At the same time my group and I are examining closely other problems about consolidation by stages as well as seeing what has been the experience of other companies, especially in the United States.

I think the report about consolidated statements will be prepared in three months. I plan to discuss each item with the administrative managers for the commercial and industrial subsidiaries and then to submit it to Dr. Prelle. Next Dr. Prelle will bring the report to Dr. Peccei with our recommended consolidation policy for the final decision.

We may note some difficulties in consolidating companies such as Argentina and Brazil when exchange rates are unstable. Some authorities recommend exclusion in such cases. Generally, I believe we should use the exchange rate at the end of the accounting period to translate the foreign currency balance sheets into lire. Some average rate for the period probably should be used for the income statement.

Of course, all of this is not official—it represents only my tentative thoughts, because my department was only established a few months ago.

Earlier in 1966, under the administrative department's general direction, standard accounting instructions for determining in local currencies the operating results and financial condition of subsidiaries for internal and, possibly, consolidation purposes were issued to all overseas subsidiaries. The goal was to achieve a conservative and reasonably consistent reporting of results so that the headquarters management could better evaluate the performance of the overseas subsidiary companies. The overseas subsidiary companies were expected to continue to follow local practices for tax purposes, however. According to Dr. Viano, administrative manager of industrial subsidiaries:

The new accounting procedures are very detailed and reflect our belief that it is prudent to be conservative in accounting. Essentially, these procedures said that fixed assets—land and buildings—should be recorded at original cost. In those countries where price-level adjustments are permitted by law, these original costs could be adjusted to reflect price-level changes, if the adjustments were actually made for tax or legal purposes. Under no circumstances, however, could the book value exceed the actual market value of assets, prudently established and disregarding temporary fluctuations in the market price.

The depreciation rates for fixed assets were also standardized. A four per cent rate was selected for permanent-type factory buildings. A minimum rate of ten per cent was set for prefabricated buildings. In those cases where fixed assets were revalued to reflect price-level changes, the revaluation factor had to be applied to the related depreciation charge as well.

We established a number of procedures for other assets, also. For example, we stipulated that complementary and accessory works, such as enclosure walls, have to be depreciated at a 20 per cent rate. Furthermore, these assets can not be revalued, principally because their short life for accounting purposes already reflect an overstatement of depreciation costs. Industrial equipment purchases were classified as being either a recurring cost or a depreciable asset. The basic principle distinguishing between the two is that when the acquisition, installation, and maintenance costs for a particular type of equipment appears more or less constant for about four years, these expenditures can be considered as recurrent costs and, therefore, totally charged to profits. In all other cases the equipment is capitalized and written off over about four years. Under no circumstances is depreciable equipment revalued. . . .

Raw material inventories are to be valued at the cost of the last important purchase made under normal supply conditions: that is, from the most convenient supplier with no hurry. No revaluation for price-level changes of any kind are permitted for inventories since the valuation reflects current costs already. Finished products are valued at the last standard cost. Used machines of other makes acquired as trade-ins are given no value since it is not likely that we will fully realize their cost when we dispose of them. In the case of requisition of used Olivetti machines, the inventory cost is the expected selling price less normal gross margin, after taking modification costs into account.

Patents, goodwill, and similar intangible assets are to be amortized as quickly as possible in every single case.

Most liabilities are handled in the conventional fashion. The amount shown for tax and customer liabilities of any kind still to be verified, however, should be adequate to cover the highest claim that could be imposed on the company under the most unfavorable circumstances.

Debts payable in a foreign currency are to be booked in local currency at the exchange rate at the registration date. In those countries with fluctuating currencies, as soon as the debt is recorded, a reserve is to be established immediately through a charge to income equal to the difference between the estimated exchange rate at the maturity date and the rate on the registration day times the foreign currency amount of the debt. Of course, these estimates should be readjusted to reflect new facts. Furthermore, in those cases where repayment of a foreign debt involves high expenses at maturity, such as special taxes, these expenses should be treated like potential exchange losses: that is, recognized as expenses at the date of registration.

For income statement purposes, the profit figure is operating profit plus or minus special charges such as losses on asset dispositions, inventory revaluations, and exchange losses. Of course estimated taxes are deducted also. . . .

ING. C. OLIVETTI & C., S.p.A. (F–1)*

In 1966, one of the key problems facing the managing director of Olivetti was in developing an approach to selecting, motivating, training, and rewarding executives which would suit the changing style of management that he was attempting to introduce to the company. The environment in which the previous approach had worked no longer existed. The director of personnel said, "The country is changing, our product line is changing, and our company is growing. Our traditional executive personnel practices must change as well."

Dr. Peccei saw the problem as a three-way task—"to rationalize, to systematize, and to decentralize." He said, "When I first came to the company (1964) we were still a part of the old school where flare and personal intelligence played too big a part. Objective reasoning and rationality should be the manager's basic ways of thinking. I hope to improve the procedures by which key decisions are made and to see that decisions are made at the lowest point possible. These new goals should be accomplished by 1968."

The normal difficulty of systematizing and rationalizing personnel practices was complicated by factors particular to the Olivetti Company, and by the historical development of its executive structure. First, Olivetti operated in 145 countries with direct sales organizations in 28, and manufacturing facilities in 10. This organization required the development of an executive cadre truly capable of successfully operating throughout the world. Second, the recession of 1963 and 1964, combined with the ownership crisis of 1964, had led to a reduction in the number of white-collar personnel, thereby lowering the absolute number of new positions made available for promotions. Whereas from 1946 to 1963 the total number of employees had increased from 4,283 to 57,631, between 1963 and 1966 employment fell back to 51,630. (This takes into account the fact that 3,000 people left the company to be employed by Olivetti-General Electric.) Third, traditionally Olivetti had promoted almost entirely from within, and many of the upper echelon executives had reached their current positions at very young ages. The average age of men reporting to the managing director in Olivetti was 44, and many of these men had held their current position or one of equivalent authority for from three to five years. Certain executives feared that the situation could lead to feelings of stagnation and boredom.

The executive group

Ing C. Olivetti & Co., which is the parent company of the worldwide Olivetti group, employed slightly over 7,000 white-collar workers. For administrative purposes, the personnel department divided this group into four categories: executive, category 1, category 2, and category 3. The executive category included about 400 employees or almost 6% of the total. Of the white-collar group, category 1 amounted to about 20%, category 2 to 33%, and category 3 to 41%. This case is concerned specifically with the nearly 400 employees classified as executives.

In this executive group, functional specialization broke down as follows:

Production and technical service	46.6%
Commercial	11.9
Administrative-finance	8.9
Social services ⎫	
Personnel ⎬	8.7
Office of the president ⎭	
Associated companies	23.9

The company had made a study of some of the demographic characteristics of its executive group in 1963. Some of the results of this study were as follows:

DISTRIBUTION OF THE EXECUTIVE POPULATION BY YEAR OF BIRTH—1963

DISTRIBUTION OF THE EXECUTIVE POPULATION BY REGION OF BIRTH—1963

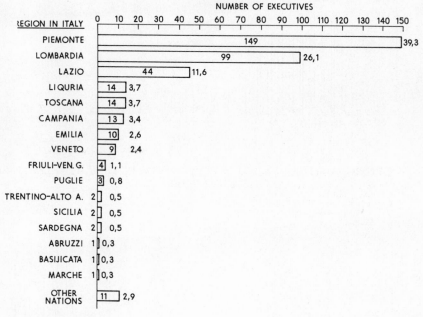

NUMBER OF EXECUTIVES

REGION IN ITALY	Number	%
PIEMONTE	149	39,3
LOMBARDIA	99	26,1
LAZIO	44	11,6
LIQURIA	14	3,7
TOSCANA	14	3,7
CAMPANIA	13	3,4
EMILIA	10	2,6
VENETO	9	2,4
FRIULI-VEN. G.	4	1,1
PUGLIE	3	0,8
TRENTINO-ALTO A.	2	0,5
SICILIA	2	0,5
SARDEGNA	2	0,5
ABRUZZI	1	0,3
BASIJICATA	1	0,3
MARCHE	1	0,3
OTHER NATIONS	11	2,9

Note : 379 total number.

SENIORITY WITHIN THE COMPANY UPON SELECTION AS EXECUTIVES—1963

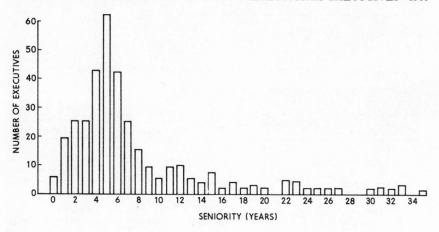

NUMBER OF EXECUTIVES

SENIORITY (YEARS)

AGE OF EXECUTIVES UPON SELECTION FOR THAT CATEGORY—1963

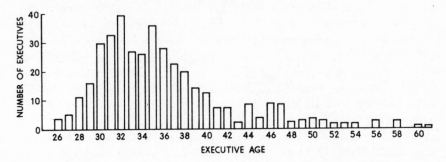

DISTRIBUTION OF THE EXECUTIVE POPULATION BY YEAR OF SELECTION AS EXECUTIVES

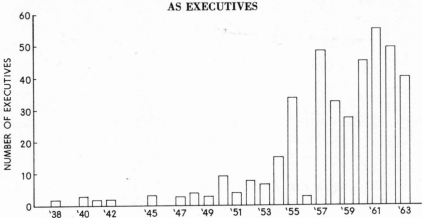

LEVELS OF EDUCATION RELATIVE TO PROMOTION TO EXECUTIVE

Number of Personnel Having Educational Qualifications as of 12/13/60		Promotions from 12/31/60–12/31/63	
		Number	Per Cent
University	485	99	20.41%
High school	2,462	24	0.97
Other	1,146	9	0.78

It is especially interesting to note the relatively young age of the executive group, their youth and low seniority when selected for an executive position, the high educational achievement, and the large proportion who were promoted to executive positions during the period 1958–1963.

The above demographic factors may be traced to the policies of Adriano Olivetti. A man intimately acquainted with both Adriano Olivetti and the

Olivetti Company observed, "The strength of Olivetti is not the organization; it is the quality of the men within it. They have the strength of morality and profound intelligence." Adriano Olivetti made it a conscious policy to seek out brilliant young men, regardless of their backgrounds, for his executive staff. During the 15 years following the war, he personally interviewed over 95% of the executives before they were hired. Sig. Innocenti, the head of personnel, said, "He sought to understand the way they thought, and the desires which they had. He was only marginally concerned with their technical expertise, and many times failed to even ask questions relating to the future job." Sig. Innocenti characterized this approach as "a search for the Renaissance man." During Adriano Olivetti's presidency only the lowest executive levels tended to be specialized. Above the immediate supervisory level there was much transferring from functional area to functional area.

Adriano Olivetti had a very strong love and concern for Italy and the Piedmont region. Much of his effort outside of business activities was devoted to regional development. This interest was reflected in the people whom he hired and in the composition of the international executive cadre. Many of the men whom he hired had originally participated in the regional planning, political, or cultural enterprises which he sponsored. This concern for regional problems extended to a profound interest in the development of a democratic Italy. During World War II, Olivetti was a major center for partisan resistance against the Nazi occupation. Much ordnance was hidden within the Olivetti factories and many of the Olivetti personnel played important parts in the movement.

Several executives said that Adriano Olivetti's procedure of measurement and rewards was very personal. One executive described the period by saying, "He chose young people in whom he had confidence, and gave them complete protection from outside criticism. None of the people who worked with him felt that he was an easy man. When we went to present results to him, we trembled. He was a severe critic, but he listened carefully. Once he made a decision he then went full steam ahead." The compensation scheme was not formalized, but the executives who were interviewed expressed the conviction that the rewards and the advancements were closely related to accomplishment. An outstanding example of this was Ing. Cappellaro. He earned Adriano Olivetti's confidence as a skillful and intelligent worker in the factory. He was then allowed to work on the development of a printing calculator and almost single-handed produced the Divisumma 14 which was the parent machine to today's printing calculator family. Reportedly he shared in the financial success of his design.

Punishment was as severe as rewards were large. As one executive put it, "From time to time, he [Adriano Olivetti] would make a man of great power disappear from the scene overnight." Although none of these people could be interviewed, it was understood that in most cases Adriano Olivetti made it financially attractive for the person to depart on his own volition. "He abhorred the use of meaningless titles and empty jobs as a sop to incompetence." Even so, many of the people so released reportedly had retained a friendly interest in both the Olivetti family and the company and returned occasionally to visit. For those with whom Adriano Olivetti disagreed in principle, there were periods of exile from the councils of power, yet such persons were often brought back in quickly. Adriano reportedly appreciated intelligent controversy and respected competence.

The changes which had occurred between 1960, when Adriano Olivetti died, and 1966 were important to the problem of executive selection and motivation. The Italian recession, the sale of the electronics business, the ownership crisis of 1964, and the reduction in white-collar personnel have already been mentioned. Dr. Peccei's aim of increasing the rationality of the decision-making process was being taken seriously by the personnel department. The head of personnel had been a close associate of Adriano Olivetti. He said:

Maybe Adriano would have developed a different solution than we have now, but we are having to meet the changing times. Rapid change is a part of our executive career. There is a trend building towards new systems of information retrieval and processing which will change many career paths. Some patterns will be speeded; others slowed down. Certainly we will develop a system which is more rationalized and controlled. Intuition and brilliance will be less important. Things will be more studied. Unfortunately a number of bright, intelligent people will think they should be moving faster, but the person who will move fast will be the team man, the executive scholar.

This forecast was being brought to fruition in many ways. In line with many other companies, the statistics showed that the current management had more formal education than previous management groups. Also the younger members of management had more education than the older members. Beyond this there were differences being introduced in the selection and training processes and in the career patterns. A pilot study was being made on the advantages to the company and to the individuals of sending executives to management training programs such as Harvard's Advanced Management Program and Columbia's management school.

There was general agreement that men were preselected at the time of hiring for future executives' roles. This did not preclude a man of real talent rising through the ranks, but, as the previous figures show, the odds were definitely against a man without a strong educational background rising to the executive level. This situation contrasted with the situation that had existed in the company 15 years earlier, as described by an Italian professor of sociology. "We were a country with limited opportunities. Olivetti was a career with unlimited opportunities for anyone with talent."

Since 1953, potential new executives had been sent to Florence to the Olivetti training school. While there, they followed the initial four-week orientation course which was given to all salesmen trainees. This course included a section dealing with the technical characteristics of the basic Olivetti products and the economic justification for the use of mechanical office equipment.

The potential executive was also given a brief introduction to competitive products and the use of Olivetti products as substitutes. Finally he was given an introduction to the Olivetti philosophy. This part included an introduction to the history of the Olivetti firm, including the development of its social philosophy, products, and corporate image. A great deal of stress was laid on the importance of each individual in carrying on the image. Dr. Alessandri, head of the training school, stated that his objective was two-fold: first, to sensitize future executives to the problems of sales; second, to help make certain that traditional Olivetti values were transmitted to new employees. Following this introduction to the Olivetti tradition, the new executive was given any specialized training which might be necessary to his task and then sent to his job.

The career patterns of Olivetti executives had been changing during the years from 1960 to 1966. Although there were still many opportunities, the nature of the opportunities was changing. In 1963, over 80% of the executive positions in Olivetti subsidiaries abroad were occupied by Italians. In 1966, this figure had dropped to under 25%. It was a conscious policy of the company to employ more foreign nationals in supervisory and executive roles. Another major change was the increasing number of levels of specialized management. Whereas previously executives often moved from one functional specialty to another, the new tendency was to leave executives in the functional specialization where they began. The personnel director said that the new complexity of the organization required several levels of functional specialists. Several executives commented that cases such as Dr. Galassi, who had been director of personnel, commercial operations, and production, and president of Olivetti Underwood, would be much more rare in the future.

Another important change which would affect future career opportunities for Olivetti executives was taking place. The Italian labor market was maturing rapidly. Many new positions were opening and intercompany mobility was slowly increasing. Prior to the 1960's, there had been a clear rule within the executive group that a position with a company required lifetime loyalty. Since over two-thirds of Italian industry had been composed of small firms, relatively few positions had been open with large private sector firms. The only real competition for executive talent had been with the state institutions and the banks. Positions in these firms had been mainly administrative in character without opportunities in either production or marketing. By 1966, however, there were many new opportunities available to the ambitious, middle-level executive. The boom years of the 1960's had brought in many foreign companies which were quite willing to hire experienced executive talent at competitive salaries. Two cases illustrated this change. Both Rank-Xerox and Minnesota Mining and Manufacturing (3M) in Italy were reportedly largely managed by ex-Olivetti personnel.

At the highest levels of management there was still some difficulty in finding openings. This resulted partly from the many interlocking directorates in Italy which made an open search hazardous. Olivetti, for example, had representatives from Fiat, IRI, and IMI on its board of directors. Fiat and IRI alone would limit greatly the possibilities of executive shifting into financial organizations and heavy industry within Italy. As of 1966, however, there were active in Italy over 10 executive-search organizations which, as they became better established, would perhaps offer a more covert method of job hunting.

Traditionally Olivetti had offered among the highest salaries in Italy to its executive and executive-trainee personnel. One of the men who had left Olivetti for another company and later returned cited his case as an example. In 1932 he was hired to work on a research and development project, but had not been satisfied with the job. He decided to leave Olivetti to work with another large industrial firm as a project engineer. In making this move he accepted a salary cut of almost 60%.

Although executive salary information was highly confidential the estimated 1966 ranges were as follows:

	Lire	Dollars
New executives with little responsibility	6,000,000 =	10,000
Chief of a service such as accounting section in a plant	7– 8,000,000 =	12–14,000
Director of medium-sized sales branch	8–10,000,000 =	14–17,000

Beyond this level there was little standardization. Salaries were negotiated individually and it was estimated that they could range up to 40,000,000 lire (below the managing director level) which is equivalent to roughly $60,000. As a basis of comparison the lowest paid white-collar worker would take home roughly 1,000,000 lire per year and a top-rated white-collar worker could approach the 6,000,000 of the executive. All salaries were reported in total to the governmental fiscal authorities; thus the executive of a large firm was unable to hide income. It was reported that managers of many smaller companies were able and willing to report lower salaries than were actually paid. This sometimes produced tax savings of up to 20% of the amount hidden.

Although luxury goods, electrical and mechanical devices, and transportation were equivalently or slightly higher-priced than in the United States, services, lodging and food seemed to be lower in cost. To the researcher, the standard of living of the executives appeared high. It appeared even higher by comparison to the level which was common for people about them.

There were a few symbols of executive status and company benefits which were more or less noticeable. The parking lot had four distinct sections and lot assignment depended on position. The office building was "Y" shaped with higher status groups on the upper levels. Office size and appointments varied with position as well. Assignment of company cars and drivers was not permanent and seemed to be made on a basis of current need. Even when an executive used the service regularly, he drew from a pool. Senior executives most often drew the more luxurious cars. Other advantages which an executive had were a separate medical insurance fund which did not require going to the company medical facility, and subscriptions to journals and magazines appropriate to professional interests.

Although the salary scale and many of these benefits had set Olivetti apart from other Italian firms for a number of years, the margin was narrowing. Olivetti was still reputed to pay about 10% above equivalent firms, but many within the company and outside felt that even this margin might soon disappear for certain jobs. Others expressed in a joking fashion that the pay differential might be a "hardship allowance" due to the cultural isolation of Ivrea.

Olivetti maintained a policy of equal pay for equal executive work throughout the world. A man transferred from one location to another could expect to receive approximately the same salary, with a dislocation allowance.

The declining relative advantage of working for Olivetti in Italy made the problem of executive selection, training, and reward important ones for the company to face. Olivetti cases F-2, F-4, and F-5 describe the attitudes, ambitions, goals, and backgrounds of three individual executives in the company.

Exhibit 1

EXECUTIVE PERSONNEL—JULY 1, 1966

Name	Current Position	Previous Work Experience	Age	Years with Olivetti	Job Location	Current Residence	Academic Studies	Place of Birth
Dr. Peccei	Managing director	Fiat	58	2	Ivrea	Rome	Economics and commerce	Turin
Dr. R. Olivetti	Director for research and development		38	11	Ivrea	Ivrea	Economics and commerce	Turin
Dr. Galassi	Director of production	Sales	54	29	Ivrea	Milan	Economics and commerce	Milan
Ing. Tufarelli	Director of industrial subsidiaries	Teaching	43	12	Ivrea	Ivrea	Civil engineering	S. Giorgio Lucano (Matera)
Dr. Rogers	Director of international relations	Import-Export insurance	56	11	Rome	Rome	Law	Trieste
Avv. Brioschi	Director of finance	IPSOA-Teaching	43	13	Ivrea	Ivrea	Law	São Paolo, Brazil
Dr. Zorzi	Director of publicity	Business Teaching journalism Editorial work	45		Milan	Milan	Letters	Verona
Sig. Innocenti	Director of industrial relations	N.A.	51	N.A.	Ivrea	Ivrea	Accounting	Florence
Dr. Prelle	Controller	N.A.	46	N.A.	Ivrea	Ivrea	Economics and commerce	Ivrea
Dr. Momigliano	Director of economic studies	Economic studies Journalism	50	N.A.	Milan	Milan	Law	Turin
Ing. Montalenti	Assistant to the president	Fiat	50	2	Ivrea	Turin	Aeronautical engineer	Turin
Ing. Sarti	Director of copying	Accounting and administration	46	N.A.	Ivrea	Turin	Electrical engineer	Bologna
Sig. Piol	Director of marketing and product planning	N.A.	35	N.A.	Ivrea	Milan	Mechanical engineer	Limana (Belluno)
Dr. Gabetti	President, Olivetti Underwood	Banking	42	8	New York	New York	Law	Turin
Dr. Lorenzotti	Director of Italian sales	Law	37	14	Milan	Milan	Law	Turin
Dr. Accornero	President, Olivetti France	N.A.	N.A.	27	Paris	Paris	N.A.	N.A.
Ing. Berla	Managing director, Olivetti Spain	Architecture	40	13	Barcelona	Barcelona	Architecture	Turin

Source: Company records.

ING. C. OLIVETTI & C., S.p.A. (F–2)*

^^

Avv. Gian Antonio Brioschi, age 42, was financial manager of Olivetti. He had been appointed to this job in June 1957. Previously he had been director of labor relations, assistant to the administrative director, and head of the sales training school in Florence. His academic background had been law.

Avv. Brioschi looks at his current job

Avv. Brioschi described his current job by saying:

I have been financial director of Olivetti during an exciting period. When I came into this job I reported to the administrative manager of the company. Dr. Pero. I had worked as his assistant previously and had gained his confidence. So he left it up to me to define my job. In 1958, Roberto Olivetti became administrative director so I reported to him, but after Adriano's death in 1960, Dr. Pero became managing director. One of his early acts was to change the organization so the job of financial manager reported directly to the managing director.

Dr. Pero had had long experience with the internal working of the company. He was very devoted to the Olivetti family and tried hard to maintain the programs which Adriano started. [Researcher's note: Another executive reported that when Dr. Pero was named managing director he said: "I hope Saint Adriano and Saint Camillo will watch over me."]

He left much of the responsibility for contact with the outside financial community to me. I guess that the most interesting experiences I have had were related to the contacts which I had with the men in the financial community. I gained important insight into the development of our own Italian economy, and I got to know many of the important men in the international financial community very well.

To understand my present feelings, you have to understand the importance of the period from 1960 to 1963 in the financial history of the Olivetti Company. During that period we had three stock issues, three bond issues and an enormous development of our short-term bank loans. Our issue of preference stock made with the help of Medio Banca was the first time that a technical and legal formula like that had been used in Italy. It was also the first time that shares of the company had been put in the hands of people who were not members of the Olivetti family or close friends of the family. I was the organization person most closely involved in seeing that this issue was handled successfully and in developing the notion of preference shares. As it turned out, the preference shares were eagerly bought up by the public. In fact, one of the biggest problems I had was to restrain, with the assistance of the normal financial media, the violent rise in price.

Now, of course, the problems are different. We have gone from financial stringency to a situation of liquidity in some areas. Now it is mainly a question of keeping contacts in the financial community and extending and tightening our financial control over our subsidiaries. It is somewhat frustrating. When the need for money is less, people care less about finance, so you feel less in the heart of things. With Adriano, there was almost continuous personal contact. It was the same thing with Pero. Now I see Dr. Peccei at least once a month, but there is much less of a tendency for the managers to get together to participate in the global decisions. I think sometimes there is a lack of horizontal coordination. We need to get the simultaneous viewpoints of more individuals so Dr. Peccei can know the ultimate implications of the decisions. Probably in the long run we will have to rely on more formal relationships. Now we are in a period of evolution.

Right now I spend about 20% of my time working with top-management personnel, about 40% of my time working with my assistants, and about 40% contacting outside people. One of my major enjoyments is watching the young people about me develop. For example, one young man who used to be my assistant is now a vice president of Turin Savings Bank [one of the largest savings institutions in Italy].

I am glad to see him get ahead so fast. Eventually, I hope we have a financial profession here in Italy. Now, by your standards, there are almost no bankers; mostly banking officers. There are no investment bankers here either. I feel that these men we are training will contribute to that goal.

Avv. Brioschi looks at his personal history and past career

Avv. Brioschi was born in Brazil of Italian parents. From the age of eight, he had lived in Italy, attending classical high school and law school in Milan. He had graduated *summa cum laude* from law school, writing his dissertation on *The Strike in Economics and Law*. This was the first of many of his writings which have been published. In 1966 he had two articles published in Italian scholarly journals. They were entitled: "The International Monetary System, Proposals for Reform" and "The Stock Market and Economic Efficiency." In addition he was currently writing an introduction to the Italian edition of *The Modern Corporation and Private Property* by Berle and Means.

Avv. Brioschi explained:

I spend about three days a week in Ivrea now, and much of the rest I spend in Milan. I have an apartment in Milan as well as one here in Ivrea. My major activities outside the office involve art, music, modern literature, and modern philosophy. I like to participate in the discussions dealing with the modern literature and modern philosophy which take place in Milan and Rome. As you know, Italy is a small country, and by now, I would say that I know many of the writers of importance here. I enjoy meeting with them whenever I can. Professors Eliot and Kissinger of Harvard started a magazine of modern European thought called *Confluence*. I was their Italian representative. Through this I became heavily involved in following the trends in intellectual thought. My interests extend to modern music and art too. I try to keep up with the openings at the better galleries as they occur, and I like to burden my mind with modern music.

Although I am Italian, my interests are international. In 1949, after I graduated from law school in labor law, and finished up a year as an assistant at the University of Milan, I attended the course in history at the Salzburg Seminar in American Studies. After that course, I was fortunate enough to receive a Fulbright Scholarship to attend Harvard Law School. I attended the law school in 1950 and 1951; then in 1952 I received a grant from the Department of Social Relations at Harvard to study the sociology of law. In March 1952 I received my LLM.

The experience I had had with the methods of education in the United States led me to Olivetti. I accepted the proposal of Adriano Olivetti to help set up a business school in Turin modeled after the Harvard Business School (with an American—mostly Harvard—faculty). I was secretary of the school, vice-director, and an instructor in Finance and Control.

By 1955, I had become convinced that I wouldn't make my career in education. I didn't have the patience to teach. Adriano Olivetti arranged for me to come to work for the Olivetti Company. My first job was still in education. I helped to set up the training school for salesmen in Florence. We had to train over 100 men a month to push our products. We had a new approach which had not been tried before in Italy. It was quite a job to make a deep impression of the spirit of Olivetti on such a large number.

After starting up the school, Adriano arranged for me to get involved in the financial and control side of the company. Through my work at the business school I had grown to enjoy that kind of work—strictly correlated to economy and law. My first job was as administrative assistant to Dr. Pero. We had a good and very informal relationship. I just went into the office, saw what was going on, what needed to be done, and did it.

In January 1956, there was a crisis in the labor relations office. Adriano Olivetti had a disagreement with the director of labor relations. The disagreement was entirely philosophical, but Adriano wanted to clear out the situation in a matter of days if not hours. I was appointed assistant to the president for labor relations. For 18 months I was responsible for dealing with the unions, developing the overall labor policy, supervising the welfare and social service facilities, and directing the training facilities. This was interesting, but didn't fit with my real final interest in finance and control. I prepared my successor and, with the agreement of Adriano Olivetti, I was taken out of that job and given my present position.

Avv. Brioschi looks at the future

In speaking of the future, Avv. Brioschi started by reviewing the path which had brought Olivetti to its present position. He said:

Adriano Olivetti's policy was to give people a variety of opportunities. Young men were challenged by putting them in jobs which were bigger than they thought they could handle and by shifting them rapidly from one function to another. He hoped to build a strong group of managers who had ideas and ideals similar to his own. He didn't want to build a dynasty, but rather a strong group of professional managers. He [Adriano Olivetti] was a creative humanist who was an entrepreneurial genius. There was a aura of inventiveness and fantasy which we shared.

Now we are in the midst of a change to a more rational world of things. We are going through a process of formalization. Our managers are becoming more professional, more oriented to one functional specialty. The opportunity for a career such as I have had might be almost nonexistent.

Personally, I will have to focus more on the development of rational procedures and on training of my subordinates. I don't think I would want necessarily to be number one in an organization. I think I would also like to work closely with a truly great man. I enjoy sharing ideas and participating in building a great organization.

The future of the company has many questions which I feel have to be asked. We must look at the general strategy of the company. How much can we expect our foreign markets to grow? In the past we have grown through capturing additional market share. Can we do this in the future, or must we content ourselves with the growth of the market in general? Will we be able to content ourselves with a modest 5%–10% growth rate when in the past we have expanded as much as 40% in a year? What is the trend of profitability for our products? To what extent can we remain dependent on the traditional electromechanical devices? Should we grow through acquisition or merger? We have made a commitment within the organization to the development of peripheral equipment. We are relying on our technical competence to build such machines. In the intense competition which we will have to face, will this be enough? What alternatives should we consider if the peripheral equipment market doesn't prove to be as great as many in the company hope?

These are some of the questions which I am asking. I don't think we have the answers. If we ask these questions properly and don't overlook the potential which is within the present organization, we have an independent and solid future. We could have a steadier, less precarious, but in some respects less exciting organization than we have had in the past.

ING. C. OLIVETTI & C., S.p.A. (F–4)*

Dr. Ugo Galassi, age 54, was general production manager for Olivetti. He had held this position since February 1966. Prior to that time he had been commercial general manager of the company, president of Olivetti Underwood, commercial manager for the Italian market, branch manager of Milan, personnel manager for the company, and in various other marketing positions. March 1966 marked the beginning of his 29th year with Olivetti. Dr. Galassi received his academic training in business and economics.

Dr. Galassi looks at his current job

In describing his current position, Dr. Galassi spoke as follows:

One of the basic problems for us is to combat the rising costs of production. Not being an engineer, I tend to rely on organizational changes to accomplish this goal and my past experience is most valuable to me in this area. Approximately 40% of my time is devoted to personnel problems. Eighty per cent of such time is spent on current problems, while the rest of the time is devoted to introduction of new policies and relations with unions.

I feel that one of my key tasks is to evaluate accurately the performance of people under me. We want to be sure to make the best use of our good people and we do have a problem in insuring for Olivetti the services of enough good people. I am supposed to concern myself only down to the second level supervisors but I try my best also to follow the younger people in our organization. I want to make sure we are getting the best people for our training schools. As a way of checking on our selection procedures, I personally interview some 5% of the workers every year.

Of course the longer range planning of personnel is most important. Dealing with the unions correctly also has a great bearing on future success of the company.

Dr. Galassi looks at his personal situation and past career

Dr. Galassi spoke of his family and earlier career as follows:

My two children are 26 and 22. The first received his Master in Economics last October, the second is a student in his third course in engineering at the Politecnico in Milan. My wife and I live in Milan so we can enjoy theater and

---

music. I also collect old paintings. Besides the fact that you can enjoy them while they are guarding your money, collecting them is one of the best hedges against inflation. My main recreations are skiing, sailing, and deep sea fishing.

I started with Olivetti as a salesman in Milan in 1938. I switched to the accounting-systems group soon afterwards. During the war, I was in Ivrea working in personnel. [Researcher's note: Others in company said that during the war Dr. Galassi played a vital role in the resistance movement and in saving company property from possible destruction.] After the war, at my request, I was sent to Milan as sales manager of the Milan-Lombardy region. I spent four years there.

In 1949, Adriano sent the vice president for commercial sales and me to the United States to begin the sales of our products there. We were the first European manufacturer of office machines to try to get dealers in the United States. I spent about two months in the United States on the first trip. Later I was sent back for another eight months to get the dealer program set up. We incorporated as Olivetti Corporation of America in February 1950, with Dino Olivetti as chief executive.

When I came back to Italy, I suggested the alliance with Machines Bull for the sale of punch card equipment. This was right up my alley with my background in accounting equipment. We thought the machines were good and the marriage was a natural. I hired some people with great enthusiasm for the new operation, such as Beltrami, Piol, and Ceccoli and by 1952 we were beginning to be successful. By 1956 we were splitting the Italian market 50–50 with IBM.

In 1953, Adriano gave me the calculating machines division and then he made me manager of all commercial activity in Italy. When I took over we had about 25% of the calculator market in Italy, and about 55% of the typewriter business. I helped lead an all-out drive which brought our share of market in these products to over 90%. My basic strategy was to study a market carefully, then build an organization in depth to exploit it. Tariffs were low at the time, so we really had to push the commercial organization. I felt we should gain command of the home market before turning to competition abroad. It worked. We had great machines, and we were able to keep prices low enough for people to afford to buy them, and competition couldn't get established.

In 1959 I was requested by Mr. Adriano Olivetti to extend my supervision to the foreign marketing operations, and later in the same year I was sent to the United States to be president of the Underwood Corporation. Lorenzotti, who had been one of my key assistants during the buildup of the commercial operation of the Olivetti Corporation of America, became my executive vice president at Underwood. You know about the mess we found there. In 1963, I came back to Italy as general commercial manager for the company; then in February, Dr. Peccei took over that position, and I became production manager.

Dr. Galassi looks at the future

Questioned about his views of the future, Dr. Galassi responded as follows:

I must preface my remarks by saying that my main purpose is doing business at a profit. This really attracts me. We receive money from the stockholders, and we have to earn money for them. It is necessary to work very hard to do this. We need specialized people, but we need to know how to manage, too. Management, for me, is knowing how to use everything possible to improve operations. A business is like a symphony. If the conductor doesn't conduct well, the band doesn't play well. Olivetti is a great company. I wish it to continue to have great success as it has so far.

As far as my specific department is concerned (i.e., production and manufacturing) I have laid down a program of automating the assembly lines, coordinating production control, and introducing on-line systems for quality control. At the same time, I have started a policy of job enlargements, to be gradually implemented, while we will proceed into personnel training.

All these various projects, properly coordinated, should make possible a reduction of the ratio of the cost of labor to the final cost of the finished product, and, as a result, should contribute to a better overall profitability.

ING. C. OLIVETTI & C., S.p.A. (F–5)*

Dr. Guido Lorenzotti, age 37, had been director of Italian commercial operations since September 1965. In this position he was responsible for all activities of the home-country sales force which accounted for 20.1% of the total company sales. Previously Dr. Lorenzotti had served as president and executive vice president of Olivetti Underwood, having earlier been regional manager in two U.S. locations and manager of the Olivetti branch in Chicago. His academic background was law. He was married and had three children.

Dr. Lorenzotti looks at his current job

Dr. Lorenzotti described his interest in his current position as follows:

There is really nothing new in this job which I hadn't experienced at Olivetti Underwood. I can see a little bit how it could contribute to my career, but not a great deal. I was probably selected for this position because I was on the winning team of Underwood, for my youth, and because the company wanted to transfer some of its U.S. experience to the Italian operation. Olivetti in Italy has 80% of the market, and it is therefore important that we hold this position. We are having the same problems of costs, merchandising, marketing, and promotion which affected American companies 30 or 40 years ago. Great changes are taking place in Italy. We are having difficulty changing fast enough. It is not that the internal organization is the greatest bulwark against change. We just can't change things outside the company. It is quite frustrating not to be able to get people to go along when we attempt to transfer some of the knowledge which the company has gained through its U.S. experience.

I was trained as a classical Italian. I was trained to think that everything worthwhile came from the humanities. I have changed. I don't negate the value of humanities, but men here in Italy should be more pragmatic. My U.S. experience helped me to balance my humanistic approach. I think the combination is good, but it does make me see the Italian condition with a different point of view. My 11 years in the States makes me a bit of a stranger here.

Perhaps America has some lessons to learn though, too. Utilitarianism is too sterile; there are many aspects of life which only the humanistic approach can help you to appreciate. People are not yet made by computer; they still have a stomach, heart, feet, ears, and sex. But here in Italy we must not fight progress. Progress is made by men, but men similar to Adam and Eve, with problems.

In Italy it is necessary to get rid of the habit of being "Yes"-men. I personally like *good* arguments that run counter to my proposals.

Reading and hearing about new sophisticated management techniques, I found that in the essence they are all directed to the same goal. Give the managers the authority to run their operation—give them more responsibility. Get the right person in the right post and stimulate him. We must use new technologies and techniques, be aware of all of them, but overall let the personalities come out. The manager must prepare his program, have it discussed and approved, but finally have the full responsibility and authority to carry it out.

This will not be completely right on paper, but what counts is that I saw it working in many great companies in the United States and I applied it successfully at Underwood.

Dr. Lorenzotti looks at his personal history and past career

Dr Lorenzotti reviewed his past history as follows:

Although I graduated in Law, my present outside activities center on getting a doctorate in political science and sociology. I have been sitting for one or two examinations each year towards this goal. I plan to write a thesis involving a sociological comparison of American and Italian managers. I hope this may inspire some self-analysis among other Italian managers. I regret having had to pursue the degree one course at a time, but the constant intellectual challenge keeps me in touch with the intellectual world and helps to keep me alive mentally.

My father was a general in the Italian army. He worked as commander of the Alpine troops of NATO with General Lee, Eisenhower, Ridgeway, and Briscoe. I studied at the Classical High School and then the University of Rome and was admitted to the bar in 1952. [Researcher's note: Out of over 3,000 who enter the school in Rome each year, only about 150 are graduated and admitted to the bar.] During school I practised law with a firm in Rome for six years.

I had been impressed by the personality and vision of Adriano Olivetti so I decided to try working for the company. I followed the standard management trainee program, including a brief assignment as a territory salesman. In the fall of 1954, Adriano Olivetti and Ugo Galassi asked me to go to the United States for a year. As it turned out, I spent a total of eleven years there. At 24, I opened the first Olivetti branch in Chicago. At 25, I became manager of the Great Lakes region including Illinois, Michigan, Indiana, and Iowa. In 1956, I was asked to open up the New York office, to operate a direct sales organization in the New York City area, and a dealer operation throughout the North Atlantic region.

Soon after the New York division was opened I was appointed as executive vice president of Olivetti-United States. Dino Olivetti, the brother of Adriano and a U.S. citizen, was president. Dino Olivetti was called back to the Italian operation in 1957, so I was left with all of the operating responsibility. When we bought Underwood in 1959, I was named as executive vice president under Dr. Galassi.

In April 1963, Dr. Galassi returned to Italy to resume his position as director of commercial activities for the company as a whole. I was named president of Olivetti Underwood. This was by far the best experience I have had, but it was a hell of a life. The brain was constantly troubled. After all the work of rebuilding Underwood, I had the reward of seeing it back on its feet.

While Dr. Lorenzotti was president of Olivetti Underwood it grew to be the largest subsidiary of Olivetti. Also the company showed a profit for the first time since 1955. At 34, Dr. Lorenzotti was one of the youngest presidents of a company listed on *Fortune's* list of the 500 largest industrial companies.

Dr. Lorenzotti looks to the future

Dr. Lorenzotti talked only a little about the future. He said:

I try not to make plans such as, "In five years I want to be the managing director." I want to keep the freedom and peace of mind which I have. I try to live so as to balance the humanistic with the practical. I try to solve problems as they arise.

We are going to have to resolve the problems of motivating change. I would say that changing the attitudes of people in Italy will be as difficult a problem for us to solve as the problems of technological change, new products, cost of distribution, and cost of production.

At this point the conversation was interrupted by a problem which Dr. Lorenzotti felt provided a graphical illustration of his point. He attempted to place an outside call on the office phone. After many minutes of frustration he hammered the receiver against the base repeatedly and said:

See what I mean!

In the United States it is perfectly reasonable to pick up a telephone and expect it to work. Here, because some time in the 1860's an Italian had an idea for a telephone, we have steadfastly refused to look outside for a new idea. You Americans have something that works well. If we can't invent, why don't we copy and get rid of this foolish system. We just won't. We have the idea that the home-grown idea is best.

You might be interested to know that I have given my children the option of becoming American. They were born in America and carry American passports. I think it is important that we Italians learn to look for ideas and opportunities everywhere. My experience in the United States was most valuable.

Getting back to the discussion of the company's future he said:

We are going to have to develop new products and make inroads into the rising cost of products and distribution. We are going to have a struggle to succeed against increasingly difficult competition. I think our traditional product lines will produce the bulk of our growth. We have some future in copying, especially as far as the Italian market is concerned, but the greatest original impact in that field is past.

I think we have a future in the peripheral equipment market, but at present, due to the variety of possibilities of solutions, the thoughts and applications are still nebulous. From an industrial point of view, we must measure our stride by the length of our leg and make certain that we proceed from the base of the strength which we have today.

ING. C. OLIVETTI & C., S.p.A. (H)*

On May 24, 1965, the stockholders annual meeting of Ing. C. Olivetti & C., S.p.A., announced the reorganization of the board of directors of the company. This reorganization came about as a result of a financial crisis within the Olivetti family and the death of Giuseppe Pero, the previous managing director and chairman of the board.[1] At that meeting the group of five companies which had purchased more than one-third of the Olivetti family's stock, giving them about 25% ownership of the company, named a new board of directors. Professor Bruno Visentini became chairman of the board, while later on the board appointed Dr. Aurelio Peccei managing director of the company.

In the Olivetti Company, Dr. Peccei was the first leader who was neither a member of the Olivetti family nor a long-time associate. He was an important executive with Fiat, managing the Fiat operations in Argentina, until 1957 when he left his full-time position at Fiat to become managing director at ITALCONSULT.[2] He retained the position of member of the steering committee of Fiat and chairman of the board of Fiat Argentina.

Upon being chosen as managing director of Olivetti, Dr. Peccei took 18 months to "extract from the confused ideas and situations within the company some principles for future action." During that 18 months, some changes were made within the company but no major changes were forced in management personnel. The only person who was brought into active management with Dr. Peccei was his assistant, Ing. Montalenti. Ing. Montalenti had been closely associated with Dr. Peccei during his work with Fiat in Argentina.

This case will focus on Dr. Peccei's plans for the future. There are three major areas to be covered: (1) his international perspective, (2) his philosophy of management, and (3) the goals he sets for the Olivetti Company.

Dr. Peccei's international perspective

Dr. Peccei's primary interest was in world affairs. He stated that he was deeply concerned about the world condition and about the fact that so few

---

[1]See Ing. C. Olivetti & C., S.p.A. (A–2) and (D) for further details.

[2]ITALCONSULT was a nonprofit consulting firm specializing in regional development. It provided technical and economic consultation on a worldwide basis.

people seemed to be genuinely concerned with the "true issues of our time."
He said:

> I fear sometimes that we in the West may be building a Maginot Line of the
> mind. That is, we may be directing our thoughts and actions towards solving
> rather unimportant problems and allowing the true issues of our time to escape
> our attention. I am fortunate to be in the position I am. There is a glamor sur-
> rounding the executive which makes people listen when he speaks. I am using
> that glamor to try to stir some thought about the challenge of the 1970's to our
> time. I am devoting a significant portion of my time to provoking a debate among
> business and government leaders concerning the challenges which we face.

In September 1965, Dr. Peccei delivered an address which he later had edited,
printed, and distributed to his acquaintances in business, government, and
education. The following section on his international perspective is a substantial abridgment of that speech:

> I believe that the highest quality that modern man must possess, especially
> when vested with high responsibilities, whether scientific, political, or productive,
> is the capacity of synthesis.
>
> Indeed, the environment in which we live is becoming increasingly complex,
> the amount of our knowledge is growing dizzily (the quasi-law of redoubling every
> ten years). If we don't know how to size up our position, if we become slaves of
> our machines, if we do not succeed in ordering our ideas and our accomplish-
> ments, everything we have created will amount to a useless wealth, even a danger.
>
> Techno-scientific progress itself, like the processes of living organisms, needs
> a regulator. Up to now a military stimulus (national defense or war prepared-
> ness) has acted as regulator, but since it contains an abnormal gene, it has
> brought the whole system to the verge of apocalyptic self-destruction.
>
> So as not to lose control of the future, the first thing to be done is to find
> a substitute for this regulator which will furnish coherent development, conceived
> of in terms of modern man, this complex being that, from a spiritual and ra-
> tional creature, has also become an economic subject. In other words, the tech-
> nological revolution must be guided in the attack on the real problems of the
> next decade: survival in the nuclear age, that is, *pacem in terris;* overpopulation;
> hunger in large parts of the world; education in the broadest sense; justice in
> liberty; better circulation and distribution of wealth produced inclusive of the
> technological patrimony itself, that is, well-being.
>
> This substitution is at the same time the prerequisite and consequence of a
> longer term global political approach, necessary for leading intelligently human
> activities during the seventies.
>
> The responsibility for defining it obviously falls on the most developed na-
> tions. It is a responsibility of world leadership which calls for establishing in
> the stride of history an overall strategy for the defense and promotion of funda-
> mental common interests.
>
> In adopting this guiding philosophy I believe that *the principal objective of
> a global policy by civilized nations must be that of enlarging and consolidating
> the area of prosperity which exists today in the world.* I employ the word pros-
> perity not because wealth is the greater blessing, even if it is difficult that im-
> material values prosper under poverty, but because we are accustomed to measur-

ing it. By increase in prosperity must therefore be understood not only the increase in individual income but also the raising of the level of life in all its aspects, a complex operation requiring human sympathy, great educational efforts and technical intervention, no less than financial resources.

To accomplish such a vast design, as is that of extending in a decade prosperity to other regions of the world, the leadership of the United States is paramount, but the full participation of Europe is indispensable. Therefore, the attainment of an advanced degree of European unity constitutes an absolute prerequisite.

Europe remains the focal point of the world. This is not only because it holds the central place in the distribution of the land masses, but because it is virtually impossible for it to be supplanted in its role as a link between the America which lives in the future and those regions which live partly in the past.

Over the many centuries of give and take with the rest of the world, Europe has accumulated a mass of instructive errors and incomparable experiences. Under Labor, Socialist, or Christian leadership today it demonstrates a singular social awareness. Since the last year it has launched important experiments in public-sector promotion of economic develpment, state participation in productive activities, and national planning.

Conseqently, the image of Europe is associated with the *idée-force* of planning, which in the seventies in one way or another will be one of the dominant elements in zones having a mixed economy.

In effect, I believe that by the end of this decade we shall be able to count on a nucleus of a united Europe which will permit it to participate actively in the development of a global policy: whether such a Europe will initially be made up of six, or six plus seven, or even ten or twelve countries is of only temporary importance and is not fundamental.

Taking these premises as a starting point, there are, as I see it, three principal lines of action to be developed for the attainment of the strategic objectives of the '70s.

In a global plan leading to development and well-being in the next decade, the fundamental action to be given effect concerns the reinforcement of relations between the United States and Europe. Since the argument is controversial, I shall do my best to clarify it as briefly as possible. I shall then indicate the two complementary lines of action which concern the Soviet zone and that of Latin America.

Above all, it is necessary to employ every means to prevent the technological and psychological gap developing between the United States and Europe from assuming impossible proportions.

According to my views, the milestone of global plan remains the North Atlantic partnership tied to European unity. It is the only solution that can ensure a continuous flow of technology and of organizational and productive experiences between the two areas, such as to maintain their respective levels in reasonable equilibrium, and, furthermore, create, by way of the exchange of goods, capital and men, interests which will act as a bulwark against any recessive tendency; and, lastly, permit over time the fusion of the communities on both shores of the Atlantic.

The essentiality of the picture and of the forces involved seems to be so evident as to make consideration of any other scheme of only ephemeral value.

In conclusion, although the way bristles with difficulties and is beset with tribulations, the important thing is to be convinced of a double truth: that the objective is attainable, and that, when we shall have a clearer vision of the affairs of the world, it will be possible to attain it in a relatively small number of years.

As an industrial manager, when there is a problem I believe in facing it and in trying to resolve it. If experience at company level can be significant, it teaches that when the objective terms of the problem are confused, almost certainly one adopts mistaken solutions; but if on the contrary we have the terms clearly in our minds, it is relatively easy to take the right decisions.

In the frame of realistic policy, the areas to be interested in development and in co-prosperity in the next decade are necessarily and only two: the Soviet area, comprising the U.S.S.R. and Eastern Europe, and the Latin American area.

The dialogue with them is not really so difficult, especially on the European side; not even with the U.S.S.R., so long as the internal political regime of each community is duly respected. The political decisions seem more difficult, but perhaps they will be rather less so when it is understood that development on both sides is synonymous with the survival of each, and that within certain limits of disparity the implementation of aid so as to bring other peoples to our standard of well-being is commercially advantageous.

Insofar as the Soviet area is concerned, simple coexistence with the West today is really too fragile and exposed to unforeseeable risks for us to be able to judge it sufficient. The road of cooperation must be followed. From the beginning of the '60s, many strides have been made along this road. Even the highest moral authorities have begun to take up positions in this sense.

No community, remembering the terrible lesson of the '40s, can be so obstinate in the defense of its own interests, of its conventional wisdom, of its own political philosophy, as to refuse to follow this road the whole way, especially when it is obvious that today, in contrast to those times, any other alternative contains the mortal danger of atomic catastrophe for all, without distinction of color, of creed, of skin.

The countries of the Soviet area appreciate that the prerequisite of their development is freer trade, but they also know that this comes into conflict with the rules of the present system of rigid planning and of bilateral trade agreements. Our headaches regarding international liquidity are as nothing compared with those of him who is obliged to conduct his foreign trade practically on barter terms.

But for the countries of the Soviet area to attain the ability to export competitively their products in much greater quantities than at present—an indispensable condition for any sharp increase in Western exports—they must resolve a veritable avalanche of complicated problems which range from the quality and specifications of the products offered to render them attractive to our sophisticated markets, to the need for greater autonomy in the processes of industrial production; from the study of modern marketing techniques to the creation *ex novo* of commercial networks; from the adoption of multilateral exchange practices to the use of modern financial instruments.

The second problem also presupposes original solutions because it concerns the very efficiency of the productive machine in the Communist countries.

I have already referred to the agonizing reappraisal being made by their leaders in the sense that, in spite of the installation of a large number of new plants, they have to accept that their industrial economy as a whole, and even more their general administrative apparatus, are entirely inadequate for the requirements of modern organized society and call for profound reform.

Hence the forthcoming launching of great plans for modernization and mechanization in which the primary stimulus which over thirty years ago had as its slogan in the U.S.S.R. "electrification," today will have that of cybernetics and automation.

But even for these plans all-out help is needed from the West. Europe could perhaps open the way, but in the end the inexhaustible organizational capacity of the United States will have to be brought in.

Let us now pass on to the last line of strategic action, that concerning Latin America. I believe it is not difficult to explain the reasons which militate in favor of the absolute priority to be given in this setting to Latin America rather than to other developing regions. As far as I am concerned, for ten years I have made a modest but indefatigable contribution to the clarification of the singular place held by Latin America for the future of the West, to the study and development of its resources, to the preparation of a coordinated policy between the United States and Europe in that continent. Today I am convinced that, if the area of well-being cannot be extended to Latin America in the near future, it will never be possible in other underdeveloped regions.

With this preface, one may recall *ad abundantiam* other objective reasons, too, which support this thesis. There are various allied factors which favor Latin America not met at present in other as yet underdeveloped regions, such as: size and geographical position, which facilitate external intervention; a cultural base homogeneous with that of the West; about 150 years of independence, which give it the advantage of several decades of experience in forms of self-government; a serious, popular support, in many countries, for the concept of government by the people; three nations, the largest, close to take-off point, and capable of acting as poles of dissemination; the regional structures, already mentioned, which constitute the web of a more highly evolved integrated system; the existence of a class of executives and civil servants, not in great numbers, but capable of increase without great difficulty; in a dual sector economy, a broad *de facto* experience of economic activities based on private initiative.

Latin America—and no other underdeveloped region—can and must, therefore, be the test-bench for the practicability of bringing a whole continent within the area of well-being.

We all know that the operation, if well planned, cannot but be successful. We have a few years to plan it and the decade from 1970 to accomplish it.

It may be observed that in my design of the world there is no reference to Africa, Asia, and China—more than half of mankind. I firmly believe—and that not solely for irrepressible demands of a moral kind—that now, as man has forced the secret of the atom and is applying himself to making other conquests of universal importance, the destiny of all countries is henceforth indivisible and that human society can no longer tolerate long periods of profound injustice and uncivilized differences. I also believe that the wealthy nations must in the future help much more than in the past those people more derelict than any other.

However, we should be culpable of unpardonable lack of realism if we were to imagine that by our aid, even if supplied in growing measure and better coordinated, they could change fundamentally their lot over the next ten or fifteen years in the way we think will happen in Latin America.

The transformation of Afro-Asian communities in the modern sense is clearly an objective for a second period, and not for that less essential. The prerequisite for facing up to it—just as is European unity for the objectives for the '70s—will be the consolidation of a large area of prosperity from Siberia to Patagonia, from the Nile Delta to Alaska. Since we are talking here of the greatest enterprise ever faced by mankind, preparations must be laid as never seen before; then indeed all the resources that can be made available by the areas of well-being must be mobilized.

This then is an objective for the '80s, when the gross product of the area of well-being that we have here imagined will be in the order of $3,000 billion a year.

To conclude, I wish to warn once more that we must have no illusions. Only by a general vision of the problems and by making a great effort to understand the enormous forces let loose around us and only on the condition that peoples and governments—especially those vested with the greatest responsibilities—give proof of maturity and firmness can we look fearlessly onward to the end of this second millenium.

It is a horizon very near to us now. For the most part our sons will be living then, and with them six or seven billion other human beings.

Since only very few will spin through space as professional cosmonauts, everyone else will have to find some way to live together on this old planet with much less incomprehension and intolerance than today.

Philosophy of management

Dr. Peccei spoke on several occasions about his philosophy of management. He said:

When I arrived at Olivetti, I detected that many patterns of operating had crystallized. New ideas were being held down by old habits which had to be broken. Too many people were living with the experiences of the past, assuming that the old solutions could be put to use on our current problems. Much too much thought was given to the question of how to present facts and to whom they should be presented rather than to the facts themselves. Of course many of the ideas and relationships which were cherished were still good and applicable, but not for long. Our industry is too dynamic.

My main task was to break up the structure so that ideas could circulate and new managers could develop their talents. I fear that many of our managers were still inclined toward centralized decision making. After so many years of family rule and with the period of indecision following Adriano's death, they had not learned to assume responsibility. They expected someone else to make the final decision. When I arrived, we were still of the old school where flair and personal intelligence played too big a part. Not enough emphasis was placed on the necessity for objectivity and rational analysis. I believe that the assumption of responsibility, the ability to be objective, and the use of rational analysis are the marks of a manager.

As a newcomer to the company and to this kind of business, I felt that one of my early tasks was to build up managers. They had to be taught to assume personal responsibility and to utilize their natural talents. We have a brilliant group of managers but most had no formal training in the modern methods of business operations.

In many ways the fact that I am not technically minded is an advantage in the process of building up managers. I can ask the managers to give me answers to the questions which I pose, and they can have a great deal of assurance that I will listen to their analysis and not try to second guess them. I try to give directions based on broad guidelines.

On specific issues, I try to let the manager assume full responsibility, including coordination with other functions where necessary. If my marketing manager comes to me to offer a plan of action, I try to judge his program on the basis of the facts and analysis which he presents. I assume that he has coordinated with others in the company who might possibly be affected. Only if there are serious side effects on other groups which he has not taken into account will I change his program.

One problem which we have had in the past is the lack of formal coordination. I believe that in a company the size of ours we must have scheduled meetings to insure communication. As you know, I am directly responsible for the commercial area now. Through this position, I am trying to set an example to the other executives. Whenever I am in Italy I hold a meeting once a week with the men in the commercial area to keep track of the new developments and problems. In my position as managing director, I hold monthly meetings with the functional managers. It is my hope that these formal meetings will relieve the load on the informal discussions.

As you can see the information and communication problem is one of my major concerns. We are not open enough yet. Some of the managers are not yet willing to expose the problems and concerns in the "functional" areas to the other managers. We still have to build up trust. I am afraid that this characteristic results from the attitude of some of the previous leaders who wanted to keep most vital information under cover. The feeling was that only a very select few should have access to the overall data of the company. The secrecy led to inaccuracy, jealousy, and fear. My first step to overcome this problem is an attempt to bring objective data into the open and to get the facts which an individual requires to do his job properly into his hands.

I am trying to give the executives more of the big picture. In late 1964 and again in 1965, I held a meeting with all of the executives to tell them about what we had done and what we were going to try to do during the next year. If the men know where the company is going, they will be better able to integrate their efforts with their colleagues.

In the future I plan to have regular meetings where colleagues will report on innovations within Olivetti. For example, we will give the group a report on our program of executive training and we will hold a meeting to tell the men about what we shall be doing in the future in the United States.

I hope these new methods of communication will help. We are smaller than many divisions of General Electric, so it shouldn't be too hard to introduce change into the company. Although we are large for Italy, measured on the scale of a worldwide, multinational company, we still have great flexibility.

In order to improve the flexibility and to get the managers better information, we have started to complete evaluation and restructuring of our information system. In the past we have had to rely on hunch where we should have had standard information coming up on a regular basis. Because of lack of technical expertise and as a part of the program of delegating responsibility, I have assigned a man to make a thorough study of this problem. He is not a specialist, but he is competent technically and has been given authority to seek out the best help available. He will be getting much of his inspiration from the systems which you have developed in the United States. I am sure that when we get the system operating, it will be one of the best available and will be appropriate to our needs. I hope that we can realistically expect to have the system in operation by 1969.

As you can see, this is an ambitious program. We do not have the balanced system which we should have. We still have a considerable way to go in developing a truly professional management team, but we have some of the best raw material to work with. As we go toward the new goals, I hope we can retain many of the things which made Olivetti great. I hope we can keep our social mindedness, our sense of taste and culture. I don't think that these are incompatible with the scientific management concepts which I am trying to introduce.

The researchers talked with Dr. Peccei about how he compared himself with Adriano Olivetti. He said:

Adriano Olivetti was a truly great man—born a leader and naturally endowed with many gifts. If I may humbly compare myself with him at all, he was an entrepreneur and I am a manager. In the modern world, it is my view that managers rank higher than entrepreneurs; they are less moved by self-interest, they wish to affect more people. The profit motivation is not a goal, it is a tool. It should be thought of as a tool in conducting a business and not as a motivating force.

When coming for a spell to Olivetti, I refused to buy Olivetti stock. I did not wish to be influenced by quick profit. My salary is quite sufficient. My objective was to render service to a particularly worthy company and the profit motive *per se* could be distorting, although in the end the Olivetti profitability was totally restored. Adriano Olivetti was an enlightened leader, a dedicated social and political worker. His dedication was to the community life. I myself am more interested in global development. I am more interested in man regardless of where he lives. I wouldn't care to dedicate myself to this or that community when I know that things at large are going out of hand, as I believe they are. I prefer to dedicate myself to the community of man. I believe that is what Adriano Olivetti would do if he were living now. The context has changed from the provincialism in Italy after the war.

We, the managers of large corporations, especially the international corporations, nowadays have deep commitments not only towards our companies (the inside circle represented by their stockholders and personnel, and the outside circle made up by their customers, suppliers and creditors, and the community), but also with respect to society at large, its progress, and its future.

Goals for the company

One evening after a discussion with Dr. Peccei about the problems and philosophies outlined previously, the researchers asked about the goals which he had set for the company. He left the room and then returned with a memo which he had prepared for distribution among the executives. He then said:

If I were a young man in the company, I would be enthusiastic about the new ideas which we are working on. It is early yet. We are just starting to develop our professional approach. We are looking at the U.S. experience for guidance, of course. You have the best management which we will have to adapt to our level here in the company. As a company, we are competing everywhere in the world and need to have the very best. We must apply the most advanced techniques in a way which is appropriate to us.

The next few years are years in which we can produce fundamental change. We can do this because we are in the process of changing from a family company to a publicly owned corporation, because we are in a rapidly changing industry, and because we are multinational in structure.

I hope as you do this case project you will see that we are trying to live up to our objectives. By and large, I think we can accomplish the goals.

Let me read the goals for you and give you some of the reasons behind them:

1. We must rationalize our organizational structure. As you know, Olivetti grew greatly during the 50's and early 60's. It was haphazard growth, which affected our structure and our personnel. Now we must develop a structure which will aid us in meeting our commitments.

2. We must be quicker and more effective in the introduction of new products. I see the last part of the '60s as being as great a period of growth as the early '60s, but in a more controlled fashion. I think we will achieve some of that growth through the development of peripheral equipment. This will be accomplished through the development of standard components which could be the building blocks for a complete system of peripheral equipment.

3. We must offset the higher costs which we anticipate by getting higher productivity. Hopefully we can achieve an absolute cost reduction which will improve our competitive position. This will be the responsibility of the research and development group and the manufacturing group.

4. We must achieve higher volume without increasing appreciably our payroll in the Piedmont region of Italy. The labor market here cannot support further significant expansion.

5. We must improve the training of executives. The machine is somewhat taking the place of the production workers, yet our training programs are focused for them. We will now place heavy emphasis on training middle and top managers, initially in management courses at American graduate schools of business. We will expand our programs for lower managers. This will involve a large expansion of our Technical Institute.

6. We must reshape our long-term 3- to 5-year corporate planning process and our yearly and up-to-three years budgets to provide a more forceful management tool. We will develop consolidated statements for our worldwide operations; we shall progress in the trend toward more full disclosure of financial data.

7. Our information system must be rethought, with the best skills available, to provide more accurate and timely information for all levels of management. As we have grown, our communication methods have not kept pace with the organization.

8. We must reorganize our commercial organization to fight complacency and to help develop new product ideas. We must not be complacent even though

we sell one-third of all the calculators and one-fourth of all the typewriters sold in the world. We combined marketing and product planning as a first step in this direction.

9. We must consolidate our number one rank in machine tools here in Italy through increased emphasis on numerical control machines.

10. We must improve our sales support and customer service. This may even include the development of a European leasing service to help our customers finance the purchase of major systems.

11. We must develop a spirit and a mentality of multinationality, including more non-Italian management personnel, a more international basis of financing, and a better worldwide rationalization of production.

12. We will have to strengthen our position in the United States. This will include strict adherence to the guidelines for U.S. companies, new industrial facilities, and a presence which will be more representative of the Olivetti tradition.

13. We will take a hard look at the potential of the U.S.S.R. We will learn how to form a bridge between the two worlds.

14. We must consolidate our position in Latin America so as to maintain our leadership role.

15. We must bring the factory in Spain up to the level of other European facilities in order to allow them to compete effectively.

16. We must keep up in the United Kingdom, possibly even strengthening our position there. There are good possibilities if Britain associates with the European Common Market. Also the shift to decimal currency will have an important effect on our business.

17. We must contribute to Italy's development. We understand that Olivetti is one of the important driving forces in Italy. While being aware of our role as a multinational company, we must remember that Olivetti started here and has a responsibility to Italy.

Right now, I would say that Fiat is the best-managed Italian company. It is conservative, prudent, and efficient. In production it is second to none. In other areas it is not yet as scientific as it should be. I think Olivetti has a chance of outstripping Fiat. If we accomplish the goals which we have set, Olivetti can become one of the leaders in Europe and *the* best Italian company.